MW00390718

LexisNexis Law School Publishing Advisory Board

Paul Caron
Professor of Law
Pepperdine University School of Law
Herzog Summer Visiting Professor in Taxation
University of San Diego School of Law

Bridgette Carr
Clinical Professor of Law
University of Michigan Law School

Olympia Duhart
Professor of Law and Director of Lawyering Skills & Values Program
Nova Southeastern University, Shepard Broad Law School

Samuel Estreicher
Dwight D. Opperman Professor of Law
Director, Center for Labor and Employment Law
NYU School of Law

Steven I. Friedland
Professor of Law and Senior Scholar
Elon University School of Law

Carole Goldberg
Jonathan D. Varat Distinguished Professor of Law
UCLA School of Law

Oliver Goodenough
Professor of Law
Vermont Law School

Paul Marcus
Haynes Professor of Law
William and Mary Law School

John Sprankling
Distinguished Professor of Law
McGeorge School of Law

INTERNATIONAL ENVIRONMENTAL LAW: CASES, MATERIALS, AND PROBLEMS
Second Edition

INTERNATIONAL ENVIRONMENTAL LAW: CASES, MATERIALS, AND PROBLEMS

Second Edition

Thomas J. Schoenbaum
Harold S. Shefelman Distinguished Professor of Law, University of Washington

Michael K. Young
President and Professor of Law, University of Washington

ISBN: 978-1-4224-7029-9
Looseleaf ISBN: 978-1-4224-8150-9
eBook ISBN: 978-0-3271-7827-9

Library of Congress Cataloging-in-Publication Data

Schoenbaum, Thomas J., author.
International environmental law : cases, materials, and problems / Thomas J. Schoenbaum, Harold S. Shefelman Distinguished Professor of Law, University of Washington, Michael K. Young, President and Professor of Law, University of Washington. -- Second edition.
p. cm.
ISBN 978-1-4224-7029-9 (hardbound)
1. Environmental law, International--Cases. I. Young, Michael K., 1949- author. II. Title.
K3585.S365 2014
344.04'6--dc23

2014035063

This publication is designed to provide authoritative information in regard to the subject matter covered. It is sold with the understanding that the publisher is not engaged in rendering legal, accounting, or other professional services. If legal advice or other expert assistance is required, the services of a competent professional should be sought.

LexisNexis and the Knowledge Burst logo are registered trademarks of Reed Elsevier Properties Inc., used under license. Matthew Bender and the Matthew Bender Flame Design are registered trademarks of Matthew Bender Properties Inc.

Copyright © 2014 Matthew Bender & Company, Inc., a member of LexisNexis. All Rights Reserved.

No copyright is claimed by LexisNexis or Matthew Bender & Company, Inc., in the text of statutes, regulations, and excerpts from court opinions quoted within this work. Permission to copy material may be licensed for a fee from the Copyright Clearance Center, 222 Rosewood Drive, Danvers, Mass. 01923, telephone (978) 750-8400.

NOTE TO USERS
To ensure that you are using the latest materials available in this area, please be sure to periodically check the LexisNexis Law School web site for downloadable updates and supplements at www.lexisnexis.com/lawschool.

Editorial Offices
121 Chanlon Rd., New Providence, NJ 07974 (908) 464-6800
201 Mission St., San Francisco, CA 94105-1831 (415) 908-3200
www.lexisnexis.com

MATTHEW◆BENDER

Preface to Second Edition

We take pleasure to offer this Casebook on International Environmental Law as a classroom learning tool that can be covered in the confines of a three-hour course on the subject. We have assembled these materials with the idea that the book should not be a scholarly work that is encyclopedic in scope but rather should be as practical and compact as possible. To this end, we put a premium on brevity and have included only basic primary materials and notes in the book. We think it is very important for the students to be familiar with more extensive primary materials as well so we are publishing a **Document Supplement** as a separate volume. The documents in the **Document Supplement** are keyed to each of the 10 chapters in the Casebook so the student can read and refer to the documents necessary to understand each topic as he or she is covering the substantive book chapter.

We have carefully ordered the Chapters in the Casebook so the student will acquire the background necessary to understand each subsequent topic in turn. We also presume the student will have no background in either Public International Law or Environmental Law; thus, we include some materials on these topics as well. Of course, it would help understanding if the student has some background in one or both of those two important subjects.

We believe the problem method is a good teaching technique, so we include problems in each Chapter that are designed to stimulate class discussion and understanding. But the professor of course may want to skip some (or all) of the problems or substitute his or her own problems for ours. Thus we offer the problems as optional tools to be covered or not as the professor who is in charge of the course decides is appropriate.

This work is obviously designed as a teaching tool. We have accordingly largely excluded secondary materials from the published work. Of course there are many important and stimulating secondary works that we hope the students consult during the course of studying the subject. To this end at the beginning of the book we provide Suggestions for Further Reading which cite both general works on International Environmental Law and works that are keyed to each of the 10 Chapters of the book.

Although this work is dubbed "second edition," it is in reality a wholly new start, differing greatly from the first edition. Although three of the co-authors of the first edition, Don Anton, Jon Charney, and Philippe Sands, for various reasons could not participate in doing this edition, the authors are grateful for their ideas and valuable prior contributions, and wish to express our deep thanks and admiration for their work in this field.

We always appreciate hearing from and having suggestions from colleagues.

Thomas J. Schoenbaum, email: tjschoen@uw.edu

Michael K. Young, email: president@uw.edu

Seattle, Washington

November 18, 2013

Suggestions for Further Reading in International Environmental Law*

Although International Environmental Law is a relatively new field, many outstanding books and articles have appeared on every subject of the field. The scholarship in this area is outstanding but voluminous. In this memorandum, we are confined for practical reasons to listing selected books and articles that we think will be helpful to students seeking additional sources of information.

General Works

To begin with, we think highly of many of the books that cover the entire field of International Environmental Law. We recommend especially the following:

Birnie, Patricia, Alan Boyle, and Catherine Redgwell, *International Law and the Environment*, 3d ed. (Oxford: Oxford Univ. Press, 2009).

Bodansky, Daniel, Jutta Brunee, and Ellen Hey, eds., *The Oxford Handbook of International Environmental Law* (Oxford: Oxford Univ. Press, 2007).

Kiss, Alexander and Dinah Shelton, *International Environmental Law* (Leiden and Boston: Martinus Nijhoff, 2007).

Sands, Philippe and Jacqueline Peel, *Principles of International Environmental Law*, 3d ed. (New York: Cambridge Univ. Press, 2012).

Chapter 1: Introduction and Background

Adams, Todd B., *Is There a Legal Future for Sustainable Development in Global Warming? Justice, Economics, and Protecting the Environment*, 16 GEO. INT'L ENVTL. L. REV. 77 (2003).

Adelman, David E., *The Art of the Unsolvable: Locating the Vital Center of Science for Environmental Law & Policy*, 37 ENVTL. L. 925 (2007).

Benedickson, Jaime, et al., eds., *Environmental Law and Sustainability After Rio* (Northampton, MA: Edward Elger Publishing, Inc., 2011).

Beyerlin, Ulrich and Thilo Marauhn, *International Environmental Law* (Portland, OR: Hart Publishing, 2011).

Blodgett, Mark S., Richard J. Hunter, Jr., and Hector R. Lozada, *A Primer on International Environmental Law: Sustainability as a Principle of International Law and Custom*, 15 ILSA J. INT'L & COMP. L. 15 (2008).

Bratspies, Rebecca M., *Rethinking Decisionmaking in International Environmental Law: A Process-Oriented Inquiry into Sustainable Development*, 32 YALE J. INT'L L. 363 (2007).

Dernbach, John C., *Creating the Law of Environmentally Sustainable Economic Development*, 28 PACE ENVTL. L. REV. 614 (2011).

Dernbach, John C., *Targets, Timetables, and Effective Implementing Mechanisms: Necessary Building Blocks for Sustainable Development*, 27 WM. & MARY ENVTL. L. & POL'Y REV. 79 (2002).

* The authors would like to thank Jessica L. Montgomery and Craig Henson, JD, 2013, for their research help preparing these materials.

Suggestions for Further Reading

Desai, Bharat H., *Institutionalizing International Environmental Law* (Ardsley, NY: Transnational Publishers, Inc., 2004).

Drumbl, Mark A., *Poverty, Wealth, and Obligation in International Environmental Law*, 76 TUL. L. REV. 843 (2002).

Esty, Daniel C., *Breaking the Environmental Law Logjam: The International Dimension*, 17 N.Y.U. ENVTL. L.J. 836 (2008).

Kotzé, Louis J., *Global Environmental Governance: Law and Regulation for the 21st Century.* Northampton (MA: Edward Elgar Publishing, Inc., 2012).

Marong, Alhaji B.M., *From Rio to Johannesburg: Reflections on the Role of International Legal Norms in Sustainable Development*, 16 GEO. INT'L ENVT'L. L. REV. 21 (2003).

Ørebech, Peter, et al., *The Role of Customary Law in Sustainable Development* (New York: Cambridge Univ. Press, 2005).

Rao, P.K., *International Environmental Law and Economics* (Malden, MA: Blackwell Publishers Inc., 2002).

Stark, Barbara, *Sustainable Development and Postmodern International Law: Greener Globalization?*, 27 WM. & MARY ENVTL. L. & POL'Y REV. 137 (2002).

Yang, Tseming and Robert V. Percival, *The Emergence of Global Environmental Law*, 36 ECOLOGY L.Q. 615 (2009).

Chapter 2: General International Environmental Law

Abate, Randall S., *Dawn of a New Era in the Extraterritorial Application of U.S. Environmental Statutes: A Proposal for an Integrated Judicial Standard Based on the Continuum of Context*, 31 COLUM. J. ENVTL. L. 87 (2006).

Applegate, John S., *The Taming of the Precautionary Principle*, 27 WM. & MARY ENVTL. L. & POL'Y REV. 13 (2002).

Bodansky, Daniel, *Is There an International Environmental Constitution?*, 16 IND. J. GLOBAL LEGAL STUD. 565 (2009).

Bruch, Carl, *Is International Environmental Law Really Law?: An Analysis of Application in Domestic Courts*, 23 PACE ENVTL. L. REV. 423 (2006).

Churchill, Robert R. and Geir Ulfstein, *Autonomous Institutional Arrangements in Multilateral Environmental Agreements: A Little-Noticed Phenomenon in International Law*, 94 AM. JUR. INT'L L. 623 (2000).

Driesen, David M., *Thirty Years of International Environmental Law: A Retrospective and Plea for Reinvigoration*, 30 SYRACUSE J. INT'L L. & COM. 353 (2003).

Dycus, Stephen, *Nuclear War: Still the Greatest Threat to the Environment*, 25 VT. L. REV 753 (2001).

Ehrmann, Markus, *Procedures of Compliance Control in International Environmental Treaties*, 13 COLO. J. INT'L ENVTL. L. & POL'Y 377 (2002).

Farber, Daniel A., *Probabilities Behaving Badly: Complexity Theory and Environmental Uncertainty*, 37 U.C. DAVIS L. REV. 145 (2003).

Fitzmaurice, Malgosia, *Contemporary Issues in International Environmental Law* (Northampton, MA: Edward Elgar Publishing, Inc., 2009).

Foster, Caroline E., *Science and the Precautionary Principle in International Courts and Tribunals: Expert Evidence, Burden of Proof and Finality* (New York: Cambridge Univ. Press, 2011).

Suggestions for Further Reading

Gray, Kevin R., *International Environmental Impact Assessment: Potential for a Multilateral Environmental Agreement*, 11 COLO. J. INT'L. ENVT'L. L. & POL'Y 83 (2000).

Gillroy, John Martin, *Adjudication Norms, Dispute Settlement Regimes and International Tribunals: The Status of "Environmental Sustainability" in International Jurisprudence*, 42 STAN. J. INT'L L. 1 (2006).

Kalas, Peggy Rodgers, *International Environmental Dispute Resolution and the Need for Access by Non-State Entities*, 12 COLO. J. INT'L ENVT'L. L. & POL'Y 191 (2001).

Kerbrat, Yann, and Sandrine Maljeau-Dubois, eds., *The Transformation of International Environmental Law* (Portland, OR: Hart Publishing, 2011).

Lin, Albert C., *The Unifying Role of Harm in Environmental Law*, 2006 WIS. L. REV. 897.

Mayer, Don, *The Precautionary Principle and International Efforts to Ban DDT*, 9 S.C. ENVT'L. L.J. 135 (2002).

Nash, Jonathan Remy, *Too Much Market? Conflict Between Tradable Pollution Allowances and the "Polluter Pays" Principle*, 24 HARV. ENVTL. L. REV. 465 (2000).

Onzivu, William, *International Environmental Law, the Public's Health, and Domestic Environmental Governance in Developing Countries*, 21 AM. U. INT'L L. REV. 597 (2006).

Percival, Robert V., *Who's Afraid of the Precautionary Principle?*, 23 PACE ENVTL. L. REV. 21 (2006).

Rinceanu, Johanna, *Enforcement Mechanisms in International Environmental Law: Quo Vandunt? Homo Sanus in Natura Sana*, 15 J. ENVTL. L. & LITIG. 147 (2000).

Voigt, Christina, *Sustainable Development as a Principle of International Environmental Law: Resolving Conflicts between Climate Measures and WTO Law* (Boston, MA: Martinus Nijhoff Publishers, 2009).

Chapter 3: State Responsibility for Transboundary Environmental Harm

Buhi, Jason and Lin Feng, *The International Joint Commission's Role in the United States-Canada Transboundary Air Pollution Control Regime: A Century of Experience to Guide the Future*, 11 VT. J. ENVTL. L. 107 (2009).

Cassar, Angela Z. & Carl E. Bruch, *Transboundary Environmental Impact Assessment in International Watercourse Management*, 12 N.Y.U. ENVTL. L.J. 169 (2003).

Dornbos, Jeffrey S., *All (Water) Politics Is Local: A Proposal for Resolving Transboundary Water Disputes*, 22 FORDHAM ENVTL. L. REV. 1 (2010).

George, Gerald F., *Environmental Enforcement Across National Borders*, 21 NAT. RESOURCES & ENV'T 3 (2006).

Guruswamy, Lakshman, *State Responsibility in Promoting Environmental Corporate Accountability*, 21 FORDHAM ENVTL. L. REV. 209 (2010).

Hall, Noah D., *Transboundary Pollution: Harmonizing International and Domestic Law*, 40 U. MICH. J. L. REFORM 681 (2007).

Hess, Gerald F., *The Trail Smelter, the Columbia River, and the Extraterritorial Application of CERCLA*, 18 GEO. INT'L ENVTL. L. REV 1 (2005).

Hsu, Shi-Ling and Austen L. Parrish, *Litigating Canada-U.S. Transboundary Harm:*

International Environmental Lawmaking and the Threat of Extraterritorial Reciprocity, 38 VA. J. INT'L L. 1 (2007).

Kelly, Ryan P. and Margaret R. Caldwell, *Ten Ways States Can Combat Ocean Acidification (and Why They Should)*, 37 HARV. ENVTL. L. REV. 57 (2013).

Kiss, Alexandre, State Responsibility and Liability for Nuclear Damage, 35 DENV. J. INT'L L. & POL'Y 67 (2006).

Knox, John H., *Assessing the Candidates for a Global Treaty on Transboundary Environmental Impact Assessment*, 12 N.Y.U. ENVTL. L.J. 153 (2003).

Knox, John H., *The Myth and Reality of Transboundary Environmental Impact Assessment*, 96 AM. J. INT'L L. 291 (2002).

Mank, Bradford, *Can Plaintiffs Use Multinational Environmental Treaties as Customary International Law to Sue Under the Alien Tort Statute?*, 2007 UTAH L. REV. 1085.

Mégret, Frédéric, *The Problem of an International Criminal Law of the Environment*, 36 COLUM. J. ENVTL. L. 195 (2011).

McIntyre, Owen, *The Role of Customary Rules and Principles of International Environmental Law in the Protection of Shared International Freshwater Resources*, 46 NAT. RESOURCES J. 157 (2006).

Okawa, Phoebe N., *State Responsibility for Transboundary Air Pollution in International Law* (New York: Oxford Univ. Press, 2000).

Parrish, Austen L., Trail Smelter Deja Vu: Extraterritoriality, International Environmental Law, and the Search for Solutions to Canadian-U.S. Transboundary Water Pollution Disputes, 85 B.U. L. REV. 363 (2005).

Percival, Robert V., *Liability for Environmental Harm and Emerging Global Environmental Law*, 25 MD. J. INT'L L. 37 (2010).

Pratt, Laura A.W., *Decreasing Dirty Dumping? A Reevaluation of Toxic Waste Colonialism and the Global Management of Transboundary Hazardous Waste*, 35 WM. & MARY ENVTL. L. & POL'Y REV. 581 (2011).

Robinson-Dorn, Michael J., *The Trail Smelter: Is What's Past Prologue? EPA Blazes New Trail for CERCLA*, 14 N.Y.U. ENVTL. L.J. 233 (2006).

Sachs, Noah, *Beyond the Liability Wall: Strengthening Tort Remedies in International Environmental Law*, 55 U.C.L.A. L. REV. 837 (2008).

Waugh, Theodore, *Where Do We Go from Here: Legal Controls and Future Strategies for Addressing the Transportation of Hazardous Waste Across International Borders*, 11 FORDHAM ENVTL. L.J. 477 (2000).

Chapter 4: Climate Change and Protection of the Atmosphere

Abate, Randall S., Massachusetts v. EPA *and the Future of Environmental Standing in Climate Change Litigation and Beyond*, 33 WM. & MARY ENVTL. L. & POL'Y REV. 121 (2008).

Attapattu, Sumudu, *Global Climate Change: Can Human Rights (and Human Beings) Survive This Onslaught?*, 20 COLO. J. INT'L ENVTL. L. & POL'Y 35 (2008).

Bancal, Jean-Charles, *The "Financial Mechanism" & "Flexible Mechanisms" of the United Nations Framework Convention on Climate Change: Faced with Climate Change, the Global Environment Facility and the Carbon Market Take Leading Roles*, 3 APPALACHIAN NAT. RESOURCES L.J. 1 (2009).

Suggestions for Further Reading

Black, Elizabeth C., *Climate Change Adaptation: Local Solutions for a Global Problem*, 22 GEO. INT'L ENVTL. L. REV. 359 (2010).

Boyd, William, *Climate Change, Fragmentation, and the Challenges of Global Environmental Law: Elements of a Post-Copenhagen Assemblage*, 32 U. PA. J. INT'L L. 457 (2010).

Burleson, Elizabeth, *Climate Change Consensus: Emerging International Law*, 34 WM. & MARY ENVTL. L. & POL'Y REV. 543 (2010).

Butti, Luciano, *The Tortious Road to Liability: A Critical Survey on Climate Change Litigation in Europe and North America*, 11 SUSTAINABLE DEV. L. & POL'Y 32 (2011).

Christopher, Caleb W., *Success by a Thousand Cuts: The Use of Environmental Impact Assessment in Addressing Climate Change*, 9 VT. J. ENVTL. L. 549 (2008).

Carlarne, Cinnamon, *Climate Change Policies an Ocean Apart: E.U. and U.S. Climate Change Policies Compared*, 14 PENN ST. ENVTL. L. REV. 435 (2006).

Cole, Daniel H., *Climate Change, Adaptation, and Development*, 26 U.C.L.A. J. ENVTL. L. & POL'Y 1 (2008).

Craig, Robin Kundis, *"Stationarity is Dead" — Long Live Transformation: Five Principles for Climate Change Adaptation Law*, 34 HARV. ENVTL. L. REV. 9 (2010).

Dembach, John C. and Seema Kakade, *Climate Change Law: An Introduction*, 29 ENERGY L.J. 1 (2008).

DeSombre, Elizabeth R., *The Experience of the Montreal Protocol: Particularly Remarkable, and Remarkably Particular*, 19 U.C.L.A. J. ENVTL. L. & POL'Y 49 (2001).

Doelle, Meinhard, *From Hot Air to Action? Climate Change, Compliance and the Future of International Environmental Law* (Toronto: Thomson Carswell, 2005).

Ferrey, Steven, *Corporate Responsibility and Carbon-Based Life Forms*, 35 B.C. ENVTL. AFF. L. REV. 419 (2008).

Gerrard, Michael B., *What the Law and Lawyers Can and Cannot Do About Global Warming*, 16 SOUTHEASTERN ENVTL. L.J. 33 (2007).

Kysar, Douglas A., *Climate Change, Cultural Transformation, and Comprehensive Rationality*, 31 B.C. ENVTL. AFF. L. REV. 555 (2004).

McGee, Jr., Henry W., *Litigating Global Warming: Substantive Law in Search of a Forum*, 16 FORDHAM ENVTL. L. REV. 371 (2005).

Osofsky, Hari M., *Climate Change Litigation as Pluralist Legal Dialogue?*, 26A STAN. ENVTL. L. REV. 181 (2007).

Osofsky, Hari M., *Is Climate Change "International"? Litigation's Diagonal Regulatory Role*, 49 VA. J. INT'L L. 585 (2009).

Osofsky, Hari M., *The Future of Environmental Law and Complexities of Scale: Federalism Experiments with Climate Change Under the Clean Air Act*, 32 WASH. U. J. L. & POL'Y 79 (2010).

Osofsky, Hari M., *The Geography of Climate Change Litigation: Implications for Transnational Regulatory Governance*, 83 WASH. U. L. Q. 1789 (2005).

Owen, Dave *Climate Change and Environmental Assessment Law*, 33 COLUM. J. ENVTL. L. 57 (2008).

Suggestions for Further Reading

Peloso, Chris, *Crafting an International Climate Change Protocol: Applying the Lessons Learned from the Success of the Montreal Protocol and the Ozone Depletion Problem*, 25 J. LAND USE & ENVTL. L. 305 (2010).

Ruhl, J.B., *Climate Change Adaptation and the Structural Transformation of Environmental Law*, 40 ENVTL. L. 363 (2010).

Stewart, Richard B., Michael Oppenheimer, and Bryce Rudyk, *Building Blocks for Global Climate Protection*, 32 STAN. ENVTL. L.J. 341 (2013).

van Asselt, Harro and Joyeeta Gupta, *Stretching Too Far? Developing Countries and the Role of Flexibility Mechanisms Beyond Kyoto*, 28 STAN. ENVTL. L.J. 311 (2009).

Vandenbergh, Michael P. and Mark A. Cohen, *Climate Change Governance: Boundaries and Leakage*, 18 N.Y.U. ENVTL. L.J. 221 (2010).

Wiener, Jonathan B., *Something Borrowed for Something Blue: Legal Transplants and the Evolution of Global Environmental Law*, 27 ECOLOGY L. Q. 1295 (2001).

Chapter 5: Environment, International Trade and Investment

Barrett, Jr., John A., *The Global Environment and Free Trade: A Vexing Problem and a Taxing Solution*, 76 IND. L.J. 829 (2001).

Burleson, Elizabeth, *From Fragmentation to Innovation Coordination*, 24 GEO. INT'L ENVTL. L. REV. 477 (2012).

Burleson, Elizabeth and Winslow Burleson, *Innovation Cooperation: Energy Biosciences and Law*, 2011 U. ILL. L. REV. 651 (2011).

Carlarne, Cinnamon, *The Kyoto Protocol and the WTO: Reconciling Tensions Between Free Trade and Environmental Objectives*, 17 COLO. J. INT'L ENVTL. L. & POL'Y 45 (2006).

Chang, Howard F., *Toward a Greener GATT: Environmental Trade Measures and the Shrimp-Turtle Case*, 74 S. CAL. L. REV. 31 (2000).

Driesen, David M., *What is Free Trade?: The Real Issue Lurking Behind the Free Trade and Environment Debate*, 41 VA. J. INT'L L. 279 (2001).

Endres, Jody M., *Clearing the Air: The Meta-Standard Approach to Ensuring Biofuels Environmental and Social Sustainability*, 28 VA. ENVTL. L.J. 73 (2010).

Frischmann, Brett, *A Dynamic Institutional Theory of International Law*, 51 BUFF. L. REV 679 (2003).

Gaines, Sanford, *The WTO's Reading of the GATT Article XX Chapeau: A Disguised Restriction on Environmental Measures*, 22 U. PA. J. INT'L ECON. L. 739 (2001).

Ghei, Nita, *Evaluating the WTO's Two Step Test for Environmental Measures Under Article XX*, 18 COLO. J. INT'L ENVTL. L. & POL'Y 117 (2007).

Gonzalez, Carmen G., *Genetically Modified Organisms and Justice: The International Environmental Justice Implications of Biotechnology*, 19 GEO. INT'L ENVTL. L. REV. 583 (2007).

Goyal, Anupam, *The WTO and International Environmental Law: Towards Conciliation* (New Delhi: Oxford Univ. Press, 2006).

Grosko, Brett, *Genetic Engineering and International Law: Conflict or Harmony? An Analysis of the Biosafety Protocol, GATT, and the WTO Sanitary and Phytosanitary Agreement*, 20 VA. ENVTL. L.J. 295 (2001).

Howse, Robert, *The Appellate Body Rulings in the Shrimp/Turtle Case: A New Legal*

Baseline for the Trade and Environment Debate, 27 COLUM. J. ENVTL. L. 491 (2002).

Kennedy, Kevin C., *Why Multilateralism Matters in Resolving Trade-Environment Disputes*, 7 WIDENER L. SYMP. J. 31 (2001).

Knox, John H., *The Judicial Resolution of Conflicts Between Trade and the Environment*, 28 HARV. ENVTL. L. REV. 1 (2004).

Lallas, Peter L., *The Role of Process and Participation in the Development of Effective International Environmental Agreements: A Study of the Global Treaty on Persistent Organic Pollutants (POPs)*, 19 U.C.L.A. J. ENVTL. L. & POL'Y 83 (2001).

Mintz, Joel A., *Two Cheers for Global POPs: A Summary and Assessment of the Stockholm Convention on Persistent Organic Pollutants*, 14 GEO. INT'L ENVTL. L. REV. 319 (2001).

Scott, Joanne, *International Trade and Environmental Governance: Relating Rules (and Standards) in the EU and the WTO*, 15 EUR. J. INT'L L. 307 (2004).

Shaffer, Gregory C., *The World Trade Organization Under Challenge: Democracy and the Law and Politics of the WTO's Treatment of Trade and Environment Matters*, 25 HARV. ENVTL. L. REV. 1 (2001).

Silva-Send, Nilmini, *Climate Change Disputes at the World Trade Organization: National Energy Policies and International Trade Liability*, 4 SAN DIEGO J. CLIMATE & ENERGY L. 195 (2013).

Steinberg, Richard H., ed., *The Greening of Trade Law: International Trade Organizations and Environmental Issues* (Lanham, MD: Rowan & Littlefield Publishers, Inc., 2002).

Stewart, Terence P. and David S. Johanson, *A Nexus of Trade and the Environment: The Relationship Between the Cartagena Protocol on Biosafety and the SPS Agreement of the World Trade Organization*, 14 COLO. J. INT'L ENVTL. L. & POL'Y 1 (2003).

Thomas, Chantal, *Should the World Trade Organization Incorporate Legal and Environmental Standards?*, 61 WASH. & LEE L. REV. 347 (2004).

VanderZwaag, David L., *The Precautionary Approach and the International Control of Toxic Chemicals: Beacon of Hope, Sea of Confusion and Dissolution*, 33 HOUS. J. INT'L L. 605 (2011).

Vinuales, Jorge E., *Legal Techniques for Dealing with Scientific Uncertainty in Environmental Law*, 43 VAND. J. TRANSNAT'L L. 437 (2010).

Vranes, Erich, *Trade and the Environment: Fundamental Issues in International Law, WTO Law, and Legal Theory* (New York: Oxford Univ. Press, 2009).

Chapter 6: Freshwater Resources

Baillat, Aline, *International Trade in Water Rights: The Next Step* (London: IWA Publishing, 2010).

Bernauer, Thomas and Anna Kalbhenn, "The Politics of International Freshwater Resources." *The International Studies Encyclopedia* (Washington D.C.: The International Studies Assn., 2010).

Bruch, Carl, ed., *Public Participation in the Governance of International Freshwater Resources* (Tokyo: United Nations Univ. Press, 2005).

Suggestions for Further Reading

Burchi, Stefano and Kerstin Mechlem, *Groundwater in International Law: Compilation of Treaties and Other Legal Instruments* (Rome: FAO, 2005).

De Chazournes, Laurence Boisson, Christina Leb, and Mara Tignino, eds., *International Law and Freshwater: The Multiple Challenges* (Northampton, MA: Edward Elgar Publishing, 2013).

Dickson, Barnabas and Jon Hutton, eds., *Endangered Species Threatened Convention: The Past, Present and Future of CITES, the Convention on International Trade in Endangered Species of Wild Fauna and Flora* (London: Routledge, 2013).

Dinar, Shlomi, *International Water Treaties: Negotiation and Cooperation Along Transboundary Rivers* (New York: Routledge, 2007).

Earle, Anton, Anders Jägerskog, and Joakim Öjendal, eds., *Transboundary Water Management: Principles and Practice* (New York: Earthscan, 2010).

Eckstein, Gabriel, *Protecting a Hidden Treasure: The UN International Law Commission and the International Law of Transboundary Ground Water Resources*, 5 AM. UNIV. SUSTAINABLE DEV. L. & POL'Y 5 (2005).

Fernandez, Linda, *Solving Water Pollution Problems Along the US-Mexico Border*, 7 ENV'T. & DEV. ECON. 715 (2002).

Fischhendler, Itay, *Legal and Institutional Adaptation to Climate Uncertainty: A Study of International Rivers*, 6 WATER POL'Y 281 (2004).

Giordano, Meredith A., *Managing the Quality of International Rivers: Global Principles and Basin Practice*, 43 NAT. RESOURCES J. 111 (2003).

Giordano, Meredith A. and Aaron T. Wolf, *Sharing Waters: Post-Rio International Water Management*, 27 NATURAL RESOURCES FORUM 163 (2003).

Hildering, Antoinette, *International Law, Sustainable Development and Water Management* (Delft, Netherlands: Eburon, 2004).

Iza, Alejandro, ed., *"International Water Governance: Conservation of Freshwater Ecosystems: Volume 1: International Agreements, Compilation and Analysis"* (Gland, Switzerland: IUCN 2004).

McCaffrey, Stephen *The Contribution of the UN Convention on the Law of the Non-Navigational Uses of International Watercourses*, 1.3 INT'L J. OF GLOBAL ENVT'L. ISSUES 250 (2001).

McCaffrey, Stephen, *"The Need for Flexibility in Freshwater Treaty Regimes."* 27 NAT. RESOURCES F. 156 (2003).

McIntryre, Owen, *The Role of Customary Rules and Principles of International Environmental Law in the Protection of Shared International Freshwater Resources*, 46 NAT. RESOURCES J. *157 (2006).*

Paisley, Richard, *Adversaries into Partnerships: International Water Law and the Equitable Sharing of Downstream Benefits*," 3 MELBOURNE J. OF INT'L L. 280 (2002).

Parrish, Austen, *Trail Smelter Deja Vu: Extraterritoriality, International Environmental Law, and the Search for Solutions to Canada-US Transboundary Water Pollution Disputes*, 85 BOSTON U. L. REV. (2005).

Priscoli, Jerome Delli, *Managing and Transforming Water Conflicts* (New York: Cambridge Univ. Press, 2009).

Weiss, Brown Edith, Laurence Boisson de Chazournes, and Nathalie Bernasconi-

Osterwalder. *Fresh Water and International Economic Law* (New York: Oxford Univ. Press 2005).

Chapter 7: Protection of the Marine Environment

Alcock, Frank, "UNCLOS, Property Rights, and Effective Fisheries Management." *Managing Institutional Complexity: Regime Interplay and Global Environmental Change*. Eds. Sebastian Oberthür and Olav Schram Stokke (Cambridge, MA: MIT Press, 2011).

Baird, Rachel, Meredith Simons, and Tim Stephens, *Ocean Acidification: A Litmus Test for International Law*, 3 CARBON & CLIMATE L. REV. 459 (2009).

Balton, David A. and Holly R. Koehler, *Ocean and Fisheries Law: Reviewing the United Nations Fish Stocks Treaty*, 7 SUSTAINABLE DEV. L. & POL'Y 5 (2006).

Boyle, Alan, *Further Development of the Law of the Sea Convention: Mechanisms for Change*, 54 INT'L & COMP. L. Q. 563 (2005).

Chung, Suh-Yong, *Is the Convention-Protocol Approach Appropriate for Addressing Regional Marine Pollution?: The Barcelona Convention System Revisited*, 13 PENN ST. ENVTL. L. REV. 85 (2004).

Crothers, G.T. and Lindie Nelson, *High Seas Fisheries Governance: A Framework for the Future?*, MARINE RESOURCE ECON. 21.4 (2006): 341.

Cullis-Suzuki, Sarika and Daniel Pauly, *Failing the High Seas: A Global Evaluation of Regional Fisheries Management Organizations*, 34 MARINE POL'Y 1036 (2010).

Davies, Andrew J., J. Murray Roberts, and Jason Hall-Spencer, *Preserving Deep-Sea Natural Heritage: Emerging Issues in Offshore Conservation and Management*, 138 BIOLOGICAL CONSERVATION 299 (2007).

Jacobsson, Mans, *The International Liability and Compensation Regime for Oil Pollution from Ships — International Solutions for a Global Problem*, 32 TULANE MAR. L.J. 1 (2007).

Kaye, Stuart, *Implementing High Seas Biodiversity Conservation: Global Geopolitical Considerations*, 28 MARINE POL'Y 221 (2004).

Klein, Natalie S., *Dispute Settlement in the UN Convention on the Law of the Sea* (New York: Cambridge Univ. Press, 2005).

Knudsen, Olav F. and Björn Hassler, *IMO Legislation and Its Implementation: Accident Risk, Vessel Deficiencies and National Administrative Practices*, 35 MARINE POL'Y 201 (2011).

Nelson, L.D.M., *The Settlement of Disputes Arising from Conflicting Outer Continental Shelf Claims*, 24 INT'L J. OF MARINE & COASTAL L. 409 (2009).

Rothwell, Donald and Tim Stephens, *The International Law of the Sea* (Oxford: Hart Publishing, 2010).

Schoenbaum, Thomas J., *Liability for Damages in Oil Spill Accidents: Evaluating the USA and International Law Regimes in the Light of Deepwater Horizon*, 24 J. OF ENVT'L. L. 395 (2012).

Schoenbaum, Thomas J., *The Deepwater Horizon Oil Spill in the Context of the Public International Law Regimes for the Protection of the Marine Environment: A Comparative Study*, 25 U.S.F. MAR. L.J. 25 1 (2012).

Sumaila, Ussif Rashid, et al., *Potential Costs and Benefits of Marine Reserves in the High Seas*, 345 MARINE ECOLOGY PROGRESS SERIES 305 (2007).

Tan, Alan Khee-Jin, *Vessel-Source Marine Pollution: the Law and Politics of International Regulation*. New York: Cambridge Univ. Press, 2006.

Wang, Hanling, *Ecosystem Management and Its Application to Large Marine Ecosystems: Science, Law, and Politics*, 35 OCEAN DEV. & INT'L L. 41 (2004).

Warner, Robin, *Protecting the Oceans Beyond National Jurisdiction: Strengthening the International Law Framework*. Vol. 3. Leiden, Netherlands: Brill, 2009.

Chapter 8: Protection of Biological Diversity

Abensperg-Traun, Max, *CITES, Sustainable Use of Wild Species and Incentive-Driven Conservation in Developing Countries, with an Emphasis on Southern Africa*, 142 BIOLOGICAL CONSERVATION 948 (2009).

Chivian, Eric, and Aaron Bernstein, eds., *Sustaining Life: How Human Health Depends on Biodiversity* (New York: Oxford Univ. Press, 2008).

Dickson, Barnabas, *International Conservation Treaties, Poverty and Development: The Case of CITES*, 74 NAT. RESOURCE PERSPECTIVES 1 (2002).

Gehring, Thomas and Eva Ruffing, *When Arguments Prevail over Power: The CITES Procedure for the Listing of Endangered Species*, 8 GLOBAL ENVTL. POL. 123 (2008).

Greiber, Thomas, et al. *An Explanatory Guide to the Nagoya Protocol on Access and Benefit-Sharing* (Gland, Switzerland: IUCN, 2012).

Joseph, Reji *International Regime on Access and Benefit Sharing: Where are We Now?*, 12 ASIAN BIOTECHNOLOGY & DEV. REV. 77 (2010).

Kamau, Evanson, Bevis Fedder, and Gerd Winter, *The Nagoya Protocol on Access to Genetic Resources and Benefit Sharing: What Is New and What Are the Implications for Provider and User Countries and the Scientific Community?*, 6 L. & DEV. J. 248 (2010).

Kamau, Evanson C., and Gerd Winter, eds*., Genetic Resources, Traditional Knowledge and the Law: Solutions for Access and Benefit Sharing* (London: Earthscan, 2009).

Laikre, Linda, et al, *Neglect of Genetic Diversity in Implementation of the Convention on Biological Diversity*, 24 CONSERVATION BIOLOGY 86 (2010).

Lenzen, M., et al, *International Trade Drives Biodiversity Threats in Developing Nations*, 486 NATURE 109 (2012).

Loreau, Michel, et al., *Diversity Without Representation*, 442 NATURE 245 (2006).

McManis, Charles, *Biodiversity and the Law: Intellectual Property, Biotechnology and Traditional Knowledge* (London: Earthscan, 2012).

Naeem, Shahid, J. Emmett Duffy, and Erika Zavaleta, *The Functions of Biological Diversity in an Age of Extinction*, 336 SCI. 1401 (2012).

Nagle, John, *The Effectiveness of Biodiversity Law*, 24 J. OF LAND USE AND ENVTL. L. 203 (2009).

Najam, Adil, "Negotiating Desertification." *Governing Global Desertification: Linking Environmental Degradation, Poverty and Participation* (Aldershot, UK: Ashgate, 2006).

Nasi, R., et al., *CBD Technical Series No. 33: Conservation and Use of Wildlife-Based Resources: the Bushmeat Crisis* (Montreal: Secretariat of the Convention on Biological Diversity, 2008).

Phelps, Jacob, et al., *Boosting CITES*, 330 SCI. 1752 (2010).

Suggestions for Further Reading

Reeve, Rosalind, *Wildlife Trade, Sanctions and Compliance: Lessons from the CITES Regime*, 82 INT'L AFFAIRS 881 (2006).

Sajeva, Maurizio, et al., *Regulating Internet Trade in CITES Species*, 27 CONSERVATION BIOLOGY 429 (2013).

Sand, Peter H., *Japan's 'Research Whaling' in the Antarctic Southern Ocean and the North Pacific Ocean in the Face of the Endangered Species Convention (CITES)*, REV. OF EUROPEAN COMMUNITY & INT'L ENVTL. L. 17.1 (2008): 56–71.

Stringer, Lindsay, *Can the UN Convention to Combat Desertification Guide Sustainable Use of the World's Soils?*, 6 FRONTIERS IN ECOLOGY & THE ENV'T 138 (2008).

Sutherland, W.J., et al., *One Hundred Questions of Importance to the Conservation of Global Biological Diversity*, 23 CONSERVATION BIOLOGY 557 (2009).

Chapter 9: Polar Regions

Baird, Rachel, *CCAMLR Initiatives to Counter Flag State Non-Enforcement in Southern Ocean Fisheries*, 36 VICTORIA U. OF WELLINGTON L. REV. 733 (2005).

Bargagli, R., *Environmental Contamination in Antarctic Ecosystems*, 400 SCI. OF THE TOTAL ENV'T 212 (2008).

Bastmeijer, Kees, *"A Long Term Strategy for Antarctic Tourism: The Key to Decision Making within the Antarctic Treaty System?" Polar Tourism: Human, Environmental and Governance Dimensions*. Eds. Patrick Maher, Emma Stewart, and Michael Lück (Elmsford, NY: Cognizant Communication Corp., 2011).

Byers, Michael and Suzanne Lalonde, *Who Controls the Northwest Passage*, 42 VANDERBILT J. OF TRANSNAT'L L. 1133 (2009).

Chown, Steven L., et al., *Challenges to the Future Conservation of the Antarctic*, 337 SCI. 158 (2012).

Dodds, Klaus, *Governing Antarctica: Contemporary Challenges and the Enduring Legacy of the 1959 Antarctic Treaty*, 1 GLOBAL POL'Y 108 (2010).

Fabra, Adriana and Virginia Gascón, *The Convention on the Conservation of Antarctic Marine Living Resources (CCAMLR) and the Ecosystem Approach*, 23 INT'L J. OF MARINE & COASTAL L. 567 (2008).

Gascón, Virginia and Rodolfo Werner, *CCAMLR and Antarctic Krill: Ecosystem Management Around the Great White Continent*, 7 SUSTAINABLE DEV. L. & POL'Y 14 (2006).

Hassan, Daud, *Climate Change and the Current Regimes of Arctic Fisheries Resources Management: An Evaluation*, 40 J. MAR. L. & COM. 511 (2009).

Herber, Bernard P., *Bioprospecting in Antarctica: The Search for a Policy Regime*, 42 POLAR REC. 139 (2006).

Holmes, Stephanie, *Breaking the Ice: Emerging Legal Issues in Arctic Sovereignty*, 9 CHI. J. INT'L L. 323 (2008).

Jarashow, Mark, Michael B. Runnels, and Tait Svenson, *UNCLOS and the Arctic: The Path of Least Resistance*, 30 FORDHAM INT'L L.J.1587 (2006).

Jensen, Oystein, *Arctic Shipping Guidelines: Towards a Legal Regime for Navigation Safety and Environmental Protection?*, 44 POLAR REC. 107(2008).

Koivurova, Timo, *Limits and Possibilities of the Arctic Council in a Rapidly Changing Scene of Arctic Governance*, 46 POLAR REC. 146 (2010).

Suggestions for Further Reading

Koivurova, Timo and David Vanderzwaag, *The Arctic Council at 10 Years: Retrospect and Prospects*, 40 U. OF BRITISH COLUMBIA L. REV. 121 (2007).

Koivurova, Timo, *Environmental Protection in the Arctic and Antarctic: Can the Polar Regimes Learn From Each Other?*, 33 INT'L J. OF LEGAL INFO. 204 (2005).

Lennon, Erika, *A Tale of Two Poles: A Comparative Look at the Legal Regimes in the Arctic and the Antarctic*, 8 SUSTAINABLE DEV. L. & POL'Y 32 (2007).

Pharand, Donat, *The Arctic Waters and the Northwest Passage: A Final Revisit*, 38 OCEAN DEV. & INT'L L. 3 (2007).

Rayfuse, Rosemary, *Protecting Marine Biodiversity in Polar Areas Beyond National Jurisdiction*, 17 REV. OF EUROPEAN COMMUNITY AND INT'L ENVTL. L. 3 (2008).

Rothwell, Donald *The Arctic in International Law: Time for a New Regime?* (2008) (ANU College of Law Research Paper 08-37).

Young, Oran, R. *Arctic in Play: Governance in a Time of Rapid Change*, 24 INT'L J. OF MARINE & COASTAL L. 423 (2009).

Chapter 10: The Environmental Responsibility of Non-State Actors

Baughn, C. Christopher and John C. McIntosh, *Corporate Social and Environmental Responsibility in Asian Countries and Other Geographical Regions*, 14 CORP. SOC. RESP. & ENVTL. MGMT. 189 (2007).

Bernstein, Steven, *Legitimacy in Global Environmental Governance*, 1 J. OF INT'L L. & INT'L REL. 139 (2004).

Betsill, Michele Merrill and Elizabeth Corell, eds., *NGO Diplomacy: The Influence of Nongovernmental Organizations in International Environmental Negotiations* (Cambridge, MA: The MIT Press, 2008).

Carrasco, Enrique R. and Alison K. Guernsey, *The World Bank's Inspection Panel: Promoting True Accountability Through Arbitration*, 41 CORNELL INT'L L.J. 594 (2008).

Cashore, Benjamin, et al., *Can Non-State Governance 'Ratchet Up' Global Environmental Standards? Lessons from the Forest Sector*, 16 REV. OF EUROPEAN COMMUNITY & INT'L ENVTL. L. 158 (2007).

Cashore, Benjamin, *Legitimacy and the Privatization of Environmental Governance: How Non — State Market — Driven (NSMD) Governance Systems Gain Rule-Making Authority*, 15 GOVERNANCE 503 (2002).

Clapp, Jennifer, *Global Environmental Governance for Corporate Responsibility and Accountability*, 5 GLOBAL ENVTL. POL. 23 (2005).

Clark, Dana, Jonathan A. Fox, and Kay Treakle, eds. *Demanding Accountability: Civil-Society Claims and the World Bank Inspection Panel* (Lanham, MD: Rowman & Littlefield, 2003).

Fisher, Dana R. and Jessica F. Green, *Understanding Disenfranchisement: Civil Society and Developing Countries' Influence and Participation in Global Governance for Sustainable Development*, 4(3) GLOBAL ENVTL. POL. 65 (2004).

Gemmill, Barbara, and Abimbola Bamidele-Izu, "The Role of NGOs and Civil Society in Global Environmental Governance." *Global Environmental Governance: Options & Opportunities*. Eds. D. C. Esty and M. H. Ivanova (New Haven, CT: Yale Center for Environmental Law and Policy, 2002).

Glasbergen, Pieter, Frank Biermann, and Arthur PJ Mol, eds., *Partnerships, Gover-*

nance and Sustainable Development: Reflections on Theory and Practice (Edward Elgar Publishing, 2007).

Gutner, Tamar, *Explaining the Gaps Between Mandate and Performance: Agency Theory and World Bank Environmental Reform*, 5 GLOBAL ENVTL. POL. 10 (2005).

Hale, Thomas, "World Bank Inspection Panel." *The Handbook of Transnational Governance: Institutions and Innovations*. Eds. Thomas Hale and David Held (Hoboken, NJ: Wiley, 2011).

Heledd Jenkins and Natalia Yakovleva, *Corporate Social Responsibility in the Mining Industry: Exploring Trends in Social and Environmental Disclosure*, 14 J. OF CLEANER PRODUCTION 271 (2006).

Levy, David Laurence, and Peter John Newell, eds., *The Business of Global Environmental Governance* (Cambridge, MA: The MIT Press, 2005).

Melnyk, Steven A. Robert P. Sroufe, and Roger Calantone, *Assessing the Impact of Environmental Management Systems on Corporate and Environmental Performance*, 21 J. OF OPERATIONS MGMT. 329 (2003).

Nielson, Daniel L. and Michael J. Tierney, *Delegation to International Organizations: Agency Theory and World Bank Environmental Reform*, 57 INT'L ORG. 241 (2003).

Oldenziel, Joris, Joseph Wilde-Ramsing, and Patricia Feeney, *10 Years on: Assessing the Contribution of the OECD Guidelines for Multinational Enterprises to Responsible Business Conduct* (Paris: OECD Watch, 2010).

Prakash, Aseem and Matthew Potoski, *Racing to the Bottom? Trade, Environmental Governance, and ISO 14001* , 50 AM. J. OF POL. SCI. 350 (2006).

Prakash, Aseem and Matthew Potoski, *Investing Up: FDI and the Cross-Country Diffusion of ISO 14001 Management Systems*, 51 INT'L STUD. Q. 723 (2007).

Table of Contents

Table of Contents

Table of Contents

Table of Contents

Table of Contents

Table of Contents

Table of Contents

Table of Contents

Table of Contents

Table of Contents

Table of Contents

Table of Contents

Table of Contents

Table of Contents

Table of Contents

Table of Contents

Table of Contents

Table of Contents

Chapter 1

INTRODUCTION AND BACKGROUND

Section I. INTERNATIONAL ENVIRONMENTAL LAW DEFINED

Rather than an autonomous subject of the law, international environmental law is most properly regarded as an important branch of the larger topic of public international law, as the application of public international law concepts and methods to international environmental problems. Public international law is commonly defined as the sets of legal rules and concepts that apply to the relations between nation-states and intergovernmental organizations, as well as international rules that apply to individuals and legal persons. Thus, international environmental law can be defined as the body of international legal rules, institutions, and concepts that apply or touch upon the protection or use of natural resources as well as the broader global environment, such as the oceans and the atmosphere, and that govern the relations between states and other subjects of international law in addressing international environmental problems.

Despite the fact that we define international environmental law as the application of public international law to international environmental problems, we believe that it is appropriate to study international environmental law as a distinct subject because of the latter subject's special characteristics and the sheer volume of international instruments and institutions concerned with aspects of the international environment. In addition, the history of the development of international environmental law is quite unique; we recount this history in the next section.

Section II. THE HISTORY AND DEVELOPMENT OF INTERNATIONAL ENVIRONMENTAL LAW

A. The Beginning: 1972 to 1992

International Environmental Law, the application of international law to global and transboundary environmental problems, is one of the newest branches of the field of Public International Law. It is quite remarkable how quickly the international law of the environment has developed. As recently as the 1960s, there were only a few dozen multilateral agreements addressing environmental problems; and most of these instruments dealt with ocean resources or particular endangered species of birds and animals. States lacked adequate national laws to deal even with domestic environmental degradation, and lawyers were unfamiliar with the terms "environment" and "ecology." As late as 1989, no index of any leading treatise or casebook on Public International Law contained any mention of the words "environment" or "pollution."[1]

Although scholars[2] trace the beginning of international environmental law to the *Bering Sea Fur-Seals Case (Great Britain v. United States)*[3] in 1898, the modern beginning of international environmental law can be traced to the 1972 Stockholm Conference on the Human Environments, convened by the United Nations' General Assembly.[4] The Stockholm Conference adopted three landmark non-binding instruments: a resolution on desirable new institutional and financial arrangements that ultimately led to the founding of the United Nations' Environmental Programme (UNEP); a declaration of guiding environmental principles; and an Action Plan setting forth 109 substantive recommendations for specific international actions to protect the environment.[5] These three documents were seminal; the United Nations' Environment Programme (UNEP) was established by the United Nations' General Assembly[6] in 1972, the first international institution to have a mandate specifically to enhance and to protect the global environment.

We set forth the most influential part of the Stockholm Conference, the Declaration of Principles. As we shall see in Chapter 2 of this book, many of these non-binding principles have developed into legal norms with binding effect. Here we offer only an historical treatment of this important declaration.

DECLARATION OF THE UNITED NATIONS CONFERENCE ON THE HUMAN ENVIRONMENT
U.N. Doc. A/CONF.48/14/Rev.1 (Stockholm, 5–16 June 1972), pp. 3–5

The United Nations Conference on the Human Environment,

Having met at Stockholm from 5 to 16 June 1972,

Having considered the need for a common outlook and for common principles to inspire and guide the peoples of the world in the preservation and enhancement of the human environment,

---

[1] Philippe Sands, *Environment, Community and International Law*, 30 Harv. Int'l L.J. 393, 394 n.3 (1989).

[2] *See* Philippe Sands, *Environmental Protection in the Twenty-First Century: Sustainable Development and International Law*, in Norman J. Vig & Regina S. Axelrod (eds.), The Global Environment: Institutions, Law and Policy 116m 123 (1999).

[3] 1 Moore's Int'l Arb. Awards 755, reprinted in 1 Envtl L. Rep. 43 (1999). This arbitration led to a landmark treaty: Treaty for the Preservations and Protection of Fur Seals (Washington D.C., 1911).

[4] G.A. Res. 2398 (XXIII) (Dec. 3, 1968).

[5] U.N. Doc. A/Conf.48/14 (July 3, 1972).

[6] G.A. Res. 2995 (Dec. 15, 1972).

I

Proclamation

Proclaims that:

1. Man is both a creature and a molder of his environment, which gives him physical sustenance and affords him the opportunity for intellectual, moral, social and spiritual growth. In the long and tortuous evolution of the human race on this planet a stage has been reached when, through the rapid acceleration of science and technology, man has acquired the power to transform his environment in countless ways and on an unprecedented scale. Both aspects of man's environment, the natural and the man-made, are essential to his well-being and to the enjoyment of basic human rights — even the right to life itself.

2. The protection and improvement of the human environment is a major issue which affects the well-being of peoples and economic development throughout the world; it is the urgent desire of the peoples of the whole world and the duty of all Governments.

*   *   *

4. In developing countries most of the environmental problems are caused by under-development. Millions continue to live far below the minimum levels required for a decent human existence, deprived of adequate food and clothing, shelter and education, health and sanitation. Therefore, the developing countries must direct their efforts to development, bearing in mind their priorities and the need to safeguard and improve the environment. For the same purpose, the industrialized countries should make efforts to reduce the gap between themselves and the developing countries. In the industrialized countries, environmental problems are generally related to industrialization and technological development.

5. The natural growth of population continuously presents problems for the preservation of the environment, and adequate policies and measures should be adopted, as appropriate, to face these problems. Of all things in the world, people are the most precious. It is the people that propel social progress, create social wealth, develop science and technology and, through their hard work, continuously transform the human environment. Along with social progress and the advance of production, science and technology, the capability of man to improve the environment increases with each passing day.

*   *   *

7. To achieve this environmental goal will demand the acceptance of responsibility by citizens and communities and by enterprises and institutions at every level; all sharing equitably in common efforts. Individuals in all walks of life as well as organizations in many fields, by their values and the sum of their actions, will shape the world environment of the future. Local and national governments will bear the greatest burden for large-scale environmental policy and action within their jurisdictions. International co-operation is also needed in order to raise resources to support the developing countries in carrying out their responsibilities in this field.

A growing class of environmental problems, because they are regional or global in extent or because they affect the common international realm, will require extensive co-operation among nations and action by international organizations in the common interest. The Conference calls upon Governments and peoples to exert common efforts for the preservation and improvement of the human environment, for the benefit of all the people and for their posterity.

II

Principles

The Conference states the common conviction that:

Principle 1

Man has the fundamental right to freedom, equality and adequate conditions of life, in an environment of a quality that permits a life of dignity and well-being, and he bears a solemn responsibility to protect and improve the environment for present and future generations. In this respect, policies promoting or perpetuating *apartheid*, racial segregation, discrimination, colonial and other forms of oppression and foreign domination stand condemned and must be eliminated.

Principle 2

The natural resources of the earth, including the air, water, land, flora and fauna and especially representative samples of natural ecosystems, must be safeguarded for the benefit of present and future generations through careful planning or management, as appropriate.

Principle 3

The capacity of the earth to produce vital renewable resources must be maintained and, wherever practicable, restored or improved.

Principle 4

Man has a special responsibility to safeguard and wisely manage the heritage of wildlife and its habitat, which are now gravely imperiled by a combination of adverse factors. Nature conservation, including wildlife, must therefore receive importance in planning for economic development.

Principle 5

The non-renewable resources of the earth must be employed in such a way as to guard against the danger of their future exhaustion and to ensure that benefits from such employment are shared by all mankind.

* * *

Principle 8

Economic and social development is essential for ensuring a favourable living and working environment for man and for creating conditions on earth that are necessary for the improvement of the quality of life.

Principle 9

Environmental deficiencies generated by the conditions of under-development and natural disasters pose grave problems and can best be remedied by accelerated development through the transfer of substantial quantities of financial and technological assistance as a supplement to the domestic effort of the developing countries and such timely assistance as may be required.

*   *   *

Principle 11

The environmental policies of all States should enhance and not adversely affect the present or future development potential of developing countries, nor should they hamper the attainment of better living conditions for all, and appropriate steps should be taken by States and international organizations with a view to reaching agreement on meeting the possible national and international economic consequences resulting from the application of environmental measures.

Principle 12

Resources should be made available to preserve and improve the environment, taking into account the circumstances and particular requirements of developing countries and any costs which may emanate from their incorporating environmental safeguards into their development planning and the need for making available to them, upon their request, additional international technical and financial assistance for this purpose.

Principle 13

In order to achieve a more rational management of resources and thus to improve the environment, States should adopt an integrated and co-ordinated approach to their development planning so as to ensure that development is compatible with the need to protect and improve environment for the benefit of their population.

*   *   *

Principle 16

Demographic policies which are without prejudice to basic human rights and which are deemed appropriate by Governments concerned should be applied in those regions where the rate of population growth or excessive population concentrations are likely to have adverse effects on the environment of the human environment and impede development.

* * *

Principle 20

Scientific research and development in the context of environmental problems, both national and multinational, must be promoted in all countries, especially the developing countries. In this connexion, the free flow of up-to-date scientific information and transfer or experience must be supported and assisted, to facilitate the solution of environmental problems; environmental technologies should be made available to developing countries on terms which would encourage their wide dissemination without constituting an economic burden on the developing countries.

Principle 21

States have, in accordance with the Charter of the United Nations and the principles of international law, the sovereign right to exploit their own resources pursuant to their own environmental policies, and the responsibility to ensure that activities within their jurisdiction or control do not cause damage to the environment of other States or of areas beyond the limits of national jurisdiction.

Principle 22

States shall co-operate to develop further the international law regarding liability and compensation for the victims of pollution and other environmental damage caused by activities within the jurisdiction or control of such States and to areas beyond their jurisdiction.

Principle 23

Without prejudice to such criteria as may be agreed upon by the international community, or to standards which will have to be determined nationally, it will be essential in all cases to consider the systems of values prevailing in each country, and the extent of the applicability of standards which are valid for the most advanced countries but which may be inappropriate and of unwarranted social cost for the developing countries.

Principle 24

International matters concerning the protection and improvement of the environment should be handled in a co-operative spirit by all countries, big and small, on an equal footing. Co-operation through multilateral or bilateral arrangements or other appropriate means is essential to effectively control, prevent, reduce and eliminate adverse environmental effects resulting from activities conducted in all spheres, in such a way that due account is taken of the sovereignty and interests of all States.

Principle 25

States shall ensure that international organizations play a coordinated, efficient and dynamic role for the protection and improvement of the environment.

NOTES AND QUESTIONS

1. ***Human rights and the environment.*** Note that Principle 1 of the Stockholm Declaration is phrased in terms of human rights. Despite the brevity and ambiguity of Principle 1, it marks the beginning of a human rights approach to protection of the environment. Principle 1 has helped promote the enactment of environmental amendments to constitutions of states all over the world. At present, by the authors' count, some 93 states have enacted environmental rights' constitutional provisions in their national constitutions. *See* Constitutions of the Countries of the World (Gilbert H. Flanz, ed), 21 looseleaf volumes (Oceana Publications, 1971 to present). In subsequent chapters of this book we cover human rights and the environment in more detail. Principle 1 has influenced lawyers and courts to create a lively jurisprudence concerning the relationship between human rights and the protection of the environment.

2. ***Mankind's duties to protect environmental quality.*** Principles 2 to 5 declare that mankind has certain duties and responsibilities to protect the environment. This part of the declaration emphasizes wise resource management and influenced the development of the principle of intergenerational equity: that present generations must ensure the environmental quality of future generations.

3. ***Developing countries and protection of the environment.*** Principles 8, 9, 11, 12, 13, 20, and 23 concern the role of developing countries and environmental protection. Developing countries voiced several concerns about the global initiative to protect the environment: first, they voiced fears that the developed world would use protection of the environment to inhibit their development by placing environmental conditions on international aid programs; second they questioned whether environmental quality standards would be used as a protectionist device to limit imports of products and services from developing countries; third, they resented the fact that developing countries were not given an adequate role in decisions concerning the new field of international environmental protection. At the 1972 Stockholm Conference, Indira Ghandi, the Prime Minister of India, stated that "we do not wish to impoverish the environment any further and yet we cannot forget for a moment the grim poverty of large numbers of people. Are not poverty and need the greatest polluters? . . . When [people] themselves feel deprived, how can we urge the preservation of animals? How can we speak to those who live in villages and in slums about keeping the oceans, rivers and the air clean when their own lives are contaminated at the source?"[7] Martin Khor of the Third World Network also argued that "the North is historically primarily responsible for depleting and polluting the world's resources and therefore should take a correspondingly major

---

[7] Ghandi, *Life Is One and the World Is One*, Environment Stockholm (1972), reprinted in *The Unfinished Revolution*, 28 Bulletin of the Atomic Sciences 35, 36 (1972).

responsibility in bearing the costs of adjustment."[8] The disagreements between developing countries and the developed world as well as attempted reconciliation efforts will be a continuing theme in this book.

4.   *The "Harm Prevention Principle."* Principle 21 is termed the "harm prevention principle" and has had a major influence on international environmental law. We cover this development in Chapter 2.

5.   *The "Further Development" Principle*. Principle 22 looks to the further development of international laws relating to liability and compensation for pollution damage. This principle has inspired the development of extensive new legal regimes on state and individual responsibility for transboundary pollution damage and pollution of areas beyond national jurisdiction. We cover this law in Chapters 3 and 6.

6.   *The duty to cooperate*. Principles 24 and 25 set out a duty to cooperate among states and including international organizations to solve international environmental problems.

As the following extract from a 1995 Report to the UN Commission on Sustainable Development explains, the *duty to cooperate* contains additional implicit principles:

> The duty of States to cooperate is well-established, as exemplified by . . . the UN Charter and the UN Declaration on Principles of International Law. It applies on the global, regional and bilateral levels and often requires prior information, consultation and negotiation. The principle of global partnership can be seen as a more recent reformulation of the obligation to cooperate.

*   *   *

> The principle of cooperation in the spirit of global partnership not only refers to cooperation among States, but should also be extended to non-State entities, ranging from business associations through non-governmental organizations to the academic world.

> The principle of duty to cooperate in the spirit of global partnership can be subdivided into three major components: (a) common concern of humankind; (b) common but differentiated responsibilities; and (c) special treatment of developing countries, including small island developing States and countries with economies in transition.

> a. Common concern of humankind

> The notion of common concern on the part of the international community, and of States as its principal actors, has traditional roots. It found its original expression in various forms, like common interest and international concern, in fields such as the protection of human rights and self-determination of peoples. The foundation of the concept is the recognition

---

[8] Martin Khor, *The North South Battles That Dominate Earth Summit*, EARTH SUMMIT BRIEFINGS 1 (Third World Network, 1992).

of a legitimate interest of the international community to concern itself with certain issues and values which, by their nature, affect the community as a whole. The scientifically-based reality of ecological interdependence, and the concomitant recognition of the global nature of environmental problems, made it only a logical step to apply the concept of common concern to the environment of the planet, or elements thereof.

The concept of the common concern of humankind might signal that the protection of the global environment can no longer be considered to be solely within the competence of individual sovereign nations. The concept could imply the right and duty of the international community, and thus of each State, to act in a manner which reflects this concern.

*   *   *

b. Common but differentiated responsibilities

. . . [T]his principle recognizes that States have common but differentiated responsibilities in the context of the different contributions to global environmental degradation. States whose societies impose a disproportionate pressure on the global environment and which command high levels of technological and financial resources, bear a proportionally higher degree of responsibility in the international pursuit of sustainable development.

In practical terms, the principle of common but differentiated responsibilities is translated into the explicit recognition that different standards, delayed compliance time tables or less stringent commitments may be appropriate for different groups of countries.

*   *   *

c. Special treatment of developing countries, small island developing States and countries with economies in transition

. . . The principle of the special treatment of developing countries finds its elaboration in the principle of global partnership and in the recognition of the differentiated responsibilities among countries.

*   *   *

The special situation of developing countries, necessitates the transfer of technology and of financial resources to them, and the strengthening of capacity-building within them. This has been recognized by several conventions.

*   *   *

The category of States with economies in transition emerged on the international agenda after the reorganization of the former Soviet Union at the end of the 1980s . . . , at which time [the international community] recognized their specific environmental and economic problems, including high levels of industrialization, outdated technologies, inefficient and wasteful production patterns, extreme pollution levels in heavily industrialized areas, and widespread public health problems. This led to a special provision in the Climate Change Convention providing "a certain degree of flexibility" in "implementing" particular commitments under the Convention.

It can be argued that the principle of special treatment of countries with economies in transition is not well defined and does not imply substantial rights for preferential treatment. The "competitive advantage" of economies in transition appears to be not so much preferential legal rights as a significant potential for investment opportunities to achieve environmental improvements.

United Nations Commission on Sustainable Development, *Report of the Expert Group Meeting on Identification of Principles of International Law for Sustainable Development*, Geneva, Switzerland, 26–28 September 1995, Background Paper Prepared by the Division for Sustainable Development for the Commission on Sustainable Development Fourth Session 18 April–3 May 1996, New York.

THE DEVELOPMENT OF INTERNATIONAL ENVIRONMENTAL LAW BETWEEN THE STOCKHOLM CONFERENCE AND THE UNITED NATIONS CONFERENCE ON ENVIRONMENT AND DEVELOPMENT (1992)

The 1972 Stockholm Conference and the founding of UNEP acted as catalysts for new initiatives to develop international environmental law. The most important of the many initiatives during this time are the following:

1. *1978 UNEP Draft Principles of Conduct in the Field of Environment.* In 1962, the United Nations General Assembly had approved a landmark resolution declaring that States have "sovereign rights" over the natural resources within their borders. See General Assembly Resolution on Permanent Sovereignty over Natural Resources, G.A. Res. 1803 (XVII), 17 U.N. GAOR Supp. (No. 17) at 15, U.N. Doc. A/5217 (1962). (Reprinted in the **Document Supplement**). In 1978, the United Nations Environment Programme (UNEP) followed this up with the UNEP Draft Principles of Conduct in the Field of the Environment for the Guidance of States in the Conservation and Harmonious Utilization of Natural Resources Shared by Two or More States ("the Draft Principles"). (Reprinted in the **Document Supplement**). These Draft Principles represent an important contribution to the development of norms governing transboundary resources. The Draft Principles were developed by a UNEP Intergovernmental Working Group of 17 States, which was later expanded to include 28 States. See UNEP Docs., UNEP/IG.2/4 and UNEP/IG.10/2. UNEP was able to overcome strong resistance by states to the Draft Principles by agreement that the Principles would consist of non-legally binding recommendations, but without prejudicing the ability of the Draft Principles to become binding as it gained acceptance through subsequent practice. *See* Andronico Adede, *United Nations Efforts Toward the Development of an Environmental Code of Conduct for States Concerning Harmonious Utilization of Shared Natural Resources*, 43 ALB. L. REV. 488, 492, 512 (1979).

The final document, adopted by consensus by the UNEP Governing Council (even though Brazil, Colombia and Mexico declared they were unable to join the consensus), contains 15 draft principles. UNEP Doc. UNEP/IG.12 UNEP, reprinted in 1 INT'L LEGAL MATERIALS 1091 (1978), adopted by UNEP Governing Council Decision 6/14, U.N. GAOR, 33d Sess., Supp. 25, at 154, U.N. Doc. A/33/25 (1978), noted in G.A. Res. 186, U.N. GAOR, 34th Sess., Supp. 46, at 128, U.N. Doc. A/34/46 (1980). Despite the contention surrounding the adoption of the 15 Draft Principles, with the benefit of hindsight it is easy to discern how they anticipate the principles that would be agreed to in later international instruments. Principles 1 and 2 elaborate the duty of states to "cooperate", including through "bilateral and multicultural agreements", with a view "to controlling, preventing, reducing or eliminating adverse environmental effects" that may result from the "use of transboundary resources." Principle 3 broadly tracks Principle 21 of the Stockholm Declaration and provides for explicit application in connection with transboundary resources.

Principle 4 anticipates international developments in the late 1980s and 1990s in connection with environmental impact assessment by indicating that states should, "before engaging in any activity with respect to a shared natural resource", assess "risk[s] . . . significantly affecting the environment" within a state, of another state or states sharing the transboundary resource. Principles 5 and 6 set out duties of information of exchange, consultation and notification, which are, under Principle 7, to be carried out in "good faith and in the spirit of good neighbourliness." Principles 8, 9, and 10 elaborate principles on scientific studies, emergency action, and services of international organizations. Settlement of disputes and state responsibility and liability in connection with transboundary resources are governed by Principles 11 and 12. Principle 13 deals with non-discrimination in environmental decision-making and Principle 14 provides for equal rights of access to judicial and administrative proceedings of non-nationals. Principle 15 addresses the link between environment and development by providing that the Draft Principles "should be interpreted in such a way as to enhance and not to affect adversely development . . ." In 1980, the U.N. General Assembly adopted G.A. Resolution 35/48 (reprinted in the **Document Supplement**) on the Historical Responsibility of States for the Preservation of Nature for Present and Future Generations (30 Oct. 1980), which declares the responsibility of States to preserve natural resources for future generations.

2. *UNEP Programme for the Development and Periodic Review of Environmental Law (Montevideo Programme).* From the beginning the development of international environmental law was high on the agenda of UNEP. A major advance in this regard was the so-called Montevideo Programme launched by UNEP. In a speech delivered in October 2001, Shafqat Kakakhel, Deputy Executive Director of UNEP, outlined the inception and subsequent development of UNEP's influential Montevideo Programme as follows:

> In 1981, a group of senior government officials, experts in environmental law, representing Governments from around the world, met in Montevideo to develop a long-term, strategic guidance for UNEP in the field of environmental law. The resulting work was adopted by the Governing Council of UNEP in 1982 and became the Montevideo Programme for the Development and Periodic Review of Environmental Law.

The Montevideo Programme has a particular focus on enhancing the effectiveness of environmental law, addressing the following areas: Implementation, Compliance and Enforcement; Capacity-building; Prevention and Mitigation of Environmental Damage; Avoidance and Settlement of International Environmental Disputes; Development of International Environmental Law; Harmonization and Coordination; Public Participation and Access to Information; Information Technology; and Innovative Approaches to Environmental Law. The Montevideo Programme also addresses certain topical issues: fresh water resources; coastal and marine ecosystems; soils; forests: biological diversity; pollution prevention and control; production and consumption patterns; environmental emergencies and natural disasters. In addition, the Programme covers certain related fields, including: trade; security and the environment; and military activities and the environment.

Under the Montevideo Programme, a number of global environmental conventions have been developed under UNEP's auspices. These include the 1985 Vienna Convention for the Protections of the Ozone Layer, the 1987 Montreal Protocol on Substances that Deplete the Ozone Layer, the 1989 Basel Convention on the Control of Transboundary Movements of Hazardous Wastes and Their Disposal, the 1992 Convention on Biological Diversity, the 1998 Rotterdam Convention on the Prior Informed Consent Procedure for Certain Hazardous Chemicals and Pesticides in International Trade, and the 2001 Stockholm Convention on Persistent Organic Pollutants.

Shafqat Kakakhel, *The Role of International Organizations in the Development of Environmental Law: A Case of UNEP*, remarks given at the International Conference on International Law in the New Millennium: Problems and Challenges Ahead (New Delhi, 4–7 October 2001). For the full text of the Montevideo Programme, see Programme for the Development and Periodic Review of Environmental Law for the First Decade of the Twenty-first Century, as set out in annex I to the report of the Meeting of Senior Government Officials Expert in Environmental Law to Prepare a Programme of Work for the Development and Periodic Review of Environmental Law for the First Decade of the Twenty-first Century, UNEP Doc. UNEP/Env.Law/4/4, Annex I, adopted by UNEP Governing Council Decision 23/23 (9 February 2001).

3. *World Charter for Nature.* In September 1975 Mobutu Sese Seko, the President of Zaire, speaking at the 12th General Assembly of the International Union for the Conservation of Nature (IUCN), made a challenge and an offer to those gathered from around the world. The President said: "the seas, the oceans, the upper atmosphere belong to the human community. . . . One cannot freely overuse [such] international resources. . . . That is why if I had any advice for you, I would suggest the establishment of a Charter of Nature. . . . Insofar as Zaire is concerned, we are ready to help you succeed. . . . If we were asked to be a pilgrim for environmental protection, this we would be willing to be." WOLFGANG E. BURHENNE AND WILL A. IRWIN, THE WORLD CHARTER FOR NATURE: A BACKGROUND PAPER 14 (Erich Schmidt Verlag, 1983).

The IUCN accepted the challenge and appointed a task force of members of its Commission on Environmental Law and independent experts to elaborate such a Charter for Nature. Taking the Universal Declaration of Human Rights as a model, the task force worked through meetings and correspondence to produce a draft Charter for consideration by the 1978 IUCN General Assembly and subsequently by all of IUCN's membership. In November 1979, the IUCN transmitted the final Draft Charter to the President of Zaire for his consideration. In June 1980, Zaire's Permanent Representative to the United Nations transmitted the Draft World Charter for Nature to the U.N. Secretary-General with a request that it be included on the agenda of the 35th Session of the General Assembly. In October 1980, the General Assembly adopted a resolution inviting member states to send their views on the Draft Charter to the Secretary-General. U.N.G.A. Res. 35/7 (30 October 1980). Comments were received from 50 states and, interestingly, the Draft Charter was strongly supported by developing countries in a marked change from the hesitant environmental position of many developing states at the 1972 Stockholm Conference. (Ibid., at 14–15).

In 1982, the U.N. General Assembly adopted the World Charter for Nature (reprinted in the **Document Supplement**), which sets forth "principles of conservation by which all human conduct affecting nature is to be guided and judged." U.N.G.A. Res. 37/7 (28 October 1982), *reprinted in* 23 INT'L LEGAL MATERIALS 455 (1983). The Charter was adopted by a vote of 111 in favor, 18 abstentions, and 1 vote against (the United States). As Professor Sands has observed: "[t]he Charter . . . is a non-binding instrument drafted in general language, which lessens the likelihood that it, or parts of it, could crystallize into rules of customary law." PHILIPPE SANDS, PRINCIPLES OF INTERNATIONAL ENVIRONMENTAL LAW 42 (Vol. I) (Manchester Univ. Press, 1995). Even so, as Sands comments, many of the provisions of the World Charter for Nature are now reflected in treaties and are, to that extent, normatively binding. Id. at 43. Moreover, given that: (i) the Universal Declaration on Human Rights served as the model for the World Charter, (ii) the Universal Declaration was drafted in similar broad terms, and (iii) it subsequently went on to become in large part customary international law, the following comments of Professor Richard Falk bear consideration:

> . . . [T]he original articulation of international human rights in the form of the Universal Declaration of Human Rights . . . was not *initially* perceived to be a significant development . . . . This enumeration of [human rights] standards was at most conceived as an admonishment to governments, and more relevantly, as a kind of heterogeneous wish list . . . . In effect, at birth the Declaration amounted to a rather innocuous and syncretic statement of consensus about desirable social goals and future aspirations for humanity as a whole. . . . Also, it should be appreciated that by using the language of "declaration" and by avoiding all pretensions of implementation, a clear signal was given that the contents were not to be treated as . . . authoritative and binding.

RICHARD A. FALK, HUMAN RIGHTS HORIZONS: THE PURSUIT OF JUSTICE IN A GLOBALIZING WORLD 37–38 (Routledge, 2000). The same could largely be said of the World Charter for Nature in an environmental context. Only time will tell whether the Charter will turn out to be the same sort of polar star as the Universal Declaration has been in international affairs. For a cogent analysis of the normative status of the Universal Declaration see OSCAR SCHACHTER, INTERNATIONAL LAW IN THEORY AND PRACTICE 336–339 (Martinus-Nijhoff Publishers, 1991).

4. *World Conservation Strategy (1980)/Caring for the Earth (1991).* These two influential documents, one published in 1980 and the other in 1991, were the result of ongoing collaboration between the IUCN, UNEP, and the Worldwide Fund for Nature (WWF). The 1980 World Conservation Strategy (WCS) was designed to demonstrate to policy makers and the general public "that development — the satisfaction of human needs and the improvement of the quality of human life — depends upon conservation, and that conservation depends equally upon development. The Strategy aims to help advance the achievement of sustainable development through the conservation of living resources." DAVID A. MUNRO, PREFACE IN ROBERT ALLEN, HOW TO SAVE THE WORLD: STRATEGY FOR WORLD CONSERVATION 9 (Barnes and Noble Books, 1980). Accordingly, the WCS helped to further establish the concept of sustainable development on the international agenda. The WCS also led to the preparation of national and subnational conservation strategies in over fifty states. *See e.g.,* J.F. Garner, *World Conservation Strategy* (Great Britain), [1983] J. PLAN. & ENVTL L. 580; *A National Conservation Strategy for Australia* (Australian Government Publishing Service, 1984).

The three prime objectives of the WCS were: "(a) to maintain essential ecological processes and life support systems, (b) to preserve genetic diversity, and (c) to ensure the sustainable utilization of species and ecosystems." WORLD CONSERVATION STRATEGY: LIVING RESOURCE CONSERVATION FOR SUSTAINABLE DEVELOPMENT (IUCN, UNEP, WWF, 1980). Professor Lynton Caldwell succinctly details the WCS as follows:

> The World Conservation Strategy as a published document is essentially a statement of goals and targets. Divided into three categories, the first states the objectives of conservation and the requirements for their achievement; the second lists the priorities for international action. Under the international category, the document specifies a need for developments in law and international assistance, for programs specifically directed toward tropical forests and arid lands, for a global program for the protection of genetic resource areas (such as biosphere reserves), and, finally, for priorities for the international commons. . . . Strategies at the regional level were advocated for international river basins and seas . . . , and regional arrangements and priorities for sustainable development . . . were recommended. . . .

LYNTON K. CALDWELL (WITH PAUL WEILAND), INTERNATIONAL ENVIRONMENTAL POLICY: FROM THE TWENTIETH TO TWENTY-FIRST CENTURY 343 (Duke Univ. Press, 3d ed., 1996). For further information about the WCS see Thomas E. Lovejoy, *A Strategy for Survival*, 8 UNITERRA 6 (Sept/Oct, 1980); *A World Conservation Strategy*, 33 UNESCO COURIER 36 (May 1980). *See also* ROBERT ALLEN, HOW TO SAVE THE WORLD; STRATEGY FOR WORLD CONSERVATION (Barnes and Nobel Books 1980) for an expanded version of the WCS published for a general readership.

The 1991 Caring for the Earth (CFE) was designed to "restate current thinking about conservation and development," to "extend and emphasize the message of the

World Conservation Strategy" and to serve as a "Second World Conservation Strategy Project" through a wider process of consultation. CARING FOR THE EARTH: A STRATEGY FOR SUSTAINABLE LIVING II, 1, 3 (IUCN, UNEP, WWF, October 1991).

5. *The World Commission on Environment and Development: the "Brundtland" Report and the Report of the Legal Experts Group.* Perhaps the biggest milestone on the "road to Rio" was the 1987 release of the Report (reprinted in part in the **Document Supplement**) prepared by the World Commission on Environment and Development (WCED), commonly known as the Brundtland Report after the Norwegian Prime Minister, Gro Harlem Brundtland, who chaired the WCED. U.N. GAOR, 42d Sess., U.N. Doc. A/42/427, Annex (1987) reprinted as OUR COMMON FUTURE (Oxford Univ. Press, 1987). The Brundtland Report highlights the nature of three interlocking global crises — an environmental crisis, a development crisis, an energy crisis — challenging the ability of the Earth's current population to meet its needs without compromising the ability of future and growing generations to meet their own needs. A major reason why the Brundtland Report met with a universally favorable reception was that it sounded the theme of sustainable development: "[O]nly growth can eliminate poverty. Only growth can create the capacity to solve environmental problems. But growth cannot be based on overexploitation of the resources. . . . It must be managed to enhance the resource base on which [all] countries all depend." Gro Harlem Brundtland, *Global Change and Our Common Future, in* CHERYL SIMON SILVER (WITH RUTH S. DEFRIES), ONE EARTH, ONE FUTURE: OUR CHANGING GLOBAL ENVIRONMENT 150 (National Academy of Sciences, 1990). The Brundtland Report is divided into three parts: Common Concerns, Common Challenges and Common Endeavors. The Brundtland Report was preceded by the publication in 1986, of an influential report of Legal Principles for Environmental Protection and Sustainable Development (reprinted in the **Document Supplement**), adopted by the Experts Group on Environmental Law of the World Commission on Environment and Development, U.N.Doc. WECD/86/23 18-20 June 1986). The Legal Experts Group Report consists of 22 non-binding principles directed to states setting out their duties to protect the environment.

B.   From Rio de Janeiro (1992) to Johannesburg (2002)

The frenzy of activity by international bodies in the wake of the 1972 Stockholm Conference bore fruit when, in 1992, the United Nations General Assembly formally endorsed the Brundtland Report and called for an "Earth Summit" of world leaders: the United Nations Conference on Environment and Development (UNCED). UNCED, which met for two weeks in Rio de Janeiro in June, 1992, was a huge success. UNCED fulfilled its mission to adopt important binding international agreements to combat environmental problems. The success of UNCED established a tradition of convening Earth Summits every 10 years.

We turn to the main developments of the 1992 UNCED Summit.

1. The 1992 United Nations Conference on Environment and Development

On December 22, 1989, the U.N. General Assembly passed a resolution calling for a United Nations Conference on Environment and Development (UNCED). The General Assembly identified nine environmental issues of major concern: (a) the protection of the atmosphere; (b) protection of freshwater resources; (c) protection of the marine environment; (d) protection of land resources; (e) conservation of biological diversity; (f) environmentally sound management of biotechnology; (g) environmentally sound management of wastes; (h) improvement of living and working environments; and (i) protection of human health and improvement of the quality of life. See United Nations Conference on Environment and Development, GA Res. 44/228, 44 UN GAOR Supp. (No. 49) at 151, UN Doc. A/44/49 (1989).

The General Assembly also outlined many complex and broad ranging objectives for UNCED, including: (a) examine the changes in the state of the environment since the 1972 Stockholm Conference; (b) identify strategies for concerted action to deal with major environmental issues; (c) recommend measures to be taken at the national and international levels to protect and enhance the environment through the implementation of policies for sustainable and environmentally sound development; (d) promote the further development of international environmental law; (e) examine ways and means to improve cooperation in environmental protection activities; (f) arrive at specific agreements and commitments to deal with major environmental issues; (g) examine the relationship between environmental degradation and international economic activity; (h) identify ways and means of providing additional financial resources to developing countries for environmentally sound development; (i) recommend effective modalities for favorable access and transfer of environmental technologies; and (j) review the role of the United Nations' system in dealing with the environment. *Ibid.*

The UNCED Conference, (popularly known as the "Earth Summit") met in Rio de Janeiro from June 3 to 14, 1992, including representatives from 178 nations, 115 heads of state, and adopted three non-binding international instruments and three landmark international agreements.

The binding international agreements:

- The United Nations Framework Convention on Climate Change
- The United Nations Convention on Biological Diversity
- The United Nations Convention to Combat Desertification (deferred and opened for signature in 1994).

The non-binding international instruments:

- The Rio Declaration on Environment and Development, a political declaration of a general nature;
- The Non-legally Binding Authoritative Statement of Principles for a Global Consensus on the Management, Conservation and Sustainable Development of All Types of Forests.

- Agenda 21, a voluminous catalogue of recommendations on the most diverse aspects of environmental and developmental policies, comprising a preamble and forty chapters covering nearly 500 pages. These three documents were officially transmitted to the General Assembly of the United Nations, which "endorsed" them by Resolution 47/190 of December 22, 1992.

UNITED NATIONS CONFERENCE ON ENVIRONMENT AND DEVELOPMENT, THE GLOBAL PARTNERSHIP FOR ENVIRONMENT AND DEVELOPMENT: A GUIDE TO AGENDA 21 6–17
(United Nations, Geneva, April 1992) (emphasis omitted)

Agenda 21 is a comprehensive programme of action . . . adopted by Governments at [UNCED]. It provides a blueprint for action in all areas relating to sustainable development of the planet, from 1992 into the 21st Century. Agenda 21 calls for changes in the economic development activities of all human beings — changes that are based on a new understanding of the impact of human behavior on the environment. . . .

Agenda 21 is addressed to Governments, to the agencies, organizations and programmes of the United Nations system, to other intergovernmental and non-governmental organizations, to constituency groups and to the public at large, all of whom must be involved, in various ways, in its implementation. These programmes are grouped around a series of themes, each of which represents an important dimension of an overall strategy for a global transition.

*   *   *

The first theme [of Agenda 21] — Sustainable Development — is the revitalization of growth with sustainability. The causes of most environmental problems in the world have their origins in the development process or in its failures and inadequacies, and — only through better management of this process that these problems can be addressed. Equally, environmental considerations impose new constraints on traditional modes and patterns of development.

*   *   *

The quality of the human condition and hopes for a better future — continue to be diminished in large parts of the world by a combination of poverty, malnutrition, demographic pressures, unemployment, lack of health care, wasteful uses of energy, pollution and degradation of air, water and land resources.

A dual approach of poverty alleviation combined with changes in lifestyles of the rich to those that are less polluting and wasteful is essential to reaching sustainable development. . . .

*   *   *

The fundamental imperative is to achieve sustainable living for people all over the world and for generations to come.

The second theme of Agenda 21 — Just World — entails coordinated actions to reduce substantially and ultimately eradicate poverty worldwide, to ensure healthy and equitable livelihoods, and to achieve in all countries consumption patterns that drastically reduce the deterioration of the environment, while leaving "space" for the growing of economies of the developing world.

*   *   *

The quality of life for humans depends critically on the physical, social and economic conditions of the villages, towns and cities in which they live. Today, some 1.5 billion people live in urban settlements. This number is expected to increase rapidly in the years ahead. . . . A breakdown of urban services, the spread of slums and social decline may well pose the most immediate threat to the environment and human well-being in many countries.

The management of human settlements in a manner that avoids these risks by raising the quality of shelter, water supply, energy and transportation and other service and dealing with the problems of urban pollution and the management of increasing solid wastes and sewage is an essential component of Agenda 21. This third theme, [that] of a Habitable World, is central to ensuring a habitable, healthy, and sustainable living environment for all.

*   *   *

The demands that humans make on resources are in many cases unsustainable, in that these resources are already being depleted at a rapid rate. While changing consumption patterns to more efficient and responsible levels and reducing demographic pressures will contribute to containing some of these demands, it is essential that more environmentally sound ways of utilizing resources be developed to meet society's needs. Renewable resources must be managed, not mined.

*   *   *

The efficient use of resources forms the basis of [Agenda 21's] fourth theme of a Fertile World. These action programmes focus on the urgency to reverse the destruction of renewable resources and to implement strategies for the sustainable use of land, fresh water, biological and genetic resources, biotechnology and energy. This must be done in a manner that raises productivity and meets rising demands on agriculture and forests while ensuring the sustainable management of fragile ecosystems, such as deserts and drought-prone areas, mountain ecosystems, coastal areas and Island States. The central thrust of these Agenda 21 action programmes is to incorporate the multi-sectoral nature of land, water, energy and biotic resource development into socio-economic development, and the multi-interest utilization of these resources for agriculture, forestry, industry, urban development, inland fisheries, transportation, recreation and other activities.

*   *   *

An important component in an overall strategy for resource management relates to strategies and institutional arrangements for ensuring the responsible and fair use of resources outside national boundaries. Regional and global conventions aimed at these ends need to be supported by proactive programmes which give effect to them.

[Agenda 21's] fifth theme of Global and Regional Resources includes action programmes dealing with the atmosphere, oceans and seas, as well as with living marine resources. The global climate and weather, hydrological and carbon cycles, and most physical processes on land are heavily influenced by atmospheric and oceanic process. The Earth's capacity to sustain and nourish life depends primarily on the qualities and composition of its atmosphere. Human activities have now reached the extent to which they are altering the atmosphere's balancing systems that make life on Earth possible. The risks are clearly of critical, perhaps decisive importance to the human future and thus require the application of the precautionary principle.

*   *   *

The use of resources and process of production necessarily generate waste. With rising production and the continuance of wasteful and destructive consumption patterns, economic development at the local, national and global levels could well be overwhelmed by the waste and pollutions it produces. . . .

*   *   *

Reducing waste generation, recycling wastes into productive activities, finding safe ways of disposing the wastes that remain and dealing with illegal trade in hazardous wastes are essential to [Agenda 21's sixth theme of] managing chemicals and waste in a healthy and habitable Clean World.

*   *   *

The above six themes of Agenda 21 form the basis of substantive action programmes designated to foster the sustainable use of natural resources for human development, while ensuring equitable living standards and quality — life in a clean and sustaining environment. An essential ingredient for success and an early realization of these goals is the active and full participation of all relevant groups, including women, youth, indigenous people and their communities, non-governmental organizations, farmers, local authorities, trade unions, business and industry and the science and technological community. . . .

*   *   *

In order to implement Agenda 21, a variety of essential means must be made available to all nations. The integrations of environment and development must be reflected in a reorientation of attitudes, in changes in decision-making and in the data and information systems for planning, implementation and monitoring. . . .

*   *   *

. . . The successful implementation of Agenda 21 will require a substantial flow of new and additional financial resources to developing countries to enable them to achieve environmentally sound and sustainable development and participate fully in international environmental cooperation. Cost estimates of Agenda 21 programme areas should be regarded as indicative rather than as definitive budgets. . . .

Based on individual programme area cost estimate, the new and additional international financing requirement for implementing Agenda 21 comes to an average annual level of $125 billion, if all activities were initiated immediately and implemented fully in the 1993–2000 period. This level of funding would amount to no less that 1 percent of GNP of the developed countries. In addition to this, the expenditure of the national Governments of the developing countries and their private sectors would amount to some $550 billion. . . .

Agenda 21 is an action programme for a sustainable future of the human family. It is a critical step towards ensuring that, within the lifetime of someone born today, the world will become a more just, secure and prosperous habitat for all of humanity. . . . It is based on the premise that sustainable development is not just an option but an imperative, in both environmental and developmental terms, and that while the transition to sustainable development will be difficult, it is entirely feasible. . . .

NOTES

1. *The Global Environment Facility (GEF) and Funding Sustainable Development.* One of the central incentives for developing country support for Agenda 21 was the commitment from donor countries that there would be "new and additional" financial resources made available for financing the "incremental" or additional costs of international environmental protection. *See,* Overview of Agenda 21 and Implementation Mechanisms, U.N. Doc. A/CONF.151/PC/100/Add.1. In 1991, the Global Environmental Facility (GEF) was created as a $1 billion pilot program in the World Bank. In 1994, the GEF became an independent organization with the World Bank supplying administrative services and acting as trustee. The GEF, which derives its funds from developed countries, provides grants and concessional funding to implement the three UNCED conventions and certain other UNEP programs and conventions. As of the end of 2013, GEF has provided $11.5 billion in grants and leveraged some $57 billion in co-financing for 3, 215 projects in 165 countries. In addition, the GEF has made some 16, 030 small grants to community-based organizations totaling $653.2 million. What factors are appropriate for measuring the "incremental costs" that are associated with international environmental actions?

In its original draft version, *Agenda 21* contained an estimated cost of implementing every Chapter. *See Draft Agenda 21, reprinted in* NICHOLAS A. ROBINSON, ED., I AGENDA 21 & THE UNCED PROCEEDINGS 59–613 (Oceana Publications, 1992). The total cost of implementing *Agenda 21* in developing countries was then estimated to be $600 billion annually to the year 2000. Donor countries, however, finally prevailed in having these costs deleted from the final version of the text.

2. *The Commission on Sustainable Development.* The Commission on Sustainable Development (CSD) was created in December 1993 to ensure effective follow-up of UNCED and to monitor and report on implementation of the Earth Summit agreements at the local, national, regional, and international levels. U.N. Doc. E/1993/207 (12 February 1993). The CSD is a functional commission of the UN Economic and Social Council (ECOSOC), with 51 members. Its Herculean roles and responsibilities were set out by the U.N. General Assembly in requesting ECOSOC

to create the Commission. *See* Resolution on Institutional Arrangements to Follow-Up the United Nations Conference on Environment and Development, G.A. Res. 47/191, U.N. GAOR, 47th Sess., Supp. No. 49, at 141, U.N. Doc. A/47/49 (1992), which is reprinted in the **Document Supplement**.

In making the request the General Assembly assigned the following duties to the CSD:

(a) To monitor progress in the implementation of Agenda 21 and activities related to the integration of environmental and developmental goals throughout the United Nations system through analysis and evaluation of reports from all relevant organs, organizations, programmes, and institutions of the United Nations system dealing with various issues of environment and development, including those related to finance;

(b) To consider information provided by Governments, for example, in the form of periodic communications or national reports regarding the activities they undertake to implement Agenda 21, the problems they face, such as problems related to financial resources and technology transfer, and other environment and development issues they find relevant;

(c) To review the progress in the implementation of the commitments set forth in Agenda 21, including those related to the provision of financial resources and transfer of technology;

(d) To review and monitor regularly progress towards the United Nations target of 0.7 per cent of the gross national product of developed countries for official development assistance; this review process should systematically combine the monitoring of the implementation of Agenda 21 with the review of financial resources available;

(e) To review on a regular basis the adequacy of funding an mechanisms, including efforts to reach the objective agreed in chapter 33 of Agenda 21, including targets where applicable;

(f) To receive and analyze relevant input from competent non-governmental organizations, including the scientific and the private sector, in the context of the overall implement of Agenda 21;

(g) To enhance the dialogue, within the framework of the United Nations, with non-governmental organizations and the independent sector, as well as other entities outside the United Nations system;

(h) To consider, where appropriate, information regarding the progress made in the implementation of environmental conventions, which could be made available by the relevant conferences of parties;

(i) To provide appropriate recommendations to the General Assembly, through the Economic and Social Council, on the basis of an integrated consideration of the reports and issues related to the implementation of Agenda 21; . . .

The staggering responsibilities with which the CSD is charged make the modest resources it has to do the job pale into insignificance. Monitoring, as in most international situations, is on the basis of voluntary self-reporting by states, and states have unfettered discretion about when and what to report.

In July 1997, the U.N. General Assembly convened a 19th Special Session — known as "Earth Summit +5" — to appraise the implementation of Agenda 21. The Assembly reaffirmed that Agenda 21 remains the fundamental program of action for achieving sustainable development. Overall, however, it found that environmental trends were worsening:

> Many polluting emissions, notably of toxic substances, greenhouse gases and waste volumes are continuing to increase although in some industrialized countries emissions are decreasing. Marginal progress has been made in addressing unsustainable production and consumption patterns. Insufficient progress has also been identified in the field of environmentally sound management and adequate control of transboundary movements of hazardous and radioactive wastes. Many countries undergoing rapid economic growth and urbanization are also experiencing increasing levels of air and water pollution, with accumulating impacts on human health. Acid rain and transboundary air pollution, once considered a problem only in the industrialized countries, are increasingly becoming a problem in many developing regions. In many poorer regions of the world, persistent poverty is contributing to accelerated degradation of natural resources and desertification has spread. In countries seriously affected by drought and/or desertification, especially those in Africa, agricultural productivity is uncertain and continues to decline, thereby hampering their efforts to achieve sustainable development. Inadequate and unsafe water supplies are affecting an increasing number of people worldwide, aggravating problems of ill health and food insecurity among the poor. Conditions in natural habitats and fragile ecosystems, including mountain ecosystems, are still deteriorating in all regions of the world, resulting in diminishing biological diversity. At the global level, renewable resources, in particular fresh water, forests, topsoil and marine fish stocks, continue to be used at rates beyond their viable rates of regeneration; without improved management, this situation is clearly unsustainable.

UN Nineteenth Special Session Press Release (1997), *see* http://www.un.org/esa/earthsummit.

PROBLEM 1-1
THE MOVEMENT TO "STOP AGENDA 21"

Agenda 21, a non-binding environmental "wish list," was formally adopted by the attendees at the United Nations Conference on Environment and Development at Rio de Janeiro in 1992. Agenda 21 consists of 40 chapters and about 500 pages of text. Agenda 21 is divided into four sections as follows:

Section I: Social and Economic Dimensions

Section II: Conservation and Management of Resources for Development

Section III: Strengthening the Role of Major Groups

Section IV: Means of Implementation

The heart of Agenda 21 is Section II, which covers all major environmental issues, such as protection of the atmosphere, conservation of biological diversity, protection of the oceans, protection of freshwater and sound management of different kinds of wastes. The most controversial parts of Agenda 21 are the sections dealing with land resources and ecosystems.

Beginning about 2008, a movement began to "stop Agenda 21" on the ground that this document subverts private property rights and the Constitution of the United States. In its January/February 2012 issue (Vol. 2, issue 1), the magazine *"Blaze"* charged that Agenda 21 is "a global scheme to wipe out the wealth and freedoms of U.S. citizens."

In 2012, resolutions to "stop Agenda 21" were introduced in eight state legislatures — Alabama, Arizona, Georgia, Kansas, Louisiana, Minnesota, New Hampshire, and Tennessee. An Alabama law known as SB477 was enacted "to prohibit the State of Alabama and its political subdivisions from adopting and developing environmental and developmental policies that, without due process, would infringe or restrict the private property rights of the owner of the property."

In May 2013, both the House of Representatives and the Senate of the State of Missouri passed veto-proof bills to stop Agenda 21. This law, An Act to amend chapter 1, RSMo, by adding thereto one new section on certain policies that infringe on private property rights, reads in relevant part as follows:

> 2. Neither the State of Missouri nor any political subdivision shall adopt or implement policy recommendations that deliberately or inadvertently infringe or restrict private property rights without due process, as may be required by policy recommendations originating in, or traceable to Agenda 21, adopted by the United Nations in 1992 at its Conference on Environment and Development or any other international law or ancillary plan of action that contravenes the Constitution of the United States or the Missouri Constitution.
>
> 3. Since the United Nations has accredited and enlisted numerous nongovernmental and intergovernmental organizations to assist in the implementation of its policies relative to Agenda 21 around the world, the State of Missouri and all political subdivisions are prohibited from entering into any agreement with, or expending any sum of money for, receiving funds from, contracting services from, or giving financial aid to those nongovernmental and intergovernmental organizations as defined in Agenda 21.

Read the excerpt from Agenda 21 in the **Document Supplement** and answer the following questions:

1. As an international instrument, what is the importance or function of Agenda 21?

2. Agenda 21 was adopted as a non-binding document; but even if it were a treaty, would it be self-executing?

3. Can a state law such as the Missouri law quoted above have any legal impact on Agenda 21?

4. Does Agenda 21 endanger or violate any provision of the Constitution of the United States or Amendments V or XIV (right to property) or the U.S. Bill of Rights?

5. Is the Missouri law designed to have political rather than legal impact?

6. Would you vote in favor of the Missouri law?

2.   The World Summit on Sustainable Development: Johannesburg, 2002

Ten years after the successful UNCED Summit, the United Nations convened a World Summit on Sustainable Development (WSSD) in Johannesburg, South Africa in 2002. The WSSD was held against the background that progress in meeting the goals set at the UNCED was extremely slow: world poverty was endemic and global environmental degradation was increasing. The WSSD, which was boycotted by the United States, adopted no important new international agreement. The major outcome of the WSSD was a negotiated Plan of Implementation and a Political Declaration. The WSSD called for:

- Significant cuts in the rate of extinction of plants and animals
- The establishment of a solidarity fund to wipe out poverty
- Substantial increases of financial aid; rich countries are urged to give 0.7% of national income to developing countries
- Improved access to affordable energy
- Substantial increase in renewable energy sources
- Restoration of depleted fisheries
- Stronger international governance

We provide an excerpt from the WSSD final declaration:

JOHANNESBURG DECLARATION ON SUSTAINABLE DEVELOPMENT, REPORT OF THE WORLD SUMMIT ON SUSTAINABLE DEVELOPMENT
A/CONF.199/20 (26 Aug–4 Sept 2002)

From our Origins to the Future

1. We, the representatives of the peoples of the world, assembled at the World Summit on Sustainable Development in Johannesburg, South Africa from 2 to 4 September 2002, reaffirm our commitment to sustainable development.

2. We commit ourselves to build a humane, equitable and caring global society cognizant of the need for human dignity for all.

3. At the beginning of this Summit, the children of the world spoke to us in a simple yet clear voice that the future belongs to them, and accordingly challenged all of us to ensure that through our actions they will inherit a world free of the indignity and indecency occasioned by poverty, environmental degradation and patterns of unsustainable development.

4. As part of our response to these children who represent our collective future, all of us, coming from every corner of the world, informed by different life experiences, are united and moved by a deeply-felt sense that we urgently need to create a new and brighter world of hope.

5. Accordingly, we assume a collective responsibility to advance and strengthen the interdependent and mutually reinforcing pillars of sustainable development — economic development, social development and environmental protection — at local, national, regional and global levels.

6. From this Continent, the Cradle of Humanity, we declare, through the Plan of Implementation and this Declaration, our responsibility to one another, to the greater community of life and to our children.

7. Recognizing that humankind is at a crossroad, we have united in a common resolve to make a determined effort to respond positively to the need to produce a practical and visible plan that should bring about poverty eradication and human development.

From Stockholm to Rio de Janeiro to Johannesburg

8. Thirty years ago, in Stockholm, we agreed on the urgent need to respond to the problem of environmental deterioration. Ten years ago, at the United Nations Conference on Environment and Development, held in Rio de Janeiro, we agreed that the protection of the environment, and social and economic development are fundamental to sustainable development, based on the Rio Principles. To achieve such development, we adopted the global programme, Agenda 21, and the Rio Declaration, to which we reaffirm our commitment. The Rio Summit was a significant milestone that set a new agenda for sustainable development.

9. Between Rio and Johannesburg the world's nations met in several major conferences under the guidance of the United Nations, including the Monterrey Conference on Finance for Development, as well as the Doha Ministerial Conference. These conferences defined for the work a comprehensive vision for the future of humanity.

10. At the Johannesburg Summit we achieved much in bringing together a rich tapestry of peoples and views in a constructive search for a common path, towards a world that respects and implements the vision of sustainable development. Johannesburg also confirmed that significant progress has been made towards achieving a global consensus and partnership amongst all the people of our planet.

The Challenges we Face

11. We recognize that poverty eradication, changing consumption and production patterns, and protecting and managing the natural resource base for economic and social development are overarching objectives of, and essential requirements for sustainable development.

12. The deep fault line that divides human society between the rich and the poor and the ever-increasing gap between the developed and developing worlds pose a major threat to global prosperity, security and stability.

13. The global environment continues to suffer. Loss of biodiversity continues, fish stocks continue to be depleted, desertification claims more and more fertile land, the adverse effects of climate change are already evident, natural disasters are more frequent and more devastating and developing countries more vulnerable, and air, water and marine pollution continue to rob millions of a decent life.

14. Globalization has added a new dimension to these challenges. The rapid integration of markets, mobility of capital and significant increases in investment flows around the world have opened new challenges and opportunities for the pursuit of sustainable development. But the benefits and costs of globalization are unevenly distributed, with developing countries facing special difficulties in meeting this challenge.

15. We risk the entrenchment of these global disparities and unless we act in a manner that fundamentally changes their lives, the poor of the world may lose confidence in their representatives and the democratic systems to which we remain committed, seeing their representatives as nothing more that sounding brass or tinkling cymbals.

Our Commitment to Sustainable Development

16. We are determined to ensure that our rich diversity, which is our collective strength, will be used for constructive partnership for change and for the achievement of the common goal of sustainable development.

17. Recognizing the importance of building human solidarity, we urge the promotion of dialogue and cooperation among the world's civilizations and peoples, irrespective of race, disabilities, religion, language, culture and tradition.

18. We welcome the Johannesburg Summit focus on the indivisibility of human dignity and are resolved through decisions on targets, timetables and partnerships to speedily increase access to basic requirements such as clean water, sanitation, adequate shelter, energy, health care, food security and the protection of bio-diversity. At the same time, we will work together to assist one another to have access to financial resources, benefit from the opening of markets, ensure capacity building, use modern technology to bring about development, and make sure that there is technology transfer, human resource development, education and training to banish forever underdevelopment.

19. We reaffirm our pledge to place particular focus on, and give priority attention to, the fight against the worldwide conditions that pose severe threats to the sustainable development of our people. Among these conditions are: chronic hunger; malnutrition; foreign occupation; armed conflicts; illicit drug problems; organized crime; corruption; natural disasters; illicit arms trafficking; trafficking in persons; terrorism; intolerance and incitement to racial, ethnic, religious and other hatreds;

xenophobia; and endemic, communicable and chronic diseases, in particular HIV/AIDS, malaria and tuberculosis.

20. We are committed to ensure that women's empowerment and emancipation, and gender equality are integrated in all activities encompassed within Agenda 21, the Millennium Development Goals and the Johannesburg Plan of Implementation.

21. We recognize the reality that global society has the means and is endowed with the resources to address the challenges of poverty eradication and sustainable development confronting all humanity. Together we will take extra steps to ensure that these available resources are used to the benefit of humanity.

22. In this regard, to contribute to the achievement of our development goals and targets, we urged developed countries that have not done so to make concrete efforts towards the internationally agreed levels of Official Development Assistance.

23. We welcome and support the emergence of stronger regional groupings and alliances, such as the New Partnership for Africa's Development (NEPAD), to promote regional cooperation, improved international cooperation and promote sustainable development.

24. We shall continue to pay special attention to the developmental needs of Small Island Developing States and the Least Developed Countries.

25. We reaffirm the vital role of the indigenous peoples in sustainable development.

26. We recognize sustainable development requires a long-term perspective and broad-based participation in policy formulation, decision-making and implementation at all levels. As social partners we will continue to work for stable partnerships with all major groups respecting the independent, important roles of each of these.

27. We agree that in pursuit of their legitimate activities the private sector, both large and small companies, have a duty to contribute to the evolution of equitable and sustainable communities and societies.

28. We also agree to provide assistance to increase income generating employment opportunities, taking into account the International Labour Organization (ILO) Declaration of Fundamental Principles and Rights at Work.

29. We agree that there is a need for private sector companies to enforce corporate accountability. This should take place within a transparent and stable regulatory environment.

30. We undertake to strengthen and improve governance at all levels, for the effective implementation of Agenda 21, the Millennium Development Goals and the Johannesburg Plan of Implementation.

Multilateralism is the Future

31. To achieve our goals of sustainable development, we need more effective, democratic and accountable international and multilateral institutions.

32. We reaffirm our commitment to the principles and purposes of the UN Charter and international law as well as the strengthening of multilateralism. We support the leadership role of the United Nations as the most universal and representative organization in the world, which is best placed to promote sustainable development.

33. We further commit ourselves to monitor progress at regular intervals towards the achievement of our sustainable development goals and objectives.

Making it Happen!

34. We are in agreement that this must be an inclusive process, involving all the major groups and governments that participated in the historic Johannesburg Summit.

35. We commit ourselves to act together, united by a common determination to save our planet, promote human development and achieve universal prosperity and peace.

36. We commit ourselves to the Johannesburg Plan of Implementation and to expedite the achievement of the time-bound, socio-economic and environmental targets contained therein.

37. From the African continent, the Cradle of Humankind, we solemnly pledge to the peoples of the world, and the generations that will surely inherit this earth, that we are determined to ensure that our collective hope for sustainable development is realized.

NOTES AND QUESTIONS

1. *Still at the crossroads?* As you read the "commitment to sustainable development" made by states at Johannesburg (especially paragraphs 18 to 20 of the Declaration) what is most striking to you? These commitments seem in accord with the Declaration's recognition that humankind "is at a cross-roads" in responding to "poverty eradication and human development," but what does it add to existing political commitments and to environmental protection? Why is it that the Summit's principal focus is "on the indivisibility of human dignity"? Did the Summit succeed in advancing new ground on sustainable development or was there a regression compared to earlier political declarations?

2. *Evaluation of the Johannesburg Summit.* Like previous environmental summit meetings, the Johannesburg World Summit on Sustainable Development adopted a declaration and an action plan, the Declaration on Sustainable Development and the Plan of Implementation.[9] The Johannesburg Plan of Implementation is reprinted in the **Document Supplement**. As you read over the main lines of the

---

[9] UN Report of the WSSD, UN Doc. A/Conf. 199/20 (2002).

results of the meeting, what was the main accomplishment? Were any new ideas advanced? Was protection of the natural environment the focus of the meeting, or did newer concerns come to the fore?

C. The United Nations Conference on Sustainable Development, 2012: Rio +20

To mark the 20th anniversary of the landmark 1992 Rio de Janeiro Conference on Environment and Development, the United Nations convened a United Nations Conference on Sustainable Development hosted by Brazil in Rio de Janeiro in June, 2012. This second "World Summit on Sustainable Development" had two themes: (1) "the green economy in the context of sustainable development"; and (2) "the institutional framework for sustainable development." The conference designated seven priority areas for discussion: decent jobs, food security, energy, sustainable cities, clean drinking water, oceans, and disaster readiness. At the close of the conference, a non-binding document was adopted: "The Future We Want." The conference called for the strengthening of the United Nations Environment Program (UNEP) so that it may become the "leading environmental authority" in the world. Accordingly UNEP should have universal membership, greater financing, and more engagement with other United Nations bodies.

The conference defined sustainable development as follows:

"Sustainable development meets the needs of the present without compromising the ability of future generations to meet their own needs." Sustainable development, which should be the guiding principle for long-term global development, rests on three pillars: economic development; social development; and environmental protection.

Excerpts from the final report of the conference are as follows:

REPORT OF THE UNITED NATIONS CONFERENCE ON SUSTAINABLE DEVELOPMENT
A/Conf. 216/16 (Rio De Janeiro, 20–22 June 2012)

*   *   *

II. Renewing political commitment

A. Reaffirming the Rio Principles and past action plans

14. We recall the Stockholm Declaration of the United Nations Conference on the Human Environment adopted at Stockholm on 16 June 1972.

15. We reaffirm all the principles of the Rio Declaration on Environment and Development, including, inter alia, the principle of common but differentiated responsibilities, as set out in principle 7 of the Rio Declaration.

B. Advancing integration, implementation and coherence: assessing the progress to date and the remaining gaps in the implementation of the outcomes of the major summits on sustainable development and addressing new and emerging challenges

*   *   *

19. We recognize that the 20 years since the United Nations Conference on Environment and Development in 1992 have seen uneven progress, including in sustainable development and poverty eradication. We emphasize the need to make progress in implementing previous commitments. We also recognize the need to accelerate progress in closing development gaps between developed and developing countries, and to seize and create opportunities to achieve sustainable development through economic growth and diversification, social development and environmental protection. To this end, we underscore the continued need for an enabling environment at the national and international levels, as well as continued and strengthened international cooperation, particularly in the areas of finance, debt, trade and technology transfer, as mutually agreed, and innovation entrepreneurship, capacity-building, transparency and accountability. We recognize the diversification of actors and stakeholders engaged in the pursuit of sustainable development. In this context, we affirm the continued need for the full and effective participation of all countries, in particular developing countries, in global decision-making.

*   *   *

III.   Green economy in the context of sustainable development and poverty eradication

56. We affirm that there are different approaches, visions, models and tools available to each country, in accordance with its national circumstances and priorities, to achieve sustainable development in its three dimensions which is our overarching goal. In this regard, we consider green economy in the context of sustainable development and poverty eradication as one of the important tools available for achieving sustainable development and that it could provide options for policymaking but should not be a rigid set of rules. We emphasize that it should contribute to eradicating poverty as well as sustained economic growth, enhancing social inclusion, improving human welfare and creating opportunities for employment and decent work for all, while maintaining the healthy functioning of the Earth's ecosystems.

57. We affirm that policies for green economy in the context of sustainable development and poverty eradication should be guided by and in accordance with all the Rio Principles, Agenda 21 and Johannesburg Plan of Implementation and contribute towards achieving relevant internationally agreed development goals, including the Millennium Development Goals.

58. We affirm that green economy policies in the context of sustainable development and poverty eradication should:

a) Be consistent with International law;

b) Respect each country's national sovereignty over their natural resources taking into account its national circumstances, objectives, responsibilities, priorities and policy space with regard to the three dimensions of sustainable development;

c) Be supported by an enabling environment and well-functioning institutions at all levels with a leading role for governments and with the participation of all relevant stakeholders, including civil society;

d) Promote sustained and inclusive economic growth, foster innovation and provide opportunities, benefits and empowerment for all and respect for all human rights;

e) Take into account the needs of developing countries, particularly those in special situations;

f) Strengthen international cooperation, including the provision of financial resources, capacity-building and technology transfer to developing countries;

g) Effectively avoid unwarranted conditionalities on official development assistance (ODA) and finance;

h) Not constitute a means of arbitrary and unjustifiable discrimination of a disguised restriction on international trade, avoid unilateral action to deal with environmental challenges outside the jurisdiction of the importing country, and ensure that environmental measures addressing transboundary or global environment problems, as far as possible, are based on an international consensus;

i) Contribute to closing technology gaps between developed and developing countries and reduce the technological dependence of developing countries using all appropriate measures;

j) Enhance the welfare of indigenous peoples and their communities, other local and traditional communities and ethnic minorities, recognizing and supporting their identity, culture and interests, and avoid endangering their cultural heritage, practices and traditional knowledge, preserving and respecting non-market approaches that contribute to the eradication of poverty;

k) Enhance the welfare of women, children, youth, persons with disabilities, smallholder and subsistence farmers, fisherfolk and those working in small and medium-sized enterprises, and improve the livelihoods and empowerment of the poor and vulnerable groups in particular in developing countries;

l) Mobilize the full potential and ensure the equal contribution of both women and men;

m) Promote productive activities in developing countries that contribute to the eradication of poverty;

n) Address the concern about inequalities and promote social inclusion, including social protection floors;

o) Promote sustainable consumption and productive patterns;

p) Continue efforts to strive for inclusive, equitable development approaches to overcome poverty and inequality.

*   *   *

VI. Means of implementation

252. We affirm that the means of implementation identified in Agenda 21, the Programme for the Further Implementation of Agenda 21, the Johannesburg Plan of Implementation, the Monterrey Consensus of the International Conference on Financing for Development and the Doha Declaration on Financing for Development are indispensable for achieving the full and effective translation of sustainable development commitments into tangible sustainable development outcomes. We reiterate that each country has primary responsibility for its own economic and social development and that the role of national policies, domestic resources and development strategies cannot be overemphasized. We reaffirm that developing countries need additional resources for sustainable development. We recognize the need for significant mobilization of resources from a variety of sources and the effective use of financing, in order to promote sustainable development. We acknowledge that good governance and the rule of law at the national and international levels are essential for sustained, inclusive and equitable economic growth, sustainable development and the eradication of poverty and hunger.

A. Finance

253. We call on all countries to prioritize sustainable development in the allocation of resources in accordance with national priorities and needs, and we recognize the crucial importance of enhancing financial support from all sources for sustainable development for all countries, in particular developing countries. We recognize the importance of international, regional and national financial mechanisms, including those accessible to subnational and local authorities, to the implementation of sustainable development programmes, and call for their strengthening and implementation. New partnerships and innovative sources of financing can play a role in complementing sources of financing for sustainable development. We encourage their further exploration and use, alongside the traditional means of implementation.

254. We recognize the need for significant mobilization of resources from a variety of sources and the effective use of financing, in order to

give strong support to developing countries in their efforts to promote sustainable development, including through actions undertaken in accordance with the outcome of the United Nations Conference on Sustainable Development and for achieving sustainable development goals.

255. We agree to establish an intergovernmental process under the auspices of the General Assembly, with technical support from the United Nations system and in open and broad consultation with relevant international and regional financial institutions and other relevant stakeholders. The process will assess financing needs, consider the effectiveness, consistency and synergies of existing instruments and frameworks, and evaluate additional initiatives, with a view to preparing a report proposing options on an effective sustainable development financing strategy to facilitate the mobilization of resources and their effective use in achieving sustainable development objectives.

256. An intergovernmental committee, comprising 30 experts nominated by regional groups, with equitable geographical representation, will implement this process, concluding its work by 2014.

257. We request the General Assembly to consider the report of the intergovernmental committee and take appropriate action.

258. We recognize that the fulfillment of all commitments related to ODA is crucial, including the commitments by many developed countries to achieve the target of 0.7 percent of gross national product (GNP) for ODA to developing countries by 2015, as well as a target of 0.15 to 0.20 per cent of GNP for ODA to the least developed countries. To reach their agreed timetable, donor countries should take all necessary and appropriate measures to raise the rate of aid disbursements in order to meet their existing commitments. We urge those developed countries that have not yet done so to make additional concrete efforts towards the target of 0.7 percent of GNP for ODA to developing countries, including the specific target of 0.15 to 0.20 per cent of GNP for ODA to the least developed countries, in accordance with their commitments. To build on progress achieved in ensuring that ODA is used effectively, we stress the importance of democratic governance, improved transparency and accountability, and managing for results. We strongly encourage all donors to establish, as soon as possible, rolling indicative timetables that illustrate how they aim to reach their goals, in accordance with their respective budget allocation process. We stress the importance of mobilizing greater domestic support in developed countries towards the fulfillment of their commitments, including through raising public awareness, providing data on the development impact of aid provided and demonstrating tangible results.

B. Technology

269. We emphasize the importance of technology transfer to developing countries and recall the provisions on technology transfer, finance, access to information and intellectual property rights as agreed in the

Johannesburg Plan of Implementation, in particular its call to promote, facilitate and finance, as appropriate, access to the development, transfer and diffusion of environmentally sound technologies and corresponding know-how, in particular to developing countries, on favourable terms, including on concessional and preferential terms, as mutually agreed. We also take note of the further evolution of discussions and agreements on these issues since the adoption of the Plan of Implementation.

270. We stress the importance of access by all countries to environmentally sound technologies, new knowledge, know-how and expertise. We further stress the importance of cooperative action on technology innovation, research and development. We agree to explore modalities in the relevant forums for enhanced access to environmentally sound technologies by developing countries.

NOTES AND QUESTIONS

1. *Contrast the 1992 and 2012 World Summits in Rio de Janeiro.* In 2012 were any new proposals made or discussed? Were any new ideas advanced in 2012? Would you be in favor of a new World Summit in 2022?

2. *The concept of sustainable development continues to be the watchword of international environmental conferences.* We cover the legal meaning of this concept in the next chapter. Birnie, Boyle, and Redgwell in their book, INTERNATIONAL LAW AND THE ENVIRONMENT 54 (3d ed. 2009) comment that "Twenty years on from the Brundtland Report we are still little nearer to in internationally agreed understanding of what constitutes sustainable development in any detail, and the concept itself has proved almost infinitely malleable." Do you agree?

3. *The WSSD documents refer to the Millennium Development Goals of the United Nations.* In 2000, the UN General Assembly adopted Resolution 55/2, setting out goals for the new Millennium to be achieved by the target date of 2015. These Millennium Development Goals are: "To end extreme poverty; To achieve universal primary education; To promote gender equality and the empowerment of women; To reduce child mortality; To improve maternal health; To combat HIV/AIDS; To ensure environmental sustainability; and to develop a global partnership for development." This UN Millennium Development Project is independent of the WSSD process but clearly related to it. How do these two significant efforts fit with each other?

Section III.   INTERNATIONAL ENVIRONMENTAL GOVERNANCE

Governance refers to the establishment and implementation of governmental policies without government. The development of a vast body of international environmental law during the past 40 years has been accompanied by a corresponding development of international institutions — primarily intergovernmental organizations — responsible to some degree for global environmental governance. As intergovernmental organizations, however, they have only limited capacity to influence policy; the actual establishment and implementation of policy is in the hands of the states-parties who are their members.

The United Nations Environment Programme (UNEP) is the central intergovernmental organization charged with the task of environmental governance. UNEP was established by UN General Assembly resolution 2997 (XXVII) of 15 December 1972. UNEP, based in Nairobi, has a full-time Secretariat of about 300 and, while its staff has secure funding, most of UNEP's activities are funded by voluntary contributions. UNEP's Governing Council of 58 members, elected by the General Assembly for four-year terms, taking into account equitable regional representation, reports to the UN Economic and Social Council. Every year, UNEP convenes the ministerial level Global Ministerial Environmental Forum, which reviews important emerging policy issues in the field of environment and debates environmental policy.

Although UNEP has a mandate to help formulate policy to deal with the entire range of global environmental problems, in reality its influence is haphazard and incomplete. In fact, there is no globally competent international authority for environmental governance. As a result, international environmental law has grown incrementally through the creation of hundreds of independent Multilateral Environmental Agreements (MEAs) and International Environmental Agreements (IEAs), each of which represent autonomous governing regimes that are typically controlled by the respective Conference of the Parties (COP) for each regime.

In addition, important policy governance is exercised by other UN bodies with authority over certain areas and issues. The UN regional commissions, especially the UN Economic Commission for Europe, have undertaken important initiatives within its region, notably the 1979 Convention on Long Range Transboundary Air Pollution and the 1991 Espoo Convention on Environmental Impact Assessment in a Transboundary Context. Many United Nations' specialized agencies play key roles in international environmental governance: the International Maritime Organization (IMO) administers some 30 treaties concerning protection of the marine environment; the Food and Agriculture Organization (FAO) administers many fisheries agreements and collaborates with UNEP on key conventions on chemicals and pesticides. Additional UN units with environmental mandates include the World Health Organization (WHO), the International Atomic Energy Agency (IAEA), the International Labour Organization (ILO), the United Nations Educational, Scientific and Cultural Organization (UNESCO) and the World Meteorological Society.

Two key environmental governance bodies established in the wake of the 1992 United Nations Conference on Environment and Development are also outside the ambit of UNEP. The United Nations Commission on Sustainable Development (CSD) was created in 1992 by the United Nations General Assembly[10] as a functional commission of the UN Economic and Social Council. The Commission's mandate is to monitor the integration of environmental and development goals throughout the UN system; to coordinate intergovernmental decision-making; to oversee the implementation of Agenda 21; and to make recommendations on new arrangements needed to advance sustainable development. The Commission meets

---

[10] G.A. Res. 47/191 (Dec. 22, 1992).

annually for two to three weeks each year. Because it has no power of implementation, it has been largely ineffective. In addition, most of the issues it considers are substantially addressed in other fora controlled by MEAs. A second important institution is the Global Environment Facility (GEF), which was established as a permanent financing mechanism to provide developing countries with "grants and concessional funding to meet the agreed full incremental cost of measures to achieve global benefits"[11] of various global environmental agreements. The GEF is governed by an Assembly, a Council and the Secretariat, and is located at the World Bank in Washington DC. UNEP is one of three "implementing agencies" of GEF, but has no actual control over funding policies.

UNEP has no charter or constitutive document; it was established by the following UN General Assembly Resolution:

INSTITUTIONAL AND FINANCIAL ARRANGEMENTS FOR INTERNATIONAL ENVIRONMENTAL COOPERATION (1972)
G.A. Res. 2997 (XXVII), U.N. DOC. A/8370 U.N. GAOR, 27th Sess., Supp. 30, at 42 (1973)

The General Assembly,

Convinced of the need for prompt and effective implementation by Governments and the international community of measures designed to safeguard and enhance the environment for the benefit of present and future generations of man,

Recognizing that responsibility for action to protect and enhance the environment rests primarily with Governments and, in the first instance, can be exercised more effectively at the national and regional levels,

Recognizing further that environmental problems of broad international significance *fall* within the competence of the United Nations system,

Bearing in mind that international co-operative programmes in the field of the environment must be undertaken with due respect for the sovereign rights of States and in conformity with the *Charter of the United Nations,* and principles of international law,

Mindful of the sectoral responsibilities of the organizations in the United Nations system,

Conscious of the significance of regional and subregional co-operation in the field of the environment and of the important role of the regional economic commissions and other regional intergovernmental organizations,

Emphasizing that problems of the environment constitute a *new* and important area for international cooperation and that the complexity and interdependence of such problems require new approaches,

Recognizing that the relevant international scientific and other professional

---

[11] Instrument for the Establishment of the Restructured Global Environment Facility (1994), 33 ILM 1273 (1994).

communities can make an important contribution to international co-operation in the field of the environment,

Conscious of the need for processes within the United Nations system which would effectively assist developing countries to implement environmental policies and programmes that are compatible with their development plans and to participate meaningfully in international environmental programmes,

Convinced that, in *order* to be effective, international co-operation in the field of the environment requires additional financial and technical resources,

Aware of the urgent need for a permanent institutional arrangement with the United Nations system for the protection and improvement of the environment,

Taking note of the report of the Secretary-General on the United Nations Conference on the Human Environment.

I
Governing Council of the United Nations Environment Programme

1. *Decides* to establish a Governing Council of the United Nations Environment Programme, composed of fifty-eight members elected by the General Assembly for three-year terms on the following basis:

    a. Sixteen seats for African States;

    b. Thirteen seats for Asian States;

    c. Six seats for Eastern European States;

    d. Ten seats for Latin American States;

    e. Thirteen seats for Western European and other States

2. *Decides* that the Governing Council shall have the following main functions and responsibilities:

    a. To promote international co-operation in the field of the environment and to recommend, as appropriate, policies to this end;

    b. To provide general policy guidance for the direction and co-ordination of environmental programmes within the United Nations system;

    c. To receive the periodic reports of the Executive Director of the United Nations Environment Programme, referred to in section II, paragraph 2, below, on the implementation of environmental programmes within the United Nations system;

    d. To keep under review the world environmental situation in order to ensure that emerging environmental problems of wide international significance receive appropriate and adequate consideration by Governments;

    e. To promote the contribution of the relevant international scientific and other professional communities to the acquisition, assessment and exchange of environmental knowledge and information and, as appropriate, to the technical aspects of the formulation and implementation of environmental programmes within the United Nations system;

f. To maintain under continuing review the impact of national and international environmental policies and measures on developing countries, as well as the problem of additional costs that may be incurred by developing countries in the implementation of environmental prgrammes and projects, and to ensure that such programmes and projects shall be compatible with the development plans and priorities of those countries;

g. To review and approve annually the programme of utilization of resources of the Environment Fund referred to in section III below;

3. *Decides* that the Governing Council shall report annually to the General Assembly through the Economic and Social Council, which will transmit to the Assembly such comments on the report as it may deem necessary, particularly with regard to questions of co-ordination and to the relationship of environmental policies and programmes within the United Nations system to overall economic and social policies and priorities;

II
Environment Secretariat

1. *Decides* that a small secretariat shall be established in the UN to serve as a focal point for environmental action and co-ordination within the United Nations system in such a way as to ensure a high degree of effective management;

2. *Decides* that the environment secretariat shall be headed by the Executive Director of the United Nations Environment Programme, who shall be elected by the General Assembly on the nomination of the Secretary-General for a term of four years and who shall be entrusted, inter alia, with the following responsibilities:

a. To provide substantive support to the Governing Council of the United Nations Environment Programme;

b. To co-ordinate, under the guidance of the Governing Council, environmental programmes within the United Nations system, to keep their implementation under review and to assess their effectiveness;

c. To advise, as appropriate and under the guidance of the Governing Council, intergovernmental bodies of the United Nations system on the formulation and implementation of environment programmes;

d. To secure the effective co-operation of, and contribution from, the relevant scientific and other professional communities in all parts of the world:

e. To provide, at the request of all parties concerned, advisory services for the promotion of international co-operation in the field of the environment;

f. To submit to the Governing Council, on his own initiative or upon request, proposals embodying medium-range and long-range planning for United Nations programmes in the field of the environment;

g. To bring to the attention of the Governing Council any matter which he deems to require consideration by it;

h. To administer, under the authority and policy guidance of the Governing Council, the Environment Fund referred to in section III below;

i. To report on environmental matters to the Governing Council;

j. To perform such other functions as may be entrusted to him by the Governing Council;

3. *Decides* that the costs of servicing the Governing Council and providing the small secretariat referred to in paragraph 1 above shall be borne by the regular budget of the United Nations and that operational programme costs, programme support and administrative costs of the Environment Fund established under section II below shall be borne by the Fund;

III
Environment Fund

1. *Decides* that, in order to provide for additional financing for environmental programmes, a voluntary fund shall be established, with effect from 1 January 1973, in accordance with existing United Nations financial procedures;

2. *Decides* that, in order to enable the Governing Council of the United Nations Environment Programme to fulfill its policy-guidance role for the direction and co-ordination of environmental activities., the Environment Fund shall finance wholly or partly the costs of the new environmental initiatives undertaken within the United Nations system — which will include the initiatives envisaged in the *Action Plan for the Human Environment/43* adopted by the United Nations Conference on the Human Environment, with particular attention to integrated projects, and such other environmental activities as may be decided upon by the Governing Council — and that the Governing Council shall review these initiatives with a view to taking appropriate decisions as to their continued financing;

An idea of the main work of UNEP can be gained by the following excerpt.

UNITED NATIONS ENVIRONMENT PROGRAMME
Annual Report, 54–67 (2007)

ENVIRONMENTAL GOVERNANCE

Since its establishment in 1972, UNEP has been closely involved with governments, assisting them to develop and apply environmental law, from the global convention level down to national environmental legislation. Long-term strategic guidance for this work is provided by the Montevideo Programme for the Development and Periodic Review of Environmental Law. Established in 1982, each decade of Montevideo Programmes has provided a long-term strategic approach for the development and implementation of UNEP's international environmental law programme. UNEP is currently implementing Montevideo Programme III, the Programme for the first decade of the twenty-first century and has already started working on the development of the next programme. For this purpose, an expert meeting was organized in September 2007, followed by a Consultative Meeting of Government Officials and Experts on a Programme for the Development and Periodic Review of Environmental Law (Montevideo Programme), held in November at UNEP's headquarters in Nairobi. Officials and experts were invited to consider emerging issues identified through the UNEP-led GEO process as well as the Millennium Ecosystem Assessment process, and to identify the direction for the further implementation of the current Programme (III) and possible components of the next programme.

The Montevideo Programme for the Development of Environmental Law provides an important policy framework for UNEP's normative and operational activities, and guides UNEP's work in the field under the Bali Strategic Plan for Technology Support and Capacity Building. During the year, UNEP has continued to provide advisory services and technical assistance programmes to various national stakeholders, such as parliamentarians, judges and magistrates, customs officials, lawyers, negotiators and NGOs, on general and specific areas of environmental management, policy and law. These training courses and workshops inform participants about policy, legal and institutional developments in the field of environmental law at international and national levels; promote greater interest in and commitment to using environmental law as an instrument for translating sustainable development policies into action; enhance capacity for effective compliance with, implementation of and enforcement of multilateral environmental agreements; and enable participants to share experiences and information and take initiative on a more informed basis in their home countries in the development and implementation of environmental law.

Activities conducted under the current Montevideo Programme III during the year included studies, reports and expert meetings on specific environmental law areas identified in the Programme as needing development. An Experts meeting on Liability and Compensation was held in January in Geneva to consider the possibility of developing guidance materials for governments. The meeting reviewed draft guidelines on liability and compensation at the national level. A study on ecosystem services and environmental law was also conducted, with a focus on financing measures to resolve environmental problems and the link between environmental degradation and poverty.

BUILDING LEGAL CAPACITY

An area where UNEP has always had a strong national as well as regional and global impact is in the field or environmental law. The Eighth biannual Global Training Programme on Environmental Law and Policy, was held at the UNEP headquarters in November 2007. The agenda was designed to cover both international and national environmental law, policy and institutional issues through presentations and discussions, simulation exercises and mock negotiation sessions. Participants also made presentations on their country experiences in the development and implementation of national environmental laws and institutions, and on policy and action taken to implement various Multilateral Environmental Agreements (MEAs). Sixty-seven participants attended the training, mainly from ministries responsible for the environment and Permanent Missions to UNEP in Nairobi from both developed and developing countries and countries with economies in transition. The participants represented 62 countries; 16 from Africa, 23 from Asia and the Pacific, 11 from Europe and 12 from Latin America and the Caribbean.

SUPPORTING THE MEAS

UNEP continues to provide legal advisory services in the context of processes for the development of global and regional legal environmental instruments. Substantive support was provided to meetings of the Parties of the Chemicals-related MEAs (i.e., Basel, Rotterdam, and Stockholm Conventions), as well as to the third meeting of legal and technical experts from the eastern Africa region for the development of a Protocol on land-based sources of pollution.

UNEP also provides secretariat services to intergovernmental panels and other processes. A notable example is the provision of joint secretariat services with the World Meteorological Organization (WMO) to the Intergovernmental Panel on Climate Change and its bureau and working groups, including facilitating the participation of developing countries and countries with economies in transition. In 2007, UNEP provided support to the 26th and 27th Sessions of the IPCC, which resulted in the approval and adoption of the IPCC Fourth Assessment Report. Other inputs provided by UNEP to the work of MEAs include the presentation of the UNEP official report to the relevant COP/MOPs as well as the organization of side events, both in respect of UNEP-administered MEAs as well as other relevant MEAs, such as UNFCCC and UNCCD. UNEP also continues to update Register of International Treaties and Other Agreements in the Field of Environment in six UN languages that will be distributed to all Governments and relevant organizations in March 2008. The updated register will contain changes in the status of ratification and signature of more than 50 environmental treaties for which UN and specialized agencies act as the depository.

UNEP has developed issue-based modules to encourage and facilitate the coherent implementation of MEAs at national level. The modules, variously developed by IUCN and UNEP-WCMC, focus on issues of common concern across different biodiversity-related agreements, including inland waters, sustainable use, climate change and biodiversity, invasive alien species, and protected areas. Each module provides a structured overview of how a certain topic is treated across different agreement by identifying and grouping implementation requirements. By clustering obligations of different agreements under certain activities, the modules facilitate communication at the national level and improve implementation of obligations through enhanced cross-sectoral understanding and cooperation. This is regarded as particularly relevant and effective for efforts made at the national level for achievement of the 2010 Biodiversity Target. The modules have been applied widely in various regions.

Each biodiversity convention (including CITES, CMS, CBD, and Ramsar) generates large quantities of data, documents and other forms of information. Much of this information addresses common biodiversity-related themes and activities. However, because it is not inter-linked or organized in a consistent and harmonized manner, grasping 'the big picture' and ensuring that the conventions are mutually supportive can be extremely difficult. In order to address these issues, UNEP is undertaking a project on Knowledge Management for Biodiversity-related MEAs, which aims to promote the strategic use of information and promote interoperability of information datasets related to biodiversity-related conventions. Under the project, an Internet portal has been developed at UNEP-WCMC that enables users to access key documents relating to the implementation of MEAs, such as decisions and resolutions, strategic plans, lists of Parties and national focal point information.

Another component of the project focuses on harmonization of national reporting for biodiversity-related MEAs. As governments accede to an increasing number of MEAs, the preparation of national reports becomes more of a burden, particularly due to often complex reporting formats as well as a lack of communication and cooperation between focal points for different agreements. The project addresses these challenges by indentifying the common core reporting elements among biodiversity-related MEAs, including through the development of thematic modules for joint reporting between a small number of MEAs. The products of the Knowledge Management Project, being implemented by UNEP-WCMC, have been shared with a number of Parties and interested individuals. The results of the first phase of the project will be disseminated at the meetings of the governing bodies of various MEAs during 2008.

ENGAGING CIVIL SOCIETY

Engagement with the major groups of civil society is essential in generating global and regional consensus and in building processes for policy deliberations. During the year under review, UNEP organized the traditional regional civil society consultation meetings as part of its Global Civil Society Forum cycle. These are held in conjunction with regional civil society fora to enhance capacity among civil society organizations (CSOs) from the South, and countries with economies in transition, in the field of environmental sustainability. The Global Civil Society Forum cycle comprises Regional Consultative Meetings in each of the six UNEP regions in preparation for the annual Global Civil Society Forum (GCSF), held prior to the Governing Council / Global Ministerial Environment Forum Conference on Sustainable Development as an associated meeting. The cycle provides a platform for exchange and consultation about key environmental issues to be addressed by the Member States during the GC/GMEF, and facilitates the input of major groups into the GC/GMEF and other international fora in the field of environment and international environmental governance.

The eighth Global Civil Society Forum was organized from 3 to 4 February 2007 in Nairobi, Kenya, in conjunction with the UNEP GC/GMEF. The meeting discussed the policy issues of the GC/GMEF, the draft GC/GMEF decisions, and UNEP's modalities for engaging with CSOs. A Global Civil Society Statement on policy issues was circulated to delegations prior to the GC/GMEF as an official document in the six UN languages. In dialogue with UNEP's Executive Director, prominent issues such as climate change and CSOs' important role in the search for global responses were discussed. The participation of major groups into the GC/GMEF was further enhanced with representatives invited to attend all the Ministerial Roundtables during the GC/GMEF, plenary sessions of the GMEF on globalization and UN reform, the Committee of the Whole and the Mercury Contact Group. At the GC/GMEF, written statements were distributed on chemicals management, globalization, gender, war, militarism and environment, water, and on specific major groups, such as business and industry, and workers and trade unions. Oral statements from the various major groups were also made in the GC/GMEF plenary and in the Ministerial Roundtables. This demonstrates that the voice of major groups is increasingly being incorporated into policy discussions at UNEP.

During 2007, six Civil Society Regional Consultation Meetings were organized in preparation for the 9th Global Civil Society Forum and 10th Special Session of the GC/GMEF in 2008, with a particular thematic focus on the key findings of GEO-4; mobilizing finance to meet the climate challenge; the UNEP medium-term strategy 2010–2013; enhancing major group participation in UNEP's governance level; and international environmental governance. The meetings were attended by a total of 236 participants from 84 countries, of whom 40 per cent were female. The year also saw, for the first time, the participation of all nine major groups of civil society at the regional meetings.

NOTES AND QUESTIONS

1. *Developing international environmental law*. The UNEP has been in the forefront of an effort to formulate and enhance the development of international environmental law. In the **Document Supplement**, we reprint a UNEP Background Study on Possible Components of the Programme for the Development and Periodic Review of Environmental Law for the First Decade of the Twenty-First Century (4 September 2000). This study documents the growth of international environmental law and identifies gaps and weaknesses. What major problems are identified in this study? The themes sounded in this study will be addressed in this book. In 2009 the Governing Council of UNEP adopted Montevideo IV, the Fourth Programme for the Development and Periodic Review of Environmental Law. UNEP/GC/25/INF/15,   *available   at*   http://www.unep.org/delc/Portals/119/ MontevideoIV.pdf. This document identifies seven principal challenges for international environmental law: (1) climate change; (2) poverty; (3) access to drinking

water and sanitation; (4) ecosystem conservation and protection; (5) environmental emergencies and natural disasters; (6) pollution prevention and control; and (7) promotion of new environmental technologies.

2. ***The role and mandate of UNEP.*** At the nineteenth session of the UNEP Council in 1997, the ministers agreed on the Nairobi Declaration on the role and mandate of UNEP. This Declaration, which was approved by the United Nations General Assembly meeting in a special session in New York in 1997, is reprinted in the **Document Supplement.**

3. ***Enhancing international environmental governance.*** International Environmental Law suffers from what Edith Brown Weiss has termed "treaty congestion,"[12] an undue multiplication of treaties and resultant legal regimes, each with their own secretariats and conferences of parties that meet each year to debate policy and take decisions. Each treaty regime has a mandate to address a particular issue. The issues range greatly in their importance and priority, from climate change to the quality of the ballast water carried in ships. Governance of international environmental quality is fragmented as well into hundreds of largely independent regimes that vary greatly in their effectiveness with very little coordination. The governance system is highly inefficient with gaps and duplication of effort. UNEP and the Commission on Sustainable Development, which are themselves duplicative, struggle to rationalize and harmonize this international system and to address emerging challenges. What can be done to create better governance? A UNEP Consultant Group[13] has proposed five options for better governance[14]:

- Enhance the authority of UNEP by granting UNEP explicit coordination authority to "cluster" MEAs to eliminate duplication and spur efficient operations; grant UNEP more secure and greater funding.

- Create a new "umbrella" governance agency on top of existing agencies that would have the power to coordinate the system of governance.

- Transform UNEP into an new World Environment Organization that would be a specialized agency of the United Nations with authority over designated existing MEAs.

- Create a Sustainable Development Council at the United Nations that would be a subsidiary United Nations body on the model of the UN Human Rights Council.

- Streamline and enhance the existing system of MEAs to eliminate duplication and spur efficiency.

Although there is broad agreement on the deficiencies of the international

---

[12] Edith Brown Weiss, *International Environmental Law: Contemporary Issues and the Emergence of a New World Order*, 81 GEO. L.J. 675, 697–702 (1993).

[13] See the website: http://www.unep.org/environmentalgovernance.

[14] Steven Bernstein and Jutta Brunnee, Options for Broader Reform of the Institutional Framework for Sustainable Development (ISFD: Structural, Legal, and Financial Aspects (2012), *available at* http://www.uncsd2012.org/content/documents/322IFSD%20FIVE%20OPTIONS%20REPORT%20-%20FINAL%20VERSION%201%20NOV%20for%20posting.pdf.

environmental governance architecture and the need for reform, there is no consensus in the international community on what type of reform is best. What is your opinion?

4. *Clustering MEAs.* All the proposals for reform would "cluster" MEAs to some degree. Clustering MEAs has different meanings. MEAs could be clustered by geographical location so that different MEA secretariats could better work together. Thematic clustering of MEAs would divide MEAs into thematic groups and mandate coordination of the resulting groups of MEAs. Conference of the Parties' meetings could also be clustered so meetings of related MEAs take place back-to-back and in the same locations. Memoranda of Understanding could be signed between mutually supportive MEAs to improve exchange of information and efficiency.

5. *Universal membership.* Should UNEP reforms include provision for universal membership and assessed dues? Should the head of UNEP be elected by the membership? (At present the Executive General of UNEP is nominated by the Secretary-General of the United Nations and elected by the UN General Assembly). What kind of decisionmaking process is appropriate for UNEP?

6. *Civil society organizations.* Non-governmental organizations and other civil society organizations are presently admitted as observers to meetings of many MEAs. Should NGOs be granted a more explicit policy-making role?

7. *Democratic deficit.* Some scholars argue that international environmental organizations are undemocratic in the way they take decisions.[15] Is this a fair charge? International law functions by assuming that each state system participating in the law creation and administration process has adequately aggregated its interests in relation to a given subject matter through its national decisionmaking process, whether democratic or not, and these different national interests are then aggregated in the international system by negotiation and agreement and then by decisionmaking of international bodies. Andrew Strauss and Richard Falk have proposed the creation of a global peoples' assembly to promote democracy on the world level: *On the Creation of a Global Peoples Assembly: Legitimacy and the Power of Popular Sovereignty*, 36 STAN. J. INT'L L. 191 (2000). Is this realistic?

Section IV.   SCIENCE AND TECHNOLOGY

Scientific considerations underlie environmental law in three ways. First, although the environmental lawyer is a layman as far as science is concerned, he or she should understand a modicum of what science tells us about the natural systems of the earth and how they are impacted by anthropomorphic activities. Second, science provides crucial information on the impact of man's activities on natural systems and the environment, and scientific research can shed light on the extent to which human health and well-being are endangered by pollution and other forms of environmental degradation. Third, science and technology may provide solutions

---

[15] *See, e. g.*, James Crawford, *Democracy and the Body of International Law*, in GREGORY H. FOX AND BRAD R. ROTH (eds.), DEMOCRATIC GOVERNANCE AND INTERNATIONAL LAW (Cambridge: Cambridge University Press, 2000).

to some environmental problems. For example, environmental science can provide options for cleaning up pollution and preventing environmental degradation.

A. The Science of Ecology

Because of space exploration in the twentieth century, mankind for the first time gazed on the planet earth as a whole from space. We saw oceans and continents without man-made territorial boundaries, a large, dynamic blue ball flecked with white clouds. The entire earth is what scientists call an ecosystem, a community of living things interacting with each other and with the physical environment. The concept of ecology was first developed by Ernst Haeckel in the nineteenth century. Haeckel became interested in the relationship of living organisms with their surroundings. He named his study ecology for the Greek work for "house" — *oikos* — and added the ending *logy*, which comes from the Greek word *logos* — word, reason or cause. Thus, ecology literally means the study of the "houses" of the natural world and their reasons or causes. This underscores the fact that all living things have an "address," particular niches that they call "home."

From the standpoint of ecology, nature is a great estate in which living organisms of countless types are interacting with each other and with the physical environment in an immense and complicated web of interrelationships. Ecologists study the interactions involved between organisms and with the physical environment that sustains them. Living organisms are arranged into populations, member of the same species that live together in the same area at the same time. Populations are, in turn, arranged into communities; a community consists of populations of different species that live and interact within a specific area. The different communities of the planet earth are, in turn, organized into what we call the biosphere, the relatively thin portion on the surface of earth that supports living things. The organisms of the biosphere depend on one another and on the other three divisions of the planet earth, which we call the atmosphere, the hydrosphere, and the lithosphere. The atmosphere is a thin envelope of gases surrounding earth; the hydrosphere is the earth's supply of water; and the lithosphere is the rock and soil of the crust of the earth.

In order to function, ecosystems require energy. The energy that powers the ecosystems of earth ultimately comes from the sun. Living organisms cannot themselves create the energy that they require; they must capture energy from their environment. Plants are the key to this process since through photosynthesis plants can absorb the radiant energy of the sun and convert it into the chemical energy contained in food molecules, which animals must eat to obtain the energy they need to live and reproduce. Ecologists study the flow of energy through ecosystems. From the point of view of energy flow, the organisms of a community can be divided into producers, consumers, and decomposers. Producers are those living things that can perform photosynthesis. Through photosynthesis the bodies of producers become a potential food source for other organisms. Animals are the consumers in the system; they derive their energy from the producers. Decomposers, especially bacteria and fungi, break down organic material and use the decomposition products to supply themselves with energy. In the process the chemical energy components essential to living things are recycled and made available to support new life.

The earth and the biosphere are essentially a closed, dynamic system from which matter cannot escape. Materials crucial to the functioning of the biosphere are continually recycled through energy flows and by means of four important processes, the carbon cycle, the nitrogen cycle, the phosphorus cycle, and the hydrologic cycle. All proteins essential for life contain carbon, so living things must have access to carbon. There are multiple carbon cycles, some short-term and some that take millions of years. Carbon is naturally present in small amounts in the atmosphere, dissolved in sea water and in rocks such as limestone. The short term carbon cycle is begun through photosynthesis when plants incorporate carbon from the atmosphere and fix it into complex chemical compounds, such as sugar. These compounds are used as fuel for cell respiration by the producer that made them, or by a consumer that eats the plant, or by a decomposer that breaks down the remains of a producer or consumer. This cell respiration returns carbon to the atmosphere. A similar carbon cycle occurs in the marine environment to return carbon to sea water. In addition, the Earth maintains longer-term carbon cycles in which great amounts of carbon remain fixed for many years — sometimes millions of years — in the remains of plants and animals. For example, carbon fixed in the wood of trees may not be recycled into abiotic environments for hundreds of years. Moreover, great quantities of carbon fixed millions of years ago by long dead plants and animals remain fixed in the form of what we call fossil fuels — oil, coal, and natural gas. In nature, this fossilized carbon is recycled extremely slowly; but human activities over the past century have dramatically speeded up the recycling of this carbon through the burning of fossil fuels.

Nitrogen and phosphorus, also required by living things, are similarly recycled between the biotic and the abiotic environment through the interactions of producers, consumers and decomposers. And though the hydrologic cycle, water, also indispensable for living things, is continuously circulated from the oceans to the atmosphere to the land and back to the oceans. Water also evaporates from soil, streams, rivers, and lakes. The transpiration of plants also adds great amounts of water to the atmosphere.

Although the earth as a whole is an ecosystem, we are more familiar with the many various types of ecosystems that exist on the earth. Ecologists classify ecosystems according to their dominant physical characteristics and their plant and animal life. Major earth biomes are Tundra; Taiga (northern evergreen forests); Temperate Forests; Temperate Grasslands; Chaparral; Deserts; Savanna (tropical grasslands); Tropical Rain Forests; Estuaries; Freshwater Ecosystems; Marine Ecosystems; and Mountain Ecosystems. All of these could be subdivided into smaller ecosystem types; an ecosystem can be as large as the entire earth or as small as a child's terrarium.

Ecosystems are important because when it comes to the natural world, living organisms and their physical environment are all interconnected so that if even one element is disturbed or removed unexpected impacts may follow. For example, Lake Victoria in East Africa formerly was teeming with about 250 kinds of native fish, many species unique to the lake. In the 1960s, an exotic, the Nile perch, was introduced into the lake. This seemed like a good idea at the time; Nile perch, which are native to several African rivers systems but not Lake Victoria, were in high demand for sport and as a high-end export. Nile perch grow rapidly to attain weights of 200 kg. or more. It was thought that introduction of the Nile perch would benefit the local economy. What happened instead was that the Nile perch, a voracious predator, drove almost all of the native fish to extinction, so that now only three varieties of fish are commonly found in the lake. The Nile perch, having exhausted the supplies of other fish, now resort to cannibalism to survive. In addition, since native fish that fed on algae now are extinct, Lake Victoria is increasingly choked with algae, which reproduce unchecked, die, sink to the bottom and, upon decomposing, cause oxygen depletion, which in turn causes eutrophication of the lake. So as a result of the introduction of one new element into the lake's ecosystem, massive environmental problems have occurred. Not only has the environment suffered but also the people, who have lost access to traditional varieties of fish. The Nile perch is caught and mainly prepared for export, so fish has largely disappeared from the diets of the people living around the lake.

What does that mean for the environmental lawyer? International organizations debate sustainable development and pollution as political issues, but the science of ecology teaches us that more than politics is involved. The science of ecology makes us realize that human beings are but a part of the biosphere and that we have a great stake in assuring the continuation of its essential processes. Moreover, we are essentially engaged in a great experiment never before conducted to see how and to what extent the activities or over 7 billion human beings now living on the planet earth can coexist with the earth's natural cycles. We should not make this experiment a contest to see who wins; in the end we know it is the earth that will win any competition. Science, then, teaches us to have a modicum of humility as we go about our business.

B. Science as a Guide to Decisionmaking

A second aspect of science is that scientific studies can provide the information we need to understand the impact of anthropogenic activities on the environment and on human health and well-being. Scientific research is regarded as important to many international environmental regimes, ranging from, for example, the United Nations Framework Convention on Climate Change (1992) to the Oslo-Paris (OSPAR) Convention (preventing marine pollution in the North Sea) (1992). Theoretically scientific information can tell us where to draw the line — where to refrain from over-development; where to set the parameters to assure clean water and clean air; and how to protect resources that are essential to the functioning of ecosystems. But we must realize that the relationship between science and decisionmaking is frequently not so straightforward. First, scientific information is frequently ambiguous or uncertain when it comes to predicting the future. For example, a consensus of scientists tell us that climate change is now occurring, but science cannot explain precisely what mechanisms are involved, how fast this is occurring, or to what extent climate change is caused by anthropogenic factors as opposed to natural factors. Science also does not provide precise answers about what to do about climate change. When it comes to pollution, scientific studies may tell us the risks involved with respect to various levels of pollution, but science does not tell us precisely what standard to set or how to achieve it. Thus, while scientific information about the impact of development is essential, it does not tell us what must be done. The standards we set for environmental quality and the solutions we devise are, in the end, political determinations.

C. Science and Technology as Solutions

Science and technology can also provide solutions to environmental problems. For example, the engineering solutions to climate change include carbon separation, the "cleaning" of fossil fuels to remove most of the carbon dioxide gas before combustion; post process capture of carbon dioxide gases; carbon sequestration; and various ideas to remove carbon dioxide from the earth's atmosphere. One technical method advanced to remove carbon from the atmosphere involves sowing the world's oceans with urea to spur the growth of phytoplankton, whose life processes remove carbon dioxide from the atmosphere. Similarly, water that is polluted may be treated; scrubbers and other engineering devices may be employed to diminish air pollution. Such technological solutions to environmental degradation abound. But technological solutions to environmental problems have obvious limitations. Technology has sometimes unpleasant and unforeseen side effects; technology imposes economic costs and may not wholly or permanently solve the problem. Thus, pollution prevention may be preferable to pollution removal through technology. Pollution prevention refers to a mix of policies and idea for reducing or eliminating waste streams at their source by modifying production processes; promoting the use of non-toxic or less toxic substances; implementing conservation techniques; and reusing materials rather that relegating them to the waste stream.

For the most part we will find that international environmental regimes do not mandate specific technological solution, but leave this to the particular parties to the regimes. Mandating technology has its advantages but there are drawbacks. For example, the OSPAR Convention (1992) and the Convention on Long Range Transboundary Air Pollution (1979) both mandate "best available" technology. Studies have found, however, that mandating specific technology has two impacts: first the diffusion of available technology is enhanced; second, the development of new technology is retarded. As Steinar Andresen and Jon Birger Skjaerseth have concluded: "Technology can be either a blessing or a curse for the environment and resource management."[16]

Section V.   ENVIRONMENTAL ETHICS

Environmental ethics is a relatively new branch of philosophy that explores the moral relationship between human beings and the natural world, especially living things. The ethical criteria involved may be derived from religious or secular ideas and are commonly derived from both fields. Major religions may be interpreted to have varying mandates with respect to the natural world as follows:

---

[16] *Science and Technology*, in DANIEL BODANSKY, JUTTA BRUNNEE, AND ELLEN HAY, THE OXFORD HANDBOOK OF INTERNATIONAL ENVIRONMENTAL LAW 182, 183 (Oxford: Oxford University Press, 2007).

- Judeo-Christian ethics recognizes mankind's "domination" over nature, but passages in Genesis may be interpreted to mean that mankind's dominion is a kind of stewardship that demands our respect for nature and living things.[17]

- Islam, founded in the seventh century by God through the prophet Mohammed, accepts the Judeo-Christian tradition as authoritative and therefore the Islamic worldview is similar. The 1983 Islamic Principles for the Conservation of the Natural Environment[18] affirms that mankind is manager of the earth and its resources, not a proprietor, but a beneficiary, very close to the Judeo-Christian stewardship concept.

- Hinduism, a major religion in India, teaches that at the core of all reality there is only one Reality or Being. All beings are therefore a manifestation of the one essential Being — called Brahman. Thus the suffering of one life form is the suffering of all others so that respect for life and conservation are mandated of Hinduism.[19]

- Buddhism believes in the interconnectedness and interdependence of all living beings and that happiness is to be found in the restraint of desire so that care, compassion, and respect may be said to characterize the Buddhist ethic toward the natural world.[20]

- Chinese Taoism teaches that mankind must adapt to the Tao (the way or path), which may be interpreted as a mandate for sustainable development.[21]

Secular theories of environmental ethics emanate from the writings of Ralph Waldo Emerson and Henry David Thoreau in the nineteenth century. One of the most powerful statements of environmental ethics is the "land ethic" of Aldo Leopold. Writing in 1949, Leopold stated that "all ethics so far evolved rest upon a single premise: that the individual is a member of a community of interdependent parts. The land ethic simply enlarges the boundaries of the community to include soils, plants, animals, or collectively, the land."[22] Edward O. Wilson roots environmental ethics in the practical need for mankind to assure its own survival. Wilson chastises what he calls human "exemptionalism", the idea that "since humankind is transcendent in intelligence and spirit so must our species have been released from the iron laws of ecology that bind all other species. No matter how serious the problem, civilized human beings, by ingenuity, force of will, and who knows, what,

---

[17] *See* Lynn White, Jr., *The Historical Roots of Our Ecological Crisis*, 155 SCIENCE 1203–07 (1967).

[18] *Basic Paper on Islamic Principles for the Conservation of the Natural Environment* (International Union for the Conservation of Nature and the Government of Saudi Arabia, 1983), *available at*, https://portals.iucn.org/library/efiles/documents/EPLP-020.pdf, accessed 3 October 2012.

[19] *See* Arne Naess, *A Defence of the Deep Ecology Movement*, 6 (3) ENVITL. ETHICS 265–70 (1984).

[20] H.H. THE DALAI LAMA, BUDDHIST PERSPECTIVES ON THE ECOCRISIS (Kandy, Sri Lanka: Buddhist Publication Society, 1987).

[21] *See* Richard Sylvan and David Bennett, *Taoism and Deep Ecology*, 1988 ECOLOGIST 18.

[22] ALDO LEOPOLD, A SAND COUNTY ALMANAC AND SKETCHES HERE AND THERE, 203–04 (Oxford: Oxford University Press, 1949).

will find a solution."[23] Wilson maintains that we should rather study the laws of ecology and nature: "By learning to understand the dynamic of these systems, we can make better forecasts and make better laws and policies than we ever could previously."[24]

The "transcendentalist" movement in the United State inspired by Ralph Waldo Emerson's 1836 Essay, "Nature" and Henry David Thoreau's "Walden Pond" saw the natural world as essential to man's appreciation of beauty and spirituality. Emerson states in "Nature" that "in the wilderness I find something more dear and connate than in streets and villages. In the tranquil landscape, and especially in the distant line of the horizon, man beholds somewhat as beautiful as his own nature."

One of the most profound ideas of the natural world is attributed to Chief Seattle of the Suquamish Tribe (1854):

> This we know
>
> The Earth does not belong to man
>
> Man belongs to the Earth
>
> All things are connected
>
> Like the blood that unites one family
>
> What befalls the Earth
>
> Befalls the sons and daughters of the Earth
>
> Man did not weave the web of life
>
> He is merely a strand in it
>
> Whatever he does to the web
>
> He does to himself

NOTES AND QUESTIONS

1. *Three primary categories.* Susan L. Smith maintains that "Environmentalists can be distinguished by ideology into three primary categories. Traditional 'conservationists' prefer a managerial approach to continued development of natural resources. Those who adhere to a 'preservationist' philosophy advocate preserving the remaining natural resources. 'Deep ecologists' require a total redefinition of man's relationship to nature in favor of minimizing human impact on nature."[25]

Which of these three best describe your ethical position?

2. *A new statement of environmental ethics.* In the 1990s, Maurice Strong, a Canadian former Under Secretary-General of the United Nations, and Mikhail

---

[23] Edward O. Wilson, *Is Humanity Suicidal?*, N.Y. TIMES, May 30, 1993, at 15, 16.

[24] *Ibid.*

[25] Susan L. Smith, *Ecologically Sustainable Development: Integrating Economics, Ecology, and Law*, 31 WILLAMETTE L. REV. 261, 299 (1995).

Gorbachev, former premier of the Soviet Union, both members of the Club of Rome, decided to formulate a modern statement of environmental ethics. A cross-cultural, cross-ethnic drafting committee was formed composed of people from all over the world. Meeting for six years, this independent committee promulgated a modern statement of environmental ethics called *The Earth Charter* (March 2000), which we reprint in the **Document Supplement**. Read over The Earth Charter. Do you agree with the ideas expressed?

Section VI. ENVIRONMENTAL POLITICS AND ECONOMICS

A. Theories of Interdependence

Why do states enter into international environmental agreements, especially multilateral environmental agreement (MEAs)? The field of international relations offers several competing theories to explain the behavior of states. First is called "Realism", or as formulated by Kenneth Waltz[26], Neo-Realism or Structural Realism. The key idea of Realism is that the key actors in the world are states and that the international system at its core is anarchic in the sense that there can be no authoritative international institutions that constrain states in the pursuit of their interests. But what, then, explains the proliferation of international regimes? In the 1980s, a theory known as Neo-Liberal Institutionalism or Regime Theory was developed, primarily by Robert Keohane[27] and S. D. Krasner[28] to explain the rise of international institutions. The institutionalists accept the idea that the international system is dominated by states pursuing their own interests, but add that self-interested states (even powerful ones) engage in macro-economic analysis and are willing to sacrifice some of their autonomy in order to establish "institutions" or "regimes" — principles, norms, rules, and decisionmaking procedures that constrain states-parties behavior on a mutual basis — where the gains from cooperation exceed the gains from unilateral action. Some scholars have advanced additional theories of international relations. "Liberal-internationalism" holds that non-state actors play a large role, and that states have broad mutual interests in securing the rule of law and solving world problems.[29] "Constructivist" scholars are critics of the "institutionalist" focus on interest-based explanations for the creation of regimes. They point out that states' interests can be shaped by regimes themselves, and that regimes are social structures where states acquire shared knowledge, material resources and engage in shared practices.[30]

The "institutionalist" thesis holds that a state will agree to constrain its behavior only if the net benefits of the agreement exceed its costs. But a state constraining its behavior will derive net benefits only if a sufficient number of other states agree

---

[26] Kenneth N. Waltz, Theory of International Politics, Ch. 1 (New York: McGraw Hill, 1979).

[27] Robert O. Keohane, After Hegemony: Cooperation and Discord in the World Economy (Princeton: Princeton University Press 1984).

[28] S.D. Krasner (ed.), International Regimes (Ithaca, New York: Cornell University Press, 1983).

[29] Ann-Marie Slaughter, A New World Order (Princeton: Princeton University Press, 2004).

[30] Alexander Wendt, *Constructing International Politics*, 10 Int'l Security 71, 73 (1995/96).

to constrain their behavior. Will this happen and under what conditions? In any environmental regime, isn't there an overwhelming incentive to Pollute rather than Abate — to be a "free rider" if possible? As Scott Barrett points out, according to "institutionalist" theory the decision whether or not to join an international regime is a form of "prisoners' dilemma," the classic game in which both parties win only by cooperating, but there is an overwhelming incentive to "defect," to eschew cooperation.[31] Is this the case when it comes to joining international environmental law regimes?

Barrett suggests a classroom game to test institutionalist cooperation theory that we like to play with our students. Two cards are distributed to each student in the class, one marked "red" and other marked "blue." The student is asked to return only one card of his or her choice to the professor without anyone seeing which card they return. Students are told to suppose they will get $15 if they keep their red card, but they will obtain $1 for every red card handed in by any student. In a class of 25 students each one will have to make a calculation: Will my return be greater by keeping my red card or by turning it in to the professor? All the students will win if they cooperate and turn in their red cards; but there is a great temptation to defect and keep the red card worth $15.

Is this an adequate explanation why states create and enter into regimes, or do you agree more with the liberal and constructivist explanations that creating a regime is not just a matter of a self-interest calculation?

B.   The Problem of Social Costs

Economic concepts enter into the law of the environment as they affect national environmental policies. The most important economic concept we must master is the problem of social costs. From an economic standpoint, the environment can be regarded as a commons, a common property resource open to all. Any common property resource open to all will tend to become overused, and ultimately may become useless to all. The point was made graphically by Garrett Hardin in his classic essay, The Tragedy of the Commons (1968).[32] Hardin asks us to picture a pasture open to all. In such a case, a rational herdsman (or woman) will keep as many cattle as possible on the commons pasture. He/she will make the following calculation when it comes to whether to add one more animal to his/her herd grazing on the commons: "My positive utility in adding another animal is close to plus one because I can keep all the proceeds from the sale of this animal. Yes, there is a negative component to adding one more animal; the commons may be overgrazed. But this does not matter because the effects of this negative component are shared by all who use the commons; and my share will be very small." Thus the rational herdsman will always add one more animal to graze on the commons even though he knows it will lead to the ruin of the commons. This is the "tragedy of the commons."

---

[31] Scott Barrett, *An Economic Theory of International Environmental Law*, in Daniel Bodansky, Jutta Brunnee, and Ellen Hey, The Oxford Handbook of International Environmental Law 231, 237 (Oxford: Oxford University Press, 2007).

[32] Garrett Hardin, *The Tragedy of the Commons*, 162 Science 1243 (1968).

How can we deal with the problem of social costs and avoid the "tragedy of the commons"? There are three obvious solutions. First, some higher authority (government) could simply limit the number of animals that can graze on the common. There are obvious problems connected with this solution, such as dealing with differences of even "science-based" opinions on how many animals the commons can accommodate and equity considerations in allocating the available animal slots, but finally a decision is handed down from on high, and all must accept it.

A second method of saving the commons is for the higher authority to pay people not to add additional animals beyond the carrying capacity of the commons. Obviously, this solution is not very practical and is fraught with ethical and economic difficulties. Subsidization of the users of the commons to save the commons will not usually be possible.

A third solution is to allow the commons to be open to all but to impose a charge on those who graze their animals on the commons. This charge will fall on the users of the commons based on the number of animals and proportional to the rate of use of the commons and can be calibrated to ensure the vitality of the commons itself.

Let us now evaluate each of these solutions from the standpoint of microeconomics. To an economist, each potential user of the commons is an economic producer acting within an economic system. In an ideal economic system — one in which there is perfect competition — each producer of an economic good will bear the costs of his production (costs set by the market) and will reap a profit if the market determines that the good he produces is worth more than the costs that went into its production. For the economist, therefore, the "tragedy of the commons" is caused by the fact that the herdsmen do not bear the total of the costs of their economic activity. A substantial part of the cost of adding the extra animal is borne by others — the users of the commons. The costs borne by others in this situation may be termed external costs. So for the economist the solution to avoid the "tragedy of the commons" is to internalize the external costs so that each herdsman will bear the total cost of his activity for which he derives the total benefit; then he will make a true, economically rational decision as to whether to add another animal to his herd.

To an economist, only one of the three solutions above will make sense. Putting an arbitrary limit on the number of animals that may use the commons is not a good idea for two main reasons: It is a coercive, "command and control" decision that (1) collides with the freedom of the individual economic actors and (2) replaces the market as the criteria for determining what is produced with government fiat. The second solution — subsidization of producers — is also bad since this also interferes with the market's ability to allocate costs and make production decisions.

Thus, the economic-based solution to the "tragedy of the commons" is to determine the actual cost to each producer of using the commons and to impose that cost on each herdsman in the form of a user charge. This seems to be the ideal solution and is consistent with free-market economics in that payment of the user charge will ensure that each herdsman pays the full cost of grazing his cattle on the commons and the decision is left to each producer whether to incur those costs.

Furthermore, we can use the same theoretical framework — internalizing external costs of production — to deal with all manner of polluting activities and environmental degradation. Economic activity should not be permitted unless the economic producer involved bears all the costs associated with his activity. Economic producers are in effect using a commons — the atmosphere or lakes, rivers, and oceans — when they pollute. The solution to environmental degradation that is consistent with free-market economics, therefore, is to impose effluent charges for water pollution and emission charges on pollution of the air.[33] This theory of "externalities" holds that as long as external costs exist and are not internalized through monetary charges the result is economically inefficient. This inefficiency is eliminated by charging a fee equivalent the environmental degradation associated with the particular activity.

But on refection, internalization of the external costs is easier said than done, especially when it comes to external costs of pollution and environmental degradation. Take the case of air pollution. Cost internalization theory dictates that the atmosphere is a commons so we must internalize the costs of pollution so that the polluter pays 100% of the costs of his activity. This is termed the "Polluter-Pays Principle," which we cover in the next chapter. But how is the cost of environmental degradation to be measured? Some of the cost — perhaps the economic damage to surrounding buildings — can be measured, but damage to surrounding ecosystems and even damage to human health caused by the pollution will be difficult to determine and impossible to measure in economic terms. In addition, a powerful case can be made that internalization of 100% of the external costs is too stringent and unfair. Typically the costs of removing or treating pollution vary with the stringency of controls required. It is easy and relatively inexpensive to remove perhaps 60% of the pollution, but sophisticated and expensive controls may be needed to approach 100% removal. In economic terms the marginal costs of pollution control tend to rise with the degree to which pollution removal is mandated. At some point the costs of removing a unit of pollution will exceed the social benefits. Moreover, society undeniably benefits from a polluter's economic activity; society derives benefits in terms of jobs, products, and economic activity. An economist would argue therefore that external costs of pollution should be internalized only to the extent that social costs of the pollution exceed the social benefits of the pollution to society.[34] All this goes to show that cost internalization as a solution to pollution and environmental degradation presents controversial issues that reasonable people may not agree upon.

Further criticisms of cost internalization as the societal cure for environmental degradation were raised by R.H. Coase in his classic essay, "The Problem of Social Cost," in 1960.[35] Coase raised three fundamental points which put externality theory and the Polluter Pays Principle into question. First, Coase pointed out that

---

[33] The economist who first came up with these insights was A.C. Pigou. *See* PIGOU, WEALTH AND WELFARE (1912) and THE ECONOMICS OF WELFARE (1920). Pigou's solution is taken up by "Chicago School" free market economists. *See* MILTON AND ROSE FRIEDMAN, FREE TO CHOOSE 207 (1980).

[34] WILLIAM F. BAXTER, PEOPLE OR PENGUINS: THE CASE FOR OPTIMAL POLLUTION (New York, Columbia University Press, 1974).

[35] 3 J. LAW & ECON. 1 (1960).

— from the point of view of economic efficiency — the problem of externalities is a "problem of a reciprocal nature." Coase attacked the idea that pollution externalities were one-sided, and that there is always a "polluter" and a "victim of pollution." Rather, Coase argued, many if not most externality situations are nuisance cases: two legitimate activities are occurring, but they cannot both be conducted without getting in each other's way. For example, a cement plant is built near a residential subdivision, and its operations cause injury from dust, smoke, and vibrations emanating from the plant. Coase argued that in such a case it is wrong to give automatically the right to be free of external costs to the residential subdivision because it may be cheaper — and therefore more economically efficient — to move or modify the subdivision rather than to forego the $45 million invested in the cement plant and the 300 workers who will lose their jobs.

Second, Coase argued that in externality situations it really does not matter to which party the right is assigned, what matters only is that the right be clearly assigned to one party or another. In that case, Coase maintained, as far as economic efficiency is concerned, free market bargaining may be employed to solve the problem of social costs without government intervention. In the cement plant example, if the right is assigned to the cement plant to pollute, the landowners will either bargain to pay the cement plant to control its pollution; or they will decide to move and use their land for some other purpose. If, on the other hand, the right is assigned to the landowners to be free of pollution, the cement plant will bargain to pay the landowners damages or will close down or eliminate its polluting activities. Either way, Coase maintained, the most economically efficient result will be arrived at through free market bargaining.[36]

Third, Coase maintained that the reason why bargaining does not actually occur in many pollution and nuisance situations is not because of any flaw in his theory of social costs, but because of the high "transaction costs" that may be involved — in our cement plant situation the number of landowners affected maybe too great to allow them to band together to create a bargaining situation. So Coase argued that the problems of social costs and the "tragedy of the commons" are not really about externalities, but rather about transaction costs. If it were not for the transaction costs, externalities would be easy to deal with in a way that achieves an optimally economically efficient solution.

From this discussion it is readily apparent that, while there a certain identity of interests between economic analysis of pollution and avoidance of environmental degradation, there are also important divergences, and that economic-based solutions to the problem of social costs, while useful, may not be sufficient to preserve environmental values. The nub of the divergence between economic analysis and environmental analysis is the difference in their purposes or ends: The economist's formulation of externality theory presumes the only goal is economic efficiency, while the environmentalist's aim is to preserve the natural world and the functioning of ecosystems. The economist's values can be reduced to monetary

---

[36] The cement plant example is an actual case, Boomer v. Atlantic Cement Co, 257 N.E.2d 870 (N.Y. 1970). In this case the court granted an injunction against the operation of the cement plant, but ordered that it be vacated upon the payment of permanent compensation to plaintiffs of damages sufficient to compensate them for the total economic loss to their property (past, present, and future).

terms, while the environmentalist's values cannot.

This may be the reason why in a given situation environmentalists may argue in favor of "command and control" governmental regulations to control the social costs of environmental degradation, but economists may be opposed. But one leading economist who argued that it was necessary to go beyond economic-based instruments to control environmental degradation was Ezra J. Mishan of the London School of Economics:

> [S]pillover [externalities] effects tend to be underestimated. Many . . . important spillover effects are irreversible. The destruction of scenic beauty, the poisoning of rivers, streams or the atmosphere may be regarded as permanent in terms of man's life span. If spillovers cause permanent damage the losses suffered by future generations must also be brought into the calculus. Once brought in they strengthen the case for government intervention, rather than for negotiation between opposing groups and for total prohibition of more suspect spillovers, rather than for their reduction.[37]

Are there limits to the economic efficiency criterion? We may ask with the poet William Blake:

> Can Wisdom be put in a silver rod?

> Or Love In a Golden Bowl?

With this background, we can analyze both the correspondence and the tensions between environmental and economic solutions to the problem of how to handle the social costs of environmental degradation. In the following excerpt the Organization for Economic Cooperation and Development (OECD), an intergovernmental organization based in Paris consisting of 34 developed country members, including the United States, advocates economic-based regulatory programs to combat environmental degradation.

None of these solutions is perfect; all have drawbacks as well as advantages.

ORGANIZATION FOR ECONOMIC COOPERATION AND DEVELOPMENT
Recommendation on the Use of Economic Instruments in Environmental Policy
31 January 1991 — C(90)177/FINAL

I. Types of Economic Instruments to which the Guidelines Apply

1.   Economic instruments have the potential to be applied to a wide range of environmental and natural resources issues. The present guidelines deal with the use or economic instruments defined hereunder. In addition, there are other types of economic instruments such as enforcement incentives, fines, non-compliance fees, administrative charges, performance bonds, damage compensation, etc. which may

---

[37] Mishan, *The Economics of Disamenity*, 14 NAT. RESOURCES. J. 54, 82 (1974).

have a role in environmental policy but are not considered here. Furthermore, the guidelines focus primarily on pollution issues although economic instruments also have considerable potential for application in the form of resource pricing.

Charges and Taxes

h. Emissions charges or taxes are payments on the emission of pollutants into air or water or onto or into soil and on the generation of noise. Emission charges or taxes are calculated on the basis of the quantity and type of pollutant discharged.

i. User charges or taxes are payments for the costs of collective treatment of effluent or waste.

j. Product charges or taxes are levied on products that are harmful to the environment when used in production processes, consumed or disposed of. Product charges or taxes can act as a substitute for emission charges or taxes when charging directly for emissions is not feasible. They may be applied to raw materials, intermediate or final (consumer) products. Product tax differentiation may be designed for the same purpose.

Marketable Permits

k. Marketable permits are quotas, allowances or ceilings on pollution emission levels of specified polluters that, once allocated by the appropriate authority, can be traded subject to a set of prescribed rules. Hence, marketable permits provide an incentive for dischargers releasing less pollution than their limits allow, to trade the differences between actual discharges and allowable discharges to other dischargers which then have the right to release more than allowed by initial limits. Under different approaches, these trades can take place within a plant, within a firm, among different firms or possibly between countries. The objective is to reach the overall pollution ceiling with maximum efficiency. Equally, marketable permits can be used as a device to encourage efficient use of natural resources such as scarce water supplies.

Deposit-Refund Systems

l. With deposit-refund systems, a deposit is paid on the acquisition of potentially polluting products. When pollution is avoided by returning the products or their residuals, a refund follows.

Financial Assistance

m. Various forms of financial assistance can be granted to polluters as help and/or as an inducement to abate their polluting emissions. As a general rule, financial assistance is incompatible with the Polluter-Pays Principle, except in a few specific cases, for example, when in compliance with the exceptions to the Polluter-Pays Principle as defined in the two Council Recommendations [C(72)128 and C(74)223] or when applied in the framework of appropriately designed redistributive charging systems.

There may also be circumstances where payments can be made to reinforce other measures designed to achieve appropriate natural resource use.

II. Criteria for Choice of Instruments

n. Economic instruments constitute one category amongst others of instruments designed to achieve environmental goals. They can be used as a substitute or as a complement to other policy instruments such as regulations and co-operative agreements with industry, in some instances, for economic and administrative reasons, direct regulation and control are appropriate when, for example, it is imperative that the emission of certain toxic pollutants or the use of hazardous products or substances be wholly prohibited. In other instances, economic instruments can supplement regulations in order to strengthen the enforcement of standards designed to protect public health.

o. The choice or environmental policy instruments can be made against five sets of criteria:

  i. Environmental effectiveness: The environmental effectiveness of economic instruments is mainly determined by the ability of polluters to react. The primary objective of economic instruments is to provide a permanent incentive to pollution abatement technical innovation, and product substitution.

  ii. Economic efficiency: In a broad sense, economic efficiency is achieved by an optimal allocation of resources; in a limited but more operational sense, it implies that the economic cost of complying with environmental requirements in minimized.

  iii. Equity: Distributive consequences vary according to the types of policy instruments applied. For example, pollution charges or taxes entail additional payment on the discharge of "residual" pollution; additionally their distributive impact would depend upon how the revenue is used. Similarly, with marketable permits, the distributional effects will differ according to their initial allocation.

  iv. Administrative feasibility and cost: All types of policy instruments involve implementation and enforcement structures. This relates in particular to the ease and cost of monitoring discharges and the number of target groups involved and also upon the nature of existing legal and institutional settings.

  v. Acceptability: It is of crucial importance that target groups be informed and consulted on the economic instruments imposed on them. In general, the success of any (economic) instrument requires certainty and stability over time with respect to their basic elements.

p. Regarding the choice of specific economic instruments, the following elements should be taken into consideration:

Emission charges or taxes can be given particular consideration for stationary pollution sources and where marginal abatement costs vary across polluters (the wider the variation, the greater the cost-saving potential). Other criteria are: the feasibility of monitoring emission (through direct monitoring or proxy variables); the ability of polluters to react to the charge; the ability of public authorities to develop a consistent framework for charges; the potential for technical innovation.

User charges are relevant when collective disposal and treatment facilities can be operated, e.g. for waste water, industrial and household waste.

Product charges or taxes can be particularly effective when applied to products that are consumed or used in large quantities and in diffuse patterns. Products subject to charges should be readily identifiable.

Deposit-refund systems can be considered for products or substances which can be reused, recycled or which should be returned for destruction. Because deposit refund schemes can be expensive and complicated to operate, it is important that products be easy to identify and to handle and that users and consumers should also be willing to take part in the scheme.

Marketable permit systems offer particular advantages in situations in which: the marginal costs of compliance with a uniform standard vary significantly across the regulated target group; when there is a fixed objective which one wants to achieve at minimum economic cost; the number of sources involved is large enough to establish a well-functioning, competitive market for permits, within a designated geographical area.

III. Guidelines for Implementing Economic Instruments

q. When considering the adoption of economic instruments, it is important to assess the cost and benefits of all policy alternatives. In particular, the development, implementation and enforcement of economic instruments should take due consideration of the issues defined hereunder.

Clear Framework and Objectives

r. First and foremost, the framework and objectives of the economic instrument must be clear, in particular, the following points should be specified: whether the economic instrument operates in combination with or as an alternative to direct regulation; whether it precedes regulations in order to speed up compliance; whether the revenues are used for general purposes or earmarked for specific environmental or other measures, in the case of charges or taxes, the objective of providing incentives should not be confused with the revenue-raising purpose.

IV. Fields of Possible Application of Economic Instruments

Water Pollution

26. Water pollution is particularly amenable to emission (effluent) and user charges or taxes as effluent discharge from stationary sources are relatively easy to monitor.

27.   Product charges or taxes may be applied in the case of products that will pollute surface or ground water before, during or after consumption. Examples of possible applications relate to detergents, fertilizers and pesticides. If the objective of the product charge or tax is to discourage consumption, the quantity of the products consumed should be highly sensitive to prices. The availability of cleaner substitutes could considerably increase the success of product charges or differentiated taxes (such as detergents with and without phosphates). Product charges or taxes can also be used as a proxy for emission charges or taxes (e.g. charge on the use of polluting products in production processes).

28.   Marketable permits could be applied to point sources as well as to combinations of point sources and non-point sources. In the case of point source/non-point source situations, point sources could obtain additional rights by reducing the pollution burden from non-point sources.

29.   Deposit-refund systems can play an indirect role in water management. Many potentially polluting substances (for example pesticides) are packed in non-returnable containers. During disposal of the containers the remnants of these substances are released into the environment and might pollute surface and ground water. Such remnants can be properly processed when containers are returned to the producer.

30.   Pollutants which are discharged in large quantities by many dischargers, and which are easy to calculate or monitor or for which a common denominator exists (BOD, COD), and more easily be subjected to emission charges or taxes thant pollutants that occur in great variety and small amounts (heavy metals, toxic substances). For the latter, product charges or taxes could be considered. Because of the complexity of the matter a multi-phase approach is necessary, starting with those pollutants that are easiest to handle and lead to substantial improvements.

31.   The main target groups for economic instruments in the field of water quality policy are industry (chemical, metal, food, pulp and paper, mining, etc.), agriculture, and households.

32.   With regard to industry, emission (effluent) charges or taxes could be applied where: 1) industry can effectively reduce emissions in response to the charge or tax; 2) technical innovation is likely to be encouraged; and 3) when the level of emissions can reasonably be monitored.

33.   Agricultural pollution from point sources (such as intensive animal husbandry units) can often be controlled by regulatory means, complemented, where effective, by economic instruments in the form of effluent charges or taxes.

Air Pollution

34.   In the field of air pollution control, emission charges or taxes may be considered as a complement or a substitute to regulation. For administrative reasons (in particular, monitoring of emissions), emission charges or taxes are more easily applicable to large volume pollutants and large stationary sources.

35.   As energy production and use is a major cause of air pollution, energy pricing should take environmental factors into account; this can be done by applying

product charges or taxes, in particular charges on fuels in the form of a surcharge on or a variation of the excise duties on fossil fuels. Product charges or taxes can be used as a proxy for emission charges or taxes, for instance when pollution is diffuse, when there are many, small (mobile) sources. There is a strong tradition, especially in the transport sector, for taxation of mobile sources, and these should be adapted in line with environmental objectives.

36.   Creating price differentiation between traditional products and cleaner substitutes can be done by a combination of surcharges and discounts on the price of such products in a broadly revenue-neutral way.

37.   Marketable permits can be considered in order to create market conditions for new and modified installations and regarding air pollution characteristics of some products (e.g. cars). Producers could be allowed to trade credits by exceeding standards or meeting them earlier than required, providing that equal or better environmental conditions are achieved.

38.   Deposit-refund systems can be applied to products that contain potentially polluting substances in closed circuits (e.g. refrigerators and air conditioners containing CFC's). After return, such products can be properly scrapped, or recycled.

39.   In the case of air pollution, the main target groups for applying economic instruments are industry, energy and transport. For industry, the same constraints applicable to water pollution (paragraph 31) should be taken into account. For the energy sector, particular attention should be paid to proper integration of energy and environmental policies through appropriate pricing of energy resources.

40.   Integration of transport and environmental policies is also of particular relevance. Not only should transport pricing and taxation take into account environmental factors, but also specific economic instruments could be introduced, such as pricing/taxation of fuels reflecting, as far as possible, the ultimate environmental damage caused. Motor-vehicles could also be subjected to environmental charges or taxes. Congestion charges or taxes, primarily designed to alleviate traffic problems, could contribute to reducing air pollution. Finally, charging for the use of transport infrastructures (road pricing and other tolls) should also integrate environmental concerns, when appropriate.

Waste Management

41.   Financing (user) charges should aim at a proper collection, processing and storage of waste or at the cleanup of old hazardous waste sites. Incentive charges or taxes can have multiple purposes which should be recognized when designed. A first purpose might be to minimize (voluminous and/or toxic) waste generation in production and consumption processes. A second purpose might be to discourage production and consumption of (voluminous and/or toxic) waste-intensive products and to promote more "friendly" substitutes. Thirdly, economic instruments can be introduced to promote recycling which saves depletable resources, including space for waste dumping.

42.   Emission (disposal) charges taxes should be based either on the volume and/or

on the toxicity (or other harmful characteristics) of waste elements. In the latter case, waste containing many substances will cause calculation and monitoring problems. Because of possible evasion, emission charges or taxes can only be applied if it is easy to control dischargers. In most cases, user charges, i.e. payment for waste collection and the use of waste disposal facilitates, can be applied.

43.   Product charges or taxes can be considered in the case of products that will generate waste in the production or consumption phases (e.g. plastic bags). They act as proxies in those cases where a direct charging for waste is not effective or efficient. Materials which cannot be recycled or re-used could be subjected to charges or taxes.

44.   In the cases where a return of used products to collection or storage sites is important, a deposit-refund system can be considered. This is desirable when such products can be re-used or recycled (bottles, crates) or when such products contain potentially polluting substances (batteries, cars). A product subject to a deposit-refund system should exist in large quantity and the necessary collection system should be manageable.

45.   Main target groups for economic instruments in waste management are industry, agriculture, households and the waste handling sector, be it public or private. Industry may be subject to economic instruments, either because they produce products that will create waste problems when used or disposed of, or generate voluminous or toxic wastes. Agricultural waste such as animal manure could also be charged for.

Applying Economic Instruments to International and Global Environmental Problems

51.   Economic instruments can be considered for tackling international and global environmental problems, such as acid rain, global warming and stratospheric ozone depletion, in the most cost-effective manner.

52.   Carbon dioxide is the main factor causing global warming, but emissions cannot be removed by any end-of-pipe treatment currently available. However, since emissions are proportional to the carbon content of the fuels being burned, a charge or tax on carbon would be identical to an emission charge or tax on carbon dioxide. The charge or tax on carbon could be translated into a product charge or tax on fossil fuels given information about the carbon content of these fuels. Likewise, the tax system may be adapted, for example through a taxation of the sulphur content of fuels. General measures such as energy taxes or charges should, in conformity with other policy objectives, encourage increased energy efficiency, thereby lowering related environmental impacts.

53.   Marketable permits can also be considered. If the goal is to hold emissions constant, some existing emission sources could be allowed to increase emissions, and new sources could be allowed to emit, provided that they can get some other source to reduce emissions by at least an equivalent amount. Alternatively, increases in emissions could be offset by investments which increase the environment's ability to absorb the emissions (in the case of carbon dioxide).

54. Target groups vary from problem to problem. For instance, a limited number of firms produce CFCs and these could be subjected to charges or marketable permits. For practical reasons, marketable permits would have to apply to producers and importers only. Large emission sources of carbon like electricity producers could be allocated marketable permits or be made subject to carbon charges or taxes. Small sources like households could also be subject to a carbon charge or tax (for example, on gasoline and home heating fuels).

PROBLEM 1-2
CHOICE OF LEGAL INSTRUMENTS TO COMBAT CARBON EMISSIONS

The United States relies upon a "mix" of legal instruments to reduce emissions of carbon dioxide and other so-called "greenhouse gases." Consider the following types of legal requirements:

1) A regulation requiring electrical generating facilities to reduce carbon dioxide emissions to comply with a national emission standard of 1,100 lb. CO_2/MWh gross over a 12-month operation period. Compliance with this standard will require the application of new technologies known as carbon capture and storage (CCS).

2) A grant made to three private electrical generating companies in the amount of $70 million under the American Recovery and Reinvestment Act of 2009, in order to fund their research into CCS technology.

3) A regulation requiring the installation of mechanical "scrubbers" to remove CO_2 from the flue gas of coal-fired power plants.

4) Tax credits to individuals and corporations that purchase defined renewable energy technology for installation in office and multifamily buildings.

5) Corporate average fuel economy (CAFÉ) standards for car and light trucks requiring an average performance of 37.8 miles per gallon.

6) All manufacturing and electrical generating facilities must pay a tax of 10 cents per ton CO_2 emitted.

7) Electrical generating facilities must comply with a "cap and trade" program designed to reduce emissions of CO_2. Once the "cap" is set, emission allowances will be issued to all eligible parties. No emissions of CO_2 will be permitted unless the emitter holds an emission allowance which covers the amount of carbon emitted. The buying and selling of carbon allowances is freely permitted. The cap and trade program is thus designed to put a price on the emissions of carbon into the atmosphere.

Which of these programs are economic instruments favored by the OECD? Which are command and control regulations? Which are subsidies? Why does the OECD favor the use of economic instruments? What is the problem with greater use of economic instruments? Why are they not widely used in the United States and in many other countries?

NOTES AND QUESTIONS

1.   ***Instrument choice.*** The choice of what regulatory instruments to select for international environmental law treaties and regimes is an important issue. The three basic varieties of regulatory instruments are (1) command and control; (2) economic instruments; and (3) information-based instruments.[38] Command and control regulation specifies in detail required prohibited conduct, including such matters as the quantitative limit of pollution allowed; and requirements for the adoption of specific technologies and solutions, such as best available technology (BAT) or product and process method (PPM) requirements. Economic instruments impose a price or opportunity cost on each unit of pollution, waste, stress, or resource consumption by regulated actors. Economic instruments do not proscribe conduct so much as create economic incentives to steer behavior in the right direction. Economic instruments include environmental taxes or fees; tradable pollution rights; property rights in natural resources; subsidies; and liability under a strict liability standard for environmental harm caused. Information-based schemes include ecolabels and other product-based information; public disclosure; environmental impact assessment and environmental goal setting, management, auditing and reporting requirements. Why does the OECD recommend greater use of economic instruments? Which of the three do you think is best? Do we need a mix of all three?

2.   ***Vertical environmental regimes.*** On the international plane international institutions usually do not have the authority to regulate directly private economic actors. Direct regulation is usually up to the state-parties to the particular regime. international environmental instruments usually may not prescribe what category of regulation state-parties must adopt, so the choice of instrument is usually left to each state party in vertical international regimes. Should states have discretion in adopting the means to achieve a mandated environmental result, or should international instruments always prescribe BAT or PPM requirements?

3.   ***Horizontal environmental regimes.*** Some international environmental regimes govern horizontal relations between states regarding certain issues, such as protection of endangered species and restrictions on the movement of hazardous waste. For example the Convention on International Trade in Endangered Species of Wild Fauna and Flora (CITES) restricts trade in endangered species and the Basil Convention on the Control of Transboundary Movements of Hazardous Wastes places controls on exports of hazardous wastes to developing countries. Such trade measures are command and control regulations. Additional command and control measures that might be adopted between states might include PPM requirements. To what extent are economic instruments and information-based measures appropriate in horizontal relations between states? For example, subsidy payments may be made to developing countries to enable them to join and to carry out an international regime. States may be granted property rights in natural resources; an example of this is the recognition that each coastal state has an Exclusive Economic Zone of 200 nautical miles. Additional economic solutions are to create pollution trading schemes among participating states and to impose liability

---

[38] *See* Richard B. Stewart, *Instrument Choice*, in DANIEL BODANSKY, JUTTA BRUNNEE, & ELLEN HEY, THE OXFORD HANDBOOK OF INTERNATIONAL ENVIRONMENTAL LAW 147 (Oxford; Oxford University Press, 2007).

for environmental damage between states. States may create an information-based regime by imposing, for example, a requirement of prior informed consent on the export of certain products, as exemplified by the Cartagena Protocol on Biosafety. Instrument choice is a pervasive issue in international environmental law.

Chapter 2

GENERAL INTERNATIONAL ENVIRONMENTAL LAW

Section I. INTRODUCTION

International Environmental Law is a distinctive branch of Public International Law that States and international organizations have created to deal with the international aspects of conservation and protection of natural resources, natural processes, and the natural environment. This body of law is quite new; most international environmental norms have been developed only in the last 40 years. General International Environmental Law is the body of principles, doctrines, and legal concepts that cut across all areas of the subject.

A. The Contours of International Environmental Law

Because the field of International Environmental Law is quite new and due to the pervasiveness of environmental problems, the contours of international environmental law are ill-defined. In general terms international environmental law addresses three categories of concerns: (1) environmental degradation that has potentially global impacts; (2) transboundary environmental and resources impacts; and (3) environmental problems of areas and resources located beyond national jurisdictions. But we emphasize that international law is neither a self-contained system nor a coherent body of international law. What we term international environmental law may also sometimes be categorized as international human rights law, international law of the sea, international finance law, international trade law, and so on. For example, in 2000, when Chile restricted access of fishing vessels to Chilean ports, the European Community filed a complaint against Chile at the World Trade Organization charging that Chile was acting inconsistently with its obligations under Articles V and IX of the General Agreement on Tariffs and Trade.[1] Chile, however, turned this international trade dispute into an international maritime and environmental dispute by filing a complaint with the international Tribunal for the Law of the Sea (ITLOS), charging that the European Community was acting inconsistently with its obligation under the United Nations Convention on the Law of the Sea to ensure conservation of swordfish stocks. In the event, Chile and the European Community happily reached a negotiated settlement: Chile restored access to its ports in return for the

---

[1] *Chile — Measures Affecting the Transit and Importation of Swordfish, Request for Consultations by the European Communities*, Doc. WT/DS193/1 (April 26, 2000).

European Community's agreement to implement new conservation measures for swordfish stocks.[2]

Thus we reiterate that international environmental law is, as cogently stated by Alan Boyle, "nothing more, or less, than the application of international law to environmental problems and concerns."[3]

B. Public International Law

For those without a background in Public International Law, a brief recap of this complex subject is in order. Public International Law is a legal system that is distinct from national law that deals with relations among states and between states and international organizations and governs certain specified activities of individuals and corporations as well. This body of law takes into account the fact that the world is divided politically into some 200 states, each of which enjoy the attribute of sovereignty, exclusive legislative, executive, and judicial jurisdiction over activities within its territory. Because of the universal political and legal recognition of sovereignty, and because there is no world sovereign, Public International Law relies on distinctive law-making methods that put states at the center of norm-creation.

Public International Law recognizes three primary and two subsidiary methods of norm-creation. The primary sources of international law are (1) treaties; (2) customary law; and (3) general principles of law. The recognized subsidiary sources of law are (1) writings of scholars and experts and (2) decisions of international tribunals. This enumeration of the sources of international law is derived from Article 38 of the Statute of the Permanent Court of International Justice, adopted in 1920, and is now enshrined in Article 38(1) of the Statute of International Court of Justice. This formulation remains the only universally accepted authoritative statement of the sources of international law. We briefly consider each of these in turn before moving on to some distinctive adaptations of these sources in international environmental law.

1. Treaties

Treaties are by far the most common source of international law norms. A treaty may be defined simply as a written or oral agreement between states, or between states and international organizations, or between international organizations that is governed by international law. In English treaties are called by many names: conventions, protocols, agreements, covenants, and pacts; but this terminology is legally immaterial. All are "treaties" under international law.

Many important aspects of treaty-making are governed by national laws, and each nation's law in this regard is distinct. For example, U.S. constitutional law

---

[2] Case Concerning the Conservation and Sustainable Exploitation of Swordfish Stocks in the South-eastern Pacific Ocean (Chile v. European Union), Order, International Tribunal for the Law of the Sea, Case No. 7, 16 December 2009.

[3] Alan Boyle, *Relationship Between International Environmental Law and Other Branches of International Law*, Chapter 7, in DANIEL BODANSKY, JUTTA BRUNNEE & ELLEN HEY (eds.), THE OXFORD HANDBOOK OF INTERNATIONAL ENVIRONMENTAL LAW 125, 127 (Oxford: Oxford University Press, 2007).

accepts two separate methods of entering into treaties. First, a treaty may be negotiated and ratified by the President and the executive branch with the advice and consent of two-thirds of the members of the Senate of the United States. Second, U.S. constitutional practice accepts as treaties executive agreements by the President acting within his or her foreign affairs power. The President may enter into an executive agreement with a foreign state in conjunction with a law enacted by Congress. An instance of the exercise of this power is the North American Free Trade Agreement, which was accompanied by the passage of domestic laws. The President may also enter into an executive agreement without asking Congress to enact an implementing law. Thus, President Carter on January 19, 1981, concluded the Algiers Accord with Iran, a presidential agreement that terminated claims of U.S. nationals against Iran in exchange for release of U.S. hostages held by Iran. The Algiers Accord was upheld by the Supreme Court in *Dames and Moore v. Regan*, 453 U.S. 654 (1981).

But it is axiomatic that treaties are governed by international law. The most important formulation of the international law of treaties is the Vienna Convention on the Law of Treaties (VCLT) (1969), which is a "treaty on treaties." The VCLT entered into force in 1980; the United States is not a party to the VCLT, but was a signatory and accepts its provisions as customary international law.

The VCLT applies to written agreements between states. Most importantly, the VCLT Article 26 provides that "every treaty in force is binding upon the parties to it and must be performed in good faith." This states the rule of *"pacta sunt servanda"* — in the international sphere, agreements between states must be kept. A party to a treaty may not invoke the provisions of its national laws to justify its failure to perform a treaty obligation (VCLT Art. 27).

Treaties may be concluded between two states — bilaterally — or between several states — multilaterally. The most important treaties in international environmental law, and most of the treaties we will study in this course, are multilateral environmental treaties. There is no official count or record of international environmental treaties, but one informal service, the International Environmental Agreements Database Project at the University of Oregon[4] counts, as of 2012, a total of 1077 multilateral environmental agreements between governments and international organizations or non-state actors. About 80% of these treaties have been concluded since 1972.

Treaties are normally negotiated by authorized representatives of states, frequently at an international conference under the auspices of an international organization. The consent of a state to be bound by a treaty may be expressed in several ways: signature, exchange of instruments constituting the treaty, ratification, acceptance, approval, accession, or any other agreed means (VCLT, Art. 11). Most commonly, signing a treaty indicates only approval of the text and the intention to submit the treaty to the national law treaty ratification process. Thus, a multilateral treaty may take many years to be ratified by parties that have signed it; and ratifications will occur at different times for different states. For this reason, most treaties have a provision on entry into force; multilateral treaties commonly

---

[4] *Available at* http://iea.uoregon.edu/, accessed 13 October 2012.

specify that a minimum number of states must ratify the treaty for it to enter into force.

The VCLT contains many important rules pertaining to treaties, covering reservations (Arts. 19–23); the application of successive treaties relating to the same subject matter (Art. 30); the interpretation of treaties (Arts. 31–33); the amendment and modification of treaties (Arts. 39–41); and the invalidity, termination, and suspension of treaties (Arts. 42–72). These important matters are commonly studied in courses on Public International Law and for the most part cannot be extensively studied here. One issue we will confront in many of the chapters of this book, however, is the matter of breach — the failure to observe a treaty obligation. The VCLT, Article 60, distinguishes between a simple breach and what is termed a "material breach," which is defined as "(a) a repudiation of a treaty not sanctioned by the present Convention; or (b) the violation of s provision essential to the accomplishment of the object or purpose of the treaty." We will see that in practice in the area of international environmental law, this distinction is blurred, and multilateral environmental treaties tend to have provisions dealing with breaches and failures to observe obligations so that important treaties treat the matter of breach in varying ways. The issue of breach of a treaty, however, does give rise to state responsibility to cease the breach and in some instances entails the obligation to compensate another state for injuries. We deal with the important matter of state responsibility in environmental matters in Chapter 3.

2. Multilateral Environmental Agreements (MEAs)

International Environmental Law favors a certain type of treaty regime known as multilateral environmental agreements or MEAs. An MEA is typically a treaty that creates a framework for future action through established permanent institutions, including a full-time secretariat, scientific and technical bodies, and a Conference of the Parties (CoP) that meets periodically to debate and to conclude additional measures and agreements. This treaty model is considered necessary to deal with difficult environmental problems because (1) knowledge and the scope of international environmental problems change and expand over time; and (2) states frequently find it difficult to take immediate action at an initial international conference on an international environmental problem, so that only limited agreement is possible, and major policy actions must be deferred. The CoP arrangement allows state-parties to a treaty to take progressively greater steps to address a pressing but politically difficult environmental problem.

There are several reasons why MEAs are employed to deal with environmental problems. The traditional type of one-off treaty can be used to effect a political settlement, but environmental treaties are concluded for the purpose of dealing with ongoing environmental problems. What is necessary to deal with an international environmental problem is an institutional regime that can institute cooperative efforts over time, and an umbrella agreement that can spur consensus building and take later actions to deal with an environmental problem that is a moving target. MEAs provide a solution to this quest.

The earliest form of CoP was introduced by the Convention on Wetlands of International importance, Especially as Waterfowl Habitat (the Ramsar

Convention) (1971). The Ramsar Convention's CoP was only an advisory body, however. The first full-blown MEA-CoP convention was the Convention on International Trade in Endangered Species of Wild Flora and Fauna (CITES) (1973). Since 1973, multiple MEA-CoP conventions have been created to deal with loss of biodiversity, pollution of the atmosphere, land degradation, chemicals and hazardous wastes, and protection of the marine environment. We cover many of these conventional regimes in this book. The most well-known MEA-CoP is the United Nations Framework Convention on Climate Change United Nations (UNFCCC) (1992), which we analyze in Chapter 4.

The powers of CoPs vary with each conventional regime. In some cases the CoPs have actual lawmaking authority. For example, Article 2.9 of the Montreal Protocol (1987) to the Convention on the Protection of the Ozone Layer (Vienna Convention) (1985) provides that binding adjustments to the phase-out schedule for the ozone-depleting substances that are subject to the Protocol may be made by a two-thirds majority decision. Although such powers are exceptions, CoPs typically exercise many important functions, including (1) adopting treaty amendments and protocols for later ratification by the state-parties; (2) taking non-binding, "soft law" policy decisions by resolution; (3) exercising supervisory powers; (4) adopting treaty interpretations; and (5) implementing non-compliance, law enforcement, and dispute resolution procedures.

Largely as a result of MEAs, norm development in the field of international environmental law is substantially different than in other areas of international law. About 200 MEA regimes operating largely autonomously from each other create and adopt norms consciously employing a step-by-step strategy to achieve policy aims. Environmental treaty systems constantly strive to create new norms principally through the adoption of regular treaty amendments and protocols and by policy decisions taken by technical bodies and standing committees.[5]

3.   Customary International Law

Customary international environmental law remains important despite the growth of treaty law. Even multilateral treaties have limitations, notably the slow pace of ratifications and accessions and the fact that treaties bind only those states that accept them. Customary law, on the other hand, may provide rules of law that have universal application. This is particularly important when it comes to addressing global environmental issues.[6] In the area of customary international law, acquiescence is considered sufficient to accept a rule, so that states may be bound by a rule that has crystallized without their explicit consent. Nevertheless, the application of a customary rule depends on some form of consent, so that a state that makes persistent objection to a customary rule will not be bound by the rule.[7]

---

[5] Thomas Gehring, *Treaty-Making and Treaty Evolution*, Chapter 20, *in* DANIEL BODANSKY, JUTTA BRUNNEE & ELLEN HEY (eds.), THE OXFORD HANDBOOK INTERNATIONAL ENVIRONMENTAL LAW 467 (Oxford: Oxford University Press, 2007).

[6] *See* Jonathn I. Charney, *Universal International Law*, 87 AM. J. INT'L L. 529 (1993).

[7] PATRICIA BIRNIE, ALAN BOYLE & CATHERINE REDGWELL, INTERNATIONAL LAW AND THE ENVIRONMENT, 3d ed. 22 (Oxford: Oxford University Press, 2009).

This fact remains a distinct limitation to the creation of a body of universal international law rules.

Two requisites are necessary for the creation of a customary international law rule.

The first element is showing of state practice observing the rule in question. State practice, to quote the RESTATEMENT (THIRD) OF THE FOREIGN RELATIONS LAW OF THE UNITED STATES, section 102, comment b (1986), "includes diplomatic acts and instructions as well as public measures and other governmental acts and official statements of policy, whether they are unilateral or undertaken in cooperation with other states . . . ." Inaction may constitute state practice, as when a state acquiesces in acts of another state that affect its rights. The practice necessary to create customary law may be of comparatively short duration, but . . . it must be "general and consistent." A practice can be general even if it is not universally followed; there is no precise formula to indicate how widespread a practice must be, but it should reflect wide acceptance among the states particularly involved in the relevant activity. Failure of a significant number of states to adopt a practice can prevent a principle from becoming general law though it might become "particular customary law" for the participating states.

The second element required is a showing of what is termed *opinio juris sive necessitatis*. The Restatement comment c defines this element as follows: "For a practice of states to become a rule of customary international law it must appear that the states follow the practice from a sense of legal obligation (*opinio juris sive necessitatis*); a practice that is generally followed but which states feel free to disregard does not contribute to customary law. A practice initially followed by states as a matter of courtesy or habit may become law when states generally come to believe they are under a legal obligation to comply with it. It is often difficult to determine when that transformation into law has taken place. Explicit evidence of a sense of legal obligation (e.g., by official statements) is not necessary; *opinio juris* may be inferred from acts or omissions."

4. General Principles of Law

The source *general principles of law* refers to legal rules and concepts that find general acceptance in the national legal systems of the world. Since these rules are derived from national laws, consent to their application in the international legal system is presumed. General principles of law are often used by international tribunals to fill in gaps in the law.

5. Case Law

The application and interaction of these sources of law are the subjects of the following cases.

NORTH SEA CONTINENTAL SHELF CASES (FEDERAL REPUBLIC OF GERMANY v. DENMARK) (FEDERAL REPUBLIC OF GERMANY v. NETHERLANDS)

International Court of Justice
1969 I.C.J. Rep. 3 (20 February 1969)

[This famous case involved the delimitation of the continental shelf in the North Sea, an area rich in deposits of oil and gas. The map reproduced below is an integral part of the judgment of the court. The solid lines represent delimitations agreed between the United Kingdom, Norway, Denmark and the Netherlands. Germany and Denmark had agreed on a partial lateral boundary represented by the line B-A on the map. Germany and the Netherlands had agreed on a partial lateral boundary represented by the line C-D on the map. In 1966 Denmark and the Netherlands agreed on line E-F to divide their shares of the shelf based on the idea that the equidistance principle gave Germany the share of the shelf based upon the lines Declaration on D-E and E-B. Germany objected to the 1966 agreement as well as the application of the equidistance principle, which Germany regarded as unfair.]

THE NORTH SEA AREA (map)

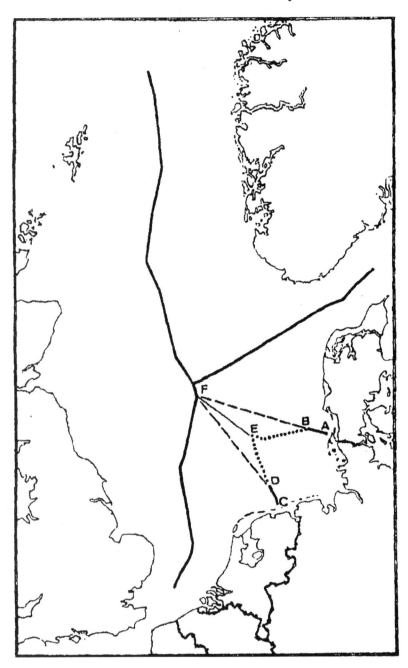

8. [I]n the case of a concave or recessing coast, such as that of the Federal Republic on the North Sea, the effect of the use of the equidistance method is to pull the line of the boundary inwards, in the direction of concavity. Consequently, where two such lines are drawn at different points on a concave coast, they will, if the curvature is pronounced, inevitable meet at a relatively short distance from the coast, thus

causing the continental shelf area they enclose, to take the form approximately of a triangle with its apex to seaward and, as it was put on behalf of the Federal Republic, "cutting off" the coastal State from the further areas of the continental shelf outside of and beyond this triangle. The effect of concavity could of course equally be produced for a country with a straight coastline if the coasts of adjacent countries protruded immediately on either side of it. In contrast to this, the effect of coastal projections, or of convex or outwardly curving coasts such as are, to a moderate extent, those of Denmark and the Netherlands, is to cause boundary lines drawn on an equidistance basis to leave the coast on divergent courses, thus having a widening tendency on the area of continental shelf off that coast.

25. The Court now turns to the legal position regarding the equidistance method. The first question to be considered is whether the 1958 Geneva Convention on the Continental Shelf is binding for all the Parties in this case — that is to say whether, as contended by Denmark and the Netherlands, the use of this method is rendered obligatory for the present delimitations by virtue of the delimitations provision (Article 6) of that instrument, according to the conditions laid down in it. Clearly, if this is so, then the provisions of the Convention will prevail in the relations between the Parties, and would take precedence of any rules having a more general character, or derived from another source.

26. The relevant provisions of Article 6 of the Geneva Convention, paragraph 2 of which Denmark and the Netherlands contend not only to be applicable as a conventional rule, but also to represent the accepted rule of general international law on the subject of continental shelf delimitation as it exists independently of the Convention, read as follows:

> "1.   Where the same continental shelf is adjacent to the territories of two or more States whose coasts are opposite each other, the boundary of the continental shelf appertaining to such States shall be determined by agreement between them. In the absence of agreement, and unless another boundary line is justified by special circumstances, the boundary is the median line, every point of which is equidistant from the nearest point of the baselines from which the breadth of the territorial sea of each State is measured.

> 2.   Where the same continental shelf is adjacent to the territories of two adjacent State, the boundary of the continental shelf shall be determined by agreement between them. In the absence of agreement, and unless another boundary line is justified by special circumstances, the boundary shall be determined by application of the principle of equidistance for the nearest points of the baselines from which the breadth of the territorial sea of each State is measured."

The Convention received 46 signatures and, up-to-date, there have been 39 ratifications or accessions. It came into force on 10 June 1964, having received the 22 ratifications or accessions required for that purpose (Article 11), and was therefore in force at the time when the various delimitations of continental shelf boundaries described earlier (paragraphs 1 and 5) took place between the Parties. But, under the formal provisions of the Convention, it is in force for any individual State only in so far as, having signed it within the time-limit provided for that purpose, that State has also subsequently ratified it; or, not having signed within that time-limit, has subsequently acceded to the Convention. Denmark and the Netherlands have both signed and ratified the Convention, and are parties to it, the former since 10 June 1964, the latter since 10 March 1966. The Federal Republic was one of the signatories of the Convention, but has never ratified it, and is consequently not a party.

27. It is admitted on behalf of Denmark and the Netherlands that in these circumstances the Convention cannot, as such, be binding on the Federal Republic, in the sense of the Republic being contractually bound by it. But it is contended that the Convention, or the regime of the Conventions, and in particular Article 6, has become binding on the Federal Republic in another way, — namely because, by conduct, by public statements and proclamations, and in other ways, the Republic has unilaterally assumed the obligations of the Convention; or has manifested its acceptance of the conventional regime; or has recognized it as being generally applicable to the delimitation of continental shelf areas. It has also been suggested that the Federal Republic had held itself out as so assuming, accepting or recognizing, in such a manner as to cause other States, and in particular Denmark and the Netherlands, to rely on the attitude thus taken up.

30. Having regard to these considerations of principle, it appears to the Court that only the existence of a situation of estoppel could suffice to lend substance to this contention, — that is to say if the Federal Republic were now precluded from denying the applicability of the conventional regime, by reason of past conduct, declarations, etc., which not only clearly and consistently evinced acceptance of that regime, but also had caused Denmark or the Netherlands, in reliance on such conduct, detrimentally to change position or suffer some prejudice. Of this there is no evidence whatever the present case.

37. It is maintained by Denmark and the Netherlands that the Federal Republic, whatever its position may be in relation to the Geneva Convention, considered as such, is in any event bound to accept delimitation on an equidistant-special circumstances basis, because the use of this method is not in the nature of a merely conventional obligation, but is or must now be regarded as involving, a rule that is part of the *corpus* of general international law; — and, like other rules of general of customary international law, is binding on the Federal Republic automatically later. This contention has both a positive law and a more fundamentalist aspect. As a matter of positive law, it is based on the work done in this field by international legal bodies, on State practice and on the influence attributed to the Geneva Convention itself, — the claim being that these various factors have cumulatively evidenced or been creative of the *opinio juris sive necessitatis*, requisite for the formation of new rules of customary international law. In its fundamentalist aspect, the view put forward derives from what might be called the natural law of the continental shelf, in the sense that the equidistance principle is seen as a necessary expression in the field of delimitation of the accepted doctrine of the exclusive appurtenance of the continental shelf to the nearby coastal State, and therefore as having an *a priori* character of so to speak juristic inevitability.

44. In the present case, although both sides relied on the prolongation principle and regarded it as fundamental, they interpreted it quite differently. Both

interpretations appear to the Court to be incorrect. Denmark and the Netherlands identified natural prolongation with closest proximity and therefrom argues that it called for an equidistance line: the Federal Republic seemed to think it implied the notion of the just and equitable share, although the connection is distinctly remote. (The Federal Republic did however invoke another idea, namely that of the proportionality of a State's continental shelf area to the length of its coastline, which obviously does have an intimate connection with the prolongation principle, and will be considered in its place.) As regards equidistance, it clearly cannot be identified with the notion of natural prolongation or extension, since, as has already been stated (paragraph 8), the use of the equidistance method would frequently cause areas which are the natural prolongation or extension of the territory of one State to be attributed to another, when the configuration of the latter's coast makes the equidistance line swing out laterally across the former's coastal front, cutting it off from areas situated directly before that front.

46. The conclusion drawn by the Court from the foregoing analysis is that the notion of equidistance as being logically necessary, in the sense of being an inescapable *a priori* accompaniment of basic continental shelf doctrine, is incorrect. It is said not to be possible to maintain that there is a rule of law ascribing certain areas to a State as a matter of inherent and original right without also admitting the existence of some rule by which those areas can be obligatorily delimited. The Court cannot accept the logic of this view. The problem arises only where there is a dispute and only in respect of the marginal areas involved. The appurtenance of a given area, considered as an entity, in no way governs the precise delimitation of its boundaries, any more than uncertainty as to boundaries can affect territorial rights.

47. A review of the genesis and development of the equidistance method of delimitation can only serve to confirm the foregoing conclusion. Such a review may appropriately start with the instrument, generally known as the "Truman Proclamation," issued by the Government of the United States on 28 September 1945. Although this instrument was not the first or only one to have appeared, it has in the opinion of the Court a special status. Previously, various theories as to the nature and extent of the rights relative to or exercisable over the continental shelf had been advanced by jurists, publicists and technicians. The Truman Proclamation however, soon came to be regarded as the starting point of the positive law on the subject, and the chief doctrine it enunciated, namely that of the coastal State as having an original, natural, and exclusive (in short a vested) right to the continental shelf off its shores, came to prevail over all others, being now reflected in Article 2 of the 1958 Geneva Convention on the Continental Shelf. With regard to the delimitation of lateral boundaries between the continental shelves of adjacent States, a matter which had given rise to some consideration on the technical, but very little on the juristic level, the Truman Proclamation stated that such boundaries "shall be determined by the United States and the State concerned in accordance with equitable principles." These two concepts, of delimitation by mutual agreement and delimitation in accordance with equitable principles, have underlain all the subsequent history of the subject. They were reflected in various other State proclamations of the period, and after, and in the later work on the subject.

48. It was in the International Law Commission of the United Nations that the

question of delimitation as between adjacent States was first taken up seriously as part of a general juridical project; for outside the ranks of the hydrographers and cartographers, questions of delimitation were not much thought about in earlier continental shelf doctrine. Juridical interest and speculation was focused mainly on such questions as what was the legal basis on which any rights at all in respect of the continental shelf could be claimed, and what was the nature of those rights. As regards boundaries, the main issue was not that of boundaries between States but of the seaward limit of the area in respect of which the coastal State could claim exclusive rights of exploitation. As was pointed out in the course of the written proceedings, States in most cases had not found it necessary to conclude treaties or legislate about their lateral sea boundaries with adjacent States before the question of exploiting the natural resources of the seabed and subsoil arose; — practice was therefore sparse.

49. In the records of the International Law Commission, which had the matter under consideration from 1950 to 1956, there is no indication at all that any of its members supposed that it was incumbent on the Commission to adopt a rule of equidistance because this gave expression to, and translated into linear terms, a principle of proximity inherent in the basic concept of the continental shelf, causing every part of the shelf to appertain to the nearest coastal State and to no other, and because such a rule must therefore be mandatory as a matter of customary international law. Such an idea does not seem ever to have been propounded. Had it been, and had it had the self-evident character contended for by Denmark and the Netherlands, the Commission would have had no alternative but to adopt it, and its long continues hesitations over this matter would be incomprehensible.

60. The conclusions so far reached leave open, and still to be considered, the question whether on some basis other than that of an *a priori* logical necessity, i.e., through positive law processes, the equidistance principle has come to be regarded as a rule of customary international law, so that it would be obligatory for the Federal Republic in that way, even though Article 6 of the Geneva Convention is not, as such, opposable to it. For this purpose it is necessary to examine the status of the principle as it stood when the Convention was drawn up, as it resulted from the effect of the Convention; but it should be clearly understood that in the pronouncements the Court makes on these matters it has in view solely the delimitation provisions (Article 6) of the Convention, not other parts of it, nor the Convention as such.

61. The first of these questions can conveniently be considered in the form suggested on behalf of Denmark and the Netherlands themselves in the course of the oral hearing, when it was stated that they had not in fact contended that the delimitation article (Article 6) of the Convention "embodied already received rules of customary law in the sense that the Convention was merely declaratory of existing rules." Their contention was, rather, that although prior to the Conference, continental shelf law was only in the formative stage, and State practice lacked uniformity, yet "the process of the definition and consolidation of the emerging customary law took place through the work of the International Law Commission, the reaction of governments to that work and the proceedings of the Geneva Conference"; and this emerging customary law became "crystallized in the adoption of the Continental Shelf Convention by the Conference."

62. Whatever validity this contention may have in respect of at least certain parts of the Convention, the Court cannot accept it as regards the delimitation provision (Article 6), the relevant parts of which were adopted almost unchanged from the draft of the International Law Commission that formed the basis of discussion at the Conference. The status of the rule in the Convention therefore depends mainly on the processes that led the Commission to propose it. These processes have already been reviewed in connection with the Danish-Netherlands contention of an *a priori* necessity for equidistance, and the Court considers this review sufficient to show that the principle of equidistance, as it now figures in Article 6 of the Convention, was proposed by the Commission with considerable hesitation, somewhat on an experimental basis, at most *de lege ferenda*, and not at all *de lege lata* or as an emerging rule of customary international law. This is clearly not the sort of foundation on which Article 6 of the Convention could be said to have reflected or crystallized such a rule.

70. The Court must now proceed to the last stage in the argument put forward on behalf of Denmark and the Netherlands. This to the effect that even if there was at the date of the Geneva Convention no rule of customary international law in favour of the equidistance principle, and no such rule was crystallized in Article 6 of the Convention, nevertheless such a rule has come into being since the Convention, partly because of its own impact, partly on the basis of subsequent State practice, — and that this rule, being now a rule of customary international law binding on all States, including therefore the Federal Republic, should be declared applicable to the delimitation of the boundaries between the Parties' respective continental shelf areas in the North Sea.

71. In so far as this contention is based on the view that Article 6 of the Convention has had the influence, and has produced the effect, described, it clearly involves treating that Article as a norm-creating provision which has constituted the foundation of, or has generated a rule which, while only conventional or contractual in its origin, has since passed into the general *corpus* of international law, and is now accepted as such by the *opinio juris*, so as to have become binding even for countries which have never, and do not, become parties to the Convention. There is no doubt that this process is a perfectly possible one and does from time to time occur: it constitutes indeed one of the recognized methods by which new rules of customary international law may be formed. At the same time this result is not lightly to be regarded as having been attained.

74. As regards the time element, the Court notes that it is over ten years since the Convention was signed, but that it is even now less than five since it came into force in June 1964, and that when the present proceedings were brought it was less than three years, while less than one had elapsed at the time when the respective negotiations between the Federal Republic and the other two Parties for a complete delimitation broke down on the question of the application of the equidistance principle. Although the passage of only a short period of time is not necessarily, or of itself, a bar to the formation of the a new rule of customary international law on the basis of what was originally a purely conventional rule, an indispensable requirement would be that within the period in question, short though it might be, State practice, including that of States whose interests are specially affected, should have been both extensive and virtually uniform in the sense of the provision invoked;

— and should moreover have occurred in such a way as to show a general recognition that a rule of law of legal obligation is involved.

75. The Court must now consider whether State practice in the matter of continental shelf delimitation has, subsequent to the Geneva Convention, been of such a kind as to satisfy this requirement. Leaving aside cases which, for various reasons, the Court does not consider to be reliable guides as precedents, such as delimitations effected between the present Parties themselves, or not relating to international boundaries, some fifteen cases have been cited in the course of the present proceedings, occurring mostly since the signature of the 1958 Geneva Convention, in which continental shelf boundaries have been delimited according to the equidistance principle — in the majority of the cases by agreement, in a few others unilaterally — or else the delimitation was foreshadowed but has not yet been carried out. Amongst these fifteen are the four North Sea delimitations United Kingdom/Norway-Denmark-Netherlands, and Norway/Denmark already mentioned in paragraph 4 of this Judgment. But even if these various cases constituted more than a very small proportion of those potentially calling for delimitation in the world as a whole, the Court would not think it necessary to enumerate or evaluate them separately, since there are *a priori*, several grounds which deprive them of weight as precedents in the present context.

76. To begin with, over half the States concerned, whether acting unilaterally or conjointly, were or shortly became parties to the Geneva Convention, and were therefore presumably, so far as they were concerned, acting actually or potentially in the application of the Convention. From their action no inference could legitimately be drawn as to the existence of a rule of customary international law in favour of the equidistance principle. As regards those States, on the other hand, which we not, and have not become parties to the Convention, the basis of their action can only be problematical and must remain entirely speculative. Clearly, they were not applying the Convention. But from that no inference could justifiably be drawn that they believed themselves to be applying a mandatory rule of customary international law. There is not a shred of evidence that they did and, as has been seen (paragraphs 22 and 23), there is no lack of other reasons for using the equidistance method, so that acting, or agreeing to act in a certain way, does not of itself demonstrate anything of a juridical nature.

77. The essential point in this connection — and it seems necessary to stress it — is that even if these instances of action by non-parties to the Convention were much more numerous than they in fact are, they would not, even in the aggregate, suffice in themselves to constitute the *opinio juris*; — for, in order to achieve this result, two conditions must be fulfilled. Not only must the acts concerned amount to a settled practice, but they must also be such, or be carried out in such a way, as to be evidence of a belief that this practice is rendered obligatory by the existence of a rule of law requiring it. The need for such a belief, i.e., the existence of a subjective element, is implicit in the very notion of the *opinio juris sive necessitatis*. The States concerned must therefore feel that they are conforming to what amounts to a legal obligation. The frequency, or even habitual character of the acts is not in itself enough. There are many international acts, e.g., in the field of ceremonial and protocol, which are performed almost invariably, but which are motivated only by

consideration of courtesy, convenience or tradition, and not by any sense of legal duty.

81. The Court accordingly concludes that if the Geneva Convention was not in its origins or inception declaratory of a mandatory rule of customary international law enjoining the use of the equidistance principle for the delimitation of continental shelf areas between adjacent States, neither has its subsequent effect been constitutive of such a role; and that State practice up-to-date has equally been insufficient for the purpose.

83. The legal situation therefore is that the Parties are under no obligation to apply either the 1958 Convention, which is not opposable to the Federal Republic, or the equidistance method as a mandatory rule of customary law, which it is not; but as between States faced with an issue concerning the lateral delimitation of adjacent continental shelves, there are still rules and principles of law to be applied; and in the present case it is not the fact either that rules are lacking, or that the situation is one for the unfettered appreciation of the Parties. Equally, it is not the case that if the equidistance principle is not a rule of law, there has to be as an alternative some other single equivalent rule.

88. The Court comes next to the rule of equity. The legal basis of that rule in the particular case of the delimitation of the continental shelf as between adjoining States has already been stated. It must however be noted that the rule rests also on a broader basis. Whatever the legal reasoning of a court of justice, its decisions must by definition be just, and therefore in that sense equitable. Nevertheless, when mention is made of a court dispensing justice or declaring the law, what is meant is that the decision finds its objective justification in considerations lying not outside by within the rules, and in this field it is precisely a rule of law that calls for the application of equitable principles. There is consequently no question in this case of any decision *ex aequo et bono*, such as would only be possible under the conditions prescribed by Article 38, paragraph 2, of the Court's Statute. Nor would this be the first time that the Court has adopted such an attitude, as is shown by the following passage from the Advisory Opinion give in the case of *Judgments of the Administrative Tribunal of the I.L.O. upon Complaints made against Unesco (I.C.J. Reports 1956, at p. 100)*:

> "In view of this Court need not examine the allegation that the validity of the judgments of the Tribunal is vitiated by excess of jurisdiction on the ground that it awarded compensation *ex aequo et bono*. It will confine itself to stating that, in the reasons given by the Tribunal in support of its decision on the merits, the Tribunal said: 'That redress will be ensured *ex aequo et bono* by the granting to the complainant of the sum set forth below.' It does not appear from the context of the judgment that the Tribunal thereby intended to depart from principles of law. The apparent intention was to say that, as the precise determination of the actual amount to be awarded could not be based on any specific law, the Tribunal fixed what the Court, in other circumstances, has described as the true measure of compensation and the reasonable figure of such compensation (*Corfu Channel* case, Judgment of December 15th, 1949, *I.C.J. Reports 1949, p. 249*)."

89. It must next be observed that, in certain geographical circumstances which are quite frequently met with, the equidistance method, despite its known advantages, leads unquestionably to inequity, in the following sense:

(a)   The slightest irregularity in a coastline is automatically magnified by the equidistance line as regards the consequences for the delimitation of the continental shelf. Thus it has been seen in the case of concave or convex coastlines that if the equidistance method is employed, then the greater the irregularity and the further from the coastline the area to be delimited, the more unreasonable are the results produced. So great an exaggeration of the consequences of a natural geographical feature must be remedied or compensated for as far as possible, being of itself creative of inequity.

(b)   In the case of the North Sea in particular, where there is no outer boundary to the continental shelf, it happens that the claims of several States converge, meet and intercross in localities where, despite their distance from the coast, the bed of the sea still unquestionably consists of continental shelf. A study of these convergences, as revealed by the maps, shows how inequitable would be the apparent simplification brought about by a delimitation which, ignoring such geographical circumstances, was based solely on the equidistance method.

90. If for the reasons equity excludes the use of the equidistance method in the present instance, as the sole method of delimitation, the question arises whether there is any necessity to employ only one method for the purposes of a given delimitation. There is no logical basis for this, and no objection need be felt to the idea of effecting a delimitation of adjoining continental shelf areas by the concurrent use of various methods. The Court has already stated why it considers that the international law of continental shelf delimitation does not involve any imperative rule and permits resort to various principles or methods, as may be appropriate, or a combination of them, provided that by the application of equitable principles, a reasonable result is arrived at.

91. Equity does not necessarily imply equality. There can never be any question of completely refashioning nature, and equity does not require that a State without access to the sea should be allotted an area of continental shelf, any more than there could be a question of rendering the situation of a State with an extensive coastline similar to that of a State with a restricted coastline. Equality is to be reckoned with in the same plane, and it is not such natural inequalities as these that equity could remedy. But in the present case there are three States whose North Sea coastlines are in fact comparable in length and which, therefore, have been given broadly equal treatment by nature except that the configuration of one of the coastlines would, if the equidistance method is used, deny to one of these States treatment equal or comparable to that given the other two. Here indeed is a case where, in a theoretical situation of equality within the same order, an inequity is created. What is unacceptable in this instance is that a State should enjoy continental shelf rights considerable different from those of its neighbours merely because in the one case the coastline is roughly convex in form and in the other it is markedly concave, although those coastlines are comparable in length. It is therefore not a question of totally refashioning geography whatever the facts of the situation but, given a geographical situation of quasi-equality as between a number of States, of abating

the effects of an incidental special feature from which an unjustifiable difference of treatment could result.

94. In balancing the factors in question it would appear that various aspects must be taken into account. Some are related to the geological, others to the geographical aspect of the situation, others again to the idea of the unity of any deposits. These criteria, though not entirely precise, can provide adequate bases for decision adapted to the factual situation.

98. A final factor to be taken account of is the element of a reasonable degree of proportionality which a delimitation effected according to equitable principles ought to bring about between the extent of the continental shelf appertaining to the States concerned and the lengths of their respective coastlines, — these being measured according to their general direction in order to establish the necessary balance between States with straight, and those with markedly concave or convex coasts, or to reduce very irregular coastlines to their truer proportions. The choice and application of the appropriate technical methods would be a matter for the parties.

101. For these reasons,

THE COURT,

by eleven vote to six,

Finds that in each case,

(A) the use of the equidistance method of delimitation not being obligatory as between the Parties; and

(B) there being no other single method of delimitation the use of which is in all circumstances obligatory;

(C) the principles and rules of international law applicable to the delimitation as between the Parties of the areas of the continental shelf in the North Sea which appertain to each of them beyond the partial boundary determined by the agreements of 1 December 1964 and 9 June 1965, respectively, are as follows:

    (1)   delimitation is to be effected by agreement in accordance with equitable principles, and taking account of all the relevant circumstances, in such a way as to leave as much as possible to each Party all those parts of the continental shelf that constitute a natural prolongation of its land territory into and under the sea, without encroachment on the natural prolongation of the land territory of the other;

    (2)   if, in the application of the preceding sub-paragraph, the delimitation leaves to the Parties areas that overlap, these are to be divided between them in agreed proportions or, failing agreement, equally, unless they decide on a regime of joint jurisdiction, user, or exploitation for the zones of overlap or any part of them;

(D) in the course of the negotiations, the factors to be taken into account are to include:

    (1)   the general configuration of the coasts of the Parties, as well as the presence of any special or unusual features;

(2) so far as known or readily ascertainable, the physical and geological structure, and natural resources, of the continental shelf areas involved;

(3) the element of a reasonable degree of proportionality, which a delimitation carried out in accordance with equitable principles ought to bring about between the extent of the continental shelf areas appertaining to the coastal State and the length of its coast measured in the general direction of the coastline, account being taken for this purpose of the effects, actual or prospective, of any other continental shelf delimitations between adjacent States in the same region.

NOTES AND QUESTIONS

1. *Entangled treaty and custom.* How does the ICJ distinguish the codification, the crystallization, and the progressive development of international law? Does it make a difference? Consider the following comments by Professor Oscar Schachter:

. . . Our starting point must be the well recognized consideration under which a treaty rule may be considered as customary law namely:

(1) where the treaty rule is declaratory of pre-existing customary law [codification];

(2) where the treaty rule is found to have crystallized customary law in process of formulations;

(3) where the treaty rule has been found to have generated new customary law subsequent to its adoption [progressive development];

These three sets of conditions have been enunciated by the International Court, most notably in the North Sea Continental Shelf Cases. . . .

However, differences have arisen in respect of their application. One view — probably a majority opinion — holds that all three conditions require adequate proof of state practice and *opinio juris* outside of the application of the treaty in question. A different position — less precisely expressed — considers that in some circumstances the act of adopting the treaty and the ratifications and adherences of States constitute State practice and evidence of *opinio juris* for purposes of customary law. This would hold particularly for treaties of a declaratory character, but not only for them. A third view suggests that when a rule is included in a multilateral convention adopted at a conference of States and a number of interested States act in conformity with that rule and no States object to it, there is a strong presumption that the rule has become customary law, even though the treaty has not obtained the necessary adherences necessary for its entry into force. A fourth position goes beyond this and maintains that an international conference of States, such as that on the Law of the Sea, may decide by consensus that treaty rules enshrine customary norms binding on states from the moment of their adoption by the conference.

Oscar Schachter, *Entangled Treaty and Custom*, in INTERNATIONAL LAW AT A TIME OF PERPLEXITY: ESSAYS IN HONOUR OF SHABTAI ROSENNE, YORAM DINSTEIN 718–719

(Martinus Nijhoff, 1989).

2. ***Practice and opinio juris.*** It is said that customary international law is a product of state practice and *opinio juris*. Why are they important for creating law? What evidence is needed to establish the necessary state practice and *opinio juris*? How do you explain that apparent chronological paradox raised by the I.C.J. in the *North Sea Continental Shelf Cases* that states creating new customary rules must believe that those rules already exist, and that their practice, therefore, is in accordance with the law? How can a juridical entity such as a state have an *opinio juris*? How is a treaty relevant in proving customary international law? Numerous attempts have been made to provide compelling answers to these questions. In order to provide yourself with familiarity with these theoretical problems, see MICHAEL BYRES, CUSTOM, POWER AND THE POWER OF RULES 130–46 (Cambridge Univ. Press, 1999); ANTHONY D'AMATO, Ed., INTERNATIONAL LAW ANTHOLOGY 51–101 (Anderson Publishing Co., 1994); MARTTI KOSKENNIEMI, Ed., SOURCES OF INTERNATIONAL LAW 251–356 (Asgate Publishing Co., 2000); Luigi Condorelli, *Custom*, in INTERNATIONAL LAW: ACHIEVEMENTS AND PROSPECTS 197–211, MOHAMMED BEDJAOUI, Ed. (UNESCO & Martinus Nijhoff, 1991).

3. ***Making or breaking customary law.*** Can state practice inconsistent with an acknowledged customary norm lead to the formation of new law? Judge Rosalyn Higgins observes:

> One of the special characteristics of international law is that violations of law can lead to the formation of new law. Of course, this characteristic is more troublesome for those who regard law as rules, and less troublesome for those who regard law as process. But . . . there still remains the question of how the 'rules' . . . change through time. And, in so far as these rules . . . are based on custom, then there is the related question of what legal significance is to be given to practice that is inconsistent with the perceived rules. . . .

> *   *   *

> What exactly causes a norm to lose its quality as law? Conceptually, this question is, of course, the same as that to be put regarding the formation of custom. To ask what is evidence of practice required for the loss of the obligatory quality of a norm is the mirror of evidence of practice required for the formation of the norm in the first place. . . .

> If a customary rule loses its normative quality when it is widely ignored, over a significant period of time, does this not lead to a relativist view of the substantive content of international law, with disturbing implications?

> *   *   *

> . . . [O]ne must not lose sight of the fact that it is the practice of the vast majority of states that is critical both in the formulation of new norms and in their development and change and possible death. . . .

> New norms require both practice and *opinio juris* before they can be said to represent customary international law. And so it is with the gradual

death of existing norms and their replacement by others. The reason why the prohibition on torture continues to be a requirement of customary international law, even though it is widely abused . . . [is] because *opinio juris* as to its normative status continues exist. No state, not even a state that tortures, believes that the international law prohibition is undesirable and that it is not bound by the prohibition. . . .

Rosalyn Higgins, *International Law and the Avoidance, Containment and Resolution of Disputes*, 230 RECUEIL DES COURS 9, 44–48 (1991-V), *reprinted sub nom. with minor amendment as*, ROSALYN HIGGINS, PROBLEMS & PROCESS: INTERNATIONAL LAW AND HOW WE USE IT 19–22 (Oxford Univ. Press, 1994).

4.   *Equity as a general principle of law.* According to the RESTATEMENT (THIRD) OF THE FOREIGN RELATIONS OF THE UNITED STATES (1986), section 102, comment I, general principles are sources of international law that are secondary to treaties and customary law. The Restatement states:

General principles common to systems of national law may be resorted to as an independent source of law. That source of law may be important when there has not been practice by states sufficient to give the particular principle status as customary law and the principle has not been legislated by general international agreement.

The Restatement, comment m states that "Reference to principles of equity, in the sense of what is fair and just, is common to major legal systems, and equity has been accepted as a principle of international law in several contexts. . . ."

5.   *The subsidiary sources of international law.* Note how the Court in the North Sea cases uses the subsidiary sources of international law — opinions of experts and decisions of international tribunals — in its Judgment. The International Law Commission was established by resolution of the United Nations General Assembly in 1947 for the purpose of addressing and solving problems related to international law and promoting the codification and progressive development of international law. The Commission consists of 34 members elected by the General Assembly. The Commission meets annually and compiles an Annual Report on its work. The Court cited and relied upon the work and opinions of the Commission in its Judgment. The Court also drew upon prior decisions of the International Court of Justice and its predecessor, the Permanent Court of International Justice, in formulating its opinion. Although there is no requirement of *stare decisis* and consequently no doctrine of precedent in international law, international tribunals obtain interpretive ideas and strive for consistency with decisions and judgments in prior cases. The rule announced by the Court in the North Sea cases — delimitation is to be effected by agreement in accordance with equitable principles — has become treaty law: the United Nations Convention on the Law of the Sea (1982) states (Articles 74 and 83) that delimitation of both the exclusive economic zones and the continental shelves of states with opposite and adjacent coasts shall be effected by agreement in order to achieve an equitable solution. In this instance, a general principle of international law as announced in the jurisprudence of the International Court of Justice has become a rule of treaty law.

6. *New approaches to establishing custom and opinio juris.* While the International Court of Justice has reaffirmed[8] the approach employed in the *North Sea Continental Shelf* cases regarding the creation of a rule of customary international law, subsequent ICJ judgments have accepted additional sources as evidence of the content of a customary rule and *opinio juris.* For example, in the case concerning *Military and Paramilitary Activities in and Against Nicaragua (Nicaragua v. United States of America)*, 1986 I.C.J. Rep. 14, the International Court accepted as evidence of customary law rules on the use of force and non-intervention contained in the Charters of the United Nations and the Organization of American States. In addition, the Court accepted as *opinio juris* resolutions adopted by international organizations, notably the Conference of American States, the Conference on Security and Cooperation in Europe, and the General Assembly of the United Nations. The International Court of Justice recognized the existence of a body of customary international law that is derived from and virtually identical to important treaty obligations contained in documents such as the United Nations Charter. It thus appears that multilateral treaties and resolutions of international organizations, particularly those with broad and diverse membership, are now recognized to play a dominant role in the development of international law. Is this to be welcomed or a cause of concern?

Now we turn to a case in which the International Court of Justice focused on the impact of emerging norms of international environmental law.

LEGALITY OF THE THREAT OR USE OF NUCLEAR WEAPONS
(Advisory Opinion)
International Court of Justice
1996 I.C.J. Rep. 226

On the legality of the threat or use of nuclear weapons,

THE COURT, . . . *gives the following Advisory Opinion:*

1. The question upon which the advisory opinion of the Court has been requested is set forth in resolution 49/75 K adopted by the General Assembly of the United Nations (hereinafter called the "General Assembly") on 15 December 1994. * * * Resolution 49/75 K . . . reads as follows:

> *"The General Assembly, Conscious* that the continuing existence and development of nuclear weapons pose serious risks to humanity, *Mindful* that States have an obligation under the Charter of the United Nations to refrain from the threat or use of force against the territorial integrity or political independence of any State.
>
> *Recalling* its resolutions 1653 (XVI) of 24 November 1961, 33/71 B of 14 December 1978, 34/83 G of 11 December 1979, 35/152 D of 12 December 1980, 36/92 1 of 9 December 1981, 45/59 B of 4 December 1990 and 46/37 D

---

[8] Case Concerning Military and Paramilitary Activities in and Against Nicaragua (Nicaragua v. United States of America), 1986 I.C.J. Rep 14, para. 185.

of 6 December 1991, in which it declared that the use of nuclear weapons would be a violation of the Charter and a crime against humanity.

Welcoming the progress made on the prohibition and elimination of weapons of mass destruction, including the Convention on the Prohibition of the Development, Production and Stockpiling of Bacteriological (Biological) and Toxin Weapons on Their Destruction and the Convention on the Prohibition of the Development, Production, Stockpiling and Use of Chemical Weapons and on Their Destruction,

Convinced that the complete elimination of nuclear weapons is the only guarantee against the threat of nuclear war,

Noting the concerns expressed in the Fourth Review Conference of the Parties to the Treaty on the Non-Proliferation of Nuclear Weapons that insufficient progress had been made towards the complete elimination of nuclear weapons at the earliest possible time,

Recalling that, convinced of the need to strengthen the rule of law in international relations, it has declared the period 1990–1999 the United Nations Decade of International Law,

Noting that Article 96, paragraph 1, of the Charter empowers the General Assembly to request the International Court of Justice to give an advisory opinion on any legal question,

Recalling: the recommendation of the Secretary-General, made in his report entitled 'An Agenda for Peace', that United Nations organs that are authorized to take advantage of the advisory competence of the International Court of Justice turn to the Court more frequently for such opinions,

Decides, pursuant to Article 96, paragraph 1, of the Charter of the United Nations, to request the International Court of Justice urgently to render its advisory opinion on the following question: 'Is the threat or use of nuclear weapons in any circumstance permitted under international law?'

20. The Court must . . . address certain matters arising in relation to the formulation of the question put to it by the General Assembly. The English text asks: "Is the threat or use of nuclear weapons in any circumstance permitted under international law?" . . .

21. The use of the word "permitted" in the question put by the General Assembly was criticized before the Court by certain States on the ground that this implied that the threat or the use of nuclear weapons would only be permissible if authorization could be found in a treaty provision or in customary international law. Such a starting point, those States submitted, was incompatible with the very basis of international law, which rests upon the principles of sovereignty and consent; accordingly, and contrary to what was implied by use of the "permitted," States are free to threaten or use nuclear weapons unless it can be shown that they are bound no to do so by reference to a prohibition in either treaty law or customary international law. Support for this contention was found in dicta of the Permanent Court of International Justice in the *"Lotus"* case that "restrictions upon the independence of States cannot . . . be presumed" and that international law leaves

to States "a wide measure of discretion which is only limited in certain cases by prohibitive rules" (*P.C.I.J., Series A, No. 10*, pp. 18 and 19). Reliance was also placed on the dictum of the present Court in the case concerning *Military and Paramilitary Activities in and against Nicaragua (Nicaragua v. United States of America)* that:

> "in international law there are no rules, other than such rules as may be accepted by the State concerned, by treaty or otherwise, whereby the level of armaments of sovereign State can be limited" (*I.C.J. Reports 1986*, p. 135, para. 269).

For other States, the invocation of these dicta in the *"Lotus"* case was inapposite; their status in contemporary international law and applicability in the very different circumstances of the present case were challenged. It was also contended that the above-mentioned dictum of the present Court was directed to the *possession* of armament and was irrelevant to the threat or use of nuclear weapons.

Finally, it was suggested that, were the Court to answer the question put by the Assembly, the word "permitted" should be replaces by "prohibited."

22. The Court notes that the nuclear-weapon States appearing before it either accepted, or did not dispute, that their independence to act was indeed restricted by the principles and rules of international law, more particularly humanitarian law . . . , as did the other States which took part in the proceedings.

Hence, the argument concerning the legal conclusions to be drawn from the use of the word "permitted," and the questions of burden of proof to which it was said to give rise, are without particular significance for the disposition of the issues before the Court.

23. In seeking to answer the question put to it by the General Assembly, the Court must decide, after consideration of the great corpus of international law norms available to it, what might be the relevant applicable law.

27. In both their written and oral statements, some States furthermore argued that any use of nuclear weapons would be unlawful by reference to existing norms relating to the safeguarding and protection of the environment, in view of their essential importance.

Specific references were made to various existing international treaties and instruments. These included Additional Protocol I of 1977 to the Geneva Conventions of 1949, Article 35, paragraph 3, of which prohibits the employment of "methods or means of warfare which are intended, or may be expected, to cause widespread, long-term and severe damage to the natural environment"; and the Convention of 18 May 1977 on the Prohibition of Military or Any Other Hostile Use of Environmental Modification Techniques, which prohibits the use of weapons which have "widespread, long-lasting or severe effects" on the environment (Art. 1). Also cited were Principle 21 of the Stockholm Declaration of 1972 and Principle 2 of the Rio Declaration of 1992 which express the common conviction of the States concerned that they have a duty "to ensure that activities within their jurisdiction or control do not cause damage to the environment of other States or of areas beyond the limits of national jurisdiction."

These instruments and other provisions relating to the protection and safeguarding of the environment were said to apply at all times, in war as well as in peace, and it was contended that they would be violated by the use of nuclear weapons whose consequences would be widespread and would have transboundary effects.

28. Other States questioned the binding legal quality of these precepts of environmental law; or, in the context of the Convention on the Prohibition of Military or Any Other Hostile Use of Environmental Modification Techniques, denied that it was concerned at all with the use of nuclear weapons in hostilities; or, in the case of Additional Protocol I, denied that they were generally bound by its terms, or recalled that they had reserved their position in respect of Article 35, paragraph 3, thereof.

It was also argued by some States that the principal purpose of environmental treaties and norms was the protection of the environment in time of peace. It was said that those treaties made no mention of nuclear weapons. It was also pointed out that warfare in general, and nuclear warfare in particular, were not mentioned in their texts and that it would be destabilizing to the rule of law and to confidence in international negotiations if those treaties were now interpreted in such a way as to prohibit the use of nuclear weapons.

29. The Court recognizes that the environment is under daily threat and that the use of nuclear weapons could constitute a catastrophe for the environment. The Court also recognizes that the environment is not an abstraction but represents the living space, the quality of life and the very health of human beings, including generations unborn. The existence of the general obligation of States to ensure that activities within their jurisdiction and control respect the environment of other States or of areas beyond national control is now part of the corpus of international law relating to the environment.

30. However, the Court is of the view that the issues is not whether the treaties relating to the protection of the environment are or not applicable during an armed conflict, but rather whether the obligations stemming from these treaties were intended to be obligations of total restraint during military conflict.

The Court does not consider that the treaties in question could have intended to deprive a State of the exercise of its right of self defense under international law because of its obligations to protect the environment. Nonetheless, States must take environmental considerations into account when assessing what is necessary and proportionate in the pursuit of legitimate military objectives. Respect for the environment is on of the elements that go to assessing whether an action is in conformity with the principles of necessity and proportionality.

This approach is supported, indeed, by the terms of Principle 24 of the Rio Declaration, which provides that:

"Warfare is inherently destructive of sustainable development. States shall therefore respect international law providing protection for the environment in times of armed conflict and cooperate in its further development, as necessary."

31. The Court notes furthermore that Articles 35, paragraph 3 and 55 of Additional Protocol I provide additional protection for the environment. Taken together, these provisions embody a general obligation to protect the natural environment against widespread, long-term and severe environmental damage; the prohibition of methods and means of warfare which are intended, or may be expected, to cause such damage; and the prohibition of attacks against the natural environment by way of reprisals.

These are powerful constraints for all the States having subscribed to these provisions.

32. General Assembly resolution 47/37 of 25 November 1992 on the Protection of the Environment in Times of Armed Conflict is also of interest in this context. It affirms the general view according to which environmental considerations constitute one of the elements to be taken into account in the implementation of the principles of the law applicable in armed conflict: it states that "destruction of the environment, not justified by military necessity and carried out wantonly, is clearly contrary to existing international law." Addressing the reality that certain instruments are not yet binding on all States, the General Assembly is this resolution *[a]ppeals* to all States that have not yet done so to consider becoming parties to the relevant international conventions."

In its recent Order in the *Request for a Examination of the Situation in Accordance with Paragraph 63 of the Court's Judgment of 20 December 1974 in the Nuclear Tests (New Zealand France) Case*, the Court stated that its conclusion was "without prejudice to the obligations of States to respect and protect the natural environment" (*Order of 22 September 1995, I.C.J. Reports 1995*, p. 306, para. 64). Although that statement was made in the context of nuclear testing, it naturally also applies to the actual use of nuclear weapons in armed conflict.

33. The Court thus finds that while the existing international law relating to the protection and safeguarding of the environment does not specifically prohibit the use of nuclear weapons, it indicates important environmental factors that are properly to be taken into account in the context of the implementation of the principles and rules of the law applicable in armed conflict.

34. In the light of the foregoing the Court concludes that the most directly relevant applicable law governing the question of which it was seised, is that relating to the use of force enshrined in the United Nations Charter and the law applicable in armed conflict which regulates the conduct of hostilities, together with any specific treaties on nuclear weapons that the Court might determine to be relevant.

35. In applying this law to the present case, the Court cannot however fail to take into account certain unique characteristics of nuclear weapons.

The Court has noted the definitions of nuclear weapons contained in various treaties and accords. It also notes that nuclear weapons are explosive devices whose energy results from the fusion or fission of the atom. By its very nature, that process, in nuclear weapons as they exist today, releases not only immense quantities of heat and energy, but also powerful and prolonged radiation. According to the material before the Court, the first two causes of damage are vastly more powerful that the damage caused by other weapons, while the phenomenon of radiation is said to be peculiar to nuclear weapons. These characteristics render the nuclear weapons cannot be contained in either space or time. They have the potential to destroy all civilization and the entire ecosystem of the planet.

The radiation released by a nuclear explosion would affect health, agriculture, natural resources and demography over a very wide area. Further, the use of nuclear weapons would be a serious danger to future generations. Ionizing radiation has the potential to damage the future environment, food and marine ecosystem, and to cause genetic defects and illness in future generations.

36. In consequence, in order correctly to apply to the present case the Charter law on the use of force and the law applicable in armed conflict, in particular humanitarian law, it is imperative for the Court to take account of the unique characteristics of nuclear weapons, and in particular their destructive capacity, their capacity to cause untold human suffering, and their ability to cause damage to generations to come.

* * *

64. The Court will now turn to an examination of customary international law to determine whether a prohibition of the threat or use of nuclear weapons as such flows from that source of law. As the Court has stated, the substance of that law must be "looked for primarily in the actual practice and *opinio juris* of States" (*Continental Shelf (Libyan Arab Jamahiriya / Malta), Judgment, (I.C.J. Reports 1985*, p. 29, para 27).

65. States which hold the view that the use of nuclear weapons is illegal have endeavored to demonstrate the existence of a customary rule prohibiting this use. They refer to a consistent practice of non-utilization of nuclear weapons by States since 1945 and they would see in that practice the expression of an *opinio juris* on the part of those who possess such weapons.

66. Some other States, which assert the legality of the threat and use of nuclear weapons in certain circumstances, invoked the doctrine and practice of deterrence in support of their argument. They recall that they have always, in concert with certain other States, reserved the right to use those weapons in the exercise of the right to self defense against an armed attack threatening their vital security interests. In their view, if nuclear weapons have not been used since 1945, it is not on account of an existing or nascent custom but merely because circumstances that might justify their use have fortunately not arisen.

67. The Court does not intend to pronounce here upon the practice known as the "policy of deterrence." It notes that it is a fact that a number of States adhered to that practice during the greater part of the Cold War and continue to adhere to it. Furthermore, the Members of the international community are profoundly divided on the matter of whether non-recourse to nuclear weapons over the past fifty years constitutes the expression of an *opinio juris*. Under these circumstances the Court does not consider itself able to find that there is such an *opinio juris*.

68. According to certain States, the important series of General Assembly resolutions, beginning with resolution 1653 (XVI) of 24 November 1961, that deal with nuclear weapons and that affirm, with consistent regularity, the illegality of nuclear weapons, signify the existence of a rule of international customary law which prohibits recourse to those weapons. According to other States, however, the resolutions in question have no binding character on their own account and are not declaratory of any customary rule of prohibition of nuclear weapons; some of these States have also pointed out that this series of resolutions not only did not meet with the approval of all of the nuclear-weapon States but of many other States as well.

69. States which consider that the use of nuclear weapons is illegal indicated that those resolutions did not claim to create any new rules, but were confined to a confirmation of customary law relating to the prohibition of means or methods of warfare which, by their use, overstepped the bounds of what is permissible in the conduct of hostilities. In their view, the resolutions in question did no more than apply to nuclear weapons the existing rules of international law applicable in armed conflict; they were no more than the "envelope" or *instrumentum* containing certain pre-existing customary rules of international law. For those States it is accordingly of little importance that the *instrumentum* should have occasioned negative votes, which cannot have the effect of obliterating those customary rules which have been confirmed by treaty law.

70. The Court notes that General Assembly resolutions, even if they are not binding, may sometimes have normative value. They can, in certain circumstances, provide evidence important for establishing the existence of a rule or the emergence of an *opinio juris*. To establish whether this is true of a given General Assembly resolution, it is necessary to see whether on *opinio juris* exists as to its normative character. Or a series of resolutions may show the gradual evolution of the *opinio juris* required for the establishment of a new rule.

71. Examined in their totality, the General Assembly resolutions put before the Court declare that the use of nuclear weapons would be "a direct violation of the Charter of the United Nations"; and in certain formulations that such use "should be prohibited." The focus of these resolutions has sometimes shifted to diverse related matters; however, several of the resolutions under consideration in the present case have been adopted with substantial numbers of negative votes and abstentions; thus, although those resolutions are a clear sign of deep concern regarding the problem of nuclear weapons, they still fall short of establishing the existence of an *opinio juris* on the illegality of the use of such weapons.

72. The Court further notes that the first of the resolutions of the General Assembly expressly proclaiming the illegality of the use of nuclear weapons, resolution 1653 (XVI) of 24 November 1961 (mentioned in subsequent resolutions), after referring to certain international declarations and binding agreements, from the Declaration of St. Petersburg of 1868 to the Geneva Protocol of 1925, proceeded to qualify the legal nature of nuclear weapons, determine their effects, and apply general rules of customary international law to nuclear weapons in particular. That application by the General Assembly of general rules of customary law to the particular case of nuclear weapons indicates that, in its view, there was no specific rule of customary law which prohibited the use of nuclear weapons; if such a rule

had existed, the General Assembly could simply have referred to it and would not have needed to undertake such an exercise of legal qualification.

73. Having said this, the Court points out that the adoption each year by the General Assembly, by a large majority, of resolutions recalling the content of resolution 1653 (XVI), and requesting the member States to conclude a convention prohibiting the use of nuclear weapons in any circumstance, reveals the desire of a very large section of the international community to take, by a specific and express prohibition of the use of nuclear weapons, a significant step forward along the road to complete nuclear disarmament. The emergence, as *lex lata*, of a customary rule specifically prohibiting the use of nuclear weapons as such is hampered by the continuing tensions between the nascent *opinio juris* on the one hand, and the still strong adherence to the practice of deterrence on the other.

*   *   *

105. For these reasons,

THE COURT,

*   *   *

(2) *Replies* in the following manner to the question put by the General Assembly:

A. Unanimously,

There is in neither customary nor conventional international law any specific authorization of the threat or use of nuclear weapons;

B. By eleven votes to three,

There is in neither customary nor conventional international law any comprehensive and universal prohibition of the threat or use of nuclear weapons as such:

C. Unanimously,

A threat or use of force by means of nuclear weapons that is contrary to Article 2, paragraph 4, of the United Nations Charter and that fails to meet all the requirements of Article 51, is unlawful;

D. Unanimously,

A threat or use of nuclear weapons should also be compatible with the requirements of the international law applicable in armed conflict, particularly those of the principles and rules of international humanitarian law, as well as with specific obligations under treaties and other undertakings which expressly deal with nuclear weapons;

E. By seven votes to seven, by the President's casting vote:

It follows from the above-mentioned requirements that the threat or use of nuclear weapons would generally be contrary to the rules of international law applicable in armed conflict, and in particular the principles and rules of humanitarian law;

However, in view of the current state of international law, and of the elements of fact at its disposal, the Court cannot conclude definitively whether the threat or use of nuclear weapons would be lawful or unlawful in an extreme circumstances of self defense, in which the very survival of a State would be at stake[.]

NOTES AND QUESTIONS

1.   ***The changed approach to customary international law.*** Compare the ICJ's views on the role of state practice and *opinio juris* in relation to treaties and resolutions of international organizations in the *Nuclear Weapons Advisory Opinion* and the *North Sea Continental Shelf* cases. What are the differences? Why the difference in approach? Which approach do you think is best?

2.   ***Environmental protection and armed conflict.*** Is international environmental law suspended during periods and in places of armed conflict? If not, is the use of nuclear weapons, which obviously would have a devastating impact on environment, legal under any circumstances? The ICJ made five different rulings in the Nuclear Weapons Advisory Opinion case. Are the rulings internally consistent? The final part of the Court's ruling is generally known as a *"non liquet"* by international lawyers. This phrase, which comes from Roman law, means literally "not clear" in the sense that there is no applicable law so the question must remain undecided. Does the *non liquet* follow logically from the Court's prior rulings?

3.   ***Claims for environmental damage during armed conflict.*** During the Gulf War in 1991, the Iraqi military detonated more than 700 Kuwaiti oil wells and opened valves at several oil terminals causing massive pollution of the surrounding lands and waters. In response, the United Nations Security Council passed Resolution 687, which stated that Iraq was liable for all direct losses, including "environmental damage and the depletion of natural resources." The Security Council established the United Nations Claims Commission, which took a series of decisions to adjudicate and to pay claims, including environmental claims from individuals and countries. The UNCC operated until July 30, 2005, with a full time staff of 240 people. During the 12 years of its operation, the UNCC adjudicated over 2.68 million claims, awarding over $300 billion in compensation to governments, companies and individual claimants. See ALEXANDRE KISS AND DINAH SHELTON, GUIDE TO INTERNATIONAL ENVIRONMENTAL LAW 253–73 (Leiden, The Netherlands: Koninklijke Brill NV, 2007) for a thorough discussion of the law of environmental protection and armed conflict.

Section II.   "SOFT LAW"

Scholars and courts recognize a hierarchy of norms of international law.[9] The most prominent norms are rights and obligations *jus cogens* and *erga omnes. Jus cogens* refers to certain human rights norms that are "peremptory" and undeniable by any state,[10] such as the prohibitions against slavery, genocide, official torture,

---

[9] Ulrich Beyerlin, *Different Types of Norms in International Environmental Law*, Chapter 18, in DANIEL BODANSKY, JUTTA BRUNNEE & ELLEN HEY (eds.), THE OXFORD HANDBOOK OF INTERNATIONAL ENVIRONMENTAL LAW 425, 426 (Oxford: Oxford University Press, 2007).

[10] Vienna Convention on the Law of Treaties, Art. 53.

and racial discrimination.[11] *Jus cogens* does not yet play a role in international environmental law. The term *erga omnes* refers to certain obligations that are owed by states to the international community as a whole; thus every state has a legal interest in the observance of such norms and may sue to enforce them.[12] *Erga omnes* norms obviously include *jus cogens*[13], but the concept *erga omnes* is broader, applying as a practical matter to international regimes that find universal acceptance. Certain international environmental regimes, such as the Montreal Protocol (1987) to the Convention on the Protection of the Ozone Layer (1985), are *de facto erga omnes* regime. Thus, we shall see that the concept *erga omnes* plays a role in international environmental law. However, the mass of international law and international environmental law norms, although not *jus cogens* or *erga omnes*, are "hard law" obligations that have unquestioned binding effect. As we have seen, treaty law is regarded as stronger and as more authoritative than the other recognized sources of international law.

At the bottom of the hierarchy of international law norms is what is known as "soft law," norms that are recognized as having "compliance pull," but which are non-binding or inherently flexible obligations. Although soft law is a feature of general international law, the extensive development of soft law norms is a unique feature of international environmental law and consequently merits extensive discussion.

Three universes of soft law norms may be distinguished. First, soft law norms may be found in a host of authoritative but explicitly non-binding resolutions and pronouncements of international organizations and other international bodies. The central soft law document of this type is the Rio Declaration of Environment and Development (1992),[14] which is reproduced in full in the following section of this book. The Rio Declaration codified such important international law normative principles as sustainable development; the obligation not to cause environmental damage to other states or areas beyond the limits of national jurisdiction; the obligation to cooperate to conserve and protect the environment; the precautionary principle; the polluter pays principle; and the obligation to use environmental impact assessment for activities that are likely to have a significant adverse impact on the environment, among many others. Note that not all of these norms are general; some norms are quite precise, such as the requirement to undertake environmental impact assessments.

A second type of soft law obligation consists of binding norms in international environmental treaties that create open ended flexibility for states' compliance. An example of such a norm are the several provisions in the United Nations Convention on Biological Diversity (1992), that qualify the obligation of state-parties to undertake *ex-situ* and *in-situ* conservation of natural resources with the phrase "as far as possible and appropriate." This wording reduces the binding nature of

---

[11] Siderman de Blake v. Republic of Argentina, 965 F.2d 699, 715–17 (9th Cir. 1992).

[12] Barcelona Traction Case (Belgium v. Spain), 1970 ICJ Rep. 3, para. 33.

[13] Application of Reservations to the Convention on the Prevention and Punishment of Genocide (Bosnia Herzegovina v. Yugoslavia), 1996 ICJ Rep. 595, para. 616.

[14] Report of the United Nations Conference on Environment and Development, A/CONF. 151/26/ Rev.1 (Vol. 1), Annex I, pp. 3–8 (June 3–14, 1992).

conservation activities to an obligation to carry out only what the state concerned desires to do, setting out what amounts to only a soft law obligation. We will meet many soft law obligations of this type in this course.

A third variety of soft law obligation is rules and standards promulgated by non-governmental industrial, environmental, and consumer protection associations in the public interest that may be adopted voluntarily by private companies and organizations. An important example of such rules are those promulgated by the International Organization for Standardization (ISO) in Geneva, which is a private international standards institution founded in 1946 to facilitate international trade. The ISO is a worldwide federation of 148 national standards bodies. ISO standards are developed by technical committees and the ISO 14000 standards mandate important environmental norms for consumer products and for environmental management systems for companies.

Why is soft law so frequently employed in the area of international environmental law? Among the reasons for this practice are the following[15]:

- States lack the political will to enter into binding obligations, but national leaders wish to take some action to address a pressing environmental problem so the solution is a non-binding or flexible accord.

- Intergovernmental organizations lack the capacity to adopt binding decisions, so to express their will they make recommendations or declarations.

- The institutions created by multilateral environmental agreements, such as conferences of parties, may not be able to agree on a binding text, but can agree on a non-binding declaration.

- The subject matter at hand may be such that a soft law instrument is more appropriate and easier to negotiate.

- Soft law instruments can include the participation of key non-governmental participants.

- Domestic political barriers may preclude binding treaty obligations.

- Business enterprises are more likely to respond positively to private, voluntary standards rather than government regulation of their business activities and products.

A famous example of an important soft law text that was adopted in lieu of a binding treaty is the Copenhagen Accord on Climate Change of 2009, which was agreed at the close of the 15th Conference of the Parties to the United Nations Framework Convention on Climate Change and which was immediately accepted by 114 parties. The Copenhagen Accord, which is non-binding, adopts the goal that the increase in global temperature should be kept below 2 degrees Celsius through "deep cuts" in greenhouse gas emissions by states-parties. We take up the Copenhagen Accord in Chapter 4 of this book.

How do you evaluate the proliferation of soft law instruments in international environmental law? Although such norms are frequently criticized as ineffective, in fact, such norms may have an important positive impact. For example, the

---

[15] *See* Alexandre Kiss and Dinah Shelton, Guide to International Environmental Law 9–10 (2007).

Copenhagen Accord induced 141 countries to make pledges to comply with aspects of the accord, including significant pledges by China and India, large emitters of greenhouse gases. This level of participation would have been impossible to attain with a binding agreement.

A.   Principles of International Environmental Law

The most discussed and most controversial soft law international environmental norms are so-called principles of international environmental law. Among the several authoritative formulations of such principles by international bodies, the most important formulation and the one that subsumes virtually all the others is the Rio Declaration on Environment and Development at the United Nations Conference on Environment and Development in 1992. In the next section of this book, we tell the story of the long development of the Rio Declaration principles, but here we set the Rio Declaration out in full in order to develop an understanding of their meaning and significance.

B.   The Rio Declaration

RIO DECLARATION ON ENVIRONMENT AND DEVELOPMENT, REPORT OF THE UNITED NATIONS CONFERENCE ON ENVIRONMENT AND DEVELOPMENT
A/CONF.151/26/Rev.1 (Vol. I) (3–14 June 1992), Annex I, pp. 3–8

Principle 1

Human beings are at the centre of concerns for sustainable development. They are entitled to a healthy and productive life in harmony with nature.

Principle 2

States have, in accordance with the Charter of the United Nations and the principles of international law, the sovereign right to exploit their own resources pursuant to their own environmental and development policies, and the responsibility to ensure that activities within their jurisdiction or control do not cause damage to the environment of other States or to areas beyond the limits of national jurisdiction.

Principle 3

The right to development must be fulfilled so as to equitably meet developmental and environmental needs of present and future generations.

Principle 4

In order to achieve sustainable development, environmental protection shall constitute an integral part of the development process and cannot be considered in isolation from it.

Principle 5

All States and all people shall cooperate in the essential task of eradicating poverty as an indispensable requirement for sustainable development, in order to decrease the disparities in standards of living and better meet the needs of the majority of the people of the world.

Principle 6

The special situation and needs of developing countries, particularly the least developed and those most environmentally vulnerable, shall be given special priority. International actions in the field of environment and development should also address the interests and needs of all countries.

Principle 7

State shall cooperate in a spirit of global partnership to conserve, protect and restore the health and integrity of the Earth's ecosystems. In view of the different contributions to global environmental degradation, States have common but differentiated responsibilities. The developed countries acknowledge the responsibility that they bear in the international pursuit of sustainable development in view of the pressures their societies place on the global environment and of the technologies and financial resources they command.

Principle 8

To achieve sustainable development and a higher quality of life for all people, States should reduce and eliminate unsustainable patterns of production and consumption and promote appropriate demographic policies.

Principle 9

States shall cooperate to strengthen endogenous capacity-building for sustainable development by improving scientific understanding through exchanges of scientific and technological knowledge, and by enhancing the development, adaptation, diffusion and transfer of technologies, including new and innovative technologies.

Principle 10

Environmental issues are best handled with the participation of all concerned citizens, at the relevant level. At the national level, each individual shall have appropriate access to information concerning the environment that is held by public authorities, including information on hazardous materials and activities in their communities, and the opportunity to participate in decision-making processes. States shall facilitate and encourage public awareness and participation by making information widely available. Effective access to judicial and administrative proceedings, including redress and remedy, shall be provided.

Principle 11

States shall enact effective environmental legislation. Environmental standards, management objectives and priorities should reflect the environmental and developmental context to which they and apply. Standards applied by some countries may be inappropriate and of unwarranted economic and social cost to other countries, in particular developing countries.

Principle 12

States should cooperate to promote a supportive and open international economic system that would lead to economic growth and sustainable development in all countries, to better address the problems of environmental degradation. Trade policy measures for environmental purposes should not constitute a means of arbitrary or unjustifiable discrimination or a disguised restriction on international trade. Unilateral actions to deal with environmental challenges outside the jurisdiction of the importing country should be avoided. Environmental measures addressing transboundary or global environmental problems should, as far as possible, be based on an international consensus.

Principle 13

States shall develop national laws regarding liability and compensation for the victims of pollution and other environmental damage. States shall also cooperate in an expeditious and more determined manner to develop further international law regarding liability and compensation for adverse effects on environmental damage caused by activities within their jurisdiction or control to areas beyond their jurisdiction.

Principle 14

States should effectively cooperate to discourage or prevent the relocation and transfer to other States of any activities and substances that cause severe environmental degradation or are found to be harmful to human health.

Principle 15

In order to protect the environment, the precautionary approach shall be widely applied by States according to their capabilities. Where there are threats of serious or irreversible damage, lack of full scientific certainty shall not be used as a reason for postponing cost-effective measures to prevent environmental degradation.

Principle 16

National authorities should endeavour to promote the internalization of environmental costs and the use of economic instruments, taking into account the approach that the polluter should, in principle, bear the cost of pollution, with due regard to the public interest and without distorting international trade and investment.

Principle 17

Eenvironmental impact assessment, as a national instrument, shall be undertaken for proposed activities that are likely to have a significant adverse impact on the environment and are subject to a decision of a competent national authority.

Principle 18

States shall immediately notify other States of any natural disasters or other emergencies that are likely to produce sudden harmful effects on the environment of those States. Every effort shall be made by the international community to help States so afflicted.

Principle 19

States shall provide prior and timely notification and relevant information to potentially affected States on activities that may have a significant adverse transboundary environmental effect and shall consult with those States at an early stage and in good faith.

Principle 20

Women have a vital role in environmental management and development. Their full participation is therefore essential to achieve sustainable development.

Principle 21

The creativity, ideals and courage of the youth of the world should be utilized to forge a global partnership in order to achieve sustainable development and ensure a better future for all.

Principle 22

Indigenous people and their communities, and other local communities have a vital role in environmental management and development because of their knowledge and traditional practices. States should recognize and duly support their identity, culture and interests and enable their effective participation in the achievement of sustainable development.

Principle 23

The environment and natural resources of people under oppression, domination and occupation shall be protected.

Principle 24

Warfare is inherently destructive of sustainable development. States shall therefore respect international law providing protection for the environment in times of armed conflict and cooperate in its further development, as necessary.

Principle 25

Peace, development and environmental protection are interdependent and indivisible.

Principle 26

States shall resolve all their environmental disputes peacefully and by appropriate means in accordance with the Charter of the United Nations.

Principle 27

States and people shall cooperate in good faith and in a spirit of partnership in the fulfillment of the principles embodied in this Declaration and in the further development of international law in the field of sustainable development.

RIO PRINCIPLE ONE — HUMAN RIGHTS AND THE ENVIRONMENT

We devote much of the rest of this chapter to the actualization of these Rio Principles of "soft law." But to begin with we wish to emphasize the importance of Rio Principle 1, which famously asserts that human beings are "entitled to a healthy and productive life [lives] in harmony with nature." The word "entitled" is very close to declaring that human beings have "rights" to a healthy environment. Is there such a right, and, if so, what are the implications of a human rights approach to protection of the environment?

International human rights law is established not only by customary international law but by a multitude of international institutions, treaties, and other international instruments. First, on the global level there are UN Charter organs, such as the Human Rights Council and UN Human Rights treaty organs, such as the Human Rights Committee under the UN Covenant on Civil and Political Rights, and other similar bodies under other human rights treaties. These human rights committees are not judicial tribunals and have no direct power to enforce their decisions, but under some human rights treaties complaints can be filed by individuals and NGOs. Human rights violations can be challenged also, sometimes more effectively, in the regional human rights systems, the European Court of Human Rights, the Inter-American Commission and Court of Human Rights, and the African Commission and Court of Human Rights.

The United Nations Human Rights Council has focused attention to the relationship between a safe and healthy environment and human rights. For example, the Council in its Resolution 7/23 of March 2008, and Resolution 10/4 of March 2009, focused on climate change, noting that climate-related effects will have a range of direct and indirect implications for the enjoyment of many of the rights guaranteed in the Universal Declaration of Human Rights, one of the United Nations' most important formulation of human rights.

There are three main dimensions of the relationship between protection of the environment and human rights: first, protection of the environment — water and air quality and environmental services — is a necessary prerequisite to the enjoyment of a wide range of human rights. Second, certain human rights, such as the right to information, the right to public participation, non-discrimination, and access to justice, are rights found in many multilateral and bilateral environmental treaties. Thus, there is an undeniable overlap between the international law of human rights and international environmental law. Third, we may be moving toward the recognition that a safe and healthy environment is a human right in itself. Principle 1 of the Rio Declaration proclaims that man has a fundamental right to freedom, equality, and adequate conditions of life, in an environment of a quality that permits a life of dignity and well-being. The UN General Assembly has declared (Resolution 4594) that all individuals are entitled to live in an environment adequate for their health and well-being. For a comprehensive introduction to this theme, see DONALD K. ANTON AND DINAH L. SHELTON, ENVIRONMENTAL PROTECTION AND HUMAN RIGHTS (Cambridge: Cambridge University Press, 2011).

We will see that many multilateral environmental treaties contain provisions that echo human rights pronouncements in human rights instruments. Procedural human rights, such as the right to information, to participate in decisionmaking, and to access to justice are commonly found in environmental treaties.

The substantive linkage between human rights and the protection of the environment was famously recognized by Judge Weeremantry of the International Court of Justice in his separate opinion in the Gabcikovo-Nagymaros Case (Hungary v. Slovakia), 1997 I.C.J. Rep. 7, 93:

> The protection of the environment is . . . a vital part of contemporary human rights doctrine, for it is a *sine qua non* for numerous human rights such as the right to health and the right to life itself. It is scarcely necessary to elaborate on this, as damage to the environment can impair and undermine all the human rights spoken of in the Universal Declaration and other human rights instruments.

In certain instances protection of the environment may justify filing a complaint in one of the international systems for the protection of human rights or invoking a human rights protection in an national constitution.

Express recognition of the right to a healthy environment is contained in two international human rights systems, the African and Inter-American rights systems. Article 24 of the African Charter of Human Rights provides that "All people shall have the right to a generally satisfactory environment favourable to their development." [21 I.L.M. 58, 60 (1982)]. The Inter-American rights system, Protocol of San Salvador, Article 11, provides that "Everyone shall have the right to live in a healthy environment and to have access to basic public services." [Additional Protocol to the American Convention on Human Rights in the Area of Economic, Social and Cultural Rights, 28 ILM 161 (1988)]. However, these rights are declaratory and aspirational, not enforceable by an individual petition.

In 2007, the United Nations General Assembly approved the UN Declaration on the Rights of Indigenous Peoples, which in Article 29 declares a "right to conservation and protection of the environment." This Declaration, however, is a non-binding, aspirational document.

In certain cases, however, rights related to the right to a healthy environment may be relied upon to vindicate an individually recognized human right. In the

European Court of Human Rights Article 8 of the European Convention on Human Rights, which establishes a right to respect for family and home has been used to stop pollution and to demand compensation for damages.

In *Lopez Ostra v. Spain*, App. No. 16798/90, 20 Eur. H.R. Rep. 277 (1994), the European Court of Human Rights ruled that Spain was guilty of violating the human rights of Lopez Ostra, a Spanish national living in Lorca (Murcia), whose home was severely impacted by pollution emanating from tannery facilities built close by. The tannery plants were permitted and subsidized by the Spanish government and were allowed to operate in such a fashion as to cause health problems to Ostra and his family. The court ruled that there was evidence that Spain was in violation of Article 8 of the European Convention on Human Rights, which states:

1. Everyone has the right to respect for his private and family life, his home and his correspondence.

2. There shall be no interference by a public authority with the exercise of this right except such as is in accordance with the law and is necessary in a democratic society in the interests of national security, public safety or the economic well-being of the country, for the prevention of disorder or crime, for the protection of health or morals, or for the protection of the rights and freedoms of others.

In the *Ostra case*, the European Court of Human Rights awarded compensatory damages for environmental harm.[16]

In certain cases minorities living within states have protested logging and environmental degradation as violations of rights to culture guaranteed by international human rights instruments. For example, rights to cultural values is featured in Article 27 of the Universal Declaration of Human Rights; Article 27 of the International Covenant on Civil and Political Rights; Article 13 of the American Declaration of Human Rights; and Article 15 of the International Covenant on Economic, Social and Cultural Rights. In the case of *Landsman v. Finland*, UN Communication CCPR/C/58/D/671/1995, reindeer breeders of Sami ethnic origin complained the UN Human Rights Committee that logging and the construction of roads approved by the Finnish government were causing an adverse impact on their reindeer herding operations, which are part of their cultural heritage. Although the Committee found on the facts that there was no breach of Article 27 of the International Covenant on Civil and Political Rights, the Committee warned that large scale exploitations of the environment in the future could constitute violations of cultural rights guaranteed by the International Covenant.

In the *Awas Tingni Case*[17], the Inter-American Court of Human Rights vindicated indigenous peoples' rights and rendered a decision in favor of protecting biodiversity. This case involved a concession granted by the government of Nicaragua to a foreign company to log the traditional lands of the Awas Tingni community. Even though the Awas Tigni did not have official legal title to the lands

---

[16] Other Article 8 cases include *Fadeyeva v. Russia* (2005) and *Taksin v. Turkey* (2004).

[17] The Mayagna (Sumo) Awas Tingni Community v. Nicaragua (2001).

in question, the Court ruled that the right to enjoy property affirmed in the American Convention on Human Rights includes the right of indigenous peoples to enjoy their traditional lands and associated natural resources.

In some countries human rights guarantees in national constitutions may be used to vindicate environmental rights. For example, the Indian Constitution protects human health (Article 47); the natural environment (Articles 48 and 51); and the right to life (Article 2). Article 32 of the Constitution grants citizens standing to sue directly in the Supreme Court for violations of constitutional rights. In several cases the Indian Supreme Court has interpreted the right to life and other rights to protect environmental values. E.g., *Vellore Citizens Welfare Reform v. Union of India* [1996 All India Rep. 2715], a suit to abate pollution from sources discharging industrial wastes in violation of their permits.

What are the advantages and disadvantages of a human rights approach to combating environmental degradation?

NOTE: THE LEGAL STATUS OF THE RIO PRINCIPLES

What is the legal status of these principles? As lawyers, we are not accustomed to dealing with norms that are as general and all-encompassing as the Rio principles. Since these principles were promulgated explicitly as non-binding norms, we may have a tendency to dismiss them out of hand as visionary ideals having no normative force. But the formulation of the principles may give us pause. The common wording "shall" and "should" implies normative force of some kind. Moreover, the fact that these principles were unanimously proclaimed at a United Nations conference attended by some 194 states and over 100 heads of state means that they intended to command our attention.

A first step in understanding the Rio principles is to realize that there is a distinction between what are termed "principles" of law, on one hand, and "rules" of law, on the other. This distinction was most famously drawn by Ronald Dworkin in his book, TAKING RIGHTS SERIOUSLY 24–26 (London: Duckworth, 1977) as follows:

> The difference between legal principles and legal rules is a logical distinction. Both sets of norms point to particular decisions about legal obligations in particular circumstances, but they differ in the character of the direction they give. Rules are applicable in an all-or-nothing fashion. If the facts a rule stipulates are given, the rule is valid, in which case the answer it gives must be accepted, or it is not, in which case it contributes nothing to the decision.

> A principle states a reason that argues in one direction, but does not necessitate a particular decision. . . . There may be other principles or policies arguing in the other directions. . . . All that is meant when we say that a particular principle is a *principle of law*, is that the principle is one which officials must take into account, if it is relevant, as a consideration inclining in one way or another.

Thus, a principle, "while still importing a legal obligation, is . . . different from a rule. Rules either dictate a result or do not apply. Principles, on the other hand, can point toward a result and remain relevant even if they do not prevail. Where a number of principles of law are relevant and intersect or conflict, the decision-maker comes under an obligation to balance their competing objectives and to reach a decision in conformity, to the maximum extent possible, with both principles. Principles and rules are related in that rules operationalise the social goal for which a principle argues."[18]

In addition, Judge Rudiger Wolfrum, President of the International Tribunal for the Law of the Sea, has stated that legal principles, as incorporated into policy documents have a three-fold function: such principles are designed "to guide the policy of States, to channel subsequent negotiations on international agreements into a particular direction, or to influence the development of international customary law."[19]

Now read over the Rio principles closely. How would you classify them; do they fall into substantive categories? What interests do they represent in addition to environmental interests?

Consider each principle from the point of view of ease of application and compliance. Which principles pose little problem or difficulty to United States' policy makers? Which pose the most problems?

All of the Rio principles are important, and we will meet virtually all of these principles in some form in the succeeding chapters of this book. But in the remainder of this section we concentrate on the principles that are deemed by scholars and practitioners as the core principles of international environmental law: (1) the "prevention of environmental harm" principle (Principle 2); (2) the sustainable development principle (Principles 1, 4, 5, 7, 8, 9, 12, 20, and 24); (3) the precautionary principle (Principle 15); (4) the intergenerational equity principle (Principle 3); (5) the environmental impact assessment principle (Principle 17); and (6) the polluter pays principle (Principle 16).

1.　The Harm Prevention Principle

Principle 2 looks in two directions. On the one hand this principle recognizes the "sovereign rights" of states to exploit natural resources within their territories; on the other hand, this principle proclaims that states have the "responsibility" to ensure that activities within their jurisdiction or control do not cause environmental damage to other states or to areas beyond national jurisdiction. The first half of Principle 2 does not really break new ground; it merely affirms that states enjoy territorial sovereignty under international law. The second half of Principle 2 is known as the harm prevention principle.

The second half of Principle 2 constitutes a limit on the exercise of sovereignty. The harm prevention principle is sometimes stated in its Latin form: *sic utere tuo,*

---

[18] Robyn Briese, *Precaution and Cooperation in the World Trade Organization: An Environmental Perspective*, 22 AUSTR. Y.B. INT'L L. 113, 117 (2002).

[19] Rudiger Wolfrum, *International Environmental Law: Purposes, Principles, and Means of Ensuring Compliance*, In F.L. MORRISON & R. WOLFRUM (eds.), INTERNATIONAL, REGIONAL AND NATIONAL ENVIRONMENTAL LAW 3, 6 (The Hague: Kluwer International, 2000)

ut alienum non laedas, a sign of its antiquity. Unlike some of the Rio principles, the harm prevention principle has a long history and is universally accepted as a customary rule. The chief antecedent of the prevention of environmental harm rule is the *Trail Smelter Arbitration*,[20] a case in which the arbitral tribunal awarded monetary damages for transboundary pollution to the United States and prescribed a regime for the control of future emissions from a Canadian smelter. The *Trail Smelter* tribunal relied in part on an earlier transboundary pollution case decided by the Supreme Court of the United States, *Georgia v. Tennessee Copper Co.*, 206 U.S. 230 (1907). Thus the prevention of environmental harm rule is well-established.

In a case we covered previously in this book, the *Nuclear Weapons Advisory Opinion*, the ICJ affirmed that: "The existence of the general obligation of states to ensure that activities within their jurisdiction and control respect the environment of other states and of areas beyond national control is now part of the corpus of international law relating to the environment." (para. 29). This conclusion is well-settled.

Although the prevention of environmental harm principle is an obligatory rule of customary international law, the juxtaposition of the prevention principle with the sovereign right of exploitation means that neither half of Principle 2 is absolute. The prevention principle should not therefore be construed as an absolute "no harm" requirement; rather what is called for is a correct balance: states should exercise their right to exploit responsibility by preventing significant transboundary harm. Principle 2 does not provide explicit guidance on how the balance should be struck. This means that the precise normative contours of the prevention of environmental harm principle must be worked out by international tribunals, treaty-makers, and the International Law Commission. The International Law Commission has adopted detailed articles implementing Principle 2 and establishing the contours of the responsibility of states in this regard. International Law Commission, *Articles on the Prevention of Transboundary Harm for Hazardous Activities* (2001), submitted to the General Assembly of the United Nations.

We cover and analyze these Articles on transboundary harm and the jurisprudence relating to the harm prevention principle in Chapter 3 on State Responsibility for Transboundary Pollution.

2. Sustainable Development

The principle of sustainable development is a complex, integrative concept that pervades both the Rio principles (*See* Principles 1, 3, 4, 5–9; 20–22, 24, and 27), and international environmental law as a whole. However, the meaning and importance of this principle is highly controversial. The concept of sustainable development originated with the Brundtland Commission Report, *Our Common Future* (1987),[21] which was the central document produced by the World Commission on Environment and Development, which was created by United Nations General Assembly Resolution in 1983. The term "sustainable development" was coined in the

---

[20] 33 Am. J. Int'l L. 162 (1939) and 35 Am. J. Int'l L. 684 (1941).

[21] World Commission on Environment and Development, *Our Common Future* (Oxford: Oxford University Press, 1987).

Brundtland Report to overcome the reluctance of many developing countries to join an effort to protect the global environment and to create a new body of international environmental law. The Brundtland Commission's mission was to unite countries to pursue a common effort to protect the global environment, and the concept of sustainable development proved to be a key to achieve virtually universal agreement to pursue environmental aims. The Brundtland Commission's definition of sustainable development reflects these origins. Sustainable development is defined as development that meets the needs of the present without compromising the needs of future generations. Sustainable development means that the essential needs of the world's poor should be paramount; and that limitations should be imposed by the state of technology and social concerns on the environment's ability to meet present and future needs.[22] Considering official formulations since the Brundtland Commission's Report, the concept of sustainable development may be stated to contain the following elements[23]:

- Sustainable utilization patterns of production and consumption;

- Integration of environmental protection and economic development;

- The right to development of developing countries;

- Inter-generational equity;

- Procedural fairness such as environmental impact assessment and public participation in decisionmaking.

What is the status of the concept of sustainable development in international law? Consider the following case.

CASE CONCERNING THE GABČÍKOVO-NAGYMAROS PROJECT (HUNGARY v. SLOVAKIA)
1997 I.C.J. 7, 77–78, 88–108 (footnotes renumbered)

[The International Court of Justice, in 1997, had occasion to directly consider how to balance the need for economic development with environmental protection. In *Case Concerning the Gabcikovo-Nagymaros Project* (Hungary v. Slovakia), 1997 I.C.J. 92, Hungary purported to terminate a treaty with Slovakia by which the parties had agreed to build and operate a dam and system of locks on the Danube River. The project as originally envisioned was supposed to significantly contribute to the economies of both states by increasing shipping access to and trade with the region and by powering two large hydroelectric power plants. The parties recognized that the project also raised serious threats to the surrounding environment and included treaty provisions obligating the parties to ensure that water quality was not diminished and "for the protection of nature."

By 1989, Hungary had suspended work on the project because new evidence had come to light about greater adverse environmental consequences than originally anticipated and growing domestic public opposition to the project. In 1992, Hungary notified Slovakia that it was terminating the treaty. Slovakia itself eventually

---

[22]   *Ibid.* at 43.

[23]   ALAN BOYLE & DAVID FREESTONE, INTRODUCTION, ALAN BOYLE & DAVID FREESTONE (eds.), INTERNATIONAL LAW AND SUSTAINABLE DEVELOPMENT 8–16 (Oxford: Oxford University Press, 1999).

constructed a modified system of locks known as Variant C and put it into operation. Once the project came on-line it dramatically reduced the flow of the Danube River downstream into Hungary. As a result, Hungary insisted, *inter alia*, that Slovakia restore the Danube to the situation it was in prior to putting Variant C into operation. Slovakia refused.

In 1993, the parties agreed to submit their dispute to the ICJ. The Court ruled that Hungary had breached the 1977 treaty by suspending work on the project and that the breach could not be excused on the ground of "ecological necessity." The Court also held that Slovakia was responsible for the interference with Hungary's interests in the Danube through the operation of Variant C. The ICJ concluded that the 1977 treaty was still in force and directed the parties to enter into good faith negotiations to reach a workable solution. In the course of its judgment the Court acknowledged the existence of international environmental norms and directed the parties to consider the principles of sustainable development in trying to reconcile the competing environmental and development aspects of the situation. The Court stated:]

140. It is clear that the Project's impact upon, and its implications for, the environment are of necessity a key issue. The numerous scientific reports which have been presented to the Court by the Parties — even if their conclusions are often contradictory — provide abundant evidence that this impact and these implications are considerable.

In order to evaluate the environmental risks, current standards must be taken into consideration. This is not only allowed by the wording of Articles 15 and 19, but even prescribed, to the extent that these articles impose a continuing — and thus necessarily evolving — obligation on the parties to maintain the quality of water of the Danube and to protect nature.

The Court is mindful that, in the field of environmental protection, vigilance and prevention are required on account of the often irreversible character of damage to the environment and of the limitations inherent in the very mechanism of reparation of this type of damage.

Throughout the ages, mankind has, for economic and other reasons, constantly interfered with nature. In the past, this was often done without consideration of the effects upon the environment. Owing to new scientific insights and to a growing awareness of the risks for mankind — for present and future generations — of pursuit of such interventions at an unconsidered and unabated pace, new norms and standards have been developed, set forth in a great number of instruments during the last two decades. Such new norms have to be taken into consideration, and such new standards given proper weight, not only when States contemplate new activities but also when continuing with activities begun in the past. This need to reconcile economic development with protection of the environment is aptly expressed in the concept of sustainable development.

For the purposed of the present case, this means the Parties together should look afresh at the effects on the environment of the operation of the Gabcikovo power plant. In particular they must find a satisfactory solution for the volume of water to be released into the old bed of the Danube and into the side-arms of both sides of the river.

[In a separate opinion, Vice-President of the Court Weeramantry significantly elaborated on the legal role of sustainable development in international law. Weeramantry explained:]

This case raises a rich array of environmentally related legal issues. A discussion of some of them is essential to explain my reasons for voting as I have in this very difficult decision. Three issues on which I wish to make some observations, supplementary to those of the Court, are the role played by the principle of sustainable development in balancing the competing demands of development and environmental protection; the protection given to Hungary by what I would describe as the principle of continuing environmental impact assessment; and the appropriateness of the use of *inter partes* legal principles, such as estoppel, for the resolution of problems with an *erga omnes* connotation such as environmental damage.

The Concept of Sustainable Development

Had the possibility of environmental harm been the only consideration to be taken into account in this regard, the contentions of Hungary could well have proved conclusive.

Yet there are other factors to be taken into account — not the least important of which is the developmental aspect, of the Gabcikovo scheme is important to Slovakia from the point of view of development. The Court must hold the balance even between the environmental considerations and the developmental considerations raised by the respective Parties. The principle that enables the Court to do so is the principle of sustainable development.

The Court has referred to it as a concept in paragraph 140 of its Judgment. However, I consider it to be more than a mere concept, but as a principle with normative value which is critical to the determination of this case. Without the benefits of its insights, the issues involved in this case would have been difficult to resolve.

Since sustainable development is a principle fundamental to the determination of the competing considerations in this case, and since, although it has attracted attention only recently in the literature of international law, it is likely to play a major role in determining important environmental disputes of the future, it calls for consideration in some detail. Moreover, this is the first occasion on which it has received attention in the jurisprudence of this Court.

When a major scheme, such as that under consideration in the present case, is planned and implemented, there is always the need to weigh considerations of development against environmental considerations, as their underlying juristic bases — the right to development and the right to environmental protection — are important principles of current international law.

In the present case we have, on the one hand, a scheme which, even in the attenuated form in which it now remains, is important to the welfare of Slovakia and its people, who have already strained their own resources and those of their predecessor State to the extent of over two billion dollars to achieve these benefits. Slovakia, in fact, argues that the environment would be improved through the operation of the project as it would help to stop erosion of the river bed, and that the scheme would be an effective protection against floods. Further, Slovakia has traditionally been short of electricity and the power generated would be important to its economic development. Moreover, if the project is halted in its tracks, vast structural works constructed at great expense, even prior to the repudiation of the Treaty, would be idle and unproductive, and would pose an economic and environmental problem in themselves.

On the other hand, Hungary alleges that the project produces, or is likely to produce, ecological damage of many varieties, including harm to river bank fauna and flora, damage to fish breeding, damage to surface water quality, eutrophication, damage to the groundwater régime, agriculture, forestry and soil, deterioration of the quality of drinking water reserves, and sedimentation. Hungary alleges that many of these dangers have already occurred and more will manifest themselves, if the scheme continues in operation. In the material placed before the Court, each of these dangers is examined and explained in considerable detail.

How does one handle these considerations? Does one abandon the project altogether for fear that the latter consequences might emerge? Does one proceed with the scheme because of the national benefits it brings, regardless of the suggested environmental damage? Or does one steer a course between, with due regard to both considerations, but ensuring always a continuing vigilance in respect of environmental harm?

It is clear that a principle must be followed which pays due regard to both considerations. Is there such a principle, and does it command recognition in international law? I believe the answer to both questions is in the affirmative. The principle is the principle of sustainable development and, in my view, it is an integral part of modern international law. It is clearly of the utmost importance, both in this case and more generally.

I would observe, moreover, that both Parties in this case agree on the applicability to this dispute of the principle of sustainable development. . . .

Their disagreement seems to be not as to the existence of the principle but, rather, as to the way in which it is to be applied to the facts of this case. . . .

The problem of steering a course between the needs of development and this necessity to protect the environment is a problem alike of the law of development and of the law of the environment. Both these vital and developing areas of law require, and indeed assume, the existence of a principle with harmonizes both needs.

To hold that no such principle exists in the law is to hold that current law recognizes the juxtaposition of two principles which could operate in collision with each other, without providing the necessary basis of principle for their reconciliation. The untenability of the supposition that the law sanctions such a state of normative anarchy suffices to condemn a hypothesis that leads to so unsatisfactory a result.

Each principle cannot be given free rein, regardless of the other. The law necessarily contains within itself the principle of reconciliation. That principle is the principle of sustainable development.

This case offers a unique opportunity for the application of that principle, for it arises from a Treaty which had development as its objective, and has been brought to a standstill over argument concerning environmental considerations.

The people of both Hungary and Slovakia are entitled to development for the furtherance of their happiness and welfare. They are likewise entitled to the preservation of their human right to the protection of their environment. Other cases raising environmental questions have been considered by this Court in the context of environmental pollution arising from such sources as nuclear explosions, which are far removed from development projects. The present case thus focuses attention, as no other case has done in the jurisprudence of this Court, on the question of the harmonization of developmental and environmental concepts.

Sustainable Development as a Principle of International Law

After the early formulations of the concept of development, it has been recognized that development cannot be pursued to such a point as to result in substantial damage to the environment within which it is to occur. Therefore development can only be prosecuted in harmony with the reasonable demands of environmental protection. Whether development is sustainable by reason of its impact on the environment will, of course, be a question to be answered in the context of the particular situation involved.

It is thus the correct formulation of the right to development that that right does not exist in the absolute sense, but is relative always to its tolerance by the environment. The right to development as thus refined is clearly part of modern international law. It is compendiously referred to as sustainable development.

The concept of sustainable development can be traced back, beyond the Stockholm Conference of 1972, to such events as the Founex meeting of experts in Switzerland in June 1971;[24] the conference on environment and development in Canberra in 1971; and United Nations General Assembly resolution 2849 (XXVI). It received a powerful impetus from the Stockholm Declaration which, by Principle 11, stressed the essentiality of development as well as the essentiality of bearing environmental considerations in mind in the developmental process. Moreover, many other Principles of that Declaration[25] provided a setting for the development of the concept of sustainable development[26] and more than one-third of the Stockholm Declaration related to the harmonization of environment and development. . . . The Stockholm Conference also produced an Action Plan for the Human Environment.[27]

---

[24] *See* SUSTAINABLE DEVELOPMENT IN INTERNATIONAL LAW, WINFRIED LANG (ed.), 1995, p. 143.

[25] For example, Principles 2, 3, 4, 5, 8, 9, 12, 13, and 14.

[26] These principles are thought to be based to a large extent on the Founex Report — see SUSTAINABLE DEVELOPMENT AND INTERNATIONAL LAW, WINIFRIED LANG (ed.), supra, p. 144.

[27] Action Plan for the Human Environment, UN Doc. A/ CONF.48/14/Rev. 1. *See especially* Chapter

The international community had thus been sensitized to this issue even as early as the early 1970s, and it is therefore no cause for surprise that the 1977 Treaty, in Articles 15 and 19, made special reference to environmental considerations. Both Parties to the Treaty recognized the need for the developmental process to be in harmony with the environment and introduced a dynamic element into the Treaty which enabled the Joint Project to be kept in harmony with developing principles of international law.

Since then, it has received considerable endorsement from all sections of the international community, and at all levels.

Whether in the field of multilateral treaties,[28] international declarations;[29] the foundation documents of international organizations;[30] the practices of international financial institutions;[31] regional declarations and planning documents;[32] or State practice,[33] there is a wide and general recognition of the concept. The Bergen ECE Ministerial Declaration on Sustainable Development of 15 May 1990, resulting from

II which devoted its final section to development and the environment.

[28] For example, the United Nations Convention to Combat Desertification (The United Nations Convention to Combat Desertification in those Countries Experiencing Serious Droughts and/or Desertification, Particularly in Africa), 1994, Preamble, Art. 9(1); the United Nations Framework Convention on Climate Change, 1992, (XXXI ILM (1992) 849, Arts. 2 and 3); and the Convention on Biological Diversity (XXXI ILM (1992) 818, Preamble, Arts. 1 and 10 — "sustainable use of biodiversity").

[29] For example, the Rio Declaration on Environment and Development, 1992, emphasizes sustainable development in several of its Principles (e.g., Principles 4, 5, 7, 8, 9, 20, 21, 22, 24 and 27 refer expressly to "sustainable development" which can be described as the central concept of the entire document); and the Copenhagen Declaration, 1995 (paras. 6 & 8), following on the Copenhagen World Summit for Social Development, 1995.

[30] For example, the North American Free Trade Agreement (Canada, Mexico, United States) (NAFTA, Preamble, XXXII ILM (1993), p. 289); the World Trade Organization (WTO) (paragraph 1 of the Preamble of the Marrakesh Agreement of 15 April 1994, establishing the World Trade Organization speaks of the "optimal use of the world's resources in accordance with the objective of sustainable development" — XXXIII ILM (1994), pp. 1143–1144); and the European Union (Art. 2 of the ECT).

[31] For example, the World Bank Group, the Asian Development Bank, The African Development Bank, the Inter-American Development Bank, and the European Bank for Reconstruction and Development all subscribe to the principle of sustainable development. Indeed, since 1993, the World Bank has convened an annual conference related to advancing environmentally and socially sustainable development (ESSD).

[32] For example, the Langkawi Declaration on the Environment, 1989, adopted by the "Heads of Government of the Commonwealth representing a quarter of the world's population" which adopted "sustainable development" as its central theme; Ministerial Declaration on Environmentally Sound and Sustainable Development in Asia and the Pacific, Bangkok, 1990 (Doc. 38a, p. 567); and Action Plan for the Protection and Management of the Marine and Coastal Environment of the South Asian Seas Region, 1983 (para. 10 — "sustainable, environmentally sound development").

[33] For example, in 1990, the Dublin Declaration by the European Council on the Environmental Imperative stated that there must be an acceleration of effort to ensure that economic development in the Community is "sustainable and environmentally sound" (*Bulletin of the European Communities*, 6-1990, Ann. II, p. 18). It urged the Community and Member States to play a major role to assist developing countries in their efforts to achieve "long-term sustainable development" (*ibid.*, p. 19). It said, in regard to countries of Central and Eastern Europe, that remedial measures must be taken "to ensure that their future economic development is sustainable" (*ibid*). It also expressly recited that:

"As Heads of State or Government of the European Community, . . . [w]e intend that action by the Community and its Member States will be developed . . . on the principles of a meeting of Ministers from 34 countries in the ECE region, and the Commissioner for the Environment of the European Community, addressed "The challenge of sustainable development of humanity" (para. 6), and prepared a Bergen Agenda for Action which included a consideration of the Economics of Sustainability, Sustainable Energy Use, Sustainable Industrial Activities, and Awareness Raising and Public Participation. It sought to develop "sound national indicators for sustainable development" (para. 13 (b)) and sought to encourage investors to apply environmental standards required in their home country to investments abroad. It also sought to encourage UNEP, UNIDO, UNDP, IBRD, ILO, and appropriate international organizations to support member countries in ensuring environmentally sound industrial investment, observing that industry and government should co-operate for this purpose (para. 15 (f))[34] A Resolution of the Council of Europe, 1990, propounded a European Conservation Strategy to meet, inter alia, the legitimate needs and aspirations of all Europeans by seeking to base economic, social and cultural development on a rational and sustainable use of natural resources, and to suggest how sustainable development can be achieved. . . .

The concept of sustainable development is thus a principle accepted not merely by the developing countries, but one which rests on a basis of worldwide acceptance.

In 1987, the Brundtland Report brought the concept of sustainable development to the forefront of international attention. In 1992, the Rio Conference made it a central feature of its Declaration and it has been a focus of attention in all questions relating to development in the developing countries.

The principle of sustainable development is thus a part of modern international law by reason not only of its inescapable logical necessity, but also by reason of its wide and general acceptance by the global community.

The concept has a significant role to play in the resolution of environmentally related disputes. The components of the principle from well-established areas of international law — human rights, State responsibility, environmental law, economic and industrial law, equity, territorial sovereignty, abuse of rights, good neighbourliness — to mention a few. It has also been expressly incorporated into a number of binding and far-reaching international agreements, thus giving it binding force in the context of those agreements. It offers an important principle for the resolution of tensions between two established rights. It reaffirms in the arena of international law that there must be both development and international protection, and that neither of these rights can be neglected.

The general support of the international community does not of course mean that each and every member of the community of nations has given its express and specific support to the principle — nor is this a requirement for the establishment of a principle of customary international law.

As Brierly observes:

---

sustainable development and preventive and precautionary action" (*Ibid.*, Conclusions of the Presidency, Point 1.36, pp. 17–18).

[34] BASIC DOCUMENTS OF INTERNATIONAL ENVIRONMENTAL LAW, HARALD HOHMANN (ed.), Vol. 1, 1992, p. 558.

> "It would hardly ever be practicable, and all but the strictest of positivists admit that it is not necessary, to show that every state has recognized a certain practice, just as in English law the existence of a valid local custom or custom of trade can be established without proof that every individual in the locality, or engaged in the trade, has practiced the custom. This test of general recognition is necessarily a vague one; but it is of the nature of customary law, whether national or international . . ."[35]

Evidence appearing in international instruments and State practice (as in development assistance and the practice of international financial institutions) likewise amply supports a contemporary general acceptance of the concept.

Recognition of the concept could thus, fairly, be said to be worldwide.[36]

Some Wisdom from the Past Relating to Sustainable Development

There are some principles of traditional legal systems that can be woven into the fabric of modern environmental law. They are especially pertinent to the concept of sustainable development which was well recognized in those systems. Moreover, several of these systems have particular relevance to this case, in that they relate to the harnessing of streams and rivers and show a concern that these acts of human interference with the course of nature should always be conducted with due regard to the protection of the environment. In the context of international wisdom generally, there is much to be derived from ancient civilizations and traditional legal systems in Asia, the Middle East, Africa, Europe, the Americas, the Pacific and Australia — in fact, the whole world. This is a rich source which modern environmental law has left largely untapped.

As the Court has observed, "Throughout the ages mankind has, for economic and other reasons, constantly interfered with nature." (Para. 140.)

The concept of reconciling the needs of development with the protection of the environment is thus not new. Millennia ago these concerns were noted and their twin demands well reconciled in a manner so meaningful as to carry a message to our age.

I shall start with a system with which I am especially familiar, which also happens to have specifically articulated these two needs — development and environmental protection — in its ancient literature. I refer to the ancient irrigation-based civilization of Sri Lanka. It is a system which, while recognizing the need for development and vigorously implementing schemes to this end, at the same time specifically articulated the need for environmental protection and ensured that the technology it employed paid due regard to environmental considerations. This concern for the environment was reflected not only in its literature and its technology, but also in its legal system, for the felling of certain forests was prohibited, game sanctuaries were established, and royal edicts decreed that the natural resources of water was to be used to the last drop without any wastage.

---

[35] J. Brierly, The Law of Nations, 6th ed. 1963, p. 61.

[36] See, further, L. Kramer, EC Treaty and Environmental Law, 2nd ed., 1995, p. 63, analyzing environmental connotation in the word "sustainable" and tracing it to the Brundtland Report.

This system, some details of which I shall touch on, is described by Arnold Toynbee in his panoramic survey of civilizations. Referring to it as an "amazing system of waterworks," Toynbee describes how hill streams were tapped and their water guided into giant storage tanks, some of them four thousand acres in extent. Below each great tank and each great channel were hundreds of little tanks, each the nucleus of a village.

The concern for the environment shown by this ancient irrigation system has attracted study in a recent survey of the Social and Environmental Effects of Large Dam., which observes that among the environmentally related aspects of its irrigation systems were the "erosion control tank" which dealt with the problem of silting by being so designed as to collect deposits of silt before they entered the main water storage tanks. Several erosion control tanks were associated with each village irrigation system. The significance of this can well be appreciated in the contest of the present case, where the problem of silting has assumed so much importance.

Another such environmentally related measure consisted of the "forest tanks" which were built in the jungle above the village, not for the purpose of irrigating land, but to provide water to wild animals.

This system of tanks and channels, some of them two thousand years old, constitute in their totality several multiples of the irrigation works involved in the present scheme. They constituted development as it was understood at the time, for they achieved in Toynbee's words, "the arduous feat of conquering the parched plains of Ceylon for agriculture." Yet they were executed with meticulous regard for environmental concerns, and showed that the concept of sustainable development was consciously practised over two millennia ago with much success.

Under this irrigation system, major rivers were dammed and reservoirs created, on a scale and in a manner reminiscent of the damming which the Court saw on its inspection of the dams in this case. This ancient concept of development was carried out on such a large scale that, apart from the major reservoirs, of which there were several dozen, between 25,000 and 30,000 minor reservoirs were fed from these reservoirs through an intricate network of canals.

The philosophy underlying this gigantic system, which for upwards of two thousand years served the needs of man and nature alike, was articulated in a famous principle laid down by an outstanding monarch that "not even a little water that comes from the rain is to flow into the ocean without being made useful to man." According to the ancient chronicles, these works were undertaken "for the benefit of the country," and "out of compassion for all living creatures." This complex of irrigation works was aimed at making the entire country a granary. They embodied the concept of development par excellence.

Just as development was the aim of this system, it was accompanied by a systematic philosophy of conservation dating back to at least the third century, B.C. the ancient chronicles record that when the King (Devanampiya Tissa 247-207 B.C.) was on a hunting trip (around 223 B.C.), the Arahat Mahinda, son of the Emperor Asoka of India, preached to him a sermon on Buddhism which converted the king. Here are excerpts from that sermon:

"O great King, the birds of the air and the beasts have as equal a right to live and move about in any part of the land as thou. The land belongs to the people and all living beings; thou are only the guardian of it."

This sermon, which indeed contained the first principle of modern environmental law — the principle of trusteeship of earth resources — caused the king to start sanctuaries for wild animals — a concept which continued to be respected for over twenty centuries. The traditional legal system's protection of fauna and flora, based on this Buddhist teaching, extended well into the 18th century.

The sermon also pointed out that even birds and beasts have a right to freedom from fear.

The notion of not causing harm to others and hence *sic utere tuo ut alienum non laedas* was a central notion of Buddhism. It translated well into environmental attitudes. "Alienum" in this context would be extended by Buddhism to future generations as well, and to other component elements of the natural order beyond man himself, for the Buddhist concept of duty had an enormously long reach.

This marked concern with environmental needs was reflected also in royal edicts, dating back to the third century B.C., which ordained that certain primeval forests should on no account be felled. This was because adequate forest cover in the highlands was known to be crucial to the irrigation system as the mountain jungles intercepted and stored the monsoon rains. They attracted the rain which fed the river and irrigation systems of the country, and were therefore considered vital.

Environmental considerations were reflected also in the actual work of construction and engineering. The ancient engineers devised an answer to the problem of silting (which has assumed much importance in the present case), and they invented a device (the bisokotuwa or valve pit), the counterpart of the sluice, for dealing with this environmental problem, by controlling the pressure and the quantity of the outflow of water when it was released from the reservoir. Weirs were also built, as in the case of the construction involved in this case, for raising the levels of river water and regulating its flow.

This juxtaposition in this ancient heritage of the concepts of development and environmental protection invites comment immediately from those familiar with it. Anyone interested in the human future would perceive the connection between the two concepts and the manner of their reconciliation.

Not merely from the legal perspective does this become apparent, but even from the approaches of other disciplines.

Thus Arthur C. Clarke, the noted futurist, with that vision which has enabled him to bring high science to the service of humanity, put his finger on the precise legal problem we are considering when he observed: "the small Indian Ocean island . . . provides textbook examples of many modern dilemmas: development versus environment," and proceeds immediately to recapitulate the famous sermon, already referred to, relating to the trusteeship of land, observing, "For us King Devanampiya Tissa was told three centuries before the birth of Christ, we are its guardians — not its owners."

The task of the law is to convert such wisdom into practical terms — and the law has often lagged behind other disciplines in so doing. Happily for international law, there are plentiful indications, as recited earlier in the opinion, of that degree of "general recognition among states of a certain practice as obligatory to give the principle of sustainable development the nature of customary law.

This reference to the practice and philosophy of a major irrigation civilization of the pre-modern world illustrates that when technology on this scale was attempted it was accompanied by a due concern for the environment. Moreover, when so attempted, the necessary response from the traditional legal system, as indicated above, was one of the affirmative steps for environmental protection, often taking the form of royal decrees, apart from the practices of a sophisticated system of customary law which regulated the manner in which the irrigation facilities were to be used and protected by individual members of the public.

The foregoing is but one illustrative example of the concern felt by prior legal systems for the preservation and protection of the environment. There are other examples of complex irrigation systems that have sustained themselves for centuries, if not millennia.

*   *   *

Many more instances can be cited of irrigation cultures which accorded due importance to environmental considerations and reconciled the rights of present and future generations. I have referred to some of the more outstanding. Among them, I have examined one at greater length, partly because it combined vast hydraulic development projects with a meticulous regard for environmental considerations, and partly because both development and environmental protection are mentioned in its ancient records. That is sustainable development par excellence; and the principles on which it was based must surely have a message for modern law.

Traditional wisdom which inspired these ancient legal systems was able to handle such problems. Modern legal systems can do no less, achieving a blend of the concepts of development and of conservation of the environment, which alone does justice to humanity's obligations to itself and to the planet which is its home. Another way of viewing the problem is to look upon it as involving the imperative of balancing the needs of the present generation with those of posterity.

In relation to concern for the environment generally, examples may be cited from nearly every traditional system, ranging from Australasia and the Pacific Islands, through Amerindian and African cultures to those of ancient Europe. When Native Americans wisdom, with its deep love of nature, ordained that no activity affecting the land should be undertaken without giving thought to its impact on the land for sever generations to come; when African tradition viewed the human community as threefold — past, present and future — and refused to adopt a one-eyed vision of concentration on the present; when Pacific tradition despised the view of land as merchandise that could be bought and sold like a common article of commerce, and viewed land as a living entity which lived and grew with the people and upon whose sickness and death the people likewise sickened and died; when Chinese and Japanese culture stressed the need for harmony with nature; and when Aboriginal custom, while maximizing the use of all species of plant and animal life, yet decreed that no land should be used by man to the point where it could not replenish itself, these varied cultures were reflecting the ancient wisdom of the human family which the legal systems of the time and the tribe absorbed, reflected and turned into principles whose legal validity cannot be denied. Ancient Indian teaching so respected the environment that it was illegal to cause wanton damage, even to an enemy's territory in the course of military conflict.

Europe, likewise, had a deep-seated tradition of love for the environment, a prominent feature of European culture, until the industrial revolution pushed these concerns into the background. Wordsworth in England, Thoreau in the United States, Rousseau in France, Tolstoy and Chekhov in Russia, Goethe in Germany spoke not only for themselves, but represented a deep-seated love of nature that was instinct in the ancient traditions of Europe — traditions whose gradual disappearance these writers lamented in their various ways. Indeed, European concern with the environment can be traces back through the millennia to such writers as Virgil, whose Georgics, composed between 37 and 30 B.C., extols the beauty of the Italian countryside and pleads for the restoration of the traditional agricultural life of Italy, which was being damaged by the drift to the cities.

This survey would not be complete without a reference also to the principles of Islamic law that inasmuch as all land belongs to God, land is never the subject of human ownership, but is only held in trust, with all the connotations that follow of due care, wise management, and custody for future generations. The first principle of modern environmental law — the principle of trusteeship of earth resources — is thus categorically formulated in this system.

The ingrained values of any civilization are the source from which its legal concepts derive, and the ultimate yardstick and touchstone of their vitality. This is so in international and domestic legal systems alike, save that international law would require a worldwide recognition of those values. It would not be wrong to state that the love of nature, the desire for its preservation, and the need for human activity to respect the requisites for its maintenance and continuance are among those pristine and universal values which command international recognition.

The formalism of modern legal systems may cause us to lose sight of such principles, but the time has come when they must once more be integrated into the corpus of the living law. As stated in the exhaustive study of The Social and Environmental Effects of Large Dams, already cited, "We should examine not only what has caused modern irrigation systems to fail; it is much more important to understand what has made traditional irrigation societies to succeed." Observing that various societies have practised sustainable irrigation agriculture over thousands of years, and that modern irrigation systems rarely last more than a few decades, the authors pose the question whether it was due to the achievement of a "congruence of fit" between their methods and "the nature of land, water and climate." Modern environmental law needs to take not of the experience of the past in pursuing this "congruence of fit" between development and environmental imperatives.

By virtue of it representation of the main forms of civilization, this Court constitutes a unique forum for the reflection and the revitalization of those global legal traditions. There were principles ingrained in these civilizations as well as embodied in their legal systems, for legal systems include not merely written legal systems but traditional legal systems as well, which modern researchers have shown to be no less legal systems than their written cousins, and in some respects even more sophisticated and finely tuned that the latter.

Living law which is daily observed by members of the community, and compliance with which is so axiomatic that it is taken for granted, is not deprived of the character of law by the extraneous test and standard of reduction to writing. Writing is of course useful for establishing certainty, but when a duty such as the duty to protect the environment is so well accepted that all citizens act upon it, that duty is part of the legal system in question.

Moreover, when the Statute of the Court described the sources of international law as including the "general principles of law recognized by civilized nations," it expressly opened a door to the entry of such principles into modern international law.

Traditional Principles that can assist in the Development of Modern Environmental Law

As modern environmental law develops, it can, with profit to itself, take account of the perspectives and principles of traditional systems, not merely in a general way, but with reference to specific principles, concepts, and aspirational standards.

Among those which may be extracted from the systems already referred to are such far-reaching principles as the principle of trusteeship of earth resources, the principle of intergenerational rights, and the principle that development and environmental conservation must go hand in hand. Land is to be respected as having a vitality of its own and being integrally linked to the welfare of the community. When it is used by humans, every opportunity should be afforded to it to replenish itself. Since flora and fauna have a niche in the ecological system, they must be expressly protected. There is a duty lying upon all members of the community to preserve the integrity and purity of the environment.

Natural resources are not individually, but collectively, owned, and a principle of their use is that they should be used for the maximum service of people. There should be no waste, and there should be a maximization of the use of plant and animal species, while preserving their regenerative powers. The purpose of development is the betterment of the condition of the people.

Most of them have relevance to the present case, and all of them can greatly enhance the ability of international environmental law to cope with problems such as these if and when they arise in the future. There are many routes of entry by which they can be assimilated into the international legal system, and modern international law would only diminish itself were it to lose sight of them — embodying as they do the wisdom which enabled the works of man to function for centuries and millennia in a stable relationship with the principles of the environment. This approach assumes increasing importance at a time when such a harmony between humanity and its planetary inheritance is a prerequisite for human survival.

Sustainable development is thus not merely a principle of modern international law. It is one of the most ancient of ideas in the human heritage. Fortified by the rich insights that can be gained from millennia of human experience, it has an important part to play in the service of international law.

NOTES AND QUESTIONS

1. *Is sustainable development a rule of customary international law?* The juridical status of the sustainable development principle is highly controversial. In the *Case Concerning Pulp Mills on the River Uruguay (Argentina v. Uruguay)*, Judgment of 20 April 2010,[37] the International Court of Justice, which ruled that Uruguay had breached procedural obligations owed to Argentina with respect to the construction and operation of two pulp mills on the Uruguay river, which borders the two countries, did not mention the sustainable development principle, but decided the case on the basis of a 1975 agreement between the two countries known as the 1975 Statute. In a separate concurring and dissenting opinion, ICJ Judge Cancado Trinidade faulted the Court for not deciding the case on the basis of general principles of international law, among them the principle of sustainable development. His opinion states in part as follows:

> 133. The 1992 Rio Declaration on Environment and Development gave considerable projection to the formulation of sustainable development tuned to the fulfillment of the necessities of present and future generations (Principle 3), whilst the 1993 Vienna Declaration and Programme of Action focused on sustainable development in relation to distinct aspects of International Human Rights Law (Part I, para. 27), also bearing in mind the satisfaction of current and future needs of protection (Part II, para. 17). Sustainable development disclosed an ineluctable temporal dimension, in bringing to the fore present and future generations altogether.

> 138. This outlook, bringing together the protection of the environment and the protection of human rights, continues to be cultivated today, at the end of the first decade of the twenty-first century. Numerous international instruments have captured today the *rationale* of sustainable development. Contemporary expert writing is also gradually recognizing its relevance; while a great part of that writing continues, somewhat hesitantly, to refer to sustainable development as a "concept," there are also those who seem today to display their preparedness and open-mindedness to admit that it has turned out to be a general principle of International Environmental Law.[38] On the occasion of the reform of the United Nations, by the end of 2005, in addition to the two documents already mentioned in the present

---

[37] 2010 ICJ Rep. 14.

[38] *Cf., e.g.,* Ph. Sands, *Principles of International Environmental Law*, 2nd ed., Cambridge University Press, 2003, pp. 252, 260 and 266; C. Voigt, *Sustainable Development as a Principle of International Law*, Leiden, Nijhoff, 2009, pp. 145, 147, 162, 171 and 189. As States cannot rely on scientific uncertainties to justify inaction, in face of possible risks of serious harm to the environment, the precautionary principle has a role to play, as much as "the principle of sustainable development"; P. Birnie, A. Boyle and C. Redgwell, *International Law and the Environment*, 3rd ed., Oxford University Press, 2009, p. 163.

separate opinion (para. 45, *supra*), the *Millennium Development Goals* were also adopted, endorsing the "principles of sustainable development "(in the plural).[39]

140. In the light of the considerations above, the present outcome of the case of the *Pulp Mills* leaves, in this respect, much to be desired, on three accounts, namely: first, in relation to the insufficiency of the arguments of the contending Parties on, concretely, the *social impacts* of the pulp mills, despite having addressed sustainable development; secondly, in respect of the insufficiency of attention on the part of the Court to the particular point at issue; and thirdly, with regard to the absence of any express acknowledgement by the Court of the guiding role of general principles of International Environmental Law.

2. *A counter-argument.* The conclusion that the principle of sustainable development is a binding norm of customary international law or general international law is disputed, famously, by Vaughan Lowe. In his article, *Sustainable Development and Unsustainable Arguments*,[40] Professor Lowe, after quoting the ruling of the court in the *Case Concerning the Gabcikovo-Nagymaros Dam (Hungary v. Slovakia)*, states as follows:

> There is a caution and a delicate ambiguity in phrasing of the passage. The Court affirms the 'development' of 'new norms and standards' and asserts that the norms have to be taken into consideration and the standards given proper weight — phrasing that suggests that the norms do not bind as rules of law bind, and that the standards are not mandatory. But the reference to sustainable development follows in a separate sentence, where it is described as the expression of a need to reconcile economic development with environmental protection. It is not at all clear that sustainable development is among the norms and standards to which the previous sentence refers. Nor is the juridical status of the concept clear.[41]

Professor Lowe, in response to Judge Weeramantry's conclusion that the principle of sustainable development is "a part of modern international law," asks, "What is the evidence for a claim that sustainable development has that status?"[42] Lowe then argues that the principle of sustainable development is not and cannot be a binding rule of law. "There is, in the catalogue of treaty provisions, declarations and so on that use the term 'sustainable development', a lack of clear evidence that the authors regarded the concept as having the force of a rule or principle of customary international law.[43] Lowe also points out that the meaning of the term sustainable development is unclear, and that this phrase is an "umbrella term to label a group of congruent norms."[44] Yet Lowe argues that the concept sustainable

---

[39] Targets 7.A and 7.B of the *Millennium Development Goals.*

[40] In Alan Boyle & David Freestone, eds., International Law and Sustainable Development 19 (Oxford: Oxford University Press, 1999).

[41] *Ibid.* at 20.

[42] *Ibid.* at 21.

[43] *Ibid.* at 24.

[44] *Ibid.* at 26.

development has normative force as a "modifying norm," a "rule of reason," an injunction to take "an equitable approach to conflicts between development and environment."[45]

Which view do you agree with, the opinions of Judges Weeramantry and Trinidade or the criticisms of Professor Lowe?

3.   *An Environmental Sustainability Index.* Is it possible to correct the ambiguity of the concept of sustainable development by devising some kind of index for sustainable development? At the World Economic Forum in Davos, Switzerland, in 2000, a task force unveiled the Environmental Sustainability Index (ESI), a proposed method to evaluate each nation's achievement of sustainability.[46] The ESI measures five components:

- Environmental systems: Are air quality, water quality, water quantity, biodiversity, and land quality maintained at healthy levels?

- Environmental stresses and risks: are risk factors being managed?

- Human vulnerability: Does the human population have access to clean water, electricity, health services and food supplies?

- Social and institutional capacity: Do political institutions offer the capacity to manage and reconcile environmental risks?

- Global stewardship: Does the country engage in international cooperation and embrace the aim to avoid harmful effects on other countries?

Is this kind of index helpful?

4.   In their classic book, INTERNATIONAL LAW AND ENVIRONMENT 116 (3d ed., 2009), Pat Birnie, Alan Boyle, and Catherine Redgwell, comment: "one of the main attractions of sustainable development as a concept is that both sides in any legal argument will be able to rely on it." Do you agree?

3.   The Precautionary Principle

The precautionary principle is a feature of many declarations by authoritative international bodies and is stated in many treaties, where it is variously formulated to suit the particular circumstances at hand. For example, the World Trade Organization (WTO) Agreement on Sanitary and Phytosanitary Measures, which permits a member state to impose import restrictions on products that pose a risk to human, animal, or plant life or health after a risk assessment based on scientific evidence, states (Article 5.8) that "in cases where relevant scientific evidence is insufficient, a Member may provisionally adopt sanitary or phytosanitary measures on the basis of available pertinent information." The application of such precautionary standards is binding treaty law in this and many other international instruments. But can we also say that precaution or the very general precautionary principle as formulated in Principle 15 of the Rio Declaration is binding customary international law?

---

[45]   *Ibid.* at 36.

[46]   Steve Charnovitz, *Environmental Sustainability Index Likely to Become Important Management Tool*, 23 INT'L ENVTL. REP. 174 (2000) (BNA).

Consider the following cases:

CASE CONCERNING PULP MILLS ON THE RIVER URUGUAY (ARGENTINA v. URUGUAY)
International Court of Justice
2010 I.C.J. Rep. 14

Separate Opinion of JUDGE CANCADO TRINIDADE

[This case arose out of the construction of two pulp mills authorized by the government of Uruguay on River Uruguay, which is the boundary river between Argentina and Uruguay. Argentina alleged the breach of certain procedural and substantive obligations contained in a 1975 agreement between the two countries, termed the 1975 Statute. The Court ruled that Uruguay had breached certain procedural duties owed to Argentina under the 1975 Statute but had not breached any substantive obligations. Judge Trinidade wrote a separate opinion in which he expressed some disagreement with the Court's opinion].

63. Over the years, the precautionary principle has been emerging also in consideration of contentious cases lodged with this Court, in the form of invocations to it by the contending parties in the course of international legal proceedings. Thus, in the (second) *Nuclear Tests* case (underground testing, *New Zealand v. France*), the Court was faced (in the proceedings concerning its Order of 22 September 1995) with New Zealand's contention that, under conventional and customary international law, there was an obligation to conduct an environmental impact assessment before carrying out nuclear tests, and an obligation to provide prior evidence that planned nuclear tests

> "will not result in the introduction of such material to [the] environment, in accordance with the 'precautionary principle' very widely accepted in contemporary international law" (*I.C.J. Reports 1995*, p. 290, para. 5).

In any circumstances — New Zealand insisted — the "precautionary principle" required an environmental impact assessment "as a precondition for undertaking the activities, and to demonstrate that there was no risk associated with them" (*ibid.*, p. 298. Para. 34).

64. More than two decades earlier, in the (first) Nuclear Tests case (atmospheric testing, *Australia and New Zealand v. France*), in an oral argument before the ICJ, of 24 May 1973, advanced in a language which seemed ahead of its time, counsel for New Zealand began by warning that the intensification of nuclear weapons testing in the 1950s presented "the dangers of radio-active fall-out to the health of present and future generations," accompanied by a growing awareness of the "grave threat" that the continuation of such a situation raised "ultimately to the very survival of mankind." He then invoked the "danger to mankind" and the need "to minimize the risk to health," the need of protection of "the peoples of the area," mankind's hope to secure its own welfare, the growth of "a regional consciousness." The use of this language in an argument before the Court, as early as 1973, seems to have passed unnoticed even in contemporary expert writing on the subject. Yet, with foresight, it reveals the importance of the awakening of conscience as to the need to resort to

precaution, beyond prevention. Finally, in the same statement, counsel for New Zealand, recalling the (then) recently adopted final document of the Stockholm United Nations Conference on the Human Environment (with emphasis on Principle 21), laid emphasis on the "heightened sense of international responsibility for environmental policies," and asserted the existence of "a moral duty" to the "benefit of all mankind," to be complied with, so as to "meet the requirements of natural justice" of the surrounding risk and of the health hazards affecting "the whole population" and the "rights of peoples," and added that "an activity that is inherently harmful is not made acceptable even by the most stringent precautionary measures."

66. In the more recent *Gabcikovo-Nagymaros Project case (Hungary v. Slovakia)*, the ICJ took note of Hungary's invocation of the "precautionary principle" *(Judgement, I.C.J. Reports 1997*, p. 62, para. 97), and recognized that "both Parties agree on the need to take environmental concerns seriously and to take the required precautionary measures, but they fundamentally disagree on the consequences this has for the joint Project" *(ibid,*. p. 68, para. 113). The ICJ unfortunately refrained from acknowledging the precautionary principle as such, and from elaborating on the legal implications ensuing therefrom.

67. The Court had a unique opportunity to do so, in the present case of the *Pulp Mills*, when *both* contending Parties, Uruguay and Argentina, expressly referred to both the preventive principle and the precautionary principle. Yet, the Court, once again, preferred to guard silence on this relevant point. It escapes my comprehension why the ICJ has so far had so much precaution with the precautionary principle. I regret to find that, since 1973, the Court has not displayed more sensitiveness to the invocation of precaution before it, when it comes to protecting human beings and their environment, even well before the corresponding precautionary principle began to take shape in contemporary International Environmental Law.

The Principles of Prevention and Precaution Together

93. In the domain of environmental protection, just as there are international instruments, as we have seen, that give expression to the principle of prevention, there are also those which lean towards the precautionary principle, like, e.g., the 1985 Vienna Convention for the Protection of the Ozone Layer (preamble and Article 2(1), and the 1997 Montreal Protocol on Substances that Deplete the Ozone Layer (preamble), among others). Yet, the aforementioned Vienna Convention for the Protection of the Ozone Layer determines also prevention, besides precaution (Article 2 (2) (b)). References to both principles, together, are also found, at regional level, e.g., in the 1991 OAU Bamako Convention on the Ban of the Import into Africa and the Control of Transboundary Movement and Management of Hazardous Wastes within Africa (Article 4 (3) (f)), in the 1992 Convention for the Protection of the Marine Environment of the North-East Atlantic (OSPAR Convention, Article 2 (2) (a)), and in the 1992 Convention on the Protection of the Marine Environment of the Baltic Sea (Article 3 (1) and (2)).

94. In fact, some of the environmental law Conventions referred to in the file of the present case of the Pulp Mills give expression to both the principle of prevention

and the precautionary principle. It is the case, e.g., of the 1992 Convention on Biological Diversity, which reflects the principle of prevention (preamble and Article 3) as well as the precautionary principle (preamble), and of its 2000 Cartagena Protocol on Biosafety (preamble and Articles 2 and 4). It is also the case of the 2001 Convention on Persistent Organic Pollutants (POPs Convention), which invokes both preventive (preamble) and precautionary (preamble and Article 1).

95. Other examples, to the same effect, are afforded by the 1992 United Nations Framework Convention on Climate Change (preamble and Article 3 (3)), and the 1997 Kyoto Protocol to the United Nations Framework Convention on Climate Change (preamble). These are just a few illustrations, not intended, of course, to be exhaustive. They display, however, the intended linkage between preventive and precautionary measures, so as to enhance environmental protection. The two principles, far from excluding each other, serve their purposes together. The phraseology whereby they are give expression is not uniform, but the rationale of one and the other is clearly identifiable.

96. May I only add that the precautionary principle, in my view, is not to be equated with over-regulation, but more properly with reasonable assessment in face of probable risks and scientific uncertainties. This may take the form of carrying out complete environmental impact assessments, and of undertaking further studies on the environmental issues at stake, as well as careful environmental risk analysis, before the issuance of authorizations. At the end, it has to do with common sense.

97. In effect, in the present case of the *Pulp Mills (Argentina v. Uruguay)*, both the complainant and the respondent States invoked the aforementioned general principles of International Environmental Law. This is hardly surprising (being in the best tradition of international legal thinking in Latin America), and it promptly brings to the fore — for the consideration of the obligations under the 1975 Statue of the River Uruguay — the general rule of treaty interpretation, set forth in Article 31 the 1969 Vienna Convention on the Law of Treaties. The constitutive elements of that general rule, enunciated in Article 31 (1) — namely, the text (ordinary meaning of the terms), the context, and the object and purpose of the treaty — are those which currently more often appear in the interpretation of treaties such elements are set forth jointly in the same formulation, thus pointing out the unity of the process of treaty interpretation.

98. Article 31 (2) of the 1969 Vienna Convention indicates the elements comprised by the context of a treaty, while Article 31 (3) adds further elements to be taken into account, *together with the context*; amongst such additional elements, Article 31 (3) refers to "any relevant" rules of international law applicable in the relations between the parties." In the present case, if any such rules are found in other (multilateral) treaties ratified or adhered to by the two Parties at issue, they can be accounted as an *element of interpretation*, for the purposes of application of the 1975 Statute of the River Uruguay.

99. Yet, treaties are living instruments, and the development of international law itself have effect upon the application of the treaty at issue; such a treaty ought then to be considered in the light of international law at the moment its interpretation is called for. General principles of law are thus to be taken into account, and it is significant that the contending Parties in the present case, pertaining to Interna-

tional Environmental Law, do not have any basic disagreement on this particular principle may not coincide. It is further significant, in this respect, that both Argentina and Uruguay refer, for example, to the principles of prevention and of precaution, as well as to the concept of sustainable development (which permeated the whole of environmental protection), though their reading of such principles and concept by the two Parties in the context of the present case is not the same.

Principle of Prevention

100. As to the *principle of prevention*, both Parties referred to its *formulation*, embodied in Principle 21 of the 1972 Stockholm Declaration on the Human Environment, i.e., the principle of prevention as pertaining to the responsibility incumbent upon States to ensure that activities performed within their jurisdiction or control do not cause damage to the environment of other States (also Principle 2 of the Rio Declaration on Environment and Development) or of areas beyond the limits of national jurisdiction. Moreover, as to its *legal status*, both Parties agreed on the customary nature of the principle of prevention; they diverged, however, as to the scope of the principle in the present case.

101. In its memorial, Argentina identified the principle of prevention as part of the law applicable to the present dispute under the 1975 Statute (para. 3.188). Uruguay, for its part, claimed, in its Counter-Memorial, that the principle of prevention under international law — and as embodied in the 1975 Statute — imposes in its view an obligation of conduct (due diligence) rather than an obligation of result (requiring full avoidance of pollution) (paras. 4.68–4.69); it added that prevention, *in casu*, ought to be assessed by reference to Article 7 (1) of the United Nations Convention on International Watercourses, which provides that States shall "take all appropriate measures to prevent the causing of significant harm to other watercourse States" (para. 4.67).

102. In its Reply, Argentina dismissed Uruguay's narrower interpretation of Article 41 of the Statute and claimed that "[t]he obligation to prevent significant damage to the other party, to the quality of the waters and to the ecosystem of the River Uruguay and the areas affected by it has its own particular features," to the assessed in light of the "regime for overall protection" established by the 1975 Statute (para. 4.45). Uruguay, in turn, in its Rejoinder, retorted that "it is not plausible to suggest that anything more can be read into the Statute than was subsequently codified by the ILC in the Watercourse Convention," as the object and purpose of Articles 36, 41, 42 and 56 *(a)* (4) of the 1975 Statute was "to give effect to the obligation [of due diligence] to prevent transboundary damage in the Uruguay River" (para. 5.53). In sum, Argentina gave a broader interpretation to the principle of prevention, though both Argentina and Uruguay significantly relied upon such principle, recognizing its relevance in the *cas d'espèce*.

Precautionary Principle

103. Moving on to the *precautionary principle*, once again both contending Parties referred to this principle as well, and based their distinct arguments in this respect, to start with on its *formulation* as embodied in the 1992 Rio Declaration on

Environment and Development (Principle 15), namely:

"In order to protect the environment, the precautionary approach shall be widely applied by States according to their capabilities. Where there are threats of serious or irreversible damage, lack of full scientific certainty shall not be used as a reason for postponing cost-effective measures to prevent environmental degradation."

In its Memorial, Argentina argued that "the 1975 Statute must be interpreted and applied in the light of the precautionary principle as a rule of international law" (para. 5.13). Furthermore, counsel for Argentina expressed the hope that the Court would in the present case "declare Principle 15 to reflect customary law."

104. To Uruguay, in turn, the precautionary principle is "a 'soft law' principle," which ought to be taken into account when interpreting treaties in accordance with Article 31 (3) *(c)* of the Vienna Convention on the Law of Treaties. Even so — Uruguay added — that principle "does not appear to meet the requirements of customary international law," and international case law has not yet treated it as "an obligatory rule of customary law." In any case, in its view, Argentina "failed to identify any significant risk" in respect of which measures were to be taken pursuant to the precautionary principle.

105. As to the *applicability* of the principle, Argentina, on its part, submitted in its Memorial that the precautionary principle should guide the interpretation of the 1975 Statute (para. 5.13). The principle would be applicable in the *cas d'espèce* as a result of the remaining areas of "scientific uncertainty" (as to the environmental impact of the Botnia plant) and the corresponding "risk" of serious or irreversible damage. Areas of scientific uncertainty would include "the implications of reverse flow for the concentration of pollutants, wind direction, climate change and the likely impact of the presence of pollutants on the fish in the river" (paras. 5.17–5.18).

106. Uruguay, in turn, reckoned, in its Rejoinder, that the principle at issue played a role in the interpretation of certain environmental law treaties (para. 5.66), but argued that it was not relevant in the context of the present dispute, first, because there was no scientific uncertainty in the operation of pulp mills, and also, because risks associated with their operation "are monitored comprehensively and can be empirically tested" so that any uncertainties be removed or dealt with (para. 5.58). Argentina, for its part, recalled, in its Memorial, that pursuant to Principle 15 of the 1992 Rio Declaration *(supra)* , [t]he precautionary principle is applicable to the protection of the environment once there exists a "risk of serious or irreversible harm" (para. 5.24). Uruguay retorted, in its Counter-Memorial, that there was in its view no reason to believe that the pulp mills might cause "serious or irreversible harm" to the environment, and, in particular, to the water quality of the River Uruguay (para. 4.81).

107. Last but not least, as the *content* of the precautionary principle, Argentina sustained in its Memorial that, within the framework of the 1975 Statute, such principle means that "the parties to the 1975 Statute are required to notify each other of all the probable environmental consequences of their actions which may cause serious or irreversible damage *before* such actions are authorized or undertaken" (para. 5.14). Precaution would thus require the parties to the 1975

Statute "to comply with their obligation of notification and consultation before authorizing the construction" of pulp mills (para. 5.14) and — it added in its Reply — to take account of "the risks of harm in the design, preparation and implementation of any project or 'form of use' relating to the River Uruguay and the areas affected by it" (para. 4.54). Argentina, thus, did not agree with Uruguay's view that the principle at issue would only apply in case of risks of "serious or irreversible harm" (cf. *supra*).

108. Argentina's claim on the basis of the precautionary principle was thus twofold: *(a)* it was first linked to its general allegation that Uruguay violated the procedural obligations laid down in the 1975 Statute, especially by commencing construction and operation of the mill before having informed Argentina of all the "*probable* environmental consequences" of actions which might cause environmental harm; and *(b)* the precautionary principle, in its view, required Uruguay not to authorize the construction and operation of the mill before having conducted comprehensive studies on the river's capacity to dispel pollutants.

109. In the oral proceedings, counsel for Argentina invited the ICJ to apply the principle, in view of

"the fact that Uruguay, faced with Argentina's claims in 2004 and 2005 and 2006, as to the limited capacity of the river to cope with the intended new pollutants, should have postponed its authorization until it had a good basis for concluding that the river could effectively disperse of these pollutants,"

Bearing in mind that, in the present case, what precaution meant was "further studies, complete assessments," rather than "acting on the basis of unfounded assumptions about the flow of the river." In addition, counsel for Argentina argued that the risks posed by the Botnia mill ha[d] not been controlled."

110. Uruguay, in its turn, submitted, in its Counter-Memorial, that it would have complied with the precautionary principle "if it were applicable" to the present dispute. The principle at issue, in the terms of the 1992 Rio Declaration, requires States "not to use scientific uncertainty to postpone 'cost-effective measures to prevent environmental degradation' " (para. 4.82); that much Uruguay would have accomplished. Yet — Uruguay added — Argentina misinterpreted the precautionary principle by suggesting that it required "measures that address risks that are remote, unlikely to result in significant harm, or purely hypothetical" (para. 4.83). Such in interpretation would, in its view, be contradicted by "the very reference to 'cost-effective measures' in Principle 15" of the Rio Declaration. Moreover, in Uruguay's view, States only have a responsibility to act on the basis of the precautionary principle when there is "some objective scientific basis for predicting the likelihood of significant harmful effects, some 'reason to believe' or 'reasonable grounds for concern' " (para. 4.83): Argentina seemed — to Uruguay — not to have presented and "significant or credible evidence" in this respect, nothing that would amount to "serious or irreversible damage."

111. Uruguay further added, in its Rejoinder, that Argentina misconstrued "the role of the precautionary principle in relation to uncertainty and risk," in having suggested that "the more unlikely a risk the more uncertain it becomes and thus the greater the role for the precautionary principle" (para. 5.61); the principle at issue,

in Uruguay's view, can only find application when there is some evidence that the risk exists (para. 5.61). In sum, according to Uruguay, "[t]he real issue is not whether environmental risk has been eliminated, but whether it has been properly managed and minimized to the fullest extent possible using cost-effective measures" (para. 5.62); having provided evidence that it had taken

> "all the measures that are reasonable and necessary to counter the Botnia plant's actual potential — however small — for serious adverse effects on the river in the real world, then there remains no basis for suggesting that the precautionary principle has any further role to play" (para. 5.61).

112. From the exchange of views above, between Argentina and Uruguay, it so results that there does not emerge therefrom a clear distinction between a general principle and customary law, as formal "sources" of the applicable law in the *cas d'espèce*. Yet, it appears significant to me that Uruguay even though arguing that constitutive elements of the principle at issue were not in its view consubstantiated in the present case, never questioned or denied the existence or material content of the principle concerned. In sum, the *existence* itself of the *principles* of prevention and of precaution, general principles of law proper to International Environmental Law, was admitted and acknowledged by the contending Parties themselves, Uruguay and Argentina.

113. Only the ICJ did not acknowledge, nor affirmed *[sic]* the existence of those principles, nor elaborated on them, thus missing a unique occasion for their consolidation in the present domain of contemporary international law. The fact that the Court's Judgment silenced on them *[sic]* does not mean that the principles of prevention and of precaution do not exist. They do exist and apply, and are, in my view, of the utmost importance as part of the *jus necessarium*. We can hardly speak of International Environmental Law nowadays without those general principles. The Court had a unique occasion, in the circumstances of the case of the *Pulp Mills*, to assert the applicability of the preventive as well as the precautionary principles; it unfortunately preferred not to do so, for reasons which go beyond, and escape, my comprehension.

NOTES AND QUESTIONS

1.   In the *Pulp Mills Case*, Argentina and Uruguay both invoked the precautionary principle, but in different ways. What was the argument on each side and what is the correct approach to the interpretation of the precautionary principle

2.   In his opinion, Judge Trinidade invokes Article 31 of the Vienna Convention on the Law of Treaties to require the application of general principles of international law. Article 31 states as follows:

> 1.   A treaty shall be interpreted in good faith in accordance with the ordinary meaning to be given to the terms of the treaty in their context and in the light of its object and purpose.

> 2.   The context for the purpose of the interpretation of a treaty shall comprise, in addition to the text, including its preamble and annexes:

(a) any agreement relating to the treaty which was made between all the parties in connection with the conclusion of the treaty,

(b) any instrument which was made by one or more parties in connection with the conclusion of the treaty and accepted by the other parties as an instrument related to the treaty.

3. There shall be taken into account, together with the context:

(a) any subsequent agreement between the parties regarding the interpretation of the treaty or the application of its provision;

(b) any subsequent practice in the application of the treaty which establishes the agreement of the parties regarding its interpretation;

(c) any relevant rules of international law applicable in the relations between the parties.

4. A special meaning shall be given to a term if it is established that the parties so intended.

Article 32 of the Vienna Convention of the Law of Treaties states that "Recourse may be had to supplementary means of interpretation, including the preparatory work of the treaty and the circumstances of its conclusion, in order to confirm the meaning resulting from the application of Article 31, or to determine the meaning when the interpretation according to Article 31:

(a) leaves the meaning ambiguous or obscure; or

(b) leads to a result which is manifestly absurd or unreasonable.

Do you agree with Judge Trinidade's analysis with respect to Article 31?

3. In an earlier stage of the Pulp Mills Case, Argentina invoked the precautionary principle to argue that the ICJ should have adopted "provisional measures," ordering Uruguay to stop all construction and operational activities on the pulp mills pending the outcome of the litigation. Argentina argued that the precautionary principle requires the promoter of a potentially harmful activity to prove that there is no risk of harm. This would reverse the usual burden of proof and would mean that an applicant could simply raise a hypothetical risk and the burden of proof would shift to the other side. Is this a good idea? In the event, the ICJ refused provisionary measures in the Pulp Mills Case because the applicant, Argentina, failed to establish a serious risk. *See Case Concerning Pulp Mills on the River Uruguay*, Order 13 July 2006 (Provisional Measures), ICJ Reports 133 (2006), paras. 72–77. Should the precautionary principle be interpreted to shift the burden of proof?

4. Do you agree with Judge Trinidade that the ICJ majority should have invoked the harm prevention and the precautionary principles in deciding the *Pulp Mills Case?*

5. ***The juridical status of the precautionary principle***. Some scholars argue that the precautionary principle in its formulation in Rio principle 15 is a binding

norm of international customary law,[47] but there is no authoritative judgment of an international tribunal declaring it so. In the *Pulp Mills Case*, the ICJ avoided basing its judgment on the precautionary principle or any general principle of international law. The World Trade Organization Appellate Body in the case *European Communities — Measures Concerning Meat and Meat Products (Hormones Case)*, WT/DS26 and 48/AB/R, adopted 13 February 1998, famously stated that "the status of the precautionary principle in international law continues to be the subject of debate among academics, law practitioners, regulators and judges. . . . Whether it has been widely accepted . . . as a principle of general or customary international law is less than clear." (para. 123). The Appellate Body did not accept that argument of the European Communities that the precautionary principle is a rule of customary international law, stating that it would be "imprudent" to do so. Nevertheless, the Appellate Body noted "some aspects of the relationship of the precautionary principle to the [WTO Sanitary and Phytosanitary Agreement]." (para. 124). This ruling is typical. Although international tribunals hesitate to apply the precautionary principle as a rule of customary law, they are willing to find in treaty law particular provisions that incorporate the precautionary principle. In addition, drafters of environmental treaties are influenced by Principle 15 to insert treaty language drawn from the precautionary principle. In this way, the precautionary principle has normative force.

6.   Some states (a small but important number) accept the precautionary principle as a matter of *national* law. For example, in *Leatch v. National Parks and Wildlife Service and Shoalhaven City Council*, 81 LGERA 270 (1993), the Land and Environment Court of New South Wales, Australia, Judge Stein, employed the precautionary principle to revoke a license to build a road that would have posed risks to an endangered species of frog. The Supreme Court of India also accepts the precautionary principle. In *Vellore Citizens Welfare Forum v. Union of India* (1996) 5 SCC 647, the Supreme Court cited the precautionary principle as a reason to compel the control of pollution emitted by tanneries. But the precautionary principle is not a feature of United States' law apart from statute.

7.   Authoritative international bodies cite and incorporate the precautionary principle into particular as well as general international instruments. Do you believe the Rio principle 15 is or will become a binding rule of customary law in the future?

4. Intergenerational Equity

Principle 3 of the Rio Declaration is the principle of intergenerational equity. The meaning of this principle, in the eloquent formulation of Edith Brown Weiss, is "that each generation is entitled to inherit a robust planet that on balance is at least as good as that of previous generations."[48] Brown Weiss proposes three facets of intergenerational equity: (1) each generation should be required to conserve the diversity of the natural and cultural resource base, so that it does not unduly restrict the options available to future generations in solving their problems and

---

[47] *See* Birnie, Boyle and Redgwell, op. cit. at 160.

[48] Edith Brown Weiss, *Our Rights and Obligations to Future Generations for the Environment*, 84 AM. J. INT'L L. 198, 200 (1990).

satisfying their own values; (2) each generation should be required to maintain the quality of the planet so that it is passed on in no worse condition than that in which it was received; and (3) each generation should provide its members with equitable rights of access to the legacy of past generations and should conserve this access for future generations.[49]

Certainly everyone will agree with these aims. Yet in practice we know they are injunctions that are difficult to keep. For example, those of us today who are enjoying the consumption of fossil fuels do not spend much time worrying about the consequences of this consumption for those human beings who will inhabit the planet 100 years from now. The principle of intergenerational equity reminds us that the present generation has a responsibility to those who come after us.

But what is the normative force of the principle of intergenerational equity? First and foremost, this principle should inspire national laws and international agreements that take into account future generations. But is there any more to the principle than that? Does the principle have force as a rule of law?

As a rule to be applied by international tribunals there are obvious problems. Procedurally, who will enforce "rights" vested in future generations? By definition there are no determinate persons to whom the rights attach. Thus, procedurally, the obligations of Intergenerational equity are duties for which there are no correlative existing right holders. Moreover, when it comes to defining the substantive context of intergenerational equity, a court may have to make a pronouncement that amounts to judicial legislation. Understandably, no international tribunal has been willing to do this.

One famous national court decision employed intergenerational equity as the rationale of an important decision. We read this next.

OPOSA v. FULGENCIA S. FACTORAN, Jr.
Supreme Court of the Philippines
G.R. No. 101083. 224 SCRA 792 (1993)
Reprinted 33 I.L.M. 173 (1994)

[In this case plaintiffs — all minors represented by their parents — and the Philippine Ecological Network, Inc., a non-profit association, brought suit against Factoran, Jr., the Secretary of the Department of Environment and Natural Resources (DENR) in order to compel DENR to cancel all timber license agreements and to cease issuing new licenses because the logging activities were causing unacceptable deforestation of a scenic area known as Mount Apo. The trial court dismissed this action, and the plaintiffs petitioned the Supreme Court to reverse this ruling].

This petition bears upon the right of Filipinos to a balanced and healthful ecology which the petitioners dramatically associate with the twin concepts of 'inter-generational responsibility' and 'inter-generational justice'. Specifically, it touches on the issue of whether the said petitioners have a cause of action to 'prevent the misappropriation or impairment' of Philippine rainforests and 'arrest the unabated

---

[49] Ibid. at 203.

hemorrhage of the country's vital life-support systems and continued rape of Mother Earth'.

Plaintiffs further assert that the adverse and detrimental consequences of continued deforestation are so capable of unquestionable demonstration that the same may be submitted as a matter of judicial notice. This notwithstanding, they expressed their intention to present expert witnesses as well as documentary, photographic and film evidence in the course of the trial.

. . . .

Before going any further, We must first focus on some procedural matters. Petitioners instituted Civil Case No. 90-777 as a class suit. The original defendant and the present respondents did not take issue with this matter. Nevertheless, we hereby rule that the said civil case is indeed a class suit. The subject matter of the complaint is of common and general interest not just to several, but to all citizens of the Philippines. Consequently, since the parties are so numerous, it becomes impracticable, if not totally impossible, to bring them all before the court. We likewise declare that the plaintiffs therein are numerous and representative enough to ensure the full protection of all concerned interests. Hence, all the requisites for the filing of a valid class suit under Section 12, Rule 3 of the Revised Rules of Court are present both in the said civil case and in the instant petition, the latter being but an incident to the former.

This case, however, has a special and novel element. Petitioners-minors assert that they represent their generation as well as generations yet unborn. We find no difficulty in ruling that they can, for themselves, for others of their generation and for succeeding generations, file a class suit. Their personality to sue in behalf of the succeeding generations can only be based on the concept of intergenerational responsibility insofar as the right to a balanced and healthful ecology is concerned. Put a little differently, the minors' assertion of their right to a sound environment constitutes, at the same time, the performance of their obligation to ensure the protection of that right for the generations to come.

The *locus standi* of the petitioners having thus been addressed, we shall now proceed to the merits of the petition.

We do not agree with the trial court's conclusion that the plaintiffs failed to allege with sufficient definiteness a specific legal right involved or a specific legal wrong committed, and that the complaint is replete with vague assumptions and conclusions based on unverified data. A reading of the complaint itself belies these conclusions.

The complaint focuses on one specific fundamental legal right — the right to a balanced and healthful ecology which, for the first time in our nation's constitutional history, is solemnly incorporated in the fundamental law. Article II, section 16 of the 1987 Constitution explicitly provides:

> Sec. 16. The State shall protect and advance the right of the people to a balanced and healthful ecology in accord with the rhythm and harmony of nature

This right unites with the right to health which is provided for in the preceding section of the same article:

> Sec. 15. The state shall protect and promote the fight to health of the people and instill health consciousness among them.

While the right to a balanced and healthful ecology is to be found under the Declaration of Principles and State Policies and not under the Bill of Rights, it does not follow that it is less important than any of the civil and political rights enumerated in the latter, Such a right belongs to a different category of rights altogether for it concerns nothing less than self-preservation and self-perpetuation — aptly and fittingly stressed by the petitioners — the advancement of which may even be said to predate all governments and constitutions.The right to a balanced and healthful ecology carries with it the correlative duty to refrain from impairing the environment.

[E]ven before the ratification of the 1987 Constitution, specific statues already paid special attention to the 'environmental right' of present and future generations. On 6 June 1977, PD No. 1151 (Philippine Environmental Policy) and PD No. 1152 (Philippine Environmental Code) were issued. The former 'declared a continuing policy of the State (a) to create, develop, maintain and improve conditions under which man and nature can thrive in productive and enjoyable harmony with each other, (b) to fulfill the social, economic and other requirements of present and future generations of Filipinos, and (c) to insure the attainment of an environmental quality that is conducive to a life of dignity and well-being (Section 1). As its goal, it speaks of the responsibilities of each generation as trustee and guardian of the environment for succeeding generations. (Section 2). The latter statute, on the other hand, gave flesh to the said policy.

Thus, the right of the petitioners and all those they represent to a balanced and healthful ecology is clear as the DENR's duty — under its mandate and by virtue of its powers and functions under the EO No. 192 and the Administrative Code of 1987 — to protect and advance the said right.

A denial or violation of that right by the other who has the correlative duty or obligation to respect or protect the same gives right to a cause of action.

NOTES AND QUESTIONS

1.   In the *Oposa Case*, one justice, Justice Feliciano, concurred in the judgment but raised two questions of concern. First, Justice Feliciano stated that

> *Locus standi* is not a function of petitioners claim that their suit is properly regarded as a class suit. I understand *locus standi* to refer to the legal interest which a plaintiff must have in the subject matter of the suit. Because of the very broadness of the class here involved — membership in this 'class' appears to embrace everyone living in the country whether now or in the future — it appears to me that everyone who may be expected to benefit from the course of action petitioners seek to require public respondents to take, is vested with the necessary *locus standi*. The Court may be seen therefore to be recognizing beneficiaries' right of action in the

field of environmental protection, as against both the public administrative agency directly concerned and the private persons or entities operating in the field . . . of activity involved.

Justice Feliciano went on to say that the implication of this ruling "is left for future determination in an appropriate case." Second, Justice Feliciano raised questions about the substantive holding in the case: "the Court is in effect saying that section 15 (and section 16) of Article II of the Constitution are self-executing and judicially enforceable even in their present form. The implications of this doctrine will have to be explored in future cases." Justice Feliciano nevertheless concurred in the Judgment "because the protection of the environment, including the forest cover of our territory, is of extreme importance for our country. The doctrines set out in the Court's decision issued today should, however, be subjected to closer examination." *Oposa v Factoran*, 224 SCRA at 804–06.

2.   In United States law the matter of standing is separate from the right to bring a class action. To satisfy standing a plaintiff must show (1) injury-in-fact, an invasion of a legally protected interest that is concrete and particularized; (2) there must be a causal connection between the injury and the conduct complained of in the sense that the injury must be "fairly traceable" to the challenged action; and (3) it must be likely that the injury will be redressed by a favorable decision. *See Lujan v. Defenders of Wildlife*, 504 U.S. 555 (1992); *Massachusetts v. Environmental Protection Agency*, 549 U.S. 497 (2007). The right to file a class suit is controlled by multiple factors specified in Rule 23 of the Federal Rules of Civil Procedure. Furthermore, provisions of state constitutions in the United States that grant a right to international quality are held to be non-self executing, and particular norms of environmental quality are dependent on legislative enactment. *See e.g., Commonwealth of Pennsylvania v. National Gettysburg Battlefield Tower, Inc*, 311 A.2d 588 (Pa. 1973).

3.   The *Oposa Case* has been cited world-wide for its ruling on intergenerational equity. There is no record of a subsequent ruling in the case, and the logging that was the subject of the lawsuit was not stopped. Antonio G.M. La Viña, writing in the Philippine Law Journal, states that, despite the plaintiffs' legal victory, no logging contracts were cancelled and that "it cannot be denied that the physical changes in the site have altered Mount Apo forever and that the communities that relied on . . . Mount Apo for their economic, cultural, and religious needs [can] no longer do so." 69 PHIL. LJ. 127, 143 (1994), *available at* http://plj.upd.edu.ph/wp-content/uploads/plj/PLJ%20volume%2069/20Healthful%20Ecology.pdf, accessed 3 October 2012.

4.   As Birnie, Boyle, and Redgwell have pointed out (INTERNATIONAL LAW AND THE ENVIRONMENT at 121), no international tribunal has expressly recognized the rights of future generations as a binding principle of law.

5.   The Environmental Impact Assessment Principle

Rio Principle 17 specifies that environmental impact assessment, as a tool for evaluating the impact of development projects on the environment, "shall" be employed as "a national instrument" of environmental policy. According to Principle 17, environmental impact assessment must be undertaken for "proposed activities that are likely to have a significant adverse impact of the environment." Principle 17 finds its origin in United States law; the requirement to conduct on environmental impact assessment for proposed activities that are likely to have a significant effect on the environment is virtually identical to the wording of the U.S. National Environmental Policy Act (NEPA) of 1969, 42 U.S.C. § 4321 *et seq.*

The international law of environmental impact assessment is contained in the Convention on Environmental Impact Assessment in a Transboundary Context of 25 February 1991 (the Espoo Convention).[50] The Espoo Convention covers such matters as the criteria for determining whether an environmental impact assessment is required and notification of the affected parties (Article 3); the preparation and content required in an environmental impact assessment (Article 4); consultation and the process of decisionmaking (Article 5); the criteria for making a final decision on the activity (Article 6); the post-project analysis (Article 7); and bilateral and multilateral cooperation (Article 8). Guidelines for environmental impact assessment were concluded and promulgated by the United Nations Environment Programme, see UNEP Goals and Principles or Environmental Impact Assessment (1987).

It is now beyond dispute that the principle of environment impact assessment is a binding rule of general and customary international law. State practice indicates that an environment impact assessment must be carried out by national authorities and by international organizations when as activity under their control poses a potentially significant risk to the environment.[51] The first case to make this unequivocally clear is what we read next.

CASE CONCERNING PULP MILLS ON THE RIVER URUGUAY (ARGENTINA v. URUGUAY)
International Court of Justice
2010 I.C.J. Rep. 14

[This dispute arose out of the construction and operation of two pulp mills in Uruguay in a border region on the River Uruguay opposite the Argentine city of Fray Bentos. A first pulp mill project (known as the CMB (ENCE) mill) was undertaken by a Spanish company and was authorized by Uruguayan authorities in 2005, but in 2006, the project's promoters announced their intention not to build the mill at the planned site. A second pulp mill project known as Orion was undertaken by Botnia, S.A., at a site a few kilometers downstream from the CMB (ENCE) site. An application to build the Orion (Botnia) mill was submitted in 2003, to Uruguayan authorities and to the bilateral (Argentina/Uruguay) Comision Administradora del Rio Uruguay (Administrative Commission for the River Uruguay) (CARU), and this plant was built and began operation in November 2007. In 2006, Uruguay authorized the construction of a port terminal adjacent to the Orion (Botnia) mill and authorized Botnia to extract and to use water from the river for industrial purposes. Argentina opposed the building and operation of the Orion mill. The legal

---

[50] *Available at* http://www.unece.org/fileadmin/DAM/env/eia/documents/legaltexts/conventiontextenglish.pdf, accessed 3 October 2012.

[51] See the MOX Plant Case (Provisional Measures) ITLOS No. 10 (2000).

framework for the dispute was a treaty concluded in 1975 known as the 1975 Statute, which established a regime for the use of the River Uruguay, which was designated as the boundary between Argentina and Uruguay in a bilateral treaty in 1961. Article 60 of the 1975 Statute designated the International Court of Justice (ICJ) as the authority for settling disputes. Argentina filed an application to the ICJ against Uruguay in 2006. The dispute concerned two points: whether Uruguay complied with its procedural obligations under the 1975 Statute; and whether Uruguay had complied with its substantive obligations under the 1975 Statute. The ICJ handed down its decision on the merits of the case in 2010, finding that Uruguay had breached certain procedural obligations under the 1975 Statute but had not breached its substantive obligations. Among the procedural obligations breached, the ICJ considered the environmental assessment requirement.]

Uruguay's obligation to notify the plans to the other party

112. The Court notes that, under the terms of Article 7, second paragraph, of the 1975 Statute, if CARU decides that the plan might cause significant damage to the other party or if a decision cannot be reached in that regard, "the party concerned shall notify the other party of this plan through the said Commission."

Article 7, third paragraph, of the 1975 Statute sets out in detail the content of this notification, which

"shall describe the main aspects of the work and . . . any other technical data that will enable the notified party to assess the probable impact of such works on navigation, the régime of the river or the quality of its waters."

113. In the opinion of the Court, the obligation to notify is intended to create the conditions for successful co-operation between the parties, enabling them to assess the plan's impact on the river on the basis of the fullest possible information and, if necessary, to negotiate the adjustments needed to avoid the potential damage that it might cause.

115. The obligation to notify is therefore an essential part of the process leading the parties to consult in order to assess the risks of the plan and to negotiate possible changes which may eliminate those risks or minimize their effects.

116. The Parties agree on the need for a full environmental impact assessment in order to assess any significant damage which might be caused by a plan.

121. In the present case, the Court observes that the notification to Argentina of the environmental impact assessment for the CMB (ENCE) and Orion (Botnia) mills did not take place through ARU, and that Uruguay only transmitted those assessments to Argentina after having issued the initial environmental authorizations for the two mills in question. Thus in the case of CMB (ENCE), the matter was notified to Argentina on 27 October and 7 November 2003, whereas the initial environmental authorization had already been issued on 9 October 2003. In the case of Orion (Botnia), the file was transmitted to Argentina between August 2005 and January 2006, whereas the initial environmental authorization had been granted on 14 February 2005. Uruguay ought not, prior to notification, to have issued the initial environmental authorizations and the authorizations for construction on the basis of

the environmental impact assessment submitted to DINAMA. Indeed by doing so, Uruguay gave priority to its own legislation over its well-established customary rule reflected in Article 27 of the Vienna Convention on the Law of Treaties, according to which "[a] party may not invoke the provisions of its internal law as justification for its failure to perform a treaty."

122. The Court concludes from the above that Uruguay failed to comply with its obligation to notify the plans to Argentina through CARU under Article 7, second and third paragraphs, of the 1975 Statute.

(a) *Environmental Impact Assessment*

203. The Court will now turn to the relationship between the need for an environmental impact assessment, where the planned activity is liable to cause harm to a shared resource and transboundary harm, and the obligations of the Parties under Article 41 *(a) and (b)* of the 1975 Statute. The Parties agree on the necessity of conducting an environmental impact assessment. Argentina maintains that the obligations under the 1975 Statute viewed together impose an obligation to conduct an environmental impact assessment prior to authorizing Botnia to construct the plant. Uruguay also accepts that it is under such an obligation. The Parties disagree, however, with regard to the scope and content of the environmental impact assessment that Uruguay should have carried out with respect to the Orion (Botnia) mill project. Argentina maintains in the first place that Uruguay failed to ensure that "full environmental assessments [had been] produced, prior to its decision to authorize the construction . . ."; and in the second place that "Uruguay's decisions [were] . . . based on unsatisfactory environmental assessments," in particular because failed to take account of all potential impacts from the mill, even though international law and practice require it, and refers in this context to the 1991 Convention on Environmental Impact Assessment in a Transboundary Context of the United Nations Economic Commission for Europe (hereinafter the "Espoo Convention") (*UNTS*, Vol. 2989, p. 309), and the 1987 Goals and Principles of Environmental Impact Assessment of the United Nations Environment Programme (hereinafter the "UNEP Goals and Principle") (UNEP/WG.15214 *Annex (1987)*. Uruguay accepts that in accordance with international practice, an environmental impact assessment of the Orion (Botnia) mill was necessary, but argues that international law does not impose any conditions upon the content of such an assessment, the preparation of which being a national, not international, procedure, at least where the project in question is not one common to several States. According to Uruguay, the only requirements international law imposes on it are that there must be assessments of the project's potential harmful transboundary effects on people, property and the environment of other States, as required by State practice and the International Law Commission 2001 draft Articles on Prevention of Transboundary Harm from Hazardous Activities, without there being any need to assess remote or purely speculative risks.

204. It is the opinion of the Court that in order for the Parties properly to comply with their obligations under Article 41 *(a) and (b)* of the 1975 Statute, they must, for the purposes of protecting and preserving the aquatic environment with respect to activities which may be liable to cause transboundary harm, carry out an environmental impact assessment. As the Court has observed in the case concerning the

Dispute Regarding Navigational and Related Rights.

> "there are situations in which the parties' intent upon conclusion of the treaty was, or may be presumed to have been, to give the terms used — or some of them — a meaning or content capable of evolving, not one fixed once and for all, so as to make allowance for, among other things, developments in international law" (*Dispute Regarding Navigational and Relate Rights (Costa Rica v. Nicaragua). Judgment, I.C.J. Reports 2009*, p. 242, para. 64).

In this sense, the obligation to protect and preserve, under Article 41 *(a) and (b)* of the Statute, has to be interpreted in accordance with a practice, which in recent years has gained so much acceptance among States that it may now be considered a requirement under general international law to undertake an environmental impact assessment where there is a risk that the proposed industrial activity may have a significant adverse impact in a transboundary context, in particular, on a shared resource. Moreover, due diligence, and the duty of vigilance and prevention which it implies, would not be considered to have been exercised, if a party planning works liable to affect the régime of the river or the quality of its waters did not undertake an environmental impact assessment on the potential effects of such works.

205. The Court observes that neither the 1975 Statute nor general international law specify the scope and content of an environmental impact assessment. It points out moreover that Argentina and Uruguay are not parties to the Espoo Convention. Finally, the Court notes that the other instrument to which Argentina refers in support of its arguments, namely, the UNEP Goals and Principles, is not binding on the Parties, but, as guidelines issues by an international technical body, has to be taken into account by each Party in accordance with Article 41 *(a)* in adopting measures within its domestic regulatory framework. Moreover, this instrument provides only that the "environmental effects in an EIA should be assessed with a degree of detail commensurate with their likely environmental significance" (Principle 5) without giving any indications of minimum core components of the assessment. Consequently, it is the view of the Court that it is for each State to determine in its domestic legislation of in the authorization process for the project, the specific content of the environmental impact assessment required in each case, having regard to the nature and magnitude of the proposed development and its likely adverse impact on the environment as well as to the need to exercise due diligence in conducting such an assessment. The Court also considers that an environmental impact assessment must be conducted prior to the implantation of a project. Moreover, once operations have started and, where necessary, throughout the life of the project, continuous monitoring of its effects on the environment shall be undertaken.

206. The Court has already considered the role of the environmental impact assessment in the context of the procedural obligations of the Parties under the 1975 Statute (paragraphs 119 and 120. It will now deal with the specific points in dispute with regard to the role of this type of assessment in the fulfillment of the substantive obligations of the Parties, that is to say, first, whether such an assessment should have, as a matter of method, necessarily considered possible

alternative sites, taking into account the receiving capacity of the river in the area where the plant was to be built and, secondly, whether the populations likely to be affected, in this case both the Uruguay and Argentine riparian populations, should have, or have in fact, been consulted in the context of the environmental impact assessment.

(i) The siting of the Orion (Botnia) mill at Fray Bentos

207. According to Argentina, one reason why Uruguay's environmental impact assessment is inadequate is that it contains no analysis of alternatives for the choice of the mill site, whereas the study of alternative sites is required under international law (UNEP Goals and Principles, Espoo Convention, IFC Operational Policy 4.01). Argentina contends that the chosen site is particularly sensitive from an ecological point of view and unconducive to the dispersion of pollutants "[b]ecause of the nature of the waters which will receive the pollution, the propensity of the site to sedimentation and eutrophication, the phenomenon of reverse flow and the proximity of the largest settlement on the River Uruguay."

208. Uruguay counters that the Fray Bentos site was initially chosen because of the particularly large volume of water in the river in that location, which would serve to promote effluent dilution. Uruguay adds that the site is moreover easily accessible for river navigation, which facilitates delivery of raw materials, and local manpower is available there. Uruguay considers that, if there is an obligation to consider alternative sites, the instruments invoked for that purpose by Argentina do not require alternative locations to be considered as part of an environmental impact assessment unless it is necessary in the circumstances to do so. Finally, Uruguay affirms that in any case it did so and that the suitability of the Orion (Botnia) site was comprehensively assessed.

209. The Court will now consider, first, whether Uruguay failed to exercise due diligence in conducting the environmental impact assessment, particularly with respect to the choice of the location of the plant and, secondly, whether the particular location chosen for the siting of the plant, in the case Fray Bentos, was unsuitable for the construction of a plant discharging industrial effluent of this nature and on this scale, or could have a harmful impact on the river.

210. Regarding the first point, the Court has already indicated that the Espoo Convention is not applicable to the present case (see paragraph 205 above); while with respect to the United Nations eradication of poverty Goals and Principles to which Argentina has referred, whose legal character has been described in paragraph 205 above, the Court recalls that Principle 4 *(c)* simply provides that an environmental impact assessment should include, at a minimum, "[a] description of practical alternatives, as appropriate." It is also to be recalled that Uruguay has repeatedly indicated that the suitability of the Fray Bentos location was comprehensively assessed and that other possible sites were considered. The Court further notes that the IFC's Final Cumulative Impact Study of September 2006 (hereinafter "CIS") shows that in 2003 Botnia evaluated four locations in total at La Paloma, at Paso de los Toros, at Nueva Palmira, and at Fray Bentos, before choosing Fray Bentos. The evaluations concluded that the limited amount of fresh water in La Paloma and its importance as a habitat for birds rendered it unsuitable, while for

Nueva Palmira its consideration was discouraged by its proximity to residential, recreational, and culturally important areas, and with respect to Pase de los Toros insufficient flow of water during the dry season and potential conflict with competing water uses, as well as a lack of infrastructure belie Argentina's argument that an assessment of possible sites was not carried out prior to the determination of the final site.

211. Regarding the second point, the Court cannot fail to note that any decision on the actual location of such a plant along the River Uruguay should take into account the capacity of the waters of the river to receive, dilute and disperse discharges of effluent from a plant of this nature and scale.

212. The Court notes, with regard to the receiving capacity of the river at the location of the mill, that the Parties disagree on the geomorphological and hydrodynamic characteristics of the river in the relevant area, particularly as they relate to river flow, and how the flow of the river, including its direction and its velocity, in turn determines the dispersal and dilution of pollutants. The differing views put forward by the Parties with regard to the river flow may be due to the different modeling systems which each has employed to analyse the hydrodynamic features of the River at the Fray Bentos location. Argentina implemented a three-dimensional modeling that measured speed and direction at ten different depths of the river and used a sonar — an Acoustic Doppler Current Profiler (hereafter "ADCP") — to record water flow velocities for a range of depths for about a year. The three-dimensional system generated a large number of data later introduced in a numerical hydrodynamic model. On the other hand, Botnia based its environmental impact assessment on a bi-dimensional modeling — the RMA2. The EcoMetrix CIS implemented both three-dimensional and bi-dimensional models. However, it is not mentioned whether an ADCP sonar was used at different depths.

213. The Court sees no need to go into a detailed examination of the scientific and technical validity of the different kinds of modeling, calibration and validation undertaken by the Parties to characterize the rate and direction of flow of the waters of the river in the relevant area. The Court notes however that both Parties agree that reverse flows occur frequently and that phenomena of low flow and stagnation may be observed in the concerned area, but that they disagree on the implications of this for the discharges from the Orion (Botnia) mill into this area of river.

214. The Court considers that in establishing its water quality standards in accordance with Articles 36 and 56 of the 1975 Statute, CARU must have taken into account the receiving capacity and sensitivity of the waters of the river, including in the areas of the river adjacent to Fray Bentos. Consequently, in so far as it is not established that the discharges of effluent of the Orion (Botnia) mill have exceeded the limits set by those standards, in terms of the level of concentrations, the Court finds itself unable to conclude that Uruguay has violated its obligations under the 1975 Statute. Moreover, neither of the Parties has argued before the Court that the water quality standards established by CARU have not adequately taken into consideration the geomorphological and hydrological characteristics of the river and capacity of its waters to disperse and dilute different types of discharges. The Court is of the opinion that, should such inadequacy be detected, particularly with

respect to certain areas of the river such as at Fray Bentos, the Parties should initiate a review of the water quality standards set by CARU and ensure that such standards clearly reflect the characteristics of the river and are capable of protecting its waters and its ecosystem.

(c). Consultation of the affected populations

215. The Parties disagree on the extent to which the populations likely to be affected by the construction of the Orion (Botnia) mill, particularly on the Argentine side of the river, were consulted in the course of the environmental impact assessment. While both Parties agree that consultation of the affected populations should form part of an environmental impact assessment, Argentina asserts that international law imposes specific obligations on States in this regard. In support of this argument, Argentina points to Articles 2.6 and 3.8 of the Espoo Convention, Article 13 of the 2001 International Law Commission draft Articles on Prevention of Transboundary Harm from Hazardous Activities and Principles 7 and 8 of the UNEP Goals and Principles. Uruguay considers that the provisions invoked by Argentina cannot serve as a legal basis for an obligation to consult the affected populations and adds that in any event the affected populations had indeed been consulted.

216. The Court is of the view that no legal obligation to consult the affected populations arises for the Parties for the instruments invoked by Argentina.

217. Regarding the facts, the Court notes that both before and after the granting of the initial environmental authorization, Uruguay did undertake activities aimed at consulting the affected populations, both on the Argentine and the Uruguayan sides of the river. These activities included meetings on 2 December 2003 in Rio Negro, and on 26 May 2004 in Fray Bentos, with participation of Argentine non-governmental organizations. In addition, on 21 December 2004, a public hearing was convened in Fray Bentos which, according to Uruguay, addressed among other subjects, the

> "handling of chemical products in the plant and in the port; the appearance of acid rain, dioxins, furan, and other polychlorates of high toxicity that could affect the environment; compliance with the Stockholm Convention; atmospheric emissions of the plant; electro-magnetic and electrostatic emissions; [and] liquid discharges into the river."

Inhabitants of Fray Bentos and nearby regions of Uruguay and Argentina participated in the meeting and submitted 138 documents containing questions or concerns.

218. Further, the Court notes that between June and November 2005 more than 80 interviews were conducted by the Consensus Building Institute, a non-profit organization specializing in facilitated dialogues, mediation, and negotiation, contracted by the IFC. Such interviews were conducted *inter alia* in Fray Bentos, Gualeguaychú, Montevideo, and Buenos Aires, with interviewees including civil society groups, non-governmental organizations, business associations, public officials, tourism operators, local business owners, fishermen, farmers and plantation owners on both sides of the river. In December 2005, the draft CIS and the report

prepared by the Consensus Building Institute were released, and the IFC opened a period of consultation to receive additional feedback from stakeholders in Argentina and Uruguay.

219. In light of the above, the Court finds that consultation by Uruguay of the affected populations did indeed take place.

NOTES AND QUESTIONS

1.   Note that in the *Pulp Mills Case* neither Argentina nor Uruguay was a party to the Espoo Convention, and the 1975 Statute did not explicitly require an environmental impact assessment, but the ICJ nevertheless ruled that the environmental impact assessment process applied. Was this holding correct? On what basis could the 1975 Statute be interpreted to include the environmental impact assessment requirement? Consider Article 31 (3)(c) of the Vienna Convention on the Law of Treaties.

2.   In paragraph 204 of the Opinion, the ICJ declared that the environmental impact assessment process is a binding norm of "general environmental law." Did the ICJ provide an adequate analysis of this finding? Was this finding based on the fact that environmental impact assessment is customary international law or a general principle of law?

3.   What is the content of the environmental impact assessment process under customary international law? The Court cites especially the UNEP Goals and Principles and the Espoo Convention. Can it be assumed that the customary international law is identical or similar to these documents?

4.   When is the environmental impact assessment process applicable? Did the Court clarify this issue?

5.   To what extent will an international tribunal exercise judicial review over the various steps in the environmental assessment process?

6.   The Polluter-Pays Principle

The polluter-pays principle is a rule concerning the allocation of the cost of pollution. According to this principle the social or external costs of pollution should be internalized back to the polluter, the source of the pollution. The first authoritative formulation of the polluter-pays principle occurred in 1972, when the Organization for Economic Cooperation and Development (OECD) formally adopted the following policy statement[52]:

> The principle to be used for allocating costs of pollution prevention and control measures to encourage rational use of scarce environmental resources and to avoid distortions in international trade and investment is the so-called "Polluter-Pays Principle." This Principle means that the polluter should bear the expenses of carrying out measures decided by

---

[52] Recommendation on Guiding Principles Concerning Economic Aspects of Environmental Policies, C (72) 128 (1972).

public authorities to ensure that the environment is in an acceptable state. In other words, the cost of these measures should be reflected in the cost of goods and services which cause pollution in production and/or consumption. Such measures should not be accompanied by subsidies that would create significant distortions in international trade and investment.

The OECD, in adopting this Principle, was aware that environmental policies and standards varied greatly among its members and, while the OECD encourages the harmonization of environmental standards, the pollution-pays principle is a method of avoiding disruption of international trade patterns and distortions in the allocation of resources even with a diversity of environmental standards among nations.

In 1974, the OECD published its Recommendation on the Implementation of the Polluter-Pays Principle.[53] This document reaffirmed the earlier OECD recommendation and asked its membership to uniformly observe the polluter-pays principle, and "not to assist the polluters by means of subsidies, tax advantages, or other measures."

The polluter-pays principle is embodied in Rio Principle 16. To what extent is the polluter-pays principle a rule of law with normative force? Consider the following case.

VELLORE CITIZENS WELFARE FORUM v. UNION OF INDIA
Supreme Court of India
1996 All India Reporter, 2715 Opinion of the Court

SINGH J:

1. This petition — public interest — under Article 32 of the Constitution of India has been filed by Vellore Citizens' Welfare Forum and is directed against the pollution which is being caused by enormous discharge of untreated effluent by the tanneries and other industries in the State of Tamil Nadu. It is stated that the tanneries are discharging untreated effluent into agricultural fields, roadsides, waterways and open lands. The untreated effluent is finally discharged in River Palar which is the main source of water supply to the residents of the area. According to the petitioner the entire surface and subsoil water of River Palar has been polluted, resulting in non-availability of potable water to the residents of the area. It is stated that the tanneries in the State of Tamil Nadu have caused environmental degradation in the area. According to the preliminary survey made by the Tamil Nadu Agricultural University Research Center, Vellore, nearly 35,000 hectares of agricultural land in the tanneries belt has become either partially or totally unfit for cultivation. It has been further stated in the petition that the tanneries use about 170 types of chemicals in the chrome tanning processes. The said chemicals include sodium chloride, lime, sodium sulphate, chlorium sulphate, fat, liquor, ammonia and sulphuric acid besides dyes which are used in large

---

[53] Recommendation on the Implementation of the Polluter-Pays Principle, C (74) 223 (1974).

quantities. Nearly 35 litres of water is used for processing one kilogram of finished leather, resulting in dangerously enormous quantities of toxic effluents being let out in the open by the tanning industry. These effluents have spoiled the physical-chemical properties of the soil and have contaminated groundwater by percolation. According to the petitioner, an independent survey conducted by Peace members, a non-governmental organisation, covering 13 villages of Dindigul and Peddiar Chatram Anchayat Unions, reveals that 350 wells out of total of 467 used for drinking and irrigation purposes have been polluted. Women and children have to walk miles to get drinking water. . . .

4. The affidavits filed on behalf of the State of Tamil Nadu and the Board clearly indicate tht the tanneries and other polluting industries in the State of Tamil Nadu are being persuaded for the last about 10 years to control the pollution generated by them. They were given option either to construct common effluent treatment plants for a cluster of industries or to set up individual pollution control devices. The Central Government agreed to give substantial subsidies for the construction of Common Effluent Treatment Plants. It is a pity that till date most of the tanneries operating in the State of Tamil Nadu have not taken any step to control the pollution caused by the discharge of effluent. . . .

11. Some of the salient principles of 'Sustainable Development', as culled out from Brundtland Report and international documents, are Inter-Generational Equity, Use and Conservation of Natural Resources, Environmental Protection, the Precautionary Principle, Polluter Pays Principle, Obligation to Assist and Cooper-ate, Eradication of Poverty and Financial Assistance to the developing countries. We are, however, of the view that 'The Precautionary Principle' and 'The Polluter Pays Principle' are essential features of 'Sustainable Development'. The 'Precau-tionary Principle' — in the context of the municipal law — means: (i) where there are threats of serious and irreversible damage, lack of scientific certainty should not be used as a reason for postponing measures to prevent environmental degradation. (ii) the 'onus of proof' is on the actor or the developer/industrialist to show that his action is environmentally benign.

12. 'The Polluter Pays Principle' has been held to be a sound principle by this Court in Indian Council for Enviro-Legal Action v. Union of India [(1996) 3 SCC 212; 91996) 2 JT (SC) 196, above, p. 256]. The Court observed (SCC p. 246, para. 65): '. . . we are of the opinion that any principle evolved in this behalf should be simple, practical and suited to the conditions obtaining in this country'. The Court ruled that: (SCC p. 246, para. 65)' . . . once the activity carried on is hazardous or inherently dangerous, the person carrying on such activity is liable to make good the loss caused to any other person by his activity irrespective of the fact whether he took reasonable care while carrying on his activity. The rule is premised upon the very nature of the activity carried on'. Consequently the polluting industries are 'absolutely' liable to compensate for the harm caused by them to villagers in the affected area, to the soil and to the underground water and hence, they are bound to take all necessary measures to remove sludge and other pollutants lying in the affected areas'. The 'Polluter Pays Principle' as interpreted by this Court means that the absolute liability for harm to the environment extends not only to compensate the victims of pollution but also the cost of restoring the environmental degradation. Remediation of the damaged environment is part of the process of

'Sustainable Development' and as such the polluter is liable to pay the cost to the individual sufferers as well as the cost of reversing the damaged ecology.

25. Keeping in view the scenario discussed by us in this judgment, we order and direct as under:

1. The Central Government shall constitute an authority under Section 3(3) of the Environment (Protection) Act 1986 and shall confer on the said authority all the powers necessary to deal with the situation created by the tanneries and other polluting industries in the State of Tamil Nadu. The authority shall be headed by a retired Judge of the High Court and it may have other members — preferably with expertise in the field of pollution control and environment protection — to be appointed by the Central Government. The Central Government shall confer on the said authority the powers to issue directions under Section 5 of the Environment Act and for taking measures with respect to the matters referred to in clauses (v), (vi), (vii), (viii), (ix), (x) and (xii) of sub-section (2) of Section 3. The Central Government shall constitute the authority before September 30, 1996.

2. The authority so constituted by the Central Government shall implement the 'Precautionary Principle' and the 'Polluter Pays Principle.' The authority shall, with the help of expert opinion and after giving opportunity to the polluters concerned, assess the loss to the ecology/ environment in the affected areas and shall also identify the individuals/ families who have suffered because of the pollution and shall assess the compensation to be paid to the said individuals/families. The authority shall further determine the compensation to be recovered from the polluters as cost of reversing the damaged environment. The authority shall lay down just and fair procedure for completing the exercise.

NOTES AND QUESTIONS

1.   In the *Vellore Case* the court explicitly imported what it believed was a rule of international law into the national law of India. Was the court correct in its judgment that the polluter pays principle is a rule of international law? Consider the way Rio Principle 16 is worded; is this a binding rule of law? No international tribunal has considered polluter-pays as more than an aspirational policy statement. BIRNIE, BOYLE & REDGWELL, INTERNATIONAL LAW AND THE ENVIRONMENT, 3d edition, state that "Principle 16 simply lacks the normative character of a rule of law. Moreover, while some treaties require parties to 'apply the polluter pays principle,' others use the softer language of guidance." (pp. 322–23). In the United States, courts have rejected the application of the polluter pays principle and the precautionary principles as independent rules of law. *See Beanal v. Freeport-McMoran*, 969 F. Supp. 362 (E.D. La. 1997), *aff'd*, 197 F.3d 161 (5th Cir. 1999); *Amlon Metals v. FMC*, 775 F. Supp. 668 (S.D.N.Y. 1991).

2.   The Polluter-Pays Principle adopts a policy of full internalization of the costs of pollution. The concept of internalization of costs comes from environmental economic theory which holds that economic efficiency may be enhanced if economic actors are compelled to bear the cost of their activities, including social costs. But full pollution cost internalization is not optimal from an economic standpoint. Economic theory holds that efficiency is optimized if the social costs of pollution are

internalized to the point where the marginal cost of pollution control is just equal to the marginal benefit of pollution abatement. Thus full internalization of the costs of pollution is inefficient. However, in order to apply the most economically efficient level of pollution control, it is necessary to know both the damages resulting from pollution and the cost of pollution control; this poses great difficulties since many social costs of pollution are beyond economic calculation, and the costs of controls vary with time and technology choice.

3.   Do you expect that the Polluter Pays Principle will become a general rule of international law some day? If so, would not international tribunals have to function as pollution control administrations like the court in the *Vellore Case*?

7.   The Duty to Notify

Principle 19 of the Rio Declaration states that states "shall provide prior and timely notification and relevant information to potentially affected states on activities that may have a significant adverse transboundary environmental effect." (*See also* Principle 18). In the wake of the Chernobyl nuclear disaster in 1986, the Soviet Union was strongly criticized by many states for its failure to give timely notice of the accident and the transboundary impacts the Soviet government knew were likely to occur. The Soviet leaders subsequently admitted that they should have supplied such information. Leading commentators Patricia Birnie and Alan Boyle argue that "state practice and case law support an obligation [on the part of states] to give timely notification to states at risk so they can take appropriate protective measures." PATRICIA W. BIRNIE & ALAN E. BOYLE, INTERNATIONAL LAW AND THE ENVIRONMENT 136 (Oxford: Oxford University Press, 2002).

8.   The Duty to Cooperate in Good Faith

Principle 27 of the Rio Declaration requires states (and peoples) to cooperate in good faith to achieve the aims of the Declaration and in the further development of international environmental law. The duty to cooperate appears in numerous treaties and other international instruments, for example in Principle 24 of the Stockholm Declaration and in Principle 6 of the UNEP Draft Principles of Conduct in the Field of Environment for the Guidance of States in the Conservation and Harmonious Utilization of Natural Resources Shared by Two or More States (1977). The duty to cooperate appears in virtually every international environmental instrument and may be said to be a customary law as well as a treaty law obligation of international environmental law. Affaire du Lac Lanoux (France v. Spain), XII U.N. Rep. Int'l Arb. Awards 281 (19 November 1956) [France; which proposed to build a hydroelectric power facility using water diverted from Lake Lanoux, was obligated to consult with Spain, an affected state.]

Does the duty to cooperate in the solution of common environmental problems include a duty to come to agreement or to arrive at a solution?

9.   The Duty of Public Participation

Principle 10 of the Rio Declaration speaks to the duty of public participation in decisions affecting the environment: "States shall facilitate and encourage public awareness and participation by making information widely available. Effective access to judicial and administrative proceedings, including redress and remedies, shall be provided." In the absence of a treaty provision, however, no court has declared public participation to be a right under customary international law.

Provisions echoing Principle 10 are common in international environmental instruments. The most important legally binding embodiment of Principle 10 is the Aarhus Convention on Access to Information, Public Participation in Decision-Making, and Access to Justice in Environmental Matters (1998). The Aarhus Convention, which was sponsored by the UN Economic Commission for Europe, has 46 Parties including the European Union. This Convention establishes the right of every member of the public to receive information from public authorities within a short time period. The Convention also establishes a right to public participation in decisionmaking and the right to challenge public decisions that affect the environment.

Read the provisions of the landmark Aarhus Convention in the **Document Supplement**. The United States is not a party to this Convention. Would you favor ratification by the United States?

QUESTION

This section has provided an analysis of nine "soft law" norms taken from the Rio Declaration, perhaps the most important "soft law" document. How do you evaluate "soft law" as a tool of international environmental law?

Section III.   INTERNATIONAL LAW AND DOMESTIC LAW

There is debate among lawyers whether international law and domestic law (sometimes called "municipal law") constitute one legal system or two separate systems of law. The former "monist" view is both legal orders constitute a single system of law and that international law is "higher" law so that domestic law must give way in the event of a conflict. The latter "dualist" view, on the other hand, holds that international law and domestic law constitute separate and distinct legal orders altogether and each operates in its own sphere. Thus a dualist would hold that it is possible to apply one rule in the international sphere, while a different rule must hold in domestic law.[54]

Both the monist and the dualist position are extremes, and virtually all states harmonize international and domestic law to some degree in their respective constitutions. Of course this means that the relationship between international and domestic law varies from state-to-state.

---

[54] For more on this debate, see MARK WESTON JANIS, INTERNATIONAL LAW 87–88 (5th ed. 2008).

To comply with the injunction of the Vienna Convention on the Law of Treaties (1969), Article 26, the *pacta sunt servanda* rule, that "[e]very treaty in force in binding upon the parties to it and must be performed by them in good faith," nation-states have the obligation to implement ("transform") a treaty to which they have agreed into their respective domestic legal orders. This implementation or transformation process differs from state-to-state. In parliamentary states[55] (as well as autocratic states), the transformation process is relatively simple, since the government that consented to the treaty is also fully in charge politically; thus the domestic implementation of a treaty is automatic, as long as the government in question approves.

In the United States the transformation of a treaty into domestic law is more complicated. To begin with, U.S. practice recognizes two general categories of treaties in the international law sense: (1) treaties that are ratified by the President with the advice and consent of at least two-thirds of the membership of the Senate of the United States[56] and (2) executive agreements negotiated by the President under his foreign affairs power. The latter power of the President has been upheld by the Supreme Court many times. *See United States v. Belmont*, 301 U.S. 324 (1937); *United States v. Curtiss-Wright*, 299 U.S. 304 (1936); and *Dames & Moore v. Regan*, 453 U.S. 654 (1981). There is an interesting debate over the interchangeability of the treaty power and the executive agreement power that is beyond the purview of this book, and the U.S. State Department has issued guidelines that the executive should follow in deciding whether to use the treaty power or an executive agreement in a given case. *See* 11 *Foreign Affairs Manual*, Chapter 700, 721.3 (2006), which codifies State Department Circular 175 of December 13, 1955. The controversy over which instrument to employ has not arisen in the context of international environmental law.

U.S. practice distinguishes between two ways a treaty may be transformed into domestic law. In *Foster & Elam v. Neilson*, 27 U.S. 253 (1829), Chief Justice Marshall explained that ratified U.S. treaties are on two types: self-executing treaties that are the law of the land by their terms alone and non-self-executing treaties, which require implementation through an act of Congress to become domestic law. Virtually all environmental treaties are non-self executing and must be transformed through laws enacted by Congress. Both self-executing treaties and those executed by an act of Congress are supreme over state law by virtue of the Supremacy Clause, Article VI of the U.S. Constitution.

In the event of a conflict between a provision in a treaty and a federal law, which prevails? Although conflicts are possible, they are rare. The rule of the *Charming Betsy, Murray v. Schooner Charming Betsy*, 6 U.S. 64, 118 (1804) states that "[A]n act of Congress ought never to be construed to violate the law of nations if any other possible construction remains." In those rare cases where there is conflict, the Supreme Court has said that since federal statutes and treaties have equal status, the last-in-time prevails. *Breard v. Greene*, 523 U.S. 371, 376 (1998) *(per curiam);*

---

[55] In the United Kingdom, the executive has the power to negotiate treaties, but only an act of Parliament can incorporate a treaty into English law. *See* IAN BROWNIE, PRINCIPLES OF PUBLIC INTERNATIONAL LAW 45 (6th ed. 2003).

[56] U.S. Constitution, Article II(2).

The Chinese Exclusion Cases, 130 U.S. 581, 600 (1889); *Whitney v. Robertson*, 124 U.S. 190, 194 (1888). The last-in-time rule looks in two directions: A later enacted statute is superior to a prior treaty, and a later self-executing treaty is superior to a prior statute.

As to customary international law rules and general principles of international law, the Supreme Court stated in the *The Paquete Habana Case:* "International law is part of our law, and must be ascertained and administered by the courts of justice of appropriate jurisdiction, as often as questions of right depending upon it are duly presented for their determination."[57] However, it is unsettled whether the last-in-time rule applies when it comes to a customary law rule. Many scholars and lawyers argue that a customary law rule, even if last-in-time, cannot override an act of Congress.[58]

What is the status of state law with respect to the treaty power? Consider the following cases.

STATE OF MISSOURI v. HOLLAND
252 U.S. 416 (1920)

Mr. Justice Holmes delivered the opinion of the Court.

This is a bill in equity brought by the State of Missouri to prevent a game warden of the United States from attempting to enforce the Migratory Bird Treaty Act of [252 U.S. 416, 431] July 3, 1918, c. 128, 40 Stat. 755, and the regulations made by the Secretary of Agriculture in pursuance of the same. The ground of the bill is that the statute is an unconstitutional interference with the rights reserved to the States by the Tenth Amendment, and that the acts of the defendant done and threatened under that authority invade the sovereign right of the State and contravene its will manifested in statutes. The State also alleges a pecuniary interest, as owner of the wild birds within its borders and otherwise, admitted by the Government to be sufficient, but it is enough that the bill is a reasonable and proper means to assert the alleged quasi sovereign rights of a State.

On December 8, 1916, a treaty between the United States and Great Britain was proclaimed by the President. It recited that many species of birds in their annual migrations traversed many parts of the United States and Canada, that they were if great value as a source of food and in destroying insects injurious to vegetation, but were in danger of extermination through lack of adequate protection. It therefore provided for specified closed seasons and protection in other forms, and agreed that the two powers would take or propose to their lawmaking bodies the necessary measures for carrying the treaty out, 39 Stat. 17 02. The above mentioned act of July 3, 1918, entitled an act to give effect to the convention, prohibited the killing, captured or selling any of the migratory birds included in the terms of the

---

[57] 175 U.S. 677, 700 (1900).

[58] *See* Curtis A. Bradley and Jack L. Goldsmith, *Customary International Law as Federal Common Law: A Critique of the Modern Position*, 110 Harv. L. Rep. 815 (1997). *See also* Maier, *The Authoritative Sources of Customary International Law in the United States*, 10 Mich. J. Int'l L. 450, 464–73 (1989).

treaty except as permitted by regulations compatible with those terms, to be made by the Secretary of Agriculture. Regulations were proclaimed on July 31, and October 25, 1918. 40 Stat. 1812, 1863. It is unnecessary to go into any details, because, as we have said, the question raised is the general one whether the treaty and statute are void as an interference with the rights reserved to the States.

To answer this question it is not enough to refer to the Tenth Amendment, reserving the powers not delegated to the United States, because by Article 2, Section 2, the power to make treaties is delegated expressly, and by Article 6 treaties made under the authority of the United States, along with the Constitution and laws of the United States made in pursuance thereof, are declared the supreme law of the land. If the treaty is valid there can be no dispute about the validity of the statute under Article I, Section 8, as a necessary and proper means to execute the powers of the Government. The language of the Constitution as to the supremacy of treaties being general, the question before us is narrowed to an inquiry into the ground upon which the present supposed exception is placed.

It is said that a treaty cannot be valid if it infringes the Constitution, that there are limits, therefore, to the treaty-making power, and that one such limit is that what an act of Congress could not do unaided, in derogation of the powers reserved to the States, a treaty cannot do. An earlier act of Congress that attempted by itself and not in pursuance of a treaty to regulate the killing of migratory birds within the States had been held bad in the District Court. *United States v. Shauver*, 214 Fed. 154. *United States v. McCullagh*, 221 Fed. 299. Those decisions were supported by arguments that migratory birds were owned by the States in their sovereign capacity for the benefit of their people, and that under cases like *Geer v. Connecticut*, 161 U.S. 519, 16 Sup. Ct. 600, this control was one that Congress had no power to displace. The same argument is supposed to apply now with equal force. Whether the two cases cited were decided rightly or not they cannot be accepted as a test of the treaty power. Acts of Congress are the supreme law of the land only when made in pursuance of the Constitution, while treaties are declared to be so when made under the authority of the United States. It is open to question whether the authority of the United States means more than the formal acts prescribed to make the convention. We do not mean to imply that there are no qualifications to the treaty-making power; but they must be ascertained in a different way. It is obvious that there may be matters of the sharpest exigency for the national well being that an act of Congress could not deal with but that a treaty followed by such an act could, and it is not lightly to be assumed that, in matters requiring national action, 'a power which must belong to and somewhere reside in every civilized government' is not to be found. *Andrews v. Andrews*, 188 U.S. 14 (1903). What was said in that case with regard to the powers of the States applies with equal force to the powers of the nation in cases where the States individually are incompetent to act. We are not yet discussing the particular case before us but only are considering the validity of the test proposed. With regard to that we may add that when we are dealing with words that also are a constituent act, like the Constitution of the United States, we must realize that they have called into life a being the development of which could not have been foreseen completely by the most gifted of its begetters. It was enough for them to realize or to hope that they had created an organism; it has taken a century and has cost their successors much sweat and blood to prove that they created a nation. The case before us must be considered in the light of our whole experience and not merely in that of what was said a hundred years ago. The treaty in question does not contravene any prohibitory words to be found in the Constitution. The only question is whether it is forbidden by some invisible radiation from the general terms of the Tenth Amendment. We must consider what this country has become in deciding what that amendment has reserved.

The State as we have intimated found its claim of exclusive authority upon an assertions of title to migratory birds, an assertion that is embodied in statute. No doubt it is true that as between a State and its inhabitants the State may regulate the killing and sale of such birds, but it does not follow that its authority is exclusive of paramount powers. To put the claim of the State upon title is to lean upon a slender reed. Wild birds are not in the possession of anyone; and possession is the beginning of ownership. The whole foundation of the State's rights is the presence within their jurisdiction of birds that yesterday had not arrived, tomorrow may be in another State and in a week a thousand miles away. If we are to be accurate we cannot put the case of the State upon higher ground than that the treaty deals with creatures that for the moment are within the state borders, that it must be carried out by officers of the United States within the same territory, and that but for the treaty the State would be free to regulate this subject itself.

As most of the laws of the United States are carried out within the States and as many of them deal with matters which in the silence of such laws that State might regulate, such general grounds are not enough to support Missouri's claim. Valid treaties of course 'are as binding within the territorial limits of the States as they are elsewhere throughout the dominion of the United States.' *Baldwin v. Franks*, 120 U.S. 678, 7 S. Sup. Ct. 656, 657. No doubt the great body of private relations usually falls within the control of the State, but a treaty may override its power.

Here a national interest of very nearly the first magnitude is involved. It can be protected only by national action in concert with that of another power. The subject matter is only transitorily within the State and has no permanent habitat therein. But for the treaty and the statute there soon might be no birds for any powers to deal with. We see nothing in the Constitution that compels the Government to sit by while a food supply is cut off and the protectors of our forests and our crops are destroyed. It is not sufficient to rely upon the States. The reliance in vain, and were it otherwise, the question is whether the United States is forbidden to act. We are of opinion that the treaty and statute must be upheld.

Decree *affirmed.*

MR. JUSTICE VAN DEVANTER and MR. JUSTICE PITNEY dissent.

COMMONWEALTH OF AUSTRALIA v. STATE OF TASMANIA (THE TASMANIAN DAM CASE)
High Court of Australia
1 July 1983
158 Commonwealth Law Reports 1

[In this case the Government of Tasmania, an Australian state, approved the construction of the Franklin Dam, a large hydroelectric dam on the Gordon River by the Tasmanian Hydroelectric Commission in a wilderness area in southwest Tasmania. The dam was opposed by environmentalists and many people in the country, but in 1982, the Government of Tasmania passed laws allowing the dam to proceed, and preliminary preparations were begun. In 1974, the Commonwealth of Australia had deposited its instrument of ratification of the Convention for the Protection of the World Natural Heritage (The World Heritage Convention), a multilateral environmental agreement with 74 parties sponsored by the United Nations Educational, Scientific and Cultural Organization (UNESCO), in force since 1975. The Commonwealth of Australia, which wanted to stop the construction of the Tasmanian Dam, secured the designation of the dam site and the surrounding area as a World Heritage area — the Western Tasmania Wilderness — listed under the World Heritage Convention. The Commonwealth also passed domestic legislation and regulations protecting the area. The State of Tasmania requested that the area be withdrawn from World Heritage listing authorized construction of the dam. The Commonwealth of Australia brought suit in the Australian High Court to stop construction of the dam, which was now prohibited by treaty law and by federal laws and regulation. The State of Tasmania contended that the federal laws and regulations were unconstitutional. The High Court of Australian is designated as the constitutional court to decide questions of federal relations in Australia. By a vote of 4 to 3, the seven judges of the High Court ruled that the Commonwealth laws, the relevant provisions of the National Parks Act, and accompanying regulations prohibiting the construction of the dam were within the external affairs power of the Commonwealth under section 51 (xxix) of the Constitution. This case is the most famous and influential environmental case in Australian history].

The power to make laws for the peace, order and good government of the Commonwealth with respect to external affairs authorizes the Parliament to make laws with respect to external affairs which govern conduct, in as well as outside, Australia. The core of Tasmania's case was that the construction of the dam and the regulation of the south-west area of Tasmania were purely domestic or internal affairs of the State. However, it is elementary that Australia's external affairs may be also internal affairs (see *Burgess; New South Wales* v. *The Commonwealth* ('the *Sea and Submerged lands Case*'); and *Koowarta*); examples are control of traffic in drugs of dependence, diplomatic immunity, preservation of endangered species and preservation of human rights.

The circumstances which bring a law within the power have not been stated exhaustively. It was recognized in *Burgess*, and is even clearer now, that along with other countries, Australia's domestic affairs are becoming more and more involved with those of humanity generally in its various political entities and groups. Increasingly, use of the external affairs power will not be exceptional or extraordinary but a regular way in which Australia will harmonize its internal order with the world order. The Constitution in its references to external affairs (s. 51(xxix)) and to matters arising under treaties or affecting consuls or representatives of other countries (s. 75) recognizes that while most Australians are residents of States as well as of the Commonwealth, they are also part of humanity. Under the Constitution Parliament has the authority to take Australia into the 'one world', sharing its responsibilities as well as its cultural and natural heritage.

The power extends to the execution of treaties by discharging obligations or obtaining benefits, but it is not restricted to treaty implantation. The power would be available for example where, without any treaty, Australia wished to assist in an overseas famine. No doubt the Parliament could authorize acquisition of food in Australia (albeit on just terms, in accordance with s. 51(xxxi)) for relief of the famine and could legislate to prevent hoarding and profiteering in regard to the food remaining in Australia.

Although external affairs are mostly concerned with our relationships with other nation States, they are not exclusively so concerned. There may be circumstances where Australia's relationship with persons or groups who are not nation States, is part of external affairs. The existence of powerful transnational corporations, international trade unions and other groups who can affect Australia, means that Australia's external affairs, as a matter of practicality, are not confined to relations with other nation States.

In *Koowarta*[59] the majority considered that if the subject was one of international concern this brought it within the external affairs power. For the reasons I have given it is not necessary that the subject be one of concern demonstrated by the other nation States generally. For example, concern expressed by the world's scientific community or a significant part of it over action or inaction in Australia might be enough to bring a matter within Australian external affairs. However, even if international concern is not always necessary, it is sufficient. External concern over human rights violations often extends internal affairs into external affairs.

It is preferable that the circumstances in which a law is authorized by the external affairs power be stated in terms of what is sufficient, even if the categories overlap, rather than in exhaustive terms. To be a law with respect to external affairs it is sufficient that it: (a) implements any international law, or (b) implements any treaty or convention whether general (multilateral) or particular, or (c) implements any recommendation or request of the United Nations organization or subsidiary organizations such as the World Health Organization, the United Nations Education, Scientific and Cultural Organization, the Food and Agriculture Organization or the International Labour Organization, or (d) fosters (or inhibits) relations between Australia or political entities, bodies or persons within Australia and other nation States, entities, groups or persons external to Australia, or (e) deals with circumstances or things outside Australia, or (f) deals with circumstances or things inside Australia of international concern.

---

[59] (1982) 153 CLR 168.

The fact that a subject becomes part of external affairs does not mean that the subject becomes, as it were, as a separate, plenary head of legislative power. If the only basis upon which a subject becomes part of external affairs is a treaty, then the legislative power is confined to what may reasonably be regarded as appropriate for implementation of provisions of the treaty. This does not mean that either all of the provisions must be implements or else none can be implemented. It does not mean that there must be any rigid adherence to the terms of the treaty. Again, if the subject of external affairs is some circumstance, the legislative power will extend to laws which could reasonably be regarded as appropriate for dealing with that circumstance.

The world's cultural and natural heritage is, of its own nature, part of Australia's external affairs. It is the heritage of Australians, as part of humanity, as well as the heritage of those where the various items happen to be. As soon as it is accepted that the Tasmanian wilderness area is part of world heritage, it follows that its preservation as well as being an internal affair, is part of Australia's external affairs.

Federal clause. The federal clause (art. 34) in the Convention is not material. It seemed to be common ground that Art. 34 does not determine which organ in a federal State should discharge its obligation; this requires examination of its own constitution. If the provisions of a treaty are within the competence of the federal legislature then the article has no relevant operation (see Bernier, *International Legal Aspects of Federalism* (1973), p. 172: Looper, '"Federal State" Clauses in Multilateral Instruments', *British Yearbook of international Law*, vol. 32 (1955–1956), p. 162; Liang, 'Colonial Clauses and Federal Clauses in United Nations Multilateral Instruments'. *American Journal of International Law*, vol. 45 (1951), p. 108).

NOTES AND QUESTIONS

1. *Missouri v. Holland* proved to be a controversial case, not because of its subject matter — protection of migratory birds — so much for its implications. Is there any limit to the treaty power? Senator John Bricker of Ohio, a conservative, sought to overturn *Missouri v. Holland* by enacting an amendment to the Constitution, known as the Bricker Amendment. One version of the Bricker Amendment introduced in 1953, stated that:

1. A provision of a treaty which conflicts with this Constitution shall not be of any force or effect.

2. A treaty shall become effective as internal law in the United States only through legislation which would be valid in the absence of treaty.

3. Congress shall have the power to regulate all executive and other agreements with any foreign power or international organization. All such agreements shall be subject to the limitations imposed on treaties by this article.

The Eisenhower Administration, which opposed this amendment because it would have limited executive authority, helped to defeat this proposed amendment by promising that it would not seek to become a party to any more human rights treaties. *See Hearings Before a Subcomm. of Senate Judiciary Committee on S.J.*

Res. 1 and S.J. Res. 43, 83d Cong. 834 (1953).

2.   Justice Holmes is considered by many to be one of the most famous men ever to serve on the Supreme Court of the United States. What do you think of his writing style?

3.   Are there any limits on the federal government's authority to enter into treaties or executive agreements? In *Reid v. Covert*, 354 U.S. 1, 5 (1957), the Supreme Court stated that "no agreement with a foreign nation can confer power on the Congress, or on any other branch of Government, which is free from the restraints of the Constitution." What is the meaning of this restraint on the treaty power? Should the federal government be able to invoke the treaty power to enact a law that goes beyond its enumerated and implied powers under the U.S. Constitution?

4.   In *Bond v. United States*, 131 S. Ct. 2355 (2011), the Supreme Court of the United States ruled unanimously that the petitioner had standing to challenge a federal statute under which he was convicted that enforces the Chemical Weapons Convention impermissibly intrudes upon areas of police powers reserved to the states under the Tenth Amendment to the U.S. Constitution. On remand, Bond's conviction under a statute implementing the Convention was affirmed, 681 F. 3d 149 (3d Cir. 2012). Bond's conduct was ruled to violate 18 U.S.C. §§ 229(a)(1), 229F (1)(A), 7(A), and 7(B), which forbid the use of a chemical that can cause death or permanent harm to another unless such use is for peaceful purposes. In 2013, the Supreme Court granted certiorari for the second time to examine the question of the extent of the treaty power and whether the rule in *Missouri v. Holland* should be modified in some way. The petitioner, Bond, argues that *Missouri v. Holland* should be overruled and that the courts should be permitted to engage in a case-by-case invalidation of the treaty power if they believe the conduct forbidden by the treaty or statute in question is too "local" to be regulated by the federal government. The Solicitor General, on the other hand, argues on behalf of the United States that this rule would hamstring U.S. treaty negotiators and throw into question the United States as a reliable treaty partner to foreign governments. *See* Note, 107 Am. J. Int'l L. 912–13 (2013). How should the Supreme Court rule in this case?

In the event, the Supreme Court unanimously reversed the conviction of Carol Anne Bond under the Chemical Weapons Implementation Act (CWIA). *Bond v. United States*, 134 S. Ct. 2077 (2014). The six-justice majority did not reach the question of the continuing validity of *Missouri v. Holland*. The majority ruled that the CWIA should not be interpreted to reach a purely local crime normally reserved to state and not federal jurisdiction. Justices Scalia, Thomas, and Alito concurred on different grounds: they disputed Justice Holmes' statement in *Missouri v. Holland* that "if [a] treaty is valid, there can be no dispute about the validity of the [implementing] statute under Article I, Section 8, as a necessary means to execute the powers of the Government." The concurring opinion argued that the Treaty Power — the implementation of treaties — is limited by the terms of Article I, section 8 of the Constitution, and the President cannot make a treaty and thereby confer powers on the Congress to legislate going beyond Article I, section 8, or in violation of the Tenth Amendment. Thus, the conviction should be overturned because the CWIA is unconstitutional, a law that goes beyond the limits of Article I, section 8. Who is correct, Justice Holmes or the three concurring judges in the *Bond* case? Article II, section 2, which confers the treaty-making power on the President, does not include any power to implement or execute treaties made. But Article I, section 8 grants Congress the power "[t]o make all Laws which shall be necessary and proper for carrying into Execution the foregoing Powers [enumerated in Article I] *and all other Powers vested by this Constitution in the Government . . . or in any . . . Officer thereof.*" Does not this grant of authority reach beyond what is necessary and proper for purposes of Article I, to include also what is necessary and proper to execute the treaty power granted to the President under Article II? If so, would not the CWIA pass constitutional muster?

5.   Compare the treaty power in the United States with the treaty power in Australia. Is there a similarity?

Section IV.   THE ENFORCEMENT AND EFFECTIVENESS OF INTERNATIONAL ENVIRONMENTAL LAW

In this book, we will study scores of multilateral environmental agreements (MEAs) and international environmental agreements (IEAs). As we have seen, virtually none of these accords are one-off international instruments. They are, rather, continuing political and legal regimes. The world of international environmental law is characterized by hundreds of largely independent institutions authorized by an MEA or a IEA to deal with a discrete environmental problem, ranging from climate change to the protection of cetaceans. There is difficulty finding common themes amid the diversity and fragmentation that characterizes the field of international environmental law. It is also difficult to judge the worth of the massive effort that has gone into protecting the global environment over the past 40 years.

When it comes to judging the worth of any international environmental regime, we naturally ask, are the norms contained in the particular MEA or IEA enforced? Does the particular MEA or IEA have any teeth or is it simply a pious pronouncement that is conveniently ignored even by those states that accept it? If there is no clear enforcement mechanism, we might conclude that the effort and expense of setting up and perpetuating the regime in question is largely or completely a waste of time and money.

But we will see that enforcement and effectiveness of MEAs and IEAs are not simple matters. In domestic law, enforcement is rather straightforward, at least in developed countries that enjoy the rule of law. If a law is concluded, there are mechanisms of enforcement in place — the executive and judicial branches of government — to assure its effectiveness. In the international sphere, however, the enforcement institutions that exist in domestic law are absent. The enforcement process of international environmental law is both complex and cumbersome. In the remaining two sections of this chapter, we come to grips with this complexity.

To understand the situation of enforcement and effectiveness of international environmental law we need a framework for analysis. Fortunately we can draw on the seminal work of Edith Brown Weiss and Harold K. Jacobson, who, in their 1998 book, ENGAGING COUNTRIES: STRENGTHENING COMPLIANCE WITH INTERNATIONAL ENVIRONMENTAL ACCORDS (Cambridge, Mass.: IT Press, 1998), published a path-breaking study of the mechanisms of MEAs and IEAs necessary for their proper enforcement and effectiveness.

Brown Weiss and Jacobson point out that enforcement of MEAs and IEAs must be analyzed differently from domestic law. Enforcement in international law is not a unitary concept but must be divided conceptually into separate elements. When a treaty is concluded on the international law plane, enforcement becomes a process involving the following parts: (1) implementation; (2) compliance; (3) dispute settlement; and (4) effectiveness. We briefly address each of these in turn.

Implementation. The first step in enforcing an MEA or IEA is to transform the international instrument in question into national law. Unless the international instrument is self-executing, this must be done through enactment of a national law or at least the adoption of new administrative regulations. In any case to be effective and to comply with obligations under international law, the national law or regulation must be consistent with the treaty.

Compliance. It is important to realize that compliance is distinct from implementation in international law. Compliance means that the state in question must actually carry out the obligations specified in the treaty in question. Compliance requires more than the passage of a national law or administrative regulations. Compliance means that the procedural and substantive norms specified in the treaty must actually be attained or performed. Compliance measures whether the state in question has carried out all its obligations under international law.

Non-compliance is, of course, the negative of compliance. There are generally two forms of non-compliance: intentional and unintentional non-compliance (where a state may not have the capacity to comply or may believe in good faith that it has complied with its obligations under a treaty instrument). We must take both forms of non-compliance into consideration.

Dispute settlement. Sometimes there will be a difference of opinion over a particular obligation under a MEA or IEA. A state may believe it has performed its obligations; other treaty parties may disagree. Dispute settlement refers to the method under international law to resolve this difference of opinion. Dispute settlement may also be used to enforce a treaty obligation against a state that intentionally breaches a treaty obligation.

Effectiveness. The concept of effectiveness is a value judgment on whether the regime in question has ameliorated the conditions or solved the problem that was the reason for its creation. Effectiveness may be rated against the objectives of the treaty in question or against the conditions that led to the treaty. Note that theoretically there may be 100% implementation and compliance with a treaty, but the treaty may still be ineffective to solve the condition or problem it addresses.

Thus the difficulty of enforcing a treaty is very complex. If we conclude that a treaty is ineffective, it may be because (1) the treaty itself was not strict enough; or (2) the treaty was not implemented fully by at least some of the parties; or (3) there was intentional or unintentional non-compliance by some parties. Finally, a treaty may be ineffective because key states refused to become parties. Thus enforcement and effectiveness problems of MEAs and IEAs may have complex or multiple causes.

The following case is a success story of enforcement of treaty obligations. The treaty in question concerned the treaty regime of the Convention for the Protection of the Mediterranean Sea against Pollution (Barcelona Convention) of 1976, and a Protocol to that treaty agreed in 1996. The Barcelona Convention is one of 13 "Regional Seas Programme" treaty regimes, most under the auspices of the United Nations Environment Programme. We cover the Regional Seas Programme in Chapter 7. Here we deal only with issues of implementation and compliance.

SYNDICAT PROFESSIONNEL COORDINATION DES PÊCHEURS DE L'ÉTANG DE BERRE ET DE LA RÉGION v. ÉLECTRICITÉ DE FRANCE (EDF)
Case C-213/03
European Court of Justice (now the Court of Justice of the
European Union)
15 July 2004

Judgment

1

By order of 6 May 2003, received at the Court on 19 May 2003, the Cour de cassation (Court of Cassation) (France) referred to the Court for a preliminary ruling under Article 234 EC two questions on the interpretation of Article 6(3) of the Protocol for the Protection of the Mediterranean Sea against Pollution from Land-based Sources, signed in Athens on 17 May 1980, approved by Council Decision 83/101/EEC of 28 February 1983 (OJ 1983 L 67, p. 1) (hereinafter 'the Protocol'), and of Article 6(1) of the Protocol as amended at the Conference of Plenipotentiaries held in Syracuse on 7 and 8 March 1996, which amendments were approved by Council Decision 1999/801/EC of 22 October 1999 (OJ 1999 L 322, p. 18) (hereinafter 'the amended Protocol').

2

Those questions were raised in proceedings between the Syndicat professionnel coordination des pêcheurs de l'étang de Berre et de la région (hereinafter 'the Syndicat') and Électricité de France Chamas (France) into the Étang de Berre.

Legal framework

3

The Convention for the Protection of the Mediterranean Sea against Pollution, signed in Barcelona on 16 February 1976 (OJ 1977 L 240, p. 3) (hereinafter 'the Convention'), was entered into by the European Economic Community by Council

Decision 77/585/EEC of 25 July 1977 (OJ 1977 L 240, p. 1).

4

Article 2(a) of the Convention defines the term 'pollution' as follows:

'. . . the introduction by man, directly or indirectly, of substances or energy into the marine environment resulting in such deleterious effects as harm to living resources, hazards to human health, hindrance to marine activities including fishing, impairment of quality for use of sea water and reduction of amenities.'

5

Article 4(1) of the Convention states:

'The Contracting Parties shall individually or jointly take all appropriate measures in accordance with the provisions of this Convention and those Protocols in force to which they are party to prevent, abate and combat pollution of the Mediterranean Sea area and to protect and enhance the marine environment in that area.'

6

Article 8 of the Convention provides:

'The Contracting Parties shall take all appropriate measures to prevent, abate and combat pollution of the Mediterranean Sea area caused by discharges from rivers, coastal establishments or outfalls, or emanating from any other land-based sources within their territories.'

7

Similarly, Article 1 of the Protocol provides that:

'The Contracting Parties . . . shall take all appropriate measure to prevent, abate, combat and control pollution of the Mediterranean Sea area caused by discharges from rivers, coastal establishments or outfalls, or emanating from any other land-based sources within their territories.'

8

Article 3 of the Protocol states:

'The area to which this Protocol applies (hereinafter referred to as the "Protocol Area") shall be:

. . .

(c) saltwater marshes communicating with the sea.'

9

Article 4(1)(a) provides that the Protocol is to apply to 'polluting discharges reaching the Protocol area from land-based sources within the territories of the Parties, in particular;

- directly, from outfalls discharging into the sea or through coastal disposal;

- indirectly, through rivers, canals or other watercourses, including underground watercourses, or through run-off'.

10

Under Article 6(1) and (3) of the Protocol:

1. The Parties shall strictly limit pollution from land-based sources in the Protocol Area by substances or sources listed in Annex II to this Protocol.

. . .

3. Discharges shall be strictly subject to the issue, by the competent national authorities, of an authorization taking due account of the provisions of Annex III.

11

Article 7(1) of the Protocol provides:

'The Parties shall progressively formulate and adopt, in co-operation with the competent international organizations, common guidelines and, as appropriate, standards or criteria dealing in particular with:

. . .

(e) specific requirements concerning the quantities of the substances listed in Annexes 1 and II discharged, their concentration in effluents and methods of discharging them.'

12

It is clear from paragraphs 11 and 13 of Section 1 of Annex II to the Protocol that the system laid down in Article 6 of the Protocol covers 'substances which have, directly or indirectly, an adverse effect on the oxygen content of the marine environment, especially those which may cause eutrophication' and 'substances which, though of a non-toxic nature, may become harmful to the marine environment or may interfere with any legitimate use of the sea owing to the quantities in which they are discharged'.

13

Section B of Annex II states:

'The control and strict limitation of the discharge of substances referred to in section A above must be implemented in accordance with Annex III.'

14

Annex III to the Protocol sets out the factors to be taken into account 'with a view to the issue of an authorization for the discharge of wastes containing substances referred to in Annex II . . .'. Contracting Party States must therefore take into account the 'characteristics and composition of the waste', the characteristics of waste constituents with respect to their harmfulness', the 'characteristics of discharge site and receiving marine environment', the 'availability of waste technologies' and, finally, the 'potential impairment of marine ecosystems and sea-water uses'.

15

Article 3(d) of the amended Protocol which corresponds to Article 3(c) of the Protocol, provides that the area to which the Protocol applies includes:

(d) Brackish waters, coastal salt waters including marshes and coastal lagoons, and ground waters communicating with the Mediterranean Sea'.

16

Article 6(1) of the amended Protocol provides:

'Point source discharges into the Protocol area, and releases into water or air that reach and may affect the Mediterranean area, as defined in Article 3(a), (c) and (d) of this Protocol, shall be strictly subject to authorization or regulation by the competent authorities of the Parties, taking due account of the provisions of this Protocol and Annex II thereto, as well as the relevant decisions or recommendations of the meetings of the Contracting Parties.'

The dispute in the main proceedings and the questions referred for a preliminary ruling

19

The Étang de Berre, located in France, is a saltwater marsh of 15 000 hectares which communicates directly with the Mediterranean Sea.

20

The Syndicat complained to EDF on several occasions of damage to the aquatic environment of the Étang de Berre, primarily as the result of fresh water from the Durance which is artificially discharged into the Étang whenever the turbines of the hydroelectric power station at Saint-Chamas are in operation.

21

On 1 September 1999, the Syndicat brought interlocutory proceedings against EDF before the Tribunal de grande instance de Marseille (Marseilles Regional Court) (France) alleging unlawful conduct and seeking an order that the hydroelectric power station at Saint-Chamas be shut down subject to a periodic penalty payment for non-compliance. In particular, the Syndicat claimed that EDF was discharging water from that power station without having obtained the prior authorization provided for in Article 6(3) of the Protocol.

22

The court hearing the application for interim measures at first instance dismissed it by order of 25 October 1999. While it acknowledged the disturbance caused by the operation of the hydroelectric power station's turbines, it took the view that:

'As regards the implementation of Community law, in particular the Barcelona Convention and the Athens Protocol . . . , the questions of their direct effect on individuals also raises issues which do not fall within the jurisdiction of the court adjudicating on the substance.

Since the question whether EDF's operation of the hydroelectric power station at Saint-Chamas constitutes a manifestly unlawful disturbance, that is to say, unlawful conduct within the meaning generally understood in the case-law, gives rise to issues which are too serious to allow the court hearing the application for interim measures to intervene and put an end to three decades of operations, such a decision being of great import in that it would have extremely serious consequences for, inter alia, production and the security of the region's electricity system . . .'

23

The Syndicat lodged an appeal against that judgment before the Cour d'appel (Court of Appeal) d'Aix-en-Provence (France), which dismissed the appeal by a judgment of 21 September 2000. The Cour d'appel took the view inter alia that 'the various Articles [of the Protocol] are interdependent' and that Article 6(3)' cannot be read in isolation, so that no authorization to discharge can legitimately and usefully be applied for by EDF on the basis of the Protocol as long as the French State has not defined the applicable technical criteria, since no response could be given'.

24

The Syndicat appealed on a point of law against that judgment, relying in particular on the infringement by EDF of Article 6(3) of the Protocol, application of which was wrongly ruled out by the Cour d' appel.

25

Under these conditions, the Cour de Cassation decided to stay the proceedings and refer the following two questions to the Court of Justice for a preliminary ruling:

    '1.   Must Article 6(3) of the Athens Protocol . . . , which has become Article 6(1) in the revised version, be held to have direct effect, so that any interested party my rely on it before the national courts in an action to halt discharges of water which are not authorized in accordance with the procedure and criteria which it prescribes?

2. Must the same provision be interpreted to mean that it prohibits the discharge into a saltwater marsh communicating with the Mediterranean Sea of substances which, although not toxic, adversely affect the oxygen content of the marine environment, without an authorization issued by the complement authorities of the Member States, taking into account the provisions of the abovementioned Protocol and of Annex III C thereto (now Annex II)?'

Direct effect of Articles 6(3) of the Protocol and 6(1) of the amended Protocol

Observations of the parties

31

EDF maintains that the various provisions of the Protocol are interdependent, making it impossible to recognize Article 6(3) as having direct effect even if it does lay down a clear and precise stipulation.

32

Article 6(1) of the Protocol sets the objective to 'strictly limit' pollution by substances or sources listed in Annex II (including substances which have an adverse effect on oxygen content). To that end, Article 6(2) requires that the parties implement 'jointly or individually', as appropriate, 'suitable programmes and measures'. Finally, Article 6(3) requires that discharges be subject to an 'authorization taking due account of the provisions of Annex III'. The obligation to 'take due account' is very vague and could, in the absence of details, lead to all discharges being subject to an authorization merely because they involve one of the substances listed in Annex II to the Protocol. That requirement, however, would be entirely disproportionate as regards the objective of the Protocol.

33

EDF also relies on Article 7(1) of the Protocol, concerning 'common . . . standards or criteria' to be formulated before an authorization system is put in place. However, those standards and criteria have not yet been defined for the discharges in question.

34

In addition, inasmuch as the Community is party to the Convention and to the Protocol, the standards to be laid down for their implementation may principally be at Community level. However, there is as yet no directive relating to discharges of fresh water and silt into a saltwater marsh.

35

The Syndicat, the French Government and the Commission for their part submit that Article 6(3) of the Protocol has direct effect, relying on the case-law of the Court (see inter alia Case 12/86 *Demirel* [1987] ECR 3719, paragraph 14).

36

Regard being had to its wording and to its purpose and nature, Article 6(3) of the Protocol contains a clear, precise and unconditional obligation to subject discharges of the substances covered by Annex II to the Protocol to the prior issue of an authorization is not subject, in its implementation or effects, to any reservation or to the adoption of any subsequent measure. In addition, Annex III to the Protocol, to which Article 6(3) refers, lists all the factors of which account must be taken with a view to the issue of an authorization.

37

According to the Commission, the absence of measures, programmes and guidelines adopted jointly does not have the effect of paralysing implementation of the Protocol or preventing the issue of discharge authorizations, but increases the discretion of the Member States in issuing those authorizations, the exercise of which is open to judicial review.

39

According to the settled case-law of the Court, a provision in an agreement concluded by the Community with a non-member country must be regarded as being directly applicable when, regard being had to its wording and to the purpose and nature of the agreement, the provision contains a clear and precise obligation which is not subject, in its implementation or effects, to the adoption of any subsequent measure (see inter alia *Demirel*, cited above, paragraph 14, and Case C-171/01 *Wählergruppe Gemeinsam* [2003] ECR 1-4301, paragraph 54).

40

In order to determine whether Article 6(3) of the Protocol satisfies those criteria, it is first necessary to examine its wording.

41

That provision clearly, precisely and unconditionally lays down the obligation for Member States to subject discharges of the substances listed in Annex II to the Protocol to the issue by the competent national authorities of an authorization taking due account of the provisions of Annex III.

42

As the Commission rightly points out, the fact that the national authorities have discretion in issuing authorizations under the criteria set out in Annex III in no way diminishes the clear, precise and unconditional nature of the prohibition on discharges without prior authorization that results from Article 6(3) of the Protocol.

43

That finding is supported by the purpose and nature of the Protocol.

44

It is clear from Articles 1 and 4 of the Protocol that its purpose is to prevent, abate, combat and eliminate pollution of the Mediterranean Sea area caused by discharges from rivers, coastal establishments or outfalls, or emanating from any other land-base sources within their territories. To that end, reiterating the undertakings given pursuant to Articles 4 and 8 of the Convention, Article 1 of the Protocol requires the Contracting Parties to take 'all appropriated measures'.

45

By establishing a system of prior authorization by the competent national authorities for the discharge of the substances listed in Annex II to the Protocol, Article 6(3) contributes to the elimination by Member States of pollution from land-based sources in the area covered by the Protocol. Recognition of the direct effect of the provision in question can only serve the purpose of the Protocol, as recalled above, and reflect the nature of the instrument, which is intended, *inter alia*, to prevent pollution resulting from the failure of public authorities to act.

46

The foregoing considerations also apply to the interpretation of Article 6(1) of the amended Protocol. The reference therein to 'the relevant decisions or recommendations of the meetings of the Contracting Parties', which the competent national authorities must take into account, does not call in question the clear, precise and unconditional nature of the prohibition on discharges without authorization. In addition, the amendments approved by Decision 1999/801 in no way alter the purpose or nature of the Protocol.

47

In the light of the foregoing, the answer to the first question must be that both Article 6(3) of the Protocol and Article 6(1) of the amended Protocol, following its entry into force, have direct effect, so that any interested party is entitled to rely on those provisions before the national courts.

Scope of Articles 6(3) of the Protocol and 6(1) of the amended Protocol

48

As the Syndicat, the French Government and the Commission have rightly observed, Annex III to the Protocol, referred to in Article 6(3) thereof, which lists the factors to be taken into account with a view to the issues of authorizations for the discharge of waste, itself refers to Annex II, which sets out the substances contained in the waste in question. These include, in paragraph 11, 'substances which have, directly or indirectly an adverse effect on the oxygen content of the marine environment, especially those which may cause eutrophication' and, in paragraph 13, 'substances which, though of a non-toxic nature, use of may become harmful to the marine environment or may interfere with any legitimate use of the sea owing to the quantities in which they are discharged'.

49

Paragraphs 11 and 13 clearly do not make the requirement of prior authorization for the discharge of the substances to which they refer conditional on their toxicity.

50

The conclusion must be the same as regards the scope of Article 6(1) of the amended Protocol.

51

Pursuant to that provision, it is all 'point source discharges into the Protocol Area [which includes, pursuant to Article 3(d) of the amended Protocol, marshes communicating with the Mediterranean Sea] and releases into water or air that reach and may affect the Mediterranean Area', and no longer merely discharges of the substances listed in Annex II to the Protocol, which will henceforth be 'strictly subject to authorization or regulation by the competent authorities', which are to take account *inter alia* of the provisions of the amended Protocol and of Annex II thereto.

52

In the light of the foregoing, the answer to the second question must be that both Article 6(3) of the Protocol and Article 6(1) of the amended Protocol must be interpreted as prohibiting, without an authorization issued by the national competent authorities, the discharge into a saltwater marsh communicating with the Mediterranean Sea of substances which, although not toxic, have an adverse effect on the oxygen content of the marine environment.

NOTES AND QUESTIONS

1. ***European Union Law.*** The European Union provides an important example of how international law may be enforces through the doctrine of direct effect of a treaty in domestic law. The European Union (EU) is, however, unique. The EU is a political and economic union of 28 states that is the result of a series of treaties going back to the 1950s. On December 1, 2009, the Treaty of Lisbon went into effect, consolidating these various treaties into a constitutional instrument titled the Treaty on the Functioning of the European Union (TFEU). The European Union has developed strong supra-national institutions, the Commission, which acts as an executive body, and a Council of Ministers and Parliament, which have the power to pass secondary legislation — called directives and regulations — and to approve treaties. Regulations and many treaties have direct effect in the national legal orders of the member states without the necessity of implementing legislation. The EU also has a powerful court, the European Court of Justice (officially named as of 2009, the Court of Justice of the European Union), which sits in Luxembourg. Note that it is compulsory under EU law for the highest court of a member state to refer a question of EU law (Community law) to the European Court of Justice. This ensures development of uniform law on the EU level.

2. ***Direct Effect.*** Outside of the EU, direct enforcement of MEAs or IEAs or of general international law is very rare. National courts will enforce national laws, and virtually all MEAs and IEAs are non-self-executing; they require implementation by enactment of a national law to become effective in the domestic legal order. Even when a treaty is transformed into national law, national courts will enforce not the treaty itself but the national law of implementation. Suppose, for example, the United States has ratified a regional seas convention to protect the Atlantic Ocean and has also approved a Protocol controlling pollution from land-based sources. If and environmental interest group brought suit in a U.S. District Court to directly enforce the Protocol, what would be the result? Comparing the ruling of a U.S. court to the ruling in the EDF case, which is better?

3. ***Effectiveness.*** Would you judge the Protocol that was the subject of the EDF case to be effective? Note that the parties to the Barcelona Convention and its Protocol include many Mediterranean states that are not EU members. Thus even with the EU doctrine of direct effect, this treaty regime may not be sufficient to attain its objectives. In addition, note that even with 100% implementation and compliance with the Barcelona Treaty regime, the Mediterranean may still be polluted if the regulations under this regime are too weak. States embracing international law norms can only achieve at most what they actually agree to do. Stronger action may be needed to solve the problem of pollution of the Mediterranean Sea. Treaties are only as effective as parties make them.

Section V. COMPLIANCE AND DISPUTE SETTLEMENT

Especially in the last 20 years there has been enormous attention and interest in the problem of compliance with respect to MEAs and IEAs. The 1992 United Nations Conference on Environment and Development in Rio de Janeiro highlighted the fact that MEAs needed better compliance mechanisms. Dispute settlement is also important to enforce compliance or to resolve a problem of interpretation that impedes compliance. The literature on compliance with international environmental law instruments is enormous. *See especially* EDITH BROWN WEISS & HAROLD K. JACOBSON, ENGAGING COUNTRIES: STRENGTHENING COMPLIANCE WITH INTERNATIONAL ENVIRONMENTAL ACCORDS (Cambridge, Mass.: MIT Press, 1999), which examines in detail compliance with five important international treaties and studies the compliance strategies of several important states. *See also*, Ronald B. Mitchell, *Compliance Theory: Compliance, Effectiveness and Behaviour Change in International Environmental Law*; Jorgen Wettestad, *Monitoring and Verification*; and Jan Klabbers, *Compliance Procedures*, all in DANIEL BODANSKY, JUTTA BRUNNEE, & ELLEN HEY (eds.), THE OXFORD HANDBOOK OF INTERNATIONAL ENVIRONMENTAL LAW at pages 893, 974, and 995, respectively (Oxford: Oxford University Press, 2007).

Compliance and dispute settlement are major themes throughout this book. Here we provide an overview and introduction. When we talk of compliance we tend to refer to the traditional adversarial approach to non-compliance — either sue the non-complying party to seek damages and a court order to comply or resort to self-help/countermeasures against the recalcitrant state. To be sure this is part of compliance even with respect to MEAs and IEAs. The breach of a treaty implicates the laws of state responsibility, which makes states liable for damages in some cases and permits even an international tribunal to order compliance. We cover this law of state responsibility in Chapter 3.

But very often when it comes to MEAs and IEAs, the adversarial approach is not the best way to deal with countries that fail to meet their treaty obligations. Very often what is needed is a pro-active, managerial approach that tries to head-off and prevent non-compliance. Preventing non-compliance requires a comprehensive system of (1) reporting of information pertinent to the issue of compliance; (2) verification of the reported information; and (3) assessment of progress toward compliance. The best response to an actual situation of non-compliance may be a non-adversarial, non-judicial, management approach that induces the party to come into compliance. Managerial, non-adversarial mechanisms are very common in MEAs and IEAs, particularly those which include developing countries. Some of the non-adversarial mechanisms to induce compliance include capacity-building, technical assistance, technology transfer, and financial assistance.

Dispute settlement is also handled distinctively in MEAs and IEAs. We have already seen several important examples of dispute settlement and we will see many more in the succeeding chapters of this book. First, although both the international Court of Justice and International Tribunal for the Law of the Sea have constituted special panels and procedures to hear environmental disputes, and the Permanent Court of Arbitration has adopted optional rules for the environmental disputes[60], there is no central international tribunal for international environmental law. We will see that the fragmented nature of international environmental law means that each treaty regime has its own dispute settlement procedure, and often there are radical differences between regimes. This disharmony may become important because a single dispute may implicate two or three MEA regimes as well

---

[60] Optional Rules for the Conciliation of Disputes Relating to the Environment and/or Natural Resources (2002)

as legal regimes in other areas such as international trade law. We have already seen one example of this, the swordfish dispute between the European Union and Chile. Because there are so many often competing, parallel legal regimes, each with its own institutions and norms, dispute settlement in international environmental law can be quite interesting.

Nevertheless, dispute settlement is becoming more important in international environmental law. We will see in the following materials that the earliest environmental treaties had no provision for dispute settlement, while many later treaties contain complex, comprehensive systems for dispute settlement. The reason for the complexity is that some state-parties negotiating such treaties resisted mandatory, comprehensive dispute settlement and accordingly introduced qualifying and exception clauses into the system. Examples of this that we will study include the innovative dispute settlement system of the United Nations Convention on the Law of the Sea, which we cover in Chapter 7, and the important dispute settlement provisions of the Protocol on Environmental Protection to the Antarctic Treaty (1991), which we will cover in the notes below.

We first analyze and compare some compliance and dispute settlement procedures contained in MEAs in the following document:

Compliance and Dispute Settlement Provisions in the WTO and in Multilateral Environmental Agreements The World Trade Organization Committee on Trade and Environment Note by the WTO and UNEP Secretariats
WT/CTE/191 (June 6, 2001)

[In the excerpt that follows we omit the discussion of compliance and dispute settlement in WTO trade agreements].

COMPLIANCE AND DISPUTE SETTLEMENT PROVISIONS IN MULTI-LATERAL ENVIRONMENTAL AGREEMENTS

A. GENERAL COMMENTS

4.   The obligations in MEAs have been tailored to reflect differing environmental, economic, social, institutional and technological factors. They may variously seek to regulate trade in a particular category of product (such as wildlife), to protect States from substances harmful to their domestic environment (such as hazardous waste), to protect global commons such as the ozone layer of the global climate system, or to address other environmental problems. From the point of view of MEAs, compliance and dispute settlement systems are determined primarily by the character of the underlying problems they each seek to address, as well as the conception, objective and approach of the particular MEA.

5.   MEAs contain specific obligations, some of which are procedural, such as the requirement to report, and others that are substantive, such as to cease or control an activity. These specific obligations are placed in a broad normative framework by the preambles, objectives and principles embodied in these treaties.

6. Most MEAs contain elaborated and flexible procedures to promote compliance, and for the avoidance of disputes. This reflects the nature of international cooperation in the environmental field, which seeks to enhance cooperation between countries in view of scientific uncertainty and the nature of commitments directed at achieving broad environmental objectives.

7. The focus of the MEAs is on procedures and mechanisms to assist Parties to remain in compliance and to avoid disputes, not on the use of provisions for the settlement of disputes. To date, none of the formal dispute settlement provisions in the MEAs discussed below have been invoked. The conception in designing MEA compliance and dispute settlement systems is based on the fact that non-compliance with MEAs affects the environment or the global commons, and that Parties to the MEAs are generally reluctant to challenge another Party when the evidence of direct injury is not apparent.

8. Instead of focusing on bilateral disputes, Parties to MEAs have explored innovative approaches to address the issue of compliance, with the objective of preventing non-compliance in advance, and of promoting compliance. It is recognized that in most case, when a State is in non-compliance, this is not because of a willful violation, but rather because of a lack of ability to comply. Therefore, the best way to address non-compliance is through the provision of assistance, rather than through punitive measures. This is particularly true when addressing compliance issues related to developing countries.

(a) Compliance

9. In the context of MEAs, compliance has several dimensions. First of all, compliance goes beyond implementation. Whereas implementation refers to measures that States take to make international treaties effective in their domestic law, compliance refers to whether States in fact adhere to the provisions of the treaties and to the implementing measures that they have instituted. Determining the extent of compliance is a matter of judgment that must be made on a case-by-case basis.

10. MEA procedures and mechanisms on compliance include a range of instruments, which can be divided into measures that serve to facilitate and assist Parties in complying with a Convention's provisions (for example, financial and technical assistance), and measures that address the situation in which the Parties are not in compliance with the provisions set out in the treaty, and which impose consequences as a last resort (for example, suspension of certain benefits).

11. MEA procedures and mechanisms on compliance are part of compliance systems that include both national and multilateral mechanisms. The examination of selected MEAs below (in Section II.B) demonstrates that MEAs contain a variety of compliance-related provisions. These include provisions that require Parties to report, notify and provide certain information; establish multilateral review mechanisms; provide financial and technical assistance; encourage the transfer of technology; establish differentiated responsibilities; and set up disincentives to address cases of non-compliance.

12. Obligations to report, notify and provide certain information are an important

measure to encourage compliance with MEA obligations. They promote the effective identification of problems, assist in the assessment of compliance, and hence encourage transparency. Reporting also enables parties to assess the particular effects of their measures, and therefore helps to evaluate progress towards meeting the objective of the MEA.

13.   MEAs often include provisions establishing multilateral mechanisms for the review, inspection, verification, and/or monitoring of efforts to implement and comply with treaty obligations. Some MEAs require their Conference of the Parties (COP), standing committees, or other subsidiary bodies to review and report on compliance-related issues. The Montreal Protocol on Substances that Deplete the Ozone Layer, for example, establishes an institutional mechanism for determining and responding to cases of alleged non-compliance. To promote compliance, these mechanisms may in some cases offer recommendations, or suggest other flexible and non-confrontational solutions, to help achieve the objectives of the MEA.

14.   To help Parties to move towards compliance, MEAs may include provisions establishing incentives to comply, such as financial and technical assistance. Mechanisms such as the Global Environment Facility and the Montreal Protocol Multilateral Fund, for example, have together disbursed over a billion dollars to assist developing countries in meeting their obligations under environmental agreements. Similarly, many MEAs establish mechanisms to provide Parties with technical assistance to prepare reports, develop national legislation, or identify and implement other measures to comply with treaty obligations.

15.   Technology transfer has also been identified as a measure to help promote compliance with MEA obligations. The United Nations Framework Convention on Climate Change, for example, notes that the extent to which developing countries parties will effectively implement their commitments will depend on the effective implementation of commitments in the treaty related to transfer of technology.

16.   Differentiated obligations for developing and least-developed countries, based on the notion of common but differentiated responsibility, are also included in the many MEAs. These may include grace periods, differentiated reporting require-ments, and other forms of flexibility allowing obligations to be implemented in accordance with national circumstances and development priorities and capabilities.

17.   Some MEAs also include measures that operate as disincentives to respond to cases in which Parties are not in compliance with treaty obligations. These measures include suspension of certain rights and privileges under the agreement and, in some MEAs, the use of trade-related measures. These measures are, however, used only rarely and are usually complemented with other efforts to promote compliance.

18.   An international mandate for the development of "mechanisms for promoting compliance" arose from the 1992 United Nations Conference on Environment and Development (UNCED), Agenda 21.[61] In February 2001, the 21st Governing Council of UNEP renewed and extended the organization's mandate to develop

---

[61] *Agenda 21*, Chapter 8, Section (e), para. 8.21.

guidelines on compliance and enforcement in MEAs.[62]

19.   The approach adopted in MEAs towards compliance has been characterized as a flexible one, allowing Parties to find a suitable response and choose a variety of solutions. In some cases, MEAs provide a role for civil society in these processes.[63] Furthermore, it has been considered to be a collective approach, rather than building upon the bilateral relationship between the non-complying State and the directly injured other State.

(b)   Dispute settlement

20.   While MEAs generally focus on promoting compliance, they may also include provisions for settling disputes, should they arise. As with provisions relating to compliance, dispute settlement systems differ according to the varying conception, objectives and approaches of individual MEAs. Generally, MEAs emphasize flexible, cooperative, consensus-building mechanisms, such as negotiations and mediation, to promote fulfillment of treaty obligations, rather than the use of more formal methods of dispute settlement.

21.   MEA dispute settlement provisions thus generally follow a progression including negotiations, good offices, mediation, conciliation, arbitration and judicial settlement. These different dispute settlement provisions can broadly be distinguished by their legal outcome: non-binding measures such as negotiation, consultation, mediation, enquiry and conciliation versus binding measures such as arbitration and judicial settlement.

22.   Negotiation and consultation are the first measures to be taken in most environmental agreements in the event that disputes arise concerning the interpretation or application of an agreement. These mechanisms allow for the exchange of views between Parties to a disagreement with the objective of finding a solution. These measures do not involve third State or institutions, but focus on solving the dispute between the Parties concerned.

23.   Some environmental agreements recommend mediation in order to facilitate cooperation between the Parties concerned. The role of the mediator is usually

---

[62] Decision 21/27 on Compliance and Enforcement of MEAs requests the Executive Director of UNEP to continue to prepare draft Guidelines for consideration at the seventh special session of the Governing Council in February 2002. A definition of compliance suggested by the UNEP Working Group on Compliance and Enforcement of Environmental Conventions is that: "compliance is the position of a Party with regard to its obligations under a MEA. It refers to whether Parties fulfill their commitments under international agreements." The two draft Guidelines (on *Options for Enhancing Compliance with MEAs*; and *for Effective National Enforcement, International Cooperation, and Coordination in Combating Violations of MEAs*) were reviewed by an Advisory Group of Experts on Compliance and Enforcement (Nairobi, 13–15 November 2000), and have been submitted to Governments, Conventions Secretariats and other relevant bodies for further review; the draft Guidelines will be further revised for consideration in the Working Group on Compliance and Enforcement.

[63] In the context of CITES, for example, non-governmental organizations play an important role in providing technical and scientific support to the Secretariat, the Parties and the various CITES Committees to ensure that the Convention is implemented successfully. The Stockholm Convention recognizes the important contribution that the private sector and NGOs can make to the objectives of the Convention to eliminate emissions and discharges of persistent organic pollutants.

assigned to another Party to the agreement, the Secretariat or a specific Committee of the Convention. For example, the Montreal Protocol and the Convention on Biological Diversity state that if the Parties concerned cannot reach agreement by negotiation, they may jointly seek the good offices of, or request mediation by, a third Party. Rather than providing for mediation as a second step after negotiation has failed, some MEAs provide mediation as an alternative choice.[64]

24.   Most MEAs contain provisions for conciliation. Conciliation often combines elements of fact-finding and mediation. The provisions regarding conciliation differ in their nature. While many MEAs only provide for voluntary conciliation, some of them include mandatory conciliation (e.g. the Vienna Convention and the Convention on Biodiversity). In addition, most MEAs provide for the establishment of a "Conciliation Commission" to settle disputes.[65] Commissions may make proposals for the resolution of the dispute, which the Parties concerned in the dispute shall consider in good faith. Conciliation procedures, whose main objectives are to establish the facts of the dispute, do not lead to binding decisions.

25.   As a last resort, MEAs often include the possibility of resorting to arbitration and/or submission of the dispute to the International Court of Justice (ICJ). The circumstances under which a Party can resort to arbitration or to the ICJ vary between MEAs. Some MEAs entitle Parties to submit a declaration accepting compulsory dispute settlement through submission to the ICJ and/or arbitration. Other MEAs also explicitly mention the possibility that the Parties to a dispute can mutually agree on arbitration or submission to the ICJ.

26.   As noted above, the use of formal dispute settlement mechanisms in MEAs to resolve disputes is rare. This reflects the nature of environmental problems, which are often multilateral rather than bilateral in nature. It also reflects the emphasis in MEAs on measures to assist Parties to remain in compliance, and to address cases of non-compliance through multilateral reviews, recommendations by various treaty bodies, technical and financial assistance, and other forms of international cooperation.

B.   COMPLIANCE AND DISPUTE SETTLEMENT PROVISIONS IN SELECTED MULTILATERAL ENVIRONMENTAL AGREEMENTS

1.   International Commission for the Conservation of Atlantic Tunas (ICCAT)

(a)   Compliance Provisions

27.   The International Commission for the Conservation of Atlantic Tunas provides for various measures to ensure compliance. According to Article IX:I of ICCAT, the Contracting Parties agree to submit to periodic statements of action. Further, the Parties are required to collaborate with each other with a view to the adoption of suitable effective measures to ensure application of ICCAT provisions and, in

---

[64] See for example the Rotterdam and Stockholm Conventions.

[65] See for example, the Convention on Biological Diversity, the Montreal Protocol, the Cartagena Protocol, the UNFCCC, the Rotterdam Convention, and the Stockholm Convention.

particular, to set up a system of international enforcement to be applied to the Convention area in which a State is entitled under International law to exercise jurisdiction over fisheries.[66] Additionally, the Parties have adopted recommendations pursuant to the Bluefin Tuna Resolution[67] and the Swordfish Action Plan Resolution[68] for compliance measures.

(b)   Dispute settlement provision

28.   The International Commission for the Conservation of Atlantic Tunas does not contain any provisions concerning dispute settlement.

2.   Convention on International Trade in Endangered Species of Wild Fauna and Flora (CITES)

(a)   Compliance provisions

29.   The compliance system of CITES is established in treaty text and subsequent Resolutions and Decisions of the COP, as well as by various notifications to the Parties, reports of the Secretariat and the activities of the Convention's subsidiary bodies. CITES was one of the first MEAs to include an extensive information system and reporting requirements. This system has been further developed in a CITES Resolution as well as in different guidelines.[69] CITES Parties are, for example, required to maintain trade records and to prepare periodic reports on their implementation.[70] Information provided for the Parties through annual reports is processed in a database maintained by UNEP and the World Conservation Monitoring Centre (WCMC). The CITES Secretariat also compiles a Report on Alleged Infractions for the COP to assist Parties in gathering information on certain violations or problem with compliance.[71]

30.   The CITES also includes a number of multilateral processes to review and monitor compliance with the agreement. In practice, monitoring is carried out by the Animals and Plant Committee[72] and by the CITES Secretariat. Some NGOs have elaborated a trade monitoring programme such as TRAFFIC (the Trade Records Analysis of Flora and Fauna in Commerce), which provides technical and scientific support to the Secretariat, the Parties and the various CITES Committees to ensure that the Convention is implemented successfully.

31.   This system is complemented by a Standing Committee that was established

---

[66] Article IX.3 of ICCAT.

[67] Resolution by ICCAT Concerning an Action Plan to Ensure Effectiveness of the Conservation Program for Atlantic Bluefin Tuna, 2 October, 1995.

[68] Resolution by ICCAT Concerning an Action Plan to Ensure Effectiveness of the Conservation Program for Atlantic Swordfish, June 22, 1996.

[69] See for example, Resolution 11.17.

[70] Article VIII.7 of CITES

[71] Decision 11.137.

[72] Resolution Conf. 11.1.

at the Sixth and Ninth COP.[73] It consists of Parties that are elected from each of the six geographic regions. The Committee assesses cases of lack of compliance or implementation that are reported to it by the Secretariat. Based upon these reports, the Committee makes non-binding recommendations to the Parties.[74] The Standing Committee meets regularly to discuss a range of issues related to the Convention, and sometimes the CITES Secretariat brings before it information on illicit trade problems. It is the COP, however, that takes decisions on infractions of CITES provisions.

32.   When the CITES Secretariat receives information that a species listed in Appendix I or II is being adversely affected by trade, or that the provisions of the Convention are not being effectively implemented, it communicates that information to the designated management authority of the Party or Parties concerned.[75] When a Party to CITES receives this communication it shall inform the Secretariat of any relevant facts and, where appropriate, propose remedial action. An important tool for receiving information is also the possibility of in-country inspection. Where a Party considers an inquiry to be desirable, such inquiry shall be carried out by person authorized by the Party. The information provided by the Party, or by the inquiry, shall be reviewed at the next COP, which may make any recommendation it deems appropriate.[76]

33.   For the past 15 years, CITES decisions of the Parties and Standing Committee have been used to recommend in a non-binding way the suspension of trade with countries that fail to comply, after prior warning, with the provisions of the Convention.[77] The criteria for recommending a suspension of trade are the presence of significant trade and the absence of domestic measures to enforce the CITES provisions as required by Article VIII. According to information provided by the CITES Secretariat, the practice of recommending trade sanctions has worked well in obtaining the enactment of national legislation related to the Convention and the submission of required reports. The possibility of a recommendation to suspend trade often draws high-level political attention to CITES issues and results in action being taken quickly to enact legislation, develop work plans, control legal/illegal trade, or improve the basis for government decision-making.

34.   Parties can request and receive assistance from the CITES Secretariat at any time to enact appropriate legislation or prepare required reports. Once compliance has been obtained, the relevant trade suspension recommendation is withdrawn. Generally, the practice of applying recommendations to suspend trade in order to bring about compliance with the Convention has never been challenged. A proposed decision by the Parties would extend trade suspension recommendations to those countries that fail to submit annual national reports, as required by Article VIII.7(a), for three consecutive years.

---

[73] *Ibid.*

[74] Establishment of the Standing Committee of the Conference of the Parties, Resolution of the Parties Conf 9.1., Annex I.

[75] Article XIII.I of CITES.

[76] *Ibid.*, Article XIII.2.

[77] General trade suspension recommendations have been made against El Salvador, Italy, Greece, Grenada, Guyana, Senegal and Thailand. Strict shipment controls have been recommended for Bolivia.

35.   The CITES compliance review process is formal in that it stems from the Convention text itself (Articles VIII, XI and XIII) as well as from Resolutions and Decisions of the Parties. Article VIII.I requires Parties to take appropriate measures to enforce the provisions of the Convention and to prohibit trade in violation thereof. This has been interpreted as a requirement for adequate legislation. Article VIII.7 requires the submission of annual biennial reports. Pursuant to Article XI.3, the COP shall review the implementation of the Convention at its meetings and, where appropriated, make recommendations for improving the effectiveness of the Convention. Under Article XIII and based on information provided by the Secretariat that (a) an Appendix I or II species is being affected adversely by trade, or (b) the provisions of the Convention are not being effectively implemented, the Conference of the Parties or the Standing Committee may make whatever recommendations it deems appropriate (e.g., that trade in CITES-listed species should be suspended with a particular Party). The National Legislation Project (Resolution Conf. 8.4), Significant Trade Review process (Resolution Conf. 8.9), Infraction Report to COP (Decision 11.137) and, most recently, annual report requirement (Resolution Conf. 11.17 and Decision 11.37) have a link to decisions of the COP or Standing Committee to recommend the suspension of trade.

36.   The Secretariat's principal reports on the National Legislation Project and Alleged Infractions and Other Problems of Implementation of the Convention are not submitted to the Standing Committee (although it will commonly receive reports of an interim nature on those subjects), but to meetings of the Conference of the Parties. The information contained within those reports may lead the COP to take a decision, usually by consensus and, in any case by a two-thirds majority, to recommend that Parties not trade with a particular country.

37.   The above is a vital point: it is the Parties themselves who agree to such a recommendation. Such decisions by the COP are very often tempered with a period of grace, within which the Party potentially subject to a recommendation for cessation of trade will be expected to rectify the implementation problem. In the vast majority of cases, this will be a period of time during which the Party will be expected to enact new and stronger domestic legislation. The Standing Committee becomes involved in the process by being tasked with hearing from the Secretariat whether the relevant Party has complied or not. If it has not, the COP's recommendation for a cessation of trade will take effect. If it has complied, the Standing Committee will confirm such compliance and the cessation of trade recommendation is not put into effect. The legal basis for such measures is contained within Article XIII of the Convention. That article also makes clear the authority of, and the process by which, the Secretariat will conduct its work to identify species being adversely affected by trade and problems of implementation of the Convention.

38.   It might also be worthy of note that CITES benefits from the Interpol Working Group on Wildlife Crime and the World Customs Organization/CITES Working Group, both of which act as semi-formal (in that they have not been allocated this task by the COP, although it has stressed the importance of liaison with ICPO and WCO) review bodies that spend considerable time in examining enforcement, compliance and implementation of the Convention. Parties to CITES also benefit from the capacity building activities of both groups. CITES has also

made use of the work done by the National Police Agency of the Netherlands, described in Notification to the Parties No. 1999/13, which reviewed reports on Alleged Infractions and Other Problems of Implementation of the Convention. The report covered aspects of the reporting process, implementation review, compliance review and effectiveness review.

39.   CITES foresees a Trust Fund and other measures to facilitate compliance. Capacity building has been financially strengthened at the last COP.

(b) Dispute settlement provisions

40.   Any dispute which could arise between two or more Parties with respect to the interpretation or application of CITES provisions is subject to negotiation between the Parties involved in the dispute.[78] If the dispute cannot be resolved in this manner, the Parties may, by mutual consent, submit the dispute to arbitration, in particular that of the Permanent Court of Arbitration at the Hague.[79] In this case, the Parties submitting the dispute shall be bound by arbitral decision.

3.   Convention for the Conservation of Antarctic Marine Living Resources (CCAMLR)

(a)   Compliance provisions

41.   Under CCAMLR, Parties have to take appropriate measures within their competence to ensure compliance with the provisions of the Convention, and with conservation measures adopted by the Commission for the Conservation of Antarctic Marine Living Resources (the "Commission"), to which the Party is bound in accordance with Article IX.[80] The Commission has been established in accordance with Article VII of the Convention and it draws the attention of all Parties to any activity which, in the opinion of the Commission, may affect the implementation by another Party or divert from the objectives of, or compliance with, the Convention.[81]

42.   CCAMLR also sets up certain notification and reporting elements. Parties are required to report regularly to the Commission on measures that have been taken to ensure compliance with CCAMLR provisions, including the imposition of sanctions for any violation, as well as on steps taken to implement the conservation measures adopted by the Commission.[82] Parties undertake to exert appropriate efforts, consistent with the Charter of the United Nations, to the end that no one engages in any activity contrary to the objective of the Convention, and have to inform the Commission of any such activity which come to their attention.[83] The

---

[78] Article XVIII.I of CITES.

[79] *Ibid.*, Article XIII.2.

[80] Article XXI.I of CCAMLR

[81] *Ibid.*, Article X.2.

[82] *Ibid.*, Articles XX.3 and XXL

[83] *Ibid.*, Article XXII.

Commission publishes and maintains a record of all the measures reported to it.

43.   In addition, compliance is also subject to a CCAMLR inspection process, which has been in place since 1989. To this end, the Commission has established the Standing Committee on Observation and Inspection (SCOI), which considers and prepares advice to the Commission on matters related to inspection and on compliance measures that are taken.

44.   In order to prevent non-compliance, the Convention states that a non-Contracting Party vessel which has been sighted engaging in fishing activities in Convention Area is presumed to be undermining the effectiveness of CCAMLR conservation measures. Information regarding such sightings shall be transmitted immediately to the Commission. Moreover, when a non-contracting party vessel enters a port of any Contracting Party, it shall be inspected by any authorized Contracting Party official who is knowledgeable about CCAMLR conservation measures, and shall not be allowed to land or transship any fish until this inspection has taken place.[84]

45.   To verify compliance with conservation measures, CCAMLR inspectors, designated by the Parties, regularly conduct inspections of fishing and research vessels of CCAMLR flag States in the Convention Area. The inspection reports are submitted to the Commission, which forwards them to the flag States of the vessels inspected. Flag States are required to report to the Commission on prosecutions and sanctions imposed as a consequence of the inspection of their vessels. The Commission has established the SCOI, which considers and prepares advice to the Commission on all matters related to inspections undertaken and steps taken by Members to enforce compliance with the Convention's conservation measures.

46.   In addition, a Contracting Party may only issue a licence to fish in the Convention Area to vessels flying its flag, if it is satisfied with its ability to exercise its responsibilities under the Convention and its conservation measures. Each Party shall verify, through inspections, compliance with the licence conditions. In the event that there is evidence that the vessel has not fished in accordance with the conditions of its licence, the Contracting Party shall investigate the infringement and, if necessary apply appropriate sanctions in accordance with its national legislation.[85]

(b)   Dispute settlement provisions

47.   Any dispute that could arise between two or more Contracting Parties concerning the interpretation or application of CCAMLR is subject to consultations among those Parties. The Parties can choose between negotiation, enquiry, mediation, conciliation, arbitration, judicial settlement or other peaceful means to resolve the dispute.[86] With the consent of all Parties to the dispute, an unresolved dispute can be referred to the ICJ or to arbitration for settlement; but failure to reach responsibility for continuing to seek to resolve it by other peaceful means. In

---

[84] Conservation Measure 1188/XVII.

[85] Conservation Measure 119/XVII.

[86] Article XXV of CCAMLR.

cases where the dispute is referred to arbitration, the arbitral tribunal shall be constituted as provided in the Annex for an arbitral tribunal to CCAMLR.

4.   The Montreal Protocol on Substances that Deplete the Ozone Layer

(a)   Compliance provisions

48. The Montreal Protocol is an example of a long-standing and developed formal compliance mechanism. It foresees various reporting and review procedures, according to which the Parties are required to provide the Secretariat with certain data on their production, imports and exports of controlled substances.[87]

49.   Article 8 of the Montreal Protocol requires the Parties to establish procedures and institutional mechanisms for determining non-compliance with the Protocol, and for treatment of Parties found to be in non-compliance. This led to the establishment of an Implementation Committee in 1990.[88] The Committee consists of ten Parties elected for two years and oversees compliance. Complaints brought before the Implementation Committee may be initiated by any Party to the Protocol that suspects another Party of non-compliance or by self-reporting by a Party defaulting on its obligations, as well as by the Secretariat. The functions of the Committee are to receive, consider and report on any submission made by one or more Parties and any information or observation forwarded by the Secretariat in connection with the preparation of the report referred to in Article 12 of the Montreal Protocol. The Implementation Committee may collect information relating to a Party's compliance in its territory, but only if the Party concerned has requested it to do so.[89] The Committee has no power to make direct recommendations to a Party, but it can make certain recommendations to the Meeting of the Parties to adopt a decision calling for steps to bring about full compliance with the Protocol, including measures to assist a Party's compliance and to further the Protocol's objectives.

50.   The Fourth Meeting of the Parties adopted an indicative list of measures that might be taken by the Meeting of the Parties in respect to non-compliance with the Protocol. The Implementation Committee has the competence to determine the facts and possible causes of non-compliance.[90] If a finding of non-compliance is entered against a Party, the Montreal Protocol provides a number of mechanisms that are available to bring the Party back into compliance. These mechanisms include appropriate assistance, including technical and financial assistance, issuing of cautions and suspensions in accordance with the applicable rules of international

---

[87] Article 7 of the Montreal Protocol.

[88] In 1990, the Second Meeting of the Parties adopted non-compliance procedures in Annex III to the Protocol and established an Implementation Committee.

[89] Report on the work of the *ad hoc* Working Group of Legal and Technical Experts on Non-Compliance with the Montreal Protocol, Appendix 7(e), UNEP/OzL.Pro/WG.4/1/3 (1998), adopted in the Report of the Tenth Meeting of the Parties to the Montreal Protocol, UNEP/OzL.Prol.10/9 (1998).

[90] Report of the Tenth Meeting of the Parties to the Montreal Protocol, UNEP/OxLPro/10/9 (1998).

law concerning suspension of the operation of a treaty[91], of specific rights and privileges under the Protocol, whether or not subject to time limits, including those concerned with industrial rationalization, production, consumption, trade[92] and transfer of technology, financial mechanisms and institutional arrangements.[93]

51.   In addition, there exists a Multilateral Fund, contributed to by developed country Parties, to meet the agreed incremental costs of developing countries implementing the control measures of the Protocol. The Multilateral Fund operates under the authority of an Executive Committee and relies upon implementing agencies (e.g., UNEP, UNDP, UNIDO and the World Bank) to carry out the projects that it funds.[94] To date, this fund has disbursed US$1.25 billion in funds for projects aimed at phasing out the use of ozone-depleting technologies and substances in developing countries, while the Global Environment Facility (GEF) has disbursed about US$160 million for a similar purpose to the countries with economies in transition, mainly in Eastern Europe.

(b)   Dispute settlement provisions

52.   The dispute settlement procedures of the Montreal Protocol, which are found in the Vienna Convention for the Protection of the Ozone Layer, have become the prototype for the recent elaboration of provisions through which to resolve disputes in MEAs. The Protocol's flexible, multi-track hierarchy of procedures allows a Party to select the procedural or institutional mechanisms that best conform to its interests.

53.   The procedures for dispute settlement under the Montreal Protocol are provided for in Article 11 of the Vienna Convention for the Protection of the Ozone Layer. In the event of a dispute between Parties concerning interpretation of application of the Protocol, the involved Parties are to seek solution by negotiation. If the Parties concerned cannot reach agreement by negotiation, they may jointly seek good offices of, or request mediation by, a third Party.[95] For those disputes not resolved in accordance with either Article 11.1 or Article 11.2 of the Vienna Convention, a Party may declare that it accepts one or both of the following means of dispute settlement as compulsory: (1) arbitration in accordance with procedures adopted by the Conference of the Parties at its first meeting; and/or (2) submission of the dispute to the ICJ. However, if the Parties have not accepted the same or any procedure, the dispute shall be submitted to a Conciliation Commission which is created at the request of one of the Parties to the dispute. The Commission shall be composed of an equal number appointed by each Party concerned and a Chair chosen jointly by the Members appointed by each Party. It shall render a final and recommendatory award, which the Parties shall consider in good faith.[96]

---

[91]   See Articles 60-64 of the Vienna Convention on the Law of Treaties.

[92]   For example, Russia and the Ukraine have been subjected to trade measures.

[93]   Report of the Fourth Meeting of the Parties to the Montreal Protocol, Annex V.

[94]   Jacob Werksman, "Compliance and Transition: Russia's Non-Compliance Tests the Ozone Regime," *Zeitschrift für Ausländisches Recht und Völkerrecht* (1996), p. 18.

[95]   Article 11.2 of the Vienna Convention on the Law of Treaties.

[96]   *Ibid.*, Article 11.5.

5. Basel Convention on the Control of Transboundary Movements of Hazardous Wastes and their Disposal

(a)   Compliance provisions

54.   The Basel Convention provides for notification, reporting and verification. Parties have to transmit a report to the COP containing information on implementation measures and other relevant information.[97]

55.   According to Article 19 of the Basel Convention, a Party that has reason to believe that another Party is acting or has acted in breach of its treaty obligations may inform the Secretariat thereof and shall simultaneously and immediately inform directly, or through the Secretariat, the Party against whom the allegations are made. The Secretariat has to submit all relevant information to the Parties. The Parties are required to employ appropriate means to cooperate in order to assist developing countries in the implementation of certain provisions.[98]

56.   As there are not yet any provisions that specify what happens after such verification has been made, the Parties are working towards developing a compliance mechanism. In June 1998, the Sub-Group of Legal and Technical Experts indentified some principles for a regime for monitoring implementation of and compliance with the Convention.[99] This led to the mandate of the Legal Working Group to constitute a compliance mechanism to be administered by a body to monitor implementation and compliance and that shall recommend effective ways to promote implementation and compliance. The mechanism shall be non-confrontational, transparent, cost-effective, preventative in nature, as well as flexible. Further, the conclusion was reached that the regime would be established through a decision of the Conference of the Parties rather than through an amendment of the Convention itself.[100]

(b)   Dispute settlement provisions

57.   Article 20 sets out the scope of dispute settlement under the Basel Convention, which apply to a dispute concerning interpretation, application, or compliance with the Basel Convention. Parties shall see the settlement of the dispute through negotiation or any other peaceful means of their own choice. If this is not successful and if the Parties agree, the dispute is to be submitted to: (1) the ICJ; or (2) arbitration in accordance with the provisions outlined in Annex VI of the Convention. Upon ratification, or at any time thereafter, a State may declare that it recognizes as compulsory, and in relation to any Party accepting the same obligation, submission of the dispute to either the ICJ or arbitration. Failure to reach common agreement as to whether to submit the dispute the ICJ or to

---

[97] Article 13.3 of the Basel Convention

[98] *Ibid.*, Article 10.3.

[99] Report of the Consultative Sub-Group of Legal and Technical Experts on the Work of its Third Session, 24 June 1998, UNEP/CHW/LSG/3/5.

[100] *Ibid.*

arbitration does not absolve the Parties from the responsibility of continuing to seek resolution through negotiation.

58.   The arbitration provisions of the Basel Convention are outlined in its Annex VI. The tribunal is to draw up its own rule of procedure and render its decision in accordance with international law and with the provisions of the Convention. It may take all appropriate measures to establish the facts of the dispute and shall render a decision within a specified time-limit. The award of the arbitral tribunal shall be accompanied by a statement of reason and be final and binding on the Parties to the dispute.

6.   Convention on Biological Diversity (CBD)

(a)   Compliance provisions

59. The Convention on Biological Diversity does not have a formal compliance procedure; there is no formal assessment of the compliance of Parties or non-parties. Article 26 requires Parties to present to the COP reports on measures which they have taken to implement the Convention's provisions and their effectiveness in meeting its objectives. Financial assistance, including through a financial mechanism, is provided for in Articles 20, 221 and 39 of the Convention on Biological Diversity.

(b)   Dispute settlement provisions

60.   The dispute settlement provisions of the Convention on Biological Diversity are set out in Article 27. In the event of a dispute between contracting Parties concerning the interpretation or application of the Convention, the Parties shall seek solution by negotiation. If they are unable to reach agreement by negotiation, they may jointly seek the good offices of, or request mediation by, a third Party.[101] A Party can also make a written declaration to the depositary accepting a compulsory dispute resolution by arbitration, by the ICJ or both, when negotiation or mediation have failed. Either of these judicial procedures is intended to lead to a binding decision. The procedures for arbitration are set out in Part I of Annex II to the CBD.

61.   In the event of a conflict between two Parties, the arbitral provisions provide for the standard three-member Panel, as described under the Montreal Protocol and the Basel Convention. If more Parties are involved, Parties having the same interest are to nominate a common arbitrator. If the dispute is taken to the ICJ, the Statutes of the ICJ apply to the procedures. If the dispute is not submitted themselves to binding settlement through adequate declarations, the dispute must be submitted to conciliation. Conciliation does not lead to a binding decision, unless the Parties agree otherwise, but the proposals for resolution of the dispute must be considered in good faith. The procedures for the five-member Conciliation Commission are set out in Part 2 of Annex II to the CBD.

---

[101] Article 27.2 of the CBD.

NOTES AND QUESTIONS

1. ***Evaluating compliance and dispute settlement procedures.*** What is the worth of the compliance and dispute settlement procedures in the various MEAs in the reading above? Are there common elements in the compliance provisions discussed? Of the various mechanisms, which in your opinion is the best? Which are the most deficient?

2. ***Varieties of dispute settlement.*** There are many forms of dispute settlement: negotiation; good offices; mediation; conciliation and fact finding; expert determination; arbitration, which can be either binding or non-binding; and litigation. With respect to litigation, international law offers several different tribunals. We will see international environmental litigation in the international Appellate Body of the World Trade Organization.

3. ***Varieties of disputes.*** The character of disputes that may arise in international environmental law varies endlessly. For example, a dispute arising under the United Nations Convention on Biological Diversity may involve such matters as patents, genetic resources, traditional knowledge and technology, plant or animal varieties, the environment broadly speaking, and food production.

PROBLEM 2-1
NEGOTIATING A COMPLIANCE REGIME FOR THE NAGOYA PROTOCOL

The Nagoya Protocol on Access to Genetic Resources and the Fair and Equitable Sharing of Benefits Arising from Their Utilization is a protocol to the Convention on Biologically Diversity (CBD) negotiated by the parties to the CBD in 2011. The Nagoya Protocol responds to one of the key objectives of the CBD, which was to foster the "fair and equitable sharing of benefits arising from the utilization of genetic resources." The conservation idea underlying the Nagoya Protocol is that by promoting the use of genetic resources and associated traditional knowledge and by strengthening the opportunities for fair and equitable sharing of benefits from their use, incentives will be created to conserve biological diversity. Accordingly the Nagoya Protocol obliges each party to take legislative, administrative or policy action to ensure fair and equitable benefit-sharing (Art. 5). To implement this obligation, parties are required to enact laws ensuring that access to genetic resources within their territories will be subject to securing prior informed consent (PIC) on mutually agreed terms (MAT) from local and indigenous communities (Art. 15, 16, and 18). Parties are required to set up administrative authorities and checkpoints to ensure that PIC and MAT are observed (Art. 17). An internationally recognized "certificate of compliance" shall serve as evidence that the genetic resource to which it is attached has been accessed in accordance with PIC and MAT (Art. 17.3). Article 30 of the Nagoya Protocol provides that "institutional measures to promote compliance . . . and to address non-compliance" will be developed by the parties.

The CBD regime is accepted by 193 parties, but not the United States. Suppose you attend the meeting at which the compliance regime is to be negotiated; what kind of compliance regime would you support?

1. Should the compliance regime contain provisions relating to individuals and private company compliance with Articles 15–18, or only provisions relating to the parties' compliance?

2. What variety of compliance institution is appropriate? Should indigenous and local communities have a right to membership on a compliance institution?

3. Should compliance procedures be non-adversarial and non-judicial?

4. Should the compliance procedure be binding or advisory in nature?

5. Should compliance be connected to dispute settlement?

How would your views on these issues vary if you were a representative from Switzerland? From Malaysia? From Brazil? From Tanzania? From China?

PROBLEM 2-2
STOPPING JAPAN FROM KILLING WHALES

Japan and Australia as well as 57 other states (including the United States) are members of the International Whaling Commission (IWC) as parties to the International Convention for the Regulation of Whaling (ICRW) (1946). Article VIII of the Convention states that

> Notwithstanding anything contained in this Convention any Contracting Party may grant to any of its nationals a special permit authorizing that national to kill, take and treat whales for purposes of scientific research subject to such restrictions as to number and subject as the Contracting Government sees fit, and the killing, taking and treating of whales shall be exempt from the operation of this Convention.

In 1985, the IWC voted to impose zero catch limits on commercial whaling, enacting a moratorium on all commercial whaling. In addition, the IWC approved an Indian Ocean Sanctuary and a Southern Ocean Sanctuary within which all commercial whaling is prohibited.

Japan, which initially objected to the moratorium, withdrew its objection in 1987, and announced the Japan Whale Research Program under Special Permit in the Antarctic (JARPA). JARPA was continued until the 2004/05 whaling season, taking from 300 to 400 minke whales in the Southern Ocean each year. In 2005, Japan announced the second phase of its whale research program, JARPA II.

Australia has objected every year to Japan's JARPA program within and outside the IWC meetings and has repeatedly urged Japan to cease its lethal research on whales. The IWC has passed resolutions demanding that Japan suspend its lethal research in favor of non-lethal research methods. There is also abundant evidence that the "research" conducted by Japan is minimal, and whale meat is sold commercially in Japan. Japan has refused to alter JARPA II, and on May 28, 2010, the Government of Australia announced its intention to file suit against Japan in an international tribunal.

Where did Australia file suit against Japan? Australia had at least three choices in the matter even without Japan's consent to be sued. First, why did Australia not file suit against Japan under the ICRW? A problem may be that the ICRW, like many early environmental treaties, has no provision for dispute settlement. Second, both Japan and Australia are parties to the United Nations Convention on the Law of the Sea (UNCLOS). Australia could have filed suit against Japan in the International Tribunal for the Law of the Sea (ITLOS). But Australia and New Zealand had previously filed suit against Japan in ITLOS alleging breach of certain articles of UNCLOS with regard to Japan's overfishing of Southern Bluefin Tuna, and the ITLOS tribunal declined jurisdiction because the matter of conservation of tuna was within the mandate of the Commission for the Conservation of Southern Bluefin Tuna under a 1993 treaty. *See Southern Bluefin Tuna (Australia and New Zealand v. Japan)*, International Tribunal for the Law of the Sea, 39 I.L.M. 1359 (2000). Third, both Australia and Japan have accepted the compulsory jurisdiction of the International Court of Justice under the "optional" clause, Article 36(2) of the Court's Statute. In the event, Australia chose option 3, the ICJ. Was this the best choice?

We return to consideration of this problem in Chapter 7.

Chapter 3

STATE ENVIRONMENTAL RESPONSIBILITY AND TRANSBOUNDARY HARM

Section I. INTRODUCTION

International Environmental Law originated out of the need to formulate rules of conduct in cases of transboundary pollution. Until the twentieth century, no rules of law existed that obliged state or private entities to prevent or pay damages in cases of transboundary environmental harm. Any payment, if made, was considered *ex gratia*, since the polluting activities giving rise to the harm were completely lawful. The case that sparked change to fill this legal vacuum was the *Trail Smelter Arbitration* between the United States and Canada that arose because of sulphur dioxide emissions from a smelter located in Trail, British Columbia, just across the Canadian border from the state of Washington in the United States. We read the report of the arbitral tribunal in the *Trail Smelter Case* below in this chapter.

The *Trail Smelter Case* can be compared with the so-called Harmon Doctrine that emphasizes state sovereignty over natural resources. In the nineteenth century Mexico complained to the United States that ranchers and farmers were diverting the waters of the Rio Grande River to such an extent that downstream Mexican communities were being "annihilated." Letter from Minister Matias Romero, October 12, 1894, reprinted in Foreign Relations of the United States 395 (1894). At the request of the U.S. Secretary of State, Richard Olney, the Mexican claim to waters of the Rio Grande was referred to U.S. Attorney General Judson Harmon for a formal legal opinion. Harmon, relying on Chief Justice John Marshall's dictum in *Schooner Exchange v. McFaddon*, 11 U.S. 116, 136 (1812), that the jurisdiction of every nation within its own territory is necessarily exclusive and absolute, stated that "[t]he fundamental principle of international law is the absolute sovereignty of every nation, as against all others, within its own territory." While considerations of "comity" may lead to a different result, "the rules, principles, and precedents of international law impose no liability or obligation upon the United States." Opinion of Attorney General Harmon, 21 Op. Atty Gen. 274, 281–83 (1895).

The issue of transboundary pollution was addressed at the Stockholm Conference of 1972 and at the Rio de Janeiro/UNCED meeting in 1992. As we have seen, Stockholm Principle 21, which was formulated as Rio Principle 2, declares that states have "responsibility to ensure that activities within their jurisdiction or control do not cause damage to the environment of other states or to areas beyond the limits of national jurisdiction." This formulation, known as the Harm Prevention Principle, extends the duty to prevent harm to areas beyond the limits of national jurisdiction, the oceans and outer space. The Harm Prevention Principle is derived from the Trail Smelter Arbitration and similar cases. Standing behind the Harm

Prevention Principle is a concept drawn from civil law — the Roman law — tradition: the Latin legal maxim, "*utere tuo ut alienum non laedas*" (conduct your activities so as not to harm others). As we have seen, the International Court of Justice in its advisory opinion of 8 July 1996, in the *Legality of the Threat or Use of Nuclear Weapons Case*, stated that the Harm Prevention Principle "is now part of the corpus of international law relating to the environment."

We will see in this chapter, however, that, despite the efforts of many expert bodies — including the prestigious International Law Commission — public international law has yet to create an effective global régime of liability for transboundary environmental damage.

In this chapter we consider, first, some of the most notable cases involving transboundary environmental damages; then we take up the most important legal instruments that attempt to codify the international law of transboundary harms both in general and in specifically defined contexts; and finally we consider the impact of the 1991 Espoo Convention on Environmental Assessment in a Transboundary Context. We consider three different kinds of transboundary environmental problems: (1) a nuclear accident; (2) border pollution; and (3) an industrial accident.

Section II.   CASES

There is a dearth of cases in international tribunals concerning transboundary environmental damages. Although many cases of pollution and accidents have occurred, states are reluctant to litigate over damages. A case in point is the Chernobyl nuclear disaster in the Soviet Union in 1986, the worst nuclear disaster in history, which had a world-wide impact. But no state lodged any claim for damages incurred in this disaster. The leading transboundary pollution damage case is still the Trail Smelter Arbitration, which we now consider.

A.   Border Pollution

TRAIL SMELTER CASE (UNITED STATES v. CANADA)
3 U.N. Rep. Int'l Arb.Awards 1905, 1938–81 (1949) (citations omitted)[1]

In 1896, a smelter was started under American ownership near the locality known as Trail, British Columbia. In 1906, a Canadian mining company, today known as Teck Cominco, acquired the smelter. As early as 1925 there were suggestions that sulphur dioxide (SO_2) emissions from the smelter at Trail were causing damage in the state of Washington in the United States to, among other things, crops, timber and livestock.

In June 1927 the U.S. government first communicated with the Canadian Government on the matter, and in December 1927 the U.S. proposed to Canada that the matter be referred to the International Joint Commission (IJC) established by

---

[1] Adapted from Phillipe Sands, Richard Tarasofskyand Mary Weiss (Eds.), IIA Principles of International Environmental Law: Documents In International Environmental Law, 85087 (Manchester Univ. Press, 1994).

Article IX of the 1909 Boundary Waters Treaty, 36 Stat. 2448, T.S. No. 548. In August 1928 the matter was formally referred to the IJC. On February 28, 1931, the Commission adopted a unanimous report and awarded the United States $350,000 in damages to compensate U.S. interests up to and including January 1932. The Commission also made recommendations concerning the damages arising after January 1932 and means to reduce further sulphur emissions. *See* Cairo A.R. Robb, ed., 1 INT'L ENVTL. L. REP. 240–43 (1999) for the text of the IJC report. The report failed to secure the acceptance of both states, but Canada did pay the U.S. the $350,000 sum awarded. *Trail Smelter Case*, 3 U.N. REP INT'L ARB.AWARDS 1905, 1945–46 (1949).

In February 1933 the U.S. complained to Canada that further damage was occurring. On April 15, 1935 a Convention for the final settlement of the dispute and establishing an Arbitral Tribunal for that purpose was signed.[2] Under Article III, the Tribunal was asked to answer four questions in resolving the dispute:

1. Whether the damage caused by the Trail smelter in the state of Washington had occurred since 1 January 1932 and if so then what indemnity should be due?

2. If the answer to the first part of question 1 is affirmative, should it be required to refrain from causing such damage in the future?

3. What régime if any should be adopted and maintained by the Trail smelter?

4. What indemnity or compensation should be paid arising from the determinations of the Tribunal?

Under Article IV, the Tribunal was instructed to "apply the law and practice followed in . . . the United States of America as well as international law and practice" and to "give consideration to the desire of the . . . parties to reach a solution just to all parties concerned."

In a 1938 decision, the Tribunal rendered a final answer to the first question in the affirmative and temporary answers to the second and third questions. *See* 3 U.N. REP. INT'L ARB. AWARDS 1911–1937 (1949); 33 AM. J. INT'L. L. 182 (1939). Final answers to the second, third and fourth questions were given in the Tribunal's 1941 decision extracted below. As to the damage and indemnity issues in the first question, the Tribunal awarded $62,000 for damage to cleared and uncleared land (other than land used for timber), and $16,000 for damage to uncleared land used for timber. The award was predicated on the U.S. law of damages. The Tribunal rejected the U.S. claim for damage to livestock (the U.S. had failed to prove injury from the fumes from the Trail smelter), damage to property in the town of Northport (lack of proof), damage to business enterprises ('too indirect, remote and uncertain to be appraised and not such for which an indemnity can be awarded'). The Tribunal also rejected the U.S. claim for damages from the 'injurious effects' to the Columbia River caused by the disposal of waste slag.

The Tribunal held that it was "unnecessary to decide whether the facts proven

---

[2] *Convention for the Final Settlement of the Difficulties Arising Through Complaints of Damage Done in the State of Washington by Fumes Discharged from the Smelter of the Consolidated Mining and Smelting Company*, Trail, British Columbia, 49 Stat. 3745 (1935), T.S. No. 893, 162 L.N.T.S. 74.

did or did not constitute an infringement or violation of the sovereignty of the United States under international law independent of the [Arbitration] Convention" since the Convention only submitted to the Tribunal the question of damages caused by the Trail smelter in the state of Washington, and it interpreted the Convention such that it was not the intention of the Parties, as expressed in the words "damages caused by the Trail Smelter" to include moneys expended by the U.S. in investigating the problems. For the same reason the Tribunal rejected the claim for interest on the earlier payment of $350,000.

* * *

On April 16, 1988, the Tribunal reported its "final decision" on Question No. 1, as well as its temporary decision on Questions No. 2 and No.3, and provided for a temporary regime thereunder. [This decision] will be referred to . . . as the "previous decision."

[In the previous decision], the Tribunal answered Question No. 1 as follows:

Damage caused by the Trail Smelter in the State of Washington has occurred since the first day of January, 1932, and up to October 1, 1937, and the indemnity to be paid therefore is seventy-eight thousand dollars ($78,000), and is to be complete and final indemnity and compensation for all damage which occurred between such dates . . . . The fact of existence of damage, if any, occurring after October 1, 1937, and the indemnity to be paid therefore, if any, the Tribunal will determine in its final decision.

Answering Questions No. 2 and No. 3, the Tribunal decided that, until a final decision should be made, the Trail Smelter should be subject to a temporary régime . . . and a trial period was established to a date not later than October 1, 1940, in order to enable the Tribunal to establish a permanent régime based on a "more adequate and intensive study," since the Tribunal felt that the information that had been placed before it did not enable it to determine at the time with sufficient certainty upon a permanent régime.]

DECISION

* * *

[By JAN HOSTIE, CHARLES WARREN & R.A.E. GREENSHIELDS:] The tribunal herewith reports its final decisions.

I

The controversy is between two Governments involving damage occurring, or having occurred, in the territory of one of them [U.S.] and alleged to be due to an agency situated in the territory of the other [Canada].

The Columbia River has its source in the Dominion of Canada. At a place in British Columbia named Trail, it flows past a smelter located in a gorge, where zinc and lead are smelted in large quantities. From Trail, its course is easterly and then it swings in a long curve to the international boundary line, at which point it is running, in a south-westerly direction; and its course south of the boundary continues in that general direction. The distance from Trail to the boundary line is about seven miles as the crow flies or about eleven miles, following the course of the river. At Trail and continuing down to the boundary and for a considerable distance below the boundary, mountains rise on either side of the river in slopes of various angles and heights. . . . The width of the valley proper is between one and two miles. . . .

* * *

As to climatic conditions, it may be stated that the region is, in general, a dry one though not what is termed "arid." . . .

* * *

The direction of the surface wind is, in general, from the northeast down the river valley, but this varies at different times of day and in different seasons.

* * *

The history of what may be termed the economic development of the area may be briefly stated as follows: Previous to 1892, there were few settlers in this area, but homesteading and location of farms received an impetus, particularly on the east side of the river, at the time when the construction of the Spokane and Northern Railway was undertaken, which was completed between the City of Spokane and Northport in 1892, and extended to Nelson in British Columbia in 1893. . . .

* * *

The most important industry in the area formerly was the lumber industry. It had its beginning with the building, of the Spokane and Northern Railway. Several saw mills were constructed and operated, largely for the purpose of furnishing the ties to the railway. In fact, the growing trees — yellow pine, Douglas fir, larch, and cedar — were the most valuable asset to be transformed into ready cash. In the early days, the area was rather heavily wooded, but the timber has largely disappeared and the lumber business is now of small size. . . .

As to agricultural conditions, it may be said that farming is carried on in the valley and upon the benches and mountain slopes and in the tributary valleys. The soils are of a light, sandy nature, relatively low in organic matter, although in the tributary valleys the soil is more loamy and fertile. In some localities, particularly on the slopes, natural sub-irrigation affords sufficient moisture; but in other regions irrigation is desirable in order to produce favorable results. . . .

In general, the crops grown on the farms are alfalfa, timothy, clover, grain cut green for hay, barley, oats, wheat, and a small amount of potatoes. . . . The crops, in general, are grown for feed rather than for sale, though there is a certain amount of wheat and oats sold. . . .

Milch cattle are raised to a certain extent and they are grazed on the wild grasses on the hills and mountains in the summer months, but the dairying business depends on existence of sufficient land under cultivation as an adjunct to the dairy to provide adequate forage for the winter months.

In early days, it was believed that, owing to soil and climatic conditions, this locality was destined to become a fruit-growing region, and a few orchards were planted. For several reasons, of which it is claimed that fumigation is one, orchards have not thrived. . . .

II.

*   *   *

From 1925, at least to 1937, damage occurred in the State of Washington, resulting from the sulphur dioxide emitted from the Trail Smelter as stated in the previous decision.

*   *   *

Since the Tribunal has, in its previous decision, answered Question No. 1 with respect to the period from the first day of January, 1932, to the first day of October, 1937, it now answers Question No. 1 with respect to the period 1 from the first day of October, 1937, to the first day of October 1940, as follows:

(1) No damage caused by the Trail Smelter in the State of Washington has occurred since the first day of October, 1937, and prior to the first day of October, 1940, and hence no indemnity shall be paid therefore.

The second question under Article III of the Convention is as follows:

In the event of the answer to the first part of the preceding question being in the affirmative, whether the Trail Smelter should be required to refrain fromcausing damage in the State of Washington in the future, and, if so, to what extent?

Damage has occurred since January 1, 1932, as fully set forth in the previous decision. To that extent the first part of the preceding question has thus been answered in the affirmative.

As has been said above, the report of the International joint Commission . . . contained a definition of the word "damage," excluding "occasional damage that may be caused by SO_2 fumes being carried across the international boundary in air pockets or by reason of unusual atmospheric conditions," as far, at least, as the duty of the Smelter to reduce the presence of that gas in the air was concerned.

The correspondence between the two Governments during the interval between that report and the conclusion of the Convention shows that the problem thus raised was what parties had primarily in mind in drafting Question No. 2. Whilst Canada wished for the adoption or the report, the United States stated that it could not acquiesce in the proposal to limit consideration of damage to damage as defined in the report. . . . The view was expressed that "so long as fumigations occur in the State of Washington with such frequency, duration and intensity as to cause injury," the conditions afforded "grounds of complaint on the part of the United States, regardless of the remedial works . . . and regardless of the effect of those works."

. . .

The first problem which arises is whether the question should be answered on the basis of the law followed in the United States or on the basis of international law. The Tribunal, however, finds that this problem need not be solved here as the law followed in the United States in dealing with the quasi-sovereign rights or the States of the Union, in the matter of air pollution, whilst more definite, is in conformity with the general rules of international law.

Particularly in reaching its conclusions as regards this question as well as the next, the Tribunal has given consideration to the desire of the high contracting parties "to reach a solution just to all parties concerned."

As Professor Eagleton puts in (*Responsibility of Slates in International Law* 1928, p. 80): "A State owes at alltimes a duty to protect other States against injurious acts by individuals from within its jurisdiction." A great number of such general pronouncements by leading authorities concerning the duty of a State to respect other States and their territory have been presented to the Tribunal. These and many others have been carefully examined. . . . [T]his principle, as such, has not been questioned by Canada. But the real difficulty often arises rather when it comes to determine what, *pro subjectamaterie*, is deemed to constitute an injurious act.

A case concerning, as the present one does, territorial relations, decided by the Federal Court of Switzerland between the Cantons of Soleure and Argovia, may serve to illustrate the relativity of the rule. Soleure brought a suit against her sister State to enjoin use of a shooting establishment which endangered her territory. The court, in granting the injunction, said: "This right (sovereignty) excludes . . . not only the usurpation and exercise of sovereign rights (of another State) . . . . but also an actual encroachment which might prejudice the natural use of the territory and the free movement of its inhabitants." As a result of the decision, Argovia made plans for the improvement of the existing installations. These, however, were considered. as insufficient protection by Soleure. The Canton of Argovia then moved the Federal Court to decree that the shooting be again permitted after completion of the projected improvements. This motion was granted. "The demand of the Government of SoIeure," said the court, "that all endangerment be absolutely abolished apparently goes too far." The court found that all risk whatever had not been eliminated, as the region was flat and absolutely safe shooting ranges were only found in mountain valleys; that there was a federal duty for the communes to provide facilities for military target practice and that "no more precaution may be demanded for shooting ranges near the boundaries of two Cantons than are required for shooting ranges in the interior of a Canton." . . .

No case of air pollution dealt with by an international tribunal has been brought to the attention of the Tribunal nor does the Tribunal know of any such case. The nearest analogy is that of water pollution. But, here also, no decision of an international tribunal has been cited or has been found.

There are, however, as regards both air pollution and water pollution, certain decisions of the Supreme Court of the United States which may legitimately be taken as a guide in this field of international law, for it is reasonable to follow by analogy, in international cases, precedents established by that court in dealing with controversies between States of the Union or with other controversies concerning the quasi-sovereign rights or such States, where no contrary rule prevails in international law and no reason for rejecting such precedents can be adduced from the limitations of sovereignty inherent in the Constitution of the United States.

In the suit of the State of Missouri v. the State of Illinois (200 U.S. 496, 521) concerning the pollution, within the boundaries of Illinois, of the Illinois River, an affluent of the Mississippi flowing into the latter where it forms the boundary between that State and Missouri, an injunction was refused. "Before this court ought to intervene," said the court, "the case should be of serious magnitude, clearly and fully proved, and the principle to be applied should be one which the court is prepared deliberately to maintain against all considerations on the other side. . . ." The court found that the practice complained of was general along the shores of the Mississippi River at that time, that it was followed by Missouri itself and that thus a standard was set up by the defendant which the claimant was entitled to invoke.

As the claims of public health became more exacting and methods for removing impurities from the water were perfected, complaints ceased. It is significant that Missouri sided with Illinois when the other riparian of the Great Lakes' system sought to enjoin it to desist from diverting the waters of that system into that of the Illinois and Mississippi for the very purpose of disposing of the Chicago sewage.

In the more recent suit of the State of New York against the State of New Jersey (256 U.S. 296, 309), concerning the pollution of New York Bay, the injunction was also refused for lack of proof, some experts, believing that the plans which were in dispute would result in the presence of "offensive odors and unsightly deposits," other equally reliable experts testifying that they were confidently of the opinion that the waters would be sufficiently purified. The court, referring to Missouri v. Illinois, said: ". . . the burden upon the State of New York of sustaining the allegations of its bill is much greater than that imposed upon a complainant in an ordinary suit between private parties. Before this court can be moved to exercise its extraordinary power under the Constitution to control the conduct of one State at the suit of another, the threatened invasion of rights must be of serious magnitude and it must be established by clear and convincing evidence."

What the Supreme Court says there of its power under the Constitution equally applies to the extraordinary power granted this Tribunal under the Convention. What is true between States of the Union is, at least, equally true concerning the relations between the United States and the Dominion of Canada.

In another recent case concerning water pollution (283 U.S. 473), the complainant was successful. The City of New York was enjoined, at the request of the State of New Jersey, to desist, within a reasonable time limit, from the practice of disposing of sewage by dumping it into the sea, a practice which was injurious to the coastal waters of New Jersey in the vicinity of her bathing resorts.

In the matter of air pollution itself, the leading, decisions are those of the Supreme Court in the State of Georgia v. Tennessee Copper Company and Ducktown Sulphur, Copper and Iron Company, Limited. Although dealing with a suit against private companies, the decisions were on questions cognate to those here at issue. Georgia stated that it had in vain sought relief from the State of Tennessee, on whose territory the smelters were located, and the court defined the nature of the suit by saying: "This is a suit by a State for an injury to it in its capacity of quasi-sovereign. In that capacity, the State has an interest independent of and behind the titles of its citizens, in all the earth and air within its domain."

On the question whether an injunction should be granted or not, the court said (206 U.S. 230):

> It (the State) has the last word as to whether its mountains shall be stripped of their forests and its inhabitants shall breathe pure air. . . . It is not lightly to be presumed to give up quasi-sovereign rights for pay and. . . . If that be its choice, it may insist that an infraction of them shall be stopped. This court has not quite the same freedom to balance the harm that will be done by an injunction against that of which the plaintiff complains that it would have in deciding between two subjects of a single political power. Without excluding the considerations that equity always takes into account . . . it is a fair and reasonable demand on the part of a sovereign that the air over its territory should not be polluted on a great scale by sulphurous acid gas, that the forests on its mountains, be they better or worse, and whatever domestic destruction they may have suffered, should not be further destroyed or threatened by the act of persons beyond its control, that the crops and orchards on its hills should not be endangered from the same source. . . . Whether Georgia, by insisting upon this claim, is doing more harm than good to her own citizens, is for her to determine. The possible disaster to those outside the State must be accepted as a consequence of her standing upon her extreme rights.

Later on, however, when the court actually framed an injunction, in the case of the Ducktown Company (237 U.S. 474, 477) (an agreement on the basis of an annual compensation was reached with the most important of the two smelters, the Tennessee Copper Company), they did not go beyond the decree "adequate to diminish materially the present probability of damage to its (Georgia's) citizens."

Great progress in the control of fumes has been made by science in the past few years and this progress should be taken into account.

The Tribunal, therefore, finds that the above decisions, taken as a whole, constitute an adequate basis for its conclusions, namely, that, under the principles of international law, as well as the law of the United States, no State has the right to use or permit the use of its territory in such a manner as to cause injury by fumes in or to the territory of another or the properties or persons therein, when the case is of serious consequence and the injury is established by clear and convincing evidence.

The decisions of the Supreme Court of the United States which are the basis of these conclusions are decisions in equity and a solution inspired by them, together with the regime hereinafter prescribed, will, in the opinion of the Tribunal, be "just to all parties concerned," as long, at least, as the present conditions in the Columbia River Valley continue to prevail.

Considering the circumstances of the case, the Tribunal holds that the Dominion of Canada is responsible in international law for the conduct of the Trail Smelter.

Apart from the undertakings in the Convention it is, therefore, the duty of the Government of the Dominion of Canada to see to it that this conduct should be in conformity with the obligation of the Dominion under international law as herein determined.

The Tribunal, therefore, answers Question No. 2 as follows: (2) So long as the present conditions the Columbia River Valley prevail, the Trail Smelter shall be required to refrain from causing any damage through fumes in the State of Washington; the damage herein referred to and its extent being such as would be recoverable under the decisions of the Courts of the United States in suits between private individuals. The indemnity for such damage should be fixed in such manner as the Governments, acting under Article XI of the Convention, should agree upon.

The third question under Article III of the Convention is as follows: "In the light of the answer to the preceding question, what measures or regime if any, should be adopted and maintained by the Trail Smelter?"

Answering this question in the light of the preceding one, since the Tribunal has, in its previous decision, found that damage caused by the Trail Smelter occurred in the State of Washington since January 1, 1932, and since the Tribunal has, in its previous decision, found that damage caused by the Trail Smelter has occurred in the State of Washington since January 1, 1932, and since the Tribunal is of opinion that damage may occur in the future unless the operations of the Smelter shall be subject to some control, in order to avoid damage occurring, the Tribunal now decides that a régime or measure of control shall be applied to the operations of the Smelter and shall remain in full force unless and until modified in accordance with the provisions hereinafter set forth. . . .

*   *   *

In order to prevent the occurrence of sulphur dioxide in the atmosphere in amounts, both as to concentration, duration and frequency, capable of causing damage in the State of Washington, the operation of the Smelter and the maximum emission of sulphur dioxide from its stacks shall be regulated as provided in the following regime. [The tribunal then elaborated a comprehensive set of regulatory requirements.]

The fourth question under Article III of the Convention is as follows:

> What indemnity or compensation, if any, should be paid on account of any decision or decisions rendered by the Tribunal pursuant to the next two preceding Questions?

The Tribunal is of opinion that the prescribed regime will probably remove the causes of the present controversy and, as said before, will probably result in preventing any damage of a material nature occurring in the State of Washington in the future.

But since the desirable and expected result of the regime or measure of control hereby required to be adopted and maintained by the Smelter may not occur, and in its answer to Question No. 2, the Tribunal has required the Smelter to refrain from causing damage in the State of Washington in the future, as set forth therein from the Tribunal answers Question No. 4 and decides that on account of decisions rendered by the Tribunal in its answers to Question No. 2 and Question No. 3 there shall be paid as follows: (a) if any damage as defined under Question No. 2 shall have occurred since October 1, 1940, or shall occur in the future, whether through failure on the part of the Smelter to comply with the regulations herein prescribed or notwithstanding the maintenance of the regime, an indemnity shall be paid for such damage but only when and if the two Government. shall make arrangements for the disposition of claims for indemnity under the provisions of Article XI of the Convention; (b) if as a consequence of the decision of the Tribunal in its answers to Question No. 2 and Question No. 3, the United States shall find it necessary to maintain in the future an agent or agents in the area in order to ascertain whether damage shall have occurred in spite of the regime prescribed herein, the reasonable cost of such investigations not in excess of $7,500 in any one year shall be paid to the United States as a compensation, but only if and when the two Governments determine under Article XI of the Convention that damage has occurred in the year in question, due to the operation of the Smelter, and "disposition of claims for indemnity for damage" has been made by the two Governments; but in no case shall the aforesaid compensation be payable in excess of the indemnity for damage; and further it is understood that such payment is hereby directed by the Tribunal only as a compensation to be paid on account of the answers of the Tribunal to Question No. 2 and Question No. 3 (as provided for in Question No. 4) and not as any part of indemnity for the damage to be ascertained and to be determined upon by the two Governments under Article XI of the Convention.

The Tribunal expresses the strong hope that any investigations which the Governments may undertake in the future, in connection with the matters dealt with in this decision, shall be conducted jointly.

NOTES AND QUESTIONS

1.   *Measure of damages.* The United States claimed damages in relations to a number or items in the Trail Smelter case. Among other things, the U.S. sought to recover damages caused by the nuisance created by the Trail Smelter for material injury to: (i) cleared land used for crops, (ii) cleared land not used for crops, (iii) cleared land used as pasture land, (iv) uncleared land used for merchantable timber, (v) the "wrong done the United States in violation of sovereignty," and (vi) the costs of investigation. The rulings of the Tribunal in relation to these claims have been conveniently summarized[3] as follows:

1

As to cleared land used for crops,

The Tribunal adopted as the measure of indemnity to be applied on account of damage in respect of cleared land used for crops, the measure of damage which the American courts apply in cases of nuisance or trespass of the type here involved, ie, the amount of reduction in the value of use or

---

[3] Adapted from PHILLIPE SANDS, RICHARD TARASOFSKY & MARY WEISS (eds.), PRINCIPLES OF INTERNATIONAL ENVIRONMENTAL LAW: DOCUMENTS IN INTERNATIONAL ENVIRONMENTAL LAW 87 (Manchester, UK: Manchester University Press, 1994).

rental value of the land caused by pollution. In the case of farm land, such reduction in the value of the use is, in general, the amount of the reduction of the crop yield arising from injury to crops, less the cost of marketing the same, the latter factor being under the circumstances of this case of negligible importance. The failure of farmers to increase their seeded land in proportion to such increase in other localities, may also be taken into consideration.

2
As to damage to cleared land not used for crops,

With respect to damage to cleared land not used for crops the Tribunal adopted as the measure of indemnity, the measure of damage applied by American courts, ie, the amount of reduction in the value of the use or rental value of the land.

3
As to damage to cleared land used as pasture land,

The Tribunal ruled that there was no evidence of any marked suscepti- bility of wild grasses to pollution and very little evidence to prove the respective amounts of uncleared land devoted to wild grazing grass and barren or shrub land, or to prove the value thereof, which would be necessary in order to estimate the value of the reduction of the use of such land.

4
As to damage in respect of uncleared land used for merchantable timber,

The Tribunal adopted as the measure of indemnity to be applied on account of damage in respect of uncleared land used for merchantable timber, the measure of damages applied by American courts, ie, that since the destruction of merchantable timber will generally impair the value of the land itself, the measure of damage should be the reduction in the value of the land itself due to such destruction of timber.

With regard to damage due to destruction and impairment of growing timber not of merchantable size, the Tribunal adopted the measure of damages applied by American courts, ie, the reduction in value of the land itself due to such destruction and impairment.

With regard to damages in respect of business enterprises, the Tribunal ruled that such damages "due to reduced economic status" of residents in the area are "too indirect, remote, and uncertain to be appraised and that no indemnity can be awarded. None of the cases cited by counsel . . . sustain the proposition that indemnity can be obtained for an injury to or reduction in a man's business due to inability of his customers or clients to buy, which inability or impoverishment is caused by a nuisance. Such damage, even if proved, is too indirect and remote to become the basis, in law, for an award of indemnity."

The Tribunal also ruled: "The Convention does not warrant the inclusion of the cost of investigation under the heading of damage. . . . [B]oth the text of the Convention and the history of its conclusion disprove any intention of including them therein."

2. *Diplomatic protection.* The *Trail Smelter* case involved private interests in the United States complaining about activity of private interests in Canada. Several factors caused the government of the United States to take the matter up with the government of Canada. First, legal opinion at the time held that neither a court in British Columbia nor in the state of Washington would exercise jurisdiction over the matter. The law of British Columbia was believed to follow *British South Africa Company v. Companhia de Moçambique*, [1893] A.C. 602, which held that *in rem* actions were local in nature, and therefore, British Columbian Courts would require the suit to be brought where the land was situated, i.e., Washington. But there was doubt that a court in Washington would assert jurisdiction; the dispute predated the "minimum contacts" test of *International Shoe Co. v. Washington*, 326 U.S. 310 (1945), and the subsequent enactment of state long-arm statutes. Thus, private interests in the state of Washington did not litigate the matter privately, but rather requested the U.S. government to claim damages on their behalf by invoking the doctrine of diplomatic protection.

The doctrine of diplomatic protection authorizes a state to assert a right to damages under international law on behalf of its nationals against another state. If the state exercising diplomatic protection recovers damages, it is up to the discretion of the state to decide what amount, if any, is to be distributed to the nationals on whose behalf diplomatic protection was exercised. Indeed, it is possible for a state to waive — on behalf of itself and its nationals — otherwise valid claims to reparation. This is what happened in the 1951 Treaty of Peace with Japan, in which the United States and the Allied Powers waived all claims arising out of actions taken by Japan and its nationals during World War II. *See* Arts. 14(b) and 19(a), Treaty of Peace with Japan, Sept. 8, 1951, 3 UST 3169, 136 UNTS 45. *See also Dames & Moore v. Regan*, 453 U.S. 654, 679–80 (1981) ("the United States has repeatedly exercised its sovereign authority to settle the claims of its nationals against foreign countries"); and *Asociacion de Reclamantes v. United States*, 735 F.2d 1517, 1523 (D.C. Cir. 1984) ("Once it has espoused a claim, a sovereign has wide-ranging discretion in disposing of it. It may compromise it, seek to enforce it, or waive it entirely"), *cert. denied*, 470 U.S. 1051 (1985).

3. *The standard of liability.* According to the *Trail Smelter* Tribunal, it is a violation of international law for a state to permit activities in its territory to cause injury to the territory of another state "when the case is of serious consequence and the injury is established by clear and convincing evidence." The Tribunal did not suggest that the harm must be reasonably foreseeable before a state could be held responsible. Should this be an additional requirement? How can a state regulate activities that it is not and could not reasonably have been aware of or known? Missing as well in the Tribunal's decision is any ruling whether liability should be based upon negligence or fault or strict liability.

a. *Seriousness.* How serious must the damage caused by an activity be before it is prohibited by international law? The tribunal also stated that "the Trail Smelter shall be required to refrain from causing any damage through fumes in the State of

Washington; the damage herein referred to and its extent being such as would be recoverable under the decision of courts of the United States in suits between private individuals?" This statement may not be entirely correct. In the United States, an action for trespass may be maintained without any proof of actual damage. *See* WILLIAM L. PROSSER, LAW OF TORTS 66 (4th ed., 1971). *But see Martin v. Reynolds Metal Co*, 342 P.2d 790, 794 (Or. 1959) (There is a point where "the intrusion [of invisible, airborne particles] is so trifling that the law will not consider it and the principle *de minimis non curat lex* is applicable."). In international law, however, the rule is that damages must be serious to be actionable. As Phoebe Okowa explains:

> [T]he duty to prevent transboundary harm . . . embodies a *de minimis* test. A state is not required to prevent all harm; only that which is *appreciable, significant or substantial.* . . . As a consequence:
>
>> In relation to contamination from industrial and other stationary sources [of pollution, it is generally accepted that in a world where states must physically coexist a measure of environmental contamination must be tolerated. In the absence of specific air quality standards the determination of tolerable harm is problematic. In the practice of states, judicial decisions, and the literature, it is clear that not all harm is prohibited.

PHOEBE OKOWA, STATE RESPONSIBILITY FOR TRANSBOUNDARY AIR POLLUTION IN INTERNATIONAL LAW, 79–83 (Oxford Univ. Press, 2000). *See also* Kamen Sachariew, *The Definition of Thresholds of Tolerance for Transboundary Environmental Injury Under International Law: Development and Present Status*, 37 NETH. INT'L L. REV. 193 (1990).

b. *Clear and convincing evidence*. In stating a "clear and convincing" standard of proof, the Tribunal in *Trail Smelter* was referring both to the serious injury and to the need to prove a causal link between the injury and the activity involved.

A TRAIL SMELTER UPDATE

One reason why the *Trail Smelter Arbitration* was possible was the close working relationship between the United States and Canada on matters of pollution and environmental protection. Note that even before the *Trail Smelter case*, Canada and the U.S. had signed the Boundary Waters Treaty of 1909, which established the International Joint Commission (IJC) to discuss common problems of pollution. In fact, the Trail Smelter problem was first referred to the IJC and resulted in an important initial decision in the case. After *Trail Smelter*, Canada and the U.S. strengthened their environmental cooperation, signing the Great Lakes Water Quality Agreement of 1978, and the Canada-U.S. Air Quality Agreement of 1991, amended 2000.

The government of Canada, whose environmental affairs are overseen by a Minister of Environment, has established a Canadian Council of Ministers of the Environment (CCME), which includes ministers from the various provinces and territories as well as the central government: Under Canada's Environmental

Protection Act (1988), the CCME has authority to set Canada-wide air quality standards and consistent emission standards. The CCME in fact sets these standards in close coordination with the U.S. Environmental Protection Agency (EPA). Thus, the Trail Smelter, which is now owned by Teck Cominco Metals, ltd., must now comply with strict emission standards very similar to those enforced in the United States by the states and the U.S. EPA.

For a contemporary view of the *Trail Smelter case*, see REBECCA BRATSPIES & RUSSELL MILLER (eds), TRANSBOUNDARY HARM IN INTERNATIONAL LAW: LESSONS FROM THE TRAIL SMELTER ARBITRATION (New York: Cambridge University Press, 2006).

In 1999, however, a new dispute arose between the United States and Canada concerning the Trail smelter. From 1905 to 1995, slag-waste from the smelting of lead and zinc from the smelter was dumped into the Columbia River, ten miles north of the Washington state border. Pollution from the slag drifted downstream and into Lake Roosevelt in the U.S., causing severe transboundary contamination.

In 1999, the Colville Tribes, whose reservation borders Lake Roosevelt, petitioned the U.S. EPA to assess the environmental contamination in the Columbia River and Lake Roosevelt. The EPA completed their investigation *in* 2003, determining that the upper Columbia River site was eligible for inclusion on the National Priorities List under the Comprehensive Environmental Response, Compensation and liability Act (CERCLA), 42 U.S.C. § 9601 *et seq*. This list is known as the "Superfund List" because sites included on this list are eligible for CERCLA ordered and financed remedial action. (42 U.S.C. § 9605(a)). The government of Canada and the U.S. Department of State became involved in this case because of the possible extraterritorial application of CERCLA to Canada and to a Canadian company.

Nevertheless, in 2003, the U.S. EPA issued a unilateral administrative order commanding Teck Cominco, the owner of the smelter, to conduct a remedial investigation and to implement a clean-up plan. Teck Cominco, however, did not comply with this order, and the U.S. EPA, apparently on the advice of the State Department, took no action to enforce it.

Two citizens, Joseph Pakootas and Donald Mitchell, joined by the Colville Tribes, thereupon sued Teck Cominco to enforce the EPA/s order. In this suit, Teck Cominco, supported by the government of Canada, moved to dismiss the case based on lack of subject matter and personal jurisdiction. The U.S. District Court denied this motion and its decision was affirmed by the Court of Appeals for the Ninth Circuit. *Pakootas v. Teck Cominco*, 452 F.3d 1066 (9th Cir. 2006). The Ninth Circuit ruled that the EPA's order was not regulatory, but was remedial, and, because the Superfund Site was located in the U.S., the EPA was not attempting an extraterritorial application of CERCLA. The Supreme Court of the United States denied certiorari. 552 U.S. 1095 (2008).

Meanwhile, Teck Cominco and the EPA settled their dispute in 2006, by signing a "contractual agreement" (pointedly not a consent decree) requiring Teck Cominco to take action to clean up the site. The EPA in turn agreed not to sue Teck Cominco for penalties (which amounted to over $24 million) or injunctive relief resulting from non-compliance with the original EPA order.

The plaintiffs, Joseph Pakootas et al., then amended their complaint and brought suit to claim the penalties that the EPA could have claimed against Teck Cominco for non-compliance with the EPA order. In this suit the District Court granted Teck Cominco's motion to dismiss based on lack of subject matter jurisdiction and the Court of Appeals for the Ninth Circuit affirmed this ruling. *Pakootas v. Teck Cominco*, 646 F.3d 1214 (9th Cir. 2011). The court ruled that CERCLA section 9613(h) stripped the federal courts of jurisdiction over CERCLA remedial actions; the court further ruled that an exception to this bar for penalty actions did not apply: the power of judicial review over penalty actions did not extend to citizen suits for past violations of EPA orders as in the case at bar.

Note that the Ninth circuit in these cases avoided the important and controversial question of the extraterritorial application of CERCLA.

Should U.S. pollution laws such as CERCLA have extraterritorial application? On the issue of extraterritorial application of U.S. regulatory laws, courts commonly distinguish between "non-market" and "market" violations. Market violations are infringements of economic laws such as the antitrust laws. In such cases the courts apply an "effects" test, which holds that the laws apply to conduct occurring outside the U.S., if the conduct has significant effects in the U.S. market. *See, e.g., United States v. Aluminum Company of America*, 148 F.2d 416 (2d Cir. 1945). With respect to "non-market" laws such as environmental statutes, however, the courts rule that absent clear expression of Congressional intent in favor of extraterritorial application, such laws do not apply to extraterritorial conduct. *See, e.g., Arc Ecology v. United States Department of the Air Force*, 294 F. Supp. 2d 1152 (N.D. Cal. 2003) [CERCLA does not apply to former U.S. bases in the Philippines]. Of all the U.S. environmental laws, only the National Environmental Policy Act (NEPA), 42 U.S.C. § 4321 *et seq.* has been held to have limited extraterritorial application. *Compare, e.g., Environmental Defense Fund v. Massey*, 986 F. 2d 528 (D.C. Cir. 1993) (National Science Foundation directed to comply with NEPA regarding food wastes disposal in Antarctica); and *NEPA Coalition v. Aspin*, 837 F. Supp. 466 (D.D.C. 1993) (NEPA does not apply to U.S. military bases in Japan).

With respect to the U.S. EPA's order against Teck Cominco, some U.S. interests voiced fear of retaliatory action by Canadian environmental bodies against U.S. companies. Is this fear realistic?

UNITED NATIONS ECONOMIC COMMISSION FOR EUROPE BACKGROUND DOCUMENT FOR WORKSHOP ON TRANSBOUNDARY POLLUTION TO BE HELD IN BUDAPEST
21–22 May 2007

[This Document sets out relatively recent cases of transboundary pollution and relates the legal consequences. In addition, the document covers the Directive on Environmental Liability adopted by the European Community (now the European Union), which binds all 28 member states of the EU.]

The Sandoz accident, Basel Switzerland 1986

On the first of November 1986, the storage facilities of the chemical giant company Sandoz in Basel caught fire. Insecticides stored in these facilities heavily contaminated the fire fighting water. The fire fighting water was released straight into the Rhine river. The poisoned water plume travelled down the river killing all kind of organisms. The fire took place in the weekend. The Swiss official in charge only informed French and German colleagues via the local warning system by telephone. He did not call in the international alarming system. Moreover the Swiss alarming office did not dispose a telex. So no information about the accident was issued to the downstream alarming centres. Water intakes on the left bank between Basel and Strasbourg were not closed in time. Two days passed before the Swiss informed the international warning centres according the convened format. Fortunately the fire got the attention of the German TV stations.

Thanks to these stations German authorities and enterprises on the right river bank could limit or stop their water intake in time. During the pass of the poisoned wave, the intakes for drinking water and other purposes were temporally closed. In the Netherlands the weirs in the Lower Rhine were opened to direct the poisoned water body as quick as possible to the North Sea.

Legal settlement and developments

Before the poisoned wave had disappeared in the North Sea, the ministers of the Rhine states met in Switzerland on 12th November for mutual exchange of experiences about the accident and lessons learned. They decided to improve the international alarming and warning system and agreed to harmonise regulations preventing sudden occurring pollution like the Sandoz accident within their territory. The ministers charged the International Rhine Commission to elaborate the agreed measures. They convened a conference in December 1986 to discuss the elaboration results and the views of the different Rhine states about a further reduction of the pollution.

The ministers also discussed the compensation of damage caused by the accident.

The December conference took measures to prevent sudden pollution like the Sandoz accident. Industries have to construct basins in which liquids (including fire fighting water) can timely be stored. The liquids have to be treated. Water has to meet the current emission standards before it can be discharged in the rivers. Telefax and later on e-mail became standard in the Rhine alarming and warning system. The tasks and understandings between the regional, national and international warning system were evaluated and newly defined.

The ministers also adopted new long-term objectives for the Rhine:
- higher species like the salmon should return to the Rhine by 2000;
- future use of Rhine water for public water supply must be possible with simple production methods;
- reduction of the pollution to a level that sediments can be applied on the land or dumped into the sea without harmful consequences for aquatic life.

Based on these objectives, the Rhine states agreed on a general reduction of the pollution by 50% in ten years, and on initiative of the North Sea states a 70% reduction for some heavy metals and dioxin in 1987. At the same time the Rhine states approved the rehabilitation plan "Salmon 2000." The 2003 message: the salmon is back in the Rhine. The objective to reduce the Rhine pollution by 50% has been realised for more than 80% of the problematic substances.

The Baia Mare tailing dam accident, Romania-Hungary, 2000

A stock company called AURUL SA, jointly owned by Esmeralda, Exploration Limited, Australia, and the Romanian CompaniaNationala a MetalelorPretiosasisiNeferoase (REMIN) was established in 1992. The company processed solid wastes from earlier mining activity to recover precious metals, especially gold and silver in Baia Mare, Romania. In 1993, the company obtained an environmental permit from the Ministry of Waters, Forests and Environmental Protection. In 1997, after receiving the Site Construction Permit from the Maramures County Council, construction of the recovering plant commenced. In 1999, the operational permit, based on documentation contained in an environmental impact assessment (EIA), was obtained. The company started operation in May 1999 by processing an existing 30-year-old tailing dam (Meda dam) located near Baia Mare city, to the west, close to the residential area. On 30 January 2000, the dam at the Aurul tailing pond overflowed and washed away a stretch of embankment wall 25 metres long and 2.5 metres deep. Approximately 100,000 m.t. of tailings water with an estimated — 120 tons of cyanide and heavy metal load began to flow into the nearby Lapus River, which is a tributary of the Szamos River and from there into the Tisza River and the Danube upstream of Belgrade and finally entered the Black Sea. On 2 February 2000, at 1:30 a.m., the spillage from the Aurul tailing dam was stopped, and the decontamination of the affected area, around 14 ha, started.

The acute transboundary pollution had the potential of having a severe negative impact on biodiversity, the rivers' ecosystems, drinking water supply and socio-economic conditions of the local population. A 30-40 kilometre long contaminated pollution plume wiped out aquatic flora and the fauna of the central Tisza River. The cyanide plume was measurable at the Danube delta, four weeks later and 2000 km away from the spill source. Acute effects, typical for cyanide, occurred for long stretches of the river system down to the confluence of the Tisza with the Danube: phyto- and zooplankton were down to zero when the cyanide plume passed and fish were killed in the plume or immediately after. Rare and unique species both of flora and of fauna have been endangered. The Hungarian authorities provided estimates of the total amount of fish killed in excess of one thousand tons, whereas the Romanian authorities reported that the amount of dead fish reported was very small. According to the Yugoslavian authorities. a large amount of dead fish appeared in the Yugoslavian part of the Tisza River as well. No major fish kills were reported from the Danube.

Timely information exchange and precautionary measures were taken by the Romanian, Hungarian and Yugoslavian authorities, including a temporary closure of the Tisza-lake side dams, mitigation and reducement of the risk and impact of the spill. Villages close to the accident site were provided with alternative water sources.

Aurul SA recommenced trial operation on June 13, 2000, upon obtaining government approval. In 2005, the company received an operation permit from the Romanian Environmental Ministry for the period of three years.

Legal settlement and further developments

The International Task Force established for the investigation of the accident concluded its report in December 2000 that the accident was caused by the use of an inappropriate design of the tailing dam facility, by the acceptance of that design by the permitting authorities; and by inadequate monitoring and dam construction, operation and maintenance.

The Hungarian State started a civil compensation case at the Capital Court of Budapest in April 2001 against AurulSA, for damages for 28,596.000.000 HUF (143 million USD) and for enforcing safety measures at the site. The Capital Court in its decision of 30 April 2005 as a temporary measurement prohibited the company to operate the facility with more than 15% of its capacity. In its final decision the Capital Court ruled on 8 May 2006 that the defendant Transgold SA (the successor of AurulSA) is responsible for the accident and ordered the company to ensure several safety measures at the facility; furthermore it confirmed its previous decision as to prohibit the operation with more than 15% of its capacity. The decision became binding on 13. December 2006. Note however that the case will continue concerning the amount of compensation to be paid.

Civilians — mostly anglers — have also started civil proceedings against the company in 2000, but their case was suspended until the court case of the State will be completed. Criminal proceedings, which commenced after the accident, are also suspended.

In the meantime, the former Aurul Company started insolvency procedures in Romania and as a result, the Romanian Administrative Court ordered on 10 April 2006 that the company is in the state of bankruptcy and suspended all ongoing cases against it.

One of the parent companies, the Australian based Esmeralda Exploration Ltd. was suspended from trading on the Australian Stock Exchange in February 2000, and reinstated in the final quarter of 2001. The directors of Esmeralda appointed an Administrator in March 2000, and started a so-called *administration* procedure, which aim was to give the opportunity for any aggrieved party to come forward and make his claim for damages. The Hungarian State lodged a proof of debt in the administration of Esmeralda Exploration for about A$ 179 million in 2000, which has been dealt with in such a manner that it does not represent a contingent liability on the accounts of Esmeralda Exploration. The Administrators passed control of Esmeralda Exploration back to its directors on 27 September 2000. A new corporate entity Transgold SA took over the operation of the plant in 2001 and all hard-rock resources and other assets previously held by Aurul SA. Transgold is now 50%-owned by Esmeralda Exploration and 45%-owned by the Romanian Government via Remin SA and 5%-owned by other Romanian shareholders. Transgold is planning the refurbishment of a 500,000 tons/year SAG Mill that will provide the necessary hard-rock preparation for the ongoing operation of the tailings plant. This will enable the Transgold plant to treat its own bard-rock material in addition to tailings material."

Discussion on the issue of state responsibility started between the governments of Hungary and Romania in 2000, but did not result in lodging an official claim against the Romanian State in front of international tribunals.

The Songhua river pollution, China — Russia, 2005

The Songhua River is Harbin's main. water source. Harbin is the capital of Heilongjiang province in north-eastern of China. On 13 November 2005, an explosion took place at Jilin Chemical Industrial Co. plant (a PetroChina benzene factory) at Jilin, a city about 380 kilometres up river from Harbin. The explosion led to a discharge of approximately 100 tonnes of chemicals including mainly benzene, into the river Songhua. The Songhua River runs into the Amur River and then enters into Russia. As a consequence of the accident, five people were reportedly killed, 70 injured and 10.000 evacuated. The peak concentration of nitrobenzene tested at 33 times over the permissible level at Harbin, yet on the same day, the concentration of benzene was below the permissible level and aniline was not detected. The contamination plume stretched for 80 kilometres when passing through Harbin and it extended to 150 kilometres when it passed through Jiamusi on 10 December 2005. Authorities were reportedly increasing water flows to dilute pollutants and providing bottled water for the population in Harbin. After the accident, the water quality was monitored at 30 monitoring stations and information was provided to downstream authorities. China and Russia agreed on a joint monitoring team, and joint sampling at the pollution plume position was carried out twice a day. On the basis of the Joint Emergency Response Monitoring Plan on Water Quality of the Songhua River signed between China and Russia, both countries will strengthen joint monitoring.

To prevent pollution from reaching fresh water intakes for the city of Khabarovsk further downstream a dam was built on a branch of the Heilongjiang River. In Russia, drinking water was immediately cut off and water samples were taken from the Amur River. A month after the accident a four-person UNEP team visited China on a field mission in order to visit affected sites on the Songhua River and to meet and discuss the incident with local and national Chinese officials. The UNEP report of the mission notes that lessons learned from the incident should be incorporated into policy, legislation and enforcement. The report particularly calls attention to communication and information sharing, response time and effectiveness and finally to environmental contingency planning. The United Nations Environment Programme suggests that both China and Russia provide access to independent and impartial sampling and chemical analysis of the river spill.

Legal settlement and further developments

On 21 February 2006 Zhou Shengxian, Chinese minister of the State Environmental Protection Administration (SEPA) and Russian minister of natural resources, Yuri Trutnev, signed a formal agreement to jointly monitor the water quality of transboundary rivers. The agreement originated in December 2005 when Russian President Vladimir Putin and Chinese Prime Minister Wen Jiabao consented to jointly tackle the Songhua River chemical spill. At the meeting, Russia and China also agreed to conclude a treaty on the protection of trans-border rivers, which would regulate how compensation for damages should be paid. Without such an agreement, Russia cannot claim any compensation for the Chinese pollution. Both sides also agreed to set up a joint working group to jointly monitor the Amur River and its tributaries.

Under Chinese law, companies can only be fined a maximum of 1 million yuan (125.000 U.S. dollars) for causing pollution. The SEPA found the company guilty of contravening the Environmental Protection Law and two articles of the law on Prevention and Control of Water Pollution and charged the highest possible amount of fine to the company in January 2007. Professor Wang Jin from the Peking University filed a lawsuit one month after the incident, demanding compensation of 10 billion yuan (1.25 billion U.S. dollars) from the company to restore the environment, but its application was rejected by the court.

In January 2007 Beijing adopted a plan that includes spending 13.4 billion yuan (US$ 1.7 billion) to clean up the Songhua River and put in place pollution controls by 2010.

There are no indications that Russia would like to commence an international procedure against China for compensation.

The E.U. Directive on environmental liability

The European Community adopted a regime with Directive 2004/35/EC establishing a framework for environmental liability based on the "polluter pays" principle, with a view to preventing and remedying environmental damage.[4] The Directive entered into force on 30 April 2004 and it is to be transposed into national legislation by 30 April 2007.[5]

The Directive establishes a common framework for liability with a view to preventing and remedying damage to animals, plants, natural habitats, water resources, and damage affecting the land.[6] The liability scheme applies to certain

---

[4] Directive 2004/35/EC of the European Parliament and of the Council of 21 April 2004 on environmental liability with regard to the prevention and remedying of environmental damage.

[5] The Directive was already modified with Directive *2006/21/EC* and the deadline for its transposition is 1 May 2008.

[6] It is important to note that the Directive does not cover maritime oil disasters and nuclear accidents. Oil spills by tankers at sea are covered by the 1992 International Convention on Civil Liability for Oil Pollution Damage and the 1992 International Convention on the Establishment of an International Fund for Compensation for Oil Pollution Damage. This regime channels liability to ship owners who have very few possibilities to exonerate themselves. The ship owner's civil liability is complemented by the IOPC Fund, which covers damage beyond the limit where the ship owner has to pay. Nuclear activities are covered by several international civil liability conventions. These conventions too, are based on strict liability. They mainly deal with traditional damage, but in addition allow governments to cover environmental damage, albeit in a less co-ordinated way.

specified occupational activities and to other activities in cases where the operator is at fault or negligent. The public authorities are also responsible for ensuring that the operators responsible take or finance the necessary preventive or remedial measures themselves. Under the terms of the Directive, environmental damage is defined as direct or indirect damage to the aquatic environment covered by Community water management legislation; direct or indirect damage to species and natural habitats protected at Community level by the 1979 Birds Directive or by the 1992 Habitats Directive; direct or indirect contamination of the land which creates a significant risk to human health.[7]

The principle of liability applies to environmental damage and imminent threat of damage resulting from occupational activities, where it is possible to establish a causal link between the damage and the activity in question. The Directive distinguishes between two complementary situations: occupational activities specifically mentioned in the Directive and other occupational activities. The first liability scheme applies to the dangerous or potentially dangerous occupational activities listed in Annex ill to the Directive. These are mainly agricultural or industrial activities requiring a licence under the Directive on integrated pollution prevention and control, activities which discharge heavy metals into water or the air, installations producing dangerous chemical substances, waste management activities (including landfills and incinerators) and activities concerning genetically modified organisms and micro-organisms. Under this first scheme, the operator may be held responsible even if he is not at fault The second liability scheme applies to all occupational activities other than those listed in Annex III to the Directive, but only where there is damage, or imminent threat of damage to species or natural habitats protected by Community legislation. In this case, the operator will be held liable only if he is at fault or negligent. The Directive provides for a certain number of exemptions from environmental liability, i.e. the liability scheme does not apply in the case of damage or imminent damage resulting from armed conflict, natural disaster, activities covered by the Treaty establishing the European Atomic Energy

---

[7] This is the official short summary of the definition as contained in the official website of the European Union, see in http://europa.eu/scadplus/leg/en/lvb/128120.htm.The actual text of the Directive is worded as follows: Article 2.

1. "environmental damage" means:

(a) damage to protected species and natural habitats, which is any damage that has significant adverse effects on reaching or maintaining the favourable conservation status of such habitats or species. The significance of such effects is to be assessed with reference to the baseline condition, taking account of the criteria set out in Annex I; Damage to protected species and natural habitats does not include previously identified adverse effects which result from an act by an operator which was expressly authorised by the relevant authorities in accordance with provisions implementing Article 6(3) and (4) or Article 16 of Directive 92/43/EEC or Article 9 of Directive 79/409fEEC or, in the case of habitats and species not covered by Community law, in accordance with equivalent provisions of national law on nature conservation.

(b) water damage, which is any damage that Significantly adversely affects the ecological., chemical and/or quantitative status and/or ecological potential, as defined in Directive 2000/60/EC, of the waters concerned, with the exception of adverse effects where Article 4(7) of that Directive applies;

(c) land damage, which is any land contamination that creates a significant risk of human health being adversely affected as a result of the direct or indirect introduction in, on or under land. of substances, preparations. organisms or micro-organisms.

Community, national defence or international security activities or activities covered by the international conventions listed in Annex IV.

Where there is an imminent threat of environmental damage, the competent authority designated by each Member State will require the operator to take the necessary preventive measures, or will take such measures itself and recover the costs incurred at a later date.

NOTE ON STATE ENVIRONMENTAL RESPONSIBILITY

The three cases discussed in the UN ECE Background Document are typical. Note that none of the three involved any legal action against the state which was the source of the damage. Why not?

The Sandoz accident implicated two treaties involving pollution of the Rhine River: the Berne Convention (1963) set up an International Commission for the Protection of the Rhine against Pollution to address the serious problems of the river's pollution. The Rhine Chemical Convention (1976) increased the Commission's powers and set standards for chemical substances in the river. Article 7 of the Chemical Convention requires the parties to ensure by all necessary legislative and administrative measures that the storage of hazardous substances will not endanger the Rhine. Article 11 of the Convention provides for mandatory warning of an accidental spill. Did the Swiss government violate these provisions? After the Sandoz spill the Rhine Conventions were upgraded by the state-parties.

After the spill Sandoz spent 10 million Swiss francs to set up a Rhine Fund to sponsor scientific research on the Rhine and its ecology. Over 1,100 damage claims were paid, most covered by insurance. Criminal actions were brought against certain individuals, and Switzerland upgraded its oversight of hazardous substances. For a comprehensive treatment, see Alfred Rest, The Sandoz Blaze and the Pollution of the Rhine in Regard to Public International law, Private International Law and National Liability Issues, 1 Milieu Aansprakellijkheid 59 (1987).

The European Union has taken action to deal with accidents involving hazardous substances. The so-called Seveso III Directive of 4 July 2012, O.J. L 197/1, 24 July 2012, requires all EU member states to adopt domestic legislation to prevent and to have in place emergency procedures to inform the public and to deal with accidental spills of chemicals. In addition, the EU Directive on Environmental Liability provides for possible damage recovery. This Directive, however, is effective as EU law, not as general international law.

International Law has failed to develop a general legal regime of state environmental responsibility for transboundary harm despite the *Trail Smelter* case and the Harm Prevention Principle.

Nevertheless, there are many examples of international practice recognizing a duty on the part of states to avoid, minimize, and provide reparation for transboundary losses or injuries:

a. In 1972, Canada claimed compensation from the United States when a Liberian-registered oil tanker unloading at Cherry Point, Washington, leaked 12,000 gallons of crude oil, fouling beaches in British Columbia.

Before the United States could respond to the claim, the owner of the tanker agreed to pay damages. *See* Handl, *State Liability for Accidental Transnational Environmental Damage by Private Persons*, 74 AM.J. INT'L'L. 525, 544–45 (1980).

b. In 1974, a Dutch court granted compensation to Dutch plaintiffs damaged by pollution emitted by a French state-owned company. *See* J. LAMMERS POLLUTION OF INTERNATIONAL WATERCOURSES 196–205 (1984).

c. In the *Gut Dam* case the water levels of Lake Ontario were raised and U.S. property owners suffered injury because of a dam built by Canada across the international boundary on the St. Lawrence River. To settle these claims, the United States and Canada agreed to establish an international arbitral claims tribunal. 17 U.S.T. 1566, T.I.A.S. No. 6114, 4I.L.M. 473 (1965). The tribunal ruled that a 1903 agreement between Canada and the U.S. obligated Canada to compensate affected U.S. property owners, and Canada paid compensation. Gut Dam Arbitration (United States v. Canada), 8 I.L.M.118 (1969).

d. The United States made payment to injured parties when in 1954 nuclear tests carried out in the Marshall Islands caused Injury to Japanese fishermen on the high seas outside the nuclear testing zone. The United States also compensated the inhabitants of the Marshall Islands for personal injuries and property damage suffered during the tests. 8 M. WHITMAN, DIGEST OF INTERNATIONAL LAW 764–67(1967).

In many such cases, a state will make *ex gratia* compensation without admitting a legal duty to do so.

We now explore an alternative method of dealing with transboundary environmental problems and pollution — establishing bilateral border environmental institutions and border agreements tailored to the specific border problems that may arise between neighboring nations.

The United States has established long-standing cooperative institutions, agreements and working relationships with both Canada and Mexico to deal with border environmental problems. As we have already seen in connection with the *Trail Smelter Case*, the United States and Canada now closely align their regulatory laws and policies and bilateral institutions function quite well to alleviate border problems and to apply principle 21/2 between the two countries.

We now turn to the southern border of the United States to examine the relationship with Mexico. Since Mexico is very different from Canada and the environmental problems are also very different, the United States and Mexico have established a different set of agreements and institutions to deal with transboundary environmental problems.

In the problem that follows, we explore the bilateral relationship of transborder environmental cooperation between the United States and Mexico.

PROBLEM 3-1
WASTEWATER POLLUTION ALONG THE MEXICAN BORDER

For many years, sewage and wastewater originating in Tijuana, Mexico on the border with California and discharged into the Tijuana River has been fouling wells and crops located downriver in the San Ysidro valley in California. In order to relieve this pollution, Mexico and the United States collaborated to build an ocean outfall pipe to discharge much of the wastewater at sea. But by the early 1960s, the system became overloaded. The pollution of the river increased and sewage from the ocean outfall contaminated San Diego beaches. The river pollution was so bad that, in a New York Times article on August 22, 1990, V.C. Ackerman, a U.S. Border Patrol agent, was quoted as saying: "[The pollution] melts the wax off your boots if you step into it."

The state of California, the city of San Diego and the U.S. EPA in the 1990s grew especially concerning about this increasing transborder pollution problem and its environmental and economic impact on San Diego and the San Ysidro valley.

What do you recommend be done to ameliorate this situation?

1. Should the United States invoke Rio Principle 2 and the Trail Smelter case and demand compensation from Mexico? *If* this is done, how do you think Mexico would respond?

2. Should the United States bring an action against Mexico in an international tribunal? If so, what tribunal would have jurisdiction?

3. Would you recommend that the U.S. EPA, the state of California, or the city of San Diego file suit in the Mexican courts seeing damages and injunctive relief? Mexico's law concerning water resources is the Ley de Aguas Nacionales, 1992, amended in 2004; Mexico's water pollution regulations are administered by SEMARNAT (Secretaria de Medio Ambiente y Recursos Naturales) (http://www.semarnat.gob.mx). Over 78% of municipal wastes and over 88% of industrial wastes generated in Mexico are released untreated into waterways. Mexico is a civil law country and judicial review of administrative actions is rare; agency decisions are virtually always handled through administrative appeals. According to Corina Warfield *et al, Improving Coastal Water Quality in Mexico* (2004), Mexican law does not provide for citizens' environmental suits. With regard to enforcement, Mexico is characterized by "a weak judiciary and few avenues for enforcement of environmental laws" (p. 15). The central government has no authority to collect fines from municipalities that do not comply with environmental regulations.

4. Should suit be filed against Mexico in the United States? Under the U.S. Foreign Sovereign Immunities Act (FSIA), 28 U.S.C. § 1602 *et seq.*, although foreign sovereigns are generally immune from suit, there is an exception if a foreign state's non-commercial acts or omissions cause tortious injury in the United States. But a "discretionary function" doctrine protects against lawsuits under the FSIA to contest policy judgments of a foreign state. E.g., *Olsen ex rel. Sheldon v. Government of Mexico*, 729 F.2d 641 (9th Cir. 1984). Furthermore, the tortious act or omission must occur

within the United States. In *In re Sedco*, 543 F. Supp. 561 (S.D. Tex. 1982), which involved a suit to recover damages due to pollution in Texas stemming from the blow-out of an offshore oil well operated by the Mexican National Oil Company in Mexican waters in the Gulf of Mexico, the court ruled that the suit was barred because the tort did not occur "in whole" within the United States.

5. The United States and Mexico have established an International Boundary and Water Commission (IBWC), 22 U.S.C. §§ 277–278b, which is charged with settling "all differences that may arise between the two governments with respect to interpretation and application of the [US-Mexico Water Treaty (1944)] subject to the approval of the two governments." This specifically includes the construction and maintenance of sanitation and sewage facilities. Is this the appropriate forum to raise the issue of pollution from Tijuana?

6. In July 1990, after difficult negotiations, the U.S. and Mexican IBWC commissioners signed an agreement to build a sewage treatment plant on the Tijuana River on the U.S. side of the border with the majority of the cost paid by the United States. *Clean Water Partnership, IBWC Minute No. 283*, 8 July 1990. After many delays, in 2011, this facility, the South Bay International Wastewater Treatment Plant, achieved full operations, treating up to 25 million gallons of wastewater per day (mgd) to secondary treatment levels.[8] The SBIWTP can be upgraded to treat up to 100 mgd. Now four wastewater treatment plants are operating to treat Tijuana wastewater on the Tijuana River, and the excess is treated by the SBIWTP to a degree as high or higher than San Diego's wastewaters.

7. In 1992, the North American Free Trade Agreement (NAFTA) was signed by the United States, Canada and Mexico. Also agreed at this time were (1) the Integrated Environmental Plan for the Mexico-U.S. Border Area (Border Plan); (2) the trilateral North American Agreement on Environmental Cooperation; and (3) a North American Development Bank. The United States and Mexico also created a Border Environment Cooperation Commission that is to work closely with the IBWC.

8. *The North American Agreement on Environmental Cooperation. (NAAEC).*

Under the NAAEC, the three countries agreed to the following obligations:

Article 3: Level of Protection

Recognizing the right of each party to establish its own levels of domestic environmental protection and environmental development policies and priorities, and to adopt or modify accordingly its environmental laws and regulations, each Party shall ensure that its laws and regulations

---

[8] Primary treatment causes solids to sink to the bottom and grease, oil and lighter solids to float; these are then removed; secondary treatment, in addition, involves removal of dissolved suspended biological matter (human waste, food wastes, soaps and detergents); tertiary treatment involves microfiltration and removal of heavy metals and other impurities.

provide for high levels of environmental protection and shall strive to continue to improve those laws and regulations.

Article 4: Publication

1. Each party shall ensure that its laws, regulations, procedures and administrative rulings of general application respecting any matter covered by this Agreement are promptly published or otherwise made available in such a manner as to enable interested persons and Parties to become acquainted with them.

2. To the extent possible, each Party shall:

    (a) publish in advance any such measure that it proposes to adopt; and

    (b) provide interested persons and Parties with a reasonable opportunity to comment on such proposed measures.

Article 5: Government Enforcement Action

1. With the aim of achieving high levels of environmental protection and compliance with its environmental laws and regulations, each Party shall effectively enforce its environmental laws and regulations through appropriate government action.

2. Each Party shall ensure that judicial, quasi-judicial or administrative enforcement proceedings are available under its law to sanction or remedy violations of its enforcement laws and regulations. . . .

Article 6: Private Access to Remedies

1. Each Party shall ensure that interested persons may request the Party's competent authorities to investigate alleged violations of its environmental laws and regulations and shall give such requests due consideration in accordance with law.

2. Each Party shall ensure that persons with a legally recognized interest under its law in a particular matter have appropriate access to administrative quasi-judicial or judicial proceedings for the enforcement of the Party's environmental laws and regulation.

3. Private access to remedies shall include rights, in accordance with the Party's law, such as:

    (a) to sue another person under that Party's jurisdiction for damages;

    (b) to seek sanctions or remedies such as monetary penalties, emergency closures or orders to mitigate the consequences of violations of its environmental laws and regulations; laws and regulations in order to protect the environment or to avoid environmental harm; or

    (d) to seek injunctions where a person suffers, or may suffer, loss, damage or injury as a result of conduct by another person under that Party's jurisdiction contrary to that Party's environmental laws and regulations or from tortious conduct.

Is the NAAEC useful for solving transboundary pollution such as that in Problem 3-1? Consider the following analysis:

The [NAAEC] set up the North American Commission for Environmental Cooperation (NACEC), which consists of a Council, a Secretariat, and a Joint Public Advisory Committee (JPAC). The Council is the NACEC's governing body, and comprises cabinet level or equivalent representatives of the Parties, or their designees. The Secretariat is NACEC's administrative arm, headed by an Executive Director appointed by the Council. The Director in turn supervises a professional staff which is supposed to be selected solely on the basis or merit. The JPAC is, as its name implies, a purely advisory body that provides advice to the Council and input to the Secretariat.

Although the [NAAEC] assigns a variety of functions to the Council and the Secretariat, perhaps the most important deal with proceedings to address alleged failures by Parties to adequately enforce their environmental laws. The Agreement provides a mechanism whereby non-governmental organizations (" 'NGOs") and private parties can make submissions to the Secretariat asserting party that a Party is failing to effectively enforce its environmental laws. The Secretariat is authorized to review these claims, and in some cases prepare a "factual record" that will presumably document whether the allegations of weak enforcement are well founded. Although the factual record itself does not bring with it any legal consequences, it could form the basis for formal consultation proceedings, discussed further below, that in turn could ultimately lead to sanctions against an offending Party. There is an expectation that the publication of a factual record critical of a Party's enforcement program will generate pressure for voluntary improvements.

Any party may commence formal consultation with another Party over whether there has been a "persistent pattern of failure by that other Party to effectively enforce its environmental law." If the Parties are thereafter unable to resolve the matter between themselves, and the matter touches on activities involving business competition or trade among the Parties, the Council can refer the matter to an arbitral panel comprised of five independent experts. The Panel must determine whether there has been a pattern of failure to enforce, and if so make recommendations that shall normally be that the Party complained against adopt and implement an action plan sufficient to remedy the pattern of non enforcement.

If the Party complained against fails to timely adopt an adequate action plan, the Panel must impose its own action plan, and may impose a monetary penalty at its discretion. Further, if the Party complained against fails to implement an approved or adopted action plan, the Panel must impose a monetary penalty. A penalty assessment can be as high as .007 percent of the total trade in goods between the Parties in the most recent year for which data are available. Penalty assessments may be enforced via suspension of NAFTA trade benefits to the offending Party, or against Canada via direct collection procedures in Canadian courts.

David S. Baron, *NAFTA and the Environment-Making the Side Agreement Work*, 12 Ariz. J. Int'l & Comp. L. 603, 606–10 (1995) (footnotes omitted).

In 20 years of operations, the Secretariat of the NAAEC has received about 100 citizen submissions on enforcement matters (SEMS), and has published a factual record in about 20 cases, but the arbitration and penalty provisions of the NAAEC have never been used. Why not?

A second environmental agreement, the bilateral Border Environmental Cooperation Agreement (BECA), builds upon the 1992 Border Plan. It particularly emphasizes efforts to build the environmental infrastructurein the U.S.-Mexico border region through a process of cooperative planning and funding of necessary projects. It gives priority to projects relating to water pollution, wastewater treatment, and municipal solid waste. It establishes two new institutions: the Border Environment Cooperation Commission (BECC), and the North American Development Bank (NADB).

The BECA also outlines the relationship of the new institutions with the IBWC, which it acknowledges "plays an important role in efforts to preserve the health and vitality of the river waters of the border region" BECA, Preamble. The Mexican and U.S. Commissioners of the IBWC serve as *ex officio* members of the BECC's Board of Directors, and the continued independence of the IBWC is guaranteed. The BECC and the IBWC are to "cooperate, as appropriate, with each other in planning, developing and carrying, out border sanitation and other environmental activities." BECA, Sec. 6(c).

The Mexico-U.S. Border Plan is now in full swing, and an Environmental Program has been adopted for implementation by 2020. The Border Program aims to implement controls on air and water pollution as well as address waste disposal problems all along the 2000-mile border between the United States and Mexico. For details, see http://www.epa.gov/region9/strategicplan/border.html. This program is largely financed by the United States and the North American Development Bank.

NOTE ON TRANSBOUNDARY POLLUTION EMANATING FROM THE UNITED STATES

Both the U.S. Clean Air Act and the Clean Water Act contain provisions for dealing with air and water pollution emanating from the United States. (We postpone the Clean Air Act provision for the chapter in this book on Protection of the Atmosphere). Section 310 of the Clean Water Act, 33 U.S.C. sec. 1320, provides that if the U.S. EPA administrator finds that water pollution emanating from the United States "endangers the health or welfare of persons in a foreign country," he or she may call a hearing at the request of the Secretary of State. A five-member hearing Board will then be empaneled to compel reports from any pollution source and to make recommendations in the matter. The EPA administrator has authority to enforce this recommendation, if necessary, in federal court. This procedure is available, however, only if the foreign country involved has granted the same rights to U.S. citizens under its laws. This procedure has never been used.

CONCLUSIONS

This section has examined general international law standards for the prevention of transboundary environmental degradation and the existing arrangements (or lack of arrangements) for imposing liability and responsibility on states for transboundary pollution emitted from their territory. We find that despite the existence of the Trail Smelter precedent and the related Stockholm Principle 21 and Rio Principle 2, no general international law regime exists that mandates the prevention of transboundary pollution or provides an avenue for the recovery of damages suffered as a result of transboundary pollution.

Transboundary environmental degradation is most frequently handled on a bilateral basis except within the European Union, which as a political and economic union has passed binding Directives on the matter.

Certain states, most notably the United States, Mexico, and Canada, have established extensive bilateral agreements, institutions and working relationships to deal with border environmental problems on a continuous, cooperative basis.

B. The Duty to Notify/Warn

THE CORFU CHANNEL CASE
(UNITED KINGDOM v. ALBANIA)
(Merits)
[1949] I.C.J. 4, 12–23

[On October 22nd, 1946, two British cruisers and two destroyers, coming from the south, entered the North Corfu Strait. The channel they were following, which was in Albanian waters, was regarded as safe: it had been swept in 1944 and check-swept in 1945. One of the destroyers, the *Saumarez*; when off Saranda, struck a mine and was gravely damaged. The other destroyer, the *Volage*, was sent to her assistance and, while towing her, struck another mine and was also seriously damaged. Forty-five British officers and sailors lost their lives, and 42 others were wounded.

An incident had already occurred in these waters on May 15, 1946: an Albanian battery had fired in the direction of two British cruisers. The United Kingdom Government had protested, stating that innocent passage through straits is a right recognized by international law; the Albanian Government had replied that foreign warships and merchant vessels had no right to pass through Albanian territorial waters without prior authorization; and on August 2, 1946, the United Kingdom Government had replied that if, in the future, fire was opened on a British warship passing through the channel, the fire would be returned. Finally, on September 21, 1946, the Admiralty in London had cabled to the British Commander-in-Chief in the Mediterranean to the following effect: "Establishment of diplomatic relations with Albania is again under consideration by His Majesty's Government who wish to know whether the Albanian Government have learnt to behave themselves. Information is requested whether any ships under your command have passed through the North Corfu Strait since August and, if not, whether you intend them to do so shortly."

After the explosions on October 22nd, the United Kingdom Government sent a Note to Tirana announcing its intention to sweep the Corfu Channel shortly. The reply was that this consent would not be given unless the operation in question took place outside Albanian territorial waters and that any sweep undertaken in those waters would be a violation of Albania's sovereignty. The sweep effected by the British Navy took place on November 12th/13th 1946, in Albanian territorial waters and within the limits of the channel previously swept. Twenty-two moored mines were cut; they were mines of the German GY type.][9]

THE COURT . . . *delivers the following Judgment:*

*   *   *

By the first part of the Special Agreement, the following question is submitted to the Court:

"(I) Is Albania responsible under international law for the explosions which occurred on the 22nd October 1946 in Albanian waters and for the damage and loss of human life which resulted from them and is there any duty to pay compensation?"

On October 22nd, 1946, a squadron of British warships, the cruisers Mauritius and Leander and the destroyers Saumarez and Volage, left the port of Corfu and proceeded northward through a channel previously swept for mines in the North Corfu Strait. The cruiser Mauritius was leading, followed by the destroyer Saumarez; at a certain distance thereafter came the cruiser Leander followed by the destroyer Volage. Outside the Bay of Saranda, Saumarez struck a mine and was heavily damaged. Volage was ordered to give her assistance and to take her in tow. Whilst towing the damaged ship, Volage struck a mine and was much damaged. Nevertheless, she succeeded in towing the other ship back to Corfu.

Three weeks later, on November 13th, the North Corfu Channel was swept by British minesweepers and twenty two moored mines were cut. Two mines were taken to Malta for expert examination. During the minesweeping operation it was thought that the mines were of the German GR type, but it was subsequently established that they were of the German GY type.

*   *   *

It is clear that knowledge of the mine laying cannot be imputed to the Albanian Government by reason merely of the fact that a minefield discovered in Albanian territorial waters caused the explosions of which the British warships were the victims. It is trite, as international practice shows, that a State on whose territory or in whose waters an act contrary to international law has occurred, may be called upon to give an explanation. It is also true that that State cannot evade such a request by limiting itself to a reply that it is ignorant of the circumstances of the act and of its authors. The State may, up to a certain point, be bound to supply particulars of the use made by it of the means of information and inquiry at its

---

[9] Taken from *Summaries of Judgments, Advisory Opinions and Orders of the International Court to Justice* 1948–1991, U.N. Doc. ST/LEG/SER.F/l (1992), pp. 3–4.

disposal. But it cannot be concluded from the mere fact of the control exercised by a State over its territory and waters that that State necessarily knew, or ought to have known, of any lawful act perpetrated therein, not yet that it knew, or should have known, the authors. This fact, by itself and apart from other circumstances, neither involves *prima facie* responsibility nor shifts the burden of proof.

On the other hand, the fact of this exclusive territorial control exercised by a State within its frontiers has a bearing upon the methods of proof available to establish the knowledge of that State as to such events. By reason of this exclusive control, the other State, the victim of a breach of international law, is often unable to furnish direct proof of facts giving rise to responsibility. Such a State should be allowed a more liberal recourse to inferences of fact and circumstantial evidence. This indirect evidence is admitted in all systems of law and its use is recognized by international decisions. It must be regarded as of special weight when it is based on a series of facts linked together and leading logically to a single conclusion.

The Court must examine therefore whether it has been established by means of indirect evidence that Albania has knowledge of mine laying in her territorial waters independently of any connivance on her part in this operation. The proof may be drawn from inferences of fact, provided that they leave no room for reasonable doubt. The elements of fact on which these inferences can be based may differ from those which are relevant to the question of connivance.

In the present case, two series of facts, which corroborate one another, have to be considered: the first relates to Albania's attitude before and after the disaster of October 22nd, 1946; the other concerns the feasibility of observing minelaying from the Albanian coast.

1. It is clearly established that the Albanian Government constantly kept a close watch over the waters of the North Corfu Channel, at any rate after May 1946. This vigilance is proved by the declaration of the Albanian Delegate in the Security Council on February 19th, 1947 . . . and especially by the diplomatic notes of the Albanian Government concerning the passage of foreign ships through its territorial waters. This vigilance sometimes went so far as to involve the use of force. . . .

As the Parties agree that the minefield had been recently laid, it must be concluded that the operation was carried out during the period of close watch by the Albanian authorities in this sector. This conclusion renders the Albanian Government's assertion of ignorance a priori somewhat improbable.

*   *   *

Another indication of the Albanian Government's knowledge consists in the fact that that Government did not notify the presence of mines in its waters, at the moment when it must have known this, at the latest after the sweep on November 13th, and further, whereas the Greek Government immediately appointed a Commission to inquire into the events of October 22nd, the Albanian Government took no decision of such a nature, nor did it proceed to the judicial investigation incumbent, in such a case, on the territorial sovereign.

This attitude does not seem reconcilable with the alleged ignorance of the Albanian authorities that the minefield had been laid in Albanian territorial waters.

It could be explained if the Albanian Government, while knowing of the minelaying, desired the circumstances of the operation to remain secret.

2. As regards the possibility of observing minelaying from the Albanian coast, Court regards the following facts, relating to the technical conditions of a secret mine laying and to the Albanian surveillance, as particularly important.

The Bay of Saranda and the channel used by shipping through the Strait are, from their geographical configuration, easily watched; the entrance of the bay is dominated by heights offering excellent observation points, both over the bay and over the Strait; whilst the channel throughout is close to the Albanian coast. The laying of a minefield in these waters could hardly fail to have been observed by the Albanian coastal defenses.

On this subject, it must first be said that the mine laying operation itself must have required a certain time. . . . The report of the Experts [of the Court] reckons the time that the minelayers would have been in the waters, between Cape Kiephali and St. George's Monastery, at between two and two and a half hours. This is sufficient time to attract the attention of the observation posts. . . .

The Court cannot fail to give great weight to the opinion of the Experts who examined the locality in a manner giving every guarantee of correct and impartial information. Apart from the existence of a look-out post at Cape Denta, which has not been proved, the Court, basing itself on the declarations of the Albanian Government that look-out posts were stationed at Cape Kiephali and at George's Monastery, refers to the following conclusions in the Experts' report: (1) that in the case of minelaying from the North towards the South, the minelayers would have been seen from Cape Kiephali; (2) in the case of minelayers from the South, the minelayers would have been seen from Cape Kiephali at George's Monastery.

From all the facts and observations mentioned above, the Court draws the conclusion that the laying of the minefield which caused the explosions on October 22nd, 1946, could not have been accomplished without the knowledge of the Albanian Government.

The obligations resulting for Albania from this knowledge are not disputed between the Parties. Counsel for the Albanian Government expressly recognized that *[translation]* "if Albania had been informed of the operation before the incidents of October 22nd and in time to warn the vessels and shipping in general of the existence of mines in the Corfu Channel, her responsibility would be involved. . . ."

The obligations incumbent upon the Albanian authorities consisted in notifying, for the benefit of shipping in general, the existence of a minefield in Albanian territorial waters and in warning the approaching British warships of the imminent danger to which the minefield exposed them. Such obligations are based, not on the Hague Convention of 1907, No. VIII, which is applicable in time of war, but on certain general and well-recognized principles, namely: elementary considerations of humanity, even more exacting in peace than in war; the principle of the freedom of maritime communication; and every State's obligation not to allow knowingly its territory to be used for acts contrary to the rights of other States.

In fact, Albania neither notified the existence of the minefield, nor warned the British warships of the danger they were approaching.

But Albania's obligation to notify shipping of the existence of mines in her waters depends on her having obtained knowledge of that fact in sufficient time before October 22nd; and the duty of the Albanian coastal authorities to warn the British ships depends on the time that elapsed between the moment that these ships were reported and the moment of the first explosion.

* * *

In fact nothing was attempted by the Albanian authorities to prevent the disaster. These grave omissions involve the international responsibility of Albania.

The Court therefore reaches the conclusion that Albania is responsible under international law for the explosions which occurred on October 22, 1946, in Albanian waters, and for the damage and loss of human life which resulted from them and that there is a duty upon Albania to pay compensation to the United Kingdom.

NOTES AND QUESTIONS

1. **Relevance to International Environmental Law.** The *Corfu Channel case* is of obvious importance to the duty of states to warn or notify of known environmental dangers even though it did not involve an environmental problem *per se*. In addition to the benefit of shipping, the I.C.J. also based its conclusion on grounds of much wider application: (i) elementary considerations of humanity, and (ii) the knowing harmful use of territory. *See also Case Concerning Military and Paramilitary Activities in and Against Nicaragua* (Nicaragua v. United States) (Merits), [1986] I.C.J. 14.

2. **UK actions and Albanian sovereignty.** A second question submitted to the Court was whether the U.K had violated the sovereignty of Albania on October 22, 1946 by transiting the Corfu strait with warships. The Court found that British vessels were exercising their right of innocent passage and thus had not violated Albanian sovereignty. [1949] I.C.J. 4, 26–32. What about the British minesweeping action on November 12 and 13, 1946 carried out against the express wishes of Albania? *See* [1949] I.C.J. 4, 32–35.

3. **Damages.** The Court subsequently assessed damages against Albania in the amount of approximately £850,000. [1949] I.C.J. 244, 250. The judgment remained unsatisfied for over 40 years despite the U.N. Charter obligation on states to comply with decisions of the Court. U.N. Charter, Art. 94. Compensation was finally paid as a result of a settlement agreement on May 8, 1992.

NOTE ON THE OBLIGATION TO INFORM, WARN, CONSULT, AND COOPERATE WITH RESPECT TO TRANSBOUNDARY ENVIRONMENTAL HARM

Recall that Rio Principles 18 and 19 require timely notification and relevant information to affected states with regard to transboundary environmental situations; that this duty is rule of customary law is reinforced by the ICJ decision in the *Corfu Channel case*. This obligation allows potentially affected states to take necessary action in an environmental emergency. Affected states can also request consultations with the source state on a proposed activity that may affect the shared environment. The duty of cooperation is recited in Rio Principle 27; the duty to cooperate is routinely stated as well in multilateral and bilateral environmental agreements and international environmental instruments. It *may* be stated unequivocally that states have duties under international law to fully inform, warn, consult, and cooperate in good faith to deal constructively with transboundary environmental problems.

C.   Areas Beyond National Jurisdictions

THE NUCLEAR TESTS CASE (AUSTRALIA v. FRANCE)
(Interim Measures)
[1973] I.C.J. 99, 99-106

THE INTERNATIONAL COURT OF JUSTICE,

*   *   *

Having regard to the Application by Australia the in the Registry of the Court on 9 May 1973, instituting proceedings against France in respect of a dispute concerning the holding of atmospheric tests of nuclear weapons by the French Government in the Pacific Ocean, and asking the Court to adjudge and declare that the carrying out of further atmospheric nuclear weapon tests in the South Pacific Ocean is not consistent with applicable rules of international law, and to order that the French Republic shall not carry out any further such tests,

Makes the following Order:

1. Having regard to the request dated 9 May 1973 and filed in the Registry the same day, whereby the Government of Australia, relying on Article 33 of the General Act of 1928 for the Pacific Settlement of International Disputes and on Article 41 of the Statute and Article 66 of the Rules of Court, asks the Court to indicate, pending the final decision in the case brought before it by, the Application of the same date, the following interim measures of protection:

> "The provisional measures should be that the French Government should desist from any further atmospheric nuclear tests pending the Judgment of the Court in this case";

*   *   *

6. Whereas by a letter dated 16 May 1973 from the Ambassador of France to the Netherlands, handed by him to the Registrar the same day, the French government stated that it considered that the Court was manifestly not competent in the case and that it could not accept the Court's jurisdiction, and that accordingly the French Government did not intend to appoint an agent, and requested the Court to remove the case from its list;

*   *   *

11. Noting that the French Government was not represented at the hearings; and whereas the non-appearance of one of the States concerned cannot by itself constitute all obstacle to the indication of provisional measures;

*   *   *

13. Whereas on a request for provisional measures the Court need not, before indicating them, finally satisfy itself that it has jurisdiction on the merits of the case, and yet ought not to indicate such measures unless the provisions invoked by the Applicant appear, prima facie, to afford a basis on which the jurisdiction of the Court might be founded;

*   *   *

15. Whereas, according to the letter of 16 May 1973 handed to the Registrar by the French Ambassador to the Netherlands, the French Government considers, *inter alia*, that the General Act of 1928 was an integral part of the League of Nations system and, since the demise of the League of Nations, has lost its effectivity and fallen into desuetude; that this view of the matter is confirmed by the conduct of States in regard to the General Act of 1928 since the collapse of the League of Nations; that, in consequence, the General Act cannot serve as a basis for the competence of the Court to deliberate on the Application of Australia with respect to French nuclear tests; that in any event the General Act of 1928 is not now applicable in the relations between France and Australia and cannot prevail over the will clearly and more recently' expressed in the declaration of 20 May 1966 made by the French Government under Article 36, paragraph 2 of the Statute of the Court — that paragraph 3 of that declaration excepts from the French Government's acceptance of compulsory jurisdiction "disputes concerning activities connected with national defence"; and that the present dispute concerning French nuclear tests in the Pacific incontestably falls within the exception contained in that paragraph;

16. Whereas in its oral observations the Government of Australia maintains, inter alia, that various matters, including certain statements of the French Government, provide indications which should lead the Court to conclude that the General Act of 1928 is still in force between the parties to that Act; that the General Act furnishes a basis for the Court's jurisdiction in the present dispute which is altogether independent of the acceptances of compulsory jurisdiction by Australia and by France under Article 36, paragraph 2, of the Statute; that France's obligations under the General Act with respect to the acceptance of the Court's jurisdiction cannot be considered as having been modified by any subsequent declaration made by her unilaterally under Article 36, paragraph 2 of the Statute; that if the reservation in paragraph 3 of the French declaration of 20 May 1966 relating to "disputes concerning activities connected with national defence" is to be regarded as one having an objective content, it is questionable whether nuclear weapon development falls within the concept of national defence; that if this reservation is to be regarded as a self-judging reservation. it is invalid, and in consequence France is bound by the terms of that declaration unqualified by the reservation in question;

17. Whereas the material submitted to the Court leads it to the conclusion, at the

present stage of the proceedings, that the provisions invoked by the Applicant appear, *prima facie* to afford a basis on which the jurisdiction of the Court might be founded; and whereas, the Court will accordingly proceed toexamine the Applicant's request for the indication of interim measures of protection;

*   *   *

22. Whereas the claims formulated by the Government of Australia in its Application are as follows:

  (i)   The right of Australia and its people, in common with other States and their peoples, to be free from atmospheric nuclear weapon tests by any country is and will be violated

 (ii)   The deposit of radio-active fall-out on the territory — of Australia and its dispersion in Australia's airspace without Australian consent:

    (a)   violates Australian sovereignty over its territory;

    (b)   impairs Australia's independent right to determine what acts shall take place within its territory and in particular whether Australia and its people shall be exposed to radiation from artificial sources;

(iii)   the interference with ships and aircraft on the high seas and in the superjacent airspace, and the pollution of the high seas by radioactive fall-out, constitute infringements of the freedom of the high seas;

*   *   *

24. Whereas by the terms of Article 41 of the Statute the Court may indicate interim measures of protection only when it considers that circumstances so require in order to preserve the rights of either party;

*   *   *

27. Whereas the Government of Australia also alleges that the atmospheric nuclear explosions carried out by France in the Pacific have caused widespread radio-active fall-out on Australian territory and elsewhere in the southern hemisphere, have given rise to concentrations of radio-nuclides in foodstuffs and in man, and have resulted in additional radiation doses to persons living in that hemisphere and in Australia in particular; that any radio-active material deposited on Australian territory- will be potentially dangerous to Australia and its people and any injury caused thereby would be irreparable; that the conduct of French nuclear tests in the atmosphere creates anxiety and concern among the Australian people; that any effects of the French nuclear tests upon the resources of the sea or the conditions of the environment can never be undone and would be irremediable by any payment of damages; and any, infringement by France of the rights of Australia and her people to freedom of movement over the high seas and superjacent airspace cannot be undone;

28. Whereas the French Government, in a diplomatic Note dated 7 February 1973 and addressed to the Government of Australia, the text of which was annexed to the Application in the present case, called attention to Reports of the Australian National Radiation Advisory Committee from 1967 to 1972, which all concluded that the fall-out from the French tests did not constitute a danger to the health of the

Australian population; whereas in the said Note the French Government further expressed its conviction that in the absence of ascertained damage attributable to its nuclear experiments, they did not violate any rule of international law, and that if the infraction of the law was alleged to consist in a violation of a legal norm concerning the threshold of atomic pollution which should not be crossed, it was hard to see what was the precise rule on which Australia relied;

29. Whereas for the purpose of the present proceedings it suffices to observe that the information submitted to the Court, including Reports of the United Nations Scientific Committee on the Effects of Atomic Radiation between 1958 and 1972, does not exclude the possibility that damage to Australia might be shown to be caused by the deposit on Australian territory of radio-active fall-out resulting from such tests and to be irreparable;

30. Whereas in the light of the foregoing considerations the Court is satisfied that it should indicate interim measures of protection in order to preserve the right claimed by Australia in the present litigation in respect of the deposit of radio-active fallout on her territory;

*   *   *

33. Whereas the decision given in the present proceedings in no way prejudges the question of the jurisdiction of the Court to deal with the merits of the case, or any questions relating to the admissibility of the Application, or relating to the merits themselves, and leaves unaffected the right of the French Government to submit arguments in respect of those questions;

*   *   *

Accordingly,

THE COURT

Indicates, by 8 votes to 6, pending its final decision in the proceedings instituted on 9 May 1973 by Australia against France, the following provisional measures:

> The Governments of Australia and France should each of them ensure that no action of any kind is taken which aggravate or extend the dispute submitted to the Court or prejudice the rights of the other Party in respect of the carrying out of whatever decision the Court may render in the case; and, in particular, the French Government should avoid nuclear tests causing the deposit of radioactive fall-out on Australian territory;

NUCLEAR TEST CASE (AUSTRALIA v. FRANCE)
(Merits)
[1974] I.C.J. 253, 267–72

THE COURT *delivers the following Judgment:*

*   *   *

43. It is well recognized that declarations made by way of unilateral acts concerning

legal or factual situations, may have the effect of creating legal obligations. Declarations of this kind may be, and often are, very specific. When it is the intention of the State making the declaration that should become bound according to its terms, that intention confers on the declaration the character of a legal undertaking, the State being thenceforth legally required to follow a course of conduct consistent with the declaration. An undertaking of this kind, if given publicly, and with an intent to be bound, even though not made within the context of international negotiations, is binding. In these circumstances, nothing in the nature of a *quid pro quo* nor any subsequent acceptance of the declaration, nor even any reply or reaction from other States, is required for the declaration to take effect, since such a requirement would be inconsistent with the strictly unilateral nature of the juridical act by which the pronouncement by the State was made.

44. Of course, not all unilateral acts imply obligation; but a State may choose to take up a certain position in relation to a particular matter with the intention of being bound — the intention is to be ascertained by interpretation of the act. When States make statements by which their freedom of action is to be limited, a restrictive interpretation is called for.

45. With regard to the question of form, it should be observed that this is not a domain in which international law imposes any special or strict requirements. Whether a statement is made orally or in writing makes no essential difference, for such statements made in particular circumstances may create commitments in international law, which does not require that they should be couched in written form. Thus the question of form is not decisive. As the Court said in its Judgment on the preliminary objections in the case concerning the *Temple of Preah Vihear*:

> "Where . . . as is generally the case in international law, which places the principal emphasis on the intentions of the parties, the law prescribes no particular form, parties are free to choose what form they please provided their intention clearly results from it."*(International Court of Justice Reports 1961*, p. 31.)

The Court further stated in the same case: ". . . the sole relevant question is whether the language employed in any given declaration does reveal a clear intention . . ." *(ibid.,* p. 32).

46. One of the basic principles governing the creation and performance of legal obligations, whatever their source, is the principle of good faith. Trust and confidence are inherent in international cooperation, in particular in an age when this co-operation in many fields is becoming increasingly essential. Just as the very rule of *pacta sunt servanda* in the law of treaties is based on good faith, so also is the binding character of an international obligation assumed by unilateral declaration. Thus interested States may take cognizance of unilateral declarations and place confidence in them, and are entitled to require that the obligations thus created be respected.

*   *   *

47. Having examined the legal principles involved, the Court will now turn to the particular statements made by the French Government. The Government of Australia has made known to the Court at the oral proceedings its own interpre-

tation of the first such statement. . . . As to subsequent statements, reference may be made to what was said in the Australian Senate by the Attorney-General on 26 September 1974. . . . In reply to a question concerning reports that France had announced that it had finished atmospheric nuclear testing, he said that the statement of the French Foreign Minister on 25 September . . . "falls far short of an undertaking that there win be no more atmospheric tests conducted by the French Government at its Pacific Tests Centre" and that France was "still reserving to itself the right to carry out atmospheric nuclear tests" so that "In legal terms, Australia has nothing from the French Government which protects it against any further atmospheric tests."

48. It will be observed that Australia has recognized the possibility of the dispute being resolved by a unilateral declaration, of the kind specified above, on the part of France, and its conclusion that in fact no "commitment" or "firm, explicit and binding undertaking" had been given is based on the view that the assurance is not absolute in its terms, that there is a "distinction between an assertion that tests will go underground and an assurance that no further atmospheric tests win take place," that "the possibility of further atmospheric testing taking place after the commencement of underground tests cannot be excluded" and that thus "the Government of France is still reserving to itself the right to carry out atmospheric nuclear tests." The Court must however form its own view of the meaning and scope intended by the author of a unilateral declaration which may create a legal obligation, and cannot in this respect be bound by the view expressed by another State which is in no way a party to the text.

49. Of the statements by the French Government now before the Court, the most essential are clearly those made by the President of the Republic. There can be no doubt, in view of his functions, that his public communications or statements, oral or written, as Head of State, are in international relations acts of the French State. His statements, and those of members of the French Government acting under his authority, tip to the statement made by the Minister of Defence (of 11 October 1974), constitute a whole. Thus, in whatever form these statements were expressed, they must be held to constitute an engagement of the State, having regard to their intention and to the circumstances in which they: were made.

50. The unilateral statements of the French authorities were made outside the Court, publicly and *erga omnes*, even though the first of them was communicated to the Government of Australia. As was observed above, to have legal effect, there was no need for these statements to be addressed to a particular State, nor was acceptance by any other State required. The general nature and characteristics of these statements are decisive for the evaluation of the legal implications, and it is to the interpretation of the statements that the Court must now proceed. The Court is entitled to presume, at the outset, that these statements were not made *in vacuo* but in relation to the tests which constitute the very object of the present proceedings, although France has not appeared in the case.

51. In announcing that the 1974 series of atmospheric tests would be the last, the French Government conveyed to the world at large, including the Applicant, its intention effectively to terminate these tests. It was bound to assume that other States might take note of these statements and rely on their being effective. The

validity of these statements and their legal consequences must be considered within the general framework of the security of international intercourse, and the confidence and trust which are so essential in the relations among States. It is from the actual substance of these statements, and from the circumstances attending their making, that the legal implications of the unilateral act must be deduced. The objects of these statements are clear and they were addressed to the international community as a whole, and the Court holds that they constitute an undertaking possessing legal effect. The Court considers that the President of the Republic, in deciding upon the effective cessation of atmospheric tests, gave an undertaking to the international community to which his words were addressed. It is true that the French Government has consistently maintained, for example in a Note dated 7 February 1973 from the French Ambassador in Canberra to the Prime Minister and Minister for Foreign Affairs of Australia, that it "has the conviction that its nuclear experiments have not violated any rule of international law," nor did France recognize that it was bound by any role of international law to terminate its tests, but this does not affect the legal consequences of the statements examined above. The Court finds that the unilateral undertaking resulting from these statements cannot be interpreted as having been made in implicit reliance on an arbitrary power of reconsideration. The Court finds further that the French Government has undertaken an obligation the precise nature and limits of which must be understood in accordance with the actual terms in which they have been publicly expressed.

*   *   *

59. Thus the Court finds that no further pronouncement is required in the present case. It does not enter into the adjudicatory functions of the Court to deal with issues *in abstracto*, once it has reached the conclusion that the merits of the case no longer fall to be determined. The object of the claim having clearly disappeared, there is nothing on which to give judgment.

*   *   *

60. Once the Court has found that a State has entered into a commitment concerning its future conduct it is not the Court's function to contemplate that it will not comply with it. However, the Court observes that if the basis of this Judgment were to be affected, the Applicant could request an examination of the situation in accordance with the provisions of the Statute; the denunciation by France, by letter dated 2 January 1974, of the General Act for the Pacific Settlement of International Disputes, which is relied on as a basis of jurisdiction in the present case, cannot by itself constitute an obstacle to the presentation of such a request.

*   *   *

62. For these reasons,

THE COURT

by nine votes to six,

finds that the claim of Australia no longer has any object and that the Court is therefore not called upon to give a decision thereon.

NOTES AND QUESTIONS

1. *Customary law.* In this case, Australia and New Zealand contended that the French atmospheric nuclear testing was a breach of customary international law. In its Memorial, Australia argued:

> 444. It will thus be evident that there is ample justification for a finding by the Court that there exists a rule of customary international law to the effect that atmospheric nuclear testing is unlawful.

> * * *

> 448. The feature common to all the specific expressions and confirmations of the rule as indicated above is that they are couched in terms of an *erga omnes* obligation and not in terms of an obligation owed to particular States. The duty to refrain from atmospheric nuclear testing is stated in absolute terms, rather than in terms relative to the incidence of the effect of nuclear testing upon particular States. The duty is thus owed to the international community; it is a duty of every State towards every other State. For this reason and — to use the very language of the Court in the *Barcelona Traction* case — because "of the importance of the rights involved, *all States can be held to have a legal interest in their protection"* (*International Court of Justice Reports 1970*, at p. 33) (italics added).

> 449. The Australian Government therefore submits that it undoubtedly has a legal interest in the protection of its right to claim from the French Government the observance of the obligation to abstain from conducting atmospheric nuclear tests; that it has *locus standi* to obtain a declaratory judgment to this effect; and that its Application is already, under this heading, fully admissible.

> 450. In making this statement, the Government of Australia. cannot refrain from also observing that, if it must be recognized that every State possesses a legal interest in the protection of the right involved in the present case, Australia has a higher title than most States to claim such protection, since by reason of its geographical situation and the deposit of fall-out from French tests in the southern hemisphere, Australia is more directly affected than many other States by the harmful effects that the rule of general international law prohibiting atmospheric nuclear tests is designed precisely to prevent. If Australia is not entitled to protect the right here in question, what other State would be entitled to do so? And one of the most essential general rules of today's international law would become devoid of any effective content.

> * * *

> 454. The question remains, of course, of the legal consequences of the effect. The Government of Australia has already, in the course of the oral hearings on interim measures (21 May 1973, pp. 186-188, supra), given some indication of the factors which establish that French conduct leading to nuclear fall-out on Australian soil is internationally unlawful. The Government of Australia repeats that its case rests upon several bases: on

the mere fact of trespass, on the harmful effects associated with trespass, and on the impairment of its independent right to determine what acts shall take place within its territory. In this connection, the Government of Australia wants to emphasize that the mere fact of trespass, the harmful effects which flow from such fallout and the impairment of its independence, each clearly constitute a violation of the affected State's sovereignty over and in respect of its territory. . . .

Nuclear Tests Cases (Australia v. France), I.C.J. Pleadings 249, 334–36 (Vol. I). Is this argument valid? Did the tests cause legally cognizable damage? Should Australia be admitted to claim to represent the common interest of the entire international community?

2.   *Atmospheric and underground testing*. France has refrained from *atmospheric* nuclear tests since making its unilateral declaration. In July 1995, however, it announced its plans to resume a series eight of underground nuclear tests at the Maurora and Fangataufa Atolls in the South Pacific after a moratorium of three years. The decision was met with protests worldwide, including by international lawyers. *See* Don Anton, *International and Environmental Lawyers Worldwide Join to Challenge the Lawfulness of the Resumption of Nuclear Testing by France*, 12 ENVTL & PLANNING L.J. 299 (1995). In the lead-up to testing, a French vulcanologist, Pierre Vincent, raised serious environmental concerns about the fracturing of the atolls from repeated underground nuclear explosions, resulting in the gradual release of radioactivity into the sea. In his view, there was a "high risk" that unique environmental factors, which predisposed the area to instability — coupled with a nuclear explosions — could cause large parts of the atoll to sheer away, leading to a "spill-out" of dangerous radioactivity.

On August 8, 1995, New Zealand Prime Minister Bolger announced that New Zealand would undertake to halt French nuclear tests by action in the International Court of Justice and on August 21, 1995, New Zealand filed a "Request for an Examination of the Situation" with the I.C.J. in accordance with the reservation of jurisdiction by the Court in its 1974 judgment, *Nuclear Tests Case (New Zealand v. France)*, [1974] I.C.J. 457, 477, para. 63 (identical to para. 60 reproduced above in the Australia v. France judgment). On September 22, 1995, the Court, by a vote of 12 to 3, dismissed New Zealand's request on the ground that the 1974 Judgment related to *atmospheric* not *underground* nuclear testing. The Court noted that this dismissal was without prejudice to the obligations of States in general to protect the natural environment. *Request for an Examination of the Situation in Accordance with Paragraph 63 of the Court's Judgment of 20 December 1974 in the Nuclear Tests (New Zealand v. France) Case*, [1995] I.C.J. 288. Was this the correct decision? *See* Barbara Kwiatowski, *New Zealand v. France Nuclear Tests: The Dismissed Case of Lasting Significance*, 37 VA. J. INT'L L. 107 (1996); Catherine Giraud, *French Nuclear Testing in the Pacific and the 1995 International Court of Justice Decision*, 1 ASIA PACIFIC J. ENVTL L. 125 (1996).

NOTE ON TRANSBOUNDARY HARM BEYOND THE LIMITS OF NATIONAL JURISDICTIONS

The Nuclear Test case is important because it concerns in part the issue of transboundary harm to areas beyond national jurisdiction. What state has standing to bring an environmental claim to prevent or to recover damage to areas beyond national jurisdiction? Is this a duty owed to all — an *ergo omnes* obligation? Should it be? In some cases the ICJ has ruled that an *actio popularis* is appropriate because the obligation is owed generally. *See Barcelona Traction Light and Power Company (Belgium* v. *Spain)* [1970] I.C.J. Rep. 4.

In the Nuclear Test Case (Merits), four dissenting member of the Court castigated the majority judges for pronouncing on the case without first determining jurisdiction. These judges ruled the Court had jurisdiction and should have rendered a decision on the merits in the case. They also ruled that the issue of *actio popularis* was properly before the Court. Do you agree?

It is notable that neither the majority opinion nor any individual opinion in the case mentions Principle 21 of the Stockholm Declaration, which extended the protection against transboundary harm to areas beyond national jurisdiction. Why not?

Section III.   CODIFICATIONS AND SPECIALIZED TREATY REGIMES

As the preceding section has demonstrated, no comprehensive liability regime for the prevention or recovery of damages for transboundary harm has been created under international law. Is the creation of such a regime possible or even desirable? Three reasons may be advanced in favor of a more robust international law regime to deal with transboundary harm: the existence of a comprehensive regime would undeniably have a deterrent effect; victims of transboundary harm would gain compensation; and such a regime would complement the existing panoply of regulatory environmental treaties.

Over the years many attempts have been made by international bodies to formulate a comprehensive international law regime on the topic of transboundary harm. Despite much effort and much spilled ink no general formulation has been accepted by states; they are simply unwilling to be subjected to what they consider open-ended environmental liability. Thus, we shall see that only 15 multilateral agreements providing for the recovery of damages for transboundary harm have been agreed, and only seven of these are in force.

Before we turn to these 15 specialized international agreements, we consider the codifications approved by one international body, the prestigious International Law Commission (ILC), which was formed by resolution of the UN General Assembly in 1947, and which consists of 34 experts on international law elected for four year terms by the UN General Assembly. The ILC Statute charges this body to formulate rules that contribute to the progressive development of international law.

A.   Principles of State Responsibility for Environmental Harm

To what extent is a state responsible under general principles of state responsibility under international law to prevent environmental degradation and to pay compensation if such degradation should occur? This section explores state responsibility in general terms. There is no comprehensive international agreement recognizing or laying down international norms of state responsibility for environmental damage. Codifications over the years by the ILC, however, have authoritatively addressed this issue.

In order to facilitate analysis, consider the following problem.

PROBLEM 3-2
THE CHERNOBYL NUCLEAR REACTOR INCIDENT

On April 26, 1986, the nuclear reactor at the Chernobyl Nuclear Power Plant in the Soviet Union (now Ukraine) experienced a critical loss of coolant and exploded after a catastrophic meltdown. As a result, a cloud of radioactive emissions was released into the atmosphere, spreading quickly over much of the Soviet Union and Western Europe. Large amounts of radioactive fallout occurred not only near the plant but also beyond. Over 50,000 persons were immediately evacuated from villages surrounding the plant. The radioactive cloud of material crossed into Western Europe, affecting first, the countries of Scandinavia, then Germany, Austria, Switzerland, Yugoslavia, and Italy. Although no immediate deaths occurred outside the Soviet Union, in many Western European countries contaminated food supplies had to be destroyed; many grazing animals were declared unfit for human consumption, and meat and dairy production was disrupted for some months. Despite the efforts of authorities to minimize the adverse effects of the radioactivity, scientists estimated that that the Chernobyl incident was responsible for excess deaths from cancer and other illnesses ranging from 14,000 to 475,000 worldwide.

The cause of the Chernobyl incident was found to be an experiment undertaken by plant officials designed to determine how long the reactor would continue to produce electricity in the case of an unexpected power cut-off. During this experiment technicians deliberately lowered the reactors' power level and shut down the plant's emergency cooling system in violation of Soviet safety regulations. The result of this "experiment" was the biggest nuclear safety disaster on record. In addition, the Soviet Union, obsessed with secrecy, tried to keep news of this disaster quiet and made no announcement or warning to the outside world.

Despite suffering millions of dollars in damages to crops, livestock, dairy and egg production as well as untold damage to the environment and human health, no state and no foreign person made a claim against the Soviet Union in connection with this incident. Why not?

Suppose a similar incident happened today. Consider the following questions.

1.   Read the International law Commission's Draft Articles on the Responsibilities of States for Internationally Wrongful Acts.

   a.   Do these Draft Articles apply to the case at hand?

b. What is the status of these Draft Articles? Are they legally binding? The General Assembly of the United Nations "took note" of these Draft Articles in Resolution 56/83 (Dec. 2001).

Background and specific questions. The ILC's Draft Articles on the Responsibility of States for Internationally Wrongful Acts, 2001, which are reprinted in the **Document Supplement**, are the product of over 50 years of work by international scholars. Note that these Draft Articles are intended to apply to any and all breaches of an international obligation by a state. But they do not set out the norms or elements of any breach of an international obligation that gives rise to state responsibility. The Draft Articles do not define or even address the elements of any substantive legal obligation. Rather these Draft Articles presume a breach of an international obligation and cover such matters as whether the conduct giving rise to the breach can be attributed to a state; the responsibility of a state in connection with an act of another state; circumstances precluding wrongfulness; and the consequences of a wrongful act.

Thus these Draft Articles are termed "secondary" rules of law; the substantive obligations that they entail and the specific norms and elements required to be proved for a breach of such norms are "primary" rules that must be independently formulated as treaty or customary international law. Of course such primary substantive rules will differ greatly from one another.

Does the Chernobyl incident involve a breach of a primary rule of international law?

If so, do Articles 12 and 13 of the Draft Articles apply?

Are the Articles in the Chapter on Attribution relevant to this Problem? Can the conduct involved be attributed to the State on whose territory the incident occurred? Keep in mind the Corfu Channel case, which is authority that failure to act, an omission — with knowledge — is attributable to the responsibility of the state involved.

Is there any circumstance precluding wrongfulness (*see* Chapter V of the Draft Articles)?

What are the legal consequences involved — the content of the international responsibility — under Part Two of the Draft Articles?

2. Consider next the applicability of the International Law Commission's Draft Articles on International liability for the Injurious Consequences of Acts Not Prohibited by International law, 1996, reprinted in the **Document Supplement.**

Background and specific questions. These Draft Articles bear a curious title; one might ask how conduct that is not prohibited by law can give rise to liability! Note that, unlike the ILC's Draft Articles on State Responsibility, these Draft Articles set out primary rules of law.

Do the rules apply to the case we are considering?

Is there liability under Article 5?

Do these Draft Articles do a good job of defining the elements that give rise to liability? What specific conduct gives rise to liability? Is fault required or is this strict liability without fault? Is it clear what kind of damage is compensable? Do the Draft Articles require a causal nexus between the damage suffered and the conduct involved?

These Draft Articles — unsurprisingly — were much criticized, and in 1997, the ILC in effect repudiated them by announcing that it would embark on a new effort to deal with the topic of transboundary harm, separating the topic into two parts: (1) prevention of harm and (2) liability. We consider these documents next.

3.   Consider the applicability of the International Law Commission's Draft Articles on Prevention of Transboundary Harm from Hazardous Activities, 2001, reprinted in the **Document Supplement**.

Background and specific questions. The new effort by the ILC to address transboundary harm separated state responsibility from state liability; do you agree with this separation? Does this formulation accord with Principle 21 of the Stockholm Declaration and Principle 2 of the Rio Declaration?

What is the scope of application of these Draft Articles?

Is the duty of prevention absolute or is this a due diligence obligation? James Crawford has observed that "different primary rules of international law impose different standards ranging from due diligence to strict liability. . . . There does not seem to be any general principle or presumption about the role of fault in relation to any primary rule." . . . JAMES CRAWFORD, THE INTERNATIONAL LAW COMMISSION'S ARTICLES ON STATE RESPONSIBILITY: INTRODUCTION, TEXT AND COMMENTARIES 13 (Cambridge: Cambridge University Press, 2002).

Do the Draft Articles require notification in the case of an emergency?

4.   Consider the applicability of the International Law Commission's Draft Principles on the Allocation of Loss in the Case of Transboundary Harm arising out of Hazardous Activities, 2006, reprinted in the **Document Supplement**.

Background and specific questions. These Draft Principles, while recognizing the necessity of specific regimes for liability in specific instances of transboundary harm, attempted to set out general principles of the international law of liability.

What is their scope of application? (Principle 1).

What is "damage"? (Principle 2).

Is environmental harm compensable? To what extent? (Principles 2 and 3).

What are the obligations of the responsible state? (Principles 4 to 8).

To what extent do the Draft Principles look to the development of specific international liability regimes? (Principle 7).

5.   What kind of specific liability regime or regimes is appropriate? Consider the example of the Convention on International Liability for Damage Caused by Space Objects (1972), reprinted in the Document Supplement. Is this a good model for environmental liability conventions? This Convention was invoked by Canada

against the Soviet Union when, in 1971, the Soviet nuclear powered satellite Cosmos 954 crashed and broke into thousands of pieces over an area of the North West Territories of Canada. Canada made a claim against the Soviet Union for environmental damages in the amount of $14 million. After several years of discussions, the Soviets paid Canada the sum of $3 million, claiming Canada's claim for clean-up was excessive. *See Claim against the USSR for Damage Caused by Soviet Cosmos 954*, 18 I.L.M. 899 (1979).

6. In the field of nuclear energy several specialized conventions have been concluded concerning liability for damages:

- Paris Convention on Third Party Liability in the Field of Nuclear Energy (1960), with Amending Protocols 1964, 1982, and 2004.

- Supplementary Convention to the Paris Convention (1963) with Amending Protocols 1964, 1982, and 2004.

- Convention on the Liability of Operators of Nuclear Ships (1962) (not yet in force).

- International Atomic Energy Agency Vienna Convention on Civil Liability for Nuclear Damage (1963) and Amending Protocol 1997 (both in force), reprinted in the Document Supplement.

- International Atomic Energy Agency Convention on Supplementary Compensation for Nuclear Damage (1997) (not yet in force).

At the time of the Chernobyl accident, the Soviet Union was not a party to these Conventions; this was one reason the Soviet Union denied liability. These Conventions are concluded on the basis of the following principles:

- Strict liability to the nuclear operator

- Exclusive liability of the nuclear operator

- Compensation without discrimination based'on nationality, domicile or residence

- Mandatory financial coverage of the operator's liability

- Exclusive jurisdiction in the courts of the state where the accident occurs

- Limitation of liability in amount and in time

The Paris Convention and the IAEA Vienna Convention are linked by a 1988 Joint Protocol.

The definition of damage under these Conventions covers property, health, and loss of life but does not cover environmental damage. Following Chernobyl steps were taken to increase the limits of liability under these Conventions. Amending Protocols in 2004 added compensation for environmental damage and economic losses. New limits of liability were set: operators are liable for at most 600 million SDRs; the amount of liability may be less depending on what protocol the installation state has ratified. The operator is required to maintain insurance to cover the amount of liability. The U.S. has accepted only the 1997 Convention, which is not yet in force. Under the U.S. Price Anderson Act (42 U.S.C. §§ 2011, 2022–2286i, 2296a–2296g-4), the liability of the nuclear operator is limited to $10.5

billion. Do these Conventions and the Price Anderson Act amount to public subsidies of nuclear power?

NOTE ON THE DUTY TO NOTIFY AND ASSIST IN CASE OF A NUCLEAR ACCIDENT

The tragedy of the Chernobyl accident led to two new agreements to facilitate response to a nuclear accident. The first, the Convention on Early Notification of a Nuclear Accident (1986) applies whenever a release of radioactive material from a nuclear reactor occurs or is likely to occur that may result in an international transboundary release. In such an event, a State party is obliged to "forthwith notify" those states which are or may be physically affected as well as the International Atomic Energy Agency as to the nature, time, and exact location of the release. (Art. 2a) In addition, the state in which the release occurred must "promptly" provide information as to the facility involved, the assumed or established cause, the characteristics of the release, information on meteorological and hydrological, conditions necessary for forecasting the extent of the release, protective measures taken or planned, the predicted behaviour of the release, and the possible development of emergency situations. Such information must be updated as appropriate. (Art. 2b and Art. 5). A second agreement, the Convention on Assistance in Case of a Nuclear Accident or Radiological Emergency (1986), requires cooperative action in the case of a nuclear accident or radiological release and the rendering of assistance as needed through the International Atomic Energy Agency.

B.   Specialized International Agreements Providing for Liability for Transboundary Environmental Harm

In addition to the field of nuclear energy, some 10 international regimes have been concluded that provide damages in particular types of cases of transboundary environmental harm. These are:

- Convention on Civil Liability for Oil Pollution Damage Resulting from the Exploration for and Exploitation of Seabed Mineral Resources (1977) (not in force).

- Convention on Civil Liability for Damage Caused During Carriage of Dangerous Goods by Road, Rail and Inland Navigation Vessels (1989) (not in force).

- International Convention on Civil liability for Oil Pollution Damage (1992, replaced 1969 Convention). (122 ratifications).

- International Convention on the Establishment of an International Fund for Oil Pollution Damage (1992, replaced 1971 Convention). (105 parties).

- Lugano Convention on Civil liability for Damage Resulting from Activities Dangerous to the Environment (1993) (not in force, 0 ratifications).

- Protocol on Civil Liability and Compensation for Damage Caused by the Transboundary Effects of Industrial Accidents on Transboundary Waters (2003) (not in force).

• Convention on Liability and Compensation in Connection with Carriage of Hazardous and Noxious Substances by Sea (1999) (not in force).

• Basel Protocol on liability and Compensation for Damage Resulting from Transboundary Movements of Hazardous Wastes (1999) (not in force).

• International Convention on Civil Liability for Bunker Oil Pollution Damage (2001) (in force 2008).

• Annex VI to the Protocol on Environmental Protection to the Antarctic Treaty, Liability Arising from Environmental Emergencies (1991) (not in force).

Note that many of these agreements have not received sufficient ratifications and are consequently not in force. All of the liability conventions in force, like the nuclear liability conventions, channel liability to private parties. States remain unwilling to subject themselves to liability either under a general international law regime or under a specialized liability regime. States are willing to ratify regulatory regimes but not a corresponding liability regime. For example, The United Nations Economic Commission for Europe's Convention on the Transboundary Effects of Industrial Accidents (1992) requires states to be prepared to respond to industrial accidents and disasters involving hazardous substances; they are also required to take measures to prevent such disasters and to fully inform the public and affected states in the event of such as disaster. But the Lugano Convention (1993), which provides liability and compensation in cases involving industrial accidents, has not received any ratification and is not in force.

Stockholm Principle 22 and Rio Principle 13 enjoin states to develop international law rules on liability and compensation for transboundary harm, but this injunction is so far largely in vain.

QUESTION

Suppose a serious industrial accident occurred in the United States having serious transboundary effects in Mexico — would any international law liability scheme apply?

Section IV.   ENVIRONMENT IMPACT ASSESSMENT IN A TRANSBOUNDARY CONTEXT

In Chapter 2, we covered environmental impact assessment as a principle of international law as stated in Rio Principle 11. The embodiment of international law on environmental impact assessment is the Espoo Convention on Environmental Impact in a Transboundary Context (1991).

PROBLEM 3-3
BUILDING A NUCLEAR POWER PLANT ON THE AUSTRIAN BORDER

Austria is known as the most anti-nuclear country in Europe. In 1979, Austrian voters rejected nuclear power forever, and Austria currently bans even imports of electricity generated by nuclear power plants outside Austria. Austrians boast that their country is *100%* nuclear-free. However, Austria's neighbor and fellow European Union member, the Czech Republic is committed to expanding nuclear power. Two nuclear power plants — Temelin and Dukovany — already operate near the Austrian border. Now authorities in the Czech Republic are planning to construct four new nuclear reactors near the Austrian border. The Austrian government has protested this decision both to Prague and to Brussels (the headquarters of the EU), but to no avail. Czech officials state that "the final decision on the nuclear power plants will be made in Prague, not Vienna or Brussels." The Czech Republic officials have said that " 'safe nuclear power is the only option for us."

Both Austria and the Czech Republic have ratified the Espoo Convention on Environmental Impact in a Transboundary Context (1991). What duties does this Convention impose on the Czech Republic in connection with the construction of additional nuclear reactors to generate electricity? Can this Convention be used by Austria to stop the construction of the new reactors? What are the options for dispute settlement?

Consider the following provisions of the Espoo Convention.

CONVENTION ON ENVIRONMENTAL IMPACT ASSESSMENT IN A TRANSBOUNDARY CONTEXT
Espoo (Finland), on 15 February 1991

The Parties to this Convention,

Aware of the interrelationship between economic activities and their environmental consequences,

Affirming the need to ensure environmentally sound and sustainable development,

Determined to enhance international co-operation in assessing environmental impact in particular in a transboundary context,

Have agreed as follows:

*   *   *

Article 2

GENERAL PROVISIONS

1. The Parties shall, either individually or jointly, take all appropriate and effective measures to prevent, reduce and control significant adverse transboundary environmental impact from proposed activities.

2. Each Party shall take the necessary legal, administrative or other measures to implement the provisions of this Convention, including, with respect to proposed activities listed in Appendix I that are likely to cause significant adverse transboundary impact, the establishment of an environmental impact assessment procedure that permits public participation and

preparation of the environmental impact assessment documentation described in Appendix II.

3. The Party of origin shall ensure that in accordance with the provisions of this Convention an environmental impact assessment is undertaken prior to a decision to authorize or undertake a proposed activity listed in Appendix I that is likely to cause a significant adverse transboundary impact.

4. The Party of origin shall, consistent with the provisions of this Convention, ensure that affected Parties are notified of a proposed activity listed in Appendix I that is likely to cause a significant adverse transboundary impact.

5. Concerned Parties shall, at the initiative of any such Party, enter into discussions on whether one or more proposed activities not listed in Appendix I is or are likely to cause a significant adverse transboundary impact and thus should be treated as if it or they were so listed. Where those Parties so agree, the activity or activities shall be thus treated. General guidance for identifying criteria to determine significant adverse impact is set forth in Appendix III.

6. The Party of origin shall provide, in accordance with the provisions of this Convention, an opportunity to the public in the areas likely to be affected to participate in relevant environmental impact assessment procedures regarding proposed activities and shall ensure that the opportunity provided to the public of the affected Party is equivalent to that provided to the public of the Party of origin.

7. Environmental impact assessments as required by this Convention shall, as a minimum requirement, be undertaken at the project level of the proposed activity. To the extent appropriate, the Parties shall endeavour to apply the principles of environmental impact assessment to policies, plans and programmes.

8. The provisions of this Convention shall not affect the right of Parties to implement national laws, regulations, administrative provisions or accepted legal practices protecting information the supply of which would be prejudicial to industrial and commercial secrecy or national security.

9. The provisions of this Convention shall not affect the right of particular Parties to Implement, by bilateral or multilateral agreement where appropriate, more stringent measures than those of this Convention.

10. The provisions of this Convention shall not prejudice any obligations of the Parties under international law with regard to activities having or likely to have a transboundary impact.

Article 3

NOTIFICATION

1. For a proposed activity listed in Appendix I that is likely to cause a significant adverse transboundary impact, the Party of origin shall, for the purposes of ensuring adequate and effective consultations under Article 5, notify any Party which it considers may be an affected Party as early as possible and no later than when informing its own public about that proposed activity.

2. This notification shall contain, inter alia:

   (a) Information on the proposed activity, including any available information on its possible transboundary impact;

   (b) The nature of the possible decision; and

   (c) An indication of a reasonable time within which a response under paragraph 3 of this Article is required, taking into account the nature of the proposed activity; and may include the information set out in paragraph 5 of this Article.

3. The affected Party shall respond to the Party of origin within the time specified in the notification, acknowledging receipt of the notification, and shall indicate whether it intends to participate in the environmental impact assessment procedure.

4. If the affected Party indicates that it does not intend to participate in the environmental impact assessment procedure, or if it does not respond within the time specified in the notification, the provisions in paragraphs 5, 6, 7 and 8 of this Article and in Articles 4 to 7 will not apply. In such circumstances the right of a Party of origin to determine whether to carry out an environmental impact assessment on the basis of its national law and practice is not prejudiced.

5. Upon receipt of a response from the affected party indicating its desire to participate in the environmental impact assessment procedure, the Party of origin shall, if it has not already done so, provide to the affected Party:

   (a) Relevant information regarding the environmental impact assessment procedure, including an indication of the time schedule for transmittal of comments; and

   (b) Relevant information on the proposed activity and its possible significant adverse transboundary impact.

6. An affected Party shall, at the request of the Party of origin, provide the latter with reasonably obtainable information relating to the potentially affected environment under the jurisdiction of the affected Party, where such information is necessary for the preparation of the environmental impact assessment documentation. The information shall be furnished promptly and, as appropriate, through a joint body where one exists.

7. When a Party considers that it would be affected by a significant adverse transboundary impact of a proposed activity listed in Appendix I, and when

no notification has taken place in accordance with paragraph 1 of this Article, the concerned Parties shall, at the request of the affected Party, exchange sufficient information for the purposes of holding discussions on whether there is likely to be a significant adverse transboundary impact If those Parties agree that there is likely to be a significant adverse transboundary impact, the provisions of this Convention shall apply accordingly. If those Parties cannot agree whether there is likely to be a significant adverse transboundary impact, any such Party may submit that question to an inquiry commission in accordance with the provisions of Appendix IV to advise on the likelihood of significant adverse transboundary impact, unless they agree on another method of settling this question.

8. The concerned Parties shall ensure that the public of the affected Party in the areas likely to be affected be informed of, and be provided with possibilities for making comments or objections on, the proposed activity, and for the transmittal of these comments or objections to the competent authority of the Party of origin, either directly to this authority or, where appropriate, through the Party of origin.

Article 4

PREPARATION OF THE ENVIRONMENTAL IMPACT ASSESSMENT DOCUMENTATION

1. The environmental impact assessment documentation to be submitted to the competent authority of the Party of origin shall contain, as a minimum, the information described in Appendix ll.

2. The Party of origin shall furnish the affected Party, as appropriate through a joint body where one exists, with the environmental impact assessment documentation. The concerned Parties shall arrange for distribution of the documentation to the authorities and the public of the affected Party in the areas likely to be affected and for the submission of comments to the competent authority of the Party of origin, either directly to this authority or, where appropriate, through the Party of origin within a reasonable time before the final decision is taken on the proposed activity.

Article 5

CONSULTATIONS ON THE BASIS OF THE ENVIRONMENTAL IMPACT ASSESSMENT DOCUMENTATION

The Party of origin shall, after completion of the environmental impact assessment documentation, without undue delay enter into consultations with the affected Party concerning, inter alia, the potential transboundary impact of the proposed activity and measures to reduce or eliminate its impact. Consultations may relate to:

(a) Possible alternatives to the proposed activity, including the no-action alternative and possible measures to mitigate significant adverse transboundary impact and to monitor the effects of such measures at the expense of the Party of origin;

(b) Other forms of possible mutual assistance in reducing any significant adverse transboundary impact of the proposed activity; and

(c) Any other appropriate matters relating to the proposed activity.

The Parties shall agree, at the commencement of such consultations, on a reasonable timeframe for the duration of the consultation period. Any such consultations may be conducted through an appropriate joint body, where one exists.

Article 6

FINAL DECISION

1. The Parties shall ensure that, in the final decision on the proposed activity, due account is taken of the outcome of the environmental impact assessment, including the environmental impact assessment documentation, as well as the comments thereon received pursuant to Article 3, paragraph 8 and Article 4, paragraph 2, and the outcome of the consultations as referred to in Article 5.

2. The Party of origin shall provide to the affected Party the final decision on the proposed activity along with the reasons and considerations on which it was based.

3. If additional information on the significant transboundary impact of a proposed activity, which was not available at the time a decision was made with respect to that activity and which could have materially affected the decision, becomes available to a concerned Party before work on that activity commences, that Party shall immediately inform the other concerned party or Parties. If one of the concerned Parties so requests, consultations shall be held as to whether the decision needs to be revised.

Article 7

POST-PROJECT ANALYSIS

1. The concerned Parties, at the request of any such Party, shall determine whether, and if so to what extent, a post-project analysis shall be carried out, taking into account the likely significant adverse transboundary impact of the activity for which an environmental impact assessment has been undertaken pursuant to this Convention. Any post-project analysis undertaken shall include, in particular, the surveillance of the activity and the determination of any adverse transboundary impact. Such surveillance and determination may be undertaken with a view to achieving the objectives listed in Appendix V.

2. When, as a result of post-project analysis, the Party of origin or the affected Party has reasonable grounds for concluding that there is a significant adverse transboundary impact or factors have been discovered which may result in such an impact, it shall immediately inform the other Party. The concerned Parties shall then consult on necessary measures to reduce or eliminate the impact.

Article 15

SETTLEMENT OF DISPUTES

1. If a dispute arises between two or more Parties about the interpretation or application of this Convention, they shall seek a solution by negotiation or by any other method of dispute settlement acceptable to the parties to the dispute.

2. When signing, ratifying, accepting, approving or acceding to this Convention, or at any time thereafter, a Party may declare in writing to the Depositary that for a dispute not resolved in accordance with paragraph 1 of this Article, it accepts one or both of the following means of dispute settlement as compulsory in relation to any Party accepting the same obligation:

   (a) Submission of the dispute to the International Court of Justice;

   (b) Arbitration in accordance with the procedure set out in Appendix VII.

3. If the parties to the dispute have accepted both means of dispute settlement referred to in paragraph 2 of this Article, the dispute may be submitted only to the International Court of Justice, unless the parties agree otherwise.

Appendix I:

LIST OF ACTIVITIES

1. Crude oil refineries (excluding undertakings manufacturing only lubricants from crude oil) and installations, for the gasification and liquefaction of 500 metric tons or more of coal or bituminous shale per day.

2. (a) Thermal power stations and other combustion installations with a heat output of 300 megawatts or more, and

   (b) Nuclear power stations and other nuclear reactors, including the dismantling or decommissioning of such power stations or reactors (except research installations for the production and conversion of fissionable and fertile materials whose maximum power does not exceed 1 kilowatt continuous thermal load)

3. (a) Installations for the reprocessing of irradiated nuclear fuel

   (b) Installations designed:

     –   For the production or enrichment of nuclear fuel;

     –   For the processing of irradiated nuclear fuel or high-level radioactive waste;

     –   For the final disposal of irradiated nuclear fuel;

     –   Solely for the final disposal of radioactive waste; or

     –   Solely for the storage (planned for more than 10 years) of irradiated nuclear fuels or radioactive waste in a different site than the production site.

4.   Major installations for the initial smelting of cast iron and steel for the production of non-ferrous metals.

5.   Installations for the extraction of asbestos and for the processing and transformation of asbestos and products containing asbestos: for asbestos-cement products, with an annual production of more than 20 000 metric tons finished product for friction material with an annual production of more than 50 metric tons finished product and for other asbestos utilization of more than 200 metric tons per year.

6.   Integrated chemical installations

7.   (a) Construction of motorways, express roads and lines for long-distance railway traffic and of airports with a basic runway length of 2 100 metres or more.

     (b)   Construction of a new road of four or more lanes, or realignment and/or widening of an existing road of two lanes or less so as to provide four or more lanes, where such new road or realigned and/or widened section of road, would be 10 km or more in continuous length

8.   Large-diameter pipelines for the transport of oil, gas or chemicals.

9.   Trading ports and also inland waterways and ports for inland-waterway traffic which permit the passage of vessels of over 1,350 metric tons.

10.   (a) Waste-disposal installations for the incineration, chemical treatment or landfill of toxic and dangerous wastes,

     (b)   Waste-disposal installations for the incineration or chemical treatment of non-hazardous waste with a capacity exceeding 100 metric tons per day

11.   Large dams and reservoirs

12.   Groundwater extraction activities or artificial groundwater recharge schemes where the annual volume of water to be abstracted or recharged amounts to 10 million cubic metres or more.

13.   Pulp, paper and board manufacturing of 200 air-dried metric tons or more per day

14.   Major quarries, mining, on-site extraction and processing of metal ores or coal

15.   Offshore hydrocarbon production. Extraction of petrochemical and natural gas for commercial purposes where the amount extracted exceeds 500

metric tons/day in the case of petroleum and 500 000 cubic metres/day in the case of gas.

16. Major storage facilities for petroleum petrochemical and chemical products.

17. Deforestation of large areas

18. (a) Works for the transfer of water resources between river basins where this transfer aims at preventing possible shortages of water and where the amount of water transferred exceeds 100 million cubic metres/year: and

    (b) In all other cases, works for the transfer of water resources between river basins where the multi-annual average flow of the basin of abstraction exceeds 2 000 million cubic metres/year and where the amount of water transferred exceeds 5 per cent of this flow In both cases transfers of piped drinking water are excluded

19. Waste-water treatment plants with a capacity exceeding 150 000 population equivalent

20. Installations for the intensive rearing of poultry or pigs with more than 85000 places for broilers,

    – 60 000 places for hens,

    3 000 places for production pigs (over 30 kg) or

    – 900 places for sows.

21. Construction of overhead electrical power lines with a voltage of 220 kV or more and a length of more than 15 km.

22. Major installations for the harnessing of wind power for energy production (wind farms).

APPENDIX II

CONTENT OF THE ENVIRONMENTAL IMPACT ASSESSMENT
DOCUMENTATION

Information to be included in the environmental impact assessment documentation shall, as a minimum, contain, in accordance with Article 4:

(a) A description of the proposed activity and its purpose;

(b) A description, where appropriate, of reasonable alternatives (for example, locational or technological) to the proposed activity and also the no-action alternative;

(c) A description of the environment likely to be significantly affected by the proposed activity and its alternatives;

(d) A description of the potential environmental impact of the proposed activity and its alternatives and an estimation of its significance;

(e) A description of mitigation measures to keep adverse environmental impact to a minimum;

(f) An explicit indication of predictive methods and underlying assumptions as well as the relevant environmental data used;

(g) An identification of gaps in knowledge and uncertainties encountered in compiling the required information;

(h) Where appropriate, an outline for monitoring and management programmes and any plans for post-project analysis; and

(i) A non-technical summary including a visual presentation as appropriate (maps, graphs, etc.).

APPENDIX III

GENERAL CRITERIA TO ASSIST IN THE DETERMINATION OF THE ENVIRONMENTAL SIGNIFICANCE OF ACTIVITIES NOT LISTED IN APPENDIX I

1. In considering proposed activities to which Article 2, paragraph 5, applies,the concerned Parties may consider whether the activity is likely to have a significant adverse transboundary impact in particular by virtue of one or more of the following criteria:

   (a) Size: proposed activities which are large for the type of the activity;

   (b) Location: proposed activities which are located in or close to an area of special environmental sensitivity or importance (such as wetlands designated under the Ramsar Convention, national parks, nature reserves, sites of special scientific interest, or sites of archaeological, cultural or historical importance); also, proposed activities in locations where the characteristics of proposed development would be likely to have significant effects on the population;

   (c) Effects: proposed activities with particularly complex and potentially adverse effects, including those giving rise to serious effects on humans or on valued species or organisms, those which threaten the existing or potential use of an affected area and those causing additional loading which cannot be sustained by the carrying capacity of the environment.

2. The concerned Parties shall consider for this purpose proposed activities which are located close to an international frontier as well as more remote proposed activities which could give rise to significant, transboundary effects far removed from the site of development.

APPENDIX IV

INQUIRY PROCEDURE

1. The requesting Party or Parties shall notify the secretariat that it or they submit(s) the question of whether a proposed activity listed in Appendix I is likely to have a significant adverse transboundary impact to an inquiry

commission established in accordance with the provisions of this Appendix. This notification shall state the subject-matter of the inquiry. The secretariat shall notify immediately all Parties to this Convention of this submission.

2. The inquiry commission shall consist of three members. Both the requesting party and the other party to the inquiry procedure shall appoint a scientific or technical expert, and the two experts so appointed shall designate by common agreement the third expert, who shall be the president of the inquiry commission. The latter shall not be a national of one of the parties to the inquiry procedure, nor have his or her usual place of residence in the territory of one of these parties, nor be employed by any of them, nor have dealt with the matter in any other capacity.

3. If the president of the inquiry commission has not been designated within two months of the appointment of the second expert, the Executive Secretary of the Economic Commission for Europe shall, at the request of either party, designate the president within a further two-month period.

4. If one of the parties to the inquiry procedure does not appoint an expert within one month of its receipt of the notification by the secretariat, the other party may inform the Executive Secretary of the Economic Commission for Europe, who shall designate the president of the inquiry commission within a further two-month period. Upon designation, the president of the inquiry commission shall request the party which has not appointed an expert to do so within one month. After such a period, the president shall inform the Executive Secretary of the Economic Commission for Europe, who shall make this appointment within a further two-month period.

5. The inquiry commission shall adopt *its* own rules of procedure.

6. The inquiry commission may take all appropriate measures in order to carry out its functions.

7. The parties to the inquiry procedure shall facilitate the work of the inquiry commission and, in particular, using all means at their disposal, shall:

    (a) Provide it with all relevant documents, facilities and information; and

    (b) Enable it, where necessary, to call witnesses or experts and receive their evidence.

8. The parties and the experts shall protect the confidentiality of any information they receive in confidence during the work of the inquiry commission.

9. If one of the parties to the inquiry procedure does not appear before the inquiry commission or fails to present its case, the other party may request the inquiry commission to continue the proceedings and to complete its work. Absence of a party or failure of a party to present its case shall not constitute a bar to the continuation and completion of the work of the inquiry commission.

10. Unless the inquiry commission determines otherwise because of the particular circumstances of the matter, the expenses of the inquiry

commission, including the remuneration of its members, shall be borne by the parties to the inquiry procedure in equal shares. The inquiry commission shall keep a record of all its expenses, and shall furnish a final statement thereof to the parties.

11. Any Party having an interest of a factual nature in the subject-matter of the inquiry procedure, and which may be affected by an opinion in the matter, may intervene in the proceedings with the consent of the inquiry commission.

12. The decisions of the inquiry commission on matters of procedure shall be taken by majority vote of its members. The final opinion of the inquiry commission shall reflect the view of the majority of its members and shall include any dissenting view.

13. The inquiry commission shall present its final opinion within two months of the date on which it was established unless it finds it necessary to extend this time limit for a period which should not exceed two months.

14. The final opinion of the inquiry commission shall be based on accepted scientific principles. The final opinion shall be transmitted by the inquiry commission to the parties to the inquiry procedure and to the secretariat.

APPENDIX V

POST-PROJECT ANALYSIS

Objectives include:

(a) Monitoring compliance with the conditions as set out in the authorization or approval of the activity and the effectiveness of mitigation measures;

(b) Review of an impact for proper.management and in order to cope with uncertainties;

(c) Verification of past predictions in order to transfer experience to future activities of the same type.

APPENDIX VI

ELEMENTS FOR BILATERAL AND MULTILATERAL CO-OPERATION

1. Concerned Parties may set up, where appropriate, institutional arrangements or enlarge the mandate of existing institutional arrangements within the framework of bilateral and multilateral agreements in order to give full effect to this Convention.

2. Bilateral and multilateral agreements or other arrangements may include:

(a) Any additional requirements for the implementation of this Convention, taking into account the specific conditions of the subregion concerned;

(b) Institutional, administrative and other arrangements, to be made on a reciprocal and equivalent basis;

(c) Harmonization of their policies and measures for the protection of the environment in order to attain the greatest possible similarity in standards and methods related to the implementation of environmental impact assessment;

(d) Developing, improving, and/or harmonizing methods for the identification, measurement, prediction and assessment of impacts, and for post-project analysis;

APPENDIX VII

ARBITRATION

1. The claimant Party or Parties shall notify the secretariat that the Parties have agreed to submit the dispute to arbitration pursuant to Article 15, paragraph 2, of this Convention. The notification shall state the subject-matter of arbitration and include, in particular, the Articles of this Convention, the interpretation or application of which are at issue. The secretariat shall forward the information received to all Parties to this Convention.

2. The arbitral tribunal shall consist of three members. Both the claimant Party or Parties and the other Party or Parties to the dispute shall appoint an arbitrator, and the, two arbitrators so appointed shall designate by common agreement the third arbitrator, who shall be the president of the arbitral tribunal. The latter shall not be a national of one of the parties to the dispute, nor have his or her usual place of residence in the territory of one of these parties, nor be employed by any of them, nor have dealt with the case in any other capacity.

3. If the president of the arbitral tribunal has not been designated within two months of the appointment of the second arbitrator, the Executive Secretary of the Economic Commission for Europe shall, at the request of either party to the dispute, designate the president within a further two-month period.

4. If one of the parties to the dispute does not appoint an arbitrator within two months of the receipt of the request, the other party may inform the Executive Secretary of the Economic Commission for Europe, who shall designate the president of the arbitral tribunal within a further two-month period. Upon designation, the president of the arbitral tribunal shall request the party which has not appointed an arbitrator to do so within two months. After such a period, the president shall inform the Executive Secretary of the Economic Commission for Europe, who shall make this appointment within a further two-month period.

5. The arbitral tribunal shall render its decision in accordance with international law and in accordance with the provisions of this Convention.

6. Any arbitral tribunal constituted under the provisions set out herein shall draw up its own rules of procedure.

7. The decisions of the arbitral tribunal, both on procedure and on substance, shall be taken by majority vote of its members.

8. The tribunal may take all appropriate measures in order to establish the facts.

9. The parties to the dispute shall facilitate the work of the arbitral tribunal and, in particular, using all means at their disposal, shall:

   (a) Provide it with all relevant documents, facilities and information; and

   (b) Enable it, where necessary, to call witnesses or experts and receive their evidence.

10. The parties and the arbitrators shall protect the confidentiality of any information they receive in confidence during the proceedings of the arbitral tribunal.

11. The arbitral tribunal may, at the request of one of the parties, recommend interim measures of protection.

12. If one of the parties to the dispute does not appear before the arbitral tribunal or fails to defend its case, the other party may request the tribunal to continue the proceedings and to render its final decision. Absence of a party or failure of a party to defend its case shall not constitute a bar to the proceedings. Before rendering its final decision, the arbitral tribunal must satisfy itself that the claim is well founded in fact and law.

13. The arbitral tribunal may hear and determine counter-claims arising directly out of the subject-matter of the dispute.

14. Unless the arbitral tribunal determines otherwise because of the particular circumstances of the case, the expenses of the tribunal, including the remuneration of its members, shall be borne by the parties to the dispute in equal shares. The tribunal shall keep a record of all its expenses, and shall furnish a final statement thereof to the parties.

15. Any Party to this Convention having an interest of a legal nature in the subject-matter of the dispute, and which may be affected by a decision in the case, may intervene in the proceedings with the consent of the tribunal.

16. The arbitral tribunal shall render its award within five months of the date on which it is established unless it finds it necessary to extend the time limit for a period which should not exceed five months.

17. The award of the arbitral tribunal shall be accompanied by a statement of reasons. It shall be final and binding upon all parties to the dispute. The award will be transmitted by the arbitral tribunal to the parties to the dispute and to the secretariat. The secretariat will forward the information received to all Parties to this Convention.

NOTES AND QUESTIONS

1. The Espoo Convention has 45 parties, including all the members of the European Union. Note the list of activities to which the Convention may apply; this list was revised in an amendment procedure in 2004. If the Convention is applicable, note the procedural steps that are required before a source state can approve a project with potential transboundary impact. What are the criteria for application of the Convention? If a dispute arises over this issue, how is it resolved?

2. What are the criteria for the content of the environmental Impact assessment? Suppose a dispute arises over the adequacy of the environmental impact assessment; how is this resolved? *See* Article 15. (Austria has selected both methods of dispute settlement set out in Article 15(2); the Czech Republic has not made any selection).

3. Who makes the final decision on the project? Can this decision be challenged by the potentially affected state?

4. What is the power of the potentially affected state to influence decisions concerning the project after the project has been completed?

5. Compare the provisions of the Espoo Convention to the Draft ILC Articles on Prevention of Transboundary Harm from Hazardous Activities; Does the latter have a greater scope? Does the Espoo Convention require more precise procedures?

Chapter 4

PROTECTION OF THE ATMOSPHERE AND THE CLIMATE

Section I. INTRODUCTION

The Intergovernmental Panel on Climate Change defines the atmosphere as

> The gaseous envelope surrounding the Earth. The dry atmosphere consists almost entirely of nitrogen (78.1%) and oxygen (20.9%), together with a number of trace gases, such as argon (0.93%, helium and radiatively active greenhouse gases such as carbon dioxide (0.035%) and ozone. In addition, the atmosphere contains the greenhouse gas water vapor, whose amounts are highly variable but typically about 1%. The atmosphere also contains clouds and aerosols.[1]

Physically the atmosphere extends upwards from the earth's surface, and is divided vertically into four layers on the basis of temperature changes with the altitude: (1) the troposphere up to about 12 kilometers; (2) the stratosphere up to about 50 kilometers; (3) the mesosphere up to about 80 kilometers; and (4) the thermosphere up to about 100 kilometers, the boundary with the emptiness of space. Of course, there is no sharp scientific boundary between the atmosphere and space, but above 100 kilometers, only 0.00003% of the atmosphere remains. Because of gravity approximately 80% of the air mass of the atmosphere exists in the troposphere and most of the rest of air exists in the stratosphere; above 50 kilometers air pressure is only about 0.1%. Scientists refer to the atmosphere up to 50 kilometers as the "lower atmosphere," while the remaining two spheres are called the "upper atmosphere." The atmosphere moves and circulates around the surface of the Earth driven by complex forces; this is called "atmospheric circulation."

While many problems of degradation of the atmosphere are local or national in scope, international concerns arise — along with the necessity of international law — in connection with three serious matters.

First, air pollution, the introduction of harmful substances into the atmosphere, in many cases not only causes local and national concern, but may have important international adverse effects as well. Common pollutants such as nitrogen oxides (NOx), sulfur oxides (SOx), carbon monoxide (CO), particulate matter (PM), ozone (O3), and persistent inorganic and volatile organic compounds that are spread by

---

[1] Intergovernmental Panel on Climate Change, *Fourth Assessment Report 2007*, at Glossary, p. 941, *available at* http://www.ipcc.ch/pdf/glossary/ar4-wg1.pdf.

strong horizontal winds may have an adverse transboundary effect on human health and natural systems. Since the atmosphere is a unitary medium, pollution may be transported to areas far from the source of their emissions. For example, in 2010, approximately 10% of the "smog" on the West coast of the United States was estimated to have come from China.[2] Transboundary pollution is no longer simply a border problem: long-range transboundary pollution is a growing problem all over the globe.

Second, chlorofluorocarbons (CFCs), halons, and halocarbon compounds emitted into the troposphere tend to rise into the stratosphere causing ozone depletion. This is a major concern because a natural layer of ozone at altitudes of 15 to 40 kilometers acts as a filter preventing harmful ultraviolet radiation from reaching the surface of the Earth, where it may cause cancer in humans and harmful impacts on ecosystems.

Third, according to the United Nations Intergovernmental Panel on Climate Change[3] and virtually all atmospheric scientists, anthropogenic emissions of compounds such as carbon dioxide, methane, and nitrous oxide are changing the balance between solar radiation that is absorbed by the Earth and that radiated into space. Increased retention of solar radiation in the Earth's atmosphere has the potential to cause a "greenhouse effect," changes in the climate of the Earth.

In this chapter we cover these three problems in turn. But first we present an overview of the international law of protection of the atmosphere. In chapter three we learned how the customary international law of state responsibility for transboundary harm developed out of border air pollution problems. An influential national law case was the case of *Georgia v. Tennessee Copper Company et al.*, which resulted in two opinions of the Supreme Court of the United States[4] holding that a state has an interest in protecting natural resources — such as air quality — within its jurisdiction, and that significant transboundary air pollution may be enjoined as a public nuisance. These rulings were transposed into customary international law by the *Trail Smelter* arbitration case[5], which established that a state bears responsibility for significant transboundary air pollution damage caused by an emission source within its territory. This "harm prevention principle" was later confirmed as Principle 21 of the Stockholm Declaration and has since become an important customary law rule.[6]

As we discovered in chapters two and three, however, the harm prevention principle as a customary rule is not specific enough either to prevent or to provide a remedy for most transboundary air pollution. The harm prevention principle is particularly inadequate to combat long-range transboundary air pollution because of the difficulty of establishing causation. Thus, in order to combat effectively transboundary air pollution, more specific treaties establishing international air

---

[2] Emissions from Asia put U.S. cities over the ozone limit. http://www.nature.com/news/emissions-from-asia-put-us-cities-over-the-ozone-limit-1.10161, visited 3 November 2012.

[3] *Op cit.*

[4] 206 U.S. 230 (1907) and 237 U.S. 474 (1915).

[5] Trail Smelter (United States v. Canada) Award, 1941, 3 U.N.R.I.A.A. 1905.

[6] *See* Chapter 2.

pollution norms are required. We begin with an overview of the applicable treaty regimes.

Shinya Murase, Professor at Sophia University in Tokyo, who has made a comprehensive study of the international instruments that address protection of the atmosphere, summarizes this body of law as follows:

a. Multilateral conventions and binding instruments on transboundary air pollution[7]

- ECE Convention on Long-Range Transboundary Air Pollution (1979, entered into force 1983); Monitoring and Evaluation Protocol (1984); Sulphur Protocol (1985); NOx Protocol (1988); Volatile Organic Compounds Protocol (1991); Sulphur Protocol (1994); Aarhus Protocol on Heavy Metals (1998); Aarhus Protocol on Persistent Organic Pollutants (1998); Gothenburg Protocol to Abate Acidification, Eutrophication and Ground-Level Ozone (1999)

- ECE Agreement concerning the Adoption of Uniform Conditions of Approval and Reciprocal Recognition of Approval for Motor Vehicle Equipment and Parts (1958); ECE Agreement concerning the Establishing of Global Technical Regulations for Wheeled Vehicles, Equipment and Parts etc. (1998)

- ECE Convention on Environmental Impact Assessment in a Transboundary Context (1991)

- ECE Convention on the Transboundary Effects of Industrial Accidents (1992, 2000)

- European Communities Council Directive No.801779 on Air Quality Limit Values (15 July 1980); EC Large Combustion Directive (1988/2001/EC); EU National Emission Ceilings Directive (2001/81/EC); European Communities Council Directive No.85/203 on Air Quality Standards for Nitrogen Dioxide (1985); Directive 2007/46/EEC establishing a framework for the approval of motor vehicles and their trailers, and of systems, components and separate technical units intended for such vehicles) and its Annexes; Regulations EC 44312009, EU 59512009, EU 510/2011, and EU 582/2011 on the CO_2 emission limits for passenger cars, light commercial vehicles and heavy duty vehicles (buses and trucks); EU Directive 2006/40/EC, aimed at reducing greenhouse gas emissions from mobile air conditioning systems in motor vehicles.

- ICAO Regulations: The 16th Annex (Environmental Protection) of the 1944 Chicago Convention on International Civil Aviation ("Aircraft Engine Emissions Standards and Recommended Practices," 1980)

- lMO Global Standards for air pollution emissions from ships: Annex VI (air pollution) of MARPOL 73/78.

---

[7] Unpublished paper on file with the authors, reprinted with permission of Murase Shinya, August 13, 2013, p. 4–5.

– The ASEAN Agreement on Transboundary Haze Pollution (2002, 2003)

– Stockholm Convention on Persistent Organic Pollutants (POPs) (2004)

– The Framework Convention for the Protection of the Environment for Sustainable Development in Central Asia (2006)[8]

b. Bilateral conventions on transboundary air pollution

– Canada-U.S. Memorandum of Intent concerning Transboundary Air Pollution (1980)

– Mexico-U.S. Agreement to Cooperate in the Solution on Environmental Problems in the Border Area (1983)[9]

– Canada-U.S. Air Quality Agreement (1991)

– Czech-German Agreements (1992, 1994, 2000 and 2004)[10]

c. Multilateral conventions on global atmospheric problems

– Vienna Convention for the Protection of the Ozone Layer (1985); Montreal Protocol on Substances that Deplete the Ozone Layer (1987)

– UN Framework Convention on Climate Change (UNFCCC, 1992); The Kyoto Protocol to the UNFCCC (1997)

Even without analysis, the weaknesses of this *potpourri* of conventional regimes are apparent. The international instruments listed were concluded by well-intentioned groups, but to deal with specific problems. No coordination exists between various legal regimes, and there has been no effort to fill in gaps or to step back and take a comprehensive approach to protection of the atmosphere. Multilateral and bilateral agreements on air quality are concentrated in Europe and North America, although transboundary air pollution may well be more of a problem in other parts of the world. Of the two multilateral regimes on global atmospheric problems, one — the Vienna Convention/Montreal Protocol — is regarded as a success, while the other — the effort to stem climate change — is beset with serious problems.

In January 2014, a study of air pollution in the United States[11] determined that between 3 and 10% of all air pollution in the Western United States can be traced to emissions in Asia, particularly China. This finding confirms that wind-blown atmospheric pollution is not merely a national problem but is a global problem as

---

[8] This is not yet in force. Parties are: Kazakhstan, Kyrgyz, Tajikistan, Turkmenistan, and Uzbekistan. Article 8 provides for "Air pollution." http://ekh.unep.org/ISDC09/ISDC_210607/docs/01_preservation%20of%20the%20environment_ru.doc.

[9] I.L.M. Vol. 22 (1983), pp. 1025ff.

[10] The 1994 Agreement provides for implementation of joint environmental pilot projects for flue gas cleaning in coal-fired power plants. The 2000 and 2004 Agreements provide for joint implementation of a "Clean Air Fund" and other pilot projects in the Czech Republic, aimed at reducing transboundary air pollution impacts in Germany; The 2004 Agreement specifically refers to "joint implementation" under the UNFCCC/Kyoto Protocol.

[11] Jintai Lin *et al.*, *China's International Trade and Air Pollution in the United States, Proceedings of the National Academy of Sciences,* January 16, 2014, *available at* http://www.pnas.org/content/early/2014/01/16/1312860111, visited 3 February 2014.

well. The Earth's atmosphere, which we tend to take for granted, is in peril. What is needed is a global, universally applicable legal regime that comprehensively addresses and establishes international guidelines to protect the Earth's atmosphere as the common heritage and the common concern of mankind.

NOTES AND QUESTIONS

1.   Note that treaty law concerning protection of the atmosphere from transboundary pollution has developed especially in Europe and in North America. In most of the world, therefore, there are no effective international regimes to protect the atmosphere. In global treaties to protect the atmosphere, only developed countries have enforceable obligations. In accordance with the principle of common but differentiated responsibilities for environmental protection, should these imbalances be ameliorated? If they are not, what will be the consequence?

2.   Professor Murase at this writing is a member of the prestigious UN International Law Commission. In his paper, quoted above, he notes that, beginning in the late 1980s, there arose a movement to codify an "international law of the atmosphere," an international instrument that would take a comprehensive approach to protection of the atmosphere. The UN Commission on Sustainable Development conducted a study on "Protection of the Atmosphere[12]" in preparation for the Johannesburg Environmental Summit in 2002. In September, 2010, the World Clean Air Congress, composed of non-governmental organizations from 40 countries, adopted a Declaration[13] titled "One Atmosphere," which seeks to encourage the integration of international climate and pollution policies and called for a new "law of the Atmosphere" similar to the UN Convention on the Law of the Sea. Professor Murase advocates action by the International Law Commission to draft a new international instrument for the protection of the atmosphere:

> The atmosphere is the planet's largest single natural resource; it is indispensable to the survival of humankind. Degradation of the conditions of the atmosphere has long been a matter of serious concern to the international community. While a number of relevant conventions dealing with transnational and global atmospheric issues have been concluded, they remain a patchwork of instruments. Substantial gaps exist in terms of geographic coverage, regulated activities, regulated substances, and, most importantly, applicable principles and rules. This piecemeal or incremental approach has created particular limitations for the protection of the atmosphere, which by its very nature warrants holistic treatment. There is no convention at present that covers the entire range of atmospheric environmental problems in a comprehensive and systematic manner. The Commission can therefore make a significant contribution by codifying and progressively developing the legal principles and rules applicable to the whole range of atmospheric problems on the basis of state practice and jurisprudence. While the final form of the Commission's work may be

---

[12] Report of the Secretary-General, E/CN.17/2001/PC/12 (Mar. 2, 2001).

[13] *See* http://www.iuappa.com/newsletters/VancouverDeclaration.pdf, visited 3 November 2012.

considered at a later stage, the present proposal envisages a framework convention similar to Part XII of the United Nations Convention of the Law of the Sea."[14]

What do you think of this idea? The International Law Commission, whose mission is the progressive development of international law, formally accepted this proposal in 2013, and has established protection of the atmosphere as an agenda item with Professor Murase as Special Rapporteur. In coming sessions, the ILC will debate and endeavor to formulate a series of guidelines acceptable to all states concerning protection of the Earth's atmosphere. Professor Murase[15] has enumerated the following four goals of this project:

> First, the project aims to identify the status of customary international law established or emerging, examining gaps and overlaps, if any, in existing law relating to the atmosphere. Second, it is to provide appropriate guidelines for harmonization and coordination among treaty regimes within and outside international environmental law. Third, the proposed draft guidelines will help clarify a framework for the harmonization of national laws and regulations with international rules, standards, and recommended practices and procedures relating to protection of the atmosphere. Fourth, the project is to establish guidelines on the mechanisms and procedures for cooperation among States in order to facilitate capacity-building in the field of transboundary and global protection of the atmosphere.

Section II.   LONG RANGE TRANSBOUNDARY POLLUTION

Acid rain is the prototype of long-range transboundary pollution. Acid rain — more properly acid deposition — occurs when certain pollutants, primarily sulfur oxides and nitrogen oxides, undergo chemical reactions in the atmosphere and are transformed into mild sulfuric and nitric acids. When these acids return to earth as rain, snow, dew, fog, drizzle, and sleet, they can disrupt ecosystems and acidify waterways. Acid rain affects large areas all over the world. We know the basic chemistry of acid deposition: nitrogen oxides in the atmosphere are oxidized to form nitrogen dioxide (H_2O, which is transformed into nitric acid according to the following equation: $2NO_2 + H_2O$ (water) $= HNO_2 + HNO_3$ (nitric acid). Similarly, carbon dioxide is transformed into carbonic acid by the following chemical reaction: $CO_2 + H_2O$ (water) $= H_2CO_3$ (carbonic acid). Sulfur oxides are oxidized in the atmosphere and then form sulfuric acid according to the following chemical reaction: $SO_3 + H_2O$ (water) $= H_2SO_4$ (sulfuric acid).

Although the basic chemistry of acid deposition is straightforward, the atmospheric processes creating acidification are complex and the damage process is difficult to predict because several pollutants are typically active at the same time and their effects may be cumulative. Because of the long-range of the pollutants involved, it is difficult to pinpoint their sources and receptors. Most states are both

---

[14] Unpublished paper, op. cit.

[15] *First Report on the Protection of the Atmosphere, International Law Commission,* 67th session, February 15, 2014, on file with the author.

sources and receptors of acid deposition, but the mix of these is often a source of dispute.

Consider the following problem and the materials that follow.

PROBLEM 4-1
CREATING A REGIME TO COMBAT LONG-RANGE
TRANSBOUNDARY AIR POLLUTION

States X and Z are neighboring states separated by a variable stretch of ocean waters. State X, which is located to the west of State Z, is a developing country which places a priority on economic development and has relatively weak environmental laws. As a result, coal burning electric generating facilities and factories that burn coal and other fossil fuels in State X spew great amounts of sulfur oxides and carbon dioxide into the air. Vehicles in State X do not have to comply with stringent air quality standards, and nitrogen oxides, ozone and particulate matter commonly pollute the air. State Z contends that the emission of these pollutants in State X is the source of the pollutants which travel on westerly winds and constitute a principal part of the air pollution that is endemic in State Z, which is a developed country with strict air pollution control laws. State X disputes the contentions of State Z, arguing that there is no proof that the pollutants emitted in State X are responsible for the air pollution in State Z. Officials from State X and Z have discussed these problems for years without arriving at any solutions.

What would you suggest be done? Consider the following materials.

A.　North America

Marilynn K. Roberts, *Acid Rain Regulation: Federal Failure and State Success*
8 VA. J. NAT. RES. L. 220, 230–35 (1988) (footnotes omitted)[16]

National Ambient Air Quality Standards for Criteria Pollutants

The basic regulatory mechanism of the Clean Air Act is National Ambient Air Quality Standards (NAAQS] for criteria pollutants. Because Congress was concerned mainly with protecting human health and controlling large stationary sources when it passed the Clean Air Act (CAA), the focus is on local ambient air, or in other words. outdoor air at ground level. The NAAQS convert the Act's general qualitative mandates into quantitative expressions of pollution concentrations. The pollutants controlled under the NAAQS program, called criteria pollutants, are those nontoxic pollutants considered by the EPA Administrator to "cause or contribute to air pollution which may reasonably be anticipated to endanger human health or welfare."

There are two types of standards under the NAAQS program: primary standards, designed to protect human health, and secondary standards, designed to

---

[16] Reprinted by permission.

protect the public welfare. Primary NAAQS are set at concentration levels that protect human health and provide a margin of safety. Primary standards are to be based on health considerations alone, without regard to cost or to the technological feasibility of compliance. The responsibility for meeting the standards is delegated to the states, which are directed to adopt, subject to EPA approval. State Implementation Plans (SIPs) that provide for "implementation. maintenance, and enforcement" of the standards. The primary standards are to be achieved no later than three years after SIP approval.

Secondary NAAQS should "protect the public welfare from any known or anticipated adverse effects associated with the presence of such air pollutant in the ambient air." Public welfare "includes, but is not limited to, effects on soils, waters, crops, vegetation, man made materials, animals, wildlife, weather visibility, and climate, damage to and deterioration of property, and hazards to transportation, as well as effects on economic values and on personal comfort and well-being." This definition of public welfare mirrors the list of known or anticipated effects of acid deposition. Although secondary standards are set at levels that allow less pollution than primary standards, they are treated as goals: instead of specific deadlines for compliance, they are to be achieved within "a reasonable time."

Current sulfur dioxide and nitrogen oxide standards are not sufficiently stringent to control acid deposition. Present levels of acid deposition in the United States are high in spite of the claim that state SIP reports show almost ninety-eight percent of counties comply with both standards. In 1980, U.S. industries emitted approximately 27 million tons of sulfur dioxide and 21 million tons of nitrogen oxides. The Office of Technology Assessment has estimated future emissions permitted by existing air pollution laws and concluded that emissions of sulfur and nitrogen oxides "are likely to remain high for at least the next half century," despite the application of stringent controls to new plants under the New Source Performance Standard (NSPS) program.

The fact that the current ambient standards for sulfur dioxide are not controlling acid deposition is not surprising, because they were not designed to do so. The CAA is concerned with ambient air pollution, not with deposition of pollutants. The Act assumes that control of pollutant concentration will control damage, but ignores the fact that acid deposition damage is related to total pollution load, i.e., the aggregate amount entering the system, rather than to ambient concentration.

Furthermore, the chemical pollutants that cause acid deposition are controlled under the CAA only in precursor form as sulfur dioxide and oxides of nitrogen. Regulation of acid deposition requires control of sulfates and nitrates because it is these transformation products that acidify the environment. This control could be accomplished under existing provisions of the Clean Air Act by the EPA Administrator's designation of sulfates and nitrates as criteria pollutants, and adoption of an ambient standard based upon consideration of acid deposition. This direct control would eliminate the difficult proof of causation currently plaguing affected areas.

It is unlikely that acid rain transformation products will be regulated as criteria pollutants. The process of designation of criteria pollutants is long and complicated, and EPA Administrators have listed only seven pollutants as criteria pollutants.

Attempts to persuade the EPA Administrator to list sulfates and nitrates as criteria pollutants have been unsuccessful.

State Implementation Plans and the Interstate Pollution Provision

The NAAQS and other CAA requirements are enforced by the states through State Implementation Plans (SIPs). SIPs, intended to be comprehensive and to incorporate actual pollution control programs necessary to meet and maintain the NAAQS, must be approved by the EPA. If a state does not promulgate a SIP, or if, in the EPA's judgment, a proposed SIP is not adequate to meet NAAQS, the EPA has the authority to promulgate the SIP itself.

Under the CAA, states must adopt ambient air quality standards for criteria pollutants. They may adopt the NAAQS or more restrictive air quality standards. The EPA divides each state into Air Quality Control Regions, and the state monitors each region's air quality. If air quality in an area meets the criteria, it is labeled an "attainment" area; if it does not, it is labeled "non attainment"

To determine how each region is to meet the required concentrations of the criteria pollutants, the responsible agencies monitor pollution levels and perform computer modeling of actual and projected source emissions. This process culminates in recommendations for limitation of emissions at certain sources. These limitations are enforced by use of source permits containing technology based control requirements.

The process appears thorough, but it misses three key problems associated with acid deposition control. First, each state is only required to meet NAAQS for criteria pollutants. Sulfates and nitrates are not listed as criteria pollutants. States are thus not obligated to set pollution standards, to monitor, nor to control sulfates and nitrates.

A further problem with the SIP program is the latitude the EPA has accorded states regarding their SIPs. The EPA may allow states to revise their SIPs as air quality conditions change, either by relaxing standards or by requiring more controls to meet standards. The EPA has recently given states wide latitude in the development and modification of SIPs for sulfur dioxide. Even though ambient standards are only marginally protective, in 1981 the EPA approved SIP revisions that allowed United States' sulfur dioxide emissions to increase by more than one million tons per year.

A third problem with the SIP program which renders the CAA ineffective at controlling acid deposition is the independent nature of state enforcement, a key concept within the Clean Air Act. As long as NAAQS are not violated, a state may freely choose standards for existing emission sources, with little or no consideration of the impact of those emissions on other states. Although in theory the Clean Air Act requires examination of the interstate impact of pollution, in practice that impact is ignored. Emission limitations may be stringent in one state and lax in another, preventing the state with stricter requirements (and therefore probably higher utility and industrial costs) from reaping the full environmental benefits of these control measures.

To a limited extent, the CAA recognizes that one state's emissions can cause pollution problems in a different state. Section 110 of the Act requires SIPs to prohibit emissions from stationary sources that "prevent attainment or maintenance by any other State of any such national primary or secondary ambient air quality standard," or that may interfere with another state's plans to prevent significant deterioration and protect visibility. To provide a mechanism of enforcement against a polluter state, Congress created a petition process in Section 126, the interstate pollution abatement provision. Section 126 allows a state or any political subdivision to petition the EPA Administrator to remedy interstate pollution.

This CAA provision for protection against interstate pollution has proved to be almost meaningless. By the time a criteria pollutant (such as SO_2) from a source reaches a border and enters another state, it is usually changed into one of its transformation products (such as SO4). Since it is no longer a criteria pollutant, no standard exists to limit or prohibit it, and EPA recognizes no remedy for the receptor state and its citizens against the source state. The CAA structure, concentrating on control of local sources to meet local air quality standards, leaves long-range transport pollution problems largely unaddressed.

Furthermore, petitioners under Section 126 are often unable to produce sufficient proof of causation to satisfy requirements that attach legal responsibility for emissions to culpable sources. According to the EPA, there are no acceptable models which accurately trace deposition resulting from long-range transport from single or aggregated source regions. The limitations of computer modeling techniques make it nearly impossible to show that sulfur dioxide emissions from one state, and specifically from one source, significantly affect another state's air quality. In addition. modeling techniques and assumptions can be manipulated by the source, by the source state, or by the EPA to emphasize factors that yield results indicating compliance. As long as there is a rational basis for the modeling assumptions, regulatory action based upon the modeling will be upheld.

The International Pollution Provision of the CAA

Acid deposition has been the source of much controversy between the United States and Canada, but the international pollution provision of the Clean Air Act [Section 115] has not been used successfully to control acid deposition. This section creates a process by which the EPA Administrator may require a state to decrease emissions that "cause or contribute to air pollution which may reasonably be anticipated to endanger health or welfare in a foreign country." The EPA Administrator must be convinced that the foreign country accords the U.S. similar treatment regarding air pollution, and then notify the governor of the alleged offending state of these findings. This notice serves as a finding that the state's SIP must be revised to reduce emissions.

The issue of causation would probably pose significant difficulty if the EPA were to act on Section 115. The meaning of "cause or contribute to" an endangerment of health or welfare in another country has not been elaborated upon nor clarified in regulations, and remains quite imprecise. Once again, a law that appeared full of promise has proved ineffective In practice. The prevailing view of commentators is that the provision will be ineffective if enforced by an Administrator with no strong commitment to resolving international pollution problems and the resulting political tensions.

HER MAJESTY THE QUEEN IN RIGHT OF ONTARIO v. U.S. ENVIRONMENTAL PROTECTION AGENCY
912 F.2d 1525 (D.C. Cir. 1990)

BUCKLEY, CIRCUIT JUDGE:

The question before us is whether the Environmental Protection Agency has any present obligation to take action under section 115 of the Clean Air Act, which establishes a procedure for the prevention of air pollutants in the United States from causing harm in the form of acid deposition to the public health and welfare in Canada. The Province of Ontario and a number of States and environmental groups have petitioned the EPA for a rulemaking that would essentially set in motion section 115's international pollution abatement procedures. We conclude, first, that section 115 does not require the EPA to initiate those procedures until it is able to identify the specific sources in the United States of pollutants that cause harm in Canada; and second, we are satisfied that the EPA is not as yet able to do so.

I. BACKGROUND

Section 115(a) of the Clean Air Act provides in relevant part as follows:

> Whenever the Administrator, upon receipt of reports, surveys or studies from any duly constituted international agency has reason to believe that any air pollutant or pollutants emitted in the United States cause or contribute to air pollution which may reasonably be anticipated to endanger public health or welfare in a foreign country . . . , the Administrator shall give formal notification thereof to the Governor of the State in which such emissions originate.

42 U.S.C. § 7415(a) (1982). The Administrator's finding that pollution emitted in the United States contributes to such air pollution is referred to as an "endangerment finding."

> Under section 115(b), the notice to the Governor of the State in which such emissions originate is deemed to be a finding that its State Implementation Plan ("SIP") under the Clean Air Act is inadequate and must be revised to the extent necessary "to prevent or eliminate the endangerment." Id. § 7415(b); see id. § 7410(a)(2)(H)(ii). (SIP's impose controls upon individual polluters with in each State sufficient to ensure that national ambient air quality standards are met.) This process is referred to as the "SIP revision" procedure.

*   *   *

II. DISCUSSION

* * *

Section 115(a) provides that "[w]henever" the Administrator, based on certain reports or studies, has "reason to believe" that an air pollutant emitted in the United States causes or contributes to air pollution that may reasonably be anticipated to endanger health or welfare in a foreign country, he "shall give formal notification thereof to the Governor of the State in which such emissions originate." 42 U.S.C. § 7415(a) (emphasis added). The words "whenever" the Administrator "has reason to believe" imply a degree of discretion underlying the endangerment finding, Once that finding is made, however, the remedial action that follows is both specific and mandatory - the Administrator "shall" notify the Governor of the specific State emitting the pollution and require it to revise its SIP.

The statute thus creates a specific linkage between the endangerment finding and the remedial procedures: Once the endangerment finding is made, the SIP revision process must follow. As a result, if there is insufficient information to enable the Administrator to implement those remedies, the promulgation of an endangerment finding alone would largely be pointless. For this reason, the EPA's view that the Administrator must have sufficient evidence correlating the endangerment to sources of pollution within a particular. State before he can exercise his discretion to make endangerment findings is both reasonable and consistent with the statute.

Our view of the EPA's interpretation is further supported by section 115(b), which mandates a revision of the polluting State's SIP. Under subsection (b), the Administrator's notice to the Governor represents a finding that the State's SIP must be revised "with respect to so much of the . . . plan as is inadequate to prevent or eliminate the endangerment referred to in subsection (a) of this section." 42 U.S.C. § 7415(b) (emphasis added). This provision reinforces the linkage between the endangerment finding and the remedy that Congress has prescribed. If the EPA does not have a sufficient base of knowledge to trace endangering pollutants to sources within specific States, then a simple endangerment finding would leave subsection (b) without effect. The unitary approach adopted by the EPA avoids that result.

* * *

We are, of course, fully aware that more than nine years have elapsed since Administrator Castle advised Secretary of State Muskie and Senator Mitchell of his conclusion that pollutants from sources in the United States were endangering the public welfare in Canada. But we are also aware of the unusual complexity of the factors facing the agency in determining the effects of acid rain and in tracing the pollutants from the point of deposition back to their sources. In fact, it was for the purpose, among others, of developing a better understanding of the acid rain phenomenon that Congress enacted the Acid Precipitation Act of 1980, 42 U.S.C. §§ 8901–8912 (1982).

This statute initiated a ten-year program, commonly known as the National Acid Precipitation Assessment Program ("NAPAP") that is designed to identify the causes and sources of acid rain. to evaluate its environmental, social, and economic effects, and to asses potential methods of control. *See* 42 U.S.C. § 8903. We note that the final NAPAP report is due in December 1990. At oral argument the EPA pointed to this study as evidence of specific research being conducted that could enable the agency to take action under section 115; the EPA also asserted that the report should provide it with a sufficient basis to make a reasoned decision on the petitioners' rulemaking petitions.

It is in part on the basis of this information that we conclude that the EPA's delay in acting on the petitions has been neither arbitrary) nor capricious, nor contrary to law.

NOTE ON THE CONTROL OF INTERNATIONAL AND INTERSTATE POLLUTION UNDER THE CLEAN AIR ACT

Marilynn K. Roberts, in an article published some 26 years ago, presciently analyzed the local nature of the U.S. Clean Air Act and the difficulty of using this Act to combat interstate and international air pollution. What is the picture now, many years later? Happily, progress has occurred.

A.   The EPA has successfully injected life into section 110 [42 USC sec. 7410] of the Clean Air Act, which is now known as the "Good Neighbor" provision of the Act. After some two decades of legal struggles, in 2014, the Supreme Court of the United States, by a vote of 6 to 2, approved EPA's comprehensive implementation of the CAA's Good Neighbor Provision in the case, *Environmental Protection Agency v. EME Homer City Generation*, 134 S. Ct. 1584 (2014). The Supreme Court approved EPA's Transport Rule, promulgated in 2011 to curtail NOX and SO2 emissions of 27 upwind States to achieve downwind attainment of three different NAAQS, including particulate matter, measured on a daily basis. *See* 76 Fed. Reg. 48208-48209. Under the Transport Rule, an upwind State could be said to "contribute significantly" to downwind non-attainment to the extent its exported pollution both (1) produced one percent or more of a NAAQS in at least one downwind State and (2) could be eliminated cost-effectively, as determined by EPA. Upwind States would be obliged to eliminate only emissions meeting both of these criteria. States must now implement the Transport Rule into their State Implementation Plans (SIPs); if they do not, the EPA is authorized to prepare a compulsory Federal Implementation Plan (FIP). The Supreme Court majority approved the EPA's authority in this regard.

B.   The implementation of concern for international air pollution also took almost two decades of legal struggles. The culmination of this struggle was the Canada-US Agreement on Air Quality (1991), to which we turn next.

CANADA-UNITED STATES AGREEMENT ON AIR QUALITY
30 I.L.M. 676 (Ottawa, 1991)

The Government of the United States of America and the Government of Canada, hereinafter referred to as the Parties,"

Convinced that transboundary air pollution can cause significant harm to natural resources of vital environmental, cultural and economic importance, and to human health in both countries;

Desiring that emissions of air pollutants from sources within their countries not result in significant transboundary air pollution;

Convinced that transboundary air pollution can effectively be reduced through cooperative or coordinated action providing for controlling emissions of air pollutants in both countries;

Recalling the efforts they have made to control air pollution and the improved air quality that has resulted from such efforts in both countries;

Intending to address air-related issues of a global nature, such as climate change and stratospheric ozone depletion, in other fora;

Reaffirming Principle 21 of the Stockholm Declaration, which provides that "States have, in accordance with the Charter of the United Nations and the principles of international law, the sovereign right to exploit their own resources pursuant to their own environmental policies, and the responsibility to ensure that activities within their jurisdiction or control do not cause damage to the environment of other States or of areas beyond the limits of national jurisdiction";

Noting their tradition of environmental cooperation as reflected in the Boundary Waters Treaty of 1909, the Trail Smelter Arbitration of 1941, the Great Lakes Water Quality Agreement of 1978, as amended, the Memorandum of Intent Concerning Transboundary Air Pollution of 1980, the 1986 Joint Report of the Special Envoys on Acid Rain, as well as the; ECE Convention on Long-Range Transboundary Air Pollution of 1979;

Convinced that a healthy environment is essential to assure the well-being of present and future generations in the United States and Canada, as well as of the global community;

Have agreed as follows:

* * *

Article IV
Specific Air Quality Objectives

1. Each Party shall establish specific objectives, which it undertakes to achieve, for emissions limitations or reductions of such air pollutants as the Parties agree to address. Such specific objectives will be set forth in annexes to this Agreement.

2. Each Party's specific objectives for emissions limitations or reductions of sulfur dioxide and nitrogen oxides, which will reduce transboundary flows of these acidic deposition precursors, are set forth in Annex 1.

* * *

Article VII
Exchange of Information

1. The Parties agree to exchange, on a regular basis arid through the Air Quality Committee established under Article VIII, information on:

(a) monitoring;

(b) emissions;

(c) technologies, measures and mechanisms for controlling emissions;

(d) atmospheric processes; and

(e) effects of air pollutants, as provided in Annex

2. Notwithstanding any other provisions of this Agreement, the Air Quality Committee and the International Joint Commission shall not release, without the consent of the owner, any information identified to them as proprietary information under the laws of the place where such information has been acquired.

Article VIII
The Air Quality Committee

1. The Parties agree to establish and maintain a bilateral Air Quality Committee to assist in the implementation of this Agreement. The Committee shall be composed of an equal number of members representing each Party. It may be supported by subcommittees, as appropriate.

2. The Committee's responsibilities shall include:

(a) reviewing progress made in the implementation of this Agreement, including its general and specific objectives;

(b) preparing and submitting to the Parties a progress report within a year after entry into force of this Agreement and at least every two years thereafter;

(c) referring each progress report to the International Joint Commission for action in accordance with Article IX of this Agreement; and

(d) releasing each progress report to the public after its submission to the Parties.

3. The Committee shall meet at least once a year and additionally at the request of either Party.

Article IX
Responsibilities of the International Joint Commission

1. The International Joint Commission is hereby given, by a Reference pursuant to Article IX of the Boundary Waters Treaty, the following responsibilities for the sole purpose of assisting the Parties in the implementation of this Agreement:

(a) to invite comments, including through public hearings as appropriate, on each progress report prepared by the Air Quality Committee pursuant to Article VIII;

(b) to submit to the Parties a synthesis of the views presented pursuant to sub-paragraph (a), as well as the record of such views if either Party so requests; and

(c) to release the synthesis of views to the public after its submission to the Parties.

2. In addition, the Parties shall consider such other joint references to the International Joint Commission as may be appropriate for the effective implementation of this Agreement.

*   *   *

Article XI

Consultations

The Parties shall consult, at the request of either Party, on any matter within the scope of this Agreement. Such consultations shall commence as soon as practicable, but in any event not later than thirty days from the date of receipt of the request for consultations, unless otherwise agreed by the Parties.

Article XII

Referrals

With respect to cases other than those subject to Article XIII, if, after consultations in accordance with Article XI, an issue remains concerning a proposed or continuing action, activity, or project that is causing or would be likely to cause significant transboundary air pollution, the Parties shall refer the matter to an appropriate third party in accordance with agreed terms of reference.

Article XIII
Settlement of Disputes

1. If, after consultations in accordance with Article XI, a dispute remains between the Parties over the interpretation or the implementation of this Agreement, they shall seek to resolve such dispute by negotiations between them. Such negotiations shall commence as soon as practicable, but in any event not later than ninety day. from the date of receipt of the request for negotiation, unless otherwise agreed by the Parties.

2. If a dispute is not resolved through negotiation, the Parties shall consider whether to submit that dispute to the International Joint Commission in accordance with either Article IX or Article X of the Boundary Waters Treaty. If, after such consideration, the Parties do not elect either of those options, they shall, at the request of either Party, submit the dispute to another agreed form of dispute resolution.

Annex 1

SPECIFIC OBJECTIVES CONCERNING SULPHUR DIOXIDE MID NITROGEN OXIDES

1. Sulfur Dioxide

A. For the United States [applies only in the 48 contiguous states and D.C.]

1. Reduction of annual sulfur dioxide emissions by approximately 10 million tons from 1980 levels in accordance with Title IV of the Clean Air Act i.e., reduction of annual sulfur dioxide emissions to approximately 10 million tons below 1980 levels by 2000 (with the exception of sources repowering with qualifying clean coal technology in accordance with section 409 of the Clean Air Act, and sources receiving bonus allowances in accordance with section 405(a) (2) and (3) of the Clean Air Act).

2. Achievement of a permanent national emission cap of 8.95 million tons of sulfur dioxide per year for electric utilities by 2010, to the extent required by Title IV of the Clean Air Act.

3. Promulgation of new or revised standards or such other action under the Clean Air Act as the Administrator of the U.S. Environmental Protection Agency (EPA) deems appropriate, to the extent required by section 406 of the Clean Air Act Amendments of 1990 (P. L. 101 - 549), aimed at limiting sulfur dioxide emissions from industrial sources in the event that the Administrator of EPA determines that annual sulfur dioxide emissions from industrial sources may reasonably be expected to exceed 5.6 million tons.

B. For Canada:

1. Reduction of sulfur dioxide emissions in the seven eastern most Provinces to 2.3 million tons per year by 1994 and the achievement of a cap on sulfur dioxide emissions in the seven easternmost Provinces at 2.3 million tons per year from 1995 through December 31, 1999.

2. Achievement of a permanent national emissions cap of 3.2 million tons per year by 2000.

2. Nitrogen Oxides

A. For the United States: [territorial limitations as per sulfur dioxide]

With a view to a reduction of total annual emissions of nitrogen oxides by approximately 2 million tons from 1980 emission levels by 2000:

1. Stationary Sources

Implementation of the following nitrogen oxides control program for electric utility boilers to the extent required by Title IV of the Clean Air Act:

    (a) By January 1, 1995, tangentially fired boilers must meet an allowable emission rate of 0.45 lb/mmBtu and dry bottom wall-fired boilers must meet an allowable emission rate of 0.50 lb/mmBtu (unless the Administrator of EPA determines that these rates cannot be achieved using low SOx burner technology).

    (b) By January 1, 1997, EPA must set allowable emission limitations for:

        – wet bottom wall-fired boilers;

        – cyclones;

        – units applying cell burner technology; and

        – all other types of utility boilers.

2. Mobile Sources

Implementation of the following mobile source nitrogen oxides control program to the extent required by Title II of the Clean Air Act:

*   *   *

B. For Canada:

1. Stationary Sources

    (a) As an interim requirement, reduction, by 2000, of annual national emissions of nitrogen oxides from stationary sources by 100,000 tons below the year 2000 forecast level of 970,000 tons.

    (b) By January 1, 1995, development of further annual national emission reduction requirements from stationary sources to be achieved by 2000 and/or 2005.

2. Mobile Sources

    (a) Implementation of a more stringent mobile source nitrogen oxides control program for gasoline powered vehicles with standards no less stringent than the following: . . .

3. Compliance Monitoring

A. Utility Units

1. For the United States

Requirement that, by January 1, 1995, each new electric utility unit and each electric utility unit greater than 25 HWe existing on the date of enactment of the Clean Air Act Amendments of 1990 (November 15, 1990) emitting sulfur dioxide or nitrogen oxides install and operate continuous emission monitoring systems or alternative systems approved by the Administrator of EPA, to the extent required by section 412 of the Clean Air Act.

2. For Canada

Requirement that, by January 1, 1995, Canada estimate sulfur dioxide and nitrogen oxides emissions from each new electric utility unit and each existing electric utility unit greater than 25 MWe using a method of comparable effectiveness to continuous emission monitoring, as well as investigate the feasibility of using and implement, where appropriate, continuous emission monitoring systems.

3. For Both parties

The Parties shall consult, as appropriate, concerning the implementation of the above.

B. Other Major Stationary Sources

Requirement that the Parties work towards utilizing comparably effective methods of emission estimation for sulfur dioxide and nitrogen oxides emissions from all major industrial boilers and process sources, including smelters.

Prevention of Air Quality Deterioration and Visibility

Recognizing the importance of preventing significant air quality deterioration and protecting visibility, particularly for international parks, national, state, and provincial parks, and designated wilderness areas:

A. For the United States

Requirement that the United States maintain means for preventing significant air quality deterioration and protecting visibility, to the extent required by Part C of Title I of the Clean Air Act, with respect to sources that could cause significant transboundary air pollution.

B. For Canada:

Requirement that Canada, by January 1, 1995, develop and implement means affording levels of prevention of significant air quality deterioration and protection of visibility comparable to those in paragraph A above, with respect to sources that could cause significant transboundary air pollution.

OZONE ANNEX (2000)

In December 2000 Canada and the United States adopted what is known as the Ozone Annex to the 1991 Canada-United States Air Quality Agreement. This Annex provides for joint cooperative regulation of transboundary pollutants leading to high levels of ground level Ozone (O3).

Annex 3: Specific Objectives Concerning Ground-level Ozone Precursors

Part I — Purpose

The objective of the annex is to control and reduce, in accordance with the provisions herein, the anthropogenic emissions of nitrogen oxides (NOx) and volatile organic compounds (VOC) that are precursors to the formation of ground-level 02ne and that contribute to transboundary air pollution, thereby helping both countries attain their respective air quality goals over time to protect human health and the environment. The Parties' goal is that in the long term and in a stepwise approach, taking into account advances in scientific knowledge, atmospheric concentrations not exceed:

1. For Canada, the Canada Wide Standard (CWS) for Ozone; and

2. For the United States, the National Ambient Air Quality Standards for Ozone.

Part II — Pollutant Emission Management Area

Each Party hereby designates a Pollution Emission Management Area (PEMA), to which obligations in this Annex shall apply in accordance with the provisions herein.

1. For Canada, the area of 301,330km2 that covers all of the Canadian territory south of about the 48th parallel beginning east of Lake Superior to the Ottawa River, and south of the corridor that extends from the Outaouals Region east to Quebec City, as definitively designated on the map at Appendix 1 to this Annex.

2. For the United States, the area comprising the states of Connecticut, Delaware, Illinois, Indiana, Kentucky, Maine, Maryland, Massachusetts, Michigan, New Hampshire, New York, New Jersey, Ohio, Pennsylvania, Rhode Island, Vermont, West Virginia, and Wisconsin, and the District of Columbia, as indicated on the illustrative map at Appendix 2 to this Annex.

Part III — Specific Obligations

A. For Canada:

1. With respect to mobile sources of NOx and VOC emissions, Canada shall control and reduce its emissions of NOx and VOC in accordance with the following obligations:

    1. Continue the application of the following emission control measures:

        1. Emission standards for new light-duty vehicles, light-duty trucks, heavy-duty vehicles, heavy-duty engines and motorcycles: Motor Vehicle Safety Act (and successor legislation), Schedule V of the Motor Vehicle Safety Regulations: Vehicle Emissions (Standard 1100), SOR/97-376, (28 July, 1997).

        2. The Recreational Marine Engine Memorandum of Understanding between Environment Canada and manufacturers of spark-ignited marine engines to supply the Canadian market with engines designed to comply with U.S. federal spark-ignited marine engine emissions standards starting with the 2001 model year.

B. For the United States:

1. Specific NOx Reduction Commitments

    a. The United States shall require States that are located in the PEMA and that are subject to EPA's NOx regulation (referred to as the "NOx SIP Call") to implement that regulation in accordance with 40 Code of Federal Regulations (CFR) sections 51.121 and 51.122 including any modifications as a result of any court decision. The NOx SIP Call requires States to ensure that seasonal NOx emissions do not exceed specified levels ("budgets").

    b. The United States shall implement a motor vehicle control program in the PEMA that meets the requirements of 40 CFR Part 80, Subpart D (reformulated gasoline), 40 CFR Part 86 (control of emissions from new and in-use highway vehicles and engines); and 40 CFR Part 80, section 80.29 (controls and prohibitions on diesel fuel quality).

    c. The United States shall implement standards for non-road engines in the PEMA as provided for in 40 CFR Part 87 (aircraft), Part 89 (compression-ignition engines), Part 90 (spark ignition engines), Part 92 (locomotives), and Part 94 (marine engines).

2. Specific VOC Reduction Commitments

    a. The United States shall implement controls in the PEMA that reduce VOC emissions as required by 40 CFR Part 59, Subpart B (automobile repair coatings), Subpart C (consumer and commercial products), and Subpart D (architectural coatings).

    b. The United States shall implement controls on hazardous.air pollutants in the PEMA that also reduce VOC emissions as required by 40

CFR Part 63. This includes the following Subparts:

Part IV — Anticipated Additional Control Measures and Indicative Reductions

In addition to the obligations set forth in Part III above, each Party currently implements or anticipates implementing additional measures that are expected to contribute to overall reductions of NOx and VOC emissions. For illustrative purposes only, additional control measures currently in place and anticipated additional control measures are set forth below, as are predicted overall emission reduction rates.

A. For Canada:

1. National Reductions

    In order to achieve, by 2010, the CWS for Ozone (65 ppb a-hour average 4th highest averaged over 3 years), Canada intends to develop and implement further reductions of *emissions* of NOx and VOc.

2. Area-Specific Reductions

    In Ontario, a 45% reduction of NOx and VOC emissions from 1990 levels is expected to be required to meet the CWS for Ozone, assuming comparable reductions in the U.S. PEMA. In the Ontario portion of the PEMA, measures to reduce VOC emissions from small to medium sized solvent users will be developed. In the Quebec portion of the PEMA, measures to reduce NOx and VOC *emissions* from existing light and heavyduty vehicles will be considered.

3. Quantitative Estimates

    The emission reduction obligations identified in Part III.A above are estimated to reduce annual NOx emissions in the PEMA from 1990 levels by 39% by 2007 and 44% by 2010 and annual VOC emissions in the PEMA from 1990 levels by 18% in 2007 and 20% in 2010. Once all the measures identified in Part III.A are implemented, in conjunction with the anticipated national and area-specific reductions identified above, it is expected that emissions reductions will be greater than currently estimated.

B. For the United States:

1. National Reductions

    The United States has developed or intends to develop and implement standards to further reduce emissions of NOx and VQC, including:

    1. Tier 2 vehicle and fuel sulphur standards

    2. Tier 3 standards for nonroad compression ignition engines

    3. Heavy-duty engine standards

    4. Recreational vehicle standards

2. Area-Specific Reductions

The United States has implemented and intends to continue to implement NOx and VOC control measures in specific areas as required by applicable provisions of the Clean Air Act. The area specific measures include: NOx and VOC reasonably available control technology, marine vessel loading, treatment storage and disposal facilities, municipal solid waste landfills, onboard refuelling, residential wood combustion, vehicle inspection/ maintenance, and reformulated gasoline. In addition to these measures, under Clean Air Act mandates, U.S. states have already adopted or will be required to adopt additional measures for particular areas in the PEMA in order to meet the applicable National Ambient Air Quality Standards for Ozone.

3. Quantitative Estimates

The emission reduction obligations identified in Part III.B above, in conjunction with the anticipated national and area-specific reductions identified above, are estimated to reduce annual NOx emissions in the PEMA from 1990 levels by 27% by 2007 and 36% by 2010 and annual VOC emissions in the PEMA from 1990 levels by 35% in 2007 and 38% in 2010. Further, the emission reduction obligations identified in Part III.B above in conjunction with the anticipated national and area-specific reductions identified above, are estimated to reduce ozone season NOx emissions in the PEMA from 1990 levels by 35% by 2007 and 43% by 2010 and ozone season VOC emissions in the PEMA from 1990 levels by 39% in 2007 and 36% in 2010.

NOTE ON TRADING SO₂ ALLOWANCES

Trading sulfur dioxide allowances is the hallmark of the EPA's Acid Rain Program. The market-based sulfur dioxide allowance trading program allows electric utility companies to adopt the most cost-effective strategy to reduce SO_2 emissions at units in their systems. Affected utilities are required to install systems that continuously monitor emissions of SO_2, nitrogen oxides, and other related pollutants in order to track progress, ensure compliance, and provide credibility to the trading component of the program.

An allowance authorizes a utility or industrial source to emit one ton of SO_2 during a given year. At the end of each year, an emission source must hold an amount of allowances equal to its annual emissions. If the utility is short of allowances, the utility must purchase allowances at least equal to its emissions; if it is long in allowances, the excess may be sold on the open market. But regardless of the amount of allowances the utility holds, it cannot exceed the limits set under Title I of the Clean Act to protect the public health.

The allowance program began in 1995. The EPA makes annual allocations of allowances based on the average fossil fuel consumed from 1985 through 1987. Additional allowances were added in 2000 when the group of affected sources was expanded to include all units over 25 MW in generating capacity. In addition, allowances are available under three EPA reserve programs. In Phase I, units could gain extra allowances by installing qualifying control technology that has the capacity to remove at least 90% of the unit's SO_2 emissions. A second reserve program provides allowances as incentives for units achieving SO_2 emissions reductions through customer-oriented conservation measures or renewable energy generation. A third reserve sets allowances available for auctions, which are held annually every March by the EPA. Beginning in 2010, the Clean Air Act puts a cap of 8.95 million on the number of allowances issued each year. This effectively caps emissions at 8.95 tons annually.

Allowances are fully marketable commodities which may be bought, sold, or traded by any individual or corporation or governing body. The allowance trading program allows utility companies to decide the most cost-effective way to comply with the acid rain provisions of the Clean Air Act. Utilities can reduce emissions through conservation programs, increasing reliance on renewable energy, switching to lower sulfur fuel, employing control technologies, or developing alternative compliance strategies.

All stakeholders — businesses, utility companies, and environmentalists — appear to accept this trading scheme.

JOINT STATEMENT MARKING THE 20TH ANNIVERSARY OF THE US-CANADA AIR QUALITY AGREEMENT

On March 14, 2011 — U.S. Environmental Protection Agency Administrator Lisa Jackson and Environment Minister Peter Kent marked the 20th anniversary of the U.S. — Canada Air Quality Agreement today, an agreement that has significantly reduced acid rain and smog.

"Protecting public health and safeguarding the environment are EPA's top priorities. Thanks to the cooperation between our nations over the last 20 years, Canada and the United States have made great strides in the ongoing effort to reduce harmful air pollution and prevent serious health challenges for our people," said EPA Administrator Lisa P. Jackson. "Our joint efforts to clean up the air we breathe have saved lives and protected American and Canadian families from asthma and other respiratory illness, removed acid from rain and smog from air, and set the foundation for continued work together on our shared challenges."

"When Canada and the United States signed the Air Quality Agreement in 1991, transboundary movement of air pollution from industrial activities on both sides of border resulted in acid rain causing serious damage to our environment and in smog posing a serious threat in the air we breathe. After twenty years of cooperation, emissions causing acid rain have been cut in half and emissions causing smog have been cut by one-third in the region covered under this agreement," said Minister Kent.

In the United States, since the signing of the Air Quality Agreement, national and regional programs have dramatically reduced emissions of pollutants that contribute to the formation of acid rain, smog, and fine particle pollution. As of 2010, the U.S. national Acid Rain Program has reduced emissions of sulfur dioxide by 67 percent from 1990 levels. Power plant emissions of nitrogen oxides have decreased by over two-thirds from 1990 to 2010 under the U.S. Acid Rain Program and other regional programs.

These reductions have contributed to significant improvements in air quality on both sides of the border. Reductions in fine particle levels resulting from the U.S. Acid Rain Program are estimated to yield Significant human health benefits including 20,000-50,000 lives saved each year.

In Canada, emissions of the key pollutants that contribute to smog, acid rain and poor air quality have seen significant declines since 1990. Emissions of sulfur oxides (SOx) declined by about 54%, mainly due to reductions from base metal smelters which were down 72% and fossil fuel-fired electricity generating utilities which decreased by 45%.

Since the addition of the Ozone Annex to the agreement in 2000, Canada has been able to reduce nitrogen oxides emissions by a third in the southern and central Ontario and southern Quebec transboundary region defined under the agreement.

The combination of these initiatives has also resulted in particulate matter emission reductions of 34 percent. Particulate matter is a major contributor to human health affects and has been linked to respiratory illnesses such as chronic bronchitis and asthma, to cardiac illness, and to premature death.

B. Europe

THE CONVENTION ON LONG-RANGE TRANSBOUNDARY AIR POLLUTION (1979)

The most detailed international regime for the control of long-range transboundary air pollution is the Convention on long-Range Transboundary Air Pollution (CLRTAP) (1979), sponsored by the United Nations Economic Commission for Europe (ECE), a framework convention outlining a set of principles, as well as mechanisms for negotiating and implementing concrete standards for the abatement of transboundary air pollution. For the provisions of CLRTAP, see the Document Supplement. The CLRTAP currently has 51 parties, including the United States and Canada, but its actively participating states are European, including the member states of the European Union as well as other states such as the Russian Federation. The CLRTAP has a permanent Secretariat in Geneva and the parties meet annually at sessions of the Executive Body to review ongoing work and to plan future actions, and to adopt a Workplan for the coming year, which is delegated to the Steering Body and the secretariat. CLRTAP's subsidiary bodies — the Working Group on Effects, a Working Group on Strategies and Review, a Steering Body, and the Implementation Committee, report to the Executive Body.

CLRTAP takes a multispeed approach to controlling air pollution by adopting protocols dealing with specific pollution issues and leaving it up to each of the 51 parties to choose which protocols to join. Since its formation in 1979, CLRTAP has adopted eight protocols, which constitute eight subregimes each with its own parties, which meet and adopt amendments to the protocols that raise air quality standards or address specific problems. CLRTAP's current priority is to extend and implement its most recent protocols to the entire ECE region with emphasis on Eastern Europe, the Caucasus, Central Asia, and South-east Europe. The CLRTAP is charged with controlling all types of air pollution, not only acid deposition.

The eight protocols adopted by the CLRTAP parties are as follows:

- The 1984 Geneva Protocol on Long-Term Financing of the Cooperative Program for Monitoring and Evaluation of the Long-Range Transmission of Air Pollutants in Europe (EMEP Protocol). This protocol is an instrument for international cost-sharing and forms the backbone for review and assessment of air pollution in Europe. 34 states and the European Union are parties.

- The 1985 Helsinki Protocol on the Reduction of Sulfur Emissions or Their Transboundary Fluxes by at least 30 percent. Under this protocol, 21 parties reduced 1980 sulfur emissions by more than 50%.

- The 1988 Sofia Protocol Concerning the Control of Emissions of Nitrogen Oxides or Their Transboundary Fluxes. 23 parties agreed to freeze their NO emissions as a first step, and as a second step the parties agreed to reduce NO emissions applying an effects-based approach.

- The 1984 Oslo Protocol on Further Reduction of Sulfur Emissions. 29 parties.

- The 1991 Geneva Protocol Concerning the Control of Emissions of Volatile Organic Compounds or Their Transboundary Fluxes. 24 parties.

- The 1998 Aarhus Protocol on Heavy Metals. 31 parties. This protocol targets cadmium, lead and mercury.

- The 1998 Aarhus Protocol on Persistent Organic Pollutants (POPS). 31 parties. This protocol targets 16 substances, eleven pesticides, two industrial chemicals and three by-product contaminants.

- The 1999 Gothenburg Protocol to Abate Acidification, Eutrophication and Ground-Level Ozone.

How does the CLRTAP compare with the US-Canada program? Consider the following analysis:

COMPARISON OF THE EUROPEAN AND U.S. APPROACHES TOWARDS ACIDIFICATION, EUTROPHICATION AND GROUND LEVEL OZONE
Commission of the European Union
4 October 2004

INTRODUCTORY OVERVIEW

This case study compares the EU and U.S. approaches to the regional air quality problems of acidification. eutrophication and ground-level ozone. Acidifying and eutrophying pollutants originate primarily from anthropogenic emissions of sulphur dioxide (SO_2), nitrogen oxides (NOx.) and ammonia (NH_3). Most of SO_2 and NO_x are emitted to the atmosphere from combustion of fossil fuel in power plants. industrial plants, residential heating, commercial and service sectors. Road transport. shipping and aircraft are significant sources of NOX. emissions. NH_3 emissions are related to agricultural activities.

Ground-level ozone is formed when NO_X and VOCs are subject to photochemical activity. Emissions of VOC are emitted from combustion and also by evaporation of fuels and solvents from stationary sources as well as traffic. Natural emissions. in particular hydrocarbon from vegetation. also contribute to the photochemical activity. Ground level ozone in both Europe and North America affects human health and leaf injury in plants. and causes damages on materials — particularly organic materials. Episodes with high levels of ozone occur mainly during the summer and especially in the southern parts of Europe and the eastern and western portions of the U.S. and where the emissions of precursors are high.

The above pollutants contribute to the formation of secondary particles (PM_{10}/ $PM_{2.5}$), and human health effects. Descriptions of the chemical processes and the effects are given in Annex 1.

COMPARISON OF THE TWO APPROACHES

To fully understand and compare the achievements in these various jurisdictions, it is important to understand the general philosophy behind acidification, eutrophication, and ozone regulation.

Acidification and Eutrophication in the EU

Efforts to address acidification and eutrophication include emissions reductions for SO_2, NOX, and NH_3. The regulations to control acidifying and eutrophying pollutants in Europe are aimed at addressing the combined effects of SO_2, NO_X and NH_3. This is because in Europe emissions from traffic as well as from agriculture — in addition to stationary sources — contribute significantly to acidification and eutrophication. This is in contrast to the U.S., where focus is on SO_2 from stationary sources. The emissions of these pollutants are also involved in the formation of particles (secondary particles), which makes the transport over long distances possible. and also influence the PM pollution implicated in human health problems NH_3 is mainly an environmental problem in the Northern- and Central parts of Europe. The reductions of NH_3 emissions have until now been rather limited.

Controls on long-range transport. Since acidifying, eutrophying, and ozone forming air pollutants — gases and articles — can be transported over long distances, e.g., thousands of kilometres, across national/state boundaries and cause damaging effects far away, the EU has addressed these impacts by setting in place controls over emissions that cut across all Member State jurisdictions. Nonetheless, parts of Europe are separated to some extent in relation to these air pollution problems, e.g. Scandinavia and the Mediterranean countries, and this factor has led to regional differentiation of emissions reduction targets for certain pollutants.

In Europe, these emissions reduction targets and measures have evolved via discussion, collaboration, and commitment among the different countries in the context of the UNECE Convention of Long-Range Transport of Air Pollution (CLRTAP). A series of CLRTAP Protocols on emissions reductions were agreed among various European countries. starting with SO_2, in the early 1980s and expanded to include NOx, VOCs, PM and NH_3. Within the EU, Directives were developed for regulation of stationary acid mobile sources, in support of the

Protocols. The recent Gothenburg Protocol was implemented for the EU countries by the NEC Directive, which sets more stringent national emissions ceilings than were agreed under the Protocol.

Use of command-and-controls approaches, with some application of emissions trading in specific countries. In the EU, regulation has been largely based on so-called "command and control," and still seems mainly to be so. A very important element in the EU legislation is the Large Combustion Plant Directive which sets emission limit values for SO_2, NO, and dust. First adopted in 1988. it was updated in 2001, in parallel with the adoption of mandatory national emissions ceilings for SO_2, NO_x, VOCs and NH_3, via the NEC Directive. The IPPC Directive which requires best available techniques for pollution control at major industrial installations is another important measure that includes large livestock rearing operations. and thus also addresses NH_3.

In addition, a few European countries have applied economic instruments in this area. For example, the Netherlands has initiated emissions trading for NO_x. Several other countries, e.g. Sweden. Denmark, France, and the Netherlands. have applied emission taxes and charges to special sectors and for specific pollutants such as SO_2, and NO_x. emissions.

In the early years of EU standard setting in the area of air quality, bureaucrats have generally convened in more or less closed. sessions to advise and take decisions. However, in the past decade, individual scientists, the World Health Organisation. NGOs and the industry have been much more involved in the work of developing standards and measures at EU as well as national levels.

SO_2, NOx, NH_3 reduction targets set for each country. Protocols under the CLRTAP aimed at reducing emissions of SO_2, NO_x, and NH_3, were based on the critical loads[17] concept. This concept was used for negotiations in Europe of emissions reductions in the individual countries based on integrated assessment modeling (RAINS[18]). The aim was to protect the major part of the sensitive ecosystems against acidification and eutrophication. In practice, the recent agreement (the Gothenburg Protocol and NEC Directive) aimed at a 50% reduction of the area of unprotected ecosystems, compared to the situation in 1990.

Acidification and Eutrophication in the U.S.

Efforts to address acidification primarily focused on SO_2 with other requirements for NO_x reductions. The scientific understanding in the U.S. during the late 1980s suggested that SO_2 was the largest contributor to acid rain and the electricity sector was estimated to account for two-thirds of the SO_2 emissions, so the program was primarily aimed at SO_2 emissions from these sources. Therefore, the primary effort, through Title IV of the 1990 CAAA, was aimed at reducing SO_2, emissions from the electricity sector. U.S. efforts have also included NO_x, reductions through Title IV. These reductions have been implemented alongside a set of parallel requirements

---

[17] A quantitative estimate of an exposure to one or more pollutants below which significant harmful effects on specified sensitive elements of the environment do not occur according to present knowledge.

[18] http://www.iiasa.ac.at/rains/.

addressing NOx emissions contributing to local ozone nonattainment.

Controls on long-range transport. Similar to the EU, the U.S., has addressed the impacts of acid rain formation by addressing emissions that cut across jurisdictions. For the U.S., these controls often include emission reductions from bordering or "upwind" states. For example, efforts to address SO_2, emissions that contribute to Acid Rain in the U.S. were addressed through a nationwide program.

The critical loads approach

In 1988, the CLRTAP parties appointed a new working group to develop a common critical-loads approach and to evolve abatement strategies based on that approach. The essence of the critical loads approach is that reductions of emissions are to be negotiated with a view to the effects of air pollutants, rather than by selling an equal percentage of reduction for all countries. The aim is to reduce, in a cost-effective manner: the emissions of air pollutants to levels where the critical loads will not be exceeded. This concept provided an acceptable, effects-based scientific approach for strategies for the abatement of air pollution. Each country was to make maps, showing the critical loads and levels for various areas, receptors, and pollutants in its own territory. The resulting data was assembled into Europe-wide maps showing exceedances of the critical loads and level. Computer models for integrated assessment enabled comparisons to be made of the cost-effectiveness of various strategies for achieving specified interim targets for environmental quality and the protection of health. Agreements were then reached on the reduction of emissions (interim targets) strategies for the abatement of emissions. and the reductions to be allocated among the various countries in the form of national ceilings for emissions.

The first result of the critical loads approach was the 1994 Second Sulphur Protocol, which came into Force in 1988. It sets differing requirements for each country - the aim being to attain the greatest possible effect for the environment at the least overall cost. It also includes some specific requirements for large combustion plants. The text for basic obligations says that "parties shall control and reduce their sulphur emissions in order to protect human health and the environment from adverse effects:" and ensure that sulphur depositions do not, in the long term, exceed critical loads. The scientific analysis of the protocol showed that in order to comply with the long-term goal was to be attained; the emissions of sulphur should be reduced by at least 90 per cent The countries commit under the protocol to reduce total European emissions of sulphur by 50 per cent by 2000, and 58 per cent by 2010, in relation to the level in 1980.

In the meantime eutrophication was observed on sensitive ecosystems, e.g., raised bogs, moors, lakes and coasts-near seas. In addition, ground-level ozone was now realised as an environmental problem in relation to health as well as damages on vegetation. NO_x plays an important role in both cases. The 1988, Protocol on the control of nitrogen oxides, which came into force in 1991, provides that emissions after 1994 should not exceed the 1987 level. It does not call for reduction, but defines the basis for a next step involving measures to reduce emissions, taking into account internationally accepted critical loads. Twelve signatories pointed out the weakness of this protocol by proposing separately, in a joint declaration, to reduce their NO_x, emissions by 30 per cent by 1998 at the latest. By 1994 the European emissions were reduced by about 16 per cent in relation to the 1987 levels. From the reported emission data it appeared however that three countries that had ratified the Protocol, Greece, Luxembourg, and Spain — had not managed even to freeze emissions. And of the 12 that were aiming at a 30 percent reduction only four or five had succeeded.

Technological Innovation

In Europe, very strong political and public pressure in connection with the debate about "forest death" in the 1970s led to "command-and-control" regulatory action in several countries, and this helped to spur some technological innovation. For example, in Germany, a 1983 ordinance gave electricity companies a very short deadline to comply with new and very strict emission limit values. This first led to adding of lime to the flue gas. Later, desulphurization technology became available to the companies. The final result was higher reduction efficiencies than had first been anticipated.

Economic incentives such as emission taxes have also played a role in encouraging technological innovation in several European countries. A study to evaluate economic incentives in France and Sweden concluded that the Swedish programme with a rather high NO_x charge, and with return of the money to the firms in proportion to the production of energy, was the most effective. The administrative cost was only 0,2-0,3% of the revenue. The Swedish NO_x charge provided a strong incentive both for fuel switching, modifications to combustion engineering and the installation of specific abatement equipment such as catalytic converters and selective non-catalytic reduction. The Swedish NO_x charge has also implied a strong incentive to use the equipment, to fine tune combustion and other processes in such a way as to minimise emissions. This led to a reduction in the average emission factor from 0.41 to 0.25 kg NO_x/MWh between 1992 and 2000.

European efforts to achieve emission reductions have also provided impetus for energy efficiency innovations. From 1994 to 1998, EU generation from Combined Heat and Power (CHP) increased from 9% of gross electricity generation to 11%, 7% short of the EU indicative target of 18% by 2010. Penetration of CHP in Denmark and the Netherlands is particularly high (more than 50%) as a result of government support. Liberalisation of energy markets in Finland and the United Kingdom has stimulated investment in CHP, However, lower electricity prices may act against more investment in CHP plants, which are capital intensive. This has already been the case in Germany where CHP generation has decreased.

The U.S. Acid Rain Trading Program has led to technological innovation in two regards. First, rail deregulation lowered the costs of low sulphur coal, making this an economic compliance option for many generators. The flexibility of the acid rain trading program enabled facilities to take advantage of this opportunity, lowering allowance prices and compliance costs for participants.

Second, the costs of scrubber technology in Phase I came down from a total cost of $0.51 per kg to $0.32 per kg, largely due to reductions in the fixed and variable operation and maintenance costs from improved instrumentation and control, reducing the parasitic loss of power and manpower requirements, and a 25 percent increase in the utilization of scrubbed plants (Popp, 2001). This higher utilization of scrubbed plants resulted from the fact that scrubber operating costs are lower than allowance costs, and because plants burning low sulphur coals now faced a premium fuel cost over the higher sulphur coals burned by scrubbed plants. On the other hand, the NO_x standards were based on implementation of low-NOx burners. Because the Alternative Emission Limit compliance option allowed plants to comply even if the limit wasn't achieved with installation of the technology, there was little incentive to take the risks needed to develop alternative compliance methods.

Costs Versus Benefits

For Europe as a whole, the total cost of reaching the emission ceilings is expected to be about 70 billion euros (US$ 75 billion) a year. This includes the cost of several other European initiatives that will contribute to meeting the emission ceilings, such as the European Union directives. The benefits of meeting the Protocol's emission ceilings have been estimated at roughly 200 billion euros (US$ 214 billion) a year. These benefits largely result from significant reductions in the negative effects of ozone and particulate matter on human health.

The benefit by reduction of SO_2 has been estimated (ExternE) at 6100 $/t SO_2, of which the major part (4000-5000 $/t SO_2) is related to human health and especially secondary particles. The benefit by reduction of NO_x has been estimated at 5000 $/t NO_x of which the major part (3000-4000 $/t NOx) is related to human health and especially secondary particles.

In the U.S., the annual benefits of the acid rain SO_2 regulations ($78 to $79 billion dollars) far exceeded the costs ($1 to $2 billion dollars) during the early years of the acid rain trading program (OMB, 2003). Similarly, acid rain NO_x regulations resulted in annual benefits of $1 to $5 billion and costs of $372 million (OMB, 2003). These values are not directly comparable with the estimates for achieving the NECs, described above, since achieving the NECs includes reductions of NO_x and VOC in addition to SO_2.

CONCLUSIONS

While a full comparative analysis between the two regions was limited due to a variety of factors, it is possible to highlight several conclusions for the comparison that we were able to conduct. A number of the conclusions from the consideration of the acidification, eutrophication and ozone formation case study can help illuminate potential areas for next steps on air quality control. Below are some of the key conclusions from the comparison of the emissions control approaches. emissions reductions, environmental achievements, and costs in the two regions.

- The EU achieved remarkable emission reduction results through a command and control approach, while the U.S. has opted to utilize market-based mechanisms to a greater extent than in the EU-15. The U.S. has utilized emissions trading systems to control Acid Rain and in some areas for emissions related to ozone, Each approach has been uniquely tailored to the given emission of concern and the impacts associated with those emissions, Canada and Japan have largely utilized command and control approaches for controlling SO_2 emissions.

- A limited number of EU countries have utilized market-based mechanisms, including emissions taxes and charges. but this *is* not a policy of the EU as a whole. The most successful tax/charge programmes in Europe (e.g. Sweden) were based on relatively high rates and returned most of the money to the companies in relation to the production achieved.

- Critical loads is a concept used more generally in the EUD than in the U.S. The concept has been at the heart of much of the EU goals setting process, The U.S., on the other hand, has no such formal concept for establishing emissions goals, but has done it using a variety of separate concepts. One reason for choosing the critical loads concept in Europe was that the uncertainties in the relationship between deposition and effects were so large that the role of cost-benefit analysis has been limited. However, the critical loads concept was also used for the negotiation in relation to the most effective emission reductions in the different European countries.

- Both EU-15 and U.S. emissions of NO_x SO_2, and VOCs are higher than those of Canada and Japan. In 2001, U.S. emissions of all three were higher than the EU-15. Further, emissions of the pollutants contributing to acidification are considerably higher per capita and in relation to GDP in the U.S. than in the EU-15. This can have implications for both the effectiveness of the EU air quality rules in light of growing GDP and population, the decoupling of the economy from the environment, and the EU's ability to reduce emissions further.

- Both regions have achieved significant reductions since 1980 of emissions that contribute to acidification, eutrophication, and ozone formation. Greater SO_2 and NO_x. reductions have been achieved in the EU-15 (78 and 26 percent) than in the U.S. (39 and 18 percent) since 1980. Likewise Japan and Canada have seen dramatic declines in SO_2 emissions over the period. Japanese SO_2 emissions fell by 82 percent between 1970 and 1992 and by 3 percent between 1990 and 1999. Between 1980 and 2000, Canada's SO_2 emissions had been lowered by 45 percent. Greater VOC reductions have been achieved in the U.S. (42 percent) than in the EU-I5 (40 percent) since 1980.

- Emissions of SO_2 and NO_x from energy industries have declined in both regions since 1980. The EU-15 has achieved a reduction in SO_2 and NOx of 76 and 50 percent, respectively, from these sources. U.S. SO_2 and NOx emission have declined by 38 and 30 percent. Respectively, over this time period. Most of the emissions reductions in both regions have occurred since 1990.

- The intensity of emissions (in kg/MWh) from energy industries is lower in the EU-15 than in the U.S. Since 1990, the EU-15 has achieved a greater decline in SO_2 intensity (70 percent compared with 47 percent), while the U.S. has achieved a slightly greater reduction in the NO_x intensity (42 percent compared with 40 percent).

- The U.S. has achieved greater reductions in NO_x emissions from transport, but total transport emissions are still higher than those in the EU-I5. The

EU-15 has achieved greater reductions in transport emissions since the 1990s, while the U.S. has seen a constant decline. Emissions per unit of travel for road vehicles (kt/km/vehicle) are higher in the U.S. than the EU-15-0,39 and 0,30 for NO_x, respectively.

- Both regions have achieved greater NO_x reductions from road transport than other transport since 1980.

- Large reductions in sulphate deposition have occurred in both regions; however, some areas in both countries suffer from high levels of sulphate deposition. Limited progress has been made on nitrate deposition in both regions.

- NH_3 is mainly an environmental problem in the Northern and Central parts of Europe. NH_3 is not a key issue in the legislation in the U.S.[19]

- Progress has been made in reducing ground level ozone formation in both regions; however, ozone formation is still a problem in many parts of the two regions.

- Technological innovation has occurred to some extent in both regions over the studied period. Some analysis has found that this is a result of the choice of environmental policy in the respective locations. Further analysis targeted at this particular issue may yield greater insight on the impact of these policies on technological innovation.

- Analysis in both Europe and the U.S. have found that the benefits (in economic valuation) have outweighed the costs of a number of air quality controls. For example, the total cost of reaching the emission ceilings is expected to be about 70 billion euros (US$ 75 billion) a year, compared with the benefits estimated at roughly 200 billion euros (USS 214 billion) a year. Likewise, the annual benefits of the U.S. Acid Rain SO_2 regulations ($78 to $79 billion dollars) far exceeded the costs ($1 to $2 billion dollars) during the early years of the acid rain trading program.

- A recent analysis found that environmental controls in Europe had not placed European industries at a competitive disadvantage vis a vis operations in other countries. A similar analysis was not available to compare competitiveness issues in the U.S.

- The transparent system of the U.S. Acid Rain Program in which non-compliance and penalties are well understood led to a near-perfect record of compliance. Because all participating units must have working CEMs, there is no question as to the number of allowances that are needed for compliance. It became less expensive for firms to comply with the requirements than to avoid compliance by seeking the various forms of modifications that characterize traditional regulatory programs in the U.S. such as exemptions, exceptions, or relaxations of the program's requirements.

---

[19] Efforts have been made during this project to determine concretely why ammonia emissions are more of an issue in the EU than in the U.S. No policy documents were found in the U.S. outlining the rationale. The issue is likely to be more of a state-by-state issue and thus relevant control efforts would be found in state documents which were outside the scope of this project.

• In theory, emissions trading programs such as the U.S. SO provisions under Title IV require greater up-front design efforts versus command-and-control approaches, but a smaller government role in implementation. In addition, the required administrative tasks differ across the two approaches. Instead of the inspection and enforcement role that is typical under a command-and-control regime, under cap-and-trade, the government role largely shifts to ensuring that continuous emissions monitoring systems are in working order and managing the data. Actual costs to EPA to implement the Acid Rain Program during the five years following the Clean Air Act Amendments carne to $44 million, or 4 percent of total costs to implement the Clean Air Act in the same period.

NOTES AND QUESTIONS

1.   Both the US-Canada Air Quality Agreement and the CLRTAP are international environmental success stories. Why is international cooperation possible in these two instances?

2.   List the major differences between the US-Canada Air Quality Agreement regime and the CLRTAP. What are the advantages and disadvantages of each approach? What elements do you admire; which elements are open to criticism?

3.   *The critical loads approach.* A *critical load* is the maximum amount of acidifying deposition that an ecosystem can tolerate in the long term without being damaged. Although the United States does not employ a critical loads approach, the EPA has analyzed the environmental conditions in the eastern United States in the Appalachian and Adirondack mountain region. For the period 2008 to 2010, 30% of the lakes and streams examined received levels of combined sulfur and nitrogen deposition that exceeded the critical load. This is an improvement over the 1989 to 1991 period, during which 55% of the lakes and streams exceeded the critical load. *United States-Canada Air Quality Agreement Progress Report 2012* (US-Canada Air Quality Committee), p. 58.

4.   *The Swedish tax program.* Sweden taxes NO_x emissions from all industrial boilers, stationary combustion engines and gas turbines with useful energy production of at least 25 GWh. Currently about 250 plants (375 boilers) are subject to the tax, which is levied at a rate of $4 per kg. of NO_x. The plants subject to the tax emit about 14,000 tons of NOx per year, which amount is approximately 5% of total NOx emissions in Sweden. The scheme is managed by the Swedish Environmental Protection Agency, which, after deducting an administrative charge of between 0.2-0.3% of revenues, refunds the balance of the money to the taxpayers in proportion to their production of "useful energy," which, for power plants and district heating plants, is equal to the energy sold, and for other industries is defined as steam, hot water, or electricity produced in the boiler and used in production processes or heating of factory buildings. The Swedish NO_x charge is a strong incentive to fine tune combustion and other processes to minimize emissions. The Swedish tax system seems to have had the desired effect. Between 1992, when the tax was first levied, and 2000, emissions of kg. of NO_x per MWh of produced energy fell from 0.41 to 0.25, and, although the number of plants subject to the tax doubled in this period, total NO_x emissions fell from 15305 tons in 1992, to 12, 664

tons in 2000. *See* EU Commission, *Assessment of the Effectiveness of European Air Quality Policies and Measures: Acidification and Eutrophication* 8 (2004).

5.   *Emissions of SO$_2$, NOx and VOCs per capita and per unit of GDP.* While both the EU and the U.S. have achieved dramatic reductions in percentage terms of major air pollutants, U.S. emissions of SO$_2$, NOx, and VOCs per capita and per unit of GDP are approximately twice as great as those in the EU; a major reason for this discrepancy is that per capita energy in the U.S. is 12.9 MWh per capita, compared to 6.0 MWh per capita in the EU.

6.   *Future actions.* Have these two international regimes reached the limit of the possible reductions in air pollutants? What policy initiatives should be undertaken in the future?

C.   Other Regions

Although all areas of the world experience varying degrees of transboundary air pollution, outside of North America and Europe, air pollution is subject only to national laws and transboundary air pollution is subject only to customary international law norms. One lone exception is the ASEAN Agreement on Transboundary Haze Pollution (2002), in force 2003, for 10 nations of the Association of Southeast Asian Nations (ASEAN). This Agreement was signed after forest fires primarily in Indonesia caused widespread haze pollution in Southeast Asia in 1997 and 2001. These forest fires were set as part of land clearing operations in rubber and palm oil plantations to get rid of old trees and to clear land for new plantations. Indonesia, where most of the fires take place each year, did not ratify this treaty until 2012. The fact that Indonesia is now a party to the Haze Agreement has given rise to new hope that the Haze Agreement will have its desired effect.

Despite the Haze Agreement, fires continue to be set and as a result, haze is a common feature each summer in Malaysia, Singapore, Brunei, and Thailand. In June 2012, Malaysia media reported that the Petronas Twin Towers in Kuala Lumpur were often shrouded in smoky haze. Consider the following provisions of the Haze Agreement. What are the weaknesses of this Agreement?

NOTE ON ASIAN SMOG

Smog and air pollution in Asia are approaching epic levels and constitute not only a major public health problem, but also a threat to food production, tourism and economic expansion. According to the World Health Organization (http://www.who.int/phe/health_topics/outdoorari/databases/en.html), China and middle income countries in the Western Pacific region have the highest number of deaths per capita — 172 per 100,000 people — from indoor and outdoor air pollution in the world. According to *The Lancet* (vol. 377, no. 9769, p. 885), more than 2.1 million people in Asia die prematurely from air pollution, mostly from the minute particles of diesel soot and gases emitted from cars and trucks, from burning forests, and from coal-burning power plants. The Shanghai Academy of Social Sciences, in a report in March 2014, (http://www.sass.org.cn), stated that Asian air pollution is now affecting climate around the world and make cities such as Beijing very dangerous.

About 20 percent of air pollution on the west coast of the United States now emanates from China and Asia.

The Observer (March 28, 2014, at 1) reports that dense smog in Southeast Asian countries is now an annual event known as "the burning season," early spring when farmers clear lands. In March 2014, satellites clearly identified hundreds of plumes of smoke emanating from palm oil plantations and rain forests emanating primarily from the vast island of Sumatra, Indonesia, and drifting across Myanmar, Thailand, Cambodia, Laos, and as far away as the Philippines and Papua New Guinea. Asia, *The Observer* reports, is now the epicenter of global air pollution; each year between January and March a "brown cloud" regularly covers the upper atmosphere over Asia, with unknown impacts for the rest of the planet. In 2014, across Southeast Asia, schools, airports, and roads have been closed as a result of air pollution, and more than 50,000 people have been treated for asthma, bronchitis, and other respiratory illnesses in Sumatra alone.

ASEAN AGREEMENT ON TRANSBOUNDARY HAZE POLLUTION (2002)

Article 2
Objective

The objective of this Agreement is to prevent and monitor transboundary haze pollution as a result of land and/or forest fires which should be mitigated, through concerted national efforts and intensified regional and international co-operation. This should be pursued in the overall context of sustainable development and in accordance with the provisions of this Agreement.

Article 3
Principles

The Parties shall be guided by the following principles in the implementation of this Agreement:

1. The Parties have, in accordance with the Charter of the United Nations and the principles of international law, the sovereign right to exploit their own resources pursuant to their own environmental and developmental policies, and the responsibility to ensure that activities within their jurisdiction or control do not cause damage to the environment and harm to human health of other States or of areas beyond the limits of national jurisdiction.

2. The Parties shall, in the spirit of solidarity and partnership and in accordance with their respective needs, capabilities and situations, strengthen co-operation and co-ordination to prevent and monitor trans-boundary haze pollution as a result of land and/or forest fires which should be mitigated.

3. The Parties should take precautionary measures to anticipate, prevent and monitor tranboundary haze pollution as a result of land and/or forest fires which should be mitigated, to minimize its adverse effects. Where there are

threats of serious or irreversible damage from transboundary haze pollution, even without full scientific certainty, precautionary measures shall be taken by Parties concerned.

4. The Parties should manage and use their natural resources, including forest and land resources, in an ecologically sound and sustainable manner.

5. The Parties, in addressing transboundary haze pollution, should involve, as appropriate, all stakeholders, including local communities, non-governmental organizations, fanners and private enterprises.

Article 4
General Obligations

In pursuing the objective of this Agreement, the Parties shall:

1. Co-operate in developing and implementing measures to prevent and monitor transboundary haze pollution as a result of land and/or forest fires which should be mitigated, and to control sources of fires, including by the identification of fires, development of monitoring, assessment and early warning systems, exchange of information and technology, and the provision of mutual assistance.

2. When the transboundary haze pollution originates from within their territories, respond promptly to a request for relevant information or consultations sought by a State or States that are or may be affected by such transboundary haze pollution, with a view to minimizing the consequences of the transboundary haze pollution.

3. Take legislative, administrative and/or other measures to implement their obligations under this Agreement.

*   *   *

Article 9
Prevention

Each Party shall undertake measures to prevent and control activities related to land and/or forest fires that may lead to transboundary haze pollution, which include:

a. Developing and implementing legislative and other regulatory measures, as well as programmes and strategies to promote a zero burning policy to deal with land and/or forest fires resulting in transboundary haze pollution;

b. Developing other appropriate policies to curb activities that may lead to land and/or forest fires;

c. Identifying and monitoring areas prone to occurrence of land and/or forest fires;

d. Strengthening local fire management and firefighting capability and co-ordination to prevent the occurrence of land and/or forest fires;

e. Promoting public education and awareness-building campaigns and strengthening community participation in fire management to prevent land and/or forest fires and haze pollution arising from such fires; Promoting and utilizing indigenous knowledge and practices in fire prevention and management; and

f. Ensuring that legislative, administrative and/or other relevant measures are taken to control open burning and to prevent land clearing using fire.

ASEAN Agreement on Transboundary Haze Pollution (2002), *available at* http://haze.asean.org/?page_id=185. *See further* Koh Kheng-Lian & Nicholas A Robinson, *Ten Years After Rio: Implementing Sustainable Development*, 6 SING. J. INT'L & COMP. L. 640, 654–58, Appendix II (2002); Kenneth Lim Tao Chung, Loh Li Qin, Angela Thiang Pei Yun, *Southeast Asian and International Law*, 7 SING. J. INTL & COMP. L. 603, 639–40 (2003).

NOTE AND QUESTION

The ASEAN Haze Pollution Agreement was concluded under the auspices of UNEP to deal with the severe haze coming from forest and land fires — many set intentionally — in Southeast Asia. This Agreement adopts a preservation approach. What are the parties' obligations under the Agreement? Will this Agreement accomplish its purpose?

The ASEAN states also established a Coordinating Center that can render assistance if needed; but a party must first request assistance. An ASEAN Haze Control Fund was established to provide money for transfer of technology and firefighting assistance. A Conference of the Parties was established to monitor the implementation of the Agreement.

Considering the Canada-US Air Quality Agreement and the Convention on Long Range Transboundary Air Pollution, what new obligations would you suggest to the parties to the ASEAN Haze Pollution Agreement?

Section III. PROTECTING THE OZONE LAYER

A. Introduction

Ozone (O3), a compound consisting of three atoms of oxygen, is a pale blue gas with an acrid smell that is very toxic to organic materials and is therefore dangerous to breathe. Ozone, along with NOx gases and hydrocarbons, is produced by combustion, and, when encountered near ground level, is commonly known as the pollutant, photochemical smog. Ozone plays a much different role, however in the upper atmosphere. Ozone is formed naturally in the stratosphere when oxygen molecules (02) are split apart by short wave solar radiation. Three free atoms of oxygen then combine to form ozone. Simultaneously, photochemical reactions catalyzed by NOx gases in the stratosphere remove ozone at a rate approximately equal to its formation. As a result, a natural ozone cycle exists in the stratosphere, where ozone is constantly created and destroyed. Stratospheric ozone plays a much different planetary role than ground-level ozone. Stratospheric ozone forms a naturally protective layer shielding the Earth from harmful shortwave ultraviolet solar radiation. Stratospheric ozone, although found in concentrations that average only about 10 parts per million by volume, acts as natural filter absorbing and blocking the sun's shortwave ultraviolet radiation (UV-B). If the ozone layer did not exist and UV-B were to reach the Earth, instances of cancer and cataracts in humans would dramatically increase and ecosystem and plant fertility would be adversely affected. Therefore stratospheric ozone depletion is a problem with the potential to affect all nations and all persons and all life on the planet Earth.

Concern over the ozone layer has been on the international agenda since the 1960s, when it was considered that high-flying supersonic aircraft might pose a danger to the ozone layer. In 1975, Sherwood Rowland and Mario Molina of the University of California published a paper showing that chlorofluorocarbons (CFCs) widely used in homes and industry — as propellants in spray cans, in cooling systems, in foam blowing, and as solvents in the electronics industry — endanger the ozone layer. CFCs are synthetically produced inert gases, non-toxic, odorless, and non-flammable. Used and emitted at the surface of the Earth, they have the potential of rising into the stratosphere after many years, where the ultraviolet rays of the sun will break them apart, releasing stray atoms of chlorine (Cl). These atoms then combine with ozone according to the chemical reaction:

$$Cl + O_3 = ClO + O_2$$

Thus the encounter of ozone with a free atom of chlorine transforms the ozone into chlorine oxide and oxygen.

> If a single atom of oxygen is further encountered by the chlorine oxide a further reaction may occur:

$$ClO + O = Cl + O_2$$

This reaction frees the atom of chlorine which can thus repeat the first reaction above destroying more ozone. Since CFCs may remain in the stratosphere for 40 to 150 years, a single chlorine atom may by repeated reactions remove as many as 100,000 ozone molecules from the stratosphere during its atmospheric lifetime. Thus even a small amount of CFCs can have a dramatic impact on the composition of the atmosphere. Many other ozone-depleting gases can have a similar impact: methane (CH_4), nitrous oxide (N_2O), carbon monoxide (CO), halons, used primarily in fire extinguishers, methylbromide, used in pesticides, carbon tetrachloride, and other chemicals commonly in use. In addition, some chemicals used as substitutes for CFCs, such as hydrochlorofluorocarbons (HCFCs), have been found to have ozone-depleting properties. For an account of the science leading up to the discovery of the ozone depletion problem, see JOHN GRIBBON, THE HOLE IN THE SKY (1989).

Despite the mounting scientific evidence concerning anthropogenic substances and ozone layer depletion, the international community first took note of the problem in 1977 with the publication by the World Meteorological Society (WMO) and UNEP of a report, titled, "Modification of the Ozone layer Due to Human Activities and Some Possible Geophysical Consequences" (WMO and UNEP, 1977). This led to an intergovernmental meeting in Washington D.C. in 1977, during which representatives from 32 countries adopted a "World Plan of Action on the Ozone Layer."

In the 1980s, discussions continued without results. Then in 1985, scientists from the British Antarctic Survey, who had been monitoring stratospheric ozone since the 1950s, discovered that stratospheric ozone had been decreasing over Antarctica since the 1970s, and that an expanding ozone "hole" formed each winter over the Antarctic continent. Something was clearly disrupting the natural ozone cycle in the stratosphere. Particularly in Antarctica and to some extent in the Arctic, frigid temperatures hasten the chlorine ozone-depleting cycle by removing nitrogen oxides, which strongly interfere with this cycle. (Nitrogen oxides can themselves destroy ozone, but their presence also ameliorates the chlorine ozone depletion cycle).

The British Survey team's evidence galvanized the international community into action, and in 1985, the Vienna Convention for the Protection of the Ozone layer (Vienna Convention) was adopted at a plenipotentiary conference sponsored by UNEP. The Vienna Convention is a binding framework treaty that obligates the parties to cooperate by conducting research and exchanging information as well as to take unspecified actions to reduce or prevent human activities within their jurisdiction "should it be found that these activities have or are likely to have adverse effects resulting from modification or likely modification of the ozone layer." (Art. 2).

The Vienna Convention (Art. 6) created a Conference of the Parties charged with meeting to review the implementation of the Convention. Read the provisions of the Vienna Convention, which is reprinted in the Document Supplement. Note that the Conference of the Parties is given a mandate (Arts. 9 and 10) to act as a legislature that adopts amendments and protocols to the basic Convention. The Vienna Convention also created an Ozone Secretariat charged with implementing the Convention. Note also that the Preamble of the Convention adopts a precautionary approach, the first international convention to do so. The precautionary approach was appropriate at the time because the scientific hypotheses of Rowland and Molina explained above were not fully confirmed until 1988.

Negotiations for an action protocol to the Vienna Convention began in 1986. In that year the U.S. National Aeronautics and Space Administration (NASA) produced spectacular infrared maps of the Antarctic ozone hole and estimated that a 3% increase in CFC emissions would deplete the ozone layer by about 10% by the year 2050; the U.S. EPA published and estimate of 40 million excess skin cancer cases and 12 million more eye cataracts over the next century in the United States alone if CFC emissions continued at recent rates. In advance of formal meetings delegates from major countries attended informal workshops that contributed to consensus building. There were serious disagreements among countries — between developed and developing countries; between developed countries that produced CFCs and those that did not; and between the European Union and the United States. By February 1987, negotiators produced a sixth draft protocol and consensus began to develop among scientists that the ozone layer was in danger of depletion; among NGOs; among the media who were demanding action; and even among much of industry who had decided to cooperate or at least not to actively oppose action. For the history of the negotiations, see MOSTAFA K. TOLBA, GLOBAL DIPLOMACY: NEGOTIATING ENVIRONMENTAL AGREEMENTS FOR THE WORLD 1973–92, 62–74 (1998).

B. The Montreal Protocol on Substances that Deplete the Ozone Layer (1987)

The Montreal Protocol on Substances that Deplete the Ozone Layer (1987) was concluded and signed by 46 states and entered force in 1989. The 1987 Montreal Protocol (1) obligated Article 2 parties (developed states) to set firm targets for reducing and eliminating consumption and production of a range of ozone-depleting substances; (2) established a 10-year delay for Article 5 (developing states) in complying with the phase-out of ozone-depleting substances; and (3) banned trade in controlled substances with non-parties (Art. 4).

The Montreal Protocol also provided for Meetings of the Parties (MOPs) at least once each year to review and strengthen the ozone regime. At this writing, 25 MOPs have occurred, and the Montreal Protocol, which now has 197 parties, has evolved and adapted to new situations to the point that it is scarcely recognizable as the regime begun in 1987. Three mechanisms are used to update the ozone regime:

1. *Adjustments.* The Montreal Protocol has a unique adjustment mechanism in Art. 2, para. 9 that allows the parties to respond quickly to new scientific information and agree to accelerate reductions already agreed. These adjustments, if approved by two-thirds of the parties, are binding on all parties. To date there have been several major adjustments of the Protocol.

2. *Amendments.* Article 9 para. 4 of the Vienna Convention provides for amendments to the ozone regime to allow the parties to control additional chemicals and for other purposes. There have been four amendments to the Protocol: the London Amendment (1990); the Copenhagen Amendment (1992); the Montreal Amendment (1997); and the Beijing Amendment (1999).

3. *Decisions.* At the MOPs, the parties may take formal decisions by two-thirds majority of those parties present and voting. See Rules of Procedure for meetings of the Conference of the Parties to the Vienna Convention and Meetings of the Parties to the Montreal Protocol, Art. 40. To date over 720 Decisions have been taken by the Montreal MOP. For the text of such decisions, as well as the Adjustments and Amendments, see Handbook for the *Montreal* Protocol on Substances that Deplete the Ozone Layer (Ozone Secretariat, United Nations Environment Programme, Ninth Edition, 2012).

A brief history of the evolution of the Montreal Protocol is as follows:

LONDON AMENDMENT AND ADJUSTMENTS: Delegates to the second meeting of the parties to the Montreal Protocol (MOP 2), which took place in London in 1990, tightened control schedules and agreed to add 10 more CFCs to the list of ODS, as well as carbon tetrachloride (CTC) and methyl chloroform. To date, 196 parties have ratified the London Amendment. MOP 2 also established the Multilateral Fund for the Implementation of the Montreal Protocol (MLF), which meets the incremental costs incurred by Article 5 parties in implementing the Protocol's control measures and finances clearinghouse functions, including technical assistance, information, training, and the costs of the MLF Secretariat. The Fund is replenished every three years, and has received contributions of over US$ 2.91 billion since its inception.

COPENHAGEN AMENDMENT AND ADJUSTMENTS: At MOP 4, held in Copenhagen, Denmark, in 1992, delegates tightened existing control schedules and added controls on methyl bromide, hydrobromofluorocarbons and hydrochloronuorocarbons (HCFCs). MOP 4 also agreed to enact non-compliance procedures and to establish an Implementation Committee. The Implementation Committee examines cases of possible non-compliance by parties, and makes recommendations to the MOP aimed at securing full compliance. To date, 196 parties have ratified the Copenhagen Amendment.

MONTREAL AMENDMENT AND ADJUSTMENTS: At MOP 9, held in Montreal, Canada, in 1997, delegates agreed to a new licensing system for the import and export of ODS, in addition to tightening existing control schedules. They also agreed to ban trade in methyl bromide with non-parties to the Copenhagen Amendment. To date, 190 parties have ratified the Montreal Amendment.

BEIJING AMENDMENT AND ADJUSTMENTS: At MOP 11, held in Beijing, China, in 1999, delegates agreed to controls on bromochloromethane and additional controls on HCFCs, and to reporting on methyl bromide for quarantine and pre-shipment (QPS) applications. At present, 178 parties have ratified the Beijing Amendment.

MOP 15 AND FIRST EXTRAORDINARY MOP: MOP 15, held in Nairobi, Kenya, in 2003, resulted in decisions on issues including the implications of the entry into force of the Beijing Amendment. However, disagreements surfaced over exemptions allowing the use of methyl bromide beyond 2004 for critical uses where no technically or economically feasible alternatives were available. Delegates could not reach agreement and took the unprecedented step of calling for an "extraordinary" MOP. The first Extraordinary Meeting of the Parties to the Montreal Protocol (ExMOP 1) took place in March 2004, in Montreal, Canada. Parties agreed to critical-use exemptions (CUEs) for methyl bromide for 2005, with the introduction of a "double-cap" concept distinguishing between old and new production of methyl bromide central to this compromise. Parties agreed to a cap on new production of 30% of parties' 1991 baseline levels, meaning that where the capped amount was insufficient for approved critical uses in 2005, parties were required to use existing stockpiles.

MOP 16 AND EXMOP 2: MOP 16 took place in Prague, the Czech Republic, in 2004. Work on methyl bromide exemptions for 2006 was not completed and parties decided to hold a second ExMOP. ExMOP 2 was held in July 2005, in Montreal, Canada. Parties agreed to supplementary levels of CUEs for 2006. Under this decision, parties also agreed that: cues allocated domestically that exceed levels permitted by the MOP must be drawn from existing stocks; methyl bromide stocks must be reported; and parties must "endeavor" to allocate CUEs to the particular use categories specified in the decision.

COP 7/MOP 17: MOP 17 was held jointly with the Seventh Conference of the Parties to the Vienna Convention (COP 7) in Dakar, Senegal, in December 2005. Parties approved essential-use exemptions for 2006 and 2007, supplemental CUEs for 2006 and CUEs for 2007. Other decisions included a US$470.4 million replenishment of the MLF for 2006–2008, and agreement on terms of reference for a feasibility study on developing a monitoring system for the transboundary movement of controlled ODS.

MOP 18: MOP 18 took place in New Delhi, India, from 30 October to 3 November 2006. Parties adopted decisions on, *inter alia*: future work following the Ozone Secretariats workshop on the Special Report of the Intergovernmental Panel on Climate Change and the Technology and Economic Assessment Panel (TEAP); difficulties with CFC phase-outs faced by some Article 5 parties manufacturing CFC-based metered-dose inhalers (MDIs); treatment of stockpiled ODS; and a feasibility study on developing a system for monitoring the transboundary movement of ODS.

MOP 19: MOP 19 took place in Montreal, Canada, in September 2007. Delegates adopted decisions on: an accelerated phase-out of HCFCs; critical-use nominations for methyl bromide; and monitoring transboundary movements of, and illegal trade in, ODS. Parties also adopted an adjustment accelerating the phase out of HCFCs.

COP 8/MOP 20: MOP 20 was held jointly with COP 8 in Doha, Qatar, in November 2008. Parties agreed to replenish the MLF with US$490 million for 2009–2011 and adopted other decisions concerning, *inter alia*: the environmentally sound disposal of ODS; approval of 2009 and 2010 CUEs for methyl bromide; and compliance and reporting issues. This meeting was the Protocol's first paperless meeting.

MOP 21: MOP 21 took place in Port Ghalib, Egypt, in November 2009 and adopted decisions on: alternatives to HCFCs; Institutional strengthening; essential uses; environmentally sound management of ODS banks; methyl bromide; and data and compliance issues. Delegates considered, but did not agree to, a proposal to amend the Montreal Protocol to include hydrofluorocarbons (HFCs) submitted by the Federated states of Micronesia and Mauritius.

MOP 22: MOP 22 took place in Bangkok, Thailand in November 2010 and adopted decisions on, *inter alia*: the terms of reference for the TEAP study on the MLF replenishment and for the evaluation of the financial mechanism; and assessment of technologies for ODS destruction. Delegates considered, but did not agree to, two proposals to amend the Montreal Protocol to address HFCs, one submitted by the U.S., Mexico and Canada, and another submitted by the Federated States of Micronesia.

COP 9/MOP 23: COP 9/MOP 23 took place in Bali, Indonesia in November 2011 and adopted decisions on, *inter alia*, a US$450 million replenishment of the MLF for the 2012–2014 period; issues related to exemptions; updating the nomination process and recusal guidelines for the TEAP; the treatment of ODS to service ships; and additional information on alternatives. Delegates considered, but did not agree to, two proposed amendments to the Montreal Protocol to address HFCs, one submitted by the U.S., Mexico, and Canada, and the other submitted by the federated States of Micronesia.

MOP 24: This meeting took place in Geneva, Switzerland in November 2012 and noted that the ozone layer is beginning to recover, but it will take at least 50 years to reach its original thickness. Information was made available on alternatives to various ozone-depleting chemicals.

MOP 25: This meeting took place in Bangkok during October 2013. The parties noted the linkage between the United Nations Framework Convention on Climate Change and the Montreal Protocol. The parties debated whether to amend the Montreal Protocol to list HFCs (hydrofluorocarbons), which is a potent greenhouse gas but is responsible for only 0.7% of ozone depletion. No action was taken on the issue of HFCs.

CURRENT ODS CONTROL SCHEDULES: Under the amendments and adjustments to the Montreal Protocol, non-Article 5 parties were required to phase out production and consumption of: halons by 1994; CFCs, CTC, hydrobromochlorofluorocarbons and methyl chloroform by 1996; bromochloromethane by 2002; and methyl bromide by 2005. Article 5 parties were required to phase out production and consumption of hydrobromochlorofluorocarbons by 1996, bromochloromethane by 2002, and CFCs, halons and CTC by 2010. Article 5 parties must still phase out production and consumption of methyl chloroform and methyl bromide by 2015. Under the accelerated phase-out of HCFCs adopted at MOP 19, HCFC production and consumption by non-Article 5 parties was frozen in 2004 and is to be phased out by 2020, while in Article 5 parties, HCFC production and consumption is to be frozen by 2013 and phased out by 2030 (with interim targets prior to those dates, starting in 2015 for Article 5 parties). There are exemptions to these phase-outs to allow for certain uses lacking feasible alternatives.

THE MONTREAL PROTOCOL ON SUBSTANCES THAT DEPLETE THE OZONE LAYER

As adjusted and amended by the Second Meeting of the Parties

(London, 27–29 June 1990)

And by the Fourth Meeting of the Parties

(Copenhagen, 23–25 November 1992)

And further adjusted by the Seventh Meeting of the Parties

(Vienna, 5–7 December 1995)

And further adjusted and amended by the Ninth Meeting of the Parties

(Montreal, 15–17 September 1997)

And by the Eleventh Meeting of the Parties

(Beijing, 29 November–3 December 1999)

And further adjusted by the Nineteenth Meeting of the Parties

(Montreal, 17–21 September 2007)

[Read the provisions of this Protocol, which is reprinted in full in the Document Supplement. Pay particular attention to the Control Measures in the following articles:

Article 2A. CFCs

Article 2B. Halons

Article2C. Other fully halogenated CFCs

Article 2D. Carbon tetrachloride

Article 2E. 1, 1, 1-Trichloroethane (Methyl chloroform)

Article 2F. Hydrochlorofluorocarbons

Article 2G. Hydrobromofluorocarbons

Article 2H. Methyl bromide

Article 21. Bromochloromethane

These are the substances currently controlled under the Protocol. We reproduce the current Schedules of Control for these substances as follows:]

Annex A - Group I: Chlorofluorocarbons (CFC-11, CFC-12, CFC-113, CFC-114 and CFC-115)

Applicable to production and consumption

Non-Article 5(1) Parties		*Article 5(1) Parties*	
Base level:	1986.	Base level:	Average of 1995–97.
Freeze:	July 1, 1989.	Freeze:	July 1, 1999.
75 per cent reduction	January 1, 1994.	50 per cent reduction	January 1, 2005.
100 per cent reduction	January 1, 1996 (with possible essential use exemptions).	85 per cent reduction	January 1, 2007.
		100 per cent reduction	January 1, 2010 (with possible essential use exemptions).

CFCs (Annex A/I) Production/Consumption Reduction Schedule

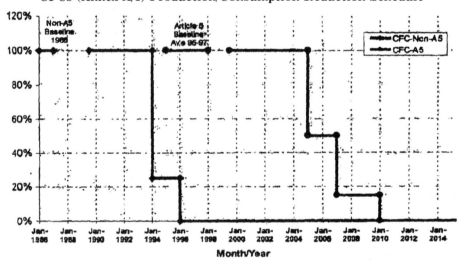

Annex A - Group II: Halons (halon 1211, halon 1301 and halon 2402)

Applicable to production and consumption

Non-Article 5(1) Parties		*Article 5(1) Parties*	
Base level:	1986.	Base level:	Average of 1995–97.
Freeze:	January 1, 1992.	Freeze:	January 1, 2002.
100 per cent: reduction	January 1, 1994 (with possible essential use exemptions).	50 per cent: reduction	January 1, 2005.
		100 per cent: reduction	January 1, 2010 (with possible essential use exemptions).

Halon (Annex A/II) Production/Consumption Reduction Schedule

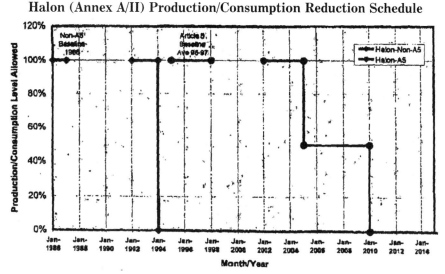

Annex B - Group I: Other fully halogenated CFCs (CFC-13, CFC-111, CFC-112, CFC-211, CFC-212, CFC-213, CFC-214, CFC215, CFC-216, CFC-217)

Applicable to production and consumption

Non-Article 5(1) Parties		*Article 5(1) Parties*	
Base level:	1989.	Base level:	Average of 1998–2000.
20 per cent: reduction	January 1, 1993.	20 per cent: reduction	January 1, 2003.
75 per cent: reduction	January 1, 1994.	85 per cent: reduction	January 1, 2007.
100 per cent: reduction	January 1, 1996 (with possible essential use exemptions).	100 per cent: reduction	January 1, 2010 (with possible essential use exemptions).

Other CFCs (Annex B/I) Production/Consumption Reduction Schedule

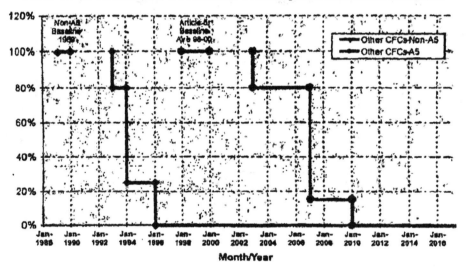

Annex B - Group II: Carbon tetrachloride

Applicable to production and consumption

Non-Article 5(1) Parties

Base level:	1989.
85 per cent: reduction	January 1, 1995.
100 per cent: reduction	January 1, 1996 (with possible essential use exemptions).

Article 5(1) Parties

Base level:	Average of 1998–2000.
85 per cent: reduction	January 1, 2005.
100 per cent: reduction	January 1, 2010 (with possible essential use exemptions).

Carbon tetrachloride (Annex B/II) Production/Consumption Reduction Schedule

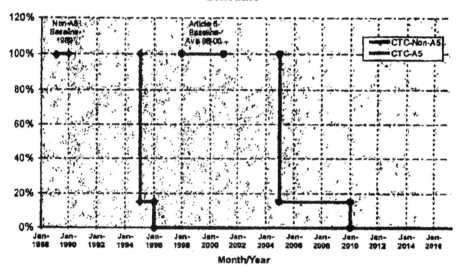

Annex B - Group III: 1,1,1-trichloroethane (methyl chloroform)

Applicable to production and consumption

Non-Article 5(1) Parties

Base level:	1989.
Freeze:	January 1, 1993.
50 per cent: reduction	January 1, 1994.
100 per cent: reduction	January 1, 1996 (with possible essential use exemptions).

Article 5(1) Parties

Base level:	Average of 1998–2000.
Freeze:	January 1, 2003.
30 per cent: reduction	January 1, 2005.
70 per cent: reduction	January 1, 2010.
100 per cent: reduction	January 1, 2015 (with possible essential use exemptions).

Methyl chloroform (Annex B/III) Production/Consumption Reduction Schedule

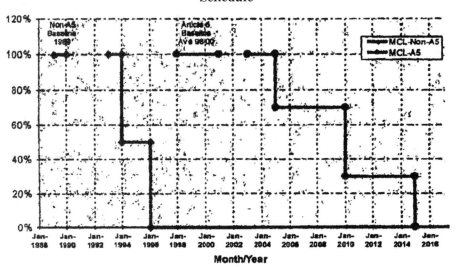

Annex C - Group I: HCFCs (consumption)

Non-Article 5(1) Parties: Consumption

Base level:	1989 HCFC consumption + 2.8 per cent of 1989 CFC consumption.
Freeze:	1996.
35 per cent reduction	January 1, 2004.
75 per cent reduction	January 1, 2010.
90 per cent reduction	January 1, 2015.
99.5 per cent reduction	January 1, 2020, and thereafter, consumption restricted to the servicing of refrigeration and air-conditioning equipment existing at that date.
100 per cent reduction	January 1, 2030.

Article 5(1) Parties: Consumption

Base level:	Average 2009–10.
Freeze:	January 1, 2013.
10 per cent reduction	January 1, 2015.
35 per cent reduction	January 1, 2020.
67.5 per cent reduction	January 1, 2025.
97.5 per cent reduction (averaged over ten years 2030–40)	January 1, 2030, and thereafter, consumption restricted to the servicing of refrigeration and air-conditioning equipment existing at that date.
100 per cent reduction	January 1, 2040.

HCFCs (Annex C/I) Consumption Reduction Schedule

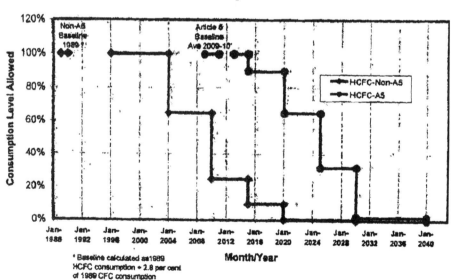

Annex C - Group I: HCFCs (production)

Non-Article 5(1) Parties: Production		*Article 5(1) Parties: Production*	
Base level:	Average of 1989 HCFC production + 2.8 per cent of 1989 CFC production and 1989 HCFC consumption + 2.8 per cent of 1989 CFC consumption.	Base level:	Average 2009–10.
Freeze:	January 1, 2004, at the base level for production.	Freeze:	January 1, 2013.
75 per cent: reduction	January 1, 2010.	10 per cent: reduction	January 1, 2015.
90 per cent: reduction	January 1, 2015.	35 per cent: reduction	January 1, 2020.
99.5 per cent: reduction	January 1, 2020, and thereafter, production restricted to the servicing of refrigeration and air-conditioning equipment existing at that date.	67.5 per cent reduction	January 1, 2025.
100 per cent: reduction	January 1, 2030.	97.5 per cent: reduction (averaged over ten years 2030–40)	January 1, 2030, and thereafter, consumption restricted to the servicing of refrigeration and air-conditioning equipment existing at that date.
		100 per cent: reduction	January 1, 2040.

HCFCs (Annex C/I) Consumption Reduction Schedule

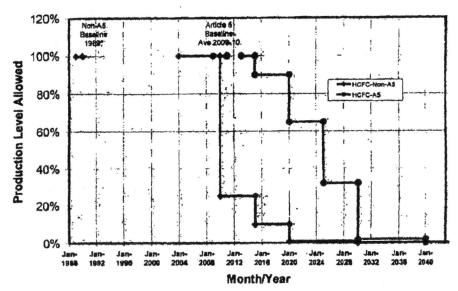

* Baseline calculated as average of 1989 HCFC
production + 2.8 per cent of 1989 CFC
production and 1989 HCFC consumption + 2.8
per cent of 1989 CFC consumption

Annex C - Group II: HBFCs

Applicable to production and consumption

Non-Article 5(1) Parties		*Article 5(1) Parties*	
100 per cent: reduction	January 1, 1996 (with possible essential use exemptions).	100 per cent: reduction	January 1, 1996 (with possible essential use exemptions).

Annex C - Group III: Bromochloromethane

Applicable to production and consumption

Non-Article 5(1) Parties		*Article 5(1) Parties*	
100 per cent: reduction	January 1, 2002 (with possible essential use exemptions).	100 per cent: reduction	January 1, 2002 (with possible essential use exemptions).

Annex E - Group I: Methyl bromide

Applicable to production and consumption, amounts used for quarantine and preshipment applications exempted.

Non-Article 5(1) Parties

Base level:	1991
Freeze:	January 1, 1995.
25 per cent: reduction	January 1, 1999.
50 per cent: reduction	January 1, 2001.
70 per cent: reduction	January 1, 2003.
100 per cent: reduction	January 1, 2005 (with possible critical use exemptions).

Article 5(1) Parties

Base level:	Average of 1995–98
Freeze:	January 1, 2002.
20 per cent: reduction	January 1, 2005.
100 per cent: reduction	January 1, 2015 (with possible critical use exemptions).

Methyl bromide (Annex E) Production/Consumption Reduction Schedule

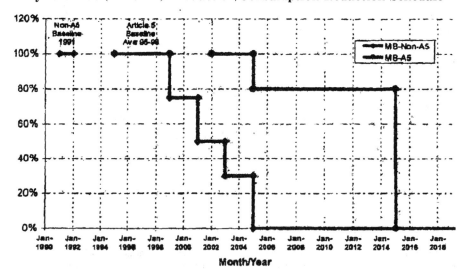

C. Major Elements of the Ozone Regime

1. The Multilateral Fund

The London Amendment at MOP 2 concluded a new Article 10 that establishes a Multilateral Fund under the Montreal Protocol. Article 10A provides for transfer of technology. These two articles are considered essential to the Protocol's success. Consider the following articles:

THE MONTREAL PROTOCOL ON SUBSTANCES THAT DEPLETE THE OZONE LAYER

Article 10: Financial mechanism

1. The Parties shall establish a mechanism for the purposes of providing financial and technical co-operation, including the transfer of technologies to Parties operating under paragraph 1 of Article 5 or this Protocol to enable their compliance with the control measures set out in Articles 2A to 2E and Article 21, and any control measures in Article 2F to 2H that are decided pursuant to paragraph 1 *bis* of Article 5 of the Protocol. The mechanism, contributions to which shall be additional to other financial transfers to Parties operating under that paragraph, shall meet all agreed incremental costs of such Parties in order to enable their compliance with the control measures of the Protocol. An indicative list of the categories of incremental costs shall be decided by the meeting of the Parties.

2. The mechanism established under paragraph 1 shall include a Multilateral Fund. It may also include other means of multilateral, regional and bilateral cooperation.

3. The Multilateral Fund shall:

    a. Meet, on a grant or concessional basis as appropriate, and according to criteria to be decided upon by the Parties, the agreed incremental costs;

    b. Finance clearing-house functions to:

        i. Assist Parties operating under paragraph 1 of Article 5, through country specific studies and other technical co-operation, to identify their needs for co-operation;

        ii. Facilitate technical co-operation to meet these identified needs;

        iii. Distribute, as provided for in Article 9, information and relevant materials, and hold workshops, training sessions, and other related activities, for the benefit of Parties that are developing countries; and

        iv. Facilitate and monitor other multilateral, regional and bilateral co-operation available to Parties that are developing countries;

    c. Finance the secretarial services of the Multilateral Fund and related support costs.

4. The Multilateral Fund shall operate under the authority of the Parties who shall decide on its overall policies.

5. The Parties shall establish an Executive Committee to develop and monitor the implementation of specific operational polices guidelines and administrative arrangements, including the disbursement of resources, for the purpose of achieving tile objectives or the Multilateral Fund. The Executive Committee shall discharge its tasks and responsibilities, specified in its terms of reference as agreed by the Parties, with the co-operation and assistance of the International Bank for Reconstruction and Development (World Bank), the United Nations Environment Programme, the United Nations Development Programme or other appropriate agencies depending on their respective areas of expertise. The members of the Executive Committee, which shall be selected on the basis of a balanced representation of the Parties operating under paragraph 1 of Article 5 and of the Parties not so operating, shall be endorsed by the Parties.

6. The Multilateral Fund shall be financed by contributions from Parties not operating under paragraph 1 of Article 5 in convertible currency or, in certain circumstances, in kind and/or in national currency, on the basis of the United Nations scale of assessments. Contributions by other Parties shall be encouraged. Bilateral and, in particular cases agreed by a decision of the Parties, regional co-operation may, up to a percentage and consistent with any cr1teria to be specified by decision of the Parties, be considered as a contribution to the Multilateral Fund, provided that such co-operation, as a minimum:

   a. Strictly relates to compliance with the provisions of this Protocol;

   b. Provides additional resources; and

   c. c. Meets agreed incremental costs.

7. The Parties shall decide upon the programme budget of the Multilateral Fund for each fiscal period and upon the percentage of contributions of the individual Parties thereto.

8. Resources under the Multilateral Fund shall be disbursed with the concurrence of the beneficiary Party.

9. Decisions by the Parties under this Article shall be taken by consensus whenever possible. If all efforts at consensus have been exhausted and no agreement reached, decisions shall be adopted by a two-thirds majority vote of the Parties present and voting, representing a majority of the Parties operating under paragraph 1 of Article 5 present and voting and a majority or the Parties not so operating present and voting.

10. The financial mechanism set out in this Article is without prejudice to any future arrangements that may be developed with respect to other environmental issues.

Article 10A: Transfer of technology

Each Party shall take every practicable step, consistent with the programmes supported by the financial mechanism, 10 ensure:

a. that the best available, environmentally safe substitutes and related technologies are expeditiously transferred to Parties operating under paragraph 1 of Article 5; and

b. that the transfers referred to in subparagraph (a) occur under fair and most favourable conditions.

QUESTIONS

What is the purpose of the Multilateral Fund? How is the Fund managed? How are decisions taken with regard to the Fund?

2. Assessment Panels

The Montreal Protocol establishes three Assessment Panels to advise the Ozone secretariat and the Parties. These are: (1) the Technology and Economic Assessment Panel (TEAP); (2) the Scientific Assessment Panel (SAP); and (3) the Environmental Effects Assessment Panel (EEAP). The Assessment Panels are considered indispensable to good decisionmaking by the institutions of the ozone regime.

UNITED NATIONS ENVIRONMENT PROGRAMME OZONE SECRETARIAT

Assessment Panels

The Assessment Panel have been the pillars of the ozone protection regime since the very beginning of the implementation of the Montreal Protocol. Through provision of independent technical and scientific assessments and information, the Panels have helped the Parties reach informed decisions that have made the Montreal Protocol a world-recognized success.

UNEP initiated the process of setting up the assessment panels in 1988, pursuant to Article 6 of the Montreal Protocol, to assess the scientific issues of ozone depletion, environmental effects of ozone depletion, and the status of alternative substances and technologies and their economic implications.

Four panels, namely the panels for Scientific, Environmental Effects, Technology, and Economic Assessments were formally established and approved at the First Meeting of the Parties to the Montreal Protocol in 1989 where their first set of Terms of Reference were adopted. Shortly after the Second Meeting of the Parties in 1990, the Panels for Technical Assessment and the Panels for Economic Assessment were merged into one Panel called the Technology, and Economic Assessment Panel (TEAP), which together with the Scientific Assessment Panel (SAP) and the Environmental Effects Assessment Panel (EEAP) make up the three assessment panels active today.

In accordance with Article 6 of the Montreal Protocol and Subsequent decisions of the Parties, the. three panels carry out a periodic assessment at least every 4 years. The first assessment reports were published in 1989 and since then major periodic assessments have been published by all three panels in 1991, 1994, 1998, 2002, 2006 and 2010. For each periodic assessment, the key findings of the panels are synthesized into a short report. The next synthesis report for the 2010 assessment is expected to be published at the end of May 2011.

The TEAP is also tasked by the Parties every year to assess and evaluate various technical issues including evaluating nominations for essential use exemptions for CFCs and halons, and nominations for critical use exemptions for methyl bromide TEAP's annual reports are a basis for the Parties' informed decision-making and TEAP also review the status of alternatives and technologies on an annual basis. The TEAP operates with six Technical Options Committees (TOCs):

- Chemicals Technical Options Committee (CTOC)

- Flexible and Rigid Foams Technical Options Committee (FTOC)

- Halons Technical Options Committee (HTOC)

- Medical Technical Options Committee (MTOC)

- Methyl Bromide Technical Options Committee (MBTOC)

- Refrigeration, Air-Conditioning and Heat Pumps Technical Options Committee (RTOC)

Other temporary subsidiary bodies (e.g. task forces) are established and dissolved according to the needs for specialized assessments as required by the Parties.

3.   The Non-Compliance Procedure

An innovative Non-Compliance Procedure was added to the Montreal Protocol by Decision X/10 in 1998, adopted pursuant to Article 8 of the Protocol.

NON-COMPLIANCE PROCEDURE (1998)

[Source: Annex II of the report of the Tenth Meeting of the Parties]

The following procedure has been formulated pursuant to Article 8 of the Montreal Protocol. It shall *apply* without prejudice to the operation of the settlement of disputes procedure laid down in Article 1 of the Vienna Convention.

1. If one or more Parties have reservations regarding another Party's implementation of its obligations under the Protocol, those concerns may be addressed in writing to the Secretariat. Such a submission shall be supported by corroborating information.

2. The Secretariat shall, within two weeks of its receiving a submission, send a copy of that submission to the party whose implementation of a particular provision of the Protocol is at issue. Any reply and information in support thereof are to be submitted to the Secretariat and to the Parties involved within three months of the date of the dispatch or such longer period as the circumstance of any particular case may require. If the Secretariat has not

received a reply from the Party three months after sending it the original submission, the Secretariat shall send a reminder to the Party that it has yet to *provide* its reply. The Secretariat shall, as soon as the reply and information from the Party are available, but not later than six months after receiving the submission, transmit the submission, the reply and the information, if any, provided by the Parties to the implementation Committee referred to in paragraph 5, which shall consider the matter as soon as practicable.

3. Where the Secretariat, during the course of preparing its report, becomes aware of possible non-compliance by any Party with its obligations under the Protocol, it may request the Party concerned to furnish necessary information about the matter. If there is no response from the Party concerned within three months or such longer period as the circumstances of the matter may require or the matter is not resolved through administrative action or through diplomatic contacts, the Secretariat shall include the matter in its report to the Meeting of the Parties pursuant to Article 12 (c) of the Protocol and inform the implementation Committee, which shall consider the matter as soon as practicable.

4. Where a Party concludes that, despite having made its best, bona fide efforts, it is unable to comply fully with its obligations under the Protocol, it may address to the Secretariat a submission in writing, explaining, in particular, the specific circumstances that it considers to be the cause of its noncompliance. The Secretariat shall transmit such submission to the Implementation Committee which shall consider it as soon as practicable.

5. An Implementation Committee is hereby established. It shall consist of 10 Parties elected by the Meeting of the Parties for two years, based on equitable geographical distribution. Each Party so elected to the Committee shall be requested to notify the Secretariat, within two months of its election, of who is to represent it and shall endeavour to ensure that such representation remains throughout the entire term of office. Outgoing Parties may be re-elected for one immediate consecutive term. A Party that has completed a second consecutive two year term as a Committee member shall be eligible for election again only after an absence of one year from the Committee. The Committee shall elect its own President and Vice-President. Each shall serve for one year at a time. The Vice-President shall, in addition, serve as the rapporteur of the Committee.

6. The Implementation Committee shall, unless it decides otherwise, meet twice a year. The Secretariat shall arrange for and service its meetings.

7. The functions of the Implementation Committee shall be:

    a. To receive, consider and report on any submission in accordance with paragraphs 1, 2 and 4;

    b. To receive, consider and report on any information or observations forwarded by the Secretariat in connection with the preparation of the reports referred to in Article 12 (c) of the Protocol and on any other information received and forwarded by the Secretariat concerning compliance with the provisions of the Protocol;

    c.   To request, where it considers necessary, through the Secretariat, further information on matters; under its consideration;

    d.   To identify the facts and possible causes relating to individual cases of non-compliance referred to the Committee, as best it can, and make appropriate recommendations to the Meeting of the Parties;

    e.   To undertake, upon the invitation of the Party concerned, information-gathering in the territory of that Party for fulfilling the functions of the Committee;

    f.   To maintain, in particular for the purposes of drawing up its recommendations, an exchange of information with the Executive Committee of the Multilateral Fund related to the provision of financial and technical cooperation, including the transfer of technologies to Parties operating under Article 5, paragraph 1, of the Protocol.

8.   The Implementation Committee shall consider the submissions, information and observations referred to in paragraph 7 with a view to securing an amicable solution of the matter on the basis of respect for the provisions of the Protocol.

9.   The Implementation Committee shall report to the Meeting of the Parties, including any recommendations it considers appropriate. The report shall be made available to the Parties not later than six weeks before their meeting. After receiving a report by the Committee the Parties may, taking into consideration the circumstances of the matter, decide upon and call for steps to bring about full compliance with the Protocol, including measures to assist the Parties' compliance with the Protocol, and to further the Protocol's objectives.

10.   Where a Party that is not a member of the Implementation Committee is identified in a submission under paragraph 1, or itself makes such a submission, it shall be entitled to participate in the consideration by the Committee of that submission.

11.   No Party, whether or not a member of the Implementation Committee, involved in a matter under consideration by the Implementation Committee, shall take part in the elaboration and adoption of recommendations on that matter to be included in the report of the Committee.

12.   The Parties involved in a matter referred to in paragraphs 1, 3 or 4 shall inform, through the Secretariat, the Meeting of the Parties of the results of proceedings taken under Article 11 of the Convention regarding possible non-compliance, about implementation of those results and about implementation of any decision of the Parties pursuant to paragraph 9.

13.   The Meeting of the Parties may, pending completion of proceedings initiated under Article 11 of the Convention, issue an interim call and/or recommendations.

14.   The Meeting of the Parties may request the Implementation Committee to make recommendations to assist the Meeting's consideration of matters of possible non-compliance.

15. The members of the Implementation Committee and any Party involved in its deliberations shall protect the confidentiality of information they receive in confidence.

16. The report, which shall not contain any information received in confidence, shall be made available to any person upon request. All information exchanged by or with the Committee that is related to any recommendation by the Committee to the Meeting of the Parties shall be made available by the Secretariat to any Party upon its request; that Party shall ensure the confidentiality of the information it has received in confidence.

QUESTIONS

How are possible violations and non-compliance by parties discovered? Who has a right to complain about non-compliance? What are the functions of the Compliance Committee? Is this procedure sufficient? Are there any penalties for non-compliance? Should there be? If so, what would you suggest?

4. Critical Use and Essential Use Exemptions

By decision of the Parties, two types of exemptions may be granted on a temporary basis upon application to the Technology and Assessment Panel (TEAP) of the Montreal Protocol for uses of controlled substances: essential uses and critical uses. Essential uses are those related to health; for example, the TEAP has granted the EU and others essential use exemptions permitting HCFCs in metered dose inhalers used for the treatment of asthma and chronic obstructive pulmonary disease. But the most controversial exemptions are critical use exemptions that are requested for economic reasons. For many years, the United States has requested and been granted critical use exemptions for methyl bromide. We examine this process next.

CRITICAL USE EXEMPTIONS FOR METHYL BROMIDE

Methyl bromide is a broad spectrum pesticide used to control pest insects, nematodes, weeds, pathogens, and rodents. It is an odorless, colorless gas at normal temperatures and pressures, but under moderate pressure methyl bromide can be handled as a liquid, weighing 14.4lb/gallon. Methyl bromide is manufactured from naturally occurring bromide salts which are found either in underground brine deposits or in above-ground areas like the Dead Sea.

Methyl bromide is used primarily in agriculture as a soil fumigant. When used as a fumigant, methyl bromide gas is usually injected into the soil at a depth of 12 to 24 inches before a crop is planted. This injection will kill a majority of soil pathogens. In order to slow the movement of methyl bromide into the atmosphere during the injection, the treated soil is covered with plastic tarps. But when these tarps are removed, normally 24 to 72 hours after the injection, methyl bromide will leak into the atmosphere. In tomato production in Florida, tarps are usually left in place for the entire growing season, some 60 to 120 days. But studies show that from 50% to 95% of methyl bromide used eventually enters the atmosphere. Methyl bromide is used in connection with many fruit and vegetable crops, especially strawberries and tomatoes.

Methyl bromide is also used as a commodity treatment as part of post-harvest pest control. When used in this way, the gas is injected into a closed chamber containing the commodities treated, primarily grapes, raisins, nuts, cherries, and other fruits and vegetables. Some commodities are treated multiple times in this way during storage and shipment.

As a structural fumigant, methyl bromide is used to fumigate buildings for termites, warehouses and food processing facilities for insects and rodents, and ships and other transportation vehicles for various pests.

Methyl bromide is highly toxic, affecting not only target pests but non-target organisms as well. It must be handled with great care and, because it dissipates rapidly into the atmosphere, is most dangerous at the site of application. Human exposure to methyl bromide can result in central nervous system damage, respiratory system failure, as well as specific and severe damage to lungs, eyes, and skin.

Methyl bromide is considered to be a significant ozone-depleting substance that is addressed by the Montreal Protocol ratified by 197 parties, including the United States, which have agreed on specific reduction steps that lead to the phase-out of production and importation of methyl bromide. (See the foregoing materials).

The United States EPA, acting under Section 604 of the Clean Air Act Amendments of 1990, in July 1992, issued a final rule (57 Fed. Reg. 33754) accelerating the phase-out of ozone-depleting substances. The July 1992 rule required producers of Class I substances (chlorofluorocarbons (CFCs), halons, carbon tetrachloride, and methyl chloroform) to gradually reduce their production of these chemicals and to phase them out completely by January 1, 2000 (2002 for methyl chloroform), During the interim before total phase-out, the EPA controlled production and export of these chemicals by issuing allowances or permits to manufacturers; these allowances could be traded. The rule required a corresponding phaseout of consumption, defined as production plus imports minus exports. On February 11, 1992, the EPA, responding to enhanced requirements under the Montreal Protocol, announced (58 Fed. Reg. 65018) that the phase-out of the production of CFCs, halons, carbon tetrachloride, and methyl chloroform would be accelerated to December 31, 1995. This regulation added hydrobromofluorocarbons (HBFCs) to the class I list of chemicals that must be phased out by this date. In 1998, amendment of the Clean Air Act required the phase-out of methyl bromide as a class I ozone-depletion substance. In final rulemaking on June 1, 1999, and November 28, 2000, the EPA required the production and import of methyl bromide to be set to 75% of the 1991 baseline. In 2001, production and import were further reduced to 50% of the baseline; in 2003 this was reduced to 30%, leading to a complete phase-out of production and import of methyl bromide by the end of 2005.

Under U.S. law, the phase-out of production and consumption of ozone-depleting substances comes under two provisions of the Clean Air Act: 42 USC sec. 7671c deals with class I substances; 42 USC sec. 7671d applies to class II substances. Both of these sections authorize the EPA to promulgate regulations and to grant certain exemptions for essential uses, medical devices, aviation safety, export to developing countries (with a later phase-out obligation) that are parties to the Montreal Protocol, national security, and fire safety. However, the exemption process is complex. Each year the EPA places a notice in the Federal Register (for example, see 76 Fed. Reg. 44001, of July 22, 2011) soliciting applications for essential use and other exemptions. Each application must contain detailed specified information about the exact quantities to be used, the role of use to society, steps to minimize use, alternatives to use, and recycling and stockpiling. Under the Montreal Protocol, the EPA, before granting permission for the exempted use, must forward the nominated exemptions to the Ozone Secretariat, where they are transmitted to the Technical and Economic Assessment Panel (TEAP) and its appropriate committee, which reviews the nomination and makes recommendations to the Parties to the Montreal Protocol. The Parties consider these recommendations at their annual meeting before making a final decision. Under this process, the only essential use exemptions granted to the United States in recent years involve CFCs for medical devices used to treat asthma and chronic obstructive pulmonary diseases. (See 76 Fed. Reg. at 44002).

A special exemption process applies to methyl bromide, which is a class I ozone-depleting substance under U.S. law. 42 USC sec. 7671c (6) allows the EPA, "to the extent consistent with the Montreal Protocol," after notice and opportunity for public comment and after consultation with other interested departments of the federal government, including the Department of Agriculture, to "exempt the production, importation, and consumption of methyl bromide for critical uses." Pursuant to this section, each year the EPA publishes in the Federal Register a notice soliciting applications for critical use exemptions of methyl bromide. (For example, see the 2013 Critical Use Exemption Notice proposal of December 14, 2012). The framework rule for methyl bromide exemptions is 69 Fed. Reg. 76982 (Dec. 23, 2004). After receiving nominations for critical use exemptions for methyl bromide, the EPA forwards the nomination package to the Ozone Secretariat, which transmits the package to the Methyl Bromide Technical Options Committee (MBTOC) of the TEAP, which reviews the nominations and makes recommenda- tions *to* the Montreal Parties for a final decision.

The EPA this year has received requests for critical use exemptions from 15 categories of uses: commodities; cucurbits, eggplant, fruit, nut and flower nurseries, food facilities, forest seedlings, ham, orchard replanting, ornamental plantings, peppers, post-harvest treatment, strawberry growers, strawberry nurseries, sweet potato slips, and tomatoes.Under the Montreal Protocol, two Decisions of the Parties apply to guide the decision of the MBTOC as to their recommendation.

First, is Decision IX/6 which states as follows:

The *Ninth Meeting of the Parties* decided in *Dec. IX/6:*

1. To *apply* the following criteria and procedure in assessing a critical methyl bromide use for the purpose of control measures in Article 2 of the Protocol:

    a. That a use of methyl bromide should qualify as "critical" only if the nominating Party determines that:

     i.   The specific use is critical because the lack of availability of methyl bromide for that use would result in a significant market disruption; and

    ii.   There are no technically and economically feasible alternatives or substitutes available to the user that are acceptable from the standpoint of environment and health and are suitable to the crops and circumstances of the nomination;

  b.   That production and consumption, if any, of methyl bromide for critical users should be permitted only if:

     i.   All technically and economically feasible steps have been taken to minimize the critical use and any associated emission of methyl bromide;

    ii.   Methyl bromide is not available in sufficient quantity and quality from existing stocks of banned or recycled methyl bromide, also bearing in mind the developing countries' need for methyl bromide;

    iii.   It is demonstrated that an appropriate effort is being made to evaluate, commercialize and secure national regulatory approval of alternatives and substitutions, taking into consideration the circumstances of the particular nomination and the special needs of Article 5 Parties, including lack of financial and expert resources, institutional capacity, and information. Non-Article 5 Parties must demonstrate that research programmes are in place to develop and deploy alternatives and substitutes. Article 5 Parties must demonstrate that feasible alternatives shall be adopted as soon as they are confirmed as suitable to the Party's specific conditions and/or that they have applied to the Multilateral Fund or other sources for assistance in identifying, evaluating, adapting and demonstrating such options;

2.   To *request* the Technology and Economic Assessment Panel to review nominations and make recommendations based on the criteria established in paragraphs 1 (a) (ii) and 1 (b) of the present decision;

3.   That the present decision will *apply to* Parties operating under Article 5 and Parties not so operating only after the phase-out date applicable to those Parties.

Second, under Decision Ex. I/4 (9f), Parties nominating critical use exemptions are requested to submit an accounting framework with information on stocks of the substance in question.

Data on the granting of critical use exemptions (CUEs) is as follows:

Amounts of MB exempted for CUE uses in the strawberry fruit industry from 2005 to 2011. Solid lines indicate the trend in CUE methyl bromide. Dashed lines indicate quantity of methyl bromide nominated by the Parties in either 2010 or 2011 and the dotted line the final recommendation by MBTOC

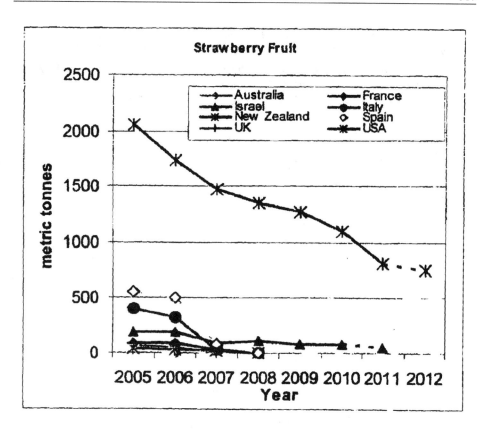

*Amounts of MB exempted for CUE uses in mills and food processing
facilities from 2005 to 2011. Solid lines indicate trend in CUE methyl
bromide. Dashed lines indicate quantity methyl bromide nominated by
the Party in either 2010 or 2011.*

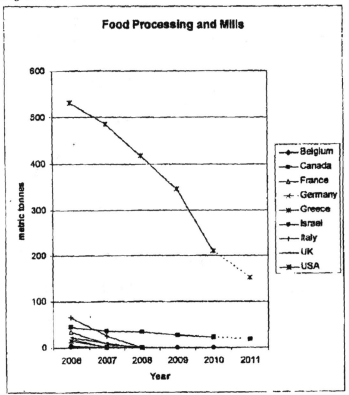

PROBLEM 4-2
A CRITICAL USE EXEMPTION (CUE) FOR METHYL BROMIDE

Each year the Parties to the' Montreal Protocol have granted the United States
CUEs for methyl bromide, but in decreasing amounts. According to the EPA,
methyl bromide has contributed about 4% to the ozone's depletion in the last 20
years. Of this, about 2.5% can be attributed to agricultural fumigation activities. The
continued use of methyl bromide as an agricultural pesticide can contribute 5 to
15% of future ozone depletion if it is not totally phased out.

    1.   Suppose you are an attorney for strawberry growers in California. Your
        clients deem it essential to use certain weed and pest sprays in connection
        with their businesses. They have long relied on methyl bromide but have
        also used various pesticides, including methyl iodide. In the United States
        pesticides are subject to regulation by the EPA under the Federal
        Insecticide, Fungicide and Rodenticide Act (FIFRA) as well as under
        various state laws. In 2010, both California and the EPA began rulemaking
        proceedings against the pesticide iodomethane — a trade name for methyl
        iodide — which is not an ozone-depleting substance but which, allegedly, is

a danger to public health and the environment. In 2012, the sole producer of iodomethane, Arysta Life Sciences North America, LLC, announced that it was voluntarily requesting cancellation of the registration of iodomethane under FIFRA, and thus iodomethane will be withdrawn from the U.S. market and may not be used in the U.S. after December 31, 2012. Certain other chemicals that are alternatives to methyl bromide are also under review in the U.S. and in other countries, notably, chloropicrin, dazomet, and metham sodium. A registration application for another substitute chemical — chemical dimethyl disulphide — is pending in the U.S., the EU, and Australia, but has not yet been approved. As attorney for strawberry growers in California, make the case for a critical use exemption to be filed with the EPA and that qualifies under the Montreal Protocol.

2. Suppose you are an attorney for Save the Ozone Layer, Ltd., an international environmental NGO. Make the case against a critical use exemption for methyl bromide.

3. Suppose you are staff attorney for Representative J.J. Politico, a member of Congress from California, where most of the U.S. strawberry growers are located. Mr. Politico wants to know why the U.S. EPA administrator, who is subject to Congressional confirmation, has to go, as he puts it, "begging on her hands and knees to some international group that I have never heard about or want to hear about to get permission to grant an exemption under American law." Mr. Politico hands you a proposed bill drafted by an attorney for one of his constituent strawberry growers. The proposed bill, titled the "U.S. Agriculture Sector Relief Act" which would amend 42 U.S.C. § 7671c to allow critical use exemptions for methyl bromide to be granted automatically for all the uses that were found critical in 2005. Under this bill, the EPA Administrator would not have to ask any international body for permission to grant a critical use exemption under U.S. law. Mr. Politico, who is unfamiliar with the Montreal Protocol, asks you to draft an opinion evaluating this bill. What is your response?

4. On July 18, 2012, David D. Doniger, Policy Director and Senior Attorney, Climate and Clean Air Program of the Natural Resources Defense Council, testified before the Subcommittee on Energy and Power of the Committee on Energy and Commerce of the U.S. House of Representatives at a Hearing on the U.S. Agricultural Sector Relief Act, as follows:

Thank you Chairman Whitfield and Ranking Member Rush for the opportunity to testify on behalf of the Natural Resources Defense Council on the proposed "U.S. Agricultural Sector Relief Act of 2012." Founded in 1970, NRDC is a national nonprofit environmental organization of scientist, lawyers, and environmental specialists with more than 1.3 million members and online activists, served from offices in New York, Washington, Chicago, San Francisco, Los Angeles, and Beijing. I am policy director of NRDC's Climate and Clean Air Program. I have been with NRDC twice, from 1978 through 1992 and from 2001 to the present. In the 1990s I served as director of climate change policy in the EPA Office of Air and Radiation. Relevant to the topic of today's hearing, I have worked on the phase-out of ozone-destroying chemicals for more than a quarter century.

There are few greater success stories than the global effort to phase out the ozone-damaging chemicals. Every American, and every citizen on this Earth, relies on the ozone layer to block dangerous ultraviolet radiation that causes skin cancer, cataracts, immune disorders and other diseases. The treaty to protect the ozone layer, known as the Montreal Protocol, has enjoyed bipartisan support from five presidents beginning with Ronald Reagan, so have the ozone layer protection provisions of the Clean Air Act. They are saving literally millions of Americans, and tens of millions of people around the world, from death and disease. They are also preventing billions of dollars in UV-related crop losses and other economic damages.

Yet the ozone shield is still being weakened by ozone-depleting chemicals that increase our exposure to dangerous UV radiation. Millions of Americans — including farmers — must work everyday in the sun. Millions more — from school children to seniors — spend hours of their days out of doors. Millions of concerned parents check the UV Index and cover their kids with sunscreen before letting them go out in the sun.

That brings us to methyl bromide. Methyl bromide is the most powerful ozone-depleter still in widespread use. All of the other more potent ozone-destroying chemicals have been successfully eliminated — *worldwide*. Methyl bromide is also highly toxic, with inhalation or dermal exposure causing a wide range of acute and chronic effects, including death.

Mr. Chairman, I will not mince words. You are considering a bill to further slow the snail-like pace of the transition from this dangerous chemical — a bill that will lead to more skin cancers, more cataracts, more immunological disease, and more crop losses due to ozone-destruction and UV radiation, as well as more illness from direct exposure. Contrary to the bill's grandiose title, this bill will not broadly benefit "the U.S. agricultural sector." Indeed, thousands of farmers growing other crops will suffer more UV-related crop losses as a result. Instead, this bill will benefit only a small sliver of strawberry growers and few others who have profited handsomely by abusing the "critical use exemption" for the better part of a decade.

No industry has had more time and more leeway to transition from dangerous ozone-destroying chemicals than this one. The auto industry replaced CFCs in car air conditioners in less than four years. The electronics industry replaced ozone-depleting solvents in circuit board manufacture in less time than that. The air conditioning and refrigeration industry and the fire protection industry got rid of their potent ozone-depleters in well under a decade. Indeed, some of these industries have gone through two rounds of transitions to safer chemicals in the last 20 years. And all of these industries have been able to produce better, more energy-efficient, and more profitable products.

But methyl bromide stands apart. The producer and the users of this chemical have dragged their feet on replacing this dangerous compound for two decades. Let's review:

The phase-out of methyl bromide was supposed to be completed by 2001 pursuant to the 1990 Clean Air Act Amendments. With a decade of lead-time, growers and other users should have invested in developing and field testing other agents and other agricultural practices, like every other industry did. Their effort was minimal. And their minimal effort was rewarded by pushing the deadline back to 2005, in conjunction with amendments to the Montreal Protocol to phase out methyl bromide worldwide. A post-2005 exemption was allowed for so-called "critical uses," but all observers then thought this would be just a small percentage of historical ("baseline") methyl bromide use, just as the "essential use" exemptions for other ozone-destroying chemicals had been only a small fraction of their baselines.

Indeed, other countries with comparable agricultural conditions played by those rules, submitting critical use exemption requests, if any at all, that reflected small fractions of their historical methyl bromide use levels. Only the U.S. took a different tack. In 2003, U.S. growers and others sought exemptions totaling some 15,000 tons, more than *60%* of country's baseline use in the early 1990s. The U.S. government requested more than 10,000 tons of exemptions, and nearly broke the back of the Montreal Protocol. For the first time in its history, the parties were unable to come to a consensus decision. For the first time, there was an impasse that could not be resolved without calling an extraordinary meeting of the parties.

For eight years running, the United States alone has requested more than 90% of all exemptions. Over this period, nearly every other developed nation has eliminated its need for methyl bromide. Specifically, every other strawberry- and tomato-growing country with Mediterranean-like growing conditions — including Italy, Spain, Greece, and Australia — has moved beyond use of methyl bromide. Even Mexico — the California strawberry growers' only competitor — is committed to end its use of methyl bromide this year.[20]

Throughout this period, and here again today, the California strawberry growers have led the pack in coming to Congress playing the hardship violin. In fact, however, California strawberry growers have done very well during the whole experience, according to a recent peer-reviewed economic study by Erin N. Mayfield and Catherine Shelley Norman, published in the Journal of Environmental Management.[21] They have expanded their strawberry acreage and increased their yields dramatically despite significant reductions in methyl bromide allocations: California strawberry acreage in 2010 had increased 83% over 1991 levels and 16% over 2004. Yields per acre in 2010 increased 29% over 1991 levels and 14% over 2004. California's share of U.S. production also increased during this period, from about 80% in 1991 to more than 90% in 2010. U.S. grower prices and total crop values adjusted for inflation also increased during the exemption years.

---

[20] "The Government of Mexico has committed to achieve the complete phase-out of MB by the end of 2012. "United Nations Environment Programme, Executive Committee of the Multilateral Fund for the implementation of the Montreal Protocol, Sixty-sixth Meeting, Montreal, 16–20 April 2012," Project Proposal: Mexico, National methyl bromide phase-out plan (third tranche), ¶ 9, http://www.multilateralfund.org/66/English/1/6641.pdf.

[21] Mayfield & C. Norman, *Moving away from methyl bromide: Political economy of pesticide transition for California strawberries since 2004,* Journal of Environmental Management, Vol. 106, pp. 93–101 (2012), *available at* http://www.sciencedirect.com/science/article/pii/S0301479712001909, and attached to this testimony.

The expansion of the strawberry acreage treated with methyl bromide is extremely troubling because it breaks a commitment made by the U.S. government not to allow such expansion. For instance, the "National Management Strategy for Methyl Bromide, United States of America, December 2005" states: "An important way that the United States addresses the issue of avoiding increases in MeBr use is our policy to disallow any increases in acreage or throughout that CUE applicants might include in their CUE request."[22] This turns out to have been a hollow promise.

The growers' complaints often center on the claim of unfair competition from Mexico. Throughout this period, however, Mexican growers used less methyl bromide per acre than their California counterparts, and Mexico, as I mentioned, has committed to stop using methyl bromide this year. Mayfield and Norman note that although strawberry imports from Mexico increased as the overall U.S. strawberry market grew, Mexico's share of total U.S. consumption did not Increase significantly, and U.S. growers' strawberry exports to Canada rose by almost as much as imports from Mexico.

Mayfield and Norman also note that the economic analysis supporting the critical use nomination for 2014 — an analysis prepared by the strawberry growers — indicates that a range of alternatives to methyl bromide are effective and available at comparable cost and without yield losses. Notably, these results do not depend on methyl iodide, which was withdrawn from the market by its manufacturer earlier this year.

As it turns out, the industry is still sitting on a stockpile of methyl bromide made before 2005 and stored in railroad cars in various communities around the country. Believe me, tank cars of highly toxic methyl bromide baking in the sun on rail sidings are not something I'd want in my community, or rolling through my Congressional district, yet few people know if they enjoy that privilege. As of today, the stockpile still exceeds 1,200 tons — three-time the U.S. critical use nomination for 2014.

Why is the stockpile important? Because the rules of the road under the treaty are that a country may request permission to manufacture new methyl bromide to serve critical use needs only if it has exhausted its stockpiles. The industry attempted to conceal that stockpile from both the public and the government, and this led to the U.S. government's initially misrepresenting to the other Montreal Protocol parties in 2003 that there would be no stockpile left in 2005. But the true stockpile, divulged only later in response to an NRDC lawsuit, was nearly 13,000 tons — more than the entire amount the U.S. claimed to need for 2005. The methyl bromide stockpile has been used — illegally, in our view — for crops that no longer qualify as critical uses, such as golf course turf grass, and to exceed the critical use limits on crops such as strawberries. Each year since 2004, the stockpile has been larger than the next year's total critical use request. That is true for 2013 and 2014. The deception over the stockpile, once revealed, almost caused the breakdown of the treaty process, and the existence of a continuing stockpile is still a major irritant between the parties today.

---

[22] http://www.epa.gov/ozone/mbr/downloads/MeBrNatMgmtStrat.pdf, p. 4.

NRDC acknowledges that the amounts of U.S. critical use exemptions have been coming down, however belatedly. Many growers and other users have finally taken up alternative chemicals and alternative pest management practices, so that we have now come to the point where the only field use for which a critical use nomination is still being made in 2014 is California strawberries. Together with several structural and commodity uses, the total U.S. exemption request is down to slightly more than 400 tons, as compared to nearly 10,000 tons in 2005. This progress, though long delayed, is noteworthy and must continue. Further progress is possible even in the short run, through practices such as greater use of impermeable films (something other countries have already adopted) and by continued adoption of alternatives.

In short, the process is working. Now is not the time to tamper with the methyl bromide phase-out requirements under Montreal Protocol and the Clean Air Act. Mr. Chairman, the bill before you would pointlessly weaken curbs on this dangerous ozone-destroying chemical, threaten the recovery of the ozone layer, and further strain our relations with other countries that are already experienced with U.S. abuse of critical use exemptions. The bill does reckless damage in at least three major ways:

First, the bill would permanently define as "critical uses" all of the uses that were labeled critical in 2005, regardless of the fact that the vast majority of those crops and applications have successfully transitioned to alternatives and no longer even use methyl bromide. Absurdly, the bill would make golf course turf grass a "critical use," even though the Bush administration's agriculture department dropped it from the list in 2006. Why in the world does it make sense to revive and freeze into law an utterly out-dated list of "critical uses"?

Second, since growers and other applicants are seeking exemptions for a chemical that is otherwise already banned under both domestic and international law, and since they are in the best position to innovate and test alternatives, they quite properly now bear the burden of showing the need for methyl bromide and the absence of economically practical alternatives. But the bill would turn that burden around. It would allow applicants to submit their wish lists for exemptions without providing any data in support. Even though this chemical is already supposed to be banned, the bill would then require EPA to shoulder the burden of developing the data to support any reduction from the growers' or other applicants' requests. As the growers would be quick to point out, EPA does not run farms, and EPA does not run alternatives testing programs.

Absent the resources and access to data, EPA would have little choice but to forward the applicants' wish lists to the parties for consideration. Even from the growers' perspective, this would be a fool's errand. It is difficult enough for the U.S. to gain approval for its out-sized exemption requests when it can bring a reasonably robust case forward for technical scrutiny by the other parties. It actually helps the U.S. win approval for exemptions to have shown that the government has exercised some judgment and discipline in framing its requests, and that the U.S. is *not* asking for everything its domestic applicants may have wanted.

Third, the bill would blast an enormous new loophole into the Clean Air Act and our pesticide safety laws, by allowing any individual user to write his own ticket for up to 20 tons of methyl bromide simply by asserting the existence of an emergency. *Emergency* is conveniently defined to mean any situation where someone wants to use more methyl bromide than is available under a critical use exemption, and where he declares that there is no alternative. The bill would allow a hundred 20-ton emergency exemptions per year, up to a total of 2,000 tons per year (the amount of critical use exemptions in 2011). This would be a massive abuse of the emergency exemption provision under the Montreal Protocol, which has been invoked only twice so far (once by Australia and once by Canada) in genuine emergencies.

This is a bad bill, and an unneeded bill. It would harm public health, harm other farmers, and indeed even harm the farmers it is intended to help. The process is working. This Committee should let well enough alone.

Do you think that Mr. Doniger is correct and persuasive in his views?

The "U.S. Agricultural Sector Relief Act of 2012," was not enacted into law, so the critical use exemption process described above remains in place. Each year the EPA calls for critical use exemption applications, which are authorized to be granted under section 604(d) of the Clean Air Act, 42 U.S.C. § 7671c(d). An EPA representative then goes before the MBTOC to make the case for a critical use exemption. The MBTOC has allowed progressively lower exemptions, and the EPA has acted consistently with their determinations. According to the EPA's web site, recent methyl bromide CUEs (expressed as a percentage of the U.S. baseline) are as follows:

2012: amount nominated — 4.6%; amount authorized — 4.0%

2013: amount nominated — 2.5%; amount authorized — 2.2%

2014: amount nominated — 1.7%; amount authorized — 1.7%

2015: amount nominated — 1.5%; amount authorized — to be determined.

In *November*, 2012, Daniel A. Reifsnyder, on behalf of the United States, made the following statement to the 24th Meeting of the Parties of the Montreal Protocol:

Remarks

Daniel A. Reifsnyder

Deputy Assistant Secretary, Bureau of Oceans and International Environmental and Scientific Affairs

24th Meeting of the Parties to the Montreal Protocol on Substances that Deplete the Ozone Layer Geneva, Switzerland

November 12, 2012

Thank you, Mr. Chair. We have made considerable progress in reducing our reliance on methyl bromide, and are now requesting less than 2% of our baseline level of consumption. This progress has been made through painstaking research and testing of new alternatives, different application methods, and changes to cropping systems. This progress has not been easy or inexpensive, but it has been worth the effort to get there.

U.S. agriculture is vital in providing our citizens with a diverse, nutritious, and affordable food supply and is a central pillar of our economy. We need to ensure the progress we are making does not impede our efforts to provide food to millions of people.

In this context, this year we are faced with a particular challenge with the withdrawal of Iodomethane from the U.S. market. This represents the loss of a significant new alternative that was already reducing our reliance on methyl bromide. As we indicated at the Open-Ended Working Group (OEWG), losing this alternative Is a substantial change, and it may require us to submit a supplemental CUE nomination for consideration next year to address its loss. We are also interested in exploring how Parties might be able to have MBTOC review their needs in the event of a loss of a key alternative.

We are still assessing the impacts of the loss of iodomethane, and will do so in a comprehensive manner. We reserve our right to submit a 2014 supplemental CUE because of the loss of iodomethane.

Turning to recommendations of the Methyl Bromide Technical Options Committee (MBTOC), we have two substantial concerns with its recommendations. First, MBTOC acknowledges there are no feasible alternatives for ham, but has nevertheless imposed cuts on our nomination. U.S. food safety regulations have zero tolerance for mites in this product, so reliable fumigation with the only available alternative is needed, and we do not agree with MBTOCs recommended cut to this nomination.

Similarly, we do not agree with MBTOC's recommendations regarding our California 2 strawberry nomination. The basis for MBTOC's cuts is unclear. For example, our nomination represents our most critical needs for those fields that have high pest pressures. There is no research to support the notion that organic production of strawberries in California on fields with high pest pressures is technically and economically feasible. Quite the contrary, it seems like a recipe for failure.

Similarly, fields with high pest pressure may need to use sufficiently high rates of alternatives that would cause our farmers to exceed regulatory constraints that are set by the State of California.

We therefore request that for both our artisanal ham and strawberry nominations the Parties approve the full amount of our nomination, and we are submitting a draft decision to this effect.

We intend to meet bilaterally with those MBTOC members here this week to discuss technical issues raised in its recommendations.

We appreciate MBTOC's efforts in revising the MB CUE Handbook. We agree that the Handbook should be updated to reflect the decisions of the Parties, without interpretation. EX/MOP Decision I/4 allows MBTOC to make factual updates of the handbook incorporating the specific language of the decisions of the Parties. Otherwise, updates require approval from the Parties.

This is directly relevant to two issues of concern we have with the Handbook. First, MBTOC is altering the economic guidelines, which were carefully negotiated at an Extraordinary Meeting of the Parties. Those should not be interpreted by MBTOC.

They should not be changed for the revised handbook. Second, we do not agree with language in the second paragraph on page 14 In Section 2.6.1 suggesting that MBTOC recommendations are made at the subcommittee level. While we fully agree that it is appropriate for MBTOC to bring together experts to review nominations in particular areas of expertise MBTOC is one committee and ultimately needs to come to a recommendation of the full committee.

Does this statement alter your views as to whether the U.S. Clean Air Act should be amended to allow critical use exemptions to methyl bromide and other ozone-depleting substances to be granted more freely and unilaterally under U.S. law? Mr. Reifsnyder's request on behalf of the United States was granted, but only at the 4.0% level, not the requested level of 4.6%.

PROBLEM 4-3
CONTROLLED SUBSTANCES IN AIR-CONDITIONING AND REFRIGERATION APPLIANCES

At the time of the signing of the Montreal Protocol in 1987, hydrochlorofluoro-carbons (HCFCs) were considered possible substitutes for the main ozone-depleting gases, CFCs. But HCFCs, although less damaging to the ozone layer than CFCs, still contain ozone-destroying chlorine, and in 1992, the Montreal Protocol was amended to establish a schedule for phasing out HCFCs. Read Article 2F of the Montreal Protocol in the Document Supplement; see the schedules for the phase-out of HCFCs in the foregoing materials. The phase-out of HCFCs is implemented in U.S. law through Title VI of the Clean Air Act and rulemaking by the EPA. Industrial countries, including the United States, must reduce consumption and production of HCFCs to 75% below the established baseline by 2010; to 90% below the baseline by 2015; and to 99.5% below the baseline by 2020, culminating in complete elimination by 2030. Developing countries must freeze production and consumption in 2013, and add stepwise reductions as follows: 10% below the 2009–10 production baseline by 2015; 35% below by 2020; 67.5% below by 2025; and complete elimination by 2040.

HCFCs are class II substances under the Clean Air Act subject to the phase-out targets under section 605 of the Act. The phase-out framework of the EPA uses a "worst-first" approach that focused first on HCFC-22, HCFC-141b, and HCFC-142b. In 2003, the EPA phased out HCFC-141b and froze the production and consumption of HCFC-22 and HCFC-142b. By final rule effective January 1, 2010, the EPA banned the sale or distribution of air-conditioning and refrigeration appliances containing HCFC-22, HCFC-142b, and blends of these substances. EPA enforces the phase-out framework by issuing marketable allowances (one allowance per each kilogram of HCFC) based on historical production and import activity. When a company produces or imports a type of HCFC, it expends an allowance for each kilogram of the HCFC produced or imported. If a company expends allowances to make HCFCs, and then exports those HCFCs, the producer company will receive allowances representing the amount exported. *See* 40 C.F.R. Part 82.

HCFC-22, also known as R-22, has been the refrigerant of choice for residential heat pump and air-conditioning systems for more than four decades. At present, about 140 million central air units in the United States that use HCFC-22 are in use. However, HCFC-22 is an ozone-depleting gas as well as a greenhouse gas that contributes to climate change. The atmospheric concentration of HCFC-22 is 218 parts per trillion, more than double the amount two decades ago. In addition, the manufacture of HCFC-22 results in a by-product, HFC-23, that contributes significantly to climate change. A number of alternatives to HCFC-22 exist that do not deplete the ozone layer, including R-410A, the most popular choice, R 134a, R-404A, and R-407C. The transition away from HCFC-22 to systems that use other refrigerants has required a redesign of heat pump and air-conditioning systems. New systems, which are more energy-efficient than the older systems, incorporate compressors and other components specifically designed for use with replacement refrigerants. So if a new outdoor "condensing" unit is installed, it is likely that a new indoor unit (an evaporator) will also be required. With these new product changes, testing and servicing must also change.

With respect to existing air-conditioning and refrigeration units, these can continue to be serviced using HCFC-22 for repairs, but the Clean Air Act prohibits discharging HCFC into the atmosphere during servicing or repair. After 2020, existing units can be serviced or repaired using only recycled or reclaimed HCFC-22. Between 2010 and 2020, chemical manufacturers may produce or import HCFCs only to service existing units.

1. You are an attorney in private practice. One of your clients contacts you to ask your opinion on her new business plan. Your client, Sheila, is an executive with a local heating and cooling company. Sheila explains to you that "because of all the cumbersome environmental regulations in her industry, the prices of refrigerants like HCFC-22 are going through the roof. A canister of refrigerant selling for $55 in 2009," she tells you, "is now selling for $140." She says she has composed a business plan to buy refrigerant at cheaper prices. Her plan, she explains, is to import HCFC canisters from China and India, where much lower prices prevail. "This is the only way to defeat all these crazy regulations," she says. The world market is booming, she explains; China and India produce enormous quantities of HCFC-22, and it is available under the marketing name, "Freaky Freon." Sheila is sure that, "with the hard economic time we are in, people are not investing in new systems, and they need refrigerants that are compatible with their old systems." Advise Sheila on the lawfulness of her business plan.

2. You are a homeowner in need of upgrading your air-conditioning unit. You call a local heating and cooling company to inquire about installing a new system. The manager of the shop tells you that a replacement compressor for an old HCFC system costs from $1,200 to $1,500, but a totally new system will cost three times as much. He tells you that to comply with new environmental regulations "if you buy an old HCFC compressor, I will have to sell it to you empty, but I will come by the next day and fill it up with HCFC." You ask him why, and he tells you, "I can't sell you a new machine

with HCFC, but I can service your old machine — no problem." Advise on the legality of this practice.

3. Your old air conditioning unit needs servicing. The repairman tells you that to fix your unit, he will vent the old coolant and put in a totally fresh installment of coolant. You are aware that the coolant is HCFC and that it is illegal to vent HCFCs into the atmosphere. You ask the repairman if he can avoid venting the coolant. He tells you that he has no way of recapturing or recycling the old coolant and "it is worthless anyway." He tells you it is much quicker, easier, and cheaper for you if he simply vents the old coolant. What should you do?

PROBLEM 4-4
USING THE MONTREAL PROTOCOL TO FIGHT CLIMATE CHANGE

The Montreal Protocol was famously called by former UN Secretary General, Kofi Annan, "perhaps the single most successful international agreement to date."[23] Not only has the Protocol reduced the production and consumption of 97 ozone depleting substances by some 98%, setting the ozone layer on the path to recovery, but, since many ozone-depleting gases, such as CFCs and HCFCs, are also greenhouse gases, the Montreal has reduced more greenhouse gases than the Kyoto Protocol and the UN climate change treaty regime. While the climate change regime struggles to reduce greenhouse gas emissions, the Montreal Protocol regime operates by regulating production, consumption, and international trade in designated products.

Should the Montreal Protocol be used as an instrument to reduce additional greenhouse gases? A prime candidate for action in this regard is reducing the production and consumption of hydrofluorocarbons (HFCs), which are predominantly alternatives to ozone-depleting substances (ODS) being phased out under the Montreal Protocol, HFCs are now widely used for air-conditioning and refrigeration and their use is growing at a rate of about 15% per year. Although HFCs do not damage the ozone layer, they are "super greenhouse gases" with several times the global warming potential as the main greenhouse gas, carbon dioxide. If left unchecked, HFC emissions will rise to amount to as much as 19% of carbon dioxide equivalent emissions by 2050. A 2011 UNEP Report, *HFCs: A Critical Link in Protecting Climate and the Ozone Layer*, concludes that the radiative forcing potential of HFCs will be as much as one-quarter of that of CO_2 emissions since 2000 by 2050. Non-greenhouse, non-ODS alternatives are readily available for all current uses of HFCs. In a report by the U.S. EPA, *Benefits of Addressing HFCs under the Montreal Protocol, June 2012*, p. 10, the EPA summarized its findings on alternatives to HFCs as follows: "To date, U.S. EPA has reviewed over 400 substitutes in the refrigeration and air-conditioning; fire suppression; foam blowing; solvent cleaning; aerosols; adhesives; coatings and inks; sterilants; and tobacco expansion sectors. Most substitutes have been found acceptable, although in some cases restrictions are applied to protect the environ-

---

[23] *Key Achievements of the Montreal Protocol to Date* (2003), *available at* http://ozone.unep.org/ Publications/MP Key Achievements-E.pdf, visited 3 November 2012.

ment and human health." The EPA has a program called SNAP (Significant New Alternatives Program) which has issued several rulemakings on preferred alternative use options using substances without ozone-depletion potential or global warming potential.

At the 2012 Meeting of the Parties of the Montreal Protocol, the U.S., Canada, and Mexico presented a proposal to amend the Montreal Protocol to include HFCs as a regulated substance.

Summary Points: North American HFC Submission to the Montreal Protocol

Key elements of the North American proposal:

- lists 20 HFCs as a new Annex F, including two substances sometimes referred to as HFOs.

- Recognizes that there may not be alternatives for all HFC applications and therefore utilizes a gradual phasedown mechanism with a plateau, as opposed to a phaseout.

- Establishes provisions for developed country (non-Article 5) and developing country (Article 5) phasedown of production and consumption (*see* figure below).

  o The baseline for Article 5 countries is calculated based on HCFC consumption and production respectively averaged over years 2005–2008, recognizing there are HFC data limitations in some countries.

  o For non-Article 5 countries, the baseline is determined from a combination of HFC plus 85% of HCFC consumption and production respectively averaged over years 2005–2008.

HFC Reduction Steps for Article 5 and Non-Article 5 Countries (% of baseline)

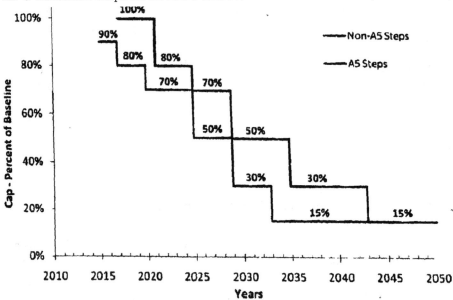

- Uses weighting by Global warming Potential for HCFCs and HFCs as compared to typical Montreal Protocol practice of Ozone Depleting Potential.

- Includes provisions to limit HFC-23 byproduct emissions resulting from the production of HCFC-22 in each production line beginning in 2014. The provisions are intended for production lines that do not have an approved project under the Clean Development Mechanism to control emissions of HFC-23.

- Requires licensing of HFC imports and exports, and bans Imports and exports to non-Parties.

- Requires reporting on production and consumption of HFCs, and HFC-23 byproduct emissions.

- Makes eligible for funding under the Montreal Protocol's Multilateral Fund the phasedown of HFC production and consumption as well as the reduction of HFC-23 byproduct emissions.

Cumulative Environmental Benefits:

- Total cumulative benefits from the HFC amendment proposal estimated by the U.S. Government amount to reductions of more than 98,000 million metric tons of carbon dioxide equivalent (MMTCO$_2$ eq) through 2050.

  ○ Cumulative benefits of the HFC phasedown amount to reductions of 2,700 MMTCO$_2$ eq through 2020, and about 87,200 MMTCO$_2$ eq through 2050.

  ○ Cumulative benefits from HfC-23 byproduct emissions controls amount to an additional 1,300 MMTCO$_2$ eq by 2020 and 11,600

MMTCO$_2$ eq through 2050.

Relationship to HCFC phaseout:

- This amendment is designed to be compatible with the HCFC phaseout.

- The proposal recognizes that HFCs are alternatives in many existing HCFC applications, so baseline levels are set to accommodate some level of transition from HCFCs to HFCs.

- The suite of known alternative chemicals, new technologies, and improved process/handling practices can significantly reduce HFC consumption while simultaneously supporting the HCFC phaseout.

Relationship with the United Nations Framework Convention on Climate Change (UNFCCC):

- The proposal is intended to support overall global efforts aimed at climate system protection.

- The proposal constitutes an amendment to the Montreal Protocol and could be complemented by a related decision by the UNFCCC confirming the Montreal Protocol approach.

- The proposal leaves unchanged the provisions of the UNFCCC / Kyoto Protocol that govern HFC emissions. Parties could follow Montreal Protocol obligations to meet certain UNFCCC obligations.

NOTE AND QUESTIONS

Proposals to amend the Montreal Protocol to regulate HFCs have been on the table for some years, and in 2012, the North American proposal was favored by 108 parties, but formal discussion has been blocked by important countries, including China, Brazil, and India, who say that HFCs are not ozone depleting and as greenhouse gases should be subject to the UN Framework Convention on Climate Change and the Kyoto Protocol. Questions are also raised about such matters as the availability of alternatives and costs.

Should the Montreal Protocol be amended according to the North American proposal? Should the Multilateral Fund under the Montreal Protocol be upgraded to pay the incremental costs of the HFC phase-out?

D.   Evaluating the Montreal Protocol

By any measure the Montreal Protocol is a successful international law regime. With 197 parties it has achieved universal membership. As of 2012, 25 years after its inception, the Montreal Protocol has reduced ozone depleting substances by some 98%, and the ozone layer, although the Antarctic ozone layer hole opened to its largest extent in September 2006, is on its way to recovery. If the current Montreal Protocol regime is maintained, the ozone layer should fully recover during the last half of the present century.

In addition to protecting the ozone layer, additional benefits include: (1) reduced health risks; (2) development of new technologies; (3) energy savings; and (4) pollution prevention. Why has the Montreal Protocol enjoyed such success? Can you identify the main factors behind this success? By contrast the climate change treaty regime, which we consider in the next section, is in disarray.

In the readings that follow, we present a variety of perspectives evaluating the Montreal Protocol.

OZONE ACTION
Protecting our atmosphere for generations to come
25 years of the Montreal Protocol
United Nations Environmental Programme, 2012

Protecting our Atmosphere for Generations to Come

When future generations look back at our times, what might they consider the most significant sustainable development actions we have taken, with far-reaching benefits?

We can only speculate, but the saving the ozone layer will surely be among those they will recognise. It is an extraordinary and still on-going success story of governments. experts and ordinary people coming together, responding to scientific findings, and acting resolutely to protect all life on Earth from the Sun's harmful ultraviolet rays.

Present generations are also struggling to address another global environmental problem — the problem of climate change.

The Montreal Protocol on Substances that Deplete the Ozone Layer provides an inspiring example where the global community is truly succeeding in reaching sustainable development objectives. It has been recognized as contributing to the realization of Millenium Development Goal 7, environmental sustainability.

As we mark the 25th anniversary of the Montreal Protocol the once endangered ozone layer is recovering. It is expected to return to pre-1980 levels by mid-century, assuming all countries continue to meet their compliance commitments.

The credit for this remarkable achievement in intergovernmental cooperation and environmental governance is widely shared. It was possible thanks to the passion, dedication and hard work of thousands of individuals in government, the private sector, Academia, and civil society. Their efforts have literally helped save the protective ozone shield on our sky — and prevented millions of cases of skin cancer and cataracts and it also has made a significant contribution to climate change.

In a quarter century of successful implementation, the Protocol has been continuously strengthened to cover the phase out of nearly 100 ozone depleting substances. It is the world's most widely ratified treaty with 197 signatories. Its Multilateral Fund has enabled an unprecedented transfer of ozone friendly technologies to developing countries assisted by a powerful network of well-trained national ozone officers in every country of the world. This unique on the-ground asset has been critical for ensuring that the Montreal Protocol has delivered on its promises.

The Protocol is widely hailed as a classic case of science-based policy making and action to protect a global commons. The officials, diplomats, corporate leaders and others who negotiated the Protocol built on cutting edge science.

Three scientists — Paul Crutzen, Sherwood Rowland and Mario Molina — shared the 1995 Nobel Prize for chemistry for their trail-blazing work done in the mid-1970s. A decade later, in 1985, the discovery of the Antarctic 'ozone hole' created news headlines and galvanized international action that culminated in Montreal in September 1987.

While much has been accomplished in this time, there is still unfinished business.

Efforts to protect the ozone layer and to combat climate change are mutually supportive. The most recent adjustments to the Montreal Protocol, adopted in 2007, accelerate the phase out of hydrochlorofluorocarb6ns, or HCFCs. These gases — widely used for refrigeration and air-conditioning — not only damage the ozone layer, but also warm the planet. The level of climate benefits that can be achieved depends on what chemicals and technologies replace HCFCs. Their phase out thus offers a unique opportunity to acquire cutting-edge technologies that not only eliminate ozone depleting chemicals, but also saves energy and maximizes climate benefits.

Looking back on the accomplishments made so far under this treaty, I hope that the Montreal Protocol community can use the same energy, ingenuity and sense of urgent optimist to help the world solve its environmental challenges.

Financing Technology Transfer and Industrial Transformation for Ozone and Climate Benefits

One hundred and forty-eight of the Montreal Protocol's 197 Parties are Article 5 countries (whose annual per capita consumption and production of ozone depleting substances or ODS is less than 0.3 kg). In 1990, an amendment of the Protocol established the Multilateral Fund to provide Article 5 countries with finance, technical assistance and technological support to assist them to phase-out their consumption and production of ODS.

Over the past 22 years, over US$ 2.8 billion has been approved by the Multilateral Fund's Executive Committee to support over 6,800 projects and activities. Funding has been approved — or is already committed — for the complete phase-out of all ODS excluding HCFCs. The recipient Article 5 countries have permanently eliminated over 98% of ODS consumption and production excluding HCFCs.

This has not only resulted in ozone layer benefits but also significant benefits for the climate. Projects supported by the Multilateral Fund have not simply provided capacity building but have fundamentally and rapidly transformed a range of diverse ODS consuming industries including the air-conditioning, refrigeration, industrial cleaning, fire fighting, aerosol and fumigation sectors, in a cost-effective manner.

Keep the Commitment and With the Future

During the past 25 years, the Parties to the Montreal Protocol on Substances that Deplete the Ozone layer have continued to improve the legal framework and administrative mechanisms of the Protocol, and to promote the protection of the ozone layer and phase out ozone depleting substances (ODS) using scientific, technical; administrative and economic approaches. They have collectively achieved remarkable results, and the Protocol has become a model for Implementing International environmental conventions.

In my view, there are several major reasons for this success.

* First, under a common vision of protecting the ozone layer, all Parties support and cooperate with each other adhering to a consistent spirit of consultation, especially following the principle of common but differentiated responsibility.

* Second, Parties involved in the decision process continue to pay attention to independent scientific, environmental, technological and economic feasibility assessments, and have developed a more impartial and practical implementation schedule.

* Third, the establishment of a special Multilateral Fund committed to providing assistance and support to developing countries.

* Fourth, setting up global and regional networks for OzoneAction, through the strengthening of relevant international organizations, implementing agencies and capacity building of each country's ozone agency.

* Fifth, the introduction of advanced environmental protection and energy saving technology for the sustainable development of industry has led to a win-win situation, benefiting both the economy and the environment.

By 1 January 2010, the world's developing countries achieved the comprehensive phase-out of CFCs, halons and carbon tetrachloride and the other major ODS. This is the Montreal Protocol's greatest success in the past 25 years.

In September 2007, at the conclusion of the 20th anniversary of the Protocol, an accelerated phaseout plan of HCFCs was adopted, and objectives of the participating Parties in next 20 years clarified. Although the substantial phase-out of HCFCs has only just begun, we are delighted to see that industry is applying the new alternative technologies. These technologies will not only eliminate damage to the ozone layer, but also reduce adverse effects on climate.

At the same time, we know very well that promoting new technologies is not a simple technical transformation. It requires hard work from government and industry. There are only a few months to go before the HCFC freeze year of 2013. I sincerely hope that all Parties will continue to cooperate so that the freeze target is successful.

As a Party to the Montreal Protocol since 1991, the Chinese Government has always strictly abided by the obligations of the Protocol, and has actively phased out ODS. During the past 20 years, China has gradually developed comprehensive policies, regulations and a management system for the protection of the ozone layer.

It has constantly strengthened compliance through capacity building in various sectors and levels of Government, and has developed an effective management mechanism.

Assessment Panels: Hard Evidence for Right Decisions

The Assessment Panels were created by a Meeting of Parties (MOP) decision in 1989 to advise the Parties on the changing scientific, technical and economical understanding of the ozone layer depletion issue.

The architects of the Protocol realized that scientific understanding of ozone depletion would improve over time and that the original control measures could prove to be inadequate. At the same time, they realized that technology innovation would likely make future controls more technically and economically feasible, and much easier to achieve than industry believed at the time. So a process of on-going assessment of science, technology and economics was built into the Montreal Protocol and still continues to serve the Parties.

The 25th anniversary of the Montreal Protocol is a good opportunity to acknowledge and thank all past and current members of the three Assessment Panels, namely Science, Environment Effects and Technology and Economics.

Each Panel has played a critical role in the Protocol. As a former co-chair of the Technology Assessment Panel (TEAP), I want to share my perspective on factors I consider critical for the success of the assessment process.

The first factor is the quality of its membership. Sound expert advice ensures the Panels' credibility. The assessment process depends on the members' knowledge which has to be substantive and diverse enough to cover different technologies, sectors and applications. They also have to cover particular circumstances of different countries and regions.

Most of the TEAP, Technical Options Committee (TOC) and Subsidiary Body members come from affected industries. The industry has been a constructive partner: many corporations offered their experts as TEAP, TOC and Subsidiary Body members. This contribution of employees' time and sponsorship of travel expenses have been crucial to TEAP's success. The Montreal Protocol Trust Fund supported developing country experts' participation in meetings.

Within the Panel itself, the composition of members is important when considering technology transfer flows and regional global situation regarding the status of new technologies. A technology solution appropriate for one region may not be feasible elsewhere. This balance enables TEAP to asses better the extent to which alternatives are technically and economically feasible throughout the world.

Technology transfer during the first 20 years was clearly a North to South process. And TEAP has had a critical mass of international experts to provide the advice that Parties needed. Now, the manufacturing of chemicals and products has shifted to the South. We can see the importance of South-South technology transfer: these are shaping the International market of products containing ODS and alternatives.

Section IV. CLIMATE CHANGE

A. Our Changing Climate

The climate of the Earth is produced by complex interactions between the atmosphere, the oceans, ice caps, living organisms and even rocks and sediments. The Earth's climate is in reality a set of innumerable natural systems with complex regional variations. The climate system of Earth has five principal components: the atmosphere, oceans, cryosphere, biosphere, and geosphere. These systems interact to produce a balance between incoming solar radiation and radiation emitted to space by the Earth and the atmosphere. The Earth's climate has always been subject to natural variations. Analysis of cores of undisturbed sediment from the ocean floor and ice from Antarctica show that over the past several million years the Earth has alternated between ice ages and interglacial periods with a rhythm controlled by the way the Earth orbits the sun. Since the last ice age period ended about 12,000 years ago, the Earth's climate has been relatively stable, at least over the last 1000 years.[24] In the twentieth century, however, the climate began a warming trend that seems to be accelerating. The U.S. National Climactic Data Center (NCDC), a unit of the National Oceanic and Atmospheric Administration, has constructed the following model of climate change over the last 1000 years:

Report on Climate Model Simulations of the Past 1000 Years

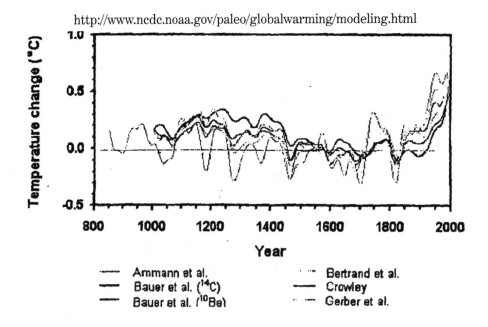

http://www.ncdc.noaa.gov/paleo/globalwarming/modeling.html

Model estimates of variations in Northern Hemisphere temperature over the last 1000 years. All time-series smoothed using a 40-year low-pass filter. Model anomalies adjusted to have the same mean over 1500–1899. Model simulations

---

[24] Thomas J. Crowley, *Causes of Climate Change over the Past 1000 Years*, 289 SCIENCE 270 (2000).

from Bauer et al. (2003) compare two different estimates of solar activity based on radiocarbon (14C) and beryllium-10 (10Be).

The NCDC in its report states that, although solar and volcanic forcing can explain the natural climate variations over the last 1000 years, "neither solar nor volcanic forcing can explain the dramatic warming of the late 20th century."

The Intergovernmental Panel on Climate Change (IPCC) is the leading international body for the assessment of all aspects of climate change. The IPCC was established by the United Nations Environment Programme (UNEP) and the World Meteorological Organization (WMO) in 1988 to provide the world with a clear, authoritative and scientific view on the current state of knowledge of climate change and its potential social, economic and environmental impacts. The IPCC's establishment was approved by the General Assembly of the United. Nations. The IPCC is open to all member countries of the UN, and thousands of scientists from all over the world participate in its work on a voluntary basis. Currently, 195 countries are members of the IPCC. Governments participate in the review process of IPCC reports and in the sessions where the reports are considered and approved. The IPCC Secretariat functions in Geneva at the headquarters of the WMO.

The IPCC has three working groups: Working Group I considers the physical and scientific basis of climate change; Working Group II considers impacts, adaptation and vulnerability to climate change; Working Group III considers mitigation of climate change.

To date the IPCC has published five assessment reports on climate change, the latest — the Fifth Assessment Report — in 2013–14. In its Fifth Assessment Report 2013, Working Group I concluded that warming in the climate system of the Earth is "unequivocal" and that human influence on the climate system is "clear."

THE FIFTH CLIMATE ASSESSMENT REPORT OF THE INTERGOVERNMENTAL PANEL ON CLIMATE CHANGE, 2013–2014

In 2008 the IPCC took a decision to draft a Fifth Climate Assessment Report. The Fifth Assessment Report (known as AR5) was released in four parts between September 2013 and November 2014. AR5, which is available at http://www.ipcc.ch, is made up of reports by Working Groups I, II, and III as well as a Synthesis Report. AR5 contains: (1) a new set of scenarios for climate change; (2) dedicated chapters on sea level change, the carbon cycle, and climate phenomena such as El Niño; (3) much greater regional detail on climate change impacts, and adaptation and mitigation interactions; and (4) risk management and response actions. The AR5 concludes that, because of climate change, ice caps are melting, sea ice in the Arctic is collapsing, water supplies are coming under stress, heat waves and heavy rains are intensifying, coral reefs are dying, and fish and other wildlife are migrating north or going extinct. The oceans are rising at a pace that threatens coastal communities in many countries. The world's oceans are becoming more acidic as they absorb carbon from the atmosphere and as run-off from land.

An important element of AR5 is the Working Group III Report, *Climate Change 2014: Mitigation of Climate Change*, released in April 2014. This report concludes that to avoid dangerous interference with the climate system, we have to move away from business as usual. Scenarios for climate change show that to have a likely chance of limiting the increase in global mean temperature to two degrees Celsius, means lowering global greenhouse gas emissions by 40 to 70 percent compared with 2010 by mid-century, and to near zero by the end of this century. (The Report analyzed over 1200 scenarios from the scientific literature). Estimates of the cost of climate change mitigation vary widely. In a business-as-usual scenario, global economic growth averages 1.6 to 3 percent per year. The Report puts the cost of "ambitious mitigation" at about 0.6 percent per year.

IPCC WORKING GROUP I: CONTRIBUTION TO THE IPCC FIFTH ASSESSMENT REPORT, CLIMATE CHANGE 2013, THE PHYSICAL SCIENCE BASIS

Background

Working Group I is co-chaired by Qin Dahe of the China Meteorological Administration, Beijing, China, and Thomas Stocker of the University of Bern, Switzerland. The Technical Support Unit of Working Group I is hosted by the University of Bern and funded by the Government of Switzerland.

At the 28th Session of the IPCC held in April 2008, the members of the IPCC decided to prepare a fifth Assessment Report (AR5). A Scoping Meeting was convened in July 2009 to develop the scope and outline of the AR5. The resulting outlines for the three Working Group contributions to the AR5 were approved at the 31st Session of the IPCC in October 2009.

The Summary for Policymakers of the IPCC WGI AR5 was approved at the Twelfth Session of IPCC Working Group I meeting in Stockholm, Sweden, 23 to 26 September 2013 and was released on 27 September.

The Final Draft of the Working Group I report (version distributed to governments on 7 June 2013), including the Technical Summary, 14 chapters and an Atlas of Global and Regional Climate Projections, was released online in unedited form on Monday 30 September 2013. Following copy editing, layout, final checks for errors, and adjustments for changes in the Summary for Policymakers, the full report of Working Group I was published online in January 2014 and will be published in book form by Cambridge University Press.

The Working Group I assessment comprises some 2,500 pages of text and draws on millions of observations and over 2 million gigabytes of numerical data from climate model simulations. Over 9,200 scientific publications are cited, more than three quarters of which have been published since the last IPCC assessment in 2007.

IPCC PRESS RELEASE

27 September 2013

Human influence on climate clear, IPCC report says

STOCKHOLM, 27 September — **Human influence on the climate system is clear. This is evident in most regions of the globe, a new assessment by the Intergovernmental Panel, on Climate Change (IPCC) concludes.**

It is extremely likely that human influence has been the dominant cause of the observed warming since the mid-20th century. The evidence for this has grown, thanks to more and better observations, an improved understanding of the climate system response and improved climate models.

Warming in the climate system is unequivocal and since 1950 many changes have been observed throughout the climate system that are unprecedented Over decades to millennia. Each of the last three decades has been successively warmer at the Earth's surface than any preceding decade since 1850, reports the Summary for Policymakers of the IPCC Working Group I assessment report, *Climate Change 2013: the Physical Science Basis*, approved on Friday by member governments of the IPCC in Stockholm, Sweden.

"Observations of changes in the climate system are based on multiple lines of independent evidence. Our assessment of the science finds that the atmosphere and ocean have warmed, the amount of snow and ice has diminished, the global mean sea level has risen and the concentrations of greenhouse gases have increased," said Qin Dahe, Co-Chair of IPCC Working Group I.

Thomas Stocker, the other Co-Chair of Working Group I said: "Continued emissions of greenhouse gases will cause further warming and changes in all components of the climate system. Limiting climate change will require **substantial and sustained** reductions of greenhouse gas emissions."

"Global surface temperature change for the end of the 21st century is projected to be likely to exceed 1.5°C relative to 1850 to 1900 in all but the lowest scenario considered, and likely to exceed 2°C for the two high scenarios," said Co-Chair Thomas Stocker. "Heat waves are very likely to occur' more frequently and last longer. As the Earth warms, we expect to see currently wet regions receiving more rainfall, and dry regions receiving less, although there will be exceptions," he added.

Projections of climate change are based on a new set of four scenarios of future greenhouse gas concentrations and aerosols, spanning a wide range of possible futures. The Working Group I report assessed global and regional-scale climate change for the early, mid-, and later 21st century.

"As the ocean warms, and glaciers and ice sheets reduce, global mean sea level will continue to rise, but at a faster rate than we have experienced over the past 40 years," said Co-Chair Qin Dahe. The report finds with high confidence that ocean warming dominates the increase in energy stored in the climate system, accounting for more than 90% of the energy accumulated between 1971 and 2010.

Observed globally averaged combined land and ocean surface temperature
anomaly 1850–2012

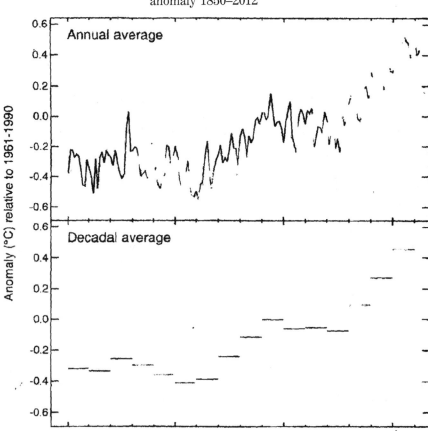

The Fifth Assessment Report makes the following additional points:

Ocean: Ocean warming dominates the increase in energy stored in the climate system, accounting for more than 90% of the energy accumulated between 1971 and 2010.

Cryosphere: Over the last two decades, the Greenland and Antarctic ice sheets have been losing mass, glaciers have continued to shrink almost worldwide, and Arctic sea ice and Northern Hemisphere spring snow cover have continued to decrease in extent.

Sea level: The rate of sea level rise since the middle of the nineteenth century has been larger than the mean rate during the previous two millennia. Over the period 1901 to 2010, global mean sea level rose by 0.19 m.

Carbon and other biogeochemical cycles: The atmospheric concentrations of carbon dioxide, methane and nitrous oxide have increased to levels unprecedented in at least the last 800,000 years. CO_2 concentrations have increased by 40% since pre-industrial times, primarily from fossil fuel emissions and secondarily from land

use change emissions. The ocean has absorbed about 30% of the emitted anthropogenic carbon dioxide, causing ocean acidification.

Global mean sea level rise

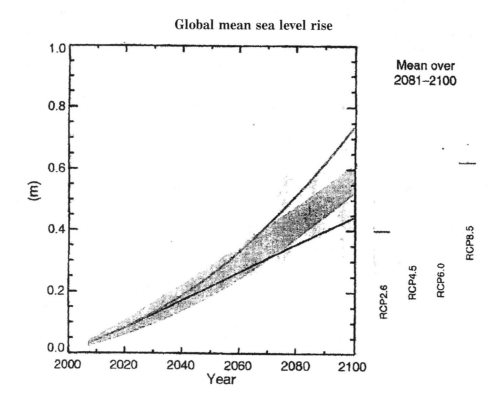

Atmospheric CO₂

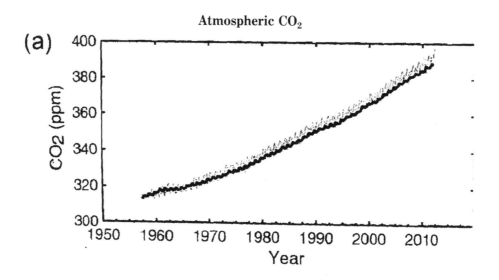

NOTES AND QUESTIONS

1.   The IPCC's conclusions with respect to the reality of climate change are supported by official reports of the United States' and other governments and data compiled by scientists and private organizations. For example, the U.S. NOAA report, State of the Climate for 2012, National Climatic Data Center, released on 8 January 2013, *available at* http://www.ncdc.noaa.gov/sotc/national/2012/13#over, accessed 14 January 2013, states (p. 2) as follows:

> In 2012, the contiguous United States (CONUS) average annual temperature of 55.3 degrees F was 3.2 degrees F above the 20th century average, and was the warmest year in the 1895–2012 period of record for the nation. The 2012 annual temperature was 1.0 degree F warmer than the previous record warm year of 1998. Since 1895, the CONUS has observed a long-term temperature Increase of about 0.13 degree F per decade.

In summary this data means that the 20th century average CONUS temperature was 52.1 degrees F, and that 2012 broke the 1998 record by an extraordinary amount. Temperature differences between years are usually measured in fractions of a degree; breaking the record by a full degree is highly unusual.

2.   ***Evidence of climate change.*** The key evidence that the world is in the throes of climate change comes from data on global and regional average temperatures as well as from data concerning sea ice, changes in sea levels, and glaciers. Consider the following data compiled by NOAA:

Global Temperature Anomaly (Degrees Celsius)

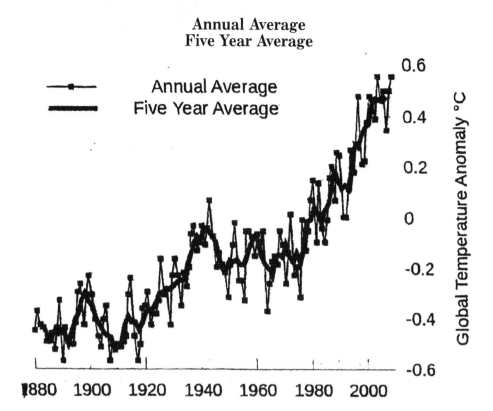

Figure 1. September Monthly Average Arctic Sea Ice Extent, 1979–2012

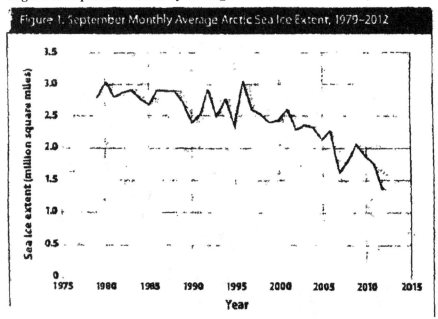

Global Average Absolute Sea level Change, 1880–2011

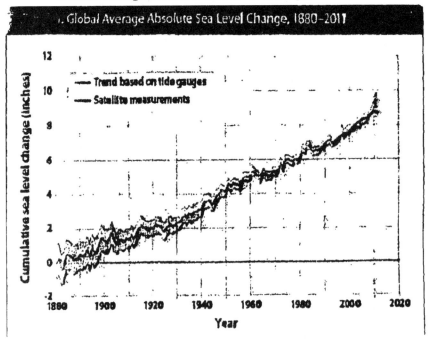

Average Cumulative Mass Balance of "Reference" Glaciers Worldwide, 1945–2010

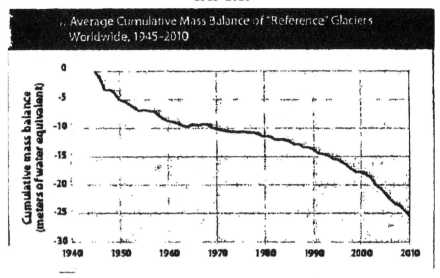

Change in Latitude of Bird Center of Abundance, 1966–2005

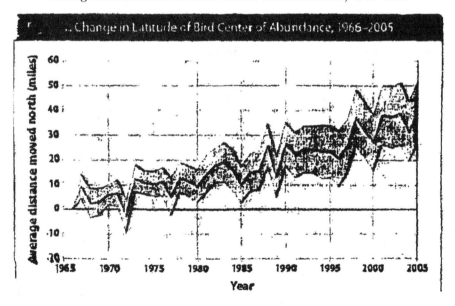

3. *Comparisons of ocean temperatures.* The Scripps Institution of Oceanography based in San Diego has conducted a comprehensive study of sea temperatures in the world's oceans, comparing this data with data compiled by the historic voyage of the HMS Challenger (1872–76). Although the Challenger data set covers only some 300 temperature soundings (measurements from the sea surface down to the deep ocean), this information sets a baseline for temperature change in the world's oceans. The Scripps Institution temperature data is collected every 10 days

from nearly 3,500 free-drifting floats around the world, compiling more than 100,000 temperature-salinity profiles each year across the world's oceans. The Scripps data shows a .33-degree Celsius (.59-degree Fahrenheit) average increase in the upper portions of the oceans to 700 meters (2,300 feet) in depth. The increase is largest at the ocean surface, .59-degree Celsius (1.1-degree Fahrenheit), decreasing to .12-degree Celsius (.22-degree Fahrenheit) at 900 meters (2,950 feet) depth. *See* Scripps Institution of Oceanography, Press Release, April 1, 2012, *available at* https://scripps.ucsd.edu/news/1858, accessed 5 January 2013.

4. ***Dissenting voices.*** A minority of scientists challenge the idea that large-scale climate change is taking place. Perhaps the most prominent of these scientists is Richard S. Lindzen, professor of meteorology at the Massachusetts Institute of Technology, who argues that changes in cloud cover will occur to counter the increases in the Earth's surface temperature. Professor Lindzen's theory is known as the "iris effect," because he posits a natural cloud phenomenon similar to the iris of the eye, which opens at night to let in more light. Lindzen posits that temperature increases on the surface of the Earth will produce increased rainfall, especially in the tropics, which will leave less moisture in the air to produce the high, thin cirrus clouds that naturally reduce the cooling of the Earth. The decrease in cloud cover will allow more solar radiation to escape the Earth's surface, providing a natural cooling mechanism to counter any increase In the Earth's surface temperature. *See* Richard S. Lindzen & Yong-Sang Choi, *On the Observational Determination of Climate Sensitivity and Its Implications*, 47 (4) ASIA-PACIFIC J. OF ATMOSPHERE SCI. 377 (2011). Most scientists are highly skeptical of Lindzen's theory. But Lindzen says, "If I'm right, we'll have saved money; if I'm wrong, we'll know in 50 years and can do something." N.Y. TIMES, May 2, 2012, at 5.

Is Professor Lindzen's argument convincing?

5. ***Scientific uncertainty.*** A number of scientific uncertainties may be raised concerning the observed data regarding climate change. For example, some researchers argue that the cause of the observed data may be minute increases in the sun's heat output, which is known to vary during the course of average 11-year sunspot cycles. A second uncertainty issue is that we do not know enough about the role of clouds, which is one of the most important determinants of climate. Professor Lindzen's hypothesis may be confirmed or additional findings with respect to may show that negative feedback mechanisms exist that will naturally moderate climate change. Third, some scientists argue that climate science relies on drawing conclusions from patchy information. Even in the industrialized world, we have reliable climate data only for the past 50 to 100 years. We therefore lack good-quality, long-term, internally inconsistent information on our changing climate. *See* Climatology, *Changing Science*, THE ECONOMIST, 10 December 2005, at 81–82.

Public policy makers are largely non-scientists. These men and women are called upon to make important political and economic decisions based upon the data compiled by scientists, who sometimes disagree. How should scientific uncertainly be handled with respect to public policy concerning climate change?

For an excellent video on climate change, see Ben Saboonchian, *Climate of Change*, Environmental Stewardship & Sustainability, University of Washington, n.d. Web. 22 Sept. 2013, *available at* https://f2.washington.edu/ess/climate-of-change.

B.   Causes of Climate Change

The climate of Earth, as we have seen, depends on the balance between the solar energy entering and leaving the planet's system. This simple statement belies the inherent complexity of the Earth's climate system. Not only are there natural variations in the solar energy reaching the Earth, but the conditions on the Earth itself influence the rates of solar energy absorption and retention and radiation of this energy into space. Innumerable "feedback loops" influence climate: feedback loops that increase the absorption or retention of solar energy operate are positive and increase warming while negative feedback loops block incoming solar energy or reflect it into space. For example, a major volcano eruption has negative feedback to climate in that a certain quantity of incoming solar radiation is blocked from reaching the Earth's surface and is reflected back into space. Low clouds and bright surfaces such as ice reflect the sun's energy back into space; but high cirrus clouds allow sunlight to pass through easily, but tend to trap rising heat. The oceans and other dark surfaces on the Earth tend to absorb solar energy and are thus positive feedback systems. The difference between the radiant energy received by the Earth and the energy radiated back into space is known as "radiative forcing," which is a measure of the influence a factor has in altering the balance of incoming and outgoing energy in the Earth-atmosphere system. A positive radiative forcing agent tends to warm the climate of Earth, while a negative radiative forcing agent has the opposite effect. Fortunately for life on the Earth, positive radiative forcing agents warm the planet. On average about one-third of the solar radiation reaching the Earth is radiated back into space; most of the solar radiation is absorbed by the atmosphere, the lands and the oceans.

Scientists investigating the causes of climate change focus, first, on the Earth's atmosphere, which is composed of 78% nitrogen, 21% oxygen, and 1% other gases. Certain gases naturally present in the atmosphere — water vapor, carbon dioxide, methane, ozone, and nitrous oxide — constitute positive radiative forcing agents that trap solar energy so that it is not radiated back into space. Together these gases produce a "blanket" or "greenhouse" effect, warming the planet by about 35 degrees C. We are aware, however, that at least since the beginning of the industrial revolution, the amount and variety of greenhouse gases — gases which trap or hold heat better than dry air — has been increasing. The principal such greenhouse gases are carbon dioxide (CO_2), methane (CH4), nitrous oxide (N20), chlorofluorocarbons (CFCs), hydrochlorofluorocarbons (HCFCs), Perfluorocarbons (PFCs), and Sulfur hexafluoride (SF6). Especially in the 20th century, the concentration of all of these substances in the Earth's atmosphere has increased dramatically. (*See* http://www.epa.gov/climatechange/science/causes.html).

Carbon dioxide is the principal greenhouse gas. Carbon, which is essential to life on Earth, is cycled through complex exchanges between the Earth's biosphere, geosphere, hydrosphere, and atmosphere. The Earth's carbon cycle is extremely complicated and exists in two versions: fast and slow. The fast carbon cycle begins with plants, which have the capacity to take carbon from the atmosphere and incorporate it into their cells through the process of photosynthesis. This produces the chemical reaction — CO_2 + H2O = CH2O + O2. The plant's carbon is then recycled when the plant breaks down sugar to produce energy, when the plant dies and decays, when the plant is eaten by animal or a man, or when the plant is consumed by fire. In any case most of the carbon is returned to the atmosphere by the chemical equation — CH2O + O2 = CO_2 + H2O. The slow carbon cycle, in contrast, recycles carbon over 100 to 200 million years. In the slow carbon cycle, carbon from the atmosphere that falls in rain or carbon from dead plants and animals reaches the oceans and the lithosphere where under pressure it forms sedimentary rocks such as shale and limestone or — if abundant — forms deposits of oil, natural gas, and coal. This carbon is stored for long periods in the Earth or under the seas until it eventually is recycled into the atmosphere by volcanic activity or tectonic plate movements. Since the beginning of the industrial revolution, and particularly in the 20th century, human activities — the recovery and burning of fossil fuels — have dramatically altered the "slow" carbon cycle, increasing the carbon dioxide present in the Earth's atmosphere.

The amount of carbon dioxide in the Earth's atmosphere averages only 0.03 to 0.04%, but the amount of CO_2 in the atmosphere has increased because of human activities from an estimated natural amount of about 280 parts per million (ppm) by volume at the beginning of the industrial revolution to 394.39 ppm in December 2012.[25] Furthermore, the concentrations of CO_2 in the atmosphere are increasing at an accelerating rate, adding about 3 ppm per year. Meanwhile, global emissions of carbon dioxide were at historically record highs in both 2011 and 2012. The radiative forcing impact of this increase in atmospheric CO_2 is undeniable. For this reason, the IPCC as well as the international legal instruments we will examine have identified atmospheric emissions of carbon dioxide and other greenhouse gases as the primary cause of climate change.

The second cause of climate change the international community has identified *is* land use changes, or as officially termed, land use, land-use change and forestry (LULUCF). Cutting down forests and other vegetation for urbanization, agriculture, and roads removes what are in effect carbon "sinks" defined as reservoirs that store carbon for an indefinite period of time. LULUCF activities disrupt the "fast" carbon cycle, which not only decreases the rate of natural carbon capture and storage, but also may increase emissions of CO_2 into the atmosphere as the vegetative cover removed decays or is burned.

Skeptics may protest that, since we know that the Earth's climate is subject to natural variations, what proof is there that anthropomorphic activities — emissions of greenhouse gases and cutting down forests — is causing climate change? After all, the observed climate changes may be the result primarily of natural phenomena.

The U.S. EPA has developed three indicators to show that the climate change phenomenon that we are experiencing is not due to natural factors but is caused by human activities.

---

[25] The measurements of CO_2 are made by NOAA at Mauna loa, Hawaii. *See* http://www.esrl.noaa.gov/gmd/ccgg/trends.

First, scientists have been able to construct models of the Earth's climate going back 800,000 years using ice core data from Antarctica. By comparing this history of the Earth's climate with natural variations in atmospheric carbon dioxide, it can be conclusively shown that a relatively high concentration of carbon dioxide in the atmosphere is a highly important determinant of global temperatures and climate. As the following table shows, the correlation between temperature and atmospheric concentrations of carbon dioxide is virtually identical:

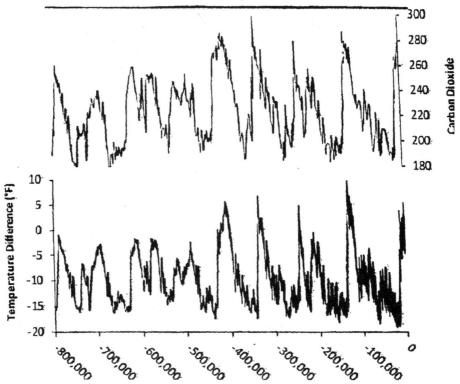

Years Before Present:

Estimates of the Earth's changing carbon dioxide (CO_2) concentration (top) and Antarctic temperature (bottom), based on analysis of ice core data extending back 800,000 years. Until the past century, natural factors caused atmospheric CO_2 concentrations to vary within a range of about 180 to 300 parts per million by volume (ppmv). Warmer periods coincide with periods of relatively high CO_2 concentrations. NOTE: The past century's temperature changes and rapid CO_2 rise (to 390 ppn in 2010) are not shown here.

Second, EPA models of climate change using only natural forces differ from the observed data concerning current climate conditions:

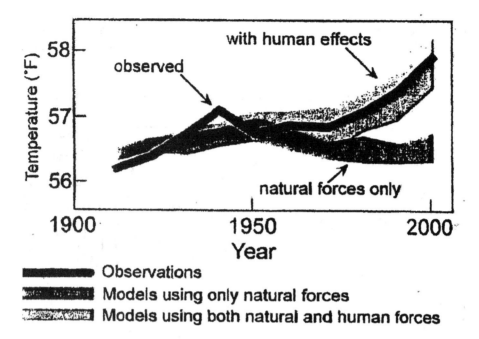

Third, human changes in land use have significantly altered the Earth's reflectivity, which contributes to changes in climate. By comparison, during the same time period, there has been little change in the natural solar radiation reaching the Earth. The following chart compares the changes in global surface temperature due to land use changes compared to the natural solar radiation reaching Earth. Elevated global surface temperatures cannot be explained by natural factors alone.

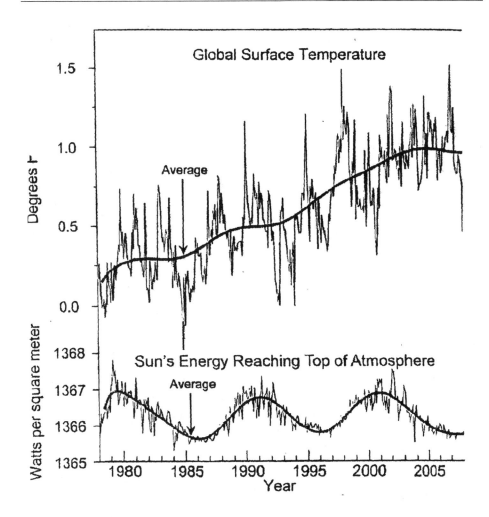

Thus, most scientists, governments and the international community have concluded that anthropogenic factors — primarily the burning of fossil fuels, industrial activities, and land use clearing — have resulted in climate change and that the Earth's climate is sensitive to increased levels of greenhouse gases in the atmosphere.

This conclusion is drawn by the following excerpt from the IPCC Fourth Assessment Climate Change Report.

INTERGOVERNMENTAL PANEL ON CLIMATE CHANGE, FOURTH ASSESSMENT REPORT, CLIMATE CHANGE, SUMMARY FOR POLICY MAKERS

https://www.ipcc.ch/pdf/assessment-report/ar4/syr/ar4_syr_spm.pdf,   pp. 36–38 (2007)

Global GHG emissions due to human activities have grown since pre-industrial times, with an increase of 70% between 1970 and 2004.[26]

Carbon dioxide (CO_2) is the most important anthropogenic GHG. Its annual emissions have grown between 1970 and 2004 by about 80%, from 21 to 38 gigatonnes (Gt), and represented 77% of total anthropogenic GHG emissions in 2004. The rate of growth of CO_2-eq emissions was much higher during the recent 10-year period of 1995-2004 (0.92 $GtCO_2$-eq per year) than during the previous period of 1970-1994 (0.43 $GtCO_2$-eq per year).

Carbon dioxide-equivalent (CO_2-eq) emissions and concentrations

GHGs differ in their warming influence (radiative forcing) on the global climate system due to their different radiative properties and lifetimes in the atmosphere. These warming influences may be expressed through a common metric based on the radiative forcing of CO_2,

- *CO_2-equivalent emission* is the amount of CO_2 emission that would cause the same time-integrated radiative forcing, over a given time horizon, as an emitted amount of a long-lived GHG or a mixture of GHGs. The equivalent CO_2 emission is obtained by multiplying the emission of a GHG by its Global Warming Potential (GWP) for the given time horizon.[27] For a mix of GHGs it is obtained by summing the equivalent CO_2 emissions of each gas. Equivalent CO_2 emission is a standard and useful metric for comparing emissions of different GHGs but does not imply the same climate change responses.

- *CO_2-equivalent concentration* is the concentration of CO_2 that would cause the same amount of radiative forcing as a given mixture of CO_2 and other forcing components.[28]

The largest growth in GHG emissions between 1970 and 2004 has come from energy supply, transport and industry, while residential and commercial buildings, forestry (including deforestation) and agriculture sectors have been growing at a lower rate.

The effect on global emissions of the decrease in global energy intensity (-33%)

---

[26] Includes only carbon dioxide (CO_2), methane (CH_4), nitrous oxide (N2O), hydrofluorocarbons (HFCs), perfluorocarbons (PFCs) and sulphurhexafJuoride (SF_6), whose emissions are covered by the UNFCCC. These GHGs are weighted by their 100-year Global Warming Potentials (GWPs), using values consistent with reporting under the UNFCCC.

[27] This report uses 100-year GWPs and numerical values consistent with reporting under the UNFCCC.

[28] Such values *may* consider only GHGs, or a combination of GHGs and aerosols.

during 1970 to 2004 has been smaller than the combined effect of global income growth (77%) and global population growth (69%); both drivers of increasing energy-related CO_2 emissions. The long-term trend of declining CO_2 emissions per unit of energy supplied reversed after 2000.

Differences in per capita income, per capita emissions and energy intensity among countries remain significant. In 2004, UNFCCC Annex I countries held a 20% share in world population, produced 57% of the world's Gross Domestic Product based on Purchasing Power Parity (GDP_{ppp}) and accounted for 46% of global GHG emissions.

Drivers of climate change

Changes in the atmospheric concentrations of GHGs and aerosols, land cover and solar radiation alter the energy balance of the climate system and are drivers of climate change. They affect the absorption, scattering and emission of radiation within the atmosphere and at the Earth's surface. The resulting positive or negative changes in energy balance due to these factors are expressed as radiative forcing[29], which is used to compare warming or cooling influences on global climate.

Human activities result in emissions of four long-lived GHGs: CO_2, methane (CH.), nitrous oxide (N20) and halocarbons (a group of gases containing fluorine, chlorine or bromine). Atmospheric concentrations of GHGs increase when emissions are larger than removal processes.

Global atmospheric concentrations of CO_2, CH4 and N2O have increased markedly as a result of human activities since 1750 and now far exceed pre-industrial values determined from ice cores spanning many thousands of years. The atmospheric concentrations of CO_2 and equivalent in 2005 exceed by far the natural range over the last 650,000 years. Global increases in CO_2 concentrations are due primarily to fossil fuel use, with land-use change providing another significant but smaller contribution. It is very likely that the observed increase in CH4 concentration is predominantly due to agriculture and fossil fuel use. The increase in N2O concentration is primarily due to agriculture.

The global atmospheric concentration of CO_2 increased from a pre-industrial value of about 280ppm to 379ppm in 2005. The annual CO_2 concentration growth rate was larger during the last 10 years (1995–2005 average: 1.9ppm per year) than it has been since the beginning of continuous direct atmospheric measurements (1960–2005 average: 1.4ppm per year), although there is year-to-year variability in growth rates.

The global atmospheric concentration of CH_4 has increased from a pre-industrial value of about 715ppb to 1732ppb in the early 1990s, and was 1774ppb in 2005. Growth rates have declined since the early 1990s, consistent with total emissions

---

[29] *Radiative forcing* is a measure of the influence a factor has in altering the balance of incoming and outgoing energy in the Earth-atmosphere system and is an index of the importance of the factor as a potential climate change mechanism. In this report radiative forcing values are for changes relative to preindustrial conditions defined at 1750 and are expressed in watts per square metre *(W/m2)*.

(sum of anthropogenic and natural sources) being nearly constant during this period.

The global atmospheric $N_2 0$ concentration increased from a pre-industrial value of about 270ppb to 319ppb in 2005.

Many halocarbons (including hydrofluorocarbons) have increased from a near-zero pre-industrial background concentrations primarily due to human activities.

There is *very high confidence* that the global average net effect of human activities since 1750 has been one of warming, with a radiative forcing of +1.6 [+0.6 to +2.4] W/m^2.

The combined radiative forcing due to increases in CO_2, CH_4 and N_2O is +2.3 [+2.1 to +2.5] *W/m2*, and its rate of increase during the industrial era is *very likely* to have been unprecedented in more than 10,000 years. The CO_2 radiative forcing increased by 20% from 1995 to 2005, the largest change for any decade in at least the last 200 years.

Anthropogenic contributions to aerosols (primarily sulphate, organic carbon, black carbon, nitrate and dust) together produce a cooling effect, with a total direct radiative forcing of -0.5 [-0.9 to -0.1] W/m^2 and an indirect cloud albedo forcing of -0.7 [-1.8 to -0.3] W/m^2. Aerosols also influence precipitation.

In comparison, changes in solar irradiance since 1750 are estimated to have caused a small radiative forcing of +0.12 [+0.06 to +0.30] W/m^2.

Climate sensitivity and feedbacks

The equilibrium climate sensitivity is a measure of the climate system response to sustained radiative forcing. It is defined as the equilibrium global average surface warming following a doubling of CO_2 concentration. Progress enables an assessment that climate sensitivity is *likely* to be in the range of 2 to 4.5°C with a best estimate of about 3°C and is *very unlikely* to be less than 1.5°C Values substantially higher than 4.5°C cannot be excluded, but agreement of models with observations is not as good for those values.

Feedbacks can amplify or dampen the response to a given forcing. Direct emission of water vapour (a greenhouse gas) by human activities makes a negligible contribution to radiative forcing. However, as global average temperature increases, tropospheric water vapour concentrations increase and this represents a key positive feedback but not a forcing of climate change. Water vapour changes represent the largest feedback affecting equilibrium climate sensitivity and are now better understood. Cloud feedbacks remain the largest source of uncertainty. Spatial patterns of climate response are largely controlled by climate processes and feedbacks. For example, sea-ice albedo feedbacks tend to enhance the high latitude response.

Warming reduces terrestrial and ocean uptake of atmospheric CO_2, increasing the fraction of anthropogenic emissions remaining in the atmosphere. This positive carbon cycle feedback leads to larger atmospheric CO_2 increases and greater climate change for a given emissions scenario, but the strength of this feedback effect varies markedly among models.

C.　Sources of Emissions of Greenhouse Gases

1.　Global emissions by gas

Global emissions of greenhouse gases (GHG) increase each year and are at record levels. As of 2013, annual global emissions of carbon dioxide alone stand at about 35,000 megatons (1 megaton is equal to 1 million tons). Emissions of carbon dioxide (CO_2) have increased from about 5000 megatons in 1950 to about seven times that level in 2013. Carbon dioxide emissions, which are produced by burning GHG fossil fuels, deforestation, and decay of biomass, constitute about 77% of global GHG emissions. Methane (CH4) accounts for some 14% of global GHG emissions and comes from agricultural activities, waste management, and energy use. Nitrous oxide, due mainly from agriculture and fertilizer use, contributes about 8% to the total GHG emissions. Fluorinated gases (hydrofluorocarbons, perfluoro-carbons, and sulfur hexafluoride) from industrial processes, refrigeration, and the use of a variety of consumer products, constitute about 1% of global GHG emissions. In addition, emissions of certain non-gases — "black carbon," solid particles and aerosols — also affect the climate.

Three principal human activities are responsible for GHG emissions: (1) energy production and use; (2) deforestation and land use changes; and (3) agricultural practices. Energy production and use that involves burning fossil fuels — coal, petroleum and natural gas — accounts for most GHG emissions. Worldwide, about 86% of energy comes from burning fossil fuels. Coal is the worst offender; mining coal results in methane emissions and burning coal emits carbon dioxide. Burning petroleum emits about two-thirds as much GHG as burning coal and natural gas emissions are about one-half that of coal, but are still substantial Deforestation, the most important type of land use change, contributes to GHG emissions in two ways: forests are carbon sinks, they naturally remove carbon from the atmosphere; and burning forests causes carbon emissions. Almost one-half of the forests that originally covered the land area of Earth are gone; each year another 16 million hectares of forests disappear. Forests now cover about 25% of the Earth's total land area; over 50% in the tropics. But only about 22% of Earth's old growth forests remain. Seven countries account for over 60% of Earth's forests: Russia, Brazil, Canada, the United States, China, Indonesia, and the Democratic Republic of the Congo. (*See* Rate of Deforestation, http://www.globalchange.umich.edu/ globalchange2/current/lectures/deforest/deforest.html).

Agricultural practices contribute to GHG emissions; bare soil emits methane and nitrous oxide; enteric fermentation of farm animals emits methane; biomass burning produces carbon dioxide, methane and nitrous oxide; rice production produces methane; and manure management practices produce methane and nitrous oxide.

Cutting GHG emissions involves substantial changes in these three human activities.

- Substantial decreases in the rate of burning of fossil fuels and switching to alternative sources of energy production.

- Substantial slowing or reversing the rate of deforestation in the world.

- Adopting organic methods of agricultural production on a large scale. Organic agriculture integrates trees, hedgerows and pastures with fields for crops; organic fertilizers replace chemical fertilizers, and less intensive tillage is employed.

How likely is this to occur?

2.   Global emissions by source

The principal human activities that produce GHG gases include:

- Energy supply (26%) from the burning of fossil fuels — coal, natural gas, and oil for electricity and heat).

- Industry (19%) from the burning of fossil fuels for industrial processes, particularly in the chemical and metallurgical industries.

- Land use, land-use change, and forestry practices (17%).

- Agriculture (14%) produces GHG emissions from fertilizer use, biomass burning, and management of soils.

- Transportation (13%) uses fossil fuels for road, rail, air, and marine transportation.

- Commercial and residential buildings (8%) use fossil fuels for on-site energy generation and for cooking in homes.

- Waste and wastewater practices (3%) produce emissions of GHG through landfills and waste incineration.

3.   Global emissions by country

The top 10 countries that together are responsible for approximately 67% of global GHG emissions (expressed in megatons of CO_2 equivalent emissions) are:

- China   9,441
- United States   6,539
- Indonesia   2,290
- India   2,273
- Russian Federation   1,963
- Japan   1,203
- United Kingdom   1,144
- Germany   1,078
- Canada   750
- Mexico   710

NOTES AND QUESTIONS

1. *Per capita carbon emissions.* Listing GHG emissions by country obscures the fact that per capita GHG emissions differ widely among countries. The nation with the highest per capita carbon emissions in the world is Qatar (44 metric tons); the U.S. per capita emissions is 19.0. Many developed nations, Japan, the UK, and Germany range from 8.5 to 9.6 metric tons of CO_2 emissions per capita. China stands at 5.0, while India is 1.4. Is per capita GHG emissions a better measure of a nation's commitment to low-carbon emissions than gross per country statistics?

2. *Carbon intensity.* Another measure of a nation's commitment and progress toward reducing emissions is carbon intensity, the amount of CO_2 emissions per unit of GDP. Nations differ widely in carbon intensity[30]:

European Union:	213
United States:	374
Japan	281
Russian Federation	510
India	377
China	754

Between 2005 and 2012, China reduced its carbon intensity by 15%; the U.S. reduction during this time period was 2.3%. For the world as a whole the rate of carbon intensity improvement in 2011–2012 was 0.7%.

3. *Land use and deforestation.* Every country in the world is responsible for some GHG emissions. The totals above do not account for emissions of GHG related to changes in land use and deforestation. The U.S. EPA (*see* http://epa.gov/climatechange) estimates that land use changes and deforestation can account for about 5 billion metric tons of CO_2 emissions, amounting to about 16% of the emissions from fossil fuel sources. Such land use changes and deforestation is particularly acute in parts of Africa, Asia, and South America.

NOTE ON U.S. GREENHOUSE GAS EMISSIONS

In the United States, carbon dioxide emissions from burning fossil fuels, transportation, industrial processes, and waste disposal practices constitute 84% of GHG emissions. Methane emissions resulting from the production and transport of coal, livestock and agricultural practices and the decay of organic wastes in landfills account for 10% of GHG emissions. Nitrous oxide emitted from agricultural and industrial activities amount to 4% of GHG emissions, and fluorinated gases used in refrigeration and industrial processes account for 2% of GHG emissions.

By sector U.S. emissions of GHG result from the production of electricity (34%); transportation (27%); industry (21%); commercial and residential activities (11%); and agriculture (7%). In forestry, the United States is a net carbon sink in that more CO_2 is absorbed than is emitted into the air.

---

[30] Price Waterhouse Coopers, Low Carbon Economy Index 2012, available at http://www.pwc.co.uk, accessed 3 January 2013.

Since 1990, U.S. emissions of GHG have increased approximately 12%. *See* http://www.epa.gov/climatechange.

D. Future Emissions Scenarios, Future Climate Projections, and Potential Impacts

With the aid of climate models, computer programs that apply physical laws to calculate how climate has changed in the past and may change in the future, various governmental agencies and international organizations have made projections as to future emissions scenarios, future climate change, and likely impacts of the present climate trends. Such future projections are inherently speculative, but represent the best scientific thinking on the problems the future may bring. Perhaps the most authoritative future projections have been published by the Intergovernmental Panel on Climate Change in its Fifth Assessment Report.

INTERGOVERNMENTAL PANEL ON CLIMATE CHANGE, FIFTH ASSESSMENT REPORT, CLIMATE CHANGE, SUMMARY FOR POLICYMAKERS

[The Report presents four scenarios for the future depending on differing standards of emissions controls. In the best possible case, with strict controls, warming will rise by as little as half a degree Fahrenheit by 2100; the middle scenarios show increases in the 3 to 4 degree range; in the worst case the rise in temperature will be between 5 and nearly 9 degrees.]

- A large fraction of anthropogenic climate change resulting from CO_2 emissions is irreversible on a multi-century to millennial time scale, except in the case of a large net removal of CO_2 from the atmosphere over a sustained period. Surface temperatures will remain approximately constant at elevated levels for many centuries after a complete cessation of net anthropogenic CO_2 emissions. Due to the long time scales of heat transfer from the ocean surface to depth, ocean warming will continue for centuries. Depending on the scenario, about 15 to 40% of emitted CO_2 will remain in the atmosphere longer than 1,000 years.

- It is *virtually certain* that global mean sea level rise will continue beyond 2100, with sea level rise due to thermal expansion to continue for many centuries. The few available model results that go beyond 2100 indicate global mean sea level rise above the pre-industrial level by 2300 to be less than 1 m for a radiative forcing that corresponds to CO_2 concentrations that peak and decline and remain below 500 ppm. For a radiative forcing that corresponds to a CO_2 concentration that is above 700 ppm but below 1500 ppm, the projected rise is 1 m to more than 3 m *(medium confidence)*.

- Sustained mass loss by ice sheets would cause larger sea level rise, and some part of the mass loss might be irreversible. There is *high confidence* that sustained warming greater than some threshold would lead to the near-complete loss of the Greenland ice sheet over a millennium or more, causing a global mean sea level rise of up to 7 m.

NOTE ON POTENTIAL IMPACTS OF CLIMATE CHANGE

The IPCC report deals with the global and international impacts of climate change. If the impacts discussed in the report come to pass, many new problems of international relations will emerge. Threats to food security and water resources in many parts of the world could lead to conflicts among people and nations, International problems of equity will arise as certain countries will be more affected than others. Climate change could trigger humanitarian crises and trigger mass population movements creating "climate refugees" around the world. Rising ocean waters may threaten island communities and whole island nations could disappear, For example, the Maldives in the Indian Ocean is a collection of some 1,190 islands, none of which is higher than 15 feet above sea level. The entire population of the Maldives, some 214,000 people, could be forced to move by rising waters.

Climate change has the potential therefore to affect national security and to increase the number of international conflicts.

The U.S. EPA has gathered data on the potential different impacts of climate change on different areas of the world. The highlights of these regional impacts are as follows:

Impacts on Africa

- Africa is one of the most vulnerable continents to climate variability and change because of multiple existing stresses and low adaptive capacity. Existing stresses include poverty, political conflicts, and ecosystem degradation.

- By 2050, between 350 million and 600 million people are projected to experience increased water stress due to climate change.

- Climate variability and change is projected to severely compromise agricultural production, including access to food, in many African countries and regions.

- Toward the end of the 21st century, projected sea level rise will likely affect low-lying coastal areas with large populations,

- Climate variability and change can negatively impact human health. In many African countries, other factors already threaten human health. For example, malaria threatens health in southern Africa and the East African highlands.

Impacts on Asia

- Glaciers in Asia are melting at a faster rate than ever documented in historical records. Melting glaciers increase the risks of flooding and rock avalanches from destabilized slopes.

- Climate change is projected to decrease freshwater availability in central, south, east, and southeast Asia, particularly in large river basins. With population growth and increasing demand from higher standards of living, this decrease could adversely affect more than a billion people by the 2050s.

- Increased flooding from the sea and, in some cases, from rivers, threatens coastal areas, especially heavily populated delta regions in south, east, and southeast Asia.

- By the mid-21st century, crop yields could increase up to 20% in east and southeast Asia. In the same period, yields could decrease up to 30% in central and south Asia.

- Sickness and death due to diarrheal disease are projected to increase in east, south, and southeast Asia due to projected changes in the hydrological cycle associated with climate change.

Impacts on Australia and New Zealand

- Water security problems are projected to intensify by 2030 in southern, and eastern Australia, and in the northern and some eastern parts of New Zealand.

- Significant loss of biodiversity is projected to occur by 2020 in some ecologically rich sites, including the Great Barrier Reef and Queensland Wet Tropics.

- Sea level rise and more severe storms and coastal flooding will likely impact coastal areas. Coastal development and population growth in areas such as Cairns and Southeast Queensland (Australia) and Northland to Bay of Plenty (New Zealand), would place more people and infrastructure at risk.

- By 2030, increased drought and fire is projected to cause declines in agricultural and forestry production over much of southern and eastern Australia and parts of eastern New Zealand.

- Extreme storm events are likely to increase failure of floodplain protection and urban drainage and sewerage, as well as damage from storms and fires.

- More heat waves may cause more deaths and more electrical blackouts,

Impacts on Europe

- Wide-ranging impacts of climate change have already been documented in Europe. These impacts include retreating glaciers, longer growing seasons, species range shifts, and heat wave-related health Impacts.

- Future impacts of climate change are projected to negatively affect nearly all European regions. Many economic sectors, such as agriculture and energy, could face challenges.

- In southern Europe, higher temperatures and drought may reduce water availability, hydropower potential, summer tourism, and crop productivity.

- In central and eastern Europe, summer precipitation is projected to decease, causing higher water stress. Forest productivity is projected to decline. The frequency of peatland fires is projected to increase.

- In northern Europe, climate change is initially projected to bring mixed effects, including some benefits such as reduced demand for heating, increased crop yields, and increased forest growth. However, as climate change continues, negative impacts are likely to outweigh benefits. These include more frequent winter floods, endangered ecosystems, and increasing ground instability.

Impacts on Latin America

- By mid-century, increases in temperature and decreases in soil moisture are projected to cause savanna to gradually replace tropical forest in eastern Amazonia.

- In drier areas, climate change will likely worsen drought, leading to salinization (increased salt content) and desertification (land degradation) of agricultural land. The productivity of livestock and some important crops such as maize and coffee is projected to decrease, with adverse consequences for food security. In temperate zones, soybean yields are projected to increase.

- Sea level rise is projected to increase risk of flooding, displacement of people, salinization of drinking water resources, and coastal erosion in low-tying areas.

- Changes in precipitation patterns and the melting of glaciers are projected to significantly affect water availability for human consumption, agriculture, and energy generation.

Impacts on North America

- Warming in western mountains is projected to decrease snowpack, increase winter flooding, and reduce summer flows, exacerbating competition for over-allocated water resources.

- Disturbances from pests, diseases, and lire are projected to increasingly affect forests, with extended periods of high fire risk and large increases in area burned.

- Moderate climate change in the early decades of the century is projected to increase aggregate yields of rain-fed agriculture by 5–20%, but with important variability among regions. Crops that are near the warm end of their suitable range or that depend on highly utilized water resources will likely face major challenges.

- Increases in the number, intensity, and duration of heat waves during the course of the century are projected to further challenge cities that currently experience heat waves with potential for adverse health impacts. Older populations are most at risk.

- Climate change will likely increasingly stress coastal communities and habitats, worsening the existing stresses of development and pollution.

Impacts on Polar Regions

- Climate changes will likely reduce the thickness and extent of glaciers and ice sheets.

- Changes in natural ecosystems will likely have detrimental effects on many organisms including migratory birds, mammals, and higher predators.

• In the Arctic, climate changes will likely reduce the extent of sea ice and permafrost, which can have mixed effects on human settlements. Negative impacts could include damage to infrastructure and changes to winter activities such as ice fishing and ice road transportation. Positive impacts could include more navigable northern sea routes.

• The reduction and melting of permafrost, sea level rise, and stronger storms may worsen coastal erosion.

• Terrestrial and marine ecosystems and habitats are projected to be at risk to invasive species, as climatic barriers are lowered in both polar regions.

Impacts on Small Islands

• Small islands, whether located in the tropics or higher latitudes, are already exposed to extreme events and changes in sea level. This existing exposure will likely make these areas sensitive to the effects of climate change.

• Deterioration in coastal conditions, such as beach erosion and coral bleaching, will likely affect local resources such as fisheries, as well as the value of tourism destinations.

• Sea level rise is projected to worsen inundation, storm surge, erosion, and other coastal hazards. Those impacts would threaten vital infrastructure, settlements, and facilities that support the livelihood of island communities.

• By mid-century, on many small islands (such as the Caribbean and Pacific), climate change is projected to reduce already limited water resources to the point that they become insufficient to meet demand during low-rainfall periods.

• Invasion by non-native species is projected to increase with higher temperatures, particularly in mid- and high-latitude islands.

The U.S. EPA[31] has detailed the potential future impacts of climate change on the United States. By the year 2100, average global temperatures are expected to increase by 2-degrees F to 11.5 degrees F, depending on the level of future GHG emissions. Past and present-day GHG emissions will affect climate far into the future since many GHG stay in the Earth's atmosphere for long periods of time. Thus, even a radical decrease in GHG emissions, would not entirely stop the global warming that is already in process. Patterns of temperature increases, precipitation, and climate events will vary across regions, but the potential impacts of climate change is expected to affect especially the following sectors:

1. *Coastal areas.* Coastal areas of the United States and around the world may be affected by climate change in a variety of ways.

   • Sea level rise (predicted to be between 20 to 39 inches) may cause coastal flooding.

   • Greater frequency and intensity of storms, storm surge, and precipitation.

---

[31] http://www.epa.gov/climatechange/impacts-adaptation/.

- Warming coastal temperatures may cause shifts in the suitable habitats of temperature-sensitive species of fish and other marine life.

- Ocean waters will absorb more carbon dioxide and become more acidic, which may adversely affect marine habitats such as corals and adversely affect some marine species.

2. *Agriculture and food supply.* Agriculture and fisheries are highly dependent upon specific climatic conditions. While carbon dioxide and increased temperature may benefit some areas, many areas will experience drought. Heat waves and drought may adversely affect livestock. The ranges of many fish and shellfish species may change markedly and warmer conditions may increase the prevalence of certain diseases.

3. *Forests.* One-third (751 million acres) of the land area of the United States is covered with forests. Warmer climate conditions may affect the growth and productivity of forests in unknown ways. Species of trees may shift in their range or may be affected by wetter or dryer climate conditions. Forest disturbances may increase in the form of outbreaks of disease, insect infestations, wildfires, and storms.

4. *Ecosystems.* Climate change may lead to dramatic ecological changes, such as range shifts, extinctions, and food web disruptions. Fragile ecosystems are particularly at risk.

5. *Transportation.* Climate change may affect different modes of transportation.

   - Roadways. Higher temperatures may cause roadways to buckle; exposure to flooding and extreme weather events may shorten the useful life of certain roadways.

   - Railways. Higher temperatures may necessitate more repairs on rail tracks and speed restrictions to avoid derailments. Certain railways may be prone to flooding.

   - Subways. Subway infrastructure may have to be rebuilt or raised to avoid flooding.

   - Air transportation. Some airports located in coastal areas, such as LaGuardia in New York, may be at risk. Air transport may be adversely affected by extreme heat and storms.

   - Marine transportation. Shipping may be adversely affected by declines in water levels of canals and inland waterways. Sea lanes may shift. On the other hand, shipping could benefit by warmer temperatures that reduce sea ice; for example, warmer temperatures in the Arctic may open the possibility of a Northwest Passage.

   - Ports and infrastructure. Port and harbor works may be vulnerable to coastal flooding and storm events.

6. *Water resources.* The water cycle is a delicate balance of precipitation, evaporation and all the steps in between. Warmer temperatures will increase the rate of evaporation of water into the atmosphere, increasing the capacity of the atmosphere to hold water. Storms as a result may be

more frequent and more severe. The amount of total precipitation may increase, although some areas will become dryer and some wetter than before. More precipitation will fall as rain rather than snow. There will accordingly be presently unpredictable impacts on water availability and water quality. Changes in water resources will have follow-on impacts upon many matters such as ecosystems, agriculture, energy supply, and human health.

7. *Human health.* Warmer temperatures will impact human health in a number of ways. Summers will be hotter with more cases of heat stroke and dehydration; extreme weather events may increase; the frequency of days with unhealthy levels of ground-level ozone and fine air-borne particulate matter may increase; and changes in allergens may occur. Climate-sensitive diseases may increase.

8. *Energy impacts.* There may be several impacts on energy resources and energy supplies from climate change. Warmer temperatures may lead to more electricity use and peak energy demand. Power plants require large amounts of water for cooling, and changes in precipitation and the timing of snowmelt may affect the availability of such water supplies. Many coastal power plants in the United States are less than three feet above sea level and may be subject to coastal flooding. Power lines and energy infrastructure may be adversely affected by weather events and flooding. Hydroelectric power facilities may be affected by changing weather patterns and water flows.

9. *Societal impacts.* Warmer temperatures and climate change will affect certain people more than others, creating problems of societal equity. Geographic location will be a major determinant of who is impacted the most; urban and coastal populations may be affected more than other areas. Society will have to cope with problems of equity and vulnerability of people affected by climate change.

THE ROLE OF LAWYERS ADVISING CLIENTS ON CLIMATE CHANGE

Many law firms have established practice groups on Climate Change and Clean Technology in order to serve their clients and to advise them on how to deal with climate change issues. As our climate changes, virtually every business will have to develop a detailed response strategy tailored to its business and its customers as well as the demands of government, investors and the public.

First, climate change will undoubtedly result in new types of regulatory measures that businesses will need to meet. Since climate change is a moving target, regulatory changes will likely be episodic and involve both long-term and short-term standards. Second, in addition to complying with required regulations, a business will have to consider the impact of climate change on its own business and its customers and determine how climate change will impact its business. Third, the company will have to consider its societal image and how it should manage its affairs to satisfy both investors and society. Companies must pay attention to societal projects such as the *Investor Network on Climate Risk*, composed of over 50 institutional investors managing in excess of $3.7 trillion in assets. Another national coalition of investors, environmental groups and non-governmental organization has formed Ceres, which published a 2006 report, *Corporate Governance and Climate Change: Making the Connection*[32] that evaluated 100 leading global companies on their climate change practices. Another coalition of public interest groups have published *The Carbon Disclosure Project*,[33] a survey of the top 500 U.S. companies on their climate risk disclosures. This group has published a *Global Framework/or Climate Disclosure*, a statement of information investors expect from companies on their climate *change* policies and risks. Other indexes published include the *Dow Jones Sustainability Index*[34]; *Business Ethics 100*[35]; *and Fortune's Most Admired.*[36] Investors and the public now are asking companies for specific information on their climate change risks and how they are dealing with them.

How should a company respond to these developments? The Climate Change Practice Group at Jenner & Block, LLP, is advising clients to (1) organize a company team to manage climate change matters; (2) prepare and adopt climate change company policies; (3) evaluate the practices of the company and recommend and implement improvements; (4) inquire into the "green" practices of suppliers and *contractors;* (5) inventory and consider how best to deal with GHG emissions within your business; and (6) require legal counsel review of all company disclosures that deal with climate change matters. Lynn Grayson, *Climate Change: Why it Matters for your Business*, 21 THE CORPORATE COUNSELOR 1 (May 2007).

E.   Options for Dealing with Climate Change: Adaptation and Mitigation

That the global climate is warming seems incontrovertible. The magnitude of the warming is unclear. Human activity seems to be the main driver of the climate change we are experiencing. The major question is what if anything, can or should be done. The international legal regime on climate change draws a fundamental distinction between the concepts of adaptation and mitigation of climate change.

1.   Adaptation

Adaptation to climate change is defined by the IPCC as "adjustments to natural or human systems in response to actual or expected climate stimuli or their effects which moderates harm or exploits beneficial opportunities."[37] In other words, adaptation to climate change is distinct from mitigation efforts to stop climate change; rather, adaptation accepts climate change and considers what can and must be done to moderate its adverse effects and to take advantage of its beneficial effects. The IPCC Working Group II is charged with investigating and making

---

[32] http://www.ceres.org.

[33] https://www.cdp.net/en-US/Pages/HomePage.aspx.

[34] http://www.sustainability-indices.com/.

[35] http://www.business-ethics.com.

[36] http://money.cnn.com/magazines/fortune/.

[37] https://unfccc.int/documentation/items/2643.php.

recommendations on all aspects of adaptation: its latest report, *Climate Change 2014: Working Group II: Impacts, Adaptation and Vulnerability* (2014), reviews in comprehensive fashion efforts to adapt to climate change in a variety of sectors.

The United Nations Framework Convention on Climate Change (UNFCCC) (1992), which is reprinted in the Document Supplement, Article 4.1 (e), titled "Commitments," states that the parties to the Convention "shall cooperate in preparing for adaptation to the impacts of climate change." To fulfill this mandate, the UNFCCC Secretariat has formulated five components of adaptation activities[38]:

- Observation. The first step to adaptation is closely observing, monitoring, and analyzing climate change impacts on various economic and environmental sectors and resources.

- Assessment. Adaptation assessment is the process of identifying options to adapt to climate change and evaluating them in terms of their availability, costs, benefits, effectiveness, efficiency, and feasibility.

- Implementation. The third step in adaptation is the selection of specific adaptation actions and their implementation.

- Monitoring and evaluation. During and after the implementation of adaptation actions, the actions taken must be monitored, evaluated, and revised as necessary. In this way, adaptation is a continuous, flexible, ongoing process.

Adaptation is an important topic at meetings of the Conference of Parties (COP) of the UNFCCC. Among the many actions taken by the COP, the most important adaptation decisions are;

- At COP 12, in Nairobi, Kenya, the parties to the UNFCCC mandated the UNFCCC Subsidiary Body for Scientific and Technological Advice (SBSTA) to formulate a guidance document for adaptation. The result of this initiative is the Nairobi Work Programme,[39] which is an ongoing process to assist especially developing countries to take adaptation actions.

- The Cancun Adaptation Framework.[40] The Bali Action Plan, adopted at COP 13 in Bali, Indonesia, December 2007, identified adaptation as one of the key building blocks required for future response to climate change. At the 2010 Cancun COP, the parties adopted the Cancun Adaptation Framework (CAF) to guide the formulation of national adaptation plans by parties. The CAF also created a new COP Adaptation Committee.

- In Doha, Qatar in December 2012, the COP 18 approved the workplan of the COP Adaptation Committee and called for completion of the process of formulating National Adaptation Plans by parties to the UNFCCC.

Thus, adaptation to climate change is an active, ongoing international effort.[41] Several funding mechanisms support the formulation and implementation plans of

---

[38] https://unfccc.int/focus/adaptation/items/6999.php.

[39] http://unfccc.int/adaptation/workstreams/nairobi_work_programme/items/3633.php.

[40] https://unfccc.int/adaptation/items/5852.php.

[41] For proposed principles of adaptation law, see Robin Kundis Craig, *"Stationarity is Dead"* —

developing countries, including the Green Climate Fund, created by COP 16, the Special Climate Change Fund administered by the Global Environment Facility (GEF), the World Bank,[42] and a Special Adaptation Fund managed by an Adaptation Fund Board of 16 parties.

What will be the cost of climate change adaptation? According to a World Bank Report — Economics of Adaptation to Climate Change (2009),[43] adaptation for developing countries alone will cost US $75–100 billion each year for the period 2010 to 2050. This study systematically analyzes costs for all developing countries for major economic sectors using country-level data sets and assessing the costs of adaptation for ecosystem services.

The costs of adaptation for developed countries will be immense. No reliable estimate of costs of adaptation exists for the U.S. or the EU, but the UNFCCC estimates that by 2030 the costs for developed countries will be as high as US $105 billion each year.[44]

PROBLEM 4-5
FORMULATING A CLIMATE CHANGE ADAPTATION PLAN FOR THE UNITED STATES

The United States and other developed countries will have to formulate and pay for adaptation to climate change without the benefit of financial help from international climate funds. On June 11, 2011, Lisa Jackson, the Administrator of the EPA, issued a Policy Statement on Climate Change Adaptation,[45] which stated: "I am directing that an EPA climate-change adaptation plan be developed and implemented to integrate climate adaptation into the agency's programs, policies, rules, and operations." Suppose Ms. Jackson called you into her office and asked you to take charge of her task force on this issue. How would you go about formulating a Climate Change Adaptation Plan for the United States? What are the greatest vulnerabilities to climate change in the U.S.? What regions and sectors will potentially feel the greatest impact? What elements of an adaptation plan would you suggest for the United States? How should the United States go about preparing such a plan?

2. Mitigation

Mitigation of climate change is defined as human intervention to reduce either emissions of greenhouse gases (abatement) or to increase sinks of carbon and other greenhouse gases (sequestration).[46] Scientists and economists agree that no single

---

Lang Live Transformation: Five Principles for Climate Change Adaptation Law, 34 HARV. ENVTL L. REV. 9 (2010).

[42] http://worldbank.org/climatechange.

[43] http://www.worldbank.org/eacc.

[44] *See* IMPERIAL COLLEGE LONDON, GRANTHAM INSTITUTE FOR CLIMATE CHANGE, ASSESSING THE COSTS OF ADAPTATION TO CLIMATE CHANGE 9–10 (2009).

[45] http://www.epa.gov/climatechange/Downloads/impacts-adaptation/adaptation-statement.pdf.

[46] http://unfccc.int/focus/mitigation/items/7169.php. Various engineering schemes have been proposed to mitigate climate change: launching a fleet of ships to whiten clouds by spraying salt mist into the

strategy exists that will moderate climate change; instead a multiplicity of solutions must be implemented. One such proposal is called the "wedge approach" which proposes dividing the graphic triangle between the present upward trend of global GHG emissions and the desired flat path where emissions level off-into a series of wedges, each of which involves a different mitigation strategy.[47]

(a)   Abatement Strategies

Most of the emphasis on climate change mitigation has been placed on abatement strategies. Abatement without sacrificing economic growth and well-being is a great challenge. Three general categories of governmental actions are possible to abate GHG emissions.

(i)   *Direct government support.* Using fiscal policy tools such as grants and tax credits government may directly support climate-friendly technologies. For example, the U.S. provides a tax credit to consumers who buy certain all-electric vehicles; wind and solar power have received similar tax credits as well as outright grants from the U.S. Department of Energy. The U.S. also supports carbon capture and storage technologies being developed by private companies. Under the U.S. DOE's Carbon Sequestration Program, companies such as Duke Power have received multi-million dollar grants to capture and store carbon deep underground in order to reduce carbon dioxide emissions from coal-powered electrical generating facilities. The Department of Energy's National Energy Technology Laboratory has been allocated $70 million from the U.S. American Recovery and Reinvestment Act of 2009, to use for various carbon storage and sequestration projects and to create regional training centers with the goal of creating a carbon sequestration qualified workforce in the United States. On the international level, more than 120 countries founded the International Renewable Energy Agency (IRENA) in 2009, in order to promote renewable energy technologies on a global basis.[48]

(ii) *Government technical requirements, standards and regulations.* Government may foster climate-friendly actions by the private sector by mandating controls or certain technologies. "Command and control" can be used to mandate the use of specific technology to control GHG emissions, energy efficiency standards and to implement product standards and operational methods that reduce GHG emissions. For example, government may mandate specific emission control technology,

---

atmosphere; sewing the seas with iron particles to encourage the growth of plankton; and sending a swarm of mirrors into space to reflect incoming sunlight. *See* Stephen Battersby, *Can We Engineer a Fix to Our Climate Problems?*, WASHINGTON POST, 6 November 2012, at E1.

[47] Robert Socolow and Steve Pacala, *Stabilization Wedges*, 305 SCI. 968 (2004). Socolow and Pacala propose six wedges, greater efficiency, decarbonized electricity, decarbonized fuels, fuel displacement by low-carbon electricity, methane management, and increasing natural carbon sinks. Each wedge is broken down into subwedges: for example, decarbonized electricity is broken down into nuclear power, renewable energy, employing coal substitution technology, and employing carbon capture and storage technology.

[48] *See* http://irena.org.

cleaner diesel engines, reducing methane emissions from rice fields by requiring them to be drained more often, and capturing methane at landfills. Government can also mandate product standards related to products themselves or production processes to promote energy efficiency. Regulatory standards can be developed also to promote renewable energy. For example, Germany ensures the viability of solar energy facilities by requiring minimum "feed-in" tariffs to assure producers of solar energy that they will receive an adequate monetary return when they sell the power they generate to electric utility companies. The feed-in tariffs are funded by adding a surcharge on conventional electricity that adds about 1 euro each month to the average German electric bill.

(iii) *Market-based incentive approaches.* Using market-based incentives, governments set firm environmental goals but defines them in terms of performance and their end results, leaving the private sector free to pursue financial self-interest by choosing their individual response and compliance strategies. Market-based incentives can be used for two purposes: (1) to improve energy efficiency with respect to present use of fossil fuels; and (2) to create incentives for greater use of alternative and renewable sources of energy. As applied to climate change, two categories of market incentives stand out:

- *Carbon taxes.* Carbon taxes are now employed in many countries, especially in British Columbia and in various European countries. Everywhere carbon taxes are deployed they substantially reduce carbon emissions not by mandating control technology but by creating incentives for businesses and individuals to take action to reduce their carbon footprints, and their tax bills. A carbon tax promotes energy efficiency and promotes the use of renewable and alternative sources of energy. A carbon tax also raises money for government that can be used to reduce other kinds of taxation, such as income and business taxes. The point of a carbon tax is to internalize environmental externalities from the burning of fossil fuels, to drive investment into renewable energy, and to encourage innovation in energy use. A carbon charge will ripple through the entire economy raising prices for users of energy, but allowing businesses and individuals to do whatever they can to avoid or minimize the tax.

- *Cap and trade.* A second market-based incentive approach is to set a price on carbon emissions by fixing a cap on total emissions, creating a system of allowances to cover the emissions under the cap, and create a market for trading the allowances at a price determined by the market. Cap and trade creates a new commodity — carbon allowances — and puts a price on carbon. The cap means that covered emitters must either cut down their emissions or go into the market to buy the allowances they need to cover them. This creates an incentive to reduce emissions, to become more efficient in using fossil fuels or to switch to renewables. Businesses that are able to reduce their carbon emission below the allowances they own can sell their allowances and make money; some businesses may find it more profitable to simply buy the extra allowances they need. The net effect of cap and trade therefore is to provide flexibility regarding how, when, and where to reduce emissions so that businesses may minimize their economic costs. This flexibility can be enhanced by giving businesses "banking and borrowing" privileges so that carbon allowances can be shifted over across years. The initial allowances under a cap and trade program may be either given away or auctioned by government. Granting allowances free to emitters is not well-suited though is politically tempting; free allowances are simply subsidies to firms receiving them resulting in windfall profits through government largesse. The United States has prior experience in operating successful cap and trade programs. In the 1980s cap and trade was used by EPA to successfully eliminate the use of leaded gasoline in cars across the U.S. Since 1990, cap and trade is being used to reduce emissions of sulfur dioxide in the United States. Cap and trade was also used by EPA to phase out emissions of ozone destroying chemicals. *See* Joel Kurtzman, *The Low Carbon Diet: How the Market Can Curb Climate Change*, 88 (5) FOREIGN AFFAIRS 114 (2009).

Of the three enumerated GHG abatement policies the United States employs only the first two, and market-based incentives are uncommon in most of the rest of the world as well. A major drawback of market-based incentives is that when they are employed unilaterally, the country using them is placed at a distinct economic disadvantage internationally. A country employing carbon taxes or cap and trade or both will have higher energy prices; international competitors will then have great advantages: (1) products imported from countries with no restraints on emissions will carry lower prices; and (2) in third country markets products from countries with no economic price on carbon will outsell products from countries which put a price on carbon through taxes or cap and trade. Thus, what is needed for market-based incentive programs to work is to deploy them on a global basis. For example, if China, the U.S. and the EU combined coordinate their carbon tax programs and to create linked cap and trade schemes for carbon, other countries would be constrained to join, creating a global carbon emission reduction scheme and a world price for carbon emissions with a level playing field internationally for all countries.

(b)   Sequestration Strategies

The second way to reduce GHG in the atmosphere is to increase carbon and GHG sinks through land use strategies. Sequestration typically involves (1) afforestation — creating new forestlands; (2) reforestation — replanting lands previously forested; and (3) preventing deforestation — preserving existing forestlands. An estimated 15 to 20% of the GHG emissions caused by human activity are the result of the degradation and destruction of forests.[49] Forest

---

[49] Statement of David Kaimowitz of the Centre for International Forestry Research, quoted in THE ECONOMIST, December 10, 2005, at 82.

destruction is ongoing, however, mainly in developing countries so that sequestration strategies, if they are to make a difference, must be international in scope. In the materials below, we cover these international efforts. Theoretically carbon sequestration strategies to preserve forests can be incorporated into the market-based approaches described above. For example, offsets could be incorporated into carbon emissions cap and trade schemes. Offsets are activities undertaken directly or indirectly by an emitter to counteract the environmental damage caused by releasing GHG. For example, a refinery in Texas could gain an offset allowance for its carbon emissions by setting up a reforestation program in the Amazon — or even in Texas. Such offsets are welcome additions to cap and trade or tax programs that add to their flexibility and carry desirable results. Of course offset programs must comply with standards of effectiveness and be subject to objective audits.

3. Cost of Mitigation

Calculating the costs of mitigation of climate change in relation to the benefits presents major difficulties. The (marginal) benefits of mitigation are unclear, and the (marginal) costs of mitigation are problematic and controversial. In addition, the damages of climate change are expected in the distant future while many of the costs must be incurred today. Damages furthermore are speculative and will be borne primarily by future generations, while the costs have to be borne in the present.

While there are many cost estimates of mitigation, few are authoritative. The most authoritative and discussed cost estimate to date is Lord Nicholas Stern *et al.*, *The Stern Review of the Economics of Climate Change* (2006), a report to the Prime Minister and the Chancellor of the Exchequer of the United Kingdom. The chief author of this report is Sir Nicholas Stern, formerly the chief economist of the World Bank, who is now a high-ranking official in the UK government. Using economic models, the Stern Review estimates that the cost of inaction (business as usual) will be equivalent to 5% to 20% of global GDP each year by 2050; and the cost of "prompt and strong action" to avoid these costs will amount to 1% of global GDP each year. The Review thus concludes that "the costs of stabilizing the climate are significant but manageable; delay would be dangerous and much more costly." (p. vii). The Review further concludes that "Climate change demands an international response, based on a shared understanding of long-term goals and agreement on frameworks for action." (p. viii).

The Stern Review is criticized on several grounds. On the costs side, some economists charge that the estimated costs are too high, but others say the estimate is too low because the deployment of necessary new technologies will be more expensive than Lord Stern assumes. *See* THE ECONOMIST, Special Report, December 5, 2009, at 10. On the benefits side, economists criticize the Stern Report for using a discount rate of nearly zero. Since the costs of mitigation are front-loaded and the benefits far distant, they advocate a discount rate for the benefits as high as 10%, reducing them substantially. Economists also argue that mitigation efforts will not stop climate change but will at best only slow the effects, so that the resulting benefits of mitigation will be much lower than Lord Stern makes out. An additional criticism is that Lord Stern compared total costs and total benefits, while good economic analysis would rather compare marginal costs to marginal benefits. *See* Richard S.J. Tol & G.W. Yohe, *The Stern Review of the Economics of Climate Change: A Comment, in* H.J. SCHELLENHUBER *ET AL.*, AVOIDING DANGEROUS CLIMATE CHANGE 291–298 (2006).

4. Case Study: The European Union Emissions Trading Scheme

The European Union (EU) operates the most ambitious GHG emission trading system in the world as a major component of its GHG emission reduction strategy. The EU's Emission Trading Scheme (EU-ETS) has operated since 2005. The EU-ETS is a cap and trade system that covers all 28 EU member states as well as Iceland, Liechtenstein and Norway.

The EU-ETS was begun by the issuance of a Directive under EU law[50]; the initial Directive has been amended several times[51] and supplemented by the issuance of regulations[52] and decisions.[53] Under EU law, the EU-ETS is implemented through National Allocation Plans (NAPs) operated by each member state. The EU-ETS has proceeded in three phases, the third of which began January 1, 2013 and continues, through 2020. Initially the EU-ETS covered only CO_2 emissions but in 2013, certain nitrous oxide emissions were also included.

Under the EU-ETS a cap is set for CO_2 and NO emissions with a linear decrease in the cap of 1.74% per year. Some 13,000 installations are subject to the EU-ETS: oil refineries, power plants over twenty megawatts (MW) in capacity, coke ovens, iron and steel plants, and cement, glass, lime, brick, ceramics, and pulp and paper facilities. Installations subject to the cap comprise about 43% of the EU's total GHG emissions. Economic sectors not covered include transportation (except for aviation, which is subject to the EU-ETS), office buildings and smaller emitting facilities.

Installations covered by the ETS are required to hold and use emission allowances, each one of which represents a permit to emit one ton of CO_2 or other GHG. The emission allowances are allocated each year and are freely tradable. Emission allowance trading using market principles creates economic incentives to reduce GHG emissions and rewards efficiency by minimizing emission control costs. Sources of emissions have flexibility in deciding whether or how they wish to abate their emissions.

---

[50] Council Directive 2003/87/EC.

[51] Council Directives 2004/101/EC; Council Directive 2008/101/EC; and Council Directive 2009/29/EC.

[52] Commission Regulation (EU) No. 219/2009; and Commission Regulation (EU) No. 1031/2010.

[53] Commission Decision 2006/780/EC of 16 November 2006; and Commission Decision 2007/5S9/EC of 18 July 2007.

THE EUROPEAN COMMISSION, THE EU EMISSIONS TRADING SCHEME
16–22 (2009)

How does emissions trading benefit companies and the environment?

Companies A and B both emit 100,000 tonnes of CO_2 per year. Let us say their governments give each of them emission allowances for 95 000 tonnes, leaving them to find ways to cover the shortfall of 5 000 allowances. This gives them a choice between reducing their emissions by 5 000 tonnes; purchasing 5 000 allowances in the market or taking a position somewhere in between. Before deciding which option to pursue they compare the costs of each. Let us imagine that the market price of an allowance at that moment is € 20 per tonne of CO_2. Company A calculates that cutting its emissions will cost it € 10 per tonne, so it decides to do this because it is cheaper than buying the necessary allowances. Company A even decides to take the opportunity to reduce its emissions not by 5 000 tonnes but by 10 000. Company B is in a different situation. Its reduction costs € 30 per tonne, i.e., higher than the market price so it decides to buy allowances instead of reducing emissions.

Company A spends €100 000 on cutting its emissions by 10 000 tonnes at a cost of € 10 per tonne, but then receives € 100 000 from selling the 5 000 allowances it no longer needs at the market price of € 20 each. This means it fully offsets its emission reduction costs by selling allowances whereas without the emissions trading scheme it would have had a net cost of € 50 000 to bear assuming that it cut emissions by only the 5 000 tonnes necessary.

Company B spends € 100 000 on buying 5 000 allowances at a price of € 20 each. In the absence of the flexibility provided by the ETS, it would have had to cut its emissions by 5 000 tonnes at a cost of € 150 000. Emissions trading thus brings a total cost saving of € 100 000 for the companies in this example. Since Company A chooses to cut its emissions (because this is the cheaper option in its case), the allowances that Company B buys represent real emissions reduction even if Company B did not reduce its own emissions.

Allocation of allowances from 2013

Under the revision of the EU ETS that took effect in 2013, a single EU-wide cap on emission allowances replaced the current system of 28 national caps implemented through national allocation plans (NAPs).

Experience gained from Phase 1 of the EU ETS indicates that this more harmonised approach will provide stronger guarantees that the EU's greenhouse gas emission reduction targets for 2020 will be achieved. It should also be more effective in minimising the cost of meeting the targets.

The single EU cap on allowances needs to be set at a level that is both cost-effective and consistent with achieving the emission reduction targets. The cap will start at the mid-point of the 2008 to 2012 period and be reduced in a linear fashion by 1.74% each year until 2020 and beyond. This means that by 2020 the number of allowances available will be 21% below the level of verified emissions in

2005, thus making a very substantial contribution to the attainment of the EU's overall greenhouse gas emission targets for that year.

This clear up-front announcement of the size and frequency of the cap's reduction for many years ahead provides market operators with a long-term perspective and the necessary predictability on which they can base decisions to invest in emission reductions.

Auctioning will become the basic principle for allocating allowances from 2013, in place of the current system whereby the vast majority of allowances is given away for free by governments. This change reflects the fact that auctioning creates a stronger incentive for businesses to take early action to reduce emissions, complies better with the 'polluter pays' principle and will increase the efficiency, transparency and simplicity of the EU ETS.

The power generation sector will in principle have to buy all of its allowances from 2013 since experience shows that power generators have been able to pass on the notional cost of emission allowances to their customers even when they are free. However under certain conditions some Member States will have the option of derogating from this rule temporarily for existing power plants. They will be able to grant such plants up to 70% of their allowances for free in 2013, but this proportion will have to decrease progressively to zero in 2020.

Installations undertaking the capture, transport and geological storage of greenhouse gases will also have to buy all of their allowances from 2013 but will not have to surrender allowances for the emissions stored.

For other sectors there will be a progressive transition to auctioning, starting with a 20% share of allowances auctioned in 2013 and rising to 70% in 2020 with a view to reaching full auctioning by 2027. However, exceptions to the principle of auctioning could be made for certain energy-intensive industries if their competitiveness were judged to be at risk.

Given the significant weight of power generation in the EU ETS, it is estimated that more than 50% of total allowances will be auctioned from 2013.

Auctions will be held by national governments but will be open to buyers from anywhere in the EU. The Commission will adopt rules on the design and execution of auctions by 30 June 2010 to ensure they are carried out in an open, transparent and non-discriminatory way.

88% of the allowances to be auctioned will be distributed among Member States on the basis of their share of verified emissions from EU ETS installations in 2005. 10% will be distributed only to the least wealthy Member States as an additional source of revenue to help them invest in reducing the carbon intensity of their economies and adapting to climate change. The remaining 2% will be distributed as a 'Kyoto bonus' to Member States which by 2005 had reduced their greenhouse gas emissions by at least 20% of levels in their Kyoto Protocol base year (Bulgaria, Czech Republic, Estonia, Hungary, Latvia, Lithuania, Poland, Romania, Slovakia).

It is estimated that auctioning could raise an EU-wide total of €30–50 billion per year by 2020, depending on the carbon price. Governments have agreed that they should use at least 50% of this income to combat climate change, in both Europe and developing countries.

Preventing 'carbon leakage'

Exceptions to the auctioning of emission allowances could be made for energy-intensive industries if their competitiveness were judged to be at risk due to laxer emissions constraints in other parts of the world.

This could be the case if, for instance, no satisfactory global climate agreement were reached or if some third countries decided not to adhere to it. Such a development could tempt Europe-based industries to relocate to less carbon-constrained jurisdictions with the result that European jobs would be lost and global greenhouse gas emission would increase — a phenomenon known as "carbon leakage."

To prevent this, energy-intensive sectors and sub-sectors judged to be potentially at risk will be determined by the Commission by the end of 2009, on the basis of an agreed set of criteria. The Commission will then reassess the situation in the light of a new global climate change agreement and propose any adjustments considered necessary. These proposals could, for example, involve adjusting the proportion of allowances that sectors should receive free of charge, or extend the EU-ETS to cover importers of products competing with those from European sectors considered at risk of carbon leakage.

Ensuring compliance

Appropriately for a market-based instrument that puts a price on carbon, the EU ETS incorporates a robust framework of measures to ensure compliance that also gives a central role to economic incentives.

After each calendar year, installations must surrender a number of allowances equivalent to their verified CO_2 emissions in that year. These allowances are then cancelled so they cannot be used again. Those installations with allowances left over can sell them or save them for future use.

Installations that do not surrender enough allowances to cover their emissions in the previous year are penalised. They have to obtain additional allowances to make up the shortfall in the following year, are 'named and shamed' by having their names published, and must pay a dissuasive fine for each excess tonne of CO_2 emitted. The penalty, set initially at E 40 per tonne, is now E 100 per tonne. From 2013) it will rise in line with the annual rate of inflation in the Eurozone (the group of EU countries using the euro as their currency).

Some Member States have also laid down additional dissuasive sanctions at national level for any infringements of the EU ETS rules.

Monitoring, reporting and verifying emissions

Each installation in the EU-ETS must have a permit from its competence authority for its emissions of all six greenhouse gases controlled by the Kyoto

Protocol. A condition for granting the permit is that the operator is capable of monitoring and reporting the plant's emissions. A permit is different from an allowance; the permit sets out the emission monitoring and reporting requirements for an installation, whereas allowances are the scheme's tradable unit.

Operators must report their emissions of the greenhouse gases covered by the EU ETS after each calendar year. The European Commission has issued a set of monitoring and reporting guidelines to be followed.

The reports have to be checked by an independent verifier on the basis of criteria set out in the ETS legislation, and are made public. Operators whose emission reports for the previous year are not verified as satisfactory are not allowed to sell allowances until a revised report is approved by a verifier.

Transaction registries

Allowances are not printed but held in accounts in electronic registries set up by Member States. Through legislation the European Commission has set up a standardised and secured system of registries based on UN data exchange standards to track the issue, holding, transfer and cancellation of allowances. Provisions on the tracking and use of credits from CDM and JI projects in the EU system are also included.

The registries system is similar to a banking system which keeps track of the ownership of money in accounts but does not look into the deals that lead to money changing hands.

The system is overseen by a central administrator at EU *level* who, through an independent transaction log, checks each transaction for any irregularities. Any irregularities detected prevent a transaction from being completed until they have been remedied.

The EU registries system is linked to the international registries system used under the Kyoto Protocol.

Trading in practice

The legal framework of the EU ETS does not lay down how and where trading in allowances should take place. Companies and other participants in the market trade directly with each other or buy and sell through one of the several organised exchanges in Europe, or via any of the intermediaries that have sprung up to take advantage of this new market.

The price of allowances is determined by supply and demand. The market in allowances has developed strongly. In the scheme's first year of operation, 2005, at least 362 million allowances (tonnes of CO_2) were traded, with a value of around €7.2 billion. Trading volume rose to 1 billion allowances in 2006, 1.6 billion in 2007 and almost 3.1 billion in 2008, according to Point Carbon, a consultancy which tracks and analyses the carbon market. European trading constituted some 73% of the global turnover in CO_2 allowances and credits, which was worth €92.4 billion in 2008.

The EU ETS has thus established itself as the engine of the global carbon market that is becoming a powerful tool for reducing greenhouse gas emissions cost-effectively.

Creating demand for third-country credits

The Clean Development Mechanism (CDM) and the Joint Implementation (JI) instrument enable developed countries that have binding emission reduction or limitation targets under the Kyoto Protocol to invest in emission-saving projects in third countries. The emission credits generated by these projects can be purchased by companies In the EU ETS to offset a proportion of their emissions, in the same way as allowances.

The CDM covers projects in developing nations. Reductions are potentially eligible to receive credits called certified emission reductions (CERs). JI applies to projects in countries that have agreed to an emission target under the Protocol — industrialised countries and countries with economies in transition. JI projects yield credits known as emission reduction units (ERUs).

The EU ETS is the world's first trading system to recognise most of these credits as equivalent to emission allowances (1 EUA = 1 CER = 1 ERU) and allow them to be traded within the system[54]

All credits except those from nuclear facilities and from land use, land-use change and forestry activities may be accepted.

The launch of the EU ETS three years before the start of the Protocol's first commitment period (2008–2012) thus provided certainty to investors in the rapidly emerging market for CDM and JI projects. This has encouraged additional investment in these projects, thus promoting the transfer of environmentally sound technologies to help the host countries meet their sustainable development goals.

For EU companies participating in the EU ETS, the recognition of CDM and JI credits increases the range of options available for limiting their emissions, improves the liquidity of the market and can potentially lower the price of allowances, thus reducing compliance costs.

The strong demand for emission credits has led major European banks and other financial institutions in both the private and public sectors to become active in providing finance for prospective emission reduction projects. In addition, many international carbon funds have been setup.

During Phase 2 from 2008 to 2012, businesses in the EU ETS are able to buy credits for a total of around 1.4 billion tonnes of CO_2 — a yearly average of 280 million tonnes — to help offset their emissions. (In addition, a number of EU governments plan to buy credits totalling around 550 million tonnes of CO_2 to help meet their Kyoto obligations, and have budgeted some €2.9 billion for these purchases. This use of credits is supplemental to their domestic action to limit emissions, as agreed by UNFCCC parties at Marrakech in 2001).

From 2013, rules on the use of credits will depend on the conclusion of a

---

[54] Directive 2004/101/EC.

satisfactory international climate agreement for the post-2012 period. Until that is the case, operators will be able to carry over to Phase 3 any credits not used in Phase 2, plus a limited additional quantity. The overall effect will be that use of credits will be limited to no more than 50% of the EU emission reductions to be made between 2008 and 2020.

Once a satisfactory international agreement has been concluded, the European Commission may propose to allow additional access to credits as well as the use of any new types of project credits or other mechanisms created under the agreement. From January 2013 onwards, however, only credits from third countries that have ratified the new agreement or from new types of project approved by the Commission will be eligible for use in the EU ETS.

Linking up with other emissions trading systems

The EU sees a key role for an effective global carbon market in helping to deliver cost-effectively the emission cuts that will be needed under a post-2012 climate agreement. Building this global market will require domestic carbon markets to be linked.

The EU ETS has been extended to Iceland, Liechtenstein and Norway since the start of 2008 and is open to linking with other compatible mandatory cap-and-trade systems that would not undermine its environmental integrity. The creation in 2007 of the International Carbon Action Partnership[55] of which the European Commission and several EU Member States are founder members, will help to support this process.

The EU's vision is to create a carbon market among member countries of the Organisation for Economic Co-operation and Development (OECD) by 2015 and then to expand this to include the big emerging economies from around 2020. The company-level cap-and-trade systems that have been put in place in Switzerland, New Zealand and the north-eastern U.S. states, the plans to set up such systems in Japan. Australia and California and the interest being shown in establishing a U.S. federal system are all welcome developments in this context.

To support cap-and-trade systems around the world, the EU is sharing the lessons learnt from the EU ETS and the results of independent monitoring and evaluation with all interested parties and stakeholders.

NOTES AND QUESTIONS

1.   *The Cap.* How and by whom is the cap calculated under the EU-ETS? The EU aims to lower total carbon emissions of covered sectors to 21% below the sectors' 2005 emissions by 2020. Will this be accomplished?

2.   *Allocations of allowances.* How are allowances allocated under the EU-ETS? For the optimum operation of the system, should allowances be given away for free or sold by auction? How should new entrants be accommodated?

---

[55] www.icapcarbonaction.com.

3.   *Windfall profits.* In the early years of the operation of the EU-ETS, many emitters were mistakenly allocated many more emission allowances than they needed, creating opportunities for windfall profits, especially because the initial allowances were distributed without charge. *See Carbon Trading: Cleaning Up*, THE ECONOMIST, May 6, 2006, at 75. Has this failing been corrected?

4.   *Fraud.* The EU-ETS has had to deal with fraud. In 2010, swindlers used fake emails to obtain access to electronic certificates that represented quantities of greenhouse gases; they then sold the certificates through trading accounts registered in Denmark and Britain, netting over 3 million euros.

5.   *Banking and borrowing.* During the third period of the EU-ETS there is no restriction on banking or borrowing. Allowances are issued annually but they are valid for covering emissions in any year within the trading period 2013–2020.

6.   *International Offsets.* What provision is there in the EU-ETS for international offset credits?

7.   *The carbon market.* The EU-ETS puts a price on carbon. Individuals, NGOs, and non-EU companies are free to buy and sell carbon allowances in the open market. Is the EU-ETS open to links to carbon trading markets around the world?

8.   *Carbon leakage.* To address the problem of carbon leakage, companies and industries deemed subject to carbon leakage will receive a free allocation of allowances. Under Article 10a of the revised ETS Directive, a sector is deemed to be exposed to a significant risk of carbon leakage if:

- The extent to which the sum of direct and indirect additional costs induced by the implementation of the directive would lead to an increase of production cost, calculated as a proportion of the Gross Value Added, of at least 5%; and

- The trade intensity (imports and exports) of the sector with countries outside the EU is above 10%.

A sector is also deemed to be exposed to a significant risk of carbon leakage if (1) the sum of direct and indirect additional costs is at least 30%; or (2) the non-EU trade intensity is above 30%.

Is this sufficient to protect against carbon leakage?

9.   *Transaction costs under the EU-ETS.* EU businesses subject to the EU-ETS incur substantial transaction costs — costs that necessarily arise in the course of participating in the emission trading system. These include: (1) application costs; (2) implementation of emissions management; (3) monitoring; (4) reporting; (5) abatement measures; (6) trading measures; and (7) strategy planning.

10.   *The Aviation directive.* The aviation sector was included in EU-ETS beginning January 1, 2012, under the provisions of EU Directive 2008/101/EC. The EU-ETS applies to all flights arriving at or departing from any EU airport.

11.   *Goals for 2020.* The EU goal for 2020 is to reduce total GHG emissions by 20% compared to 1990 levels, to get 20% of its energy from renewable energy sources and to reduce its energy consumption to 20% below projected levels.

NOTE ON THE APPLICATION OF THE EU-ETS TO INTERNATIONAL AVIATION

EU Directive 2008/101/EC extended the ETS to airlines (including those headquartered in non-EU countries) that operate flights arriving or departing at airports in 30 European countries. International airlines that operate in Europe therefore must annually redeem carbon-dioxide allowances commensurate with the volume of their recorded carbon emissions or pay a penalty price. In 2009, three major U.S. airlines and the Air Transport Association of America filed suit in the High Court of Justice of England and Wales seeking to quash the regulations implementing this Directive. The English court, in accordance with EU law, sought a preliminary ruling from the Court of Justice of the European Union (ECJ) on the matter of EU law, certifying the following four questions:

1. Are the claimants entitled to rely on customary norms of international law; the provisions of the Chicago Convention,[56] the Kyoto Protocol,[57] or the Open Skies Agreement[58] as benchmarks against which to judge the Directive's validity?

2. Is the Directive invalid for contravening one or more of the customary law norms?

3. Is the Directive invalid for contravening a treaty norm?

4. Is the Directive invalid for unilaterally applying the ETS to international aviation activities governed by the standards found in global conventions or promulgated by the International Civil Aviation Organization (ICAO)?

The ECJ, on 12 December 2012, upheld the regulations and the Aviation Directive against this legal challenge. Case C-366/10, *Air Transp. Ass'n of Am. v. Secretary of State for Energy and Climate Change (ECJ)*, *available at* http://curia. europa.eu, accessed 2 April 2013.

As a threshold matter, the ECJ ruled that under Article 216(2) of the Treaty on the Functioning of the European Union, international agreements concluded by the EU are binding upon EU institutions and prevail over acts of the EU. Thus the validity of an act of the EU, such as a Directive, may be affected by the fact that it is incompatible with international law. But rules of international law may defeat an EU act only where the provisions of the treaty in question "appear, as regards their content, to be unconditional and sufficiently precise." (paras. 52–55).

The ECJ found that the Directive was compatible with the treaties in question. Since the ETS is not a tax or a charge on airport fuel, it does not contravene Article 11 of the Open Skies Agreement. The ECJ also ruled that there was no inconsistency between the Directive and the environmental standards under the Chicago Convention, the Kyoto Protocol or ICAO. (paras. 148–56).

---

[56] Convention on International Civil Aviation, Dec. 7, 1944, as amended, 15 U.N.T.S. 295, ICAO Doc. 7300/9 (2006).

[57] Kyoto Protocol to the United Nations Framework Convention on Climate Change, Dec. 11, 1997, 2303 U.N.T.S. 148.

[58] EU-US Air Transport Agreement, Apr. 30, 2007, as amended March 25, 2010, 28 U.S.T. 5367.

As to the customary law norms in question — norms recognizing the sovereignty of states over their airspace; the illegitimacy of claims to sovereignty over the high seas; and the freedom to fly over the high seas, the ECJ stated that the Aviation Directive did not impinge on such norms because the application of the ETS occurs only when aircraft voluntarily land in the territory of one of the Member States covered by the Directive. Thus, the application of the Directive is founded on the physical presence of aircraft in the EU area. It makes no difference that the relevant events occur partly outside EU territory. (paras. 127–29).

The Aviation Directive obviously presents important economic and political issues as well as legal issues. Under a U.S. law[59] enacted in 2012, in opposition to the extraterritorial feature of the Aviation Directive, the U.S. Secretary of Transportation has the authority to forbid U.S. carriers from participating in the ETS where such a ban is determined by the Secretary to be in the public interest; and to take such action as may be necessary to hold U.S. carriers harmless from liability under the ETS. The Secretary is also empowered to conduct international negotiations on the issue with a view to finding a global solution.

How should this row be settled? Should the U.S. file an interstate action against the EU? It may do so at the ICAO, before the US-EU Joint Committee or at the World Trade Organization.

EVALUATING THE EUROPEAN UNION'S EMISSIONS TRADING SCHEME

Phase III of the EU's Emission Trading Scheme, which runs from 2013 to 2120, is beset with major problems. The revised ETS Directive, 2009/29/EC, makes substantial changes and allows free allocation of allowances to all sectors except installations for the production of electricity. Industrial sectors are allocated free allowances on the basis of product benchmarks. Commission Decision of 27 April 2011 determining transition Union-wide rules for harmonized free allocation of emission allowances.

In 2013, the price for carbon allowances in the EU crashed (hitting a low of 2.63 euros per ton in April 2013) because of a glut of allowances on the market. This huge oversupply is attributed to the large number of allowances for sale in the EU that stem from reduction schemes in other countries under the EU scheme of linking the EU ETS with global schemes such as the Clean Development Mechanism, Joint Implementation and other nations' cap and trade schemes. EU companies are now banking these low-priced, surplus allowances for use after 2020, when the ETS Phase IV is expected to begin.

On July 16, 2013, the EU Parliament approved an emergency measure to delay the auctioning of the 900 million allowances scheduled for 2013–2015 until 2019–2020. This was a measure to restore sanity to the carbon allowance market, but is regarded as only a temporary fix. Discussions are underway as of the end of 2013 on a major structural reform of the EU ETS so that it can operate properly.

---

[59] The European Union Emissions Trading Scheme Prohibition Act of 2011, Pub. L. No. 112-200, 126 STAT. 1477 (2012), codified at 49 U.S.C. § 40101 note.

The future of the EU Aviation Emission Directive is also in doubt. On 4 October 2013, the International Civil Aviation Organization (ICAO) voted to rebuff the EU, stating that no country has the right to levy unauthorized charges on international airlines. The EU has suspended the effectiveness of the Aviation Emissions Directive to 2016. The ICAO has also called for a global plan to reduce aviation GHG emissions for adoption at its meeting in 2016, to be effective in 2020.

Thus the EU ETS is now in a period of transition and its future structure is uncertain.

F.   The Ethics of Climate Change and the Divide Between the Developed and Developing World

Concern over environmental justice arose in the 1980s as communities of color challenged agency environmental decisions on the basis of distributional and participatory inequities. Adaptation and mitigation of climate change raise similar domestic issues[60] and, in addition, major international issues of equity come to the fore. In this section we introduce the ethics of climate change on the international level, the deep divide between industrial and developing countries that runs through all international negotiations on climate change and is reflected in the international agreements on climate change that we will analyze in the sections below.

Retributive and distributive justice and fairness are consistent themes in international climate change forums. Developing countries and coalitions such as the Pacific Island Developing States (PIDS) and the larger Alliance of Small Island States (AOSIS) lobby for ambitious mitigation actions by developed states as well as financial aid and technology transfer from developed states for adaptation and capacity-building. As a result, climate change financial instruments have proliferated, including not only the Global Environmental Fund (GEF), which developing states distrust because it is controlled by the industrial countries, but also the Fast-Start Finance Module, the Long-Term Finance Fund, the Green Climate Fund, the Least Developing Countries Fund, the Adaptation Fund, and the Special Climate Change Fund.[61] Through these and other funding mechanisms, billions of dollars are dispensed each year to developing countries to fund various climate change-related projects.

What are the ethical responsibilities of the industrial world toward developing countries?

Developing countries charge that the developed world is the cause of climate change and that retributive justice demands that developing countries take mitigation actions to prevent future climate change. Developing countries also demand that developing countries pay for the consequences of climate change on their territories and societies. These ethical responsibilities of developed countries are analyzed by Eric A. Posner and David Weisbach in their book, CLIMATE CHANGE

---

[60] *See e.g.*, DENIS G. ARNOLD (ed.), THE ETHICS OF CLIMATE CHANGE (Cambridge: Cambridge University Press, 2011).

[61] *See* http://www.unfccc.int/financeportal.

JUSTICE (Princeton: Princeton University Press, 2010), which concludes that, while climate change aid is appropriate, climate change should not be employed as a vehicle for distributive justice, distributing wealth from rich to poor countries. (p. 191).

Do developed countries bear responsibility for climate change beyond technology transfer and financial aid? Specifically should developed countries compensate developing countries for loss and damages from the impacts of climate change? This issue was broached for the first time at the Doha Conference of the Parties (COP-I8) of the UNFCCC in December 2012. Consider the following COP-decision:

DOHA CONFERENCE OF THE PARTIES TO THE UNFCCC
Decision 3/CP.18 of 8 December 2012, *available at*, http://unfccc.int/resource/docs/2012/cop18/eng/08a01.pdf

> Approaches to address loss and damage associated with climate change impacts in developing countries that are particularly vulnerable to the adverse effects of climate change to enhance adaptive capacity

The Conference of the Parties,

Recognizing the need to strengthen international cooperation and expertise in order to understand and reduce loss and damage associated with the adverse effects of climate change, including impacts related to extreme weather events and slow onset events,

Highlighting the important and fundamental role of the Convention in addressing loss and damage associated with climate change impacts, especially in developing countries that are particularly vulnerable to the adverse effects of climate change, including by promoting leadership, collaboration and cooperation, at the national, regional and international levels and for a broad range of sectors and ecosystems, in order to enable coherent and synergistic approaches to address such loss and damage,

Reaffirming the need for Parties to take precautionary measures, in accordance with the principles and provisions of the Convention, to anticipate, prevent or minimize the causes of climate change and mitigate its adverse effects, and underlining that the lack of full scientific certainty should not be used as reason for postponing action,

Appreciating the progress made in the implementation, and the importance of the continuation, of the work programme to address the loss and damage associated with the adverse effects of climate change,

Acknowledging ongoing initiatives relevant to loss and damage associated with the adverse effects of climate change at the national, international and regional levels and that there is a need to scale up these efforts, including by enhancing support and coordination in the broader context of climate-resilient sustainable development,

1. *Acknowledges the need to enhance support, including finance, technology and*

capacity-building, for relevant actions;

2. *Notes* that a range of approaches, methods and tools is available to assess the risk of and to respond to loss and damage associated with the adverse effects of climate change, and that their selection depends upon regional, national and local capacity, context and circumstances, and involves the engagement of all relevant stakeholders;

3. *Also notes* that there are important linkages between extreme weather events and slow onset events, and the importance of building comprehensive climate risk management approaches;

4. *Agrees* that comprehensive, inclusive and strategic responses are needed to address loss and damage associated with the adverse effects of climate change;

5. *Also agrees* that the role of the Convention in promoting the implementation of approaches to address loss and damage associated with the adverse effects of climate change includes, *inter alia*, the following:

  (a) Enhancing knowledge and understanding of comprehensive risk management approaches to address loss and damage associated with the adverse effects of climate change, including slow onset impacts;

  (b) Strengthening dialogue, coordination, coherence and synergies among relevant stakeholders;

  (c) Enhancing action and support, including finance, technology and capacity-building, to address loss and damage associated with the adverse effects of climate change;

6. *Invites* all Parties, taking into account common but differentiated responsibilities and respective capabilities and specific national and regional development priorities, objectives and circumstances, to enhance action on addressing loss and damage associated with the adverse effects of climate change, taking into account national development processes, by undertaking, *inter alia*, the following:

  (a) Assessing the risk of loss and damage associated with the adverse effects of climate change, including slow onset impacts;

  (b) Identifying options and designing and implementing country-driven risk management strategies and approaches, including risk reduction, and risk transfer and risk-sharing mechanisms;

  (c) The systematic observation of, and data collection on, the impacts of climate change, in particular slow onset impacts, and accounting for losses, as appropriate;

  (d) Implementing comprehensive climate risk management approaches, including scaling up and replicating good practices and pilot initiatives;

  (e) Promoting an enabling environment that would encourage investment and the involvement of relevant stakeholders in climate risk management;

  (f) Involving vulnerable communities and populations, and civil society, the private sector and other relevant stakeholders, in the assessment of and response to loss and damage;

(g)   Enhancing access to, sharing and the use of data, at the regional, national and subnational levels, such as hydrometeorological data and metadata, on a voluntary basis, to facilitate the assessment and management of climate-related risk;

7. Requests developed country Parties to provide developing country Parties with finance, technology and capacity-building, in accordance with decision I/CP.16 and other relevant decisions of the Conference of the Parties;

8. Decides to establish, at its nineteenth session, institutional arrangements, such as an international mechanism, including functions and modalities, elaborated in accordance with the role of the Convention as defined in paragraph 5 above, to address loss and damage associated with the impacts of climate change in developing countries that are particularly vulnerable to the adverse effects of climate changes.

NOTES AND QUESTIONS

1.   This COP 18 decision seems to go beyond aid from developed countries for adaptation and mitigation by developing countries and takes the view that compensation for loss and damage from climate change is due as a matter of right to developing countries. What kind of international instrument did the COP 18 call for to address this issue?

2.   Following up Decision 3/CP.18, the Parties adopted Decision -/CP.19 at the Warsaw COP in 2013, establishing the Warsaw International Mechanism for Loss and Damage Associated with Climate Change Impacts in Developing Countries in order to "address loss and damage associated with the adverse impacts of climate change . . . in a comprehensive, integrated and coherent manner." (Para. 5). This Decision (para. 14) "requests" developed country Parties "to provide developing country Parties with finance, technology, and capacity building."

3.   Is there an ethical or a legal case for compensation for losses and damages? Do developing countries have a case to recover losses and damages under customary international law?

G.   The United Nations Framework Convention on Climate Change (UNFCCC)

Scientists are now predicting that if the world remains on its present course in terms of allowing carbon dioxide and other greenhouse gases to accumulate in the atmosphere, the Earth's climate will warm on the average between 2 to 6 degrees C by the end of the present century. Since the phenomenon that we now call the "greenhouse effect" and the ability of GHG to cause climate warming has been known for over a century,[62] why was the alarm over global warming so slow in coming? Not until the 1980s did scientists and governments seek to raise consciousness about the problem of climate change and its possible impacts. Two key reasons for the delay in recognizing the global warming threat were (1) global

---

[62] MARK MASLIN, GLOBAL WARMING 23–25 (Oxford: Oxford University Press, 2004).

temperature data between 1940 and 1980, and (2) the lack of public awareness of environmental problems before the late 1970s.[63] The first reason is perhaps the most important: between 1940 and 1980, global temperatures were below average, and some scientists even predicted an imminent "little Ice age."[64] But scientists now attribute this cool period to the influence of the sunspot cycle.[65] In the 1980s global temperatures began their precipitous rise, which still continues, and prominent scientists quickly made the connection between warming temperatures and the increase of GHG in the atmosphere. The scientific warnings fell on fertile ground because the 1980s also saw the rise of worldwide environmental consciousness, the formation of environmental NGOs, and more environmental stories in the media.[66]

One of the earliest international conferences on global warming was convened by the government of Canada in 1988, in Toronto, which sounded a warning that, "Humanity is conducting an unintended, uncontrolled, globally pervasive experiment whose ultimate consequence could be second only to a global nuclear war."[67] In 1988 the IPCC was formed and, in December of that year, the United Nations General Assembly passed a landmark resolution: Protection of the Global Climate for Present and Future Generations of Mankind, G.A. Res. 43/53 (December 6, 1988). From 1989 to 1992, a flurry of international meetings and conferences prepared the way for the 1992 United Nations Conference on Environment and Development in Rio de Janiero, which adopted as its centerpiece agreement, the United Nations Framework Convention on Climate Change (UNFCCC). The UNFCCC has achieved universal participation; 194 states and the European Union are parties, and its annual Conference of the Parties (COP) has served as the principal forum for international climate change policy since 1992.

The text of the UNFCCC is reprinted in the Document Supplement. Note that the UNFCCC divides the parties into three groups: (1) Annex I parties — industrialized parties plus parties such as the Russian Federation, the Baltic states, and several central and eastern European states with economies in transition; (2) Annex II parties — industrialized OECD states but not the countries with economies in transition; and (3) Non Annex I parties — all other parties including mainly developing countries. In addition 49 parties classed as least developing countries by the United Nations are given special consideration in the UNFCCC.

Read the UNFCCC and answer the following questions:

1. *Objective.* What is the declared objective of the UNFCCC? (Art. 2). Is this sufficient? Does this mean that the parties to the UNFCCC envisage allowing climate change to take place to some extent? Is there a time

---

[63] *Id.* at 27.

[64] *Id.* at 27–28.

[65] *Id.*

[66] *See generally* John Gribbin, Hothouse Earth: The Greenhouse Effect and Gaia (London: Grove Weidenfeld, 1989).

[67] Quoted in Daniel Bodansky, *The United Nations Framework Convention on Climate Change: A Commentary,* 18 Yale J. Int'l. L. 451, 461 (1993).

frame for action under the UNFCCC? As of 2013, global GHG emissions are some 32% higher than when the UNFCCC was concluded. As we have seen, the atmospheric level of CO_2 now stands at 395 parts per million (ppm) and is increasing at a rate of about 3 ppm each year. Many scientists state that a "safe" level of CO_2 is about 350 ppm, which would be higher than the pre-industrial amounts, but would safely prevent further change.[68]

2. *Principles.* Consider the Principles of the UNFCCC. These bear a distinct resemblance to the global responsibility principles of the Rio Declaration. Are any of these principles action-forcing? Do they provide parameters for future work of the parties?

3. *Commitments.* Article 4.1 of the UNFCCC obligates the parties to make national inventories of GHG emissions and sinks, cooperate on a wide variety of fronts to deal with climate change, promote training and public awareness, and take climate change considerations into account in decisionmaking. Article 4.2 contains commitments directly related to mitigation of climate change. Article 4.2 (a) to (f) establishes commitments only for Annex I parties. Is a uniformity of approach required by Annex I parties? Read carefully paragraphs (a) and (b) of Article 4.2. Is there a clear or strong commitment to dealing with GHG emissions and sinks? Articles 4.3 to 4.10 concern Non-Annex I developing country parties and the relationship between developing and developed parties. What are the specific commitments of Non-Annex I parties?

4. *Research and systematic observation.* (Article 5). Which parties bear the greatest burden under this article?

5. *Training and Public Awareness.* (Article 6). This article appears to place equal burdens on all parties.

6. *Conference of the Parties.* (Article 7). A key to understanding the UNFCCC is the fact that it is a framework convention that establishes an international process to deal with climate change and that with the benefit of additional information and greater political will, progressively greater action will be taken to solve the problem. The Conference of the Parties (COP) as the "supreme body" of the Convention is crucial to the future evolution of the climate change regime and to its future success. The COP is a forum for information reporting, negotiations, and concluding future commitments. The COP, which meets annually, will hold its 20th meeting (COP-20) in 2014. Each conference of the parties takes certain substantive and procedural decisions to advance the climate change regime. In the materials that follow we will largely deal with the work of the COP since 1992.

7. *Secretariat.* (Article 8). What are the functions of the Secretariat? The permanent Secretariat of the UNFCCC is headquartered in Bonn,

---

[68] Statement of James Hanson of NASA to the American Geophysical Union Conference in San Francisco, December 2007, as reported by Bill McKibben, *Remember This: 350 Parts Per Million,* WASHINGTON POST, 15 December 2007, at A15.

Germany and constitutes about 500 full-time staff.

8. *The Subsidiary Body for Scientific and Technological Advice (SBSTA) and the Subsidiary Body for Implementation (SBI).* (Articles 9 and 10). The parties to the UNFCCC have established numerous subsidiary bodies, but these two bodies, which are established by the Convention itself, are among the most important. What is the function of these bodies?

9. *Financial Mechanism.* (Article 11). What is the function of the Financial Mechanism? The COP has established a variety of additional funding mechanisms. Note that Article 21 on Interim Arrangements entrusts the GEF with the operation of the Financial Mechanism on an interim basis. The GEF is still central to many of the financial aspects of climate change, but many developing countries distrust the GEF and additional funding sources have been created without the GEF's involvement.

10. *Implementation Communications.* (Articles 12 and 13). These two articles speak to the process of implementation of the UNFCCC. Note the distinction between developing and Annex I parties.

11. *Settlement of Disputes.* (Article 14). This article has never been used.

12. *Adoption of Amendments and Protocols.* (Articles 15, 16, and 17). What is the difference between amendments and protocols? What is the process for adoption of amendments? Does an adopted amendment bind a party who has not specifically accepted it? Is a protocol adopted by the COP binding upon parties who have not specifically accepted it?

13. *Right to Vote.* (Article 18). In the COP how is voting conducted? Does the European Union have a right to vote independent from its member states?

H. The Kyoto Protocol

The first Conference of the Parties (COP-1) after the conclusion of the UNFCCC was held in Berlin in 1995. The most important outcome of COP-1 was agreement on the Berlin Mandate, which, after a review of the adequacy of UNFCCC Article 4.2(a) and (b) on industrialized countries' emission commitments stated as follows:

The Berlin Mandate

Conference of Parties

Review of adequacy of Article 4, para 2(a) and (b) [industrialized-country emission commitments],

including proposals related to a protocol and decisions on follow-up.

The Conference of Parties, having reviewed [the commitments] and concluded that these are not adequate, agrees to begin a process to enable it to take appropriate action for the period beyond 2000, including the strengthening of the commitments of Annex I Parties . . .

2. The process will, *inter alia:*

(a) Aim, as the priority in the process of strengthening the commitments in Article 4.2 (a) and (b) of the Convention, for developed country/other parties included in Annex I, both

　• to elaborate policies and measures, as well as

　• to set quantified limitation and reduction objectives with specified time-frames, such as 2005, 2010 and 2020, for their anthropogenic emissions by sources and removals of sinks by greenhouse gases not controlled by the Montreal Protocol taking into account the differences in starting points and approaches, economic structures and resource bases, the need to maintain strong and sustainable economic growth . . .

(b) Not introduce any new commitments for Parties not included in Annex I, but reaffirm existing commitments in Article 4.1 and continue to advance the implementation of these commitments in order to achieve sustainable development . . .

(c) Take into account any result from the review . . .

(d) Consider, as provided in Article 4.2(e), the coordination among Annex I Parties, as appropriate, of relevant economic and administrative instruments . . .

(e) Provide for the exchange of experience on national activities in areas of interest, particularly those identified in the review and synthesis and available national communications: and

(f) Provide for a review mechanism.

3. The process will be carried out in the light of the best available scientific information and assessment on climate change and its impacts, as well as relevant technical, social and economic information, including, *inter alia*, IPCC reports . . .

4. The process will include in its early stages an analysis and assessment, to identify possible policies and measures for Annex I Parties . . . [and] . . . could identify environmental and economic impacts and the results that could be achieved with regard to time horizons such as 2005, 2010 and 2020.

5. The protocol of the Alliance of Small Island States [AOSIS — proposing a 20% reduction in industrialized-country emissions by 2005] . . . should be included for consideration in the process.

6. The process should begin without delay and be conducted as a matter of urgency . . . to ensure completion of the work as early as possible in 1997 with a view to adopting the results at the third session of the Conference of the Parties.

After the Berlin Mandate, the parties to the UNFCCC established a negotiating body, the Ad Hoc Group on the Berlin Mandate (AGBM), which after several negotiating sessions, concluded what became the Kyoto Protocol, which was approved by the parties at COP-3 in Kyoto, Japan in December 1997.

Read carefully the Kyoto Protocol, which is reprinted in the **Document Supplement**, and answer the following questions:

1. *Substantive obligations.* Articles 2, 3, 5, and 7 of the Kyoto Protocol contain substantive obligations for the Annex I parties to the UNFCCC. What are these obligations? Why were Annex I parties singled out? Was this in accordance with the Berlin Mandate?

2. *Quantified emission limitation or reduction commitment.* The central obligation of the Kyoto Protocol is Article 3, which goes beyond the obligations in UNFCCC Article 4 by requiring quantified GHG emission limitations or reductions for Annex I parties. What GHGs are covered by this commitment? (See Annex A). Inclusion of three synthetic GHGs was controversial. HFCs, PFCs and SF6 are primarily used as substitutes for the stratospheric ozone-depleting substances controlled by the Montreal Protocol.

3. *Base years.* What are the base years against which the quantified emission limitations or reductions are measured? (Articles 3.7 and 3.8).

4. *Differentiated commitments.* Note the list of required emission reductions in Annex B of the Kyoto Protocol differentiates substantially between Annex I countries. Parties with commitments under Annex B have emission targets that are expressed in terms of allowed emissions or "assigned amounts." The allowed emissions are divided into Assigned Amount Units (AAUs).

Annex B

Quantified emission limitation or reduction commitment (percentage of base year or period)

Party	
Australia	108
Austria	92
Belgium	92
Bulgaria*	92
Canada	94
Croatia*	95
Czech Republic*	92
Denmark	92
Estonia*	92
European Community	92
Finland	92
France	92
Germany	92
Greece	92
Hungary *	94
Iceland	110
Ireland	92
Italy	92

Japan	94
Latvia*	92
Liechtenstein	92
Lithuania*	92
Luxembourg	92
Monaco	92
Netherlands	92
New Zealand	100
Norway	101
Poland*	94
Portugal	92
Romania*	92
Russian Federation*	100
Slovakia*	92
Slovenia*	92
Spain	92
Sweden	92
Switzerland	92
Ukraine*	100
United Kingdom of Great Britain and Northern Ireland	92
United States of America	93

* Countries that are undergoing the process of transition to a market economy.

5. *Total mandated reduction in* GHG *under the Kyoto Protocol.* Assuming perfect compliance with the Kyoto Protocol, what is the total mandated reduction from 1990 GHG emission levels? (Article 3.1).

6. *Compliance period.* Note that rather than a single-year, fixed date for attainment of the emission reduction targets, the Protocol establishes a multiyear period of 2008–2012. (Article 3.1). The purpose of this provision was to give parties flexibility in meeting their target obligations.

7. *Accounting for sinks.* Taking into account land use, land use change and forestry (LULUCF) was controversial at Kyoto because of the measurement problems involved. Many parties believed that taking LULUCF into account would simply dilute the necessity for GHG emission reductions. However, the Protocol takes sequestration from land use change into account. The Kyoto Protocol Article 3.3 requires each Annex I party to use "net changes" in GHG emissions and removals by sinks resulting from direct human-induced land-use change and forestry activities *since 1990* to calculate compliance with its targeted limitation or reduction commitment.

Note that this accounting for sinks is limited to net afforestation, reforestation, and deforestation activities. *Preservation of existing forests therefore may not be used under this provision.* This provision rewards those parties that are increasing their sinks and penalizes parties whose sinks are decreasing.

Article 3.7 of the Protocol ameliorates this penalizing impact somewhat by providing that Annex I parties whose land-use and forestry constituted a net source of GHG emissions in 1990 (those which were deforesting in 1990) shall include those emissions in its base year calculation, which has the effect of raising their allowed emissions during the commitment period.

Article 3.4 of the Protocol adds an additional twist: prior to COP-1, parties must provide to the Subsidiary Body for Scientific and Technical Advice (SBSTA) data to establish its level of carbon stocks in 1990 so that estimates can be made of changes in carbon stocks in subsequent years. Under Article 3.4 an Annex I party may elect to include additional LULUCF activities to meet their 2008–2012 commitment obligations. Such additional LULUCF activities may include forest management, cropland management, grazing land management, and revegetation. *Thus, when LULUCF activities under Articles 3.3 and 3.4 result in a net removal of GHGs, an Annex I party can issue GHG Removal Units (RMUs[69]) on the basis of these activities as part of meeting its commitment under Article 3.1.* Note that changes in carbon stock, which are elective in the first commitment period, must be included in commitment periods subsequent to 2008–2012.

PROBLEM 4-6
HOW TO DETERMINE A KYOTO PROTOCOL PARTY'S "ASSIGNED AMOUNT UNITS"

Article 3 (1) of the Kyoto Protocol (KP) states that Parties included in Annex I must ensure that their aggregate carbon dioxide equivalent (CO_2 eq) emissions of Annex A GHG "do not exceed their assigned amounts," calculated pursuant to their quantified emission limitation and reduction commitments inscribed in Annex B. How are "assigned amount units" calculated?

Article 3(7) states that "in the first quantified emission limitation and reduction period, from 2008 to 2012, the assigned amount for each Party included in Annex I shall be equal to the percentage inscribed for it in Annex B of its aggregate anthropogenic carbon dioxide equivalent emissions of the gases listed in Annex A in 1990, or the base year or period determined in accordance with paragraph 5 above, multiplied by 5."

The referenced paragraph 5 gives Annex I Parties that are undergoing the process of transition to a market economy a choice whether to choose 1990 as a base year or another year in accordance with the COP decision 9/CP.2.

Definition and function of "assigned amount"

An assigned amount unit (AAU) is a term of art in the KP. In the UNFCC Kyoto Protocol Reference Manual, p. 118, an assigned amount unit is: "[a] Kyoto unit representing an allowance to emit one metric tonne of carbon dioxide equivalent.

---

[69] One RMU is equal to 1 ton of CO_2, which can be counted toward meeting a Kyoto target.

AAUs are issued up to a level of a Party's initial assigned amount. *At the end of the commitment period, each Party must ensure that its total Annex A emissions over the commitment period are less or equal to its total assigned amount."* (emphasis supplied).

Calculation of assigned amount

A Party's assigned amount is calculated as follows [UNFCCC Reference Manual, p. 55]: "The exact quantity of each Party's assigned amount in CO_2 eq must be calculated prior to the commitment period or within one year of the entry into force of the Kyoto Protocol for that Party, whichever is later. A Party's initial assigned amount shall be calculated by multiplying its Annex A emissions in its base year by its target in Annex B multiplied by 5."

The first step in calculating a Party's initial AAU is to determine the Party's base year. Most Annex I Parties have a mandatory base year of 1990 (1995 for HFCs, PFCs and SF).

Certain Parties in transition have selected different base years: Bulgaria: 1988; Hungary: the average of years 1985–1987; Poland: 1988; Romania: 1989; and Slovenia: 1986). *Note — it is in a party's interest to select a base year in which GHG emissions were as great as possible.*

> Note: during the commitment period a KP Party's AAU will be modified (plus or minus) by other provisions of the KP: Art. 3(3), 3(4), and 3(7) for LULUCF; Art. 6 for JI; Art. 12 for CDM; and Art. 17 for trading AAUs.

PROBLEM 4-7
TAKING ADVANTAGE OF THE SINK PROVISIONS OF THE KYOTO PROTOCOL

Country A is an Annex I party subject to the Kyoto Protocol. Country A is located in a tropical zone and during the 1980s and early 1990s, large areas of Country A were deforested. Country A is developing economically and its GHG emissions greatly increased even after it accepted the Kyoto Protocol in 1997. In order to meet its Kyoto commitment, Country A decided that, rather than stemming GHG emissions, it would take maximum advantage of Articles 3.3, 3.4, and 3.7 of the Kyoto Protocol. What strategy should Country A have adopted to maximize the advantages of these three articles?

The COP-7 in Marrakesh in 2001, adopted the Marrakesh Accords,[70] which provide guidance to the parties in accounting for LULUCF. Note that Country A, if it chose to take advantage of the Article 3.4 option, could have calculated LULUCF as an annual flow rate of carbon sequestered or emitted. The LULUCF rules allow Country A to claim carbon credits from business-as-usual forest management. Is this good policy? Should "additionality" — carbon sequestration above normal carbon intake of existing forests — be required? Note also that as forests age there is a declining rate of carbon sequestration.

---

[70] COP-7 Decision 2/CMP 7, Modalities, Rules, and Guidelines relating to Land Use, Land-Use Change, and Forestry Activities under the Kyoto Protocol.

8. *The European Union "bubble."* Read carefully Article 4 of the Kyoto Protocol. In 1997, the EU had 15 member states. Does this provision make it easier for the 15 EU member states to comply with the limitation and reduction commitments of Article 3? In 2013, the EU has expanded to 28 member states. Can the "EU bubble" be expanded to include additional EU member states? Can non-EU Annex I parties take advantage of Article 4?

9. *Joint Implementation (JI).* Read carefully Article 6 of the Kyoto Protocol. Joint implementation (JI) is a market-based mechanism under the Kyoto Protocol whereby one Annex I party can obtain credit for a reduction or removal project in another Annex I country. Joint implementation offers Annex I parties a flexible and cost efficient means of fulfilling a part of their Kyoto commitments. Joint implementation requires a bilateral investment agreement between two Annex I parties as a precondition (Article 6.1(a). Pursuant to such an agreement, the investor Annex I party or a company under its jurisdiction then implements a project in the territory of the host Annex I country that either reduces GHG emissions or enhances GHG sinks. The project involved must provide a GHG reduction or a sink enhancement that is additional to any that would otherwise occur (Article 6.1(b)).

There are two separate procedures for verifying and authorizing the issuance of the Emission Reduction Units (ERUs) that are the outcome of JI.[71] Under the Track 1 procedure, the host party may issue the ERUs certifying that they are additional to what would otherwise occur. But to be eligible for Track 1 approval the host party must fulfill several eligibility requirements: The host must (1) be a party to the Kyoto Protocol; (2) its assigned commitment amounts under Kyoto must be calculated and recorded pursuant to Articles 3.7 and 3.8 of the Protocol; (3) it must have in place national systems for estimation of anthropogenic emissions and sinks as well as a national registry as required by Articles 5.1 and 7.4 of the Protocol; (4) it must have submitted its most recent inventory and supplemental information under Articles 5.2 and 7.1 of the Protocol. Track 1 is a "simplified" procedure which allows the host party to verify JI. If the host party does not meet the eligibility requirements for Track I, the verification of the reductions must be submitted to the Joint Implementation Supervisory Committee (JISC) established under the Protocol. Under this so-called Track 2 procedure, the transfer of the ERUs must receive independent verification by an entity approved by the JISC before they may be issued by the host party.

Note that a private company in Country A may have an incentive to participate in a JI project in Country B as an international investment. The private company may, for example, buy electric generating facilities in Country B, and, after modernizing them, operate them at a profit. The private company can then sell the ERUs earned from JI to Country A, which will buy the ERUs in order to meet its Kyoto commitment.

---

[71] JI Guidelines, Decision 13, CMP-l (2005).

10. *Clean Development Mechanism (CDM).* Read carefully Article 12 of the Kyoto Protocol. The Clean Development Mechanism (CDM) is another market-based flexibility mechanism which facilitates compliance with Kyoto commitments by Annex I parties. CDM, like JI, presumes the existence of a bilateral investment agreement, in the case of CDM between an Annex I party and a Non-Annex I party (usually a developing country). Under the framework of such bilateral investment agreement, a private company (or the Annex I country itself) implements an emission reduction project in the Non-Annex I country. The investment project may fall into two different categories. Category one would be a project that reduces GHG emissions, for example a rural electrification project using solar panels or the installation of energy efficient boilers. Category two would be a project involving afforestation or reforestation activities to enhance carbon sinks in the Non-Annex I country. Either category of project produces Certified Emission Reductions (CERs), units of tons of carbon credits that may be used by the Annex I party toward meeting its Kyoto Article 3 commitment. In order to generate CERs the CDM credit must be approved by the Designated National Authorities in the Non-Annex I country and be submitted to and gain the approval of the CDM Executive Board, a Kyoto Protocol institution.

The CDM is designed to foster sustainable development and to achieve emission reductions in developing countries that have no commitments themselves under the Kyoto Protocol. A CDM project must provide emission reductions that are additional to what would have otherwise occurred. Public funding of a CDM project must not result in the diversion of official development assistance. With respect to Category one, projects involving nuclear power are not eligible. With respect to Category two, projects involving sinks, preserving existing forests will not qualify for CDM; only projects involving afforestation or reforestation are eligible. In addition, Annex I parties are limited in how much they can use CERs to satisfy their Kyoto commitments: an Annex I party may use CERs for up to 1% of its emissions in its base year, for each of the five years of the 2008-2012 commitment period.

Note that private companies that participate in CDM projects will generate CERs that can then be sold to Annex I governments seeking Kyoto credits.

CDM has generated much investment in developing countries, especially in China. Many CDM projects involve transfer of significant technology to developing countries. About 3000 CDM projects each year deliver about 500 million CERs each year.

As we have seen in the previous subsection, the EU Linking Directive that complements the EU Trading Directive establishing the EU-ETS, allows affected installations to generate GHG emission credits through CDM and JI projects.

Is it in the interests of developing countries to attract CDM projects? What should developing countries do to attract CDM projects?

11. *Emission Trading (ET). Read carefully Article 17 of the Kyoto Protocol.* Target-based Emission Trading (ET) is a third important market-based flexibility mechanism under the Kyoto Protocol. This article authorizes Annex I parties that have commitments under Annex B of the Protocol to use trading to meet emission target commitments under Article 3. Article 17 cautions, however, that ET shall be "supplemental to domestic actions" to comply with Article 3 commitments.

ET allows Annex I parties that have emission units to spare — emission units permitted but not used — to sell them to countries that are over their targets. Japan has been a major purchaser of ET units. In order to address the danger that a party may mistakenly oversell its units, Annex I parties are required to maintain a reserve of ERUs, CERs, AAUs and/or RMUs in its national registry. This reserve, which is called the "commitment period reserve," must not drop below 90% of the party's assigned amount or 100% of five times its most recently reviewed inventory, whichever is lowest.

Only Annex I parties that are also parties to the Kyoto Protocol and have assigned emission and reduction commitments under Annex B of the Protocol may participate in Emission Trading.

12. *Obligations for all UNFCCC parties.* Article 10 of the Kyoto Protocol is the only provision that contains substantive obligations for all parties to the UNFCCC. What are these obligations? Does this article go beyond what is already required under the UNFCCC?

13. *Financial obligations.* Article 11 of the Kyoto Protocol concerns financial obligations of Annex I parties in order to assist developing country parties with compliance with Kyoto Protocol Article 10.

14. *Institutions.* Institutional provisions are contained in Kyoto Protocol Articles 9, 13, 14, 15, and 16. Note the central role of the Conference of the Parties in Articles 9 and 13. Subsequent to 1997, the COP serves as the Meeting of the Parties of the Kyoto Protocol (CMP). Parties to the UNFCCC that are not parties to the Protocol, like the United States, are able to participate in the CMP as observers. The first CMP was held in Montreal, Canada in conjunction with COP-11 in 2005.

15. *Compliance.* Article 18 of the Kyoto Protocol mandates the development of compliance procedures and mechanisms.

16. *Disputes.* Article 19 makes the dispute settlement provision of the UN-FCCC applicable to the Kyoto Protocol.

17. *Final provisions.* Articles 20 to 28 concern matters such as amendments, entry into force, voting, reservations, withdrawal, and official languages. Canada withdrew from the Kyoto Protocol in 2011.

18. Note the synergism between the Kyoto Protocol and the Montreal Protocol on Substances that Deplete the Ozone Layer. Such substances as HCFCs and HFCs are both ozone-destroying gases and potent GHGs. The Montreal Protocol as amended phases out HCFCs by 2030, but takes no action against HFCs. Should there be more linkage and coordination between the Montreal Protocol and the UNFCCC regime?

19. The Kyoto Protocol entered into force on February 16, 2005. 191 parties signed and ratified the Kyoto Protocol. The United States signed the Protocol but did not ratify.

20. The United States was the only UNFCCC Annex I party that did not adhere to the Kyoto Protocol. The United States therefore did not have any obligations or commitments under the Kyoto Protocol. Canada joined the Kyoto Protocol but withdrew in 2011.

PROBLEM 4-8
OPTIONS FOR COMPLYING WITH THE KYOTO PROTOCOL

Country Z is an Annex I party under the UNFCCC, has ratified the Kyoto Protocol, and has an emission limitation and reduction commitment under Annex B. Country Z seeks to comply with its commitment in the most efficient way possible considering its particular economic characteristics.

1. Each Annex I party must submit national greenhouse gas inventory data to the UNFCCC. Secretariat in common format each year in the form of a National Report.

2. Each Annex I party subject to the Kyoto Protocol maintains a registry system that tracks and records the "Kyoto units" it holds in its national registry.

3. What are the options by which Country Z can comply with its commitment? Consider the following:

   a. Emission reductions (AAUs)

   b. Removal units (RMUs)

   c. Emission Reduction Units (ERUs)

   d. Certified Emission Reduction Units (CERs)

   e. Article 17 of the Protocol is a framework whereby ERUs, CERs, AAUs, and RMUs may be transferred among Annex I parties.

4. Country Z also operates a domestic emissions trading scheme at the national level. May domestic industries subject to its domestic emissions trading scheme satisfy their obligations under national law by holding AAUs, ERUs, CERs, or RMUs created under the Kyoto Protocol?

I. Compliance with the Kyoto Protocol

AN INTRODUCTION TO THE KYOTO PROTOCOL COMPLIANCE MECHANISM
http://unfccc.int/kyoto_protocol/compliance/items/3024.php

The Kyoto Protocol compliance mechanism is designed to strengthen the Protocol's environmental integrity, support the carbon markers credibility and ensure transparency of accounting by Parties. Its objective is to facilitate, promote and enforce compliance with the commitments under the Protocol. It is among the most comprehensive and rigorous systems of compliance for a multilateral environmental agreement. A strong and effective compliance mechanism is key to the success of the implementation of the Protocol.

The Compliance Committee is made up of two branches: a facilitative branch and an enforcement branch. As their names suggest, the facilitative branch aims to provide advice and assistance to Parties in order to promote compliance, whereas the enforcement branch has the responsibility to determine consequences for Parties not meeting their commitments. Both branches are composed of 10 members, including one representative from each of the five official UN regions (Africa, Asia, Latin America and the Caribbean, Central and Eastern Europe, and Western Europe and Others), one from the small island developing States, and two each from Annex I and non-Annex I Parties. The Committee also meets in a plenary composed of members of both branches, and a bureau, made up of the chairperson and vice-chairperson of each branch, supports its work. Decisions of the plenary and the facilitative branch may be taken by a three-quarters majority, while decisions of the enforcement branch require, in addition, a double majority of both Annex I and non-Annex Parties.

Through its branches, the Committee considers questions of implementation which can be raised by expert review teams under Article 8 of the Protocol, any Party with respect to itself, or a Party with respect to another party (supported by corroborating information). Each party designates an agent who signs submissions containing such questions, as well as comments. The bureau of the Committee allocates a question of implementation to the appropriate branch, based on their mandates. In addition, at any time during its consideration of a question of implementation, the enforcement branch may refer a question of implementation to the facilitative branch.

The enforcement branch is responsible for determining whether a Party included in Annex I (Annex I Party) is not in compliance with its emissions targets, the methodological and reporting requirements for greenhouse gas inventories, and the eligibility requirements under the mechanisms. In ease of disagreements between a Party and an expert review team, the enforcement branch shall determine whether to apply adjustments to greenhouse gas inventories or to correct the compilation and accounting database for the accounting of assigned amounts.

The mandate of the facilitative branch is to provide advice and facilitation Parties in implementing the, Protocol, and to promote compliance by Parties with their Kyoto commitments. It is responsible for addressing questions of implementation by Annex I Parties of response measures aimed at mitigating climate change in a way that minimizes their adverse impacts on developing countries and the use by Annex I Parties of the mechanisms as "supplemental" to domestic action. Furthermore, the facilitative branch may provide "early warning" of potential non-compliance with emission targets, methodological and reporting commitments relating to greenhouse gas inventories, and commitments on reporting supplementary information in a Party's annual inventory.

The Committee must take into account any degree of flexibility allowed by the CMP for Annex I Parties undergoing the process transition to a market economy. In addition, the facilitative branch is to take into consideration the common but differentiated responsibilities of the Parties, and the circumstances pertaining to questions before it.

In the case of the enforcement branch, each type of non-compliance requires a specific course of action. For instance, where the enforcement branch has determined that the emissions of a Party have exceeded its assigned amount, it must declare that that Party is in non-compliance and require the Party to make up the difference between its emissions and its assigned amount during the second commitment period, plus an additional deduction of 30%. In addition, it shall require the Party to submit s a compliance action plan and suspend the eligibility of the Party to make transfers under emissions trading until the Party is reinstated.

No such correspondence exists in the case of the facilitative branch, which can decide to provide advice and facilitation of assistance to individual Parties regarding the implementation of the Protocol, facilitate financial and technical assistance to any Party concerned, including technology transfer and capacity building and/or formulate recommendations to the Party concerned.

In the enforcement branch, questions of implementation will be resolved within approximately 35 weeks from receipt by branch of the question of implementation. In time-sensitive requests, including those relating to eligibility to participate in the mechanisms, the expedited procedures involving shorter periods will apply. Apart from the three-week deadline given to complete its preliminary examination, no fixed deadlines are provided for the facilitative branch.

The branches of the Compliance Committee will base their deliberations on reports from expert review teams, the subsidiary bodies, Parties and other official sources. Competent intergovernmental and non-governmental organizations may submit relevant factual and technical information to the relevant branch after the preliminary examination.

There are detailed procedures with specific timeframes for the enforcement branch, including the opportunity for a Party facing the Compliance Committee to make formal written submissions and request a hearing where it can present its views and call on expert testimony.

Any Party not complying with reporting requirements must develop a compliance action plan as well, and Parties that are found not to meet the criteria for participating in the mechanisms will have their eligibility withdrawn. In all cases, the enforcement branch will make a public declaration that the Party is in non-compliance and will also make public the consequences to be applied.

If a Party's eligibility is withdrawn or suspended, it may request, either through an expert review team or directly to the enforcement branch, to have its eligibility restored if it believes it has rectified the problem and is again meeting the relevant criteria.

In the case of compliance with emission targets, Annex I Parties have 100 days after the expert review of their final annual emissions inventory has finished to make up any shortfall in compliance (e.g. by acquiring AAUs, CERs, ERUs or RMUs through emissions trading). If, at the end of this period, a Party's emissions are still greater than its assigned amount, the enforcement branch will declare the

Party to be in non-compliance and apply the consequences outlined above.

As or general rule, decisions taken by the two branches of the Committee cannot be appealed. The exception is a decision of the enforcement branch relating to emissions targets. Even then, a Party can only appeal if it believes it has been denied due process.

Background Paper on Information on Trends in Relation to the Commitments Under Article 3, Paragraph 1, of the Kyoto Protocol Found in Reports of the In-Depth Reviews of the Fifth National Communications of Parties Included in Annex I
Note by the secretariat

COMPLIANCE COMMITTEE

CC/FB/12/2012/2

11 October 2012

I. Introduction

A. Mandate

1. At its sixth meeting, the facilitative branch agreed to continue its discussions on how it can carry out its responsibility to provide advice and facilitation "with the aim of promoting compliance and providing for early warning of potential non-compliance" under section IV, paragraph 6 (a), of the procedures and mechanisms relating to compliance under the Kyoto Protocol at its next meeting. The branch also decided to consider how it could make use of the wealth of information found in expert review team (ERT) reports that are forwarded to members and alternate members of the Compliance Committee pursuant to section VI, paragraph 3, of the procedures and mechanisms to the extent that the information is relevant to the mandate of the branch. To facilitate discussions on these matters, the branch requested the secretariat to prepare a background paper providing the branch with a compilation and assessment of information on trends in relation to the commitments under Article 3, paragraph 1, of the Kyoto Protocol found in reports of the in-depth reviews of national communications of Parties included in Annex I that have been submitted as of 1 January 2010.

2. At its seventh meeting, the facilitative branch agreed to keep the matter on how it can carry out its responsibilities to provide advice and facilitation "with the aim of promoting compliance and providing for early warning of potential non-compliance" under section IV, paragraph 6 (a), of the procedures and mechanisms relating to compliance under the Kyoto Protocol on the agenda of its eighth meeting. In this regard, the branch also agreed to consider, at its eighth meeting, observations made by ERTs in the in-depth reviews (IDRs) of the fifth national

communications (NC5s) of Parties included in Annex I in relation to greenhouse gas emission projections until 2020.

GHG emission projections with respect to meeting commitments for reducing GHG emissions under the Kyoto Protocol

15.   According to Parties' projections and the observations made by ERTs in the IDRs of NC5s, 22 Parties are expected to meet their targets under the Kyoto Protocol by domestic actions alone (Australia, Bulgaria, Croatia (on basis of projections reported in the NC5), Czech Republic, Estonia, the European Union, Finland, France, Germany, Greece, Hungary, Iceland, Latvia, Lithuania, Monaco, Poland, Romania, the Russian Federation, Slovakia, Sweden, Ukraine and United Kingdom); New Zealand is expected to meet its Kyoto Protocol target through domestic action and the use of credits from Article 3, paragraph 3, activities; and 14 Parties are expected to meet their targets under the Kyoto Protocol only by a combination of domestic measures and the use of Kyoto Protocol mechanisms (Austria, Belgium, Denmark, Ireland, Italy, Japan, Liechtenstein, Luxembourg, Netherlands, Norway, Portugal, Slovenia, Spain and Switzerland). With respect to Canada, the ERT noted that the projections indicate that Canada cannot meet its KP target with current implemented domestic actions and that LULUCF activities under Article 3, paragraph 3, and those elected under Article 3, paragraph 4, as well as the use of the Kyoto mechanisms are not expected to contribute significantly to meeting the KP target and plans for further reductions were not reported.

16.   The ERTs raised particular issues with regard to some Parties. In relation to Canada, the ERT noted with strong concern that on the basis of information provided in its NC5 and during the review, Canada could potentially become non-compliant with its commitments under Article 3, paragraph I, of the Kyoto Protocol. Regarding Croatia, according to the estimates made by the ERT during the review using the figures provided in the IRR and the emission projections reported in the NC5, projected total GHG emissions in 2010 are above the Kyoto Protocol targets. Thus, the ERT noted that, according to these estimates, Croatia may not be in a position to meet its KP target.- With respect to Austria, it was not clear to the ERT how Austria is going to meet its Kyoto Protocol target: while with respect to Italy it remained unclear to the ERT how Italy will meet its Kyoto Protocol target.

17.   In addition to the use of flexibility mechanisms, the accounting for activities under Article 3, paragraph 3, is important for the following 10 Parties (Austria, Denmark, Ireland, Japan, Netherlands, New Zealand, Norway, Slovenia, Spain and Switzerland).

18.   According to the ERTs, the majority of Parties that intend to make use of Kyoto Protocol mechanisms provided explicit or implicit information on how their use of the mechanisms under Articles 6.12 and 17 of the Kyoto Protocol is supplemental to domestic action. Only Japan, Liechtenstein, Luxembourg and Slovenia did not provide this information.

19.   The IDRs of NC5s also showed that some Parties included in Annex I have improved their projections, either in terms of completeness or with respect to the

consideration of 'with additional measures' scenarios, as compared to their projections in NC4s. This might also reflect the situation that some of the policies and measures implemented in the lead-up to the submission of the NC4s required more time to be fully implemented and for their effect to become visible in the emission trends of Parties.

20.   Looking towards future developments, it is expected that the sixth national communications (NC6s), which Parties included in Annex I are requested to submit to the secretariat by I January 2014, may provide even more comprehensive and reliable data with respect to GHG emissions projections taking into account effects of the global economic downturn and recovery.

NOTES AND QUESTIONS

1.   The first commitment period under the Kyoto Protocol ended on December 31, 2012, and, somewhat surprisingly, the compliance scorecard is better than many expected.

2.   Flexibility mechanisms were crucial to compliance by many important Kyoto parties. The European Union 15 easily complied with its 8% reduction commitment, but several EU member states were not in compliance.

3.   The biggest user of the flexibility provisions of the Kyoto Protocol is Japan, whose GHG emissions are substantially in excess of its 1990 base levels. Despite this Japan came into compliance by using RMUs, CERs, and billions of dollars of AAUs (over 100 million Kyoto Protocol units) from Russia, Latvia, and Hungary.

4.   In 2006, Friends of the Earth, Canada, an NGO, submitted a communication to the Kyoto Protocol Compliance Committee accusing Canada of violating the UNFCC in three respects: (1) Not having established measures that would lead to a reversal of the long-term trend of increasing GHG emissions in order to stabilize atmospheric GHG concentrations, contrary to Article 4.2(a) and (b), in conjunction with *Article* 2; (2) Not having adopted and implemented measures to adapt to the impacts of climate change, contrary to Article 4.1(b); and (3) Not having submitted its 4th National Communication, contrary to Articles 12 and 4 and Decision 4/CP8. Canada was also accused of violating the Kyoto Protocol by not having (1) made demonstrable progress by 2005 in achieving its 6% reduction target for 2008-2012, as required by Article 3.2; and (2) submitted its report on demonstrable progress, contrary to Articles 7.2 and 7.3, with Article 3.2 and Decision 22/CP7. In 2011, Canada withdrew from the Kyoto Protocol, effective 15 December 2012.

EVALUATING THE KYOTO PROTOCOL

Data submitted to the Compliance Committee of the UNFCCC indicate that only about five relatively small states will miss their Kyoto Protocol targets under Article 3. Four of these are EU members covered by the Article 4 EU bubble. One of the non-complying states, Canada, has withdrawn from the Protocol. Thus, compliance with the Protocol is very high; Annex I parties have taken their international obligations seriously and to this extent the Protocol's mandated reductions have been achieved. In addition, the Kyoto Protocol's flexibility mechanisms have been a success. A majority of parties have used these mechanisms to some extent to comply with the Protocol. Indeed, without the flexibility mechanisms, many more states would not have complied with their Article 3 commitments. CDM has been a particular success, although one state, China, has garnered most of the benefit. But CDM projects in China, according to a senior official of China's National Development and Reform Commission, is likely to enable China to reduce its annual GHG emissions by about 300 million tons per year.[72]

However, in terms of effectiveness in grappling with the problem of increasing GHG emissions and disappearing carbon sinks, the Kyoto Protocol and the UNFCCC are not successful. GHG emissions continue to rise and are about 32% higher in 2013 than in the base year of 1990. Three reasons stand out as to why the Kyoto Protocol has not solved the problem of climate change. First, the mandate of the Protocol was insufficient; even with perfect compliance, the Protocol was designed to lower GHG emissions from 37 parties by only about 5%. Second, the Annex I country that was the largest emitter at the time the Kyoto Protocol was signed, the United States, did not participate. Instead of reducing GHG emissions as mandated by the Protocol, the United States in 2013 has annual GHG emissions about 12% higher than in 1990. Third, the biggest reason for Kyoto's inadequacy, is that since the Protocol was signed, emissions of GHG from Non-Annex I parties, who have no Kyoto commitments, have skyrocketed and are now greater than the GHG emissions of Annex I parties.

Thus, although the Kyoto Protocol cannot be termed a failure, it was manifestly inadequate to deal with the problem of climate change. The future challenge for the 195 parties to the UNFCCC is to improve the climate change international regime to deal with the true scope of the problem. The key to fulfilling the objective of the UNFCCC and stabilizing the rise in global temperatures, therefore, depends on future decisions of the 195 parties to the UNFCCC.

The two most universally ratified international agreements in history, the Montreal Protocol and the UNFCCC, have thus had quite different results. Whereas the Montreal Protocol is regarded as successful, and the ozone layer is expected to recover, the UNFCCC and the Kyoto Protocol have been inadequate to slow climate change. What are the reasons for the differences between the two regimes? Can lessons of the Montreal Protocol be applied to improve the UNFCCC regime?

J.   The Copenhagen Accord: A New Approach

With the 2012 deadline for the expiration of the Kyoto Protocol drawing near, the Conference of the Parties to the UNFCCC and the Meeting of the Parties to the Kyoto Protocol felt a sense of urgency to agree on a post-Kyoto climate accord. At the UNFCCC COP-13 in Bali, Indonesia in 2007, the Bali Road Map and the Bali Action Plan[73] were concluded in order to chart the way toward a binding climate agreement that would take effect after Kyoto. The Bali Action Plan was

---

[72] Takamitsu Sawa, *A Way Past Kyoto's Hot Air,* JAPAN TIMES, 13 December 2006, at 15.

[73] Decision 1/CP.13 (2007).

regarded as a breakthrough at the time because it was agreed to take:

"Enhanced national/international action on mitigation of climate change, including . . . consideration of:

(i) Measurable, reportable and verifiable nationally appropriate mitigation commitments or actions, including quantified emission limitation and reduction objectives, by all developed country Parties . . . ;

(ii) Nationally appropriate mitigation actions by developing country Parties in the context of sustainable development, supported and enabled by technology, financing, and capacity-building, in a measurable, reportable and verifiable manner."

The key breakthrough for many UNFCCC parties, especially the United States, was that Non-Annex I developing country parties to the UNFCCC had agreed to take concrete actions. Hopes were high when COP-15 convened in Copenhagen, Denmark in 2009 that agreement on a post-Kyoto climate change regime was within reach. Heads of state, including U.S. President Obama, announced their intention to attend the Copenhagen meeting in the expectation of signing a landmark agreement.

The Copenhagen meeting and COP-15, however, failed to produce a binding agreement. The divide between developing and developed countries was evident from the start. Non-Annex I parties to the UNFCCC rejected any binding GHG reduction commitments and demanded large payments and transfer of technology from developed countries to pay for adaptation and mitigation actions.

On the last day of the Copenhagen meeting, which was attended by over 100 heads of state, key nations, mainly the United States and China, crafted a non-binding political declaration — now known as the Copenhagen Accord — and presented it to the conference participants. The COP-15 rejected any formal adoption of the Accord, but agreed to "take note" of this document.

THE COPENHAGEN ACCORD
FCCC/CP/2009/L.7, 18 December 2009

The Heads of State, Heads of Government, Ministers, and other beads of the following delegations present at the United Nations Climate Change Conference 2009 in Copenhagen: *[List of Parties]*.

In pursuit of the ultimate objective of the Convention as stated in its Article 2.

Being guided by the principles and provisions of the Convention.

Noting the results of work done by the two Ad hoc Working Groups,

Endorsing decision x/CP.l5 on the Ad hoc Working Group on Long-term Cooperative Action and decision x/CMP.5 that requests the Ad hoc Working Group on Further Commitments of Annex I Parties under the Kyoto Protocol to continue its work,

Have agreed on this Copenhagen Accord which is operational immediately.

1. We underline that climate change is one of the greatest challenges of our

time. We emphasise our strong political will to urgently combat climate change in accordance with the principle of common but differentiated responsibilities and respective capabilities. To achieve the ultimate objective of the Convention to stabilize greenhouse gas concentration in the atmosphere at a level that would prevent dangerous anthropogenic interference with the climate system, we shall, recognizing the scientific view that the increase in global temperature should be below 2 degrees Celsius, on the basis of equity and in the context of sustainable development, enhance our long-term cooperative action to combat climate change. We recognize the critical impacts of climate change and the potential impacts of response measures on countries particularly vulnerable to its adverse effects and stress the need to establish a comprehensive adaptation programme including international support.

2.   We agree that deep cuts in global emissions are required according to science, and as documented by the IPCC Fourth Assessment Report with a view to reduce global emissions so as to hold the increase in global temperature below 2 degrees Celsius, and take action to meet this objective consistent with science and on the basis of equity. We should cooperate in achieving the peaking of global and national emissions as soon as possible, recognizing that the time frame for peaking will be longer in developing countries and bearing in mind that social and economic development and poverty eradication are the first and overriding priorities of developing countries and that a low-emission development strategy is indispensable to sustainable development.

3.   Adaptation to the adverse effects of climate change and the potential impacts of response measures is a challenge faced by all countries. Enhanced action and international cooperation on adaptation is urgently required to ensure the implementation of the Convention by enabling and supporting the implementation of adaptation actions aimed at reducing vulnerability and building resilience in developing countries, especially in those that are particularly vulnerable, especially least developed countries, small island developing States and Africa. We agree that developed countries shall provide adequate, predictable and sustainable financial resources, technology and capacity-building to support the implementation of adaptation action in developing countries.

4.   Annex I Parties commit to implement individually or jointly the quantified economy-wide emissions targets for 2020, to be submitted in the format given in Appendix I by Annex I Parties to the secretariat by 31 January 2010 for compilation in an INF document. Annex I Parties that are Party to the Kyoto Protocol will thereby further strengthen the emissions reductions initiated by the Kyoto Protocol. Delivery of reductions and financing by developed countries will be measured, reported and verified in accordance with existing and any further guidelines adopted by the Conference of the Parties, and will ensure that accounting of such targets and finance is rigorous, robust and transparent.

5. Non-Annex I Parties to the Convention will implement mitigation actions, including those to be submitted to the secretariat by non-Annex I Parties in the format given in Appendix II by 31 January 2010, for compilation in an INF document, consistent with Article 4.1 and Article 4.7 and in the context of sustainable development. Least developed countries and small island developing

States may undertake actions voluntarily and on the basis of support. Mitigation actions subsequently taken and envisaged by Non-Annex I Parties, including national inventory reports, shall be communicated through national communications consistent with Article 12.1 (b) every two years on the basis of guidelines to be adopted by the Conference of the Parties. Those mitigation actions in national communications or otherwise communicated to the Secretariat will be added to the list in appendix II. Mitigation actions taken by Non-Annex I Parties will be subject to their domestic measurement, reporting and verification the result of which will be reported through their national communications every two years. Non-Annex I Parties will communicate information on the implementation of their actions through National Communications, with provisions for international consultations and analysis under clearly defined guidelines that will ensure that national sovereignty is respected. Nationally appropriate mitigation actions seeking international support will be recorded in a registry along with relevant technology, finance and capacity building support. Those actions supported will be added to the list in appendix II. These supported nationally appropriate mitigation actions will be subject to international measurement, reporting and verification in accordance with guidelines adopted by the Conference of the Parties.

6.   We recognize the crucial role of reducing emission from deforestation and forest degradation and the need to enhance removals of greenhouse gas emission by forests and agree on the need to provide positive incentives to such actions through the immediate establishment of a mechanism including REDD-plus, to enable the mobilization of financial resources from developed countries;

7.   We decide to pursue various approaches, including opportunities to use markets, to enhance the cost-effectiveness of, and to promote mitigation actions. Developing countries, especially those with low emitting economies should be provided incentives to continue to develop on a low emission pathway.

8.   Scaled up, new and additional, predictable and adequate funding as well as improved access shall be provided to developing countries, in accordance with the relevant provisions of the Convention, to enable and support enhanced action on mitigation, including substantial finance to reduce emissions from deforestation and forest degradation (REDD-plus), adaptation, technology development and transfer and capacity-building, for enhanced implementation of the Convention. The collective commitment by developed countries is to provide new and additional resources, including forestry and investments through international institutions, approaching USD 30 billion for the period 2010–2012 with balanced allocation between adaptation and mitigation. Funding for adaptation will be prioritized for the most vulnerable developing countries, such as the least developed countries, small island developing States and Africa. In the context of meaningful mitigation actions and transparency on implementation, developed countries commit to a goal of mobilizing jointly USD 100 billion dollars a year by 2020 to address the needs of developing countries. This funding will come from a wide variety of sources, public and private, bilateral and multilateral, including alternative sources of finance, New multilateral funding for adaptation will be delivered through effective and efficient fund arrangements, with a governance structure providing for equal representation of developed and developing countries. A significant portion of such funding should flow through the Copenhagen Green Climate Fund.

9.   To this end, a High Level Panel will be established under the guidance of and accountable to the Conference of the Parties to study the contribution of the potential sources of revenue including alternative sources of finance, towards meeting this goal.

10.   We decide that the Copenhagen Green Climate Fund shall be established as an operating entity of the financial mechanism of the Convention to support projects, programme, policies and other activities in developing countries related to mitigation including REDD-plus, adaptation, capacity-building, technology development and transfer.

11.   In order to enhance action on development and transfer of technology we decide to establish a Technology Mechanism to accelerate technology development and transfer in support of action on adaptation and mitigation that will be guided by a country -driven approach and be based on national circumstances and priorities.

12.   We call for an assessment of the implementation of this Accord to be completed by 2015, including in light of the Convention's ultimate objective. This would include consideration of strengthening the long-term goal referencing various matters presented by the science, including in relation to temperature rises of 1.5 degrees Celsius.

SUMMARY OF MAIN POINTS OF THE COPENHAGEN ACCORD

1.   A political, non-binding international agreement may not be the optimum outcome, but it is better than no agreement at all.

2.   Goal: to limit the rise in global temperatures to less than 2 degrees Celsius.

3.   Establish long-term cooperative action to achieve "deep cuts" in emissions "as soon as possible" but within a time frame that is longer for developing countries.

4.   Developed countries will provide "adequate, predictable and sustainable financial resources, technology and capacity-building" to support adaptation actions in developing countries.

5.   Annex I parties will commit to implement quantified emission target reduction targets for 2020.

6.   Non-Annex I parties will implement "mitigation actions" that are subject to domestic measurement, reporting, and verification.

7.   Recognition of the need to reduce emissions of greenhouse gases from deforestation and to enhance removals of greenhouse gases by forests through "positive incentives" such as "mobilization of financial resources from developed countries."

8.   Markets and incentives will be employed to promote and enhance the cost-effectiveness of mitigation actions.

9.   A commitment for funding "approaching" USD 30 billion for the period 2010 to 2012 for adaptation and mitigation; and a goal of USD 100 billion

per year by 2020 "to address the needs of developing countries."

10. The Copenhagen Green Climate Fund is established as a new operating entity of the Financial Mechanism of the UNFCCC.

11. A new Technology Mechanism is established to develop and transfer technology.

RESPONSE TO THE COPENHAGEN ACCORD

The Copenhagen Accord calls for both Annex I and Non-Annex I parties to respond to the UNFCCC Secretariat by 31 January 2010. Annex I parties are to state their quantified, economy-wide emission reduction targets for 2020 along with selecting their individual base year for such cuts. Non-Annex I parties are invited to state simply their intended "actions."

As of this writing, 138 countries, including the 28 member EU, have engaged with the Copenhagen Accord in some manner.[74] Countries have engaged in different ways: some have "associated with the Accord"; some have "associated with the targets"; some have simply submitted action; some have stated that they are "supportive." Eight states have communicated that they do not support the Accord.

As listed on the web site of the UNFCCC, 15 Annex I parties plus the 28 member EU have formally responded to the call for quantified, economy-wide emission targets for 2020. 44 Non-Annex I parties have specifically listed actions they intend to take to reduce GHG emissions.

APPENDIX I (SELECTED ENTRIES)

Annex I Parties.	*Quantified economy-wide emissions targets for 2020*	
	Emissions reduction in 2020	Base year
United States of America	In the range of 17%, in conformity with anticipated U.S. energy and climate legislation, recognizing that the final target will be reported to the Secretariat in light of enacted legislation.	2005

Note: The pathway set forth in pending legislation would entail a 30% reduction in 2025 and a 42% reduction in 2030, in line with the goal to reduce emissions 83% by 2050

---

[74] https://unfccc.int/meetings/copenhagen_dec_2009/items/5262.php.

The EU and its Member States are committed to an independent quantified economy-wide emissions reduction target of 20% by 2020, compared to 1990 levels. This target could be increased to 30% under the conditions set out by the European Council of December 2009.

Therefore, the EU and its Member States wish to inform about these commitments in the format set out by Appendix 1 to the Copenhagen Accord:

Annex I Parties*	*Quantified economy-wide emissions targets for 2020*	
	Emissions reduction in 2020	Base year
EU and its Member States (Belgium, Bulgaria, Czech Republic, Denmark, Germany, Estonia, Ireland, Greece, Spain, France, Italy, Cyprus, Latvia, Lithuania, Luxembourg, Hungary, Malta, Netherlands, Austria, Poland, Portugal, Romania, Slovenia, Slovakia, Finland, Sweden, United Kingdom) acting in common	20% / 30%**	1990

Note: In 2014, the EU — amid much criticism — revised its ambitious commitment as follows

1. The target for renewable energy use was set at 27% by 2030 (the EU is legally bound to achieve 20 percent by 2020).

2. The 2030 target for GHG reduction was set at 40% (the EU is obligated to reduce GHG emissions by 20% by 2020).

As of 2014, the EU has reduced emissions of GHG (compared to 1990 levels) by 18%, and has, during this time, raised its GDP by about 45%.

———————

BOTSCHAFT VON JAPAN   HIROSHIMASTR 6

1078 BERLIN/GERMANY

The Embassy of Japan in Germany presents its compliments to the secretariat of the United Nations Framework Convention on Climate Change and has the honour to inform the latter of the willingness of the Government of Japan to be associated with the Copenhagen Accord of 18 December 2009.

The Embassy of Japan has the honour to submit to the secretariat information on its quantified economy-wide emissions target for 2020 in the format given in

Appendix I of the Accord as below.

Annex: Parties	Quantified economy-wide emissions targets for 2020	
	Emissions reduction in 2020	Base year
Japan	25% reductionwhich is premised on the establishment of a fair and effective Japan internationalframework in which. all major economies participate: and on agreement by those economies on ambitious targets	1990

The Embassy of Japan in Germany avails itself of this opportunity to renew to the secretariat of the, United Nations Framework Convention on Climate Change the assurance of its highest consideration.

Berlin, January 26, 2010

To the,

Secretariat of the United Nations Framework Convention Change

Change

Bonn

Note: After a new government took power in Japan in 2011, Japan revised its Copenhagen pledge; Japan pledges to reduce GHG emissions for 2020 to 3.8 percent from 2005 levels.

中国国家发展和改革委员会应对气候变化司

DEPARTMENT OF CLIMATE CHANGE, NATIONAL DEVELOPMENT & REFORM COMMISSION OF CHINA

No. 38, Yue Tan Nan Jie, Beijing, 100824, China, Tel: +86-10-68505862, Fax: +86-10-68505881

28 January 2010

Executive Secretary UNFCCC Secretariat

Bonn, Germany

Fax: +49-228-8151997

Dear Mr. Yvo de Boer,

I have the honor to communicate to you the information on China's autonomous domestic mitigation actions as announced, for information to the UNFCCC Parties, as follows:

China will endeavor to lower its carbon dioxide emissions per unit of GDP by 40–45% by 2020 compared to the 2005 level, increase the share of non-fossil fuels in primary energy consumption to around 15% by 2020 and increase forest coverage by 40 million hectares and forest stock volume by 1.3 billion cubic meters by 2020 from the 2005 levels.

Please note that the above-mentioned autonomous domestic mitigation actions are voluntary in nature and will be implemented in accordance with the principles and provisions of the UNFCCC, in particular Article 4, paragraph 7.

This Communication is made in accordance with the provisions of Articles 12, paragraph 1 (b), Article 12, paragraph 4 and Article 10, paragraph 2(a).

Sincerely yours,

SU Wei
Director General
Department of Climate Change
National Development and Reform Commission of China
(National Focal Point)

GOVERNMENT OF INDIA
MINISTRY OF ENVIRONMENT & FORESTS

Executive Secretary

United Nations Framework Convention on Climate Change

P.O. Box 260124

D-53153, Bonn, Germany

Fax- +49-228-8151997

30 January 2010

Dear Mr Yvo de Boer

I have the honour to communicate to you the information on India's domestic mitigation actions as follows:

India will endeavour to reduce the emissions[75] intensity of its GOP by 20–25% by 2020 in comparison to the 2005 level.

Please note that the proposed domestic actions are voluntary in nature and will not have a legally binding character. Further, these actions will be implemented in accordance with the provisions of the relevant national legislations and policies as well as the principles and provisions of the UNFCCC, particularly its Article 4, paragraph 7.

This Communication is made in accordance with the provisions of Article 12 paragraph 1(b), Article 12 paragraph 4 and Article 10 paragraph 2(a) of the UNFCCC.

Sincerely yours

Rajani Ranjan Rashmi
Joint Secretary
Ministry of Environment & Forests
Government of India
(National Focal Point)

---

[75] The emissions from agriculture sector will not form part of the assessment of emissions intensity.

PARYAVARAN BHAWAN, C.G.O. COMPLEX, LODHI ROAD, NEW DELHI 110 003

KETUA HARIAN

DEWAN NASIONAL PERUBAHAN IKLIM

Our Ref. : E-03/EC-NCCC/0l/2010

Subject : Indonesia Voluntary Mitigation Actions

Dear Mr. de Boer,

Jakarta, January 30th 2010
To.
Mr. Yvo de Boer Executive Secretary
United Nations Framework Convention on
Climate Change
P.O. Box 260124 D 53153 Bonn-Germany

With reference to my letter dated 19 January 2010, I have the honor to reiterate Indonesia's association with Copenhagen Accord that in our view served as a very important milestone in our common endeavor in addressing the challenges of climate change.

For information to the UNFCCC Parties, please find the information of our voluntary Mitigation Actions, in the format set forth in Appendix II of the Copenhagen Accord, as follow:

Nationally Appropriate Mitigation Actions	Emission Reduction
The Reduction will be achieved, inter alia, through the following action: 1. Sustainable Peat Land Management 2. Reduction in Rate of Deforestation and Land Degradation 3. Development of Carbon Sequestration Projects in Forestry and Agriculture 4. Promotion of Energy Efficiency 5. Development of Alternative and Renewable Energy Sources 6. Reduction in Solid and Liquid Waste	26% by 2020

NOTES AND QUESTIONS

1.   Note the flexibility in the responses to the Copenhagen Accord. Parties can select their own base year and reduction as well as how this will be achieved. India and China express their reductions in terms of energy intensity — GHG per unit of GDP.

2.   How does the Copenhagen Accord compare with the UNFCCC approach to negotiate binding international agreements?

3.   The Peterson Institute of International Economics has evaluated the Copenhagen national pledges against a "business-as-usual" scenario (BAU) — the path we are currently on.[76] The BAU analysis captured all national policies enacted through mid-year 2009. Under BAU global greenhouse gas emissions will grow from 45 billion tons in 2005 to 56 billion tons in 2020, to 113 billion tons by 2100. By the end of the century GHG concentrations reach 1,055 ppm (up from current 393 ppm), and global temperatures will rise more than 4 degrees Celsius. Against this trajectory, the national pledges currently listed in the Copenhagen Accord would reduce emissions to between 49.7 and 51.5 billion tons in 2020, which is 7 to 11% below BAU. Limiting climate change to a goal of below 2 degrees Celsius will depend on further actions to be taken after 2020.

4.   The Copenhagen Accord calls for a review of pledged national actions by 2015. Since the UNFCCC parties did not formally adopt the Accord, who will conduct this review and under what auspices will it be done?

K.   Reducing Emissions from Deforestation and Forest Degradation (REDD)

REDD, an acronym for Reducing Emissions from Deforestation and Forest Degradation, is "an effort to create financial value for the carbon stored in forests, offering incentives for developing countries to reduce emissions from forested lands and invest in low-carbon paths to sustainable development."[77] REDD Plus, a related concept, adds the idea that forests in developing countries should be managed sustainably to enhance ecosystems and to provide livelihoods for local people, while respecting the rights of indigenous peoples.[78] REDD-Plus makes clear that concern for deforestation and forest degradation is not just about reducing carbon emissions; it must also address the welfare of people who live in forested areas. REDD and REDD-Plus are attracting great interest because two important environmental aims coincide in connection with this concept: preservation of ecosystems and biological diversity and slowing climate change. Moreover, all previous international efforts to stem deforestation have failed. REDD is a new approach that holds great promise.

---

[76] *See Evaluating Copenhagen: Does the Accord meet the Challenge?*, http://www.iie.com/realtime/?p=1173, accessed 2 November 2010.

[77] http://unfccc.int/methods/redd/redd_web_platform/items/4531.php.

[78] *Id.*

1.   The Development and Elements of REDD-Plus

REDD became an agenda item for the Parties to the UNFCCC through the efforts of Costa Rica and Papua New Guinea at COP 11 held at Montreal in 2005. Many developing countries have extensive tropical forests within their borders that not only are important repositories of biological diversity but also act as natural carbon "sinks," fixing and storing vast amounts of carbon annually through photosynthesis. The ongoing deforestation of these areas involves a double "whammy" for climate change: not only are carbon sinks eliminated, the burning of these areas result in carbon emissions into the atmosphere. It is estimated that about 17% of annual carbon emissions come from deforestation activities.[79] Thus, preservation of forests and slowing the rate of deforestation and forest degradation should be an important part of climate change policy. But, as we have seen, up to now this has been a lacuna in the UNFCCC legal regime. Under the provisions of the UNFCCC only Annex I Parties may obtain credit for land use sinks under the LULUCF program. Furthermore, the Clean Development Mechanism extends credits for afforestation and reforestation, but not for preserving forests or avoiding forest degradation. REDD thus fills this gap in the UNFCCC. Moreover, REDD goes beyond climate change since it is the first internationally enforceable effort to address the problem of deforestation and forest degradation in developing countries.

REDD and REDD-Plus have been developed progressively by successive COPs since its inception in 2005. The Bali Action Plan adopted by COP 14 in 2008, called for new "policy approaches and positive incentives on issues related to reducing emissions from deforestation and forest degradation in developing countries; and conservation [and] sustainable management of forest carbon stocks in developing countries."[80] The Copenhagen Accord agreed at COP 15 in 2009, recognized the "crucial role" of reducing carbon emissions from deforestation and forest degradation as a component of international action to combat climate change.

The key decision to implement REDD Plus was taken by COP 16 in 2010, which adopted the following Decision which is known as the "Cancun Mandate."

OUTCOME OF THE AD HOC WORKING GROUP ON LONG-TERM COOPERATIVE ACTION UNDER THE CONVENTION
UNFCCC DECISION 1/CP.16 (2010)

The Parties,

Affirming that, in the context of the provision of adequate and predictable support to developing country Parties, Parties should collectively aim to slow, halt and reverse forest degradation and forest loss, in accordance with national circumstances, consistent with the ultimate objectives of the Convention as stated in Article 2,

Also affirming the need to promote broad country participation in all phases

---

[79] The current rate of global deforestation is about 13 million hectares per year.

[80] Decision 1/CP.14, para. 1(b)(iii).

described in paragraph 73 below, including through the provision of support that takes into account existing capacities,

68. Encourage all Parties to find effective ways to reduce the human pressure on forests that results in greenhouse gas emissions, including actions to address drivers of deforestation;

69. Affirm that the implementation of the activities referred to in paragraph 70 below should be carried out in accordance with Appendix I to this Decision, and that the safeguards referred to in paragraph 2 of Appendix I should be promoted and supported;

70. Encourage developing country Parties to contribute to mitigation actions in the forest sector by undertaking the following activities, as deemed appropriate by each Party and in accordance with their respective capabilities and national circumstances:

(a) Reducing emissions from deforestation;

(b) Reducing emissions from forest degradation;

(c) Conservation of forest carbon;

(d) Sustainable management of forests;

(e) Enhancement of forest carbon stocks;

71. Request developing country Parties aiming to undertake the activities referred to in paragraph 70 above, in the context of the provision of adequate and predictable support, including financial resources and technical and technological support to developing country Parties, in accordance with national circumstances and respective capabilities, to develop the following elements:

(a) A national strategy or action plan;

(b) A national forest reference emission level and/or forest reference level or, if appropriate, as an interim measure, subnational forest reference emission levels, in accordance with national circumstances . . . .

(c) A robust and transparent national forest monitoring system for the monitoring and reporting of the activities referred to in paragraph 70 above, with, if appropriate, subnational monitoring and reporting as an interim measure, in accordance with national circumstances . . . .

(d) A system for providing information on how the safeguards referred to in Appendix I to this Decision are being addressed . . . .

72. Also request developing country Parties, when developing and implementing their national strategies or action plans, to address, *inter alia*, the drivers of deforestation and forest degradation, land tenure issues, forest governance issues, gender considerations, and the safeguards identified in paragraph 2 of Appendix I to this Decision, ensuring the full and effective participation of relevant stakeholders, inter alia, indigenous peoples and local communities;

73. Decide that the activities undertaken by Parties referred to in paragraph 70 above, should be implemented in phases, beginning with the development of national strategies or action plans, policies and measures, and capacity-building,

followed by the implementation of national policies and measures and national strategies or action plans that could involve further capacity-building, technology development and transfer and results-based demonstration activities, and evolving into results-based actions that should be fully measured, reported and verified;

76. Urge Parties, in particular developed country Parties, to support, through multilateral and bilateral channels, the development of national strategies or action plans, policies and measures and capacity-building, followed by the implementation of national policies and measures and national strategies or action plans that could involve further capacity building, technology development and transfer and results-based demonstration activities, including consideration of the safeguards referred to in paragraph 2 of Appendix I of this Decision, taking into account the relevant provisions on finance, including those relating to reporting on support;

77. Request the Ad Hoc Working Group on Long-Term Cooperative Action under the Convention to explore financing options for the full implementation of the results-based actions referred to in paragraph 73 above and to report on progress made, including any recommendations for draft decisions on this matter, to the Conference of the Parties . . . .

Appendix I — Guidance and Safeguards for [REDD]

    2. The activities referred to in paragraph 70 of this Decision should:

        a. Contribute to the achievement of the objective set out in Article 2 of the Convention;

        b. Contribute to the fulfillment of the commitments set out in Article 4, paragraph 3 of the Convention;

        c. Be country-driven and be considered options available to Parties;

        d. Be consistent with the objective of environmental integrity and take into account the multiple functions of forests and other ecosystems;

        e. Be undertaken in accordance with national development priorities, objectives and circumstances and capabilities and should respect sovereignty;

        f. Be consistent with Parties' national and sustainable development needs and goals;

        g. Be implemented in the context of sustainable development and reducing poverty, while responding to climate change;

        h. Be consistent with the adaptation needs of the country;

        i. Be supported by adequate and predictable financial and technology support, including support for capacity-building;

        j. Be results-based;

        k. Promote sustainable management of forests;

    3. When undertaking the activities referred to in paragraph 70 of this Decision, the following safeguards should be promoted and supported:

        a. That actions complement or are consistent with the objectives of national forest programs and relevant international conventions and agreements;

b. Transparent and effective national forest governance structures, taking into account national legislation and sovereignty;

c. Respect for knowledge and rights of indigenous peoples and local communities, by taking into account relevant international obligations, national circumstances and laws, and noting the United Nations has adopted the United Nations Declaration on the Rights of Indigenous Peoples;

d. The full and effective participation of relevant stakeholders, in particular indigenous peoples and local communities, in the actions referred to in paragraphs 70 and 72 of this Decision;

e. That actions are consistent with the conservation of natural forests and biological diversity, ensuring that the actions referred to in paragraph 70 of this Decision are not used for the conversion of natural forests, but are instead used to incentivize the protection and conservation of natural forests and their ecosystem services, and to enhance other social and environmental benefits;

f. Actions to address the risks of reversals;

g. Actions to reduce displacement of emissions.

The Cancun Mandate for REDD-Plus was carried forward by COP 17 by the following Decision, known as the "Durban Platform for Enhanced Action."

OUTCOME OF THE WORK OF THE AD HOC WORKING GROUP ON LONG-TERM COOPERATIVE ACTION UNDER THE CONVENTION
UNFCCC DECISION 2/CP.17 (2011)

The Parties,

63. Agree that, regardless of the source or type of financing, the activities referred to in Decision 1/CP.16, paragraph 70, should be consistent with the relevant provisions included in Decision 1/CP.16, including the safeguards in its Appendix I, in accordance with the relevant decisions of the Conference of the Parties;

64. Recall that for developing country Parties undertaking the results-based actions referred to in Decision 1/CP.16, paragraphs 73 and 77, to obtain and receive results-based finance, these actions should be fully measured, reported and verified, and developing country Parties should have the elements referred to in Decision 1/CP.16, paragraph 71, in accordance with any decisions taken by the Conference of the Parties on this matter;

65. Agree that results-based finance provided to developing country Parties that is new, additional, and predictable may come from a wide variety of sources, public and private, bilateral and multilateral, including alternative sources;

66. Consider that, in the light of the experience gained from current and future demonstration activities, appropriate market-based approaches could be developed by the Conference of the Parties to support the results-based actions by developing

country Parties referred to in Decision 1/CP.16, paragraph 73.

67. Note that non-market-based approaches, such as joint mitigation and adaptation approaches for the integral and sustainable management of forests as a non-market alternative that supports and strengthens governance, the application of safeguards as referred to in Decision 1/CP.16, Appendix I, paragraph 2(c–e), and the multiple functions of forests, could be developed.

In 2013, the COP 19 meeting in Warsaw adopted what is known as "the Warsaw Framework for REDD Plus."[81]

Two Warsaw decisions concerned financial matters:

Decision 9/CP.19 — Establishing a work program on results-based finance for REDD-Plus activities referred to in Article 70 of Decision 1/CP.16; and Decision -/CP.19 on the coordination of finance and support for the implementation of mitigation activities in the forest sector undertaken by developing countries.

Decision 13/CP.19 concerned guidelines and procedures for determining technical assessment of forest reference emission levels submitted by developing country Parties.

Decision 15/CP.19 concerned guidelines for addressing the drivers of deforestation and forest degradation.

Decision 11/CP.19 concerned modalities for national forest monitoring systems.

Decision 14/CP.19 concerned modalities for national measuring, reporting and verification.

Decision 12/CP.19 concerned modalities for the timing and frequency of reporting on safeguards.

NOTES AND QUESTIONS

1.   As of 2014, the major components of REDD-Plus are in place; appropriate decisions have been taken and primary issues addressed by the COP. Note that the implementation of REDD-plus will take place in three phases (para. 73 of Decision 1/CP.16).

2.   Paragraph 70 of Decision 1/CP.16 outlines five separate but related activities to be undertaken by developing country Parties. What are these activities? Note that forest degradation is to be distinguished from deforestation. The latter term measures the area denuded of trees, while forest degradation refers to the necessity of maintaining the quality of existing forests, their ecosystems, biological diversity, soil, and other characteristics.

3.   Note that Decision 1/CP.16 calls on developing country Parties (paras. 71 and 72) to adopt specific action policies in exchange for "adequate and predictable [financial] support."

---

[81] The text of all decisions are available on the UNFCCC website.

4.   What is the purpose of requiring safeguard actions as outlined in the Appendix?

5.   What duties are incumbent upon developed country Parties under these decisions?

6.   *Implementation issues.* The implementation of REDD-Plus will involve many difficult issues, such as the following:

   a.   *Additionality.* How can it be assured that REDD activities constitute a departure from business as usual? This is addressed in part by the Warsaw Framework decision on forest emission reference levels.

   b.   *Measuring, reporting, and verification.* Modalities must be developed for international standards for independent and objective measuring, reporting, and verification of REDD activities. This issue is addressed by a Warsaw Framework decision.

   c.   *Objective assessment and tracking of compliance with safeguards.* The safeguard issue is also addressed by the Warsaw Framework.

   d.   *Drivers of forest degradation and deforestation.* The Warsaw Framework also requires that the underlying causes of forest degradation and deforestation be addressed. These drivers will be different in each country.

   e.   *Permanence.* How can the permanence of the anti-deforestation and anti-degradation measures be assured?

   f.   *Rights of indigenous peoples.* To succeed, REDD-Plus will have to contribute to the social, economic, and cultural advancement of indigenous people and local communities.

   g.   *Leakage.* The term *leakage* refers to emissions of GHG that occur outside a project area but occur as a result of REDD activity. Leakage can result from either an activity shift or a market shift. How should REDD account for leakage?

   h.   *Forest governance.* How will REDD-Plus assure that tree plantations — palm oil plantations and industrial tree farms — are not the consequence of REDD activities?

7.   The implementation of REDD-Plus will not be a simple matter. Many difficult issues must be addressed and overcome. To succeed, REDD cannot be just about forestry; it must be embedded into the whole economic fabric of the regions and nations involved across numerous economic sectors. Are you optimistic this will occur or will this effort fail?

2.   Institutions and Demonstration Projects

In order to assist developing countries to participate in REDD and REDD-Plus the United Nations' UNREDD Programme was launched in 2008, as a consortium of the Food and Agriculture Organization (FAO), the United Nations Development Programme (UNDP), and the United Nations Environment Programme (UNEP). The UNREDD Programme, whose Secretariat is in Geneva, supports efforts in 46 partner countries to (1) direct financial support to design and implement national

REDD and REDD-Plus initiatives and (2) to support these national programs through analyses, supplying data, and technical advice. As of July 2012, total funding for these efforts totaled USD 117.6 million.[82]

The UNREDD Programme works closely with two programs administered by the World Bank, the Forest Investment Program (FIP), founded in 2008 to assist 48 least developing countries meet their REDD commitments, and the Forest Carbon Partnership Facility (FCPF). The mission of the FCPF is to demonstrate how REDD-Plus can be applied at the country level. The FCPF administers a Readiness Fund to assist developing countries to prepare their national strategies, to develop national forest emission reference levels, and to design measurement, reporting, and verification systems as required under REDD-Plus mandate. The FCPF will also assist in developing management systems that include the required safeguards.

The fundamental idea behind REDD-Plus is to provide financial incentives to developing countries to avoid deforestation and to manage forests in a sustainable, eco-friendly manner. A key part of the run up to the deployment of REDD-Plus has been the establishment of demonstration projects as called for by the COP. For example, in 2009, Norway and Guyana signed a Memorandum of Understanding and a Joint Concept Note pledging that the countries will work together on a REDD-Plus project that will be a replicable model for future projects of this type. To implement these agreements, the government of Guyana formulated a legal framework for action, including a REDD-Plus Governance Development Plan (RGDP) outlining key activities and adopting a rules-based forest-governance, accountability, and enforcement system. The government of Norway created a financial mechanism, the Guyana REDD-Plus Investment Fund (GRIF), under the management of the World Bank's International Development Association (IDA), whose function is to manage and monitor payments for Forest Climate Services, support REDD-Plus activities, attract and fund low-carbon investments in Guyana, and establish benefit sharing arrangements for indigenous workers. As of December 2012, the GRIF has disbursed a total of USD 115 million to the government of Guyana. In January, 2013, an NGO, Rainforest Alliance published an independent report on the Guyana REDD project; this team audited the project on the basis of ten verification indicators:[83]

1. Transparent and effective multi-stakeholder consultations continue and evolve — not met.

2. Participation of all affected and interested stakeholders — partially met.

3. Protection of the rights of indigenous peoples — not met.

4. Transparent and accountable oversight of financial support — partially met.

5. Initial structure for independent forest monitoring — met.

6. Continuing stakeholder consultations on the European Union Forest Law process — met.

---

[82] http://www.un-redd.org/AboutUN-REDDProgramme/tabid/102613/Default.aspx.

[83] http://www.redd-monitor.org/2013/01/17/.

7. Continuing development of a national inter-sectoral system for coordinated land use — partially met.

8. Continuing stakeholder consultation on the Extractive Industries Transparency Initiative — partially met.

9. Agreement on specific measures to reduce forest degradation — not met.

10. Mapping of priority areas for biodiversity — met.

In a joint statement in December 2012, the governments of Norway and Guyana "recognized the potential for improvement in the areas identified in the verification report" and agreed to reform efforts.[84] *See also* Christine Gruning and Laura Susanne Shuford, *Case Study: Guyana REDD-Plus Investment Fund* (GRIF) (Frankfurt School, UNEP Collaborating Centre for Climate & Sustainable Energy Fairness, 2012).

What are the main challenges facing REDD and REDD-Plus?

3.   Where Will the Money Come from?

Most importantly, how can REDD and REDD-Plus be financed? The full deployment of REDD-Plus as the chief legal and financial tool to address deforestation in developing countries will cost untold billions each year. Two categories of alternatives are discussed as options for financing REDD-Plus: public, non-market-based financing and private, market-based financing.

(a)   Non-market based financing

REDD-Plus may be financed through public compensation funds made available through bilateral and multilateral arrangements between donor organizations — developed nations and international organizations — and individual developing countries. Like the Norway-Guyana REDD-Plus Project, a developed nation or a multilateral fund such as the World Bank's FIC, would enter into a long-term agreement with a developing country to disburse funding in return for the developing country's administration of an anti-deforestation and anti-forest degradation program that meets the guidelines set out by the UNFCCC.

(b)   Market-based financing

Market-based financing of REDD-Plus occurs when a REDD-Plus project can be "securitized," creating tradable carbon credits that are attractive to investors. To create tradable REDD-Plus carbon credits a developing country would institute a REDD-Plus program consisting of various projects that meet the UNFCCC guidelines, then would seek certification of the carbon emissions reductions represented by these projects in order to create a certain amount of tradable carbon credits to sell in the carbon markets. The "common currency" of tradable carbon credits is one metric ton of CO_2 emissions. Other GHG — methane, nitrous oxide, sulfur hexafluoride, hydrofluorocarbons, and perfluorocarbons, can be securitized as well by converting them into their equivalent in CO_2; these are

---

[84] *Id.*

referred to in terms of metric tons of CO_2 E, where "E" stands for "equivalent." Once securitized the carbon emission credits may be sold to investors on one of the carbon credit trading markets.

Two categories of carbon credit trading markets exist at present: the mandatory (also called compulsory) market and the voluntary market. The mandatory market exists to accommodate trading by entities that are under a legal obligation to own carbon trading credits to cover their GHG emissions. If such entities do not have sufficient carbon credits they are obliged to purchase them; if they have more than enough they can sell unneeded carbon credits. The largest mandatory carbon market now operating is the EU-ETS, which we studied earlier in this chapter. In the United States a small mandatory market is operating: the Regional Greenhouse Gas Initiative (RGGI), a legal compact of several New England and Mid-Atlantic states to reduce GHG emissions from electric generating facilities. Small mandatory markets exist in certain other countries, notably New Zealand, Australia, and Japan.

At present no mandatory market accepts REDD-Plus carbon credits so these must be sold on the voluntary carbon credit markets. Six voluntary carbon credit trading markets exist: the Chicago Climate Exchange, the European Energy Exchange, the NASDAQ OMX, PowerNext, the Commodity Exchange — Bratislava, and the European Climate Exchange. The largest of these is the Chicago Climate Exchange with a trading volume is about 700 million metric tons of CO_2 E. Trading in these voluntary carbon credit markets is voluntary but legally binding. Many predict a steep rise in volume in these voluntary markets and some see a trillion dollar trading volume by 2020. Of course another option for trading carbon credits in the U.S. is the "over-the-counter market" — direct trades between entities or with a brokerage business.

At present the voluntary carbon trading markets are unregulated; thus, in order to sell carbon credits it is essential to obtain third-party verification that the carbon emission reductions represented by the carbon credits are legally binding and, in the case of REDD, meet UNFCCC standards. Several organizations exist which offer objective verification and certification of REDD project credits. These organizations are private, non-profit companies that have been formed to operate for this purpose. Perhaps the best-known such company is the Verified Carbon Standard (VCS) based in Washington DC. For a fee, VCS will investigate and certify a carbon emission saving project and determine the number of tradable carbon credits, referred to as VCUs — voluntary carbon units. VCUs — each representing one metric ton of CO_2 E — can be sold after certification on one of the voluntary carbon trading markets.

Why should an individual or company purchase or invest in VCUs in the voluntary carbon markets? Consider the following reasons:

- Companies may seek to enhance their brands by emphasizing sustainability practices and environmental citizenship.
- Businesses may purchase VCUs to meet internally set voluntary corporate GHG reduction targets and offset goals.
- A company may purchase VCUs to attract investors.

- A company may want to accumulate carbon credits to prepare for and acquire experience for possible future regulation.

- An individual or company may wish to speculate in the carbon credit markets.

- A business may want to purchase VCUs to gain experience to influence possible future legislation.

- A business may purchase VCUs in order to cover its "carbon footprint" so that it can publicize the fact that it is "carbon neutral."

PROBLEM 4-9
A LAW STUDENT CONTEMPLATES INVESTING IN THE VOLUNTARY CARBON MARKETS

Susan is a law student in a major U.S. university. Having taken a course in International Environmental Law, she has studied carefully the climate change issues, REDD-Plus, and the rise of trading volumes of carbon credits in the voluntary carbon markets. She is aware of the new REDD-Plus program and she is convinced that in the future buying and selling carbon credits will become a big business and the price of VCUs will rise exponentially. Although Susan is burdened by student loan debt, she sees a way out: she is thinking of scraping together all the funds she can and investing in VCUs. She is convinced that she will make a huge profit within a few short years once REDD projects get off the ground. Susan comes to you to ask your advice before she invests. What will you tell her?

PROBLEM 4-10
PROMOTING REDD-PLUS IN INDONESIA

Indonesia has become the third largest emitter of GHG in the world behind China and the United States. Approximately 85% of Indonesia's GHG emissions are due to deforestation, forest degradation, and forest fires. Indonesia contains over one-half of the world's tropical peatlands, which are extremely rich in carbon and are being widely cleared and converted to palm oil plantations, fast-growing tree plantations for pulp and paper, and large-scale irrigated rice and agricultural lands. Logging and the conversion of forests into agricultural land is a major problem. The rate of deforestation in Indonesia is one of the highest in the world, almost 2% annually.[85]

In response to the Copenhagen Accord, the government of Indonesia pledged a GHG emission reduction of 26% by 2020, and further indicated that if international financing is available, an additional reduction of 15% was possible. In order to implement this pledge, Indonesia has enacted a National Action Plan for Reducing Greenhouse Gas Emissions (Rencana Nasional Penurunan Emisi Gas Rumah Kaca — RAN-GRK) that will provide the basis for actions that will directly reduce GHG emissions in five sectors, including forestry and peatland. A wide variety of policy instruments may be employed by the government to attain its goals, including

---

[85] NATHALIE OLSEN & JOSHUA BISHOP, THE FINANCIAL COSTS OF REDD: EVIDENCE FROM BRAZIL AND INDONESIA, ii–iv (Gland, Switzerland: IUCN, 2009).

regulations and standards, taxes and charges, tradable permits, voluntary agreements, and subsidies and incentives.

Such a National Action Plan for Indonesia as a Non-Annex I developing country is in accordance with the UNFCCC COP-13 Decision 1/CP.13 (the Bali Action Plan), which encourages the development of "nationally appropriate mitigation actions by developing country Parties in the context of sustainable development, supported and enabled by technology, financing, and capacity-building, in a measurable, reportable, and verifiable manner."

Economic analyses have determined the opportunity costs for various kinds of forests and peatland in Indonesia. Peatland conservation has a very low opportunity cost because the costs of conversion are high and the economic returns are low. The highest opportunity cost of REDD in Indonesia occurs where forest conservation competes with palm oil production. The opportunity costs of forestland conservation range from USD 0.49/ton CO_2 for small holder farming in Sumatra up to USD 19.6/ton CO_2 for palm oil tree farming in certain especially favorable areas.

Suppose you are an official of the Indonesian government who seeks financing for conservation plans under the RAN-GRK to preserve specific forest and peatland areas. You have heard about a nonprofit company based in California, Code REDD (http://www.coderedd.org), that seeks to catalyze the market for REDD and REDD-Plus projects. Code REDD investigates REDD projects and, if appropriate, grants a Certificate of Approval for specific REDD projects with the view to making them attractive to private investors. Your investigation shows also that Wildlife Works (http://www.wildlifeworks.com), a California non-profit company, bills itself as an organization that "uses the emerging marketplace for REDD-Plus carbon offsets to preserve forests all over the world." Recently the company Allianz, based in Munich, Germany, one of the largest financial service companies in the world, purchased a 10% share in Wildlife Works. Allianz and several other large companies have joined a "REDD alliance" with a view to purchasing verified carbon credits approved by Code REDD and either selling them on the EU-ETS or banking them for later sale after the possible creation of an international marketplace for the sale and purchase of REDD carbon credits. Allianz is a company that prides itself on the fact that it intends to be "carbon neutral" in its worldwide operations. To do so, Allianz purchases Certified REDD project carbon credits from time-to-time.

Formulate the elements of a plan for a REDD-Plus project that the government of Indonesia might market to private investors.

L.　The United States' Implementation of Its Copenhagen Pledge

The United States, which led the effort to establish the Copenhagen Accord, pledged a reduction of GHG emissions "in the range of 17%" by 2020, using a base year of 2005. The United States is the second largest GHG emitting country; since 1990, U.S. emissions have grown approximately 12%. The United States was the only Annex I country not to ratify the Kyoto Protocol and so never had any binding obligation to reduce its GHG emissions. The United States is, of course, bound by the provisions of the UNFCCC and participates in the annual meetings of the

Conference of the Parties. The Inventory of United States' Greenhouse Gas Emissions and Sinks, filed by the U.S. EPA is *available at* http://unfccc.int/national_reports/annex_i_ghg_inventories/national_inventories_submissions/items/8108.php.

In 2009, the U.S. House of Representatives of the United States passed the American Clean Energy and Security Act, which would have created a cap-and-trade greenhouse gases limitation and reduction system for the United States, but this legislative initiative did not pass the U.S. Senate and did not become law. As a result, no significant climate change legislation has been enacted at the federal level in the United States. The effort to stem climate change has played out mainly in the courts, the U.S. Environmental Protection Agency, and in the individual U.S. states.

In 2007, the Supreme Court of the United States, by a vote of 5 to 4, decided the landmark case, Massachusetts v. Environmental Protection Agency.

MASSACHUSETTS v. ENVIRONMENTAL PROTECTION AGENCY
549 U.S. 497 (2007)

JUSTICE STEVENS delivered the opinion of the Court.

A well-documented rise in global temperatures has coincided with a significant increase in the concentration of carbon dioxide in the atmosphere. Respected scientists believe the two trends are related. For when carbon dioxide is released into the atmosphere, it acts like the ceiling of a greenhouse, trapping solar energy and retarding the escape of reflected heat. It is therefore a species — the most important species — of a "greenhouse gas."

Calling global warming "the most pressing environmental challenge of our time," a group of States, local governments and private organizations, alleged in a petition for certiorari that the Environmental Protection Agency (EPA) has abdicated its responsibility under the Clean Air Act to regulate the emissions of four greenhouse gases, including carbon dioxide. Specifically, petitioners asked us to answer two questions concerning the meaning of § 202(a)(l) of the Act: whether EPA has the statutory authority to regulate greenhouse gas emissions from new motor vehicles; and if so, whether its stated reasons for doing so are consistent with the statute. In response, EPA, supported by 10 intervening States and six trade associations, correctly argued that we may not address those two questions unless at least one petitioner has standing to invoke our jurisdiction under Article III of the Constitution.

I

Section 202(a)(1) of the Clean Air Act, as added by Pub. L. 89-272, § 101(8), 79 Stat. 992, and as amended by, *inter alia*, 84 Stat. 1690 and 91 Stat. 791, 42 U.S.C. § 7521(a)(1), provides:

"The [EPA] Administrator shall by regulation prescribe (and from time to time revise) in accordance with the provisions of this section, standards applicable to the emission of any air pollutant from any class or classes of new motor vehicles or new motor vehicle engines, which in his judgment cause, or contribute to, air pollution which may reasonably be anticipated to endanger public health or welfare. . . ."[86]

The Act defines "air pollutant" to include "any air pollution agent or combination of such agents, including any physical, chemical, biological, radioactive . . . substance or matter which is emitted into or otherwise enters the ambient air," § 7602(g). "Welfare" is also defined broadly: among other things, it includes "effects on . . . weather . . . and climate." § 7602(h).

When Congress enacted these provisions, the study of climate change was in its infancy.[87] In 1959, shortly after the U.S. Weather Bureau began monitoring atmospheric carbon dioxide levels, an observatory in Mauna Loa, Hawaii, recorded a mean level of 316 parts per million. This was well above the highest carbon dioxide concentration — no more than 300 parts per million — revealed in the 420,000-year-old ice-core record.[88] By the time Congress drafted § 202(a)(1) in 1970, carbon dioxide levels had reached 325 parts per million.

In the late 1970's, the Federal Government began devoting serious attention to the possibility that carbon dioxide emissions associated with human activity could provoke climate change. In 1978, Congress enacted the National Climate Program Act, 92 Stat. 601, which required the President to establish a program to "assist the Nation and the world to understand and respond to natural and man-induced climate processes and their implications," *id.*, § 3. President Carter, in turn, asked the National Research Council, the working arm of the National Academy of Sciences, to investigate the subject. The Council's response was unequivocal: "If carbon dioxide continues to increase, the study group finds no reason to doubt that climate changes will result and no reason to believe that these changes will be negligible. . . . A wait-and-see policy may mean waiting until it is too late."

Congress next addressed the issue in 1987, when it enacted the Global Climate Protection Act, Title XI of Pub. L. 100-204, 101 Stat. 1407, note following 15 U.S.C. § 2901. Finding that "manmade pollution-the release of carbon dioxide, chlorofluorocarbons, methane, and other trace gases into the atmosphere-may be producing a long-term and substantial increase in the average temperature on Earth,"

---

[86] The 1970 version of § 202(a)(1) used the phrase "which endangers the public health or welfare" rather than the more-protective "which may reasonably be anticipated to endanger public health or welfare." See § 6 (a) of the Clean Air Amendments of 1970, 84 Stat. 1690. Congress amended § 202(a)(1) in 1977 to give its approval to the decision in Ethyl Corp. v. EPA, 541 F.2d 1, 25 (CADC 1976) (en banc), which held action to prevent harm, even if the regulator is less than certain that harm is otherwise inevitable." See § 401(d)(a) of the Clean Air Act Amendments of 1977, 91 Stat. 791; see also H. R. Rep. No. 95-294, p. 49 (1977).

[87] The Council on Environmental Quality had issued a report in 1970 concluding that "[m]an may be changing his weather." Environmental Quality: The First Annual Report 93. Considerable uncertainty remained in those early years, and the issue went largely unmentioned in the congressional debate over the enactment of the Clean Air Act. But see 116 Cong. Rec. 32914 (1970) (statement of Sen. Boggs referring to Council's conclusion that "[a]ir pollution alters the climate and may produce global changes in temperature").

[88] See Intergovernmental Panel on Climate Change, Climate Change 2001: Synthesis Report, pp. 202–203 (2001).

§ 1102(1), 101 Stat. 1408, Congress directed EPA to propose to Congress a "coordinated national policy on global climate change," § 1103(b), and ordered the Secretary of State to work "through the channels of multilateral diplomacy" and coordinate diplomatic efforts to combat global warming, § 1103(c). Congress emphasized that "ongoing pollution and deforestation may be contributing now to an irreversible process" and that "[n]ecessary actions must be identified and implemented in time to protect the climate." § 1102(4).

II

On October 20, 1999, a group of 19 private organizations filed a rulemaking petition asking EPA to regulate "greenhouse gas emissions from new motor vehicles under § 202 of the Clean Air Act." Petitioners maintained that 1998 was the "warmest year on record"; that carbon dioxide, methane, nitrous oxide, and hydrofluorocarbons are "heat trapping greenhouse gases"; that green-house gas emissions have significantly accelerated climate change; and that the IPCC's 1995 report warned that "carbon dioxide remains the most important contributor to [man-made] forcing of climate change." The petition further alleged that climate change will have serious adverse effects on human health and the environment.

On September 8, 2003, EPA entered an order denying the rulemaking petition. 68 Fed. Reg. 52922. The agency gave two reasons for its decision: (1) that contrary to the opinions of its former general counsels, the Clean Air Act does not authorize EPA to issue mandatory regulations to address global climate change, and (2) that even if the agency had the authority to set greenhouse gas emission standards, it would be unwise to do so at this time.

III

Petitioners, now joined by intervenor States and local governments, sought review of EPA's order in the United States Court of Appeals for the District of Columbia Circuit. Although each of the three judges on the panel wrote a separate opinion, two judges agreed "that the EPA Administrator properly exercised his discretion under § 202(a)(1) in denying the petition for rule making." 415 F.3d 50, 58 (2005). The court therefore denied the petition for review.

IV

Article III of the Constitution limits federal-court jurisdiction to "Cases" and "Controversies." Those two words confine "the business of federal courts to questions presented in an adversary context and in a form historically viewed as capable of resolution through the judicial process." Flast v. Cohen, 392 U.S. 83, 95 (1968).

The parties' dispute turns on the proper construction of a congressional statute, a question eminently suitable to resolution in federal court. Congress has moreover authorized this type of challenge to EPA action. See 42 U.S.C. § 7607(b)(1). That authorization is of critical importance to the standing inquiry: "Congress has the power to define injuries and articulate chains of causation that will give rise to a case or controversy where none existed before." Lujan, 504 U.S., at 580 (Kennedy, J., concurring in part and concurring in judgment). "In exercising this power, however, Congress must at the very least identify the injury it seeks to vindicate and relate the injury to the class of persons entitled to bring suit." Ibid. We will not, therefore, "entertain citizen suits to vindicate the public's nonconcrete interest in the proper administration of the laws." Id., at 581.

EPA maintains that because greenhouse gas emissions inflict widespread harm, the doctrine of standing presents an insuperable jurisdictional obstacle. We do not agree. At bottom, "the gist of the question of standing" is whether petitioners have "such a personal stake in the outcome of the controversy as to assure that concrete adverseness which sharpens the presentation of issues upon which the court so largely depends for illumination." Baker v. Carr, 369 U.S. 186, 204 (1962). As Justice Kennedy explained in his Lujan concurrence:

> "While it does not matter how many persons have been injured by the challenged action, the party bringing suit must show that the action injures him in a concrete and personal way. This requirement is not just an empty formality. It preserves the vitality of the adversarial process by assuring both that the parties before the court have an actual, as opposed to professed, stake in the outcome, and that the legal questions presented . . . will be resolved, not in the rarified atmosphere of a debating society, but in a concrete factual context conducive to a realistic appreciation of the consequences of judicial action." 504 U.S., at 581 (internal quotation marks omitted).

To ensure the proper adversarial presentation, *Lujan* holds that a litigant must demonstrate that it has suffered a concrete and particularized injury that is either actual or imminent, that the injury is fairly traceable to the defendant, and that it is likely that a favorable decision will redress that injury. See *id.*, at 560–561. However, a litigant to whom Congress has "accorded a procedural right to protect his concrete interests," *id.*, at 572, n. 7 — here, the right to challenge agency action unlawfully withheld, § 7607(b)(1) — "can assert that right without meeting all the normal standards for redressability and immediacy," *ibid.* When a litigant is vested with a procedural right, that litigant has standing if there is some possibility that the requested relief will prompt the injury-causing party to reconsider the decision that allegedly harmed the litigant.

Well before the creation of the modern administrative state, we recognized that States are not normal litigants for the purposes of invoking federal jurisdiction. As Justice Holmes explained in Georgia v. Tennessee Copper Co., 206 U.S. 230, 237 (1907), a case in which Georgia sought to protect its citizens from air pollution originating outside its borders:

> "The case has been argued largely as if it were one between two private parties; but it is not. The very elements that would be relied upon in a suit between fellow-citizens as a ground for equitable relief are wanting here. The State owns very little of the territory alleged to be affected, and the damage to it capable of estimate in money, possibly, at least, is small. This is a suit by a State for an injury to it in its capacity of *quasi*-sovereign. In that capacity the State has an interest independent of and behind the titles

of its citizens, in all the earth and air within its domain. It has the last word as to whether its mountains shall be stripped of their forests and its inhabitants shall breathe pure air."

Just as Georgia's "independent interest . . . in all the earth and air within its domain" supported federal jurisdiction a century ago, so too does Massachusetts' well-founded desire to preserve its sovereign territory today.

When a State enters the Union, it surrenders certain sovereign prerogatives. Massachusetts cannot invade Rhode Island to force reductions in greenhouse gas emissions, it cannot negotiate an emissions treaty with China or India, and in some circumstances the exercise of its police powers to reduce in-state motor-vehicle emissions might well be pre-empted. See Alfred L. Snapp & Son, Inc. v. Puerto Rico ex rel. Barez, 458 U.S. 592, 607 (1982) ("One helpful indication in determining whether an alleged injury to the health and welfare of its citizens suffices to give the State standing to sue parens patriae is whether the injury is one that the State, if it could, would likely attempt to address through its sovereign lawmaking powers").

These sovereign prerogatives are now lodged in the Federal Government, and Congress has ordered EPA to protect Massachusetts (among others) by prescribing standards applicable to the "emission of any air pollutant from any class or classes of new motor vehicle engines, which in [the Administrator's] judgment cause, or contribute to, air pollution which may reasonably be anticipated to endanger public health or welfare." 42 U.S.C. § 7521(a)(1). Congress has moreover recognized a concomitant procedural right to challenge the rejection of its rulemaking petition as arbitrary and capricious. § 7607(b)(1). Given that procedural right and Massachusetts' stake in protecting its quasi-sovereign interests, the Commonwealth is entitled to special solicitude in our standing analysis.[89]

---

[89] THE CHIEF JUSTICE accuses the Court of misreading *Georgia v. Tennessee Copper Co.*, 206 U.S. 230 (1907), see *post*, at 3–4 (dissenting opinion), and "devis[ing} a new doctrine of state standing," *id.*, at 15. But no less an authority than Hart & Wechsler's The Federal Courts and the Federal System understands *Tennessee Copper* as a standing decision. R. Fallon, D. Meltzer, & D. Shapiro, Hart & Wechsler's The Federal Courts and the Federal System 290 (5th ed. 2003). Indeed, it devotes an entire section to chronicling the long development of cases permitting States "to litigate as *parens patriae* to protect quasi-sovereign interests — i.e., public or governmental interests that concern the state as a whole." *Id.*, at 289; see, *e.g., Missouri v. Illinois*, 180 U.S. 208, 240–241 (1901) (finding federal jurisdiction appropriate not only "in cases involving boundaries and jurisdiction over lands and their inhabitants, and in cases directly affecting the property rights and interests of a state," but also when the "substantial impairment of the health and prosperity of the towns and cities of the state" are at stake).

Drawing on Massachusetts v. Mellon, 262 U.S. 447 (1923), and *Alfred L. Snapp & Son, Inc. v. Puerto Rico ex rel. Barez*, 458 U.S. 592 (1982) (citing *Missouri v. Illinois*, 180 U.S. 208 (190)), THE CHIEF JUSTICE claims that we "overloo[k] the fact that our cases cast significant doubt on a State's standing to assert a quasi-sovereign interest . . . against the Federal Government." *Post*, at 5. Not so. *Mellon* itself disavowed any such broad reading when it noted that the Court had been "called upon to adjudicate, not rights of person or property, not rights of dominion over physical domain, [and) *not quasi sovereign rights actually invaded or threatened*." 262 U.S., at 484–485 (emphasis added). In any event, we held in *Georgia v. Pennsylvania R. Co.*, 324 U.S. 439, 447 (1945), that there is a critical difference between allowing a State "to protect her citizens from the operation of federal statutes" (which is what *Mellon* prohibits) and allowing a State to assert its rights under federal law (which it has standing to do). Massachusetts does not here dispute that the Clean Air Act *applies* to its citizens; it rather seeks to assert its rights under the Act. See also *Nebraska v. Wyoming*, 515 U.S. 1, 20 (1995) (holding that Wyoming had standing to bring a cross claim against the United States to vindicate its " 'quasi-

With that in mind, it is clear that petitioners' submissions as they pertain to Massachusetts have satisfied the most demanding standards of the adversarial process. EPA's steadfast refusal to regulate greenhouse gas emissions presents a risk of harm to Massachusetts that is both "actual" and "imminent." Lujan, 504 U.S., at 560 (internal quotation marks omitted). There is, moreover, a "substantial likelihood that the judicial relief requested" will prompt EPA to take steps to reduce that risk. Duke Power Co. v. Carolina Environmental Study Group, Inc., 438 U.S. 59, 79 (1978).

The Injury

The harms associated with climate change are serious and well recognized. Indeed, the NRC Report itself — which EPA regards as an "objective and independent assessment of the relevant science," 68 Fed. Reg. 52930-identifies a number of environmental changes that have already inflicted significant harms, including "the global retreat of mountain glaciers, reduction in snow-cover extent, the earlier spring melting of rivers and lakes, [and] the accelerated rate of rise of sea levels during the 20th century relative to the past few thousand years . . . ." NRC Report 16.

Petitioners allege that this only hints at the environmental damage yet to come. According to the climate scientist Michael MacCracken, "qualified scientific experts involved in climate change research" have reached a "strong consensus" that global warming threatens (among other things) a precipitate rise in sea levels by the end of the century, "severe and irreversible changes to natural ecosystems," a "significant reduction in water storage in winter snowpack in mountainous regions with direct and important economic consequences," and an increase in the spread of disease. He also observes that rising ocean temperatures may contribute to the ferocity of hurricanes

That these climate-change risks are "widely shared" does not minimize Massachusetts' interest in the outcome of this litigation. See Federal Election Comm'n v. Akins, 524 U.S. 11, 24 (1998) ("[W]here a harm is concrete, though widely shared, the Court has found 'injury in fact'"). According to petitioners' unchallenged affidavits, global sea levels rose somewhere between 10 and 20 centimeters over the 20th century as a result of global warming. These rising seas have already begun to swallow Massachusetts' coastal land.

The severity of that injury will only increase over the course of the next century: If sea levels continue to rise as predicted, one Massachusetts official believes that a significant fraction of coastal property will be "either permanently lost through inundation or temporarily lost through periodic storm surge and flooding events." Remediation costs alone, petitioners allege, could run well into the hundreds of millions of dollars.

---

sovereign' interests which are 'independent of and behind the titles of its citizens, in all the earth and air within its domain' " (quoting Tennessee Copper, 206 U.S., at 237).

Causation

EPA does not dispute the existence of a causal connection between man-made greenhouse gas emissions and global warming. At a minimum, therefore, EPA's refusal to regulate such emissions "contributes" to Massachusetts' injuries.

EPA nevertheless maintains that its decision not to regulate greenhouse gas emissions from new motor vehicles contributes so insignificantly to petitioners' injuries that the agency cannot be haled [sic] into federal court to answer for them. For the same reason, EPA does not believe that any realistic possibility exists that the relief petitioners seek would mitigate global climate change and remedy their injuries. That is especially so because predicted increases in greenhouse gas emissions from developing nations, particularly China and India, are likely to offset any marginal domestic decrease.

But EPA overstates its case. Its argument rests on the erroneous assumption that a small incremental step, because it is incremental, can never be attacked in a federal judicial forum. Yet accepting that premise would doom most challenges to regulatory action. Agencies, like legislatures, do not generally resolve massive problems in one fell regulatory swoop. See Williamson v. Lee Optical of Okla., Inc., 348 U.S. 483, 489 (1955) ("[A] reform may take one step at a time, addressing itself to the phase of the problem which seems most acute to the legislative mind").

And reducing domestic automobile emissions is hardly a tentative step. Even leaving aside the other greenhouse gases, the United States transportation sector emits an enormous quantity of carbon dioxide into the atmosphere-according to the MacCracken affidavit, more than 1.7 billion metric tons in 1999 alone. That accounts for more than 6% of worldwide carbon dioxide emissions. To put this in perspective: Considering just emissions from the transportation sector, which represent less than one-third of this country's total carbon dioxide emissions, the United States would still rank as the third-largest emitter of carbon dioxide in the world, outpaced only by the European Union and China. Judged by any standard, U.S. motor-vehicle emissions make a meaningful contribution to greenhouse gas concentrations and hence, according to petitioners, to global warming.

The Remedy

While it may be true that regulating motor-vehicle emissions will not by itself reverse global warming, it by no means follows that we lack jurisdiction to decide whether EPA has a duty to take steps to slow or reduce it. See also Larson v. Valente, 456 U.S. 228, 244, n.15 (1982) ("[A] plaintiff satisfies the redressability requirement when he shows that a favorable decision will relieve a discrete injury to himself. He need not show that a favorable decision will relieve his every injury"). Because of the enormity of the potential consequences associated with man-made climate change, the fact that the effectiveness of a remedy might be delayed during the (relatively short) time it takes for a new motor-vehicle fleet to replace an older one is essentially irrelevant. Nor is it dispositive that developing countries such as China and India are poised to increase greenhouse gas emissions substantially over the next century: A reduction in domestic emissions would slow the pace of global emissions increases, no matter what happens elsewhere.

In sum — at least according to petitioners' uncontested affidavits — the rise in sea levels associated with global warming has already harmed and will continue to harm Massachusetts. The risk of catastrophic harm, though remote, is nevertheless real. That risk would be reduced to some extent if petitioners received the relief they seek. We therefore hold that petitioners have standing to challenge the EPA's denial of their rulemaking petition.

VI

On the merits, the first question is whether § 202(a)(1) of the Clean Air Act authorizes EPA to regulate greenhouse gas emissions from new motor vehicles in the event that it forms a "judgment" that such emissions contribute to climate change. We have little trouble concluding that it does. In relevant part, § 202(a)(1) provides that EPA "shall by regulation prescribe . . . standards applicable to the emission of any air pollutant from any class or classes of new motor vehicles or new motor vehicle engines, which in [the Administrator's] judgment cause, or contribute to, air pollution which may reasonably be anticipated to endanger public health or welfare." 42 U.S.C. § 7521(a)(1). Because EPA believes that Congress did not intend it to regulate substances that contribute to climate change, the agency maintains that carbon dioxide is not an "air pollutant" within the meaning of the provision.

The statutory text forecloses EPA's reading. The Clean Air Act's sweeping definition of "air pollutant" includes "*any* air pollution agent or combination of such agents, including *any* physical, chemical . . . substance or matter which is emitted into or otherwise enters the ambient air. . . ." § 7602(g) (emphasis added). On its face, the definition embraces all airborne compounds of whatever stripe, and underscores that intent through the repeated use of the word "any."[90] Carbon dioxide, methane, nitrous oxide, and hydrofluorocarbons are without a doubt "physical [and] chemical . . . substance[s] which [are] emitted into . . . the ambient air." The statute is unambiguous.[91]

Rather than relying on statutory text, EPA invokes postenactment congressional actions and deliberations it views as tantamount to a congressional command to refrain from regulating greenhouse gas emissions. Even if such postenactment legislative history could shed light on the meaning of an otherwise-unambiguous

---

[90] *See Department of Housing and Urban Development v. Rucker, 535* U.S. 125, 131 (2002) (observing that " 'any'. . . has an expansive meaning, that is, one or some indiscriminately of whatever kind" (some internal quotation marks omitted)).

[91] In dissent, JUSTICE SCALIA maintains that because greenhouse gases permeate the world's atmosphere rather than a limited area near the earth's surface, EPA's exclusion of greenhouse gases from the category of air pollution "agent[s]" is entitled to deference under *Chevron U. S. A. Inc.* v. *Natural Resources Defense Council, Inc.* 467 U.S. 837 (1984). See *post,* at 11–13. EPA's distinction, however, finds no support in the text of the statute, which uses the phrase "the ambient air" without distinguishing between atmospheric layers. Moreover, it is a plainly unreasonable reading of a sweeping statutory provision designed to capture "*any* physical, chemical . . . substance or matter which is emitted into or otherwise enters the ambient air." 42 U.S.C. § 7602(g). JUSTICE SCALIA does not (and cannot) explain why Congress would define "air pollutant" so carefully and so broadly, yet confer on EPA the authority to narrow that definition whenever expedient by asserting that a particular substance is not an "agent." At any rate, no party to this dispute contests that greenhouse gases both "ente[r] the ambient air" and tend to warm the atmosphere. They are therefore unquestionably "agent[s]" of air pollution.

statute, EPA never identifies any action remotely suggesting that Congress meant to curtail its power to treat greenhouse gases as air pollutants. That subsequent Congresses have eschewed enacting binding emissions limitations to combat global warming tells us nothing about what Congress meant when it amended § 202(a)(1) in 1970 and 1977. And unlike EPA, we have no difficulty reconciling Congress' various efforts to promote interagency collaboration and research to better understand climate change*' with the agency's pre-existing mandate to regulate "any air pollutant" that may endanger the public welfare. See 42 U.S.C. § 7601(a)(1). Collaboration and research do not conflict with any thoughtful regulatory effort; they complement it.

While the Congresses that drafted § 202(a)(1) might not have appreciated the possibility that burning fossil fuels could lead to global warming, they did understand that without regulatory flexibility, changing circumstances and scientific developments would soon render the Clean Air Act obsolete. The broad language of § 202(a)(1) reflects an intentional effort to confer the flexibility necessary to forestall such obsolescence. See *Pennsylvania Dept. of Corrections* v. *Yeskey*, 524 U.S. 206, 212 (1998) ("[T]he fact that a statute can be applied in situations not expressly anticipated by Congress does not demonstrate ambiguity. It demonstrates breadth" (internal quotation marks omitted)). Because greenhouse gases fit well within the Clean Air Act's capacious definition of "air pollutant," we hold that EPA has the statutory authority to regulate the emission of such gases from new motor vehicles.

VII

The alternative basis for EPA's decision-that even if it does have statutory authority to regulate greenhouse gases, it would be unwise to do so at this time — rests on reasoning divorced from the statutory text. While the statute does condition the exercise of EPA's authority on its formation of a "judgment," 42 U.S.C. § 7521(a)(1), that judgment must relate to whether an air pollutant "cause[s], or contribute[s] to, air pollution which may reasonably be anticipated to endanger public health or welfare," *ibid.* Put another way, the use of the word "judgment" is not a roving license to ignore the statutory text. It is but a direction to exercise discretion within defined statutory limits.

If EPA makes a finding of endangerment, the Clean Air Act requires the agency to regulate emissions of the deleterious pollutant from new motor vehicles. *Ibid.* (stating that "[EPA] shall by regulation prescribe . . . standards applicable to the emission of any air pollutant from any class of new motor vehicles"). EPA no doubt has significant latitude as to the manner, timing, content, and coordination of its regulations with those of other agencies. But once EPA has responded to a petition for rule making, its reasons for action or inaction must conform to the authorizing statute. Under the clear terms of the Clean Air Act, EPA can avoid taking further action only if it determines that greenhouse gases do not contribute to climate change or if it provides some reasonable explanation as to why it cannot or will not exercise its discretion to determine whether they do. Ibid. To the extent that this constrains agency discretion to pursue other priorities of the Administrator or the President, this is the congressional design.

EPA has refused to comply with this clear statutory command. Instead, it has offered a laundry list of reasons not to regulate. For example, EPA said that a number of voluntary executive branch programs already provide an effective response to the threat of global warming, 68 Fed. Reg. 52932, that regulating greenhouse gases might impair the President's ability to negotiate with "key developing nations" to reduce emissions, *id.*, at 52931, and that curtailing motor-vehicle emissions would reflect "an inefficient, piecemeal approach to address the climate change issue," *ibid.*

Although we have neither the expertise nor the authority to evaluate these policy judgments, it is evident they have nothing to do with whether greenhouse gas emissions contribute to climate change. Still less do they amount to a reasoned justification for declining to form a scientific judgment. In particular, while the President has broad authority in foreign affairs, that authority does not extend to the refusal to execute domestic laws. In the Global Climate Protection Act of 1987, Congress authorized the State Department-not EPA-to formulate United States foreign policy with reference to environmental matters relating to climate. See § 1103(c), 101 Stat. 1409. EPA has made no showing that it issued the ruling in question here after consultation with the State Department. Congress did direct EPA to consult with other agencies in the formulation of its policies and rules, but the State Department is absent from that list. § 1103(b).

Nor can EPA avoid its statutory obligation by noting the uncertainty surrounding various features of climate change and concluding that it would therefore be better not to regulate at this time. See 68 Fed. Reg. 52930–52931. If the scientific uncertainty is so profound that it precludes EPA from making a reasoned judgment as to whether greenhouse gases contribute to global warming, EPA must say so. That EPA would prefer not to regulate greenhouse gases because of some residual uncertainty — which, contrary to Justice Scalia's apparent belief, post, at 5–8, is in fact all that it said, see 68 Fed. Reg. 52929 ("We do not believe . . . that it would be either effective or appropriate for EPA to establish [greenhouse gas] standards for motor vehicles at this time" (emphasis added)) — is irrelevant. The statutory question is whether sufficient information exists to make an endangerment finding.

In short, EPA has offered no reasoned explanation for its refusal to decide whether greenhouse gases cause or contribute to climate change. Its action was therefore "arbitrary, capricious, . . . or otherwise not in accordance with law." 42 U.S.C. § 7607(d)(9)(A). We need not and do not reach the question whether on remand EPA must make an endangerment finding, or whether policy concerns can inform EPA's actions in the event that it makes such a finding. Cf. Chevron U. S. A. Inc. v. Natural Resources Defense Council, Inc., 467 U.S. 837, 843–844 (1984). We hold only that EPA must ground its reasons for action or inaction in the statute.

VIII

The judgment of the Court of Appeals is reversed, and the case is remanded for further proceedings consistent with this opinion.

It is so ordered.

[CHIEF JUSTICE ROBERTS joined by JUSTICES ALITO, SCALIA, and THOMAS dissented from the Court's majority opinion. On the standing issue, the Chief Justice argued that the effects of climate change are too generalized, too uncertain, and too unlikely to be effectively redressed by domestic legislation to provide any plaintiff with standing to sue. He also argued that, even if global warming is a crisis and "the most pressing environmental problem of our time," it is a problem best addressed by the Congress and the President, not by the courts. 564 U.S. at 535. Justice Scalia in dissent argued that greenhouse gases are not agents of air pollution because substances that pollute the air do so primarily only at ground level or near the surface of the Earth and are to be distinguished from substances in the upper atmosphere like greenhouse gases. 564 U.S. at 556–60.]

NOTE

In response to *Massachusetts v. EPA*, the U.S. EPA took several actions. First, on December 7, 2009, the EPA made the following findings:[92]

Endangerment Finding: The Administrator finds that the current and projected concentrations of the six well-mixed greenhouse gases — carbon dioxide, methane, nitrous oxide, hydrofluorocarbons, perfluorocarbons, and sulfur hexafluoride — in the atmosphere threaten the public health and welfare of current and future generations.

Cause or Contribute Finding: The Administrator finds that the combined emissions of these well-mixed greenhouse gases from new motor vehicles and new motor vehicle engines contribute to the greenhouse gas pollution which threatens public health and welfare.

Second, the EPA issued a so-called Tailpipe Rule, 75 Fed. Reg. 25,324 (May 7, 2010), which set greenhouse gas emission standards for cars and light trucks as part of joint rulemaking with fuel economy standards issued by the National Highway Traffic Safety Administration. This rulemaking of mobile sources under the Clean Air Act triggered mandatory rulemaking of stationary sources of greenhouse gas emissions — iron and steel and electrical generating facilities, for example. *See* 42 U.S.C. §§ 7475 and 7479(1). This provided authority for the EPA to issue a so-called Timing Rule, 75 Fed. Reg. 17,004 (April 2, 2010), which announced that major stationary emitters of greenhouse gases would soon be subject to new greenhouse gases permitting regulations. Next the EPA promulgated the so-called Tailoring Rule, 75 Fed. Reg. 31,514 (June 3, 2010), which stated that only the largest stationary sources-those exceeding 75 thousand or 100 thousand (depending on the program and the project) of CO_2 e per year would be subject to the new regulations.

The EPA's Endangerment Finding as well as the Tailpipe, Timing and Tailoring Rules were immediately challenged by a coalition of states and industry groups.

---

[92] These findings were made pursuant to the statutory authority in 42 U.S.C. § 7521(a)(1). *See* http://www.epa.gov/climatechange/Downloads/endangerment/EndangermentFinding_FAQs.pdf.

The EPA's findings and rules were upheld in *Coalition for Responsible Regulation v. EPA*, 684 F.3d 102 (D.C. Cir. 2012).

Third, the EPA on January 8, 2014, proposed stringent new limits on emissions of GHG from new coal-fired and gas-fired electrical generating facilities under section 111 of the Clean Air Act, 42 U.S.C. § 7411. (Federal Register, January 8, 2014, available at www.federalregister.gov/article/2014/01/08). On June 2, 2014, the EPA issued proposed new GHG emission limits from existing electrical power plants. (Federal Register, June 2, 2014, available at www.federalregister.gov/article/2014/02/06). These two proposals are the heart of the EPA's Clean Power Program, which aims to secure a 30% CO2 emission reduction from fossil fuel generation by 2030, using a 2005 baseline. Industry and Republican lawmakers criticized these proposals as excessive. Senator Mike Enzi (R, Wyo) charged that "the Administration has set out to kill coal and its 800,000 jobs."

In June 2014, the Supreme Court in *Utility Air Regulatory Group v. Environmental Protection Agency*, 189 L. Ed. 2d 372 (2014), upheld (four justices separately concurring in part and dissenting in part) EPA's authority to issue the "Triggering Rule" that held that new motor vehicle GHG emission standards triggered new stationary source permitting requirements under the Clean Air Act. Thus, the Supreme Court's holding in *Massachusetts v. EPA*, which concerned Title II of the Clean Air Act (mobile sources), carries over to Title I of the Act, which applies to stationary sources. The Court, however, struck down the EPA's "Tailoring Rule," which was issued under Clean Air Act Title V to limit the classes of stationary sources subject to the PSD (prevention of significant deterioration) provisions of the Act. The court ruled that the Triggering Rule did not carry over to require PSD stationary sources that otherwise would not be subject to regulation to be covered as to their GHG emissions. However, this decision leaves the EPA free to regulate some 83% of stationary sources nationwide responsible for GHG emissions.

In June of 2013, the Obama Administration announced a major new initiative on climate change.

1.　The President's Climate Action Plan

THE PRESIDENT'S CLIMATE ACTION PLAN EXECUTIVE OFFICE OF THE PRESIDENT
June 2013

I. Deploying Clean Energy

Cutting Carbon Pollution from Power Plants. Power plants are the largest concentrated source of emissions in the United States, together accounting for roughly one-third of all domestic greenhouse gas emissions. We have already set limits for arsenic, mercury, and lead, but there is no federal rule to prevent power plants from releasing as much carbon pollution as they want. Many states, local governments, and companies have taken steps to move to cleaner electricity sources. More than 35 states have renewable energy targets in place, and more than 25 have set energy efficiency targets.

Despite this progress at the state level, there are no federal standards in place to reduce carbon pollution from power plants. In April 2012, as part of a continued effort to modernize our electric power sector, the Obama Administration proposed a carbon pollution standard for new power plants. The Environmental Protection Agency's proposal reflects and reinforces the ongoing trend towards cleaner technologies, with natural gas increasing its share of electricity generation in recent years, principally through market forces and renewables deployment growing rapidly to account for roughly half of new generation capacity installed in 2012.

With abundant clean energy solutions available, and building on the leadership of states and local governments, we can make continued progress in reducing power plant pollution to improve public health and the environment while supplying the reliable, affordable power needed for economic growth. By doing so, we will continue to drive American leadership in clean energy technologies, such as efficient natural gas, nuclear, renewables, and clean coal technology.

II. Building a 21st-Century Transportation Sector

Increasing: Fuel Economy Standards; Heavy-duty vehicles are currently the second largest source of greenhouse gas emissions within the transportation sector. In 2011, the Obama Administration finalized the first-ever fuel economy standards for Model Year 2014–2018 for heavy-duty trucks, buses, and vans. These standards will reduce greenhouse gas emissions by approximately 270 million metric tons and save 530 million barrels of oil. During the President's second term, the Administration will once again partner with industry leaders and other key stakeholders to develop post-2018 fuel economy standards for heavy-duty vehicles to further reduce fuel consumption through the application of advanced cost-effective technologies and continue efforts to improve the efficiency of moving goods across the United States.

The Obama Administration has already established the toughest fuel economy standards for passenger vehicles in U.S. history. These standards require an average performance equivalent of 54.5 miles per gallon by 2025, which will save the average driver more than $8,000 in fuel costs over the lifetime of the vehicle and eliminate six billion metric tons of carbon pollution — more than the United States emits in an entire year.

Developing and Deploying Advanced Transportation Technologies; Biofuels have an important role to play in increasing our energy security, fostering rural economic development, and reducing greenhouse gas emissions from the transportation sector. That is why the Administration supports the Renewable Fuels Standard, and is investing in research and development to help bring next-generation biofuels on line. For example, the United States Navy and Departments of Energy and Agriculture are working with the private sector to accelerate the development of cost-competitive advanced biofuels for use by the military and commercial sectors. More broadly, the Administration will continue to leverage partnerships between the private and public sectors to deploy cleaner fuels, including advanced batteries and fuel cell technologies, in every transportation mode. The Department of Energy's eGallon informs drivers about electric car operating costs in their state — the national average is only $1.14 per gallon of gasoline equivalent, showing the promise for consumer pocketbooks of electric-powered vehicles. In addition, in the coming months, the Department of Transportation will work with other agencies to further explore strategies for integrating alternative fuel vessels into the U.S. flag fleet. Further, the Administration will continue to work with states, cities and towns through the Department of Transportation, the Department of Housing and Urban Development, and the Environmental Protection Agency to improve transportation options, and lower transportation costs while protecting the environment in communities nationwide.

III. Cutting Energy Waste in Homes, Businesses, and Factories

Reducing Energy Bills for American Families and Businesses: Energy efficiency is one of the clearest and most cost-effective opportunities to save families money, make our businesses more competitive, and reduce greenhouse gas emissions. In the President's first term, the Department of Energy and the Department of Housing and Urban Development completed efficiency upgrades in more than one million homes, saving many families more than $400 on their heating and cooling bills in the first year alone. The Administration will take a range of new steps geared towards achieving President Obama's goal of doubling energy productivity by 2030 relative to 2010 levels:

- **Establishing a New Goal for Energy Efficiency Standards**: In President Obama's first term, the Department of Energy established new minimum efficiency standards for dishwashers, refrigerators, and many other products. Through 2030, these standards will cut consumers' electricity bills by hundreds of billions of dollars and save enough electricity to power more than 85 million homes for two years. To build on this success, the Administration is setting a new goal: Efficiency standards for appliances and federal buildings set in the first and second terms combined will reduce carbon pollution by at least 3 billion metric tons cumulatively by 2030 — equivalent to nearly one-half of the carbon pollution from the entire U.S. energy sector for one year — while continuing to cut families' energy bills.

- **Reducing Barriers to Investment in Energy Efficiency**: Energy efficiency upgrades bring significant cost savings, but upfront costs act as a barrier to more widespread investment. In response, the Administration is committing to a number of new executive actions. As soon as this fall, the Department of Agriculture's Rural Utilities Service will finalize a proposed update to its Energy Efficiency and Conservation Loan Program to provide up to $250 million for rural utilities to finance efficiency investments by businesses and homeowners across rural America. The Department is also streamlining its Rural Energy for America program to provide grants and loan guarantees directly to agricultural producers and rural small businesses for energy efficiency and renewable energy systems.

In addition, the Department of Housing and Urban Development's efforts include a $23 million Multifamily Energy Innovation Fund designed to enable affordable housing providers, technology firms, academic institutions, and philanthropic organizations to test new approaches to deliver cost-effective residential energy. In order to advance ongoing efforts and bring stakeholders together, the Federal Housing Administration will convene representatives of the lending community and other key stakeholders for a mortgage roundtable in July to identify options for factoring energy efficiency into the mortgage underwriting and appraisal process upon sale or refinancing of new or existing homes.

- **Expanding the President's Better Buildings Challenge:** The Better Buildings Challenge, focused on helping American commercial and industrial buildings become at least 20 percent more energy efficient by 2020, is already showing results. More than 120 diverse organizations, representing over 2 billion square feet are on track to meet the 2020 goal: cutting energy use by an average 2.5 percent annually, equivalent to about $58 million in energy savings per year. To continue this success, the Administration will expand the program to multifamily housing - partnering both with private and affordable building owners and public housing agencies to cut energy waste. In addition, the Administration is launching the Better Buildings Accelerators, a new track that will support and encourage adoption of State and local policies to cut energy waste, building on the momentum of ongoing efforts at that level.

IV. Reducing Other Greenhouse Gas Emissions

Curbing Emissions of Hydrofluorocarbons: Hydrofluorocarbons (HFCs), which are primarily used for refrigeration and air conditioning, are potent greenhouse gases. In the United States, emissions of HFCs are expected to nearly triple by 2030, and double from current levels of 1.5 percent of greenhouse gas emissions to 3 percent by 2020.

To reduce emissions of HFCs, the United States can and will lead both through international diplomacy as well as domestic actions. In fact, the Administration has already acted by including a flexible and powerful incentive in the fuel economy and carbon pollution standards for cars and trucks to encourage automakers to reduce HFC leakage and transition away from the most potent HFCs in vehicle air conditioning systems. Moving forward, the Environmental Protection Agency will use its authority through the Significant New Alternatives Policy Program to encourage private sector investment in low-emissions technology by identifying and approving climate-friendly chemicals while prohibiting certain uses of the most harmful chemical alternatives. In addition, the President has directed his Administration to purchase cleaner alternatives to HFCs whenever feasible and transition over time to equipment that uses safer and more sustainable alternatives.

Reducing Methane Emissions; Curbing emissions of methane is critical to our overall effort to address global climate change. Methane currently accounts for roughly 9 percent of domestic greenhouse gas emissions and has a global warming potential that is more than 20 times greater than carbon dioxide. Notably, since 1990, methane emissions in the United States have decreased by 8 percent. This has occurred in part through partnerships with industry, both at home and abroad, in which we have demonstrated that we have the technology to deliver emissions reductions that benefit both our economy and the environment. To achieve additional progress, the Administration will:

- **Developing an Interagency Methane Strategy:** The Environmental Protection Agency and the Departments of Agriculture, Energy, Interior, Labor, and Transportation will develop a comprehensive, interagency methane strategy. The group will focus on assessing current emissions data, addressing data gaps, identifying technologies and best practices for reducing emissions, and identifying existing authorities and incentive-based opportunities to reduce methane emissions.

- **Pursuing a Collaborative Approach to Reducing Emissions:** Across the economy, there are multiple sectors in which methane emissions can be reduced, from coal mines and landfills to agriculture and oil and gas development. For example, in the agricultural sector, over the last three years, the Environmental Protection Agency and the Department of Agriculture have worked with the dairy industry to increase the adoption of methane digesters through loans. incentives, and other assistance. In addition, when it comes to the oil and gas sector, investments to build and upgrade gas pipelines will not only put more Americans to work, but also reduce emissions and enhance economic productivity.

Preserving the Role of Forests in Mitigating Climate Change: America's forests play a critical role in addressing carbon pollution, removing nearly 12 percent of total U.S. greenhouse gas emissions each year. In the face of a changing climate and increased risk of wildfire, drought, and pests, the capacity of our forests to absorb carbon is diminishing. Pressures to develop forest lands for urban or agricultural uses also contribute to the decline of forest carbon sequestration. Conservation and sustainable management can help to ensure our forests continue to remove carbon from the atmosphere while also improving soil and water quality, reducing wildfire risk, and otherwise managing forests to be more resilient in the fact of climate change. The Administration is working to identify new approaches to protect and restore our forests, as well as other critical landscapes including grasslands and wetlands, in the face of a changing climate.

WORKING WITH OTHER COUNTRIES TO COMBAT CLIMATE CHANGE

Negotiating Global Free Trade in Environmental Goods and Services: The U.S. will work with trading partners to launch negotiations at the World Trade Organization towards global free trade in environmental goods, including clean energy technologies such as solar, wind, hydro and geothermal. The U.S. will build on the consensus it recently forged among the 21 Asia-Pacific Economic Cooperation (APEC) economies in this area. In 2011, APEC economies agreed to reduce tariffs to 5 percent or less by 2015 on a negotiated list of 54 environmental goods. The APEC list will serve as a foundation for a global agreement in the WTO, with participating countries expanding the scope by adding products of interest. Over the next year, we will work towards securing participation of countries which account for 90 percent of global trade in environmental goods, representing roughly $481 billion in annual environmental goods trade. We will also work in the Trade in Services Agreement negotiations towards achieving free trade in environmental services.

Phasing Out Subsidies that Encourage Wasteful Consumption of Fossil Fuels:

The International Energy Agency estimates that the phase-out of fossil fuel subsidies — which amount to more than $500 billion annually — would lead to a 10 percent reduction in greenhouse gas emissions below business as usual by 2050. At the 2009 G-20 meeting in Pittsburgh, the United States successfully advocated for a commitment to phase out these subsidies, and we have since won similar commitments in other fora such as APEC. President Obama is calling for the elimination of U.S. fossil fuel tax subsidies in his Fiscal Year (FY) 2014 budget, and we will continue to collaborate with partners around the world toward this goal.

Leading Global Sector Public Financing Towards Cleaner Energy: Under this Administration, the United States has successfully mobilized billions of dollars for clean energy investments in developing countries, helping to accelerate their transition to a green, low-carbon economy. Building on these successes, the President calls for an end to U.S. government support for public financing of new coal plants overseas, except for (a) the most efficient coal technology 'available in the world's poorest countries in cases where no other economically feasible alternative exists, or (b) facilities deploying carbon capture and sequestration technologies. As part of this new commitment, we will work actively to secure the agreement of other countries and the multilateral development banks to adopt similar policies as soon as possible.

Strengthening Global Resilience to Climate Change: Failing to prepare adequately for the impacts of climate change that can no longer be avoided will put millions of people at risk, jeopardizing important development gains, and increasing the security risks that stem from climate change. That is why the Obama Administration has made historic investments in bolstering the capacity of countries to respond to climate-change risks. Going forward, we will continue to:

- Strengthen government and local community planning and response capacities, such as by increasing water storage and water use efficiency to cope with the increased variability in water supply

- Develop innovative financial risk management tools such as index insurance to help smallholder farmers and pastoralists manage risk associated with changing rainfall patterns and drought

- Distribute drought-resistant seeds and promote management practices that increase farmers' ability to cope with climate impacts.

Mobilizing Climate Finance: International climate finance is an important tool in our efforts to promote low-emissions, climate-resilient development. We have fulfilled our joint developed country commitment from the Copenhagen Accord to provide approximately $30 billion of climate assistance to developing countries over FY 2010–FY 2012. The United States contributed approximately $7.5 billion to this effort over the three year period. Going forward, we will seek to build on this progress as well as focus our efforts on combining our public resources with smart policies to mobilize much larger flows of private investment in low-emissions and climate resilient infrastructure.

Leading Efforts to Address Climate Change through International Negotiations

The United States has made historic progress in the international climate negotiations during the past four years. At the Copenhagen Conference of the United Nations Framework Convention on Climate Change (UNFCCC) in 2009, President Obama and other world leaders agreed for the first time that all major countries, whether developed or developing, would implement targets or actions to limit greenhouse emissions, and do so under a new regime of international transparency. And in 2011, at the year-end climate meeting in Durban, we achieved another' breakthrough: Countries agreed to negotiate a new agreement by the end of 2015 that would have equal legal force and be applicable to all countries in the period after 2020. This was an important step beyond the previous legal agreement, the Kyoto Protocol, whose core obligations applied, to developed countries, not to China, India, Brazil or other emerging countries. The 2015 climate conference is slated to play a critical role in defining a post-2020 trajectory. We will be seeking an agreement that is ambitious, inclusive and flexible. It needs to be ambitious to meet the scale of the challenge facing us. It needs to be inclusive because there is no way to meet that challenge unless all countries step up and play their part. And it needs to be flexible because there are many differently situated parties with their own needs and imperatives, and those differences will have to be accommodated in smart, practical ways.

At the same time as we work toward this outcome in the UNFCCC context, we are making progress in a variety of other important negotiations as well. At the Montreal Protocol, we are leading efforts in support of an amendment that would phase down HFCs; at the International Maritime Organization, we have agreed to and are now implementing the first-ever sector-wide, internationally applicable energy efficiency standards; and at the International Civil Aviation Organization, we have ambitious aspirational emissions and energy efficiency targets and are working towards agreement to develop a comprehensive global approach.

2. Action by the States

Virtually every U.S. state and many U.S. local governments have enacted laws[93] to reduce greenhouse gas emissions. A complete inventory of such state laws is beyond the scope of this book, but the principle initiatives will be briefly addressed:

- *Cap and trade programs.* The Western Climate initiative (WCI) was begun in 2007 as a cooperative effort by several western states and Canadian provinces to coordinate GHG gas reduction programs. California acted independently to create a cap and trade program with the objective of reducing total GHG emission levels to 1990 levels by 2020. The cap and trade rules apply to electric power plants and industrial plants that emit 25,000 metric tons of CO_2 equivalent (CO_2 e) per year, about 360 businesses. California held its first auction of GHG allowances on November 14, 2012. The California program is operated by the California Air Resources Board under the authority of Cal. Health & Safety Code seq. 38500 et seq.

---

[93] *See* http://www.c2es.org/us-states-regions/key-legislation.

A second cap and trade program is the Regional Greenhouse Gas Initiative (RGHGI), a cooperative effort among the states of Connecticut, Delaware, Maine, Maryland, Massachusetts, New Hampshire, New York, Rhode Island, and Vermont. Together these states have capped and will reduce CO_2 emissions from the power sector 10% by 2018. RGHGI held its first auction of CO_2 allowances in 2008. The operating entity of RGHGI is RGHGI, Inc., a non-profit corporation specially created for this task. *See* http://www.rggi.org.

- *Economy-wide* GHG *reduction programs.* Hawaii and Minnesota have enacted economy-wide programs with the goal of achieving GHG reductions.

- *Climate action plans.* Connecticut, Maine and Colorado have enacted climate action plans.

- *Greenhouse gas reporting.* Several states, such as California and Wisconsin, have enacted GHG reporting mandates.

- *Greenhouse gas performance standards for electric power plants.* California, Washington and Minnesota have enacted performance standards for electrical generating facilities.

- *Greenhouse gas performance standards for vehicles.* California, New Jersey, Washington have enacted strict GHG performance standards applicable to vehicles.

State standards risk being preempted by EPA regulations under the Clean Air Act. State initiatives also must pass muster under certain provisions of the Constitution of the United States, such as the Commerce Clause, the Supremacy Clause, and the Compact Clause. Regional programs that include Canadian provinces may impinge on the foreign affairs power of the federal government. *See* Steven Ferrey, *Goblets of Fire: Potential Constitutional Impediments to the Regulation of Global Warming*, 34 ECOLOGY L.Q. 835 (2008).

In October 2013, the governors of California, Oregon, and Washington and the Environment Minister of British Columbia announced the Pacific Coast Action Plan on Climate and Energy, a new, nonbinding initiative to set a price on carbon emissions for big polluters in the four jurisdictions. The idea behind PCAP is to link the four states to trading of carbon allowances. California presently requires large polluters to buy the right to emit CO_2; and British Columbia has had a tax on carbon since 2008. Now Oregon and Washington are seeking to join and to link up with these schemes.

3. Additional Climate Change Legal Tools

A variety of other legal tools are advanced to challenge GHG emissions and to stem climate change. The City of New York, several states, and private land trusts brought an action against four private power companies charging them with violating the federal common law of nuisance and asking the court to set a CO_2 cap for each defendant, but this action was dismissed as preempted by the U.S. Clean Air Act regulations. *American Electric Power Co. Inc. v. Connecticut*, 131 S. Ct. 2527 (2011). Some scholars believe the public trust doctrine may be used under common law to combat climate change. *See, e.g.*, Edgar Washburn and Alejandra Nunez, *Is the Public Trust a Viable Mechanism to Regulate Climate Change?*, 2012 NAT. RESOURCES & ENVT. 23. Tort law scholars predict an upsurge in common law and statutory tort claims to recover damages for climate change. *See* Robert F. Blomquist, *Comparative Climate Change Torts*, 46 VAL. U. L. REV. 1053 (2012).

Efforts to address climate change through common law claims have met with little success. *See Climate Change Lawsuits Get Chilly Reception*, MARTEN LAW ENVIRONMENTAL NEWS, June 19, 2012. Is it realistic to believe that climate change can be reversed through filing lawsuits for injunctions and damages based on common law theories?

M.   The Doha Gateway: The Second Commitment Period of the Kyoto Protocol

After the Copenhagen COP, the climate change regime met in Cancun, Mexico (COP-16) in 2010, and in Durban, South Africa (COP-17) in 2011. At COP-17, the parties adopted three measures of interest primarily to developing country parties: the Green Climate Fund to receive the funding pledged at Copenhagen; the creation of an Adaptation Committee (composed of 16 members) with a mandate to develop adaptation efforts on a global scale; and a Technology Mechanism to transfer new technology to developing country members. COP-17 also adopted the Durban Platform (ADP) for Enhanced Action, with a mandate to negotiate a "protocol, another legal instrument or an agreed outcome with legal force as soon as possible, but no later than 2015 and to come into effect and be implemented from 2020 as well as the workplan on enhancing mitigation ambition with a view to ensuring the highest possible mitigation efforts by all Parties."[94]

At COP-18 in Doha, Qatar, the major accomplishment was to extend the Kyoto Protocol to a Second Commitment Period beginning January 1, 2013 and ending December 31, 2020 (Decision 1/CP.18).

The Meeting of the Parties to the Kyoto Protocol adopted an Amendment to Annex B of the Kyoto Protocol that extends the Kyoto Protocol beyond the expiry date of the First Commitment Period, which ended on December 31, 2012, to create a Second Commitment Period of eight additional years. This Amendment, which at this writing has not entered into force, will enter into force for those Parties accepting it, on the 90th day after the date of receipt of its acceptance of at least three-fourths of the Parties to the Kyoto Protocol. In order to avoid a gap between the First and Second Commitment Periods, which run consecutively, however, the Meeting of the Parties declared the Amendment to have "provisional application" pending its entry into force.

Under the Doha Amendment, thirty-seven developed country Kyoto Parties have expressed willingness to make legally binding GHG emission reduction commitments for the Second Commitment Period amounting to an average reduction of at least 18% below 1990 levels. In the jargon of the Amendment, these are known as "Quantified Emission Limitation or Reduction Obligations

---

[94] COP-l7, Decision 1/CP.17.

(QELROs). However, this commitment is dominated by the European Parties to the Kyoto Protocol. Under the Amendment, the EU, its 28 member states, plus Iceland, which have entered into a joint fulfillment agreement pursuant to Kyoto Protocol Article 4, accept a reduction commitment of 20%; this reduction commitment has already been made under EU law by the EU-28. The other Kyoto Parties which have expressed willingness to make a commitment for the Second Commitment Period are: Australia (-0.5% or 5% below 2000 levels); Belarus (-5 to -10%); Kazakhstan (-5%); Liechtenstein (-16%); Norway (-30 to -40%); Switzerland (-20 to -30%); and Ukraine (-24%).

Critics note that the amount of annual GHG emissions emitted by those Kyoto Parties accepting a QELRO for the Second Commitment Period amount to only about 14% of global GHG emissions. Thus, the reductions undertaken, even if they are achieved, will do little to stem the ongoing rise in global GHG emissions. Several Annex I Parties, Japan, the Russian Federation and New Zealand, rejected taking on new Kyoto Protocol commitments for the Second Commitment Period. Canada withdrew as a Party to the Kyoto Protocol in 2011.

The Kyoto Amendment adds a seventh GHG to the six listed in the KP Annex A: nitrogen trifluoride (NF3).

Parties are required by the Doha Amendment to review their Second Commitment Period QELROs by the end of 2014, with a view to increasing them.

A key issue in Doha was to define the extent to which "surplus emission allowances" — unused emission allowances from the First Commitment Period (CP1) — can be carried over to fulfill commitments made for the Second Commitment Period (CP2). It was decided that a Party can carry over 100% of its own unused allowances, but must do this by establishing a "previous period surplus reserve account (PPSRA). Surplus AAUs in a Party's PPSRA may be carried over in full; but surplus ERUs and CERs may only be carried over to CP2 up to a maximum for each of 2.5% of the relevant Party's CP1 assigned amount. CP2 Parties may buy or sell units from other CP2 Parties' PPSRA, but only up to 2% of its CP1 assigned amount. But many CP2 Parties pledged in a political declaration that they will refrain from purchasing CP1 emission units.

With regard to the issue of the availability of market mechanisms in CP2 — the Clean Development Mechanism (CDM); Joint Implementation (JI); and International Emissions Trading (IET) — a similar compromise was reached. All Parties to the Kyoto Protocol, even those not participating in CP2, may participate in CDM projects during CP2, but only CP2 Parties will be eligible to transfer or acquire the CERs that result from CDM. With respect to JI and IET, only CP2 Parties will be eligible to transfer and acquire AAUs, CERs, ERUs and other removal units which are valid in CP2.

Thus, the Kyoto Protocol carries on, though it is a shadow of its former self. All Parties must continue periodic reporting of emissions and sinks, including their afforestation, deforestation and forest management activities.

Of course, Canada and the USA, Annex I Parties that are not Parties to the Kyoto Protocol, fall outside the system entirely.

NOTES AND QUESTIONS

1. *Second Commitment Period of the Kyoto Protocol.* Adoption of the Second Commitment Period is embedded in Article 3.9 of the Kyoto Protocol. While for the First Commitment Period (2008–2012), 37 Annex I, developed country parties (excluding the USA which never ratified) were required to reduce or limit their emissions of GHG, what is the situation with respect to the Second Commitment Period? Note that Canada has withdrawn and that Japan and Russia will not take on any commitments. New Zealand will take its commitments from the UNFCCC alone, effectively withdrawing from the Protocol. Will this extension move the world forward to achieve the ultimate objective of the UNFCCC — the stabilization of GHG concentrations in the atmosphere at a level that would prevent dangerous anthropogenic interference with the climate system?

2. *Implementation gap.* There will be gap between the first and second implementation periods because the first period ended on December 31, 2012, and it will take time for the parties to ratify the amendments to Kyoto and for these amendments to come into force. To close this gap, the parties agreed to apply the Kyoto Protocol provisions on a provisional basis. COP-18/CMP-8, Decision 1/CMP.8 (2012).

3. *Carry-over from the First Commitment Period of surplus assigned amount units.* According to the CMP-8 Decision in 2012, a party may transfer all unused assigned amount units (AAUs) from the First to the Second Commitment Period. There are about 6000 megatons of CO_2 e left among Annex I parties, most from Russia, Ukraine, and some of the new EU member states. This carry-over adds about 20% of the assigned amount to the emissions capped according to the new pledges of Annex I parties. What effect will this have?

4. *Flexibility mechanisms in the Second Commitment Period.* According to the CMP-8 Decision in 2012, eligibility to take advantage of the flexibility mechanisms of the Kyoto Protocol — emission trading, joint implementation, and clean development mechanism — only accrue to those parties that have accepted a new Article B commitment for the Second Commitment Period. What impact will this have?

5. *Participation in the Second Commitment Period.* New Annex B involves parties responsible for less than 40% of developed country GHG emissions and less than 15% of global emissions.

6. *A new climate change tool — bilateral agreements.* Japan, which did not make any new commitment for the Second Commitment Period under the Kyoto Protocol, has begun a new program to mitigate climate change through bilateral agreements with developing countries. Japanese companies and the Japanese government will jointly use aid money to transfer low carbon technologies, products, systems, services and infrastructures to participating developing countries. This program, known as the Joint Crediting Mechanism (JCM) is designed to provide Japanese companies and, if necessary, the Japanese government, new carbon emission credits that may be recognized internationally. Monitoring and verification of JCM is up to bilateral joint committees established in each participating country.

N. Summary: The Future

The UNFCCC climate regime is at an important transition point. As of 2014, after 19 COP meetings, no process is in place to come close to meeting the objective of UNFCCC Article 2, stabilizing GHG emissions. Neither the UNFCCC nor the Kyoto Protocol has succeeded in retarding the upward rise of global GHG emissions. The pledges of Annex I parties for the Second Commitment Period are clearly insufficient, and the Second Commitment Period must be regarded as, at best, only a transitional agreement to more robust undertakings by all parties.

The Copenhagen Accord involves greater reductions and limitations of GHG than amendments to the Kyoto Protocol, but the Copenhagen pledges are voluntary and not subject to international supervision or verification.

Much depends on actions taken by future COP meetings. Several negotiating tracks are important in this regard.

1) *Work of the ADP.* The ADP, created in Durban in 2011, is charged with developing a new legal instrument by 2015 that would, for the first time, cover all major emitters and would enter into force in 2020. This would break with the pattern established so far of binding emission targets for developed countries but only non-binding pledges for developing countries. But one of the UNFCCC's core principles is common but differentiated responsibilities; how will this principle be integrated into a new agreement? Developing countries are willing to take only nationally appropriate mitigation actions contingent on support from developed countries. The negotiation focuses on more robust commitments from developed countries and "nationally appropriate mitigation actions by developing country Parties in the context of sustainable development, supported and enabled by technology, financing and capacity building, in a measurable, reportable and verifiable manner." Negotiation of a new and more robust 2020 agreement will be extremely difficult.

2) *Work of the Adaptation Committee.* The newly created Adaptation Committee is focused on implementation of the adaptation provisions of the UNFCCC, Articles 4.1(b), (e), (f) and Article 4.4, as well as issues relating to funding and transfer of technology for adaptation under Articles 4.8 and 4.9. A satisfactory outcome to these negotiations is essential but will be extremely difficult to attain.

3) *Funding and transfer of technology.* Developing countries call on developed parties to fulfill their Copenhagen Accord pledge of at least USD 100 billion per year. In addition, developing countries seek funding for the additional funds of the UNFCCC as well as for "losses and damages" for climate change.

4) *Reducing Emissions from Deforestation and Forest Degradation (REDD).* REDD and the issue of increasing the forest carbon stocks in developing countries remains an important agenda item. COP-18, Decision 1/CP.18 C. para. 34 recognizes the need to improve coordination in the implementation of the [REDD-Plus] activities referred to in decision 1/CP.16, paragraph 70, and to provide predictable support, including

financial resources and technical and technological support, to developing country Parties for the implementation of those activities." The Warsaw Framework adopted by the COP in 2013 prepares the way for the deployment of REDD-Plus.

PROBLEM 4-11
THE PARIS 2015 CONFERENCE OF THE PARTIES (COP 21): DRAFTING A FAIR AND BALANCED, BINDING AGREEMENT FOR THE THIRD COMMITMENT PERIOD, A CLASS SIMULATION

In 2011 the parties to the UNFCCC and the Kyoto Protocol launched negotiations on a new, comprehensive, fair and balanced, binding climate change agreement to apply during the post-2020 time period — called Third Commitment Period. This new agreement is currently being negotiated through a process called the "Durban Platform for Enhanced Action" (ADP).

To set the stage, the Kyoto Protocol involved the First Commitment Period, which ended 31 December 2012, in which 37 industrial nations and the European Union were called upon to collectively reduce GHG emissions by about 5% from 1990 levels. Although the United States did not participate, this goal was largely achieved. But a 5% reduction is considered insufficient to combat climate change. The Kyoto Amendment adopted at Doha creates a Second Commitment Period extending from 1 January 2013 to 31 December 2020, during which a smaller number of nations and the European Union have agreed to reduce GHG emissions collectively by at least 18% from 1990 levels.

The deadline for the new climate change agreement is late 2015 at the 21st meeting of the Conference of the Parties of the UNFCCC to be held on Paris, France. Preparatory meetings for this COP have already begun. The negotiation received a boost when China, the largest GHG emitter, announced that it would be willing to consider a legally binding reduction commitment for the Third Commitment Period. However, China attached five conditions: (1) that all rich countries also make substantial commitments; (2) that rich countries fulfill their financial commitments made to developing countries; (3) that rich countries agree on transfer of technology to developing countries; (4) that the negotiations move forward on the basis of the IPCC reports and determinations; and (5) that rich countries agree to deeper binding cuts than developing countries, reflecting the fact that rich countries bear more responsibility for past GHG emissions than developing countries. After this announcement, India and a number of additional developing countries said they would consider binding reduction commitments as well.

Let us conduct a class simulation of the COP 21 Paris negotiation. Various members or groups of members of the class should be assigned roles as follows:

The Chairperson of the Intergovernmental Panel on Climate Change

Delegate from China

Delegate from the United States

Delegate from the European Union

Delegate from India

Delegate from Indonesia

Delegate from Japan

Delegate from Mexico

Delegate from Saudi Arabia

Delegate from the Democratic Republic of the Congo

Delegate from Brazil

Delegate from Russia

Delegate from Australia

Delegate from Canada

Observer Delegate representing the World Wildlife Fund

The class should appoint a Reporter to note down points of agreement and disagreement. At the end of a first round of statements, the points of agreement and disagreement can be announced; further negotiations should proceed to deal with the points of disagreement. At the end of class, the Reporter will announce the outlines of a Draft Agreement. A vote can then be taken or alternatively, the Reporter can ask if there are any objections, and, if not, the Draft Agreement is adopted by consensus.

Before this exercise, consider the following Communication from the Commission of the European Union:

COMMUNICATION FROM THE COMMISSION TO THE EUROPEAN PARLIAMENT, THE COUNCIL, THE EUROPEAN ECONOMIC AND SOCIAL COMMITTEE AND THE COMMITTEE OF THE REGIONS
Brussels, 26.3.2013 COM(2013) 167 final

The 2015 International Climate Change Agreement: Shaping international climate policy beyond 2020

Consultative Communication
(2013)

INTERNATIONAL CLIMATE POLICY: STATE OF PLAY, CHALLENGES AND OPPORTUNITIES 2020-2030

The 2015 Agreement will have to bring together, by 2020, the current patchwork of binding and non-binding arrangements under the UN Framework Convention on Climate Change (Convention), into a single comprehensive regime. The EU and a number of other European countries as well as Australia agreed to join a legally binding 2nd commitment period under the Kyoto Protocol as a transitional measure between 2012 and 2020. During this same period, a further sixty countries, including the United States of America (U.S.), major emerging economies, low and middle income as well as least developed countries, have pledged to take different types of emission reduction and limitation commitments under the Convention. These pledges were triggered by the Copenhagen Climate Conference at the end of 2009 and formally submitted as pledges that are not legally binding under the Convention a year later in Cancun.

The unilateral, or "bottom up" nature of the Copenhagen-Cancun pledging process allowed for a more inclusive international approach. For the first time the U.S., China, India, Brazil, South Africa, the EU and others committed at the international level to specific domestic climate policies as part of the same initiative. However, in addition to being voluntary, a number of the pledges made by major economies are conditioned, for example on others taking more ambitious action and the availability of financial resources. Most importantly, as already mentioned, current pledges, if fully implemented, are expected to deliver less than a third of the ambition required to stay below a 2° C temperature rise.

In shaping the 2015 Agreement we will need to learn from the successes and shortcomings of the Convention, the Kyoto Protocol, and the Copenhagen — Cancun process. We will need to move beyond the North-South paradigm reflecting the world in the 1990s towards one based on mutual interdependence and shared responsibility. The 2015 Agreement will need to address the challenge of attracting the participation of all major economies, including the U.S., China, India and Brazil, that have so far resisted legally binding commitments to reduce their GHG emissions. It must build on the current frameworks to support countries in their efforts to adapt to unavoidable climate change, especially the most vulnerable. Most importantly, it must provide a bridge from the current patchwork and bottom up approach, largely based on non-binding decisions, to a legally binding agreement that effectively combines a bottom up and top down approach and that will put the world on an emissions pathway that will keep the global temperature rise below 2° Celsius.

The Agreement will have to reflect how the world has changed since climate negotiations began in 1990 and how it will continue to change as we approach 2030. It will operate in a context in which (see accompanying staff working document):

- Scientific advances have removed any reasonable doubt that we are warming the planet;

- Emerging economies are an increasing source of economic growth and GHG emissions;

- Significant sustainable development challenges remain;

- Addressing climate change also brings significant opportunities;

- Increasing global trade will continue to raise issues about production-related emissions, and preventing carbon leakage (carbon intensive activities shifting from high ambition to low ambition countries).

Question 1:

How can the 2015 Agreement be designed to ensure that countries can pursue sustainable economic development while encouraging them to do their equitable and fair share in reducing global GHG emissions so that global emissions are put on a pathway that allows us to meet the below 2°C objective? How can we avoid a repeat of the current situation where there is a gap between voluntary pledges and the reductions that are required to keep global temperature increase below 2° C?

- **Enabling the contribution of all major economies and all sectors in the global mitigation effort**

Environmental effectiveness will require contributions from all major economies and all sectors in a comparable, equitable, transparent and accountable manner that minimises the risk of carbon leakage. Securing contributions from all major economies and all sectors is therefore essential. Without such agreement, individual states and regions may continue to hold back their climate ambition in relation to what their competitors are prepared to do. To help avoid this, the 2015 Agreement could both encourage and incentivise countries to adopt ambitious commitments sooner rather than later and help level the playing field between current leaders and laggards.

Question 2:

How can the 2015 Agreement best ensure the contribution of all major economies and sectors and minimise the potential risk of carbon leakage between highly competitive economies?

- **Mainstreaming climate change and the mutual reinforcement of processes and initiatives**

Climate change policy can never stand alone but instead must support economic growth and the broader sustainable development agenda, as well as' help create new employment opportunities. Whether it addresses mitigation or adaptation, climate policy must be fully integrated or "mainstreamed" across all policy areas and form a key component in the design of energy, transport, industry, agriculture, forestry and broader sustainable development policies and strategies.

The 2015 Agreement must therefore recognise and reinforce broader sustainable development objectives and support the full integration of climate change objectives into relevant policy areas. This includes the follow-up to the Rio+20 Conference, and the review of the Millennium Development Goals (MDG) by 2015, as well as the implementation of agreements such as the Convention on Biological Diversity. This work provides an opportunity to address challenges related to climate change and its impacts on poverty eradication and the three pillars of sustainability (environmental, economic and social development), where it can provide important co-benefits. In this respect, the Commission has proposed a joint approach towards a "Decent Life for all by 2030" that brings together the work strands of the follow-up to Rio+20 and the MDG review.

Question 3:

How can the 2015 Agreement most effectively encourage the mainstreaming of climate change in all relevant policy areas? How can it encourage complementary processes and initiatives, including those carried out by non-state actors?

DESIGNING THE 2015 AGREEMENT

The negotiation round launched in Durban in 2011 reflects a fragile but crucial international consensus about the nature of the 2015 Agreement. If it is to deliver more than Kyoto, Copenhagen and Cancun have yet delivered, the 2015 Agreement must be inclusive, by containing commitments that are "applicable to all" countries, developed and developing alike. It must be ambitious, by containing commitments that are consistent with limiting global mean temperature rise to 2° C. It must be effective, by enabling the right set of incentives for implementation and compliance. It must be widely perceived as fair and equitable in the way in which it shares the effort to reduce GHG emissions and the cost of adapting to unavoidable climate change. Moreover, the 2015 Agreement must be legally binding. Only a legal form entailing a legally binding treaty will reflect the highest degree of political will required to drive the necessary level of ambition and the global transition to a low carbon economy; ensure that commitments are ratified and implemented in national law; secure the longer-term attention of governments, civil society, business and the media; and ensure the appropriate level of transparency and accountability for the commitments made.

The 2015 Agreement must focus on encouraging and enabling countries to take new and ambitious mitigation commitments. At the same time it must learn from and strengthen the current international climate regime. Many of its institutions, tools and processes, including the Green Climate Fund, the Adaptation Committee, International Assessment and Review and Consultation and Analysis, the Technology Executive Committee, Low Emission Development Strategies and National Adaptation Plans, have only just started their operation, but could contribute significantly to the design of the 2015 Agreement.

The 2015 Agreement must respond to scientific advances, including the 5th Assessment Report of the Intergovernmental Panel on Climate Change (IPCC), the summary of which is due to be finalised in October 2014, a year before the adoption of the 2015 Agreement. It will also need to be sufficiently dynamic and flexible to adjust as scientific knowledge develops further, but also as unit costs of technologies, as well as national or regional socio-economic circumstances change. The recently agreed second commitment period to the Kyoto Protocol sets an interesting precedent for dynamic regime design by defining a review process that encourages ambition to be increased or ambition gaps to be narrowed during the commitment period. At the same time, this dynamism will have to be balanced by the expectation, especially from business, for predictability and certainty.

Chapter 5

ENVIRONMENT, TRADE, AND INVESTMENT

Section I.   INTRODUCTION

International trade law is one of the fastest growing areas of international law. The last 20 years in particular have seen many new treaties concluded and many new areas of domestic trade policy submitted to international regulation. Modern trade law (extending beyond nineteenth century bilateral treaties) began shortly after the Second World War, with the negotiation of a multilateral treaty to deal with trade in goods: the *General Agreement on Tariffs and Trade* (GATT). From the 1940s until the 1980s, international trade law steadily grew, and the GATT regime attracted more members, mostly developing countries. However, it was not until the 1990s that a formal international organization to regulate trade was established, the World Trade Organization (WTO) established in 1995.

International trade law should be distinguished from the broader field of international economic law. The latter can be said to encompass, not only WTO law, but also law governing the international monetary system and currency regulation, controlled by the International Monetary Fund (IMF) and the law and policy of the World Bank concerning development aid. Indeed, the law of development itself is an area of *lex ferenda*, largely evolving from UN bodies such as the General Assembly and the UN Conference on Trade and Development (UNCTAD). The relationship between international trade and development is a fundamental issue that lies at the heart of tensions within the international economic system.

International trade law is based on theories of economic liberalism developed in Europe (and later the USA) in the eighteenth to twentieth centuries. Whilst an examination of economic theory is outside the scope of this chapter, certain points should be noted. Economic liberalism is based on some key principles that are subject to much debate. These include the assumption that wealth can be increasingly generated by free trade and that free trade requires an efficient use of resources. Efficiency is said to entail the theory of "comparative advantage": that producers (indeed, nations) should specialize in the production of goods and services that they are best able to produce. Efficiency is also said to entail minimum government intervention and regulation in international trade, and the abolition of "protectionist" measures. *Protectionism* is a vague term often used to describe a range of government policies to support and regulate essential services and domestic industry (e.g. government monopolies on services such as telecommunications, subsidies on the production of goods and services, protection from foreign competition by the use of import quotas, high tariffs and discriminatory policies and laws.) Economic liberalism thus advocates the minimal use of such measures. For a more comprehensive account of economic theory and its relationship to international trade law, see TREBILCOCK & HOWSE, THE REGULATION OF INTERNATIONAL TRADE, Ch 1 (4th ed. 2012).

Despite free trade theories lying behind international trade law, it is also true to say that these theories are hotly debated and, when translated into international treaties, subject to many and varied exceptions. Some critics of international trade law focus on the many "loopholes" which allow protectionist policies to be maintained in many areas. Others focus on the concerns of developing countries and the ways in which international trade law inhibits their development.

The controversy over the impact of international trade on the environment began to make headlines about 20 years ago and shows no sign of diminishing, In fact, this conflict is part of a larger set of issues: the impact of trade and globalization on civil society. Various groups and organizations charge that fostering free trade has the capacity to undermine workers' rights, human health and many other values. The wrath of the environmentalists has singled out one intergovernmental agency, the World Trade Organization (WTO), which administers an extensive set of international agreements on trade, the most prominent of which is the General Agreement on Tariffs and Trade, 1994. The WTO also administers a compulsory dispute settlement system under which any of the 159 Members of the WTO can complain against other Members and obtain an adjudication regarding any "nullification or impairment" of trade benefits. The WTO's dispute settlement body has handled several high-profile trade-environment cases. In this Chapter, we explore the main lines of the ongoing conflicts.

The "link" between international trade and protection of the environment bears explanation. In the popular mind, and even among some specialists, the topic of the WTO and the environment dominates discussion. One finds criticism such as the following:

> The WTO has been a disaster for the environment. Threats — often by industry but with government support — of WTO-illegality are being used to chill environmental innovation and to undermine multilateral environmental agreements. Already WTO threats and challenges have undermined or threatened to interfere with U.S. Clean Air rules, the U.S. Endangered Species Act, Japan's *[sic]* Kyoto (global warming) Treaty implementation, a European toxics and recycling law, U.S. long horned beetle infestation policy, EU ecolabels, U.S. dolphin protection, and an EU humane trapping law.

Things only stand to get worse . . .

This criticism implies that the link between trade and the environment is one of overlap and opposition. Upon analysis, this is not the case.

First, international trade and protection of the environment are both essential for the welfare of mankind. In the vast majority of cases, these two values do not come into conflict. On the contrary, they are mutually supportive. As stated in Agenda 21, adopted at the UN Conference on Environment and Development in 1992,

Environment and trade policies should be mutually supportive. An open multilateral trading system makes possible a more efficient allocation and use of resources and thereby contributes to an increase in production and incomes and to lessening demands on the environment. It thus provides additional resources needed for economic growth . . . and improved environmental protection. A sound environment, on the other hand, provides the ecological and other resources needed to sustain growth and underpin continuing expansion of trade.

Second, taking active steps to protect the environment is beyond the scope of authority allotted to the WTO under international law. The WTO's function is limited to administering the WTO agreements. Thus, the WTO deals only with trade, not protection of the environment. The WTO agreements apply to measures protecting the environment only where and insofar as they have an impact on international trade. Relatively few environmental measures fall into this category.

Third, nothing in the WTO Agreements requires that free trade be accorded priority over environmental protection. Rather, the preamble to the WTO Agreement acknowledges that expansion of production and trade must allow for "the optimal use of the world's resources in accordance with the objective of sustainable development, seeking both to protect and preserve the environment and to enhance the means for doing so in a manner consistent with their respective needs and concerns at different levels of economic development."

Thus, what is sought is balance between the two objectives of free trade and environmental protectionism. In addition, the WTO is sensitive to uncovering measures that purport to be for environmental reasons but are a subterfuge for serving other interests, such as protection of domestic producers.

Accordingly, many WTO agreements contain conditional exceptions for environmental measures.

The GATT 1994 states as follows in Article XX:

Subject to the requirement that such measures are not applied in a manner which would constitute a means of arbitrary or unjustifiable discrimination between countries where the same conditions prevail, or a disguised restriction on international trade, nothing in this Agreement shall be construed to prevent the adoption or enforcement by any contracting party of measures:

*   *   *

(b)   necessary to protect human, animal or plant life or health;

*   *   *

(g)   relating to the conservation of exhaustible natural resources if such measures are made effective in conjunction with restrictions on domestic production or consumption.

The General Agreement on Trade in Services (GATS) contains an identical exception to GATT Article XX(b). The Agreement on Trade-Related Aspects of Intellectual Property Rights (TRIPS Agreement) states that "Members may exclude from patentability inventions, the prevention within their territory of the commercial exploitation of which is necessary . . . to protect human, animal or plant life or health or to avoid serious prejudice to the environment." The Agreement on Subsidies and Countervailing Measures (SCM Agreement) exempts certain environmental subsidies. The Agreement on Technical Barriers to Trade (TBT Agreement) states that protection of the environment is a "legitimate objective" that allows a WTO Member to enact high standards of protection. The Agreement on the Application of Sanitary and Phytosanitary Measures (SPS Agreement) sets out criteria to supplement GATT XX(b) to govern the validity of national measures passed to protect humans, plants and animals from contaminants, disease-carrying organisms, and pests.

* * *

The WTO established a Committee on Trade and Environment (CTE) in 1995. The CTE was charged with making appropriate recommendations on "the need for rules to enhance the positive interaction between trade and environment measures for the promotion of sustainable development." The CTE was asked to address the following matters:

1. "the relationship between the provisions of the multilateral trading system and trade measures for environmental purposes, including those pursuant to multilateral environmental agreements";

2. "the relationship between environmental policies relevant to trade and environmental measures with significant trade effects and the provisions of the multilateral trading system";

3. "the relationship between the provisions of the multilateral trading system and: (a) charges and taxes for environmental purposes[,] (b) requirements for environmental purposes relating to products, including standards and technical regulations, packaging, labelling and recycling";

4. "the provisions of the multilateral trading system with respect to the transparency of trade measures used for environmental purposes and environmental measures and requirements which have significant trade effects";

5. "the relationship between the dispute settlement mechanisms in the multilateral trading system and those found in multilateral environmental agreements";

6. "the effect of environmental measures on market access, especially in relation to developing countries, in particular to the least developed among them, and environmental benefits of removing trade restrictions and distortions";

7. "the issue of exports of domestically prohibited goods";

8. "the relevant provisions of the Agreement on Trade-Related Aspects of Intellectual Property Rights";

9. "the work programme envisaged in Decision on Trade in Services and the Environment"; and

10. "input to the relevant bodies in respect of appropriate arrangements for relations with inter-governmental and non-governmental organizations."

However, no significant decision has been taken by the CTE, which is open to participation by all members. Consequently, the Final Declaration of the Doha Ministerial Conference in November 2001 adopted a Trade and Environment Work Programme, which includes the following:

1. The relationship between WTO rules and trade restrictions in multilateral environmental agreements;

2. Criteria for granting observer status and information exchange;

3. reduction and elimination of trade barriers for environmental goods and services; and

4. Fisheries subsidies.

In addition, the CTE was instructed to give particular attention to (1) the effect of environmental measures on market access, especially for developing countries; (2) environmental aspects of TRIPS; and (3) labelling requirements for environmental purposes.

Thus, the accommodation of protection of the environment and trade is incomplete and ongoing.

Environmentalist Trade Demands: A Critical Analysis

What is the basis of the environmentalist objection to the rules of the multilateral trading system? Daniel Esty, a distinguished critic, has identified the following four environmentalist critiques:

- Without environmental safeguards, trade may cause environmental harm by promoting economic growth that results in the unsustainable consumption of natural resources and waste production.

- Trade rules and trade liberalization often entail market access agreements that can be used to override environmental regulations unless appropriate environmental protections are built into the structure of the trade system.

- Trade restrictions should be available as leverage to promote worldwide environmental protection, particularly to address global or transboundary environmental problems and to reinforce international environmental agreements.

- Even if the pollution they cause does not spill over into other nations, countries with lax environmental standards have a competitive advantage in the global marketplace and put pressure on countries with high environmental standards to reduce the rigor of their environmental requirements.

DANIEL C. ESTY, THE GREENING OF THE GATT 42 (1994).

The Environmental Impact of Trade

Some environmentalist opposition to trade is based on the notion that international mobility of goods, services, and capital is fundamentally anti-environmental. Herman Daly, an economist, for example, has stated that free trade:

> sins against allocative efficiency by making it difficult for nations to internalize external costs; it sins against distributive justice by widening the disparity between labor and capital in high wage countries; it sins against community by demanding more mobility and by further separating ownership and control; [and] it sins against sustainable scale [by offering] a way to loosen local constraints by importing environmental services (including waste absorption) from elsewhere.

15 Loy. L.A. Int'l & Comp. L. Rev. 33, 41–42 (1992).

The facts, however, belie these charges. It is wrong to blame failure to internalize environmental costs on trade. First, there is little empirical evidence that companies relocate to take advantage of lax pollution controls. Second, countries like Brazil, with very protectionist trade policies, still fail to preserve natural resources. Commercial logging for export, for example, plays little part in the destruction of the Amazon rain forest. Instead, the basic causes are the demand for land and local agriculture and forestry practices.

A 1994 OECD study on the impact of trade on the environment found that the direct effects of trade on the environment are generally small because only a limited share of ecologically sensitive goods enter into trade and because trade is only one of many factors affecting the environment. It found:

> In general, trade is not the root cause of environmental problems, which are due to market and intervention failures. Market failures occur when markers do not reflect environmental values. Intervention failures occur when public policies do not correct for, create or exacerbate market failures. Such failures can distort the incentives for protecting the environment and can drive a wedge between the private and socially optimum rates and modes of production and consumption. Environmental economics has focused on understanding and correcting these failures at the domestic level, but such failures also occur at the international level and increasingly have global impacts. International trade can help correct market and intervention failures through providing increased funds and incentives for environmental protection and promoting efficient resource use. But, at times, international trade may exacerbate the environmental problems in the presence of market and intervention failures.

The impact of trade on the environment is complex; it may be positive, negative or neutral, depending on the economic sector and the circumstances. The OECD framework for analysis is to consider trade-related environmental impacts from two perspectives (1) market failures and (2) intervention failures. The chief categories of market failure leading to environmental degradation are (1) failure to externalize environmental costs; (2) improper valuation of ecosystems; and (3) ill-defined or open property rights regimes for certain resources. Two categories of intervention failure are (1) subsidies and (2) trade barriers.

Using these analytical tools, the positive or negative effects of trade may be identified and measured. With respect to products, trade may make a significant positive contribution by providing the opportunity for the global spread of environmental technologies and services to address particular environmental problems. Traded products may also have a negative environment effect if hazardous wastes or harmful chemicals are involved or through the sale of products from endangered species.

Trade may foster economic efficiency and growth, raising incomes and providing more money for environmental protection. If there is market or intervention failure, however, trade may lead to degradation and depletion of natural resources.

All WTO Members should keep the environmental impacts of trade and trade agreements under review. Positive and negative impacts of trade should be identified, the positive impacts enhanced, and the negative aspects eliminated. For example, in the United States, the tariff-quota on sugar imports leads to greater production of sugar by American farmers. One of the principal sugar growing areas is in south Florida, where the high water use and fertilizers necessary for the production of sugar cane have an adverse impact on the Everglades, one of the most valuable and productive U.S. ecosystems. Such trade distortions should be removed.

NOTES AND QUESTIONS

1.   Do you agree with the authors that it is desirable and possible to reconcile trade and environmental protection? Is international trade inherently detrimental to the environment? If so, would civil society be better off without trade or at least if trade is minimized. For example, the growing world economy has been accompanied by great environmental degradation. Globalization has accelerated world economic growth. At the current rate, per capita GDP will double by 2035 and quadruple by 2070. What are the arguments against trade? Are they convincing?

2.   What is the argument of the OECD Study cited in the reading? Is this study too optimistic about reconciling trade and environment?

3.   Trade measures may be used to protect the environment by freely allowing restrictions on trade to protect resources against exploitation. But the OECD Study calls this a "second best" solution. The best way to protect the environment is to correct "market failure" by an appropriate mixture of taxes and regulations and to end intervention failures such as subsidies. In this ideal state of affairs governments would use the proper environmental policies to "internalize" the full environmental costs of production and consumption under the "Polluter Pays Principle." Then trade liberalization would unambiguously raise welfare. Do you agree?

4.   Is there a positive role for trade in protecting the environment? For example, can trade agreements help to reduce or eliminate costly and environmentally destructive subsidy programs for fishing ($54 billion per year), agriculture (over $300 billion per year), and forestry? Another role for trade is to facilitate the transfer of technology and the international exchange of environmentally clean

products. Can trade also contribute to expanding the financial resources available to protect the environment?

5.   Does trade inevitably produce "pollution havens" countries that specialize in "dirty" production at low prices? If so, is trade policy, which is founded on the concept of comparative advantage, be fashioned to remove environmental degradation as an element of comparative advantage? How would you accomplish this?

6.   The 2001 WTO Ministerial Conference, held in Doha, Qatar, which initiated a still unfinished new "round" of global trade negotiations, called for several new trade initiatives to protect the environment:

- The negotiation of a new agreement liberalizing trade in environmental goods and services.

- Negotiations to limit or abolish fishing subsidies.

- Negotiations to assure that WTO trade rules will not unduly interfere with the administration of existing and future multilateral environmental agreement (MEAs). Note that Article 3(5) of the UNFCCC and Article 2(3) of the Kyoto Protocol state that measures to combat climate change shall not constitute means of arbitrary or unjustifiable discrimination or disguised restrictions on international trade.

However, as of this writing, none of these initiatives have come to fruition.

Section II.   THE INSTITUTIONS AND CORE PRINCIPLES OF INTERNATIONAL TRADE

Current policies relating to international trade had their inception in the 1940s. In 1944, as World War II was ending, allied nations, led by the United States, held a conference at Bretton Woods, New Hampshire, in order to discuss and to establish the principal international economic institutions that would be needed after the war. The outcome of this conference was, the creation of the international Monetary Fund (IMF), whose principal mission is to safeguard the stability and exchange-ability of national currencies, and the World Bank, which was established, first, to spearhead post-war economic recovery and now to alleviate world poverty. The Bretton Woods Conference also called for the creation of a new global organization to foster international trade in the post-war era. Although the charter for a new International Trade Organization (ITO) was drafted, the creation of such an organization proved politically difficult. But in 1947, 23 nations, including the United States, agreed to apply, on a provisional basis, a General Agreement on Tariffs and Trade, an international agreement setting out detailed rules on the conduct of international trade. This document, commonly called the GATT, became a de-facto international organization based in Geneva, Switzerland, when the contracting parties to the agreement used the agreement as a basis for conducting negotiations to lower tariffs and non-tariff barriers to trade and to conclude new trade agreements. After the initial GATT agreement in 1947, eight additional "rounds" of international trade negotiations were successfully concluded, culminating in the Uruguay Round, an ambitious undertaking, which not only dramatically reduced trade barriers, but created a new international trade organization, the World Trade

Organization (WTO), which went into operation on January 1, 1995, replacing the organization known as the GATT.

The Agreement Establishing the World Trade Organization was signed at Marrakesh, Morocco in 1994, and is the charter that governs the conduct of the WTO, which is based in Geneva. The Preamble of the Marrakesh Agreement states that international trade "should be conducted with a view to raising standards of living, ensuring full employment and a large and steadily growing volume of real income and effective demand, and expanding the production of, and trade in goods and services, while allowing for the optimal use of the world's resources in accordance with the objective of sustainable development, seeking both to protect and preserve the environment and to enhance the means for doing so in a manner consistent with their respective needs and concerns at different levels of development."

The Agreement Establishing the WTO includes, as annexes, many additional trade agreements, the Multilateral Trade Agreements that are binding on all WTO members. Included in these agreements are 13 agreements related to international trade in goods. These include an updated version of the General Agreement on Tariffs and Trade, which is now known a "GATT 1994." In addition, the Multilateral Trade Agreements include an agreement related to services trade: the General Agreement on Trade in Services (GATS); an agreement on intellectual property: the WTO Agreement Relating to Intellectual Property (TRIPS); and an agreement on investment: the WTO Agreement on Trade Related Investment Measures (TRIMS). These Multilateral Trade Agreements constitute the law of international trade, an important component of international economic law.

The functions of the WTO, as set out in Article III of the Agreement, are (1) to provide an institutional framework for administration of Multilateral Trade Agreements; (2) to serve as a forum for discussions and negotiations on trade matters; (3) to administer a system for the resolution of trade disputes; (4) to administer a Trade Policy Review Mechanism on the extent of compliance with trade policy rules; and (5) to coordinate relevant economic policies with the IMF and the World Bank.

The highest decisionmaking body of the WTO is the Ministerial Conference, which is normally held every two years. At this conference trade ministers from the WTO members meet and have authority to take decisions on all matters under any of the Multilateral Trade Agreements.[1] Between Ministerial Conferences, the business of the WTO is largely conducted by the General Council, which is composed of all WTO members.[2] The WTO also has many additional councils, committees, and working groups as well as a small secretariat of full-time employees.[3] The head of the WTO is a Director-General, who is chosen by the members by consensus. The Director-General, however, has no executive power independent of the members.

---

[1] Agreement Establishing the World Trade Organization, Art. IV.

[2] *Id.*

[3] *Id.* Art. VI.

The WTO, at this writing, consists of 159 members, the majority of which are states, although independent customs unions, such as the European Union, are also members. The members of the WTO include all the principal economies of the world. Decisionmaking in the WTO is commonly by consensus, although voting is possible, in which case each member has one vote and decisions are taken by majority vote, except for certain extraordinary matters.[4] A condition of membership in the WTO is an undertaking to comply with all the provisions of the Multilateral Trade Agreements[5], except for a very few, such as the WTO Agreement on Government Procurement, that are termed "Plurilateral Trade Agreements."[6]

An important function of the WTO is the resolution of trade disputes between members. All WTO members are bound by the WTO Understanding on Rules and Procedures Governing the Settlement of Disputes (DSU), which details the process of how disputes are managed. Any WTO member may complain against any other member concerning a matter related to any of the Multilateral Trade Agreements. After mandatory consultations, the dispute, if not settled, must be referred to a WTO panel to render a decision on the matter. Any party may appeal the decision of a WTO panel in a particular dispute to the WTO Appellate Body, which consists of seven persons, who normally sit in three-judge panels. The decisions of WTO panels and the Appellate Body with respect to particular disputes become official when they are adopted by the Dispute Settlement Body (DSB), which is the GATT Council sitting as the DSB. Decisions of the WTO panels and the Appellate Body are considered and adopted by the DSB under a rule of "negative consensus" — the decision must be adopted by the DSB unless there is a consensus against adoption.[7] The Dispute Settlement Mechanism of the WTO replaced an earlier dispute settlement system that was administered under the GATT 1947. The current WTO system now operates very much like a court of international trade. Since its inception in 1995, this system has handled over 400 disputes between members, and, the rate of compliance with DSB decisions is very high because non-compliance my result in trade compensation or retaliation. As a result the WTO is much busier than most international tribunals and a burgeoning jurisprudence has emerged interpreting and applying the Multilateral Trade Agreements. In this chapter we examine the most important WTO decisions involving aspects of environmental protection.

The substance of the law of international trade is contained in the Multilateral Trade Agreements, the most important of which is GATT 1994. We set out the core rules of GATT 1994 that are most relevant to environmental disputes:

---

[4] *Id.* Art. IX.

[5] *Id.* Arts. II and XVI.

[6] *Id.* Art. II

[7] DSU, Arts. 16 and 17.

GENERAL AGREEMENT ON TARIFFS AND TRADE (GATT)
(1994)

Article I
General Most-Favoured-Nation Treatment

1. With respect to customs duties and charges of any kind imposed on or in connection with importation or exportation or imposed on the international transfer of payments for imports or exports, and with respect to the method of levying such duties and charges, and with respect to all rules and formalities in connection with importation and exportation, and with respect to all matters referred to in paragraphs 2 and 4 of Article III, any advantage, favour, privilege or immunity granted by any contracting party to any product originating in or destined for any other country shall be accorded immediately and unconditionally to the like product originating in or destined for the territories of all other contracting parties.

Article III
National Treatment on Internal Taxation and Regulation

1. The contracting parties recognize that internal taxes and other internal charges, and laws, regulations and requirements affecting the internal sale, offering for sale, purchase, transportation, distribution or use of products, and internal quantitative regulations requiring the mixture, processing or use of products in specified amounts or proportions, should not be applied to imported or domestic products so as to afford protection to domestic production.

2. The products of the territory of any contracting party imported into the territory of any other contracting party shall not be subject, directly or indirectly, to internal taxes or other internal charges of any kind in excess of those applied, directly or indirectly, to like domestic products. Moreover, no contracting party shall otherwise apply internal taxes or other internal charges to imported or domestic products in a manner contrary to the principles set forth in paragraph 1.

4. The products of the territory of any contracting party imported into the territory of any other contracting party shall be accorded treatment no less favourable than that accorded to like products of national origin in respect of all laws, regulations and requirements affecting their internal sale, offering for sale, purchase, transportation, distribution or use. The provisions of this paragraph shall not prevent the application of differential internal transportation charges which are based exclusively on the economic operation of the means of transport and not on the nationality of the product.

*   *   *

Article XI
General Elimination of Quantitative Restrictions

1. No prohibitions or restrictions other than duties, taxes or other charges, whether made effective through quotas, import or export licences or other

measures, shall be instituted or maintained by any contracting party on the importation of any product of the territory of any other contracting party or on the exportation or sale for export of any product destined for the territory of any other contracting party.

Article XX
General Exceptions

Subject to the requirement that such measures are not applied in a manner which would constitute a means of arbitrary or unjustifiable discrimination between countries where the same conditions prevail, or a disguised restriction on international trade, nothing in this Agreement shall be construed to prevent the adoption or enforcement by any contracting party of measures:

(a) necessary to protect public morals;

(b) necessary to protect human, animal or plant life or health;

* * *

(f) imposed for the protection of national treasures of artistic, historic or archaeological value;

(g) relating to the conservation of exhaustible natural resources if such measures are made effective in conjunction with restrictions on domestic production or consumption. . . .

NOTES AND QUESTIONS

1. Article II of the GATT requires each member to adhere to a schedule of trade concessions that are mainly in the form of tariff bindings — maximum tariff rates they agree to apply to various categories of imported products. Over the years of trade negotiations, tariff rates have dropped so that between developed countries tariffs average less than 3% of value of the product, although some tariff rates remain high. Tariff rates of developing countries are, on the average, higher.

2. GATT Articles I and III go beyond reducing tariffs and are fundamental principles of non-discrimination. For example, considering Article I: if one WTO member grants another WTO member a trade concession in the form of a lower tariff than its GATT tariff binding, can third-party WTO members automatically claim the benefit as well without a *quid pro quo?* Considering Article III: suppose a WTO member imposes a tax on imported products that is not imposed on domestic products. Is this a violation of Article III?

3. There are important exceptions to Article I, which is known as the Most Favored Nation (MFN) principle. GATT Article XXIV provides an exception for free trade area and customs union agreements. More than 200 of such agreements are in operation between WTO members. For example, the 28-member EU/EC is a customs union for purposes of WTO law, and thus the EU members are permitted to abolish tariffs among themselves without extending this treatment to other WTO members. The North American Free Trade Agreement (NAFTA) between Mexico,

the United States, and Canada is a free trade agreement, so tariffs and other trade barriers may be abolished among NAFTA members without including the rest of the WTO. In addition, a special Enabling Clause allows developing country members of the WTO to benefit from certain trade advantages that do not have to be extended to all WTO members because they are exempt from MFN treatment.

4.　　GATT Article XI is an important article that seeks to prohibit non-tariff barriers to international trade. The fundamental thrust of WTO law is that tariffs on imported products are permissible as long as they are within the maximum tariff bindings set in the national schedules of members; but non-tariff barriers such as quotas are prohibited with very few exceptions. Nontariff barriers are looked upon as more detrimental to trade and less transparent than tariffs.

5.　　GATT Article XX is an important "general exception" to other WTO obligations. The application of Article XX was considered by the WTO Appellate Body in one of the earliest cases decided after the formation of the WTO, the so-called Gasoline Case, which we read next.

UNITED STATES — STANDARDS FOR REFORMULATED AND CONVENTIONAL GASOLINE
Report of the Appellate Body, adopted on May 20, 1996, WT/DS2/AB/R

[This case involved 1990 Amendments to the U.S. Clean Air Act that directed the U.S. Environmental Protection Agency (EPA) to promulgate new regulations concerning the composition of gasoline. These new regulations were designed to reduce vehicle emissions of air pollutants in order to improve air quality. The 1990 amendments directed the EPA to use the quality of gasoline in 1990 as a baseline to set standards for future reformulated and conventional gasoline. The trade dispute concerned EPA's final regulations concerning the 1990 baselines. The EPA regulations adopted a two-tier system for establishing such baselines: (1) domestic refiners were permitted to use individual baselines' representing the quality of their gasoline in 1990; (2) foreign refiners were required to use statutory baselines set by the EPA. Brazil and Venezuela complained to the WTO that the U.S. EPA regulations were discriminatory in violation of GATT Article III. The WTO panel ruled in favor of Brazil and Venezuela on this issue. The United States did not appeal this ruling but instead asked the WTO Appellate Body to validate the EPA regulations by applying GATT Article XX. The following is the ruling with respect to Article XX(g).]

"relating to the conservation of exhaustible natural resources"

The Panel Report took the view that clean air was a "natural resource" that could be "depleted." Accordingly, as already noted earlier, the Panel concluded that a policy to reduce the depletion of clean air was a policy to conserve an exhaustible natural resource within the meaning of Article XX(g). Shortly thereafter, however, the Panel Report also concluded that "the less favourable baseline establishments methods" were *not* primarily aimed at the conservation of exhaustible natural resources and thus fell outside the justifying scope of Article XX(g).

One problem with the reasoning in that paragraph is that the Panel asked itself whether the "less favourable treatment" of imported gasoline was "primarily aimed at" the conservation of natural resources, rather than whether the "measure," i.e., the baseline establishment rules, was "primarily aimed at" conservation of clean air. In our view, the Panel here was in error in referring to its legal conclusion on Article III instead of the measure in issue. The result of this analysis is to turn Article XX on its head Obviously, there had to be a finding that the measure provided "less favourable treatment" under Article III:4 before the Panel examined the "General Exceptions" contained in Article XX. That, however, is a conclusion of law. The chapeau of Article XX makes it clear that it is the "measures" which are to be examined under Article XX(g), and not the legal finding of "less favourable treatment."

Furthermore, the Panel, Report appears to have utilized a conclusion it had reached earlier in holding that the baseline establishment rules did not fall within the justifying terms of Articles XX(b); i.e., that the baseline establishment rules were not "necessary" for the protection of human, animal or plant life. The Panel Report, it will be recalled, found that the baseline establishment rules had not been shown by the United States to be "necessary" under Article XX(b) since alternative measures either consistent or less inconsistent with the *General Agreement* were reasonably available to the United States for achieving its aim of protecting human, animal or plant life. In other words, the Panel Report appears to have applied the "necessary" test not only in examining the baseline establishment rules under Article XX(b), but also in the course of applying Article XX(g).

A principal difficulty, in the view of the Appellate Body, with the Panel Report's application of Article XX(g) to the baseline establishment rules is that the Panel there overlooked a fundamental rule of treaty interpretation. This rule has received its most authoritative and succinct expression in the *Vienna Convention on the Law of Treaties* (the *"Vienna Convention"*) which provides in relevant part:

ARTICLE 31
General rule of interpretation

I. A treaty shall be interpreted in good faith in accordance with the ordinary meaning to be given to the terms of the treaty in their context and in the light of its object and purpose.

The "general role of interpretation" set out above has been relied upon by all of the participants and third-party participants, although not always in relation to the same issue. That general rule of interpretation has attained the status of a rule of customary or general international law. As such, it forms part of the "customary rules of interpretation of public international law" which the Appellate Body has been directed, by Article 3(2) of the *DSU*, to apply in seeking to clarify the provisions of the *General Agreement* and the other "covered agreements" of the *Marrakesh Agreement Establishing the World Trade Organization"* (the *"WTO Agreement"*). That direction reflects a measure of recognition that the *General Agreement* is not to be read in clinical isolation from public international law.

Applying the basic principle of interpretation that the words of a treaty, like the *General Agreement*, are to be given their ordinary meaning, in their context and in the light of the treaty's object and purpose, the Appellate Body observes that the Panel Report failed to take adequate account of the words actually used by Article XX in its several paragraphs. In enumerating the various categories of governmental acts, laws or regulations which WTO Members may carry out or promulgate in pursuit of differing legitimate state policies or interests outside the realm of trade liberalization, Article XX uses different terms in respect of different categories:

"necessary" — in paragraphs (a), (b) and (d); "essential" — in paragraph (j);

"relating to" — in paragraphs (c), (e) and (g); "for the protection of" — in paragraph (f);

"in pursuance of" — in paragraph (h); and "involving" — in paragraph (i).

It does not seem reasonable to suppose that the WTO Members intended to require, in respect of each and every category, the same kind or degree of connection or relationship between the measure under appraisal and the state interest or policy sought to be promoted or realized.

At the same time, Article XX(g) and its phrase, "relating to the conservation of exhaustible natural resources," need to be read in context and in such a manner as to give effect to the purposes and objects of the *General Agreement.* The context of Article XX(g) includes the provisions of the rest of the *General Agreement*, including in particular Articles I, III and XI; conversely, the context of Articles I and III and XI includes Article XX. Accordingly, the phrase "relating to the conservation of exhaustible natural resources" may not be read so expansively as seriously to subvert the purpose and object of Article III:4. Nor may Article III:4 be given so broad a reach as effectively to emasculate Article XX(g) and the policies and interests it embodies. The relationship between the affirmative commitments set out in, *e.g.*, Articles I, III and XI, and the policies and interests embodied in the "General Exceptions" listed in Article XX, can be given meaning within the framework of the *General Agreement* and its object and purpose by a treaty interpreter only on a case-to-case basis, by careful scrutiny of the factual and legal context in a given dispute, without disregarding the words actually used by the WTO Members themselves to express their intent and purpose.

The 1987 *Herring and Salmon Report*[8] . . . gave some recognition to the foregoing considerations of principle. The Panel Report [in the case at bar] quoted the following excerpt from the Herring and Salmon Report:

"as the preamble of Article XX indicates, the purpose of including Article XX(g) in the General Agreement was not to widen the scope for measures serving trade policy purposes but merely to ensure that the commitments under the General Agreement do not hinder the pursuit of policies aimed at the conservation of exhaustible natural resources."

All the participants . . . in this appeal accept the propriety and applicability of the view of the Herring and Salmon Report and the Panel Report [in the case at

---

[8] Canada — Measures Affecting Exports of Unprocessed Herring and Salmon, BISD 35S/98, para. 4.6, adopted 22 March 1988.

bar] that a measure must be "primarily aimed at" the conservation of natural resources in order to fall within the scope of Article XX(g). Accordingly, we see no need to examine this point further save, perhaps, to note that the phrase "primarily aimed at" is not itself treaty language and was not designed as a simple litmus test for exclusion or exclusion from Article XX(g),

Against this background, we turn to the specific question of whether the baseline establishment rules are appropriately regarded as "primarily aimed at" the conservation of natural resources for the purposes of Article XX(g). We consider that this question must be answered in the affirmative.

The baseline establishment rules, taken as a whole (that is, the provisions relating to establishment of baselines for domestic refiners, along with the provisions relating to baselines for blenders and importers of gasoline), need to be related to the "non-degradation" requirements set out elsewhere in the Gasoline Rule. Those provisions can scarcely be understood if scrutinized strictly by themselves, totally divorced from other sections of the Gasoline Rule which certainly constitute part of the context of these provisions. The baseline establishment rules, whether individual or statutory, were designed to permit scrutiny and monitoring of the level of compliance of refiners, importers and blenders with the "non-degradation" requirements. Without baselines of some kind, such scrutiny would not be possible and the Gasoline Rule's objective of stabilizing and preventing further deterioration of the level of air pollution prevailing in 1990, would be substantially frustrated. The relationship between the baseline establishment rules and the "non-degradation" requirements of the Gasoline Rule is not negated by the inconsistency, found by the Panel, of the baseline establishment rules with the terms of Article III:4. We consider that, given that substantial relationship, the baseline establishment rules cannot be regarded as merely incidentally or inadvertently aimed at the conservation of clean air in the United States for the purposes of Article XX(g).

"if such measures are made effective in conjunction with restrictions on domestic production or consumption"

The Panel did not find it necessary to deal with the issue of whether the baseline establishment rules "are made effective in conjunction with restrictions on domestic production or consumption," since it had earlier concluded that those rules had not even satisfied the preceding requirement of "relating to" in the sense of being "primarily aimed at" the conservation of clean air. Having been unable to concur with that earlier conclusion of the Panel, we must now address this second requirement of Article XX(g), the United States having, in effect, appealed from the failure of the Panel to proceed further with its inquiry into the availability of Article XX(g) as a justification for the baseline establishment rules.

The Appellate Body considers that the basic international law rule of treaty interpretation, discussed earlier, that the terms of a treaty are to be given their ordinary meaning, in context, so as to effectuate its object and purpose, is applicable here, too. Viewed in this light, the ordinary or natural meaning of "made effective" when used in connection with a measure — a governmental act or regulation — may be seen to refer to such measure being "operative," as "in force," or as having "come into effect." Similarly, the phrase "in conjunction with" may be read quite plainly as "together with" or "jointly with." Taken together, the second clause of Article XX(g) appears to us to refer to governmental measures like the baseline establishment rules being promulgated or brought into effect together with restrictions on domestic production or consumption of natural resources. Put in a slightly different manner, we believe that the clause "if such measures are made effective in conjunction with restrictions on domestic product or consumption" is appropriately read as a requirement that the measures concerned impose restrictions, not just in respect of imported gasoline, but also with respect to domestic gasoline. The clause is a requirement of *even-handedness* in the imposition of restrictions, in the name of conservation, upon the production or consumption of exhaustible natural resources.

There is, of course, no textual basis for requiring identical treatment of domestic and imported products. Indeed, where there is identity of treatment — constituting real, not merely formal, equality of treatment — it is difficult to see how inconsistency with Article III:4 would have arisen in the first place. On the other hand, if *no* restrictions on domestically-produced like products are imposed at all, and all limitations are placed upon imported products *alone*, the measure cannot be accepted as primarily or even substantially designed for implementing conservationist goals.[9] The measure would simply be naked discrimination for protecting locally-produced goods.

In the present appeal, the baseline establishment rules affect both domestic gasoline and imported gasoline, providing for — generally speaking — individual baselines for domestic refiners and blenders and statutory baselines for importers. Thus, restrictions on the consumption or depletion of clean air by regulating the domestic production of "dirty" gasoline are established jointly with corresponding restrictions with respect to imported gasoline. That imported gasoline has been determined to have been accorded "less favourable treatment" than the domestic gasoline in terms of Article III:4, is not material for purposes of analysis under Article XX(g). It might also be noted that the second clause of Article XX(g) speaks disjunctively of "domestic production *or* consumption."

We do not believe, finally, that the clause "if made effective in conjunction with restrictions on domestic production or consumption" was intended to establish an empirical "effects test" for the availability of the Article XX(g) exception. In the first place, the problem of determining causation, well-known in both domestic and international law, is always a difficult one. In the second place, in the field of conservation of exhaustible natural resources, a substantial period of time, perhaps years, may have to elapse before the effects attributable to implementation of a given measure may be observable. The legal characterization of such a measure is

---

[9] Some illustration is offered in the *Herring and Salmon* case which involved, *inter alia*, a Canadian prohibition of exports of unprocessed herring and salmon. This prohibition effectively constituted a ban on purchase of certain unprocessed fish by foreign processors and consumers while imposing no corresponding ban on purchase of unprocessed fish by domestic processors and consumers. The prohibitions appeared to be designed to protect domestic processors by giving them exclusive access to fresh fish and at the same time denying such raw material to foreign processors. The Panel concluded that these export prohibitions were not justified by Article XX(g). BISD 35S/98, para. 5.1, adopted 22 March 1988. See also the Panel Report in the *United States — Prohibition of Imports of Tuna and Tuna Products from Canada*, BISD 29S/91, paras. 4.10–4.12; adopted on 22 February 1982.

not reasonably made contingent upon occurrence of subsequent events. We are not, however, suggesting that consideration of the predictable effects of a measure is never relevant. In a particular case, should it become clear that realistically, a specific measure cannot in any possible situation have any positive effect on conservation goals, it would very probably be because that measure was not designed as a conservation regulation to begin with. In other words, it would not have been "primarily aimed at" conservation of natural resources at all.

The Introductory Provisions of Article XX of the General Agreement: Applying the Chapeau of the General Exceptions

Having concluded, in the preceding section, that the baseline establishment rules of the Gasoline Rule fall within the terms of Article XX(g), we come to the question of whether those roles also meet the requirements of the chapeau of Article XX. In order that the justifying protection of Article XX may be extended to it, the measure at issue must not only come under one or another of the particular exceptions — paragraphs (a) to (j) — listed under Article XX; it must also satisfy the requirements imposed by the opening clauses of Article XX. The analysis is, in other words, two-tiered: first, provisional justification by reason of characterization of the measure under XX(g); second, further appraisal of the same measure under the introductory clauses of Article XX.

The chapeau by its express terms addresses, not so much the questioned measure or its specific contents as such, but rather the manner in which that measure is applied. It is, accordingly, important to underscore that the purpose and object of the introductory clauses of Article XX is generally the prevention of "abuse of the exceptions of [what was later to become] Article [XX]." This insight drawn from the drafting history of Article XX is a valuable one. The chapeau is animated by the principle that while the exceptions of Article XX may be invoked as a matter of legal right, they should not be so applied as to frustrate or defeat the legal obligations of the holder of the right under the substantive roles of the *General Agreement*. If those exceptions are not to be abused or misused, in other words, the measures falling within the particular exceptions must be applied reasonably, with due regard both to the legal duties of the party claiming the exception and the legal rights of the other parties concerned.

The burden of demonstrating that a measure provisionally justified as being within one of the exceptions set out in the individual paragraphs of Article XX does not, in its application, constitute abuse of such exception under the chapeau, rests on the party invoking the exception. That is, of necessity, a heavier task than that involved in showing that an exception, such as Article XX(g), encompasses the measure at issue.

The chapeau, it will be seen, prohibits such application of a measure at issue (otherwise falling within the scope of Article XX(g)) as would constitute

    (a)   "arbitrary discrimination" (between countries where the same conditions prevail);

    (b)   "unjustifiable discrimination" (with the same qualifier); or

    (c)   "disguised restriction" on international trade.

The text of the chapeau is not without ambiguity, including one relating to the field of application of the standards it contains: the arbitrary or unjustifiable discrimination standards and the disguised restriction on international trade standard. It may be asked whether these standards do not have different fields of application. Such a question was put to the United States in the course of the oral hearing. It was asked whether the words incorporated into the first two standards "between countries where the same conditions prevail" refer to conditions in importing and exporting countries, or only to conditions in exporting countries. The reply of the United States was to the effect that it interpreted that phrase as referring to both the exporting countries and importing countries and as between exporting countries. It also said that the language spoke for itself, but there was no reference to third parties; while some thought that this was only between exporting countries *inter se*, there is no support in the text for that view. No such question was put to the United States concerning the field of application of the third standard — disguised restriction on international trade. But the United States put forward arguments designed to show that in the case under appeal, it had met all the standards set forth in the chapeau. In doing so, it clearly proceeded on the assumption that, whatever else they might relate to in another case, they were relevant to a case of national treatment where the Panel had found a violation of Article III:4. At no point in the appeal was that assumption challenged by Venezuela or Brazil. Venezuela argued that the United States had failed to meet all the standards contained in the chapeau. So did Norway and the European Communities as third participants. In short, the field of application of these standards was not at issue.

"Arbitrary discrimination," "unjustifiable discrimination" and "disguised restriction" on international trade may, accordingly, be read side-by-side; they impart meaning to one another. It is clear to us that "disguised restriction" includes disguised discrimination in international trade. It is equally clear that concealed or unannounced restriction or discrimination in international trade does not exhaust the meaning of "disguised restriction." We consider that "disguised restriction," whatever else it covers, may properly be read as embracing restrictions amounting to arbitrary or unjustifiable discrimination in international trade taken under the guise of a measure formally within the terms of an exception listed in Article XX. Put in a somewhat different manner, the kinds of considerations pertinent in deciding whether the application of a particular measure amounts to "arbitrary or unjustifiable discrimination," may also be taken into account in determining the presence of a "disguised restriction" on international trade. The fundamental theme is to be found in the purpose and object of avoiding abuse or illegitimate use of the exceptions to substantive rules available in Article XX.

There was more than one alternative course of action available to the United States in promulgating regulations implementing the CAA. These included the imposition of statutory baselines without differentiation as between domestic and imported gasoline. This approach, if properly implemented, could have avoided any discrimination at all. Among the other options open to the United States was to make available individual baselines to foreign refiners as well as domestic refiners. The United States has put forward a series of reasons why either of these courses was not, in its view, realistically open to it and why, instead, it had to devise and apply the baseline establishment rules contained in the Gasoline Rule.

In explaining why individual baselines for foreign refiners had not been put in place, the United States laid heavy stress upon the difficulties which the EPA would have had to face. These difficulties related to anticipated administrative problems that individual baselines for foreign refiners would have generated. This argument was made succinctly by the United States in the following terms:

> Verification on foreign soil of foreign baselines, and subsequent enforcement actions, present substantial difficulties relating to problems arising whenever a country exercises enforcement jurisdiction over foreign persons. In addition, even if individual baselines were established for several foreign refiners, the importer would be tempted to claim the refinery of origin that presented the most benefits in terms of baseline restrictions, and tracking the refinery or origin would be very difficult because gasoline is a fungible commodity. The United States should not have to prove that it cannot verify information and enforce its regulations in every instance in order to show that the same enforcement conditions do not prevail in the United States and other countries . . . The impracticability of verification and enforcement of foreign refiner baselines in this instance shows that the "discrimination" is based on serious, not arbitrary or unjustifiable, concerns stemming from different conditions between enforcement of its laws in the United States and abroad.

Thus, according to the United States, imported gasoline was relegated to the more exacting statutory baseline requirement because of these difficulties of verification and enforcement. The United States stated that verification and enforcement of the Gasoline Rule's requirements for imported gasoline are "much easier when the statutory baseline is used" and that there would be a "dramatic difference" in the burden of administering requirements for imported gasoline if individual baselines were allowed.

While the anticipated difficulties concerning verification and subsequent enforcement are doubtless real to some degree, the Panel viewed them as insufficient to justify the denial to foreign refiners of individual baselines permitted to domestic refiners.

We agree with the finding made in the Panel Report. There are, as the Panel Report found, established techniques for checking, verification, assessment and enforcement of data relating to imported goods, techniques which in many contexts are accepted as adequate to permit international trade — trade between territorial sovereigns — to go on and grow. The United States must have been aware that for these established techniques and procedures to work, cooperative arrangements with both foreign refiners and the foreign governments concerned would have been necessary and appropriate. At the oral hearing, in the course of responding to an enquiry as to whether the EPA could have adapted, for purposes of establishing individual refinery baselines for foreign refiners, procedures for verification of information found in U.S. antidumping laws, the United States said that "in the absence of refinery cooperation and the possible absence of foreign government cooperation as well," it was unlikely that the EPA auditors would be able to conduct the on-site audit reviews necessary to establish even the overall quality of refineries'

1990 gasoline. From this statement, there arises a strong implication, it appears to the Appellate Body, that the United States had not pursued the possibility of entering into cooperative arrangements with the governments of Venezuela and Brazil or, if it had, not to the point where it encountered governments that were unwilling to cooperate. The record of this case sets out the detailed justifications put forward by the United States. But it does not reveal what, if any, efforts had been taken by the United States to enter into appropriate procedures in cooperation with the governments of Venezuela and Brazil so as to mitigate the administrative problems pleaded by the United States. The fact that the United States Congress might have intervened, as it did later intervene, in the process by denying funding, is beside the point: the United States, of course, carries responsibility for actions of both the executive and legislative departments of government.

We have above located two omissions on the part of the United States: to explore adequately means, including in particular cooperation with the governments of Venezuela and Brazil, of mitigating the administrative problems relied on as justification by the United States for rejecting individual baselines for foreign refiners; and to count the costs for foreign refiners that would result from the imposition of statutory baselines. In our view, these two omissions go well beyond what was necessary for the Panel to determine that a violation of Article III:4 had occurred in the first place. The resulting discrimination must have been foreseen, and was not merely inadvertent or unavoidable. In the light of the foregoing, our conclusion is that the baseline establishment rules in the Gasoline Rule, in their application, constitute "unjustifiable discrimination" and a "disguised restriction on international trade." We hold, in sum, that the baseline establishment rules, although within the terms of Article XX(g), are not entitled to the justifying protection afforded by Article XX as a whole.

NOTES AND QUESTIONS

1.   The *Gasoline Case* provides an overview on how the WTO handles trade matters relating to environmental quality. Note that the WTO has no independent environmental mandate and is bound only by the particular environmental provisions in the WTO Agreements, such as GATT Article XX. Do you think the WTO should develop a Code of Environmental Conduct over and above the Multilateral Trade Agreements? Is this possible given the diverse membership of the WTO and its decisionmaking procedures?

2.   Note that the WTO Appellate Body turned to the Vienna Convention on the Law of Treaties for guidance. Did the Appellate Body correctly apply the Convention's article on treaty interpretation?

3.   The Gasoline Case is famous for its "reform" of Article XX(g). Does the reform adopted by the Appellate Body advance protection of the environment as a concern at the WTO?

Section III. WILDLIFE, NATURAL RESOURCES, AND POLLUTION

PROBLEM 5-1
AMAZONIA SEEKS GLOBAL ENVIRONMENTAL REFORMS

Amazonia is a WTO member country located in the tropics of Latin America. In Amazonia a new government has come to power on a platform of protection of the environment. The President of Amazonia has prepared a package of domestic environmental reforms that include: (1) protection of endangered species of wildlife as determined by the domestic law of Amazonia, which includes strict protection of all fur-bearing mammal species; (2) preservation of tropical forests including a prohibition of logging stands of designated species of tropical timber, such as *mahogany, ceiba, and ebony;* (3) a requirement that all sales of wood products must carry a Seal of Approval from the Amazonia Forest Stewardship Council that confirms that the wood comes from a sustainably managed forest; and (4) strict pollution control standards.

Together with these domestic reforms, the President of Amazonia has proposed reforms in international trade that include:

(1) a ban on the import of all furs and species of fur-bearing mammals;

(2) a ban on the importation of any wood products containing any of 12 species of tropical timber;

(3) a requirement that imported wood products of any kind must carry a Certificate of Approval from an approved organization that the wood comes from a sustainably managed forest;

(4) a ban on the imports of products from any country that does not enforce air and water pollution standards at least as stringent as Amazonia;

(5) a moratorium of three years on the exportation of wood products made from designated species of tropical timber that are in short supply in Amazonia;

(6) a ban on the exportation of raw logs from forests in Amazonia. This ban is justified on the grounds that Amazonia must encourage the development of value added domestic wood product industries and must also conserve its forests in order to participate in Amazonia's REDD-Plus (Reducing Emissions from Deforestation and Forest Degradation) program under the United Nations Framework Convention on Climate Change;

(7) a ban on the export of coal on the grounds that such a ban will cut down on the extraction and production of coal in Amazonia, thus reducing emissions of sulfur dioxide and other pollutants.

(8) Amazonia has imposed an eco-tax on the sale of cars and trucks based upon their pollution emissions; this tax applies equally to domestic-made and foreign-made vehicles, but, since Amazonia enforces strict vehicle pollution emission standards, the taxes will fall most heavily on vehicles imported from countries that have less strict pollution standards.

Consider the following materials and determine whether any of these trade restrictions violate the provisions of WTO agreements.

THE TUNA DOLPHIN CASES: A FALSE START

Before 1991, the relationship between protection of the environment and international trade was an arcane specialty that attracted little attention. In 1971, the GATT Council established a Working Group on Environmental Measures and International Trade. This group did not even meet for over 20 years.

Everything changed with the decision in the *Tuna Dolphin I* case, in which a GATT panel declared a U.S. embargo on tuna caught by fishing methods causing high dolphin mortality to be illegal. The *Tuna Dolphin I* decision produced an explosion of rhetoric in both learned journals and the popular press. It was also a very interesting clash of highly different "cultures": trade specialists versus environmentalists.

Acting under the U.S. Marine Mammal Protection Act (MMPA), the United States had adopted a unilateral ban on imports of yellowfin tuna using methods that also kill dolphins, a protected species under the MMPA. Upon Mexico's complaint to the GATT, a dispute settlement panel found that the U.S. tuna embargo violated GATT Article XI:1, which forbids measures prohibiting or restricting imports or exports. The United States sought to justify the embargo under GATT Article III:1 and III:4 because U.S. fishermen were subject to the same MMPA rules. The GATT panel rejected the U.S. argument on the grounds that Article III:1 and Article III:4 permit only regulations relating to products as such. Because the MPA regulations concerned harvesting techniques that could not possibly affect tuna as a product, the ban on tuna could not be justified. This holding was reiterated by a second GATT panel in the *Tuna Dolphin II* decision, which involved the legality of a secondary embargo of tuna products from countries that processed tuna caught by the offending countries.

Both *Tuna Dolphin* panels also concluded that neither GATT Article XX(b) nor XX(g) could justify the U.S. tuna import ban. As to Article XX(b), both panels held that the ban failed the "necessary" test. They rejected the U.S. argument that "necessary" means "needed," stating that "necessary" means that no other reasonable alternative exists and that "a contracting party is bound to use, among the measures available to it, that which entails the least degree of inconsistency" with the GATT. A trade measure taken to force other countries to change their environmental policies, and that would be effective only if such changes occurred, could not be considered "necessary" within the meaning of Article XX(b). Both panels similarly concluded that Article XX(g) was not applicable; they found that the terms "relating to" and "in conjunction with" in Article XX(g) were synonymous with "primarily aimed at," and held that unilateral measures to force other countries to change conservation policies cannot satisfy the "primarily aimed at" standard.

The GATT panels in the two Tuna Dolphin cases came to different conclusion' regarding the territorial application of Article XX(b) and (g). The Tuna Dolphin 1 panel concluded that the natural resources and living things protected under these provisions were only those within the territorial jurisdiction of the country concerned. This view, which was based on the belief that the drafters of Article XX had focused on each contracting party's domestic concerns, has been widely criticized. The Tuna Dolphin II panel, in contrast, "could see no valid reason supporting the conclusion that the provisions of Article XX(g) apply only to the conservation of exhaustible natural resources located within the territory of the contracting parry invoking the provision." Nevertheless, the panel ruled that governments can enforce an Article XX(g) restriction extraterritorially only against their own nationals and vessels.

UNITED STATES — IMPORT PROHIBITION OF CERTAIN SHRIMP AND SHRIMP PRODUCTS
Report of the Appellate Body adopted by the DSB, WT/DS58/AB/R (Nov. 6, 1998)

Introduction: Statement of the Appeal

1. This is an appeal by the United States from certain issues of law and legal interpretations in the Panel Report, United States — *Import Prohibition of Certain Shrimp and Shrimp Products.* Following a joint request for consultations by India, Malaysia, Pakistan and *Thailand on* 8 October 1996, Malaysia and Thailand requested in a communication dated 9 January 1997, and Pakistan asked in a communication dated 30 January 1997, that the Dispute Settlement Body (the "DSB") establish a panel to examine their complaint regarding a prohibition imposed by the United States on the importation of certain shrimp and shrimp products by Section 609 of Public Law 101-162 ("Section 609") and associated regulations and judicial rulings.

*   *   *

2 . . . The United States issued regulations in 1987 pursuant to the Endangered Species Act of 1973 requiring all United States shrimp trawl vessels to use approved Turtle Excluder Devices ("TEDs") or tow-time restrictions in specified areas where there was a significant mortality of sea turtles in shrimp harvesting. These regulations, which became fully effective in 1990, were modified so as to require the use of approved TEDs at all times and in all areas where there is a likelihood that shrimp trawling will interact with sea turtles, with certain limited exceptions.

3. Section 609 was enacted on 21 November 1989. Section 609(a) calls upon the United States Secretary of State, in consultation with the Secretary of Commerce, inter alia, to "initiate negotiations as soon as possible for the development of bilateral or multilateral agreements with other nations for the protection and conservation of . . . sea turtles" and to "initiate negotiations as soon as possible with all foreign governments which are engaged in, or which have persons or companies engaged in, commercial fishing operations which, as determined by the Secretary of Commerce, may affect adversely such species of sea turtles, for the purpose of entering into bilateral and multilateral treaties with such countries to protect such species of sea turtles; . . ."

113. Article XX of the GATT 1994 reads, in its relevant parts:

Article XX
General Exceptions

Subject to the requirement that such measures are not applied in a manner which would constitute a means of arbitrary or unjustifiable discrimination between countries where the same conditions prevail, or a disguised restriction on international trade, nothing in this Agreement shall be construed to prevent the adoption or enforcement by any Member of measures:

*   *   *

(b)   necessary to protect human, animal or plant life or health;

*   *   *

(g)   relating to the conservation of exhaustible natural resources if such measures are made effective in conjunction with restrictions on domestic production or consumption;

"Exhaustible Natural Resources"

127. We begin with the threshold question of whether Section 609 is a measure concerned with the conservation of "exhaustible natural resources" within the meaning of Article XX(g). The Panel, of course, with its "chapeau-down" approach, did not make a finding on whether the sea turtles that Section 609 is designed to conserve constitute "exhaustible natural resources" for purposes of Article XX(g). In the proceedings before the Panel, however, the parties to the dispute argued this issue vigorously and extensively. India, Pakistan and Thailand contended that a "reasonable interpretation" of the term "exhaustible" is that the term refers to "finite resources such as minerals, rather than biological or renewable resources." In their view, such finite resources were exhaustible "because there was a limited supply which could and would be depleted unit for unit as the resources were consumed." Moreover, they argued, if "all" natural resources were considered to be exhaustible, the term "exhaustible" would become superfluous They also referred to the drafting history of Article XX(g), and, in particular, to the mention of minerals, such as manganese, in the context of arguments made by some delegations that "export restrictions" should be permitted for the preservation of scarce natural resources. For its part, Malaysia added that sea turtles, being living creatures, could only be considered under Article XX(b), since Article XX(g) was meant for "nonliving exhaustible natural resources." It followed, according to Malaysia, that the United States cannot invoke both the Article X:(b) and the Article XX(g) exceptions simultaneously.

128. We are not convinced by these arguments. Textually, Article XX(g) is not limited to the conservation of "mineral" or "non-living" natural resources. The complainants' principal argument is rooted in the notion that "living" natural resources are "renewable" and therefore cannot be "exhaustible" natural resources. We do not believe that "exhaustible" natural resources and "renewable" natural resources are mutually exclusive. One lesson that modern biological sciences teach us is that living species, though in principle, capable of reproduction and, in that

sense, "renewable," are in certain circumstances indeed susceptible of depletion, exhaustion and extinction, frequently because of human activities. Living resources are just as "finite" as petroleum, iron ore and other non-living resources.

129. The words of Article XX(g), "exhaustible natural resources," were actually crafted more than 50 years ago, They must be read by a treaty interpreter in the light of contemporary concerns of the community of nations about the protection and conservation of the environment. While Article XX was not modified in the Uruguay Round, the preamble attached to the *WTO Agreement* shows that the signatories to that Agreement were, in 1994, fully aware of the importance and legitimacy of environmental protection as a goal of national and international policy. The preamble of the *WTO Agreement — which* informs not only the GATT 1994, but also the other covered agreements — explicitly acknowledges "the objective of *sustainable development*":

> The *Parties* to this Agreement,
>
> *Recognizing* that their relations in the field of trade and economic endeavour should be conducted *with a view to raising standards of living, ensuring full employment and* a *large and steadily growing volume of real income and effective demand*, and *expanding the production of and trade in goods and services*, while allowing for the optimal use of the world's resources in accordance with the *objective of sustainable development, seeking both to protect and preserve the environment and to enhance the means for doing so* in a manner consistent with their respective needs and concerns at different levels of economic development, . . . (emphasis added).

130. From the perspective embodied in the preamble of the *WTO Agreement*, we note that the generic term "natural resources" in Article XX(g) is not "static" in its content or reference but is rather "by definition, evolutionary." It is, therefore, pertinent to note that modern international conventions and declarations make frequent references to natural resources as embracing both living and nonliving resources. For instance, the 1982 United Nations Convention on the Law of the Sea ("UNCLOS"), in defining the jurisdictional rights of coastal states in their exclusive economic zones, provides:

Article 56

Rights, jurisdiction and duties of the coastal State in the *exclusive economic zone*

1. In the exclusive economic zone, the coastal State has:

> (a) sovereign rights for the purpose of exploring and exploiting, conserving and managing the *natural resources, whether living or nonliving*, of the waters superjacent to the sea-bed and of the sea-bed and its subsoil, . . . (emphasis added).

The UNCLOS also repeatedly refers in Articles 61 and 62 to "living resources" in specifying rights and duties of states in their exclusive economic zones. The Convention on Biological Diversity uses the concept of "biological resources." Agenda 21 speaks most broadly of "natural resources" and goes into detailed statements about "marine resources." In addition, the Resolution on Assistance to Developing Countries, adopted in conjunction with the Convention on the Conservation of Migratory Species of Wild Animals, recites:

> Conscious that an important element of development lies in the conservation and management of *living natural resources* and that migratory species constitute a significant part of these resources; . . . (emphasis added).

131. Given the recent acknowledgement by the international community of the importance of concerted bilateral or multilateral action to protect living natural resources, and recalling the explicit recognition by WTO Members of the objective of sustainable development in the preamble of the *WTO Agreement*, we believe it is too late in the day to suppose that Article XX(g) of the GATT 1994 may be read as referring only to the conservation of exhaustible mineral or other non-living natural resources. Moreover, two adopted GATT 1947 panel reports previously found fish to be an "exhaustible natural resource" within the meaning of Article XX(g). We hold that, in line with the principle of effectiveness in treaty interpretation measures to conserve exhaustible natural resources, whether *living* or *non-living*, may fall within Article XX(g).

132. We turn next to the issue of whether the living natural resources sought to be conserved by the measure are "exhaustible" under Article XX(g). That this element is present in respect of the five species of sea turtles here involved appears to be conceded by all the participants and third participants in this case. The exhaustibility of sea turtles would in fact have been very difficult to controvert since all of the seven recognized species of sea turtles are today listed in Appendix 1 of the Convention on International Trade in Endangered Species of Wild Fauna and Flora ("CITES"). The list in Appendix 1 includes "all species *threatened with extinction* which are or may be affected by trade." (emphasis added).

133. Finally, we observe that sea turtles are highly migratory animals, passing in and out of waters subject to the rights of jurisdiction of various coastal states and the high seas. In the Panel Report, the Panel said:

> . . . Information brought to the attention of the Panel, including documented statements from the experts, tends to *confirm the fact that sea turtles, in certain circumstances of their lives, migrate through the waters of several countries and the high sea* . . . . (emphasis added).

The sea turtle species here at stake, i.e., covered by Section 609, are all known to occur in waters over which the United States exercises jurisdiction." Of course, it is not claimed that *all* populations of these species migrate to, or traverse, at one time or another, waters subject to United States jurisdiction. Neither the appellant nor any of the appellees claims any rights of exclusive ownership over the sea turtles, at least not while they are swimming freely in their natural habitat — the oceans. We do not pass upon the question of whether there is an implied jurisdictional limitation in Article XX(g), and if so, the nature or extent of that limitation. We note only that in the specific circumstances of the case before us, there is a sufficient nexus between the migratory and endangered marine populations involved and the United States for purposes of Article XX(g).

134. For all the foregoing reasons, we find that the sea turtles here involved constitute "exhaustible natural resources" for purposes of Article XX(g) of the GATT 1994.

"Relating to the Conservation of Exhaustible Natural Resources"

135. Article XX(g) requires that the measure sought to be justified be one which "relat[es] to" the conservation of exhaustible natural resources. In making this determination, the treaty interpreter essentially looks into the relationship between the measure at stake and the legitimate policy of conserving exhaustible natural resources. It is well to bear in mind that the policy of protecting and conserving the endangered sea turtles here involved is shared by all participants and third participants in this appeal, indeed, by the vast majority of the nations of the world. None of the parties to this dispute question the genuineness of the commitment of the others to that policy.

137. In the present case, we must examine the relationship between the general structure and design of the measure here at stake, Section 609, and the policy goal it purports to serve, that is, the conservation of sea turtles.

138. Section 609(b)(1) imposes an import ban on shrimp that have been harvested with commercial fishing technology which may adversely affect sea turtles. This provision is designed to influence countries to adopt national regulatory programs requiring the use of TEDs by their shrimp fishermen. In this connection, it is important to note that the general structure and design of Section 609 *cum* implementing guidelines is fairly narrowly focused. There are two basic exemptions from the import ban, both of which relate clearly and directly to the policy goal of conserving sea turtles. First, Section 609, as elaborated in the 1996 Guidelines, excludes from the import ban shrimp harvested "under conditions that do not adversely affect sea turtles." Thus, the measure, by its terms, excludes from the import ban: aquaculture shrimp; shrimp species (such as *pandalid* shrimp) harvested in water areas where sea turtles do not normally occur; and shrimp harvested exclusively by artisanal methods, even from non-certified countries. The harvesting of such shrimp dearly does not affect sea turtles. Second, under Section 609(b)(2), the measure exempts from the import ban shrimp caught in waters subject to the jurisdiction of certified countries.

139. There are two types of certification for countries under Section 609(b)(2). First, under Section 609(b)(2)(C), a country may be certified as having a fishing environment that does not pose a threat of incidental taking of sea turtles in the course of commercial shrimp trawl harvesting. There is no risk, or only a negligible risk, that sea turtles will be harmed by shrimp trawling in such an environment.

140. The second type of certification is provided by Section 609(b)(2)(A) and (B). Under these provisions, as further elaborated in the 1996 Guidelines, a country wishing to export shrimp to the United States is required to adopt a regulatory program that is comparable to that of the United States program and to have a rate of incidental take of sea turtles that is comparable to the average rate of United States' vessels. This is, essentially, a requirement that a country adopt a regulatory program requiring the use of TEDs by commercial shrimp trawling vessels in areas

where there is a likelihood of intercepting sea turtles. This requirement is, in our view, directly connected with the policy of conservation of sea turtles. It is undisputed among the participants, and recognized by the experts consulted by the Panel that the harvesting of shrimp by commercial shrimp trawling vessels with mechanical retrieval devices in waters where shrimp and sea turtles coincide is a significant cause of sea turtle mortality. Moreover, the Panel did "not question . . . the fact generally acknowledged by the experts that TEDs, when properly installed and adapted to the local area, would be an effective tool for the preservation of sea turtles."

141. In its general design and structure, therefore, Section 609 is not a simple, blanket prohibition of the importation of shrimp imposed without regard to the consequences (or lack thereof) of the mode of harvesting employed upon the incidental capture and mortality of sea turtles. Focusing on the design of the measure here at stake, it appears to us that Section 609, *cum* implementing guidelines, is not disproportionately wide in its scope and reach in relation to the policy objective of protection and conservation of sea turtle species. The measures are, in principle, reasonably related to the ends. The means and ends relationship between Section 609 and the legitimate policy of conserving an exhaustible and, in fact, endangered species, is observably a close and real one, a relationship that is every bit as substantial as that which we found in *United States Gasoline* between the EPA baseline establishment rules and the conservation clean air in the United States.

142. In our view, therefore, Section 609 is a measure "relating to" the conservation of an exhaustible natural resource within the meaning of Arti **cle** XX(g) of the GATT 1994.

"If Such Measures are Made Effective in conjunction with Restrictions on Domestic Production or Consumption"

143. In *United States — Gasoline*, we held that the above-captioned clause Article XX(g), . . . is appropriately read as a requirement that the measures concerned impose restrictions, not just in respect of imported gasoline but also with respect to domestic gasoline. The clause is a requirement of *even-handedness* in the imposition of restrictions, in the name of conservation, upon the production or consumption of exhaustible natural resources.

In this case, we need to examine whether the restrictions imposed by Section 609 with respect to imported shrimp are also imposed in respect of shrimp caught by United States shrimp trawl vessels.

144. We earlier noted that Section 609, enacted in 1989, addresses the mode of harvesting of imported shrimp only. However, two years; earlier, in 1987, the United States issued regulations pursuant to the Endangered Species Act requiring all United States shrimp trawl vessels to use approved TEDs, or to restrict the duration of towtimes, in specified areas where there was significant incidental mortality of sea turtles in shrimp trawls. These regulations became fully effective in 1990 and were later modified. They now require United State shrimp trawlers to use approved TEDs "in areas and at times when there is likelihood of intercepting sea

turtles," with certain limited exceptions. Penalties for violation of the Endangered Species Act, or the regulations issued thereunder, include civil and criminal sanctions." The United States government currently relies on monetary sanctions and civil penalties for enforcement. The government has the ability to seize shrimp catch from trawl vessels fishing in United States waters and has done so in cases of egregious violations. We believe that, in principle, Section 609 is an even-handed measure.

145. Accordingly, we hold that Section 609 is a measure made effective in con junction with the restrictions on domestic harvesting of shrimp, as required by Article XX(g).

The Introductory Clauses of Article XX: Characterizing

Section 609 under the Chapeau's Standards

147. Although provisionally justified under Article XX(g), Section 609, if it is ultimately to be justified as an exception under Article XX, must also satisfy the *requirements* of the introductory clauses — the "chapeau" — of Article XX.

150. We commence the second tier of our analysis with an examination of ordinary meaning of the words of the chapeau. The precise language of the chapeau requires that a measure not be applied in a manner which would constitute a means of "arbitrary or unjustifiable discrimination between countries where the same conditions prevail" or a "disguised restriction on international trade." There are three standards contained in the chapeau: first, arbitrary discrimination between countries where the same conditions prevail; second, unjustifiable discrimination between countries where the same conditions prevail; and third, a disguised restriction on international trade. In order for the measure to be applied in a manner which would constitute "arbitrary or unjustifiable discrimination between countries where the same conditions prevail three elements must exist. First, the application of the measure must result in *discrimination.* As we stated in *United States — Gasoline*, the nature and quality of this discrimination is different from the discrimination in the treatment of products which was already found to be inconsistent with one of the. substantive obligations of the GATT 1994, such as Articles I, III or XI. Second, discrimination must be *arbitrary* or *unjustifiable* in character. We will examine this element of *arbitrariness* or *unjustifiability* in detail below. Third, this discrimination must occur *between countries where the same conditions prevail.* In *United States — Gasoline*, we accepted the assumption of the participants in the appeal that such discrimination could occur not only between different exporting Members, but also between exporting Members and the importing Members concerned. Thus, the standards embodied in the language of the chapeau are not only different from the requirements of Article XX(g); they are also different from the standard used in determining that Section 609 is violative of the substantive rules of Article XI:1 of the GATT 1994.

"Unjustifiable Discrimination"

161. We scrutinize first whether Section 609 has been applied in a manner constituting "unjustifiable discrimination between countries where the same conditions prevail." Perhaps the most conspicuous flaw in this measure's application relates to its intended and actual coercive effect on the specific policy decisions made by foreign governments, Members of the WTO, Section 609, in its application, is, in effect, an economic embargo which requires *all other exporting Members*, if they wish to exercise their GATT rights, to adopt *essentially the same policy* (together with an approved enforcement program) as that applied to, and enforced on, United States domestic shrimp trawlers. As enacted by the Congress of the United States, the *statutory* provisions of Section 609(b)(2)(A) and (B) do not, in themselves, *require* that other WTO Members adopt *essentially the same* policies and enforcement practices as the United States. Viewed alone, the statute appears to permit a degree of discretion or flexibility in how the standards for determining comparability might be applied, in practice, to other countries. However, any flexibility that may have been intended by Congress when it enacted the statutory provision has been effectively eliminated in the implementation of that policy through the 1996 Guidelines promulgated by the Department of State and through the practice of the administrators in making certification determinations.

163. The actual *application* of the measure, through the implementation of the 1996 Guidelines and the regulatory practice of administrators, *requires* other WTO Members to adopt a regulatory program that is not merely *comparable*, but rather *essentially the same*, as that applied to the United States shrimp trawl vessels. Thus, the effect of the application of Section 609 is to establish a rigid and unbending standard by which United States officials determine whether or not countries will be certified, thus granting or refusing other countries the right to export shrimp to the United States. Other specific policies and measures that an exporting country may have adopted for the protection and conservation of sea turtles are not taken into account, in practice, by the administrators making the comparability determination.

164. We understand that the United States also applies a uniform standard throughout its territory, regardless of the particular conditions existing in certain parts of the country. The United States requires the use of approved TEDs at all times by domestic, commercial shrimp trawl vessels operating in waters where there is any likelihood that they may interact with sea turtles, regardless of the actual incidence of sea turtles in those waters, the species of those sea turtles, or other differences or disparities that may exist in different parts of the United States. It may be quite acceptable for a government, in adopting and implementing a domestic policy, to adopt a single standard applicable to all its citizens throughout that country. However, it is not acceptable, in international trade relations, for one WTO Member to use an economic embargo to *require* other Members to adopt essentially the same comprehensive regulatory program, to achieve a certain policy goal, as that in force within that Member's territory, *without* taking into consideration different conditions which may occur in the territories of those other Members.

165. This suggests to us that this measure, in its application, is more concerned

with effectively influencing WTO Members to adopt essentially the same comprehensive regulatory regime as that applied by the United States to its domestic shrimp trawlers, even though many of those Members may be differently situated. We believe that discrimination results not only when countries in which the same conditions prevail are differently treated, but also when the application of the measure at issue does not allow for any inquiry into the appropriateness of the regulatory program for the conditions prevailing in those exporting countries.

166. Another aspect of the application of Section 609 that bears heavily in any appraisal of justifiable or unjustifiable discrimination is the failure of the United States to engage the appellees, as well as other Members exporting shrimp to the United States, in serious, across-the-board negotiations with the objective of concluding bilateral or multilateral agreements for the protection and conservation of sea turtles, before enforcing the import prohibition against the shrimp exports of those other Members.

167. A *propos* this failure to have prior consistent recourse to diplomacy as an instrument of environmental protection policy, which produces discriminatory impacts on countries exporting shrimp to the United States with which no international agreements are reached or even seriously attempted, a number of points must be made. First, the Congress of the United States expressly recognized the importance of securing international agreements for the protection and conservation of the sea turtle species in enacting this law. Section 609(a) *directs* the Secretary of State to:

(1) *initiate negotiations as soon as possible for the development of bilateral or multilateral agreements with other nations* for the protection and *conservation of* such species of sea turtles;

(2) *initiate negotiations as soon as possible* with all foreign governments which are engaged in, or which have persons or companies engaged in, commercial fishing operations which, as determined by the Secretary of Commerce, may affect adversely such species of sea turtles, *for the purpose of entering into bilateral and multilateral treaties with such countries to protect such species of sea turtles;*

(3) *encourage such other agreements* to promote the purposes of this section *with other nations* for the protection of specific ocean and land regions which are of special *significance to* the health and stability of such species of sea turtles;

(4) *initiate the amendment of any existing international treaty* for the protection and conservation of such species of sea turtles to which the United States is a party *in order to make such treaty consistent with the purposes and policies of this section;* and

(5) provide to the Congress by not later than one year after the date of enactment of this section:

*   *   *

(C) a full report on:

(i) the results of his efforts under this section; . . . (emphasis added).

Apart from the *negotiation of* the Inter-American Convention for the Protection and Conservation of Sea Turtles (the "Inter-American Convention") which concluded in 1996, the record before the Panel does not indicate any serious, substantial efforts to carry out these express directions of Congress.

168. Second, the protection and conservation of highly migratory species of sea turtles, that is, the very policy objective of the measure, demands concerted and cooperative efforts on the part of the many countries whose waters are traversed in the course of recurrent sea turtle migrations. The need for, and the appropriateness of, such efforts have been recognized in the WTO itself as well as in a significant number of other international instruments and declarations.

169. Third, the United States did negotiate and conclude one regional international agreement for the protection and conservation of sea turtles: The Inter-American Convention. This Convention was opened for signature on 1 December 1996 and has been signed by five countries, in addition to the United States, and four of these countries are currently certified under Section 609. This Convention has not yet been ratified by any of its signatories. The Inter-American Convention provides that each party shall take "appropriate and necessary measures" for the protection, conservation and recovery of sea turtle populations and their habitats within such party's land territory and in maritime areas with respect to which it exercises sovereign rights or jurisdiction.

171. The Inter-American Convention thus provides convincing demonstration that an alternative course of action was reasonably open to the United States for securing the legitimate policy goal of its measure, a course of action other than the unilateral and non-consensual procedures of the import prohibition under Section 609. It is relevant to observe that an import prohibition is, ordinarily, the heaviest "weapon" in a Member's armory of trade measures. The record does not, however, show that serious efforts were made by the United States to negotiate similar agreements with any other country or group of countries before (and, as far as the record shows, after) Section 609 was enforced on a world-wide basis on 1 May 1996. Finally, the record also does not show that the appellant, the United States, attempted to have recourse to such international mechanisms as exist to achieve cooperative efforts to protect and conserve sea turtles before imposing the import ban.

172. Clearly, the United States negotiated seriously with some, but not with other Members (including the appellees), that export shrimp to the United States. The effect is plainly discriminatory and, in our view, unjustifiable. The unjustifiable nature of this discrimination emerges clearly when we consider the cumulative effects of the failure of the United States to pursue negotiations for establishing consensual means of protection and conservation of the living marine resources here involved, notwithstanding the explicit statutory direction in Section 609 itself to initiate negotiations as soon as possible for the development of bilateral and multilateral agreements. The principal consequence of this failure may be seen in the resulting unilateralism evident in the application of Section 609. As we have emphasized earlier, the policies relating to the necessity for use of particular kinds of TEDs in various maritime areas, and the operating details of these policies, are all shaped by the Department of State, without the participation of the exporting

Members. The system and processes of certification are established and administered by the United States agencies alone. The decision-making involved in the grant, denial or withdrawal of certification to the exporting Members, is, accordingly, also unilateral. The unilateral character of the application of Section 609 heightens the disruptive and discriminatory influence of the import prohibition and underscores its unjustifiability.

173. The application of Section 609, through the implementing guidelines together with administrative practice, also resulted in other differential treatment among various countries desiring certification. Under the 1991 and 1993 Guidelines, to be certifiable, fourteen countries in the wider Caribbean/Western Atlantic region had to commit themselves to require the use of TEDs on all commercial shrimp trawling vessels by 1 May 1994. These fourteen countries had a "phase-in" period of three years during which their respective shrimp trawling sectors could adjust to the requirement of the use of TEDs. With respect to all other countries exporting shrimp to the United States (including the appellees, India, Malaysia, Pakistan and Thailand), on 29 December 1995, the United States Court of International Trade directed the Department of State to apply the import ban on a world-wide basis not later than 1 May 1996. On 19 April 1996, the 1996 Guidelines were issued by the Department of State bringing shrimp harvested in *all* foreign countries within the scope of Section 609, effective 1 May 1996. Thus, all countries that were not among the fourteen in the wider Caribbean /western Atlantic region had only four months to implement the requirement of compulsory use of TEDs. We acknowledge that the greatly differing periods for putting into operation the requirement for use of TEDs resulted from decisions of the Court of International Trade. Even so, this does not relieve the United States of the legal consequences of the discriminatory impact of the decisions of that Court. The United States, like all other Members of the WTO and of the general community of states, bears responsibility for acts of all its departments of government, including its judiciary.

175. Differing treatment of different countries desiring certification is also observable in the differences in the levels of effort made by the United States in transferring the required TED technology to specific countries. Far greater efforts to transfer that technology successfully were made to certain exporting countries — basically the fourteen wider Caribbean/western Atlantic countries cited earlier — than to other exporting countries, including the appellees. The level of these efforts is probably related to the length of the "phase-in" periods granted — the longer the "phase-in" period, the higher the possible level of efforts at technology transfer. Because compliance with the requirements of certification realistically assumes successful TED technology transfer, low or merely nominal efforts at achieving that transfer will, in all probability, result in fewer countries being able to satisfy the certification requirements under Section 609, within the very limited "phase-in" periods allowed them.

176. When the foregoing differences in the means of application of Section 609 to various shrimp exporting countries are considered in their cumulative effect, we find, and so hold, that those differences in treatment constitute "unjustifiable discrimination" between exporting countries desiring certification in order to gain access to the United States shrimp market within the meaning of the chapeau of Article xx.

"Arbitrary Discrimination"

177. We next consider whether Section 609 has been applied in a manner constituting "arbitrary discrimination between countries where the same conditions prevail." We have already observed that Section 609, in its application, imposes a single, rigid and unbending requirement that countries applying for certification under Section 609(b)(2)(A) and (B) adopt a comprehensive regulatory program that is essentially the same as the United States' program, without inquiring into the appropriateness of that program for the conditions prevailing in the exporting countries" Furthermore, there is little or no flexibility in how officials make the determination for certification pursuant to these provisions. In our view, this rigidity and inflexibility also constitute "arbitrary discrimination" within the meaning of the chapeau.

186. What we have decided, in this appeal is simply this: although the measure of the United States in dispute in this appeal serves an environmental objective that is recognized as legitimate under paragraph (g) of Article XX of the GATT 1994, this measure has been applied by the United States in a manner which constitutes arbitrary and unjustifiable discrimination between Members of the WTO, contrary to the requirements of the chapeau of Article XX. For all of the specific reasons outlined in this Report, this measure does not qualify for the exemption that Article XX of the GATT 1994 affords to measures which serve certain recognized, legitimate environmental purposes but which, at the same time, are not applied in a manner that constitutes a means of arbitrary or unjustifiable discrimination between countries where the same conditions prevail or a disguised restriction on international trade.

The Appellate Body recommends that the DSB request the United States to bring its measure found in the Panel Report to be inconsistent with Article XI of the GATT 1994, and found in this Report to be not justified under Article XX of the GATT 1994, into conformity with the obligations of the United States under that Agreement.

UNITED STATES — IMPORT PROHIBITION OF CERTAIN SHRIMP AND SHRIMP PRODUCTS RECOURSE TO ARTICLE 21.5

Report of the Appellate Body adopted by the DSB
WT/DS58/AB/RW (Nov. 21, 2001)

[After the adoption of the Decision in the Shrimp/Turtle case, the United States (U.S.) took two measures to comply with the mandate of the WTO. First, the U.S. revised its regulations and issued the 1999 Guidelines concerning the issuance of Certifications that must accompany the importation of shrimp into the U.S. The 1999 Guidelines adopt more flexible methods of protecting turtles. Certification is still issued on the basis that the nation has provided assurances that the rate of incidental taking is comparable to the U.S. rate. But certification may be given either on the basis that the exporting country has implemented a TEDs program or a country must demonstrate that it can protect turtles without the use of TEDs. New procedures are also a feature of the 1999 Guidelines. Second, the U.S. began efforts to negotiate an agreement on the conservation of sea turtles with states in the Indian Ocean region and offered new programs on technical assistance in the use of TEDs.

Malaysia, nevertheless, brought an action against the U.S. under Article 21.5 of the WTO Dispute Settlement Understanding (DSU), charging that the U.S. had failed to bring Section 609 into conformity with its WTO obligations.]

The Nature and the Extent of the Duty of the United States to Pursue International Cooperation in the Protection and Conservation of Sea Turtles

* * *

119. In *United States-Shrimp*, we stated that the measure at issue there resulted in "unjustifiable discrimination," in part because, as applied, the United States treated WTO Members differently. The United States had adopted a cooperative approach with WTO Members from the Caribbean/Western Atlantic region, with whom it had concluded a multilateral agreement on the protection and conservation of sea turtles, namely the Inter-American Convention. Yet the United States had not, we found, pursued the negotiation of such a multilateral agreement with other exporting Members, including Malaysia and the other complaining WTO Members in that case.

122. We concluded in *United States-Shrimp* that, to avoid "arbitrary or unjustifiable discrimination," the United States had to provide all exporting countries "similar opportunities to negotiate" an international agreement. Given the specific mandate contained in Section 609, and given the decided preference for multilateral approaches voiced by WTO Members and others in the international community in various international agreements for the protection and conservation of endangered sea turtles that were cited in our previous Report, the United States, in our view, would be expected to make good faith efforts to reach international agreements that are comparable from one forum of negotiation to the other. The negotiations need not be identical. Indeed, no two negotiations can ever be identical, or lead to identical results. Yet the negotiations must be *comparable* in the sense that comparable efforts are made, comparable resources are *invested, and* comparable energies are devoted to securing an international agreement. So long as such comparable efforts are made, it is more likely that "arbitrary or unjustifiable discrimination" will be avoided between countries where an importing Member concludes an agreement with one group of countries, but fails to do so with another group of countries.

123. Under the chapeau of Article XX, an importing Member may not treat its trading partners in a manner that would constitute "arbitrary or unjustifiable discrimination." With respect to this measure, the United States could conceivably respect this obligation, and the conclusion of an international agreement might nevertheless not be possible despite the serious, good faith efforts of the United States. Requiring that a multilateral agreement be *concluded* by the United States in order to avoid "arbitrary or unjustifiable discrimination" in applying its measure would mean that any country party to the negotiations with the United States, whether a WTO Member or not, would have, in effect, a veto over whether the

United States could fulfill its WTO obligations. Such a requirement would not be reasonable. For a variety of reasons, it may be possible to conclude an agreement with one group of countries but not another. The conclusion of a multilateral agreement requires the cooperation and commitment of many countries. In our view, the United States cannot be held to have engaged in "arbitrary or unjustifiable discrimination" under Article XX solely because one international negotiation resulted in an agreement while another did not.

130. The Panel compared the efforts of the United States to negotiate the Inter-American Convention with one group of exporting WTO Members with the efforts made by the United States to negotiate a similar agreement with another group of exporting WTO Members. The Panel rightly used the Inter-American Convention as a factual reference in this exercise of comparison. It was all the more relevant to do so given that the Inter-American Convention was the only international agreement that the Panel could have used in such a comparison. As we read the Panel Report, it is clear to us that the Panel attached a relative value to the Inter-American Convention in making this comparison, but did not view the Inter-American Convention in any way as an absolute standard. Thus, we disagree with Malaysia's submission that the Panel raised the Inter-American Convention to the rank of a "legal standard." The mere use by the Panel of the Inter-American Convention as a basis for a comparison did not transform the Inter-American Convention into a "legal standard." Furthermore, although the Panel could have chosen a more appropriate word than "benchmark" to express its views, Malaysia is mistaken in equating the mere use of the word "benchmark," as it was used by the Panel, with the establishment of a legal standard.

131. The Panel noted that while "factual circumstances may influence the duration of the process or the end result, . . . any effort alleged to be a 'serious good faith effort' must be assessed against the efforts made in relation to the conclusion of the Inter-American Convention." Such a comparison is a central element of the exercise to determine whether there is "unjustifiable discrimination." The Panel then analyzed the negotiation process in the Indian Ocean and South-East Asia region to determine whether the efforts made by the United States in those negotiations were serious, good faith efforts comparable to those made in relation with the Inter-American Convention.

132. On this basis and, in particular, on the basis of the "contribution of the United States to the steps that led to the Kuantan meeting and its contribution to the Kuantan meeting itself", the Panel concluded that the United States had made serious, good faith efforts that met the "standard set by the Inter American Convention." In the view of the Panel, whether or not the South-East Asian MOU is a legally binding document does not affect this comparative assessment because differences in "factual circumstances have to be kept in mind." Furthermore, the Panel did not consider as decisive the fact that the final agreement in the Indian Ocean and South-East Asia region, unlike the Inter-American Convention, had not been concluded at the time of the Panel proceedings. According to the Panel, "at least until the Conservation and Management Plan to be attached to the MOU is completed, the United States efforts should be judged on the basis of its active participation and its financial support to the negotiations, as well as on the basis of

its previous efforts since 1998, having regard to the likelihood of a conclusion of the negotiations in the course of 2001."

134. In sum, Malaysia is incorrect in its contention that avoiding "arbitrary and unjustifiable discrimination" under the chapeau of Article XX requires the *conclusion* of an international agreement on the protection and conservation of sea turtles. Therefore, we uphold the Panel's finding that, in view of the serious, good faith efforts made by the United States to negotiate an international agreement, "Section 609 is now applied in a manner that no longer constitutes a means of unjustifiable or arbitrary discrimination, as identified by the Appellate Body in its Report."

The Flexibility of the Revised Guidelines

*   *   *

135. Malaysia disagrees with the Panel that a measure can meet the requirements of the chapeau of Article XX if it is flexible enough, both in design and application, to permit certification of an exporting country with a sea turtle protection and conservation programme "comparable" to that of the United States. According to Malaysia, even if the measure at issue allows certification of countries having regulatory programs "comparable" to that of the United States, and even if the measure is applied in such a manner, it results in "arbitrary or unjustifiable discrimination" because it conditions access to the United States market on compliance with policies and standards "unilaterally" prescribed by the United States.

140. In United States-Shrimp, we concluded that the measure at issue there did not meet the requirements of the chapeau of Article XX relating to "arbitrary or unjustifiable discrimination" because, through the application of the measure, the exporting members were faced with "a single, rigid and unbending requirement" to adopt *essentially the same* policies and enforcement practices as those applied to, and enforced on, domestic shrimp trawlers in the United States. In contrast, in this dispute', the Panel found that this new measure is more flexible than the original measure and has been applied more flexibly than was the original measure. In the light of the evidence brought by the United States, the Panel satisfied itself that this new measure, in design and application, does *not* condition access to the United States market on the adoption by an exporting Member of a regulatory programme aimed at the protection and the conservation of sea turtles that is essentially the same as that of the United States.

143. Given that the original measure in that dispute required "essentially the same" practices and procedures as those required in the United States, we found it necessary in that appeal to rule only that Article XX did not allow such inflexibility. Given the Panel's findings with respect to the flexibility of the new measure in this dispute, we find it necessary in this appeal to add to what we ruled in our original Report. The question raised by Malaysia in this appeal is whether the Panel erred in inferring from our previous Report, and thereby finding, that the chapeau of Article XX permits a measure which requires only "comparable effectiveness."

144. In our view, there is an important difference between conditioning market access on the adoption of essentially the same programme, and conditioning market

access on the adoption of a programme *comparable in effectiveness*. Authorizing an importing Member to condition market access on exporting Members putting in place regulatory programmes *comparable in effectiveness* to that of the importing Member gives sufficient latitude to the exporting Member with respect to the programme it may adopt to achieve the level of effectiveness required. It allows the exporting Member to adopt a regulatory programme that is suitable to the specific conditions prevailing in its territory. As we see it, the Panel correctly reasoned and concluded that conditioning market access on the adoption of a programme *comparable in effectiveness*, allows for sufficient flexibility in the application of the measure so as to avoid "arbitrary or *unjustifiable discrimination*." We, therefore, agree with the conclusion of the Panel on "comparable effectiveness."

146. We note that the Revised Guidelines contain provisions that, permit the United States authorities to take into account the specific conditions of Malaysian shrimp production, and of the Malaysian sea turtle conservation programme, should Malaysia decide to apply for certification. The Revised Guidelines explicitly state that "[if] the government of a harvesting nation demonstrates that it has implemented and is enforcing a comparably effective regulatory program to protect sea turtles in the course of shrimp trawl fishing without the use of TEDs, that nation will also be eligible for certification." Likewise, the Revised Guidelines provide that the "Department of State will take fully into account any demonstrated differences between the shrimp fishing conditions in the United States and those in other nations as well as information available from other sources."

147. Further, the Revised Guidelines provide that the import prohibitions that can be imposed under Section 609 do not apply to shrimp or products of shrimp "harvested in any other manner or under any other circumstances that the Department of State. may determine, following consultations with the [United States National Marine Fisheries Services), does not pose a threat of the incidental taking of sea turtles." . . . Additionally, Section II.B(c)(iii) states that "[i]n making certification determinations, the Department shall also take fully into account other measures the harvesting nation undertakes to protect sea turtles, including national programmes to protect nesting beaches and other habitat, prohibitions on the direct take of sea turtles, national enforcement and compliance programmes, and participation in any international agreement for the protection and conservation of sea turtles." . . .

148. These provisions of the Revised Guidelines, on their face, permit a degree of flexibility that, in our view, will enable the United States to consider the particular conditions prevailing in Malaysia if, and when, Malaysia applies for certification. As Malaysia has not applied for certification, any consideration of whether Malaysia would be certified would be speculation.

149. We need only say here that, in our view, a measure should be designed in such a manner that there is sufficient flexibility to take into account the specific conditions prevailing in *any* exporting Member, including, of course, Malaysia. Yet this is not the same as saying that there must be specific provisions in the measure aimed at addressing specifically the particular conditions prevailing in *every individual* exporting Member. Article XX of the GATT 1994 does not require a Member to anticipate and provide explicitly for the specific conditions prevailing

and evolving in *every individual* Member.

150. We are, therefore, not persuaded by Malaysia's argument that the measure at issue is not flexible enough because the Revised Guidelines do not explicitly address the specific conditions prevailing in Malaysia.

153. For all these reasons, we uphold the finding of the Panel, in paragraph 6.1 of the Panel Report, that "Section 609 of Public Law 101-162, as implemented by the Revised Guidelines of 8 July 1999 and as applied so far by the [United States] authorities, is justified under Article XX of the GATT 1994 as long as the conditions stated in the findings of this Report, in particular the ongoing serious, good faith efforts to reach a multilateral agreement, remain satisfied."

CHINA — MEASURES RELATED TO THE EXPORTATION OF VARIOUS RAW MATERIALS
Report of the Appellate Body, adopted February 22, 2012
WT/DS394, 395, 398/AB/R

[This case involved complaints against China by the United States, the European Union, and Mexico concerning Chinese export restrictions on a variety of natural resources, including forms of bauxite, coke, fluorspar, magnesium, manganese, silicon carbide, silicon metal, yellow phosphorus, and zinc. These materials are required for the production of many high technology products. The complainants charged that the export restrictions kept the cost of raw materials low in China but high in the rest of the world, creating a comparative advantage for China.

Four types of Chinese export restraints were at issue: (1) export duties; (2) export quotas; (3) export licensing; and (4) minimum export price requirements.

As to the export duties, the Appellate Body upheld the panel's determination that, although export duties are permitted under the GATT, certain export duties violated China's obligations under its Accession Protocol.

On export licensing, the panel had ruled that such licensing falls within the scope of GATT Article XI:1 and that, although this Article prohibits only licensing that has a limiting or restrictive effect, China's measures have such effect because the open-ended discretion in its administration creates uncertainty. But the Appellate Body vacated this ruling as moot and of no legal effect because the issue was not within the panel's terms of reference.

As to the minimum export prices, the panel had ruled that setting minimum export prices constitutes a violation of GATT Article XI:1; but the Appellate Body vacated this ruling on the grounds the issue was not within the panel's terms of reference.

The principal issue before the WTO panel and Appellate Body was whether export quotas on natural resources and raw materials can be justified under the GATT. On this issue the Appellate Body ruled as follows]:

Article XI:2(a) of the GATT 1994

318. Article XI of the GATT 1994 provides, in relevant part:

General Elimination of Quantitative Restrictions

1. No prohibitions or restrictions other than duties, taxes or other charges, whether made effective through quotas, import or export licences or other measures, shall be instituted or maintained by any contracting party on the importation of any product of the territory of any other contracting party or on the exportation or sale for export of any product destined for the territory of any other contracting party.

2. The provisions of paragraph 1 of this Article shall not extend to the following:

    (a) Export prohibitions or restrictions temporarily applied to prevent or relieve critical shortages of foodstuffs or other products essential to the exporting contracting party[.]

322. We note that Article XI:2(a) permits such measures to be "temporarily applied to prevent or relieve critical shortages of foodstuffs or other products essential to the exporting Member." We examine the meaning of each of these concepts — "temporarily applied," "to prevent or relieve critical shortages," and "foodstuffs or other products essential" — in turn below.

323. First, we note that the term "temporarily" in Article XI:2(a) of the GATT 1994 is employed as an adverb to qualify the term "applied." The word "temporary" is defined as "[l]asting or meant to last for a limited time only; not permanent; made or arranged to supply a passing need." Thus, when employed in connection with the word "applied," it describes a measure applied for a limited time, a measure taken to bridge a "passing need." As we see it, the definitional element of "supply[ing] a passing need" suggests that Article XI:2(a) refers to measures that are applied in the interim.

324. Turning next to consider the meaning of the term "critical shortage," we note that the noun "shortage" is defined as "[d]eficiency in quantity; an amount lacking, and is qualified by the adjective "critical," which, in turn, is defined as "[o]f, pertaining to, or constituting a crisis; of decisive importance, crucial; involving risk or suspense." The term "crisis" describes "[a] turning point, a vitally important or decisive stage; a time of trouble, danger or suspense in politics, commerce, etc." Taken together, "critical shortage" thus refers to those deficiencies in quantity that are crucial, that amount to a situation of decisive importance, or that reach a vitally important or decisive stage, or a turning point.

325. We consider that context lends further support to this reading of the term "critical shortage." In particular, the words "general or local short supply" in Article XX(j) of the GATT 1994 provide relevant context for the interpretation of the term "critical shortage" in Article XI:2(a). We note that the term "in short supply" is defined as "available only in limited quantity, scarce." Thus, its meaning is similar to that of a "shortage," which is defined as "[d]eficiency in quantity; an amount lacking." Contrary to Article XI:2(a), however, Article XX(j) does not include the word "critical," or another adjective further qualifying the short supply. We must give meaning to this difference in the wording of these provisions. To us, it suggests that the kinds of shortages that fall within Article XI:2(a) are more narrowly circumscribed than those falling within the scope of Article XX(j).

326. For Article XI:2(a) to apply, the shortage, in turn, must relate to "foodstuffs or other products essential to the exporting Member." Foodstuff is defined as "an item of food, a substance used as food." The term "essential" is defined as "[a]bsolutely indispensable or necessary." Accordingly, Article XI:2(a) refers to critical shortages of foodstuffs or otherwise absolutely indispensable or necessary products. By including, in particular, the word "foodstuffs," Article XI:2(a) provides a measure of what might be considered a product "essential to the exporting Member" but it does not limit the scope of other essential products to only foodstuffs.

327. Article XI:2(a) allows Members to apply prohibitions or restrictions temporarily in order to "prevent or relieve" such critical shortages. The word "prevent" is defined as "[p]rovide beforehand against the occurrence of (something); make impracticable or impossible by anticipatory action; stop from happening." The word "relieve" means "[r]aise out of some trouble, difficulty or danger; bring or provide aid or assistance to." We therefore read Article XI:2(a) as providing a basis for measures adopted to alleviate or reduce an existing critical shortage, as well as for preventive or anticipatory measures adopted to pre-empt an imminent critical shortage.

The Panel's Evaluation of China's Export Quota on Refractory-Grade Bauxite

329. China argues that the Panel erred in finding that China had not demonstrated that its export quota on refractory-grade bauxite was "temporarily applied," within the meaning of Article XI:2(a) of the GATT 1994, to either prevent or relieve a "critical shortage." With respect to the Panel's interpretation of the term "temporarily," China supports the Panel's finding that the word "temporarily" "suggest[s] a fixed time-limit for the application of a measure." China, however, alleges that the Panel subsequently "adjusted" its interpretation of the term "temporarily" to exclude the "long-term" application of export restrictions." China argues that the term "temporarily" does not mark a "bright line" moment in time after which an export restriction has necessarily been maintained for too long. Instead, Article XI:2(a) requires that the duration of a restriction be limited and bound in relation to the achievement of the stated goal. Furthermore, China argues that the Panel erroneously found that Article XI:2(a) and Article XX(g) are mutually exclusive, and that this finding was a significant motivating factor for the Panel's erroneous interpretation of the term "temporarily" in Article XI:2(a). China submits that the two provisions are not mutually exclusive, and instead apply cumulatively.

330. We note that the Panel found that the word "temporarily" suggests "a fixed time-limit for the application of a measure," and also expressed the view that a "restriction or ban applied under Article XI:2(a) must be of a limited duration and not indefinite." We have set out above our interpretation of the term "temporarily" as employed in Article XI:2(a). In our view, a measure applied "temporarily" in the sense of Article XI:2(a) is a measure applied in the interim, to provide relief in extraordinary conditions in order to bridge a passing need. It must be finite, that is, applied for a limited time. Accordingly, we agree with the Panel that a restriction or prohibition in the sense of Article XI:2(a) must be of a limited duration and not indefinite.

331. The Panel further interpreted the term "limited time" to refer to a "fixed

time-limit" for the application of the measure. To the extent that the Panel was referring to a time-limit fixed in advance, we disagree that "temporary" must always connote a time-limit fixed in advance. Instead, we consider that Article XI:2(a) describes measures applied for a limited duration, adopted in order to bridge a passing need, irrespective of whether or not the temporal scope of the measure is fixed in advance.

332. China alleges that the Panel erred in reading the term "temporarily" to exclude the "long-term" application of export restrictions. In particular, China refers to the Panel's statements that Article XI:2(a) cannot be interpreted "to permit the long-term application of . . . export restrictions," or to "permit long-term measures to be imposed." We consider that the terms "long-term application" and "long-term measures" provide little value in elucidating the meaning of the term "temporary," because what is "long-term" in a given case depends on the facts of the particular case. Moreover, the terms "long-term" and "short-term" describe a different concept than the term "temporary," employed in Article XI:2(a). Viewed in the context of the Panel's entire analysis, it is clear, however, that the Panel used these words to refer back to its earlier interpretation of the term "temporarily applied" as meaning a "restriction or prohibition for a limited time." Because the Panel merely referred to its earlier interpretation of the term "temporarily applied" and did not provide additional reasoning, the Panel cannot be viewed as having "adjusted" its interpretation of the term "temporarily" to exclude the "long-term" application of export restrictions.

335. Turning then to the Panel's application of the term "temporarily applied" in the present case, China alleges that the Panel failed to take into consideration the fact that China's export restrictions on refractory-grade bauxite are subject to annual review. China faults the Panel for "simply assum[ing]" that China's restriction on exports of refractory-grade bauxite will be maintained indefinitely. China submits that, at the close of each year, the factual circumstances are assessed in the light of the legal standard set forth in Article XI:2(a) to establish whether the export restriction should be maintained. We note that China has made parallel claims, under Article XI:2(a), alleging an error of application, and under Article 11 of the DSU, alleging that the Panel failed to make an objective assessment of the facts. We consider China's allegation that the Panel "simply assumed" something to be more in the nature of a claim made under Article II of the DSU, and therefore address it below at the end of our analysis in this section.

336. China further argues that the Panel erred in its interpretation and application of Article XI:2(a) by presuming that export restrictions "imposed to address a limited reserve of an exhaustible natural resource" cannot be "temporary" and that a shortage of an exhaustible nonrenewable resource cannot be "critical." The Panel reasoned that, "if there is no possibility for an existing shortage ever to cease to exist, it will not be possible to 'relieve or prevent' it through an export restriction applied on a temporary basis." The Panel further stated that, "[i]f a measure were imposed to address a limited reserve of an exhaustible natural resource, such measure would be imposed until the point when the resource is fully depleted." The Panel added that "[t]his temporal focus seems consistent with the notion of 'critical', defined as 'of the nature of, or constituting, a crisis.' "

337. We do not agree with China that these statements by the Panel indicate that the Panel presumed that a shortage of an exhaustible non-renewable resource cannot be "critical" within the meaning of Article XI:2(a). The Panel noted instead, correctly in our view, that the reach of Article XI:2(a) is not the same as that of Article XX(g), adding that these provisions are "intended to address different situations and thus must mean different things." Articles XI:2(a) and XX(g) have different functions and contain different obligations. Article XI:2(a) addresses measures taken to prevent or relieve "critical shortages" of foodstuffs or other essential products. Article XX (g), on the other hand, addresses measures relating to the conservation of exhaustible natural resources. We do not exclude that a measure falling within the ambit of Article XI:2(a) could relate to the same product as a measure relating to the conservation of an exhaustible natural resource. It would seem that Article XI:2(a) measures could be imposed, for example, if a natural disaster caused a "critical shortage" of an exhaustible natural resource, which, at the same time, constituted a foodstuff or other essential product. Moreover, because the reach of Article XI:2(a) is different from that of Article XX(g), an Article XI:2(a) measure might operate simultaneously with a conservation measure complying with the requirements of Article XX(g).

344. For the above reasons, we *uphold* the Panel's conclusion that China did not demonstrate that its export quota on refractory-grade bauxite was "temporarily applied," within the meaning of Article XI:2(a) of the GATT 1994, to either prevent or relieve a "critical shortage," and we dismiss China's allegation that the Panel acted inconsistently with its duty to conduct an objective assessment of the matter as required by Article 11 of the DSU.

[Next the Appellate Body took up the issue of whether the GATT Article XX justified China's export measures with respect to the minerals and resources in question. Although the Appellate Body agreed with the panel that export duties were precluded by China's Accession Protocol, the Appellate Body examined *arguendo* the application of Article XX to both measures.]

With respect to Article XX(g) the panel had examined China's argument that the export measures were justified as conservation measures. China argued that the minerals in question were exhaustible natural resources that had to be managed and protected. China also argued that Article XX(g) should be interpreted to recognize China's sovereignty over the natural resources within its territory. China referred to the need "for developing countries to make optimum use of their resources for their development as they deem appropriate, including the processing of their raw material." (Panel Report, para. 7.356). The panel agreed that the resources in question were exhaustible natural resources, but the panel said the crucial question was whether the China's measures "relate to" a conservation program. To decide this question the panel examined the "relationship between" the measures and the conservation goal. Considering the Vienna Convention's canons of treaty interpretation, the panel ruled that Article XX (g) must be interpreted to "take into account" the principle of sovereignty over natural resources and the rights of WTO members to regulate the use of these resources to ensure sustainable development, but "Members must exercise their sovereignty over natural resources consistent with their WTO obligations." (Panel Report, paras. 7.281–383). The panel took note of GATT Article XX (i), which is a general exception that allows measures:

(i) Involving restrictions on exports of domestic materials necessary to ensure essential quantities of such materials to a domestic processing industry during periods when the domestic price of such materials in held below the world price as part of a governmental stabilization plan; Provided that such restrictions shall not operate to increase the exports of or the protection afforded to such domestic industry, and shall not depart from the provisions of this Agreement relating to non-discrimination.

The panel ruled that Article XX (g) should not be interpreted in such a way as to contradict or undermined Article XX (i) or to allow members with respect to raw materials to do indirectly what Article XX (g) prohibits, i.e., export restrictions that increase the protection of domestic industry. (Panel Report paras. 7.384–386).

The panel then examined the second part of Article XX (g), whether the export measures are made effective in conjunction with restrictions on domestic production or consumption. The European Union argued that this requirement is one of "evenhandedness," although not identical treatment, between domestic and foreign interests. The panel ruled that the domestic measures must not only be applied jointly with the export measures but must also be done to ensure the effectiveness of the domestic restrictions. China argued that export restrictions may be employed to achieve diversification of its economy and that a proportionately higher burden on foreigners is permissible. The panel ruled that a certain degree of evenhandedness is required and that "Article XX (g) cannot be invoked for GATT-inconsistent measures whose goal or effect is to insulate domestic producers from foreign competition in the name of conservation." (Panel Report, para. 7-408).

In conclusion, the panel ruled that China had not met its burden to prove that its export restrictions were made effective in conjunction with restrictions on domestic production or consumption. In order the show "evenhandedness," the panel stated that China would have to show that "the impact of the export duty or quota on foreign users is somehow balanced with some measure imposing the restrictions on domestic users and consumers." (Panel Report, para. 7.465).

[On this issue, the Appellate Body found that the panel had erred in interpreting the phrase "made effective in conjunction with" in Article XX (g) to require a showing that the purpose of the challenged export measure *must be to make effective* restrictions on domestic production or consumption. (Appellate Body Report, paras. 359–60), and thus reversed the panel's interpretation in this regard without commenting on the rest of the panel's ruling.]

The panel also considered the argument of China that the export measures were justified uinder GATT Article XX (b) in that the export restrictions are necessary to protect the health of its domestic population since they reduce the pollution emitted in the course of extraction and production of these raw materials.

The panel applied a balancing test to determine whether the export restriction were "necessary." On the one hand, the panel considered three separate elements: (1) the importance of the interests and values at issue; (2) the extent of the contribution of the measures to the achievement of the measures' objective; and (3) the trade restrictiveness of the measures, i.e., the effect on international commerce. If the analysis of these three factors yields a preliminary judgment that the measure is necessary, the panel stated it still must consider if this judgment is confirmed by comparing the challenged measures with possible alternatives suggested by the complainants. (Panel Report, paras. 7.482–92).

Applying these criteria, the panel considered separately the question of pollution from the production of "energy-intensive, highly polluting, resource-based products," on the one hand, and (2) pollution from the production of scrap metal products that may be avoided by the export measures. The panel ruled, first, that the interests at stake were of vital importance; second, but the measures in question do not make any mention of environmental or health concerns, and "we do not discern in this array of measures a comprehensive framework aimed at addressing environmental protection and health." (Panel Report, paras. 7.501–11). The panel also ruled that there was no evidence that the measures make a material contribution to reducing pollution. Third, the panel ruled that the measures in question have an important world-wide trade and economic impact. Finally, the panel stated that numerous alternatives were available to safeguard the health of the Chinese people, such as investment in more environmentally friendly technologies, promotion of recycling, increasing environmental standards, investing in infrastructure necessary to recycle scrap, stimulating greater local demand for scrap, and introducing pollution controls on primary production facilities.

For these reasons the panel ruled that China's export measures could not be justified on the basis of Article XX(b).

[The Appellate Body did not consider this ruling because China did not appeal this issue].

NOTES AND QUESTIONS

1.   At this writing the *U.S.-Shrimp/Turtle Cases* and the *China-Natural Resources Case* are the leading WTO cases on conservation of natural resources. The former case concerns import restrictions and the latter export restrictions. Note the great difference between the Reports of the Appellate Body in the *U.S.-Shrimp/Turtle Cases* and the two *U.S.-Tuna/Dolphin Cases*, both of which are unadopted GATT panel reports. For the full reports of the latter cases, see *United States — Restrictions* on *Imports of Tuna*, Report of the Panel, GATT Doc. DS21/R 3 September 1991, reprinted in 30 I.L.M. 1594 (1991); and *United States — Restrictions on Imports of Tuna*, Report of the Panel, DS29/R 16 June 1994, reprinted 33 I.L.M. 839 (1994). How would the *U.S.-Tuna/Dolphin Case* be decided today?

2.   *The China-Rare Earths Case*. In March 2014, a WTO panel handed down an opinion in the *China-Measures Related to the Exportation of Rare Earths, Tungsten and Molybdenum*, WT/DS431, 432, 433/R (Final Reports Circulated March 26, 2014), currently on appeal to the WTO Appellate Body. In this case, the U.S., EU, and Japan complained against China's export duties, export quotas, and export administration and allocation regarding rare earths, a group of 15 chemical elements, and several other important mineral resources. China's defense was based upon GATT Articles XX(b) and(g). The panel concluded (1) that the export duties in question violated paragraph 11.3 of China's Accession Protocol to the

WTO; (2) that the exceptions of Article XX do not apply to claims under China's Accession Protocol (one panelist dissenting); (3) and that (*arguendo*) China did not demonstrate that the export measures employed are justified as "necessary" to protect human animal, or plant life or health. Regarding Article XX(g), the panel ruled that measures in question involved exhaustible natural resources; that China has a right and did adopt a conservation policy; but that China did not carry its burden to show that the export measures in question are "substantially connected to the goal of conservation. Furthermore, the panel ruled that China did not show that its export quota was made effective in conjunction with restrictions on domestic production or consumption. As to the chapeau of Article XX, the panel ruled that China's export measures lacked "evenhandedness" and unjustifiably discriminated against foreign interests.

3.   ***Process and Production Methods.*** An important rule derived from the *U.S.-Tuna/Dolphin cases* was a strict GATT prohibition against import bans based on the method a product is produced or harvested. This is known as the PPM (Process and Production Methods) Rule. The announcement of this PPM Rule, more than anything else, set off the fury of environmentalists against the GATT and the multilateral trading system. The *U.S.-Shrimp/Turtle Cases* interpreted the provisions of the GATT quite differently in order to permit trade restrictions for PPMS to some degree. What GATT standards now apply to PPMs?

4.   ***The European Union (EU) Seal Products Case.*** In 2013, a WTO Panel decided a case involving an EU ban on the importation of seal products. *European Communities — Measures Prohibiting the Importation and Marketing of Seal Products*, WT/DS400, 401/R (November 25, 2013). Two EU regulations placed strict conditions on the import of seal products into the EU: (1) imports can be allowed only where the seal products result from hunts traditionally conducted by Inuit and other traditional communities (the IC condition); (2) imports are allowed from countries allowing hunting only for marine resource management (the MRM condition); and (3) imports are permitted in cases of personal hunting of seals by travelers (the travelers condition). Norway and Canada challenged this trade restriction in the WTO. Regarding the GATT norms, the Panel ruled, first, that the IC condition was inconsistent with GATT Article I:1 (Most-favored Nation) because, while very few seal products from Norway and Canada can be sold in the EU, almost all seal products from Greenland can be imported and sold because of the IC condition. Second, the Panel ruled that the three conditions violated GATT Article III: 4, national treatment, because the conditions placed on imports from Canada and Norway did not apply to seal products produced and sold within the EU itself. With regard to the application of GATT Article XX, the Panel ruled that the EU conditions were necessary to address public moral concerns regarding seal and animal welfare concerns in the EU; thus, the EU Seal Regime satisfied Article XX(a); however, the Panel ruled that the seal measures were discriminatory, failing the tests of the chapeau of Article XX.

On appeal the Appellate Body upheld the panel's finding that — *de facto* — the EU seal import regime discriminated in violation of GATT Article 1:1 because, although it is facially neutral, the structure of the IC exemption means that while virtually all seal products from Greenland qualify, the vast majority of seal products from Norway and Canada do not. The Appellate Body also upheld the panel's finding that the EU seal regime qualifies as provisionally necessary to protect public morals. The Appellate Body found that the principal objective of the seal import regime was to address public concerns on seal welfare and that the regime makes some contribution to this objective. The Appellate Body also found that the regime was "necessary" in that alternative measures were not reasonably available. However, the Appellate Body ruled that the EU seal regime failed the discrimination tests of the Article XX chapeau for the same reason discrimination was found to violate Article I: 1 — while IC seal hunts in Greenland qualify, IC hunts in Norway and Canada are considered "commercial" and do not qualify. *European Communities – Measures Prohibiting the Importation and Marketing of Seal Products*, WT/DS400,401/AB/R, Report of the Appellate Body, adopted 18 June 2014. Which side was the winner in the EU Seal Products Case?

5.   Consider the import and export restrictions in Problem 5-1.

a.   Does the import ban of furs and all species of fur-bearing mammals violate GATT Article XI? If so, is it justified by Article XX (b) or (g)? What about the chapeau?

b.   The same questions come up with respect to the ban on the import of wood products containing any of 12 species of tropical timber.

Timber and wood products are major international trade commodities and constitute an important source of income, particularly to developing countries. Data on trade in tropical timber is collected by the Timber Resources Division of the Food and Agriculture Organization (FAO) and the UNCTAD International Trade Centre. The International Tropical Timber Agreement (1994, in force 1997) created the International Tropical Timber Organization in Yokohama, Japan, which provides a forum for discussion of tropical timber trade practices. The role of international trade in deforestation is hotly debated and doubtlessly varies from country-to-country. Many states ban the export of certain species or raw logs of timber. In the United States the Lacey Act, 16 U.S.C. § 3371 *et seq.*, prohibits trade in wildlife, fish, and plants that are illegally taken. The Lacey Act, which is enforced by the U.S. Department of Agriculture and the Justice Department, puts the burden of responsibility on importing companies which may be subject to civil and criminal penalties for violations. The Lacey Act prohibits imports that are illegal under the laws of the exporting countries. In 2012, the Gibson Guitar Company pleaded "no contest" to the imposition of a $350,000 fine for importing illegally cut mahogany and rosewood from Madagascar. *See* Andrew Revkin, *A Closer Look at Gibson's Legal Troubles*, N.Y. TIMES, 10 August 2012, at 5.

c.   Does the Certificate of Approval requirement conform to the standards of GATT XX (g)?

d.   A ban on all products from countries with lax pollution laws is very broad. This is an example of a PPM requirement. Does it pass the *U.S.-Shrimp/Turtle* test?

Some commentators have stated that not enforcing pollution control laws is a kind of "dumping," selling below fair value, because not all the costs of production of the products are included in the sale price — the export price — of the products involved. See Joseph Stiglitz, *A New Agenda for Global Warming*, 3 ECONOMISTS'

Voice 1, 2 (2006). However, no GATT or WTO panel has accepted this argument, and national laws on dumping and countervailing duties do not define dumping and subsidies in this manner.

e.   Does the three-year moratorium conform to the criteria set out in the *China-Natural Resources Case*?

f.   What about the ban on the export of raw logs? Can this be justified on the basis of Article XX(g)?

g.   Can a ban on the export of coal be justified under Article XX(b)?

h.   Is the eco-tax consistent with the GATT? A closely analogous case was litigated at the GATT, the WTO's predecessor organization in 1994, in *United States — Taxes on Automobiles*, Report of the GATT Panel, DS31/R (unadopted) (October 11, 1994). This case involved the GATT consistency of various taxes imposed by the United States: (1) a luxury tax on certain kinds of automobiles; and (2) a graduated "gas guzzler" tax imposed on autos failing to meet certain fuel efficiency standards. These taxes were imposed on all autos attaining less than 22.5 miles per gallon (mpg). The tax per vehicle model varied from $1000 to $7000, depending on the mpg. (Light trucks were not subject to the tax). Also involved were so-called United States Corporate Average Fuel Economy (CAFE) standards requiring passenger autos and light trucks to meet certain average fuel economy values.

The United States defended the gas guzzler taxes as eco-taxes that would create incentives to both auto manufacturers and consumers to create and buy more fuel-efficient cars and trucks. The taxes were challenged at the GATT by the European Community on the ground they constituted a violation of GATT Article III. The EC argued that since all autos are "like products" under Article III they could not be taxed according to their mpg. The EC also argued that because most of the impact of the tax fell on imported autos, the tax was a *de facto* violation of Article III. In addition, the EC maintained that the exclusion of some vehicles, light trucks and minivans, demonstrated that the tax was not based on objective criteria.

The GATT panel rejected all of the EC's arguments. In doing so the panel applied an "aim and effects" test to ascertain whether the tax was protectionist. Since the tax was not facially discriminatory, the panel recognized that governments should examine the tax in the light of the purpose of Article III, which is "to prohibit regulatory distinctions between products applied so as to afford protection to domestic industries."

The panel examined in order the issues of (1) the 22.5 mpg threshold; (2) the use of model types for the tax assessment; and (3) the exclusion of minivans and small trucks.

In the panel's view, the 22.5 mpg threshold demonstrated that the purpose of the tax was to conserve fossil fuel and pointed out that EC companies had the technology to meet this threshold. Imposing the tax on models was permissible since the U.S. was employing valid sampling methodology; and exempting minivans and trucks was permissible since such vehicles were not inherently of U.S. origin. The panel ruled therefore that the gas guzzler tax was not in violation of GATT Article III.

The U.S. CAFE standards, originally enacted in 1975, required auto manufacturers to achieve an average of at least 27.5 mpg for their entire fleet. These standards were enforced by civil penalties of $5 per vehicle imposed on the manufacturers for each 0.1 mpg under 27.5. In ascertaining compliance, the domestically-made fleet was calculated separately from the imported fleet. The CAFE regulations excluded exported autos from the calculations.

The GATT panel found two violations of GATT Article III:4 in this scheme. First, the origin-based accounting was found to treat non-U.S. manufacturers of large autos less favorably than U.S. large auto manufacturers because non-U.S. manufacturers cannot lower their average by mixing in small U.S.-made autos. Second, the panel found the fleet averaging regulations to be a violation of GATT Article III:4 because that method "depends on several factors not directly related to the product as a product, including the relationship of ownership and control of the manufacturer/importer."

The panel also rejected the application of GATT Article XX(g) since neither the origin-based accounting nor the fleet averaging was "primarily aimed at" conservation of natural resources.

This GATT panel decision was never adopted by the GATT contracting parties and thus has no binding effect. Furthermore, the panel used a now-discredited test for the application of GATT Article XX(g). In addition, the "aim and effects" test for Article III was rejected in a later WTO Appellate Body Report, *see* Japan-Taxes on Alcoholic Beverages, WT/DS8 /AB/R (November 1, 1996).

What would be the result in the *U.S.-Taxes on Automobiles Case* today?

NOTE ON THE WTO AND TRADE IN NATURAL RESOURCES

Environmentalists charge that the rules of the WTO have a negative impact on all forms of natural resources because these rules facilitate all-out exploitation of natural resources and raw materials. In order to examine this charge let us review the application of WTO rules to natural resources. Access to natural resources is crucial for economic activity. Developed countries, such as Japan, are in many cases highly dependent on international trade for access to resources that they need for their economic wellbeing. With the *China-Raw Materials Case*, access to natural resources under the rules of international trade law came to the fore as an international issue and problem. The *China-Raw Materials Case* poses the issue as a clash between development and sustainability: to what extent can a country that is a member of the WTO adopt restrictions on exports of raw materials and natural resources under the rules of the multilateral trading system? The *China-Raw Materials Case* ruled that Chinese export duties on a large number of Chinese raw materials (except 84 products that are specifically exempted) infringe WTO rules. Does this ruling confirm the environmentalists' charge?

To what extent do WTO rules apply to raw materials? This issue was not discussed but is implicit in the *China-Raw Materials Case*. The GATT applies to trade in "products" and "imports and exports" but these terms are not defined. The

China-Raw Materials Case confirms the applicability of trade rules to raw materials. We can summarize this applicability as follows:

- The *China-Raw Materials Case* applies international trade rules to a host of raw materials and natural resources that are derived from mining activities, such as bauxite, manganese, and silicon carbonate.

- This ruling would apply to all other metals and minerals important in international trade, such as uranium and coal, which are important sources of energy.

- WTO rules apply to international trade in raw harvested fish, timber, and agricultural products. *See* the *United States-Shrimp/Turtle Cases*, reprinted above, and *GATT Panel Report, Canada — Measures Affecting Exports of Unprocessed Herring and Salmon, L/6268, adopted* 22 *March* 1988, BISD 35S/98.

- Trade in oil, natural gas, and energy-related equipment is regulated by WTO and other trade rules. Under the Energy Charter Treaty (1994) and the Trade Amendment to the Energy Charter Treaty (1998), even non-WTO members who have ratified these agreements are bound by WTO rules.

- Water that is bottled as a "product" of some type is clearly subject to trade rules. Heading 22.01 of the World Custom Union's Harmonizing Commodity Description and Coding System covers water in various forms. An undecided question is whether GATT 1994 covers diversions of water in its natural state through canals, pipelines or other conveyances. It seems doubtful that such water diversions constitute "products," but water carried in bulk aboard tanker ships may be ruled to be covered under trade rules. These are open questions. *See* EDITH BROWN WEISS *ET AL.*, FRESH WATER AND INTERNATIONAL ECONOMIC LAW 66–84 (Oxford: Oxford University Press, 2005).

The trade rules governing natural resources and raw materials concern primarily the extent to which nations may place export restrictions on natural resources. A country may want to restrict exports of natural resources for a host of different reasons, ranging from environmental protection to boosting domestic employment and economic production by requiring processing of natural resources prior to export.

The GATT generally forbids quotas or outright bans on exports, but permits export taxes and charges on exports (Article XI). But exceptionally the GATT allows export restrictions to prevent or relieve critical shortages in products essential to the exporting country (Article XI:2(a)); to conserve exhaustible natural resources (Article XX(g)); and to protect human, animal, or plant life and health (Article XX(b)). Are these sufficient to protect the natural environment and to protect sustainability?

Section IV.   MULTILATERAL ENVIRONMENTAL AGREEMENTS AND THE TRADE LAWS

About 250 multilateral environmental agreements (MEAs) exist covering almost every sector of international environmental protection. About 20 of these contain measures that restrict international trade in some manner. Trade restrictions are not central or essential to enforce multilateral environmental norms, but they can serve useful purposes:

- Trade restrictions can directly save endangered species of animals and plants.
- Trade restrictions can aid enforcement efforts.
- Trade restrictions are useful in banning harmful or hazardous products and substances.
- Trade restrictions can create incentives for nations to join an international environmental regime and to prevent free-riding.
- Trade restrictions can support compliance and enforcement.

UNITED NATIONS ENVIRONMENT PROGRAMME TRADE-RELATED MEASURES IN MULTILATERAL TRADE AGREEMENTS
(2007)

Introduction

Growing global interdependencies, both economic and environmental, increase the need for coherence and coordination in trade and environmental policies, rules, and institutions. As international rules in both the trade and environmental fields increase in geographic and substantive scope, promoting the complementary functioning and implementation of these sets of rules is crucial to achieving sustainable development objectives.[10] As noted by trade ministers at the Fourth Ministerial Conference of the WTO, held in Doha in November 2001, "an open and non-discriminatory multilateral trading system, and acting for the protection of the environment and the promotion of sustainable development can and must be mutually supportive."[11]

Maximizing the synergies between multilateral environmental agreements (MEAs) and the rules of the World Trade Organization (WTO) is particularly important in this regard. With a view to enhancing the mutual supportiveness of trade and environment, WTO Members are thus currently engaged in negotiations, pursuant to paragraph 31(i) of the Doha Ministerial Declaration, on:

---

[10] *See* United Nations Environment Programme (UNEP), "Capacity Building on Environment, Trade, and Development: Trends, Needs and Future Directions." Discussion Paper prepared for the UNEP Workshop on Capacity Building on Environment, Trade, and Development, 19–20 March 2002, Geneva.

[11] WTO Doha Ministerial Declaration, WT/MIN(01)/DEC/1, paragraph 6.

"the relationship between existing WTO rules and specific trade obligations set out in multilateral environmental agreements (MEAs). The negotiations shall be limited in scope to the applicability of such existing WTO rules as among parties to the MEA in question. The negotiations shall not prejudice the WTO rights of any Member that is not a party to the MEA in question . . ."

The relevance of the relationship between MEAs and WTO rules for enhancing mutual supportiveness of environment and trade has been clearly reflected in these negotiations. Indeed, over thirty submissions have been put forth on paragraph 31(i) since 2002. Nevertheless, progress has been limited due to fundamental divergences in relation to approach and interpretation of the terms of the above-mentioned mandate.[12] In particular, significant discussions have taken place in relation to the various types of trade-related measures established in a number of MEAs, and how these measures may qualify as "specific trade obligations" for the purposes of the negotiations.

MEAS — Their Role, Importance and Approach

The importance of international cooperation across a diversity of topics is increasingly recognized.[13] An ever more interconnected world demands multilateral approaches to trade, security, migration, and a host of other issues. In the environmental context, in particular, there is an appreciation that environmental degradation is often a global problem and, as such, requires global responses. The depletion of the ozone layer, the loss of biodiversity, and the spread of persistent organic pollutants, for instance, result from human activity in countries around the world and have impacts that extend far beyond national borders. As a result, domestic conservation and environmental management strategies alone are insufficient to conserve shared natural resources and safeguard the global ecosystem. International cooperation is not only fundamental; it has also been recognized as the best and most effective way for governments to tackle transboundary or global environmental problems.[14]

In this context, the need for MEAs will likely continue to grow.[15] MEAs offer a

---

[12] For an overview of the progress made in the trade and environment negotiations under Paragraph 31(i) of the Doha Ministerial Declaration up to the time of the Hong Kong Ministerial Conference, *see* the "Report by the Chairperson of the Special Session of the Committee on Trade and Environment to the Trade Negotiations Committee" 28 November 2005, TNITE/14.

[13] The United Nations Millennium Declaration, adopted by the UN General Assembly in 2000, recognized that, in addition to States' separate responsibilities to their individual societies, there is a collective responsibility for managing worldwide economic and social development, as well as threats to international peace and security, and that such responsibility should be exercised multilaterally.

[14] *See, e.g.,* the Johannesburg Declaration on Sustainable Development at the World Summit for Sustainable Development, September 2002. This has also been recognized in the trade context, see, e.g., the "Report of the WTO Committee on Trade and Environment to the Singapore Ministerial Conference," 12 November 1996, WT/CTE/l (CTE Singapore Report).

[15] There is no agreed definition of an "MEA" in general, though UNEP has developed working definitions for certain projects. For instance, in the context of Environment and Trade: A Handbook, MEAs were defined as environmental agreements with more than two parties. For the purpose of the present note, a definition is not required, as the six selected environmental agreements are widely recognized as MEAs.

framework for collectively addressing environmental problems on the basis of policy consensus and science. In addition, as environmental challenges become more and more complex, MEAs increasingly provide a comprehensive approach to effectively and equitably deal with those challenges. Thus, most MEAs include a broad range of provisions that take into account issues such as: the lack and inadequacy of data and other information; the need for broad stakeholder participation; the different levels at which countries have contributed to the problem and can contribute to the solution; and the need for incentives to take action.[16] In addition to addressing environmental problems, many of the measures contained in MEAs also have positive social and economic impacts. For example, the harmonization of standards and practices encouraged by many MEAs is designed to enhance environmental protection, but may also have positive effects on trade and the economy by avoiding trade distortions, facilitating the technical and legal implementation of standards and technical regulations, and assisting consumers in their decision-making.[17]

Trade, Environment and MEAs

As all economic activity is linked to some degree to the natural environment, the interaction between trade and environment is inevitable and has been addressed in both the trade and environmental context. The Preamble to the Agreement establishing the WTO, for example, recognizes that trade should "protect and preserve the environment" in a manner consistent with Members' different levels of economic development. The WTO has also recognized that not only is there no inherent policy contradiction between an open, equitable and non-discriminatory multilateral trading system and the protection of the environment, but that sustainable development requires the two systems to be mutually supportive. Specifically, in Paragraph 6 of the Doha Mandate, WTO Members noted that "the aims of upholding and safeguarding an open and non-discriminatory multilateral trading system, and acting for the protection of the environment and the promotion of sustainable development can and must be mutually supportive."

In summary, there are a number of elements that must be considered in any analysis of trade-related measures in MEAs, including the role, importance, and particular approach of MEAs, as well as the fundamental functions of trade-related measures in that context. The following analysis considers trade-related measures in the context of the overall objectives and package of measures of six specific MEAs.

CITES

i. Objectives and Overview of CITES

The principle objective of CITES, which entered into force in July 1975, is to ensure that international trade in specimens of certain wild animals and plants does

---

[16] Diverse types of measures in selected MEAs are analyzed in Section III below.

[17] *See* Stevens, Candice, *"Harmonization, trade and the environment," International Environmental Affairs* 5 (I): 42–49 (1993).

not threaten the survival of these species. Annual international wildlife trade is estimated to be worth billions of dollars and to include hundreds of millions of plant and animal specimens. Levels of exploitation of some animal and plant species are so high that unregulated trade in them, together with other factors such as habitat loss, is capable of heavily depleting or destroying their populations. CITES was thus conceived as an international effort to safeguard certain species from over-exploitation.

The CITES Preamble recognizes that wild fauna and flora are an irreplaceable part of the natural systems of the Earth that must be protected for future generations. Contracting States were also conscious, however, of the ever-growing value of wild fauna and flora from aesthetic, scientific, cultural and economic points of view. CITES therefore does not serve as an embargo on wildlife trade but subjects international trade in selected species to certain controls. It requires that the import, export, re-export and introduction from the sea of these species be authorized through a permitting system." The species covered by CITES are listed in three Appendices, depending on the level of the threat of extinction they face as a result of international trade. Appendix I includes species threatened with extinction, in which trade is only exceptionally permitted. Appendix II includes species not necessarily currently in danger of extinction but in which trade must be controlled in order to avoid utilization incompatible with their survival. Finally, Appendix III contains species that are protected in at least one country, which has asked other CITES Parties for assistance in controlling the trade: CITES is among the largest conservation agreements in existence, with over 170 Parties, and has had significant success in curbing, and arguably halting, species extinction resulting from international trade.

ii. Trade-related and Other Measures in CITES

CITES provides a regulatory framework for the international trade in specimens of certain wild animals and plants through a system of permits and certificates based on the listing of the species.[18] Thus, controls for Appendix I species those threatened with extinction — are strict, limiting their trade to exceptional circumstances that do not further endanger their survival. The import of specimens of Appendix I species for "primarily commercial purposes" is prohibited.[19] For Appendix I species, an export permit is required and shall only be granted when the following conditions are met: a) the exporting Party has advised that the export will not be detrimental to the survival of the species; b) the exporting Party is satisfied that the species has been legally acquired; c) the exporting Party is satisfied that the method of shipment for the specimens will minimize risks of injury, damage to health, and cruel treatment; and d) the exporting Party is satisfied that an import permit has been granted for the specimen. In turn, an import permit may only be granted when the following conditions have been met: a) the importing Party has advised that the import will be for purposes that are not detrimental to the survival of the species; b) the importing Party is satisfied that the recipient is suitably

---

[18] *See, e.g.,* CITES, Articles III, IV and V.

[19] CITES, Article III, para. 3(c).

equipped to care for any live specimen; and c) the importing Party is satisfied that the species will not be used for primarily commercial purposes.[20] Trade in Appendix II and III species — those not currently threatened with extinction — only requires an export permit with some of the above-mentioned characteristics or a certificate of origin in the case of certain Appendix III species.[21]

CITES also requires that permits and certificates granted under a Party's permitting system be in accordance with the Convention.[22] Each permit or certificate, for instance, must contain the title of the Convention, the name and any identifying stamp of the national Management Authority granting it, and a control number assigned by the national Management Authority. All permits and certificates should follow the standard format provided as an annex to Resolution Conf. 12.3 (Rev. COP 14). These measures encourage a harmonized system that will avoid the proliferation of different standards and contribute to effective compliance monitoring. The problems of insufficient information and lack of effective monitoring are also addressed by the CITES requirement that Parties maintain records of trade in covered species and submit periodic reports to the Secretariat.[23]

CITES also includes certain exceptions. For instance, CITES facilitates certain kinds of trade that are less likely to cause detrimental impact on wild populations through the provision of exemptions and special procedures.[24] CITES also allows trade with non-Parties to the Convention under special circumstances. Trade in listed species with non-Parties is possible when comparable documentation, which substantially conforms with the CITES requirements for permits and certificates, is issued by the competent authorities in those countries.[25] Limiting trade with non-Parties to situations where CITES requirements are met aims to further enhance the conservation objectives of CITES while simultaneously encouraging membership to the Convention. It also aims to avoid trade in listed species by non-Parties from undermining the conservation achievements of CITES Parties. It should be noted, however, that it does not prevent trade among two or more non-Parties to the Convention.

Article XIII of CITES on International Measures (i.e. the key compliance-related article), while not referring expressly to trade-related measures, does authorize the COP to recommend appropriate measures in certain cases. The COP has delegated such authority to the Standing Committee on a number of occasions. One of the measures available to the COP or Standing Committee is the recommendation that Parties temporarily suspend trade with a Party or non-Party in question. The focus of Article XIII, however, which addresses cases where species included in Appendix I or II are adversely affected by trade in specimens of that species or where CITES provisions are not being effectively implemented, is on working with the Party in question to achieve remedial action. Of the various

---

[20] *See* CITES, Article III.

[21] *See* CITES, Articles IV and V.

[22] *See, e.g.*, CITES, Article VI and VII.

[23] *See* CITES, Article VIII.

[24] See CITES, Article VII.

[25] *See* CITES, Article X.

measures to address a Party's non-compliance, and bring about full compliance with the Convention, a recommendation of a temporary suspension of commercial or all trade in specimens of one or more CITES-listed species is generally used as a last resort. The use of trade-related measures in this context would normally only occur where a Party's non-compliance is unresolved and "persistent," including cases in which a Party does not follow recommendations, take advantage of offers of assistance, agree to a compliance action plan, or comply with an agreed plan.[26]

As mentioned, CITES' trade-related measures function in the context of an integrated package of measures, which is intended to achieve effectiveness, efficiency and equity. In terms of equity, CITES contains a number of exceptions and flexibilities. CITES general trade provisions do not apply to pre-Convention specimens, personal or household effects and species bred in captivity or artificially propagated.[27] In addition, Parties have the right to opt out of specific listings by entering a reservation at the time of adherence to the Convention or, thereafter, at the time of listing. This means that, for a particular species, the State is treated as a non-Party with respect to trade if a reservation has been entered.[28] Moreover, the CITES permitting system is dynamic and can adapt to changing needs and circumstances. Appendices I and II may be amended by two-thirds of the Parties present and voting at a meeting of the COP, while Appendix III species may be submitted and withdrawn by Parties unilaterally at any time.[29]

Though not provided for in the Convention itself, another critical part of CITES is the broad range of training and technical assistance activities conducted by the Secretariat under its capacity building programme and by the Parties themselves. The main capacity building objectives are to ensure that Parties have and are able to use all of the technical information, knowledge and skills necessary for them to fulfill their responsibilities under the Convention and thus ensure the achievement of the CITES objectives.

Montreal Protocol

i. Objectives and Overview of the Montreal Protocol

The Montreal Protocol aims to protect the stratospheric ozone layer, and thus human health and the environment, by equitably controlling the production and consumption of substances that deplete it, with the ultimate objective of their elimination.[30] Following the discovery of the Antarctic ozone hole in 1985, governments recognized the need for measures to reduce the production and consumption of a number of gases harmful to stratospheric ozone — the protective layer shielding the Earth from harmful ultra-violet radiation. Certain industrial pro-

---

[26] At COP 14, CITES Parties adopted Resolution Conf. 14.3 on CITES compliance procedures (http://www.cites.org/ eng/res/14/index.shtml.).

[27] *See* CITES, Article VII.

[28] *See* CITES, Article VII.

[29] *See* CITES, Articles XV and XVI.

[30] *See* Montreal Protocol, Articles 2 and 5.8.

cesses and consumer products result in the atmospheric emission of "halogen source gases" that are known to be harmful to the ozone layer. For example, chlorofluorocarbons (CFCs), once used in almost all refrigeration and air conditioning systems, eventually reach the stratosphere and release ozone-depleting chlorine atoms. The increased UV-B radiation resulting from stratospheric ozone depletion can be extremely harmful, causing, for example, skin cancer and cataracts in humans and some animals, and inhibiting growth and photosynthesis in certain plants.[31] The Montreal Protocol, adopted in 1987, thus addresses the need to take appropriate measures to protect human health and the environment against adverse effects resulting from human activities that modify the ozone layer.[32]

To achieve these objectives, the Montreal Protocol requires Parties to establish controls on the national production and consumption of ozone-depleting substances (ODS).[33] The core of the Montreal Protocol is thus the control measures it requires Parties to impose on the production and consumption of ODS.[34] Article 2 of the Protocol defines phase-out schedules for the various categories of ODS. In addition, the Protocol was designed so that the phase-out schedules could be revised on the basis of periodic scientific and technological assessments. Following such assessments, the Protocol has been adjusted five times between 1990 and 1999 to accelerate the phase-out schedules of ozone-depleting substances. It has also been amended to introduce other kinds of control measures and to add new controlled substances to the list. It should be noted, however, that not all Parties have ratified all of these amendments. As a result of the Protocol, now ratified by over 190 states and the European Community, the total abundance of ozone-depleting gases in the atmosphere has begun to decrease in recent years and, if States continue to follow its provisions, effective levels of ozone-depleting gases should fall to early 1980s levels by the middle of this century.[35]

ii. Trade-related and other Measures of the Montreal Protocol

Although regulating trade in ODS is not the primary concern of the Montreal Protocol, it does contain trade-related measures to supplement and strengthen the controls on production and consumption. Similarly, a broad range of other measures ensure the effectiveness of the control system, including those regarding financial assistance and those promoting research, development, and exchange of information on best management technologies and possible alternatives for controlled substances.

Article 4 contains some of the Montreal Protocol's main trade-related provisions.

---

[31] *See* UNEP website, "2002 Environmental Effects Assessment — Questions and Answers About the Effects of the Depletion of the Ozone Layer on Humans and the Environment," pages 6–9 (http://www.unep.org/ozone/Public_ Information/eeapfaq2002.pdf).

[32] *See* Montreal Protocol, Preamble.

[33] *See* Fahey, D.W. "Twenty Questions and Answers About the Ozone Layer," *2002 Scientific Assessment Report*, page 28 (http://www.unep.org/ozone/pdfs/Scientific_ assess_ depletion/ll-qa.pdf).

[34] *See* UNEP website, "Action on Ozone," 2000 (http://www.unep.org/ozone/pdfs/ozone-action-en.pdf).

[35] *See* UNEP website, "Evolution of the Montreal Protocol," (http://www.unep.ch/ozone/Ratification_status/evolution_ of_ mp.shtml).

With respect to controlled substances, Article 4 prohibits the import and export to non-Parties, and establishes a process for Parties to limit the international movement of products containing controlled substances or produced with controlled substances. Nevertheless, the imports and exports of controlled substances may be permitted from, or to, any non-Party, if a meeting of the Parties determines that country to be in full compliance with the Protocol's control measures. These trade restrictions thus aim to promote broad participation in the agreement, and they seek to ensure that the environmental gains made by Parties are not undermined by activities in other countries that may not be party to the Protocol.

Article 4A concerns trade between Parties to the Montreal Protocol. In particular, it addresses the situation in which a Party is unable, despite having taken all practicable steps to comply with its obligations under the Protocol, to cease production of a controlled ozone-depleting substance for domestic consumption. In those circumstances, Article 4A ensures there is no perverse incentive to maintain that production by requiring Parties to ban the export of used, recycled and reclaimed quantities of the substance produced, other than for the purpose of destruction. Trade-related measures thus support the phase-out of controlled substances. Article 4B requires Parties to establish and implement a system for licensing the import and export of controlled substances, in order to monitor the imports and exports of ODS, prevent illegal trade, and enable data collection.[36] These information requirements, along with reporting and other measures of the Montreal Protocol, have been significant in effectively reducing global emissions of ODS.

In rare circumstances, implementation of Article 8 could result in application of trade-measures. Article 8 instructs the COP to establish the procedures and institutional mechanisms for determining non-compliance, as well as the treatment of Parties found to be in non-compliance. The non-compliance procedure adopted in 1992 focuses primarily on providing parties with the incentives and assistance they require to meet their obligations under the Protocol. Nevertheless, in certain cases of non-compliance Parties may suspend the rights of the non-complying Party to trade controlled substances and technologies with other Parties.[37]

Not only trade-related provisions but also other types of measures support the Protocol's control system. For instance, the control measures themselves provide flexibilities that seek to facilitate compliance. The formula used to determine consumption, the granting of an ozone depleting value to each covered substance, among other measures, affords countries the possibility of choosing how to best satisfy their obligations.[38] In addition, the Protocol recognizes that the burdens of

---

[36] *See* Report of the Fifteenth Meeting of the Parties to the Montreal Protocol on Substances that Deplete the Ozone Layer, UNEP/OzL.Pro.15/9, Decision XV/20 (http://www.unep.org/ozone/Meeting_Documents/mop/15mop/15mop-9.e.pdf).

[37] The use of such measures is exceedingly rare. In the sixteenth Meeting of the Parties of the Montreal Protocol in November 2004, of the sixteen decisions adopted on non-compliance, only one incorporated trade-related measures. The decision on Azerbaijan's non-compliance due to excess consumption of CFCs in 2001–2003 *urged* Azerbaijan to report 2004 consumption data and introduce a ban on the import of CFCs, in order to support complete phase out by 2005.

[38] *See* Montreal Protocol, Article 3 and Annexes A, B and C.

the control system are sometimes disproportionate for developing countries and seeks to offset some of the economic and social costs associated with ratification and compliance, For instance, the Protocol allows developing country Parties with a limited annual per capita consumption of controlled substances to defer their phase-out obligations for up to ten years.[39] Further, the Protocol establishes mechanisms for providing technological and financial assistance to these Parties as they make the transition to more ozone-friendly technologies. The London Amendments, adopted at the Second COP, require Parties to establish a mechanism of financial and technical cooperation to enable developing country Parties to comply with the Protocol. In particular, the establishment of the Multilateral Fund has ensured that adequate and consistent financing is available for developing country Parties. Moreover, developing countries' compliance was made contingent upon the effective implementation of these financial and transfer of technology provisions. As a result, these positive measures not only make trade-related measures more efficient, but also, in some cases, decrease the need for their actual use.

Basel Convention

i. Overview and Objectives of the Basel Convention

The Basel Convention addresses the challenges posed by the generation, trans boundary movement and management of hazardous wastes and other wastes. In the late 1980s, stricter environmental standards and higher disposal costs in developed countries increased the shipment of hazardous waste to countries that were not always able to adequately manage the waste. Improper management, indiscriminate dumping, and the accidental spill of wastes can result in, *inter alia*, air, water, and soil pollution that endangers entire communities, burdens countries with colossal clean up costs, and undermines prospects for development. A public outcry over the mounting evidence of uncontrolled movement and dumping of hazardous wastes, including incidents of illegal dumping in developing nations by companies from developed countries, led to the adoption of the Basel Convention in 1989.[40]

The Basel Convention came into force in 1992. Its fundamental aims are the control and reduction of transboundary movements of hazardous wastes and other wastes subject to the provisions of the Convention, the disposal and treatment of such wastes as close as possible to their source of generation, the reduction and minimization of their generation, the environmentally sound management of such wastes and the active promotion of the transfer and use of cleaner technologies.[41] One of the key elements in the Basel Convention is thus a control system for the

---

[39] *See* Montreal Protocol, Article 5.1.

[40] *See* Basel website, "Origins of the Basel Convention" (http://www.basel.int/convention/basics.html).

[41] Article 2 of the Basel Convention contains the definition of "waste," which must be read in conjunction with the definition of "disposal" in Annex IV of the Convention. A waste is "hazardous" under the Convention if it is included in Annex I (unless it does not possess any of the hazardous characteristics contained in Annex III) or if it is considered hazardous under' the domestic legislation of one of the countries involved in the transboundary movement (Basel Convention, Article I). "Other wastes" for the purposes of the Convention, are wastes that belong to any category contained in Annex II that are subject to a transboundary movement.

transboundary movement, management and disposal of such wastes that requires that transboundary movements of hazardous wastes and other wastes for disposal can only take place upon prior written notification by the State of export to the competent authority of the State of import, and upon the prior informed consent by the importing State to the import.[42] The State of export must ensure that the waste does not leave its territory until prior informed consent is received. Another central element of the Basel Convention system is the requirement for the environmentally sound management of waste, which aims to protect human health and the environment against the adverse effects which may result from such wastes by, *inter alia*, minimizing the generation of hazardous waste whenever possible. Environmentally sound management requires addressing the issue through an "integrated life-cycle approach," and integrated waste management, which involve strong controls from the generation of a waste to its collection, storage, transport, and final disposal. During its first decade, the Basel Convention was primarily devoted to setting up the legal framework for controlling the transboundary movements of hazardous wastes. At its sixth COP meeting in 2002, Parties to the Basel Convention decided to build on this framework by emphasizing the full implementation and enforcement of treaty commitments at the national level, the minimization of hazardous waste generation, as well as the importance of capacity building. It was at this COP that a mechanism for promoting implementation and compliance was established to assist Parties to comply with their obligations under the Convention and to facilitate, promote, monitor and aim to secure the implementation of and compliance with the obligations under the Convention.[43]

ii. Trade-related and other Measures of the Basel Convention

Due to the fact that the Basel Convention regulates transboundary movements of hazardous wastes and other wastes by establishing a regulatory framework for the import and export of these wastes, its implementation may have implications for the multilateral trade regime.

Article 6 of the Convention, which establishes the procedures for prior informed consent, requires Parties to notify in writing the intended country of import and countries of transit of any proposed trans boundary movement of hazardous wastes and other wastes. The notification must include information such as, *inter alia*, the reason for the waste export; the generator, exporter, intended carrier (if known), and disposer of the waste; the countries of export, transit and import of the waste, and the competent authorities; information relating to insurance; designation and physical description of the waste and information on any special handling requirements, including emergency provisions in case of accidents; and method of disposal.[44] The Party of import is obliged to respond to the notifier in writing, either consenting to the movement with or without conditions, denying permission for the

---

[42] *See* Basel Convention, Article 6.3.

[43] *See* "Report of the Conference of the Parties to the Basel Convention on the Control of Transboundary Movements of Hazardous Wastes and Their Disposal," 10 February 2003, UNEP/ CHW.6/40 (http://www.basel.int/meetings/cop/cop6/ English/Report40e.pdf).

[44] *See* Basel Convention, Annex V.A.

movement, or requesting additional information.[45] Until written consent has been received, along with a confirmation of the existence of a contract between the exporter and the disposer specifying environmentally sound management of the wastes in question, the State of export must not allow the generator or exporter to commence the transboundary movement.[46]

Other elements of the regulatory framework of the Basel Convention, such as those regarding the import, export, packaging, and labeling of hazardous and other wastes, may also have implications for the multilateral trade regime. Article 4 of the Convention sets out the general obligations for Parties, including the right of Parties to prohibit the import of hazardous wastes or other wastes to their country for disposal. Other Parties to the Convention are obliged to recognize the exercise of that right by not allowing the export of hazardous wastes and other wastes to the Parties which have established such prohibitions, if these have been notified to the other Parties through the Secretariat. Parties are also required to not allow the import and export of wastes if there is reason to believe the wastes will not be managed in an environmentally sound manner.[47]

In addition, Article 4 prohibits Parties from permitting the export of hazardous wastes or other wastes to a non-Party or to import such waste from a non-Party.[48] Nevertheless, transboundary movements to or from non-Parties are allowed as long as it is subject to a bilateral, multilateral or regional agreement or arrangement, the provisions of which are no less stringent than those of the Basel Convention and thus do not derogate from the environmentally sound management of hazardous wastes.[49]

Finally, Article 4 requires that hazardous wastes and other wastes that are the subject of a transboundary movement be packaged, labeled, and transported in conformity with generally accepted and recognized international rules and standards, as well as be accompanied by a movement document from the point at which a transboundary movement commences to the point of disposal.[50] These measures ensure environmentally sound management of wastes, while addressing information requirements and promoting harmonized identification systems.

In 1995, the Basel COP adopted at its third meeting, an amendment to the Convention that is known as the Ban Amendment, which has not yet entered into force. This amendment requires Parties listed in Annex VII of the Convention

---

[45] *See* Basel Convention, Article 6.2

[46] *See* Basel Convention, Article 6.3. Information requirements are also addressed elsewhere in the Basel Convention. For example, Article 13 of the Basel Convention requires Parties to inform those states that might be at risk in the case of an accident occurring during the transboundary movement or disposal of hazardous wastes or other wastes, which are likely to present risks to human health and the environment. The Secretariat also acts as a clearing house for decisions made by Parties not to consent totally or partially to the import or export of hazardous wastes or other wastes, as well as for reports on transboundary movements of hazardous wastes or other wastes in which Parties have been involved and other relevant information.

[47] *See* Basel Convention, Article 4.1 (a), (b), and (e).

[48] *See* Basel Convention, Article 4.5.

[49] *See* Basel Convention, Article 4.5.

[50] *See* Basel Convention, Article 4.7 (b) and (c).

(OECD, EC and Liechtenstein) to prohibit all trans boundary movements of hazardous wastes that are destined for final disposal in States not listed in Annex VII. The Ban Amendment also requires Parties listed in Annex VII to phase out by 31 December 1997 and, prohibit, as of that date, all trans boundary movements of hazardous wastes which are destined for operations which may lead to resource recovery, recycling reclamation, direct re-use or alternative uses to States not listed in Annex VII. The Ban Amendment is intended to respond to lingering problems relating to illegal traffic in waste, and the concerns expressed by some developing countries about their inability to effectively monitor and enforce their own import restriction policies.[51] Similar measures were also adopted, for instance, by African nations in the Bamako Convention in 1991. Nevertheless, the Ban Amendment has been criticized by some countries that claim it will prevent the growth of legitimate and potentially profitable recycling industries in developing countries. These Parties have also questioned why the ban should be applied to an arbitrary list of countries rather than countries that lack capacity to handle the hazardous wastes, and question the presumption that developing countries as a group lack the capacity to manage waste in an environmentally sound manner.[52]

In addition to trade-related provisions, a number of non-trade related measures are also incorporated in the Basel Convention to achieve its objectives. The Convention contains provisions, for instance, on the collection of information and on the supply of legal and technical assistance.[53] In addition, the COP meetings have developed a number of important mechanisms. For instance, the Basel Protocol on Liability, although not yet in force, was adopted at the fifth meeting of the COP to establish a comprehensive regime for liability, including both strict and fault-based liability that aims at providing for adequate and prompt compensation for damage occurring during a transboundary movement of hazardous wastes and other wastes. Another example is Article 14, which contains a commitment to establish regional or sub-regional centers for training and technology transfer that has also been built upon by the COP meetings, leading to the designation of centers all over the world.[54] The core functions of the centers include, inter alia, developing and conducting training programmes in the field of environmentally sound management of hazardous wastes, identifying, developing and strengthening mechanisms for the transfer of environmentally sound technologies, and providing assistance and advice to the Parties and non-Parties of the region at their request on any relevant matters and on the implementation of the Convention.[55] Moreover, the compliance mechanism, adopted at the sixth meeting of the COP, consists of a non-confrontational,

---

[51] *See, e.g.,* interventions by developing country representatives during the third COP meeting stressing the need for technical assistance to prevent illegal traffic into their territories, "Report of the Third Meeting of the Conference of the Parties to the Basel Convention on the Control of Trans boundary Movements of Hazardous Wastes and Their Disposal," paragraph 21 (http://www. basel. int/meetings/cop/cop1-4/cop3repe.pdf).

[52] *See. e.g.,* Earth Negotiations Bulletin, "Basel Convention COP 7 — Summary and analysis," Vol. 20 No. 18, November 2004 (http://www.iisd.ca/download/pdf/enb2018e.pdf).

[53] *See* Basel Convention, Articles 4, 13, 10 and 16.

[54] For instance, at the seventh meeting of the COP a Regional Center in Tehran, Iran was established.

[55] *See* Basel website, Regional Centers (http://www.basel.int/centers/regdescr.html).

facilitative procedure that aims to assist Parties facing compliance difficulties through advice and non-binding recommendations. The Basel Strategic Plan sets out the guidelines for the Convention's activities up to 2010, focusing on the minimization of hazardous waste generation. Particularly, the Strategic Plan focuses on developing countries establishing a vision that environmentally sound management should be accessible to all Parties and a commitment to improve their institutional and technical capabilities and further develop regional and sub-regional centers to achieve that vision.[56]

Finally, the last meeting of the COP held in December 2006, recognized that new waste streams pose new challenges which may also have trade-related implications, e.g. e-waste and computers.[57]

Rotterdam Convention

i. Overview and Objectives of the Rotterdam Convention

The Rotterdam Convention provides countries considering the importation of certain hazardous pesticides and chemicals the tools and information they need to identify potential risks and exclude chemicals they cannot manage safely.[58] In addition, if a country agrees to import chemicals, the Rotterdam Convention promotes their safe use through labelling standards, technical assistance, and other forms of support. Hazardous pesticides and other chemicals create significant risks to human health and the environment, killing or seriously affecting the health of thousands of people every year and also damaging the natural environment and many wild animal species. Governments began to address the problem in the 1980s by establishing a voluntary Prior Informed Consent (PIC) procedure and in 1998 strengthened the procedure by adopting the Rotterdam Convention, which makes PIC legally binding.[59]

The Rotterdam Convention has two primary objectives. First, it aims to promote shared responsibility and cooperative efforts among Parties in the international trade of certain hazardous chemicals in order to protect human health and the environment from potential harm.[60] Second, it seeks to contribute to the environmentally sound use of those chemicals by facilitating information exchange about their characteristics. The Rotterdam Convention initially covered 22 pesticides and 5 industrial chemicals, with the possibility of more being added by the COP.[61] Since

---

[56] *See* Basel Convention COP 6, "Strategic Plan For The Implementation Of The Basel Convention (to 2010)" (http:// www.basel.int/meetings/cop/cop6/StPlan.pdf).

[57] *See* "Report of the Conference of the Parties to the Basel Convention on the Control of Transboundary Movements of Hazardous Wastes and their Disposal on its eighth meeting," 5 January 2007, UNEP/CHW.8/16 (http://www.basel.int/meetings/cop/cop8/docs/16eREISSUED.pdf).

[58] *See* Rotterdam Convention website, "What is the Rotterdam Convention" (http://www.pic.int/home.php?type=t&id=5&sid=16).

[59] *Id.*

[60] *Id.*

[61] The Rotterdam Convention covers pesticides and industrial chemicals that have been banned or severely restricted for health or environmental reasons and that Parties have notified for inclusion in the

the Rotterdam Convention entered into force in February 2004, the first COP has already added fourteen chemicals, including several forms of asbestos, two lead additives for gasoline, and a range of hazardous pesticides.[62] There are currently 39 chemicals listed in Annex III of the Convention: 24 pesticides, 11 industrial chemicals, and severely hazardous pesticide formulations.

ii. Trade-related and other Measures of the Rotterdam Convention

The Rotterdam Convention focuses on the regulation of international trade of certain hazardous chemicals as a way to protect human health and the environment from potential harm and to contribute to their environmentally sound use. Whereas the use of both industrial and agricultural chemicals has traditionally been greatest in industrialized counties, their fastest growing market is now in developing countries.[63] Of the challenges raised by the use and management of hazardous pesticides and other chemicals, international attention has centered on the fact that many countries lack the institutional capacity to make informed decisions on chemical imports and their subsequent management, which raises concern for human health and the environment.[64] The regulatory framework for international trade in certain hazardous chemicals established by the Rotterdam Convention thus emphasizes information exchange and adequate national decision-making processes. The PIC procedure, the core of the Convention and main trade-related measure, is designed to overcome the problem of lack of adequate and precise information. It ensures that countries have accurate data on which to base their policy decisions concerning harmful effects of certain banned or severely restricted chemicals and severely hazardous pesticides. Informed choices are also fundamental for acceptable national regulations concerning the manufacture, use, and disposal of the chemicals. As a result, other measures within the Rotterdam Convention also aim to address information gaps or deficiencies. In that context, both trade-related and other measures are an integral part of the regulatory package of the Convention.

Article 10 establishes the obligations in relation to imports of substances subject to the PIC procedure. It sets forth means for formally obtaining and disseminating the decisions of Parties on future shipments of specified chemicals. Once a chemical is included in the PIC procedure, a "decision guidance document" (DGD) containing information concerning the chemical and the regulatory decisions to ban or severely restrict the chemical for health or environmental reasons is circulated to importing

---

PIC procedure. One notification from each of two specified regions triggers consideration of the addition of a chemical to the PIC procedure, while severely hazardous pesticide formulations that present risks under conditions of use in developing countries may also be nominated for inclusion in the procedure.

[62] *The* First Ministerial Conference of Rotterdam Convention was held in Geneva in September 2004.

[63] *See* Rotterdam Convention website, "95 Countries Agree On New International Convention On Dangerous Chemicals And Pesticides," *News and Highlights*, 16 March 1998 (http://www.fao.org/ WAICENT/FaoInfo/Agricult/AGP/AGPP/ Pesticid/PIC/picnews6.htm).

[64] As mentioned, in 1987 the UNEP Governing Council adopted The London Guidelines for the Exchange of Information on Chemicals in International Trade, UNEP/GC, 14/17, Annex IV. In addition, in 1985, the FAO adopted the first International Code of Conduct on the Distribution and Use of Pesticides, which established voluntary standards to aid countries without existing pesticide regulation, M/R8130, E/8.86/1/5000.

countries.[65] These countries are given nine months to prepare a response concerning the future import of the chemical. The response can consist of either a final decision (to allow import of the chemical, not to allow import, or to allow import subject to specified conditions) or an interim response, which may entail a request for additional information or assistance by the Secretariat. To ensure decisions are not made in a protectionist manner, any prohibitions or specific conditions must apply equally to domestic production.

Exporting Parties must also comply with PIC procedure requirements. Article II establishes the obligations in relation to exports of covered substances in the PIC procedures. It provides that exporting Parties are obliged to take appropriate measures to ensure that exporters within their jurisdiction comply with decisions in each response, as well as to ensure that exports to an importing Party that has not produced a response only take place if there is explicit consent or the chemical is already registered or used in that country, or six months after the Secretariat has informed Parties of the failure of the importing Party to produce a response. In addition, Article 12 establishes that even if a chemical is not included in the Convention, if it is banned or restricted within the jurisdiction of the exporting Party, that Party is obliged to provide notification of the first export after the regulatory measures and then for the first export in each calendar year, and provide the same information as it would for a covered substance. finally, Article 13 states that, without prejudice to any requirements of the importing Party, each exporting Party must require that chemicals listed in Annex III of the Convention, chemicals banned or severely restricted in its territory and chemicals subject to labeling requirements in its territory, when exported, are subject to labeling requirements that provide adequate information with regard to risks and/or hazards to human health or the environment.

As mentioned above, trade-related measures within the PIC procedure are complemented by a number of other provisions in the Rotterdam Convention. For instance, beyond the exchange of information resulting from PIC, Article 14 provides that Parties are obliged to promote the exchange of scientific, technical, economic and legal information concerning the covered chemicals, including toxicological and safety information. Also, Article 16 provides that Parties must cooperate in promoting technical assistance for the development of the infrastructure and the capacity necessary to manage chemicals to enable implementation of the Rotterdam Convention. Finally, Article 17 calls for Parties to develop and approve procedures and mechanisms for addressing compliance issues with the Convention. The Parties are currently working towards establishing the compliance procedures and mechanisms.

---

[65] *See* Rotterdam Convention, Articles 7.3 and 10.2.

Cartagena Protocol on Biosafety

i. Objectives and Overview of the Biosafety Protocol

The Cartagena Protocol on Biosafety seeks to "protect biological diversity from the potential risks posed by living modified organisms resulting from modern biotechnology," taking into account risks to human health.[66] Genetic modification, achieved by the application of recombinant DNA technology, allows for genes to be transferred in ways that are not possible in nature, which may lead to useful products and technologies.[67] Agenda 21, for example, states that modem biotechnology could significantly contribute to improving health care and enhancing food security through sustainable agricultural practices.[68] However, there is also concern about the potential risks of genetic modification for biodiversity, including potential dispersal of genetically modified organisms in the environment, potential impacts on non-target species, and potential transfer of the inserted genetic material to other organisms. Given the growth of the international market for genetically modified organisms and products made from them, an international framework to ensure their safe transfer, handling and use and to achieve an adequate balance between their potential benefits and risks is of fundamental importance.

The Cartagena Protocol on Biosafety, a supplementary agreement to the Convention on Biological Diversity (CBD), recognizes both the potential of modem biotechnology for human well-being and its potential adverse effects on biological diversity and human health.[69] Its objective is to contribute, in accordance with the precautionary approach, "to ensuring an adequate level of protection in the field of the safe transfer, handling and use of living modified organisms, taking also into account risks to human health, and specifically focusing on transboundary movements."[70] Its scope is thus limited to living modified organisms (LMOs) — biological entities capable of replicating or transferring genetic material and constituting a novel combination of genetic material obtained through use of modem biotechnology.[71] The Biosafety Protocol establishes an advance informed agreement (AIA) procedure for ensuring that countries are provided with the information necessary to make informed decisions before agreeing to the import into their territory of living modified organisms that are intended for release into the environment.[72] It also reaffirms the precautionary approach contained in Principle 15 of the Rio

---

[66] *CBD website*, "The Biosafety Protocol: Background" (http://www.cbd.int/biosafety/background.shtml).

[67] *See* Mackenzie, Ruth et al, *An Explanatory Guide to the Cartagena Protocol on Biodiversity*, IUCN, 2003 (http:// www.iucn.org/themes/law/pdfdocuments/Biosafety-guide.pdf).

[68] *Id.*

[69] *See* Biosafety Protocol, Preamble.

[70] Biosafety Protocol, Article 1.

[71] Biosafety Protocol, Article 3. Some categories of LMOs or transboundary movements were also excluded, either as general exclusions from the Protocol or as specific exclusions to the AIA procedures. *See, e.g.,* Biosafety Protocol, Article 5.

[72] *See, e.g.,* Biosafety Protocol, Article 7.

Declaration on Environment and Development.[73] In addition, the Biosafety Protocol establishes a Biosafety Clearing House to facilitate the exchange of information on living modified organisms and to assist countries in the implementation of the Protocol.

ii. Trade-related and other Measures of the Biosafety Protocol

The Biosafety Protocol, although containing a broader overall objective, primarily focuses on transboundary movements of LMOs. Thus, a number of provisions are related to trade, most significantly the measures within the AIA mechanism, but also those that refer to trade with non-Parties and to the handling, transport, identification and packaging of LMOs.

The AIA mechanism is considered the backbone of the agreement. The need to know and to take informed decisions was identified from the outset of negotiations as a crucial element for adequate biosafety in light of the possible risks of LMOs, including that they could be environmentally hazardous, cause environmental damage, or pose risks to human health. Article 7 requires the first importation of an LMO destined for intentional introduction in the environment and not identified by a decision of the Parties as unlikely to have adverse effects to comply with the AIA procedure. This procedure centers around two components: notification and decision-making.[74] Article 8 establishes the notification procedure, requiring the Party of export to notify to the Party of import, in writing, the proposed transboundary movement. The notification must contain, at least, the information specified in Annex I, which includes: the taxonomic status, common name, point of collection or acquisition, and characteristics of recipient organism or parental organisms related to biosafety; the centers of origin and centers of genetic diversity, if known, of the recipient organism and/or the parental organisms and a description of the habitats where the organisms may persist or proliferate; a description of the nucleic acid or the modification introduced, the technique used, and the resulting characteristics of the LMO; and the intended use of the LMO or products thereof.

Article 10 establishes the decision procedure, which the Party of import must follow to either approve the import, with or without conditions, prohibit it, or request additional time or information. The basis for the decision must be a risk assessment carried out in a scientifically sound manner and in compliance with requirements contained in Article 15 and Annex III of the Protocol. In addition, the Parties may establish and maintain appropriate mechanisms, measures and strategies to regulate, manage and control risks identified in the risk assessment provisions. Moreover, in order to avoid or minimize potential adverse effects, a lack of scientific certainty does not prevent Parties from taking a decision.[75]

---

[73] *See, e.g.,* Biosafety Protocol, Article 10.

[74] It should be noted that the scope of the AIA mechanism is narrower than that of the Protocol. LMOs in transit or destined for contained use, for instance, are not subject to the AIA mechanism.

[75] The Protocol contains provisions that aim to simplify the dynamic of AIA when appropriate. For example, Parties may choose to apply their own domestic regulations rather than the Protocol, as long as they are consistent with the Protocol. In addition, a Party of import may indicate that certain transboundary movements of LMOs may commence during the notification process and that certain

LMOs destined for direct use as food, feed or for processing (FFP) are not subject to the AIA mechanism but rather to a set of simplified procedures. Article II establishes a multilateral information exchange process: where a Party makes a decision on domestic use of an LMO that may be exported for FFP, it must notify the Biosafety Clearing House within fifteen days and provide the information contained in Annex II. Annex II includes such information as the name and contact details of the applicant for a decision and of the authority responsible for the decision; the name and identity of the LMO; the description of the gene modification, the technique used, and the resulting characteristics of the LMO; the approved uses of the LMO; a risk assessment report; and suggested methods for the safe handling, storage, transport and use, including packaging, labeling, documentation, disposal and contingency procedures, where appropriate. As in the AIA mechanism, Article II provides that the lack of scientific certainty does not prevent Parties from taking a decision. With respect to decision making on import of LMO-FFPs, the Party of import may follow its own domestic regulatory framework.

Other trade-related measures in the Biosafety Protocol include the provision of trade with non-Parties and handling, packaging, identification and transport requirements. Article 24 does not prohibit transboundary movements of LMOs between Parties and non-Parties, but rather sets up a flexible system to ensure the environmental objectives of Protocol are not undermined. It requires trade with non-Parties to be consistent with the objective of the Protocol, though it does not require that they follow the Protocol's specific provisions, such as AIA. Moreover, though Article 24 foresees the possibility of these movements being subject to other agreements, it does not require them to be. Article 18 establishes handling, transport, packaging and identification/documentation requirements for LMOs subject to intentional transboundary movement within the scope of the Protocol. The provision encourages harmonized systems of identification (requiring, for instance, relevant international rules and standards to be considered and certain information to be included in the accompanying documentation) and also requires that transportation takes place under conditions of safety in order to avoid adverse effects on the conservation and sustainable use of biological diversity, taking also into account risks to human health.

Although one of the Protocol's primary measures, the AIA mechanism, is related to trade, the scope of the agreement is broader, and a number of other measures complement the trade-related provisions. The scope of the Protocol is established in Article 4, which refers to the transboundary movement, transit, handling and use of all living modified organisms that may have adverse effects on the conservation and sustainable use of biological diversity, taking also into account risks to human health. Thus, the Protocol also contains measures regarding unintentional transboundary movements and the transit or passage of an LMO through the territory of a State, and its provisions apply to a variety of operations involving LMOs.[76] In addition, the Protocol provides a framework for achieving adequate implementation. Article 20, for instance, establishes a Biosafety Clearing House to facilitate the

---

LMOs are exempted from the AIA procedure altogether. Finally, Parties to the Protocol may enter into bilateral, regional and multilateral biosafety agreements provided they are consistent with the objective of the Protocol and do not result in a lower level of protection.

[76] *See, e.g.,* Biosafety Protocol, Articles 6 and 17.

exchange of scientific technical, environmental and legal information on LMOs, while also actively assisting Parties in implementing the Protocol.

Article 22 promotes implementation by requiring Parties to cooperate in the development and strengthening of human resources and institutional capacities in biosafety in developing countries. While no specific commitments are articulated,[77] a Compliance Committee was established and procedures were adopted under Article 34, which required the first meeting of the COP serving as the Meeting of the Parties to the Biosafety Protocol (COP-MOP) to develop cooperative procedures and institutional mechanisms to promote compliance and to address cases of non-compliance. The Compliance Committee may, taking into account the capacity of the Party in question, in particular that of developing countries, request or assist the Party in developing a compliance action plan, or invite the Party to submit progress reports on the measures it is taking to bring itself into compliance.[78] Depending on factors such as the cause, degree, type and frequency of non-compliance, the Committee may also recommend that the COP-MOP decide, inter alia, to provide financial or technical assistance, transfer of technology, training measures, or to issue a caution to the Party concerned.[79] As a final step, and only in cases of repeated non-compliance, the COP-MOP may decide on supplementary measures, as it deems appropriate.[80] However, it should be noted, that the COP-MOP has not yet adopted any such supplementary measures. Finally, Article 35 of the Protocol calls for an evaluation of the effectiveness of the Protocol to be undertaken at least every five years.

Stockholm Convention

i. Objectives and Overview of the Stockholm Convention

The Stockholm Convention is a global treaty focused on protecting human health and the environment from persistent organic pollutants (POPS).[81] POPs are chemicals that remain intact in the environment for long periods, become widely distributed geographically, accumulate in the fatty tissue of living organisms, and are toxic to humans and wildlife.[82] With the evidence of long-range transport of these chemicals to regions where they have never been used or produced and the consequent global threats they pose to human health and the environment, States

---

[77] Nevertheless, following the adoption of the Biosafety Protocol, the Council of the Global Environment Facility (GEF) adopted the GEF Initial Strategy on Biosafety, which is aimed at assisting countries to establish national biosafety frameworks (NBFs) to implement the Protocol. Currently, besides running the Biosafety Clearing House, UNEP-GEF is managing a development project assisting 123 countries to develop a draft NBF and eight implementation projects with the goal of establishing operational NBFs.

[78] COP-MOP I Decision BS I/7 Section VI, (1)(d)(f)(g).

[79] *Id.* at Section VI, (2)(a) and (b).

[80] *Id.* at Section VI, 2(d).

[81] *See* POPS website, "Stockholm Convention on Persistant Organic Pollutants" (http://www.pops.int/).

[82] *Id.*

recognized the need for global actions to reduce and eliminate releases of these chemicals.[83]

The Stockholm Convention, which is the first global, legally binding agreement designed to protect human health and the environment from the harmful impacts of POPs, came into force in May 2004. In order to achieve its objective, the Stockholm Convention seeks to eliminate or restrict the production and use of intentionally produced POPS.[84] It also seeks to continue minimizing and, where feasible, ultimately eliminate releases of unintentionally produced POPS.[85] In addition, the Stockholm Convention requires Parties to develop strategies for identifying POPs stockpiles and wastes and to ensure that they are managed or disposed of in an environmentally sound manner.

ii. Trade-related and other Measures of the Stockholm Convention

In line with its objectives, the core measures of the Stockholm Convention are those that require eliminating and restricting the production and use of listed chemicals.[86] The Convention contains trade-related measures to support these aims. For example, the Stockholm Convention requires Parties to limit trade in POPs to those countries that comply with the Convention's provisions, in order to ensure that all POPs existing or produced within the Parties are used and disposed of subject to its restrictions. Article 3, for instance, requires Parties to ban imports of listed chemicals, except if the import is from another Party and is destined for environmentally sound disposal or the chemical is covered by a specific exemption. Article 3 also requires all Parties to ban the export of listed chemicals to other Parties except for the purpose of environmentally sound disposal. In addition, Parties can export those chemicals to Parties subject to a specific exemption as well as to non-Parties that certify compliance with the Convention's provisions.[87] In this regard, trade-related measures constitute an important supplementary element in promoting the protection of human health and the environment from POPs.

As mentioned above, the Stockholm Convention contains a wide range of

---

[83] *See* UNEP website, "Persistant Organic Pollutants" (http://www.chem.unep.ch/pops/).

[84] Some of the POPs initially covered by the Stockholm Convention include: aldrin (a pesticide applied to soils to kill termites, grasshoppers, corn rootworm, and other insect pests); chlordane (used extensively to control termites and as a broad-spectrum insecticide on a range of agricultural crops); and DDT (widely used during World War II to protect soldiers and civilians from malaria, typhus, and other diseases spread by insects — now applied against mosquitoes in several countries to control malaria).

[85] The unintentional production of POPs refers to POPs that are unintentional by-products of industrial and other processes, including dioxins and furans.

[86] Thus far nine intentionally produced POPs are listed in Annex A (elimination) with only DDT listed in Annex B (restriction). As a dynamic agreement, however, the Stockholm Convention sets out a process whereby further chemicals can be added to the list for action, helping governments identify these chemicals and incorporating them into the appropriate treaty annexes. The Convention is also dynamic in that it recognizes that some of the covered chemicals are still widely used in developing countries and allows countries to get "specific exemptions" that enable them to eliminate production and use over time, as substitutes are phased in. For example, disease vector control is an acceptable use of DDT, though countries must comply with certain conditions, such as following World Health Organization guidelines.

[87] *See* Stockholm Convention, Article 3.2 (b). Once all specific exemptions for a POP chemical are eliminated, Parties would be required to prohibit trade in that chemical.

measures to promote the environmentally sound management of POPs. Article 5, for example, requires Parties to take measures to reduce or eliminate releases from the unintentional production of POPs, including developing national action plans to identify, characterize and address the release of these chemicals and promote the development and use of substitute or modified materials, products, and processes. In addition, Article 6 requires Parties to take measures to reduce or eliminate releases from stockpiles and wastes — a significant measure in light of the large number of waste stockpiles and contaminated sites containing persistent pesticides and PCBs, particularly in the developing world.[88] The provision also calls for close cooperation with the Basel Convention to, inter alia, establish levels of appropriate POPs destruction and determine methods for their environmentally sounds disposal. Article 8 establishes the procedures for the listing of new chemicals under the Convention.

The core measures of the Stockholm Convention are established in the context of other measures that complement, reinforce, and balance them. Such measures include provisions on information exchange and public information, as well as technical and financial assistance. Article 9, for instance, mandates Parties to facilitate or undertake the exchange of information relevant to reduction or elimination of POPs, with the aim of facilitating the implementation of the control measures and of promoting the use of alternatives, and establishes a clearinghouse mechanism within the Secretariat to facilitate POPs information exchange. Article 10 calls on Parties to, within their capabilities, promote awareness of the risks of POPs, and Article II outlines the requirements to support and further develop international programmes for conducting and financing POPs research, taking into account the special needs of developing countries. Article 12 recognizes that timely and appropriate technical assistance in response to requests is essential and calls for the establishment of regional and subregional centers for capacity building and transfer of technology to assist Parties in fulfilling their obligations under the Convention, and Article 13 establishes a financial mechanism to ensure adequate and sustainable financial resources to enable Parties to do SO.[89] Thus, trade-related measures are only an element of a broader framework of provisions established to pursue the goals established in the Convention.

Article 16 requires an evaluation of the effectiveness of the Convention to take place four years after the Convention's entry into force and periodically thereafter. Parties have agreed to complete the first effectiveness evaluation by the fourth meeting of the COP scheduled for 2009. Similar to the Rotterdam Convention, Article 17 calls for Parties to develop and approve procedures and mechanisms for addressing compliance issues. These are still under negotiation by the Parties.

---

[88] According to the FAO, about 20,000 tons of obsolete pesticides are believed to be stockpiled in Africa, with perhaps another 80,000 tons in Asia and Latin America, and at least 150,000 tons in countries of the former Soviet Union.

[89] The institutional structure of the Global Environment Facility will, on an interim basis, be the principal entity entrusted with the operation of the financial mechanism.

NOTES AND QUESTIONS

1.   No WTO member has challenged any MEA trade measure. Thus there is no case law on the compatibility of WTO trade agreements and MEAs. The negotiation begun in Doha in 2001, has gone badly and is now suspended. Thus the question of possible clashes between MEA trade restrictions and WTO norms is still a possibility.

2.   The trade provisions of MEAs restrict trade between members and non-members of the MEA regime and sometimes even between members. MEA trade provisions may thus be inconsistent with GATT Article I (MFN treatment) and GATT Article XI (quotas and import and export restrictions). Discriminatory taxes or regulations may violate GATT Article III. Thus, most MEA trade provisions must pass the tests inherent in GATT Article XX to be consistent with GATT norms.

3.   Consider the trade provisions of each of the MEAs discussed in the foregoing UNEP reading on Trade-Related MEAs: CITES, the Montreal Protocol, the Basel Convention, the Rotterdam Convention, the Biosafety Protocol, and the Stockholm Convention. Are all these MEAs consistent with GATT norms?

4.   What are the options for reconciling MEAs and WTO obligations? Consider the following ideas set out (in a private communication to the authors) by Mitsuo Matsushita, a renowned trade expert and former member of the WTO Appellate Body:

Under the circumstances as they exist today, some ways should be explored to deal with possible conflicts between WTO agreements and the MEAs. Although tentative at this stage, three approaches are suggested below. One is to use waiver under Article IX:3 of the Marrakesh Agreement. In this approach, a WTO member implementing a provision of a MEA agreement through measures which may come into conflict with provisions of a WTO agreement may seek a waiver from the WTO in accordance with the above article. If a waiver is granted, the member's obligations under the GATT 1994 or any other WTO agreement are waived to the extent of conditions incorporated in the waiver.

However, a waiver is only an *ad hoc* and temporary measure and can be granted only by 3/4 majority votes at the General Council of the WTO. Article IX:3 states that waiver is granted to deal with "exceptional circumstances." Moreover, to characterize MEAs as "exceptional" seems to be at odds with the importance of environmental policies today as incorporated into MEAs. Although the use of waiver may be necessary as a temporary measure, this is hardly a permanent solution.

Another way might be to enact a new exception to GATT Article XX. For example, a new Article XX(k) could simply provide that environmental measures necessary to implement an MEA are exempt from other provisions of the GATT. But amendment of the GATT requires unanimity or at least consensus of the entire WTO membership, and this may be difficult or impossible to achieve.

Perhaps the best option is for the WTO membership to adopt an "Understanding or Interpretation" with respect to the relationship between MEAs and GATT Articles XX(b) and (g) that states that there is a presumption in favor of the validity of any environmental measures associated with implementing an MEA. The presumption of validity would operate only under the following conditions:

(a) (a) The MEA is open to membership by all countries.

(b) (b) The parties to the MEA are representative of both major supplier and major consumer countries.

(c) The content and scope of trade measures which will be used to implement the MEA should be clearly defined. Also the procedure for executing such measures should be clear and transparent.

(d) Trade measures implementing the MEA should not be arbitrary and discriminatory with regard to countries under the same or similar conditions. Also these should not be employed in a way that they constitute a disguised restriction of international trade.

(e) The purpose of the MEA should be protection of the environment including the protection of life and health of humans, animals or plants as well as the conservation of exhaustible natural resources.

(f) Trade measures employed to implement the MEA should be related to the objectives of environmental protection and this relationship should be reasonably close and real.

(g) The scope of trade measures based on the MEA should not be too broad in proportion to the purpose of protecting environment.

An understanding or interpretation incorporating the above principles can be promulgated as a "decision" of the WTO in accordance with Article IX:1 of the Marrakesh Agreement or Article XXV of the GATT 1994. It can also be announced as a "declaration" of the WTO. In either case, however, the understanding would be non-binding and exhortative. However, it is expected that WTO members would abide by these principles. Also panels and the Appellate Body dealing with disputes in which the relationship between WTO agreements and MEAs is at issue would be expected to follow them. In this understanding or interpretation, national measures complying with the principles incorporated therein should be given a presumption of satisfying the requirements of Articles XX (b) and (g) of the GATT 1994, but the presumption can be rebutted.

What solution would you suggest?

Section V.   CLIMATE CHANGE, RENEWABLE ENERGY, AND GREEN TECHNOLOGY

In the last 60 years, international trade has increased 32-fold, and its share of world GDP is now 21%. This enormous expansion of trade has been possible not only because of international legal rules but also because of new technologies of transportation and communication. Nevertheless, the carbon "footprint" of trade is relatively small: 90% of international trade moves by ship, and maritime shipping accounts for only 11.8% of the transport sectors' total contribution to CO_2 emissions. (Aviation accounts for 11.2%, rail transport 2%, and road transport 72.6%).

International trade, on the one hand, is a key to dealing with climate change since through trade green technology and climate-friendly products can be spread around the world. But this raises the question whether the rules of the WTO concerning intellectual property and technology transfer impede or facilitate technological innovation and technology-related transactions. A broader question is what impact does international trade law have on international and national policies to mitigate and adapt to climate change?

In the materials that follow we examine the compatibility of major policies to mitigate and to adapt to climate change with the law of the multilateral trading system. We examine three general categories of climate change measures: (1) price and market mechanisms to internalize the environmental costs of GHG emissions; (2) financial mechanisms to promote the development and deployment of renewable energy and green technologies; and (3) technical requirements to promote green goods and technologies.

A.   Price and Market Mechanisms

In Chapter 4, we covered all aspects of climate change except the issues related to international trade law. In that chapter we analyzed the two major types of price and market mechanisms being employed to combat climate change: taxes on greenhouse gas emissions, especially carbon taxes; and cap and trade schemes. Both of these are market mechanisms that attempt to set a price on greenhouse gas emissions in order to internalize their environmental costs. Broadly speaking a carbon tax may be levied on two main points of application — on producers or consumers. A tax on producers is normally levied at the first point of sale (or export) of a fossil fuel; a tax on consumers is levied at the point of consumption or use. Many countries have implemented some form of carbon or energy tax.

A carbon tax is much simpler than a cap and trade scheme and has the advantage of raising money for the government concerned. An optimum carbon tax should be set at a level that fully internalizes the costs of environmental damage so that prices reflect the real environmental costs. (A carbon tax should be set to equal the marginal damage caused by the emissions). Most taxing countries, however, follow a more pragmatic approach that sets the tax rate at a level to simply influence taxpayers' behavior to achieve a given environmental objective. This pragmatic scheme is easier to implement where the cost of environmental damage is difficult to determine.

The second way of setting a price on greenhouse gas emissions is to (1) fix a cap on total emissions; (2) translate this cap into "allowed emissions" or "emission allowances" to cover emissions; and (3) create a market in which these allowances can be trade at prices set by the market. In theory domestic trading schemes can be linked to two different kinds of emission targets: an overall emission level (the cap and trade system) or an emission standard for each covered source (the rate-base system). Virtually all trading schemes now in effect employ the cap and trade system, which is easier to administer. A cap and trade system may be either mandatory or voluntary in nature. There are two ways of allocating the allowances in a cap and trade system: allocation free of charge (usually on the basis of historical emission levels) or auctioning. Most trading schemes use a combination of both methods. A trading scheme may set up two kinds of linkages to outside systems: first, direct links can be set up to allow emission allowance trading across several different emission trading systems; second, indirect links may be set up to allow project-based offsets. (An offset is the act of reducing or avoiding greenhouse gas emissions in one place in order to "offset" greenhouse gas emissions occurring somewhere else).

Most emission trading schemes allow banking of emissions to help stabilize the fluctuations of allowance prices. Banking allows allowances to be carried over from one phase to another. Borrowing is another flexibility mechanism that allows a greenhouse gas emitting entity to use allowances from a future time-period to cover current emissions.

Both a carbon tax and emission trading schemes put a price on carbon/greenhouse gas emissions. This price results in at least partial internalization of the environmental costs of emissions.

In the following reading we examine the principal WTO issues raised by carbon taxes and emission trading schemes.

TRADE AND CLIMATE CHANGE A REPORT BY THE UNITED NATIONS ENVIRONMENTAL PROGRAMME AND THE WORLD TRADE ORGANIZATION
103–110 (2009) (footnotes omitted)

[Any domestic law scheme designed to control GHG emissions will confront the problem of "leakage." Leakage occurs because industries and importers will seize on the opportunity to avoid stringent GHG regulations by a variety of tactics, chief among them: (1) importing more products from countries that do not strictly control GHG emissions; and (2) relocating factories from countries with strict GHG controls to countries with less strict controls. In both of these scenarios, a country with strict GHG controls will be at a competitive disadvantage, which will vary from industry to industry but may be very serious. What can be done about such leakage? One solution is "border tax adjustment" that levies GHG charges on all imports from countries with less than certain defined GHG controls. Such a GHG charge would be levied at the border on top of the applicable tariff due. The amount of the GHG charge could be calibrated to stop leakage and to ensure that imported products from countries that do not regulate GHG emissions would pay their fair share, at least to countries that do have strict GHG controls. But would such a system of GHG charges on imports survive the legal tests under the rules of the multilateral trading system?]

Relevant WTO rules

Several WTO disciplines may come into play if a carbon/energy tax or an emission trading scheme and/or their adjustments affect international trade. The literature has been very prolific on the extent to which GATT and WTO rules would apply to border measures based on the carbon content of products or based on the adoption of "comparable" climate change mitigation measures.

The discussion has been triggered by a number of factors, including: (i) the recent design by governments of new policy mechanisms to mitigate climate change; (ii) the concerns over competitiveness and carbon leakage and the related risk of protectionism; (iii) the absence of universal commitment to reduce greenhouse gas emissions and the related temptation to use trade measures to encourage reduction in emissions; and (iv) some perceived legal uncertainties in GATT and WTO provisions about measures on production processes (in particular "non-product related PPMs"), as they have not yet been clarified in the dispute settlement system of the WTO.

a) Rules specific to border tax adjustments

Generally speaking, two types of internal taxes may be distinguished: taxes on products (called indirect taxes) and taxes on producers (i.e. direct taxes). In its examination of BTAs, the 1970 GATT Working Party indicated that taxes directly levied on products (i.e. so-called indirect taxes, such as excise duties, sales taxes and the tax on value added) were eligible for adjustment, while certain taxes that were not directly levied on products (i.e. direct taxes such as taxes on property or income) were normally not eligible for adjustment.

In 1976, a GATT panel, in the *United States Tax Legislation (DISC)* case, confirmed, for the export side and in relation to GATT rules, the distinction between direct and indirect taxes and the ineligibility of direct taxes (on producers) for adjustment. The question of whether domestic carbon/energy taxes are eligible for border tax adjustment pursuant to GATT and WTO rules and, if so, under which conditions, is addressed in this subsection.

i) Border tax adjustments on imported products

Pursuant to GATT Article II on tariff concessions and customs duties, for a BTA on imports to be characterized as a tax adjustment and not a customs duty, the charge imposed on the imported product needs to be equivalent to the tax imposed on the "like" domestic product. In other words, there is a difference between a "border tax" and a "border tax adjustment." A "border tax" is a tax (or customs duty) imposed on imported goods, while a "border tax adjustment," is an adjustment of the taxes imposed domestically on products when the goods are imported. Therefore, GATT Article II.2 (a) allows WTO members, at any time, to impose on the importation of any product a charge equivalent to an internal tax (e.g. a border tax adjustment).

There is an extensive legal debate over the eligibility, for border adjustment, of domestic carbon/energy taxes. Some authors have also discussed whether the price paid by an industry to participate in an emission trading scheme (in the form of an obligation to hold emission allowances) could be qualified as an "internal tax or other internal charge of any kind" under GATT Article III.2, and would therefore be comparable to a carbon/energy tax for the purpose of introducing border adjustments. According to these authors, GATT and WTO rules on border tax adjustment could then become relevant.

Two GATT provisions are at the centre of the discussion on border tax adjustments in relation to carbon/energy taxes: (i) Article II.2(a) and its phrase "articles from which the imported product has been manufactured or produced in whole or in part"; and (ii) Article III.2, first sentence and the terms "applied, directly or indirectly, to like domestic products."

Article 11.2(a) allows two types of impact charges (i.e. border tax adjustments): (i) charges imposed on imported *products* that are like domestic products; and (ii) charges imposed on *articles* from which the imported product has been manufactured or produced in whole or in part. The first type could refer, for instance, to charges imposed on domestic fuels and imported "like" fuels.

Concerning the second type of charges, however, extensive discussion has taken place on the extent to which the energy inputs and fossil fuels used in the production of a particular product could be considered to be "articles from which the imported product has been manufactured or produced in whole or in part." It has been suggested by some that the wording of Article II.2 (a) may restrict the application of Article II to inputs physically incorporated into, or part of, the final product, which would therefore exclude the possibility to adjust taxes on the energy or fossil fuels used during the production of goods (other than taxes on fuels themselves).

Article II.2(a) also states that internal taxes and equivalent charges on imported products need to be imposed consistently with GATT Article III.2 and the preamble to Ad Note Article III. Under Article III.2, border adjustments on imported products is only allowed in respect of taxes "applied, directly or indirectly, to like domestic products" (i.e. indirect taxes). The meaning of the words "directly or indirectly" has been extensively debated in the literature related to adjustments of taxes on CO emissions. In particular, the focus of the debate has been the question whether, pursuant to both Articles II.2(a) and III.2, only the environmental taxes on inputs which are physically incorporated into the final product may be eligible for adjustments when the final product is imported.

It has been argued by some that the word "indirectly" contained in Article III.2 may be interpreted as allowing the use of border tax adjustments on taxes that are charged on inputs used during the production process of a particular product, i.e. applied indirectly to products. According to this argument, a tax on the energy or fuels used in the production process or the CO_2 emitted during production (neither of which are physically incorporated in the final product) could therefore be considered to be applied indirectly to products.

The GATT *Superfund* case has been mentioned in this context. In this case, the dispute panel found that a U.S. tax on certain substances (used as inputs in the production process of certain chemicals) which was imposed directly on products was eligible for border tax adjustment. It has been argued that this case confirms that the GATT allows border tax adjustments on imported products in relation to an internal tax on certain inputs used in the production process.

ii) Border tax adjustments on exported products

GATT and WTO rules permit, under certain conditions, the use of border tax adjustments on exported products. Export BTAs cannot be subject to anti-dumping duties imposed on goods that are deemed to be "dumped" (i.e. exported at less than the cost price in the domestic marker) nor can they be subject to countervailing duties that an importing country introduces to offset certain subsidies provided in the exporting country. Export BTAs do not constitute subsidies. Export BTAs are therefore neither prohibited nor "actionable" under the WTO Agreement on Subsidies and Countervailing Measures (SCM) and GATT rules. Footnote 1 of the SCM Agreement reads:

"In accordance with the provisions of Article XVI of GATT 1994 (Note to Article XVI) and the provisions of Annexes I through III of this Agreement, the exemption of an exported product from duties or taxes *borne by* the like product when destined for domestic consumption, or the remission of such duties or taxes in amounts not in excess of those which have accrued, shall not be deemed to be a subsidy." [emphasis added]

GATT Article VI:4, the Ad Note to Article XVI and footnote 1 of the SCM Agreement refer to taxes "borne by" products and not "applied to" or "subject to" as contained in GATT Article III:3. In 1970, i.e. before the SCM Agreement came into effect, the GATT Working Parry on Border Tax Adjustments took note of these differences in wording in the GATT and concluded that they had not led to any differences in interpretation of the provisions. It also noted that GATT provisions on tax adjustment applied the "principle of destination" identically to imports and exports.

Furthermore, items (e) and (g) of the Illustrative List of Export Subsidies contained in Annex I of the SCM Agreement endorse the distinction between direct and indirect taxes. Border tax adjustments on exports with respect to direct taxes are considered to be export subsidies (Item (e)) and are therefore prohibited under Article 3 of the SCM Agreement. On the other hand; border tax adjustments on exports with respect to indirect taxes are considered an export subsidy only when the BTAs are "in excess" of taxes "levied in respect of the production and distribution of like products when sold for domestic consumption" (Item (g)). Item (g) provides that the following is an export subsidy:

"The exemption or remission, in respect of the production and distribution of exported products, of indirect taxes [footnote omitted] in excess of those levied in respect of the production and distribution of like products when sold for domestic consumption."

Item (g) therefore allows, for instance, a tax on domestically produced fossil fuels to be rebated when a product is exported, provided that the rebate is not larger than the actual tax levied on "like" products "when sold for domestic consumption." Moreover, Item (g) allows border tax adjustment (if not "in excess" of taxes that are charged on like products) in relation to indirect taxes levied "in respect of the production and distribution" of like domestic products. This has been interpreted by some authors as including taxes on energy or fuel consumption, since those taxes are levied in respect of the production of the goods.

It has also been argued that carbon and energy taxes are a particular type of indirect tax and would fall under the category of "taxes occultes" (literally, "hidden taxes"). The 1970 GATT Working Party on Border Tax Adjustments included, under this category, taxes on "advertising, *energy*, machinery and transport" (emphasis added). In fact, the Working Party noted a divergence of views among delegations regarding the eligibility for adjustment of "taxes occultes" and even indicated that adjustment was not normally made for "taxes occultes" except in countries having a cascade tax. However, it has been argued by some authors that certain of the "taxes occultes" that were mentioned by the GATT Working Party are now explicitly allowed by the SCM Agreement: the Working Group listed taxes on "machinery and transport" as examples of "taxes occultes," whereas the SCM Agreement allows border tax adjustments on taxes not in excess of domestic indirect taxes in respect of the "production and distribution" of like products, which potentially could include transport taxes.

Finally, there has been extensive discussion on the extent to which Item (h) on "prior stage cumulative indirect taxes" (PSCI taxes) of the Illustrative List of Export Subsidies read together with footnote 61 to Annex II on "Guidelines on consumption of inputs in the production process" could be interpreted as implying that carbon and energy taxes are eligible for border tax adjustment on both the product and the related production process of the product.

NOTES AND QUESTIONS

1. ***Reasons for Border Tax Adjustment.*** If country A enacts a carbon or energy tax or institutes cap and trade, the economic impact will be to raise the prices of domestically-made goods and services in country A. If the country's trading partners have no corresponding tax or cap and trade system, country A may experience competitiveness problems and "carbon leakage": imports that are not subject to the tax may be cheaper than domestic products in country A, and domestic manufacturing plants in country A may relocate abroad to avoid the tax or cap and trade system. Border tax adjustment (BTA) is therefore essential to create a level playing field with trading partners.

2. ***The two faces of Border Tax Adjustment.*** Note that BTA has two elements: a payment on the import side but a rebate on the export side. The reason for this is that BTA treats carbon taxes as destination taxes payable by the consumer of the products containing carbon inputs that are consumed during the course of manufacture. Because of the rebate on the export side, exports are stimulated by BTA and may increase in volume.

3. ***Compatibility of Border Tax Adjustment with WTO rules.*** Note the controversy whether BTA passes muster according to the WTO rules. This question has never been decided and there are differing opinions on the matter. Go through the analysis yourself and decide for yourself. On the import side, the two important GATT provisions are Article III:2, which is quoted above, and Article II:2(a), which provides as follows:

> Nothing in this Article shall prevent any contracting party from imposing at any time on the importation of any product:
>
> (a) a charge equivalent to an internal tax imposed consistently with the provisions of paragraph 2 of Article III in respect of the like domestic product or in respect of an article from which the

imported product has been manufactured or produced in whole or in part.

On the export side, GATT Article XVI and the Ad Note to Article XVI are quoted in the reading in this subsection. We reprint here the relevant provisions of Annex I and Annex II of the WTO's SCM Agreement:

ANNEX I
ILLUSTRATIVE LIST OF EXPORT SUBSIDIES

(e) The full or partial exemption remission, or deferral specifically related to exports, of direct taxes[90] or social welfare charges paid or payable by industrial or commercial enterprises.[91]

(g) The exemption or remission, in respect of the production and distribution of exported products, of indirect taxes in excess of those levied in respect of the production and distribution of like products when sold for domestic consumption.

(h) The exemption, remission or deferral of prior-stage cumulative indirect taxes on goods or services used in the production of exported products in excess of the exemption, remission or deferral of like prior-stage cumulative indirect taxes on goods or services used in the production of like products when sold for domestic consumption; provided, however, that prior-stage cumulative indirect taxes may be exempted, remitted or deferred on exported products even when not exempted, remitted or deferred on like products when sold for domestic consumption, if the

---

[90] [58] For the purpose of this Agreement:

The term "direct taxes" shall mean taxes on wages, profits, interests, rents, royalties, and all other forms of income, and taxes on the ownership of real property;

The term "import charges" shall mean tariffs, duties, and other fiscal charges not elsewhere enumerated in this note that are levied on imports;

The term "indirect taxes" shall mean sales, excise, turnover, value added, franchise, stamp, transfer, inventory and equipment taxes, border taxes and all taxes other than direct taxes and import charges;

"Prior-stage" indirect taxes are those levied on goods or services used directly or indirectly in making the product;

"Cumulative" indirect taxes are multi-staged taxes levied where there is no mechanism for subsequent crediting of the tax if the goods or services subject to tax at one stage of production are used in a succeeding stage of production;

"Remission" of taxes includes the refund or rebate of taxes;

"Remission or drawback" includes the full or partial exemption or deferral of import charges.

[91] [59] The Members recognize that deferral need not amount to an export subsidy where, for example, appropriate interest charges are collected. The Members reaffirm the principle that prices for goods in transactions between exporting enterprises and foreign buyers under their or under the same control should for tax purposes be the prices which would be charged between independent enterprises acting at arm's length. Any Member may draw the attention of another Member to administrative or other practices which may contravene this principle and which result in a significant saving of direct taxes in export transactions. In such circumstances the Members shall normally attempt to resolve their differences using the facilities of existing bilateral tax treaties or other specific international mechanisms, without prejudice to the rights and obligations of Members under GATT 1994, including the right of consultation created in the preceding sentence.

Paragraph (e) is not intended to limit a Member from taking measures to avoid the double taxation of foreign-source income earned by its enterprises or the enterprises of another Member.

prior-stage cumulative indirect taxes are levied on inputs that are consumed in the production of the exported product (making normal allowance for waste).[92] This item shall be interpreted in accordance with the guidelines on consumption of inputs in the production process contained in Annex II.

ANNEX II
GUIDELINES ON CONSUMPTION OF INPUTS IN THE PRODUCTION PROCESS[93]

I

1. Indirect tax rebate schemes can allow for exemption, remission or deferral of prior-stage cumulative indirect taxes levied on inputs that are consumed in the production of the exported product (making normal allowance for waste). Similarly, drawback schemes can allow for the remission or drawback of import charges levied on inputs that are consumed in the production of the exported product (making normal allowance for waste).

2. The Illustrative List of Export Subsidies in Annex I of this Agreement makes reference to the term "inputs that are consumed in the production of the exported product" in paragraphs (h) and (i). Pursuant to paragraph (h), indirect tax rebate schemes can constitute an export subsidy to the extent that they result in exemption, remission or deferral of prior-stage cumulative indirect taxes in excess of the amount of such taxes actually levied on inputs that are consumed in the production of the exported product. Pursuant to paragraph (i), drawback schemes can constitute an export subsidy to the extent that they result in a remission or drawback of import charges in excess of those actually levied on inputs that are consumed in the production of the exported product. Both paragraphs stipulate that normal allowance for waste must be made in findings regarding consumption of inputs in the production of the exported product.

Having gone through the analysis on both the import and the export side, what is your opinion? Is BTA of a carbon tax allowed under WTO rules? Note that there is no doubt as to legality of BTA on the export side; the ambiguity exists on the import side. But if BTA is freely allowed on the export side, does this not add to the argument that it should also be permitted on the import side?

4. *Border Tax Adjustment and Cap and Trade Systems.* Even if your conclusion is that BTA is allowed for a carbon tax, what about cap and trade? In a cap and trade system the emitters subject to the system pay in the form of a price for carbon allowances. But these prices will greatly vary over time. Is it possible to

---

[92] [60] Paragraph (h) does not apply to value-added tax systems and border-tax adjustment in lieu thereof; the problem of the excessive remission of value-added taxes is exclusively covered by paragraph (g).

[93] [61] Inputs consumed in the production process are inputs physically incorporated, energy, fuels, and oil used in the production process and catalysts which are consumed in the course of their use to obtain the exported product.

have BTA for cap and trade allowances and still comply with the discipline of GATT Article III:2?

B. Financial Mechanisms to Promote Renewable Energy and Green Technology

The development of climate-friendly renewable energy and green technology may lag for various reasons. First, if carbon emissions do not have a price, firms and consumers have little incentive to reduce the externalities they involve; this "environmental externality" is not internalized and therefore operates as a subsidy to firms and consumers. Second, companies may not seek to develop new technologies because of what is called the "knowledge effect": knowledge about new technologies tends to spread quickly beyond the company that developed the new technology before the developer has the opportunity to make a profit from them. Third, innovation requires investment, and investors may not want the risk inherent in the development of new technology. In addition, many factors may retard the deployment of renewables and new technology, for example the difficulty of integrating solar and wind power into the electricity grid, which was built for fossil fuel energy.

In response to these difficulties government funding may contribute to the faster deployment and increased use of renewables and green technology. Government incentive policies may thus be used to increase the use of renewable and clean energy sources; to develop and deploy energy efficient and low carbon content goods and technologies; and to develop and deploy carbon sequestration technologies. Government support in this regard my take many forms, but three principal categories of instruments are commonly used: (1) fiscal measures, such as tax advantages; (2) price support measures, such as feed-in tariffs (a minimum guaranteed price) to encourage the generation of renewable energy sources; and (3) investment support, such as grants and demonstration projects.

Are the norms of the WTO and the multilateral trading system compatible with these governmental measures? Consider the following reading:

TRADE AND CLIMATE CHANGE: A REPORT BY THE UNITED NATIONS ENVIRONMENTAL PROGRAMME AND THE WORLD TRADE ORGANIZATION
115–118 (2009)

Relevant WTO rules

Governmental funding policies to increase the development and deployment of renewable energy sources and of low-carbon goods and technologies may have an impact on the price and production of such goods. From an international trade perspective, such policies lower the costs for producers, leading to lower product prices. In turn, lower prices may reduce exporting countries' access to the market of the subsidizing country or may increase the exports of the subsidizing country.

Moreover, some countries may provide domestic energy-consuming industries with subsidies to offset the cost of installing emission-reducing technologies, thus enabling them to maintain international competitiveness. Since the renewable energy and low-carbon technology sectors are open to international trade, WTO disciplines on subsidies (as contained in the Agreement on Subsidies and Counter-vailing Measures (SCM) may become relevant to certain support policies. Moreover, the WTO Agreement on Agriculture may be relevant: it contains a category of permissible green subsidies, known as Green Box, which could allow countries to pursue climate adaptation and mitigation measures in the area of agriculture.

The SCM Agreement aims at striking a balance between the concern that domestic industries should not be put at an unfair disadvantage by competition from goods that benefit from government subsidies, and the concern that countervailing measures to offset those subsidies should not themselves be obstacles to fair trade. The rules of the SCM Agreement define the concept of "subsidy," establish the conditions under which WTO members may or may not employ subsidies, and regulate the remedies (countervailing duties) that may be taken against subsidized imports.

The SCM Agreement also contains surveillance provisions: Article 25 requires each member to notify the WTO of all the specific subsidies it provides, and Article 26 calls for the Committee on Subsidies and Countervailing Measures to review these notifications.

Article 1 of the SCM Agreement defines a subsidy as having three necessary elements: (a) a financial contribution has been provided; (b) the contribution was made by a government or a public body within the territory of a WTO member; and (c) the contribution confers a benefit.

A "financial contribution" is defined by an exhaustive list of measures, which include direct transfers of funds (for example grants or loans), potential direct transfers of funds (such as loan guarantees), government revenue forgone (e.g. fiscal incentives through tax credits), the provision by government of goods and services other than general infrastructure, and government purchase of goods. The range of governmental measures which may be described as subsidies is broadened further by Article 1.1(a)(2), which includes any form of income or price support.

The SCM Agreement does not provide guidance on how to evaluate whether or not a "financial contribution" confers a "benefit." However, the Appellate Body ruled, in the *Canada — Aircraft* case that the existence of a benefit is to be determined by comparison with the market-place (i.e., on the basis of what the recipient of the benefit would have received in the market). Moreover, the SCM Agreement's operative provisions only apply to subsidies that are "specific" to a certain enterprise or industry or to a group of enterprises or industries, because it is assumed that non-specific subsidies will not distort the allocation of resources within the economy.

The Agreement makes a distinction between two categories of subsidies: (i) prohibited subsidies (i.e., subsidies contingent upon the export or use of domestic rather than imported products); and (ii) actionable subsidies (i.e. subsidies that cause adverse effects to the interests of other WTO members). Subsidies in the second category are open to challenge by other members only if they are believed to cause adverse effects. In either case, the complaining member may challenge the subsidizing member's subsidies in the dispute settlement.

Three types of adverse effect are identified in the Agreement: "injury" to the domestic industry of another WTO member; nullification or impairment of benefits accruing under GATT 1994; and "serious prejudice" to the interests of another member, as defined in the SCM Agreement. These adverse effects generally occur when a subsidy has a negative impact on the access to the subsidizing member's market or to a third country's market, or affects domestic producers in the home market of the complaining member.

In addition to challenging subsidies through WTO dispute settlement, a member may impose countervailing measures on imported products in order to offset the benefits of specific subsidies that have been granted upon the manufacture, production or export of those goods. However, a WTO member may not impose a countervailing measure unless three specific conditions are met: (i) it must determine that there are subsidized imports; (ii) it must establish that there is injury to the domestic industry; and (iii) it must show that there is a causal link between the subsidized imports and the injury. The SCM Agreement also includes rules on procedures for initiating and conducting investigations, and rules on the implementation and duration (normally five years) of countervailing measures.

Finally, the Agreement on Trade-Related Aspects of Intellectual Property Rights (TRIPS Agreement) may be relevant to the development and diffusion of climate friendly technologies. The essential objective of the grant and enforcement of intellectual property rights, as set out in the TRIPS Agreement, is to both promote necessary innovation and facilitate the diffusion of technology, balancing legitimate interests in a socially beneficial manner. Intellectual property protection should "contribute to the promotion of technological innovation and to the transfer and dissemination of technology, to the mutual advantage of producers and users of technological knowledge and in a manner conducive to social and economic welfare, and to a balance of rights and obligations."

While the TRIPS Agreement sets out general standards for the protection of intellectual property under national laws, achieving this "balance" in practice is a matter for domestic policymakers and legislators to establish, through an appropriate mix of law, regulation and administrative measures within the policy space defined by the TRIPS Agreement, including through the use of flexibilities in the application of TRIPS standards. Specifically concerning the promotion of climate-friendly innovation and the diffusion of climate friendly technology, patent-related measures that have been raised in policy discussions include promoting technology sharing and patent pooling, technology brokering and clearing house initiatives, more effective use of patent information tools to locate useful technologies, and the facilitation of patent examination of green technologies, as well as limitations or exceptions to patent rights such as research exceptions and specific regulatory interventions such as non-voluntary licensing, government use authorizations and disciplines or guidelines on patent licensing to promote competition. Beyond patent law, other areas of TRIPS standards are relevant to the protection of marks certifying environmentally friendly products and suppressing acts of unfair competition such as making misleading representations about the positive environmental qualities of products (so-called "greenwashing").

CANADA — CERTAIN MEASURES AFFECTING RENEWABLE ENERGY GENERATION SECTOR/CANADA — MEASURES RELATING TO THE FEED-IN TARIFF PROGRAM REPORT OF THE PANEL
WT/DS412/R, WT/DS426/R (Dec. 19, 2012)

[These cases concerned the electricity generating system of the province of Ontario, Canada and the Ontario Power Authority (OPA), the government agency that oversees this system. The Ontario electrical system is a complex hybrid whereby both public and private entities participate in the generation, transmission, distribution and retail selling of electricity. The price of electricity in Ontario is closely regulated by OPA through the Independent Electricity System Operator (IESO), a non-profit company whose Board of Directors is appointed by the Ontario government. IESO connects all participants — all generators, transmitters, distributors, industries and businesses that buy and use electricity, and local distribution companies that sell electricity to private homes. IESO monitors the system and every five minutes forecasts electricity supply and demand. IESO then collects best offers for the generation of the electricity needed, thus assuring the best price, the Market Clearing Price (MCP). Thus, prices for electricity vary greatly over time, and the price at the wholesale level — known as the HOEP (Hourly Ontario Energy Price) varies based on the costs of generation. The MCP/HOEP is an unconstrained price, and, to align economic incentives of certain generators who are required at times to dispatch electricity uneconomically because of transmission constraints, certain generators are paid Congestion Management Settlement Credits. In addition, certain generators that have contracted prices receive what are called Global Adjustments (GAs) to reconcile differences with their regulated prices. Retail electricity prices are calculated depending on all these arrangements with an additional charge to cover the cost of delivering electricity to the consumer. The Ontario electrical generating system accommodates renewable energy generators — wind, photovoltaic solar (PV), renewable biomass, biogas, landfill gas, and waterpower — through special feed-in tariffs (FITs), guaranteed prices per kWh of electricity delivered into the Ontario electricity system under 20 or 40-year contracts with OPA. The FIT Programme comprises two types of electricity streams: the FIT stream for generators with a capacity to produce more than 10 kW and the micro-FIT stream for generators with the capacity to produce less than 10 kW (small household, farm or business generators). Upon entering into a FIT or microFIT contract, the qualifying entity is required to build and maintain renewable generating facilities according to the standards set by OPA. In the development and construction of such FIT and micro FIT projects, owners are required to satisfy a Minimum Domestic Content Level — their facilities must be composed of required levels of Canadian-purchased goods and services.

Japan and the European Union complained against Canada at the WTO that these arrangements violated Canada's obligations under the GATT and the WTO's Trade-Related Investment Agreement (TRIMS), and the WTO's Subsidies and Countervailing Measures (SCM) Agreement. The United States and many other countries joined these disputes as third parties.

The WTO panel ruled that Canada's domestic content requirements were trade-related investment measures (TRIMS) falling within the scope of Article 2.1 of the TRIMS Agreement, which prohibits certain TRIMS contained in an Illustrative List annexed to Article 2.2 of the TRIMS Agreement. Paragraph l(a) of this Illustrative List of prohibited TRIMS reads as follows:

"TRIMS that are inconsistent with the obligation of national treatment provided for in paragraph 4 of Article III of the GATT 1994 include those which are mandatory or enforceable under domestic law or under administrative rulings, or compliance with which is necessary to obtain an advantage, and which require: (a) the purchase or use by an enterprise of products of domestic origin or from any domestic source, whether specified in terms of particular products, in terms of volume, or value of products, or in terms of proportion of volume or value of its local production."

The WTO panel rejected Canada's defense based upon GATT Article III:8, which exempts from national treatment "laws, regulations or requirements governing the procurement by government agencies of products purchased for governmental purposes and not with a view to commercial resale." The WTO panel found that this exemption did not apply because the electricity purchased under the FIT Programme is commercial and for resale. (para. 7.151).

The WTO panel thus ruled that Canada's FIT Programme was inconsistent with GATT Article III:4 and Article 2.1 of the TRIMS Agreement as informed by the TRIMS Illustrative List under Article 2.2 of the TRIMS Agreement.

The panel also considered whether Canada's FIT Programme was inconsistent with the WTO SCM Agreement. To decide this question, the panel had to decide if the FIT Programme involved a subsidy as defined in the SCM Agreement. Under Article I of the SCM Agreement a subsidy has three elements: (a) a financial contribution; (2) the contribution was made by a government or a public body within the territory of a WTO member; and (3) the contribution confers a benefit.

The panel found that the FIT Programme involved a financial contribution by a public body because financial contribution is defined as "government purchases [of] goods." However, the panel split on the issue of whether the financial contribution conferred a benefit. Two panel members ruled that the FIT Programme did not confer a benefit within the meaning of the SCM Agreement, Article 1.1(b). A dissenting member found the conferring of a benefit under this Article.

The majority of the panel thus rejected claims that the FIT Programme was inconsistent with SCM Agreement Articles 3.1(b) and 3.2, as a prohibited subsidy.

We reproduce the portion of the panel's opinion and the dissent concerning the benefit issue].

Whether the challenged measures confer a "benefit" within the meaning of Article 1.1(b) of the SCM Agreement

The legal standard for determining the existence of "benefit"

7.271 A financial contribution will confer a benefit upon a recipient within the meaning of Article l.l(b) of the SCM Agreement when it provides an advantage to its recipient. It is well established that the existence of any such advantage is to be determined by comparing the position of the recipient with and without the financial contribution, and that "the marketplace provides an appropriate basis for [making this] comparison." Article 14(d) of the SCM Agreement establishes guidelines for calculating the amount of subsidy in terms of benefit when there has been a government purchase of goods for the purpose of countervailing duty investigations. Although not intended to define the circumstances when a government purchase of goods will confer a benefit in disputes involving Part III of the SCM Agreement, Article 14(d) provides useful context for the analysis that is required in the present disputes. Article 14(d) reads as follows:

> [T]he provision of goods or services or purchase of goods by a government shall not be considered as conferring a benefit unless the provision is made for less than adequate remuneration, or the purchase is made for more than adequate remuneration. The adequacy of remuneration shall be determined in relation to prevailing market conditions for the good or service in question in the country of provision or purchase (including price, quality, availability, marketability, transportation and other conditions of purchase or sale).

7.272 On its face, Article 14(d) stipulates that a government purchase of goods will not confer a benefit upon a recipient unless it is made for "more than adequate remuneration," and that the adequacy of this remuneration must be evaluated in relation to the "prevailing market conditions" for the good in question in the country of purchase, including "price, quality, availability, marketability, transportation and other conditions of purchase or sale." Thus, in the context of the present disputes, Article 14(d) suggests that one way to demonstrate that the challenged measures confer a benefit is by showing that the remuneration provided to FIT generators using windpower and solar PV technology to produce the electricity purchased by the OPA is "more than adequate" compared with the remuneration the same generators would receive on the "market" for electricity in Ontario, in the light of the "prevailing market conditions." As we see it, the starting point for this analysis is the identification of the relevant "market."

7.273 In *U.S.-Upland Cotton*, the Appellate Body defined a "market" as "the area of economic activity in which buyers and sellers come together and the forces of supply and demand affect prices." Similarly, in *EC and certain member States —— Large Civil Aircraft*, the Appellate Body clarified that the "marketplace to which the Appellate Body referred in *Canada-Aircraft* reflects a sphere in which goods and services are exchanged between willing buyers and sellers." Moreover, the Appellate Body has explained that:

> The terms of a financial transaction must be assessed against the terms that would result from unconstrained exchange in the relevant market. The

relevant market may be more or less developed; it may be made up of many or few participants. . . . In some instances, the market may be more rudimentary. In other instances, it may be difficult to establish the relevant market and its results. But these informational constraints do not alter the basic framework from which the analysis should proceed. . . . There is but one standard — the market standard . . .

7.274 In the specific context of Article 14(d), however, the relevant "marketplace" need not be one that is "undistorted by government intervention" or that excludes "situations in which there is government involvement." The relevant "market" need not be a "pure" marketplace that is devoid of any degree of government intervention. Nevertheless, in previous disputes involving a government provision of goods, it has been held that where a "government's role in providing a financial contribution is so predominant that it effectively determines the price at which private suppliers will sell the same or similar goods, . . . the comparison contemplated by Article 14 would become circulars. In other words, where a government's involvement as a provider of a particular good in a given market is such that "there is no way of telling whether the recipient is 'better off' absent the financial contribution", the market that is the object of the government intervention cannot serve as an appropriate benchmark for the purpose of Article 14(d). We see no reason why the same considerations should not also apply to situations involving government purchases of goods.

7.275 Thus, as we understand the relevant jurisprudence, the "market" against which to evaluate whether a financial contribution in the form of a government purchase of goods confers a benefit need not be one that is necessarily "perfectly competitive" in the sense of economic theory. However, it must nevertheless be a market where there is effective competition, in the sense that prices for the purchased good must be established through the operation of unconstrained forces of supply and demand, and not by means of government intervention of a kind that renders "the comparison contemplated by Article 14 . . . circular." With this legal standard in mind, we turn to evaluate the merits of the parties' arguments.

The wholesale market for electricity as the relevant focus of the benefit analysis

7.276 Fundamentally, the complainants' first and main line of benefit argument is that in the absence of the FIT Programme, a competitive wholesale market for electricity in Ontario could not support commercially viable operations of the contested FIT generators because the terms and conditions, including price, that would be attached to private purchases of electricity in such a market would expose them to significantly lower revenues and higher commercial risks compared with the terms and conditions associated with participation in the FIT Programme. To substantiate this argument, the complainants advance a number of proposed competitive wholesale market electricity price benchmarks, or proxies for this benchmark, that they submit demonstrate that the FIT Programme provides "more than adequate remuneration" for the OPA's purchases of electricity under the FIT and microFIT Contracts. The complainants also focus on the long-term (20-year) guaranteed pricing that is available under the FIT Programme, arguing that no such condition would be available from a private purchaser of electricity on the relevant market. Moreover, the complainants' note that one of the key uncontested objectives of the FIT Programme is to induce new investment in renewable energy generation facilities, arguing that this alone demonstrates that relevant FIT generators would not be operating in the Ontario wholesale electricity market in the absence' of the FIT Programme.

7.277 Canada accepts that "most" of the contested FIT generators would be unable to conduct viable operations in a competitive wholesale market for electricity in Ontario. Indeed, Canada points out that one of the objectives of the FIT Programme was to encourage the construction of new renewable energy generation facilities that would not have otherwise existed. However, Canada rejects the view that this demonstrates that the OPA's purchases of electricity under the FIT Programme confer a benefit within the meaning of Article 1.1(b) of the SCM Agreement. Canada explains that the OPA's purchases of electricity, including from renewable energy generators under the FIT Programme, have been motivated by the inability of Ontario's wholesale electricity market to encourage the investment in new electricity generation facilities needed to secure a reliable and clean supply of electricity that is sufficient to meet Ontario's long-term requirements (i.e. the "missing money" problem). Canada emphasizes that given the different costs associated with the different technologies that must operate to achieve this objective, the most appropriate benchmark for the Panel's benefit analysis in relation to the FIT and microFIT Contracts must reflect what it considers to be the fundamental condition for the Government of Ontario's purchases of electricity under the FIT Programme, namely, that the electricity be produced from renewable energy sources. Thus, Canada submits that the relevant "market" comparator must be the market for electricity produced from wind and solar PV generation technologies.

7.278 The different positions held by the complainants and Canada about what should be the appropriate "market" benchmark raise a number of important questions related to the nature of competitive wholesale electricity markets and the suitability of using one or more alleged examples of such markets to determine the existence of benefit in the present disputes. It is to these questions that we now turn, starting first with the "missing money" problem.

The economics of electricity markets and the "missing money" problem

7.279 As we have previously explained electricity has some specific properties compared to other types of goods. It is intangible and, with some limited exceptions, cannot be effectively stored. It is also delivered to consumers through networks of transmission and distribution lines that can fail if the quantity demanded (known as load) is greater or less than the quantity supplied for any length of time. These properties imply that electricity must be produced at the time that it is consumed, and that the flow of electricity through a transmission grid cannot be left to the choices of individual market participants, but rather it must be centrally coordinated and controlled. Consumers, and therefore governments, regard electricity as an essential commodity because a safe, reliable and long-term supply is necessary for the smooth functioning of all modem economies. The fact that there are no close substitutes for electricity, combined with a lack of easily observable price signals on the demand side, implies that electricity demand is largely unresponsive to prices in the short run (i.e. it is relatively inelastic).

7.280 It is generally accepted that a diverse mix of generation technology is desirable on the supply side in the interest of securing a reliable and clean electricity system. Indeed, as we have explained elsewhere, the use of a range of generation technologies is a technical, economic and environmental imperative. The "conventional" technologies can be separated into base-load generation (characterized by high fixed and low marginal costs, e.g. nuclear power), intermediate generation (moderate fixed and marginal costs, e.g. oil or gas-fired steam), and peak-load generation (low fixed costs and high marginal costs, e.g. single cycle gas combustion turbines). Base-load generators are designed to operate almost always, supplying electricity to satisfy core and sustained levels of demand in most hours of the day and, importantly, keep the grid "alive." Intermediate-load plants are used to supply electricity during periods when demand is above core minimum levels, but not at its peak. These generators typically operate during the day and evening. Peak-load generators satisfy demand when it is very high, such as during the hottest days of summer, and some may operate for only a few hours per day. The ability of generators to adjust their level of output quickly, known as *dispatch ability*, tends to be lowest for base-load generators and highest for peak-load generators. Although hydroelectricity is usually classified as base load power, certain types of hydroelectric facilities can be dispatched. Electricity generation by means of solar PV and wind technology provides variable or intermittent generation, meaning that power is produced only during certain times of the day and/or night. Typically, both types of facilities have relatively high capital costs per MW of energy produced, but they have little or no variable cost. To replace part of the generating capacity that will be lost when Ontario's coal-fired plants will be decommissioned at the end of 2014, Ontario's supply mix has expanded to include renewable technologies like wind and solar PV. It is expected that these technologies will account for 11.5% of Ontario's generating capacity by 2030.

7.283 In the absence of demand that is more responsive (but not only for this reason), governments and regulators have sought to control potential/actual price volatility by intervening in the market because of the value of stable electricity prices to their economies, with the consequence that many countries have experienced insufficient investment in generation because the price achieved on their "organized" wholesale market is not allowed to rise to a level that, in the long-run, fully compensates generators for the all-in cost of their investments (including fixed and sunk costs). Private investors will not be willing to finance construction of new generation under such conditions; and in the absence of such investment, an electricity market will be unable to reliably meet future electricity demand. This is referred to as the "missing money" problem, and it affects not only more expensive solar PV and wind generation technologies, but also "conventional generating technologies, where energy-only markets do not support investment." To resolve this dilemma, "alternative mechanisms to wholesale spot markets have been required to provide incentives for long-term investment to meet forecasted demand," including power purchase agreements (as in Ontario) and "capacity" payments.

7.284 Thus, because of the specific features of electricity and the nature of competitive wholesale electricity markets, government intervention will often be necessary in order to secure an electricity supply that is safe, reliable and sustainable in the long-term.

7.308 We recall that Article 14(d) of the SCM Agreement provides useful guidance for determining whether "financial contribution[s]" in the form of "government purchases [of] goods" confer a benefit for the purpose of claims made under Part III of the SCM Agreement. According to this guidance, one way the challenged measures may be found to confer a benefit is by demonstrating that the remuneration obtained by FIT generators operating on the basis of windpower and solar PV technology under the FIT Programme is "more than adequate" compared with the remuneration the same generators would receive on the relevant "market" for electricity in Ontario, in the light of the "prevailing market conditions." Throughout these proceedings, the complainants' principal argument has been that the benchmark for "adequate remuneration" should be found in the allegedly competitive wholesale electricity market that exists in Ontario or four out-of-Province jurisdictions. However, for the reasons we have explained above, the evidence before us indicates that the wholesale electricity market that currently exists in Ontario is not a market where there is effective competition. Rather, Ontario's wholesale electricity market is perhaps better characterized as a part of an electricity system that is defined in almost all aspects by the Government of Ontario's policy decisions and regulations pertaining to the supply mix needed to ensure that Ontario has a safe, reliable and long-term sustainable supply of electricity, as well as how the costs of that system will be recuperated. We have little doubt that the HOEP results from the operation of forces of supply and demand that are significantly affected by government intervention in a way that renders it an inappropriate benchmark to conduct the present benefit analysis. In the light of the benefit standard that has thus far been applied in WTO disputes, we find that the HOEP and all of the HOEP-derivatives that the complainants have advanced, cannot serve as appropriate benchmarks for the purpose of the benefit analysis.

7.309 Importantly, the complainants have not convinced us of the premise underlying their two main lines of benefit arguments, namely, that in the absence of the FIT Programme, the FIT generators would be faced with having to operate in a competitive wholesale electricity market. The evidence before us indicates that competitive wholesale electricity markets, although a theoretical possibility, will only rarely operate in a way that remunerates the mix of generators needed to secure a *reliable* electricity system with enough revenue to cover their all-in costs, let alone a system that pursues *human health and environmental* objectives through the inclusion of facilities using solar PV and wind technologies into the supply-mix. In the specific context of Ontario, the 2002 market opening experience illustrates this point. Although intended to operate as a "classical" competitive market where generators would sell electricity at spot prices equal to marginal costs, the conditions of supply and demand that existed at that time made it impossible for the market to attract the investment in generation capacity needed to secure a reliable system of electricity supply. By saying that it was because "the established market structure did not Invite the sufficient entry of new generators . . . [that] the Government of Ontario enacted the Electricity Restructuring Act, 2004, amending the Electricity Act, 1998," Japan appears to recognize the limits of the competitive market experience in Ontario.

7.310 The complainants have referred to examples of what they consider to be competitive wholesale markets existing outside of Ontario. However, as we have explained, the evidence before us suggests that because of, at least in part, the particular conditions of supply and demand that were forecast in 2003 for Ontario up to 2020, the ECSTF found that the Alberta experience could not be reproduced in Ontario with the same degree of success. Given the significant volume of generating capacity (around 43%) that it is projected will need to be renewed, replaced or added to Ontario's electricity system by 2030, and in the light of the limitations that are inherent to competitive wholesale electricity markets, the complainants' benefit arguments fail to convince us that the recommendations of the ECSTF do not also hold true today. With respect to the three examples of allegedly competitive wholesale markets in the United States, it appears from the Hogan Report that these markets do not, in fact, provide participating generators with *all* of the revenues they need to be present on the market. As Professor Hogan explains, the New York, PJM and New England electricity systems have developed "parallel capacity markets and [require] ratepayers to pay additional capacity charges for their share of required levels of capacity, to meet resource adequacy requirements and provide the additional compensation to generators." It follows that the allegedly competitive New York, PJM and New England wholesale electricity markets do not represent examples of competitive wholesale markets that are capable, *on their own*, of attracting sufficient investment in generation capacity to secure a reliable system of electricity supply.

7.311 We note that all parties to these proceedings agree that FIT generators using solar PV and windpower technology would be unable to conduct viable operations on the basis of the equilibrium prices that could be achieved in a competitive wholesale electricity market. However, Canada has also suggested that there would be unacceptable risks to the *reliability* of Ontario's electricity system if the structure of Ontario's supply-mix were left to be settled by competitive forces of supply and demand. We tend to agree. Given the technical complexities of electricity systems, the inherent limitations of competitive wholesale electricity markets, and recalling, in particular, Ontario's failed 2002 market-opening experience, as well as the current and projected conditions of supply and demand in Ontario, we are not convinced that a *reliable* supply of electricity could be secured at present in Ontario solely through the operation of a competitive wholesale electricity market.

7.312 In our view, the application of a competitive wholesale market standard in the circumstances of the present disputes would not only insufficiently respond to the considerable challenges faced by electricity systems that are caused by the specific properties of electricity, but it would also overlook the particular situation in Ontario. Importantly, it would ignore the evidence indicating that the prevailing conditions of supply and demand in Ontario suggest that a competitive wholesale electricity market would fail to attract the degree of investment in generating capacity needed to secure a reliable supply of electricity, and that, at present, this goal can only be achieved by means of government intervention in what would otherwise be unacceptable competitive market outcomes. In these circumstances, and given the critical importance of electricity to all facets of modem life, we cannot accept that it would be appropriate to determine whether the FIT Programme and the FIT and micro FIT Contracts confer a benefit within the meaning of Article 1.1

(b) of the SCM Agreement by comparing the terms and conditions of participation in the FIT Programme with those that would be available to generators participating in a wholesale electricity market where there is effective competition.

7.313 Thus, for all of the foregoing reasons, we conclude that:

(a)   the HOEP is a price set through the interaction of supply and demand forces that in many critical aspects are significantly influenced by the supply-mix and pricing policy decisions and regulations of the Government of Ontario, and therefore, the HOEP and all of the related HOEP-derivatives the complainants have submitted as appropriate benchmarks for the purpose of the benefit analysis cannot be accepted;

(b)   the complainants have failed to convince us that, in the absence of the FIT Programme, the FIT generators would be faced with having to operate in a competitive wholesale electricity market because: (i) the economics of competitive wholesale electricity markets suggest that they will only rarely attract the degree of investment in the generation capacity needed to secure a reliable electricity system; and (ii) the weight of the evidence before us indicates that, at present, a competitive wholesale electricity market would fail to achieve this outcome in Ontario; and

(c)   in the light of our conclusions in (a) and (b), and given the critical importance of electricity to all facets of modem life, we find that the question whether the challenged measures confer a benefit within the meaning of Article 1.1(b) of the SCM Agreement cannot be resolved by applying a benchmark that is derived from the conditions for purchasing electricity in a competitive wholesale electricity market.

Final conclusions and observations on the existence of benefit

7.320 We have carefully reviewed the parties' legal and factual arguments in the light of the legal standard for determining the existence of benefit that has to date been applied in WTO dispute settlement. In the particular circumstances of these disputes, we have concluded that determining whether the challenged measures confer a benefit on the basis of a benchmark derived from a *competitive* wholesale electricity market, would mean that the FIT and microFIT Contracts could be legally characterized as subsidies by means of a comparison with a market standard that has not been demonstrated to actually exist nor one that could be reasonably achieved in Ontario — a market standard that the complainants have not contested will only rarely, if at all, attract sufficient investment in generation capacity to secure a reliable system of electricity supply even outside of Ontario. In our view, such an outcome would fail to reflect the reality of modem electricity systems, which by their very nature need to draw electricity from a range of diverse generation technologies that play different roles and have different costs of production and environmental impacts. As we have emphasized on a number of occasions, it is only in exceptional circumstances that the generation capacity needed from all such technologies will be attracted into a wholesale market operating under the conditions of effective competition. Thus, the competitive wholesale electricity market that is at the centre of the complainants' main submissions cannot be the appropriate focus of the benefit analysis in these disputes. Furthermore, for the reasons we have outlined above, the alternatives to the wholesale electricity market that have been presented to us also cannot stand as appropriate benchmarks against which to measure whether the challenged measures confer a benefit. There is therefore no basis to uphold the complainants' benefit arguments.

DISSENTING OPINION OF ONE MEMBER OF THE PANEL WITH RESPECT TO WHETHER THE CHALLENGED MEASURES CONFER A BENEFIT WITHIN THE MEANING OF ARTICLE 1.1(B) OF THE SCM AGREEMENT

A. INTRODUCTION

9.1 The Panel majority has undertaken a long and careful evaluation of the parties' arguments concerning the question whether the challenged measures confer a benefit, ultimately concluding that the complainants have failed to establish the existence of subsidization. While I agree with parts of the Panel majority's benefit analysis, I respectfully disagree with certain key aspects of its reasoning and ultimate findings. In essence, the Panel majority has found that the circumstances of ensuring a reliable supply of electricity that achieves certain objectives sought by the Government of Ontario justifies the rejection of the competitive wholesale electricity market as the relevant focus of the benefit analysis. The Panel majority has furthermore suggested that, in these circumstances, the existence of benefit could be determined by focusing upon the rate of return associated with the FIT and microFIT Contracts and comparing this with the average cost of capital in Canada for projects having a comparable risk profile.

9.2 I respectfully disagree with these findings and the alternative benefit test. The wholesale electricity market that currently exists in Ontario is recognizable as a market for the buying and selling of electricity. It is undeniable that the supply of electricity, its price and competition between electricity generators — in particular, market entry — are very heavily regulated and conditioned in the market by the Government of Ontario. The wholesale electricity market that currently exists in Ontario is therefore not the kind of market where price is determined by the unconstrained forces of supply and demand. The regulatory impacts on the market are not simply in the nature of framework regulation, within which those forces may operate. The Government of Ontario (through Hydro One) and the municipal governments (through Local Distribution Companies) account for almost all purchases of electricity made at the wholesale level. The same product, which in this case is electricity, is purchased by these entities at different prices depending upon its method of generation or particular status in the Government of Ontario's electricity supply policy, including under the FIT Programme. In these circumstances the complainants have expressed their concern that an advantage is being given to the market participants that are receiving the highest prices for the electricity they produce, namely generators using solar PV and windpower technologies operating under the FIT Programme. The Panel's task is to test that concern according to the disciplines of the SCM Agreement.

9.3 The relevant question that a Panel in a case such as this must address is whether a benefit is conferred on the recipient of the financial contribution. The wholesale electricity market in Ontario does not allow for the discovery of a single market-clearing price established through the unconstrained forces of supply and demand. In that market the Government of Ontario and the municipal governments are the chief buyers of the goods concerned. In these circumstances the Panel must consider whether there is some appropriate frame of reference for determining if a benefit is conferred in the provision of that financial contribution. In my view, the competitive wholesale market for electricity that *could* exist in Ontario is the appropriate focus of the benefit analysis. Furthermore, I am of the view that facilitating the entry of certain technologies into the market that does exist — such as it is — by way of a financial contribution can itself be considered to confer a benefit. In the light of these considerations, it follows from the arguments and evidence presented by the complainants, as well as Canada's own statements, that the challenged measures confer a benefit, within the meaning of Article 1.1 (b) of the SCM Agreement.

B. The Competitive Wholesale Electricity Market is the Relevant Focus of the Benefit Analysis

9.4 As the Panel majority explained, a financial contribution will confer a benefit within the meaning of Article 1.1 (b) of the SCM Agreement when it confers an advantage upon its recipient. It is well established that the existence of any such advantage is to be determined by comparing the position of the recipient with and without the financial contribution, and that "the marketplace provides an appropriate basis for [making this] comparison. Having found that the challenged measures amount to "financial contribution[s]" in the form of "government purchases [of] goods," it follows that the relevant "marketplace" must be the competitive market where electricity is purchased at the same level of trade as the government purchases that are challenged in the present disputes, namely, the wholesale level of trade.

9.5 The Panel majority concluded that the wholesale electricity market currently operating in Ontario cannot be used for the purpose of conducting the benefit analysis. In addition; the Panel majority found that the competitive wholesale electricity market that could, in theory, exist in Ontario could also not be used as a basis for the benefit analysis because, in the light of the prevailing conditions of supply and demand, such a market would fail to attract the generation capacity needed to secure a reliable supply of electricity for the people of Ontario. In my view, however, the fact that a competitive market might not exist in the absence of government intervention or that it may not achieve all of the objectives that a government would like it to achieve, does not mean it cannot be used for the purpose of conducting a benefit analysis. Indeed, it is because competitive markets do not often work the way that governments would like them to that governments will decide to influence market outcomes by, for example, becoming a market participant, regulating market participants or providing them with incentives (or creating disincentives) to behave in a particular way. A government might also choose to intervene in competitive market outcomes by granting subsidies, as defined in Article 1.1 of the SCM Agreement. Provided that such subsidies are not prohibited under Article 3 of the SCM Agreement, a government will be entitled to maintain such measures, subject to the remedies available to other WTO Members under

Parts III and V of the SCM Agreement where either "adverse effects" or "material injury" is proven.

9.7 On the basis of the above considerations, I now turn to examine the merits of the two lines of argument the complainants have advanced in support of their allegations of subsidization.

C. Whether the Challenged Measures Provide for "More Than Adequate Remuneration" within the Meaning of Article 14(0) of the SCM Agreement

9.8 The first line of benefit argument advanced by the complainants follows the approach that is described in the guidelines for calculating the amount of subsidy in terms of benefit contained in Article 14(d) of the SCM Agreement. Although intended to guide benefit determinations for the purpose of countervailing duty investigations, previous disputes tell us that the approach adopted by the complainants may be one way of demonstrating the existence of benefit in the present proceedings. Thus, the complainants have advanced a series of different prices for electricity, which they submit represent the price that a distributor or trader would have to pay for electricity in Ontario's current wholesale electricity market, or are a proxy for that price. As the complainants note, each of the proposed benchmark prices is outwardly lower than the prices received by solar PV and windpower projects under the FIT Programme.

9.9 Before evaluating the merits of the complainants' arguments, it is important to recall that the guidelines in Article 14(d) of the SCM Agreement stipulate that the amount of benefit may be calculated by identifying the extent to which "more than adequate remuneration" has been paid for a purchased product "in relation to prevailing market conditions" in the country of purchase. In the present disputes, the complainants have not advanced country-specific price benchmarks, but rather benchmarks based on prices established in regional intra-national markets operating in Canada, and also the United States. The complainants appear to have done so because there are no national electricity wholesale markets in Canada. In other words, the "prevailing market conditions" in the country of purchase (Canada) are such that there are no country-wide electricity markets. In my view Article 14(d) does not suggest that the prevailing market conditions can only be those of a national market. Market conditions in a regional market of a country are, relevantly, market conditions "in the country of purchase." In this light, the complainants' approach is not inconsistent with the guidelines stipulated in Article 14(d) of the SCM Agreement.

9.10 Returning to the substance of the complainant's benefit submissions, the competitive nature of the IESO-administered wholesale electricity market in Ontario was closely examined by the Panel majority, which found that the equilibrium level of the HOEP that is set in this market is directly related to the electricity pricing policy and supply-mix decisions of the Government of Ontario. I agree with this finding, The Government of Ontario's intervention in the IESO-administered wholesale market price outcomes encompasses participation not only as a purchaser of electricity, but also a generator, transmitter, distributor and price-setter (for both generators and consumers). As a result, the price outcomes of the IESO-administered wholesale market (the HOEP) are significantly distorted by the actions and policies of the Government of Ontario. For this reason, the HOEP and all related derivatives advanced by the complainants cannot be used as appropriate market benchmarks for the purpose of performing a benefit analysis under the terms of Article 14(d) of the SCM Agreement. They do not represent a price established on a competitive wholesale electricity market in Ontario.

9.11 The complainants also present the prices for electricity paid in four allegedly competitive wholesale electricity markets outside of Ontario as proxies for the wholesale market price of electricity in Ontario, and argue that these prices demonstrate that the challenged measures confer a benefit. They are prices in Alberta, Canada (the "Alberta benchmark") and prices in New York, New England, and the PJM Interconnection (the "U.S. benchmarks").

[The dissenting panel member agreed with the majority that the four proxy markets advanced by complainants, although in theory able to be used as benchmarks, may not be used as benchmarks in this case because the complainants failed to make appropriate adjustments to the prices in these out-of-province markets that would allow the panel to use them as relevant markets: "in my view, the evidence is not in a sufficient state to enable the panel to conduct the benefit analysis under the terms of Article 14(d) of the SCM Agreement in the way the Appellate Body has insisted that it should be conducted."].

D. WHETHER THE CHALLENGED MEASURES ENABLE SOLAR PV AND WINDPOWER GEN-
ERATORS TO CONDUCT VIABLE OPERATIONS AND THEREBY PARTICIPATE IN THE WHOLESALE
ELECTRICITY MARKET

9.17 The second line of benefit argument advanced by the complainants is focused on the very nature and objectives of the FIT Programme. In particular, the complainants submit that the FIT Programme was created and operates for the purpose of allowing generators of electricity from renewable sources of energy, including solar and wind, to supply electricity into the Ontario electricity system because a competitive wholesale electricity market could not support such high cost producers. Thus, the complainants argue that in the absence of the FIT Pro-gramme, solar PV and windpower generators would be unable to support commer-cially viable operations in the wholesale electricity market in Ontario.

9.18 Canada accepts that in the absence of the FIT Programme, "most" of the contested FIT generators would be unable to conduct viable operations. Thus, Canada explains that:

> Like FIT programs in other parts of the world, the Ontario FIT Program was created to induce new renewable generation. As recognized by Japan, the Ontario 'FIT Program . . . became necessary to encourage the entry into the market of renewable energy generators, most of which would not have entered the market in the absence of the FIT Program.

9.19 Moreover, referring to Ontario's episodic market opening experience in 2002, Canada states that "the market alone would not be sufficient to encourage the construction of new generation facilities able to provide the long-term supply needed by Ontario residents," adding that [a]s recognized by Japan, the OPA was created because the market structure established immediately following the dissolution of Ontario Hydro in 1998 did not invite the sufficient entry of new generators, particularly generators using alternative and renewable energy sources. Thus, the OPA was established with a mandate to:

> [R]estructure Ontario's electricity sector, to promote the expansion of electricity supply and capacity including supply and capacity from alternative and renewable energy sources. . . .

9.20 That the FIT Programme was intended to bring about the entry of new generating capacity from renewable sources of energy that would otherwise not exist in the Ontario wholesale electricity market can also be understood from the objectives of the FIT Programme described in the Ministerial Direction, which include to "[i]ncrease capacity of renewable energy supply to ensure adequate generation and reduce emissions," to "[p]rovide incentives for investment in renewable energy technologies" and "[e]nable new green industries through new investment and job creation." Similarly, the FIT Rules explain that the "fundamental objective of the FIT Program, in conjunction with the Green Energy and Green Economy Act of 2009 is to facilitate the increased development of Renewable Generating Facilities of varying sizes, technologies and configurations. . . ."

9.21 Professor Hogan confirms that renewable energy technologies are typically too expensive to be supported by the spot prices achieved on wholesale electricity markets.

9.22 According to Professor Hogan, the major costs differences between solar and windpower generating facilities compared with more "conventional" technologies exist for the following reasons:

> The relatively small scale of wind and solar facilities leads to few if any economies of scale in generation in comparison with large nuclear, coal, hydro and gas plants.

> Wind and solar facilities have relatively low capacity factors, due to their dependence on the wind and the sun, meaning that the generating facilities produce electricity for a much smaller proportion of the hours of the year or day than conventional generating technologies.

> The relatively small base of experience in operating wind and solar generating facilities means that there are fewer efficiencies in operating new facilities.

> The lack of experience in constructing wind and solar generating facilities, leading to relatively fewer efficiencies in constructing new facilities.

9.23 Thus, by contracting to purchase electricity produced from solar PV and windpower technologies under the FIT Programme at a price intended to provide for a reasonable return on the investment associated with a "typical" project, the Government of Ontario ensures that qualifying generators are remunerated at a level that allows them to recoup the entirety of their "very high" capital costs. As the complainants argue and Canada accepts, such levels of remuneration would never be achieved through the unconstrained forces of supply and demand in a competitive wholesale electricity market in Ontario. Nor could they be achieved within the constrained forces of supply and demand which actually do operate within the wholesale electricity market in Ontario, without an intervention which remunerates the facilities which generate power from solar PV and windpower technologies at a higher rate than is paid in respect of electricity generated by the other technologies. It follows that by bringing these high cost and less efficient electricity producers into the wholesale electricity market, when they would otherwise not be present, the Government of Ontario's purchases of electricity from solar PV and windpower generators under the FIT Programme clearly confer a benefit upon the relevant FIT generators, within the meaning of Article 1.1(b) of the SCM Agreement.

NOTES AND QUESTIONS

1. The Appellate Body of the WTO modified somewhat the Panel's decision in the *Canada-Renewable Energy* case. *Canada — Certain Measures Affecting the Renewable Energy Generation Sector/Canada — Measures Relating to the Feed-In Tariff Program, WT/DS412/AB/R, WT/DS426/AB/R, adopted 24 May 2013*. With respect to the issue of the relationship between GATT Article 111:8(a) and the TRIMS Agreement, the Appellate Body agreed with the Panel's conclusion that the challenged measures were inconsistent with GATT Article III:4 and the TRIMS Agreement and not covered by the derogation of GATT Article III:8(a). But the Appellate Body pointed out that, while the discriminatory domestic content regulations at issue apply to the purchase of generation equipment, the governmental purchases in question are purchases of electricity not generating equipment. Thus, since the purchases of generating equipment are made not by government but by the generating companies, Article III:8(a) does not apply. Unlike the Panel, the Appellate Body refused to conflate the purchases of generating equipment and electricity, since these "two products are not in a competitive relationship." (para. 5.78). For this separate reason the Appellate Body came to the same conclusion as the Panel — that the domestic content regulations were not within the ambit of GATT Article III:8(a).

On the subsidy issue, the Appellate Body agreed with the Panel that the measures at issue (the FIT program and related measures) constitute government purchases of goods within the meaning of SCM Agreement Article 1.1(a)(1)(iii). (para. 5.128). As to the "benefit" issue under SCM Agreement Article 1.1(b), the Appellate Body agreed with the Panel that the determination of benefit depends upon analysis of whether the recipient has received a financial contribution on terms more favorable than those available under market conditions. (para. 5.162–166). But the Appellate Body disagreed with the Panel with regard to its analysis of the relevant market for the purpose of making the benefit comparison. While the Panel found the relevant market to be electricity generated from all sources of energy, the Appellate Body determined the relevant market to be electricity generated from solar and windpower only. (para. 5.219). Thus, the prices for solar and windpower under the measure in question must be compared to market prices for solar and windpower to determine if there is a "benefit." The Appellate Body then turned to the question whether it could complete the analysis on the basis of the facts in the record to see if there is a "benefit." The Appellate Body concluded that the record lacked sufficient facts to make the required comparison. Thus the Appellate Body could not determine if the purchases confer a benefit within the meaning of SCM Agreement Article 1.1(b) and whether they constitute prohibited subsidies inconsistent with SCM Agreement Articles 3.1(b) and 3.2. (para. 5.246).

2.   Ordinarily, even if the elements of an "actionable" subsidy under the SCM Agreement are fulfilled, in order to prevail, a complainant must also prove that there are "adverse effects" under Article 5 of the SCM Agreement. In order to show "adverse effects" the complainant must show the subsidy is having a negative effect on the sale of foreign goods or services in Ontario or adversely affects access of foreign competitors to third country markets. In this case, however, since the subsidy was coupled with domestic content requirements, the subsidy is per se prohibited under Articles 3.1(b) and 3.2 of the SCM Agreement. Since the Appellate Body could not complete the analysis, however, the FIT program — minus the domestic content requirements — survived the WTO challenge.

3.   *Subsidies/or renewable energy.* The Canadian FIT program is an example of many actions taken by WTO members to assist the development of renewable energy. Since wind, solar, and other renewable energy sources are more expensive than fossil fuel sources of energy, government assistance is often required to bring renewable sources on line. The *Canada-Renewable Energy* case shows that renewable energy subsidies may be challenged under WTO law. Should there be an exception to permit such subsidies?

4.   *Energy subsidies around the world.* Fossil fuel as well as "green" energy enjoys subsidies in many countries. According to the International Energy Agency, global fossil fuel subsidies total $523 billion per year. Twelve nations account for a majority of the world's fossil fuel subsidies: Iran — $82 billion per year; Saudi Arabia — $61 billion per year; Russia, India and China — between $30 and $40 billion per year; and Venezuela, Egypt, Iraq, U.A.E., Indonesia, Mexico, and Algeria — $5–$15 billion per year. By comparison global renewable energy subsides total $88 billion per year. But renewables receive about three times as much money per energy unit generated compared to fossil fuels. In the United States, according to the U.S. Energy Information Administration, fossil fuel subsidies amount to $4 billion per year. These include $240 million for investment in Clean Coal Facilities, a tax deferral worth $980 million called "excess of percentage over cost depletion"; and an expense deduction on amortization of pollution control equipment. Renewable sources receive about $14 billion, mainly in the form of tax credits. Bjorn Lomborg, *Green Energy is the Real Subsidy Hog*, THE WALL ST. J., 12 Nov. 2013, at A15.

C.   Technical Requirements to Promote the Use of Climate Friendly Products and Green Technology

As an essential part of climate change adaptation and mitigation efforts, governments may develop and implement technical regulations — which may be either mandatory or voluntary — for products and production methods so as to bring about emission reductions and gains in energy efficiency. Such technical requirements are normally fashioned and implemented at the national level.

TRADE AND CLIMATE CHANGE: A REPORT BY THE UNITED NATIONS ENVIRONMENTAL PROGRAMME AND THE WORLD TRADE ORGANIZATION
124–128

Climate change related technical requirements may take the form of maximum levels of emissions or of energy consumption or they may specify standards for energy efficiency for both products and production methods. Such requirements are accompanied by implementation and enforcement measures, such as labelling requirements and procedures to assess conformity.

Technical requirements to promote energy efficiency, such as labelling to indicate the energy efficiency of a product, have been adopted at the national level by most developed countries, and by a growing number of developing countries. It is estimated that energy efficiency improvements have resulted in reductions in energy consumption of more than 50 per cent over the last 30 years. A number of studies show that regulations and standards in OECD countries have the potential to increase the energy efficiency of specific products, particularly electrical equipment, such as household appliances. However, a significant energy-efficiency potential remains untapped in various sectors, such as buildings, transport and industry.

Standards that aim at enhancing energy efficiency have also been developed internationally. Such international standards are often used as a basis for regulations at the national level. Currently, examples of areas where international standards may assist in the application of climate-related regulations include standards on measurement and methodology for quantifying energy efficiency and greenhouse gas emissions, and standards related to the development and use of new energy efficient technologies and renewable energy sources, such as solar power.

The type of technical requirement that is chosen depends on the desired environmental outcome. Product-related requirements may achieve indirect results depending on whether consumers choose to purchase energy efficient products and how they use these products.

On the other hand, requirements targeting production methods may result in direct environmental benefits, such as a reduction in emissions, during the production process. Moreover, standards and regulations, whether related to products or to processes, can be based either on design characteristics, or in terms of performance.

Requirements based on design characteristics determine the specific features of a product, or, with regard to production methods, set out the: specific actions to be taken, goods to be used, or technologies to be installed. Regulations based on design standards are often used when there are few options available to the polluter for controlling emissions; in this case, the regulator is able to specify the technological steps that a firm must take to limit pollution.

In contrast, performance-based requirements prescribe the specific environmental outcomes which should be achieved by products or production methods, without defining how the outcomes are to be delivered. Such requirements may be established, for instance, in terms of maximum CO_2 emission levels, maximum energy consumption levels, minimum fuel economy for cars or minimum energy performance standards for lighting products. Performance-based requirements often provide more flexibility than design-based requirements, and their costs may be lower, as firms may decide how best to meet the environmental target.

Energy labelling schemes are intended to provide consumers with data on a product's energy performance (such as its energy use, efficiency, or energy cost) and/or its related greenhouse gas emissions. Labelling schemes may also provide information on a product's entire life cycle, including its production, use and disposal. Labelling schemes have also been used by some private companies to declare the origin of an agricultural product, how many "food miles" it has travelled from where it was grown to where it will be consumed, and the emissions generated during transport.

Relevant WTO rules and work

Countries have developed a number of climate change related standards and regulations, including procedures to assess conformity. The key WTO instrument governing these measures is the Agreement on Technical Barriers to Trade (TBT). In addition, certain rules of the General Agreement on Tariffs and Trade (GATT) may be relevant, such as GATT Article I (the "Most-Favoured Nation" clause), Article III (National Treatment principle) and more specifically, Article III:4.

Other provisions of the GATT 1994 may also be relevant. For instance, Article XI requires the general elimination of quantitative restrictions on the importation or exportation of products. Article XI 2(b) introduces an exception to the general rule contained in Article XI and allows import and export prohibitions or restrictions "necessary to the application of standards or regulations for the classification, grading or marketing of commodities in international trade." Furthermore, Article XX establishes exceptions to GATT obligations which may be applicable to certain technical measures.

Coverage of the TBT Agreement

The TBT Agreement covers three sets of activities:

(i) the preparation, adoption and application of technical regulations by governments; (ii) the preparation, adoption and application of standards by standardizing bodies; and (iii) the conformity assessment procedures used to determine whether the relevant requirements in technical regulations or standards are fulfilled.

The scope of the TBT Agreement extends to all technical regulations, standards and conformity assessment procedures that apply to trade in goods, i.e. to all agricultural and industrial products. However, two areas of trade in goods are excluded from the TBT Agreement: sanitary and phytosanitary measures, which instead are subject to the provisions of the Agreement on the Application of Sanitary and Phytosanitary Measures (SPS); and government procurement specifications, which are addressed in the plurilateral Agreement on Government Procurement (GPA). Technical measures which relate to services are dealt with under Article VI.4 of the General Agreement on Trade in Services (GATS).

i) Mandatory regulations, voluntary standards and conformity assessment procedures

The TBT Agreement makes a distinction between technical regulations (with which compliance is mandatory), and standards (which are voluntary). A fair number of climate-related requirements are voluntary standards and labelling schemes, including some adopted by private entities.

Although the key legal principles are broadly similar for regulations, standards and conformity assessment procedures, there are some differences among each set of provisions, as well as important differences in the level of obligation of members with regard to mandatory regulations and voluntary standards. Indeed, as regards mandatory regulations, members have an obligation to ensure that these regulations are consistent the provisions of the TBT Agreement. On the other hand, with regard to voluntary standards, members are only required to rake "reasonable measures" to ensure, for example, that standardization bodies within their territories respect certain disciplines of the TBT Agreement.

An annex to the TBT Agreement contains the Code of Good Practice for the Preparation, Adoption and Application of Standards. This Code of Good Practice includes all the key legal principles of the TBT Agreement (e.g. non discrimination, avoidance of unnecessary obstacles to trade and harmonization). The Code can be accepted, and its provisions followed, by any standardizing body within a WTO member's territory; by any governmental regional standardizing body of which one or more members are also WTO members; and by any non-governmental regional standardizing body which has one or more members situated within the territory of a WTO member. Given the recent proliferation of private carbon labelling (in particular, "food miles" schemes), some authors have also discussed the potential relevance of the TBT Agreement to requirements of this type, which are developed and adopted by private entities (e.g., food supply chains).

Finally, given the number of energy-efficiency and emission-reduction standards that are based on performance requirements, TBT Article 2.8 is an important element. This provision states a preference for regulations based on performance — which may also be seen as less trade-restrictive measures to regulate — rather than for regulations based on design. Indeed, the idea of this provision is to allow producers to find the most cost-effective way of fulfilling the requirements of a technical regulation. What counts is the result, i.e. the performance of a product, rather than the way in which this outcome is achieved.

ii) Products, processes and production methods

A technical regulation is defined under the TBT Agreement as a document which lays down product characteristics or their related processes and production methods, including the applicable administrative provisions, with which compliance is mandatory.

The Appellate Body, in the *EC-Asbestos* and the *EC-Sardines* cases, has set forth three criteria in order to identify a technical regulation: (i) the document must apply to an identifiable product or group of products. A product does not necessarily have to be mentioned explicitly in a document for that product to be an identifiable product, as "identifiable" does not mean "expressly identified; (ii) the document must lay down one or more characteristics of the product. This has been interpreted as meaning that the term "product characteristics" includes not only features and qualities intrinsic to the product itself, but also related "characteristics," such as the means of identification, the presentation and the appearance of a product; and (iii) compliance with the product characteristics must be mandatory.

As outlined in the definitions of technical regulations and standards contained in the TBT Agreement, such requirements include documents which specify requirements relative to "processes and production methods" (PPMs) that are *related* to the product characteristics. However, the second sentence of the definition of technical regulations and standards states that they "may also include or deal exclusively with terminology, symbols, packaging, marking or labelling requirements as they apply to a product, process or production method."

The fact that the second sentence of both definitions leaves out the term "related" when "labelling" (among others) is mentioned, has been interpreted by some as providing some scope for the labelling of a non-product related process or production method (i.e. that does not leave a trace in the final product, so-called "unincorporated PPMs") to be covered by the TBT Agreement. As has been seen in the previous Subsection, a number of energy-efficiency and emission-reduction standards and labelling schemes are based on non-product related PPMs (i.e. the emissions involved in the production of a product do not leave a trace in the characteristics of the final product).

Non-discrimination and the avoidance of unnecessary barriers to trade

The TBT Agreement applies the core GATT principle of non-discrimination to each set of activities described above. Technical regulations, standards and conformity assessment procedures are to be applied to products imported from other WIO members in a manner no less favourable than that accorded to "like" (i.e. similar) products of national origin (national treatment principle) and to like products originating in any other WIO member (most-favoured nation treatment. A key question in this context is whether goods produced with different emission intensity or energy intensity may be considered "unlike" pursuant to the TBT Agreement.

Moreover, technical regulations, standards and conformity procedures must also not be prepared, adopted or applied with the intention or effect of creating unnecessary obstacles to trade. It is important to note, however, that the TBT Agreement recognizes the right of members to take regulatory measures to achieve their legitimate objectives, including: national security; the prevention of deceptive practices; protection of human health or safety, animal or plant life or health, or the environment. Thus, the protection of human, animal or plant life or health and of the environment could be relevant to an energy-efficiency or emission-reduction regulation.

The TBT Agreement also provides a number of guidelines and tests to avoid unnecessary obstacles to trade. For instance, a technical regulation would be considered an "unnecessary" obstacle to trade if it was found to be more trade-restrictive than necessary to fulfil a legitimate objective. Similarly, conformity assessment procedures should not be stricter than is necessary to give confidence that products conform with technical regulations and standards. Although the provisions of the TBT Agreement mentioned in this subsection have never been tested in the Dispute Settlement Body, it may be relevant to refer to the panels' and the Appellate Body's interpretation of the word "necessary" in the context of GATT Article XX.

The non-discrimination principle has also not been tested in the context of the TBT Agreement. However, it may be interesting to note an unadopted GATT panel report; the *United States — Automobiles* case. In this case, the panel examined three U.S. measures on automobiles: the luxury tax on automobiles, the "gas guzzler" tax on automobiles, and the Corporate Average Fuel Economy regulation (CAFE). The luxury tax of 10 per cent was imposed on the first retail sale of vehicles over US$ 30,000 (a tax paid by customers). The gas guzzler tax was an excise tax on the sale of automobiles within "model types" whose fuel economy failed to meet certain fuel-economy requirements (a tax imposed on manufacturers). The CAFE regulation required a minimum average fuel economy for passenger automobiles (or light trucks) manufactured in the United States, or sold by any importer. For companies that were both importers and domestic manufacturers, the average fuel economy was calculated separately for imported passenger automobiles and for those manufactured domestically.

The GATT panel found that both the luxury tax and the gas guzzler tax were consistent with the national treatment principle. However, it found the CAFE regulation to be inconsistent with this principle, because the separate calculations of fuel economy for the foreign vehicles discriminated against foreign cars, and because the fleet averaging requirement differentiated between imported and domestic cars on the basis of factors relating to control or ownership of producers or importers (i.e. based on origin), rather than on the basis of factors directly related to the products themselves.

Harmonization

Energy-efficiency standards and regulations and their related conformity assessment procedures may act as a barrier to trade, in particular when they differ from country to country. Differing requirements raise the cost of information, and make exporting to other markets more difficult. A solution to this obstacle is the harmonization of norms, which may be described as the adoption by several countries of common norms on the same subject, where previously each might have had its own set of requirements. Harmonization is a core principle of the TBT Agreement, and the importance of international standards is enshrined in its Preamble. The TBT Agreement strongly encourages efforts by WTO members to harmonize technical regulations, standards and conformity assessment procedures.

The TBT Agreement provides for three approaches to harmonization. First, members are to give positive consideration to accepting the technical regulations of other members as being equivalent to their own. The TBT Agreement urges countries to recognize the equivalence of the norms set by their trading partners, even when they differ from their own, provided they achieve the same final objective. Second, the Agreement encourages mutual recognition of conformity assessment results. Countries are encouraged to recognize the procedures that their trading partners use to assess compliance with regulations if they are convinced of the reliability and competence of their conformity assessment institutions.

Third, and most importantly, WTO members are urged to use international standards as a basis for their own technical regulations, standards and conformity assessment procedures, except when such international standards would be an ineffective or inappropriate means for the fulfilment of the legitimate objectives pursued. Moreover, in order to encourage members to base their regulations on international standards, the Agreement contains a "rebuttable presumption" that any technical regulation which is prepared in accordance with (and not only "based on") relevant international standards will not be considered an unnecessary obstacle to trade. In this context, the TBT Agreement also provides that members, within the limits of their resources, must play a full part in the preparation of international standards, with a view to harmonizing technical regulations.

Although a list of international standardizing bodies for the purposes of the TBT Agreement does not exist, guidance on the identification of these bodies may be found in a decision adopted in 2000 at the Second Triennial Review by the TBT Committee on principles for the development of international standards, guides and recommendations.

d) The TBT Committee and transparency requirements

Transparency is a core principle of the WTO and features in many WTO agreements, including the TBT Agreement. It is an important tool to ensure that trade flows as smoothly, predictably and openly as possible. In the TBT Agreement, WTO members are required to share information on any draft technical regulations and conformity assessment procedures that may have an impact on trade: such measures must be notified to other members. Notifications can make an important contribution towards avoiding unnecessary obstacles to trade and can provide members with the opportunity to influence proposed regulations of other members.

Moreover, a Committee on Technical Barriers to Trade, composed of representatives from each WTO member, meets three to four times a year. An official record of the discussions held during formal meetings is prepared, and is made available to the public. About half of each meeting of the TBT Committee is dedicated to the discussion of specific trade concerns that members may have in relation to technical regulations or conformity assessment procedures which have been proposed or adopted by other members. The Committee therefore provides an important forum to discuss technical requirements to mitigate climate change. Such concerns are often based on a notification of a technical regulation or conformity assessment. Usually, before raising a specific trade concern in the TBT Committee, members go through several stages of information exchange and consultation.

Most trade concerns are in relation to the implementation of transparency procedures and claims that certain measures adopted by WTO members are more trade-restrictive than necessary. In recent years, a number of measures related to the reduction of emissions of certain equipment or the improvement of energy efficiency of electrical appliances have been discussed in the TBT Committee and/or notified to other members.

For instance, in 2007 Brazil notified a draft technical regulation which sets down minimum energy performance standards for non-electric water heaters; in 2008, the European Communities notified a draft regulation that established CO_2 emission performance standards for new passenger cars; Singapore notified a regulation that stipulates that motor vehicles must be registered and labelled to provide information on their levels of fuel consumption and CO_2 emissions; and China notified several technical regulations related to the energy efficiency and energy conservation of electrical storage water heaters, copy machines and computer monitors.

Technical assistance provisions

The TBT Agreement contains detailed provisions on technical assistance to developing countries and least developed countries. These provisions are mandatory but most of them are accompanied by one or more qualifications, such as "take such reasonable measures as may be available to them" or "on mutually agreed terms and conditions," These provisions combine two sorts of obligations: obligations to advise other members, especially developing-country members, on certain issues, and obligations to provide them with technical assistance.

NOTES AND QUESTIONS

1.   The WTO Agreement on Technical Barriers to Trade (TBT) has many ramifications for international environmental law. The main operative provisions of the TBT Agreement are as follows:

Article 2
Preparation, Adoption and Application of Technical
Regulations by Central Government Bodies

With respect to their central government bodies:

2.1   Members shall ensure that in respect of technical regulations, products imported from the territory of any Member shall be accorded treatment no less favourable than that accorded to like products of national origin and to like products originating in any other country.

2.2   Members shall ensure that technical regulations are not prepared, adopted or applied with a view to or with the effect of creating unnecessary obstacles to international trade. For this purpose, technical regulations shall not be more trade-restrictive than necessary to fulfil a legitimate objective, taking account of the risks non-fulfilment would create. Such legitimate objectives are, *inter alia:* national security requirements; the prevention of deceptive practices; protection of human health or safety, animal or plant life or health, or the environment. In assessing such risks, relevant elements of consideration are, *inter alia:* available scientific and technical information, related processing technology or intended end-uses of products.

2.3   Technical regulations shall not be maintained if the circumstances or objectives giving rise to their adoption no longer exist or if the changed circumstances or objectives can be addressed in a less trade-restrictive manner.

2.4   Where technical regulations are required and relevant international standards exist or their completion is imminent, Members shall use them, or the relevant parts of them, as a basis for their technical regulations except when such international standards or relevant parts would be an ineffective or inappropriate means for the fulfilment of the legitimate objectives pursued, for instance because of fundamental climatic or geographical factors or fundamental technological problems.

2.5   A Member preparing, adopting or applying a technical regulation which may have a significant effect on trade of other Members shall, upon the request of another Member, explain the justification for that technical regulation in terms of the provisions of paragraphs 2 to 4. Whenever a technical regulation is prepared, adopted or applied for one of the legitimate objectives explicitly mentioned in paragraph 2, and is in accordance with relevant international standards, it shall be rebuttably presumed not to create an unnecessary obstacle to international trade.

2.   Article 2 of the TBT Agreement poses some difficult hurdles for technical regulations. Article 2.1 is a version of the MFN and national treatment provisions enshrined in GATT Articles I and III. Article 2.2 sets out a "not more restrictive than necessary" standard for technical regulations and enumerates the "legitimate objectives" which technical regulations may aim to fulfill. Article 2.3 requires that technical regulations be modified if the conditions giving rise to their adoption change. Article 2.4 requires members to use international standards as a first option; national standards may be used only when international standards are inappropriate to fulfill a legitimate objective. Article 2.5 is a transparency requirement.

3.   *What is a technical regulation?* A technical regulation is defined broadly by the TBT Agreement Annex 1.1 as "a document which lays down product characteristics or their related product or production methods, including the applicable administrative provisions, with which compliance is mandatory." Consider the case of *European Communities — Measures Prohibiting the Importation and Marketing of Seal Products*, WT/DS400, 401/R, Report of the Panel, 22 November 2013, which we covered earlier in this Chapter. Do you think that the EU Seal Regime that was at issue in that case meets the test of "technical regulation"? The WTO Panel in that case ruled that the EU Seal Regime was a technical regulation within the meaning of Annex 1.1. (para. 7.125). But the Appellate Body reversed this ruling on the grounds that the EU regulation in question, objectively and holistically considered, did not lay down a technical product characteristic. *European Communities – Measures Prohibiting the Importation and Marketing*

of Seal Products, WT/DS400,401/AB/R, Report of the Appellate Body, adopted 18 June 2014.

4. _Technical Standards for Labeling Tuna._ Article 2.1 of the TBT Agreement was interpreted and applied by the WTO Appellate Body in *United States — Measures Concerning the Importation, Marketing, and Sale of Tuna and Tuna Products*, WT/DS381/ AB/R, adopted June 13, 2012. At issue were U.S. standards for labeling canned tuna as "dolphin safe" under the Dolphin Protection Information Act, 16 U.S.C. § 1385. U.S. law did not permit the "dolphin safe" label to be attached to tuna caught using purse seine nets, a common Mexican fishing method. Mexico argued that its purse seine method was in compliance with the stringent requirements of the Agreement on International Dolphin Conservation Program (AIDCP) and deserved the "dolphin safe" label.

The Appellate Body ruled that the U.S. labeling standards were inconsistent with TBT Article 2.1 because Mexico had carried its burden of showing that U.S. standards *prima facie* result in less favorable treatment for Mexican tuna, and the United States had not carried its burden of showing that the less favorable treatment stemmed from a legitimate regulatory distinction as opposed to discrimination against a Mexican product. Similarly, in *United States — Measures Affecting the Production and Sale of Clove Cigarettes*, WT/DS406/AB/R, adopted on April 24, 2012, the Appellate Body ruled that to establish a violation of TBT Article 2.1, three elements must be established: (1) the measure at issue must be a technical regulation; (2) the imported and domestic products at issue must be like products; and (3) the imported product must be accorded less favorable treatment than the domestic product. But while Article 2.1 prohibits both *de jure* and *de facto* discrimination, a detrimental impact stemming exclusively from a legitimate regulatory distinction will be permitted. Thus, the mere existence of a detrimental impact on a foreign product can be justified by showing that this is the result of a legitimate regulatory distinction. In the *Clove Cigarettes Case*, however, the Appellate Body ruled that a prohibition on the sale of clove cigarettes was inconsistent with Article 2.1 because clove cigarettes and menthol cigarettes are like products, and since the U.S. permits the sale of menthol cigarettes, the U.S. cannot ban the sale of imported clove cigarettes. In *United States — Certain Country of Origin (COOL) Labeling Requirements*, WT /DS384/ AB/R, adopted on July 23, 2012, the Appellate Body, after finding a violation of Article 2.1, stated that "Article 2.1 should not be read to mean that any distinctions, particularly ones that are based exclusively on . . . particular product characteristics or on particular process and production methods, would *per se* constitute less favorable treatment under Article 2.1." Nevertheless, the Appellate Body ruled that a U.S. origin law that states that muscle cuts of meat must be from animals born, raised, and slaughtered in the U.S., was inconsistent with Article 2.1 because it modifies the conditions of competition between U.S. and foreign meat and does not stem from any legitimate regulatory distinction.

5. _TBT Agreement, Article 2.2._ In the *U.S.-Dolphin Safe Label Case* the WTO Appellate Body ruled that the U.S. had not acted inconsistently with TBT Agreement Article 2.2 in not adopting the AIDCP dolphin safe labeling scheme. In the COOL Case the panel had found a violation of Article 2.2, but the Appellate Body reversed the panel without completing the Article 2.2 analysis.

6.   *TBT Agreement, Article 2.4.* In the case, *European Communities — Trade Description of Sardines*, Report of the Appellate Body, WT/DS231/AB/R, adopted on October 23, 2002, the Appellate Body interpreted and applied Article 2.4, stating that it is up to the complaining member who seeks to establish a violation of Article 2.4 to carry the burden of proof that an international standard exists and has not been used as a basis for a national technical regulation and that the international standard is effective and appropriate to fulfill the legitimate objectives pursued by the responding member. The *EC-Sardines Case* involved an EC regulation defining fish species that can carry the name "sardines" on a food container. The EC did not use the existing international regulation as a basis for its regulation, and the Appellate Body ruled that Peru, the complaining member, successfully carried its burden of proof under Article 2.4, that the international regulation was appropriate and effective, and that the EC had failed to rebut this proof. The Appellate Body also ruled that the "legitimate objectives" referred to in Article 2.4 are those listed in Article 2.2. In the *U.S.-Dolphin Safe Label Case*, the Appellate Body ruled that to qualify as an international standardizing organization under Article 2.4, a standard-setting body must be open to all WTO members; thus the AIDCP standard was not an appropriate international standard because the AIDCP's membership was by invitation only.

PROBLEM 5-2
STATE Z ADOPTS TECHNICAL REGULATIONS MANDATING ENERGY EFFICIENT PRODUCTS AND GREEN PROCESS AND PRODUCTION METHODS

State Z, a member of the WTO, is in the forefront of the international effort to reduce greenhouse gas emissions. State Z has enacted a carbon tax payable by domestic industries and instituted a cap and trade system of carbon emission allowances. State Z has also enacted stringent energy efficiency regulations for 1256 types of consumer and industrial products ranging from washing machines to chain saws, mandating technical requirements so that the products in question are as energy efficient as possible. In enacting these technical regulations, State Z rejected following international energy efficiency standards on the ground that the international standards are impossibly loose and were devised by standards' organizations as lowest common denominator energy efficiency mandates. Last month, State Z enacted a new law that extends all domestic energy efficiency standards to imported products. Beginning next January 1, when the new law takes effect, all imported products must meet the same strict energy efficiency standards as domestic products. Now State Z is considering a second law. Concerned about carbon leakage because of its carbon tax and cap and trade programs, State Z is considering issuing new technical regulations covering process and production methods for 258 different consumer and industrial products. Beginning January 1, all domestic and imported products in these 258 categories will have to meet stringent process and production criteria to assure that in the manufacture of these products only the minimum necessary energy input is employed. These new process and production standards will thus reduce the "carbon footprint" of all 258 categories of products both domestically and internationally. The new regulations will also effectively combat carbon leakage, which puts domestic industries of State

Z at a disadvantage. The new regulations will "level the playing field," assuring that both domestic and imported products are manufactured using minimum expenditure of energy.

1. Are State Z's new product energy efficiency standards consistent with WTO agreements?

2. Are State Z's new process and production standards consistent with WTO agreements?

PROBLEM 5-3
STATE Y ADOPTS COMPREHENSIVE ENERGY LABELING REQUIREMENTS

State Y is an environmentally-minded member of the WTO and is concerned about climate change. State Y has recently enacted legislation requiring all consumer appliances sold within the state to contain labels that disclose: (1) the product's energy performance, including energy use, energy efficiency and energy cost; and (2) the size of the product's "carbon footprint" the average amount of greenhouse gas emissions that were expended in manufacturing the product.

State X, another member of the WTO opposes energy labeling and has brought a complaint against state Y at the WTO. Is State Y's labeling scheme inconsistent with WTO standards?

The TBT Committee of the WTO is an important forum for the discussion of technical regulations adopted by WTO members to mitigate climate change. Technical regulations and labeling related to climate change are tested according to the requirements of the TBT Agreement. Examples of such regulations include: fuel economy standards for vehicles, energy efficiency standards for products, and emission limits for engines. International standards bodies, including the Geneva-based International Organization for Standardization (ISO) have adopted many technical regulations for the purpose of reducing emissions of greenhouse gases. A WTO member may adopt these international standards as its national standards. Are such standards immune from attack under the TBT Agreement? If so, can the TBT Agreement be enlisted as an affirmative tool to combat climate change?

Section VI. HAZARDOUS SUBSTANCES AND WASTES

Industries and governments produce and utilize many types of hazardous and toxic substances that are dangerous to human health and the environment. Three general categories of such substances exist: (1) chemicals; (2) nuclear and radioactive substances; and (3) non-chemical dangerous substances.

Today at least 75,000 different chemicals are produced and used in pesticides, fertilizers, fuels, pharmaceuticals, plastics, and other products. Many of these chemicals pose dangers to human health and the environment.

Thirty-one countries in all parts of the world utilize nuclear power, and nine states maintain nuclear weapons programs. The utilization of nuclear materials begins with the mining and refining of uranium and extends to what is known as the "back end of the nuclear fuel cycle," the collection and disposal of nuclear wastes.

The utilization of nuclear materials poses potential dangers to human health and the environment.

Many non-chemical dangerous substances pose dangers to human health and the environment. For example, asbestos was once considered extremely useful and was deployed in building materials all over the world. But we have learned that chrysotile asbestos fibres pose a danger to human health.

The primary responsibility for dealing with hazardous chemicals, nuclear materials and hazardous substances is up to national governments, but beginning in the 1980s, important international instruments were adopted to deal with the international problems presented by these materials, and today international regulatory regimes and standards exist with respect to such materials.

Waste management, waste minimization and recycling are closely related to the problem of the production and utilization of hazardous chemicals and materials. Whatever is produced and deployed will inevitably find its way into waste streams. Thus, governments and the international community must deal with the problems of waste management of the many kinds of substances we produce and utilize. Waste management is likewise the primary responsibility of national governments; but important international instruments and regimes are functioning to deal with the international aspects of waste management.

In this section we analyze the principal international regimes instituted to regulate substances that are hazardous to human health and the environment. An important aspect of all such international regimes is restrictions on international trade. Thus, the WTO agreements and the functioning of the multilateral trading system are important concerns for all these regimes.

We begin by reading an important case on WTO standards for import bans on hazardous products.

A. Hazardous Products and the Multilateral Trading System

EUROPEAN COMMUNITIES — MEASURES AFFECTING ASBESTOS AND ASBESTOS-CONTAINING PRODUCTS REPORT OF THE APPELLATE BODY
WT/DS135/AB/R (April 5, 2001)

I. Introduction

1. Canada appeals certain issues of law and legal interpretations developed in the Panel Report in European Communities — Measures Affecting Asbestos and Asbestos-Containing Products (the "Panel Report"). The Panel was established to consider claims made by Canada regarding French Decree No. 9-1133 concerning asbestos and products containing asbestos (décret no. 96-113 relatif à l'interdiction de l'amiante, pris en application du code de travail et du code de la consommation) ("the Decree"), which entered into force on 1 January 1997.

2. Articles 1 and 2 of the Decree set forth prohibitions on asbestos and certain products containing asbestos fibres, followed by certain limited and temporary

exceptions from those prohibitions:

Article 1

I.   For the purpose of protecting workers, and pursuant to Article L. 231.7 of the Labour Code, the manufacture, processing, sale, import, placing on the domestic market and transfer under any title whatsoever of all varieties of asbestos fibres shall be prohibited, regardless of whether these substances have been incorporated into materials, products or devices.

II. For the purpose of protecting consumers, and pursuant to Article L. 221.3 of the Consumer Code, the manufacture, import, domestic marketing, exportation, possession for sale, offer, sale and transfer under any title whatsoever of all varieties of asbestos fibres or any product containing asbestos fibres shall be prohibited.

III. The bans instituted under Articles I and II shall not prevent fulfilment of the obligations arising from legislation on the elimination of wastes.

Article 2

I.   On an exceptional and temporary basis, the bans instituted under Article 1 shall not apply to certain existing materials, products or devices containing chrysotile fibre when, to perform an equivalent function, no substitute for that fibre is available which:

   • On the one hand, in the present state of scientific knowledge, poses a lesser occupational health risk than chrysotile fibre to workers handling those materials, products or devices;

   • on the other, provides all technical guarantees of safety corresponding to the ultimate purpose of the use thereof.

II. The scope of application of paragraph I of this Article shall cover only the materials, products or devices falling within the categories shown in an exhaustive list decreed by the Ministers for Labour, Consumption, the Environment, Industry, Agriculture and Transport. To ascertain the justification for maintaining these exceptions, the list shall be re-examined on an annual basis, after which the Senior Council for the Prevention of Occupational Hazards and the National Commission for Occupational Health and Safety in Agriculture shall be consulted.

VI. "Like Products" in Article III:4 of the GATT 1994

A. Background

84. In addressing Canada's claims under Article III:4 of the GATT 1994, the Panel examined whether two different sets of products are "like." First, the Panel examined whether *chrysotile asbestos fibres* are "like" certain other fibres, namely *polyvinyl alcohol fibres ("PVA"), cellulose and glass fibres* (PVA, cellulose and glass fibres are all collectively referred to, in the remainder of this Report, as "PCG

fibres"). The Panel concluded that chrysotile asbestos and PCG fibres are all "like products" under Article III:4 The Panel next examined whether *cement-based products containing chrysotile asbestos fibres* are "like" *cement-based products containing one of the PCG fibres.* The Panel also concluded that all these cement-based products are "like."

85. In examining the "likeness" of these two sets of products, the Panel adopted an approach based on the Report of the Working Party on *Border Tax Adjustments.* Under that approach, the Panel employed four general criteria in analyzing "likeness:" (i) the properties, nature and quality of the products; (ii) the end-uses of the products; (iii) consumers' tastes and habits; and, (iv) the tariff classification of the products. The Panel declined to apply "a criterion on the risk of a product," "neither in the criterion relating to the properties, nature and quality of the product, nor in the other likeness criteria. . . ."

86. On appeal, the European Communities requests that we reverse the Panel's findings that the two sets of products examined by the Panel are "like products" under Article III:4 of the GATT 1994, and requests, in consequence, that we reverse the Panel's fording that the measure is inconsistent with Article III:4 of the GATT 1994. The European Communities contends that the Panel erred in its interpretation and application of the concept of "like products," in particular, in excluding from its analysis consideration of the health risks associated with chrysotiie asbestos fibres. According to the European Communities, in this case, Article III:4 calls for an analysis of the health objective of the regulatory distinction made in the measure between asbestos fibres, and between products containing asbestos fibres, and all other products. The European Communities argues that, under Article III:4, products should not be regarded as "like" unless the regulatory distinction drawn between them "entails [a] shift in the competitive opportunities" in favour of domestic products.

* * *

97. We have previously described the "general principle" articulated in Article III as follows:

> The broad and fundamental purpose of Article III is to avoid protectionism in the application of internal tax and regulatory measures. More specifically, the purpose of Article III "is to ensure that internal measures 'not be applied to imported and domestic products so as to afford protection to domestic production.' " Toward this end, Article III obliges Members of the WTO to provide *equality of competitive conditions for imported products in relation to domestic products* . . . . Article III protects expectations not of any particular trade volume but rather of the equal competitive relationship between imported and domestic products . . . . (emphasis added)

98. As we have said, although this "general principle" is not explicitly invoked in Article III:4, nevertheless, it "informs" that provision." Therefore, the term "like product" in Article III:4 must be interpreted to give proper scope and meaning to this principle. In short, there must be consonance between the objective pursued by Article III, as enunciated in the "general principle" articulated in Article III:1, and

the interpretation of the specific expression of this principle in the text of Article III:4. This interpretation must, therefore, reflect that, in endeavouring, to ensure "equality of competitive conditions," the "general principle" in Article III seeks to prevent Members from applying internal taxes and regulations in a manner which affects the competitive relationship, in the marketplace, *between the domestic and imported products involved*, "so as to afford protection to domestic production."

99. As products that are in a competitive relationship in the marketplace could be affected through treatment of imports "less favourable" than the treatment accorded to *domestic* products, it follows that the word "like" in Article III:4 is to be interpreted to apply to products that are in such a competitive relationship. Thus, a determination of "likeness" under Article III:4 is, fundamentally, a determination about the nature and extent of a competitive relationship between and among products . . . .

*   *   *

114. Panels must examine fully the physical properties of products. In particular, panels must examine those physical properties of products that are likely to influence the competitive relationship between products in the marketplace. In the case of chrysotile asbestos fibres, their molecular structure, chemical composition, and fibrillation capacity are important because the microscopic particles and filaments of chrysotile asbestos fibres are carcinogenic in humans, following inhalation. In this respect, we observe that, at paragraph 8.188 of its Report, the Panel made the following statements regarding chrysotile asbestos fibres:

> . . . we note that the carcinogenicity of chrysotile fibres has been acknowledged for some time by international bodies. This carcinogenicity was confirmed by the experts consulted by the Panel, with respect to both lung cancers and mesotheliomas, even though the experts appear to acknowledge that chrysotile is less likely to cause mesotheliomas than amphiboles. We also note that the experts confirmed that the types of cancer concerned had a mortality rate of close to 100 per cent. We therefore consider that we have sufficient evidence that there is in fact a serious carcinogenic risk associated with the inhalation of chrysotile fibres. Moreover, in the light of the comments made by one of the experts, the doubts expressed by Canada with respect to the direct effects of chrysotile on mesotheliomas and lung cancers are not sufficient to conclude that an official responsible for public health policy would find that there was not enough evidence of the existence of a public health risk.

This carcinogenicity, or toxicity, constitutes, as we see it, a defining aspect of the physical properties of chrysotile asbestos fibres. The evidence indicates that PCG fibres, in contrast, do not share these properties, at least to the same extent. We do not see how this highly significant physical difference *cannot* be a consideration in examining the physical properties of a product as part of a determination of "likeness" under Article III:A of the GATT 1994.

115. We do not agree with the Panel that considering evidence relating to the health risks associated with a product, under Article III:4, nullifies the effect of Article XX/b) of the GATT 1994. Article XX(b) allows a Member to "adopt and

enforce" a measure, *inter alia*, necessary to protect human life or health, even though that measure is inconsistent with another provision of the GATT 1994. Article III:4 and Article XX(b) are distinct and independent provisions of the GATT 1994 each to be interpreted on its own. The scope and meaning of Article III:4 should not be broadened or restricted beyond what is required by the normal customary international law rules of treaty interpretation, simply because Article XX(b) exists and may be available to justify measures inconsistent with Article III:4. The fact that an interpretation of Article III:4, under those rules, implies a less frequent recourse to Article XX(b) does not deprive the exception in Article XX(b) of effect. Article XX(b) would only be deprived of *effect* if that provision could not serve to allow a Member to "adopt and enforce" measures "necessary to protect human . . . life or health." Evaluating evidence relating to the health risks arising from the physical properties of a product does not prevent a measure which is inconsistent with Article III:4 from being justified under Article XX(b). We note, in this regard, that, different inquiries occur under these two very different Articles. Under Article III:4, evidence relating to health risks may be relevant in assessing the *competitive relationship in the marketplace* between allegedly "like" products. The same, or similar, evidence serves a different purpose under Article XX(b), namely, that of assessing whether a Member has a sufficient basis for "adopting or enforcing" a WTO-inconsistent measure on the grounds of human health.

116. We, therefore, find that the Panel erred, in paragraph 8.132 of the Panel Report, in excluding the health risks associated with chrysotile asbestos fibres from its examination of the physical properties of that product.

133. As we have reversed both of the Panel's conclusions on "likeness" under Article III:4 of the GATT 1994, we think it appropriate to complete the analysis, on the basis of the factual findings of the Panel and of the undisputed facts in the Panel record. We have already examined the meaning of the term "like products," and we have also approved the approach for inquiring into "likeness" that is based on the Report of the Working Party in *Border Tax Adjustments* and that was also approved, though not entirely followed, by the Panel in this case. Under that the evidence is to be examined under four criteria: physical properties; end-uses; consumers' tastes and habits; and tariff classification.

1. Chrysotile and PCG fibres

134. We address first the "likeness" of *chrysotile asbestos fibres* and PCG *fibres.* As regards the physical properties of these fibres, we recall that the Panel stated that:

> The Panel notes that no party contests that the structure of chrysotile fibres is unique by nature and in comparison with artificial fibres that can replace chrysotile asbestos. The parties agree that none of the substitute fibres mentioned by Canada in connection with Article III:4 has the same structure, either in terms of its form, its diameter, its length or its potential to release particles that possess certain characteristics. Moreover, they do not have the same chemical composition, which means that, in purely physical terms, none of them has the same nature or quality. . . .

135. We also see it as important to take into account that, since 1977, chrysotile asbestos fibres have been recognized internationally as a known carcinogen because of the particular combination of their molecular structure, chemical composition, and fibrillation capacity. In that respect, the Panel noted that:

> . . . the carcinogenicity of chrysotile fibres has been acknowledged for sometime by international bodies. This carcinogenicity was confirmed by the experts consulted by the Panel, with respect to both lung cancers and mesotheliomas, even though the experts appear to acknowledge that chrysotile is less likely to cause mesotheliomas than amphiboles. We also note that the experts coned that the types of cancer concerned had a mortality rate of close to 100 per cent. We therefore consider that we have sufficient evidence that there is in fact a serious carcinogenic risk associated with the inhalation of chrysotile fibres . . . .

In contrast, the Panel found that the PCG fibres "are not classified by the WHO at the same level of risk as chrysotile." The experts also confirmed, as the Panel reported, that current scientific evidence indicates that PCG fibres do "not present the same risk to health as chrysotile" asbestos fibres.

136. It follows that the evidence relating to properties indicates that, physically, chrysotile asbestos and PCG fibres are very different. As we said earlier, in such cases, in order to overcome this indication that products are not "like," a high burden is imposed on a complaining Member to establish that, despite the pronounced physical differences, there is a competitive relationship between the products such that, *all* of the evidence, taken together, demonstrates that the products are "like" under Article III:4 of the GATT 1994,

137. The Panel observed that the end-uses of chrysotile asbestos and PCG fibres are the same "for a small number" of applications. The Panel simply adverted to these overlapping end-uses and offered no elaboration on their nature and character. We note that Canada argued before the Panel that there are some 3,000 commercial applications for asbestos fibres." Canada and the European Communities indicated that the most important end-uses for asbestos fibres include, in no particular order, incorporation into: cement-based products; insulation; and various forms of friction lining. Canada noted that 90 percent, by quantity, of French imports of chrysotile asbestos were used in the production of cement-based products." This evidence suggests that chrysotile asbestos and PCG fibres share a small number of similar end-uses and, that, as Canada asserted, for chrysotile asbestos, these overlapping end-uses represent an important proportion of the end-uses made of chrysotile asbestos, measured in terms of quantity.

138. There is, however, no evidence on the record regarding the nature and extent of the many end-uses for chrysotile asbestos and PCG fibres which are not overlapping. Thus, we do not know what proportion of all end-uses for chrysotile asbestos and PCG fibres overlap. Where products have a wide range of end-uses, only some of which overlap, we do not believe that it is sufficient to rely solely on evidence regarding the overlapping end-uses, without also examining evidence of the nature and importance of these end-uses in relation to all of the other possible end-uses for the products. In the absence of such evidence, we, cannot determine

the significance of the fact that chrysotile asbestos and PCG fibres share a small number of similar end-uses.

139. As we have already stated, Canada took the view, both before the Panel and before us, that consumers' tastes and habits have no relevance to the inquiry into the "likeness" of the fibres. We have already addressed, and dismissed, the arguments advanced by Canada in support of this contention. We have also stated that, in a case such as this one, where the physical properties of the fibres are very different, art examination of the evidence relating to consumers' tastes and habits is an indispensable — although not, on its own, sufficient — aspect of any determination that products are "like" under Article 111:4 of the GATT 1994. If there is no evidence on this aspect of the nature and extent of the competitive relationship between the fibres, there is no basis for overcoming the inference, drawn from the different physical properties, that the products are not "like." However, in keeping with its argument that this criterion is irrelevant, Canada presented *no* evidence on consumers' tastes and habits regarding chrysotile asbestos and PCG fibres.

140. Finally, we note that chrysotile asbestos fibres and the various PCG fibres all have different tariff classifications. While this element is not, on its own, decisive, it does tend to indicate that chrysotile and PCG fibres are not "like products" under Article III:4 of the GATT 1994.

141. Taken together, in our view, all of this evidence is certainly far from sufficient to satisfy Canada's burden of proving that chrysotile asbestos fibres are "like" PCG fibres under Article III:4 of the GATT 1994. Indeed, this evidence rather tends to suggest that these products are not "like products" for the purposes of Article III:4 of the GATT 1994.

2. Cement-based products containing chrysotile and PCG fibres

142. We turn next to consider whether *cement-based products* containing chrysotile *asbestos fibres* are "like" *cement based products containing PCG fibres* under Article III:4 of the GATT 1994. We begin, once again, with physical properties. In terms of composition, the physical properties of the different cement-based products appear to be relatively similar. Yet, there is one principal and significant difference between these products: one set of cement based products contains a known carcinogenic fibre, while the other does not. The Panel concluded that the presence of chrysotile asbestos fibres in cement-based products poses "an undeniable public health risk."

143. The Panel stated that the fibres give the cement-based products their specific function — "mechanical strength, resistance to heat, compression, etc." These functions are clearly based on the physical properties of the products. There is no evidence of record to indicate whether the presence of chrysotile asbestos fibres, rather than PCG fibres, in a particular cement-based product, affects these particular physical properties of the products. For instance, a tile incorporating chrysotile asbestos fibres may be more heat resistant than a tile incorporating a PCG fibre.

144. In addition, there is no evidence to indicate to what extent the incorporation

of one type of fibre, instead of another, affects the suitability of a particular cement-based product for a specific end-use. Once again, it may be that tiles containing chrysotile asbestos fibres perform some end-uses, such as resistance to heat, more efficiently than tiles containing a PCG fibre. Thus, while we accept that the two different types of cement-based products may perform largely similar end-uses, in the absence of evidence, we cannot determine whether each type of cement-based product can perform, with *equal* efficiency, all of the functions performed by the other type of cement-based product.

145. As with the fibres, Canada contends that evidence on consumers' tastes and habits concerning cement-based products is irrelevant. Accordingly, Canada submitted no such evidence to the Panel. We have dismissed Canada's arguments in support of this contention. We have also indicated that it is of particular importance, under Article III of the GATT 1994, to examine evidence relating to competitive relationships in the marketplace. We consider it likely that the presence of a known carcinogen in one of the products will have an influence on consumers' tastes and habits regarding that product. It may be, for instance, that, although cement-based products containing chrysotile asbestos fibres are capable of performing the same functions as other cement-based products, consumers are, to a greater or lesser extent, not willing to use products containing chrysotile asbestos fibres because of the health risks associated with them. Yet, this is only speculation; the point is, there is no evidence. We are of the view that a determination on the "likeness" of the cement-based products cannot be made, under Article III:4, in the absence of an examination of evidence on consumers' tastes and habits. And, in this case, no such evidence has been submitted.

146. As regards tariff classification, we observe that, for any given cement-based product, the tariff classification of the product is the same. However, this indication of "likeness" cannot, on its own, be decisive.

147. Thus, we find that, in particular, in the absence of any evidence concerning consumers' tastes and habits, Canada has not satisfied its burden of proving that cement-based products containing chrysotile asbestos fibres are "like" cement-based products containing PCG fibres, under Article III:4 of the GATT 1994.

148. As Canada has not demonstrated either that chrysotile asbestos fibres are "like" PCG fibres, or that cement-based products containing chrysotile asbestos fibres are "like" cement-based products containing PCG fibres, we conclude that Canada has not succeeded in establishing that the measure at issue is inconsistent with Article III:4 of the GATT 1994.

*   *   *

VII. Article XX(b) of the GATT 1994 and Article 11 of the DSU

155. Under Article XX(b) of the GATT 1994, the Panel examined, first, whether the use of chrysotile-cement products poses a risk to human health and, second, whether the measure at issue is "necessary to protect human . . . life or health." Canada contends that the Panel erred in law in its findings on both these issues. We will examine these two issues in turn before addressing Canada's appeal that the Panel failed to make an "objective assessment," under Article 11 of the DSU, in

reaching its conclusions under Article XX(b) of the GATT 1994.

156. We recall that Article XX(b) of the GATT 1994 reads:

> Subject to the requirement that such measures are not applied in a manner which would constitute a means of arbitrary or unjustifiable discrimination between countries where the same conditions prevail, or a disguised restriction on international trade, nothing in this Agreement shall be construed to prevent the adoption or enforcement by any Member of measures:

*   *   *

> (b) *necessary to protect human*, animal or plant *life or health;* (emphasis added).

A. *"To Protect Human Life or Health"*

157. On the issue of whether the use of chrysotile-cement products poses a risk to human health sufficient to enable the measure to fall within the scope of application of the phrase "to protect human . . . life or health" in Article XX(b), the Panel stated that it "considers that the evidence before it *tends to show* that handling chrysotile-cement products constitutes a risk to health rather than the opposite." (emphasis added). On the basis of this assessment of the evidence, the Panel concluded that:

> . . . the EC has made a prima facie case for the existence of a health risk in connection with the use of chrysotile, in particular as regards lung cancer and mesothelioma in the occupational sectors downstream of production and processing and for the public in general in relation to chrysotile-cement products. This prima facie case has not been rebutted by Canada. Moreover, the Panel considers that the comments by the experts confirm the health risk associated with exposure to chrysotile in its various uses. *The Panel therefore considers that the EC have shown that the policy of prohibiting chrysotile asbestos implemented by the Decree falls within the range* of *policies designed to protect human life or health* . . . . (emphasis added).

Thus the Panel found that the measure falls within the category of measures embraced by Article XX(b) of the GATT 1994.

158. According to Canada, the Panel deduced that there was a risk to human life or health associated with manipulation of chrysotile-cement products from seven factors. These seven factors all relate to the scientific evidence which was before the Panel, including the opinion of the scientific experts. Canada argues that the Panel erred in law by deducing from these seven factors that chrysotile-cement products pose a risk to human life or health.

159. Although Canada does not base its arguments about these seven factors on Article 11 of the DSU, we bear in mind the discretion that is enjoyed by panels as the trier of facts. In *United States — Wheat Gluten*, we said:

> . . . in view of the distinction between the respective roles of the Appellate Body and panels, we have taken care to emphasize that a panel's appreciation of the evidence falls, in principle, "within the scope *of the panel's discretion* as *the trier* of

facts." (emphasis added) In assessing the panel's appreciation of the evidence, we cannot base a finding of inconsistency under Article 11 simply on the conclusion that we might have reached a different factual finding from the one the panel reached. Rather, we must be satisfied that the panel has exceeded the bounds of its discretion, as the trier of facts, in its appreciation of the evidence. As is clear from previous appeals, we will not interfere lightly with the panel's exercise of its discretion.

160. In Korea — *Alcoholic Beverages*, we were faced with arguments that sought to cast doubt on certain studies relied on by the panel in that case. We stated:

The Panel's examination and weighing of the evidence submitted fall, in principle, within the scope of the Panel's discretion as the trier of facts and, accordingly, outside the scope of appellate review. This is true, for instance, with respect to the Panel's treatment of the Dodwell Study, the Sofres Report and the Nielsen Study. *We cannot second-guess the Panel in appreciating either the evidentiary value of such studies or the consequences, if any, of alleged defects in those studies.* Similarly, it is not for us to review the relative weight ascribed to evidence on such matters as marketing studies . . . (emphasis added).

161. The same holds true in this case. The Panel enjoyed a margin of discretion in assessing the value of the evidence, and the weight to be 'ascribed to that evidence. The Panel was entitled, in the exercise of its discretion, to determine that certain elements of evidence should be accorded more weight than other elements — that is the essence of the task of appreciating the evidence.

162. With this in mind, we have examined the seven factors on which Canada relies in asserting that the Panel erred in concluding that there exists a human health risk associated with the manipulation of chrysotile-cement products. We see Canada's appeal on this point as, in reality, a challenge to the Panel's assessment of the credibility and weight to be ascribed to the scientific evidence before it. Canada contests the conclusions that the Panel drew both from the evidence of the scientific experts and from scientific reports before it. As we have noted, we will interfere with the Panel's appreciation of the evidence only when we are "satisfied that the panel has *exceeded the bounds of its discretion*, as the trier of facts, in its appreciation of the evidence." (emphasis added). In this case, nothing suggests that the Panel exceeded the bounds of its lawful discretion. To the contrary, all four of the scientific experts consulted by the Panel concurred that chrysotile asbestos fibres, and chrysotile-cement products, constitute a risk to human health, and the Panel's conclusions on this point are faithful to the views expressed by the four scientists. In addition, the Panel noted that the carcinogenic nature of chrysotile asbestos fibres has been acknowledged since 1977 by international bodies, such as the International Agency for Research on Cancer and the World Health Organization. In these circumstances, we find that the Panel remained well within the bounds of its discretion in finding that chrysotile-cement products pose a risk to human life or health.

163. Accordingly, we uphold the Panel's finding, in paragraph 8.194 of the Panel Report, that the measure "protect[s] human . . . life or health," within the meaning of Article XX(b) of the GATT 1994.

B. "Necessary"

164. On the issue of whether the measure at issue is "necessary' to protect public health within the meaning of Article XX(b), the Panel stated:

In the light of France's public health objectives as presented by the European Communities, the Panel concludes that the EC has made a prima facie case for the non-existence of a reasonably available alternative to the banning of chrysotile and chrysotile-cement products and recourse to substitute products. Canada has not rebutted the presumption established by the EC. We also consider that the EC's position is confirmed by the comments of the experts consulted in the course of this proceeding.

165. Canada argues that the Panel erred in applying the "necessity" test under Article XX(b) of the GATT 1994 "by stating that there is a high enough risk associated with the manipulation of chrysotile-cement products that it could in principle justify strict measures such as the Decree." Canada advances four arguments in support of this part of its appeal. First, Canada argues that the Panel erred in finding, on the basis of the scientific evidence before it, that chrysotile-cement products pose a risk to human health. Second, Canada contends that the Panel had an obligation to "quantify" itself the risk associated with chrysotile-cement products and that it could not simply "rely" on the "hypotheses" of the French authorities. Third, Canada asserts that the Panel erred by postulating that the level of protection of health inherent in the Decree is a halt to the spread of asbestos-related health risks. According to Canada, this "premise is false because it does not take into account the risk associated with the use of substitute products without a framework for controlled use." Fourth, and finally, Canada claims that the Panel erred in finding that "controlled use" is not a reasonably available alternative to the Decree.

166. With respect to Canada's first argument, we note simply that we have already dismissed Canada's contention that the evidence before the Panel did not support the Panel's findings. We are satisfied that the Panel had a more than sufficient basis to conclude that chrysotile-cement products do pose a significant risk to human life or health.

167. As for Canada's second argument, relating to "quantification" of the risk, we consider that, as with the SPS Agreement, there is no requirement under Article XX(b) of the GATT 1994 to quantify, as such, the risk to human life or health. A risk may be evaluated either in quantitative or qualitative terms. In this case, contrary to what is suggested by Canada, the Panel assessed the nature and the character of the risk posed by chrysotile-cement products. The Panel found, on the basis of the scientific evidence, that "no minimum threshold of level of exposure or duration of exposure has been identified with regard to the risk of pathologies associated with chrysotile, except for asbestosis." The pathologies which the Panel identified as being associated with chrysotile are of a very serious nature, namely lung cancer and mesothelioma, which is also a form of cancer. Therefore, we do not agree with Canada that the Panel merely relied on the French authorities' "hypotheses" of the risk.

168. As to Canada's third argument, relating to the level of protection, we note

that it is undisputed that WTO Members have the right to determine the level of protection of health that they consider appropriate in a given situation. France has determined, and the Panel accepted, that the chosen level of health protection by France is a "halt" to the spread of asbestos-related health risks. By prohibiting all forms of amphibole asbestos, and by severely restricting the use of chrysotile asbestos, the measure at issue is clearly designed and apt to achieve that level of health protection. Our conclusion is not altered by the fact that PCG fibres might pose a risk to health. The scientific evidence before the Panel indicated that the risk posed by the PCG fibres is, in any case, less than the risk posed by chrysotile asbestos fibres, although that evidence did not indicate that the risk posed by PCG fibres is non-existent. Accordingly, it seems to us perfectly legitimate for a Member to seek to halt the spread of a highly risky product while allowing the use of a less risky product in its place. In short, we do not agree with Canada's third argument.

169. In its fourth argument, Canada asserts that the Panel erred in finding that "controlled use" is not a reasonably available alternative to the Decree. This last argument is based on Canada's assertion that, in United States — *Gasoline*, both we and the panel held that an alternative measure "can only be ruled out if it is shown to be impossible to implement." We understand Canada to mean by this that an alternative measure is only excluded as a "reasonably available" alternative if implementation of that measure is "impossible." We certainly agree with Canada that an alternative measure which is impossible to implement is not "reasonably available." But we do not agree with Canada's reading of either the panel report or our report in United States — *Gasoline*. In United States — *Gasoline*, the panel held, in essence, that an alternative measure did not cease to be "reasonably" available simply because the alternative measure involved *administrative difficulties* for a Member. The panel's findings on this point were not appealed, and, thus, we did not address this issue in that case.

170. Looking at this issue now, we believe that, in determining whether a suggested alternative measure is "reasonably available," several factors must be taken into account, besides the difficulty of implementation. In Thailand — *Restrictions on Importation of and Internal Taxes on Cigarettes*, the panel made the following observations on the applicable standard for evaluating whether a measure is "necessary" under Article XX(b):

The import restrictions imposed by Thailand could be considered to be "necessary" in terms of Article XX(b) only if there were no alternative measure consistent with the General Agreement, or less inconsistent with it, which Thailand could *reasonably be expected to employ to achieve its health policy objectives*. (emphasis added)

171. In our Report in Korea — *Beef*, we addressed the issue of "necessity" under Article XX(d) of the GATT 1994. In that appeal, we found that the panel was correct in following the standard set forth by the panel in United States *Section 337 of the Tariff Act of 1930*:

It was clear to the Panel that a contracting party cannot justify a measure inconsistent with another GATT provision as "necessary" in terms of Article XX(d) if an alternative measure which it could reasonably be expected to employ and which is not inconsistent with other GATT provisions is available to it. By the same token, in cases where a measure consistent with other GATT provisions is not reasonably available, a contracting party is bound to use, among the measures reasonably available to it, that which entails the least degree of inconsistency with other GATT provisions.

172. We indicated in Korea — *Beef* that one aspect of the "weighing and balancing process . . . comprehended in the determination of whether a WTO-consistent alternative measure" is reasonably available is the extent to which the alternative measure "contributes to the realization of the end pursued. In addition, we observed, in that case, that "[t]he more vital or important [the] common interests or values" pursued, the easier it would be to accept as "necessary" measures designed to achieve those ends. In this case, the objective pursued by the measure is the preservation of human life and health through the elimination, or reduction, of the well-known, and life-threatening, health risks posed by asbestos fibres. The value pursued is both vital and important in the highest degree. The remaining question, then, is whether there is an alternative measure that would achieve the same end and that is less restrictive of trade than a prohibition.

173. Canada asserts that "controlled use" represents a "reasonably available" measure that would serve the same end. The issue is, thus, whether France could reasonably be expected to employ "controlled use" practices to achieve its chosen level of health protection — a halt in the spread of asbestos-related health risks.

174. In our view, France could not reasonably be expected to employ *any* alternative measure if that measure would involve a continuation of the very risk that the Decree seeks to "halt." Such an alternative measure would, in effect, prevent France from achieving its chosen level of health protection. On the basis of the scientific evidence before it, the Panel found that, in general, the efficacy of "controlled use" remains to be demonstrated. Moreover, even in cases where "controlled use" practices are applied "with greater certainty," the scientific evidence suggests that the level of exposure can, in some circumstances, still be high enough for there to be a "significant residual risk of developing asbestos-related diseases." The Panel found too that the efficacy of "controlled use" is particularly doubtful for the building industry and for DIY enthusiasts, which are the most important users of cement-based products containing chrysotile asbestos. Given these factual findings by the Panel, we believe that "controlled use" would not allow France to achieve its chosen level of health protection by halting the spread of asbestos-related health risks. "Controlled use" would, thus, not be an alternative measure that would achieve the end sought by France.

175. For these reasons, we uphold the Panel's finding, in paragraph 8.222 of the Panel Report, that the European Communities has demonstrated a *prima facie* case that there was no "reasonably available alternative" to the prohibition inherent in the Decree. As a result, we also uphold the Panel's conclusion, in paragraph 8.223 of the Panel Report, that the Decree is "necessary to protect human . . . life or health" within the meaning of Article XX(b) of the GATT 1994.

NOTES AND QUESTIONS

1.   The *EC-Asbestos Case* involved a total import ban of a class of products. The Appellate Body's interpretation of the "necessary" test of Article XX(b) created much comment. *See, e.g.,* David A. Wirth, *Comment,* 96 AM. J. INT'L L. 435 (2002). Did the Appellate Body convincingly rebut the four arguments on this issue raised by Canada? Is the test for "necessary" a balancing test or a bright line test?

2.   In national legal systems and in the European Union, balancing tests are used to weigh the matter of the validity of local bans and environmental safeguards that impede free movement of goods in international trade. In the United States the matter is handled under the "dormant" Commerce Clause of the Constitution.

    (a)   In the United States, the Constitution requires that "The Congress shall have the power . . . To regulate commerce . . . among the several states." (U.S. Const. Art. I, sec. 8, cl. 3). The negative or "dormant" aspect of the Commerce Clause is that it prohibits economic protectionism. Thus, if a state enacts a law that impedes free movement of goods between it and other U.S. states, two frameworks are used to evaluate whether the law should stand. First, if the law in question overtly discriminates against interstate commerce, strict (rigorous) scrutiny applies, and the law will be struck down unless the state demonstrates that it has no other means to advance a legitimate state interest. Second, even if the law is not discriminatory, the law will be stricken if the burden on interstate commerce exceeds its local benefit. *See, e.g., Cotto Waxo. v. Williams,* 46 F.3d 790 (8th Cir. 1995) [upholding a Minnesota statute that prohibits the sale in the state of petroleum-based sweeping compounds]. The latter inquiry is a balancing test involving the weighing of the local benefit against the burden on interstate commerce. *See also Hampton Feedlot v. Nixon,* 249 F.3d 814 (8th Cir. 2001) [Missouri statute prohibiting price discrimination in the purchase of livestock].

    (b)   The European Union employs a balancing test to determine the validity of member states laws that impede the free movement of goods. For example, in *Kemikalieninspektionen v. Toolex Alpha,* Case C-4, 73/98, [2000] ECR (July 11, 2000), the European Court of Justice considered the legality of a Swedish law forbidding the use of trichloroethylene for industrial purposes. The Court employed a balancing test to uphold the law as justified under Article 30 of the European Community Treaty (now Article 36 of the Treaty on the Functioning of the European Union), which provides exceptions to the free movement of goods for health and environmental protection.

Did the WTO Appellate Body employ a balancing test to decide the question of whether a measure is "necessary" under GATT Article XX(b)?

3.   Consider the "like product" analysis of the Appellate Body in the *EC-Asbestos Case.* The Appellate Body broke new ground in distinguishing "like products" on the basis of their safety characteristics. Can this new doctrine be used to prohibit the import of products on the basis of how they are produced — on the basis of PPMs?

4. The *EC — Asbestos Case* involved an import ban. What about an export ban of dangerous goods? If a nation that bans certain chemicals and hazardous substances for domestic sales, enacts an export ban of such products, will this violate GATT Article XI? A GATT Working Group that was formed to consider this question was unable to come to agreement and issued a report that individual GATT members should decide this question for themselves. *See Report by the Chairman of the GATT Working Group on Export of Domestically Prohibited Goods and Other Hazardous Substances*, GATT Doc. L/6872 (1991). In the next section we look more closely at this question.

B. Hazardous Chemicals

Two global regimes address the manufacture, use and trading of toxic and hazardous chemicals. The Rotterdam Convention on the Prior Informed Consent Procedure for Certain Hazardous Chemicals and Pesticides in International Trade (1998), ratified by 143 parties (but not the United States), entered into force in 2004, and revised in 2011. The Stockholm Convention on Persistent Organic Pollutants (POPS) (2001), ratified by 178 parties (but not the United States), entered into force in 2004, and was amended in 2009. Both Conventions are reprinted in the Document Supplement.

1. The Rotterdam Convention

The Rotterdam Convention currently regulates 38 categories of chemicals and hazardous substances, including pesticides, such as DDT and dieldrin, and dangerous chemicals such as mercury compounds and asbestos, by subjecting international sales (exports and imports) of such chemicals and substances to a Prior Informed Consent (PIC) Procedure in international trade. Each party to the Convention must designate one or more Designated National Authorities (DNAs) who are to perform the administrative functions of the Convention, including the PIC Procedure. The PIC Procedure is a formal mechanism whereby importing parties make and disseminate their decisions as to whether they wish to receive future shipments of each of the chemicals listed in Annex III of the Convention. All parties are required to take a decision for each of the Annex III chemicals as to whether they wish to allow imports. Every six months, the Convention Secretariat then circulates the Import Responses (as the decisions of the importing parties are called) to all DNAs, and all Import Responses are also available on the Convention's website, http://www.pic.int. All exporting parties to the Convention are required to ensure that exports of chemicals do not occur contrary to the Import Responses.

The Rotterdam Convention's Secretariat is the FAO in Rome, Italy. The Conference of the Parties meets periodically to review the Convention, to take decisions, and to add chemicals to Annex III. The Convention facilitates the exchange of information among the parties; a Chemical Review Committee of experts reviews notifications and proposals from the parties and makes recommendations as to additions to Annex III.

Annex II to the Convention contains the criteria adopted by the parties for the listing of banned or severely restricted chemicals in Annex III. Article 9 of the Convention is a procedure for the removal of chemicals from listing under Annex

III. Annex VI of the Convention designates Arbitration for the resolution of disputes.

2. The Stockholm Convention

The Stockholm Convention focuses on POPs, persistent organic chemicals that, because of their toxicity and their persistence, pose especially dangerous problems for the environment and human health. The Stockholm Convention targets POPs that are listed either in Annex A — chemicals listed for elimination as to production, use, imports and exports; or Annex B — chemicals that are severely restricted as to acceptable uses. Article 3 of the Convention requires the parties to take stated measures to reduce or eliminate releases from intentional production and use of these listed chemicals. Article 4 is a Register of Specific Exemptions for the chemicals listed in Annexes A and B. Annex C of the Convention lists chemicals that are subject to the requirements of Article 5, which obligates the parties to take measures to reduce or eliminate releases from unintentional production.

Twelve POPs were initially listed under Annexes A, B, or C of the Stockholm Convention: aldrin (A); chlordane (A); DDT (B); dieldrin (A); endrin (A); heptachlor (A); hexachlorobenzene (A and C); mirex (A); toxaphene (A); polychlorinated biphenyls (A and C); polychlorinated dlbenzo-p-dioxins (C); and polychlorinated dibenzofurans (C). In 2009, the Conference of the Parties agreed to add nine additional chemicals to these lists. The new listing is generally binding on the parties who do not notify the Secretariat that they cannot accept a listing within one year of communication to them of the new listings. (Ten parties have declared that they must declare their acceptance of amendments). Only the government of New Zealand has declared that it cannot accept the 2009 amendments to Annexes A, B, and C.

There is an overlap between the Rotterdam and Stockholm Conventions as some chemicals, such as DDT and dieldrin, are subject to both international regimes. Since DDT is severely restricted, not banned under the Stockholm Convention, exports are subject to the PIC Procedure of the Rotterdam Convention.

NOTES AND QUESTIONS

1. *United States law.* The United States, which is not a party to either the Rotterdam or Stockholm Conventions, regulates hazardous chemicals under the Toxic Substances Control Act (TSCA), 15 U.S.C. §§ 2601–2692, for chemicals, and the Federal Insecticide, Fungicide, and Rodenticide Act (FIFRA), 7 U.S.C. §§ 136–136y, for pesticides. TSCA provides EPA with authority to regulate chemicals that present a risk to health or the environment. Section 6 of TSCA allows the EPA to restrict any chemical if it finds there is a reasonable basis to conclude there is an unreasonable risk to human health or the environment. Under TSCA section 5, notice must be given to the EPA at least 90 days prior to the manufacture or importation of any "new" chemical. Under TSCA section 12(b), 15 U.S.C. § 2611, the EPA is required to notify importing countries of the export of industrial chemicals that are subject to regulatory restrictions under U.S. law. Approximately 2000 chemicals come under this requirement. Under FIFRA section 17, 7 U.S.C. § 1360,

pesticides intended solely for exports do not have to be registered with the EPA provided the exporter obtains and submits to EPA, prior to export, a statement from the foreign purchaser acknowledging that the purchaser is aware that the product is not registered in the United States and cannot be sold there. Note that U.S. export notification requirements for chemicals and pesticides are more lenient than the PIC Procedure under the Rotterdam Convention: while the U.S. laws require notice, the Rotterdam Convention requires the importing countries' consents. Is this important? The U.S. is also not subject to the trade restrictions and bans of the Stockholm Convention. Is this a problem? Do you think the United States should ratify these two Conventions?

2. ***The European Union's REACH program.*** In 2006, the European Union adopted a new regulatory regime for chemical substances, the Registration, Evaluation, and Authorization of Chemicals (REACH), Council Regulation (EC) No. 1907/2006 (18 Dec. 2006), which covers all chemical substances both manufactured and imported. REACH required all chemicals sold in the EU to be registered and evaluated by the European Chemical Agency (ECHA), which also assesses concern to the environment and public health. Listed Substances of Very High Concern may not be used or sold unless the company involved is granted an affirmative authorization by the ECHA. REACH is generally considered much more stringent than the U.S. TSCA and FIFRA. Is a precautionary approach warranted in connection with chemicals or is this simply too burdensome for industry?

PROBLEM 5-4
STATE B ENACTS A BAN AND RESTRICTIONS ON THE EXPORT OF CERTAIN CHEMICALS

State B is a developed nation that is a member of the WTO. State B has banned the production and use of DDT within its territory. State B is a party to both the Rotterdam and the Stockholm Conventions. While under the Stockholm Convention DDT is a severely restricted chemical, State B plans to adopt a total ban on DDT exports, reasoning that since DDT is banned domestically, exports should not be permitted. State B is also concerned about exports of DDT because, in the past, imported fruits and vegetables from State C, also a WTO member, have been found to contain unacceptable levels of DDT residue.

If State B enacts a total ban on the export of DDT, going beyond what is required under the Stockholm and Rotterdam Conventions, will it be acting inconsistently with its obligations under the WTO agreements?

C. Hazardous Waste Management

1. The Basel Convention

The centerpiece of the global regime to address the international transfer of hazardous wastes is the Basel Convention on the Control of Transboundary Movements of Hazardous Wastes and their Disposal (1989), in force since 1992. The Basel Convention, which is reprinted in the Document Supplement, currently has 178 parties, not including the United States. The aims of the Basel Convention are to reduce the generation of hazardous wastes, to encourage their disposal as close as possible to the source of their generation, and to ensure that all hazardous wastes are managed in an environmentally sound manner. An estimated 300 to 500 million tons of hazardous wastes are generated each year, some 95% of which are generated in developed countries. The Basel Convention was concluded primarily to assure that transboundary movements of such wastes, particularly from developed to developing countries where the costs of disposal are typically much less than in developed countries, are carried out, if at all, under internationally agreed standards. The Basel Convention was created after an outcry concerning incidents in the 1980s, such as fly ash from Philadelphia deposited on the Kassa Island in Guinea and the illegal transport of hazardous waste from Italy to Nigeria.

The coverage of the Basel Convention is very broad. Hazardous wastes include (Article 1) a wide variety of substances listed in Annex I and for most purposes include household wastes listed in Annex II of the Convention. In addition, covered hazardous wastes include all wastes defined as such by the party of import or export. Radioactive wastes and wastes from the normal operation of ships are excluded from coverage.

The Basel Convention comes into play whenever a covered category of waste is destined for transboundary "disposal," which is broadly defined as including (Annex IV) both operations which do not lead to the possibility of recovery, reclamation or reuse and operations which do allow for the possibility of recovery, reclamation and reuse. Thus international sales of hazardous wastes for recycling come within the scope of the Basel Convention.

The Basel Convention allows transboundary movements of hazardous wastes only if the states of export does not have the appropriate facilities for treating the wastes in an environmentally sound manner, or, alternatively, if the wastes are required for recycling or recovery in the state of import. (Art. 4, para. 9). Export of wastes is prohibited to Antarctica and to any states where there is "reason to believe" that the wastes in question will not be managed in an environmentally safe manner. (Art. 4, para. 2(e)). In addition, any party to the convention has the right to prohibit the import of hazardous wastes, and that right must be respected by exporting states (Art. 4, para. 1).

The Basel Convention prohibits both imports from and exports to non-parties. (Art. 4, para. 5).

In cases where the transboundary movement of hazardous wastes is permitted — between parties — Articles 6 and 7 mandate a system of prior informed consent (PIC): the exporting state must require the generator of the waste to give notice in writing to the designated Competent Authority in the importing state who must give its express written consent to the state of export, based on detailed information provided by the exporting to the importing state. Each party to the Convention, therefore, must designate a Competent Authority to administer its obligations under the Convention. (Art. 5).

Article 11 of the Convention allows parties to enter into bilateral, regional, or multilateral agreements or arrangements with parties or non-parties regarding the transboundary movement of hazardous wastes as long as these agreements do not derogate from the environmentally sound management of hazardous wastes as required by the Basel Convention.

In the event of a transboundary movement of hazardous waste to which consent has not been given under the PIC procedure, the state of export must take back the waste if environmentally sound disposal cannot be arranged within 90 days. (Art. 8). If illegal traffic occurs on the part of the importer, the importing state must assure the disposal of the waste in an environmentally sound manner. (Art. 9).

The Basel Convention operates through a Secretariat (Art. 16) and a Conference of the Parties (Art. 15). There is close cooperation between the Secretariat of the Basel Convention and the secretariats of the Rotterdam and Stockholm Conventions.

2. The Ban Amendment

At the Conference of the Parties to the Basel Convention in 1994, the parties adopted Decision 11/12, commonly called the Ban Amendment. This decision amends the Convention to ban the export of all wastes covered by the Convention by OECD (developed) parties (including the EU and Liechtenstein) to non-OECD countries (generally developing countries). This ban includes exports of waste that are made for the purpose of recycling and recovery. The Ban Amendment has not entered into force but is generally observed.

In 1992, the OECD Council, perhaps anticipating the Ban Amendment, adopted Decision C(92)39 Concerning the Transfrontier Movement of Hazardous Waste Destined for Recovery Operations. This decision, which was supported by the United States, facilitated exports of hazardous wastes between OECD countries for purposes of recycling and reuse. The U.S. EPA has promulgated regulations implementing this decision. 40 C.F.R. §§ 262.80–262.89.

3. Liability for Damages

In 1999, the parties to the Basel Convention adopted a Protocol on Liability and Compensation for Damage Resulting from Transboundary Movements of Hazardous Wastes and their Disposal. This Protocol, which is not yet in force, imposes strict liability for damages caused by illegal movements of transboundary hazardous waste on a graduated scale that can reach a maximum of 10 million units of account.[94] In addition, fault-based liability is unlimited. Parties are required to implement these liability provisions in their national laws, and are obligated to provide mutual recognition and enforcement of judgments rendered under the Protocol.

---

[94] A unit of account is a Special Drawing Right as defined by the International Monetary Organization (currently a weighted basket of values of the U.S. dollar, the British pound sterling, the Japanese yen and the euro).

4. Regional and Bilateral Agreements

A number of regional and bilateral hazardous waste agreements have been notified to the Basel Convention Secretariat, which on its web site, http://www.basel.int, recounts these as follows:

- The (Waigani) Treaty on Hazardous and Toxic Wastes (July 1995);

- the Bamako Convention on the Ban of Import into Africa and the Control of Transboundary Movement and Management of Hazardous Wastes within Africa (January 1991);

- the Protocol of the Southeast Pacific Countries on the Control of the Transboundary Movement of Noxious Wastes and their Disposal;

- the Central American Agreement on the Transboundary Movement of Hazardous Wastes; the Protocol for the Protection of the Mediterranean Sea against Pollution resulting from Exploration and Exploitation of the Continental Shelf and the Seabed and its Subsoil;

- the OECD Council Decisions concerning the control of transfrontier movements of wastes; the Council of the European Communities Regulation (EEC) No 259/93 on the supervision and control of shipments of waste within, into and out of the European Community; and

- the Lome IV ACP-EEC Convention.

In addition, three Bilateral Agreements are referred to:

- the Agreement between the Government of Canada and the government of the United States of America concerning the Transboundary Movement of Hazardous Waste;

- the Agreement of Cooperation between the United States of America and the United Mexican States Regarding the Transboundary Shipments of Hazardous Wastes and Hazardous Substances; and

- the Agreement between the Government of the Kingdom of Sweden and the Government of the Kingdom of Morocco on the Control of the Transboundary Movements of Toxic Wastes and Other Wastes for Recovery Operations.

5. Waste Prevention, Minimization, and Recovery

The Basel Convention has two main pillars: the regulation of transboundary movements of hazardous wastes; and requiring that such wastes are managed and disposed on in an environmentally sound manner. A relatively neglected topic under the Basel Convention is waste prevention, minimization, and recovery. At the 2011 Conference of the Parties (COP-10), the member governments, meeting at Cartagena, Columbia, adopted the "Cartagena Declaration on the Prevention, Minimization, and Recovery of Hazardous and Other Wastes." This Declaration calls for a hierarchy of waste management options: (1) prevention; (2) reduction at the source; (3) recovery and reuse; and (4) final safe disposal. It remains to be seen how this Declaration will be implemented.

6. Compliance

PROBLEM 5-5
STATE A SEEKS A PROFIT FROM DISPOSING OF
HAZARDOUS WASTES

State A is a developing country party to the Basel Convention with a very low GDP. The government of State A seeks to establish a hazardous waste disposal and recycling center in order to attract contracts from other states that want to dispose of hazardous wastes. State A can profit greatly from such contracts and provide lucrative employment opportunities for its people. State A has accordingly notified its partner states that it is open for business as a place for disposal of hazardous wastes of all kinds. However, the hazardous waste center in State A is experiencing great problems. The area around the center has become contaminated and the environment and health of the surrounding area is endangered. State A officials, however, seek to conceal the true situation and publicly deny that there is any problem at their center.

What can be done to assure compliance by State A of its obligations under the Basel Convention?

Consider the following provisions of the Compliance Mechanism of the Basel Convention:

COMPLIANCE MECHANISM OF THE BASEL
CONVENTION

Chapter I

OVERVIEW OF THE BASEL COMPLIANCE MECHANISM

1. To assist Parties to comply with their Obligations under the Convention, the Basel Compliance Mechanism:

- Establishes a Committee dedicated to help Parties to implement the provisions of the Convention;

- Establishes a procedure that is non-confrontational, transparent, cost-effective, preventive and non-binding in nature;

- Pays particular attention to the special needs of developing countries and countries with economies in transition;

- Promotes cooperation between all Parties;

- Considers specific submissions with a view to determining the facts and root causes of the matter of concern;

- Assists in the resolution of compliance difficulties by providing Parties with advice, non-binding recommendations and information;

- Recommends to the Conference of the Parties further additional measures to address Parties' compliance difficulties; and

- Reviews, as directed by the Conference of the Parties, general issues of compliance and implementation under the Convention.

2. A bit of history:

- The Mechanism for Promoting Implementation and Compliance was established by Decision VII12 of the Conference of the Parties adopted in 2002.

- The Mechanism was established as a subsidiary body of the Conference of the Parties under Article 15, paragraph 5 (e) of the Convention.

3. Who are the members of the Committee?

- The Committee is comprised of 15 members: three from each of the five regional groups of the United Nations (the African group, the Asian group, the Central and Eastern European group, the Latin America and Caribbean group, and the Western Europe and Others group).

- Although the members are nominated by Governments, they serve objectively and in the best interest of the Basel Convention.

- The members have expertise relating to the Basel Convention in areas including scientific, technical, socio-economic and/or legal fields.

Chapter II

HOW TO USE THE MECHANISM

1. The Committee initiates its work by two procedures: (1) Specific Submissions, and (2) General Review

- Specific submissions can be made by:

    (a) A Party as to its own compliance difficulty ("self-submissions").

    (b) A Party as to another Party's failure to comply with the obligations under the Convention ("Party-to-Party submissions").

    (c) The Secretariat as to Party's reporting obligations under the Convention ("Secretariat submissions").

- General review can be initiated by a decision of the Conference of the Parties.

7. Information considered by the Committee

- During its review of a submission, the Committee will consider:

    (a) the information provided in the submission and in the response provided by the Party whose compliance is in question;

    (b) the responses and comments presented by the Party whose compliance is in question during the consideration of the matter;

- The Committee may determine that it requires further information and may seek such information through the following means:

    (a) Consult with other bodies of the Convention;

(b) Information gathering in the territory of relevant Party(ies) with the agreement of that (those) Party(ies);

(c) Consult with the Secretariat and draw upon its experience and knowledge base compiled under Article 16 of the Convention;

(d) Request information through the Secretariat, where appropriate in the form of a report, on matters under its consideration;

(e) Request further information from any sources and draw upon outside expertise, as it considers necessary and appropriate, either with the consent of the Party concerned or as directed by the Conference of the Parties;

(f) Review national reports of the Parties provided under Article 13 of the Convention.

- The Committee, any Party or others involved in its deliberations must protect the confidentiality of information received in confidence. A Party may indicate that all the information it provides is to be treated as confidential.

8. Remedies available to the Committee

Step 1: *Facilitation Procedure*

- The Committee considers any submission made to it with a view to determining the facts and root causes of the matter of concern and assist in its resolution. As part of this process, after coordinating with that Party, the Committee may provide a Party with advice, non-binding recommendations and information relating to (amongst other things):

    (a) establishing and/or strengthening its domestic/regional regulatory regimes;

    (b) facilitation of assistance in particular to developing countries and countries with economies in transition, including on how to access financial and technical support, such as technology transfer and capacity-building;

    (c) elaborating, as appropriate and with the cooperation of the Party or Parties faced with the compliance problems, voluntary compliance action plans, and reviewing their implementation. A voluntary compliance action plan may include benchmarks, objectives and indicators of the plan, as well as an indicative timeline for its implementation.

    (d) Any follow-up arrangements for progress reporting to the Committee, including through the national reporting procedure under article 13.

- Advice, non-binding recommendations and information other than those listed above should be provided in agreement with that Party.

Step 2: *Recommendation to the Conference of the Parties on additional measures*

- If, after undertaking the facilitation procedure, and taking into account the cause, type, degree and frequency of compliance difficulties, the Committee considers it necessary to pursue further measures to address a Party's implementation and compliance difficulties, it may recommend to the Conference of the Parties that it considers:

(a) Further support under the Convention for the Party concerned, including prioritisation of technical assistance and capacity-building and access to financial resources; or

(b) Issuing a cautionary statement and provide advice regarding future compliance in order to help Parties to implement the provisions of the Basel Convention and to promote cooperation between all Parties.

- Any of the actions above must be consistent with Article 15 of the Convention on the functions of the Conference of the Parties.

9. Decision-making

- As is the normal practice of Basel Convention bodies, every effort is taken to reach decisions on matters of substance by consensus. Where consensus cannot be reached, decisions are adopted by a two-thirds majority of the members present and voting, or by eight members, whichever is greater.

- Decisions will only be adopted if there are at least ten members of the Committee present.

Chapter IV

THE GENERAL REVIEW PROCEDURE

1. What general issues of compliance and implementation can be the subject of review?

- The Committee may, under the direction of the Conference of the Parties, review general issues of compliance and implementation relating to (amongst other things):

(a) Ensuring the environmentally sound management and disposal of hazardous and other wastes.

(b) Training customs and other personnel.

(c) Accessing technical and financial support, particularly for developing countries, including technology transfer and capacity-building.

(d) Establishing and developing means of detecting and eradicating illegal traffic, including investigating, sampling and testing.

(e) Monitoring, assessing and facilitating reporting under the Convention.

(f) The implementation of, and compliance with, specified obligations under the Convention.

2. What does the Committee do once it has conducted a review?

- Once the Committee has undertaken a review, it reports to the next ordinary meeting of the Conference of the Parties on any conclusions and/or recommendations it has developed and on its suggestions for any future work that facilitates implementation of, and compliance with, the

Basel Convention. The Conference of the Parties will consider such recommendations, and may approve them.

PROBLEM 5-6
STATE M SEEKS TO VINDICATE ITS RIGHT TO FREE TRADE IN HAZARDOUS WASTES UNDER THE WTO AGREEMENTS

State M is a member of the WTO and is a non-party to the Basel Convention. The government of State M believes that the Basel Convention regime is counterproductive in that it seeks to protect the environment but in reality it is harming the environment by impeding global movements of waste for recycling and reuse. The government of State M has refused to join the Basel Convention because it wishes to promote global free trade and recycling of hazardous and other wastes. Last month, Ace Recycling Inc., private company in State M that is in the business of recycling hazardous wastes, lost a contract to purchase such wastes from a company in State P, also a WTO member. The President of the State P company told the CEO of Recycling, Inc.: "I would love to deal with you, but I am told by my lawyers that, since my government is a party to the Basel Convention, we cannot deal with you and cannot sell you our waste even for recycling purposes because the Basel Convention prohibits my government and my company from exporting waste to your country." There is no question that Recycling, Inc. employs state-of-the-art facilities for the recycling and disposal of hazardous waste.

The government of State M seeks your advice whether to bring a complaint against State P at the WTO to vindicate its rights to free trade in waste products under the GATT. What are the chances such a complaint will succeed?

NOTES AND QUESTIONS

1. *United States law.* Is waste a "product" entitled to protection under the Commerce Clause of the Constitution of the United States? The Supreme Court, in *City of Philadelphia v. New Jersey*, 437 U.S. 617, 621–23 (1978) ruled that even "valueless" out-of-state wastes fall within the Commerce Clause definition of "commerce." Thus, in principle, waste is guaranteed free movement across state lines and implicates the constitutional protections of the Commerce Clause. In *Fort Gratiot Sanitary Landfill v. Michigan Department of Resources*, 504 U.S. 353 (1992), the Supreme Court, in a ruling under the dormant Commerce Clause, held invalid a local law that limited waste from both in-state and out-of-state sources. Similarly, in *C&A Carbone, Inc. v. Clarkston*, 511 U.S. 383 (1994), the Supreme Court overturned a local waste flow control ordinance that required trash haulers to deliver trash to a particular private waste processing facility, because it increased costs for disposal of some out-of-state waste. But in *United Haulers Association v. Oneida-Herkimer*, 550 U.S. 330 (2007), the Supreme Court upheld a county flow-control ordinance requiring trash haulers to deliver waste to a particular public processing facility. In the latter case the Supreme Court majority distinguished *Carbone* on the ground that public facilities are more benign than private ones. But the Court's majority hastened to add that it approved local flow-control ordinances "which treat in-state private business interests exactly the same as out-of-state ones, [and] do not discriminate against interstate commerce for purposes of the

dormant Commerce Clause." 550 U.S. at 341. Importantly, the Court added: "by requiring all waste to be deposited at [the local] facilities, the Counties have markedly increased their ability to enforce recycling laws. If the haulers could take their waste to any disposal site, achieving an equal level of enforcement would be much more costly, if not impossible. For these reasons, any arguable burden the ordinances impose on interstate commerce does not exceed their public benefits." 550 U.S. at 346. The Supreme Court's opinion in *United Haulers* was motivated by a balancing process in favor of allowing local restrictions to operate when their purpose and effect is to encourage waste minimization and recycling that protects the environment. *See also American Beverage Association v. Snyder*, 700 F.3d 796 (6th Cir. 2012) [upholding a state "bottle bill" requirement that returnable containers of liquid drinks possess a unique-to-Michigan mark identification label].

2. *The Walloon Waste Case.* In the European Union, the European Court of Justice in the *Walloon Waste Case, Commission v. Belgium*, Case C-2/90 [1992] ECR 1-4431 (9 July 1992), ruled that wastes, whether recyclable or non-recyclable, are *goods* for purposes of the European Community Treaty and are in principle entitled to free movement within the European Union. But the Court nevertheless ruled that, absent EU secondary legislation, a local ban on imports of wastes into Wallonia could be justified as a mandatory requirement necessary to protect the local environment, since it was undisputed that Wallonia had been confronted with a massive and abnormal influx of wastes from other regions. The Court also drew its ruling from Article 130r(2) of the EC Treaty, which requires environmental damage to be rectified at its source (the proximity principle). Thus, the EU, like the United States, recognizes that, although wastes are commerce, some local restrictions to benefit the environment are valid.

3. *United States law governing the export of hazardous waste.* Two U.S. federal laws, the Resource Conservation and Recovery Act (RCRA), 42 U.S.C. §§ 6901–6992, and the Comprehensive Environmental Response, Compensation, and Liability Act (CERCLA), 42 U.S.C. §§ 9601–9675, provide comprehensive regulation of solid waste, including hazardous waste, and establish liability for liability and response costs. The export of hazardous waste is regulated by RCRA section 3017, 42 U.S.C. § 6938, which establishes notification, consent, and manifest and reporting requirements for the export of hazardous waste. RCRA thus creates a notification, monitoring, and consent program for the export of hazardous waste from the United States. The EPA administers this law (40 C.F.R. Subparts E and H). The EPA has entered into a Memorandum of Understanding with U.S. Customs and Border Protection, which has enforcement authority to seize shipments that do not have proper documentation.

4. As a practical matter, U.S. exports of hazardous waste are minimal, amounting to only about 1% of hazardous wastes generated. The vast majority of exported hazardous waste goes to Mexico and Canada pursuant to bilateral agreements with those countries. See U.S. EPA, Regulations Governing Hazardous Waste, available, http://www.epa.gov/osw/inforesources/pubs/orientat/rom33.pdf., accessed 5 January 2013.

5. *The Metalclad Case.* In 1993, Metalclad Corporation purchased the Mexican company Confinamiento Tecnico de Residuos Industriales, S.A. de C.V.

(COTERIN) in order to build and operate a hazardous waste transfer station and landfill in Guadalcazar, San Luis Potosi. Although the federal government of Mexico and the state government of San Luis Potosi had granted COTERIN permits to construct and operate the landfill, the municipality of Guadalcazar denied Metalclad a municipal construction permit, and the governor of San Luis Potosi subsequently declared an area encompassing the landfill site to be an ecological reserve. Metalclad brought a complaint against Mexico under Chapter 11 (Investment) of the North American Free Trade Agreement (NAFTA), and the NAFTA Arbitral Tribunal convened under Chapter 11 ruled that Mexico's regulatory requirements were a violation of NAFTA Article 1105 (denial of fair and equitable treatment because of lack of transparency) and an expropriation in violation of NAFTA Article 1110. The Tribunal awarded damages plus 6% interest to Metalclad totaling USD 16,685,000. Mexico filed suit in British Columbia, the site of the arbitration proceeding, to set aside the award. The trial court, examining the case under British Columbia's International Commercial Arbitration Act, set aside the award in part, and while this case was pending before the British Columbia Court of Appeal, the parties settled for USD 15,626,260.[95] *See Metalclad Corporation v. Mexico*, ICSID Case No. ARB(AF)/97/I, 40 I.L.M. 36 (2001); and *Mexico v. Metalclad Corporation*, 2001 B.C.S.C. 664.

6.   ***Amlon Metals v. FMC Corporation, 775 F. Supp. 668 (S.D.N.Y.1991).*** Amlon contracted with FMC to ship recyclable copper residues from Baltimore to a customer in the UK. The residues were found to contain very high concentrations of organic chemicals, including xylene, in quantities over 10 times that disclosed by FMC. UK authorities were alerted and required the UK consignee to drum the wastes and to store them away from the environment, pending the return of the wastes to the United States. Amlon filed suit in the UK against FMC for damages, but the English court dismissed the case, ruling that American law applied since all the relevant actions took place in the U.S. Amlon then filed suit against FMC in New York, but the court granted a motion to dismiss, ruling that RCRA did not have extraterritorial application and did not reach damages incurred abroad. The court permitted common law claims involving fraud, strict liability, breach of warranty, and negligence to go forward, and the case was ultimately settled. *See* Lisa T. Belensky, *Cradle to Border: U.S. Hazardous Waste Export Regulations and International Law*, 17 BERKELEY J. INT'L. L. 95, 114 (1999).

Suppose the United States had been a party to the Basel Convention when this incident occurred, what remedy would the UK have against the United States? [See Article 8 of the Basel Convention, which requires the exporting country to take back the waste in the event of a violation].

---

[95] Metalclad Corp. Press Release, June 13, 2001.

BRAZIL-MEASURES AFFECTING IMPORTS OF RETREADED TYRES REPORT OF THE APPELLATE BODY
WT/DS332/AB/R (Dec. 3, 2007)

Introduction

1. The European Communities appeals certain issues of law and legal interpretations developed in the Panel Report, *Brazil — Measures Affecting Imports of Retreaded Tyres* (the "Panel Report").[96] The Panel was established to consider a complaint by the European Communities concerning the consistency of certain measures imposed by Brazil on the importation and marketing of retreaded tyres[97] with the *General Agreement on Tariffs and Trade 1994* (the "GATT 1994").

2. Before the Panel, the European Communities claimed that Brazil imposed a prohibition on the importation of retreaded tyres, notably by virtue of Article 40 of Portaria No. 14 of the Secretaria de Comércio Exterior ("SECEX") (Secretariat of Foreign Trade of the Brazilian Ministry of Development, Industry, and Foreign Trade), dated 17 November 2004 ("Portaria SECEX 14/2004"), and that this prohibition was inconsistent with Article XI:I of the GATT 1994. The European Communities also contended that certain Brazilian measures providing for the imposition of fines on the importation of retreaded tyres, and on the marketing, transportation, storage, keeping, or warehousing of imported retreaded tyres, were similarly inconsistent with Article XI:1 or, alternatively, Article III:4 of the GATT 1994. In addition, the European Communities made claims under Article III:4 of the GATT 1994 in respect of certain state measures prohibiting the marketing of, and/or imposing disposal obligations on the importers of, imported retreaded tyres. Finally, the European Communities challenged the exemption from the import prohibition on retreaded tyres and associated fines provided by Brazil to retreaded tyres originating in countries of the Mercado Común del Sur ("MERCOSUR") (Southern Common Market). The European Communities contended that these exemptions were inconsistent with Articles 1:1 and XIII:1 of the GATT 1994.

3. Brazil did not contest that the prohibition on the importation of retreaded tyres and associated fines were prima facie inconsistent with Article XI:1; or that state measures prohibiting the marketing of, and/or imposing disposal obligations on the importers of, imported retreaded tyres were prima facie inconsistent with Article III:4; or that the exemptions from both the import prohibition and associated fines

---

[96] *WT/DS332/R*, 12 June 2007.

[97] Retreaded tyres are used tyres that are reconditioned for further use by stripping the worn tread from the skeleton (casing) and replacing it with new material in the form of a new tread, and sometimes with new material also covering parts or all of the sidewalls. (See Panel Report, para. 2.1) Retreaded tyros can be produced through different methods, all indistinctively referred to as "retreading." These methods are: (i) top-capping, which consists of replacing only the tread; (ii) re-capping, which entails replacing the tread and part of the sidewall; and (iii) remoulding, which consists of replacing the tread and the sidewall including all or part of the lower area of the tyre. (See ibid., para. 2.2) The retreaded tyres covered in this dispute are classified under subheadings 4012.11 (motor cars), 4012.12 (buses and lorries), 4012.13 (aircraft), and 4012.19 (other types) of the *International Convention on the Harmonized Commodity Description and Coding System, done at Brussels*, 14 June 1983. In contrast, used tyres are classified under subheading 4012.20. New tyres are classified under heading 4011. (See *ibid.*, para. 2.4)

afforded to retreaded tyres imported from MERCOSUR countries were prima facie inconsistent with Articles I:1 and XIII:1 of the GATT 1994. Instead, Brazil submitted that the prohibition on the importation of retreaded tyres and associated fines, and state measures restricting the marketing of imported retreaded tyres, were all justified under Article XX(b) of the GATT 1994. Brazil contended that the fines associated with the import prohibition on retreaded tyres were justified also under Article XX(d) of the GATT 1994. Brazil further maintained that the exemption from the import prohibition and associated fines afforded to imports of remoulded tyres from MERCOSUR countries was justified under Articles XX(d) and XXIV of the GATT 1994.

Background and the Measure at Issue

Factual Background

118. Tyres are an integral component in passenger cars, lorries, and airplanes and, as such, their use is widespread in modem society. New passenger cars are typically sold with new tyres. When tyres need to be replaced, consumers in some countries may have a choice between new tyres or "retreaded" tyres. This dispute concerns the latter category of tyres. Retreaded tyres are used tyres that have been reconditioned for further use by stripping the worn tread from the skeleton (casing) and replacing it with new material in the form of a new tread, and sometimes with new material also covering parts or all of the sidewalls. Retreaded tyres can be produced through different methods, one of which is called "remoulding."

119. At the end of their useful life, tyres become waste, the accumulation of which is associated with risks to human, animal, and plant life and health. Specific risks to human life and health include:

> (i) the transmission of dengue, yellow fever and malaria through mosquitoes which use tyres as breeding grounds; and (ii) the exposure of human beings to toxic emissions caused by tyre fires which may cause loss of short-term memory, learning disabilities, immune system suppression, cardiovascular problems, but also cancer, premature mortality, reduced lung function, suppression of the immune system, respiratory effects, heart and chest problems.

Risks to animal and plant life and health include: "(i) the exposure of animals and plants to toxic emissions caused by tyre tires; and (ii) the transmission of a mosquito-borne disease (dengue) to animals."

120. Governments take actions to minimize the adverse effects of waste tyres. Policies to address "waste" include preventive measures aiming at reducing the generation of additional waste tyres, as well as remedial measures aimed at managing and disposing of tyres that can no longer be used or retreaded, such as landtilling, stockpiling, the incineration of waste tyres, and material recycling.

121. The Panel observed that the parties to this dispute have not suggested that retreaded tyres used on vehicles pose any particular risks compared to new tyres, provided that they comply with appropriate safety standards. Various international

standards exist in relation to retreaded tyres, including, for example, the norm stipulating that passenger car tyres may be retreaded only once. One important difference between new and retreaded tyres is that the latter have a shorter lifespan and therefore reach the stage of being waste earlier.

The Panel's Analysis of the Necessity of the Import Ban

A. *The Panel's Necessity Analysis under Article XX(b) of the GATT 1994*

133. The first legal issue raised by the European Communities' appeal relates to the Panel's finding that the Import Ban is "necessary" within the meaning of Article XX(b) of the GATT 1994. The European Communities challenges three specific aspects of the Panel's analysis under Article XX(b). First, the European Communities contends that the Panel applied an "erroneous legal standard" assessing the contribution of the Import Ban to the realization of the ends pursued by it, and that it did not properly weigh this contribution in its analysis of the necessity of the Import Ban. Secondly, the European Communities submits that the Panel did not define correctly the alternatives to the Import Ban and erred in excluding possible alternatives proposed by the European Communities. Thirdly, the European Communities argues that, in its analysis under Article XX(b), the Panel did not carry out a proper, if any, weighing and balancing of the relevant factors. We will examine these contentions of the European Communities in turn.

143. In *U.S. — Gambling*, the Appellate Body addressed the "necessity" test in the context of Article XIV of the GATS. The Appellate Body stated that the weighing and balancing process inherent in the necessity analysis "begins with an assessment of the 'relative importance' of the interests or values furthered by the challenged measure," and also involves an assessment of other factors, which will usually include "the contribution of the measure to the realization of the ends pursued by it" and "the restrictive impact of the measure on international commerce."

144. It is against this background that we must determine whether the Panel erred in assessing the contribution of the Import Ban to the realization of the objective pursued by it, and in the manner in which it weighed this contribution in its analysis of the necessity of the Import Ban. We begin by identifying the objective pursued by the Import Ban. The Panel found that the objective of the Import Ban is the reduction of the "exposure to the risks to human, animal or plant life or health arising from the accumulation of waste tyres," and noted that "few interests are more 'vital' and 'important' than protecting human beings from health risks, and that protecting the environment is no less important." The Panel also observed that "Brazil's chosen level of protection is the reduction of the risks of waste tyre accumulation to the maximum extent possible. Regarding the trade restrictiveness of the measure, the Panel rioted that it is "as trade-restrictive as can be, as far as retreaded tyres from non-MERCOSUR countries are concerned, since it aims to halt completely their entry into Brazil."

146. We note that the Panel chose to conduct a qualitative analysis of the contribution of the Import Ban to the achievement of its objective. In previous cases, the Appellate Body has not established a requirement that such a contribu-

tion be quantified. To the contrary, in EC — Asbestos, the Appellate Body emphasized that there is "no requirement under Article XX(b) of the GATT 1994 to quantify, as such, the risk to human life or health." In other words, "[a] risk may be evaluated either in quantitative or qualitative terms." Although the reference by the Appellate Body to the quantification of a risk is not the same as the quantification of the contribution of a measure to the realization of the objective pursued by it (which could be as it is in this case, the reduction of a risk), it appears to us that the same line of reasoning applies to the analysis of the contribution, which can be done either in quantitative or in qualitative terms.

147. Accordingly, we do not accept the European Communities' contention that the Panel was under an obligation to quantify the contribution of the Import Ban to the reduction in the number of waste tyres and to determine the number of waste tyres that would be reduced as a result of the Import Ban. In our view, the Panel's choice of a qualitative analysis was within the bounds of the latitude it enjoys in choosing a methodology for the analysis of the contribution.

148. The Panel analyzed the contribution of the Import Ban to the achievement of its objective in a coherent sequence. It examined first the impact of the replacement of imported retreaded tyres with *new tyres* on the reduction of waste. Secondly, the Panel sought to determine whether imported retreaded tyres would be replaced with *domestically retreaded tyres*, which led it to examine whether domestic used tyres can be and are being retreaded in Brazil. Thirdly, it considered whether the reduction in the number of waste tyres would contribute to a reduction of the risks to human, animal, and plant life and health.

Assuming, for the time being, that the Panel assessed the facts in accordance with Article 11 of the DSU, it appears to us that the Panel's analysis supports its conclusion that the Import Ban is capable of making a contribution and can result in a reduction of exposure to the targeted risks. We have now to determine whether this was sufficient to conclude that the Import Ban is "necessary" within the meaning of Article XX(b) of the GATT 1994.

150. As the Panel recognized, an import ban is "by design as trade-restrictive as can be."

151. This does not mean that an import ban, or another trade-restrictive measure, the contribution of which is not immediately observable, cannot be justified under Article XX(b). We recognize that certain complex public health or environmental problems may be tackled only with a comprehensive policy comprising a multiplicity of interacting measures.

153. We observe, first, that the Panel analyzed the contribution of the Import Ban as initially designed, without taking into account the imports of remoulded tyres under the MERCOSUR exemption. As we indicated above, this is not the only possible approach. Nevertheless, we proceed with our examination of the Panel's reasoning on that basis for the reasons we explained earlier. In the light of the evidence adduced by the parties, the Panel was of the view that the Import Ban would lead to imported retreaded tyres being replaced with retreaded tyres made from local casings, or with new tyres that are retreadable. As concerns new tyres, the Panel observed, and we agree, that retreaded tyres "have by definition a shorter

lifespan than new tyres" and that, accordingly, the Import Ban "may lead to a reduction in the total number of waste tyres because imported retreaded tyres may be substituted for by new tyres which have a longer lifespan." As concerns tyres retreaded in Brazil from local casings, the Panel was satisfied that Brazil had the production capacity to retread domestic used tyres and that "at least some domestic used tyres are being retreaded in Brazil." The Panel also agreed that Brazil has taken a series of measures to facilitate the access of domestic retreaders to good-quality used tyres, and that new tyres sold in Brazil are high-quality tyres that comply with international standards and have the potential to be retreaded. The Panel's conclusion with which we agree was that, "if the domestic retreading industry retreads more domestic used tyres, the overall number of waste tyres will be reduced by giving a second life to some used tyres, which otherwise would have become waste immediately after their first and only life." For these reasons, the Panel found that a reduction of waste tyres would result from the Import Ban and that, therefore, the Import Ban would contribute to reducing exposure to the risks associated with the accumulation of waste tyres. As the Panel's analysis was qualitative, the Panel did not seek to estimate, in quantitative terms, the reduction of waste tyres that would result from the Import Ban, or the time horizon of such a reduction. Such estimates would have been very useful and, undoubtedly, would have strengthened the foundation of the Panel's findings. Having said that, it does not appear to us erroneous to conclude, on the basis of the hypotheses made, tested, and accepted by the Panel, that fewer waste tyres will be generated with the Import Ban than otherwise.

154. Moreover, we wish to underscore that the Import Ban must be viewed in the broader context of the comprehensive strategy designed and implemented by Brazil to deal with waste tyres. This comprehensive strategy includes not only the Import Ban but also the import ban on used tyres, as well as the collection and disposal scheme adopted by CONAMA Resolution 258/1999, as amended in 2002, which makes it mandatory for domestic manufacturers and importers of new tyres to provide for the safe disposal of waste tyres in specified proportions. For its part, CONAMA Resolution 258/1999, as amended in 2002, aims to reduce the exposure to risks arising horn the accumulation of waste tyres by forcing manufacturers and importers of new tyres to collect and dispose of waste tyres at a ratio of five waste tyres for every four new tyres. This measure also encourages Brazilian retreaders to retread more domestic used tyres by exempting domestic retreaders from disposal obligations as long as they process tyres consumed within Brazil . . . . Thus, the CONAMA scheme provides additional support for and is consistent with the design of Brazil's strategy for reducing the number of waste tyres. The two mutually enforcing pillars of Brazil's overall strategy — the Import Ban and the import ban on used tyres — imply that the demand for retreaded tyres in Brazil must be met by the domestic retreaders, and that these retreaders, in principle, can use only domestic used tyres for raw material. Over time, this comprehensive regulatory scheme is apt to induce sustainable changes in the practices and behaviour of the domestic retreaders, as well as other actors, and result in an increase in the number of retreadable tyres in Brazil and a higher rate of retreading of domestic casings in Brazil. Thus, the Import Ban appears to us as one of the key elements of the comprehensive strategy designed by Brazil to deal with waste tyres, along with the import ban on used tyres and the collection and disposal scheme

established by CONAMA Resolution 25801999, as amended in 2002.

155. As we explained above, we agree with the Panel's reasoning suggesting that fewer waste tyres will be generated with the Import Ban in place. In addition, Brazil has developed and implemented a comprehensive strategy to deal with waste tyres. As a *key element* of this strategy, the Import Ban is likely to bring a material contribution to the achievement of its objective of reducing the exposure to risks arising from the accumulation of waste tyres. On the basis of these considerations, we are of the view that the Panel did not err in finding that the Import Ban contributes to the achievement of its objective.

2. The Panel's Analysis of Possible Alternatives to the Import Ban

156. In order to determine whether a measure is "necessary" within the meaning of Article XX(b) of the GATT 1994, a panel must assess' all the relevant factors, particularly the extent of the contribution to the achievement of a measure's objective and its trade restrictiveness, in the light of the importance of the interests or values at stake. If this analysis yields a preliminary conclusion that the measure is necessary, this result must be confirmed by comparing the measure with its possible alternatives, which may be less trade restrictive while providing an equivalent contribution to the achievement of the objective pursued. It rests upon the complaining Member to identify possible alternatives to the measure at issue that the responding Member could have taken. As the Appellate Body indicated in *U.S. — Gambling*, while the responding Member must show that a measure is necessary, it does not have to "show, in the first instance, that there are *no* reasonably available alternatives to achieve its objectives." We recall that, in order to qualify as an alternative, a measure proposed by the complaining Member must be not only less trade restrictive than the measure at issue, but should also "preserve for the responding Member its right to achieve its desired level of protection with respect to the objective pursued." If the complaining Member has put forward a possible alternative measure, the responding Member may seek to show that the proposed measure does not allow it to achieve the level of protection it has chosen and, therefore, is not a genuine alternative. The responding Member may also seek to demonstrate that the proposed alternative is not, in fact, "reasonably available." As the Appellate Body indicated in *U.S. — Gambling*, "[a]n alternative measure may be found not to be 'reasonably available' . . . where it is merely theoretical in nature, for instance, where the responding Member is not capable of taking it, or where the measure imposes an undue burden on that Member, such as prohibitive costs or substantial technical difficulties." If the responding Member demonstrates that the measure proposed by the complaining Member is not a genuine alternative or is not "reasonably available," taking into account the interests or values being pursued and the responding Member's desired level of protection, it follows that the measure at issue is necessary.

157. Before the Panel, the European Communities put forward two types of possible alternative measures or practices: (i) measures to reduce the number of waste tyres accumulating in Brazil; and (ii) measures or practices to improve the management of waste tyres in Brazil. The Panel examined the alternative measures proposed by the European Communities in some detail, and in each case found that the proposed

measure did not constitute a reasonably available alternative to the Import Ban. Among the reasons that the Panel gave for its rejections were that the proposed alternatives were already in place, would not allow Brazil to achieve its chosen level of protection, or would carry their own risks and hazards.

174. In evaluating whether the measures or practices proposed by the European Communities were "alternatives," the Panel sought to determine whether they would achieve Brazil's policy objective and chosen level of protection, that is to say, reducing the "exposure to the risks to human, animal or plant life or health arising from the accumulation of waste tyres" to the maximum extent possible. In this respect, we believe, like the Panel, that non-generation measures are more apt to achieve this objective because they prevent the accumulation of waste tyres, while waste management measures dispose of waste tyres only once they have accumulated. Furthermore, we note that, in comparing a proposed alternative to the Import Ban, the Panel took into account specific risks attached to the proposed alternative, such as the risk of leaching of toxic substances that might be associated to landfilling, or the risk of toxic emissions that might arise from the incineration of waste tyres. In our view, the Panel did not err in so doing. Indeed, we do not see how a panel could undertake a meaningful comparison of the measure at issue with a possible alternative while disregarding the risks arising out of the implementation of the possible alternative. In this case, the Panel examined as proposed alternatives landfilling, stockpiling, and waste tyre incineration, and considered that, even if these disposal methods were performed under controlled conditions, they nevertheless pose risks to human health similar or additional to those Brazil seeks to reduce through the Import Ban. Because these practices carry their own risks, and these risks do not arise from non-generation measures such as the Import Ban, we believe, like the Panel, that these practices are not reasonably available alternatives.

175. With respect to material recycling, we share the Panel's view that this practice is not as effective as the Import Ban in reducing the exposure to the risks arising from the accumulation of waste tyres. Material recycling applications are costly, and hence capable of disposing of only a limited number of waste tyres. We also note that some of them might require advanced technologies and know-how that are not readily available on a large scale. Accordingly, we are of the view that the Panel did not err in concluding that material recycling is not a reasonably available alternative to the Import Ban.

3. The Weighing and Balancing of Relevant Factors by the Panel

176. The European Communities argues that, in its analysis of the necessity of the Import Ban, the Panel stated that it had weighed and balanced the relevant factors, but it "has not actually done it." According to the European Communities, although the Appellate Body has not defined the term "weighing and balancing," "this language refers clearly to a process where, in the first place, the importance of each element is assessed individually and, then, its role and relative importance is taken into consideration together with the other elements for the purposes of deciding whether the challenged measure is necessary to attain the objective pursued." The European Communities reasons that, "since the Panel failed to establish . . . the extent of the actual contribution the [Import Ban] makes to the reduction of the

number of waste tyres arising in Brazil, . . . it was incapable of 'weighing and balancing' this contribution against any of the other relevant factors."

178. We begin our analysis by recalling that, in order to determine whether a measure is "necessary" within the meaning of Article XX(b) of the GATT 1994, a panel must consider the relevant factors, particularly the importance of the interests or values at stake, the extent of the contribution to the achievement of the measure's objective, and its trade restrictiveness. If this analysis yields a preliminary conclusion that the measure is necessary, this result must be confirmed by comparing the measure with possible alternatives, which may be less trade restrictive while providing an equivalent contribution to the achievement of the objective. This comparison should be carried out in the light of the importance of the interests or values at stake. It is through this process that a panel determines whether a measure is necessary.

179. In this case, the Panel identified the objective of the Import Ban as being the reduction of the exposure to risks arising from the accumulation of waste tyres. It assessed the importance of the interests underlying this objective. It found that risks of dengue fever and malaria arise from the accumulation of waste tyres and that the objective of protecting human life and health against such diseases "is both vital and important in the highest degree." The Panel noted that the objective of the Import Ban also relates to the protection of the environment, a value that it considered — correctly, in our view — important. Then, the Panel analyzed the trade restrictiveness of the Import Ban and its contribution to the achievement of its objective. It appears from the Panel's reasoning that it considered that, in the light of the importance of the interests protected by the objective of the Import Ban, the contribution of the Import Ban to the achievement of its objective outweighs its trade restrictiveness. This finding of the Panel does not appear erroneous to us.

180. The Panel then proceeded to examine the alternatives to the Import Ban proposed by the European Communities. The Panel explained that some of them could not be viewed as alternatives to the Import Ban because they were complementary to it and were already included in Brazil's comprehensive policy. Next, the Panel compared the other alternatives proposed by the European Communities — landfilling, stockpiling, incineration, and material recycling — with the Import Ban, taking into consideration the specific risks associated with these proposed alternatives. The Panel concluded from this comparative assessment that none of the proposed options was a reasonably available alternative to the Import Ban.

181. The European Communities argues that the Panel failed to make a proper collective assessment of all the proposed alternatives, a contention that does not stand for the following reasons. First, the Panel did refer to its collective examination of these alternatives in concluding that "none of these, either individually or collectively, would be such that the risks arising from waste tyres in Brazil would be safely eliminated, as is intended by the current import ban. Secondly, as noted by the Panel and discussed above, some of the proposed alternatives are not real substitutes for the Import Ban since they complement each other as part of Brazil's comprehensive policy. Finally, having found that other proposed alterna-

tives were not reasonably available or carried their own risks, these alternatives would not have weighed differently in a collective assessment of alternatives.

182. In sum, the Panel's conclusion that the Import Ban is necessary was the result of a process involving, first, the examination of the contribution of the Import Ban to the achievement of its objective against its trade restrictiveness in the light of the interests at stake, and, secondly, the comparison of the possible alternatives, including associated risks, with the Import Ban. The analytical process followed by the Panel is consistent with the approach previously defined by the Appellate Body. The weighing and balancing is a holistic operation that involves putting all the variables of the equation together and evaluating them in relation to each other after having examined them individually, in order to reach an overall judgement. We therefore do not share the European Communities' view that the Panel did not "actually" weigh and balance the relevant factors, or that the Panel made a methodological error in comparing the alternative options proposed by the European Communities with the Import Ban.

183. In the light of all these considerations, we are of the view that the Panel did not err in the manner it conducted its analysis under Article XX(b) of the GATT 1994 as to whether the Import Ban was "necessary to protect human, animal or plant life or health."

VI. The Panel's Interpretation and Application of the Chapeau of Article XX of the GATT 1994

A. *The MERCOSUR Exemption and the Chapeau of Article XX of the GATT 1994*

213. After finding that the Import Ban was provisionally justified under Article XX(b) of the GATT 1994, the Panel examined whether the application of the Import Ban by Brazil satisfied the requirements of the chapeau of Article XX.

214. The chapeau of Article XX of the GATT 1994 reads:

> Subject to the requirement that such measures are not applied in a manner which would constitute a means of arbitrary or unjustifiable discrimination between countries where the same conditions prevail, or a disguised restriction on international trade, nothing in this Agreement shall be construed to prevent the adoption or enforcement . . . of measures [of the type specified in the subsequent paragraphs of Article XX].

215. The focus of the chapeau, by its express terms, is on the application of a measure already found to be inconsistent with an obligation of the GATT 1994 but failing within one of the paragraphs of Article XX. The chapeau's requirements are two-fold. First, a measure provisionally justified under one of the paragraphs of Article XX must not be applied in a manner that would constitute "arbitrary or unjustifiable discrimination" between countries where the same conditions prevail. Secondly, this measure must not be applied in a manner that would constitute "a disguised restriction on international trade." Through these requirements, the chapeau serves to ensure that Members' rights to avail themselves of exceptions are

exercised in good faith to protect interests considered legitimate under Article XX, not as a means to circumvent one Member's obligations towards other WTO Members.

[The Appellate Body, after analyzing the chapeau, ruled that the MERCOSUR exemption and the imports of used tyres under court injunctions have resulted in the import ban being applied in a manner that constitutes arbitrary and unjustifiable discrimination and in a manner that constitutes a disguised restriction on international trade. The Appellate Body therefore ruled that the import ban was not justified under Article XX].

NOTES AND QUESTIONS

1.   The WTO panel in the *Brazil — Tyres Case* ruled that since the MERCO-SUR exemption did not result in a significant number of used tyre imports, there was no violation of the chapeau of Article XX. The Appellate Body disagreed with this ruling and found a violation of the chapeau even though the imports were not significant. Do you agree with the Appellate Body on this point?

2.   Does the Appellate Body's ruling in the *Brazil — Tyres Case* conflict with the Basel Convention?

3.   Do you think that Brazil would be able to rectify the violation of the chapeau?

D.   Nuclear and Radioactive Substances

Nuclear safety and security are now of paramount concern. The Three-Mile Island partial meltdown that occurred in Pennsylvania in the United States in 1979, the Chernobyl catastrophe in the Soviet Union in 1986, and the Fukushima, Japan tsunami and nuclear meltdown in 2011, are reminders that accidents can and will happen.

Electrical energy was generated for the first time using nuclear power in 1951. As of 2013, there are 437 operating nuclear power plants in 31 countries. The United States operates the most nuclear power plants — 104, followed by France (58), and Japan (50, not counting the four Fukushima reactors). These reactors have a total capacity of some 69,760 billion kWh. In 2013, although Germany has decided to phase out nuclear power, energy production from nuclear power is on the increase: 68 plants in 15 countries are under construction, mainly in China, Russia, and India.[98]

As of 2013, there are eight states that have declared they have stockpiles of nuclear weapons: China, France, Russia, the United Kingdom, the United States, India, Pakistan, and North Korea. Israel is widely assumed to possess nuclear weapons, and Iran may be developing nuclear weapons.

Not counting the several nuclear weapons international instruments, such as the Treaty on Nuclear Non-Proliferation (190 parties, 1968, in force 1970), which is

---

[98] http://www.euronuclear.org/info/encyclopedia/n/nuclear-power-plant.htm. 233 I.L.M. 1514 (1994).

beyond the scope of this book, there are a panoply of international agreements concerning nuclear safety and security. The two centerpieces of international agreements on nuclear safety are (1) the Convention on Nuclear Safety (CNS) (1994, in force 1996)[99] and (2) the Joint Convention on the Safety of Spent Fuel Management and on the Safety of Radioactive Waste Management (Joint Convention) (1997, in force 2002).[100]

The CNS aims to legally commit states operating nuclear power plants to a high level of safety and security. The CNS Secretariat is the International Atomic Energy Agency (IAEA) in Vienna, and the obligations of the parties are based largely on the IAEA Safety Fundamentals document titled, "Fundamental Safety Principles (SF-1)." These obligations cover such matters as siting, design, construction, operation, the availability of adequate financial and human resources, the assessment and verification of safety, quality assurance, and emergency preparedness. The CNS carries no sanctions or penalties but is an incentive instrument that aims to assure nuclear safety based upon the common interest of the parties. The principal instrument of implementation is the obligation to submit periodic national reports for "peer review" by all the parties to the CNS. For this purpose the CNS holds Review Meetings of the parties from time-to-time. As of this writing, 75 parties have ratified the CNS, and another 10 states are signatories.

The Joint Convention is the first international instrument to deal with the important problem of safety of management and storage of radioactive waste and spent fuel in countries with and without nuclear programs. Nuclear power plants generate both high-level and low-level nuclear waste. High-level nuclear waste is primarily the spent reactor fuels. Low-level nuclear waste is generated when items such as clothing and equipment become radioactive due to exposure to neutron radiation.

Nuclear fuel consists of fuel pins that are stacks of uranium oxide or mixed uranium plutonium oxide (MOX) cylindrical ceramic pellets, with diameters of 8 to 15 mm, that are encapsulated in metal tubes. The useful life of a fuel element is usually 3 to 7 years, after which it is removed from the nuclear reactor core. Since the spent fuel generates both heat and radiation, the fuel elements must be stored under water, which provides both the necessary cooling and radiation shielding. After about 12 months, the radiation has sufficiently decreased so that dry storage is possible. However, the material is still highly radioactive and must be shielded for thousands of years. Two different management strategies are available to handle spent nuclear fuel: (1) the fuel can be reprocessed to extract usable material (uranium and plutonium) for new fuel; and (2) the spent fuel can be considered simply a waste to be stored pending disposal. Both methods have safety risks. China, Japan, France, Russia, and India have chosen reprocessing, while most states, including the United States, simply treat spent fuel as waste.

From today's 437 operating nuclear power plants over 12,000 metric tons of heavy metal fuel (tHM) are unloaded each year, with annual discharges projected

---

[99] 33 I.L.M. 1514 (1994).

[100] 36 I.L.M. 1431 (1997).

to increase year-by-year. Less than one-third of this amount is reprocessed. In the over 50 years of civilian nuclear power, over 280,000 tHM of spent fuel has been generated, and some 200,000 tHM are in storage, all of which is still dangerously radioactive. By 2020, the total amount of spent fuel is predicted to amount to rise to 445,000 tHM, of which about 324,000 will still be in storage rather than reprocessed.

The Joint Convention obligates 64 parties (which include the United States) to conduct environmental assessments and to review safety requirements both at existing and proposed spent fuel and radioactive waste management facilities. The Joint Convention also covers planned and controlled releases of radioactive materials from regulated facilities. Parties are obligated to create and maintain a legislative and regulatory framework to govern radioactive waste management. The Joint Convention provides a binding national reporting system on measures being taken to implement the Convention's safety and management standards. Review meetings of the parties to the Joint Convention are held at least yearly. The Secretariat to the Joint Convention is the IAEA, and the obligations of the parties are based primarily on IAEA guidance documents.

The Joint Convention includes obligations placed upon the parties concerning the transboundary movement of nuclear waste. (Nuclear waste is not covered by the Basel Convention). The obligations in the Joint Convention are based upon the IAEA Code of Practice on the Transboundary Movement of Radioactive Waste (1990).

INTERNATIONAL ATOMIC ENERGY AGENCY, CODE OF PRACTICE ON THE INTERNATIONAL TRANSBOUNDARY MOVEMENT OF RADIOACTIVE WASTE
Adopted by the IAEA General Conference by Resolution GC(XXXIV)RES/ 530 (Sept. 21, 1990)

GENERAL

1. Every State should take the appropriate steps necessary to ensure that radioactive waste within its territory, or under its jurisdiction or control is safely managed and disposed of, to ensure the protection of human health and the environment.

2. Every State should take the appropriate steps necessary to minimize the amount of radioactive waste, taking into account social, environmental, technological and economic considerations.

INTERNATIONAL TRANSBOUNDARY MOVEMENT

3. It is the sovereign right of every State to prohibit the movement of radioactive waste into from or through its territory.

4. Every State involved in the international transboundary movement of radioactive waste should take the appropriate steps necessary to ensure that such movement is undertaken in a manner consistent with international safety standards.

5. Every State should take the appropriate steps necessary to ensure that, subject to the relevant norms of international law, the international trans boundary movement of radioactive waste takes place only with the prior notification and consent of the sending, receiving and transit States in accordance with their respective laws and regulations.

6. Every State involved in the international transboundary movement of radioactive waste should have a relevant regulatory authority and adopt appropriate procedures as necessary for the regulation of such movement.

7. No receiving State should permit the receipt of radioactive waste for management or disposal unless it has the administrative and technical capacity and regulatory structure to manage and dispose of such waste in a manner consistent with international safety standards. The sending State should satisfy itself in accordance with the receiving State's consent that the above requirement is met prior to the international transboundary movement of radioactive waste.

8. Every State should take the appropriate steps to introduce into its national laws and regulations relevant provisions as necessary for liability, compensation or other remedies for damage that could arise from the international transboundary movement of radioactive waste.

9. Every State should take the appropriate steps necessary, including the adoption of laws and regulations, to ensure that the international transboundary movement of radioactive waste is carried out in accordance with this Code.

INTERNATIONAL CO-OPERATION

10. The sending State should take the appropriate steps necessary to permit readmission into its territory of any radioactive waste previously transferred from its territory if such transfer is not or cannot be completed in conformity with this Code, unless an alternative safe arrangement can be made.

11. States should co-operate at the bilateral, regional and international levels for the purpose of preventing any international transboundary movement of radioactive waste that is not in conformity with this Code.

ROLE OF THE IAEA

The IAEA should continue to collect and disseminate information on the laws, regulations and technical standards pertaining to radioactive waste management and disposal, develop relevant technical standards and provide advice and assistance on all aspects of radioactive waste management and disposal, having particular regard to the needs of developing countries.

The IAEA should review this Code as appropriate, taking into account experience gained and technological developments.

NOTES AND QUESTIONS

1. What are the main elements of the IAEA Code of Practice? Are they sufficient? What would you suggest to provide a stronger framework?

2. Is the IAEA Code of Practice compatible with WTO obligations?

NOTE ON LIABILITY FOR NUCLEAR DAMAGE

Note that the IAEA Code of Practice mandates the adoption of "national laws and regulations . . . as necessary for liability, compensation or other remedies for damage that could arise from international transboundary movement of radioactive waste."

In 1997, a conference sponsored by the IAEA was convened to consider revising the Convention on Civil liability for Nuclear Damage adopted in Vienna in 1963. This conference produced protocols the created two international instruments:

- The 1997 Vienna Convention on Civil liability for Nuclear Damage
- The 1997 Convention on Supplementary Compensation for Nuclear Damage.[101]

The basic principles of nuclear damage liability law under these Conventions are:

- Liability is channeled to the operator of the nuclear installation (a nuclear power plant or a waste storage site). The operator is exclusively liable in the case of a nuclear accident to the exclusion of all other persons.

- The operator is liable for damages resulting from an accident at its installation or during the course of transport of nuclear materials to or from its installation.

- Liability is strict without regard to fault.

- Liability is limited in amount and in time. The statute of limitations is 10 years from the date of the nuclear incident and 300 million special drawing rights (SDRs) is the minimum amount a state must make available under its national law to compensate nuclear damage. The state is free to impose a greater limit or even unlimited liability. The Convention on Supplementary Compensation (CSC) will provide an additional 300 million SDRs in compensation, bringing the total to 600 million SDRs.

- The operator is required to maintain financial security (liability insurance) covering the limit of liability.

- Exclusive jurisdiction is channeled to the court of the party where the nuclear incident occurred to the exclusion of courts in other states.

A very important aspect of the 1997 Convention and the CSC is a new definition of "nuclear damage." Whereas the 1963 Convention defined nuclear damage as

---

[101] *See* IAEA, *The 1997 Vienna Convention on Civil Liability for Nuclear Damage and the 1997 Convention on Supplementary Compensation for Nuclear Damage-Explanatory Texts*, IAEA International Law Series No.3 (2012).

including personal injury and property damage, the 1997 Convention contains the following definitions:

(k)   "Nuclear Damage" means—

    (i)   loss of life or personal injury;

    (ii)   loss of or damage to property;

    and each of the following to the extent determined by the law of the competent court—

    (iii)   economic loss arising from loss or damage referred to in sub-paragraph (i) or (ii), insofar as not included in those sub-paragraphs, if incurred by a person entitled to claim in respect of such loss or damage;

    (iv)   the costs of measures of reinstatement of impaired environment, unless such impairment is insignificant, if such measures are actually taken or to be taken, and insofar as not included in sub-paragraph (ii);

    (v)   loss of income deriving from an economic interest in any use or enjoyment of the environment, incurred as a result or a significant impairment of that environment, and insofar as not included in subparagraph (ii);

    (vi)   the costs of preventive measures, and further loss or damage caused by such measures;

    (vii)   any other economic loss, other than any caused by the impairment of the environment, if permitted by the general law on civil liability of the competent court, in the case of sub-paragraphs (i) to (v) and (vii) above, to the extent that the loss or damage arises out of or results from ionizing radiation emitted by any source of radiation inside a nuclear installation, or emitted from nuclear fuel or radioactive products or waste in, or of nuclear material coming from, originating in, or sent to, a nuclear installation, whether so arising from the radioactive properties of such matter, or from a combination of radioactive properties with toxic, explosive or other hazardous properties of such matter.

(l)   "Nuclear incident" means any occurrence or series of occurrences having the same origin which causes nuclear damage or, but only with respect to preventive measures, creates a grave and imminent threat of causing such damage.

(m)   "Measures of reinstatement" means any reasonable measures which have been approved by the competent authorities of the State where the measures were taken, and which aim to reinstate or restore damaged or destroyed components of the environment, or to introduce, where reasonable, the equivalent of these components into the environment. The law of the State where the damage is suffered shall determine who is entitled to take such measures.

(n)   "Preventive measures" means any reasonable measures taken by any person after a nuclear incident has occurred to prevent or minimize damage referred to in sub-paragraphs (k)(i) to (v) or (vii), subject to any approval of the competent authorities required by the law of the State where the measures were taken.

(o) "Reasonable measures" means measures which are found under the law of the competent, court to be appropriate and proportionate having regard to all the circumstances . . . .

The general topic of liability for transboundary harm in the case of a nuclear accident is covered in Chapter 3 of this book.

Section VII. FOOD SAFETY, BIOTECHNOLOGY, AND ENVIRONMENTAL PROTECTION

PROBLEM 5-7
STATE A TAKES ACTION TO PROTECT HUMAN HEALTH AND ECOSYSTEMS

State A is a large, developing African country concerned about the health of its people as well as protecting its magnificent wildlife heritage. State A wants to take a precautionary approach because of the importance of these issues. The government of State A is concerned that certain products developed and commonly sold and used in industrialized countries may not be suitable for conditions in State A. State A is a member of the WTO and the United Nations, and is a party to the *Convention on Biological Diversity* (1992) as well as the *Protocol on Biosafety to the Convention on Biological Diversity* (2000).

State A has recently passed legislation to do the following:

1. Prohibits the domestic production, use and importation of all genetically modified plants, seeds, animals, and organisms of any kind. This is out of concern that such plants and seeds may disturb ecosystem in State A.

2. Prohibits the domestic sale and importation of any processed foods containing more than 1.5% of ingredients from genetically modified foodstuffs.

3. Enforces strict standards of zero tolerance for pesticide residues on imported and domestically produced fruits and vegetables. In effect, State A is moving to establish an all-organic food supply for its people.

4. Prohibits the importation of all fruits and vegetables from areas of the world where the Mediterranean fruit fly (commonly known as the Medfly) is present. The Medfly differs from the common fruit fly (Drosophila melanogaster) in that, while the common fruit fly eats fruit only after it has begun to rot, the Medfly feeds on ripening fruit and causes it to rot. The Medfly is not native to State A.

5. Prohibits the domestic production and importation of goods and textiles containing artificial fibers. Only products containing natural fibers, such as cotton, linen, and wool, may be sold in State A. The reason for this is that State A's scientists argue that, in general, artificial fibers are more flammable than natural fibers. Although admittedly some artificial fibers

are flame-resistant, State A has decided to ban all artificial fibers to facilitate administration and enforcement. Moreover, the precautionary principle dictates that safety should come first even if scientific evidence is incomplete.

In order to determine whether these measures comply with State A's obligations under international law, we must study two documents: (1) the WTO Agreement on Sanitary and Phytosanitary Measures; and (2) the Biosafety Protocol to the U.N. Convention on Biological Diversity.

A.   National Regulation of Food Safety

Protecting the safety of food and drugs and protecting the environment against harmful pests is up to national governments. In the United States, protecting the safety of food and the integrity of the environment is shared among many federal agencies, principally the Federal Food and Drug Administration, the Department of Agriculture, and the Environmental Protection Agency.

Americans spend over $1 trillion on food each year, nearly half of it in restaurants, schools, and other places outside the home. The combined efforts of the food industry and regulatory agencies are generally credited with making the U.S. food supply among the safest in the world. Nevertheless, the U.S. Centers for Disease Control and Prevention reports that each year an estimated one in six Americans — a total of 48 million people — become sick from contaminated food. Of these, an estimated 128, 000 cases require hospitalization and 3000 cases result in death.[102]

The Food and Drug Administration (FDA), which is part of the U.S. Department of Health and Human Services, under the authority of the Federal Food, Drug, and Cosmetic Act, 42 U.S.C. § 201 *et seq.*, and related statutes, is responsible for ensuring that all domestic and imported food products — except for most meat and poultry — are safe, nutritious, wholesome, and accurately labeled. In 2011, the Congress, concerned about food safety, passed the FDA Food Safety Modernization Act, the largest expansion of FDA's food safety authority since the 1930s. The FDA conducts periodic inspections not only of food facilities in the United States, but also about 200,000 foreign food facilities that are registered with the agency. An increasing percentage of the U.S. food supply comes from outside the United States.

The Food Safety and Inspection Service (FSIS) of the Department of Agriculture, under the authority of the Federal Meat Inspection Act, 21 U.S.C. § 601 *et seq.* and the Poultry Products Inspection Act, 21 U.S.C. § 451 *et seq.*, is responsible for the safety, wholesomeness, and proper labeling of most domestic and imported meat and poultry products. FDA and FSIS share responsibility for eggs under the Egg Products Inspection Act, 21 U.S.C. § 1031 *et seq.* FSIS is responsible for assuring that foreign meat and poultry plants are operating under an inspection service equivalent to the U.S. system before they can export their products to the United States.

---

[102] The Federal Food Safety System: A Primer, Congressional Research Service 1 (2012).

The Environmental Protection Agency (EPA) has statutory responsibility for ensuring that chemicals used on food crops do not endanger the public health. The EPA sets tolerances for pesticide residues levels on food commodities and animal feed. The primary regulatory statute giving the EPA this authority is the Federal Insecticide, Fungicide, and Rodenticide Act, 7 U.S.C. § 136 *et seq.*

Biotechnology is the use of plants, animals and microorganism to create new products or processes. One variety of biotechnology is gene technology, sometimes called genetic modification, where the genetic material of living things is deliberately altered to inject or remove a particular trait and allow the organism to perform new functions. Genes within a species can be modified or genes can be moved from one species to another. For example, gene technology has been used to make cotton plants resistant to insect pests.

More than 40 genetically modified (GM) crops are currently allowed in commerce in the United States.[103] Two traits are especially important: herbicide tolerance (HT) and insect resistance (Bt). HT and Bt crops are very popular with U.S. farmers, and most food staples sold in the United States, such as corn, soybeans, sugarbeets, are genetically modified. Genetic modification can be used also to alter a plant's characteristics, to increase stress resistance, or to cause the plant to produce important enzymes and hormones.

Three federal agencies have responsibility for evaluating new crop varieties using genetic modifications: (1) the Department of Agriculture, through the Biotechnology Regulatory Service Office of the Animal and Plant Health Inspection Service (APHIS), regulates all GM plants prior to commercial release. Under the authority of the Plant Protection Act, 7 U.S.C. § 7701 *et seq.*, the main concern is to make sure that the new plant will not be a threat to agriculture and to the environment. After review of the life cycle, reproductive characteristics, and the molecular, biochemical, and cellular characteristics of the plant, the APHIS will issue an Environmental Assessment and, if it approves the new plant, a Determination of Non-Regulated Status. (2) The FDA has authority to review the application to determine if there is a threat to human or animal health. (3) EPA review comes into play if the plant has pesticidal properties. Thus the EPA must approve HT and Bt plant varieties in addition to the other agencies involved.

In the European Union a complex and time-consuming process is used to approve GM plants.[104] A company that wishes to introduce a GM plant into the environment must first make application to an EU member state national authority; the application is then transferred to the European Food Safety Authority in Parma, Italy, where it is evaluated by the GMO Panel, a committee of independent scientists from all member states. The EFSA recommendation is then sent to the European Commission, who refers it to the Standing Committee on the Food Chain and Animal Health, who must approve the application by a two-thirds

---

[103] Food and Agriculture, Union of Concerned Scientists, *available at,* http://www.ucsusa.org/food_and_agriculture/.

[104] Two EU laws are especially important: the EU Directive 2001/18 on the Deliberate Release into the Environment of Genetically Modified Organisms; and EU Directive 1829/2003 on the Regulation of Genetically Modified Food and Feed.

majority. If the Standing Committee gives its approval, the Commission will transfer the matter to the Council of the EU for approval after consultation with the European Parliament. In the EU, unlike the United States, no GM fruits or vegetables have been approved; only GM maize, cotton, rapeseed, and soybeans are grown in the EU on a large scale.

National labeling laws for GM foods differ greatly. For example, in the United States, foods do not have to be labeled as to their GM content. A GM product or processed food may carry the label "natural" and be composed of GM foods.[105] In the EU, however, labels must inform the consumer if the product contains GM foods, and companies must maintain records to show the traceability of the GM foods they utilize. (*See* EU Directive 1830/2003 on the Labeling and Traceability of GM Foods).

The United States is the world's largest producer and exporter of GM foods. Without laboratory testing, GM plants and foods are difficult or impossible to distinguish from their non-GM counterparts. GM plants have a tendency to "contaminate" non-GM varieties either by natural selection (since they tend to be hardier) or by cross-pollination (since insects indiscriminately operate on both). Thus, GM plants and foods are often found in farm fields, streams of commerce, and in countries where they were not approved by law.[106]

The framework for U.S. regulation of GM seeds, plants and foods was set in the late 1980s, when the Reagan Administration charged the White House Office of Science and Technology Policy (OSTP) with drafting a federal framework policy for food biotechnology. The OSTP proposed various policy statements designed to minimize regulatory burdens on the emerging biotechnology industry. The OSTP published its Final Statement of Scope in 1992,[107] making the following points:

- The same physical and biological laws govern the response of organisms modified by modern molecular and cellular methods and those produced by classical methods.

- Information about the process used to produce a GM organism is not a useful criterion for determining whether the product requires more or less oversight.

- Crops modified by molecular and cellular methods should pose risks no different from those modified by classical methods for similar traits.

Following this Final Statement, the U.S. FDA formally announced a policy that most new foods created using biotechnology would not be subject to safety testing under the Federal Food, Drug, and Cosmetic Act.[108]

---

[105] *See* Erik Benny, *"Natural" Modifications: The FDA's Need to Promulgate an Official Definition of "Natural" That Includes Genetically Modified Organisms*, 80 GEO. WASH. L. REV. 1504, 1508–09 (2012).

[106] *See* Alison Peck, *Leveling the Playing Field in GMO Risk Assessment: Importers, Exporters, and the Limits of Science*, 28 B.U. INT'L L.J. 241, 244 (2010).

[107] Notice of Exercise of Federal Oversight Within Scope of Statutory Authority: Planned Introductions of Biotechnology Products into the Environment, 57 Fed. Reg. 6753, 6760 (Feb. 27, 1992).

[108] Notice of Statement of Policy: Foods Derived from New Plant Varieties, 57 Fed. Reg. 22, 984 (May 29, 1992).

B. Criteria Governing International Trade in Food and Associated Products

WORLD TRADE ORGANIZATION AGREEMENT ON THE APPLICATION OF SANITARY AND PHYTOSANITARY MEASURES
(1994)

[The governing agreement relating to international trade in food, pharmaceuticals and associated products is the WTO Agreement on the Application of Sanitary and Phytosanitary Measures (SPS Agreement). Annex A of this Agreement defines as a sanitary or phytosanitary measure, any measure applied:

(a) To protect animal or plant life or health within the territory of the Member from risks arising from the entry, establishment or spread of pests, diseases, disease-carrying organisms, or disease causing organisms;

(b) To protect human or animal life or health within the territory of the Member from risks arising from additives, contaminants, toxins, or disease-causing organisms in foods, beverages or feedstuffs;

(c) To protect human life or health within the territory of the Member from risks arising from diseases carried by animals, plants or products thereof, or from the entry, establishment or spread of pests; or

(d) To prevent or limit other damage within the territory of the Member from the entry or establishment or spread of pests.

Sanitary or phytosanitary measures include all relevant laws, decrees, regulations, requirements, and procedures including, *inter alia*, end product criteria; processes and production methods; testing, inspection, certification and approval procedures; quarantine treatments including relevant requirements associated with the transport of animals or plants, or with the materials necessary for their survival during transport; provisions on relevant statistical methods, sampling procedures and methods of risk assessment; and packaging and labeling requirements directly related to food safety.]

Article 2
Basic Rights and Obligations

1. Members have the right to take sanitary and phytosanitary measures necessary for the protection of human, animal or plant life or health, provided that such measures are not inconsistent with the provisions of this Agreement.

2. Members shall ensure that any sanitary or phytosanitary measure is applied only to the extent necessary to protect human, animal or plant life or health, is based on scientific principles and is not maintained without sufficient scientific evidence, except as provided for in paragraph 7 of Article 5.

3. Members shall ensure that their sanitary and phytosanitary measures do not arbitrarily or unjustifiably discriminate between Members where identical or similar conditions prevail, including between their own territory and that of other

Members. Sanitary and phytosanitary measures shall not be applied in a manner which would constitute a disguised restriction on international trade.

4. Sanitary or phytosanitary measures which conform to the relevant provisions of this Agreement shall be presumed to be in accordance with the obligations of the Members under the provisions of GATT 1994 which relate to the use of sanitary or phytosanitary measures, in particular the provisions of Article XX(b).

Article 3
Harmonization

1. To harmonize sanitary and phytosanitary measures on as wide a basis as possible, Members shall base their sanitary or phytosanitary measures on international standards, guidelines or recommendations, where they exist, except as otherwise provided for in this Agreement, and in particular in paragraph 3.

2. Sanitary or phytosanitary measures which conform to international standards, guidelines or recommendations shall be deemed to be necessary to protect human, animal or plant 'life or health, and presumed to be consistent with the relevant provisions of this Agreement and of GATT.

3. Members may introduce or maintain sanitary or phytosanitary measures which result in a higher level of sanitary or phytosanitary protection than would be achieved by measures based on the relevant international standards, guidelines or recommendations, if there is a scientific justification, or as a consequence of the level of sanitary or phytosanitary protection a Member deter mines to be appropriate in accordance with the relevant provisions of paragraphs 1 through 8 of Article 5. Notwithstanding the above, all measures which result in a level of sanitary or phytosanitary protection different from that which would be achieved by measures based on international standards, guidelines or recommendations shall not be inconsistent with any other provision of this Agreement.

* * *

Article 5
Assessment of Risk and Determination of the Appropriate

Level of Sanitary or Phytosanitary Protection

1. Members shall ensure that their sanitary or phytosanitary measures are based on an assessment, as appropriate to the circumstances, of the risks to human; animal or plant life or health, taking into account risk assessment techniques developed by the relevant international organizations.

2. In the assessment of risks, Members shall take into' account available scientific evidence; relevant processes and production methods; relevant inspection, sampling and testing methods; prevalence of specific diseases or pests; existence of pest- or disease-free areas; relevant ecological and environmental conditions; and quarantine or other treatment.

3. In assessing the risk to animal or plant life or health and determining the

measure to be applied for achieving the appropriate level of sanitary or phytosanitary protection from such risk, Members shall take into account as relevant economic factors: the potential damage in terms of loss of production or sales in the event of the entry, establishment or spread of a pest or disease; the costs of control or eradication in the territory of the importing Member; and the relative cost-effectiveness of alternative approaches to limiting risks.

4. Members should, when determining the appropriate level of sanitary or phytosanitary protection, take into account the objective of minimizing negative trade effects.

5. With the objective of achieving consistency in the application of the concept of appropriate level of sanitary or phytosanitary protection against risks to human life or health, or to animal and plant life or health, each Member shall avoid arbitrary or unjustifiable distinctions in the levels it considers to be appropriate in different situations, if such distinctions result in discrimination or a disguised restriction on international trade. Members shall cooperate in the Committee, in accordance with paragraphs 1,2 and 3 of Article 12, to develop guidelines to further the practical implementation Of this provision. In developing the guidelines, the Committee shall take into account all relevant factors, including the exceptional character of human health risks to which people voluntarily expose themselves.

6. Without prejudice to paragraph 2 of Article 3, when establishing or maintaining sanitary or phytosanitary measures to achieve the appropriate level of sanitary or phytosanitary protection, Members shall ensure that such measures are not more trade-restrictive than required to achieve their appropriate level of sanitary or phytosanitary protection, taking into account technical and economic feasibility.

7. In cases where relevant scientific evidence is insufficient, a Member may provisionally adopt sanitary or phytosanitary measures on the basis of available pertinent information, including that from the relevant international organizations as well as from sanitary or phytosanitary measures applied by other Members. In such circumstances, Members shall seek to obtain the addition information necessary for a more objective assessment of risk and review the sanitary or phytosanitary measure accordingly within a reasonable period of time.

EUROPEAN COMMUNITIES MEASURES CONCERNING MEAT AND MEAT PRODUCTS (HORMONES)

Report of the Appellate Body (adopted by the DSB on February 13, 1998) WT/DS26/AB/R and WT/DS48/AB/R (16 January 1998) (footnotes omitted)

I. Introduction: Statement of the Appeal

1. The European Communities, the United States and Canada appeal from certain issues of law and legal interpretations in the Panel Reports, EC — *Measures Concerning Meat and Meat Products (Hormones)*. These two Panel Reports, circulated to Members of the World Trade Organization ("WTO") on 18 August 1997, were rendered by two Panels composed of the same three persons. These Panel Reports are similar, but they are not identical in every respect. The Panel in the complaint brought by the United States was established by the Dispute

Settlement Body (the "DSB") on 20 May 1996. On 16 October 1996, the DSB established the Panel in the complaint brought by Canada. The European Communities and Canada agreed, on 4 November 1996, that the composition of the latter Panel would be identical to the composition of the Panel established at the request of the United States.

2. The Panel dealt with a complaint against the European Communities relating to an EC prohibition of imports of meat and meat products derived from cattle to which either the natural hormones: oestradiol-17β, progesterone or testosterone, or the synthetic hormones: trenbolone acetate, zeranol or melengestrol acetate ("MGA"), had been administered for growth promotion purposes.

*   *   *

6. The Panel circulated its Reports to the Members of the WTO on 18 August 1997. The U.S. Panel Report and the Canada Panel Report reached the same conclusions in paragraph 9.1:

(i)   The European Communities, by maintaining sanitary measures which are not based on a risk assessment, has acted inconsistently with the requirements contained in Article 5.1 of the Agreement on the Application of Sanitary and Phytosanitary Measures.

(ii) The European Communities, by adopting arbitrary or unjustifiable distinctions in the levels of sanitary protection it considers to be appropriate indifferent situations which result in discrimination or a disguised restriction on international trade, has acted inconsistently with the requirement contained in Article 5.5 of the Agreement on the Application of Sanitary and Phytosanitary Measures.

(iii) The European Communities, by maintaining sanitary measures which are not based on existing international standards without justification under Article 3.3 of the Agreement on the Application of Sanitary and Phytosanitary Measures, has acted inconsistently with the requirements of Article 3.1 of that Agreement.

In both Reports, the Panel recommended in paragraph 9.2:

. . . that the Dispute Settlement Body requests the European Communities to bring its measures in dispute into conformity with its obligations under the Agreement on the Application of Sanitary and Phytosanitary Measures.

*   *   *

III. Issues Raised in this Appeal

96. This appeal raises the following legal issues:

(a) Whether the Panel correctly allocated the burden of proof in this case;

(b) Whether the Panel applied the appropriate standard of review under the *SPS Agreement;*

(c) Whether, or to what extent, the precautionary principle is relevant in the interpretation of the *SPS Agreement;*

(d) Whether the provisions of the *SPS Agreement* apply to measures enacted before the date of entry into force of the WTO Agreement;

(e) Whether the Panel made an objective assessment of the facts pursuant to Article I of the DSU;

(f) Whether the Panel acted within the scope of its authority in its selection and use of experts, in granting additional third party rights to the United States and Canada and in making findings based on arguments not made by the parties;

(g) Whether the Panel correctly interpreted Articles 3.1 and 3.3 of the *SPS Agreement;*

(h) Whether the EC measures are "based on" a risk assessment within the meaning of Article 5.1 of the *SPS Agreement;*

(i) Whether the Panel correctly interpreted and applied Article 5.5 of the *SPS Agreement;* and

(j) Whether the Panel appropriately exercised "judicial economy" in not making findings on the consistency of the EC measures with Article 2.2 and Article 5.6 of the *SPS Agreement.*

IV. Allocating the Burden of Proof in Proceedings Under the *SPS Agreement*

97. The first general issue that we must address relates to the allocation of the burden of proof in proceedings under the *SPS Agreement*. The Panel appropriately describes this issue as one of particular importance, in view of the nature of disputes under that Agreement. Such disputes may raise multiple and complex issues of fact.

*   *   *

108. To the extent that the Panel purports to absolve the United States and Canada from the necessity of establishing a *prima facie* case showing the absence of the risk assessment required by Article 5.1, and the failure of the European Communities to comply with the requirements of Article 3.3, and to impose upon the European Communities the burden of proving the existence of such risk assessment and the consistency of its measures with Articles 5.4, 5.5 and 5.6 *without regard to whether or riot the complaining parties had already established their prima facie case*, we consider and so hold that the Panel once more erred in law.

109. In accordance with our ruling in United States — *Shirts and Blouses*, the Panel should have begun the analysis of each legal provision by examining whether the United States and Canada had presented evidence and legal arguments sufficient to demonstrate that the EC measures were inconsistent with the obligations assumed by the European Communities under each Article of the *SPS Agreement* addressed by the Panel, i.e., Articles 3.1. 3.3, 5.1 and 5.5. Only after such a *prima facie* determination had been made by the Panel may the onus be shifted to the European Communities to bring forward evidence and arguments to disprove the complaining party's claim.

V. The Standard of Review Applicable in Proceedings Under the *SPS Agreement*

*   *   *

119. We consider . . . that the issue of failure to apply an appropriate standard of review, raised by the European Communities, resolves itself into the issue of whether or not the Panel, in making the above and other findings referred to and appealed by the European Communities, had made an "objective assessment of the matter before it, including an *objective assessment of the facts* . . .". This particular issue is addressed (in substantial detail) below. Here, however, we uphold the findings of the Panel appealed by the European Communities upon the ground of failure to apply either a "deferential reasonableness standard" or the standard of review set out in Article 17.6(i) of the *Anti-Dumping Agreement.*

VI. The Relevance of the Precautionary Principle in the Interpretation of the *SPS Agreement*

*   *   *

121. The basic submission of the European Communities is that the precautionary principle is, or has become, "a general customary rule of international law" or at least "a general principle of law. Referring more specifically to Articles 5.1 and 5.2 of the *SPS Agreement*, applying the precautionary principle means, in the view of the European Communities, that it is not necessary for *all* scientists around the world to agree on the "possibility and magnitude" of the risk, nor for *all* or most of the WTO Members to perceive and evaluate the risk in the same ways. It is also stressed that Articles 5.1 and 5.2 do not prescribe a particular type of risk assessment and do not prevent Members from being cautious in their risk assessment exercise. The European Communities goes on to state that its measures here at stake were precautionary in nature and satisfied the requirements of Articles 2.2 and 2.3, as well as of Articles 5.1, 5.2, 5.4, 5.5 and 5.6 of the *SPS Agreement.*

122. The United States does not consider that the "precautionary principle" represents customary international law and suggests it is more an "approach" than a "principle. Canada, too, takes the view that the precautionary principle has not yet been incorporated into the corpus of public international law; however, it concedes that the "precautionary approach" or "concept" is "an *emerging* principle of law" which may in the future crystallize into one of the "general principles of law recognized by civilized nations" within the meaning of Article 38(1)(c) of the *Statute of the International Court of Justice.*

123. The status of the precautionary principle in international law continues to be the subject of debate among academics, law practitioners, regulators and judges. The precautionary principle is regarded by some as having crystallized into a general principle of customary international environmental law. Whether it has been widely accepted by Members as a principle of general or customary international law appears less than clear. We consider, however, that it is unnecessary, and probably imprudent, for the Appellate Body in this appeal to take a

position on this important, but abstract, question. We note that the Panel itself did not make any definitive finding with regard to the status of the precautionary principle in international law and that the precautionary principle, at least outside the field of international environmental law, still awaits authoritative formulation.

124. It appears to us important, nevertheless, to note some aspects of the relationship of the precautionary principle to the *SPS Agreement*. First, the principle has not been written into the *SPS Agreement* as a ground for justifying SPS measures that are otherwise inconsistent with the obligations of Members set out in particular provisions of that Agreement. Secondly, the precautionary principle indeed finds reflection in Article 5.7 of the *SPS Agreement*. We agree, at the same time, with the European Communities, that there is no need to assume that Article 5.7 exhausts the relevance of a precautionary principle. It is reflected also in the sixth paragraph of the preamble and in Article 3.3. These explicitly recognize the right of Members to establish their own appropriate level of sanitary protection, which level may be higher (i.e., more cautious) than that implied in existing international standards, guidelines and recommendations. Thirdly, a panel charged with determining, for instance, whether "sufficient scientific evidence" exists to warrant the maintenance by a, Member of a particular SPS measure may, of course, and should, bear in mind that responsible, representative governments commonly act from perspectives of prudence and precaution where risks of irreversible, e.g. life-terminating, damage to human health are concerned. Lastly, however, the precautionary principle does not, by itself, and without a clear textual directive to that effect, relieve a panel from the duty of applying the normal (i.e. customary international law) principles of treaty interpretation in reading the provisions of the *SPS Agreement*.

125. We accordingly agree with the finding of the Panel that the precautionary principle does not override the provisions of Articles 5.1 and 5.2 of the *SPS Agreement*.

* * *

VIII. The Requirement of Objective Assessment of the Facts by a Panel Under Article 11 of the DSU

131. The European Communities claims that the Panel has disregarded or distorted the evidence submitted by the European Communities to the Panel, as well as the opinions and statements made by the scientific experts advising the Panel. It is claimed, in other words, that the Panel has failed to make an objective assessment of the facts as required by Article 11 of the DSU, and the European Communities asks us to reverse the findings so arrived at by the Panel.

132. Under Article 17.6 of the DSU, appellate review is limited to appeals on questions of law covered in a panel report and legal interpretations developed by the panel. Findings of fact, as distinguished from legal interpretations or legal conclusions, by a panel are, in principle, not subject to review by the Appellate Body. The determination of whether or not a certain event did occur in time and space is typically a question of fact; for example, the question of whether or not Codex has adopted an international standard, guideline or recommendation on MGA is a

factual question. Determination of the credibility and weight properly to be ascribed to (that is, the appreciation of) a given piece of' evidence is part and parcel of the fact finding process and is, in principle, left to the discretion of a panel as the trier of facts. The consistency or inconsistency of a given fact or set of facts with the requirements of a given treaty provision is, however, a legal characterization issue. It is a legal question. Whether or not a panel has made an objective assessment of the facts before it, as required by Article 11 of the DSU, is also a legal question which, if properly raised on appeal, would fall within the scope of appellate review.

133. The question which then arises is this: when may a panel be regarded as having failed to discharge its duty under Article 11 of the DSU to make an objective assessment of the facts before it? Clearly, not every error in the appreciation of the evidence (although it may give rise to a question of law) may be characterized as a failure to make an objective assessment of the facts. In the present appeal, the European Communities repeatedly claims that the Panel disregarded or distorted or misrepresented the evidence submitted by the European Communities and even the opinions expressed by the Panel's own expert advisors. The duty to make an objective assessment of the facts is, among other things, an obligation to consider the evidence presented to a panel and to make factual findings on the basis of that evidence. The deliberate disregard of, or refusal to consider, the evidence submitted to a panel is incompatible with a panel's duty to make an objective assessment of the facts. The wilful distortion or misrepresentation of the evidence put before a panel is similarly inconsistent with an objective assessment of the facts.

*   *   *

[The Appellate Body, after carefully considering the evidence in the record before the Panel, concluded that, despite certain errors, such as misquoting certain experts, the Panel did not err in any significant way and, accordingly, complied with its obligation to make an objective determination of the facts.]

*   *   *

IX. Certain Procedures Adopted by the Panel

The Selection and Use of Experts

146. The European Communities considers that in its selection and use of experts, the Panel has violated Article 11.2 of the *SPS Agreement* and Articles 11, 13.2 and Appendix 4 of the DSU. We note that the Panel decided to request the opinion of experts on certain scientific and other technical matters raised by the parties to the dispute, and rather than establishing an experts review group, the Panel considered it more useful to leave open the possibility of receiving a range of opinions from the experts in their individual, capacity. The Panel stresses, among other things, that:

> We considered, however, that neither Article 11.2 of the SPS Agreement nor Article 13.2 of the DSU limits our right to seek information from *individual* experts as provided for in Article 11.2, first sentence, of the SPS Agreement and Articles 13.1 and 13.2, first sentence, of the DSU.

147. We agree with the Panel. Both Article 11.2 of the *SPS Agreement* and Article 13 of the DSU enable panels to seek information and advice as they deem appropriate in a particular case. Article 1 1.2 of the *SPS Agreement states*:

> In a dispute under this Agreement involving scientific or technical issues, a panel should seek advice from experts chosen by the panel in consultation with the parties to the dispute. To this end, the panel *may, when it deems it appropriate*, establish an advisory technical experts group. (underlining added)

Article 13 of the DSU provides, in relevant part:

1. Each panel shall have the right to seek information and technical advice from any individual or body *which it deems appropriate* . . .

2. Panels may seek information from *any relevant source and may consult experts* to obtain their opinion on certain aspects of the matter. With respect to a factual issue concerning a scientific-or *[sic]* other technical matter raised by a party to the dispute, a panel *may* request an advisory report in writing from an experts review group . . . (under-lining added),

We find that in disputes involving scientific or technical issues, neither Article 11.2 of the *SPS Agreement*, nor Article 13 of the DSU prevents panels from consulting with individual experts. Rather, both the *SPS Agreement* and the BSU leave to the sound discretion of a panel the determination of whether the establishment of an expert review group is necessary or appropriate.

* * *

X. The Interpretation of Articles 3.1 and 3.3 of the *SPS Agreement*

157. The European Communities appeals from the conclusion of the Panel that the European Communities, by maintaining SPS measures which are not based on existing international standards without justification under Article 3.3 of the *SPS Agreement*, has acted inconsistently with the requirements contained in Article 3.1 of that Agreement.

158. It will be seen below that the Panel is actually saying that the European Communities acted inconsistently with the requirements of both Articles 3.1 and 3.3 of the *SPS Agreement*, a position that flows from the Panel's view of a supposed "general rule — exception" relationship between Articles 3.1 and 3.3, a view . . . we do not share.

159. The above conclusion of the Panel has three components: first, international standards, guidelines and recommendations exist in respect of meat and meat products derived from cattle to which five of the hormones involved have been administered for growth promotion purposes; secondly, the EC measures involved here are not based on the relevant international standards, guidelines and recommendations developed by Codex, because such measures are not in conformity with those standards, guidelines and recommendations; and thirdly, the EC measures are "not justified under," that is, do not comply with the requirements of Article 3.3. *En route* to its above-mentioned conclusion, the Panel developed three

legal interpretations, which have all been appealed by the European Communities and which need to be addressed: the first relates to the meaning of "based on" as used in Article 3.1; the second is concerned with the relationship between Articles 3.1, 3.2 and 3.3 of the *SPS Agreement;* and the third relates to the requirements of Article 3.3 of the *SPS Agreement.* As may be expected, the Panel's three interpretations are intertwined.

A. *The Meaning of "Based On" as Used in Article 3.1 of the SPS Agreement*

160. Article 3.1 provides:

> To harmonize sanitary and phytosanitary measures on as wide a basis as possible, Members shall base their sanitary or phytosanitary measures on international standards, guidelines or recommendations, where they exist, except as otherwise provided for in this Agreement, and in particular in paragraph 3.

161. Addressing the meaning of "based on," the Panel constructs the following interpretations:

> The SPS Agreement does not explicitly define the words *based on* as used in Article 3.1. However, Article 3.2, which introduces a presumption of consistency with both the SPS Agreement and GATT for sanitary measures which *conform to* international standards, equates measures *based on* international standards with measures which *conform to* such standards. Article 3.3, in turn, explicitly relates the definition of sanitary measures *based on* international standards to the level of sanitary protection achieved by these measures. Article 3.3 stipulates the conditions to be met for a Member to enact or maintain certain sanitary measures which are *not* based on international standards. It applies more specifically to measures "which result in a *higher level of* sanitary . . . protection than would be achieved by measures based on the relevant international standards" or measures "which result in a *level* of sanitary . . . protection *different* from that which would be achieved by measures based on international standards." One of the determining factors in deciding, whether a measure is *based on* an international standard is, therefore, the level of protection that measure achieves According to Article 3.3 all measures which are based on a given international standard should in principle achieve the *same* level of sanitary protection. Therefore, if an international standard reflects a specific level of sanitary protection and a sanitary measure implies a *different* level, that measure cannot be considered to be *based on* the international standard to reflect the same level of sanitary protection as the *standard.* In this dispute a comparison thus needs to be made between the level of protection reflected in the EC measures in dispute and that reflected in the Codex standards for each of the five hormones at issue. (underlining added)

162. We read the Panel's interpretation that Article 3.2 "equates" measures "based on" international standards with measures which "conform to" such standards, as signifying that "based on" and "conform to" are identical in meaning. The Panel is thus saying that, henceforth, SPS measures of Members "conform to"

Codex standards, guidelines and recommendations.

163. We are unable to accept this interpretation of the Panel. In the first place, the ordinary meaning of "based on" is quite different from the plain or natural import of "conform to." A thing is commonly said to be "based on" another thing when the fanner "stands" or, is "founded" or "built" upon or "is supported by" the latter" In contrast, much more is required before one thing may be regarded as "conform[ing] to" another: the former must "comply with," "yield or show compliance" with the latter. The reference of "conform to" is to "correspondence in form or manner," to "compliance with" or "acquiescence," to "follow[ing] in form or nature. A measure that "conforms to" and incorporates a Codex standard is, of course, "based on" that standard. A measure, however, based on the same standard might not conform to that standard, as where only some, not all, of the elements of the standard are incorporated into the measure.

164. In the second place, "based on" and "conform to" are used in different articles, as well as in differing paragraphs of the same article. Thus, Article 2.2 uses "based on"; while Article 2.4 employs "conform to." Article 3.1 requires the Members to "base" their SPS measures an international standards; however, Article 3.2 speaks of measures which "conform to" international standards. Article 3.3 once again refers to measures "based on" international standards. The implication arises that the choice and use of different words in different places in the *SPS Agreement* are deliberate, and that the different words are designed to convey different meanings. A treaty interpreter is not entitled to assume that such usage was merely inadvertent on the part of the Members who negotiated and wrote that Agreement. Canada has suggested the use of different terms was "accidental" in this case, but has offered no convincing argument to support its suggestion. We do not believe this suggestion has overturned the inference of deliberate choice.

165. In the third place, the object and purpose of Article 3 run counter to the Panel's interpretation. That purpose, Article 3.1 states, is "[t]o harmonize [SPS] measures on as wide a basis as possible . . .." The preamble of the SPS Agreement also records that the Members "[d]esir[e] to further the use of harmonized' [SPSJ measures between Members on the basis of international standards, guidelines and recommendations developed by the relevant international organizations . . .." (emphasis added) Article 12.1 created a Committee on Sanitary and Phytosanitary Measures and gave it the task inter alia; of "furtherance of its objectives, in particular with respect to harmonization" and (in Article 12.2) to "encourage the use of international standards, guidelines and recommendations by all Members. It is clear to us that harmonization of SPS measures of Members on the basis of international standards is projected in the Agreement, as a goal, yet to be realized in the future. To read Article 3.1 as requiring Members to harmonize their SPS measures by *conforming those measures with international standards*, guidelines and recommendations, in *the here and now*, is, in effect, to vest such international standards, guidelines and recommendations (which are by the terms of the Codex *recommendatory* in form and nature) with obligatory force and effect. The Panel's interpretation of Article 3.1 would, in other words, transform those standards, guidelines and recommendations into binding *norms*. But, as already noted, the *SPS Agreement* itself sets out no indication of any intent on the part of the Members to do so. We cannot lightly assume that sovereign states intended to

impose upon themselves the more onerous, rather than the less burdensome, obligation by mandating *conformity* or *compliance with* such standards, guidelines and recommendations. To sustain such an assumption and to warrant such a far-reaching interpretation, treaty language far more specific and compelling than that found in Article 3 of the *SPS Agreement* would be necessary.

166. Accordingly, we disagree with the Panel's interpretation that "based on" means the same thing as "conform to."

167. After having erroneously "equated" measures "based on" an international standard with measures that "conform to" that standard," the Panel proceeds to Article 3.3. According to the Panel, Article 3.3 "explicitly relates" the "definition of sanitary measures *based on* international standards to the level of sanitary protection achieved by those measures." The Panel then interprets Article 3.3 as saying that "all measures which are based on a given international standard should *in principle* achieve the *same* level of sanitary protection" and argues *a contrario* that "if a sanitary measure implies a *different* level (from that reflected in an international standard), that measure cannot be considered to be *based on* the international standard." The Panel concludes that, under Article 3.1, "for a sanitary measure to be *based on* an international standard . . . , that *measure* needs to reflect the same level of sanitary protection as the *standard.*"

168. It appears to us that the Panel reads much more into Article 3.3 than can be reasonably supported by the actual txt of Article 3.3. Moreover, the Panel's entire analysis rests on its flawed premise that "based on," as used in Articles 3.1 and 3.3, means the same thing as "conform to" as used in Article 3.2. As already noted, we are compelled to reject this premise as an error in law. The correctness of the rest of the Panel's intricate interpretation and examination of the consequences of the Panel's litmus test however, have to be left for another day and another case.

B. *Relationship Between Articles* 3.1, 3.2 *and* 3.3 *of the SPS Agreement*

169. We turn to the relationship between Articles 3.1, 3.2 and 3.3 of the *SPS Agreement*. As observed earlier, the Panel assimilated Articles 3.1 and 3.2 to one another, designating the product as the "general rule," and contraposed that product to Article 3.3 which denoted the "exception." This view appears to us an erroneous representation of the differing situations that may arise under Article 3, that is, where a relevant international standard, guideline or recommendation exists.

170. Under Article 3.2 of the *SPS Agreement*, a Member may decide to promulgate an SPS measure that conforms to an international standard. Such a measure would embody the international standard completely and, for practical purposes, converts it into a municipal standard. Such a measure enjoys the benefit of a presumption (albeit a rebuttable one) that it is consistent with the relevant provisions of the *SPS Agreement* and of the GATT 1994.

171. Under Article 3.1 of the *SPS Agreement*, a Member may choose to establish an SPS measure that is based on the existing relevant international standard, guideline or recommendation. Such a measure may adopt some, not necessarily all, of the elements of the international standard. The Member imposing this measure does not benefit from the presumption of consistency set up in Article 3.2; but, as

earlier observed, the Member is not penalized by exemption of a complaining Member from the normal burden of showing a *prima facie* case of inconsistency with Article 3.1 or any other relevant article of *the SPS Agreement* or of the GATT 1994.

172. Under Article 3.3 of the *SPS Agreement*, a Member may decide to set for itself a level of protection different from that implicit in the international standard, and to implement or embody that level of protection in a measure not "based on" the international standard. The Member's appropriate level of protection may be higher than that implied in the international standard. The right of a Member to determine its own appropriate level of sanitary protection is an important right. This is made clear in the sixth preambular paragraph of the *SPS Agreement:*

Members,

*   *   *

Desiring to further the use of harmonized sanitary and phytosanitary measures between Members, on the basis of international standards, guidelines and recommendations developed by the relevant international organizations, including the Codex Alimentarius Commission, the International Office of Epizootics, and the relevant international and regional organizations operating within the framework of the International Plant Protection Convention, without requiring Members to change their appropriate level of protection of human, animal or plant life or health. (underlining added).

As noted earlier, this right of a Member to establish its own level of sanitary protection under Article 3.3 of the *SPS Agreement* is an autonomous right and not an "exception" from a "general obligation" under Article 3.1.

C. The Requirements of Article 3.3 of the STS Agreement

173. The right of a Member to define its appropriate level of protection is not, however, an absolute or unqualified right. Article 3.3 also makes this clear:

Members may introduce or maintain sanitary or phytosanitary measures which result in a higher level of sanitary or phytosanitary protection than would be achieved by measures based on the relevant international standards, guidelines or recommendations; if there is a scientific justification, or as a consequence of the level of sanitary or phytosanitary protection a Member determines to be appropriate in accordance with the relevant provisions of paragraphs 1 through 8 of Article 5. Notwithstanding the above, all measures which result in a level of sanitary or phytosanitary protection different from that which would be achieved by measures based on international standards, guidelines or recommendations shall not be inconsistent with any other provision of this Agreement.

174. The European Communities argues that there are two situations covered by Article 3.3 and that its SPS measures are within the first of these situations. It is claimed that the European Communities has maintained SPS measures "which result in a higher level of . . . protection than would be achieved by measures based on the relevant" Codex standard, guideline or recommendation, for which measures

"there is a scientific justification." It is also, accordingly, argued that the requirement of a risk assessment under Article 5.1 does not apply to the European
Communities. At the same time, it is emphasized that the EC measures have
satisfied the requirements of Article 2.2.

175. Article 3.3 is evidently not a model of clarity in drafting and communication.
The use of the disjunctive "or" does indicate that two situations are intended to be
covered. These are the introduction or maintenance of SPS measures which result
in a higher level of protection:

(a) "if there is a scientific justification"; or

(b) "as a consequence of the level of . . . protection a Member determines to
     be appropriate in accordance with the relevant provisions of paragraphs 1
     through 8 of Article 5"

It is true that situation (a) does not speak of Articles 5.1 through 5.8. Nevertheless,
two points need to be noted. First, the "last sentence of Article 3.3 requires that "all
measures which result in a [higher] level of . . . protection," that is to say, measures
falling within situation (a) as well as those falling within situation (b), be "not
inconsistent with any other provision of [the SPS] Agreement." Any other provision
of this Agreement", textually includes Article 5. Secondly, the footnote to Article 3.3,
while attached to the end of the first sentence, defines "scientific justification" as an
"examination and evaluation of available scientific information in conformity with
relevant provisions of his Agreement . . .." This examination and evaluation would
appear to partake of the nature of the risk assessment required in Article 5.1 and
defined in paragraph 4 of Annex A of the *SPS Agreement*.

176. On balance, we agree with the Panel's finding that although the European
Communities has established for itself a level of protection higher, or more exacting,
than the level of protection implied in the relevant Codex standards, guidelines or
recommendations, the European Communities was bound to comply with the
requirements established in Article 5.1. We are not unaware that this finding tends
to suggest that the distinction made in Article 3.3 between two situations may have
very limited effects and may, to that extent, be more apparent than real. Its involved
and layered language: actually leaves us with no choice.

177. Consideration of the object and purpose of Article 3 and of the *SPS
Agreement* as a whole reinforces our belief that compliance with Article 5.1 was
intended as a countervailing factor in respect of the right of Members to set their
appropriate level of protection. In generalized terms, the object and purpose of
Article 3 is to promote the harmonization of the SPS measures of Members on as
wide a basis as possible, while recognizing and safeguarding, at the same time, the
right and duty of Members to protect the life and health of their people. The
ultimate goal of the harmonization of SPS measures is to prevent the use of such
measures for arbitrary or unjustifiable discrimination between Members or as a
disguised restriction on international trade, without preventing Members from
adopting or enforcing measures which I are both "necessary to protect" human life
or health and "based on scientific principles," and without requiring them to change
their appropriate level of protection. The requirements of a risk assessment under
Article 5.1, as well as of "sufficient scientific evidence" under Article 2.2, are
essential for the maintenance of the delicate and carefully negotiated balance in the

SPS Agreement between the shared, but sometimes competing, interests of promoting international trade and of protecting the life and health of human beings. We conclude that the Panel's finding that the European Communities is required by Article 3.3 to comply with the requirements of Article 5.1 is correct and, accordingly, dismiss the appeal of the European Communities from that ruling of the Panel.

XI. The Reading of Articles 5.1 and 5.2 of the *SPS Agreement:* Basing SPS Measures on a Risk Assessment

178. We turn to the appeal of European Communities from the Panel's conclusion that, by maintaining SPS measures which are not based on a risk assessment, the European Communities acted inconsistently with the requirements contained in Article 5.1 of the *SPS Agreement.*

179. Article 5.1 of the *SPS Agreement* provides:

> Members shall ensure that their sanitary or phytosanitary measures are based on an assessment, as appropriate to the circumstances, of the risks to human, animal or plant life or health, taking into account risk assessment techniques developed by the relevant international organizations. (underlining added).

A. *The Interpretation of "Risk Assessment"*

180. At the outset, two preliminary considerations need to be brought out. The first: is that the Panel considered that Article 5.1 may be viewed as a specific application of the basic obligations contained in Article 2.2 of the *SPS Agreement*, which reads as follows:

> Members shall ensure that any sanitary or phytosanitary measure is applied only to the extent necessary to protect human, animal or plant life or health, is based on scientific principles and is not maintained without sufficient scientific evidence, except as provided for in paragraph 7 of Article 5. (underlining added).

We agree with this general consideration and would also stress that Articles 2.2 and 5.1 should constantly be read together. Article 2.2 informs Article 5.1: the elements that define the basic obligation set out in Article 2.2 impart meaning to Article 5.1.

181. The second preliminary consideration relates to the Panel's effort to distinguish between "risk assessment: and "risk management." The Panel observed that an assessment of risk is, at least, with respect to risks of human life and health, a scientific examination of data and factual studies; it is not in the view of the panel, a "policy" exercise involving social value judgments made by political bodies. The Panel describes the latter as "non-scientific" and as pertaining to "risk management" rather than to "risk assessment," We must stress, in this connection, that Article 5 and Annex A of the *SPS Agreement* speak of "risk assessment" only and that the term "risk management" is not to be found either in Article 5 or in any other provision of the *SPS Agreement.* Thus, the Panel's distinction, which it apparently employs to achieve or support what appears to be a restrictive notion of risk assessment, has no textual basis. The fundamental rule of treaty interpretation

requires a treaty interpreter to read and interpret the words actually used by the agreement under examination, and not words which the interpreter may fell should have been used.

1. *Risk Assessment and the Notion of "Risk"*

182. Paragraph 4 of Annex A of the *SPS Agreement* sets out the treaty definition of risk assessment:

This definition, to the extent pertinent to the present appeal, speaks of:

> . . . the evaluation of the potential for adverse effects on human or animal health arising from the presence of additives, contaminants, toxins or disease-causing organisms in food, beverages or feedstuffs. (underlining added).

183. Interpreting the above definition, the Panel elaborates risk assessment as a two-step process that "should (i) *identify* the *adverse effects* on human health (if any) arising from the presence of the hormones at issue when used as growth promoters *in meat* . . . , and (ii) if any such adverse effects exist, *evaluate* the *potential* or probability of occurrence of such effects."

184. The European Communities appeals from the above interpretation as involving an erroneous notion of risk and risk assessment. Although the utility of a two-step analysis may be debated, it does not appear to us to be substantially wrong. What needs to be pointed out at this stage is that the Panel's use of "probability" as an alternative term for "potential" creates a significant concern. The ordinary meaning of "potential" relates to "possibility" and is different from the ordinary meaning of "probability." "Probability" implies a higher degree or a threshold of potentiality or possibility. It thus appears that here the Panel introduces a quantitative dimension to the notion of risk.

185. In its discussion on a statement made by Dr. Lucier at the joint meeting with the experts in February 1997, the Panel states the risk referred to by this expert is an estimate which ". . . only represents a statistical range of 0 to 1 in a million, not a scientifically identified risk". The European Communities protests vigorously that, by doing so, the Panel is in effect requiring a Member carrying out a risk assessment to quantify the potential for adverse effects on human health.

186. It is not clear in what sense the Panel uses the term "scientifically identified risk." The Panel also frequently uses the term "identifiable risk," and does not define this term either. The Panel might arguably have used the terms "scientifically identified risk" and "identifiable risk" simply to refer to an ascertainable risk: if a risk is not ascertainable, how does a Member ever know or demonstrate that it exists? In one part of its Reports, the Panel opposes a requirement of an "identifiable risk" to the uncertainty that theoretically always remains since science can *never* provide *absolute* certainty that a given substance will not *ever* have adverse health effects. We agree with the Panel that this theoretical uncertainty is not the kind of risk which, under Article 5.1, is to be assessed. In another part of its Reports, however the Panel appeared to be using the term "scientifically identified risk" to prescribe implicitly that a certain *magnitude* or threshold level of risk be

demonstrated in a risk assessment if an SPS measure based thereon is to be regarded as consistent with Article 5.1 To the extent that the Panel purported to require a risk assessment to establish a minimum magnitude of risk, we must note that imposition of such a quantitative requirement finds no basis in the *SPS Agreement*. A panel is authorized only to determine whether a given SPS measure is "based on" a risk assessment. As will be elaborated below, this meant that a panel has to determine whether an SPS measure is sufficiently supported or reasonably warranted by the risk assessment.

2. Factors to be Considered in Carrying Out a Risk Assessment

187. Article 5.2 of the SPS *Agreement* provides an indication of the factors that should be taken into account in the assessment of risk. Article 5.2 states that:

> In the assessment of risks, Members shall take into account available scientific evidence; relevant processes and production methods; relevant inspection, sampling and testing methods; prevalence of specific; diseases or pests; existence of pest- or disease-free areas; relevant ecological and environmental conditions; and quarantine or other treatment.

The listing in Article 5.2 begins with "available scientific evidence"; this, however, is only the beginning. We note in this connection that the Panel states that, for purposes of the EC measures in dispute, a risk assessment required by Article 5.1 is "a *scientific* process aimed at establishing the *scientific* basis for the sanitary measure" a Member intends to take. To the extent that the Panel intended to refer to a process characterized by systematic, disciplined and objective enquiry and analysis, that is, a mode of studying and sorting out facts and opinions, the Panel's statement is unexceptionable. However, to the extent that the Panel purports to exclude from the scope of a risk assessment in the sense of Article 5.1, all matters not susceptible of quantitative analysis by the empirical or experimental laboratory methods commonly associated with the physical sciences, we believe that the Panel is in error. Some of the kinds of factors listed in Article 5.2 such as "relevant processes and production methods" and "relevant inspection, sampling and testing' methods" are not necessarily or wholly susceptible of investigation according to laboratory methods of, for example, biochemistry or pharmacology. Furthermore, there is nothing to indicate that the listing of factors that may be taken into account in a risk assessment of Article 5.2 was intended to be a closed list. It is essential to bear in mind that the risk that is to be evaluated in a risk assessment under Article 5.1 is not only risk ascertainable in a science laboratory operating under strictly controlled conditions, but also risk in human societies as they actually exist, in other words, the actual potential for adverse effects on human health in the real world where people live and work and die.

B. The Interpretation of "Based On"

1. A "Minimum Procedural Requirement" in Article 5.1?

188. Although it expressly recognizes that Article 5.1 does *not* contain any specific procedural requirements for a Member to base its sanitary measures on a

risk assessment, the Panel nevertheless proceeds to declare that "there is a minimum procedural requirement contained in Article 5.1." That requirement is that "the Member imposing a sanitary measure needs to submit evidence that at least it actually *took into account* a risk assessment when it enacted or maintained its sanitary measure in order for that measure to be considered as *based on* a risk assessment." The Panel goes on to state that the European Communities did not provide any evidence that the studies it referred to or the scientific conclusions reached therein *"have actually been taken into account by the competent EC institutions either when it enacted those measures (in 1981 and 1988) or at any later point in time."* (emphasis added). Thereupon, the Panel holds that such studies could not be considered as part of a risk assessment on which the European Communities based its measures in dispute. Concluding that the European Communities had not met its burden of proving that it had satisfied the "minimum procedural requirement" it had found in Article 5.1, the Panel holds the EC measures as inconsistent with the requirements of Article 5.1.

189. We are bound to note that, as the Panel itself acknowledges, no textual basis exists in Article 5 of the *SPS Agreement for* such a "minimum procedural requirement." The term "based on," when applied as a "minimum procedural requirement" by the Panel, may be seen to refer to a human action, such as particular human individuals "taking into account" a document described as a risk assessment. Thus, "take into account" is apparently used by the Panel to refer to some subjectivity which, at some time, may be present in particular individuals but that, in the end, may be totally rejected by those individuals. We believe that "based on" is appropriately taken to refer to a certain *objective relationship* between two elements, that is to say, to an *objective situation* that persists and is observable between an SPS measure and a risk assessment. Such a reference is certainly embraced in the ordinary meaning of the words "based on" and, when considered in context and in the light of the object and purpose of Article 5.1 of the *SPS Agreement*, may be seen to be more appropriate than "taking into account." We do not share the Panel's interpretative construction and believe it is unnecessary and an error of law as well.

190. Article 5.1 does not insist that a Member that adopts a sanitary measure shall have carried out its own risk assessment. It only requires that the SPS measures be "based on an assessment, as appropriate for the circumstances . . .." The SPS measure might well find its objective justification in a risk assessment carried out by another Member, or an international organization. The "minimum procedural requirement" constructed by the Panel, could well lead to the elimination or disregard of available scientific evidence that rationally supports the SPS measure being examined. This risk of exclusion of available scientific evidence may be particularly significant for the bulk of SPS measures which were put in place before the effective date of the WTO Agreement and that have been simply maintained thereafter.

191. In the course of demanding evidence that EC authorities actually "took into account" certain scientific studies, the Panel refers to the preambles of the EC Directives here involved. The Panel notes that such preambles did not mention any of the scientific studies referred to by the European Communities in the panel proceedings. Preambles of legislative or quasi-legislative acts and administrative

regulations commonly fulfil requirements of the internal legal orders of WTO Members. Such preambles are certainly not required by the *SPS Agreement;* they are not normally used to demonstrate that a Member has complied with its obligations under international agreements. The absence of any mention of scientific studies in the preliminary sections of the EC Directives does not, therefore, prove anything so far as the present case is concerned.

2. Substantive Requirement of Article 5.1-Rational Relationship Between an SPS Measure and a Risk Assessment

192. Having posited a "minimum procedural requirement" of Article 5.1, the Panel turns to the "substantive requirements" of Article 5.1 to determine whether the EC measures at issue are "based on" a risk assessment. In the Panel's view, those "substantive requirements" involve two kinds of operations: first, identifying the scientific conclusions reached in the risk assessment and the scientific conclusions implicit in the SPS measures; and secondly, examining those scientific conclusions to determine whether or not one set of conclusions matches, i.e. conforms with, the second set of conclusions. Applying the "substantive requirements" it finds in Article 5.1, the Panel holds that the scientific conclusions implicit in the EC measures do not conform with any of the scientific conclusions reached in the scientific studies the European Communities had submitted as evidence.

193. We consider that, in principle, the Panel's approach of examining the scientific conclusions implicit in the SPS measure under consideration and the scientific conclusion yielded by a risk assessment is a useful approach. The relationship between those two sets of conclusions is certainly relevant; they cannot, however, be assigned relevance to the exclusion of everything else. We believe that Article 5.1, when contextually read as it should be, in conjunction with and as informed by Article 2.2 of the *SPS Agreement*, requires that the results of the risk assessment must sufficiently warrant — that is to say, reasonably support — the SPS measure at stake. The requirement that an SPS measure be "based on" a risk assessment is a substantive requirement that there be a rational relationship between the measure and the risk assessment.

194. We do not believe that a risk assessment has to come to a monolithic conclusion that coincides with the scientific conclusion or view implicit in the SPS measure. The risk assessment could set out both the prevailing view representing the "mainstream" of scientific opinion, as well as the opinions of scientists taking a divergent view. Article 5.1 does not require that the risk assessment must necessarily embody only the view of a majority of the relevant scientific community. In some cases, the very existence of divergent views presented by qualified scientists who have investigated the particular issue at hand may indicate a state of scientific uncertainty. Sometimes the divergence may indicate a roughly equal balance of scientific opinion, which may itself be a form of scientific uncertainty. In most cases, responsible and representative governments tend to base their legislative and administrative measures on "mainstream" scientific opinion. In other cases, equally responsible and representative governments may act in good faith on the basis of what, at a given time, may be a divergent opinion coming from qualified and respected sources. By itself, this does not necessarily signal the absence of a

reasonable relationship between the SPS measure and the risk assessment, especially where the risk involved is life threatening in character and is perceived to constitute a clear and imminent threat to public health and safety. Determination of the presence or absence of that relationship can only be done on a case-to-case basis, after account is taken of all considerations rationally bearing upon the issue of potential adverse health effects.

195. We turn now to the application by the Panel of the substantive requirements of Article 5.1 to the EC measures at stake in the present case. The Panel lists the following scientific material to which the European Communities referred in respect of the hormones here involved (except MGA):

- the 1982 Report of the EC Scientific Veterinary Committee, Scientific Committee for Animal Nutrition and the Scientific Committee for Food on the basis of the Report of the Scientific Group on Anabolic Agents in Animal Production ("Lamming Report");

- the 1983 Symposium on Anabolics in Animal Production of the *Office international des epizooties* ("OIE") ("1983 OIE Symposium");

- the 1987 Monographs of the International Agency for Research on Cancer ("IARC") on the Evaluation of Carcinogenic Risks to Humans, Supplement 7 ("1987 IARC Monographs");

- the 1988 and 1989 JECFA Reports;

- the 1995 European Communities Scientific Conference on Growth Promotion in Meat Production. ("1995 EC Scientific Conference");

- articles and opinions by individual scientists relevant to the use of hormones (three articles in the journal Science, one article in the International Journal of Health Service, one report in The Veterinary Record and separate scientific opinions of Dr. H. Adlercreutz, Dr. E. Cavalieri, Dr. S.S. Epstein, Dr. J.G. Liehr, Dr. M. Metzler, Dr. Perez-Comas and Dr. A. Pinter, all of whom were part of the EC delegation at [the] joint meeting with experts).

196. Several of the above scientific reports appeared to the Panel to meet the minimum requirements of a risk assessment, in particular, the Lamming Report and the 1988 and 1989 JECFA Reports. The Panel assumes accordingly that the European Communities had demonstrated the existence of a risk assessment carried out in accordance with Article 5 of the *SPA Agreement*. At the same time, the Panel finds that the conclusion of these scientific reports is that the use of the hormones at issue (except MGA) for growth promotion purposes is "safe." The Panel states:

> . . . none of the scientific evidence referred to by the European Communities which specifically addresses the safety of some or all of the hormones in dispute when used for growth promotion, indicates that an identifiable risk arises for human health from such use of these hormones if good practice is followed. All of the scientific studies outlined above came to the conclusion that the use of the hormones at issue (all but MGA, for which no evidence was submitted) for growth promotion purposes is safe; most of

these studies adding that this conclusion assumes that good practice is followed.

197. Prescinding from the difficulty raised by the Panel's use of the term "identifiable risk," we agree that the scientific reports listed above do not rationally support the EC import prohibition.

198. With regard to the scientific opinion expressed by Dr. Lucier at the joint meeting with the experts, and as set out in paragraph 819 of the Annex to the U.S. and Canada Panel Report P, we should note that this opinion by Dr. Lucier does not purport to be the result of scientific studies carried out by him or under his supervision focusing specifically on residues of hormones in meat from cattle fattened with such hormones' Accordingly, it appears that the single divergent opinion expressed by Dr. Lucier is not reasonably sufficient to overturn the contrary conclusions reached in the scientific studies referred to by the European Communities that related specifically to residues of the hormones in meat from cattle to which hormones had been administered for growth promotion.

199. The European Communities laid particular emphasis on the 1987 IARC Monographs and the articles and opinions of individual scientists referred to above. The Panel notes, however, that the scientific evidence set out in these Monographs and these articles and opinions relates to the carcinogenic potential of entire *categories* of hormones, or of the hormones at issue *in general*. The Monographs and the articles and opinions are, in other words, in the nature of general studies of or statements on the carcinogenic potential of the named hormones. The Monographs and the articles and opinions of individual scientists have not evaluated the carcinogenic potential of those hormones when used specifically *for growth promotion purposes*. Moreover, they do not evaluate the specific potential for carcinogenic effects arising from the presence *in "food"*, more specifically, "meat or meat products" of residues of the hormones in dispute. The Panel also notes that, according to the scientific experts advising the Panel, the data and studies set out in these 1987 Monographs have been taken into account in the 1988 and 1989 JECFA Reports and that the conclusions reached by the 1987 IARC Monographs are complementary to, rather than contradictory of, the conclusions of the JECFA Reports. The Panel concludes that these Monographs and these articles and opinions are insufficient to support the EC measures at issue in this case.

200. We believe that the above findings of the Panel are justified. The 1987 IARC Monographs and the articles and opinions of individual scientists submitted by the European Communities constitute general studies which do indeed show the existence of a general risk of cancer; but they do not focus on and do not address the particular kind of risk here at stake — the carcinogenic or genotoxic potential. of the residues of those hormones found in meat derived from cattle to which the hormones had been administered for growth promotion purposes — as is required by paragraph 4 of Annex A of the SPS *Agreement*. Those general studies, are in other words, relevant but do not appear to be sufficiently specific to the case at hand.

201. With regard to risk assessment concerning MGA. the European Communities referred to the 1987 IARC Monographs. These Monographs deal with, *inter alia*, the category of progestins of which the hormone progesterone is a member.

The European Communities argues that because MGA is an anabolic agent which mimics the action of progesterone, the scientific studies and experiments relied on by the 1987 IARC Monographs were highly relevant. However, the Monographs and the articles and opinions of the individual scientists did not include any study that demonstrated how closely related MGA is chemically and pharmacologically to other progestins and what effects MGA residues would actually have on human beings when such residues are ingested along with meat from cattle to which MGA has been administered for growth promotion purposes. It must be recalled in this connection that none of the other scientific material submitted by the European Communities referred to MGA, and that no international standard, guideline or recommendation has been developed by Codex relating specifically to MGA. The United States and Canada declined to submit any assessment of MGA upon the ground that the material they were aware of was proprietary and confidential in nature. In other words, there was an almost complete absence of evidence on MGA in the panel proceedings. We therefore uphold the Panel's finding that there was no risk assessment with regard to MGA.

202. The evidence referred to above by the European Communities related to the biochemical risk arising from the ingestion by human beings of residues of the five hormones here involved in treated meat, where such hormones had been administered to the cattle in accordance with good veterinary practice. The European Communities also referred to distinguishable but closely related risks — risks arising from failure to observe the requirements of good veterinary practice, in combination with multiple problems relating to detection and control of such abusive failure, in the administration of hormones to cattle for growth promotion.

203. The Panel considers this type of risk and examines the arguments made by the European Communities but finds no assessment of such kind of risk.

Ultimately, the Panel rejects those arguments principally on a priori grounds. First, to the Panel, the provisions of Article 5.2 relating to "relevant inspection, sampling and testing methods":

> . . . do not seem to cover the general problem of control (such as the problem of ensuring the observance of good practice) which can exist for any substance. The risks related to the general problem of control do not seem to be specific to the substance at issue but to the economic or social incidence related to a substance or its particular use (such as economic incentives for abuse). These non-scientific factors should, therefore not be taken into account in a risk assessment but in *risk management.* (underlining added).

Moreover, the Panel finds that, assuming these factors could be taken into account in a risk assessment, the European Communities has not provided convincing evidence that the control or prevention of abuse of the hormones here involved is more difficult than the control of other veterinary drugs, the use of which is allowed in the European Communities. Further, the European Communities has not provided evidence that control would be more difficult under a regime where the use of the hormones in dispute is allowed under specific conditions than under the current EC regime of total prohibition both domestically and in respect of imported meat. The Panel concludes by saying that banning the use of a substance does not necessarily offer better protection of human health than other means of regulating its use.

204. The European Communities appeals from these findings of the Panel principally on two grounds: firstly, that the Panel has misinterpreted Article 5.2 of the *SPS Agreement*; secondly, that the Panel has disregarded and distorted the evidence submitted by the European Communities.

205. In respect of the first ground, we agree with the European Communities that the Panel has indeed misconceived the scope of application of Article 5.2. It should be recalled that Article 5.2 states that in the assessment of risks, Members shall take into account, in addition to "available scientific evidence," "relevant processes and production methods; [and] relevant inspection, sampling and testing methods." We note also that Article 8 requires Members to "observe the provisions of Annex C in the operation of control, inspection and approval procedures . . .." The footnote in Annex C states that "control, inspection and approval procedures include, *inter alia*, procedures for sampling, testing and certification." We consider that this language is amply sufficient to authorize the taking into account of risks arising from failure to comply with the requirements of good veterinary practice in the administration of hormones for growth promotion purposes, as well as risks arising from difficulties of control, inspection and enforcement of the requirements of good veterinary practice.

206. Most, if not all, of the scientific studies referred to by the European Communities, in respect of the five hormones involved here, concluded that their use for growth promotion purposes is "safe," if the hormones are administered in accordance with the requirements of good veterinary practice. Where the condition of observance of good veterinary practice (which is much the same condition attached to the standards, guidelines and recommendations of Codex with respect to the use of the five hormones for growth promotion) is *not* followed, the logical inference is that the use of such hormones for growth promotion purposes mayor may not be "safe." The *SPS Agreement* requires assessment of the potential for adverse effects on human health arising from the presence of contaminants and toxins in food. We consider that the object and purpose of the *SPS Agreement* justify the examination and evaluation of all such risks for human health whatever their precise and immediate origin may be. We do not mean to suggest that risks arising from potential abuse in the administration of controlled substances and from control problems need to be, or should be, evaluated by risk assessors in each and every case. When and if risks of these types do in fact arise, risk assessors may examine and evaluate them. Clearly, the necessity or propriety of examination and evaluation of such risks would have to be addressed on a case-by-case basis. What, in our view, is a fundamental legal error is to exclude, on an a priori basis, any such risks from the scope of application of Articles 5.1 and 5.2. We disagree with the Panel's suggestion that exclusion of risks resulting from the combination of potential abuse and difficulties of control is justified by distinguishing between "risk assessment" and "risk management." As earlier noted, the concept of "risk management" is not mentioned in any provision of the *SPS Agreement* and, as such, cannot be used to sustain a more restrictive interpretation of "risk assessment" than is justified by the actual terms of Article 5.2, Article 8 and Annex C of the SPS Agreement.

207. The question that arises, therefore, is whether the European Communities did, in fact, submit a risk assessment demonstrating and evaluating the existence and level of risk arising in the present case from abusive use of hormones and the difficulties of control of the administration of hormones for growth promotion purposes, within the United States and Canada as exporting countries, and at the frontiers of the European Communities as an importing country. Here, we must agree with the finding of the Panel that the European Communities in fact restricted itself to pointing out the condition of administration of hormones "in accordance with good practice" "without further providing an assessment of the potential adverse effects related to non compliance with such practice." The record of the panel proceedings shows that the risk arising from abusive use of hormones for growth promotion combined with control problems for the hormones at issue, may have been examined on two occasions in a scientific manner. The first occasion may have occurred at the proceedings before the Committee of Inquiry into the Problem of Quality in the Meat Sector established by the European Parliament, the results of which constituted the basis of the Pimenta Report of 1989. However, none of the original studies and evidence put before the Committee of Inquiry was submitted to the Panel. The second occasion could have been the 1995 EC Scientific Conference on Growth Promotion in Meat Production. One of the three workshops of this Conference examined specifically the problems of "detection and control." However, only one of the studies presented to the workshop discussed systematically some of the problems arising from the combination of potential abuse and problems of control of hormones and other substances. The study presented a theoretical framework for the systematic analysis of such problems, but did not itself investigate and evaluate the actual problems that have arisen at the borders of the European Communities or within the United States, Canada and other countries exporting meat and meat products to the European Communities. At best, this study may represent the beginning of an assessment of such risks.

208. In the absence of any other relevant documentation, we find that the European Communities did not actually proceed to an assessment, within the meaning of Articles 5.1 and 5.2 of the risks arising from the failure of observance of good veterinary practice combined with problems of control of the use of hormones for growth promotion purposes. The absence of such a risk assessment, when considered in conjunction with the conclusion actually reached by most, if not all, of the scientific studies relating to the other aspects of risk noted earlier, leads us to the conclusion that no risk assessment that reasonably supports or warrants the import prohibition embodied in the EC Directives was furnished to the Panel. We affirm, therefore, the ultimate conclusion of the Panel that the EC import prohibition is not based on a risk assessment within the meaning of Articles 5.1 and 5.2 of the *SPS Agreement* and is, therefore, inconsistent with the requirements of Article 5.1.

209. Since we have concluded above that an SPS measure, to be consistent with Article 3.3, has to comply with, *inter alia*, the requirements contained in Article 5.1, it follows that the EC measures at issue, by failing to comply with Article 5.1, are also inconsistent with Article 3.3 of the *SPS Agreement.*

XII. The Reading of Article 5.5 of the *SPS Agreement:* Consistency of Levels of Protection and Resulting Discrimination or Disguised Restriction on International Trade

210. The European Communities also appeals from the conclusion of the Panel that, by adopting arbitrary or unjustifiable distinctions in the levels of sanitary protection it considers appropriate in different situations which result in discrimination or a disguised restriction on international trade, the European Communities acted inconsistently with the requirements set out in Article 5.5 of the *SPS Agreement.*

[In this part of the opinion, the Appellate Body examined the argument that the different levels of protection applied by the EC were arbitrary and unjustifiable and disguised restrictions on international trade. The EC regulations distinguished between the natural and artificial hormones and adopted more stringent protections for certain hormones if they were being used for growth promotion. The Appellate Body, after extensive analysis, concluded as follows:]

246. Our conclusion, therefore, is that the Panel's finding that the "arbitrary or unjustifiable" difference in the EC levels of protection in respect of the hormones at issue on the one hand and in respect of carbadox and olaquindox on the other hand, "result in discrimination or a disguised restriction on international trade," is not supported either by the architecture and structure of the EC Directives here at stake or of the subsequent Directive on carbadox and olaquindox, or by the evidence submitted by the United States and Canada to the Panel. The Panel's finding is itself unjustified and erroneous as a matter of law. Accordingly, we reverse the conclusion of the Panel that the European Communities has acted inconsistently with the requirements set out in Article 5.5 of the SPS Agreement.

XIII. Appeals by the United States and Canada: Articles 2.2 and Article 5.6 of the SPS Agreement

The Panel refrained from making findings under Articles 2.2 and 5.6 of the SPS *Agreement.* In respect of Article 2.2, the Panel, having found, that the EC measures are inconsistent with Articles 3.1, 5.1 and 5.5, did not believe there was any necessity for making a finding on the consistency of the same EC measures with Article 2.2. The Panel, in so concluding, also considered that Articles 3 and 5 provide for more specific rights and obligations than the "basic rights and obligations" set out in Article 2.

*   *   *

252. We consider . . . and so hold, that the Panel did not err in refraining from making findings on Articles 2.2 and 5.6 of *the SPS Agreement.*

XIV. Findings and Conclusions

*   *   *

254. The foregoing legal findings and conclusions uphold, modify and reverse the findings and conclusions of the Panel in Parts VIII and IX of the Panel Reports, but

leave intact the findings and conclusions of the Panel that were not the subject of this appeal.

255. The Appellate Body recommends that the Dispute Settlement Body request the European Communities to bring the SPS measures found in this Report and in the Panel Reports, as modified by this Report, to be inconsistent with the SPS Agreement into conformity with the obligations of the European Communities under that Agreement.

NOTES AND QUESTIONS

1.   *The Hormones Case* is one of the most controversial and, at least in some quarters, celebrated WTO cases. Do you agree with the Appellate Body's interpretation of SPS Article 3.3 — that it should be read in tandem with Article 5.1? What do you think of the Appellate Body's interpretation of Article 5.1 and its application? The EC prevailed on Article 5.5. Why? Finally, read carefully Article 5.7. Why was this not argued by the EC?

2.   *Compliance.* When the EC did not comply with the WTO ruling in the Hormones Case within a reasonable time, an arbitrator authorized Canada to suspend trade concessions with the EU in the amount of Canadian dollars 11.3 million per year and authorized the United States to suspend trade concessions amounting to USD 116.8 million. (Under WTO rules, the level of suspension of trade concessions is dependent on the level of nullification of trade implicated by the losing party's WTO-inconsistent measure). The EU responded to the WTO decisions by commissioning further studies of the consequences of hormones in meat products. On October 27, 2003, the EU issued Directive 2003/73/EC, amending the original offending Directive 96/22/EC by incorporating new studies and findings. The amended Directive prohibited one growth hormone, oestradiol-17 beta, based on evidence that this hormone was both carcinogenic and genotoxic. The other five hormones in question — progesterone, testosterone, zeranol, acetate, and melengesterol — were provisionally prohibited since research showed they posed risks, but scientific evidence was incomplete. When the United States and Canada refused to rescind their retaliatory tariffs of EU products, the EU brought a complaint against both countries at the WTO. This complaint resulted in a new decision: *Canada/United States — Continued Suspension of Obligations in the EC — Hormones Dispute*, WT/DS320/AB/R, Report of the Appellate Body, adopted 14 November 2008. This decision was inconclusive: the Appellate Body overturned the panel's interpretation of its review authority with regard to the prohibition of oestradiol-17 beta, but refused to decide whether the EU's risk assessment complied with Article 5.1. As to the provisional bans on the other five hormones, the Appellate Body ruled that the provisional ban did not comply with the all of the four requirements of Article 5.7. Thus, the Appellate Body ruled that the recommendations adopted in the *EC — Hormones Case* "remain operative."

3.   *Biotechnology.* The EU and other members of the WTO have clashed with respect to standards for imports of biotechnology products. In 2003 the United States, Australia and Canada brought cases in the WTO against the EU to challenge the slow pace of biotechnology approvals in the EU. The EU had mandated a moratorium on biotechnology approvals between 1998 and 2003, and EU law

allowed any EU member state to adopt a safeguard measure to provisionally restrict the sale of a biotechnology product that received EU approval. The decision in this case was rendered by a WTO panel in 2006: *European Communities — Measures Affecting the Approval and Marketing of Biotech Products*, WT/DS291,292,293/R, Report of the Panel, adopted 21 November 2006. In this case the panel ruled that the EC had not acted inconsistently with Article 5.1, but the panel concluded that the EC was guilty of "undue delay" in violation of SPS Agreement Article 8. On the issue of the member state safeguards, the panel ruled that the EC had not satisfied all the requirements of SPS Article 5.7. The EU/EC did not appeal this decision and it was adopted at the WTO as binding upon the parties. Under the EU Directive 2001/18 on the Deliberate Release into the Environment of Genetically Modified Food and Feed (2001), the member state safeguard provision states that member states may prohibit cultivation of an EU approved GMO plant on a case-by-case basis but must produce evidence concerning the protection of the environment or environmental dangers. On this basis, most member state safeguards have been disapproved by the EU Commission, For example, Poland, in accordance with Polish law, prohibited the cultivation of GMO plants except in designated zones. In 2008, the EU Commission ruled that this safeguard was not in accordance with EU law because Poland had not produced any scientific studies, findings, or new evidence of dangers to the environment. EU Commission Decision 2008/62/EG (2008).

4.   *Biotechnology, food, and the environment.* Two separate concerns are involved in the approval of GM plants and foods. First, will the food products in question have short-term or long-term adverse impacts on human or animal health? Second, will the cultivation of the GM plant in question pose unacceptable risks to natural ecosystems, existing cultivated varieties or the environment? On the first issue, according to the Union of Concerned Scientists (UCS),[109] in the time frame that GM foods have been on the market, "no major human health problems have emerged in connection with genetically modified food crops." As to the impact on the environment, the UCS states that "there have been no serious environmental impacts — certainly no catastrophes — associated with the use of engineered crops in the United States." Some environmental problems have occurred. For example, in 2000 it was found that one variety of Bt corn produced high enough toxin levels to be lethal to butterfly larvae; but this variety was not widely planted and most Bt corn varieties are safe.[110]

5.   *The Biosafety Protocol.* In 2000, the Conference of the Parties to the U.N. Convention on Biological Diversity negotiated a Biosafety Protocol, an international treaty that governs the movements of living modified organisms (LMOs) resulting from the application of biotechnology from one country to another. This agreement, which entered into force in 2003, adopts certain trade restrictions applicable to LMOs (not biotechnology trade generally).

---

[109] Union of Concerned Scientists, Margaret Mellon and Jane Rissler, Food and Agriculture, Environmental Effects of Genetically Modified Food Crops, *available at* http://www.ucsusa.org/publications/publications-food-and-agriculture.html, accessed 7 January 2013.

[110] *See* Suzie Key, Julian K-C Ma & Pascal MW Drake, *Genetically Modified Plants and Human Health*, 101(6) J. ROYAL SOCIETY OF MEDICINE 290–98 (2008).

First, LMOs intended to be used for food, feed, or processing must be accompanied by documentation stating that such shipments "may contain" LMOs and are not intended for intentional introduction into the environment. Similarly, shipments of LMOs destined for "contained use" (for example, in a laboratory) must be accompanied by documentation clearly identifying them as such.

Second, for exports of LMOs intended to be introduced into the environment of the importing state (for example, microorganisms for bioremediation, seeds for planting, or live fish for release into lakes), the exporter must provide detailed information in advance to the importing state, after which the importing state may accept or deny authorization for the shipment. This is known as an Advance Informed Agreement procedure. The importing state, in taking the decision entailed in the Advance Informed Agreement procedure, is required to undertake or to require the exporter to undertake a risk assessment in a scientifically sound manner to identify and evaluate possible adverse effects of the LMO in question on the conservation and sustainable use of biological diversity, taking also into account possible adverse effects on human health. If authorized, the shipment must be accompanied by documentation specifying the identity and traits of the LMO. After approval, risk management must be carried out. The, Protocol also establishes a Biosafety Clearing House intended to assist states in the exchange of information about LMOs.

Is this Advance Informed Agreement procedure consistent with WTO obligations? The Biosafety Protocol states (Article 14) that "the Protocol shall not be interpreted as implying a change in the rights and obligations of a Party under any existing agreements."

6. ***Problem 5-7.*** Are the five measures taken by State A in Problem 10-8 consistent with State A's WTO obligations and obligations under the Biosafety Protocol?

To undertake measure 1, what requirements will State A have to satisfy?

Is measure 2 feasible?

For zero tolerance as required by measure 3, what will State A have to show?

What requirements will State A have to show for measure 4?

Will State A be successful in invoking the precautionary principle in measure 5?

NOTE ON LABELING GM FOODS

As a consumer do you wish to know if the foods you are buying contain GMOs? Does it matter that foods labeled "organic" and "natural" may contain GMOs? In 2012, California voters defeated Proposition 37, which would have required the labeling of GMOs in foods. The State of Washington defeated a similar referendum in 2013, but bills to label GMOs are pending in a number of state legislatures and one such bill was enacted into law in Connecticut in 2013. Labels for GMOs would have to pass muster under the TBT and SPS Agreements. In 2009, a giant step toward mandatory labeling of GMOs was taken when the United States dropped its opposition to labeling at the meeting of the Codex Alimentarius Commission, the principal international standard-setting body for food safety. This paved the way for adaption of international labeling standards for GMOs in food. *See* THE CODEX ALIMENTARIUS COMMISSION, PRINCIPLES FAR THE RISK ASSESSMENT OF FOODS DERIVED FROM MODERN BIOTECHNOLOGY (Rome: 2009).

A summary of the EU directive on GMO labeling is as follows (Europa: Summaries of EU Legislation, http://europa.eu/legislation_summaries/index_en.htm):

Traceability and Labelling of GMOs

The European Union guarantees the traceability and labelling of genetically modified organisms (GMOs) and products produced from these organisms throughout the food chain. Traceability of GMOs allows the monitoring and checking of information given on labels, the monitoring of effects on the environment and the withdrawal of products from the market in cases where new scientific data demonstrate that the GMOs used in the product present an environmental or health risk.

Regulation (EC) No *1830/2003* of the European Parliament and of the Council of 22 September 2003 concerning the traceability and labelling of genetically modified organisms and the traceability of food and feed products produced from genetically modified organisms and amending Directive 2001/18/EC [See amending act(s)].

SUMMARY

The European Union sets out a framework for guaranteeing the traceability of GMOs throughout the food chain, including in processed foods in which the production methods have destroyed or altered the genetically modified DNA (e.g. in oils). These rules apply not only to GMOs to be used in food, but also those intended to be used in crops (e.g. seeds).

Objectives

The European Union has two main objectives:

- to inform consumers through the compulsory labelling, giving them the freedom to choose;
- to create a "safety net" based on the traceability of GMOs at all stages of production and placing on the market. This "safety net" will facilitate the monitoring of labelling, the surveillance of the potential effects on human health or the environment and the withdrawal of products in cases of risk to human health or the environment.

GMOS

This Regulation covers:

- all products which consist of GMOs or which contain them (this includes fields as diverse as the products, which are intended for entry into the human or animal food chain, products destined for industrial processing for uses other than consumption (e.g. in the production of biofuel) or even products destined to be used ornamentally (e.g. in the production of cut flowers));

- foodstuffs and animal feed products made from GMOs.

Labelling and traceability

All the products covered by this Regulation are subject to compulsory labelling, which shall enable consumers to be better informed and will offer them the freedom to choose to buy products consisting of, containing or made from GMOs.

The specific requirements of this Regulation related to labelling shall not apply in isolation as these rules are in addition to the following rules which also concern labelling:

- the general labelling rules applicable to foodstuffs generally intended for human consumption (Directive *2000/13/EC);*
- the general labelling rules provided for the marketing of feed (Regulation (EC) No *767/2009);*
- the specific labelling rules applicable to GMO food and feed (Regulation (EC) No *1829/2003).*

Traceability enables GMOs and their products to be traced throughout the production chain. This system is based on the transmission and holding of information by each operator.

GMOs or products containing GMOS

Operators must transmit the following information in writing:

- an indication that the products consist of or contain GMOs;
- the unique identifiers assigned to the GMOs.

If the product is a mixture of GMOs, the industrial operator may submit a declaration of use of these products, together with a list of the unique identifiers assigned to all the GMOs used to constitute the mixture.

This information must also be held for five years.

The operators who place on the market a pre-packaged product consisting of or containing GMOs must, at all stages of the production and distribution chain, ensure that the words "This product contains genetically modified organisms" or "Product produced from GM (name of organism)" appear on a label of the product. In the case of products, including in large quantities, which are not packaged and if the use of a label is impossible, the operator must ensure that this information is transmitted with the product. It may take the form of accompanying documents, for example.

Products produced from GMOs

When placing a product on the market, the operator must transmit the following information in writing to the operator receiving the product:

- an indication of each food ingredient produced from GMOs;
- an indication of each raw material or additive for feeding stuffs produced from GMOs;
- if there is no list of ingredients, the product must bear an indication that it is produced from GMOs.

This information must also be held for five years.

GMO adventitious presence threshold

All food or feed products, including those intended directly for processing are subject to the labelling obligation when they consist, contain or are made from GMOs. Only traces of GMOs may be exempt from this obligation if they do not exceed the threshold of 0.9 % and if their presence is adventitious and technically unavoidable.

The Member States carry out measures for the inspection and monitoring of products, including sampling and quantitative and qualitative analyses of food and feed. These measures entail the Member States being able to withdraw from the market a product that does not meet the conditions laid down in this Regulation.

Context

This Regulation harmonises the traceability measures laid down in the legislation, particularly Directive 2001/18/EC on the deliberate release of GMOs in the environment.

Although the U.S. Food and Drug Administration (FDA) does not require mandatory labeling for GM foods, since 2010, the FDA has enforced regulations for organic food labeling as part of its National Organic Program. 7 C.F.R. section 205.102 specifies that any food product labeled "100 percent organic," "organic," or "made with organic ingredients" must comply with certain standards set out in 7 C.F.R. section 205.105. Among these standards are "excluded methods," which are defined (7 C.F.R. section 205.2) as "[a] variety of methods used to genetically modify organisms or influence their growth and development by means that are not possible under natural conditions or processes and are not considered compatible with organic food production . . . . Such methods do not include the use of traditional breeding, conjugation, fermentation, hybridization, in vitro fertilization, or tissue culture."

Thus, in the United States, foods labeled "100 percent Organic" cannot contain GMOs or synthetic growth hormones. But this label is not without some confusion: FDA organic labels come in four varieties — 100% organic; organic (meaning 95%

organic); made with organic ingredients (meaning 70% organic); and some organic ingredients (less than 70%).

Which labeling do you prefer the FDA labels or those in force in the EU?

With many countries and the *Codex Alimentarius Commission* in favor of GMO labeling, it may be only a matter of time before such labeling becomes standard in the United States.

Section VIII. INTERNATIONAL INVESTMENT LAW AND THE ENVIRONMENT

Beginning in the 1950s, nations of the world have created an extensive law of international investment consisting of bilateral investment treaties (BITs) and free trade agreements (FTAs) that contain investor provisions. Over 2500 BITs and over 200 FTAs are now in force that contain provisions governing foreign direct investment, the establishment of business enterprises in foreign countries. This body of international investment law defines the rights of foreign investors and sets out standards of treatment of investors by host nations. These investor rights typically specify "national" treatment of foreign investors and a guarantee of equitable treatment and against expropriation. These protections are enforced through provisions of BITs and FTAs that create mandatory investor-state arbitration which the investor may invoke to gain compensation from any infringement of investor rights by the host nation. Under this procedure, an investor may proceed directly against a host state in an arbitral tribunal consisting typically of three persons specially created to hear the investor claim. The arbitral tribunal has authority to make findings of fact and law and to render judgment and to award damages against the state in favor of the foreign investor. Such an award is enforceable in national courts without appeal.

Environmental NGOs argue that this process and the BIT/FTA system sometimes elevate investor rights over protection of the environment. We consider in this regard, a case decided under the investment Chapter Eleven of the North American Free Trade Agreement (NAFTA). (The text of Chapter Eleven is reprinted in the **Document Supplement**).

METALCLAD CORPORATION v. THE UNITED MEXICAN STATES
International Centre for Settlement of Investment Disputes (Additional Facility), Case No. ARB(AF)/97/1

Before the Arbitral Tribunal constituted under Chapter Eleven of the North American Free Trade Agreement, and comprised of: PROFESSOR SIR ELIHU LAUTERPACHT, QC, CBE PRESIDENT, MR. BENJAMIN R. CIVILETTI, MR. JOSE LUIS SIQUEIROS.

Date of dispatch to the parties: August 30, 2000

1. INTRODUCTION

This dispute arises out of the activities of the Claimant, Metalclad Corporation (hereinafter "Metalclad"), in the Mexican Municipality of Guadalcazar (hereinafter "Guadalcazar"), located in the Mexican State of San Luis Potosi (hereinafter "SLP"). Metalclad alleges that Respondent, the United Mexican States (hereinafter "Mexico"), through its local governments of SLP and Guadalcazar, interfered with its development and operation of a hazardous waste landfill. Metalclad claims that this interference is a violation of the Chapter Eleven investment provisions of the North American Free Trade Agreement (hereinafter "NAFTA"). In particular, Metalclad alleges violations of (i) NAFTA, Article 1105, which requires each Party to NAFTA to "accord to investments of investors of another Party treatment in accordance with international law, including fair and equitable treatment and full protection and security"; and (ii) NAFTA, Article 1110, which provides that "no Party to NAFTA may directly or indirectly nationalize or expropriate an investment of an investor of another Party in its territory or take a measure tantamount to nationalization or expropriation of such an investment ('expropriation'), except: (a) for a public purpose; (b) on a non-discriminatory basis; (c) in accordance with due process of law arid Article 1105(1); and (d) on payment of compensation in accordance with paragraphs 2 through 6." Mexico denies these allegations.

V. FACTS AND ALLEGATIONS

A. The Facilities at Issue:

28. In 1990 the federal government of Mexico authorized COTERIN to construct and operate a transfer station for hazardous waste in La Pedrera, a valley located in Guadalcazar in SLP. The site has an area of 814 hectares and lies 100 kilometers northeast of the capital city of SLP, separated from it by the Sierra Guadalcazar mountain range, 70 kilometers from the city of Guadalcazar. Approximately 800 people live within ten kilometers of the site.

29. On January 23, 1993, the National Ecological Institute (hereinafter "INE"), an independent sub-agency of the federal Secretariat of the Mexican Environment, National Resources and Fishing (hereinafter "SEMARNAP"), granted COTERIN a federal permit to construct a hazardous waste landfill in La Pedrera (hereinafter "the landfill").

B. Metalclad's Purchase of the Site and its Landfill Permits

30. Three months after the issuance of the federal construction permit, on April 23, 1993, Metalclad entered into a 6-month option agreement to purchase CO-TERIN together with its permits, in order to build the hazardous waste landfill.

31. Shortly thereafter, on May 11, 1993, the government of SLP granted COTERIN a state land use permit to construct the landfill. The permit Was issued subject to the condition that the project adapt to the specifications and technical requirements indicated by the corresponding authorities, and accompanied by the General Statement that the license did not prejudice the rights or ownership of the

applicant and did not authorize works, constructions or the functioning of business or activities.

32. One month later, on June 11, 1993, Metalclad met with the Governor of SLP to discuss the project. Metalclad asserts that at this meeting it obtained the Governor's support for the project. In fact, the Governor acknowledged at the hearing that a reasonable person might expect that the Governor would support the project if studies confirmed the site as suitable or feasible and if the environmental impact was consistent with Mexican standards.

33. Metalclad further asserts that it was told by the President of the INE and the General Director of the Mexican Secretariat of Urban Development and Ecology (hereinafter "SEDUE")[111] that all necessary permits for the landfill had been issued with the exception of the federal permit for operation of the landfill. A witness statement submitted by the President of the INE suggests that a hazardous waste landfill could be built if all permits required by the corresponding federal and state laws have been acquired.

34. Metalclad also asserts that the General Director of SEDUE told Metalclad that the responsibility for obtaining project support in the state and local community lay with the federal government.

35. On August 10, 1993, the INE granted COTERIN the federal permit for operation of the landfill. On September 10, 1993, Metalclad exercised its option and purchased COTERIN, the landfill site and the associated permits.

36. Metalclad asserts it would not have exercised its COTERIN purchase option but for the apparent approval and support of the project by federal and state officials.

C. Construction of the Hazardous Waste Landfill

37. Metalclad asserts that shortly after its purchase of COTERIN, the Governor of SLP embarked on a public campaign to denounce and prevent the operation of the landfill.

38. Metalclad further asserts, however, that in April 1994, after months of negotiation, Metalclad believed it had secured SLP's agreement to support the project. Consequently, in May 1994, after receiving an eighteen-month extension of the previously issued federal construction permit from the INE, Metalclad began construction of the landfill. Mexico denies that SLP's agreement or support had ever been obtained.

39. Metalclad further maintains that construction continued openly and without interruption through October 1994. Federal officials and state representatives inspected the construction site during this period, and Metalclad provided federal and state officials with written status reports of Its progress.

40. On October 26, 1994, when the Municipality ordered the cessation of all

---

[111] SEDUE is the predecessor organization to SEMARNAP.

building activities due to the absence of a municipal construction permit, construction was abruptly terminated.

41. Metalclad asserts it was once again told by federal officials that it had all the authority necessary to construct and operate the landfill; that federal officials said it should apply for the municipal construction permit to facilitate an amicable relationship with the Municipality; that federal officials assured it that the Municipality would issue the permit as a matter of course; and that the Municipality lacked any basis for denying the construction permit. Mexico denies that any federal officials represented that a municipal permit was not required, and affirmatively states that a permit was required and that Metalclad knew, or should have known, that the permit was required.

42. On November 15, 1994, Metalclad resumed construction and submitted an application for a municipal construction permit.

43. On January 31, 1995, the INE granted Metalclad an additional federal construction permit to construct the final disposition cell for hazardous waste and other complementary structures such as the landfill's administration building and laboratory.

44. In February 1995, the Autonomous University of SLP (hereinafter "UASLP") issued a study confirming earlier findings that, although the landfill site raised some concerns, with proper engineering it was geographically suitable for a hazardous waste landfill. In March 1995, the Mexican Federal Attorney's Office for the Protection of the Environment (hereinafter "PROFEPA"), an independent sub-agency of SEMARNAP, conducted an audit of the site and also concluded that, with proper engineering and operation, the landfill site was geographically suitable for a hazardous waste landfill.

D. Metalclad is Prevented from Operating the Landfill

45. Metalclad completed construction of the landfill in March 1995. On March 10, 1995, Metalclad held an "open house," or "inauguration," of the landfill which was attended by a number of dignitaries from the United States and from Mexico's federal, state and local governments.

46. Demonstrators impeded the "inauguration," blocked the entry and exit of buses carrying guests and workers, and employed tactics of intimidation against Metalclad. Metalclad asserts that the demonstration was organized at least in part by the Mexican state and local governments, and that state troopers assisted in blocking traffic into and out of the site. Metalclad was thenceforth effectively prevented from opening the landfill.

47. After months of negotiation, on November 25, 1995, Metalclad and Mexico, through two of SEMARNAP's independent sub-agencies (the INE and PROFEPA), entered into an agreement that provided for and allowed the operation of the landfill (hereinafter "the Convenio").

48. The Convenio stated that an environmental audit of the site was carried out from December, 1994 through March, 1995; that the purpose of the audit was to check the project's compliance with the laws and regulations; to check the project's

plans for prevention of and attention to emergencies; and to study the project's existing conditions, control proceedings, maintenance, operation, personnel training and mechanisms to respond to environmental emergencies. The Convenio also stated that, as the audit detected certain deficiencies, Metalclad was required to submit an action plan to correct them; that Metalclad did indeed submit an action plan including a corresponding site remediation plan; and that Metalclad agreed to carry out the work and activities set forth in the action plan, including those in the corresponding plan of remediation. These plans required that remediation and commercial operation should take place simultaneously within the first three years of the landfill's operation. The Convenio provided for a five-year term of operation for the landfill, renewable by the INE and PROFEPA. In addition to requiring remediation, the Convenio stated that Metalclad would designate 34 hectares of its property as a buffer zone for the conservation of endemic species. The Convenio also required PROFEPA to create a Technical-Scientific Committee to monitor the remediation and required that representatives of the INE, the National Autonomous University of Mexico and the UASLP be invited to participate in that Committee. A Citizen Supervision Committee was to be created. Metalclad was to contribute two new pesos per ton of waste toward social works in Guadalcazar and give a 10% discount for the treatment and final disposition of hazardous waste generated in SLP. Metalclad would also provide one day per week of free medical advice for the inhabitants of Guadalcazar through Metalclad's qualified medical personnel, employ manual labor from within Guadalcazar, and give preference to the inhabitants of Guadalcazar for technical training. Metalclad would also consult with government authorities on matters of remediation and hazardous waste, and provide two courses per year on the management of hazardous waste to personnel of the public, federal, state and municipal sectors, as well as social and private sectors.

49. Metalclad asserts that SLP was invited to participate in the process of negotiating the Convenio, but that SLP declined. The Governor of SLP denounced the Convenio shortly after it was publicly announced.

50. On December 5, 1995, thirteen months after Metalclad's application for the municipal construction permit was filed, the application was denied. In doing this, the Municipality recalled its decision to deny a construction permit to COTERIN in October 1991 and January 1992 and noted the "impropriety" of Metalclad's construction of the landfill prior to receiving a municipal construction permit.

51. There is no indication that the Municipality gave any consideration to the construction of the landfill and the efforts at operation during the thirteen months during which the application was pending.

58. From May 1996 through December 1996, Metalclad and the State of SLP attempted to resolve their issues with respect to the operation of the landfill. These efforts failed and, on January 2, 1997, Metalclad initiated the present arbitral proceedings against the Government of Mexico under Chapter Eleven of the NAFTA.

59. On September 23, 1997, three days before the expiry of his term, the Governor issued an Ecological Decree declaring a Natural Area for the protection of rare cactus. The Natural Area encompasses the area of the landfill. Metalclad

relies in part on this Ecological Decree as an additional element in its claim of expropriation, maintaining that the Decree effectively and permanently precluded the operation of the landfill.

60. Metalclad also alleges, on the basis of reports by the Mexican media, that the Governor of SLP stated, that the Ecological Decree "definitely cancelled any possibility that exists of opening the industrial waste landfill of La Pedrera."

61. Metalclad also asserts that a high level SLP official, with respect to the Ecological Decree and as reported by Mexican media, "expressed confidence in closing in this way, all possibility for the United States firm Metalclad to operate its landfill in this zone, independently of the future outcome of its claim before the Arbitral Tribunals of the NAFTA treaty."

62. The landfill remains dormant. Metalclad has not sold or transferred any portion of it.

63. Mexico denies each of these media accounts as they relate to the Ecological Decree.

THE TRIBUNAL'S DECISION

72. Metalclad contends that Mexico, through its local governments of SLP and Guadalcazar, interfered with and precluded its operation of the landfill. Metalclad alleges that this interference is a violation of Articles 1105 and 1110 of Chapter Eleven of the investment provisions of NAFTA.

A. Responsibility for the conduct of state and local governments

73. A threshold question is whether Mexico is internationally responsible for the acts of SLP and Guadalcazar. The issue was largely disposed of by Mexico in paragraph 233 of its post-hearing submission, which stated that" [Mexico] did not plead that the acts of the Municipality were not covered by NAFTA. [Mexico] was, and remains, prepared to proceed on the assumption that the normal rule of state responsibility applies; that is, that the Respondent can be internationally responsible for the acts of state organs at all three levels of government." Parties to that Agreement must "ensure that all necessary measures are taken in order to give effect to the provisions of the Agreement, including their observance, except as otherwise provided in this Agreement, by state and provincial governments." *(NAFTA Article 105).* A reference to a state or province includes local governments of that state or province. *(NAFTA Article 201 (2)).* The exemptions from the requirements of Articles 1105 and 1110 laid down in Article 1108(1) do not extend to states or local governments. This approach accords fully with the established position in customary international law. This has been clearly stated in Article 10 of the draft articles on state responsibility adopted by the International Law Commission of the United Nations in 1975 which, though currently still under consideration, may nonetheless be regarded as an accurate restatement of the present law: "The conduct of an organ of a State, of a territorial government entity or of an entity empowered to exercise elements of the Governmental authority, such organ having acted in that capacity, shall be considered as an act of the State under international law even if, in the particular case, the organ exceeded its competence

according to internal law or contravened instructions concerning its activity." *(Yearbook of the International Law Commission,* 1975, vol. ii, p. 61).

B. NAFTA Article 1105: Fair and equitable Treatment

74. NAFTA Article 1105(1) provides that "each Party shall accord to investments of investors of another Party treatment in accordance with international law, including fair and equitable treatment and full protection and security." For the reasons set out below, the Tribunal finds that Metalclad's investment was not accorded fair and equitable treatment in accordance with international law, and that Mexico has violated NAFTA Article 1105(1).

75. An underlying objective of NAFTA is to promote and increase cross-border investment opportunities and ensure the successful implementation of investment initiatives. *(NAFTA Article 102(1)).*

76. Prominent in the statement of principles and rules that introduces the Agreement is the reference to "transparency" *(NAFTA Article 102(1)).* The Tribunal understands this to include the idea that all relevant legal requirements for the purpose of initiating, completing and successfully operating investments made, or intended to be made, under the Agreement should be capable of being readily known to all affected investors of another Party. There should be no room for doubt or uncertainty on such matters. Once the authorities of the central government of any Party (whose international responsibility in such matters has been identified in the preceding section) become aware of any scope for misunderstanding or confusion in this connection, it is their duty to ensure that the correct position is promptly determined and clearly stated so that investors can proceed with all appropriate expedition in the confident belief that they are acting in accordance with all relevant laws.

77. Metalclad acquired COTERIN for the sole purpose of developing and operating a hazardous waste landfill in the valley of La Pedrera, in Guadalcazar, SLP.

78. The Government of Mexico issued federal construction and operating permits for the landfill prior to Metalclad's purchase of COTERIN, and the Government of SLP likewise issued a state operating permit which implied its political support for the landfill project.

79. A central point in this case has been whether, in addition to the above-mentioned permits, a municipal permit for the construction of a hazardous waste landfill was required.

80. When Metalclad inquired, prior to its purchase of COTERIN, as to the necessity for municipal permits, federal officials assured it that it had all that was needed to undertake the landfill project. Indeed, following Metalclad's acquisition of COTERIN, the federal government extended the federal construction permit for eighteen months.

81. As presented and confirmed by Metalclad's expert on Mexican law, the authority of the municipality extends only to the administration of the construction permit, ". . . to grant licenses and permits for constructions and to participate in

the creation and administration of ecological reserve zones . . . ." *(Mexican Const. Art.* 115, *Fraction V)*. However, Mexico's experts on constitutional law expressed a different view.

82. Mexico's General Ecology Law of 1988 (hereinafter "LGEEPA") expressly grants to the Federation the power to authorize construction and operation of hazardous waste landfills. Article 5 of the LGEEPA provides that the powers of the Federation extend to:

> V. [t]he regulation and control of activities considered to be highly hazardous, and of the generation, handling and final disposal of hazardous materials and wastes for the environments of ecosystems, as well as for the preservation of natural resources, in accordance with [the] Law, other applicable ordinances and their regulatory provisions.

83. LGEEPA also limits the environmental powers of the municipality to issues relating to *non*-hazardous waste. Specifically, Article 8 of the LGEEPA grants municipalities the power in accordance with the provisions of the law and local laws to apply:

> [l]egal provisions in matters of prevention and control of the effects on the environment caused by generation, transportation, storage, handling treatment and final disposal of solid industrial wastes which are *not* considered to be hazardous in accordance with the provisions of Article 137 of [the 1988] law. (Emphasis supplied).

84. The same law also limits state environmental powers to those not expressly attributed to the federal government. *Id., Article 7.*

85. Metalclad was led to believe, and did believe, that the federal and state permits allowed for the construction and operation of the landfill. Metalclad argues that in all hazardous waste matters, the Municipality has no authority. However, Mexico argues that constitutionally and lawfully the Municipality has the authority to issue construction permits.

86. Even if Mexico is correct that a municipal construction permit was required, the evidence also shows that, as to hazardous waste evaluations and assessments, the federal authority's jurisdiction was controlling and the authority of the municipality only extended to appropriate construction considerations. Consequently, the denial of the permit by the Municipality by reference to environmental impact considerations in the case of what was basically a hazardous waste disposal landfill, was improper, as was the municipality's denial of the permit for any reason other than those related to the physical construction or defects in the site.

87. Relying on the representations of the federal government, Metalclad started constructing the landfill, and did this openly and continuously, and with the full knowledge of the federal, state, and municipal governments, until the municipal "Stop Work Order" on October 26, 1994. The basis of this order was said to have been Metalclad's failure to obtain a municipal construction permit.

88. In addition, Metalclad asserted that federal officials told it that if it submitted an application for a municipal construction permit, the Municipality would have no legal basis for denying the permit and that it would be issued as a matter of course.

The absence of a clear rule as to the requirement or not of a municipal construction permit, as well as the absence of any established practice or procedure as to the manner of handling applications for a municipal construction permit, amounts to a failure on the part of Mexico to ensure the transparency required by NAFTA.

89. Metalclad was entitled to rely on the representations of federal officials and to believe that it was entitled to continue its construction of the landfill. In following the advice of these officials, and filing the municipal permit application on November 15, 1994, Metalclad was merely acting prudently and in the full expectation that the permit would be granted.

90. On December 5, 1995, thirteen months after the submission of Metalclad's application — during which time Metalclad continued its open and obvious investment activity — the Municipality denied Metalclad's application for a construction permit. The denial was issued well after construction was virtually complete and immediately following the announcement of the *Convenio* providing for the operation of the landfill.

91. Moreover, the permit was denied at a meeting of the Municipal Town Council of which Metalclad received no notice, to which it received no invitation, and at which it was given no opportunity to appear.

92. The Town Council denied the permit for reasons which included, but may not have been limited to, the opposition of the local population, the fact that construction had already begun when the application was submitted, the denial of the permit to COTERIN in December 1991 and January 1992, and the ecological concerns regarding the environmental effect and impact on the site and surrounding communities. None of the reasons included a reference to any problems associated with the physical construction of the landfill or to any physical defects therein.

93. The Tribunal therefore finds that the construction permit was denied without any consideration of, or specific reference to, construction aspects or flaws of the physical facility.

94. Moreover, the Tribunal cannot disregard the fact that immediately after the Municipality's denial of the permit it filed an administrative complaint with SEMARNAP challenging the *Convenio*. The Tribunal, infers from this that the Municipality lacked confidence in its right to deny permission for the landfill solely on the basis of the absence of a municipal construction permit.

95. SEMARNAP dismissed the challenge for lack of standing, which the Municipality promptly challenged by filing an *amparo* action. An injunction was issued, and the landfill was barred from operation through 1999.

96. In 1997 SLP re-entered the scene and issued an Ecological Decree in 1997 which effectively and permanently prevented the use by Metalclad of its investment.

97. The actions of the Municipality following its denial of the municipal construction permit, coupled with the procedural and substantive deficiencies of the denial, support the Tribunal's finding, for the reasons stated above, that the Municipality's insistence upon and denial of the construction permit in this instance

was improper.[112]

98. This conclusion is not affected by NAFTA Article 1114, which permits a Party to ensure that investment activity is undertaken in a manner sensitive to environmental concerns. The conclusion of the *Convenio* and the issuance of the federal permits show clearly that Mexico was satisfied that this project was consistent with, and sensitive to, its environmental concerns.

99. Mexico failed to ensure a transparent and predictable framework for Metalclad's business planning and investment. The totality of these circumstances demonstrates a lack of orderly process and timely disposition in relation to an investor of a Party acting in the expectation that it would be treated fairly and justly in accordance with the NAFTA.

100. Moreover, the acts of the State and the Municipality — and therefore the acts of Mexico — fail to comply with or adhere to the requirements of NAFTA, Article 1105(1) that each Party accord to investments of investors of another Party treatment in accordance with international law, including fair and equitable treatment. This is so particularly in light of the governing principle that internal law (such as the Municipality's stated permit requirements) does not justify failure to perform a treaty. *(Vienna Convention on the Law of Treaties, Arts. 26, 27)*.

101. The Tribunal therefore holds that Metalclad was not treated fairly or equitably under the NAFTA and succeeds on its claim under Article 1105.

C. NAFTA, Article 1110: Expropriation

102. NAFTA Article 1110 provides that "[n]o party shall directly or indirectly . . . expropriate an investment . . . or take a measure tantamount to . . . expropriation . . . except: (a) for a public purpose; (b) on a nondiscriminatory basis; (c) in accordance with due process of law and Article 1105(1); and (d) on payment of compensation . . ." "A measure" is defined in Article 201 (1) as including "any law, regulation, procedure, requirement or practice."

103. Thus, expropriation under NAFTA includes not only open, deliberate and acknowledged takings of property, such as outright seizure or formal or obligatory transfer of tide in favour of the host State, but also covert or incidental interference with the use of property which has the effect of depriving the owner, in whole or in significant part, of the use or reasonably-to-be-expected economic benefit of property even if not necessarily to the obvious benefit of the host State.

104. By permitting or tolerating the conduct of Guadalcazar in relation to Metalclad which the Tribunal has already held amounts to unfair and inequitable treatment breaching Article 1105 and by thus participating or acquiescing in the denial to Metalclad of the right to operate the landfill, notwithstanding the fact that

---

[112] The question of turning to NAFTA before exhausting local remedies was examined by the parties. However, Mexico does not insist that local remedies must be exhausted. Mexico's position is correct in light of NAFTA Article 1121(2)(b) which provides that a disputing investor may submit a claim under NAFTA Article 1117 if both the investor and the enterprise waive their rights to initiate or continue before any administrative tribunal or court under the law of any Party any proceedings with respect to the measure of the disputing Party that is alleged to be a breach referred to in NAFTA Article 1117.

the project was fully approved and endorsed by the federal government, Mexico must be held to have taken a measure tantamount to expropriation in violation of NAFTA Article 1110(1).

105. The Tribunal holds that the exclusive authority for siting and permitting a hazardous waste landfill resides with the Mexican federal government. This finding is consistent with the testimony of the Secretary of SEMARNAP and, as stated above, is consistent with the express language of the LGEEPA.

106. As determined earlier (see above, para 92), the Municipality denied the local construction permit in part because of the Municipality's perception of the adverse environmental effects of the hazardous waste landfill and the geological unsuitability of the landfill site. In so doing, the Municipality acted outside its authority. As stated above, the Municipality's denial of the construction permit without any basis in the proposed physical construction or any defect in the site, and extended by its subsequent administrative and judicial actions regarding the *Convenio*, effectively and unlawfully prevented the Claimant's operation of the landfill.

107. These measures, taken together with the representations of the Mexican federal government, on which Metalclad relied, and the absence of a timely, orderly or substantive basis for the denial by the Municipality of the local construction permit, amount to an indirect expropriation.

108. The present case resembles in a number of pertinent respects that of *Biloune v. Ghana Investment Centre*, 95 I.L.R.183, 207–10 (1993) (Judge Schwebel, President; Wallace and Leigh, Arbitrators). In that case, a private investor was renovating and expanding a resort restaurant in Ghana. As with Metalclad, the investor, basing itself on the representations of a government affiliated entity, began construction before applying for a building permit. As with Metalclad, a stop work order was issued after a substantial amount of work had been completed. The order was based on the absence of a building permit. An application was submitted, but although it was not expressly denied, a permit was never issued. The Tribunal found that an indirect expropriation had taken place because the totality of the circumstances had the effect of causing the irreparable cessation of work on the project. The Tribunal paid particular regard to the investor's justified reliance on the government's representations regarding the permit, the fact that government authorities knew of the construction for more than one year before issuing the stop work order, the fact that permits had not been required for other projects and the fact that no procedure was in place for dealing with building permit applications. Although the decision in *Biloune* does not bind this Tribunal, it is a persuasive authority and the Tribunal is in agreement with its analysis and its conclusion.

109. Although not strictly necessary for its conclusion, the Tribunal also identifies as a further ground for a finding of expropriation the Ecological Decree issued by the Governor of SLP on September 20, 1997. This Decree covers an area of 188,758 hectares within the "Real de Guadalcazar" that includes the landfill site, and created therein an ecological preserve. This Decree had the effect of barring forever the operation of the landfill.

110. The Tribunal is not persuaded by Mexico's representation to the contrary. The Ninth Article, for instance, forbids any work inconsistent with the Ecological

Decree's management program. The management program is defined by the Fifth Article as one of diagnosing the ecological problems of the cacti reserve and of ensuring its ecological preservation. In addition, the Fourteenth Article of the Decree forbids any conduct that might involve the discharge of polluting agents on the reserve soil, subsoil, running water or water deposits and prohibits the undertaking of any potentially polluting activities. The Fifteenth Article of the Ecological Decree also forbids any activity requiring permits or licenses unless such activity is related to the exploration, extraction or utilization of natural resources.

111. The Tribunal need not decide or consider the motivation or intent of the adoption of the Ecological Decree. Indeed, a finding of expropriation on the basis of the Ecological Decree is not essential to the Tribunal's finding of a violation of NAFTA Article 1110. However, the Tribunal considers that the implementation of the Ecological Decree would, in and of itself, constitute an act tantamount to expropriation.

112. In conclusion, the Tribunal holds that Mexico has indirectly expropriated Metalclad's investment without providing compensation to Metalclad for the expropriation. Mexico has violated Article 1110 of the NAFTA.

NOTES AND QUESTIONS

1.   Consider the legal standards protecting the rights of investors in Chapter Eleven of NAFTA. Are investors' rights an obstacle to protection of the environment?

Which provisions did the tribunal in *Metalclad* hold were violated? What other provisions of NAFTA are relevant to the protection of investors? Do these protections conflict with the goal of protecting the environment?

2.   What is the effect of Article 1114? Why did the tribunal ignore this article?

3.   In the *Metalclad case* the arbitral tribunal awarded $16,685,000 in damages. NAFTA Article 1136(6) allows a party to make a limited challenge to an award under the New York Convention. Mexico filed a challenge in court in British Columbia, the site of the arbitration. Metalclad and Mexico settled this case for a payment of $15.6 million. The Mexican government then withheld the damages paid from money owed to the state of San Luis Potosi in an effort to recoup its losses. The Mexican Supreme Court rebuffed this effort. *See* Carlos Aviles, *Corte anula descuento a recursos federales para gobierno de San Luis Potosi*, EL UNIVERSAL, 5 March 2004.

4.   Is an expropriation under NAFTA broader than a "taking" under U.S. law? Does NAFTA effectively override local environmental laws?

5.   At this writing, 80 investor-state arbitrations have been decided under Chapter 11. Damages totaling USD 405.4 million have been awarded in favor of investors in 13 cases.

Chapter 6

FRESHWATER RESOURCES

Section I.   INTRODUCTION

Water is essential to life on Earth. Human consumption currently appropriates about 54% of the world's accessible freshwater runoff. Yet worldwide over 1.1 billion people lack access to safe drinking water, and about 1.1 billion people have no access to adequate sanitation. More than one-half million children die annually due to water-borne diseases. These water deficiencies are expected to worsen in coming years. By 2050, one-fourth of the world's population will live in countries with chronic water shortages. On December 20, 2000, the UN General Assembly adopted Resolution 55/96 proclaiming the year 2003 as the International Year of Freshwater and called for better management and conservation of water resources. One of the eight goals of the UN Millennium Declaration of 2000 is to achieve by 2015 the goal of reducing by half the proportion of people in the world without access to safe drinking water. Water security is thus at the top of the international agenda as awareness grows of the links between water, energy, and food security and as water overuse and pollution affect more people every year.

According to the water conflict management data base at Oregon State University (http://www.transboundarywaters.orst.edu), there are 279 river basins across the globe that are shared by two or more countries. Increasingly, matters of water supply, pollution, navigation, flooding, and other issues of water management are international in scope. There are over 450 international agreements concerning aspects of freshwater resources. (*See* http://www.internationalwaterlaw.org/documents/intldocs/watercourse_status.html). Many such agreements have major gaps or failings; many have not been fully implemented or observed. As a result, conflicts and disputes over water abound in every part of the world. These conflicts and disputes are bound to get worse as populations and shortages increase. Climate change will cause unknown effects on the distribution and scarcity of water resources that will be felt in the future.

Water availability is a necessity for consumption as well as for economic development. Water quality must be maintained to benefit humans as well as to maintain the integrity of ecosystems around the world. Management and the resolution of international disputes over water resources are urgent imperatives.

It is more urgent than ever to create and agree upon settled principles concerning all aspects of the international law of water resources.

Section II.   WATER AS A HUMAN RIGHT

International human rights instruments proclaim that access to water is a fundamental human right.

INTERNATIONAL COVENANT ON ECONOMIC, SOCIAL AND CULTURAL RIGHTS

G.A. Res. 2200 (XXI), 21 U.N. GAOR Supp. No. 16 at 49, U.N. Doc. A/6316 (1967); 993 U.N.T.S. 3; 6 I.L.M. 360

Article 11

1. The States Parties to the present Covenant recognize the right of everyone, to an adequate standard of living for himself and his family, including adequate food, clothing and housing, and to the continuous improvement of living conditions. The States Parties will take appropriate steps to ensure the realization of this right, recognizing to this effect the essential importance of international co-operation based on free consent.

2. The States Parties to the present Covenant, recognizing the fundamental right of everyone to be free from hunger, shall take, individually and through international co-operation, the measures, including specific programmes, which are needed:

(a)   To improve methods of production, conservation and distribution of food by making full use of technical and scientific knowledge, by disseminating knowledge of the principles of nutrition and by developing or reforming agrarian systems in such a way as to achieve the most efficient development and utilization of natural resources;

(b)   Taking into account the problems of both food-importing and food-exporting countries, to ensure an equitable distribution of world food supplies in relation to need.

Article 12

1. The States Parties to the present Covenant recognize the right of everyone to the enjoyment of the highest attainable standard of physical and mental health.

2. The steps to be taken by the States Parties to the present Covenant to achieve the full realization of this right shall include those necessary for:

(a)   The provision for the reduction of the stillbirth-rate and of infant mortality and for the healthy development of the child;

(b)   The improvement of all aspects of environmental and industrial hygiene;

(c)   The prevention, treatment and control of epidemic, endemic, occupational and other diseases;

(d)   The creation of conditions which would assure to all medical service and medical attention in the event of sickness.

GENERAL COMMENT NO. 15 (2002), COMMITTEE ON ECONOMIC, SOCIAL AND CULTURAL RIGHTS
U.N. Doc. E/C.12/2002/11 (26 November 2002)
(paragraph numbers and footnotes omitted)

The right to water (Articles 11 and 12 of the International Covenant on Economic, Social and Cultural Rights)

Water is a limited natural resource and a public good fundamental for life and health. The human right to water is indispensable for leading a life in human dignity. It is a prerequisite for the realization of other human rights. The Committee has been confronted continually with the widespread denial of the right to water in developing as well as developed countries. Over a billion persons lack access to a basic water supply, while several billion do not have access to adequate sanitation, which is the primary cause of water contamination and diseases linked to water. The continuing contamination, depletion and unequal distribution of water is exacerbating existing poverty. States parties have to adopt effective measures to realize, without discrimination, the right to water, as set out in this General Comment.

The human right to water entitles everyone to sufficient, safe, acceptable, physically accessible and affordable water for personal and domestic uses. An adequate amount of safe water is necessary to prevent death from dehydration, reduce the risk of water-related disease and provide for consumption, cooking, personal and domestic hygienic requirements.

Article 11(1) specifies a number of rights emanating from, and indispensable for, the realization of the right to an adequate standard of living "including adequate food, clothing and housing." The use of the word "including" indicates that this catalogue of rights was not intended to be exhaustive. The right to water clearly falls within the category of guarantees essential for securing an adequate standard of living, particularly since it is one of the most fundamental conditions for survival. Moreover, the Committee has previously recognized that water is a human right contained in Article 11(1) (see General Comment No. 6). The right to water is also inextricably related to the right to the highest attainable standard of health (Art. 12(1)) and the rights to adequate housing and adequate food (Art. 11(1)). The right should also be seen in conjunction with other rights enshrined in the International Bill of Human Rights, foremost amongst them the right to life and human dignity.

*　　*　　*

Water is required for a range of different purposes, besides personal and domestic uses, to realize many of the covenant rights. For instance, water is necessary to produce food (right to adequate food) and ensure environmental hygiene (right to health). Water is essential for securing livelihoods (right to gain a living by work) and enjoying certain cultural practices (right to take part in cultural life). Nevertheless, priority in the allocation of water must be given to the right to water for personal and domestic uses. Priority should also be given to the water resources required to prevent starvation and disease, as well as water required to meet the core obligations of each of the Covenant rights.

The Committee notes the importance of ensuring sustainable access to water resources for agriculture to realize the right to adequate food (see General Comment No. 12). Attention should be given to ensuring that disadvantaged and marginalized fanners, including women farmers, have equitable access to water and water management systems, including sustainable rain harvesting and irrigation technology. Taking note of the duty in Article 1(2) of the Covenant, which provides that a "people may not be deprived of its means of subsistence," States parties should ensure that there is adequate access to water for subsistence farming and for securing the livelihoods of indigenous peoples.

Environmental hygiene, as an aspect of the right to health under article 12(2)(b) of the Covenant, encompasses taking steps on a non-discriminatory basis to prevent threats to health from unsafe and toxic water conditions. For example, States parties should ensure that natural water resources are protected from contamination by harmful substances and pathogenic microbes. Likewise, States parties should monitor and combat situations where aquatic eco-systems serve as a habitat for vectors of diseases wherever they pose a risk to human living environments.

*   *   *

The right to water contains both freedoms and entitlements. The freedoms include the right to maintain access to existing water supplies necessary for the right to water, and the right to be free from interference, such as the right to be free from arbitrary disconnections or contamination of water supplies. By contrast, the entitlements include the right to a system of water supply and management that provides equality of opportunity for people to enjoy the right to water.

The elements of the right to water must be adequate for human dignity, life and health, in accordance with Articles 11(1) and 12. The adequacy of water should not be interpreted narrowly, by mere reference to volumetric quantities and technologies. Water should be treated as a social and cultural good, and not primarily as an economic good. The manner of the realization of the right to water must also be sustainable ensuring that the right can be realized for present and future generations.

*   *   *

While the Covenant provides for progressive realization and acknowledges the constraints due to the limits of available resources, it also imposes on States parties various obligations which are of immediate effect. States parties have immediate obligations in relation to the right to water, such as the guarantee that the right will be exercised without discrimination of any kind . . . and the obligation to take steps . . . towards the full realization of Articles 11(1) and 12. Such steps must be deliberate, concrete and targeted towards the full realization of the right to water.

States parties have a constant and continuing duty under the Covenant to move as expeditiously and effectively as possible towards the full realization of the right to water. Realization of the right should be feasible and practicable, since all States parties exercise control over a broad range of resources, including water, technology, financial resources, and international assistance, as with all other rights in the Covenant.

There is a strong presumption that retrogressive measures taken in relation to the right to water are prohibited under the Covenant. If any deliberately retrogressive measures are taken, the State party has the burden of proving that they have been introduced after the most careful consideration of all alternatives and that they are duly justified by reference to the totality of the rights provided for in the Covenant in the context of the full use of the State party's maximum available resources.

Specific legal obligations

The right to water, like any human right, imposes three types of obligations on States parties: obligations to respect, obligations to protect and obligations to fulfill.

Obligations to respect

The obligation to respect requires that States parties refrain from interfering directly or indirectly with the enjoyment of the right to water. The obligation includes, *inter alia* refraining from engaging in any practice or activity that denies or limits equal access to adequate water; arbitrarily interfering with customary or traditional arrangements for water allocation; unlawfully diminishing or polluting water, for example through waste from State-owned facilities or through use and testing of weapons; and limiting access to, or destroying, water services and infrastructure as a punitive measure, for example, during armed conflicts in violation of international humanitarian law.

The Committee notes that during armed conflicts, emergency situations and natural disasters, the right to water embraces those obligations by which States parties are bound under international humanitarian law. This includes protection of objects indispensable for survival of the civilian population, including drinking water installations and supplies and irrigation works, protection of the natural environment against widespread, long-term and severe damage and ensuring that civilians, internees and prisoners have access to adequate water

Obligations to protect

The obligation to *protect* requires State parties to prevent third parties from interfering in any way with the enjoyment of the right to water. Third parties include individuals, groups, corporations and other entities as well as agents acting under their authority. The obligation includes, *inter alia*, adopting the necessary and effective legislative and other measures to restrain, for example, third parties from denying equal access to adequate water; and polluting and inequitably extracting from water resources, including natural sources, wells and other water distribution systems.

Where water services (such as piped water networks, water tankers, access to rivers and wells) are operated or controlled by third parties, States parties must prevent them from compromising equal, affordable, and physical access to sufficient, safe and acceptable water. To prevent such abuses an effective regulatory system must be established, in conformity with the Covenant and this General

Comment, which includes independent monitoring, genuine public participation and imposition of penalties for non-compliance.

Obligations to fulfill

The obligation to *fulfill* can be disaggregated into the obligations to *facilitate, promote* and *provide*. The obligation to *facilitate* requires the State to take positive measures to assist individuals and communities to enjoy the right. The obligation to *promote* obliges the State party to take steps to ensure that there is appropriate education concerning the hygienic use of water, protection of water sources and methods to minimize water wastage. States parties are also obliged to *fulfill (provide)* the right when individuals or a group are unable, for reasons beyond their control, to realize that right themselves by the means at their disposal.

The obligation to *fulfill* requires States parties to adopt the necessary measures directed towards the full realization of the right to water. The obligation includes, *inter alia*, according sufficient recognition of this right within the national political and legal systems, preferably by way of legislative implementation; adopting a national water strategy and plan of action to realize this right; ensuring that water is affordable for everyone; and facilitating improved and sustainable access to water, particularly in rural and deprived urban areas.

To ensure that water is affordable States parties must adopt the necessary measures that may include, *inter alia*: (a) use of a range of appropriate low-cost techniques and technologies; (b) appropriate pricing policies such as free or low-cost water; and (c) income supplements. Any payment for water services has to be based on the principle of equity, ensuring that these services, whether privately or publicly provided, are affordable for all, including socially disadvantaged groups. Equity demands that poorer households should not be disproportionately burdened with water expenses as compared to richer households.

States parties should adopt comprehensive and integrated strategies and programmes to ensure that there is sufficient and safe water for present and future generations. Such strategies and programmes may include: (a) reducing depletion of water resources through unsustainable extraction, diversion and damming; (b) reducing and eliminating contamination of watersheds and water-related eco-systems by substances such as radiation, harmful chemicals and human excreta; (c) monitoring water reserves; (d) ensuring that proposed developments do not interfere with access to adequate water; (e) assessing the impacts of actions that may impinge upon water availability and natural ecosystems watersheds such as climate changes, desertification and increased soil salinity, deforestation and loss of biodiversity; (f) increasing the efficient use of water by end-users; (g) reducing water wastage in its distribution; (h) response mechanisms for emergency situations; (i) and establishing competent institutions and appropriate institutional arrangements to carry out the strategies and programmes.

Ensuring that everyone has access to adequate sanitation is not only fundamental for human dignity and privacy, but is one of the principal mechanisms for protecting the quality of drinking water supplies and resources. In accordance with the rights to health and adequate housing . . . States parties have an obligation to progressively extend safe sanitation services, particularly to rural and deprived urban areas, taking into account the needs of women and children.

* * *

Core obligations

. . . [T]he Committee confirms that States parties have a core obligation to ensure the satisfaction of, at the very least, minimum essential levels of each of the rights enunciated in the Covenant. In the Committee's view, at least a number of core obligations in relation to the right to water can be identified, which are of immediate effect:

a. To ensure access to the minimum essential amount of water, that is sufficient and safe for personal and domestic uses to prevent disease;

b. To ensure the right of access to water, and water facilities and services on a non-discriminatory basis, especially for disadvantaged or marginalized groups;

c. To ensure physical access to water facilities or services that provide sufficient, safe and regular water; have a sufficient number of water outlets to avoid prohibitive waiting times; are at a reasonable distance from the household;

d. To ensure personal security is not threatened when having to physically access to water;

e. To ensure equitable distribution of all available water facilities and services;

f. To adopt and implement a national water strategy and plan of action addressing the whole population; the strategy and plan of action should be devised, and periodically reviewed. on the basis of a participatory and transparent process; they should include methods, such as right to water indicators and benchmarks, by which progress can be closely monitored; the process by which the strategy and plan of action are devised, as well as their content, shall give particular attention to all disadvantaged or marginalized groups;

g. To monitor the extent of the realization, or the non-realization, of the right to water;

h. To adopt relatively low-cost targeted water programmes to protect vulnerable and marginalized groups;

i. To take measures to prevent, treat and control diseases linked to water, in particular ensuring access to adequate sanitation;

For the avoidance of any doubt, the Committee wishes to emphasize that it is particularly incumbent on States parties and other actors in a position to assist, to provide "international assistance and cooperation, especially economic and technical" which enables developing countries to fulfill their core obligations . . . .

PLAN OF IMPLEMENTATION OF THE WORLD SUMMIT ON SUSTAINABLE DEVELOPMENT, REPORT OF THE WORLD SUMMIT ON SUSTAINABLE DEVELOPMENT
U.N. Doc. A/CONF.199/20 (26 August–4 September 2002), at 9

Poverty eradication

7. Eradicating poverty is the greatest global challenge facing the world today and an indispensable requirement for sustainable development, particularly for developing countries. Although each country has the primary responsibility for its own sustainable development and poverty eradication and the role of national policies and development strategies cannot be overemphasized, concerted and concrete measures are required at all levels to enable developing countries to achieve their sustainable development goals as related to the internationally agreed poverty-related targets and goals, including those contained in Agenda 21, the relevant outcomes of other United Nations conferences and the United Nations Millennium Declaration. This would include actions at all levels to:

   (a) Halve, by the year 2015, the proportion of the worlds people whose income is less than 1 dollar a day and the proportion of people who suffer from hunger and, by the same date, to halve the proportion of people without access to safe drinking water;

*   *   *

8. The provision of clean drinking water and adequate sanitation is necessary to protect human health and the environment. In this respect, we agree to halve, by the year 2015, the proportion of people who are unable to reach or to afford safe drinking water (as outlined in the Millennium Declaration) and the proportion of people who do not have access to basic sanitation, which would include actions at all levels to:

   (a) Develop and implement efficient household sanitation systems;

   (b) Improve sanitation in public institutions, especially schools;

   (c) Promote safe hygiene practices;

   (d) Promote education and outreach focused on children, as agents of behavioural change;

   (e) Promote affordable and socially and culturally acceptable technologies and practices;

   (f) Develop innovative financing and partnership mechanisms;

   (g) Integrate sanitation into water resources management strategies.

NOTES AND QUESTIONS

1. *The United Nations Millennium Declaration Goal.* Goal Number 7 of the Millennium Declaration of 2000 was to halve the proportion of people in the world without access to safe drinking water. According to the World Health Organization

this goal was reached in 2010, five years ahead of schedule. *See* http://www.who.int/topics/water/en/. But there is no guarantee that this access will be maintained in the future.

2. *World Summits on Sustainable Development.* The World Summit on Sustainable Development (Rio +10) and the World Summit on Sustainable Development (Rio +20) both called eradicating poverty the greatest global challenge facing mankind. Do you agree? Both stated that promoting access to water, water resource management, and efficient use of water are essential international goals. Both also called for water pollution prevention to reduce health hazards and to protect ecosystems are essential to sustainable development.

3. Consider the comment of the UN Committee on Economic, Social, and Cultural Rights. Does it correspond or does it differ from the goals of the World Summits on Sustainable Development?

Section III. SHARED WATER RESOURCES

About one-half of the world's fresh watercourses — rivers and lakes — are shared between two or more states. Despite the obvious potential for disagreement and conflict over interstate freshwater resources, the international law of freshwater resources has been very slow to develop. In 1963, A. P. Lester, writing in the American Journal of International Law[1], bemoaned the fact that existing principles of international freshwater law were "too few in number and too closely tied to the unique characteristics of the particular river dispute to provide elaborate norms of international . . . law."

A. International Law Rules on Shared Watercourses

1. Cases

Until quite recently, no rules of international law existed regarding the allocation or the pollution of shared watercourses. In Chapter 3 of this book, we learned of the Harmon Doctrine relating to water and other natural resources. The Harmon Doctrine refers to the opinion letter written by U.S. Attorney General Judson Harmon in answer to Mexico's protest concerning U.S. diversions of water from the Rio Grande River on June 8, 1895, which stated that the rules, principles, and precedents of international law allowed the United States complete freedom to divert the waters of an interstate river within its territory with impunity. This doctrine is known as the principle of absolute territorial sovereignty because it recognizes the right of an upper riparian state to do what it pleases with a watercourse regardless of the effect on other riparian states.

In the early years of the twentieth century watercourse agreements between riparian states were uncommon and treated limited subjects. Nevertheless, the Permanent Court of International Justice (PCIJ) interpreted treaty language to chip away at the absolute territorial sovereignty doctrine. In the *S.S. Wimbledon*

---

[1] A.P. Lester, *River Pollution in International Law*, 57 Am. J. Int'l L. 828, 830 (1963).

Case[2] in 1923, the Permanent Court of International Justice (PCIJ) ruled that Germany had no right to deny the right of passage to a ship in the Kiel Canal because under the Versailles Treaty the canal, although in German territory, was to be open to all vessels. In 1929, the PCIJ ruled in a case involving the jurisdiction of the International Commission of the Oder River,[3] which was created under the Treaty of Versailles, that riparian states have a "community of interests in a navigable river [which] becomes the basis of a common legal right, the essential features of which are the perfect equality of all riparian states in the use of the whole course of the river and the exclusion of any preferential privilege of anyone riparian in relation to others." A 1937 case, *Diversion of Water from the Meuse (Netherlands v. Belgium)*[4] involved an 1863 treaty between Belgium and the Netherlands governing diversions of water from the Meuse River. In later times both nations had enlarged their respective waterways, constructing canals, locks and dams. In 1937, the Netherlands brought a case against Belgium in the PCIJ alleging that Belgium's canal expansion projects were in violation of the treaty. Belgium counterclaimed against the Netherlands accusing that country of similar treaty violations. The Court in its judgment rejected both claims: ruling that the construction of canals and other waterworks were not implicated by the treaty as long as the treaty commitments regarding diversions of water were kept. The court in its judgment observed, however, that "Belgium is a riparian state and it is not limited to the joint section of the Meuse only but extends to the whole river."[5] Although these judicial decisions concerned navigation and treaty provisions, they pointed up the flaws in the absolute territorial sovereignty doctrine.

After 1950, in the context of the interdependence of the post-war world, international tribunals became more active in pronouncing customary international law rules in conjunction with interpreting treaty law. In this section we read three watercourse cases, all involving treaties between the litigants, but the tribunals in each case confronted and decided non-treaty issues as well.

The first case we consider involved a proposal by France to build a hydroelectric power facility using water diverted from Lake Lanoux. Waters from Lake Lanoux are the source of the Carol River, which drains into the Mediterranean after flowing through Spain. The French plan was to divert Lake Lanoux waters into the Ariège River which drains into the Atlantic Ocean. The French plan, however, was to fully restore to the Carol River all waters diverted from Lake Lanoux. Nevertheless, Spain objected to the French plan, and the two states submitted the dispute to arbitration. The second case involved a dispute between Hungary and Slovakia over a joint investment project to construct a hydroelectric power plant in the Danube River basin. This project was the subject of a treaty between Hungary and the unified state of Czechoslovakia in 1977; but in May 1992, Hungary gave notice of termination of the treaty partially on environmental grounds. The third case, which we considered in Chapter 2 as well, concerned Uruguay's decision to build two pulp mills on the boundary river with Argentina. All three cases shed light on the

---

[2] [1923] P.C.I.J. (Ser. A), No. 1.

[3] Case Relating to the Territorial Jurisdiction of the Oder River, [1929] P.C. I. J.(Ser. A) No. 23.

[4] [1937] P.C.I.J. (Ser. A/B) No. 70.

[5] *Id.* para. 309.

international law relating to shared watercourses.

AFFAIRE DU LAC LANOUX (FRANCE v. SPAIN)

XII U.N. Rep. Int'l Arb. Awards 281 (19 November 1956); LXII Revue generale de droit international public 79 (1958)
(English summary and extracts taken from [1974] II Yb. I.L.C. 194–99 (1957) and 24 INT'L L. REP. 105 (1957));
(paragraph numbers and footnotes omitted)

[By STURE PETRE, P, PLINIO BOLLA, PAUL REUTER, FERNAND DE VISSCHER and ANTONIO DE LUNA:] Lake Lanoux is situated on the south slope of the Pyrenees and on the territory of the French Republic . . . . It is fed by streams all of which rise on French territory and traverse only that territory. Its waters flow out through a single stream, the Font-Vive, which is one of the sources of the Carol River. This river, after having flowed about twenty-five kilometres . . . on French territory, crosses the Spanish boundary at Puigcerdá and continues its course in Spain for about six kilometres before joining the Segre River, which ultimately empties into the Ebro . . . .

Regulations governing the administration of the waters common to France and Spain were established by the Treaties of Bayonne and the "Additional Act to the . . . Treaties [of Bayonne] concluded on 2 December 1856, 14 April 1862 and 26 May 1866[6] . . . . [The Additional Act provides, in pertinent part:

*   *   *

Control and Enjoyment of Waters of Common Use between the Two Countries

Article 8: All standing and flowing waters, whether they are in the private or public domain, are subject to the sovereignty of the State in which they are located, and therefore to that State's legislation, except for modifications agreed upon between the two Governments.

*   *   *

Article 9: For watercourses which flow from one Country to the other . . . each Government recognizes, subject to a right of verification when appropriate, the legality of irrigations, of works and of enjoyment for domestic use currently existing in the other State, . . . with the reservation that only that volume of water necessary to satisfy actual needs will be used, that abuses must be eliminated, and that this recognition will in no way injure the respective rights of the Governments to authorize works of public utility on condition that proper compensation is paid.

*   *   *

---

[6] Translation in 56 Brit. & For. State Papers, 1865-1866226 (1870); HERTSLET, III THE MAP OF EUROPE BY TREATY 1647 (1875).

Article 11: When in one of the two states it is proposed to construct works or to grant new concessions which might change the course or the volume of which the lower . . . part is being used by the riparian owners of the other country, prior notice will be given to the highest administrative authority of the [National Government] or of the Province to which such riparian owners are subject by the corresponding authority in the jurisdiction where such schemes are proposed, so that, if they might threaten the rights of the riparian owners of the adjoining Sovereignty, a claim may be lodged in due time with the competent authorities, and thus the interests that may be involved on both sides will be safeguarded . . . .

Article 12: The downstream lands are obliged to receive from the higher lands of the neighbouring country the waters which flow naturally therefrom together with what they carry without the hand of man having contributed thereto. There may be constructed neither a dam, nor any obstacle capable of harming the upper riparian owners, to whom it is likewise forbidden to do anything which might increase the burdens attached to the servitude of the downstream lands.

*　　*　　*

Article 15: When, apart from disputes within the exclusive jurisdiction of the ordinary courts, there shall arise between riparian owners of different nationality difficulties or subjects of complaint regarding the use of water; the persons concerned shall each apply to their respective authorities, so that [the authorities] shall agree between themselves to resolve the dispute . . . .

Article 16: The highest administrative authorities of the bordering Departments and Provinces will act in concert in the exercise of their right to make regulations for the general interest and to interpret or modify their regulations whenever the respective interests are at stake, and in case they cannot reach agreement, the dispute shall be submitted to the two Governments.]

Starting in 1917, the questions of the use of the waters of Lake Lanoux was the subject of repeated exchanges of views and negotiations between the French and Spanish Governments. [For instance, when in 1917 the French authorities began investigating a scheme for diverting the waters of Lake Lanoux towards the Ariège and thence toward the Atlantic, the Spanish Government protested to the French Government that such a scheme would affect Spanish interests and requested that the scheme would not be carried out without previous notice to the Spanish Government and agreement between the two Governments. One effect of this protest was that in January 1918, the French Foreign Ministry informed the Spanish Ambassador that France would not divert the waters of Lake Lanoux toward the Ariège without previously notifying the Spanish authorities. Spain replied that that it regarded the scrupulous maintenance of the *status quo* as being guaranteed under France adopted a definite plan of diversion at which time an amicable accord would be reached by the parties. Periodic negotiations continued until World War II intervened and did not recommence until 1949, when France and Spain agreed to establish a Mixed Commission of Engineers to study the proposed

French scheme and report to the two governments.]

In [1953, and without recourse to the Mixed Commission of Engineers], the French Government adopted a development project for Lake Lanoux, submitted by Electricité de France, the main features of which were as follows:

> Without any change in the rivers and streams which now fed it, the lake would be transformed, in particular by the establishment of a dam to permit the accumulation of a volume of water which would raise its capacity from 17 to 70 million cubic meters. The water of the lake, which naturally debouches through a tributary stream of the Carol and thereby flows towards Spain, would no longer follow this course regularly. It would be employed to produce electric power through a diversion which would carry it towards the Ariège . . . . To offset this withdrawal of part of the water which feeds the Carol, an underground return tunnel would carry a [quantity of water] of the Ariège to the Carol, to which river the water would be restored in French territory . . . .

[The quantity of water to be returned to the Carol was to correspond to the actual needs of Spanish users and the Spanish Government was invited to formulate the compensation to which claims would be available under Article 9 of the Additional Act. Spain replied with a request that no work be commenced on the project until after of a meeting of the Mixed Commission of Engineers. France agreed to such a meeting of the Commission and gave an assurance that no work had been carried out or was imminent in connection with Lake Lanoux, but stressed that the assurance was given *ex gratia* because nothing in the Additional Act required works to be suspended at the request of a party. Negotiations between France and Spain continued.]

As the negotiations . . . did not yield any results, the French Government informed the Spanish Government [on] 21 March 1956 "of its determination henceforth to exercise its freedom within the area of its rights." Accordingly, the development works for Lake Lanoux . . . [commenced] on 3 April 1956.

Subsequently, . . . the French and Spanish Governments [agreed] to submit the case for arbitration [and] referred the following question to an arbitral tribunal [in the *Compromis*]:

Is the French Government justified in its contention that, in carrying out, without a preliminary agreement between the two Governments, works for the use of the waters of Lake Lanoux . . . it would not commit a violation of the provisions of the Treaty of Bayonne of 26 May 1866 and of the Additional Act of the same date?

*   *   *

The tribunal formulated the requests of the parties in the following terms:

> The Spanish Government asked the Tribunal to declare that the French Government could not carry out works for the use of the waters of Lake Lanoux in accordance with the procedures and guarantees established in the Electricité de France project, for if a preliminary agreement was not concluded between the two Governments on the development programme

for the said waters, the French Government would commit a violation of the
. . . Treat[ies] of Bayonne . . . and of the Additional Act. . . .

The French Government asked the Tribunal to adjudge and declare that [it]
was justified in its contention that by carrying out, without a preliminary
agreement between the two Governments, works for the use of the waters
of Lake Lanoux . . . it would not commit a violation of the [Treaties and
Additional Act].

After setting forth the principal arguments advanced by the Parties, the Tribunal
considered the legal aspects' of the case:

1. The public works envisaged in the French scheme are wholly situate in France;
the most important part if not the whole of the effects of such works will be felt in
French territory; they would concern waters which Article 8 of the Additional Act
submits to French territorial sovereignty . . . .

3. The present dispute can be reduced to two fundamental questions:

(A) Do the works for utilising the waters of Lake Lanoux in the
conditions laid down in the French scheme and proposals mentioned in the
Preamble of the *Compromis* constitute an infringement of the rights of
Spain recognised by the principal provisions of the Treaty of Bayonne of
May 26, 1866, and the Additional Act of the same date?

(B) If the reply to the preceding question be negative, does the execution
of the said works constitute an infringement of the provisions of the Treaty
of Bayonne of May 26, 1866, and of the Additional Act of the same date,
because those provisions would in any event make such execution subject to
a prior agreement between the two. Governments or because other rules of
Article 11 of the Additional Act concerning dealings between the two
Governments have not been observed?

As to question (A):

4. The Additional Act. of May 26, 1866, includes a section headed 'Control and
enjoyment of waters of common user between the two countries'. Besides Article 8
. . . it contains three articles which are fundamental for the present case (9, 10 and
11) . . . . Articles 9 and 10 both apply to watercourses 'which flow from one country
to the other' (successive watercourses) or which 'constitute a boundary' (contiguous
watercourses). By Article 9, each State recognises the legality of irrigations, of
works and of enjoyment for domestic use, by virtue of concessions, of title or by
prescription, existing in the other State at the moment when the Additional Act
entered into force. Under Article 18, an international Commission of Engineers was
charged with the technical operations necessary for the application of Article 9 and
other articles of the Additional Act.

The recognition of the legality of such use is subject to the following conditions:

(a) Each State may, when appropriate, require the concession, the title or the
prescription invoked by the other State to be verified by examination. The
recognition of such legality by the State which requires the verification

shall cease for any enjoyment which has not passed this latter test.

(b) The legality of each enjoyment is recognised only to the extent that the water used is necessary to satisfy actual needs.

(c) The recognition of the legality of an enjoyment is to cease in case of abuses, including abuses other than employment of water in excess of what is necessary to satisfy actual needs.

5. Article 10 provides that after having satisfied the actual needs of recognised enjoyments, the quantity of water available at low water at the point where it crosses the frontier is calculated and is then shared out in advance according to a predetermined principle of distribution.

These two Articles, 9 and 10, ought clearly both to be interpreted together without opposing one to the other, because Article 10 deals with 'available water' after the application of Article 9 concerning recognised enjoyment: the two Articles taken together exhaust the object of the regulation.

6. In effect, thanks to the restitution effected by the devices described above, none of the guaranteed users will suffer in his enjoyment of the waters (this is not the subject of any claim founded on Article 9). At the lowest water level, the volume of the surplus waters of the Carol, at the boundary, will at no time suffer a diminution; it may even, by virtue of the minimum guarantee given by France, benefit by an increase in volume assured by the waters of the Ariège flowing naturally to the Atlantic.

One might have attacked this conclusion in several different ways.

It could have been argued that the works would bring about an ultimate pollution of the waters of the Carol or that the returned waters would have a chemical composition or a temperature or some other characteristic which could injure Spanish interests. Spain could then have claimed that her rights had been impaired in violation of the Additional Act. Neither in the *dossier* nor in the pleadings in this case is there any trace of such an allegation.

7. The Spanish Government takes its stand on a different ground. In the arbitration Compromis it had already alleged that the French scheme 'modifies the natural conditions of the hydrographic basin of Lake Lanoux by diverting its waters into the Ariège and thus making the restoration of the waters of the Carol physically dependent on human will, which would involve the de facto preponderance of one Party in place of the equality of the two Parties as provided by the Treaty of Bayonne of May 26, 1866, and by the Additional Act of the same date.

. . . In the [Spanish] Memorial . . . that Government invokes Article 12 of the Additional Act. . . .

According to the Spanish Government, that provision appears to establish the conception that neither of the Parties may, without the consent of the other, modify the natural flow of the waters. The Spanish Counter Memorial . . . recognises nevertheless that: 'From the moment when human will intervenes to bring about some hydraulic development, it is an extra-physical element, which acts upon the current and changes what Nature has established.' Similarly, the 'Spanish Government does not give a fixed meaning to 'the order of Nature'; according to the

Counter Memorial . . . : 'A State has the right to utilise unilaterally that part of a river which runs through it so far as such utilisation is of a nature which will effect on the territory of another State only a limited amount of damage, a minimum of inconvenience, such as falls within what is implied by good neighbourliness.'

Actually, it seems that the Spanish argument is twofold and relates, on the one hand, to the prohibition, in the absence of the consent of the other Party, of compensation between two basins, despite the equivalence of what is diverted and what is restored, and, on the other hand, the prohibition, without the consent of the other Party, of all acts which may create by a *de facto* inequality the physical possibility of a violation of rights.

These two points must now be examined successively.

8. The prohibition of compensation between the two basins, in spite of equivalence between the water diverted and the water restored, unless the withdrawal of water is agreed to by the other Party, would' lead to the prevention in a general way of a withdrawal from a watercourse belonging to River Basin A for the benefit of River Basin B, even if this withdrawal is compensated for by a strictly equivalent restitution effected from a watercourse of River Basin B for the benefit of River Basin A. The Tribunal does not overlook the reality, from the point of view of physical geography, of each river basin, which constitutes, as the Spanish Memorial . . . maintains, 'a unit'. But this observation does not authorise the absolute consequences that the Spanish argument would draw from it. The unity of a basin is sanctioned at the juridical level only to the extent that it corresponds to human realities. The water which by nature constitutes a fungible item may be the object of a restitution which does not change its qualities in regard to human needs. A diversion with restitution, such as that envisaged by the French project, does not change a state of affairs organised for the working of the requirements of social life.

The state of modern technology leads to more and more frequent justifications of the fact that waters used for the production of electric energy should not be returned to their natural course. Water is taken higher and higher up and it is carried ever farther, and in so doing it is sometimes diverted to another river basin, in the same State or in another country within the same federation, or even in a third State. Within federations, the judicial decisions have recognised the validity of this last practice (*Wyoming v. Colorado* . . . [259 U.S. 419]) and the instances cited by Dr. J. E. Berber, *Die Rechtsquellen des internationalen Wassernutzungsrechts*, p. 180, and by M. Sauser-Hall, 'L'Utilisation industrielle des fleuves internationaux', [in] *Recueil des Cours de l'Académie de Droit international de la Haye*, 1953 vol. 83, p. 544; for Switzerland, [see] *Recueil des Arrêts du Tribunal Fédéral*, vol. 78, Part 1, pp. 14 *et seq.*).

The Tribunal therefore is of opinion that the diversion with restitution as envisaged in the French scheme and proposals is not contrary to the Treaty and to the Additional Act of 1866.

As to question (B) [stated under para. 3]:

10. In the *Compromis*, the Spanish Government had already declared that, in its opinion, the French scheme required for its execution 'the previous agreement of

both Governments, in the absence of which the country making the proposal is not at liberty to undertake the works'.

In the written as well as the oral proceedings, that Government developed this point of view, completing it by the recital of the principles which ought to govern dealings leading to such prior agreement. Two obligations, therefore, would seem to rest upon the State which desires to undertake the works envisaged, the more important being to reach a prior agreement with the other interested State; the other, which is merely accessory thereto, being to respect the other rules laid down by Article 11 of the Additional Act.

The argument put forward by the Spanish Government is stated on two planes — the Spanish Government takes its stand, on the one hand, on the Treaty and the Additional Act, on the other hand on the system of *faceries* or *compascuités* which exists on the Pyrenean frontier, as well as on the rules of international common law. The two latter sources would permit, first of all, the interpretation of the Treaty and the Additional Act of 1866, and then, in a larger perspective, the demonstration of the existence of an unwritten general rule of international law. The latter (it is contended) has precedents which would permit its establishment in the traditions of the system of *faceries*, in the provisions of the Pyrenean Treaties and in the international practice of States in the matter of the industrial use of international watercourses.

11. Before proceeding to an examination of the Spanish argument, the Tribunal believes it will be useful to make some very general observations on the nature of the obligations invoked against the French Government. To admit that jurisdiction in a certain field can no longer be exercised except on the condition of, or by way of, an agreement between two States, is to place an essential restriction on the sovereignty of a State, and such restriction could only be admitted if there were clear and convincing evidence. Without doubt, international practice 'does reveal some special cases in which this hypothesis has become reality; thus, sometimes two States exercise conjointly jurisdiction over certain territories (joint ownership, *co-imperium*, or *condominium*); likewise, in certain international arrangements, the representatives of States exercise conjointly a certain jurisdiction in the name of those States or in the name of organisations But these cases are exceptional, and international 'judicial decisions are slow to recognise their existence, especially when they impair the territorial sovereignty of a State, as would be the case in the present matter.

In effect, in order to appreciate in its essence the necessity for prior agreement, one must envisage the hypothesis in which the interested States cannot reach agreement. In such case, it must be admitted that the State which is normally competent has lost its right to act alone as a result of the unconditional and arbitrary opposition of another State. This amounts to admitting a 'right of assent', a 'right of veto', which at the discretion of one State paralyses the exercise of the territorial jurisdiction of another.

That is why international practice prefers to resort to less extreme solutions by confining itself to obliging the States to seek, by preliminary negotiations, terms for an agreement, without subordinating the exercise of their competences to the conclusion of such an agreement. Thus, one speaks, although often inaccurately, of the 'obligation of negotiating an agreement'. In reality, the engagements thus undertaken by States take very diverse forms and have a scope which varies according to the manner in which they are defined and according to the procedures intended for their execution; but the reality of the obligations thus undertaken is incontestable and sanctions can be applied in the event, for example, of an unjustified breaking off of the discussions, abnormal delays, disregard of the agreed procedures, systematic refusals to take into consideration adverse proposals or interests, and, more generally, in cases of violation of the rules of good faith *(Tacna-Arica Arbitration: Reports of International Arbitral Awards*, vol. II, pp. *921 et seq.; Case of Railway Traffic between Lithuania and Poland: P.C.I.J.*, SeriesA/B, No. 42, pp. 108 *et seq.).*

In *the* light of these general observations, and in relation to the present case, we will now examine in turn whether a prior agreement is necessary and whether the other rules laid down by Article XI of the Additional Act have been observed.

A. *The necessity for a prior agreement.*

12. First, to enquire whether the argument that the execution of the French scheme is subject to the prior agreement of the Spanish Government is justified in relation to the system of *compascuités* or *faceries* or in relation to international common law; the collected evidence would permit, if necessary, the interpretation of the Treaty and the Additional Act of 1866, or rather, according to the wider formula given in the Spanish argument, to affirm the existence of a general principle of law, or of a custom, the recognition of which, *inter alia*, is embodied in the Treaty and the Additional Act of 1866 . . . .

The Spanish Government has endeavoured to demonstrate that 'the demarcation line at the Pyrenean boundary constitutes a zone organised in conformity with a special law, customary in nature, incorporated in international law by the Boundary Treaties which have recognised it, rather than being a limitation on the sovereign rights of bordering States' . . . . The most characteristic manifestation of this customary law would be the existence of *compascuités* or *faceries* . . . which are themselves the remnant of a more extensive communal system which, in the Pyrenean valleys, was founded on the rule that matters of common interest must be regulated by agreements that have been freely debated.

But one cannot take the matter any further; it is impossible to extend the system of *compascuités* beyond the limits assigned to them by the treaties, or to deduce therefrom a notion of generalised 'communal rights' *[communauté]* which would have a legal content of some sort. As for recourse to the notion of the 'boundary zone', it cannot, by the use of a doctrinal vocabulary, add an obligation to those sanctioned by positive law.

13. The Spanish Government endeavoured to establish similarly the content of current positive international law. Certain principles which it demonstrates are, assuming the demonstration to be accepted, of no interest for the problem now under examination. Thus, if it is admitted that there is a principle which prohibits the upstream State from altering the waters of a river in such a fashion as seriously to prejudice the downstream State, such a principle would have no application to the

present case, because it has been admitted by the Tribunal, in connection with the first question examined above, that the French scheme will not alter the waters of the Carol. In fact, States are today perfectly conscious of the' importance of the conflicting interests brought into play by the industrial use of international rivers, and of the necessity to reconcile them by mutual concessions. The only way to arrive at such compromises of interests is to conclude agreements on an increasingly comprehensive basis. International practice reflects the conviction that States' ought to strive to conclude such agreements: there would thus appear to be an obligation to accept in good faith all communications and contracts which could, by a broad comparison of interests and by reciprocal good will, provide States with the best conditions for concluding agreements. This point will be referred to again later on, when enquiring what obligations rest on France and Spain in connection with the contracts and the communications preceding the putting in hand of a scheme such as that relating to Lake Lanoux.

But international practice does not so far permit more than the following conclusion: the rule that States may utilise the hydraulic power of international watercourses only on condition of a *prior* agreement between the interested States cannot be established as a custom, even less as a general principle of law. The history of the formulation of the multilateral Convention signed at Geneva on December 9, 1923, relative to the Development of Hydraulic Power Affecting More than One State, is very characteristic in this connection. The initial project was based on the obligatory and paramount character of agreements whose purpose was to harness the hydraulic forces of international watercourses. But this formulation was rejected, and the Convention, in its final form, provides (Article 1) that

> '[The present Convention] in no way alters the freedom of each State, within the framework of international law, to carry out on its territory all operations for the development of hydraulic power which it desires';

there is provided only an obligation upon the interested signatory States to join in a common study of a development programme; the execution of this programme is obligatory only for those States which have formally subscribed to it.

Customary international law, like the traditional Law of the Pyrenees, does not supply evidence of a kind to orient the interpretation of the Treaty and of the Additional Act of 1866 in the direction of favouring the necessity for prior agreement; even less does it permit us to conclude that there exists a general principle of law or a custom to this effect.

14. As between Spain and France, the existence of a rule requiring prior agreement for the development of the water resources of an international water-course can therefore result only from a Treaty. From this point of view, first the Treaty and the Additional Act of 1866 and then the Agreement of 1949 will be examined. [The tribunal concluded that neither gave rise to a rule on prior agreement].

*   *   *

B. Other obligations flowing from Article 11 of the Additional Act.

21. Article 11 of the Additional Act imposes on the States in which it is proposed

to erect works or to grant new concessions likely to change the course or the volume of a successive watercourse a double obligation. One is to give prior notice to the competent authorities of the frontier district; the other is to set up machinery for dealing with compensation claims and safeguards for all interests involved on either side.

*   *   *

It has not been disputed that France has, in regard to the development of Lake Lanoux, complied with the obligation to give notice.

22. The content of the second obligation is more difficult to determine. The 'claims' mentioned in Article 11 are related to the various rights protected by the Additional Act, but the essential problem is to ascertain how 'all the interests that may be involved on both sides' ought to be safeguarded.

It must first be determined what are the 'interests' which have to be safeguarded. A strict interpretation of Article 11 would permit the reading that the only interests are those which correspond with a riparian right. However, various considerations which have already been explained by the Tribunal lead to a more liberal interpretation. Account must be taken of all interests, of whatsoever nature, which are liable to be affected by the works undertaken, even if they do not correspond to a right. Only such a solution complies with the terms of Article 16, with the spirit of the Pyrenees Treaties, and with the tendencies which are manifested in instances of hydro-electric development in current international practice.

The second question is to determine the method by which these interests can be safeguarded. If that method necessarily involves communications, it cannot be confined to purely formal requirements, such as taking note of complaints, protests or representations made by the downstream State. The Tribunal is of the opinion that, according to the rules of good faith, the upstream State is under the obligation to take into consideration the various interests involved, to seek to give them every satisfaction compatible with the pursuit of its own interests, and to show that in this regard it is genuinely concerned to reconcile the interests of the other riparian State with its own.

It is a delicate matter to establish whether such an obligation has been complied with. But, without substituting itself for the Parties, the Tribunal is in a position to proceed to that decision on the basis of elements furnished by the negotiations.

23. In the present case, the Spanish Government reproaches the French Government for not having based the development scheme for the waters of Lake Lanoux on a foundation of absolute equality: this is a double reproach. It attacks simultaneously form and substance. As to form, it is said that the French Government has imposed its scheme unilaterally without associating the Spanish Government with it in a common search for an acceptable solution. Substantively, it is alleged that the French scheme does not maintain a just balance between French interests and Spanish interests. The French scheme, in the Spanish view, would serve perfectly French interests, especially those related to the production of electric energy, but would not take into sufficient consideration Spanish interests in connection with irrigation. According to the Spanish Government, the French Government refused to take into consideration schemes which, in the opinion of the

Spanish Government, would have involved a very small sacrifice of French interests and great advantages for the Spanish rural economy. Spain bases its arguments on the following facts in particular. In the course of the work of the Special Mixed Commission at Madrid (September 12–17, 1955), the French delegation compared three schemes for the development of Lake Lanoux and remarked on the considerable advantages which the first scheme (which was similar to the final scheme) presented, in its view, over the' other two. The Spanish delegation having no special objection in regard to the latter schemes, declared itself ready to accept either of the two. The French delegation did not feel itself able to depart from the execution of scheme No. I which was more favourable to French interests and was founded, according to the delegation, on French rights . . . .

On a theoretical basis the Spanish argument is unacceptable to the Tribunal, for Spain tends to put rights and simple interests on the same plane. Article 11 of the Additional Act makes this distinction and the two Parties have reproduced it in the basic statement of their contention at the beginning of the *Compromis:*

Considering that in the opinion of the French Government the carrying out of its scheme . . . will not harm any of the rights or interests referred to in the Treaty of Bayonne of May 26, 1866, and in the Additional Act of the same date, considering that, in the opinion of the Spanish Government, the carrying out of that scheme will harm Spanish rights and interests.

France is entitled to exercise her rights; she cannot ignore Spanish interests.

Spain is entitled to demand that her rights be respected and that her interests be taken into consideration.

As a matter of form, the upstream State has, procedurally, a right of initiative; it is not obliged to associate the downstream State in the elaboration of its schemes. If, in the course of discussions, the downstream State submits schemes to it, the upstream State must examine them, but it has the right to give preference to the solution contained in its own scheme provided that it takes into consideration in a reasonable manner the interests of the downstream State.

24. In the case of Lake Lanoux, France has maintained to the end the solution which consists in diverting the waters of the Carol to the Ariège with full restitution. By making this choice France is only making use of a right; the development works of Lake Lanoux are on French territory, the financing of and responsibility for the enterprise fall upon France, and France alone is the judge of works of public utility which are to be executed on her own territory, save for the provisions of Articles 9 and 10 of the Additional Act, which, however, the French scheme does not infringe.

On her side, Spain cannot invoke a right to insist on a development of Lake Lanoux based on the needs of Spanish agriculture. In effect, if France were to renounce all of the works envisaged on her territory, Spain could not demand that other works in conformity With her wishes should be carried out. Therefore, she can only urge her interests in order to obtain, within the framework of the scheme decided upon by France, terms which reasonably safeguard them.

It remains to be established whether this requirement has been fulfilled.

*   *   *

When one examines the question of whether France, either in the course of the dealings or in her proposals, has taken Spanish interests into sufficient consideration, it must be stressed how closely linked together are the obligation to take into consideration, in the course of negotiations, adverse interests and the obligation to give a reasonable place to these interests in the solution finally adopted. A State which has conducted negotiations with understanding and good faith in accordance with Article 11 of the Additional Act is not relieved from giving a reasonable place to adverse interests in the solution it adopts simply because the conversations have been interrupted, even though owing to the intransigence of its partner) Conversely, in determining the manner in which a scheme has taken into consideration the' interests involved, the way in which negotiations have developed, the total number of the interests which have been presented, the price which each Party was ready to pay to have those interests safeguarded, are all essential factors in establishing, with regard to the obligations set out in Article II of the Additional Act, the merits of that scheme.

Having regard to all the circumstances of the case, set out above, the Tribunal is of opinion that the French scheme complies with the obligations of Article 11 of the Additional Act.

CASE CONCERNING THE GABČIKOVO-NAGYMAROS PROJECT (HUNGARY v. SLOVAKIA)
International Court of Justice
1997 I.C.J. Rep. 7, 17–27, 76–78 (Judgment of Sept. 25)

*   *   *

The present case arose out of the signature, on 16 September 1977, by the Hungarian People's Republic and the Czechoslovak People's Republic, of a treaty "concerning the construction and operation of the Gabčikovo-Nagymaros System of Locks" (hereinafter called the "1977 Treaty"). The names of the two contracting States have varied over the years; hereinafter they will be referred to as Hungary and Czechoslovakia. The 1977 Treaty entered into force on 30 June 1978.

It provides for the construction and operation of a System of Locks by the parties as a "joint investment." According to its Preamble, the barrage system was designed to attain

> "the broad utilization of the natural resources of the Bratislava-Budapest section of the Danube river for the development of water resources, energy, transport, agriculture and other sectors of the national economy of the Contracting Parties."

The joint investment was thus essentially aimed at the production of hydroelectricity, the improvement of navigation on the relevant section of the Danube and the protection of the areas along the banks against flooding. At the same time, by the terms of the Treaty, the contracting parties undertook to ensure that the quality of water in the Danube was not impaired as a result of the Project, and that compliance with the obligations for the protection of nature arising in connection with the construction and operation of the System of Locks would be observed.

The Danube is the second longest river in Europe, flowing along or across the borders of nine countries in its 2,860-kilometre course from the Black Forest eastwards to the Black Sea. For 142 kilometres, it forms the boundary between Slovakia and Hungary. The sector with which this case is concerned is a stretch of approximately 200 kilometres, between Bratislava in Slovakia and Budapest in Hungary. Below Bratislava, the river gradient decreases markedly, creating an alluvial plain of gravel and sand sediment. This plain is delimited to the north-east, in Slovak territory, by the Malý Danube and to the south-west, in Hungarian territory, by the Mosoni Danube. The boundary between the two States is constituted, in the major part of that region, by the main channel of the river. The area lying between the Malý Danube and that channel, in Slovak territory, constitutes the Žitaný Ostrov; the area between the main channel and the Mosoni Danube, in Hungarian territory, constitutes the Szigetköz. Čunovo and, further downstream, Gabčíkovo, are situated in this sector of the river on Slovak territory, Čunovo on the right bank and Gabčíkovo on the left. Further downstream, after the confluence of the various branches, the river enters Hungarian territory and the topography becomes hillier. Nagymaros lies in a narrow valley at a bend in the Danube just before it turns south, enclosing the large river island of Szentendre before reaching Budapest.

The Danube has always played a vital part in the commercial and economic development of its riparian States, and has underlined and reinforced their interdependence, making international co-operation essential. Improvements to the navigation channel have enabled the Danube, now linked by canal to the Main and thence to the Rhine, to become an important navigational artery connecting the North Sea to the Black Sea. In the stretch of river to which the case relates, flood protection measures have been constructed over the centuries, farming and forestry practised, and, more recently, there has been an increase in population and industrial activity in the area. The cumulative effects on the river and on the environment of various human activities over the years have not all been favourable, particularly for the water regime.

Only by international co-operation could action be taken to alleviate these problems. Water management projects along the Danube have frequently sought to combine navigational improvements and flood protection with the production of electricity through hydroelectric power plants. The potential of the Danube for the production of hydroelectric power has been extensively exploited by some riparian States. The history of attempts to harness the potential of the particular stretch of the river at issue in these proceedings extends over a 25-year period culminating in the signature of the 1977 Treaty.

Article 1, paragraph 1, of the 1977 Treaty describes the principal works to be constructed in pursuance of the Project. It provided for the building of two series of locks, one at Gabčíkovo (in Czechoslovak territory) and the other at Nagymaros (in Hungarian territory), to constitute "a single and indivisible operational system of works." The Court will subsequently have occasion to revert in more detail to those works, which were to comprise, *inter alia*, a reservoir upstream of Dunakiliti, in Hungarian and Czechoslovak territory; a dam at Dunakiliti, in Hungarian territory; a bypass canal, in Czechoslovak territory, on which was to be constructed the Gabčíkovo System of Locks (together with a hydroelectric power plant with an installed capacity of 720 megawatts (MW); the deepening' of the bed of the Danube downstream of the place at which the bypass canal was to rejoin the old bed of the river; a reinforcement of flood-control works along the Danube upstream of Nagymaros; the Nagymaros System of Locks, in Hungarian territory (with a hydroelectric power plant of a capacity of 158 MW); and the deepening of the bed of the Danube downstream.

Article 1, paragraph 4, of the Treaty further provided that the technical specifications concerning the system would be included in the "Joint Contractual Plan" which was to be drawn. up in accordance with the Agreement signed by the two Governments for this purpose on 6 May 1976; Article 4, paragraph 1, for its part, specified that "the joint investment [would] be carried out in conformity with the joint contractual plan."

According to Article 3, paragraph 1,

"Operations connected with the realization of the joint investment and with the performance of tasks relating to the operation of the System of Locks shall be directed and supervised by the Governments of the Contracting Parties through . . . (. . . 'government delegates')."

Those delegates had, inter alia, "to ensure that construction of the System of Locks is . . . carried out in accordance with the approved joint contractual plan and the Project work schedule." When the works were brought into operation, they were moreover "To establish the operating and operational procedures of the System of Locks and ensure compliance therewith."

Article 4, paragraph 4, stipulated that:

"Operations relating to the joint investment [should] be organized by the Contracting Parties in such a way that the power generation plants [would] be put into service during the period 1986–1990."

Article 5 provided that the cost of the joint investment would be borne by the contracting parties in equal measure. It specified the work to be carried out by each one of them. Article 8 further stipulated that the Dunakiliti dam, the bypass canal and the two series of locks at Gabčíkovo and Nagymaros would be "jointly owned" by the contracting parties "in equal measure," Ownership of the other works was to be vested in the State on whose territory they were constructed.

The parties were likewise to participate in equal measure in the use of the system put in place, and more particularly in the use of the base-load and peak-load power generated at the hydroelectric power plants (Art. 9).

According to Article 10, the works were to be managed by the State on whose territory they were located, "in accordance with the jointly-agreed operating and operational procedures," while Article 12 stipulated that the operation, maintenance (repair) and reconstruction costs of jointly owned works of the System of Locks were also to be borne jointly by the contracting parties in equal measure.

According to Article 14,

"The discharge specified in the water balance of the approved joint contractual plan shall be ensured in the bed of the Danube [between

Dunakiliti and Sap] unless natural conditions or other circumstances temporarily require a greater or smaller discharge."

Paragraph 3 of that Article was worded as follows:

"In the event that the withdrawal of water in the Hungarian-Czechoslovak section of the Danube exceeds the quantities of water specified in the water balance of the approved joint contractual plan and the excess withdrawal results in a decrease in the output of electric power, the share of electric power of the Contracting party benefiting from the excess withdrawal shall be correspondingly reduced."

Article 15 specified that the contracting parties

"shall ensure, by the means specified in the joint contractual plan, that the quality of the water in the Danube is not impaired as a result of the construction and operation of the System of Locks."

Article 16 set forth the obligations of the contracting parties concerning the maintenance of the bed of the Danube.

Article 18, paragraph 1, provided as follows:

"The Contracting Parties, in conformity with the obligations previously assumed by them, and in particular with article 3 of the Convention concerning the regime of navigation on the Danube, signed at Belgrade on 18 August 1948, shall ensure uninterrupted and safe navigation on the international fairway both during the construction and during the operation of the System of Locks."

It was stipulated in Article 19 that;

"The Contracting Parties shall, through the means specified in the joint contractual plan, ensure compliance with the obligations for the protection of nature arising in connection with the construction and operation of the System of Locks."

Article 20 provided for the contracting parties to take appropriate measures. within the framework of their national investments, for the protection of fishing interests in conformity with the Convention concerning Fishing in the Waters of the Danube, signed at Bucharest on 29 January 1958.

According to Article 22, paragraph 1, of the Treaty, the contracting parties had, in connection with the construction and operation of the System of Locks, agreed on minor revision to the course of the State frontier between them.

* * *

It was further provided, in paragraph 2, that the revision of the State frontier and the exchange of territories so provided for should be effected "by the Contracting Parties on the basis of a separate treaty." No such treaty was concluded.

Finally a dispute settlement provision was contained in Article 27 . . . .

*   *   *

[Thus, the Project was to have taken the form of an integrated joint project with the two contracting parties on an equal footing in respect of the financing, construction and operation of the works. Its single and indivisible nature was to have been realized through the Joint Contractual Plan which complemented the Treaty. In particular, Hungary would have had control of the sluices at Dunakiliti and the works at Nagymaros, whereas Czechoslovakia would have had control of the works at Gabčíkovo.

The schedule of work had for its part been fixed in an Agreement on mutual assistance signed by the two parties on 16 September 1977, at the same time as the Treaty itself. The Agreement moreover made some adjustments to the allocation of the works between the parties as laid down by the Treaty.

Work on the Project started in 1978. On Hungary's initiative, the two parties first agreed, by two Protocols signed on 10 October 1983 (one amending Article 4, paragraph 4, of the 1977 Treaty and the other the Agreement on mutual assistance), to slow the work down and to postpone putting into operation the power plants, and then, by a Protocol signed on 6 February 1989 (which amended the Agreement on mutual assistance), to accelerate the Project.

As a result of intense criticism which the Project had generated in Hungary, the Hungarian Government decided on 13 May 1989 to suspend the works at Nagymaros pending the completion of various studies which the competent authorities were to finish before 31 July 1989. On 21 July 1989, the Hungarian Government extended the suspension of the works at Nagymaros until 31 October 1989, and, in addition, suspended the works at Dunakiliti until the same date. Lastly, on 27 October 1989, Hungary decided to abandon the works at Nagymaros and to maintain the status quo at Dunakiliti.

During this period, negotiations were being held between the parties. Czechoslovakia also started investigating alternative solutions. One of them, subsequently known as "Variant C," entailed a unilateral diversion of the Danube by Czechoslovakia on its territory some 10 kilometres upstream of Dunakiliti.

   The dispute was brought before the ICJ by way of Special Agreement between the parties under Article 40 of the Statute of the ICJ. The Special Agreement directed specific questions to the ICJ concerning:

   (a) Hungary's right to suspend and subsequently abandon certain works on the Hungarian side of the Project;

   (b) The right of the Czech and Slovak Republic to proceed to and implement a 'provisional solution' to enable the operation of the project and involving the diversion of a significant body of water from the Danube River within the Czech and Slovak Republic territory; and

   (c) the validity of Hungary's purported termination of the 1977 Treaty.

The ICJ was also requested to determine the legal consequences of its finding on the three questions. Upon judgment, the Special Agreement provided that the parties would enter into negotiations on the modalities for its execution within six months and, failing agreement in that time, either party could request the ICJ to render an additional judgment regarding the manner of execution of its decision.

In its judgment of 25 September 1997, the ICJ concluded that both parties had been at fault, finding that:

(a) Hungary had no right to suspend and abandon works;

(b) The Czech and Slovak Republic had the right to proceed to but not to implement the 'provisional solution';

(e) Hungary's purported termination of the 1977 Treaty was invalid.

Having found the 1977 Treaty to be in force, the ICJ proceeded to determine the future conduct of the parties on the basis of the 1977 Treaty, other relevant conventions to which the two states are party and the rules of general international law].

*   *   *

In this regard it is of cardinal importance that the Court has found that the 1977 Treaty is still in force and consequently governs the relationship between the Parties. That relationship is also determined by the rules of other relevant conventions to which the two States are party, by the rules of general international law and, in this particular case, by the rules of State responsibility; but it is governed, above all, by the applicable roles of the 1977 Treaty as a *lex specialis*.

The Court, however, cannot disregard the fact that the Treaty has not been fully implemented by either party for years, and indeed that their acts of commission and omission have contributed to creating the factual situation that now exists. Nor can it overlook that factual situation — or the practical possibilities and impossibilities to which it gives rise — when deciding on the legal requirements for the future conduct of the Parties.

This does not mean that facts — in this case facts which flow from wrongful conduct — determine the law. The principle *ex injuria jus non oritur* is sustained by the Court's finding that the legal relationship created by the 1977 Treaty is preserved and cannot in this case be treated as voided by unlawful conduct.

What is essential, therefore, is that the factual situation as it has developed since 1989 shall be placed within the context of the preserved and developing treaty relationship, in order to achieve its object and purpose in so far as that is feasible. For it is only then that the irregular state of affairs which exists as the result of the failure of both Parties to comply with their treaty obligations can be remedied.

What might have been a correct application of the law in 1989 or 1992, if the case had been before the Court then, could be a miscarriage of justice if prescribed in 1997. The Court cannot ignore the fact that the Gabčíkovo power plant has been in operation for nearly five years, that the bypass canal which feeds the plant receives its water from a significantly smaller reservoir formed by a dam which is built not at Dunakiliti but at Čunovo, and that the plant is operated in a run-of-the-river mode and not in a peak hour mode as originally foreseen. Equally, the Court cannot ignore the fact that, not only has Nagymaros not been built, but that, with the effective discarding by both Parties of peak power operation, there is no longer any point in building it.

As the Court has already had occasion to point out, the 1977 Treaty was not only a joint investment project for the production of energy, but it was designed to serve other objectives as well: the improvement of the navigability of the Danube, flood control and regulation of ice-discharge, and the protection of the natural environment. None of these objectives has been given absolute priority over the other, in spite of the emphasis which is given in the Treaty to the construction of a System of Locks for the production of energy. None of them has lost its importance. In order to achieve these objectives the parties accepted obligations of conduct, obligations of performance, and obligations of result.

It could be said that that part of the obligations of performance which related to the construction of the System of Locks — in so far as they were not yet implemented before 1992 — have been overtaken by events. It would be an administration of the law altogether out of touch with reality if the Court were to order those obligations to be fully reinstated and the works at Čunovo to be demolished when the objectives of the Treaty can be adequately served by the existing structures.

Whether this is indeed the case is, first and foremost, for the Parties to decide. Under the 1977 Treaty its several objectives must be attained in an integrated and consolidated programme, to be developed in the Joint Contractual Plan. The Joint Contractual Plan was, until 1989, adapted and amended frequently to better fit the wishes of the parties. This Plan was also expressly described as the means to achieve the objectives of maintenance of water quality and protection of the environment.

The 1977 Treaty never laid down a rigid system, albeit that the construction of a system of locks at Gabčíkovo and Nagymaros was prescribed by the Treaty itself. In this respect, however, the subsequent positions adopted by the parties should be taken into consideration. Not only did Hungary insist on terminating construction at Nagymaros, but Czechoslovakia stated, on various occasions in the course of negotiations, that it was willing to consider a limitation or even exclusion of operation in peak hour mode. In the latter case the construction of the Nagymaros dam would have become pointless. The explicit terms of the Treaty itself were therefore in practice acknowledged by the parties to be negotiable.

The Court is of the opinion that the Parties are under a legal obligation, during the negotiations to be held by virtue of Article 5 of the Special Agreement, to consider, within the context of the 1977 Treaty, in what way the multiple objectives of the Treaty can best be served, keeping in mind that all of them should be fulfilled.

It is clear that the Project's impact upon, and its implications for, the environment are of necessity a key issue. The numerous scientific reports which have been presented to the Court by the Parties — even if their conclusions are often contradictory — provide abundant evidence that this impact and these implications are considerable.

In order to evaluate the environmental risks, current standards must be taken into consideration. This is not only allowed by the wording of Articles 15 and 19, but even prescribed, to the extent that these articles impose a continuing — and thus necessarily evolving — obligation on the parties to maintain the quality of the water of the Danube and to protect nature.

The Court is mindful that, in the field of environmental protection, vigilance and prevention are required on account of the often irreversible character of damage to the environment and of the limitations inherent in the very mechanism of reparation of this type of damage.

Throughout the ages, mankind has, for economic and other reasons, constantly interfered with nature. In the past, this was often done without consideration of the effects upon the environment. Owing to new scientific insights and to a growing awareness of the risks for mankind — for present and future generations — of pursuit of such interventions at an unconsidered and unabated pace; new norms and standards have been developed, set forth in a great number of instruments during the last two decades. Such new norms have to be taken into consideration, and such new standards given proper weight, not only when States contemplate new activities but also when continuing with activities begun in the past. This need to reconcile economic development with protection of the environment is aptly expressed in the concept of sustainable development.

For the purposes of the present case, this means that the Parties together should look afresh at the effects on the environment of the operation of the Gabčíkovo power plant. In particular they must find a satisfactory solution for the volume of water to be released into the old bed of the Danube and into the side-arms on both sides of the river.

It is not for the Court to determine what shall be the final result of these negotiations to be conducted by the Parties. It is for the Parties themselves to find an agreed solution that takes account of the objectives of the Treaty, which must be pursued in a joint and integrated way, as well as the norms of international environmental law and the principles of the law of international watercourses. The Court will recall in this context that, as it said in the *North Sea Continental Shelf* cases:

> "[the Parties] are under an obligation so to conduct themselves that the negotiations are meaningful, which will not be the case when either of them insists upon its own position without contemplating any modification of it" (*I.C.J. Reports* 1969, p. 47, para. 85).

CASE CONCERNING PULP MILLS ON THE RIVER URUGUAY ARGENTINA v. URUGUAY
International Court of Justice
2010 I.C.J. Rep. 14 (Judgment of 20 April 2010)

[This case concerned two pulp mills, one constructed and the other to be constructed on the River Uruguay, which by treaty forms the boundary between Argentina and Uruguay. The dispute concerned the interpretation of obligations under the Statute of the River Uruguay, a treaty signed by Argentina and Uruguay in 1975. The object and purpose of the 1975 Statute was found to be "the optimum and rational utilization of the River Uruguay." (para. 75). The Statute creates a joint Administrative Commission of the River Uruguay (CARU) to manage the river.

Argentina charged Uruguay with violating both procedural and substantive obligations regarding this treaty. The jurisdiction of the International Court of Justice (IU) was founded upon Article 60 of the Statute, which states that "any dispute concerning the interpretation or application of the Treaty" shall be referred to the International Court of Justice.

The ICJ found Uruguay in violation of certain procedural obligations under the 1975 Statute:

- By failing to inform CARU of the planned works before the issuance of the initial environmental authorizations for each of the mills and for the port terminal adjacent to the mills. (para. 111).

- By failing to fulfill its obligation to negotiate and for disregarding the cooperation mechanism of CARU in connection with the construction of the mills. (para. 150).

- By failing to inform, notify and negotiate with Argentina concerning the mills. (para. 158).

Thus, Uruguay was not entitled, for the duration of the period of consultation and negotiation provided in Articles 7 to 12 of the Statute, to construct or to authorize the construction of the planned mills. (para. 143).

As to the substantive obligations under the Statute, the ICJ ruled as follows:]

1. The obligation to contribute to the optimum and rational utilization of the river' (Article 1)

170. According to Argentina, Uruguay has breached its obligation to contribute to the "optimum and rational utilization of the river" by failing to co-ordinate with Argentina on measures necessary to avoid ecological change, and by failing to take the measures necessary to prevent pollution. Argentina also maintains that, in interpreting the 1975 Statute (in particular Articles 27, 35, and 36 thereof) according to the principle of equitable and reasonable use, account must be taken of all pre-existing legitimate uses of the river, including in particular its use for recreational and tourist purposes.

171. For Uruguay, the object and purpose of the 1975 Statute is to establish a structure for co-operation between the Parties through CARU in pursuit of the shared goal of equitable and sustainable use of the water and biological resources of the river. Uruguay contends that it has in no way breached the principle of equitable and reasonable use of the river and that this principle provides no basis for favouring pre-existing uses of the river, such as tourism or fishing, over other, new uses.

173. The Court observes that Article 1, as stated in the title to Chapter I of the 1975 Statute, sets out the purpose of the Statute. As such, it informs the interpretation of the substantive obligations, but does not by itself lay down specific rights and obligations for the parties, Optimum and rational utilization is to be achieved through compliance with the obligations prescribed by the 1975 Statute for the protection of the environment and the joint management of this shared resource. This objective must also be ensured through CARU, which constitutes

"the joint machinery" necessary for its achievement, and through the regulations adopted by it as well as the regulations and measures adopted by the Parties.

2. The obligation to ensure that the management of the soil and woodland does not impair the regime of the river or the quality of its waters (Article 35)

178. Article 35 of the 1975 Statute provides that the parties:

> "undertake to adopt the necessary measures to ensure that the management of the soil and woodland and the use of groundwater and the waters of the tributaries of the river do not cause changes which may significantly impair the regime of the river or the quality of its waters."

179. Argentina contends that Uruguay's decision to carry out major eucalyptus planting operations to supply the raw material for the Orion (Botnia) mill has an impact on management of the soil and Uruguayan woodland, but also on the quality of the waters of the river. For its part, Uruguay states that Argentina does not make any arguments that are based on Uruguay's management of sailor woodland — "nor has it made any allegations concerning the waters of tributaries."

180. The Court observes that Argentina has not provided any evidence to support its contention. Moreover, Article 35 concerns the management of the soil and woodland as well as the use of groundwater and the water of tributaries, and there is nothing to suggest, in the evidentiary material submitted by Argentina, a direct relationship between Uruguay's management of the soil and woodland, or its use of ground water and water of tributaries and the alleged changes in the quality of the waters of the River Uruguay which had been attributed by Argentina to the Orion (Botnia) mill. Indeed, while Argentina made lengthy arguments about the effects of the pulp mill discharges on the quality of the waters or the river, no similar arguments have been presented to the Court regarding it deleterious relationship between the quality of the waters of the river and the eucalyptus-planting operations by Uruguay. The Court concludes that Argentina has not established its contention on this matter.

3. The obligation to co-ordinate measures to avoid changes in the ecological balance (Article 36)

181. Argentina contends that Uruguay has breached Article 36 of the 1975 Statute, which places the Parties under an obligation to co-ordinate through CARU the necessary measures to avoid changing the ecological balance of the river. Argentina asserts that the discharges from the Orion (Botnia) mill altered the ecological balance of the river, and cites as examples the 4 February 2009 algal bloom, which, according to it, provides graphic evidence of a change in the ecological balance, as well as the discharge of toxins, which gave rise, in its view, to the malformed rotifers whose pictures were shown to the Court.

182. Uruguay considers that any assessment of the Parties' conduct in relation to Article 36 of the 1975 Statute must take account of the rules adopted by CARU, because this Article, creating an obligation of co-operation, refers to such rules and does not by itself prohibit any specific conduct Uruguay takes the position that the

mill fully meets CARU requirements concerning the ecological balance of the river. and concludes that it has not acted in breach of Article 36 of the 1975 Statute.

183, It is recalled that Article 36 provides that "[the parties shall coordinate, through the Commission. the necessary measures to avoid any change in the ecological balance and to control pests and other harmful factors in the river and the areas affected by it."

184. It is the opinion of the Court that compliance with this obligation cannot be expected to come through the individual action of either Party, acting on its own, Its implementation requires co-ordination through the Commission. It reflects the common interest dimension of the 1975 Statute and expresses one of the purposes for the establishment of the joint machinery which is to co-ordinate the actions and measures taken by the Parties for the sustainable management and environmental protection of the river. The Parties have indeed adopted such measures through the promulgation of standards by CARU. These standards are to be found in Sections E3 and E4 of the CARU Digest. One of the purposes of Section E3 is "[t]o protect and preserve the water and its ecological balance." Similarly, it is stated in Section E4 that the section was developed "in accordance with . . . Articles 36, 37, 38, and 39."

185, In the view of the Court, the purpose of Article 36 of the 1975 Statute is to prevent any transboundary pollution liable to change the ecological balance of the river by co-ordinating. through CARU, the adoption of the necessary measures. It thus imposes an obligation on both States to take positive steps to avoid changes in the ecological balance, These steps consist not only in the adoption of a regulatory framework. as has been done by the Parties through CARU, but also in the observance as well as enforcement by both Parties of the measures adopted.

4. The obligation to prevent pollution and preserve the aquatic environment (Article 41)

190. Article 41 provides that:

"Without prejudice to the functions assigned to the Commission in this respect, the parties undertake:

(a)   to protect and preserve the aquatic environment and, in particular, to prevent its pollution, by prescribing appropriate rules and [adopting appropriate] measures in accordance with applicable international agreements and in keeping, where relevant, with the guidelines and recommendations of international technical bodies:

(b)   not to reduce in their respective legal systems:

1.   the technical requirements in force for preventing water pollution, and

2.   the severity of the penalties established for violations:

(c)   to inform one another of any rules which they plan to prescribe with regard to water pollution in order to establish equivalent rules in their respective legal systems."

191. Argentina claims that by allowing the discharge of additional nutrients into a river that is eutrophic and suffers from reverse flow and stagnation, Uruguay violated the obligation to prevent pollution, as it failed to prescribe appropriate measures in relation to the Orion (Botnia) mill and failed to meet applicable international environmental agreements. including the Biodiversity Convention and the Ramsar Convention. It maintains that the 1975 Statute prohibits any pollution which is prejudicial to the protection and preservation of the aquatic environment or which alters the ecological balance of the river. Argentina further argues that the obligation to prevent pollution of the river is an obligation of result and extends not only to protecting the aquatic environment proper, but also to any reasonable and legitimate use of the river, including tourism and other recreational uses.

192. Uruguay contends that the obligation laid down in Article 41 (a) of the 1975 Statute to "prevent . . . pollution" does not involve a prohibition on all discharges into the river. It is only those that exceed the standards jointly agreed by the Parties within CARU in accordance with their international obligations. and that therefore have harmful effects, which can be characterized as "pollution" under Article 40 of the 1975 Statute. Uruguay also maintains that Article 41 creates an obligation of conduct, and not of result. but that it actually matters little since Uruguay has complied with its duty to prevent pollution by requiring the plant to meet best available technology ("BAT") standards.

195. In view or the central role of this provision in the dispute between the Parties in the present case and their profound differences as to its interpretation and application, the Court will make a few remarks of a general character on the normative content of Article 41 before addressing the specific arguments of the Parties. First, in the view of the Court, Article 41 makes a clear distinction between regulatory functions entrusted to CARU under the 1975 Statute, which are dealt with in Article 56 of the Statute, and the obligation it imposes on the Parties to adopt rules and measures individually to "protect and preserve the aquatic environment and, in particular, to prevent its pollution." Thus, the obligation assumed by the Parties under Article 41, which is distinct from those under Articles 36 and 56 of the 1975 Statute, is to adopt appropriate rules and measures within the framework of their respective domestic legal systems to protect and preserve the aquatic environment and to prevent pollution. This conclusion is supported by the wording of paragraphs (b) and (c) of Article 41, which refer to the need not to reduce the technical requirements and severity of the penalties already in force in the respective legislation of the Parties as well as the need to inform each other of the rules to be promulgated so as to establish equivalent rules in their legal systems.

196. Secondly, it is the opinion of the Court that a simple reading of the text of Article 41 indicates that it is the rules and measures that are to be prescribed by the Parties in their respective legal systems which must be "in accordance with applicable international agreements" and "in keeping, where relevant, with the guidelines and recommendations of international technical bodies."

197. Thirdly, the obligation to "preserve the aquatic environment, and in particular to prevent pollution by prescribing appropriate rules and measures" is an obligation to act with due diligence in respect of all activities which take place under the jurisdiction and control of each party. It is an obligation which entails' not only

the adoption of appropriate rules and measures, but also a certain level of vigilance in their enforcement and the exercise of administrative control applicable to public and private operators, such as the monitoring of activities undertaken by such operators, to safeguard the rights of the other party. The responsibility of a party to the 1975 Statute would therefore be engaged if it was shown that it had failed to act diligently and thus take all appropriate measures to enforce its relevant regulations on a public or private operator under its jurisdiction. The obligation of due diligence under Article 41 (a) in the adoption and enforcement of appropriate rules and measures is further reinforced by the requirement that such rules and measures must be "in accordance with applicable international agreements" and "in keeping, where relevant, with the guidelines and recommendations of international technical bodies." This requirement has the advantage of ensuring that the rules and measures adopted by the parties both have to conform to applicable international agreements and to take account of internationally agreed technical standards.

198. Finally, the scope of the obligation to prevent pollution must be determined in light of the definition of pollution given in Article 40 of the 1975 Statute. Article 40 provides that: "For the purposes of this Statute. pollution shall mean the direct or indirect introduction by man into the aquatic environment of substances or energy which have harmful effects." The term "harmful effects" is defined in the CARU Digest as:

> "any alteration of the water quality that prevents or hinders any legitimate use of the water, that causes deleterious effects or harm to living resources, risks to human health or a threat to water activities including fishing or reduction of recreational activities" (Title I, Chapter I, Section 2, Article 1 *(c)* of the Digest (E3)).

199. The Digest expresses the will of the Parties and their interpretation of the provisions of the 1975 Statute. Article 41, not unlike many other provisions of the 1975 Statute, lays down broad obligations agreed to by the Parties to regulate and limit their use of the river and to protect its environment. These broad obligations are given more specific content through the co-ordinated rule-making action of CARU as established under Article S36 of the 1975 Statute or through the regulatory action of each of the parties, or by both means. The two regulatory actions are meant to complement each other: As discussed below (see paragraphs 201 to 202, and 214), CARU standards concern mainly water quality. The CARU Digest sets only general limits on certain discharges or effluents from industrial plants such as: "hydrocarbons," "sedimentable solids," and "oils and greases." As the Digest makes explicit, those matters are left to each party to regulate. The Digest provides that, as regards effluents within its jurisdiction, each party shall take the appropriate "corrective measures" in order to assure compliance with water quality standards (CARU Digest. Sec. E3: Pollution, Title 2. Chapter 5, Section 1, Article 3). Uruguay has taken that action in its Regulation on Water Quality (Decree No. 253/79) and in relation to the Orion (Botnia) mill in the conditions stipulated in the authorization issued by MVOTMA [Ministerio de Vivienda Ordenamiento Territorial y Medio Ambiente].

265. It follows from the above that there is no conclusive evidence in the record to show that Uruguay has not acted with the requisite degree of due diligence or

that the discharges of effluent from the Orion (Botnia) mill have had deleterious effects or caused harm to living resources or to the quality of the water or the ecological balance of the river since it started its operations in November 2007. Consequently, on the basis of the evidence submitted to it, the Court concludes that Uruguay has not breached its obligations under Article 41.

266. The Court is of the opinion that both Parties have the obligation to enable CARU, as the joint machinery created by the 1975 Statute, to exercise on a continuous basis the powers conferred on it by the 1975 Statute, including its function of monitoring the quality of the waters of the river and of assessing the impact of.the operation of the Orion (Botnia) mill on the aquatic environment. Uruguay, for its part, has the obligation to continue monitoring the operation of the plant in accordance with Article 41 of the Statute and to ensure' compliance by Botnia with Uruguayan domestic regulations as well as the standards set by CARU. The Parties have a legal obligation under the 1975 Statute to continue their co-operation through CARU and to enable it to devise the necessary means to promote the equitable utilization of the river, while protecting its environment.

*   *   *

THE CLAIMS MADE BY THE PARTIES
IN THEIR FINAL SUBMISSIONS

267. Having concluded that Uruguay breached its procedural obligations under the 1975 Statute (see paragraphs above), it is for the Court to draw the conclusions following from these internationally wrongful acts giving rise to Uruguay's inter-national responsibility and to determine what that responsibility entails.

268. Argentina first requests the Court to find that Uruguay has violated the procedural obligations incumbent on it under the 1975 Statute and has thereby engaged its international responsibility. Argentina further requests the Court to order that Uruguay immediately cease these internationally wrongful acts.

269. The Court considers that its finding of wrongful conduct by Uruguay in respect of its procedural obligations per se constitutes a measure of satisfaction for Argentina. As Uruguay's breaches of the procedural obligations occurred in the past and have come to an end. there is no cause to order their cessation.

270. Argentina nevertheless argues that a finding of wrongfulness would be insufficient as reparation, even if the Court were to find that Uruguay has not breached any substantive obligation under the 1975 Statute but only some of its procedural obligations. Argentina maintains that the procedural obligations and substantive obligations laid down in the 1975 Statute are closely related and cannot be severed from one another for purposes of reparation. since undesirable effects of breaches of the former persist even after the breaches have ceased. Accordingly, Argentina contends that Uruguay is under an obligation to "re-establish on the ground and in legal terms the situation that existed before [the] internationally wrongful acts were committed." To this end, the Orion (Botnia) mill should be dismantled. According to Argentina, *restitutio in integrum* is the primary form of reparation for internationally wrongful acts. Relying on Article 35 of the Interna-tional Law Commission's Articles on the Responsibility of States for Internationally

Wrongful Acts, Argentina maintains that restitution takes precedence over all other forms of reparation except where it is "materially impossible" or involves "a burden out of all proportion to the benefit deriving from restitution instead of compensation."

275. As the Court has pointed out (see paragraphs 154 to 157 above), the procedural obligations under the 1975 Statute did not entail any ensuing prohibition on Uruguay's building of the Orion (Botnia) mill. failing consent by Argentina, after the expiration of the period for negotiation. The Court has however observed that construction of that mill began before negotiations had come to an end, in breach of the procedural obligations laid down in the 1975 Statute. Further, as the Court has found, on the evidence submitted to it, the operation of the Orion (Botnia) mill has not resulted in the breach of substantive obligations laid down in the 1975 Statute (paragraphs 180, 189 and 265 above). As Uruguay was not barred from proceeding with the construction and operation of the Orion (Botnia) mill after the expiration of the period for negotiation and as it breached no substantive obligation under the 1975 Statute, ordering the dismantling of the mill would not, in the view of the Court, constitute an appropriate remedy for the breach of procedural obligations.

276. As Uruguay has not breached substantive obligations arising under the 1975 Statute, the Court is likewise unable, for the same reasons, to uphold Argentina's claim in respect of compensation for alleged injuries suffered in various economic sectors, specifically tourism and agriculture.

282. For these reasons.

THE COURT.

(I) By thirteen votes to one,

Finds that the Eastern Republic of Uruguay has breached its procedural obligations under Articles 7 to 12 of the 1975 Statute of the River Uruguay and that the declaration by the Court of this breach constitutes appropriate satisfaction;

IN FAVOUR:	*Vice-President* Tomka, *Acting President; Judges* Koroma, AI-Khasawneh, Simma, Abraham, Keith, Sepúlveda-Amor, Bennouna, Skotnikov, Cancado Trindade, Yusuf, Greenwood; *Judge* ad hoc Vinuesa:
AGAINST:	*Judge* ad hoc Torres Bernárdez;

(2) By eleven votes to three,

Finds that the Eastern Republic of Uruguay has not breached its substantive obligations under Articles 35, 36 and 41 of the 1975 Statute of the River Uruguay;

IN FAVOUR:	*Vice-President* Tomka, *Acting President: Judges* Koroma, Abraham, Keith, Sepúlveda-Amor, Bennouna, Skotnikov, Cancado Trindade, Yusuf, Greenwood: *Judge* ad hoc Torres Bernárdez;
AGAINST:	*Judges* Al-Khasawneh, Simma; *Judge* ad hoc Vinuesa;

(3) Unanimously.

Rejects all other submissions by the Parties.

NOTES AND QUESTIONS

1. ***Lake Lanoux.*** In the *Lake Lanoux arbitration*, with regard to question A, the tribunal in paragraph 6 suggests an argument concerning environmental quality that Spain failed to make. Do you think the arbitrators would have been sympathetic to this argument if made? What was Spain's argument? The tribunal was unsympathetic to Spain's argument on this point. Why? As to question B, does the tribunal's ruling go beyond the literal language of the treaty provision, which simply required notice? Was the tribunal justified in fleshing out in more detail the rights and obligations of France as the upper riparian and the rights of Spain as the lower riparian? How did the tribunal's ruling develop the international law of shared watercourses and diminish the absolute territorial sovereignty principle?

2. ***Rejecting extreme positions.*** In negotiations with Spain leading up to the Lake Lanoux arbitration, France argued in favor of the absolute territorial sovereignty principle, while Spain embraced the principle of absolute river basin integrity. Note that the arbitral panel rejected both of these extreme positions in favor of a principle that may be termed *limited territorial sovereignty.*

3. ***The Gabčikovo Dam Case.*** In this case the International Court of Justice concluded that general international law could affect the obligations of the parties to a bilateral agreement where the language of the agreement indicated the parties intention to create a "living" document that could be adapted to emerging environmental norms. Do you agree with the court that the Project's impact on the environment should be a key issue? Is there a basis in the treaty for such a ruling or is the court importing environmental norms and the principle of sustainable development into the treaty?

4. ***The Pulp Mills Case.*** Compare the agreement between Uruguay and Argentina to the agreements in the previous two cases. The 1975 Statute speaks expressly to both equitable and reasonable use of the watercourse and safeguarding water quality. This agreement also creates a bilateral commission, CARU, to implement these standards on a continuing basis. Do you agree with the court that only procedural obligations were breached by Uruguay?

2.   Codifications of International Shared Watercourses Law

Receiving its impetus from a number of serious river disputes that arose after 1945, such as those between India and Pakistan over the Indus and between Egypt and Sudan over the Nile, the International Law Association, after many years of study and debate, published the first international attempt to codify the principles relating to the law of shared watercourses. These are the *Helsinki Rules on the Uses of the Waters of International Rivers*, adopted by the International Law Association on 20 August 1966. 52 *Report of the Annual Conference of the International Law Association* 484 (1967). This document, known as the *Helsinki Rules*, is reprinted in the **Document Supplement**. On August 21, 2004, the

International Law Association, meeting in Berlin, approved an updated and expanded version of the Helsinki Rules, the *Berlin Rules on Water Resources* as a summary of current customary international law rules. The Berlin Rules, 2004 are reprinted in the **Document Supplement**. Both of these documents are non-binding expressions of international shared watercourse rules of law.

In 1970, following publication of the Helsinki Rules, the General Assembly of the United Nations[7] requested the International Law Commission to take up the study of non-navigational uses of international watercourses with a view of the progressive development of international law. In response, the ILC produced Draft Articles on Non-Navigational Uses of International Watercourses, 1994, and reported to the General Assembly. A Working Group on Water of the U.N. General Assembly convened beginning in 1996, and on 27 May 1997, the General Assembly formally approved a *Convention on the Law of the Non-Navigational Uses of International Watercourses*, U.N. Doc. A/RES/51/869, reprinted in 36 I.L.M. 700 (1997). (This Draft Convention is reprinted in the **Document Supplement**). At this writing the 1997 UN Watercourses Convention has been ratified or approved by 31 parties; it will come into force upon ratification or acceptance of 35 parties. The UN Watercourses Convention is expected to enter into force shortly, becoming binding treaty law for a significant number of states.

Meanwhile, the U.N. Economic Commission for Europe (UNECE), taking the Helsinki Rules as a starting point, undertook to draft a regional water convention. This was promulgated at Helsinki on 17 March 1992, as the *Convention on the Protection and Use of Transboundary Watercourses and International Lakes* (1992). (This Convention is reprinted in the **Document Supplement**). The UNECE Watercourses Convention is now in force for 51 mainly European parties. In 2003 the UNECE adopted an amendment to allow accession of this Convention by all United Nations members; and this amendment entered into force on 6 February 2013, turning the Convention into a global legal framework for transboundary water cooperation. (See the UNECE website, http://www.unece.org/env/water/).

Thus, on a global basis, there are four principal authoritative codifications of the international law relating to water resources: two international watercourses conventions and the non-binding Helsinki Rules (1966) and the Berlin Rules (2004): These documents, while differing in some details, are largely similar; the Conventions reflect and are based on international customary law. The two Conventions are designed to be fully compatible and mutually complementary. (*See* UNECE, *The Global Opening of the 1992 UNECE Water Convention 9* (2013)). Many states are, in fact, parties to both Conventions. The Berlin Rules, which are an update of the Helsinki Rules, are designed to be fully compatible with the Conventions, but to go beyond them to restate customary law rules.

These codifications are designed to function as frameworks of principles and guides to parties in drafting and applying bilateral and regional watercourse conventions that address issues and problems particular to local situations. The purpose of the Conventions is to strengthen transboundary water cooperation and to encourage measures for the ecologically sound management and protection of

---

[7] U.N. GAOR, 25th Sess., Supp. No. 8, U.N. Doc. A/8028 (1970).

shared water resources. As framework documents, the Conventions do not replace bilateral and multilateral water agreements for specific basins; instead, they are designed to foster their establishment and implementation.

The need for the application of these legal principles is demonstrable. Currently human consumption appropriates 54% of the world's accessible freshwater runoff. Increases of accessible water supplies are unlikely to keep up with population growth and per capita water availability is predicted to shrink in the future.[8] Water shortages already affect over 2 billion people in some 40 countries. Water security is reaching the top of the international agenda. The environmental situation is also dire: freshwater ecosystems are the most threatened of the world's biomes; some one-fifth of freshwater fish species are in decline.[9]

Although some 450 international agreements exist concerning watercourses and freshwater resources, functioning cooperative management regimes for shared watercourses exist for only about 40% of the world's international watercourses. Even in existing agreement regimes there are gaps and deficiencies:

- Some agreements are only bilateral although third states are part of the watercourse in question.

- Many agreements are too rigid and do not take into account longer term conditions and climate change.

- Some focus on certain issues and neglect other pressing problems. For example, Colombia and Venezuela share the Orinoco basin and have established cooperation on some issues, but there is no agreement covering hydropower development and water diversions from major tributaries.

- Some agreements ignore less powerful stakeholders. For example, the Fly and Sepik basins are shared by Papua New Guinea and Indonesia but delicate ecosystems are not covered and indigenous communities are not included in watercourse management.

- Some agreements have created fixed arrangements that may become outmoded. For example the 1944 United States Mexico water treaty specifies a-fixed partition of the waters involved, (we take this question up infra).

- Some agreements do not cover tributaries of major rivers.

- Many treaties neglect emergency conditions and harmful conditions such matters as flooding.

- In some instances international watercourses are managed essentially unilaterally and the states involved fail to cooperate effectively.

In many cases issues arising from shared watercourses create conflict and endanger regional peace and security. In this section we look at common issues that arise in connection with shared watercourses. We consider the application of the rules of the codifications and their potential to ameliorate these issues and

---

[8] World Wildlife Fund, *Everything You Need to Know About the UN Watercourses Convention* 5 (2010).

[9] *Id.*

problems. Consider the following *Problem* in connection with the application of the international rules of law.

PROBLEM 6-1
TURKEY, SYRIA, AND IRAQ SPAR OVER THE TIGRIS AND EUPHRATES RIVERS

The Tigris and Euphrates Rivers, the cradle of the ancient civilizations of Mesopotamia, constitute one of the great river systems of southwest Asia. The two rivers have their sources in eastern Turkey within 80 kilometers of one another. Both rivers then flow southeast into Syria (where the Tigris forms part of the Turkish-Syrian border) and on into Iraq, where they join at Al Qurnah to form the Shatt al-Arab, which flows into the Persian Gulf. The waters of the two rivers and their tributaries are essential to the prosperity and culture of the northeastern area of Syria known as Jazira, which is dependent on these waters, particularly for agriculture. The two rivers are also essential for the agricultural and industrial development of Iraq and for essential water supplies for cities and towns.

Turkey has embarked on a massive development scheme for the upper basin of the two rivers in order to aid its growing economy. Turkey is developing what is known as GAP in Turkish, the Southeast Anatolia Development Project, the construction of 21 dams and 19 hydroelectric plants on both rivers. The GAP, when fully operational will irrigate 1.65 million hectares of land and generate 1.65 billion KWh annually with an installed capacity of 7,500 MW. But when completed, the GAP will significantly reduce the downstream flows of the two rivers into Syria and Iraq.

Both Syria and Iraq have protested the construction of the GAP, which Turkey has unilaterally decided and is implementing. Envoys from the three countries have met frequently but have been unable to agree to resolve the issues involved. Turkey is willing only to guarantee Syria and Iraq small quantities of minimum flows in the two rivers, which Syria and Iraq regard as totally unacceptable. Relations between Syria and Iraq have also become strained, as Syria wants to implement its own development project, GOLD (General Organization for Land Development) that will greatly reduce the remaining flow of the Euphrates into Iraq.

Syria and Iraq, but not Turkey, are parties to the UN Watercourses Convention.

Consider and discuss the following questions after consulting the relevant provisions of the international instruments that codify international watercourses law.

1. What is the scope of application of the Berlin Rules (Art. 1); how does this compare with the scope of application of the two conventions? Note also the requirements in the Berlin Rules to give the public access to information (Art. 18); to provide education (Art. 19) and the obligation to protect and to compensate "particular communities" (Arts. 20–21). How would these rules apply to the Problem?

2. The Berlin Rules require participation by stakeholders on two levels: first participation by "persons likely to be affected" (Art. 4) and second by all basin states (Art. 10). Do the conventions require these two levels of participation?

3. The Berlin Rules require both "conjunctive" and "integrated" management. (Arts. 5 and 6). What do these terms mean? Are these requirements found in the conventions?

4. The Berlin Rules require that waters be managed "sustainably." What is the meaning of this term? Is this a feature of the conventions as well?

5. The Berlin Rules contain many obligations relating to protection of the environment, control of pollution and minimization of environmental harm. (Arts. 8, 22–28). Note that this protection extends to a duty to preserve minimum streamflows to preserve ecological integrity. (Art. 24). Is this found in either of the conventions?

6. The Berlin Rules require the avoidance of transboundary harm (Art. 16) as well as an environmental assessment process (Arts. 29–31). Are these requirements in the conventions?

7. The Berlin Rules contain many provisions relating to the obligation of basin states to cooperate, notify, consult, inform, warn, and jointly manage.

(Arts. 11, 56–67). To what extent are these obligations echoed in the conventions?

8. The Berlin Rules contain rules on state responsibility and access to remedies and to the courts. (Arts. 68–71). Are these obligations in the conventions?

9. The Berlin Rules contain obligations the parties must fulfill in extreme situations (accidents and floods and droughts) and in situations of armed conflict. (Arts. 32–35; 50–55). Are these in the conventions?

10. The Berlin Rules cover navigation (Arts. 43–49) and address groundwater (Arts. 36–42). Note that the conventions do not address navigation and that they include groundwater but have no provisions specifically relating to groundwater. In fact, the 1997 UN Watercourses Convention leaves confined groundwater out of its scope altogether.

11. Compare the dispute settlement provisions of the Berlin Rules (Arts. 72–73) and the conventions.

12. The Berlin Rules encourage the establishment of basin wide joint management institutions and arrangements. (Arts. 64–65). Are these obligations also in the conventions?

13. *Rules for the allocation of water resources.* Perhaps the most important provisions of the international instruments codifying the rules applicable to freshwaters are those dealing with the allocation of waters between basin states and among various users. Consider the various concepts expressed:

Berlin Rules. In these rules water must be allocated (Art. 12)—

- In an equitable and reasonable manner
- Without doing significant harm
- In order to attain optimal and sustainable use

Article 13 to 16 further defines these concepts, and Article 17 creates a right of access to water.

UNECE Watercourses Convention (1992) requires the parties (Art. 2)—

- To ensure the use of waters with the aim of ecologically sound and rational water management;
- To ensure that waters are used in a reasonable and equitable way;
- Taking into account possible transboundary impact.

UN Watercourses Convention (1997) requires—

- Utilization in an equitable and reasonable manner (Art. 5 and 6)
- In such a way as not to cause significant harm (Art. 7).

Thus, the key legal concepts with regard to allocating waters of shared watercourses under international law are, on the one hand, the rule of equitable and reasonable utilization; and, on the other hand, the obligation to avoid significant harm. All three formulations contain these concepts, although the 1997 UN Watercourses Convention seems to subordinate the no harm rule to the rule of equitable and reasonable utilization (*see* Art. 7(2)).

What do these rules mean? Clearly the application of these rules is a case-by-case judgment on the basis of the particular situation at hand. The Berlin Rules and the 1997 UN Watercourses Convention list particular factors that go into determining what is an equitable and reasonable use.

For an example of the considerations that go into deciding a water allocation case, consider the following decisions of the Supreme Court of the United States.

COLORADO v. NEW MEXICO ("VERMEJO I")
On exceptions to Report of Special Master 459 U.S. 176 (1982)

JUSTICE MARSHALL delivered the opinion of the Court.

This case concerns the proper apportionment between New Mexico and Colorado of the water of an interstate river. The water of the Vermejo River is at present fully appropriated by users in New Mexico. Colorado seeks to divert water for future uses. Invoking this Court's original jurisdiction under Art. III, 2 of the Constitution, Colorado brought this action far an equitable apportionment of the water of the Vermejo River. A Special Master appointed by the Court recommended that Colorado be permitted a diversion of 4,000 acre-feet per year. The case is before us on New Mexico's exceptions to the Special Master's report. [459 U.S. 176, 178]

I

The Vermejo River is a small, nonnavigable river that originates in the snow belt of the Rocky Mountains in southern Colorado and flows southeasterly into New Mexico for a distance of roughly 55 miles before it joins the Canadian River. The major portion of the river is located in New Mexico. The Colorado portion consists of three main tributaries that combine to form the Vermejo River proper approximately one mile below the Colorado-New Mexico border. At present there are no uses of the water of the Vermejo River in Colorado, and no use or diversion has ever been made in Colorado. In New Mexico, by contrast, farmers and industrial users have diverted water from the Vermejo for many years. In 1941 a New Mexico state court issued a decree apportioning the water of the Vermejo River among the various New Mexico users.

In 1975, a Colorado corporation, Colorado Fuel and Iron Steel Corp. (C. F. & I.), obtained in Colorado state court a conditional right to divert 75 cubic feet per second from the headwaters of the Vermejo River. C.F.&1. proposed a transmountain diversion of the water to a tributary of the Purgatoire River in Colorado to be used for industrial development and other purposes. Upon learning of this decree, the four principal New Mexico users — Phelps Dodge Corp. (Phelps Dodge), Kaiser Steel Corp. (Kaiser Steel), Vermejo Park Corp. (Vermejo Park), and the Vermejo Conservancy District (Conservancy District) — filed suit in the United States District Court for the District of New Mexico, seeking to enjoin any diversion by C. F. & I. that would violate their senior rights. On January 16, 1978, the District Court enjoined C. F. & I. from diverting any water from the Vermejo River in derogation of the senior water rights of New Mexico [459 U.S.176, 176] users. The court found that under the doctrine of prior appropriation, which both New Mexico and Colorado recognize, the New Mexico users were entitled to have their needs fully satisfied because their appropriation was prior in time. C. F. & I. filed a notice of appeal, and the Court of Appeals for the Tenth Circuit has stayed its proceedings during the pendency of this case before us.

In June 1978 Colorado moved for leave to file an original complaint in this Court. New Mexico opposed the motion. On April 16, 1979, we granted Colorado's motion and appointed [459 U.S. 176, 180] the Honorable Ewing T. Kerr, Senior Judge of the United States District Court for the District of Wyoming, as Special Master in this case. 441 U.S. 902. After a lengthy trial involving an extensive presentation of evidence, the Special Master submitted a report to the Court on January 9, 1982. The report was accepted for filing on February 22, 1982. 455 U.S 932.

The Special Master found that most of the water of the Vermejo River is consumed by the New Mexico users and that very little, if any, reaches the confluence with the Canadian River. He thus recognized that strict application of the rule of priority would not permit Colorado any diversion since the entire available supply is needed to satisfy the demands of appropriators in New Mexico with senior rights. Nevertheless, applying the principle of equitable apportionment established in our prior cases, he recommended permitting Colorado a transmountain diversion of 4,000 acre-feet of water per year from the headwaters of the Vermejo River. He stated:

"It is the opinion of the Master that a transmountain diversion would not materially affect the appropriations granted by New Mexico for users downstream. A thorough examination of the existing economies in New Mexico convinces the Master that the injury to New Mexico, if any, will be more than offset by the benefit to Colorado." Report of Special Master 23.

Explaining his conclusion, the Special Master noted that any injury to New Mexico would be restricted to the Conservancy District, the user in New Mexico furthest downstream, since there was sufficient water in the Vermejo River for the three other principal New Mexico water users, Vermejo Park, Kaiser Steel, and Phelps Dodge. He further found that the "Vermejo Conservancy District has never been an economically feasible operation." Ibid.

The Special Master's recommendation appears to rest on two alternative grounds: first, that New Mexico could compensate for some or all the Colorado diversion through reasonable water conservation measures; and second, that the injury, if any, to New Mexico would be outweighed by the benefit to Colorado from the diversion. In its various exceptions to his report, New Mexico challenges the Special Master's interpretation of the law of equitable apportionment. New Mexico maintains that the rule of priority should be strictly applied in this case to preclude Colorado from diverting any water from the Vermejo River. New Mexico also challenges the factual bases of the Special Master's conclusions that the recommended diversion would not materially affect New Mexico users and that any harm to New Mexico would be offset by the benefits to Colorado.

We conclude that the criteria relied upon by the Special Master comport with the doctrine of equitable apportionment as it has evolved in our prior cases. We thus reject New Mexico's contention that the Special Master was required to focus exclusively on the rule of priority. However, the report of the Special Master does not contain sufficient factual findings to enable us to assess the correctness of the Special Master's application of the principle of equitable apportionment to the facts of this case. We therefore remand with instructions to the Special Master to make further findings of fact.

II

Equitable apportionment is the doctrine of federal common law that governs disputes between States concerning their rights to use the water of an interstate stream. Kansas v. Colorado, 206 U.S. 46, 98 (1907); Connecticut v. Massachusetts, 282 U.S. 660, 670–671 (1931). It is a flexible doctrine which calls for "the exercise of an informed judgment on a consideration of many factors" to secure a "just and equitable" allocation. Nebraska v. Wyoming, 325 U.S. 589, 6, 8 (1945). We have stressed that in arriving at "the delicate adjustment of interests which must be made," ibid., we must consider all relevant factors, including:

"physical and climatic conditions, the consumptive use of water in the several sections of the river, the character and rate of return flows, the extent of established uses, the availability of storage water, the practical effect of wasteful uses on downstream areas, [and] the damage to upstream areas as compared to the benefits to downstream areas if a limitation is imposed on the former." Ibid.

Our aim is always to secure a just and equitable apportionment "without quibbling over formulas." New Jersey v. New York, 283 U.S. 336, 343 (1931). The laws of the contending States concerning intrastate water disputes are an important consideration governing equitable apportionment. When, as in this case, both States recognize the doctrine of prior appropriation, priority becomes the "guiding principle" in an allocation between competing States. Nebraska v. Wyoming, supra, at 618. But state law is not controlling. Rather, the just apportionment of interstate waters is a question of federal law that depends "upon a consideration of the pertinent laws of the contending States and all other relevant facts." Connecticut v. Massachusetts, supra, at 670–671.

In reaching his recommendation the Special Master did not focus exclusively on the rule of priority, but considered other factors such as the efficiency of current uses in New Mexico and the balance of benefits to Colorado and harm to New Mexico. New Mexico contends that it is improper to consider these other factors. It maintains that this Court has strictly applied the rule of priority when apportioning water between States adhering to the prior appropriation doctrine, and has departed from that rule only to protect an existing economy built upon junior appropriations. Since there is no existing economy in Colorado dependent upon the use of water from the Vermejo River, New Mexico contends that the rule of priority is controlling. We disagree with this inflexible interpretation of the doctrine of equitable apportionment.

Our prior cases clearly establish that equitable apportionment will protect only those rights to water that are "reasonably required and applied." Wyoming v.

Colorado, 259 U.S. 419, 484 (1922). Especially in those Western States where water is scarce, "[there] must be no waste . . . of the 'treasure' of a river . . . . Only diligence and good faith will keep the privilege alive." Washington v. Oregon, 297 U.S. 517, 527 (1936). Thus, wasteful or inefficient uses will not be protected. See Nebraska v. Wyoming, supra, at 618. Similarly, concededly senior water rights will be deemed forfeited or substantially diminished where the rights have not been exercised or asserted with reasonable diligence. Washington v. Oregon, supra, at 527–528; Colorado v. Kansas, 320 U.S. 383, 394 (1943).

We have invoked equitable apportionment not only to require the reasonably efficient use of water, but also to impose on States an affirmative duty to take reasonable steps to conserve and augment the water supply of an interstate stream. In *Wyoming v. Colorado*, Wyoming brought suit to prevent a proposed diversion by Colorado from the Laramie River. This Court calculated the dependable supply available to both States, subtracted the senior Wyoming uses, and permitted Colorado to divert an amount not exceeding the balance. In calculating the dependable supply we placed on each State the duty to employ "financially and physically feasible" measures "adapted to conserving and equalizing the natural flow." 259 U.S., at 484. Adopting a position similar to New Mexico's in this case, Wyoming objected to a requirement that it employ conservation measures to facilitate Colorado's proposed uses. The answer we gave is especially relevant to this case:

"The question here is not what one State should do for the other, but how each should exercise her relative rights in the waters of this interstate stream . . . . Both States recognize that conservation within practicable limits is essential in order that needless waste may be prevented and the largest feasible use may be secured. This comports with the all-pervading spirit of the doctrine of appropriation and takes appropriate heed of the natural necessities out of which it arose. We think that doctrine lays on each of these States a duty to exercise her right reasonably and in a manner calculated to conserve the common supply." Ibid.

We conclude that it is entirely appropriate to consider the extent to which reasonable conservation measures by New Mexico might offset the proposed Colorado diversion and thereby minimize any injury to New Mexico users. Similarly, it is appropriate to consider whether Colorado has undertaken reasonable steps to minimize the amount of diversion that will be required.

In addition, we have held that in an equitable apportionment of interstate waters it is proper to weigh the harms and benefits to competing States. In Kansas v. Colorado, where we first announced the doctrine of equitable apportionment, we found that users in Kansas were injured by Colorado's upstream diversions from the Arkansas River. 206 U.S., at 113–114, 117. Yet we declined to grant any relief to Kansas on the ground that the great benefit to Colorado outweighed the detriment to Kansas. Id., at 100–101, 113–114, 117. Similarly, in Nebraska v. Wyoming, we held that water rights in Wyoming and Nebraska, which under state law were senior, had to yield to the "countervailing equities" of an established economy in Colorado even though it was based on junior appropriations. 325 U.S., at 622. We noted that the rule of priority should not be strictly applied where it "would work more hardship" on the junior user "than it would bestow benefits" on the senior user. Id., at 619. See also Washington v. Oregon, supra, at 522. The same principle is applicable in balancing the benefits of a diversion for proposed uses against the possible harms to existing uses. See, e.g., Wyoming v. Colorado, *supra* (placing upon Wyoming, the State with senior water rights, a duty to conserve water in order to facilitate a diversion for a proposed use in Colorado); Connecticut v. Massachusetts; 282 U.S. 660 (1931); New Jersey v. New York, 283 U.S. 336 (1931).

We recognize that the equities supporting the protection of existing economies will usually be compelling. The harm that may result from disrupting established uses is typically certain and immediate, whereas the potential benefits from a proposed diversion may be speculative and remote. Under some circumstances, however, the countervailing equities supporting a diversion for future use in one State may justify the detriment to existing users in another State. This may be the case, for example, where the State seeking a diversion demonstrates by clear and convincing evidence that the benefits of the diversion substantially outweigh the harm that might result. In the determination of whether the State proposing the diversion has carried this burden, an important consideration is whether the existing users could offset the diversion by reasonable conservation measures to prevent waste. This approach comports with our emphasis on flexibility in equitable apportionment and also accords sufficient protection to existing uses.

We conclude, therefore, that in the determination of an equitable apportionment of the water of the Vermejo River the rule of priority is not the sole criterion. While the equities supporting the protection of established, senior uses are substantial, it is also appropriate to consider additional factors relevant to a just apportionment, such as the conservation measures available to both States and the balance of harm and benefit that might result from the diversion sought by Colorado.

III

Applying the doctrine of equitable apportionment, the Special Master recommended that Colorado be permitted to divert 4,000 acre-feet of water per year from the headwaters of the Vermejo River. Because all of the water of the Vermejo River is currently consumed by New Mexico appropriators, the recommended diversion would necessarily reduce the amount of water available to New Mexico.

In explaining the basis for his recommendation, the Special Master stated that the diversion would not "materially affect" existing New Mexico appropriations. This conclusion appears to reflect certain assumptions about the ability of New Mexico users to implement water conservation measures. The Special Master also concluded that any injury to New Mexico would be "more than offset" by the benefits to Colorado. Report of Special Master 23. Both the availability of conservation measures and a weighing of the harm and benefits that would result from the diversion are factors relevant to the determination of a just and equitable apportionment. However, the Special Master did not clearly state the factual findings supporting his reliance on these factors. Accordingly, we remand for additional factual findings. In particular, we request specific findings concerning the following areas:

(1) the existing uses of water from the Vermejo River; and the extent to which

present levels of use reflect current or historical water shortages or the failure of existing users to develop their uses diligently;

(2) the available supply of water from the Vermejo River, accounting for factors such as variations in streamflow, the needs of current users for a continuous supply, the possibilities of equalizing and enhancing the water supply through water storage and conservation, and the availability of substitute sources of water to relieve the demand for water from the Vermejo River;

(3) the extent to which reasonable conservation measures in both States might eliminate waste and inefficiency in the use of water from the Vermejo River;

(4) the precise nature of the proposed interim and ultimate use in Colorado of water from the Vermejo River, and the benefits that would result from a diversion to Colorado;

(5) the injury, if any; that New Mexico would likely suffer as a result of any such diversion, taking into account the extent to which reasonable conservation measures could offset the diversion.

IV

The flexible doctrine of equitable apportionment dearly extends to a State's claim to divert water for future uses. Whether such a diversion should be permitted will turn on an examination of all factors relevant to a just apportionment. It is proper, therefore, to consider factors such as the extent to which reasonable conservation measures by existing users can offset the reduction in supply due to diversion, and whether the benefits to the State seeking the diversion substantially outweigh the harm to existing uses in another State. We remand for specific factual findings relevant to determining a just and equitable apportionment of the water of the Vermejo River between Colorado and New Mexico.

It is so ordered.

COLORADO v. NEW MEXICO ("VERMEJO II")
On exceptions to Report of Special Master 467 U.S. 310 (1984)

JUSTICE O'CONNOR delivered the opinion of the Court.

In this original action, the State of Colorado seeks an equitable apportionment of the waters of the Vermejo River, an interstate river fully appropriated by users in the State of New Mexico. A Special Master, appointed by this Court, initially recommended that Colorado be permitted a diversion of 4,000 acre-feet per year. Last Term, we remanded for additional factual findings on five specific issues. 459 U.S. 176 (1982). The case is before us again on New Mexico's exceptions to these additional findings. We now conclude that Colorado has not demonstrated by clear and convincing evidence that a diversion should be permitted. Accordingly, we sustain New Mexico's exceptions and dismiss the case.

I

The facts of this litigation were set forth in detail in our opinion last Term, see id., at 178–183, and we need recount them here only briefly The Vermejo River is a small, non-navigable stream, originating in the snow belt of the Rocky Mountains. The river flows southeasterly into New Mexico for roughly 55 miles before feeding into the Canadian River. Though it begins in Colorado, the major portion of the Vermejo River is located in New Mexico. Its waters historically have been used exclusively by farm and industrial users in that State.

In 1975, however, a Colorado corporation, Colorado Fuel and Iron Steel Corp. (C. F. & I.), proposed to divert water from the Vermejo River for industrial and other uses in Colorado. As a consequence, several of the major New Mexico users sought and obtained an injunction against the proposed diversion. The State of Colorado, in turn, filed a motion for leave to file an original complaint with this Court, seeking an equitable apportionment of the Vermejo River's waters. We granted Colorado its leave to file, 439 U.S. 975 (1978), and the Court of Appeals for the Tenth Circuit stayed C. F. & I's appeal pending our resolution of the equitable apportionment issue.

We then appointed a Special Master, 441 U.S. 902 (1979), the Honorable Ewing T Kerr, Senior Judge of the United States District Court for the District of Wyoming, who held a lengthy trial at which both States presented extensive evidence. On the basis of this evidence, the Master recommended that Colorado be allowed to divert 4,000 acre-feet of water per year. His recommendation rested on two grounds: first, that New Mexico could compensate for some or all of the Colorado diversion through reasonable water conservation measures; and second, that the injury, if any, to New Mexico would be outweighed by the benefit to Colorado from the diversion.

New Mexico took exceptions, both legal and factual, to the Master's recommendation. As to the Master's view of the law of equitable apportionment, New Mexico contended that the Master erred in not focusing exclusively on the priority of uses along the Vermejo River. 159 U.S. at 181–182. The Court rejected that contention:

"We recognize that the equities supporting the protection of existing economies will usually be compelling . . . . Under some circumstances, however, the countervailing equities supporting a diversion for future use in one State may justify the detriment to existing users in another State. This may be the case, for example, where the State seeking a diversion demonstrates by clear and convincing evidence that the benefits of the diversion substantially outweigh the harm that might result. In the determination of whether the State proposing the diversion has carried this burden, an important consideration is whether the existing users could offset the diversion by reasonable conservation measures. . . ." Id., at 187–188 (footnote omitted).

In short, though the equities presumptively supported protection of the established senior uses, the Court concluded that other factors — such as waste, availability of reasonable [467 U.S. 310, 314] conservation measures, and the balance of benefit and harm from diversion — could be considered in the apportionment calculus. Ibid.

New Mexico also took issue with the factual predicates of the Master's recommendation. Specifically, it contended that Colorado had failed to prove by clear and convincing evidence that New Mexico currently uses more than its equitable share of the Vermejo River's waters. On this matter, we found the Master's report unclear and determined that a remand would be appropriate.

To help this Court assess whether Vermejo River water could reasonably be made available for diversion, the Master was instructed to make specific findings concerning:

"(1) the existing uses of water from the Vermejo River, and the extent to which present levels of use reflect current or historical water shortages or the failure of existing users to develop their uses diligently;

"(2) the available supply of water from the Vermejo River, accounting for factors such as variations in stream flow, the needs of current users for a continuous supply, the possibilities of equalizing and enhancing the water supply through water storage and conservation, and the availability of substitute sources of water to relieve the demand for water from the Vermejo River; [and]

"(3) the extent to which reasonable conservation measures in both States might eliminate waste and inefficiency in the use of water from the Vermejo River[.]"

Then, to assist this Court in balancing the benefit and harm from diversion, the Master was asked to make findings concerning:

"(4) the precise nature of the proposed interim and ultimate use in Colorado of water from the Vermejo River, and the benefits that would result from a diversion to Colorado; [and]

"(5) the injury, if any, that New Mexico would likely suffer as a result of any such diversion, taking into account the extent to which reasonable conservation measures could offset the diversion." Id., at 190 (footnote omitted).

On remand, New Mexico filed a motion to submit new evidence. Colorado opposed the motion and attested that, unless the record were reopened, it did not intend to offer any additional evidence in support of its case. The Special Master denied New Mexico's motion. Then, on the basis of the evidence previously received, he developed additional factual findings and reaffirmed his original recommendation.

II

Last Term, because our initial inquiry turned on the factors relevant to determining a just apportionment, the Court explained in detail the law of equitable apportionment. This Term, because our inquiry turns on the evidentiary material Colorado has offered in support of its complaint, we find it necessary to explain the standard by which we judge proof in actions for equitable apportionment.

The function of any standard of proof is to "instruct the factfinder concerning the degree of confidence our society thinks he should have in the correctness of factual conclusions for a particular type of adjudication." In re Winship, 397 U.S. 358, 370 (1970) (Harlan, J., concurring). By informing the factfinder in this manner, the standard of proof allocates the risk of erroneous judgment between the litigants and indicates the relative importance society attaches to the ultimate decision.

Last Term, the Court made clear that Colorado's proof would be judged by a clear-and-convincing evidence standard. Colorado v. New Mexico, 459 U.S. at 187–188, and n.13. In contrast to the ordinary civil case, which typically is judged by a "preponderance of the evidence" standard, we thought a diversion of interstate water should be allowed only if Colorado could place in the ultimate factfinder an abiding conviction that the truth of its factual contentions are "highly probable." See C. McCormick, Law of Evidence 320, p. 679 (1954). This would be true, of course, only if the material it offered instantly tilted the evidentiary scales in the affirmative when weighed against the evidence New Mexico offered in opposition.

Requiring Colorado to present clear and convincing evidence in support of its proposed diversion is necessary to appropriately balance the unique interests involved in water rights disputes between sovereigns. The standard reflects this Court's long-held view that a proposed diverter should bear most, though not all, of the risks of erroneous decision: "The harm that may result from disrupting established uses is typically certain and immediate, whereas the potential benefits from a proposed diversion may be speculative and remote." Colorado v. New Mexico, 459 U.S., at 187; see also id., at 182, n. 9. In addition, the clear-and-convincing-evidence standard accommodates society's competing interests in increasing the stability of property rights and in putting resources to their most efficient uses: "[T]he rule of priority [will] not be strictly applied where it "would work more hardship' on the junior user 'than it would bestow benefits' on the senior user . . . [though] the equities supporting the protection of existing economies will usually be compelling." Id., at 186–187. In short, Colorado's diversion should and will be allowed only if actual inefficiencies in present uses or future benefits from other uses are highly probable.

III

With these principles in mind, we turn to review the evidence the parties have submitted concerning the proposed diversion. As our opinion noted last Term, New Mexico has met its initial burden of showing "real or substantial injury" because "any diversion by Colorado, unless offset by New Mexico at its own expense, [would] necessarily reduce the amount of water available to New Mexico users." 459 U.S., at 188, n. 13. Accordingly, the burden shifted on remand to Colorado to show, by clear and convincing evidence, that reasonable conservation measures could compensate for some or all of the proposed diversion and that the injury, if any, to New Mexico would be outweighed by the benefits to Colorado from the diversion. Though the Master's findings on these issues deserve respect and a tacit presumption of correctness, the ultimate responsibility for deciding what are correct findings of fact remains with us. See Mississippi v; Arkansas, 415 U.S. 289, 291–292, 294 (1974); C. Wright, A. Miller, & E. Cooper, Federal Practice and Procedure 4054, pp. 196–197 (1978). Upon our independent review of the record, we find that Colorado has failed to meet its burden.

A

To establish whether Colorado's proposed diversion could be offset by eliminating New Mexico's nonuse or inefficiency, we asked the Master to make specific findings concerning existing uses, supplies of water, and reasonable conservation measures available to the two States. After assessing the evidence both States offered about existing uses and available supplies, the Master concluded that "current levels of use primarily reflect failure on the part of existing users to fully develop and put to work available water." Additional Factual Findings 28. Moreover, with respect to reasonable conservation measures available, the Master indicated his belief that more careful water administration in New Mexico would alleviate shortages from unregulated stockponds, fisbponds, and water detention structures, prevent waste from blockage and clogging in canals, and ensure that users fully devote themselves to development of available resources. He further concluded that "the heart of New Mexico's water problem is the Vermejo Conservancy District," id., at 20, which he considered a failed "reclamation project [that had] never lived up to its expectations or even proved to be a successful project, . . . and [that] quite possibly should never have been built." Id., at 8. Though the District was quite arguably in the "middle range in reclamation project efficiencies," id., at 20, the Master was of the opinion "that [the District's] inefficient water use should not be charged to Colorado." Ibid. Furthermore, though Colorado had not submitted evidence or testimony of any conservation measures that C. F. & I. would take, the Master concluded that "it is not for the Master or for New Mexico to say that reasonable attempts to conserve water will not be implemented by Colorado." Id., at 21.

We share the Master's concern that New Mexico may be overstating the amount of harm its users would suffer from a diversion. Water use by appropriators along the Vermejo River has remained relatively stable for the past 30 years, and this historic use falls substantially below the decreed rights of those users. Unreliable supplies satisfactorily explain some of this difference, but New Mexico's attempt to excuse three decades of nonuse in this way is, at the very least, suspect. Nevertheless, whatever the merit of New Mexico's explanation, we cannot agree that Colorado has met its burden of identifying, by clear and convincing evidence, conservation efforts that would preserve any of the Vermejo River water supply.

For example, though Colorado alleged that New Mexico could improve its administration of stockponds, fishponds, and water detention structures, it did not actually point to specific measures New Mexico could take to conserve water. Thus, ultimately all the Master could conclude was that some unspecified "education and/or regulation . . . could not help but be an effort, however small, to conserve the water supply. . . ." Id., at 18. Similarly, though Colorado asserted that more rigorous water administration could eliminate blocked diversion works and ensure more careful development of water supplies, it did not show how this would actually preserve existing supplies. Even if Colorado's generalizations were true, they would prove only that some junior users are diverting water that senior appropriators ultimately could call; they would not prove that water is being wasted or used inefficiently by those actually diverting it. In short, the administrative improvements Colorado suggests are either too general to be meaningful of involve redistribution, as opposed to preservation, of water supplies.

Colorado's attack on current water use in the Vermejo Conservancy District is inadequate for much the same reason. Our cases require only conservation measures that are "financially and physically feasible" and "within practicable limits." See, e. g., Colorado v. New Mexico, 459 U.S., at 192; Wyoming v. Colorado, 259 U.S. 419, 484 (1922). New Mexico submitted substantial evidence that the District is in the middle of reclamation project efficiencies and that the District has taken considerable independent steps including, the construction, at its own expense and on its own initiative, of a closed stockwater delivery system — to improve the efficiency of its future water use. Additional Factual Findings 20. The Master did not find to the contrary; indeed, he commended New Mexico for the substantial efforts it had taken. See ibid. Nevertheless, he accepted Colorado's general assertion that the District was not as efficient as other reclamation projects and concluded that New Mexico's inefficient use should not be charged to Colorado. But Colorado has not identified any "financially and physically feasible" means by which the District can further eliminate or reduce inefficiency and, contrary to the Master's suggestion, we believe that the burden is on Colorado to do so. A State can carry its burden of proof in an equitable apportionment action only with specific evidence about how existing uses might be improved, or with clear evidence that a project is far less efficient than most other projects. Mere assertions about the relative efficiencies of competing projects will not do.

Finally, there is no evidence in the record that "Colorado has undertaken reasonable steps to minimize the amount of the diversion that will be required." Colorado v. New Mexico, supra, at 186. Nine years have passed since C. F. & I. first proposed diverting water from the Vermejo River. Yet Colorado has presented no evidence concerning C. F. & I.'s inability to relieve its needs through substitute sources. Furthermore, there is no evidence that C. F. & I. has settled on a definite or even tentative construction design or plan, or that it has prepared an economic analysis of its proposed diversion. Indeed, C. F. & I. has not even conducted an operational study of the reservoir that Colorado contends will be built in conjunction with the proposed diversion. It may be impracticable to ask the State proposing a diversion to provide unerring proof of future uses and concomitant conservation measures that would be taken. But it would be irresponsible of us to apportion water to uses that have not been, at a minimum, carefully studied and objectively evaluated, not to mention decided upon. Financially and physically feasible conservation efforts include careful study of future, as well as prudent implementation of current, water uses. Colorado has been unwilling to take any concrete steps in this direction.

Society's interest in minimizing erroneous decisions in equitable apportionment cases requires that hard facts, not suppositions or opinions, be the basis for interstate diversions. In contrast to Justice Stevens, we do not believe Colorado has produced sufficient facts to show, by clear and convincing evidence, that reasonable conservation efforts will mitigate sufficiently the injury that New Mexico successfully established last Term that it would suffer were a diversion allowed. No State can use its lax administration to establish its claim to water. But once a State successfully proves that a diversion will cause it injury, the burden shifts to the diverter to show that reasonable conservation measures exist. Colorado has not carried this burden.

B

We also asked the Master to help us balance the benefits and harms that might result from the proposed diversion: The Master found that Colorado's proposed interim use is agricultural in nature and that more permanent applications might include use in coal mines, timbering, power generation, domestic needs, and other industrial operations. The Master admitted that "[t]his area of fact finding [was] one of the most difficult [both] because of the necessarily speculative nature of [the] benefits . . ." and because of Colorado's "natural reluctance to spend large amounts of time and money developing plans, operations, and cost schemes. . . ." Additional Factual Findings 23. Nevertheless, because the diverted water would, at a minimum, alleviate existing water shortages in Colorado, the Master concluded that the evidence showed considerable benefits would accrue from the diversion. Furthermore, the Master concluded that the injury, if any, to New Mexico would be insubstantial, if only because reasonable conservation measures could, in his opinion, offset the entire impact of the diversion. Id., at 24–28.

Again, we find ourselves without adequate evidence to approve Colorado's proposed diversion. Colorado has not committed itself to any long-term use for which future benefits can be studied and predicted. Nor has Colorado specified how long the interim agricultural use might or might not last. All Colorado has established is that a steel corporation wants to take water for some unidentified use in the future.

By contrast, New Mexico has attempted to identify the harms that would result from the proposed diversion. New Mexico commissioned some independent economists to study the economic effects, direct and indirect, that the diversion would have on persons in New Mexico. The study these economists produced was submitted at the original hearing, conducted prior to the remand, as evidence of the injury that would result from the reduction in water supplies. No doubt, this economic analysis involves prediction and forecast. But the analysis is surely no more speculative than the generalizations Colorado has offered as "evidence." New Mexico, at the very least, has taken concrete steps toward addressing the query this Court posed last Term. Colorado has made no similar effort.

Colorado objects that speculation about the benefits of future uses is inevitable and that water will not be put to its best use if the expenditures necessary to development and operation must be made without assurance of future supplies. We agree, of course, that asking for absolute precision in forecasts about the benefits and harms of a diversion would be unrealistic. But we have not asked for such precision. We have only required that a State proposing a diversion conceive and implement some type of long-range planning and analysis of the diversion it proposes. Long-range planning and analysis will, we believe, reduce the uncertainties with which equitable apportionment judgments are made. If New Mexico can develop evidence to prove that its existing economy is efficiently using water, we see no reason why Colorado cannot take similar steps to prove that its future economy could do better.

In the nine years that have passed since C. F. & I. first requested a diversion, neither it nor Colorado has decided upon a permanent use for the diverted water. It therefore is no surprise that Colorado cannot conduct studies or make predictions about the benefits and harms of its proposed diversion. Under the clear-and-convincing-evidence standard, it is Colorado, and not New Mexico, that must bear the risk of error from the inadequacy of the information available.

C

As a final consideration, the Master pointed out that approximately three-fourths of the water in the Vermejo River system is produced in Colorado. He concluded, therefore, that "the equities are with Colorado, which requests only a portion of the water which it produces." Additional Factual Findings 29. Last Term, the Court rejected the notion that the mere fact that the Vermejo River originates in Colorado automatically entitles Colorado to a share of the river's waters. Colorado v. New Mexico, 459 U.S., at 181, n. 8. Both Colorado and New Mexico recognize the doctrine of prior appropriation, id., at 179, and appropriative, as opposed to riparian, rights depend on actual use, not land ownership. See id., at 179, n. 4. It follows, therefore, that the equitable apportionment of appropriated rights should turn on the benefits, harms, and efficiencies of competing uses, and that the source of the Vermejo River's waters should be essentially irrelevant to the adjudication of these sovereigns' competing claims. Id., at 181, n. 8. To the extent the Master continued to think the contrary, he was in error.

IV

We continue to believe that the flexible doctrine of equitable apportionment extends to a State's claim to divert previously appropriated water for future uses. But the State seeking such a diversion bears the burden of proving, by clear and convincing evidence, the existence of certain relevant factors. The complainant must show, for example, the extent to which reasonable conservation measures can adequately compensate for the reduction in supply due to the diversion, and the extent to which the benefits from the diversion will outweigh the harms to existing users. This evidentiary burden cannot be met with generalizations about unidentified conservation measures and unstudied speculation aboutfuture uses. The Special Master struggled, as best he could, to balance the evidentiary requirement against the inherent limitations of proving a beneficial future use. However, we do not find enough evidence to sustain his findings. Until Colorado can generate sufficient evidence to show that circumstances have changed and that a diversion is appropriate, the equities compel the continued protection of the existing users of the Vermejo River's waters.

Accordingly, we sustain the State of New Mexico's exceptions to the Special Master's Report and Additional Factual Findings, and dismiss the case.

It is so ordered.

NOTES AND QUESTIONS

1. *Legal doctrines for the allocation of water rights.* In the United States two basic systems are used for the allocation of water rights under state law. In the Eastern, Southern and Midwestern U.S. states the riparian rights common law

system holds that water is a usufruct (right of use) associated with land ownership, and a landowner riparian to surface waters has a right to make a "reasonable use" of the waters. Under this reasonable use system: (1) water is shared by riparians on an equitable basis; (2) no single user may interfere with the reasonable use of another riparian; and (3) if there are conflicting uses, the utility of the use must outweigh the gravity of the harm.[10] Under this system, if a use is not reasonable, there is no privilege to continue the use. If two uses conflict and it is determined that both are reasonable, a court will determine the practicality of adjusting the quantity of each appropriately. If such an equitable adjustment is not possible, the court will choose priority weighing and balancing factors such as the suitability of the use to the water body; the economic and social value of the use; the harm it causes; its temporal priority; and its potential for coordination with other uses.[11] Some riparian water rights states have instituted permitting based on reasonable use to gain certainty of the amount of water it may use. In Western U.S. states the prior appropriation doctrine governs water rights. Under prior appropriation water rights are acquired by diverting water and applying it for a beneficial purpose. It is important to stress that under the prior appropriation system as well as the riparian system, the use of water involved must be beneficial and reasonable. A distinctive feature of prior appropriation is the rule of priority under which the rights of water users are ranked in terms of their temporal seniority. Note that in contradistinction to the riparian rights system, prior appropriation gives the right-holder a stated quantity of water. In the event of a water shortage, the parties at the bottom of the priority list bear the burden of the shortage. Priority dates and quantity of water rights are typically determined in adjudication, which is a court proceeding that brings all water users from the same watercourse into court together. In the *Vermejo case*, a New Mexico state court adjudicated water rights in 1941, listing the four rights holders. The most junior of these was the Vermejo Conservancy District, a federally funded reclamation district serving over 60 farms with extensive canals and reservoirs. The Conservancy also serves the Maxwell Wildlife Refuge.

2. *International law and the rule of reasonable use.* One-half of the international law rule of equitable and reasonable utilization — the reasonable use rule — is directly derived from the common law riparian system. Stephen McCaffrey, the Reporter who prepared the 1997 UN Watercourses Convention, relied upon the U.S. Supreme Court's decision in *Kansas v. Colorado*[12] to define the criteria for the international law of reasonable use:

> [T]he right to the reasonable and beneficial use of a running stream is common to all the riparian proprietors, and so, each is bound so to use his common right, as not essentially to prevent or interfere with an equally beneficial enjoyment of the common right by all the proprietors. . . . It is only for . . . deprivation of this common benefit, or for an unreasonable and unauthorized use of it, that an action will lie."[13]

---

[10] *See* Restatement (Second) of Torts § 850A (1979).

[11] *Id.*

[12] 206 U.S. 46, 104 (1907).

[13] Stephen C. McCaffrey, The Law of International Watercourses 389 (2d ed. 2007).

The international law rule therefore picks up on the criteria for unreasonableness employed at common law. Examples of unreasonable use might be: sale of water withdrawn outside the basin; pollution; waste; and excessive or inefficient use of water.

3. *The international law rule of equitable and reasonable utilization.* The international law rule combines the term "reasonable" with "equitable." According to McCaffrey, the equitable utilization part of the international law rule is derived from the U.S. Supreme Court's decisions in interstate apportionment cases such as *Vermejo I* and *Vermejo II*. Apportionment is the division of water between states. Equitable apportionment is a principle of equity; it does not mean necessarily an equal division but rather what is equitable under the circumstances. The key idea behind equitable apportionment is that it must not be done unilaterally. Equitable apportionment can only be done through cooperation and good faith negotiations between the states concerned. Thus equitable apportionment is equitable sharing of the benefits of water between basin states.

4. *The application of the international allocation rule.* A true application of the international law rules must take into account the different meanings of reasonable use and equitable utilization. Both concepts must be applied to the case of the Tigris/Euphrates basin problem as well as the "no harm" rule of international law. Note that all three components of the international law rule enjoins the parties to take into account the ecological character of the watercourse involved. Consider the factors enumerated in Article 6 of the UN Watercourses Convention and in Article 13 of the Berlin Rules. How appropriate are these factors to the allocation between Turkey, Iraq, and Syria? If you were a mediator between the parties in this case, what solutions would you suggest?

5. *Consider the Supreme Court's apportionment between New Mexico and Colorado in Vermejo I and II.* The Special Master's decision was based on two factors: first, that New Mexico could compensate for Colorado's diversion through reasonable (and needed) conservation measures; and second, that any injury to New Mexico would be outweighed by the benefit to Colorado. The Special Master therefore was taking into account economic criteria of efficiency and the allocation of water to its highest use value. Should such economic criteria have weight or even decisive weight in international law? Are economic criteria involved in the international instruments we have considered? Should they be?

6. Why precisely did the court majority in *Vermejo II* deny Colorado's requested diversion? If you were mediator in the Tigris/Euphrates case, would you apply the same standard as a matter of international law?

7. In the *Vermejo case*, Colorado wanted to undertake an out-of-basin diversion of water. Did this fact enter into the court's decision?

8. The Berlin Rules, Article 14 contains a "need-based" criterion for international water allocation. Article 17 specifies "rights-based" considerations. Should these criteria be applied in the Tigris/Euphrates allocation?

9. *Environmental flows and protection of the environment.* Study the environmental provisions of the 1997 UN Watercourses Agreement, Articles 20–25. To what extent does the treaty make provision for environmental flows in international watercourses? What are the elements of required environmental amenities?

10. ***Dispute settlement.*** Suppose Turkey were a party to the 1997 UN Watercourses Agreement. What dispute settlement mechanisms would be available to resolve the issues between Turkey, Syria, and Iraq? (*See* Art. 33).

NOTE ON DAMS AND DEVELOPMENT

In the case involving water allocations in the Tigris/Euphrates river basin Turkey's GAP development project involves constructing 21 large dams in the upper basin. For decades, dam construction has been favored by many governments as necessary for water supply, irrigation, navigation, and other developmental goals. However, many people increasingly question whether the economic, social and environmental costs of large dams are worth the benefits. In 1998, the World Bank created a World Commission on Dams (WCD) consisting of independent experts from many countries to conduct a comprehensive review of all large dams financed or supported by international aid and credit agencies with a view to setting international policies with respect to further financing of such projects. The WCD carried out case studies of large dams in five regions of the world; made 17 thematic reviews of social, economic, and environmental impact of large dams; and surveyed 125 dams in 56 countries. Regional consultations were carried out in Africa, the Middle East, East and Southeast Asia, Latin America and South Asia. In addition, 950 submissions from 79 countries and input from 70 nongovernmental organizations were considered. In 2000, the WCD published its final report: Dams and Development: A New Framework for Decision-Making (Earthscan Publication, 2000),   *available*   *at*   http://www.unep.org/dams/WCD/report/ WCD_DAMS%20report.pdf. A summary of the Report is as follows:

WORLD COMMISSION ON DAMS

The World Commission on Dams (WCD) was established by the World Bank and IUCN — The World Conservation Union in May 1998 in response to the growing opposition to large dams. Its mandate was to:

> review the development effectiveness of large dams and assess alternatives for water resources and energy development; and

> develop internationally acceptable criteria, guidelines and standards for the planning, design, appraisal, construction, operation, monitoring and decommissioning of dams.

The 12 Commission members came from a variety of backgrounds, representing a broad spectrum of interests in large dams — including governments and nongovernmental organisations (NGOs), dam operators and grass roots people's movements, corporations and academics, industry associations and consultants.

The WCD relied on extensive public consultation and commissioned a large volume of research. An associated Forum with 68 members from 36 countries representing a cross-section of interests, views and institutions was consulted during the Commission's work. The $10 million necessary to fund the Commission came from more than 50 governments, international agencies, private corporations (including many of the main dam industry multinationals), private charitable foundations and NGOs.

To conduct the most comprehensive and independent review of the world's dams to date, and base its conclusions on a solid foundation, the WCD commissioned and assessed:

in-depth case studies of eight large dams on five continents, and papers assessing the overall dam-building records of China, India and Russia;

17 thematic reviews on social, environmental, economic and financial issues; alternatives to dams; different planning approaches and environmental impact assessments;

brief reviews of 125 large dams in 56 countries;

four public hearings in different regions; and

950 submissions by interested individuals, groups and institutions.

The Commission's final report, *Dams and Development: A New Framework for Decision-Making*, was released in November 2000.

The WCD found that while "dams have made an important and significant contribution to human development, and benefits derived from them have been considerable . . . in too many cases an unacceptable and often unnecessary price has been paid to secure those benefits, especially in social and environmental terms, by people displaced, by communities downstream, by taxpayers and by the natural environment." Applying a "balance-sheet" approach to assess the costs and benefits of large dams that trades off one group's loss with another's gain is seen as unacceptable, particularly given existing commitments to human rights and sustainable development.

The WCD's final report provides ample evidence that large dams have failed to produce as much electricity, provide as much water, or control as much flood damage as their supporters originally predicted. In addition, these projects regularly suffer major cost overruns and time delays. Furthermore, the report found that:

Large dams have forced 40–80 million people from their homes and lands, with impacts including extreme economic hardship, community disintegration, and an increase in mental and physical health problems. Indigenous, tribal, and peasant communities have suffered disproportionately. People living downstream of dams have also suffered from water-borne diseases and the loss of natural resources upon which their livelihoods depended.

Large dams cause great environmental damage, including the extinction of many fish and other aquatic species, huge losses of forest, wetlands and farmland.

The benefits of large dams have largely gone to the rich while the poor have borne the costs.

The Commission provides a new framework for decision-making on water and energy projects based on recognising the rights of, and assessing the risks to, all stakeholders. Those who would be adversely affected should participate in the planning and decision-making process and have a share in project benefits. The Commission's main recommendations include the following:

> No dam should be built without the "demonstrable acceptance" of the affected people, and without the free, prior and informed consent of affected indigenous and tribal peoples.

> Comprehensive and participatory assessments of people's water and' energy needs, and different options for meeting these needs, should be developed before proceeding with any project.

> Priority should be given to maximising the efficiency of existing water and energy systems before building any new projects.

> Periodic participatory reviews should be done for existing dams to assess such issues as dam safety, and possible decommissioning.

> Mechanisms should be developed to provide reparations, or retroactive compensation, for those who are suffering from existing dams, and to restore damaged ecosystems.

The WCD prepared the first global, independent review of large dams. The process was transparent and participatory, and extensive research was conducted. The WCD found that the economic, social and environmental costs of large dams are high and often outweigh their benefits, and that alternatives for water and energy are available, viable, and often untested. The WCD put forward a series of recommendations that have relevance not just for energy and water planning, but for development planning generally.

As an internationally respected commission, the WCD's findings and recommendations can carry great weight in dam debates worldwide. What the WCD says is matched in importance by who is saying it. The WCD was co-sponsored by the World Bank. The commissioners included the Chief Executive Officer of engineering multinational company ABB and an ex-President of the International Commission on Large Dams (ICOLD), the lead professional association of the global big dam industry. The report was unanimously endorsed by all the Commissioners.

NGOs and people's movements can use the WCD report to stop or modify destructive development projects, to promote alternatives, to encourage greater accountability and performance of development processes, and to push for new models of decision-making around development planning. Some ideas for how you can use the report include:

> Educate affected communities, NGOs and the general public about the WCO's findings and recommendations. Translate materials into local languages. Organise local, regional and national workshops for NGOs, affected communities, academics, students and government representatives to discuss the report.

> Prepare analyses on whether proposed projects comply with WCD recommendations and distribute them to government agencies and funders.

Advocate for WCD recommendations to be incorporated into national laws and policies and pressure government institutions to formally endorse the recommendations.

Push the World Bank, regional development banks, export credit agencies and bilateral aid agencies to adopt WCD recommendations into their policies and follow them in practice.

Use the WCD recommendations to advocate for reparations for communities affected by existing dams.

Organise community-based processes to identify and promote non-dam alternatives for water supply, energy and flood control.

For more information, go to the WCD's website at www.dams.org and International Rivers Network's website at www.irn.org.

The reaction to the WCD Report was mixed. While many countries (i.e., Germany, Sweden, the UK) voiced support, some states totally rejected it (i.e., China and Turkey), while many states voiced mixed reactions (Norway, India, and the United States). *See* http//: http://www.unep.org/dams//.

According to the WCD web site, "The Turkish General Directorate of State Hydraulic Works alleges that the WCD was a conspiracy by the nuclear and thermal power industries. Turkey also refused to allow the WCD to study the huge Attaturk Dam in southeastern Anatolia."

3. The United States-Mexico Water Sharing Agreement

a.   The 1944 Agreement

The border area shared between the United States and Mexico is an arid region that, ironically, is the site of several important river systems. The 1,954 mile-long border runs from the Pacific Ocean overland for 141 miles along the southern border of California, where it reaches the Colorado River. The boundary then turns south and runs down the centerline of the Colorado River for 24 miles. The boundary continues overland 534 miles along the southern boundaries of Arizona and New Mexico until it reaches the Rio Grande between El Paso, Texas and Ciudad Juarez, Chihuahua. The Rio Grande then forms the easternmost 1,255 miles of the border, running south and east to the Gulf of Mexico. As increasing numbers of users on both sides of this border used water from the border rivers and their tributaries, disputes arose over entitlements to the finite water supplies involved.

In 1944, the United States and Mexico entered into the Treaty for the Utilization of the Waters of the Colorado and Tijuana Rivers and of the Rio Grande (reprinted in the **Document Supplement**).[14] This Treaty established water entitlements for both the United States and Mexico and placed the administration

---

[14] Feb. 3, 1944, 59 Stat. 1219.

of the Treaty in the International Boundary and Water Commission (IBWC), a bilateral organization that traces its history back to 1889.[15] This 1944 Treaty is still today the basic document that governs water allocation issues of shared watercourses between the United States and Mexico.

Read the provisions of the 1944 Treaty. What are the powers of the IBWC? (Arts. 2 and 24). Is there any provision in the Treaty for protection of the environment? For settlement of disputes? The Treaty contains extensive provisions regarding the construction of waterworks for water storage, flood control, the generation of hydroelectric power, and other economic purposes.

Should the Treaty be amended to take protection of the environment into account as current customary and conventional law requires?

How is water allocated under the Treaty? *See* Article 4 (Rio Grande and its tributaries); Articles 10, 11, and 15 (Colorado River); and Article 16 (Tijuana River). Article 3 contains priorities between water users; this is a guide to the IBWC if it has to provide for joint use of any of the international waters.

Rio Grande system

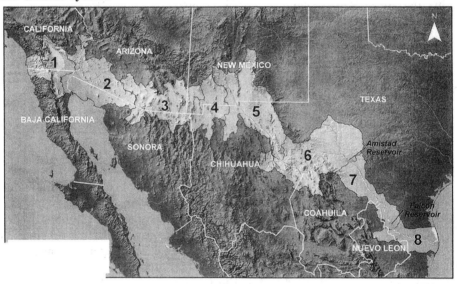

Article 4 of the Treaty allocates to Mexico (1) an amount of water equal to all the waters reaching the main channel of the Rio Grande for the San Juan and Alamo Rivers; (2) two-thirds of the flow reaching the Rio Grande Conchos, San Diego, San Rodrigo, Escondido, and Salado Rivers and the Las Vacas Arroyo, subject to the condition that the remaining one-third shall not be less than an average of 350,000 acre-feet per year; and (3) one-half of all other flows occurring in the main channel of the Rio Grande downstream from Fort Quitman. Under this Article the United States is allocated (1) an amount equal to all the waters reaching the main channel of the Rio Grande from the Pecos and Devils Rivers, Goodenough Spring and

---

[15] *See* http://www.ibwc.org.

Alamito, Terlingua, San Felipe and Pinto Creeks; (2) one third of the flow reaching the main channel of the Rio Grande from the Conchos, San Diego, San Rodrigo, Escondido, and Salado Rivers and Las Vacas Arroyo, which must not be less, as an average amount in cycles of five consecutive years, than 350,000 acre-feet annually; and (3) one-half of all other flows occurring in the main channel of the Rio Grande downstream from Fort Quitman.

Colorado River

Article 10 of the Treaty allocates to Mexico a guaranteed annual quantity of 1,500,000 acre-feet of the waters of the Colorado River, to be delivered according to schedules formulated by Mexico, as well as any other quantities that may arrive at points of diversion in Mexico (but this is capped at 1,700,000 acre-feet per year).

Tijuana River

Article 16 states that Tijuana River system waters shall be allocated on recommendations for an "equitable distribution" by the IBWC; but these recommendations are subject to the approval of the two governments.

Question

Do these allocations meet the legal standard — equitable and reasonable utilization — of the Berlin Rules and the 1997 Convention?

Temporary exceptions

Note that the Treaty allows certain temporary exceptions to the water delivery requirements. If, because of drought or serious accident, Mexico is unable to provide the U.S. with the average annual 350,000 acre-feet it guarantees to the U.S. from Mexican tributaries, it must make up any water debt incurred during the next 5-year cycle. On the other hand, if extraordinary drought or serious accident prevents the U.S. from delivering its guaranteed 1,500,000 acre-feet of Colorado River water to Mexico, the water due to Mexico will be reduced in proportion to the reduction in United States' consumptive uses.

Does this treatment of temporary exemptions meet the international law standards?

The Minute Process

Under Articles 2 and 25 of the Treaty, the IBWC is responsible for the administration of the Treaty, and must record its decisions in the form of "Minutes" written in English and Spanish. Three major crises have arisen. We consider them in turn.

b.   The Salinity Crisis

The 1944 Treaty does not deal with water quality issues. In the 1960s, salinity of the Colorado River became a major problem. The Colorado River is naturally salty and the saline content of the river was increased by saline irrigation return flows in the United States. The salinity concentration was further increased as well when the filling of Lake Powell in Utah caused less water to be released into the Colorado River downstream from Glen Canyon Dam. Out-of-basin transfers and increased municipal and industrial use of water also were responsible for the high saline levels of Colorado River water reaching Mexico. By the 1960s salinity was wreaking havoc for Mexican farmers in the Mexicali Valley as well as for drinking water supplies in Mexico.

After several years of protests and after Mexico threatened to sue the United States in the International Court of Justice, the IBWC went to work on the problem and adopted the following Minute.

PERMANENT AND DEFINITIVE SOLUTION TO THE INTERNATIONAL PROBLEM OF THE SALINITY OF THE COLORADO RIVER (ENGLISH TEXT OF MINUTE 242)
International Boundary and Water Commission United States and Mexico

Mexico, D. F.
August 30, 1973

The Commission met at the Secretariat of Foreign Relations, at Mexico, D.F., at 5:00 p.m. on August 30, 1973, pursuant to the instructions received by the two Commissioners from their respective Governments, in order: to incorporate in a Minute of the Commission the joint recommendations which were made to their respective Presidents by the Special Representative of President Richard Nixon, Ambassador Herbert Brownell, and the Secretary of Foreign Relations of Mexico, Lic. Emilio O. Rabasa for a permanent and definitive solution of the international problem of the salinity of the Colorado River, resulting from the negotiations which they, and their technical and juridical advisers, held in June, July and August of 1973, in compliance with the references to this matter contained in the Joint Communiqué of Presidents Richard Nixon and Luis Echeverría of June 17, 1972.

Accordingly, the Commission submits for the approval of the two Governments the following

RESOLUTION:

1. Referring to the annual volume of Colorado River waters guaranteed to Mexico under the Treaty of 1944, of 1,500,000 acre-feet (1,850,234,000 cubic meters):

   a) The United States shall adopt measures to assure that not earlier than January 1, 1974, and no later than July 1, 1974. the approximately 1,360,000 acre-feet (1,677,545,000 cubic meters) delivered to Mexico upstream of Morelos Dam have an annual average salinity of no more than 115 p.p.m.–30 p.p.m. U.S. count (121 p.p.m.–30 p.p.m. Mexican count) over the annual average salinity of Colorado River waters which arrive at Imperial Dam, with the understanding that any waters that may be delivered to Mexico under the Treaty of 1944 by means of the All American Canal shall be considered as having been delivered upstream of Morelos Dam for the purpose of computing this salinity.

b) The United States will continue to deliver to Mexico on the land boundary at San Luis and in the limitrophe section of the Colorado River downstream from Morelos Dam approximately 140,000 acre-feet (172,689,000 cubic meters) annually with a salinity substantially the same as that of the waters customarily delivered there.

c) Any decrease in deliveries under point l(b) will be made up by an equal increase in deliveries under point 1(a).

d) Any other substantial changes in the aforementioned volumes of water at the stated locations must be agreed to by the Commission.

e) Implementation of the measures referred to in point l(a) above is subject to the requirement in point 10 of the authorization of the necessary works.

2. The life of Minute No. 241 shall be terminated upon approval of the present Minute. From September 1, 1973, until the provisions of point l(a) become effective, the United States shall discharge to the Colorado River downstream from Morelos Dam volumes of drainage waters from the Wellton-Mohawk District at the annual rate of 118,000 acre-feet (145,551,000 cubic meters) and substitute therefor an equal volume of other waters to be discharged to the Colorado River above Morelos Dam; and, pursuant to the decision of President Echeverria expressed in the Joint Communique of June 17, 1972, the United States shall discharge to the Colorado River downstream from Morelos Dam the drainage waters of the Wellton-Mohawk District that do not form a part of the volumes of drainage waters referred to above, with the understanding that this remaining volume will not be replaced by substitution waters. The Commission shall continue to account for the drainage waters discharged below Morelos Dam as part of those described in the provisions of Article 10 of the Water Treaty of February 3, 1944.

3. As a part of the measures referred to in point l(a), the United States shall extend in its territory the concrete-lined Wellton-Mohawk bypass drain from Morelos Dam to the Arizona-Sonora international boundary and operate and maintain the portions of the Wellton-Mohawk bypass drain located in the United States.

4. To complete the drain referred to in point 3, Mexico, through the Commission and at the expense of the United States, shall construct, operate and maintain an extension of the concrete-lined bypass drain from the Arizona-Sonora international boundary to the Santa Clara Slough of a capacity of 353 cubic feet (10 cubic meters) per second. Mexico shall permit the United States to discharge through this drain to the Santa Clara Slough all or a portion of the Wellton-Mohawk drainage waters, the volumes of brine from such desalting operations in the United States as are carried out to implement the Resolution of this Minute, and any other volumes of brine which Mexico may agree to accept. It is understood that no radioactive material or nuclear wastes shall be discharged through this drain, and that the United States shall acquire no right to navigation, servitude or easement by reason of the existence of the drain, nor other

legal rights, except as expressly provided in this point.

5. Pending the conclusion by the Governments of the United States and Mexico of a comprehensive agreement on groundwater in the border areas, each country shall limit pumping of groundwaters in its territory within five miles (eight kilometers) of the Arizona-Sonora boundary near San Luis to 160,000 acre-feet (197,358,000 cubic meters) annually.

6. With the objective of avoiding future problems, the United States and Mexico shall consult with each other prior to undertaking any new development of either the surface or the groundwater resources, or undertaking substantial modifications of present developments, in its own territory in the border area that might adversely affect the other country.

7. The United States will support efforts by Mexico to obtain appropriate financing on favorable terms for the improvement and rehabilitation of the Mexicali Valley. The United States will also provide non-reimbursable assistance on a basis mutually acceptable to both countries exclusively for those aspects of the Mexican rehabilitation program of the Mexicali Valley relating to the salinity problem, including tile drainage. In order to comply with the above-mentioned purposes, both countries will undertake negotiations as soon as possible.

8. The United States and Mexico shall recognize the undertakings and understandings contained in this Resolution as constituting the permanent and definitive solution of the salinity problem referred to in the Joint Communique of President Richard Nixon and President Luis Echeverría dated June 17, 1972.

9. The measures required to implement this Resolution shall be undertaken and completed at the earliest practical date.

10. This Minute is subject to the express approval of both Governments by exchange of Notes. It shall enter into force upon such approval; provided, however, that the provisions which are dependent for their implementation on the construction of works or on other measures which require expenditure of funds by the United States, shall become effective upon the notification by the United States to Mexico of the authorization by the United States Congress of said funds, which will be sought promptly.

Thereupon, the meeting adjourned.

(signed) J. F. Friedkin	(signed) D. Herrera J.
Commissioner of the United States	Commissioner of Mexico
(signed) F. H. Sacksteder, Jr.	(signed) Fernando Rivas S.
Secretary of the United States Section	Secretary of the Mexican section

––––––––

Minute 242 is regarded as a significant accomplishment of cooperative action by the IBWC. *See* Allie Alexis Umoff, *An Analysis of the U.S-Mexico Water Treaty*, 32

U.C. Davis L. Rev. 69, 80 (2008). A U.S. IBWC 2006 Report[16] states that the salinity reductions required by Minute 242 were largely achieved, and the U.S. bore the financial burden of the clean-up and provided financial assistance to Mexico to clean up the Mexicali Valley. However, the U.S. did not assume responsibility for the economic damage to farmers in the Valley.

c.   Mexico's Water Debt

Beginning in 1992, because of years of drought in the Rio Grande Valley, Mexico fell behind in its water delivery obligations under the 1944 Treaty, and by 2002, the Mexican water debt had reached 450 billion gallons[17] of water. As a result, Texas farmers in the lower Rio Grande valley were suffering hardship and the issue erupted as a serious political issue between the two countries.[18] By 1992, the waters of the Rio Grande no longer reached the natural delta of the river flowing into the Gulf of Mexico. Environmental groups said that repayment of Mexico's water debt would help the short-term environmental problem, but they called for a long-term plan to manage the river to take into consideration the needs of the estuary and the river ecosystem. The river's severed connection with the Gulf eliminates the estuary which is essential for the life cycle of many forms of aquatic life and some components of the Gulf of Mexico fishery.[19]

In response to this crisis, the IBWC adopted the following Minute 308 on 28 June 2002.

UNITED STATES ALLOCATION OF RIO GRANDE WATERS DURING THE LAST YEAR OF THE CURRENT CYCLE (ENGLISH TEXT OF MINUTE 308)
International Boundary and Water Commission United States and Mexico

June 28, 2002
Ciudad Juarez, Chihuahua

The Commission met at the offices of the Mexican Section in Ciudad Juarez, Chihuahua at 5:00 pm on June 28, 2002 to consider the Government of Mexico's proposals concerning the United States' allocation of Rio Grande waters during the last year of the present five year cycle in the framework of Paragraph B of Article 4 of the United States Mexico Treaty for Utilization of Waters of the Colorado and Tijuana Rivers and of the Rio Grande, dated February 3, 1944.

The Commissioners made note of the conversations on this matter between United States President George W. Bush and Mexican President Vicente. Fox Quesada in Monterrey, Nuevo Leon on March 20, 2002, to their subsequent conversations and to the June 6, 2002 meeting in Washington of delegations of the

---

[16] IBWC, *Report on Salinity Operations on the Colorado River Under Minute* 242, exhibit 2 (2006).

[17] The annual Mexican obligation is 350,000 acre-feet. An acre-foot is the volume of water that would cover on acre of land to a depth of one foot, or about 326,000 gallons.

[18] *See* Texas House of Representatives, Interim News No. 77-7 (April 30, 2002).

[19] *Id*, at 3–4.

two countries at which the two Commissioners participated.

Based on the above, the Commissioners:

A. Observed that the Mexican allotment to the United States on the Rio Grande during the last year of the current cycle can be made based on the following:

a) The National Water Commission will request of the Secretariat of Foreign Relations that the Mexican Section of the Commission, on the date which the present Minute enters into force and as part of normal joint accounting of the storages of both countries at the international Amistad and Falcon dams, to join the United States Section of the Commission for the Commission to account in favor of the United States the contingency assignment of 90,000 acre-feet — af (111 Million Cubic Meters — Mm^3) subject to the following understandings:

   1. The Commission will continue its weekly preliminary accounting of the inflows, releases and storage at the international dams;

   2. At the accounting period ending October 26, 2002, the Commission will issue a joint report of new Mexican inflows to the international darns recorded since the date of entry into force of this Minute;

   3. If, by October 26, 2002, the new Mexican inflows have replaced the volume of 90,000 af (111 Mm^3) this volume will remain assigned to the United States in the Commission's final accounting and at that time, the losses attributed to conveyance of this volume to the international dams estimated at 28,845 af (35.5 Mm^3) will be accounted in favor of Mexico.

   4. If, by October 26, 2002, the new Mexican inflows have not replaced the volume of 90,000 af (111 Mm^3) the Commission will make a compensating adjustment to Mexico's favor that is equal to the difference between 90,000 af (111 Mm^3) and the quantity of Mexico's inflows.

   5. If, by October 26, 2002 and after making the aforementioned compensating adjustment and providing that Mexico's releases at the Amistad and Falcon Dams from July I to October 26, 2002 were consistent with those of the same timeframe in 2001 and yet the volume of water belonging to Mexico in storage at Amistad and Falcon dams falls below 243,213 af (300 Mm^3), a quantity that the Government of Mexico considers is needed to supply Mexico's Rio Grande communities for the following 10 months, then the Government of the United States authorizes the United States Commissioner to make available to Mexico volumes of water allotted to the United States necessary to maintain the volume of 243,213 af (300 Mm^3) in Mexico's storage, which would be repaid with Mexican source water in excess of the volume of 243,213 af (300 Mm^3).

    b)   The One-Third flows from measured Treaty Tributaries as follows:

        1.   The volume flowing into the Rio Grande between October 1, 2001 and May 31, 2002, was 13,620 af (16.80 Mm^3)

        2.   Based on an estimate by Mexico's National Water Commission of a 90 per cent probability, one-third of the volume flowing into the Rio Grande from the six Mexican tributaries could be at least 12,566 af (15.50 Mm^3) in June 1–30, 2002;

        3.   Based on the referenced probability the one-third volume flowing to the Rio Grande from the six Mexican tributaries could be 8,999 af (11.10 Mm^3) in July 1–31, 2002;

        4.   Similarly, the one-third volume flowing to the Rio Grande from the six Mexican tributaries could be at least 5,918 af (7.30 Mm^3) in August 1–31, 2002; and

        5.   Similarly, also, the one-third volume flowing to the Rio Grande from the six Mexican tributaries could be at least 15,971 af (19.70 Mm^3) in September 1–30, 2002.

B.   The Commissioners observed the information of the Government of Mexico that it intended to finance the modernization and technical enhancement for sustainability in irrigated areas of the Districts and Irrigation Units in the Rio Grande Basin, and to improve the efficiency in water use in the border cities.

C.   The Commissioners noted the information of the Government of Mexico that Mexico proposes a capital investment of $1,535,000,000 pesos in the next four years. In this period, approximately 321,041 af (396 Mm^3) could be conserved in the irrigation districts. The conserved volume could increase by 46,210 af (57.00 Mm^3) with an additional expenditure of $310,000,000 pesos.

D.   The Commissioners also observed the support of both Governments to increasing data exchange relating to the management of hydrological systems in both countries in a timely manner to enable the Commission to adopt principles and understandings under which both Governments provide the highest priority to fulfilling their respective obligations under the 1944 Water Treaty.

E.   The Commissioners also observed that the United States Department of the Treasury and Mexico's Secretariat of Treasury and Public Credit and exchanged letters on this date under which financial measure are proposed to support the water conservation projects, including those tube carried out through the North American Development Bank.

F.   The Commissioners noted the intent of the two Governments of there being review and observation by the Commission of the water conservation projects and provision of its findings to the two Governments and appropriate international funding institutions concerning the estimated volumes of salvaged waters and the measures necessary to ensure their conveyance to the Rio Grande.

G. The Commissioners considered the application of Recommendation 3 of Minute No. 307, dated March 16, 2001 in the following manner:

1. Measures of Cooperation on Drought Management — Mexico's National Water Commission will present to the International Boundary and Water Commission a progress report on its studies concerning drought management planning to support the Commission as a forum under which the proper authorities in each country may coordinate their respective drought management plans.

2. Sustainable Management of the Basin — The Commission took note of the desire of both Governments to convene a bi-national summit meeting of experts and water users from each country for the purpose of providing the proper authorities and stakeholders information concerning sustainable management of the Rio Grande Basin. Taking the recommendations of the summit into account, the two Governments will consider a binational sustainable management plan for the basin.

3. International Advisory Council — The Commission, subject to provision of financial and personnel resources to each Section by the respective governments as a step to strengthen the Commission's role in the area of sustainable management of the basin and drought management planning, will establish a forum for the exchange of information and advice to the Commission from government and non-government organizations in their respective countries.

Based on the foregoing, the Commissioners recommend the following to the two Governments, for their approval:

1. The International Boundary and Water Commission will account in favor of the United States of 90,000 acre feet — af (111 Million Cubic Meters — Mm^3) of waters assigned to Mexico in the international Amistad and Falcon Reservoirs with the understandings in Part A hereinabove.

2. The Government of the United States and the Government of Mexico will urge the appropriate international funding institutions, to which they are a party, to ensure analyses and consideration of the Commission's observations concerning the water conservation projects cited in Parts B–E. The Commission will provide its findings to the two Governments and these institutions, concerning the estimated volumes of conserved waters by these projects and the measures necessary to ensure their conveyance to the Rio Grande.

3. The two Governments will continue discussions through the Commission regarding measures to be taken concerning the deficit in the allocation of water from the Mexican tributaries.

4. The two Governments will support an increase in data exchange relating to the management of the hydrological systems in both countries in a timely manner to enable the Commission to adopt principles and understandings for application in the next cycle under which both Governments will provide the highest priority to fulfilling their respective obligations under the 1944

Water Treaty.

5. The Government of the United States and the Government of Mexico will support the Commission's application of point 3 of Minute 307 of March 16, 2001 outlined in Part G of this Minute with regard to drought management and the sustainable management of this basin.

6. This Minute shall enter into force upon approval of the Government of the United States of America and the Government of United Mexican States.

The meeting was adjourned.

_____
Carlos M. Ramirez
United States Commissioner

_____
Manuel R. Ybarra
United States Section Secretary

J. Arturo Herrera Solis
Mexican Commissioner

José de Jesús Luévano Grano
Mexican Section Secretary

With the assistance of this Minute and Minute 293 of 1995, that authorized Mexico to use some to the waters belonging to the United States stored in two international reservoirs, Mexico was able to eliminate its water debt in 2005. But the larger environmental problems remain. The Rio Grande no longer reaches the Gulf of Mexico on Mexico's eastern border with the U.S.; and the Colorado River no longer reaches its delta and the Gulf of California on the western border. What is to be done? Is the binational sustainable development plan adopted by the IBWC the answer?

d.   Environmental Flows for the Colorado River Delta

Under Article 3 of the Treaty, environmental concerns (which are not even mentioned) come last. Nevertheless, concern about the ecology of the Colorado River delta and low water flows and the impact on the environment have inspired a rethinking of the water shortage problem on the border. The uncertainties associated with climate change are also having an impact. The United States and Mexico are now taking new initiatives with respect to border water problems. The first fruit of this initiative was Minute 319 adopted by the IBWC on November 20, 2012.

Colorado River Basin

**INTERIM INTERNATIONAL COOPERATIVE MEASURES IN
THE COLORADO RIVER BASIN THROUGH 2017 AND
EXTENSION OF MINUTE 318 COOPERATIVE MEASURES
TO ADDRESS THE CONTINUED EFFECTS OF THE APRIL
2010 EARTHQUAKE IN THE MEXICALI VALLEY, BAJA
CALIFORNIA (MINUTE 319)**

International Boundary and Water Commission United States and Mexico

Coronado, California

November 20, 2012

The Commissioners met in the City of Coronado, California on November 20, 2012 at 1:00 p.m., in order to consider interim international joint cooperative measures to address water management in the Colorado River Basin.

I. BACKGROUND

The Commissioners referred to the interest of both countries in identifying cooperative opportunities that would help ensure that the Colorado River system is able to continue to meet the needs of both nations, consistent with the declarations in the August 13, 2007 Joint Statement by officials from both governments, and the Joint Declaration by the United States Secretary of the Interior and Mexico's Ambassador on January 15, 2009, which noted that, based on the principles of mutual respect and bilateral collaboration, the United States and Mexico have sought to address areas of common interest and support the efforts of the Commission to identify innovative opportunities for water conservation and environmental protection.

The Commissioners observed that in this context, in early 2008 the Commission prepared the terms of reference to be applied, established a framework for discussion, and coordinated binational work groups in order to explore opportunities for cooperation on the Colorado River, in furtherance of the provisions of the "United States-Mexico Treaty on Utilization of Waters of the Colorado and Tijuana Rivers and of the Rio Grande," signed February 3, 1944 (hereinafter the 1944 Water Treaty).

The Commissioners also referred to Minute 317, "Conceptual Framework for U.S.-Mexico Discussions on Colorado River Cooperative Actions," dated June 17, 2010, which stipulates that the Commission "shall in particular explore opportunities for binational cooperative projects that: minimize the impacts of potential Colorado River shortage conditions; generate additional volumes of water using new water sources by investing in infrastructure such as desalinization facilities; conserve water through investments in a variety of current and potential uses, including agriculture, among others; and envision the possibility of permitting Mexico to use United States infrastructure to store water."

The Commissioners recognize that various considerations exist in both countries with respect to the implementation of some of the long-term options and activities that have been identified in Minute 317 to address binational cooperative objectives and opportunities. Minute 319 represents a further agreement by the United States and Mexico to work towards addressing these considerations by implementing several of these options and activities in phases.

From the date this Minute enters into force and for an interim period through December 31, 2017 a series of temporary measures will be undertaken, including a pilot program to improve infrastructure and develop projects in Mexico, which will allow both countries to better assess the long-term opportunities and cooperative measures for water conservation, management and development.

The Commissioners referred to the interest stated by the Governments of the United States and Mexico in the preservation of the riparian and estuarine ecology of the Colorado River in its limitrophe section and delta, in accordance with the provisions of Minute 306, "Conceptual Framework for United States-Mexico Studies for Future Recommendations concerning the Riparian and Estuarine Ecology of the Limitrophe Section of the Colorado River and its Associated Delta," dated December 12, 2000.

In addition, activities will be initiated with regard to longer term planning, study, and development of future cooperative actions that could be undertaken, including discussion of potential for deliveries to Mexico of new or non-Colorado River sources that would allow Mexico to utilize additional volumes of such water after the term of this Minute.

The Commissioners further referred to Minute 318, "Adjustment of Delivery Schedules for Water Allotted to Mexico for the Years 2010 through 2013 as a Result of Infrastructure Damage in Irrigation District 014, Rio Colorado, Caused by the April 2010 Earthquake in the Mexicali Valley, Baja California," dated December 17, 2010.

II. PREVIOUS CONSULTATIONS

The Commissioners made note of the consultations held under the framework of the Commission, during which issues of mutual interest were jointly identified, as were the mechanisms for their discussion through binational work groups coordinated by the Commission, which included the participation of a wide range of agencies and organizations at the three levels of government, as well as nongovernmental and research institutions from both countries, who are stakeholders in the matters under discussion. In this context, the Commissioners referred to the binational Consultative Council created under Minute 317, composed of representatives of the Commission, the federal governments and the basin states, to facilitate consideration of the matters associated with these issues and make recommendations to the Commissioners as appropriate; the Commissioners will review the Consultative Council's activities and recommendations.

The Commissioners also noted that the topics covered during the aforementioned binational discussions included aspects such as generating and conserving additional volumes of water, salinity, variable water supplies within the Colorado River Basin, opportunities to establish Intentionally Created Mexican Allocation (ICMA) by means of Mexico deciding to defer delivery of water volumes through adjustments to its annual delivery schedule, the exchange of water, and the delivery of water for the environment; at the same time, several specific binational projects were identified that could be jointly implemented to the benefit of both countries.

III. PROPOSED MEASURES

Both countries have recognized the value of an interim period of cooperation to proactively manage the Colorado River in light of the historical and potential future increased variability due to climate change; therefore, proactive management of the Colorado River will maximize utilization of the resource during variable reservoir conditions, benefiting both countries. The Commissioners made note that based on the consultations undertaken through the binational work groups, it is in the interests of the United States and Mexico to partner in exploring various cooperative measures with regard to the management of the Colorado River system, including allowing for the creation of Intentionally Created Mexican Allocation (ICMA) when Mexico chooses to adjust its delivery schedule, sharing in the benefits of water that may be available temporarily through high elevation reservoir conditions, engaging in cooperative measures to reduce the likelihood of unprecedented drought-related reductions in water deliveries to water users in both countries, and addressing the continuing impacts of the 2010 earthquake in the Mexicali Valley. To further binational cooperation, the countries have identified the following measures to be undertaken during an interim period from the date this Minute enters into force through December 31, 2017. These measures incorporate mechanisms identified on a voluntary basis in consultations within and between both countries to explore cooperative opportunities on the Colorado River.

If by December 31, 2016, the Commission has not completed a comprehensive Minute that extends or replaces the substantive provisions of this Minute through no later than December 31, 2026, the Commissioners shall instruct their respective Principal Engineers to develop recommendations for a potential comprehensive Minute by working with and taking into consideration the advice of the Consultative Council and any other institution that each Commissioner deems necessary, by reviewing the experiences gained through implementation of this Minute and by considering the reports and other documentation that have been prepared.

For purposes of making the determinations under Section III of this Minute, the Commission will request from the United States Bureau of Reclamation (Reclamation) the August 24-Month Study, which will be used for projecting the January 1 elevations of Lake Mead. The Commission will provide the Study to Mexico's National Water Commission through the Mexican Section. The 24-Month Study refers to the operational study conducted each month by Reclamation to project future reservoir operations.

Furthermore, in the event of a mid-year review of Colorado River operations, Reclamation will provide the Commission with updated projections and if increased deliveries' are authorized to water users in the Lower Basin in the United States.: then increased deliveries will be made available to Mexico under the provisions of Section III of this Minute.

The Commissioners made note that based on the consultations undertaken and the progress on each issue and particular project, the following cooperative measures have been identified:

1. EXTENSION OF MINUTE 318 COOPERATIVE MEASURES TO ADDRESS THE CONTINUED EFFECTS OF THE APRIL 2010 EARTHQUAKE IN THE MEXICALI VALLEY, BAJA CALIFORNIA

The Commissioners, in reference to Resolution 10 of Minute 318, recognizing the potential benefits of continuing joint cooperative actions between the two countries, considered the progress achieved to date in the reconstruction of the damaged infrastructure in Mexico. Additionally, they recognized that, as of the date this

Minute is signed, the works contemplated in Minute 318 to repair infrastructure damage in Irrigation District 014, Rio Colorado, caused by the April 2010 earthquake in Mexicali, Baja California, have not been concluded.

Based upon the need to continue these repairs the Commissioners decided:

- To extend through December 31, 2017 the cooperative measures first established in Minute 318;

- That all water that was previously deferred under Minute 318 shall be referred to and accounted for and combined with any amounts deferred under Section III. I; and

- Subject to Section III.4.0 of this Minute, the maximum total amount previously stipulated in Resolution 1 of Minute 318 shall not apply.

Furthermore, the Commissioners decided the following:

- Mexico may utilize water generated under the framework of Minute 318 when Mexico requests it, including to compensate for any reduction in deliveries under Section III.3, and subject to the specific terms contained in the 1944 Water Treaty and this Minute; and

- The 2% assessment that applies to ICMA in the year of its creation will not be applied to those volumes of water deferred due to infrastructure damage in Mexico.

2. DISTRIBUTION OF FLOWS UNDER HIGH ELEVATION RESERVOIR CONDITIONS

The Commissioners considered the appropriateness of coordinating basin operations under high elevation reservoir conditions for an interim period to provide benefits to both nations. This interim cooperative approach will result in deliveries to Mexico of volumes of water in addition to the normal annual delivery of 1,500,000 acre-feet (1,850,234,000 cubic meters) stipulated in Article 10(a) of the 1944 Water Treaty when the basin is in a condition such that Lake Mead elevation is at or above 1,145 feet mean sea level (msl)-and Colorado River mainstream water is available for delivery to water users in the Lower Basin of the United States in conformance with the surplus guidelines applicable to said users that are in effect at the time this Minute enters into force. With this understanding, this interim cooperative approach will be carried out as follows:

a. In years when Lake Mead is projected to be at or above elevations specified in the following table on January 1 of the following year and Mexico has reached at least once a minimum of 80,000 acre-feet (99 million cubic meters [mcm]) of ICMA under this Minute and/or deferred delivery under Section III.I after the date of entry into force of this Minute, Mexico may increase its order for Colorado River system water as follows:

b.

Lake **Mead Elevation**	Mexico Annual **Increase**
At or above 1,145 feet msl and below 1,170 feet msl	40,000 acre-feet (49 mcm)

Lake **Mead Elevation**	Mexico Annual **Increase**
At or above 1,170 feet msl and below 1,200 feet msl	55,000 acre-feet (68 mcm)
At or above 1,200 feet msl and flood control releases are not required	80,000 acre-feet (99 mcm)
When flood control releases are required, regardless of elevation	200,000 acre-feet (247 mcm)

c. For delivery of increased flows at high elevation reservoir conditions, the Mexican Commissioner will provide a timely notification to the United States Commissioner of the schedule for increased releases, indicating the volumes, months, and delivery points in which the delivery of said volumes is desired.

d. The provisions of this Minute will not affect the operation of Article 10(b) of the 1944 Water Treaty, which provides that additional waters of the Colorado River system may be delivered to Mexico up to 200,000 acre-feet (246,697,000 cubic meters) for a total quantity not to exceed 1,700,000 acre-feet (2,096,931,000 cubic meters).

3. DISTRIBUTION OF FLOWS UNDER LOW ELEVATION RESERVOIR CONDITIONS

The Commissioners considered the appropriateness of coordinating basin operations under low elevation reservoir conditions for an interim period to provide benefits to both nations. The United States and Mexico recognize that it is in their mutual interests to mitigate and work preventatively and proactively in a program to address the potential for unprecedented reductions on the Colorado River, which would occur when major Colorado River storage reservoirs reach critical elevations. If these major reservoirs reach critical elevations as a result of prolonged drought conditions in the basin, it may no longer be operationally possible to deliver each country's full amount of Colorado River water, which would result in reductions in Colorado River deliveries that would adversely affect the interests of water users in both countries.

The Commissioners observed that in the framework of this joint cooperative process the information regarding shortage conditions has been exchanged and said conditions have been modeled jointly for the purpose of analyzing rainfall and runoff behavior. The Commissioners also observed that, for an interim period, it is appropriate to use the elevation of Lake Mead as the trigger for potential reductions as part of this program under this Minute that will provide benefits for both countries.

The Commissioners made note that under domestic operational guidelines that are applicable to United States water users in the Lower Basin, the following water delivery reductions are applied: 333,000 acre-feet (411 mcm) when the January 1 Lake Mead elevation is projected to be at or below 1,075 feet msl and at or above 1,050 feet msl; 417,000 acre-feet (514 mcm) when the January 1 Lake Mead elevation is projected to be below 1,050 feet msl and at or above 1,025 feet msl; and

500,000 acre-feet (617 mcm) when the January 1 Lake Mead elevation is projected to be below 1,025 feet msl.

Considering the above, current conditions, projected water availability; potential water shortage in the Colorado River Basin, and the benefits of preventative and proactive management, the Mexican Commissioner stated the willingness of the Government of Mexico to implement the measures that are described below, and the United States Commissioner agreed with such measures, which will operate in the following manner:

a. Water delivery reductions to Mexico: 50,000 acre-feet (62 mcm) when the January I Lake Mead elevation is projected to be at or below 1,075 feet msl and at or above 1,050 feet msl; 70,000 acre-feet (86 mcm) when the January 1 Lake Mead elevation is projected to be below 1,050 feet msl and at or above 1,025 feet msl; and 125,000 acre-feet (154 mcm) when the January 1 Lake Mead elevation is projected to be below 1,025 feet msl.

b. Prior to December 31, 2017, Mexico may adjust its order to include deliveries from ICMA or water deferred under Section III.1 up to a volume to offset the reductions described in Section III.3.a above, not to exceed a total annual delivery to Mexico of 1,500,000 acre-feet (1,850,234,000 cubic meters), on the condition that Mexico has reached at least once a minimum of 80,000 acre-feet (99 mcm) of ICMA under this Minute and/or deferred delivery under Section III.I after the date of entry into force of this Minute.

c. Whenever Lake Mead is below elevation 1,025 feet msl and it is projected to decrease to below 1,000 feet, the United States Section of the Commission shall consult with Reclamation at least annually to consider Colorado River hydrologic conditions, and notify the Commission of the results of said consultations to enable the Commission to discuss further measures that could be undertaken recognizing that reductions in both countries may need to increase when Lake Mead is below elevation 1,025 feet msl.

d. In order for the Government of Mexico to systematically track the basin conditions and prepare in a timely manner for any eventual reductions in its deliveries, the Government of the United States will provide the most current information to Mexico on basin conditions as often as required, including precipitation, streamflow, and water storage conditions in the basin and their historical behavior; the consumptive water uses for the different basin states and the historical trend; and the status of the determination of shortage conditions in the Colorado River Basin within the United States, including, on a monthly basis, the 24-Month Study.

e. In years when Lake Mead is projected to be at or below the elevations identified in Section III.3.a on January 1, the United States will furnish to Mexico, through the Commission, information on the natural causes for the projected reservoir elevation of Lake Mead.

f. Lake Mead reservoir elevations and correlation with drought indicators will 'be monitored and studied during the term of this Minute. Prior to December 31, 2017, the Commissioners shall consider the results of such monitoring and studies, to assess the pertinent future applicability of such information for potential operational agreements.

4. INTENTIONALLY CREATED MEXICAN ALLOCATION (ICMA)

The Commissioners determined that as a cooperative measure to address the growing water demand and potential low elevation reservoir conditions in the basin in the future, a program of Intentionally Created Mexican Allocation (ICMA) will be established. Mexico will be able to create ICMA by deciding to defer delivery of water volumes through adjustments to its annual delivery schedule resulting from water conservation projects or new water sources projects. ICMA would then be available for subsequent delivery. Creation, accumulation and delivery of ICMA will be subject to the following terms:

a. Mexico may use ICMA or water deferred under Section III.1 for any purpose, subject to the specific provisions of this Minute.

b. Mexico may create an annual maximum volume of ICMA of 250,000 acre-feet (308 mcm) through December 31, 2017, by making a downward adjustment to the schedule for the annual delivery to Mexico of its Article 10(a) allotment under the 1944 Water Treaty, in accordance with Section III.4 of this Minute. Any adjustment of deliveries of water deferred under Section III.1 shall count towards the annual maximum 250,000 acre-foot (308 mcm) amount.

c. The maximum volume of ICMA that Mexico may take delivery of in anyone calendar year is 200,000 acre-feet (246,697,000 cubic meters) until all of its available ICMA is used. Any delivery to Mexico of water deferred under Section III.1 shall count towards the 200,000 acre-foot (246,697,000 cubic meters) maximum annual delivery amount established in this Section III.4.c. In any given year, the total annual delivery to Mexico may not exceed 1,700,000 acre-feet (2,096,931,000 cubic meters).

d. When Lake Mead is below elevation 1,025 feet msl, Mexico may not take delivery of ICMA or water deferred under Section III.1.

e. A 3 percent reduction for evaporation shall be applied annually on December 31 to ICMA and water deferred under Section III.1 beginning in the year of creation. This reduction will not be applied in years when Lake Mead elevation is below 1,025 feet msl on January 1.

f. A 2 percent water assessment shall be applied to ICMA in the year of creation and reserved for environmental purposes in Mexico. The 2 percent assessment would not be applied to any water created through the Water for the Environment and ICMA/ICS Exchange Pilot Program described in Section III.6 or to the water deferred under Section III.1. ICS refers to Intentionally Created Surplus applicable in the United States.

g. Notwithstanding the provisions of Section IIL3.b, ICMA or water deferred under Section III.1 will not be delivered to Mexico when doing so would reduce the projected January 1 elevation of Lake Mead triggering the first water delivery reduction level (at or below 1,075 feet msl) or a subsequent water delivery reduction level (below 1,050 or below 1,025 feet msl) as provided in Section III.3.

h. Mexico may create ICMA or water deferred under Section III.I in any year except when flood control releases are being made from Lake Mead.

i. If Mexico decides to create ICMA or water deferred under Section III.1 at or above 1,145 feet msl, increased deliveries to Mexico above 1,500,000 acre-feet (1,850,234,000 cubic meters) that occur when Lake Mead is at or above 1,145 feet msl may not be converted to ICMA or considered water deferred under Section IIU. When Lake Mead is at or above 1,145 feet msl, Mexico will describe the water conservation projects or new water sources that created the ICMA or affirm that the delivery adjustment is related to the continuing impacts of the 2010 earthquake in the Mexicali Valley.

j. During flood control releases, the quantities of ICMA and water deferred under Section III.1 accumulated by Mexico, and the quantity of ICS accumulated by the United States after January I, 2013 in accordance with domestic operational guidelines, will be released proportionally based on volume. Mexico shall decide how to allocate the reduction between its accumulated balances of ICMA and water deferred under Section III. I. This provision will remain in effect after December 31, 2017 until no ICMA and water deferred under Section III.1 remain.

k. The Mexican Commissioner will provide a timely notification to the United States Commissioner of the creation of ICMA or water deferred under Section III.1 by means of a letter indicating the volumes and schedule for the creation of said ICMA or the adjustment in its delivery schedule, including a brief description of the water conservation projects or new water sources or describing that the delivery adjustment is related to the continuing impacts of the 2010 earthquake in the Mexicali Valley. The United States and Mexico will consider operational constraints to ensure that creation of ICMA or water deferred under Section III.1 does not adversely affect U.S. operations.

l. For delivery to Mexico of ICMA or volumes deferred under Section III.1, the Mexican Commissioner will submit a request for the corresponding delivery to the United States Commissioner, indicating the volumes and months in which the delivery of said volumes is required. The United States Commissioner, upon receipt of the request, will review the Colorado River system's status and. approve the order subject to available balances of ICMA or volumes deferred under Section III.I as well as operational issues identified in the review of the Colorado River system's status, taking into consideration the desire of both countries to schedule the delivery of ICMA or volumes deferred under Section III.I in such a fashion so as not to trigger the first water delivery reduction level (at or below 1,075 feet msl) or a subsequent water delivery reduction level (below 1,050 or below 1,025 feet msl) as provided in Section III.3 and to avoid potential adverse effects on United States operations. Reclamation shall forward to the Commission water accounting records that will be used by the Commission to account for the creation, delivery, and resulting balances of water deferred under Section III.1 and ICMA under Section III.4.

m. Beginning on January 1, 2018, Mexico may order delivery of ICMA and water deferred under Section III.1 only when the elevation of Lake Mead is greater than 1,075 feet msl but cannot order delivery of such water when the elevation of Lake Mead is below 1,075 feet msl; delivery of these volumes remains subject to the terms established in Sections III.4.a, c–e, g, j, 1.

n. The water deferred under Section III.1 may be converted to ICMA at Mexico's election and, when that occurs, will be subject to all of the conditions associated with ICMA as described in this Section III.4.

o. Through December 31, 2017, Mexico may accumulate a maximum combined balance of 1,500,000 acre-feet (1,850,234,000 cubic meters) of ICMA and water deferred under Section III.1.

5. SALINITY

In light of the efforts made by both governments to reach an agreement on a permanent and definitive solution to the international problem of the salinity of the Colorado River through Minute 242, "Permanent and Definitive Solution to the International Problem of the Salinity of the Colorado River," dated August 30, 1973, the Commissioners determined that any cooperative arrangement or measure that is implemented under this Minute 319 through December 31, 2017 must comply with the salinity differential between Imperial Dam and the Northerly International Boundary (NIB) as described in Resolution 1.a) of Minute 242.

With respect to the foregoing, the Commissioners observed that the implementation of certain cooperative options, such as the creation of ICMA and water deferred under Section III.1, could impact the salinity of the waters delivered at the Northerly International Boundary, and therefore require the implementation of measures to address said impacts.

In this context, based on the analysis performed by the Binational Work Group established under the Commission framework to assess the issue of salinity, the Commissioners observed the appropriateness of minimizing salinity impacts when creating ICMA and water deferred under Section III.1. To this end, the Governments of the United States and Mexico will operate their systems in order to minimize impacts on salinity due to creation of lCMA and water deferred under Section III.1 as follows:

a. Mexico may use the Wellton-Mohawk bypass drain to convey volumes it considers appropriate. The United States and Mexico will take into account operational constraints to ensure that the water conveyance does not adversely affect United States water operations.

b. During the creation of ICMA and water deferred under Section III.l, the salinity and volumes stipulated in Minute 242 will be complied with at all times, which will proceed under the following terms:

  i. Taking into account the potential impact that the adjustment in the schedule for creating ICMA and water deferred under Section III.1 may have on the salinity differential between Imperial Dam and the NIB described in Resolution 1.a) of Minute 242, the aforementioned salinity differential will be calculated as if the volume of water created as ICMA and water deferred under Section III.1 were delivered from Imperial Dam to the NIB, consistent with the Water Deliveries

Monitoring adopted in the Amended Joint Report of the Principal Engineers associated with Minute 314, "Extension of the Temporary Emergency Delivery of Colorado River Water for Use in Tijuana, Baja California," dated November 14, 2008.

ii. The volumes of water that Mexico conveys to the Wellton-Mohawk bypass drain and/or discharges directly to the channel of the Colorado River downstream from Morelos Dam as a result of the creation of ICMA or deferred delivery under Section III.1 of this Minute, will be added to and accounted for in their quantity and quality with the deliveries at the NIB in order to comply with the volumes and salinity limits stipulated in Minute 242 and the 1944 Water Treaty. To implement what is described in this paragraph, the Principal Engineers, through an exchange of letters, will document the procedure developed by the Binational Salinity Work Group.

c. For purposes of this section, those volumes of water that Mexico expressly requests to be conveyed in accordance with SectionsIII.5.a–b shall be accounted for as part of Mexico's 1944 Water Treaty allotment.

6. WATER FOR THE ENVIRONMENT AND ICMA/ICS EXCHANGE PILOT PROGRAM

The Commissioners considered that to the extent additional water supplies can be identified, it is desirable to have water for environmental purposes flow to the Colorado River limitrophe and delta ecosystem.

The Commissioners referred to Minute 306, which provided a conceptual framework for United States-Mexico studies related to the riparian and estuarine ecology of the Colorado River limitrophe and delta.

The Commissioners also made note of Minute 316, "Utilization of the Wellton-Mohawk Bypass Drain and Necessary Infrastructure in the United States for the Conveyance of Water by Mexico and Non-governmental Organizations of both Countries to the Santa Clara Wetland during the Yuma Desalting Plant Pilot Run," signed April 16, 2010, in which the Governments of the United States and Mexico, together with a binational coalition of non-governmental organizations, previously worked together in the spirit of binational cooperation to make water available for environmental benefits on a temporary basis.

The Commissioners also made note of the Environmental Work Group's efforts to identify water needs for the Colorado River limitrophe and delta. This pilot program will arrange for the means to create 158,088 acre-feet (195 mcm) of water for base flow and pulse flow for the Colorado River limitrophe and its delta by means of the participation of the United States, Mexico, and non-governmental organizations. The Commissioners further acknowledged that there remain important issues to be explored with regard to environmental water needs, including the timing and location of periodic pulse flows and base flows.

Implementation of this Minute will provide a mechanism to deliver both base flow and pulse flow during the period this Minute is in force. For purposes of the pilot program in this Minute, a volume of water will be delivered to the Riparian Corridor in a joint effort between the Government of the United States and the Government of Mexico, with the anticipated participation of a binational coalition of non-governmental organizations. Furthermore, the information developed through implementation of this Minute will be used to inform future decisions regarding binational cooperative efforts to address proactive actions in the Colorado River Delta.

The Commissioners further made note that in the discussions among the binational work groups regarding cooperation on the Colorado River, the opportunity was observed to obtain mutual benefits from joint investments by both countries in binational projects that could generate or conserve volumes of water. Based on the joint investments made, some of the water produced through these projects would be made available for environmental water needs, while other portions would be distributed between the two countries for a defined period of time in the proportion agreed upon through the Commission in this Minute. The Commissioners noted that the implementation of such a program would require the resolution of a series of issues; and that investigation of those issues through a pilot program could yield significant information.

Accordingly, the Commissioners observed that the following shall apply:

    a. During the five-year interim period (2013-2017), a joint-cooperative pilot program will be implemented to evaluate the aspects involved in creating water for the environment and an ICMA to ICS exchange project.

    b. A binational coalition of non-governmental organizations has indicated its willingness to provide water for base flow. This arrangement will be documented in a Joint Report of the Principal Engineers in accordance with the Delivery Plan referred to in this Minute.

    c. As part of this pilot program, resources for a joint investigation of the different aspects of the pilot program should be obtained. The resources for this investigation should be provided by the United States and Mexico. This investigation should:

        i. Evaluate the performance of the pilot program, including:

- its success in creating water for the environment;

- the environmental benefits derived therefrom;

- the accounting for the volumes conserved;

- the operational aspects of creating ICMA and the conversion of ICMA to ICS.

        ii. Explore options for future joint cooperative actions to create water for the environment, capitalizing on the environmental improvements achieved during the five-year period that this Minute is in force.

        iii. Test the mechanisms for the allotment and delivery of water to the Riparian Corridor in the reach between Morelos Dam and the Hardy River confluence.

        iv. Evaluate the ecosystem response, most importantly the hydrological response and, secondarily, the biological response.

The Pilot Project will be implemented as follows:

d. The United States will contribute a total amount of $21 million dollars to Mexico through the Commission for infrastructure and environmental projects in Mexico. The Commission will develop a schedule for contributions to reach this amount. The infrastructure and environmental projects include the following:

   i. water infrastructure, including the Reforma Canal lining and technical improvement projects in Module 18 of Irrigation District 014, Rio Colorado

   ii. environmental enhancement of riparian areas of the Colorado River, including its delta

   iii. other related projects

e. Mexico shall receive all waters derived from this binational pilot project subject to the following agreements for the limited term of this Minute:

   i. The United States and Mexico will implement a binational cooperative pilot program for the duration of this Minute. The binational project will generate environmental flows to benefit the riparian ecosystem and as a part of that effort a pulse flow will be implemented to the Colorado River Delta of approximately 105,392 acre-feet (130 mcm) tentatively during 2014 but no later than 2016. A portion of the funds provided in Section III.6.d above by the United States will provide funding for projects which will generate 50% of this pulse flow. The United States and Mexico shall take all such appropriate actions in their respective territories to ensure that such pulse flow reaches the intended areas of the Colorado River Delta. The sources of water to implement this flow shall be from ICMA created or water deferred under Section III.1.

   ii. To provide for the delivery of the base flow and pulse flow for environmental purposes within Mexico under this Minute, the Commissioners will direct the Consultative Council and the Environmental Work Group to prepare a Delivery Plan, which will include a schedule of monthly flows, delivery points and volumes in an amount of approximately 105,392 acre-feet (130 mcm) for pulse flow and 52,696 acre-feet (65 mcm) for base flow. The Delivery Plan will be submitted to the two Sections of the Commission for review and approval by January 31, 2014. Once approved by the Commission, the Delivery Plan will be implemented, consistent with the 1944 Water Treaty and the provisions of this Minute.

   iii. In consideration for the infrastructure investments referenced in this Section III.6, before December 31, 2017, Mexico shall take all action necessary to provide to the United States a total quantity of 124,000 acre-feet (153 mcm) of water to be converted from ICMA, water deferred under Section III.1, or from any other source for use in the United States.

f. The international accounting for the pulse flow and base flow implemented under this pilot program will be performed by the Commission, taking into consideration the information provided by Reclamation. The Commission, with the advice of the Consultative Council, will present a report to the Governments of the United States and Mexico regarding the delivery of water pursuant to the pilot program and the environmental results achieved by such deliveries.

g. A Joint Report of the Principal Engineers shall be prepared by December 31, 2018 with the results of the investigation referred to in Section III.6.c above, evaluating its success in creating water to be used for environmental and other purposes, the environmental benefits derived therefrom, the accounting for the volumes conserved, and the operational aspects of creating ICMA and the conversion of ICMA to ICS. The aforementioned report will contain the recommendations necessary for similar subsequent programs.

7. INTERNATIONAL PROJECTS

The Commissioners noted that during the talks held within the framework of Minute 317 of the Commission to discuss the opportunities for cooperation on the Colorado River, the opportunity was observed to obtain mutual benefits by undertaking construction of international projects with joint investment by both countries that would allow for water conservation or the generation of new water sources to address the growing water demands in the basin and potential shortage conditions in the basin in the future. In this context, the Commissioners observed the usefulness of immediately pursuing development of the Environmental Restoration Pilot Project at the Miguel Aleman Site. The Commissioners further observed that a number of other opportunities exist for joint cooperative projects benefitting both nations, including but not limited to those set forth below. These additional projects should be pursued concurrently with development and execution of a Minute to extend the substantive provisions of Sections III.1–6 of this Minute 319 through 2026.

The specific binational opportunities that have been identified at this time are as follows:

a. Environmental Restoration Project at the Miguel Aleman Site

In 2013, the Commission will begin implementation of a 50-acre (20-hectare) Environmental Restoration Project, with willows, cottonwoods and mesquites, at the Miguel Aleman site located in Mexico near the Colorado River limitrophe reach across from the Hunter's Hole restoration site in the United States.

The total cost of the Environmental Restoration Project is $700,000 dollars, with contributions from both countries. The distribution of works and costs between the two countries has been discussed and proposed by the Binational Environmental Work Group established under Minute 317, and should be formalized in a Joint Report of the Principal Engineers for implementation of the Project.

To develop the activities for this Environmental Restoration Project, the Commission will rely on contracting and/or consulting by environmental institutions from both countries specializing in the matter.

In addition to implementing this Environmental Restoration Project, the Commission will continue to explore other projects and joint cooperative opportunities for environmental restoration in the Colorado River Delta, considering the "Water Needs in the Colorado River Delta" report prepared by the Binational Environmental Work Group under the framework of Minute 306 and Minute 317 of the Commission.

b. Water Conservation Projects

Study and implementation of these projects will require agreement of the two countries through the Commission, and such agreement should be contained in a specific Minute of the Commission:

i.   Alamo Canal Regulating Reservoir Conservation Pilot Project

ii. Payment for Taking Agricultural Land out of Production (Fallowing)

iii. Modernization and Technical Improvements to Irrigation District 014

c. Project Associated with System Operations

Study and implementation of this project will require agreement of the two countries through the Commission, and such agreement should be contained in a specific Minute of the Commission:

i.   Conveyance of Mexican Water through the All-American Canal (AAC)

This project for consideration of the potential conveyance of Mexican water through the All-American Canal has been identified as a high priority of both the United States and Mexico, and will be the subject of expedited consideration by both countries upon the entry into force of this Minute. The Commissioners took note of the commitment of U.S. entities, led by Reclamation and the United States Section of the Commission, to establish processes and timelines to work through applicable issues that must be addressed for the construction of a connection between the All-American Canal in the United States and Mexico's Colorado River-Tijuana Aqueduct, at Pump Station 0 that, at a minimum, could be used for water deliveries to Mexico in emergency situations.

d. New Water Sources Projects

Study and implementation of these projects will require agreement of the two countries through the Commission, and such agreement should be contained in a specific Minute of the Commission:

i.   Binational Desalination Plant in Rosarito, Baja California

ii.   Beneficial Use of the New River

iii. Binational Desalination Plant near the Gulf of California (Sea of Cortez)

Finally, the Commissioners took note of the commitment of the U.S. institutions to continue the efforts during the term of this Minute for the development of studies, designs, and other analyses for the potential implementation of additional binational infrastructure that could generate significant volumes of water to benefit both countries, including but not limited to those enumerated above.

With regard to the above, the Commissioners observed that the binational work groups discussed the projects listed in the table below, which also presents the estimated volume of water that each project will generate. The current estimated cost for those projects is approximately $1,700 million dollars. There is no obligation for any financial participation by the United States, Mexico, or any other party in these projects. Nonetheless, the Commissioners took note that both governments have stated their firm willingness to continue discussion of potentially allotting resources for the development of projects for the conservation and generation of water for mutual benefit.

PROJECT	ESTIMATED ANNUAL VOLUME in thousand acre-feet (mm)
Miguel Aleman Environmental Restoration	not applicable
Alamo Canal Regulating Reservoir	3.2 (4)
Fallowing Payments	243 (300) one time
Modernization of Irrigation District 014	
First Phase	101 (125)
Subsequent Phases	519(640)
AAC-Pump Station 0 Connection	to be determined
Rosarito Desalination Plant	56 (69)
Use of the New River	38 (47)
Explore Desalination Plant in Gulf of California (Sea of Cortez)	to be determined
TOTALS	717 (885) annually 243 (300) one time

The Commissioners considered that these quantities were based on preliminary estimates by the binational groups or by the responsible institutions in one country and that they could be subject to adjustments once the details of the respective projects are developed.

The Commissioners noted the intention of the Governments of the United States and Mexico to seek agreement on the development of additional bilateral collaborative projects through an additional Minute to be negotiated during the interim five-year period of the joint cooperative pilot program covering the period between 2013 and 2017, and with the same implementation horizon until 2026 that has been indicated for a comprehensive Minute that would extend or replace the substantive provisions of this Minute.

The Commissioners considered appropriate the recommendation of the binational work groups that a portion of the water generated in the potential future binational projects be reserved for environmental purposes and that any beneficiaries of binational projects will assume appropriate responsibility for the necessary actions to comply with the salinity limits of Minute 242.

Based on the above, the Commissioners submit the following resolutions for the approval of both governments:

1. The cooperative measures first established in Minute 318 shall be extended through December 31, 2017 consistent with the provisions of this Minute, including Section III.1.

2. Distribution of flows under high elevation reservoir conditions will be carried out in accordance with the provisions of this Minute, including Section III.2.

3. Distribution of flows under low elevation reservoir conditions will be carried out in accordance with the provisions of this Minute, including Section III.3.

4. Creation and delivery of ICMA and water deferred under Section III.1 will be carried out in accordance with the provisions of this Minute, including Section III.4.

5. Operations addressing salinity regarding creation of ICMA and water deferred under Section III.1 will be carried out in accordance with the provisions of this Minute; including Section III.5.

6. The Water for the Environment and ICMA/ICS Exchange Pilot Program will be carried out in accordance with the provisions of this Minute, including Section III.6.

7. Implementation of International Projects will be carried out in accordance with the provisions of this Minute, including Section m.7.

8. The limitations as to the rates of deliveries specified in Article 15 of the 1944 Water Treaty continue to apply.

9. The United States shall be deemed to have fulfilled its delivery obligations to Mexico under the 1944 Water Treaty for 2013 through 2017, notwithstanding any reduction or adjustment of delivery schedules pursuant to this Minute.

10. The Commission will apply the procedures described in this Minute to implement the above resolutions.

11. The interim measures agreed to in Resolutions 1 to 6 of this Minute will apply through December 31, 2017. However, delivery of any remaining ICMA and/or water deferred under Section III.1 after December 31, 2017 shall be carried out in accordance with the applicable paragraphs in Section III.4.

12. The discussions pursuant to Minute 317 as referenced in Section III.7 of this Minute may consider other joint cooperative actions, taking into consideration potential benefits to both countries.

13. The provisions of this Minute shall not be regarded as a precedent for developing further necessary implementing agreements within the United States, nor for future delivery of Colorado River water allotted to Mexico annually under Article 10 of the 1944 Water Treaty, nor for future salinity management via the mechanism described in Resolution 5 above.

14. The provisions of this Minute do not affect the interpretation or application of the provisions of Article 10(b) of the 1944 Water Treaty, including reduction of water allotted to Mexico under Article 10(a) of said treaty.

15. All activities undertaken pursuant to this Minute shall be subject to the availability of funds, resources, and corresponding personnel, as well as to applicable laws and regulations in each country.

16. This Minute shall enter into force upon notification of approval by the Government of the United States of America and the Government of the United Mexican States through the respective Section of the Commission.

The meeting was adjourned.

Edward Drusina
U.S. Commissioner

erto F. Salmón Ca
ican Commission

José de Jesús Luévano Grano
Mexican Section Secretary

Sally E. Spener

U.S. Section Secretary

———

The purpose of Minute 319 is to share Colorado River shortages and surpluses and to address the needs of the Colorado River delta ecosystem. The Minute creates a pilot program to provide water to be used as environmental flows for the Colorado River delta, which has been dry for decades. Scientists believe that the pulse of water will create 2000 acres of new wetlands and provide the basis for new restoration projects. Is Minute 319 sufficient? The delta has shrunk to one-tenth its original size and receives only 0.1% of the river's water.

e.   Evaluating the 1944 Treaty Regime

With rising border populations, climate change, and new environmental consciousness, many challenges face water management policies on the southern border of the United States. Although the Treaty makes rigid water allocations, the IBWC process builds some flexibility into the administration of the Treaty regime. Ecological and environmental problems have been largely neglected for years, but both parties now have begun to address the long-term problems of this arid region.

B.   Transboundary Groundwater

Groundwater is an important and neglected subject of international environmental law. About 31% of the total freshwater in the world is groundwater, which is found in geological structures known as aquifers. Many of these aquifers have transboundary relationships. An aquifer can be said to be transboundary in scope in four different ways: (1) an aquifer may straddle the border between two or more states; (2) an aquifer located wholly in one state, may depend on a recharge zone located across the border in another state or states; (3) a hydrological relationship may exist between two or more aquifers located in different states; (4) a hydrological relationship may exist between an aquifer located in one state and a surface water body (a river or lake) located in one or more different states.

Despite the known presence of many transboundary aquifers all over the world, principles for transboundary groundwater management have been developed only very recently. In 2010, a UNESCO body, the Internationally Shared Aquifer Resource Management Initiative (ISARM) published a methodological guide outlining best practices.[20] This guidebook advocates a comprehensive approach to transboundary aquifer management and the application of technical and legal tools for the equitable, sustainable, and concerted management of shared groundwater.

Varied principles of law apply to groundwater in places around the world. Often there is little or no correlation between the law of surface waters and the law of groundwaters. Five possible theoretical approaches to groundwater law rules may be identified: (1) a rule of "capture" which gives the right to groundwater to the person who retrieves it; (2) pro-rata allocation (using some economic or equitable criterion) of groundwater among multiple users; (3) allocation attached to overlying property rights; (4) allocation based on prior appropriation; and (5) allocation based on application and permitting by public authorities.

In international law, there is little state practice with respect to groundwater; unilateralism prevails. As a result, customary international law is unsettled. Conventional law is also very sparse. The 1992 UNECE Watercourses Convention and the 1997 UN Watercourses Convention deal with groundwater only marginally. The Berlin Rules (2004) (reprinted in the **Document Supplement**) were the first international instrument to deal at length with shared groundwater issues.

---

[20] Towards the Concerted Management of Transboundary Aquifer Systems (2010), *available at* http://www.isarm.org/dynamics/modules/SFIL0100/view.php?fil_Id=311.

Following the Berlin Rules, the International Law Commission (ILC) promulgated its Draft Articles on Transboundary Aquifers (2008) (reprinted in the **Document Supplement**). In 2012, the UNECE promulgated Model Provisions on Groundwater. Consider these rules, which follow, and compare the provisions of the Berlin Rules and the ILC Draft Articles.

UNITED NATIONS ECONOMIC COMMISSION FOR EUROPE DRAFT MODEL PROVISIONS ON TRANSBOUNDARY AQUIFERS
2012

Provision 1

1. Each Party shall in its utilization of transboundary groundwaters, or while undertaking any activity in the recharge area of transboundary groundwaters, or an activity anyhow affecting transboundary groundwaters, take all appropriate measures to prevent, control and reduce any transboundary impact.

2. The Parties shall use transboundary groundwaters in an equitable and. reasonable manner, taking into account all relevant factors.

Provision 2

1. The Parties shall use [exploit] transboundary groundwaters in a sustainable manner, with a view to maximizing the long-term benefits accruing therefrom and preserving groundwater dependent ecosystems.

2. To that end, the Parties shall take into due account, in using groundwater resources, the amount of groundwater in reserve, as well as the rate of its replenishment making their best efforts to avoid that the reduction of groundwater reaches a critical level.

Provision 3

The Parties shall cooperate on the integrated management of their transboundary groundwaters and surface waters.

Provision 4

1. The Parties shall cooperate in the common identification, delineation and characterization of their transboundary groundwaters. They shall also strive for developing common conceptual models whose level of detail is owed to the complexity of the system and the pressures weighting on it.

2. The Parties shall establish programmes for the joint monitoring and assessment of their transboundary groundwaters. To this end, they shall use common or harmonized standards and methodologies, agree upon assessment criteria and key parameters which shall be regularly moni-

tored, taking into account the specific features of groundwaters, establish a groundwater monitoring network and develop appropriate hydrogeological maps, including aquifer vulnerability maps.

Provision 5

1. The Parties shall take appropriate measures to prevent, control and reduce the pollution of transboundary groundwaters, especially those reserved for drinking water supply. In this context, they shall take a precautionary approach in view of the vulnerability of groundwaters to pollution, particularly in cases of possible uncertainty about the nature and extent of groundwater bodies.

2. Such measures [may][shall] include, *inter alia*, the following:

(a) The establishment of protection zones in particular in the most vulnerable parts/critical parts/points of the recharge area of groundwaters, especially of groundwaters used or intended to be used for the provision of drinking water;

(b) The adoption of measures to prevent or limit the release of pollutants into groundwaters, such as emission limits for discharges from point sources into groundwaters;

(c) The regulation of land uses, including intensive agricultural practices, to combat pollution of groundwater from nitrates and plant protection agents;

(d) The definition of groundwater quality objectives and the adoption of groundwater quality criteria.

Provision 6

1. The Parties shall establish and implement joint or coordinated plans for the proper management of their transboundary groundwaters.

2. Such management plans shall provide, *inter alia*, for:

(a) The allocation of water uses, taking into account all relevant factors, including present and future needs, as well as needs of groundwater dependent ecosystems.

(b) The recording of the volume of water abstractions and the prescription of a requirement of prior authorization for abstraction and artificial recharge.

(c) The prescription of pumping limitations, i.e. in the form of quantification of the aggregate of annual abstraction, and of criteria for the placement of new wells [or intake facilities].

(d) The development of concerted action programmes for preserving and rehabilitating groundwater quality.

Provision 7

The Parties shall establish arrangements for the exchange of information and available data on the condition of transboundary groundwaters, including available data on the parameters prescribed in Provision 4 as well as [information on the grant of rights of use of transboundary waters accorded pursuant to their respective national legislation] [information on the status of use of transboundary groundwaters].

Provision 8

1. All planned activities which are likely to have a significant effect on transboundary groundwaters and, thereby, to have an adverse impact on another Party, shall be subject to an environmental impact assessment procedure. In addition, the Party of origin of the planned activity shall notify the other Party accordingly and, if the latter so wishes, provide the environmental impact assessment documentation and enter into consultations with that Party.

2. The obligations of paragraph 1 shall apply, *inter alia*, in cases of large-scale abstractions of groundwater from the transboundary aquifer or in case of significant artificial groundwater recharge schemes.

3. The Parties shall adopt measures aiming at raising awareness and providing access to information, public participation and access to justice with respect to the conditions of transboundary groundwaters, and the proposed activities of paragraph 1.

Provision 9

In order to implement the objectives and principles of the present Model Provisions and coordinate their cooperation, the Parties shall establish a joint body.

NOTES AND QUESTIONS

1.   The Berlin Rules cover shared aquifers in Articles 36 to 42. The UNECE Model Provisions are very brief but comprehensive. The ILC Draft Articles are quite extensive. The UN General Assembly only "took note" of the ILC Draft Articles (Resolution A/RES/124 of 11 Dec. 2008). All three contain some provisions that are common and very similar. What are these?

2.   What are the standards for maintaining the quality of groundwaters? (*See* UNECE Provision 5). *See also* the Berlin Rules Article 41. *Compare* the ILC Draft Articles, Articles 6 and 10.

3.   How should groundwaters be allocated according to these three sets of rules?

4.   UNECE Provision 9 mandates the establishment of a joint body. Is this a feature of the other international instruments?

5. The ILC Draft Articles stress sovereignty over groundwaters. Is this a feature of the other instruments? Should it be?

PROBLEM 6-2
THE SANTA CRUZ AND THE SAN PEDRO WATERSHEDS
BETWEEN THE UNITED STATES AND MEXICO

The United States and Mexico share groundwater resources along almost the entire length of the almost 2000 mile border. As many as twenty aquifers straddle the border, and many of these serve as the primary source of freshwater for people in the overlying region. Many of the border area's aquifers are threatened with depletion from overuse and deterioration.

On the border between Arizona and Sonora, Mexico, lie two key aquifers, the Santa Cruz and the San Pedro watersheds. Both aquifers communicate with overlying rivers of the same names that form an integral part of the watersheds involved. On this area of the border are two urban areas, Nogales, Sonora and Nogales, Arizona. Both aquifers are crucial for the water needs of these cities and the overlying populations, and both have been depleted by high volume pumping, and their water quality is increasingly threatened by salinity and agricultural and industrial discharges. The United States and Mexico have never penned an agreement concerning transboundary aquifers. Both countries employ a unilateral approach to groundwater exploitation that does not take the needs or use of transborder people into account. The 1944 U.S. Mexico Water Treaty is silent concerning groundwater, and only two Minutes of the IBWC have specifically addressed groundwater problems. Minute 242 of 1973 (reprinted at Section III of this chapter) limited groundwater withdrawals on both sides of the Sonora-Arizona border to specifically enumerated targets because of concern over salinity of the Colorado River. Minute 289 of 1992 expressed concern over the water quality of border groundwaters and referenced the 1992 U.S. Mexico Integrated Border Environmental Plan that calls for water monitoring and the creation of a data base on border surface and groundwater quality.

In Mexico, the regulation of water resources is reserved to the federal government under the Mexican national constitution.[21] The Mexican water authority, Comision Nacional del Agua, known as CONAGUA, subjects all users of surface or groundwater to a permitting process. By contrast, regulation of water in the United States is largely up to the states. Arizona has different regulatory schemes for surface water and groundwater. The Arizona Department of Natural Resources regulates the use of groundwater under the doctrine of "reasonable use." A landowner may pump the water underlying his land for reasonable uses on the overlying land.[22] A use of groundwater on non-overlying land is permitted only where it does not interfere with the water use of another landowner who is using the water on his overlying land.[23] Groundwater withdrawal may also be limited if it diminishes the flow of an associated surface stream. Arizona has also designated

---

[21] Article 27, Political Constitution of the United Mexican States (1917).

[22] Bristor v. Cheatham, 255 P.2d 173 (Ariz. 1953).

[23] Neal v. Hunt, 541 P.2d 559 (Ariz. 1975).

Active Management Areas where special use restrictions apply to preserve a "safe yield" of groundwater for the future.[24]

In 2006, the United States Congress enacted the United States-Mexico Transboundary Aquifer Assessment Act (P.L. No. 109-448, 120 STAT. 3328), which establishes the U.S.-Mexico Transboundary Aquifer Assessment Program (TAAP), a process for cooperation with Mexico's CONAGUA to comprehensively assess the conditions of groundwaters along the U.S.-Mexico border. In the United States the U.S. Geological Survey (USGS) is the lead agency for this work. The objectives and scope of TAAP are as follows:

UNITED STATES-MEXICO TRANBOUNDARY AQUIFER ASSESSMENT ACT
P.L. 109-448, 120 STAT. 3328 (2006)

SEC. 4. ESTABLISHMENT OF PROGRAM.

(a) In General — The Secretary, in consultation and cooperation with the Border States, the water resources research institutes, Sandia National Laboratories, and other appropriate entities in the United States and Mexico, shall carry out the United States-Mexico transboundary aquifer assessment program to characterize, map, and model trans boundary groundwater resources along the United States-Mexico border at a level of detail determined to be appropriate for the particular aquifer.

(b) Objectives — The objectives of the program are to—

(1) develop and implement an integrated scientific approach to assess trans boundary groundwater resources, including—

(A)(i) identifying fresh and saline transboundary aquifers; and

(ii) prioritizing the transboundary aquifers for further analysis by assessing—

(I) the proximity of the transboundary aquifer to areas of high population density;

(II) the extent to which the trans boundary aquifer is used;

(III) the susceptibility of the trans boundary aquifer to contamination; and

(IV) any other relevant criteria;

(B) evaluating all available data and publications as part of the development of study plans for each priority trans boundary aquifer;

---

[24] Arizona Groundwater Management Act, ARIZ. REV. STAT. ANN. §§ 45-401–636.

(C) creating a new, or enhancing an existing, geographic information system database to characterize the spatial and temporal aspects of each priority trans boundary aquifer; and

(D) using field studies, including support for and expansion of ongoing monitoring and metering efforts, to develop—

(i) the additional data necessary to adequately define aquifer characteristics; and

(ii) scientifically sound groundwater flow models to assist with State and local water management and administration, including modeling of relevant groundwater and surface water interactions;

(2) expand existing agreements, as appropriate, between the United States Geological Survey, the Border States, the water resources research institutes, and appropriate authorities in the United States and Mexico, to—

(A) conduct joint scientific investigations;

(B) archive and share relevant data; and

(C) carry out any other activities consistent with the program; and

(3) produce scientific products for each priority transboundary aquifer that—

(A) are capable of being broadly distributed; and

(B) provide the scientific information needed by water managers and natural resource agencies on both sides of the United States-Mexico border to effectively accomplish the missions of the managers and agencies.

(c) Designation of Priority Transboundary Aquifers—

(1) IN GENERAL — For purposes of the program, the Secretary shall designate as priority transboundary aquifers—

(A) the Hueco Bolson and Mesilla aquifers underlying parts of Texas, New Mexico, and Mexico;

(B) the Santa Cruz River Valley aquifers underlying Arizona and Sonora, Mexico; and

(C) the San Pedro aquifers underlying Arizona and Sonora, Mexico.

(2) ADDITIONAL AQUIFERS — The Secretary shall, using the criteria under subsection (b)(1)(A)(ii), evaluate and designate additional priority transboundary aquifers.

(d) Cooperation With Mexico — To ensure a comprehensive assessment of transboundary aquifers, the Secretary shall, to the maximum extent practicable, work with appropriate Federal agencies and other organizations to develop partnerships with, and receive input from, relevant organizations in Mexico to carry out the program.

(e) Grants and Cooperative Agreements — The Secretary may provide grants or enter into cooperative agreements and other agreements with the water resources research institutes and other Border State entities to carry out the program.

SEC. 5. IMPLEMENTATION OF PROGRAM.

(a) Coordination With States, Tribes, and Other Entities — The Secretary shall coordinate the activities carried out under the program with—

(1) the appropriate water resource agencies in the Border States;

(2) any affected Indian tribes; and

(3) any other appropriate entities that are conducting monitoring and metering activity with respect to a priority transboundary aquifer.

NOTES AND QUESTIONS

The Arizona TAAP is being carried out in cooperation with the Water Resources Research Center of the University of Arizona. The IBWC plays a coordinating role in the process. Suppose as a result of the TAAP, the State of Arizona desires to enter into an agreement with Mexico or Nogales regarding groundwater use and quality.

1. Should the U.S. and Mexico enter into a comprehensive groundwater agreement? Is this possible given the institutional asymmetries on both sides? Would the four-border states consent to a U.S.-Mexico Groundwater Agreement? Would such an agreement be constitutional given the fact that the regulation of groundwater in the U.S. is reserved to state law?

2. What if Arizona desires to enter into a groundwater agreement with Mexico. The U.S. Constitution, Art. I, section 10 states that "[n]o state shall enter into any treaty or alliance" and "no state shall, without the consent of Congress, . . . enter into any agreement or compact with another state, or with a foreign power." Would an agreement between Mexico and Arizona pass constitutional muster?

3. Suppose these political and constitutional obstacles could be overcome, which model would you suggest for substantive groundwater regulation: (1) the Bellagio Treaty (reprinted in the **Document Supplement**); (2) the ILC Draft Articles; or (3) the UNECE Principles?

Is the best solution to leave the matter of border groundwater policy to the IBWC? If so, should the IBWC take a comprehensive approach or an aquifer-by-aquifer approach to groundwater policy? Should the 1944 Treaty be amended to cover groundwater? *See* Robert C. Gavrell, *Note, The Elephant Under the Border: An Argument for a New Comprehensive Treaty for the Transboundary Waters and Aquifers of the United States and Mexico*, 16 Colo. J. Int'l Envtl L. & Pol'y 189 (2005).

Section IV.   WATER TRADE AND INTERBASIN WATER TRANSFERS

The world increasingly faces the challenge of how to assure access to water for expanding populations and economic growth while retaining sufficient freshwater *in situ* necessary for the functioning of healthy ecosystems. We think of water as a natural resource and a social good, but water is also a commodity with economic value. This "commoditization" of water has resulted in two spin-off phenomena: (1) globalization, the creation of water markets across national boundaries; and (2) privatization, the transfer of the business of supplying water to the private sector. The commoditization of water and these accompanying effects put increasing pressure on freshwater supplies necessary for ecosystems and the environment. A case in point is the Aral Sea, located in central Asia, which was a vibrant inland sea as recently as the 1960s. Now, due to large scale upstream diversions to irrigate cropland, the Aral Sea has lost its commercial fishery, 20 of 24 native fish species have disappeared, and the Sea is only 40 percent of its original size.

The commoditization, globalization and privatization of water lead ineluctably to calls for interbasin transfers of water: water transfer schemes that convey water out of one freshwater basin to be used in another basin or in a different place altogether. Such large-scale water transfers can fulfill important needs to provide water to shortage areas; globally 1.1 billion people lack access to sufficient freshwater. But water transfers may seriously damage the environment in the donor basin. Often such transfers cost more than they are worth, involve expensive government subsidies, and the benefits to the recipient basin may come at the cost of the donor basin. As a result, state water laws in the United States typically subject interbasin water transfers to permit requirements that very strictly regulate the costs and benefits of such transfers. The U.S. state of Georgia has carefully examined interbasin water transfers and requires the following criteria to be examined before a permit may be issued (Official Code of Georgia 12-5, Article 8):

a. *Donor basin considerations*

   i. *The quantity of the proposed withdrawal and the stream flow of the donor basin, with special consideration for dry years and low flow conditions.*

   ii. *The current and reasonably foreseeable future water needs of the donor basin, with special consideration for dry years and low flow conditions.*

   iii. *Protection of water quality in the donor basin, with special consideration for dry years and low flow conditions.*

   iv. *Any offsetting increases in flow in the donor basin that may be arranged through permit conditions.*

   v. *The number of downstream river miles from which water will be diverted as a result of the transfer.*

   vi. *The connection between surface water and groundwater in the donor basin, and the effect of the proposed transfer on either or both.*

b. *Receiving basin considerations*

      i. *Determination of whether or not the applicant's proposed use is reasonable, including consideration of whether the applicant has implemented water conservation practices and achieved reasonable water conservation goals.*

      ii. *Assessment of the wastewater treatment capacity of the receiving basin.*

      iii. *The supply of water presently available to the receiving basin, as well as the estimates of overall current water demand and the reasonable foreseeable future water needs of the receiving basin.*

      iv. *The beneficial impact of any proposed transfer, and the demonstrated capability of the applicant to effectively implement its responsibilities under the requested permit.*

      v. *The impact of the proposed transfer on water conservation.*

      vi. *The applicant's efforts to explore all reasonable options for use of reclaimed water and recycling of available sources to meet the needs of the receiving basin.*

      vii. *Assessment of the adequacy a/treatment capacity and current water quality conditions.*

  c. *Considerations affecting both basins*

      i. *The economic feasibility, cost effectiveness, and environmental impacts of the proposed transfer in relation to alternative sources of water supply.*

      ii. *The cumulative impacts of the current and proposed interbasin transfers in the basin.*

      iii. *The requirements of the state and federal agencies with authority related to water resources.*

      iv. *The availability of water for responding to emergencies, including drought, in the donor basin and the receiving basin.*

      v. *The impact, whether beneficial or detrimental, on offstream and instream uses.*

      vi. *The quantity, quality, location, and timing of water returned to the basin of donor basin receiving basin, and basins downstream.*

      vii. *Impact on interstate water use.*

      viii. *The cumulative effect on the donor basin and the receiving basin of any water transfer or consumptive use that is authorized or forecasted.*

      ix. *Such other factors as are reasonably necessary to carry out the purposes of Georgia law.*

The application of these criteria would obviously impede interbasin bulk transfers of water, but such transfers are increasing all over the world despite the possible disadvantages involved. Most interbasin water transfers are within a single country and thus do not implicate international law. But international bulk transfers are on the rise and may become commonplace to relieve shortages in arid areas of the world. *See generally*, World Wildlife Fund, *Pipedreams? Interbasin Water Transfers and Water Shortages* (2007); and EDITH BROWN WEISS, THE EVOLUTION OF INTERNATIONAL WATER LAW, Vol. 331 *Recueil des Cours* (New York: Brill, 2009).

On the international law level, bulk transfers of water are not regulated by cost/benefit or environmental criteria such as those in force in Georgia; rather the applicable law is international trade and investment law. First, the international sale of water, whether in bottles, tankers, pipelines or canals, is classed in international law as the sale of a "product," which is subject to the international law regime on the sale of goods in international trade, the General Agreement on Tariffs and Trade (GATT), 1994, which we covered in Chapter 5 of this book. Second, international water services offered by private companies are subject to the international law regime that governs services, the General Agreement on Trade in Services (GATS), which covers virtually all categories of international services. Third, international investments in water projects must be accorded the protections offered by bilateral investment treaties (BITS) and the investment provisions in bilateral and multilateral free trade agreements that we also covered in Chapter 5.

Although these three categories of international economic law apply to international transfers of water, the precise scope of their application is uncertain, because there have not been any definitive rulings by international tribunals or international organizations on these matters. But environmental NGOs fear that the application of international economic criteria to these international water transfers may clash with policies put in place to protect ecosystems and the environment. E.g., PETER H. GLEICK *ET AL*, THE NEW ECONOMY OF WATER (Pacific Institute, 2002).

For example, suppose a nation seeking to protect its freshwater ecosystems and environmental quality, enacts a ban on the export of water in bulk and interbasin water transfers. Such action was taken by the Canadian province of Newfoundland, which passed the Water Resource Protection Act of 1999, which prohibited the export of water subject to certain exceptions, including an environmental assessment that showed that present and future water requirements of communities and other water users would be protected; and that water quality and the water needs of ecosystems would not be compromised. A Newfoundland Ministerial Committee looking into the impact of this law, requested legal opinions regarding the possible application of international trade and investment laws. We reprint one of the legal opinions published by the Ministerial Committee.

EXPORT OF BULK WATER FROM NEWFOUNDLAND AND LABRADOR REPORT OF THE MINISTERIAL COMMITIEE EXAMINING THE EXPORT OF BULK WATER
Government of Newfoundland and Labrador, 2007

Report of the Ministerial Committee Examining the Export of Bulk Water

Following is the text of the July 1, 1999 opinion provided by Gary Horlick of the firm O'Melveny & Myers:

Introduction:

This memorandum provides an initial analysis to the questions presented by the Government of Newfoundland and Labrador on the implications of exporting water from Gisbourne Lake in the Province of Newfoundland in bottles and tankers. The issues raised are the following:

Questions Presented:

1. If the project to export bulk water from Gisbourne Lake is approved by the Newfoundland Province and subsequently a policy change occurs prohibiting such projects in the future, can Canada's trading partners ignore the policy change pursuant to NAFTA (or other trade obligations) and demand similar treatment?

2. If the policy change was effected by a change in provincial legislation, what would be the impact on the province's position with respect to Canada's trade obligations?

Analysis:

Article 309 of NAFTA provides for the treatment of import and export restrictions. It states that "no Party may adopt or maintain any prohibition or restriction on the importation of any good of another Party or on the *exportation or sale for export of any goods* destined for the territory of another Party, except in accordance with Article XI of GATT 1994, including its interpretative notes." Article XI of GATT 1994 states that parties to the Agreement may not place restrictions on export or sale for export of any product with exceptions listed in Article XI:2.[25]

Of the exceptions listed in Article XI:2, the only applicable exception to this case would be paragraph 2 (a), where water would not only have to be classified as an essential product to Canada, but also there would have to be a critical shortage of it to temporarily restrict its export.

Aside from the exceptions of the restriction of exports provided in NAFTA and GATT 1994, the issue of export restrictions can be examined under a different light: the nature of the measure adopting the ban. In this respect, the wording of Article XI:1[26] of GATT 1994 is very comprehensive: it applies to *all measures* instituted or maintained by a contracting Party prohibiting or restricting the importation,

---

[25] Article XI:2 of the GATT: The provisions of paragraph I of this Article shall not extend to the following:

(a) Export prohibitions or restrictions temporarily applied to prevent or relieve critical shortages of foodstuffs or other products essential to the exporting contracting party;

(b) Import and export prohibitions or restrictions necessary to the application of standards or regulations for the classification, grading or marketing of commodities in international trade;

(c) Import restrictions on any agricultural or fisheries product, imported in any form, necessary to the enforcement of governmental measures which operate: (. . .)"

[26] Article XI:I of the GATT, "1. No prohibition or restriction other than duties, taxes or other charges, whether made effective through quotas, imports or export licenses or other measures, shall be instituted or maintained by any contracting party on the importation of any product of the territory of any other

exportation or sale for export of products other than measures that take the form of duties, taxes or other charges. The scope of the term "other measures" that adversely affect exports is defined in part by the TRIMS Agreement, Annex, Illustrative List, in paragraph 2:

"Trade related investment measures that are inconsistent with the obligation of general elimination of quantitative restrictions provided for in Paragraph 1 of Article XI of GATT 1994 include those which are <u>mandatory</u> or <u>enforceable</u> under domestic law or under administrative rulings, or compliance with which is necessary to obtain an advantage, and which restrict . . . the exportation or sale for export by an enterprise of products, whether specified in terms of particular products, in terms of volume or value of products, or in terms of a proportion of volume or value of its local production."

An analysis of this provision combined with the wording of Article XI: 1 of GATT 1994 leads to an understanding that a Government measure that is mandatory and legally binding, *i.e.*, legislation prohibiting the export of bulk water, which avoids or prohibits the exportation or the sale for export of a product falls under the scope of Article XI:1, and is, therefore, a violation of both NAFTA and GATT obligations.

The issue of the reach of the term "other measures" within the meaning of Article XI:1 of GATT 1994 was dealt in a pre-WTO GATT case,[27] where the panel viewed the matter in the following way:

"106. (. . .) In this respect the Panel noted that Article XI:1, unlike other provisions of the General Agreement, did not refer to laws or regulations but more broadly to measures. This wording indicated clearly that any measure instituted or maintained by a contracting party which restricted the exportation or sale for export of products was covered by this provision, irrespective of the legal status of the measure."

The Panel recognized that mandatory and legally binding measures by the Government were included within the meaning of the term "other measures" of Article XI:1. The Panel also recognized that not all non-mandatory measures could be construed as measures within the meaning of Article XI:1. To discern between government measures that are and that aren't included within the meaning of Article XI:1 of GATT 1947, the Panel adopted two criteria that need to be satisfied in order to determine that a Government measure prohibiting the export or sale for export of any destined for the territory of any other contracting party, is, in fact, a violation of Article XI:1. The two criteria are: 1) reasonable grounds to believe that sufficient incentives or disincentives exist for non-mandatory measures to take effect; and 2) the operation of the measures to restrict exports is essentially dependent on government action or intervention.

Even though this panel analysis was made prior to the WTO Agreement and knowing that GATT precedents are not formally binding on WTO cases, the lack of differing subsequent cases and analysis on the subject matter leads us to believe

---

contracting party or on the exportation or sale for export of any product destined for the territory of any other contracting party."

[27] GATT Panel report adopted May, 1988, 35th Supp. BISD 116 (1989), "Japan — Trade in Semiconductors."

that this analysis would be followed if this issue was raised in a WTO resolution panel.

In view of the above, an inference can be made from the provisions in NAFTA and GATT 1994 that if the prohibition of export of bulk water from Gisbourne Lake is undertaken through legislation, then there is a contravention of Article XI:1 and Canada's trading partners have a right to challenge such measure based on the fact that the particular law or policy constitutes a barrier to trade or is inconsistent with the agreement. The one possible "fig leaf" approach would be a prohibitive export tax (100 percent?), since Canada already claims (weakly) that the export tax on softwood lumber is not inconsistent with Article XI.

Further concerns should be taken into consideration if the Province of Newfoundland is to act as a private enterprise in restricting the export of bulk water. With respect to these concerns, please refer to our memorandum of August 6, 1998 which summarizes what should be the nature of the conditions the Province sets on sale for export of bulk water and provides a broad overview of what the possible consequences of past-sale restrictions are, *i.e.*, the Province allows the sale of water for export but conditions it to be bottled only within the Province in order to generate jobs. In the event the Province of Newfoundland, acting as a private enterprise, decided to impose such a post-sale requirement restricting the exports of bulk water, Canada's trading partners would have grounds to challenge, and fair odds of winning, this export restriction as a violation of Article XI of GATT.

Question Presented:

3. If the legislative changes only dealt with environmental concerns, could Canada avoid its trade obligations under NAFTA flowing from the approval of the Gisbourne Lake project?

Analysis:

The NAFTA Agreement is one of the few treaties of its kind to address the issue of environmental implications in trade relations. Nevertheless, no specific provision is provided with respect to environmental protection and the treatment of environmental standards set by federal and sub-federal jurisdictions. In the preamble of the NAFTA, the parties agree to carry out their obligations in a manner consistent with environmental protection and conservation and to strengthen the development and enforcement of environmental laws and regulations but no clear-cut provision is provided with respect to implementation.

Article 104 of NAFTA allows the obligations of the NAFTA countries under three specified environmental agreements to take precedence over NAFTA provisions. These international agreement are:

- Convention on International Trade in Endangered Species of Wild Fauna and Flora, done at Washington, March 3, 1973, as amended June 22, 1979;

- Montreal Protocol on Substances that Deplete the Ozone Layer, done at Montreal, September 16, 1987, as amended June 29, 1990;

- Basel Convention on the Control of Transboundary Movements of Hazardous Waste and Their' Disposal, done as Basel, March 22, 1989, on its entry into force for Canada, Mexico and the United States.

Aside from these agreements, the parties affirm their obligations with respect to each other under GATT.[28]

The broad language of NAFTA's Environmental Cooperation side agreement recognizes in Article 3 the right of each Party to establish its own level of domestic environmental protection, development policies and priorities and to adopt or modify accordingly its environmental laws and regulations. Article 3 reaffirms the notion within the preamble of the side agreement that it is a sovereign right of each State to exploit their own resources pursuant to their own environmental and development policies. Further support to the idea that the adoption of environmental laws and policies is a sovereign right of each Party is found in Chapter 11; Investment, Article 1114 of NAFTA:

NAFTA:

"Nothing in this Chapter shall be construed to prevent a Party from adopting, maintaining or enforcing any measure otherwise consistent with this Chapter that it considers appropriate to ensure that investment activity in its territory is undertaken in a manner sensitive to environmental concerns."

Nonetheless, Article 1 of NAFTA's Environmental Cooperation side agreement sets out the objectives of this agreement by supporting the environmental goals and objectives of NAFTA as long as they do not create trade distortions or new trade barriers. With this in mind, if a Party prohibits the export or sale for export of a good to another Party based on an environmental standard that fails to meet the other Party's environmental standards, a dispute may arise between the Parties. Even though there is nothing in the Agreement that requires countries with a stricter environmental standard to harmonize those standards with more flexible standards of other contracting parties, disputes may arise over whether a specific environmental policy or measure is in fact a disguised trade barrier. In such a case, a dispute resolution panel would be empowered to make a determination that that particular law or policy constitutes a barrier to trade or is inconsistent with the Agreement. It is important to note that the complaining Party would bear the burden of proving that the other Party's environmental measure is inconsistent with NAFTA.

In sum, NAFTA provides contracting parties freedom to strengthen their environmental laws and enforcement efforts as long as legitimate environmental objectives are being pursued. Countries retain their sovereignty over their environmental standards although these standards can be challenged if it restrains the trade in goods, *i.e.*, prohibition of export or sale for export of bulk water, and does not reflect a genuine credible environmental concern. In such a scenario, a dispute resolution panel would be requested by the challenging Party to determine whether that

---

[28] This memorandum does not address any other international environmental agreement which may possibly cover the issue presented.

particular law or policy is based on an authentic environmental concern or if it is a disguised trade barrier that violates the NAFTA Agreement.

Question Presented:

4. If the Gisbourne Lake project is approved, what is the scope of the trade implications and do these implications apply to other Provinces aside from the Province of Newfoundland and Labrador?

Analysis:

In a scenario in which a complete environmental assessment is made and the export of bulk water from the Gisbourne Lake in the Province of Newfoundland is approved, the trade implications are closely tied to the issues, and therefore the responses, presented in the prior questions of this memorandum. The options may vary according to the circumstance and the policy to be adopted by the Province but the general implications are underscored as follows.

The Province of Newfoundland may desire to export bulk water as it pleases without any limitation or prohibition. In case the Province re-evaluates its position and decides to prohibit the export or sale for export of bulk water, it has a greater chance of being successful if: 1) the ban falls within one of the exceptions to export restriction provided for in NAFTA and GATT; or 2) the measure taken is a consequence of the Province acting as a private enterprise; or 3) the ban derives from a valid environmental law restriction. If the circumstance is not one which qualifies for an exception to the restriction on exports provided in NAFTA and GATT, the Province should evaluate the two latter options. Please keep in mind that both measures are subject to challenge by a contracting Party if the ban is viewed as a restriction to the export of bulk water and not as commercial action taken by a private enterprise or a justified environmental concern.

With respect to the issue of whether a precedent is set for the other Provinces in Canada based on the measures taken by the Province of Newfoundland, the NAFTA Agreement does not provide for a distinction in the treatment in the trade of goods between a State and a province or state. Article 301.2 of NAFTA, which addresses the principle of national treatment, uses the term state or province to indicate that such sub-federal units of jurisdiction should provide treatment no less favorable than the most favorable treatment accorded to the entire Party (i.e., nation) of which it is part.

Greater guidance can be found under Article III of GATT 1994; which provides that the contracting Parties recognize that laws, regulations and requirements affecting the internal sale, offering for sale, purchase, transportation, distribution or use of products should not be applied to imported or domestic products to afford protection to domestic production. The note to Article III (ad Article III:1) of the GATT 1994, provides that the application of Article III is subject to the provisions of the final paragraph of Article XXIV, which states that:

"12. Each contracting Party shall take such *reasonable measures* as may be available to it to ensure observance of the provisions of the GATT Agreement by the regional and local governments and authorities within its territory."

From the wording of this provision, one might argue that if reasonable measures are not available to the contracting Party to ensure that the regional and local governments and authorities within its territory observe the provisions of the GATT, then the sub-federal unit's legislation would not be violating Article III of the GATT.

However, a 1992 GATT Panel Report[29] observed in some detail the application and the drafting history of Article XXIV:12 as follows:

". . . this provision was designed to apply only to those measures by regional or local governments or authorities which the central government cannot control because they fall outside its jurisdiction under the constitutional distribution of powers. The Panel agreed with this interpretation in view of the general principle of international treaty law that a party to a treaty may not invoke the provisions of its internal law as justification for its failure to perform a treaty obligation. . . . The above-mentioned interpretation — according to which Article XXIV:12 applies only to measures by regional or local authorities which the central government cannot control under the constitutional distribution of powers — meets the constitutional difficulties which the central governments may have in ensuring the observance of the provisions of the General Agreement by regional and local authorities, but minimizes the risk that such difficulties lead to imbalances in the rights and obligations of contracting parties."

Little is left to conclude from this 1992 GATT Panel Report but that if the Province of Newfoundland legislates restricting exports of bulk water and this legislation is found to be a violation of Article XI of the GATT, then Canada, as the contracting Party to the GATT, will have to take reasonable measures to conform the Province's legislation to the provisions in the GATT unless the power to legislate on such matters falls outside of Canada's jurisdiction under the constitutional distribution of powers.

Further to providing the interpretation of the application of Article XXIV:12 of the GATT, the 1992 GATT Panel Report also observed how different provisions of different states should be treated in face of the national treatment principle.

"The Panel did not consider relevant the fact that many of the state provisions at issue in this dispute provide the same treatment to products of other states of the United States as that provided to foreign products. The national treatment provisions require contracting parties to accord to imported products treatment no less favorable than that accorded to any like domestic product, whatever the domestic origin. Article III consequently requires treatment of imported products no less favorable than that accorded to the most-favored domestic products."

In light of the above and in accordance with the principle of national treatment, if the Province of Newfoundland allows the sale for exports of bulk water, then Canada is responsible for ensuring that no other Province deny the sale for export of bulk water and that no other Province afford treatment less favorable than the

---

[29] GATT Panel Report adopted June 1992, DS23/R(1992), "United States — Measures Affecting Alcoholic and Malt Beverages."

one afforded by the Province of Newfoundland.

NOTES AND QUESTIONS

1. Consider the legal opinion by Gary Horlick and consult the relevant GATT and NAFTA provisions we covered in Chapter 5. Does Mr. Horlick's opinion mean that Newfoundland cannot stop the bulk export of its water? In the same document, Professor Donald McRae states that "Nothing in NAFTA or the WTO requires a state to exploit its natural resources. There is, thus, no obligation on Canada to permit the sale of bulk water. It can do so if it chooses. Since natural resources, including freshwater, fall within provincial jurisdiction, any decision on the sale of bulk water is a matter for each province. However, should a province authorize the sale of bulk water, then the relevant rules of NAFTA and WTO would apply." Does Horlick have a different view?

2. McRae also states: "The second consequence of permitting the sale of bulk water would be that obligations under NAFTA Chapter Eleven relating to foreign investors from the other NAFTA parties would be relevant. This would mean that, in accordance with NAFTA Article 1102, a foreign investor seeking to invest in bulk water sales would be entitled to treatment that is no less favorable than that accorded in like circumstances to domestic investors." Does Horlick agree?

3. Please refer to the NAFTA investment section of this book, Chapter 5. In 1990, a bulk water investor, Sun Belt, Inc., a California company with a Canadian subsidiary, entered into a joint venture with Snowcap Waters Ltd., a Canadian company, to export bulk water from British Columbia to California using tankers. Snowcap had obtained an export license from the provincial government. In 1991, after public protests, the government of British Columbia temporarily suspended the export license, and a moratorium of water export licenses was enacted in 1995. Both Sun Belt and Snowcap brought suit against the province in the Canadian courts, alleging revocation of a valuable contract right. In July, 1996, British Columbia reached a settlement with Snowcap, paying $245,000, but no settlement was offered to Sun Belt, which did not hold any export license. On October 12, 1999, Sun Belt filed a claim and demand for arbitration with UNCITRAL against Canada, invoking its rights under NAFTA Chapter Eleven. Sun Belt claimed damages of $10.6 billion for lost business opportunities due to the export moratorium. Sun Belt claimed that settling with Snowcap and refusing to settle with Sun Belt was discriminatory in violation of NAFTA Article 1102. Sun Belt also claimed violations of NAFTA Articles 1105 and 1110. Apparently Sun Belt never followed up this complaint, however, since the web site of the Canadian government states: 'There is no Chapter Eleven arbitration pending on this matter." *See* http://www.international.gc.ca/trade-agreements-accords-commerciaux/topics-domaines/ (visited 30 October 2013).

If this arbitration had gone ahead, what result?

Chapter 7

PROTECTION OF THE MARINE ENVIRONMENT

The world's oceans comprise about 70% of the surface of planet earth. A report published in the journal Science in 2008,[1] analyzing 17 global data sets of anthropogenic impacts on the world's oceans, found that no area of the oceans is unaffected by human activity and that over 41% of the oceans of the world are "strongly" fouled by pollutants. Only 3.7% of the oceans have small impacts from humans; these areas lie near the North and South Poles. In this chapter we address in comprehensive fashion international law concerning marine pollution, marine living resources, and protection of marine ecosystems. Because international law concerning the protection of the marine environment is part of the larger corpus of the international law of the sea, we first present a "bird's eye view" of the law of the sea as codified in the 1982 United Nations Convention on the Law of the Sea (UNCLOS). The student should read the text of UNCLOS, portions of which are reprinted in the **Document Supplement**.

Section I. THE MARINE ENVIRONMENT AND THE LAW OF THE SEA

A. The UNCLOS "Constitution" for the Law of the Sea

The provisions of UNCLOS are often compared to constitutional provisions for the law of the sea.[2] UNCLOS provides very comprehensive rules on the law of the sea: virtually every aspect of mankind's use and abuse of the world's oceans is addressed to some degree by this Convention. But despite the comprehensive nature of UNCLOS, many of its rules are unclear, ambiguous, and disputed. The full scope of UNCLOS is beyond the scope of this book, but for those who are unacquainted with this Convention, we provide a brief overview of this landmark agreement in order that the body of international law relating to protection of the marine environment may be better understood. The international law relating to protection of the marine environment must be learned in the context of the larger body of law represented by UNCLOS. And UNCLOS itself, as we shall see, addresses to some extent all aspects of protection of the marine environment, although by necessity in such a fashion as to require further agreements on more specific rules of law.[3]

---

[1] Benjamin S. Halpern et al., *A Global Map of Human Impact on Marine Ecosystems*, 319 SCIENCE 948–52 (2008).

[2] Mr. T.B. Koh of Singapore, the President of the Third United Nations Conference on the Law of the Sea first made this comment at the signing ceremony for UNCLOS.

[3] For detailed treatment of the international law of the sea and UNCLOS, see R.R. CHURCHILL & A.V.

UNCLOS, which was concluded at Montego Bay, Jamaica, December 10, 1982, was the culmination of several attempts to codify the international law of the sea in the twentieth century. In the 1930s, the League of Nations convened a conference at the Hague for the purpose of concluding an agreement on the law of the sea, but this conference adjourned without agreement. In the post-World War II period, the first United Nations Conference on the Law of the Sea (1958) concluded four separate treaties: (1) the Convention on the Territorial Sea and the Contiguous Zone; (2) the Convention on the High Seas; (3) the Convention on the Continental Shelf; and (4) the Convention on Fishing and Conservation of the Living Resources of the High Seas. A second United Nations Conference on the Law of the Sea in 1960, was unsuccessful. A third United Nations Conference on the Law of the Sea was convened by the General Assembly of the United Nations in 1973, which produced UNCLOS, the Montego Bay Treaty. On November 16, 1994, the UNCLOS formally entered into force. At this writing 161 states and the European Union are parties to UNCLOS. The United States is the only significant country that is not a party to this important Convention.

UNCLOS reversed centuries of customary law of freedom of the seas by extending formal recognition to several categories of ocean zones that are under the jurisdiction and control of coastal states; nevertheless, freedom of navigation over ocean space is largely maintained despite the recognition of such national zones.

UNCLOS comprises 320 articles and includes nine annexes and two "implementing conventions." UNCLOS is subdivided into 17 parts as follows:

Part I of UNCLOS (Art. 1) is titled "Introduction." This part sets out some important definitions of terms used in the Convention.

Part II of UNCLOS (Arts. 2–33) is devoted to the maritime zones known as the territorial sea and the contiguous zone. Every coastal state has the right to establish a territorial sea of up to 12 nautical miles (Art. 3), measured from its coastal baseline, as well as a contiguous zone of an additional 12 nautical miles where the state may enforce its customs, fiscal and other laws (Art. 33). The right of "innocent passage" of ships of all nations, including military vessels, is also defined and preserved (Arts. 17–32).

Part III of UNCLOS (Arts. 34–45) deals with maritime straits used for international navigation. This part establishes international rules and a right of "transit passage" for ships and aircraft through such straits.

Part IV of UNCLOS (Arts. 46–54) addresses the issue of archipelagic states, establishing rules for determining the baselines of such states, the measurement of the breadth of the territorial sea, the contiguous zone, and the continental shelf, the legal status of archipelagic waters, and rules for the innocent passage of ships and aircraft.

Part V of UNCLOS (Arts. 55–75) establishes the right of each coastal state to an Exclusive Economic Zone (EEZ) of up to 200 nautical miles, measured from the coastal baseline of the state. This Part also addresses the conservation and

LOWE, THE LAW OF THE SEA (3d. ed., Manchester: Manchester University Press, 1999).

utilization of living resources in this zone, a topic that will be addressed below in this chapter.

Part VI of UNCLOS (Arts. 76–85) recognizes the right of coastal states to jurisdiction and control over their Continental Shelves, the seabed and subsoil of offshore submarine areas, to distances of 200 nautical miles from the coastal states' respective baselines. UNCLOS recognizes and sets out rules for extending control of the Continental Shelf beyond 200 miles and establishes a Commission on the Limits of the Continental Shelf to make recommendations to coastal states concerning this process.

Part VII of UNCLOS (Arts. 86–120) sets out legal rules to govern the use of the High Seas, areas of the oceans beyond national jurisdiction, as well as rules relating to navigation and the conservation and use of living resources in the High Seas.

Part VIII of UNCLOS (Art. 121) deals with islands and their maritime zones.

Part IX of UNCLOS (Arts. 122–123) establishes rules concerning Enclosed and Semi-Enclosed Seas.

UNCLOS Part X (Arts. 124–132) guarantees the right of access to the sea and freedom of maritime transit to land locked states.

Part XI of UNCLOS (Arts. 133–191) creates a legal regime to govern what is called "the Area," the deep seabed beyond national jurisdictions. The Area is declared to be "the common heritage of mankind" (Art. 136)[4], and no state may claim sovereignty over any part of the Area or its resources (Art. 137). UNCLOS establishes an International Seabed Authority (ISA) as an autonomous international organization headquartered in Kingston, Jamaica, to set policy and to administer the exploitation and the protection of the Area. The ISA includes five bodies: the Assembly, the Council, the Legal and Technical Commission, the Finance Committee and the Secretariat.[5] The supreme organ of the ISA is the Assembly, which consists of all ISA members. The Assembly elects the members of the Council and other bodies, appoints the Secretary-General, who is head of the Assembly, sets the ISA's budget, approves rules and regulations after they are considered and adopted by the Council, and makes financial and technical decisions concerning deep-sea mineral exploitation. The comprehensive set of rules and regulations issued by the ISA is called the Mining Code[6], which also includes the forms necessary to apply for seabed exploration rights as well as the standard terms of exploration contracts.

Part XII of UNCLOS (Arts. 192–237) concerns protection and preservation of the marine environment; we consider these articles in detail immediately following this section.

---

[4] For a comprehensive article on the meaning of this term, see Patricia Mallia, *The Applicability of the Principle of the Common Heritage of Mankind to the Waters and Airspace Superjacent to the International Seabed Area*, 19 JIML 331 (2013).

[5] *See* http://www.isa.org.

[6] *Ibid.*

Part XIII of UNCLOS (Arts. 238–265) establishes rules for marine scientific research.

Part XIV of UNCLOS (Arts. 266–278) contains rules to govern the development and transfer of marine technology.

UNCLOS MARITIME ZONES

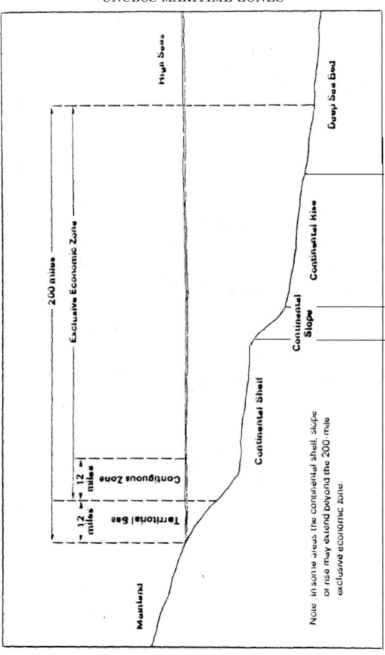

UNCLOS RULES ON THE CONSTRUCTION OF COASTAL BASELINES

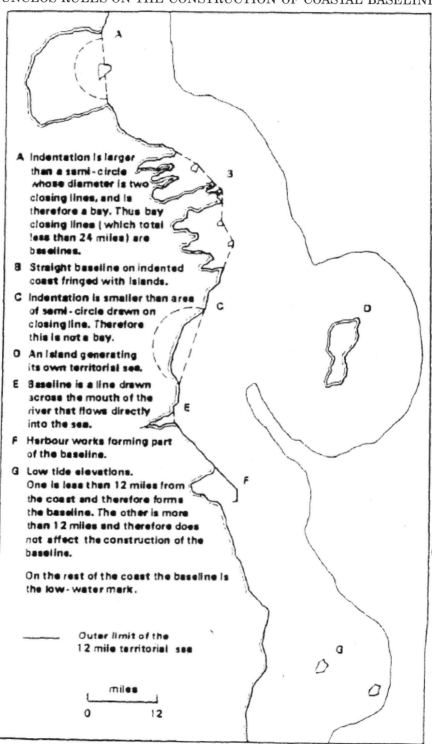

A Indentation is larger than a semi-circle whose diameter is two closing lines, and is therefore a bay. Thus bay closing lines (which total less than 24 miles) are baselines.

B Straight baseline on indented coast fringed with islands.

C Indentation is smaller than area of semi-circle drawn on closing line. Therefore this is not a bay.

O An island generating its own territorial sea.

E Baseline is a line drawn across the mouth of the river that flows directly into the sea.

F Harbour works forming part of the baseline.

G Low tide elevations. One is less than 12 miles from the coast and therefore forms the baseline. The other is more than 12 miles and therefore does not affect the construction of the baseline.

On the rest of the coast the baseline is the low-water mark.

_____ Outer limit of the 12 mile territorial sea

miles

0   12

Part XV of UNCLOS (Arts. 279–299) contains important provisions on the settlement of disputes. UNCLOS establishes a system of compulsory dispute settlement for international maritime disputes, although this system contains several important exceptions. We consider dispute settlement in detail below.

UNCLOS Part XVI (Arts. 300–304) contains general provisions on good faith and abuse of rights, disclosure of information, archaeological and historical objects found at sea, and responsibility and liability for damage. The latter provision (Art. 304) preserves the application of existing and future rules on responsibility and liability under international law.

UNCLOS Part XVII (Arts. 305–320) contains Final Provisions on matters such as entry into force of the convention, reservations (none are permitted), the relationship of UNCLOS to other international instruments, and amendment procedures.

B.　The Status of UNCLOS in United States Law

Although the United States delegation was very active in helping to formulate most of the provisions of UNCLOS, the United States voted against the final text of the Convention and at this writing is not a party to UNCLOS. The U.S. rejection of the Convention in the 1980s was based primarily upon the seabed mining regime (Part XI), which, because of mandatory technology transfer provisions and production quotas and other provisions, was regarded as unfavorable to the U.S. and other developed countries. In 1994, a new Agreement Relating to the Implementation of Part XI of the United Nations Convention on the Law of the Sea was adopted by the United Nations' General Assembly. This Agreement, which is reprinted in the **Document Supplement** and will be considered in more detail later in this chapter, restructured the ISA to give the United States veto power over key decisions, guarantees the U.S. a seat on the Council and ends mandatory production quotas and transfer of technology in favor of free market principles.[7] After the adoption of this Agreement, which is effectively an amendment to UNCLOS, Presidents Clinton, Bush, and Obama, have called on the U.S. Senate to ratify UNCLOS, but the U.S. Senate has not taken this step.

In 1983, President Ronald Reagan formally proclaimed a U.S. Exclusive Economic Zone of 200 nautical miles and announced that the United States "will recognize the rights of other states in the waters off their coasts, as reflected in the Convention," and the UNCLOS is largely observed by the United States as binding customary international law.[8] 1n 1988, President Reagan proclaimed an extension of the U.S. territorial sea to 12 nautical miles in accordance with the Convention.[9] In 1994, when President Clinton signed the 1994 Agreement, he pledged that the U.S. is committed to provisional application of the UNCLOS seabed regime, as

---

[7] *See* Bernard Oxman, *The 1994 Agreement and the Convention*, 88 Am. J. Int'l L. 687 (1994).

[8] *See* David Caron & Harry N. Schreiber, *The United States and the 1982 Law of the Sea Treaty*, 11 ASIL Insights, Issue 16 (2007).

[9] 24 U.S. Weekly Compilation of Presidential Documents 1661 (No. 52), reprinted 28 I.L.M. 284 (1989).

modified by the 1994 Agreement.[10] The U.S. is an observer at the meetings of the International Seabed Authority.

QUESTIONS

Should the United States become a party to UNCLOS? If you were a member of the Senate of the United States, would you vote in favor of ratification?

Some arguments in favor of ratification:

* Enhancement of U.S. security interests in the world's oceans

* Protection of U.S. economic and environmental interests

* Participation by U.S. in key decisions made by the UNCLOS institutions

* Participation by U.S. in process of adjudicating and processing claims over ocean resources.

Some arguments against:

* The U.S. would be bound by the mandatory dispute settlement provisions of UNCLOS and would be subject to unwarranted lawsuits in international tribunals

* The ISA is still dominated by developing countries hostile to U.S. interests

* The U.S. has little to gain by ratification since its interests are already guaranteed by customary international law.

C.   UNCLOS Part XII: Protection and Preservation of the Marine Environment

Part XII of UNCLOS contains substantive standards for the protection of the marine environment against all forms of environmental degradation. This Part also establishes an important legal framework for further agreements to deepen comprehensive protection of the marine environment. Many of the provisions of this Part are general in nature and presume the conclusion of more specific implementing agreements.

Please read carefully the UNCLOS Part XII, Articles 192 to 237, in the **Document Supplement**.

The obligations in section 1 (Arts. 192 to 196) of Part XII are quite general but they are comprehensive and important. Parties have the right to exploit natural resources in their sovereign control, but also must prevent, reduce, and control marine pollution from all sources and take "all necessary measures" to ensure that such pollution does not spread beyond national jurisdictions. The legal standard for marine pollution control that states must apply as set out in Article 194(1): States must use the "best practical means at their disposal and in accordance with their capabilities." Parties also must prevent, reduce, and control pollution resulting from the use of technologies under their jurisdiction and prevent the accidental or intentional introduction of alien or new species into the marine environment.

---

[10] Oxman, op. cit.

Article 1(4) of UNCLOS defines "pollution of the marine environment" as:

the introduction by man, directly or indirectly, of substances or energy into the marine environment, including estuaries, which results or is likely to result in such deleterious effects as harm to living resources and marine life, hazards to human health, hindrance to marine activities, including fishing and other legitimate uses of the sea, impairment of quality for use of sea water and reduction of amenities.

In addition, Article 194(5) requires parties to take measures to preserve "rare and fragile marine ecosystems" and the marine habitats of rare and endangered species. Article 195 takes a holistic approach: in taking measures to control marine pollution, parties may not transfer damage or transform one type of pollution into another.

The comprehensive obligations of Section 1 are reinforced by UNCLOS Part XII, section 2 (Arts. 197 to 201), which requires state-parties to cooperate on a global or regional level, to have contingency plans to cope with pollution, and to employ scientific criteria for the regulation of polluting activities.

Section 3 (Arts. 202–203) requires technical assistance to developing states on preferential terms to improve their capacity to protect the marine environment.

Section 4 (Arts. 204 to 206) requires states to monitor and publish the risks and effects of pollution and related activities.

Section 5 reinforces the preceding general obligations by stating separate obligations to control the various sources of marine pollution: (1) land-based sources (Art. 207); (2) pollution from continental shelf activities (Art. 208); (3) pollution from activities in the Area (Art. 209); (4) pollution from dumping (Art. 210); (5) pollution from vessels (Art. 211); and (6) pollution from the atmosphere (Art. 212).

UNCLOS requires states to adopt national standards for each source of marine pollution that are at least as strict as international standards, with the exception of land-based pollution standards, which must "take into account" international rules and the economic capacity of developing states. Standards for toxic pollutants, however, must minimize such pollution "to the fullest extent possible."

UNCLOS clearly contemplates, therefore, that state-parties will cooperate to develop international legal rules for all sources of marine pollution.

Enforcement of national and international rules is addressed by section 6 of Part XII, Articles 213 to 222. Note that enforcement of marine pollution rules is up to national authorities. Enforcement may be carried out by (1) the flag state; (2) the port state; and (3) the coastal state. Which state has priority? What are the criteria for enforcement activities by each category of state?

Note that under Articles 219 and 221, states may take the initiative to avoid or prevent pollution from unseaworthy vessels or vessels involved in marine casualties.

Section 7 (Arts. 223–233) covers safeguard measures designed to facilitate cooperation in enforcement activities. Note Article 228 and compare Article 229. Are these safeguard provisions really necessary?

Section 8 (Art. 234) is a special provision for control of pollution in ice-covered areas.

Section 9 (Art. 235) preserves the international law of state responsibility with respect to marine pollution obligations and mandates cooperation to conclude international regimes for liability and compensation for marine pollution damages.

Section 10 (Art. 236) preserves the international law of sovereign immunity for warships and government-operated ships for non-commercial purposes.

Section 11 (Art. 237) requires states to observe the obligations they assume in additional international agreements relating to protection of the marine environment. Thus UNCLOS does not purport to be a complete code, but looks toward additional international agreements addressing more specific problems of environmental protection.

Note that the provisions of Part XII build on Principle 7 of the Stockholm Declaration of 1972, (covered in Chapter 1), which urged states to take "all possible steps" to prevent hazards to human health and marine life.[11] Is Part XII consistent with the Rio Principles we covered in chapter 2, such as the Harm Prevention Principle and the Principle of Sustainable Development?

Agenda 21, Chapter 7 of the Report of the United Nations Conference on Environment and Development establishes a seven point agenda for preserving and protecting the marine environment building upon UNCLOS Part XII. Agenda 21 represents a program for future action by national governments and international organizations. We reprint this part of Agenda 21 in the **Document Supplement**.

D.   Dispute Settlement Under UNCLOS

Read carefully the provisions of UNCLOS Part XV, Articles 279 to 299.

The dispute settlement provisions of UNCLOS are very complex, reflecting difficult negotiations between those states that wanted compulsory dispute settlement and those states that did not want to be pinned down to utilize international dispute settlement procedures. Let us analyze these articles.

Article 279 obliges parties to seek and use peaceful methods of dispute settlement as required by the United Nations Charter. Note that section 1 of Part XV gives states-parties three options:

- First option: Article 280 states that parties to a dispute can agree among themselves on the appropriate means or procedure to settle their dispute.

- Second option: Article 282 states that where parties to a dispute have agreed, through a general, regional, or bilateral agreement, or otherwise, on a procedure that entails a binding decision, that procedure shall apply at the request of any party to the dispute. Note that such an agreed dispute settlement procedure takes precedence over the dispute settlement procedures under UNCLOS, in any event. We will see that this provision can be used to oust a dispute from the UNCLOS dispute system.

---

[11]   U.N. Doc. A/Conf.48/14/Rev.1 (1972).

- Third option: Article 284 provides that the parties by agreement can submit the dispute to non-binding Conciliation under the procedure established under UNCLOS Annex V or some other conciliation procedure. Note, however, that this procedure applies only if parties to a dispute agree, and the procedure leads only to a non-binding conciliation recommendation.

Section 2 of Part XV, Article 286, provides that if the state-parties have not reached any agreement on a procedure under section 1, section 2 — compulsory jurisdiction entailing a binding decision — will apply to the settlement of the dispute.

Article 287 details the compulsory procedures that will lead to a binding decision settling the dispute:

Upon each state-party's acceptance of UNCLOS or thereafter, the state-party "is free to choose, by means of a written declaration" one or more of four dispute settlement methods:

(a). The International Tribunal for the Law of the Sea (ITLOS), a specialized tribunal constituted under UNCLOS Annex VI. The ITLOS has its seat of operations in Hamburg, Germany and consists of 21 independent persons, no two of which can come from the same state, elected by two-thirds majorities by the states-parties, who serve renewable nine-year terms. The ITLOS was established in 1996, and at this writing has rendered decisions in 22 cases. *See* http://ww.itlos.org.

(b). The International Court of Justice.

(c). An Arbitral Tribunal constituted under UNCLOS Annex VII, which provides for an Arbitral Tribunal composed of five persons, who have the power to render a final and binding decision settling the dispute.

(d). A Special Arbitral Tribunal constituted in accordance with UNCLOS Annex VIII, which provides for an Arbitral Tribunal of five persons with expertise in fisheries, marine environment, marine research, or navigation. The decision of this Tribunal is "conclusive" as between the parties unless they otherwise agree.

Article 287 provides, however, that, if a state-party is not covered by a declaration in force, it will be deemed to accept Annex VII Arbitration. Thus, a state-party cannot escape binding dispute settlement, and Annex VII Arbitration is the default dispute settlement method.

If, however, states-parties having a dispute have all accepted the same one of the four above methods of dispute settlement, this method will apply. If different methods have been accepted by the states-parties to the dispute, Annex VII Arbitration will apply.

Section 3 of Part XV creates important limitations and exceptions to the compulsory dispute settlement regime of section 2.

Article 297 contains three automatic limitations to section 2.

First, disputes concerning the exercise of its sovereign rights or jurisdiction by a coastal state as granted by UNCLOS are subject to the compulsory dispute settlement procedures of section 2 only

(a) If it is alleged the coastal state has contravened UNCLOS with respect to rights of freedom of navigation, overflight, laying cables or pipelines, or lawful uses of the sea specified in UNCLOS Article 58 (stating the rights of non-coastal states in exclusive economic zones).

(b) If it is alleged that the non-coastal state exercising the freedoms of navigation, overflight, laying of cables and pipelines, has contravened laws of the coastal state that are compatible with UNCLOS or other rules of international law.

(c) If it is alleged that the coastal state has acted in contravention of international rules protecting the marine environment which are applicable in the coastal state as established by UNCLOS or through a competent international organization.

Second, marine scientific research disputes are to be settled under section 2, except that a coastal state may reject compulsory dispute settlement for a dispute involving UNCLOS Article 246 (the right of a coastal state to regulate research in its EEZ or continental shelf) or UNCLOS Article 253 (the right of a coastal state to suspend research in its EEZ or continental shelf). Such disputes must, however, be remitted to non-binding Conciliation under Annex V, but the coastal state's exercise of discretion as permitted under the UNCLOS must be respected.

Third, disputes concerning fisheries are to be settled under section 2, except that a coastal state may reject compulsory dispute settlement

for any dispute relating to its sovereign rights with respect to the living resources in the exclusive economic zone or their exercise, including its discretionary powers for determining the allowable catch, its harvesting capacity, the allocation of surpluses to other States and the terms and conditions established in its conservation and management laws and regulations.

The excluded types of fisheries disputes must, however, be submitted to Conciliation under Annex V if it is alleged that the coastal state has manifestly failed to comply with its obligation to conserve and manage living resources in its EEZ; or has arbitrarily refused to determine, at the request of another state, its allowable catch; or has arbitrarily refused to permit other states from harvesting a surplus in its EEZ, or is closing out fishing by nationals from land-locked or geographically disadvantaged states. But the Conciliation Tribunal must respect the discretion of the coastal state involved in such cases.

In addition, Article 298 of UNCLOS specifies three optional exceptions to the compulsory and binding dispute settlement under section 2 that may be invoked by states-parties to UNCLOS on accepting the Convention or at any time thereafter:

First, a states-parties may exclude any dispute involving sea boundary delimitations (Arts. 15, 74, and 83) or those involving historic bays or titles. Such disputes must, however, be submitted to Conciliation under Annex V unless they involve an unsettled territorial or sovereignty dispute.

Second, a states-parties may exclude disputes involving military activities or aircraft engaged in non-commercial service or law enforcement activities in regard to the exercise of sovereign rights or jurisdiction.

Third, a states-parties may exclude disputes that are before the United Nations Security Council.

PROBLEM 7-1
A DISPUTE BETWEEN NEIGHBORING STATES OVER MARINE POLLUTION

State *A* and State *B* are located adjacent to one another and share a common land border. The City of *X*, which is located in State *A* on the border of State *B*, operates an ocean outfall that from time to time emits raw sewage and toxic chemicals into the ocean waters shared by States *A* and *B*. In addition, a refinery in State *A* owned by the Acme Corporation, a private company, discharges oily effluent into the sea, which pollutes the maritime waters bordering States *A* and *B*. Both the ocean outfall operated by City of *X* and the refinery are in compliance with the national pollution laws of State *A*. Both State *A* and State *B* are parties to UNCLOS.

Does UNCLOS create an international cause of action in favor of State *B* against State *A*? Discuss.

PROBLEM 7-2
A DISPUTE BETWEEN NEIGHBORING STATES OVER FISHING

States *W* and *Z*, both parties to UNCLOS, are adjacent coastal states and share a common land border. A productive coastal fishery, the Banks, is located some 60 nautical miles offshore both countries and is exploited by fishing vessels of both countries. Both states *W* and *Z* have established 200 nautical mile EEZs, but the lateral maritime boundary between *W* and *Z* is disputed; both states claim the entire fishing Banks as within their respective EEZs. In addition, while state *W* has adopted and enforces strict catch limits for fishing resources on the Banks, state *Z*, a developing country, does not enforce any management standards, so that fishing stocks on the Banks are depleted despite the strict regulations applied by state *W*.

How should the dispute between state *W* and state *Z* be settled under UNCLOS? Discuss.

Section II. THE PRINCIPAL INTERNATIONAL ORGANIZATIONS INVOLVED IN PROTECTING THE MARINE ENVIRONMENT

Two international organizations sponsor conventions and international agreements concerning activities that degrade the marine environment: the International Maritime Organization (IMO), based in London, and the United Nations Environment Program, based in Nairobi, Kenya.

A.   The International Maritime Organization (IMO)

The Convention establishing the International Maritime Organization (IMO) was adopted in Geneva in 1948 and IMO first met in 1949. IMO's main task has been to develop and maintain a comprehensive regulatory framework for shipping and its ambit today includes safety, environmental concerns, legal matters, technical co-operation, maritime security, and the efficiency of shipping.

A specialized agency of the United Nations with 169 Member States and three Associate Members, IMO is based in the United Kingdom with around 300 international staff.

IMO's specialized committees and sub-committees are the focus for the technical work to update existing legislation or develop and adopt new regulations, with meetings attended by maritime experts from Member Governments, together with those from interested intergovernmental and non-governmental organizations.

The result is a comprehensive body of international conventions, supported by hundreds of recommendations governing every facet of shipping. There are, first, measures aimed at the prevention of accidents, including standards for ship design, construction, equipment, operation and manning, and the prevention of pollution by ships, and a convention on standards of training for seafarers.

Second, there are measures which recognize that accidents do happen, including rules concerning distress and safety communications, the International Convention on Search and Rescue and the International Convention on Oil Pollution Preparedness, Response and Cooperation.

Third, there are conventions which establish compensation and liability regimes — including the International Convention on Civil Liability for Oil Pollution Damage, the Convention establishing the International Fund for Compensation for Oil Pollution Damage and the Athens Convention covering liability and compensation for passengers at sea.

Inspection and monitoring of compliance are the responsibility of member States, but the adoption of a Voluntary IMO Member State Audit Scheme is playing a key role in enhancing implementation of IMO standards. The first audits under the Voluntary IMO Member State Audit Scheme were completed at the end of 2006 but the IMO Assembly has agreed a program to make this schema mandatory, with the entry into force of the mandatory audit scheme likely to be in 2015.

List of IMO Conventions

Most important IMO Conventions

International Convention for the Safety of Life at Sea (SOLAS), 1974, as amended

International Convention for the Prevention of Pollution from Ships, 1973, as modified by the Protocol of 1978 relating thereto and by the Protocol of

1997(MARPOL)

International Convention on Standards of Training, Certification and Watchkeeping for Seafarers (STCW) as amended, including the 1995 and 2010 Manila Amendments

Other conventions relating to maritime safety and security and ship/port interface

Convention on the International Regulations for Preventing Collisions at Sea (COLREG), 1972

Convention on Facilitation of International Maritime Traffic (FAL), 1965

International Convention on Load Lines (LL), 1968

International Convention on Maritime Search and Rescue (SAR), 1979

Convention for the Suppression of Unlawful Acts Against the Safety of Maritime Navigation (SUA), 1988, and Protocol for the Suppression of Unlawful Acts Against the Safety of Fixed Platforms located on the Continental Shelf (and the 2005 Protocols)

International Convention for Safe Containers (CSC), 1972

Convention on the International Maritime Satellite Organization (IMSOC), 1976

The Torremolinos International Convention for the Safety of Fishing Vessels (SFV), 1977

International Convention on Standards of Training, Certification and Watchkeeping for Fishing Vessel Personnel (STCW-F), 1995

Special Trade Passenger Ships Agreement (STP), 1971 and Protocol on Space Requirements for Special Trade Passenger Ships, 1973

Other conventions relating to prevention of marine pollution

International Convention Relating to Intervention on the High Seas in Cases of Oil Pollution Casualties (INTERVENTION), 1969

Convention on the Prevention of Marine Pollution by Dumping of Wastes and Other Matter (LC), 1972 (and the 1996 London Protocol)

International Convention on Oil Pollution Preparedness. Response and Co-operation (OPRC), 1990

Protocol on Preparedness, Response and Co-operation to pollution Incidents by Hazardous and Noxious Substances, 2000 (OPRC-HNS Protocol)

International Convention on the Control of Harmful Anti-fouling Systems on Ships (AFS), 2001

International Convention for the Control and Management of Ships' Ballast Water and Sediments, 2004

The Hong Kong International Convention for the Safe and Environmentally Sound Recycling of Ships, 2009

Conventions covering liability and compensation

International Convention on Civil Liability for Oil Pollution Damage (CLC), 1969, and its 1992 Protocol

1992 Protocol to the International Convention on the Establishment of an International Fund for Compensation for Oil Pollution Damage (FUND 1992)

Convention relating to Civil Liability in the Field of Maritime Carnage of Nuclear Material (NUCLEAR), 1971

Athens Convention relating to the Carriage of Passengers and their Luggage by Sea (PAL), 1974

Convention on Limitation of Liability for Maritime Claims (LLMC), 1976

International Convention on Liability and Compensation for Damage in Connection w1th the Carnage of Hazardous arid Noxious Substances by Sea (HNS), 1996 (and its 2010 Protocol)

International Convention on Civil Liability for Bunker Oil Pollut1on Damage, 2001

Nairobi International Convention on the Removal of Wrecks, 2007

Other subjects

International Convention on Tonnage Measurement of Ships (TONNAGE), 1969

International Convention on Salvage (SALVAGE), 1989

NOTE ON THE WORK AND WORKINGS OF THE INTERNATIONAL MARITIME ORGANIZATION

The work of the International Maritime Organization (IMO) extends beyond protection of the marine environment to include virtually all matters pertaining to shipping and the oceans. IMO's work includes maritime safety, maritime security, standards for workers in the shipping industry, and the facilitation of maritime navigation and shipping. The IMO web site is http://www.imo.org.

IMO works through an Assembly, which consists of all IMO members, and a Council of 40 members elected by the Assembly for 2-year terms. The Council members must include 10 members with the largest interest in international shipping services; 10 members with the largest interest in international seaborne trade; and 20 members with special interests in maritime transport and navigation. The work of the Assembly and Council is assisted by: (1) a Maritime Safety Committee (MSC), (2) a Marine Environmental Protection Committee (MEPC) and various subcommittees. The IMO Legal Committee may consider any legal matter involving IMO's work. In addition, a Technical Cooperation Committee aids the implementation of technical standards and solutions, and a Facilitation Committee considers how the efficiency of international shipping may be enhanced. IMO has a full-time Secretariat led by a Secretary-General.

The IMO Assembly meets every two years, although special sessions can be called. The Council is IMO's main body; the Council adopts IMO's budget, work program and makes financial decisions. IMO takes decisions commonly by consensus.

PROBLEM 7-3
ADOPTING A NEW IMO STANDARD

Suppose that an environmental NGO has drawn to the attention of your nation — a member of IMO — that an important new technological breakthrough has made it easier and cheaper to control emissions into the air of major pollutants commonly emitted by ships' engines. You understand that the general subject of air pollution from ships is covered by the International Convention for the Prevention of Pollution from Ships (1973 and 1978), known as MARPOL. Your nation believes that the technology in question should be drawn to the attention of the entire IMO membership, and that MARPOL should be amended to require the new technology as an international shipping standard.

Suppose also that your nation believes that an entirely new IMO initiative should be started to adopt international standards for the protection of coral reefs in the marine environment.

How will your nation's delegation to IMO put forward these proposals, and how might they be handled by IMO so that they become international rules of law?

1. Consider how and where to raise these matters at IMO; what do you suggest?

2. Should your delegation carefully prepare before making your intervention at IMO?

3. Your delegation's proposals may be referred to an IMO Committee or subcommittee or a Working Group may be established to develop them further. What committees will likely consider them?

4. The subcommittee or Working Group may solicit information from UN specialized agencies or from IMO member states or NGOs.

5. The subcommittee will report to the relevant full committee, to the Council or to the Assembly.

6. A draft international instrument may be reported to the Council with recommendations by the relevant subcommittee, Working Group, and committees.

7. The Council or Assembly may decide to convene an international conference to consider the matter and the draft international instrument.

8. At the conference members will discuss the proposal and the draft instrument and amendments may be adopted. Observers will be invited to the conference, including NGOs, industry representatives, and intergovernmental agencies.

9.   If the conference formally adopts (by consensus) a draft international convention or an amendment to an existing IMO convention, states may sign the convention "subject to ratification, acceptance, approval, and accession." What is the meaning of this phrase and this process? See the Vienna Convention on the Law of Treaties, 1969, Articles 12 and 18. The words "acceptance" and "approval" basically mean the same as ratification, but the process of ratification of a treaty is controlled by national constitutional law, which may require special proceedings and the passage of domestic legislation. An IMO multilateral treaty will be declared open for signature for a specified period of time. Accession is the method of adhering to a treaty by a state that did not sign while the treaty in question was open for signature.

10.   A multilateral convention will enter into force only when it has been ratified (accepted or approved) by the specified number of governments as stated in the convention.

11.   An amendment to an existing IMO convention may come into force much more quickly than a new IMO convention. In 1971, because of concern over the delay that commonly attended IMO convention amendments coming into force, the IMO Assembly adopted Resolution A.249(VII), which specifies that IMO convention amendments should come into force through a special "Tacit Acceptance Procedure." Under this procedure, which is a feature of most IMO conventions, the IMO body which adopts the amendment at the same time fixes a time period within which contracting parties to the particular convention have the opportunity to notify either their acceptance or rejection of the amendment. If they remain silent and the period of time specified expires, the amendment is considered to have been accepted by the party.[12]

12.   The enforcement of IMO conventions is up to member states; IMO has no internal enforcement power.

B.   The United Nations Environment Program (UNEP) and the Regional Seas Programmes

The United Nations Environment Program, which we covered in chapter 2, is active in combating marine pollution and dealing with maritime environmental problems through various Regional Seas Programmes. UNEP's web site contains the following description of such programs.

The Regional Seas Programme, launched in 1974 in the wake of the 1972 United Nations Conference on the Human Environment held in Stockholm, is one of UNEP's most significant achievements in the past 35 years.

The Regional Seas Programme aims to address the accelerating degradation of the world's oceans and coastal areas through the sustainable management and use of the marine and coastal environment, by engaging neighboring countries in

---

[12] *See* Oya Ozcayir, *IMO Conventions; The Tacit Consent Procedure and Some Recent Examples*, 10 JIML 204 (2004).

comprehensive and specific actions to protect their shared marine environment. It has accomplished this by stimulating the creation of Regional Seas programme prescriptions for sound environmental management to be coordinated and implemented by countries sharing a common body of water.

Today, more than 143 countries participate in 13 Regional Seas programmes established under the auspices of UNEP: Black Sea, Wider Caribbean, East Asian Seas, Eastern Africa, South Asian Seas, Persian Gulf Area, Mediterranean, North-East Pacific, Northwest Pacific, Red Sea and Gulf of Aden, South-East Pacific, Pacific, and Western Africa. Six of these programmes, are directly administered by UNEP.

The Regional Seas programmes function through Action Plans. In most cases the Action Plan is underpinned with a strong legal framework in the form of a regional Convention and associated Protocols on specific problems. Furthermore, five independent partner programmes for the Antarctic, Arctic, Baltic Sea, Caspian Sea, and North-East Atlantic Regions are members of the regional seas "family."

All programmes reflect a similar approach, yet each has been tailored by its own governments and institutions to suit their particular environmental challenges.

The work of Regional Seas Programmes is coordinated by UNEP's Regional Seas Branch based at the Nairobi Headquarters. Regional Coordination Units (RCUs), often aided by Regional Activity Centres (RACs), oversee the implementation of the programmes and aspects of the regional action plans, such as marine emergencies, information management and pollution monitoring.

Key Issues

Coastal Area Management

    Coastal Zone Management

        Environmental management has always been a key chapter of the Regional Seas action plans, beginning with the Mediterranean.

    Coastal Development

        Some 37% of the world's population lives within 100 km of a coast, a population density twice the global average.

Ecosystems and Biodiversity

    Coral reefs

        Coral reefs are among the most productive and diverse of all natural ecosystems. Recent decades have been catastrophic for them, however; some 10% of the world's reefs may already have been degraded beyond recovery and another 30% are in decline.

Marine Mammals

Many species of whales, seals and dolphins are threatened world-wide. Hundreds of thousands of dolphins and whales die each year in fishing nets.

Marine Protected Areas

The Regional Seas' Action Plans are considered to have a major role to play in the promotion of the Jakarta Mandate on Marine and Coastal Biological Diversity of the Convention on Biological Diversity (CBD) at the regional level.

UNEP Regional Seas Programme and Marine and Coastal Invasives — April 2006

The mandate can be found in CBD decisions Vl/23 1 / and VII/5. Decision Vl/23 2/ paragraph 26(e), which requested the Executive Secretary, in collaboration with the Global Invasive Species Programme (GISP) and other relevant organizations, to develop a joint programme of work on invasive alien species (IAS).

Large Marine Ecosystems (LMEs)

Large Marine Ecosystems (LMEs) are regions of ocean encompassing coastal areas from river basins and estuaries to the seaward boundaries of continental shelves and the outer margins of the major current systems. These areas of the ocean are characterized by distinct bathymetry, hydrography, productivity and trophic interaction. They provide a flexible approach to ecosystem-based management by identifying driving forces of ecosystem change, within the framework of sustainable development. UAEs are located within Regional Seas areas.

Land-based Sources of Pollution

Municipal, Industrial and agricultural wastes and run-off account for as much as 80% of all marine pollution: sewage and waste water, persistent organic pollutants (including pesticides), heavy metals, oils, nutrients and sediments.

Marine Litter

Marine litter is a comprehensive problem, with significant implications for the environment and human activity all over the world. It is found in all seas; not only in densely populated regions, but also in remote places far away from any obvious sources.

NOTE

The most extensive of the UN regional seas programmes is the oldest one, the Barcelona Convention for protection of the Mediterranean Sea. The original

Barcelona Convention dates from 1976, and entered into force in 1978. The original convention was modified by extensive amendments in 1995, and the amended document is known as the Convention for the Protection of the Marine Environment and the Coastal Region of the Mediterranean, in force since 2004 for 21 riparian states and the European Union. The Barcelona Convention (1995) is reprinted in the **Document Supplement**.

The parties to the Barcelona Convention have adopted an Action Plan for the Protection of the Marine Environment and Sustainable Development of the Coastal Area of the Mediterranean (1995) as well as protocols covering specific aspects of the Mediterranean Sea:

- Protocol for the prevention and elimination of pollution in the Mediterranean Sea by dumping from ships and aircraft or incineration at sea.

- Protocol concerning cooperation in combating pollution of the Mediterranean Sea by oil and other harmful substances in cases of emergency.

- Protocol for the protection of the Mediterranean Sea against pollution from land-based sources and activities.

- Protocol concerning specially protected areas and biological diversity in the Mediterranean.

- Protocol concerning cooperation in preventing pollution from ships and, in cases of emergency, combating pollution of the Mediterranean Sea.

- Protocol on Integrated Coastal Zone Management in the Mediterranean.

- Protocol for the Protection of the Mediterranean Sea against pollution resulting from exploration and exploitation of the continental shelf and the seabed and its subsoil.

- Protocol on the prevention of pollution of the Mediterranean Sea by transboundary movements of hazardous wastes and their disposal.

This comprehensive approach toward protection of the Mediterranean Sea depends for implementation on actions by national governments and the EU. A distinctive feature of the Barcelona Convention and its protocols is a non-adversarial, transparent, and relatively effective compliance mechanism that is aimed at providing advice and technical assistance to parties facing problems of implementation. *See* http://www.unepmap.org.

Section III. LAND-BASED MARINE POLLUTION AND INTERNATIONAL LAW

The first efforts to deal with land-based marine pollution in international law can be traced to the adoption of a regional convention, the 1974 *Convention for the Prevention of Marine Pollution from Land-Based Sources*, reprinted in 13 I.L.M. 352 (1974), known as the Paris Convention, which entered into force in 1978. The parties to the Paris Convention were developed European states, and the Convention applied to the area of the Northeast Atlantic Ocean and the North Sea. The Paris Convention established the Paris Commission to establish "best environmental practices" to serve as international standards for land-based municipal, industrial, and agricultural pollution emanating from land-based sources. In 1992, the Paris Commission was merged with the Oslo Commission created by the Oslo Convention (the Convention for the Prevention of Marine Pollution by Dumping from Ships and Aircraft (1972). In 1998, a replacement for the Paris and Oslo Conventions entered into force: the Convention for the Protection of the Marine Environment of the North-East Atlantic (the OSPAR Convention), and the two Commissions became the OSPAR Commission.

At the present time the OSPAR Convention operates as an Independent Regional Seas Programme covering the north-east Atlantic Ocean and the North Sea ranging from the North Pole to the Straits of Gibraltar. The Convention's management body, the OSPAR Commission, based in London, brings together 15 state-parties, the European Union, and observers from some 27 non-governmental organizations, representing both environmental groups and industry. The OSPAR Commission and a small Secretariat, important treaty bodies based in London, continue to work on land-based pollution as well as other problems. Over the years the OSPAR Commission has formulated and issued several hundred Decisions, Recommendations, Agreements, and Guidances concerning a wide range of aspects of land-based marine pollution. The OSPAR Convention is based upon the precautionary principle; the polluter pays principle; Best Available Techniques (BAT); and Best Environmental Practices (BEP). See the OSPAR web site, http://www.ospar.org.

Current international law norms applicable to land-based pollution may be classified into several categories.

First, customary law norms clearly apply. Foremost among these rules of customary international law is the Harm Prevention Principle, which we have already covered in chapters two and three.

This is the rule that no state has the right to use or permit the use of its territory in such a manner as to cause injury in or to the territory of another state or areas beyond national jurisdiction.[13] However, there are many problems with using this rule in a particular case. Among such problems are (1) the abstract nature of the rule; (2) the fact that liability under this rule is based on an obligation to use "due diligence," which is another vague concept. It is also uncertain how due diligence should be interpreted with respect to developing states and the principle of common but differentiated responsibilities. Is there a double standard for due diligence?

Second, the UNCLOS contains norms that apply to land-based pollution. UNCLOS Article 194 (1), (2) and (3) address aspects of land-based pollution, especially Article 194 (3), which requires state parties to minimize to the fullest possible extent "the release of toxic, harmful, or noxious substances, especially those which are persistent, from land-based sources." In addition, Article 207 of UNCLOS deals specifically with land-based pollution, and Article 213 requires states to enforce the laws and regulations adopted under Article 207. But Article 194 (1) may contain a double standard in that it says that state parties must reduce pollution using "the best practicable means at their disposal and in accordance with

---

[13] This rule is also sometimes stated in Latin: sic tuo ut alienum non laeda (use your property so as not to injure that of others).

their capabilities." Article 300 of UNCLOS creates an obligation not to exercise the rights they enjoy in a way that abuses those rights. But while the doctrine of abuse of rights may be an instrument to combat land-based pollution, the precise criteria for the application of this doctrine remain obscure.

Third, non-binding instruments are a source of law concerning land-based pollution. We have already seen that the Harm Prevention Principle, discussed above, was formulated as Principle 21 of the Stockholm Declaration and Principle 2 of the Rio Declaration. What was Principle 2 1/2 is now, of course, customary international law. An important non-binding soft law document is the Montreal Guidelines for the Protection of the Marine Environment against Pollution from Land-Based Sources (1985). The Montreal Guidelines stress the importance of "a comprehensive environmental management approach" (Guideline 10), and enumerate various measures, such as environmental impact assessment, monitoring, notification, information exchange and consultation, scientific and technical cooperation, assistance to developing countries, and the development of control strategies. The Montreal Guidelines also introduce the concept of specially protected marine areas. (Guideline 7). Another non-binding instrument is Agenda 21, Chapter 17 (1992), which requires states to take action at the national level as well as the regional and sub-regional levels and to take into account the Montreal Guidelines. Agenda 21 required the UNEP Governing Council to convene an intergovernmental meeting on the protection of the marine environment from land-based activities. (Para. 17.26). At this meeting, which was held in Washington DC in 1995, two further non-binding instruments were adopted: (1) the Washington Declaration on the Protection of the Marine Environment from Land-Based Activities and (2) the Global Programme of Action for the Protection of the Marine Environment from Land-Based Activities. In 2001 a new Montreal Declaration on the Protection of the Marine Environment from Land-Based Activities was approved.[14] For a complete summary, see UNEP/GPA (2006), *Protecting Coastal and Marine Environments from Land-Based Activities, A Guide for National Action*, available at http://www.gpa.unep.org.

It is evident that there are distinct limits to the global legal framework governing land-based marine pollution. Not only is there no global treaty, there is a paucity of hard law, and soft law instruments lack specificity. The global legal framework is not adequate to deal with the geographical and ecological differences in the oceans of the world. The global framework also cannot deal with the great diversity of states in the world.

Most experts therefore advocate regional agreements to address problems of land-based marine pollution.[15] The extensive Regional Seas Programme spearheaded by UNEP consists of thirteen regional treaties covering many areas of the world.[16] Protocols on land-based pollution are in effect in the following ocean regions under the UNEP Regional Seas Programme: the Baltic Sea, the Black Sea,

---

[14] UNEP/GPA/GR/9.

[15] *E.g.*, Yoshifume Tanaka, *Regulation of Land-Based Marine Pollution in International Law: A Comparative Analysis Between Global and Regional Legal Frameworks*, 66 ZaoRV 535, 549–50 (2006).

[16] *See* http://www.unep.org/regionalseas/Programmes/default.asp.

the Mediterranean Sea, the North-East Atlantic, the Kuwait region, the Southeast Pacific, and the Wider Caribbean Sea.

The OSPAR Convention deals with land-based pollution in Annex I, which is very short:

ON THE PREVENTION AND ELIMINATION OF POLLUTION FROM LAND-BASED SOURCES

ARTICLE 1

1. When adopting programmes and measures for the purpose of this Annex the Contracting Parties shall require, either individually or jointly, the use of

- best available techniques for point sources
- best environmental practice for point and diffuse sources including, where appropriate, clean technology.

2. When setting priorities and in assessing the nature and extent of the programmes and measures and their time scales, the Contracting Parties shall use the criteria given in Appendix 2.

3. The Contracting Parties shall take preventive measures to minimise the risk of pollution caused by accidents.

4. When adopting programmes and measures in relation to radioactive substances, including waste, the Contracting Parties shall also take account of:

(a) the recommendations of the other appropriate international organisations and agencies;

(b) the monitoring procedures recommended by these international organisations and agencies.

ARTICLE 2

1. Point source discharges to the maritime area, and releases into water or air which reach and may affect the maritime area, shall be strictly subject to authorisation or regulation by the competent authorities of the Contracting Parties. Such authorisation or regulation shall, in particular, implement relevant decisions of the Commission which bind the relevant Contracting Party.

2. The Contracting Parties shall provide for a system of regular monitoring and inspection by their competent authorities to assess compliance with authorisations and regulations of releases into water or air.

ARTICLE 3

For the purposes of this Annex, it shall, *inter alia*, be the duty of the Commission to draw up:

(a) plans for the reduction and phasing out of substances that are toxic, persistent and liable to bioaccumulate arising from land-based sources;

(b)   when appropriate, programmes and measures for the reduction of inputs of nutrients from urban, municipal, industrial, agricultural and other sources.

The details of controls on land-based pollution are handled by the OSPAR Commission, which has the authority to take Decisions and to make Recommendations to the state parties. A Decision must be adopted by at least three-fourths of the parties and is binding on the states that voted for it, while Recommendations have no binding force. OSPAR Convention, Article 13.

The OSPAR Convention specifically adopts the precautionary principle as well as the polluter pays principle in Article 2.

Is the OSPAR Convention a good model for the creation of an international legal regime to deal with land-based pollution? OSPAR appears to be an excellent model, but as the following case suggests, some controversies arise which pose difficult issues even between developed states with friendly diplomatic relations. The MOX Plant Dispute between Ireland and the United Kingdom went to arbitration under the OSPAR Convention and was litigated in the ITLOS under UNCLOS. Note that in the ITLOS opinion we reprint below, the court made no mention of the precautionary principle. This was apparently because, although the precautionary principle is specifically included in the OSPAR Convention, it is not mentioned in UNCLOS. One of the ITLOS judges, Rudiger Wolfrum, in an omitted separate opinion in the MOX Plant Case, stated that: "it is still a matter of discussion whether the precautionary principle or the precautionary approach in international environmental law has become part of international customary law." MOX Plant Case, *ITLOS Order on Request for Preliminary Measures*, 41 I.L.M. 415, 428–29 (2002). Do you agree? Why didn't ITLOS apply the precautionary principle since it is explicitly part of the OSPAR Convention?

The MOX Plant Dispute (Ireland v. United Kingdom)

The UK's Sellafield Mixed Oxide (MOX) nuclear recycling plant on the Irish Sea coast provoked a dispute between Ireland and the UK over radioactive emissions that Ireland contended caused elevated radioactivity in shellfish and finfish endangering human health. The UK rejoined that the small levels of radiation were not dangerous.

In 2001, Ireland commenced two proceedings against the UK: (1) an international arbitration proceeding under the 1992 Convention for the Protection of the Marine Environment of the North East Atlantic (OSPAR); and (2) a proceeding against the UK in the International Tribunal for the Law of the Sea.

In the OSPAR case Ireland charged that the UK was in breach of Article 9 of the OSPAR Convention by refusing to make available two reports concerning the Sellafield MOX plant.

Ireland's case before the ITLOS concerned the UK's failure to carry out a proper assessment of the potential effects of Sellafield on the marine environment as required by UNCLOS Art. 206; a failure to cooperate as required by UNCLOS Arts. 123 and 197; and a failure to take all steps necessary to protect the marine environment as required by UNCLOS Arts. 192–94, 207, 211, 213, and 217.

THE MOX PLANT CASE (IRELAND v. UNITED KINGDOM)
International Tribunal for the Law of the Sea, Case No. 10 (6 Dec. 2001)

Request for provisional measures

Present: PRESIDENT CHANDRASEKHARA RAO; VICE-PRESIDENT NELSON; JUDGES CAMINOS, MAROTTA RANGEL, YANKOV, YAMAMOTO, KOLODKIN, PARK BAMELA ENGO, MENSAH, AKL. ANDERSON, VUKAS, WOLFRUM, TREVES, MARSIT, EIRIKSSON, NDIAYE, JESUS, XU; JUDGE AD HOC SZEKELY; REGISTRAR GAUTIER

THE TRIBUNAL,

composed as above,

after deliberation,

Having regard to article 290 of the united Nations Convention on the Law of the Sea (heareinafter "the Convention") and articles 21, 25 and 27 of the Statute of the Tribunal (hereinafter "the Statute"),

Having regard to articles 89 and 90 of the Rules of the Tribunal (hereinafter "the Rules"),

Having regard to the fact that Ireland and the United Kingdom of Great Britain and Northern Ireland (hereinafter "the United Kingdom") have not accepted the same procedure for the settlement of disputes in accordance with article 287 of the Convention and are therefore deemed to have accepted arbitration in accordance with Annex VII to the Convention,

Having regard to the Notification and Statement of Claim submitted by Ireland to the United Kingdom on 25 October 2001 instituting arbitral proceedings as provided for in Annex VII to the Convention "in the dispute concerning the MOX plant, international movements of radioactive materials, and the protection of the marine environment of the Irish Sea,"

Having regard to the Request for provisional measures submitted by Ireland to the United Kingdom on 25 October 2001 pending the constitution of an arbitral tribunal under Annex VII to the Convention,

Having regard to the Request submitted by Ireland to the Tribunal on 9 November 2001 for the prescription of provisional measures by the Tribunal in accordance with article 290, paragraph 5, of the Convention,

Makes the following Order:

Whereas Ireland and the United Kingdom are States Parties to the Convention;

Whereas, on 9 November 2001, Ireland filed with the Registry of the Tribunal by facsimile a Request for the prescription of provisional measures under article 290, paragraph 5, of the Convention "in the dispute concerning the MOX plant, international movements of radioactive materials, and the protection of the marine environment of the Irish Sea" between Ireland and the United Kingdom;

Whereas, in the Notification and Statement of Claim of 25 October 2001. Ireland requested the arbitral tribunal to be constituted under Annex VII (hereinafter "the Annex VII arbitral tribunal") to adjudge and declare:

1. That the United Kingdom has breached its obligations under Articles 192 and 193 and/or Article 194 and/or Article 207 and/or Articles 211 and 213 of UNCLOS in relation to the authorisation of the MOX plant, including by failing to take the necessary measures to prevent, reduce and control pollution of the marine environment of the Irish Sea from (1) intended discharges of radioactive materials and or wastes from the MOX plant, and/or (2) accidental releases of radioactive materials and/or wastes from the MOX plant and/or international movements associated the MOX plant, and/or (3) releases of radioactive materials and/or wastes from the MOX plant and/or international movements associated the MOX plant resulting from a terrorist act;

2. That the United Kingdom has breached its obligations under Articles 192 and 193 and/or Article 194 and/or Article 207 and/or Articles 211 and 213 of UNCLOS in relation to the authorisation of the MOX plant by failing (1) properly or at all to assess the risk of terrorist attack on the MOX plant and international movements of radioactive material associated with the plant, and/or (2) properly or at all to prepare a comprehensive response strategy or plan to prevent, contain and respond to terrorist attack on the MOX plant and international movements of radioactive waste associated with the plant;

3. That the United Kingdom has breached its obligations under Articles 123 and 197 of UNCLOS in relation to the authorisation of the MOX plant, and has failed to cooperate with Ireland in the protection of the marine environment of the Irish Sea *inter alia* by refusing to share information with Ireland and/or refusing to carry out a proper environmental assessment of the impacts on the marine environment of the MOX plant and associated activities and/or proceeding to authorise the operation of the MOX plant whilst proceedings relating to the settlement of a dispute on access to information were still pending;

4. That the United Kingdom has breached its obligations under Article 206 of UNCLOS in relation to the authorisation of the MOX plant, including by

   (a) failing, by its 1993 Environmental Statement, properly and fully to assess the potential effects of the operation of the MOX plant on the marine environment of the Irish Sea; and/or

   (b) failing, since the publication of its 1993 Environmental Statement, to assess the potential effects of the operation of the MOX plant on the marine environment by reference to the factual and legal developments which have arisen since 1993, and in particular since 1998; and/or

(c) failing to assess the potential effects on the marine environment of the Irish Sea of international movements of radioactive materials to be transported to and from the MOX plant; and /or

(d) failing to assess the risk of potential effects on the marine environement of the Irish Sea arising from terrorist act or acts on the MOX plant and/or on international movements of radioactive material to and from the MOX plant.

5. That the United Kingdom shall refrain from authorizing or failing to prevent (a) the operation of the MOX plant and/or (b) international movements of radioactive materials into and out of the United Kingdom related to the operation of the MOX Plant or any preparatory or other activities associated with the operation of the MOX until such time as (1) there has been carried out a proper assessment of the environmental impact of the operation of the MOX plant as well as related international movements of radioactive materials, and (2) it is demonstrated that the operation of the MOX plant and related international movements of radioactive materials will result in the deliberate discharge of no radioactive materials, including wastes, directly or indirectly into the marine environment of the Irish Sea, and (3) there has been agreed and adopted jointly with Ireland an comprehensive strategy or plan to prevent, contain and respond to terrorist attack on the MOX plant and international movements of radioactive waste associated with the plant;

29. Whereas Ireland, in its final submissions at the public sitting held on 20 November 2001, requested the prescription by the Tribunal of the following provisional measures:

(1) that the United Kingdom immediately suspend the authorisation of the MOX plant dated 3 October, 2001, alternatively take such other measures as are necessary to prevent with immediate effect the operation of the MOX plant;

(2) that the United Kingdom immediately ensure that there are no movements into or out of the waters over which it has sovereignty or exercises sovereign rights of any radioactive substances or materials or wastes which are associated with the operation of: or activities preparatory to the operation of, the MOX plant;

(3) that the United Kingdom ensure that no action of any kind is taken which might aggravate, extend or render more difficult of solution the dispute submitted to the Annex VII tribunal (Ireland hereby agreeing itself to act so as not to aggravate, extend or render more difficult of solution that dispute); and

(4) that the United Kingdom ensure that no action is taken which might prejudice the rights of Ireland in respect of the carrying out of any decision on the merits that the Annex VII tribunal may render (Ireland likewise will take no action of that kind in relation to the United Kingdom);

. . . .

34. Considering that article 290, paragraph 5, of the Convention provides in the relevant part that:

> Pending the constitution of an arbitral tribunal to which a dispute is being submitted under this section, any court or tribunal agreed upon by the parties or, failing such agreement within two weeks tram the date of the request for provisional measures, the International Tribunal for the Law of the Sea . . . may prescribe, modify or revoke provisional measures in accordance with this article if it considers that *prima facie* the tribunal which is to be constituted would have jurisdiction and that the urgency of the situation so requires;

35. Considering that, before prescribing provisional measures under article 290, paragraph 5, of the Convention, the Tribunal must satisfy itself that prima facie the Annex VII arbitral tribunal would have jurisdiction;

36. Considering that Ireland maintains that the dispute with the United Kingdom concerns the interpretation and application of certain provisions of the Convention, including, in particular, articles 123, 192 to 194, 197, 206, 207, 211, 212 and 213 thereof;

37. Considering that Ireland has invoked as the basis of jurisdiction of the Annex VII arbitral tribunal article 288, paragraph 1, of the Convention which reads as follows: A court or tribunal referred to in article 287 shall have jurisdiction over any dispute concerning the interpretation or application of this Convention which is submitted to it in accordance with this Part;

38. Considering that the United Kingdom maintains that Ireland is precluded from having recourse to the Annex VII arbitral tribunal in view of article 282 of the Convention which reads as follows:

> If the States Parties which are parties to a dispute concerning the interpretation or application of this Convention have agreed, through a general, regional or bilateral agreement or otherwise, that such dispute shall, at the request of any party to the dispute, be submitted to a procedure that entails a binding decision, that procedure shall apply in lieu of the procedures provided for in this Part, unless the parties to the dispute otherwise agree;

39. Considering that the United Kingdom maintains that the matters of which Ireland complains are governed by regional agreements providing for alternative and binding means of resolving disputes and have actually been submitted to such alternative tribunals, or are about to be submitted;

40. Considering that the United Kingdom referred to the fact that Ireland has under article 32 of the 1992 Convention for the Protection of the Marine Environment of the NorthEast Atlantic (hereinafter "the OSPAR Convention") submitted a dispute between Ireland and the United Kingdom "concerning access to information under article 9 of the OSPAR Convention in relation to the economic 'justification' of the proposed MOX plant" to an arbitral tribunal (hereinafter "the OSPAR arbitral tribunal");

41. Considering that the United Kingdom has further stated that certain aspects of the complaints of Ireland are governed by the Treaty establishing the European Community (hereinafter "the EC Treaty") or the Treaty establishing the European Atomic Energy Community (hereinafter "the Euratom Treaty") and the Directives issued thereunder and that States Parties to those Treaties have agreed to invest the Court of Justice of the European Communities with exclusive jurisdiction to resolve disputes between them concerning alleged failures to comply with such Treaties and Directives;

42. Considering that the United Kingdom has also stated that Ireland has made public its intention of initiating separate proceedings in respect of the United Kingdom's alleged breach of obligations arising under the EC Treaty and the Euratom Treaty;

43. Considering that the United Kingdom maintains that the main elements of the dispute submitted to the Annex VII arbitral tribunal are governed by the compulsory dispute settlement procedures of the OSPAR Convention or the EC Treaty or the Euratom Treaty;

44. Considering that, for the above reasons, the United Kingdom maintains that the Annex VII arbitral tribunal would not have jurisdiction and that, consequently, the Tribunal is not competent to prescribe provisional measures under article 290, paragraph 5, of the Convention;

45. Considering that Ireland contends that the dispute concerns the interpretation or application of the Convention and does not concern the interpretation or application of either the OSPAR Convention or the EC Treaty or the Euratom Treaty;

46. Considering that Ireland further states that neither the OSPAR arbitral tribunal nor the Court of Justice of the European Communities would have jurisdiction that extends to all of the matters in the dispute before the Annex VII arbitral tribunal;

47. Considering that Ireland further maintains that the rights and duties under the Convention, the OSPAR Convention, the EC Treaty and the Euratom Treaty are cumulative and, as a State Party to all of them, it may rely on any or all of them as it chooses;

48. Considering that, in the view of the Tribunal, article 282 of the Convention is concerned with general, regional or bilateral agreements which provide for the settlement of disputes concerning what the Convention refers to as "the interpretation or application of this Convention;"

49. Considering that the dispute settlement procedures under the OSPAR Convention, the EC Treaty and the Euratom Treaty deal with disputes concerning the interpretation or application of those agreements, and not with disputes arising under the Convention;

50. Considering that, even if the OSPAR Convention, the EC Treaty and the Euratom Treaty contain rights or obligations similar to or identical with the rights or obligations set out in the convention, the rights and

obligations under those agreements have a separate existence from those under the Convention;

51. Considering also that the application of international law rules on interpretation of treaties to identical or similar provisions of different treaties may not yield the same results, having regard to, *inter alia*, differences in the respective contexts, objects and purposes, subsequent practice of parties and *travaux preparatoires*;

52. Considering that the Tribunal is of the opinion that, since the dispute before the Annex VII arbitral tribunal concerns the interpretation or application of the Convention and no other agreement, only the dispute settlement procedures under the Convention are relevant to that dispute;

53. Considering that, for the reasons given above, the Tribunal considers that, for the purpose of determining whether the Annex VII arbitral tribunal would have prima facie jurisdiction, article 282 of the Convention is not applicable to the dispute submitted to the Annex VII arbitral tribunal;

54. Considering that the United Kingdom contends that the requirements of article 283 of the Convention have not been satisfied since, in its view, there has been no exchange of views regarding the settlement of the dispute by negotiation or other peaceful means;

55. Considering that article 283 of the Convention reads as follows:

1. When a dispute arises between States Parties concerning the interpretation or application of this Convention, the parties to the dispute shall proceed expeditiously to an exchange of views regarding its settlement by negotiation or other peaceful means.

2. The parties shall also proceed expeditiously to an exchange of views where a procedure for the settlement of such a dispute has been terminated without a settlement or where a settlement has been reached and the circumstances require consultation regarding the manner of implementing the settlement;

. . . .

89. *For these reasons,*

THE TRIBUNAL

1. Unanimously,

Prescribes, pending a decision by the Annex VII arbitral tribunal, the following provisional measure under article 290 paragraph 5, of the Convention:

Ireland and the United Kingdom shall cooperate and shall for this purpose, enter into consultations forthwith in order to:

(a) exchange further information with regard to possible consequences for the Irish Sea arising out of the commissioning of the MOX plant;

(b) monitor risks or the effects of the operation of the MOX plant for the Irish Sea;

(c) devise, as appropriate, measures to prevent pollution of the marine environment which might result from the operation of the MOX plant.

2. Unanimously,

Decides that Ireland and the United Kingdom shall each submit the initial report referred to in article 95, paragraph 1, of the Rules not later than 17 December 2001, and authorizes the President of the Tribunal to request such further reports and information as he may consider appropriate after that date.

3. Unanimously,

Decides that each party shall bear its own costs.

Done in English and in French, both texts being authoritative, in the Free and Hanseatic City of Hamburg, this third day of December, two thousand and one, in three copies, one of which will be placed in the archives of the Tribunal and the others transmitted to the Government of Ireland and the government of the United Kingdom, respectively.

(Signed) P. Chandrasekhara Rao
President.

(Signed) Philippe Gautier,
Registrar.

Judges Caminos, Yamamoto Park, Akl, Marsit, Eirikksson and Jesus append a joint declaration to the Order of the Tribunal.

Vice-President Nelson, Judges Mensah, Anderson, Wolfrum, Treves, Jesus and Judge ad hoc Szekely append separate opinions to the Order of the Tribunal.

NOTES AND QUESTIONS

1. *The OSPAR Convention.* The Arbitration Tribunal[17] convened under the OSPAR Convention ruled that it had jurisdiction over the dispute between Ireland and the United Kingdom, but the majority held that Ireland's claim for information did not fall within Article 9(2) of the OSPAR Convention, which requires disclosure of "any available information . . . on the state of the maritime area, on activities or measures adversely affecting or likely to affect it, and on activities or measures introduced in accordance with the Convention." Ireland sought information on the environmental impact of the operation of the plant, while the UK disclosed only information on the discharge of radioactive materials into the Irish Sea. The majority of the arbitrators ruled that the UK's rejection of Ireland's information request did not violate the requirements of OSPAR Convention Article 9. Do you agree? In a dissenting opinion, one of the arbitrators, Gavan Griffith, found that the precautionary principle applied to this dispute, shifting the burden of proof to the UK. The majority disagreed with this approach.

---

[17] MOX Plant Case (Ireland v. United Kingdom), OSPAR Arbitration, 42 I.L.M. 1118 (2003).

2. *European Union (EU) law.* The MOX Plant dispute ended when the Commission of the European Union filed suit against Ireland in the European Court of Justice (ECJ), and the ECJ ruled that Ireland, by bringing proceedings against the UK within the framework of the international law of the sea, was in breach of Article 292 of the European Community (EC) Treaty (now Article 344 of the Treaty on the Functioning of the European Union), under which "Member States [of the EU] undertake not to submit a dispute concerning the interpretation or application of the EC Treaties to any method of settlement other than those provided for therein." Case C-459/03 Commission of the European Communities v. Ireland, Judgment of the Court (Grand Chamber) of 30 May, 2006, (2006) ECR 1-4635, reprinted 45 I.L.M. 1051 (2006). The ECJ reasoned that UNCLOS is a classic "mixed" international agreement under EU law, in that it concerns matters within the competence of the EU, such as fisheries, as well as matters, such as maritime boundary delimitation, that are within the competence of the EU Member States. Both the EU[18] and the EU Member States have acceded to the UNCLOS, and, although competence over the marine environment is shared under EU law, the EU has exclusive jurisdiction under EC Treaty Article 292 over disputes concerning UNCLOS between Member States. Is the ECJ's ruling consistent with UNCLOS Article 282? Is the ECJ's ruling inconsistent with the ruling of the ITLOS?

3. After the ECJ Judgment, the arbitral proceeding that Ireland instituted against the UK under UNCLOS Article 287 and Art. 1 of Annex VII in the Permanent Court of Arbitration in the Hague was terminated at Ireland's request. *See* MOX Plant Arbitral Tribunal Order No. 6 of 6 June 2008.

PROBLEM 7-4
NON-POINT POLLUTION IN THE SOUTH CHINA SEA

In an effort to increase food production to feed its growing population and to encourage economic development, China has promoted the massive use of fertilizers and pesticides in its agricultural sector. Some of the pesticides contain significant quantities of mercury. China also continues to rely on traditional tilling of the soil prior to planting. Soil tilling increases the quantity of agricultural runoff from rain and irrigation that drains into rivers that discharge into the sea. This Chinese policy has produced a massive increase in chemical pollution of the South China Sea. The South China Sea is a Semi-Enclosed Sea. No area within that sea is beyond 200-nautical-miles from the coastline of one of the littoral states. These chemicals cause damage to the living resources of that sea. Philippine fishermen who fish in the South China Sea within 200-nautical-miles of the Philippines coastline report a substantial decrease in fish stocks. Of those that remain, many show deformities that are caused by the mercury in pesticides, which only China uses for its agriculture in the region. The runoff deposits these pesticides into the South China Sea. The decrease in fish stocks in the South China Sea is also believed to be a result of the pesticide runoff from China. The Philippines wants to do something about this situation. The damage to the stock of fish has caused economic hardship to its fishermen and to its economy. Both China and the Philippines are parties to the

---

[18] Council Decision 98/392/EC, invoking as authority EC Treaty Art. 175(1).

1982 Law of the Sea Convention. Neither state is a party to a treaty that bans the use of these chemicals (including mercury) in agriculture or bans their deposit through land-based sources into the marine environment.

If China were to eliminate the use of mercury in its pesticides, it would probably suffer a 10% drop in its agricultural output. This would cause food shortages and, perhaps, some starvation. China could use other pesticides that would be equally effective, but it would take about five years to develop the manufacturing capabilities. Those pesticides would be more expensive to use, in addition to the cost of the construction of the necessary facilities and of training persons to use those pesticides. To do this, China would have to divert substantial funds from other sectors of its economy, causing losses in jobs and productivity or a decline in its military. China refuses to do this.

The Philippines and China have agreed to discuss the situation with the assistance of an ambassador from Indonesia. In the course of those discussions, questions regarding the legal situation have arisen, and the disputants have agreed to present their views on the subject. In particular two questions are to be addressed. They are as follows:

1. Has China violated its obligations under public international law regarding its agricultural policies?

2. What remedies are available to the Philippines if it were to decide to pursue the matter? What defenses might China have to such measures?

Students may be selected to represent China and the Philippines in this matter.

For further study see, Daud Hassan, *International Conventions Relating to Land-Based Sources of Marine Pollution Control: Applications and Shortcomings*, 16 Geo. Int'l Envtl. L. Rev. 657 (2004); Comment, *Developments in Land-Based Pollution: From Sewer to Shining Sea*, 2003 Colo J. Int'l Envtl. L. & Pol'y 61.

NOTES AND QUESTIONS

1. *Jurisdiction*. Considering the Part XV of UNCLOS and the MOX Plant Dispute, is there a possible dispute settlement forum available so that China will have to submit to compulsory dispute settlement in this case?

2. *UNCLOS norms*. Consider the provisions of UNCLOS Part XII. This is the substantive international law that applies to China's polluting activities in the South China Sea. What provisions of Part XII are applicable? Consider in particular Articles 194 (1), (2), (3), and (5); 195; 204, 205, 206, 207, 212, 213, 235, and 237.

3. *State responsibility*. May the Philippines successfully invoke international law principles of state responsibility against China? Do the International Law Commission's (ILC) Draft Articles on the Responsibility of States for Internationally Wrongful Acts (2001), approved by UN General Assembly Resolution 56/83, apply? In chapter 3 of this book we learned that the ILC's Draft Articles state secondary rules designed to apply to all kinds of international obligations regardless of their source, but these Articles must be read in association with primary, substantive law standards. In this case the primary standards are supplied by

UNCLOS Part XII. Are these substantive standards sufficient to charge China with committing internationally wrongful acts?

4. *Customary international law*. Will the Philippines successfully invoke customary international law principles against China that create liability for transboundary pollution? Consider the material covered in chapters 2 and 3 of this book, in particular:

- The *Trail Smelter Case*

- Principle 21 of the Stockholm Declaration repeated by Principle 2 of the Rio Declaration. Principle 21/2 was declared to be a rule of customary international law by the International Court of Justice in the Nuclear Weapons Advisory Opinion [1996] ICJ Rep. 226 (29), and this conclusion was reaffirmed by the Court in the Gabcikovo-Nagymaros Project Case, [1997] ICJ Rep. 7 (53). Principle 21/2 extends the ruling of the Trail Smelter Case to include areas beyond national jurisdiction.

- Is the now discredited ILC Draft Articles on International Liability for Acts Not Prohibited by International Law (1996) helpful?

- Consider also Sections 601 and 602 of the American Law Institute, Restatement (Third) of the Foreign Relations Law of the United States (1986).

- Consider the ILC Draft Articles on Prevention of Transboundary Harm from Hazardous Activities (2001). These Draft Articles require an equitable balancing of interests (*see* Articles 9 and 10). Is this helpful? Is balancing of interests a good idea when it comes to preventing harm from discharges of toxic substances such as mercury?

- Consider also the ILC Draft Principles on International Liability in Cases of Loss from Transboundary Harm Arising out of Hazardous Activities (2006).

5. *Remedies*. Suppose China were adjudged to have violated its international law obligations; what remedies should be imposed? What remedies are appropriate under international law?

6. *A global treaty on land-based marine pollution*. About 80% of marine pollution ultimately has its source on land. Is a global treaty that specifically addresses land-based marine pollution the answer? Such a treaty has been proposed: see DAVID HASSAN, PROTECTING THE MARINE ENVIRONMENT FROM LAND-BASED SOURCES OF POLLUTION: TOWARDS EFFECTIVE INTERNATIONAL COOPERATION (Burlington, VT: Ashgate Press, 2006).

7. *The United Nations Environmental Programme (UNEP) Global Programme of Action for the Protection of the Marine Environment from Land-Based Activities (GPA)*. UNEP has developed a strategy for combating land-based marine pollution on a global scale. See UNEP, The Other 70%: UNEP Marine and Coastal Strategy (Nairobi: UNEP, 2011). This UNEP initiative began in 1995 with the UNEP Washington Declaration on Protection of the Marine Environment from Land-Based Activities, which is reprinted in the **Document Supplement**. The Washington Declaration states, as a "common goal" . . . "effective action to deal with all land-based impacts on the marine environment." (para. 1). This document also calls for a "Global Programme of Action, a global, legally binding instrument for the reduction and/or elimination of emissions, discharges and, where appropriate, the elimination of the manufacture and use of the persistent organic pollutants identified in decision 18/32 of the Governing Council of the United Nations Environment Programme." (para. 17). To this end, UNEP adopted the Global Programme of Action for the Protection of the Marine Environment from Land-Based Activities (1995). The GPA recommends that states identify and assess particular problems of land-based marine pollution; establish priorities for action; set management objectives; identify, evaluate and select strategies and measures to achieve these objectives; and develop criteria for evaluating the effectiveness of strategies and measures. For information on the GPA, see http://www.gpa.unep.org. The GPA relies upon national governments to take action to achieve and enforce standards to reduce land-based marine pollution. UNEP holds periodic meetings to review progress in implementing the GPA. Meetings were held in Montreal in 2001; in Beijing in 2006; and in Manila in 2012. *See* UNEP, *Review of Implementation of the Global Programme of Action for the Protection of the Marine Environment from Land-Based Activities at the International, Regional, and National Levels,* UNEP/GPA/IGR.3/2 (9 November 2011). This review states that "Many Governments have integrated the Programme across sectors and ministries and in national budgets." But the review adds that "much remains to be done." (para. 1). UNEP's strategy is to implement the GPA through national programmes of action adopted by states. To this end, the UNEP offers technical assistance, capacity building, and training of personnel.

   8. *Regional seas programmes.* A key element of the GPA is to encourage the development of regional seas programmes to combat land-based marine pollution. There is no regional seas programme for the South China Sea. Would the establishment of such a program be beneficial? The two most advanced regional seas programmes are OSPAR, which covers the north-east Atlantic Ocean, and the Mediterranean programme established by the Convention for the Protection of the Marine Environment and the Coastal Region of the Mediterranean. OSPAR includes, as we have seen, Annex I-Prevention and elimination of pollution from land-based sources. The OSPAR Commission has authority to issue Decisions and Recommendations to implement this Annex. The Mediterranean regional seas programme was originally instituted by the Barcelona Convention of 1976 and was amended as the Convention for the Protection of the Marine Environment and the Coastal Region of the Mediterranean (Barcelona, 1995, entry into force 2004). The 1995 Barcelona Convention, which is reprinted in the **Document Supplement**, includes a Protocol for the protection of the Mediterranean Sea against pollution from land-based sources; a Protocol concerning specially protected areas and biological diversity in the Mediterranean; and a Protocol on Integrated Coastal Zone Management in the Mediterranean. The Barcelona Convention is implemented by both the contracting parties and the European Union, which is also a party, as well as by national governments.

   9. *Non-point marine pollution.* The problem of non-point pollution is not well-addressed even by the domestic laws of important states. In the United States the Clean Water Act sections 208 and 319 (33 U.S.C. § 1288 and 1329) address

non-point pollution. Section 2008 directs the states to identify areas with substantial water quality control problems and to develop plans to correct the situation. In 1987, Congress enacted section 319 of the Clean Water Act, which requires states to compile new lists of waters impaired by non-point pollution and to develop new control programs on a watershed basis. Thus, the U.S. Environmental Protection Agency leaves non-point pollution control to each individual state, and the section 208 and 319 programs have done little to solve the problem. In the late 1990s, the EPA started a controversial new initiative to combat non-point pollution: using its authority under Clean Water Act section 303 (33 U.S.C. § 1313), the EPA required states to establish "total maximum daily loads" (TMDL) for waters within their boundaries for which the effluent limitations established under the Clean Water Act section 301 (33 U.S.C. § 1311) are insufficient to meet the water quality standards applicable to such waters. The EPA has also established a TMDL-like program for toxic pollutants such as mercury under Clean Water Act, 33 U.S.C. § 1314(1). But these programs have not been fully implemented by most states.[19]

Under a TMDL program a regulator establishes the total maximum daily load of various pollutants for a particular water body. This TMDL defines the maximum amount of a pollutant that a body of water can receive from point sources as well as non-point sources. The regulator then uses modeling that allocates the allowable TMDL between point and non-point sources. A comprehensive TMDL program covers all pollutants, including nitrogen, phosphorus, and sediment allocations. In the United States the Environmental Protection Agency has established such a program for the Chesapeake Bay, which is approximately 200 miles long and between four and 30 miles wide. The water surface of Chesapeake Bay encompasses more than 2,500 square miles in Virginia, Maryland, Pennsylvania, New York, Delaware, West Virginia, and the District of Columbia. There are 50 major rivers or tributaries flowing into Chesapeake Bay. But the Chesapeake Bay TMDL program is controversial and is tied up in litigation. *See American Farm Bureau Federation v. USEPA*, 984 F. Supp. 2d 289 (M.D. Pa. 2013), currently on appeal to the United States Court of Appeals for the Third Circuit.

If land-based non-point pollution controls are inadequate even in the United States, is there hope for an international law solution to such problems?

Section IV. PROTECTION OF THE ENVIRONMENT OF THE "AREA"

The mineral riches of the seabed were discovered during the epic voyage of the HMS Challenger in 1872–76. The Challenger's dredge-hauls recovered black polymetallic nodules as well as crusts of ferromanganese materials. At present three main mineral resources are known to exist on the sea bed and its subsoil — (1) polymetallic nodules, (2) cobalt-rich ferromanganese crusts, and (3) polymetallic sulphides.

---

[19] *See* HOLLY DOREMUS ET AL., ENVIRONMENTAL POLICY LAW 808–09 (5th ed., New York: Thomson/ Foundation Press 2008).

The metals contained in deep seabed polymetallic nodules come from erosion of rocks on land which are transported into the oceans by rivers and subsequently are deposited on the ocean floor. Polymetallic nodules collect on the ocean floor in a single layer; they contain various minerals, among which are nickel, manganese, cobalt, copper, and small amounts of molybdenum, vanadium, titanium, and the rare earths. Cobalt-rich ferromanganese crusts, which are present at lesser depths than the polymetallic nodules, are a marine mineral resource that is the result of millions of years of precipitation of substances from seawater on the submerged flanks of inactive underwater volcanoes. These deposits occur throughout the world's oceans; they are potential resources for the recovery of cobalt, titanium, cerium, nickel, platinum, manganese, thallium, and tellurium. Polymetallic sulphides result from actions near plate boundaries submerged on the ocean floor. Along such plate boundaries cold, heavy seawater comes into contact with hot, molten rocks on the ocean floor. When this occurs, the seawater is heated and expands, rising rapidly, dissolving and transporting metals from the surrounding rock. The dissolved metals react with sulphur in seawater, producing a precipitate of polymetallic sulphides known as "black smokers" because they resemble black smoke rising from factory smoke stacks. These polymetallic sulphides contain copper, iron, zinc, silver, gold, and other metals in varying amounts. These deposits occur at areas about the size of a football field wherever hot springs discharge from the sea floor.

The international legal regime that governs seabed mining is contained in Part XI of the UNCLOS, Articles 133 to 191. In addition, Annex III of UNCLOS contains the Basic Conditions of Prospecting, Exploration and Exploitation in the Area. *See also* Section 4, Articles 35 to 40 of UNCLOS Annex IV, the Statute of the International Tribunal for the Law of the Sea. These articles create a special Seabed Disputes Chamber of ITLOS for the purpose of resolving disputes arising under the international seabed mining regime. (*See* UNCLOS Articles 187 to 191).

Read over the provisions of UNCLOS Part XI. In the aftermath of the signing of UNCLOS in 1982, the United States and several industrialized nations announced that they would not ratify UNCLOS because of certain provisions of Part XI.

Can you identify these problem provisions?

In 1994, consultations under the auspices of the U.N. Secretary-General produced a modification of UNCLOS Part XI designed to placate the concerns of developed states concerning the sea bed mining regime. This document — the 1994 Agreement Relating to the Implementation of Part XI of the United Nations Convention on the Law of the Sea of 10 December 1982, July 28, 1994, S. Treaty Doc. No. 103-39 (1994) — is reprinted in the **Document Supplement.** How does this document address the following problems with regard to the original Part XI:

1. Policy-making in the Seabed Authority would be carried out by a one-nation, one-vote Assembly.

2. Decision-making in the Council may be carried out without input from the United States or developed state-parties.

3. There is insufficient oversight of decisions involving major financial and budgetary implications.

4. Seabed mining will be carried out without observing market principles because Part XI permits production controls and subsidies as well as potential discriminatory treatment of mining entities.

5. Part XI mandates forced technology transfer.

6. Part XI entails possible discrimination against qualified mining applicants.

7. Part XI creates discrimination in favor of the Enterprise, the operational mining arm of the International Seabed Authority.

8. Part XI would impose undue financial and regulatory burdens on industrialized countries and private mining entities.

9. Part XI creates a system of unequal sharing of revenues from mining.

10. Under Part XI a review conference would have the power to impose treaty amendments on the United States and other nations without their consent;

Are these concerns ameliorated by the 1994 Agreement?

At the heart of the international seabed mining regime is the International Sea-bed Authority (ISA), which is located in Kingston, Jamaica. (*See* UNCLOS Articles 156 to 158). The ISA is an autonomous international organization established to organize and control all mineral development activities in the Area, defined in UNCLOS Article 1 (1) as the seabed, the ocean floor and subsoil beyond the limits of national jurisdiction, the geographical area underlying most of the world's oceans. The tasks of the ISA are set out in UNCLOS Part XI. Note that Article 136 of UNCLOS states that the resources of the Area are the common heritage of mankind, which means that they are vested in mankind as a whole, on whose behalf the ISA is empowered to act. The ISA has four main functions:

- To administer the mineral resources of the Area;

- To adopt rules, regulations and procedures for the conduct of mining activities prospecting, exploration and exploitation — of the Area;

- To promote marine scientific research in the Area (to this end the ISA administers an International Seabed Authority Endowment Fund); and

- To protect and conserve the natural resources of the area, and to prevent damage to the flora and fauna of the marine environment.

The principal organs of the ISA are an Assembly, a Council, and a Secretariat, headed by a Secretary-General. Under UNCLOS Article 163, the ISA was to have two subsidiary organs, an Economic Planning Commission and a Legal and Technical Commission. At present the function of the former Commission are being handled by the Legal and Technical Commission. In addition, the 1994 Agreement established a Finance Committee in the ISA.

The Assembly is the supreme organ of the ISA; it meets annually and in such special sessions as may be called by the Assembly. (UNCLOS, Article 159–60). Each member of the Assembly has one vote, and decisions are taken by consensus, but in the absence of consensus, decisions on matters of substance may be taken by two-thirds vote. The powers and functions of the Assembly are set out in UNCLOS Article 160.

The Council is the executive organ of the ISA (UNCLOS Articles 161–65). The Council initiates policies with respect to seabed mining and both promotes and regulates exploration and exploitation of seabed resources. The Council's task is to approve contract applications, draw up contracts, oversee their implementation, and to establish environmental and other regulatory standards. The Council is adopting a Mining Code that will provide a comprehensive regulatory regime for seabed mining. Key provisions of the ongoing Mining Code include a Regulation on Prospecting and Exploration for Polymetallic Nodules in the Area (13 July 2000); a Regulation on Prospecting and Exploration for Polymetallic Sulphides in the Area (7 May 2010); and a Regulation on Prospecting and Exploration for Cobalt-Rich Crusts in the Area (27 July 2012). The entire Mining Code may be found at http://www.isa.org.jm/en/mcode. The Council will have additional responsibilities once sea bed mining exploitation commences. The Council will oversee compliance with mining regulations and will monitor the economic effects of sea bed production. The Council will also issue directives to the Enterprise and will establish a staff of inspectors to check compliance with regulations.

The Council consists of 36 members of the ISA elected by the Assembly organized into five chambers as follows:

- Four states that are major consumers of seabed minerals including the state having the largest economy;

- Four states with the largest investment in seabed activities;

- Six developing countries with special interests (land-locked states; major importer states);

- Four states among parties that are major exporters of seabed minerals; and

- Eighteen members elected to ensure overall geographical balance.

So far the Council has taken all major decisions by consensus. If voting is necessary, procedural votes may be taken by simple majority, while decisions of substance require either a two-thirds or three-fourths majority vote.

A major feature of UNCLOS Part XI is the creation of the Enterprise (Article 170) as the operational mining entity of the ISA. Under UNCLOS Article 153, the Enterprise has the capacity to carry out mining activities as well as the transporting, processing, and marketing of minerals recovered from the Area. The Statute of the Enterprise is contained in Annex IV of UNCLOS, Articles 1–13.

The regime for seabed mining as specified in UNCLOS Article 153 is a so-called parallel system which involves either a state-owned mining company or a state-sponsored private natural or juridical person, on the one hand; and the Enterprise on the other. Each application by an entity operated or sponsored by a state party must designate a section of the Area large enough to accommodate two mining operations of approximately equal commercial value. If the application is approved, the ISA allocates one part to the applicant and the other part is designated as a reserved area, a site banking scheme to reserve areas for the future conduct of mining by the Enterprise.

At this writing the ISA has entered into 15 year exploration contracts with 13 contractors, either state-owned companies or state-sponsored contractors; another four contracts are in process. No production of seabed minerals has actually occurred under the ISA regime.

The United States is the only major industrial country that has not ratified UNCLOS. The U.S. has promulgated an alternative national legal regime for the mining of seabed minerals, the Deep Sea bed Hard Mineral Resources Act, 30 U.S.C. § 1401 et seq. This act is implemented by regulations issued by the U.S. Department of Commerce, National Oceanic and Atmospheric Administration (NOAA), 15 CFR Part 970. NOAA has issued several exploration licenses to companies under this regulatory regime.

Suppose you are the CEO of a company interested in conducting sea bed mining. Which regime would you apply to, the ISA or the U.S.?

PROBLEM 7-5
MINING THE RICHES OF THE SEA

The ABC Nautilus Mining Company is a Canadian corporation with long experience mining and processing minerals in mountain areas of North America. ABC has contacted the government of Cook Islands in the South Pacific about sponsoring ABC to carry out prospecting and exploration activities in the sea bed and subsoil of the South Pacific Ocean. ABC has obtained information that an area of about 100 square kilometers ranging from 150 to 300 kilometers off the coast of the northern Cook Islands would be an ideal area to mine polymetallic nodules and polymetallic sulphides. ABC, after exploration, may exploit this area using un-manned remote cutting machines which can be operated from a surface ship. The ore that is removed will then be conveyed to the surface by a continuous line bucket system to a processing ship which will separate the ore from valuable minerals. The rock resulting from the separation process will then be dumped back into the sea. Scientists and experts with whom ABC has consulted have stated that this mining process is safe and will have little impact on the environment. There may be some temporary disruption of the benthic layer and the undersea ecosystem and some temporary pollution resulting from an increase in the turbidity and toxicity of the water column above the mining site, but considering that the site is in the middle of the ocean far from inhabited lands and in deep waters, the impact on the marine environment will be limited and not long-lasting. ABC sees no need to use cleaner technology such as enclosed cutting tools and hydraulic suction casing to convey the ores to the surface. ABC also sees no need to replace the spent rock more carefully on the sea floor instead of jettisoning it overboard.

The government of Cook Islands has no experience is administering seabed mining ventures and is leaving the legality of this operation up to the experts of the ISA. The CEO of ABC has told the Prime Minister of Cook Islands that there is no need for him to introduce legislation or administrative regulations to govern the exploration or mining activities as everything can be covered by contract. The CEO of ABC has also stated that there is no danger of extraordinary liability on the part of Cook Islands under international law. The worst-case accident that may occur is a ship collision or fire aboard one of ABC's vessels. ABC will have insurance to cover such a casualty so Cook Islands should not worry; any such casualty will also be far from any inhabited area so there is no chance of damages.

Under the ISA's standard contract provisions, the contract with ABC will contain the following provisions:

Section 15
Safety, labour and health standards

15.1 The Contractor shall comply with the generally accepted international rules and standards established by competent international organizations or general diplomatic conferences concerning the safety of life at sea, and the prevention of collisions and such rules, regulations and procedures as may be adopted by the Authority relating to safety at sea. Each vessel used for carrying out activities in the Area shall possess current valid certificates required by and issued pursuant to such international rules and standards.

15.2 The Contractor shall, in carrying out exploration under this contract, observe and comply with such rules, regulations and procedures as may be adopted by the Authority relating to protection against discrimination in employment, occupational safety and health, labour relations, social security, employment security and living conditions at the work site. Such rules, regulations and procedures shall take into account conventions and recommendations of the International Labour Organization and other competent international organizations.

Section 16
Responsibility and liability

16.1 The Contractor shall be liable for the actual amount of any damage, including damage to the marine environment, arising out of its wrongful acts or omissions, and those of its employees, subcontractors, agents and all persons engaged in working or acting for them in the conduct of its operations under this contract, including the costs of reasonable measures to prevent or limit damage to the marine environment, account being taken of any contributory acts or omissions by the Authority.

16.2 The Contractor shall indemnify the Authority, its employees, subcontractors and agents against all claims and liabilities of any third party arising out of any wrongful acts or omissions of the Contractor and its employees, agents and subcontractors, and all persons engaged in working or acting for them in the conduct of its operations under this contract.

16.3 The Authority shall be liable for the actual amount of any damage to the Contractor arising out of its wrongful acts in the exercise of its powers and functions, including violations under article 168, paragraph 2, of the Convention, account being taken of contributory acts or omissions by the Contractor, its employees, agents and subcontractors, and all persons engaged in working or acting for them in the conduct of its operations under this contract.

16.4 The Authority shall indemnify the Contractor, its employees, subcontractors, agents and all persons engaged in working or acting for them in the conduct of its operations under this contract, against all claims and liabilities of any third party arising out of any wrongful acts or omissions in the exercise of its powers and functions hereunder, including violations under article 168, paragraph 2, of the Convention.

––––––

Is the assessment of ABC that Cook Islands need not worry about liability under international law correct? Consider the Advisory Opinion of the Sea bed Disputes Chamber below.

As to the potential environmental impacts of ABC's mining activities, a Workshop held by the ISA in collaboration with the government of Fiji in 2011, has recommended that every contract for prospecting and exploration of the seabed mineral resources should require the contractor to prepare an Environmental Impact Assessment (EIA). According to the published workshop results: Environmental Management Needs for Exploration and Exploitation of Deep Sea Minerals, ISA Technical Study No. 10, the content and process of preparing the EIA should be as follows:

Content of the Environmental Impact Statement

The applicant should provide detailed responses to all areas below that are relevant to the development proposal.

Executive summary

One of the main objectives of this section is to provide an explanation of the project for non-technical readers. Information provided in the executive summary should briefly describe:

    A. the proposed development activity and its objectives;

    B. anticipated bio-physical and socio-economic impacts (direct/indirect, reversible/irreversible) of the activity;

    C. details of remedial actions that are proposed;

    D. the benefits to be derived from the project;

    E. details of the consultation programme undertaken by the applicant, including degree of public interest; and

    F. end-use plans for the development activity.

The summary should not be more than 15 pages in length and in English. Appendices should be attached, as appropriate, to the EIS in order to provide complete information on the development proposal. These should cover the following points:

I. The Project

This should include a brief description of the deposit discovery and the exploration and test mining activities conducted to date.

Project proponent

This section should summarize the credentials of the Contractor proposing the development, including major shareholders.

Purpose of and justification for the development

The purpose of this section is to ensure that only development activities that are in line with the Authority's goals and objectives are considered for approval. This section should provide information on the viability of the proposed development activity. These details should include, but not limited to, the following:

A. the capital cost associated with the development;

B. the proponent's technological expertise and resources;

C. results of any feasibility investigations that have been carried out;

D. the extent of landowner and/or resource owner support, including a copy of the formal written approval of their consent;

E. the anticipated lifespan and development phases of the project.

II. Policy, legal and administrative framework

This section should provide information on relevant legislation, agreements or policies that are applicable to the proposed mining operation. It is separated into four sections, each covering a different aspect of the legal framework.

Applicable mining and environmental legislation, policy and agreements

The applicant should note any legislation, regulation or guidelines that apply to the management, or regulation of mining, or the environment in the Area, or any other relevant (existing or proposed) jurisdiction. This should include a note on how the proposed operation will comply with these requirements.

Other legislation, policy and regulations

Description of any other legislation, policy or regulations that do not apply specifically to mining or environment, but may be relevant to the proposal (e.g., shipping regulations, offshore mining certificates, and potentially many more inside jurisdictional boundaries).

Relevant international agreements

This subsection describes other more general international agreements that could be applicable to the operation, such as UNCLOS, CBD regulations and UNGA resolutions.

International standards, principles and guidelines

Any other non-legal standards or guidelines that may apply to best practice in the operation, e.g., Equator Principles.

III. Stakeholder consultation

This section describes any consultation(s) that may have taken place with interested parties and stakeholders with an interest in the OSM application in the period leading up to the application.

Relevant jurisdiction consultation requirements

This outlines any international or jurisdictional consultation obligations.

Stakeholders

List any relevant stakeholders or other interested parties that have been consulted.

Public consultation and disclosure programme

Description of the goals and consultation workshop meetings that have occurred prior to the preparation of the report.

IV. Description of the proposed development

All relevant details on the proposed development activity required under this section should be provided where applicable to the proposal. Details to be provided under this section may include the headings listed below.

Location

This section should include detailed location maps (drawn to scale), site layout, etc.

Associated activities

This section should include a description of any supporting activities and infrastructure required (e.g., ports, barges, transportation corridors, crew transfers, etc.).

Project components

This section should provide background information to the proposal, technologies to be employed, etc. For polymetallic nodule exploitation;, Contractors should refer to Section IV C of the Recommendations for the guidance of contractors for the: assessment of the possible environmental impacts arising from exploration for polymetallic nodules in the Area (ISBA/16/LTC/7). This section should include information on methods of exploitation site selection including alternatives investigated; relevant diagrams and drawings.

Mineral resource

This section should include the type of resource proposed for extraction (e.g; nodules, polymetallic sulphides, cobalt-rich crusts or other mineral); the type of commodity, the grade and volume. Estimates of inferred and indicated resource should be provided.

Offshore mining and support equipment

This section should include descriptions of the offshore mining and support equipment (including vessels) required to carry out the activity.

Mining

Mine plan

General mining sequence

Hazardous materials management

Description of hazardous materials

Transportation

Storage; handling and disposal

Workforce

Workforce description

Employment policy

Capacity-building objectives and commitments

Construction and operating standards

This section should outline the design codes to which the equipment will be built, as well as the health and safety standards that will be applied.

Design codes

Health and safety

Decommissioning and closure

Offshore infrastructure

Onshore facilities

V. Development timetable (Detailed schedule)

This should include the major phases of the operation, as well as the milestone dates on which relevant tasks are expected to be completed. Information on the development timetable provided under this section should clearly communicate the different phases in the development proposal. Information provided in this section should include, but not be limited to, the following:

A. The funding arrangement for proposed activity or if availability of funds is subject to this or other approvals being granted;

B. Pre-construction activities;

C. Construction schedule; staging, etc.;

D. Commissioning and operational schedules;

E. Infrastructure development schedule; and

F. Closure schedule.

VI. Description of the existing offshore environment

In this section, the applicant is to give a detailed account of knowledge of the environmental conditions at the site. It provides the baseline description of geological, oceanographic and biological conditions against which impacts will be measured and assessed.

Regional overview

Provide a general description of the environmental conditions in the broad region of the site, including major oceanographic, geological and biological setting.

Studies completed

Special considerations for site

Description of any notable characteristics of the site, whether geological, oceanographic or biological, such as hydrothermal venting, seamounts, high-surface productivity, eddies and endemic fauna.

Meteorology and air quality

Geological setting

Description of the general geologica/landscape and topographic features of the site.

Physical oceanographic setting

Description of oceanographic aspects such as currents, sedimentation rates.

Water quality

Description of water mass characteristics at the site at various depths, including nutrients, particle loads, temperature and dissolved gas profiles, etc.

Sediment characteristics

Description of substrate composition with special reference to sediment composition, pore water profiles, and grain size.

Biological environment

This section is divided by depth regime into a description of the various biological components and communities that are present in or utilize the water column and seabed in the region of the site.

Pelagic

From the surface down to 200m. This includes plankton, surface/near surface fish, such as tunas, but also utilization by seabirds and marine mammals.

Midwater

Open water from a depth of 200m down to the seafloor. This includes zooplankton, mesopelagic and bathypelagic fishes and deep-diving mammals.

Benthic

Benthic invertebrate communities, including infauna and demersal fish. This should include considerations of species richness, biodiversity, faunal densities and community structures.

Natural hazards

Description of volcanism, seismic activity, etc.

Noise

Description of ambient noise if any, influence of ongoing exploration and maritime activity.

Description of the existing onshore environment

Description of the conditions of any onshore processing operation, as well as any relevant environmental information on transit lanes/areas.

VII. Socio-economic environment

If the project area occurs within an area used by fisheries, then this needs to be described here.

Existing resource utilization

Fisheries

Marine traffic

This section describes the non-project-related marine traffic occurring within the project area.

Other

This section will deal with other uses of the project area that are not related to fisheries or marine traffic (e.g., telecommunications cables, other mineral exploitation projects, etc.).

Cultural/historical resources

This section will deal with items of cultural/historical significance that occur within the project area (e.g., shipwrecks).

Socio-economic and socio-cultural issues

Issues that may arise within and outside of the project area should be identified, including whether this is a direct or indirect outcome of the physical, biological or socio-economic effects of the proposed development activity.

Onshore socio-economic environment

It is envisaged that this section will only be applicable to projects located within EEZs.

VIII. Environmental impacts, mitigation and management measures

In this section, the applicant is to provide a detailed description and evaluation of potential impacts of the mining operation to environmental components identified previously. The format should be consistent between and within sections, so for each component a description would be included of:

A.   the nature and extent of any impact;

B.   measures that will be taken to avoid, mitigate or minimize such impact; and

C.   what unavoidable impacts will remain.

It is expected that some repetition will occur between sections, notably where an impact of the mining operation will affect several components of the environment at the site.

Description of potential impact categories

This section is an overview and description of general impact categories caused by the mining operation. This is not expected to be detailed, but introduce the major types of effect, such as habitat removal, crushing of animals, creation of sediment plumes, noise, light etc. A description should be included of any lessons learnt from activities during the exploratory phase of the programme (e.g., test mining trials).

Air quality

Description of any effect on the air quality. from the surface or subsurface operations.

Geological setting

Description of impacts the mining may have on the topography of the site or the geological or geophysical composition:

Physical oceanographic setting:

Description of effects on current speed; direction; sedimentation rates, etc.

Water quality

Description of effects such as sediment plume generation and clarity of water, particulate loading, water temperature, dissolved gas and nutrient levels etc., in all levels of the water column.

Sediment characteristics

Changes in the sediment composition, grain size, density, pore water profiles.

Biological communities

Description of the effects on individuals, communities, populations and meta-populations from the proposed activity.

Pelagic

Includes plankton, surface/ near-surface fish, such as tunas, but also seabirds and marine mammals.

Midwater

Includes zooplankton, mesopelagic and bathypelagic fishes and deep-diving mammals.

Benthic

Benthic epifaunal and infauna/invertebrate communities and demersal fish.

Natural hazards

Volcanic eruptions, seismic activity, sea floor instability and tsunami.

Noise

Noise above existing levels.

Greenhouse gas emissions and climate change

Effects of surface/ subsurface activities on GHG emissions and any activity that may affect water acidity.

IX. Maritime safety and interactions with shipping

X. Residual impacts

XI. Biosecurity

XII. Waste management

Vessel waste management, with reference to compliance with relevant conventions, legislation or principles, methods of cleaner production and energy balance.

XIII. Cumulative impacts

Here the proposer should consider the nature and extent of any interactions between various impacts where they may have cumulative effects.

XIV. On and nearshore environment

Where appropriate, this should contain a description of general issues related to transit from/to the site and port operation, etc. This subsection is to be developed in as much detail as appropriate, with emphasis on the particular circumstances of the mining operation and processing location.

XV. Socio-economic impacts

In this section, the applicant is to provide a description and evaluation of potential impacts of the mining operation to previously identified socioeconomic components. This involves fisheries, marine traffic, and possible telecommunications impacts.

XVI. Cultural/Historical resources (e.g., shipwrecks, IUCN natural world heritage sites)

XVII. Environmental management, monitoring and reporting

Sufficient information should be provided to enable the Authority to anticipate possible environmental management, monitoring and reporting requirements for an environment permit. Information listed should reflect the proponent's environmental policy (Environment Management System) and the translation of that policy to meet the requirements under this section and previous sections during different stages in the project life, i.e. from operations to decommissioning and closure. Information detailed in this section should include, but not be limited to, the headings below.

Organizational structure and responsibilities

This section should show how the Contractor's environmental team fits into its overall organizational structure. Responsibilities of key personnel should be outlined.

Environmental Management System (EMS)

It is understood that a full EMS may or may not exist at the EIS submission stage. This section should outline the standards that will be considered and/ or aligned with in developing the EMS for the project.

Environmental Management Plan (EMP)

An EMP will be submitted as a separate document for the Authority's approval prior to exploitation operations commencing. This section should provide an overview of what an EMP would entail. This section shall include, as a minimum, the following headings.

Mitigation and management

This section should summarize the actions and commitments that have arisen from the impact minimization and mitigation strategies.

Monitoring plan

This section should summarize the monitoring plan approach and programme. For development proposals associated with nodule exploitation, Contractors should take into account sections IV(D) and IV(E) of the "Recommendations for the guidance of contractors for the assessment of the possible environmental impacts arising from exploration for polymetallic nodules in the Area (ISBA/16/LTC/7)."

Closure plan

It is expected that a closure plan will be submitted as a separate document for the Authority's approval. However, this section should provide an overview of what the closure plan will entail, including decommissioning, continued monitoring and rehabilitation measures, if applicable.

NOTE

One reason why sea bed mining in the Area is not yet operational is the complex legal issues that are involved. The principal international environmental law obligations that must be observed include the following:

- Precautionary approach (Rio Principle 15; ISA Mining Code)
- Duty to preserve and protect the marine environment (UNCLOS Art. 192)
- Duty to prevent, reduce and control pollution from seabed activities (UNCLOS Art. 208)
- Best environmental practices (ISA Mining Code)
- Duty to prevent transboundary harm (Rio Principle 2; Part XII of UNCLOS)
- Duty to conserve biodiversity (UN Convention on Biological Diversity Art. 3)
- Duty to prepare a prior environmental impact assessment (UNCLOS Art. 206)
- Duty to monitor environmental impacts (UNCLOS Art. 204)

In addition, seabed mining may expose the seabed mining contractor, the sponsoring state, and even the ISA to liability for damages. Consider the following landmark opinion by the Seabed Disputes Chamber of the International Tribunal for the Law of the Sea.

RESPONSIBILITIES AND OBLIGATIONS OF STATES SPONSORING PERSONS AND ENTITIES WITH RESPECT TO ACTIVITIES IN THE AREA
International Tribunal for the Law of the Sea, Seabed Disputes Chamber, Case No. 17 (1 Feb. 2011)

ADVISORY OPINION

[On 11 May 2011, the Council of the International Seabed Authority transmitted a request to the Seabed Disputes Chamber of the International Tribunal for an Advisory Opinion on the following three questions:

What are the legal responsibilities and obligations of States Parties to the Convention with respect to the sponsorship of activities in the Area in accordance with the Convention, in particular Part XI, and the 1994 Agreement relating to the

Implementation of Part XI of the United Nations Convention on the Law of the Sea of 10 December 1982?

What is the extent of liability of a State Party for any failure to comply with the provisions of the Convention, in particular Part XI, and the 1994 Agreement, by an entity whom it has sponsored under Article 153, paragraph 2(b), of the Convention?

What are the necessary and appropriate measures that a sponsoring State must take in order to fulfill its responsibility under the Convention, in particular Article 139 and Annex III, and the 1994 Agreement?

This Request for an Advisory Opinion was occasioned by the fact that on 10 April 2008, the International Seabed Authority had received two applications for approval of a plan of work for exploration in the areas reserved for the conduct of activities by the Authority through the Enterprise or in association with developing states pursuant to UNCLOS. These two applications were sponsored respectively by the Republic of Nauru and the Kingdom of Tonga.]

Question 1

72.   The first question submitted to the chamber is as follows:

   What are the legal responsibilities and obligations of States Parties to the Convention with respect to the sponsorship of activities in the Area in accordance with the Convention, in particular Part XI, and the 1994 Agreement relating to the implementation of Part XI of the United Nations Convention on the Law of the Sea of 10 December 1982?

· · · ·

I. Sponsorship

74.   The notion of "sponsorship" is a key element in the system for the exploration and exploitation of the resources of the Area set out in the Convention. Article 153, paragraph 2, of the Convention describes the "parallel system" of exploration and exploitation activities indicating that such activities shall be carried out by the Enterprise, and, in association with the Authority, by States Parties or state enterprises or natural or juridical persons. It further states that, in order to be eligible to carry out such activities, natural and juridical persons must satisfy two requirements. First, they must be either nationals of a State Party or effectively controlled by it or its nationals. Second, they must be "sponsored by such States." Article 153, paragraph 2(b), of the Convention makes the requirement of sponsorship applicable also to state enterprises.

· · · ·

77.   The connection between States Parties and domestic law entities required by the Convention is twofold, namely, that of nationality and that of effective control. All contractors and applicants for contracts must secure and maintain the sponsorship of the State or States of which they are nationals. If another State or its nationals exercises effective control, the

sponsorship of that State is also necessary. This is provided for in Annex Ill, article 4, paragraph 3, of the Convention and confirmed in regulation 11, paragraph 2, of the Nodules Regulations and of the Sulphides Regulations.

. . . .

II. "Activities in the Area"

82. Question 1 concerns the responsibilities and obligations of sponsoring States in respect of "activities in the Area." This expression is defined in article 1, paragraph 1 (3), of the Convention as "all activities of exploration for, and exploitation of, the resources of the Area." According to article 133 (a) of the Convention, for the purposes of Part XI, the term "resources" means "all solid, liquid or gaseous mineral resources in situ in the Area at or beneath the seabed, including polymetallic nodules." The two definitions, however, do not indicate what is meant by "exploration" and "exploitation." It is important to note that according to article 133 (b), "resources, when recovered from the Area, are referred to as 'minerals.'"

83. Some indication of the meaning of the term "activities in the Area" may be found in Annex IV, article 1, paragraph 1, of the Convention. It reads as follows:

> The Enterprise is the organ of the Authority which shall carry out activities in the Area directly, pursuant to article 153, paragraph 2(a), as well as the transporting, processing and marketing of minerals recovered from the Area.

84. This provision distinguishes "activities in the Area" which the Enterprise carries out directly pursuant to article 153, paragraph 2(a), of the Convention; from other activities with which the Enterprise is entrusted, namely, the transporting, processing and marketing of minerals recovered from the Area. Consequently, the latter activities are not included in the notion of "activities in the Area" referred to in Annex IV, article 1, paragraph 1, of the Convention.

94. In light of the above, the expression "activities in the Area," in the context of both exploration and exploitation, includes, first of all, the recovery of minerals from the seabed and their lifting to the water surface.

95. Activities directly connected with those mentioned in the previous paragraph such as the evacuation of water from the minerals and the preliminary separation of materials of no commercial interest, including their disposal at sea, are deemed to be covered by the expression "activities in the Area." "Processing," namely, the process through which metals are extracted from the minerals and which is normally conducted at a plant situated on land, is excluded from the expression "activities in the Area." This is confirmed by the wording of Annex IV, article 1, paragraph 1, of the Convention as well as by information provided by the Authority at the request of the Chamber.

96. Transportation to points on land from the part of the high seas superjacent to the part of the Area in which the contractor operates cannot be included

in the notion of "activities in the Area," as it would be incompatible with the exclusion of transportation from "activities in the Area" in Annex IV, article 1, paragraph 1, of the Convention. However, transportation within that part of the high seas, when directly connected with extraction and lifting, should be included in activities in the Area. In the case of polymetallic nodules, this applies, for instance, to transportation between the ship or installation where the lifting process ends and another ship or installation where the evacuation of water and the preliminary separation and disposal of material to be discarded take place. The inclusion of transportation to points on land could create an unnecessary conflict with provisions of the Convention such as those that concern navigation on the high seas.

. . . .

III. Prospecting

98.   "Prospecting," although mentioned in Annex III, article 2, of the Convention and in the Nodules Regulations and the Sulphides Regulations, is not included in the Convention's definition of "activities in the Area" because the Convention and the two Regulations distinguish it from "exploration" and from "exploitation." Moreover, under the Convention and related instruments, prospecting does not require sponsorship. In conformity with the questions submitted to it, which relate to "activities in the Area" and to sponsoring States, the Chamber will not address prospecting activities. However, considering that prospecting is often treated as the preliminary phase of exploration in mining practice and legislation, the Chamber considers it appropriate to observe that some aspects of the present Advisory Opinion may also apply to prospecting.

IV. Responsibilities and obligations

Key provisions

99.   The key provisions concerning the obligations of the sponsoring States are: article 139, paragraph 1; article 153, paragraph 4 (especially the last sentence); and 4, paragraph 4, of the Convention (especially the first sentence).

100.   These provisions read:

Article 139, paragraph 1

States Parties shall have the responsibility to ensure that activities in the Area, whether carried out by States Parties, or state enterprises or natural or juridical persons which possess the nationality of States Parties or are effectively controlled by them or their nationals, shall be carried out in conformity with this Part. The same responsibility applies to international organizations for activities in the Area carried out by such organizations.

Article 153, paragraph 4

The Authority shall exercise such control over activities in the Area as is necessary for the purpose of securing compliance with the relevant provisions of this Part and the Annexes relating thereto, and the rules, regulations and procedures of the Authority, and the plans of work approved in accordance with paragraph 3. States Parties shall assist the Authority by taking all measures necessary to ensure such compliance in accordance with article 139.

Annex III, article 4, paragraph 4

The sponsoring State or States shall, pursuant to article 139, have the responsibility to ensure, within their legal systems, that a contractor so sponsored shall carry out activities in the Area in conformity with the terms of its contract and its obligations under this Convention. A sponsoring State shall not, however, be liable for damage caused by any failure of a contractor sponsored by it to comply with its obligations if that State Party has adopted laws and regulations and taken administrative measures which are, within the framework of its legal system, reasonably appropriate for securing compliance by persons under its jurisdiction.

"Responsibility to ensure"

. . . .

107. The central issue in relation to Question 1 concerns the meaning of the expression "responsibility to ensure" in article 139, paragraph 1, and Annex III, article 4, paragraph 4, of the Convention.

108. "Responsibility to ensure" points to an obligation of the sponsoring State under international law. It establishes a mechanism through which the rules of the convention concerning activities in the Area, although being treaty law and thus binding only on the subjects of international law that have accepted them, become effective for sponsored contractors which find their legal basis in domestic law. This mechanism consists in the creation of obligations which States Parties must fulfill by exercising their power over entities of their nationality and under their control.

109. As will be seen in greater detail in the reply to Question 2, a violation of this obligation entails "liability." However, not every violation of an obligation by a sponsored contractor automatically gives rise to the liability of the sponsoring State. Such liability is limited to the State's failure to meet its obligation to "ensure" compliance by the sponsored contractor.

110. The sponsoring State's obligation "to ensure" is not an obligation to achieve, in each and every case, the result that the sponsored contractor complies with the aforementioned obligations. Rather, it is an obligation to deploy adequate means, to exercise best possible efforts, to do the utmost, to obtain this result. To utilize the terminology current in international law, this obligation may be characterized as an obligation "of conduct" and not "of result," and as an obligation of "due diligence."

111. The notions of obligations of "due diligence" and obligations "of conduct" are connected. This emerges clearly from the Judgment of the ICJ in the Pulp Mills on the River Uruguay: "An obligation to adopt regulatory or administrative measures . . . and to enforce them is an obligation of conduct. Both parties are therefore called upon, under article 36 [of the Statute of the River Uruguay], to exercise due diligence in acting through

the [Uruguay River] Commission for the necessary measures to preserve the ecological balance of the river" (paragraph 187 of the Judgment).

112. The expression "to ensure" is often used in international legal instruments to refer to obligations in respect of which, while it is not considered reasonable to make a State liable for each and every violation committed by persons under its jurisdiction, it is equally not considered satisfactory to rely on mere application of the principle that the conduct of private persons or entities is not attributable to the State under international law (see ILC Articles on State Responsibility, Commentary to article 8, paragraph 1).

113. An example may be found in article 194, paragraph 2, of the Convention which reads: "States shall take all measures necessary to ensure that activities under their jurisdiction or control are so conducted as not to cause damage by pollution to other States and their environment . . . ."

. . . .

115. In its Judgment in the Pulp Mills on the River Uruguay case, the ICJ illustrates the meaning of a specific treaty obligation that it had qualified as "an obligation to act with due diligence" as follows:

> It is an obligation which entails not only the adoption of appropriate rules and measures, but also a certain level of vigilance in their enforcement and the exercise of administrative control applicable to public and private operators, such as the monitoring of activities undertaken by such operators . . . . (Paragraph 197)

116. Similar indications are given by the International Law Commission in its Commentary to article 3 of its Articles on Prevention of Transboundary Harm from Hazardous Activities, adopted in 2001. According to article 3, the State of origin of the activities involving a risk of causing transboundary harm "shall take all appropriate measures to prevent significant transboundary harm or at any event to minimize the risk thereof." The Commentary states:

> The obligation of the State of origin to take preventive or minimization measures is one of due diligence. It is the conduct of the State of origin that will determine whether the State has complied with its obligation under the present articles. The duty of due diligence involved, however, is not intended to guarantee that significant harm be totally prevented, if it is not possible to do so. In that eventuality, the State of origin is required . . . to exert its best possible efforts to minimize the risk. In this sense, it does not guarantee that the harm would not occur. (Paragraph 7)

The content of the "due diligence" obligation to ensure

117. The content of "due diligence" obligations may not easily be described in precise terms. Among the factors that make such a description difficult is the fact that "due diligence" is a variable concept. It may change over time as measures considered sufficiently diligent at a certain moment may become not diligent enough in light, for instance. of new scientific or technological knowledge. It may also change in relation to the risks involved in the activity. As regards activities in the Area, it seems

reasonable to state that prospecting is, "generally speaking, less risky than exploration activities which, in turn, entail less risk than exploitation. Moreover, activities in the Area concerning different kinds of mineral, for example, polymetallic nodules on the one hand and polymetallic sulphides or cobalt rich ferromanganese crusts on the other, may require different standards of diligence. The standard of due diligence has to be more severe for the riskier activities.

. . . .

V. Direct obligations of sponsoring States

121.   The obligations of sponsoring States are not limited to the due diligence "obligation to ensure." Under the Convention and related instruments, sponsoring States also have obligations with which they have to comply independently of their obligation to ensure a certain behavior by the sponsored contractor. These obligations may be characterized as "direct obligations."

122.   Among the most important of these direct obligations incumbent on sponsoring States are: the obligation to assist the Authority in the exercise of control over activities in the Area; the obligation to apply a precautionary approach; the obligation to apply best environmental practices; the obligation to take measures to ensure the provision of guarantees in the event of an emergency order by the Authority for protection of the marine environment; the obligation to ensure the availability of recourse for compensation in respect of damage caused by pollution; and the obligation to conduct environmental impact assessments.

. . . .

VI. Environmental impact assessment

141.   The obligation of the contractor to conduct an environmental impact assessment is explicitly set out in section 1, paragraph 7, of the Annex to the 1994 Agreement as follows: "An application for approval of a plan of work shall be accompanied by an assessment of the potential environmental impacts of the proposed activities . . . ." The sponsoring State is under a due diligence obligation to ensure compliance by the sponsored contractor with this obligation.

. . . .

VII. Interests and needs of developing States

151.   With respect to activities in the Area, the fifth preambular paragraph of the Convention states that the achievement of the goals set out in previous preambular paragraphs: will contribute to the realization of a just and equitable international economic order which takes into account the interests and needs of mankind as a whole and, in particular, the special interests and needs of developing countries, whether coastal or land-locked.

152. Accordingly, it is necessary to examine whether developing sponsoring States enjoy preferential treatment as compared with that granted to developed sponsoring States under the Convention and related instruments.

153. Under article 140, paragraph 1, of the Convention : Activities in the Area shall, as specifically provided for in this Part, be carried out for the benefit of mankind as a whole, irrespective of the geographical location of States, whether coastal or land-locked, and taking into particular consideration the interests and needs of developing States . . . .

154. According to article 148 of the Convention: The effective participation of developing States in activities in the Area shall be promoted as specifically provided for in this Part, having due regard to their special interests and needs, and in particular to the special needs of the land-locked and geographically disadvantaged among them to overcome obstacles arising from their disadvantaged location, including remoteness from the Area and difficulty of access to and from it.

. . . .

156. For the purposes of the present Advisory Opinion, and in particular of Question 1, it is important to determine the meaning of article 148 of the Convention. According to this provision, the general purpose of promoting the participation of developing States in activities in the Area taking into account their special interests and needs is to be achieved "as specifically provided for" in Part XI (an expression also found in article 140 of the Convention). This means that there is no general clause for the consideration of such interests and needs beyond what is provided for in specific provisions of Part XI of the Convention. A perusal of Part XI shows immediately that there are several provisions designed to ensure the participation of developing States in activities in the Area and to take into particular consideration their interests and needs.

157. The approach of the Convention to this is particularly evident in the provisions granting a preference to developing States that wish to engage in mining in areas of the deep seabed reserved for the Authority (Annex III, articles 8 and 9, of the Convention); in the obligation of States to promote international cooperation in marine scientific research in the Area in order to ensure that programmes are developed "for the benefit of developing States" (article 143, paragraph 3, of the Convention); and in the obligation of the Authority and of States Parties to promote the transfer of technology to developing States (article 144, paragraph 1, of the Convention and section 5 of the Annex to the 1994 Agreement), and to provide training opportunities for personnel from developing States (article 144, paragraph 2, of the Convention and section 5 of the Annex to the 1994 Agreement); in the permission granted to the Authority in the exercise of its powers and functions to give special consideration to developing States, notwithstanding the rule against discrimination (article 152 of the Convention); and in the obligation of the Council to take "into particular consideration the interests and needs of developing States" in recommending, and approving, respectively, rules regulations and procedures on the

equitable sharing of financial and other benefits derived from activities in the Area (articles 160, paragraph 2(f)(i), and 162, paragraph 2(o)(i), of the Convention).

158. However, none of the general provisions of the Convention concerning the responsibilities (or the liability) of the sponsoring State "specifically provides" for according preferential treatment to sponsoring States that are developing States. As observed above, there is no provision requiring the consideration of such interests and needs beyond what is specifically stated in Part XI. It may therefore be concluded that the general provisions concerning the responsibilities and liability of the sponsoring State apply equally to all sponsoring States, whether developing or developed.

159. Equality of treatment between developing and developed sponsoring States is consistent with the need to prevent commercial enterprises based in developed States from setting up companies in developing States, acquiring their nationality and obtaining their sponsorship in the hope of being subjected to less burdensome regulations and controls. The spread of sponsoring States "of convenience" would jeopardize uniform application of the highest standards of protection of the marine environment, the safe development of activities in the Area and protection of the common heritage of mankind.

> [With respect to the equality issue, the ITLOS qualified its ruling by stating that "rules setting out direct obligations of states may provide for differences between developed and developing states (para. 160). Moreover, the precautionary approach may apply differently to developing and developed states (para. 161). Developing states should also be assisted with training (para. 162).]

. . . .

Question 2

164. The second question submitted to the Chamber is as follows:

> *What is the extent of liability of a State Party for any failure to comply with the provisions of the Convention in particular Part XI, and the 1994 Agreement, by an entity whom it has sponsored under Article 153, paragraph 2(b), of the Convention?*

I. Applicable provisions

165. In replying to this question, the Chamber will proceed from article 139, paragraph 2, of the Convention, read in conjunction with the second sentence of Annex III, article 4, paragraph 4, of the Convention.

166. Article 139, paragraph 2, of the Convention reads:

Without prejudice to the rules of international law and Annex III, article 22, damage caused by the failure of a State Party or international organization to carry out its responsibilities under this Part shall entail liability; States Parties or international organizations acting together shall bear joint and several liability. A State Party shall not however be liable for damage caused by any failure to comply with this Part by a person whom it has sponsored under article 153, paragraph 2(b), if the State Party has taken all necessary arid appropriate measures to secure effective compliance under article 153, paragraph 4, and Annex III, article 4, paragraph 4.

167. Annex III, article 4, paragraph 4, second sentence, of the Convention states:

A sponsoring State shall not, however, be liable for damage caused by any failure of a contractor sponsored by it to comply with its obligations if that State Party has adopted laws and regulations and taken administrative measures which are, within the framework of its legal system, reasonably appropriate for securing compliance by persons under its jurisdiction.

168. The Chamber will further take into account articles 235 and 304 as well as Annex III, article 22, of the Convention. Lastly, it will consider, as appropriate, the relevant rules on liability set out in the Nodules Regulations and the Sulphides Regulations. In this context, the Chamber notes that the Regulations issued to date by the Authority deal only with prospecting and exploration. Considering that the potential for damage, particularly to the marine environment, may increase during the exploitation phase, it is to be expected that member States of the Authority will further deal with the issue of liability in future regulations on exploitation.

. . . .

II. Liability in general

. . . .

171. Article 139, paragraph 2, of the Convention and the related provisions referred to above, prescribe or refer to different sources of liability, namely, rules concerning the liability of States Parties (article 139, paragraph 2, first sentence, of the Convention), rules concerning sponsoring State liability (article 139, paragraph 2, second sentence, of the Convention), and rules concerning the liability of the contractor and the Authority (referred to in Annex III, article 22, of the Convention). The "without prejudice" clause in the first sentence of article 139, paragraph 2, of the Convention refers to the rules of international law concerning the liability of States Parties and international organizations. A reference to the international law rules on liability is also contained in article 304 of the Convention. The Chamber considers that these rules supplement the rules concerning the liability of the sponsoring State set out in the Convention.

. . . .

III. Failure to carry out responsibilities

175. The Chamber will now turn to the interpretation of the elements constituting liability as set out in article 139, paragraph 2, of the Convention, read in conjunction with Annex III, article 4, paragraph 4, of the Convention.

176. The wording of article 139, paragraph 2, of the Convention clearly establishes two conditions for liability to arise: the failure of the sponsoring State to carry out its responsibilities (see paragraphs 64 to 71 on the meaning of key terms); and the occurrence of damage.

177. The failure of a sponsoring State to carry out its responsibilities, referred to in article 139, paragraph 2, of the Convention, may consist in an act or an omission that is contrary to that State's responsibilities under the deep seabed mining regime.

IV. Damage

178. As stated above, according to the first sentence of article 139, paragraph 2, of the Convention, the failure of a sponsoring State to carry out its responsibilities entails liability only if there is damage. This provision covers neither the situation in which the sponsoring State has failed to carry out its responsibilities but there has been no damage, nor the situation in which there has been damage but the sponsoring State has met its obligations. this constitutes an exception to the customary international law rule on liability since, as stated in the Rainbow Warrior Arbitration (Case concerning the difference between New Zealand and France concerning the interpretation or application of two agreements, concluded on 9 July 1986 between the two States and which related to the problems arising from the Rainbow Warrior Affair, UNRIAA, 1990, vol. XX, p. 215, at paragraph 110), and in paragraph 9 of the Commentary to article 2 of the ILC Articles on State Responsibility, a state may be held liable under customary international law even if no material damage results from its failure to meet its international obligations.

179. Neither the Convention nor the relevant Regulations (regulation 30 of the Nodules Regulations and regulation 32 of the Sulphides Regulations) specifies what constitutes compensable damage, or which subjects may be entitled to claim compensation. It may be envisaged that the damage in question would include damage to the Area and its resources constituting the common heritage of mankind, and damage to the marine environment.

180. No provision of the Convention can be read as explicitly entitling the Authority to make such a claim. It may, however, be argued that such entitlement is implicit in article 137, paragraph 2, of the Convention, which states that the Authority shall act "on behalf" of mankind. Each State Party may also be entitled to claim compensation in light of the *erga omnes* character of the obligation s relating to preservation of the environment of the high seas and in the Area. In support of this view, reference may be made to article 48 of the ILC Articles on State Responsibility, which provides:

> Any State other than an injured State is entitled to invoke the responsibility of another State . . . if: (a) the obligation breached is owed to a group of States including that State, and is established for the protection of a collective interest of the group; or (b) the obligation breached is owed to the international community as a whole.

Causal link between failure and damage

181. Article 139, paragraph 2, first sentence, of the Convention refers to "damage caused," which clearly indicates the necessity of a causal link between the damage and the failure of the sponsoring State to meet its responsibilities. The second sentence of article 139, paragraph 2, of the Convention does not mention this causal link. It refers only to a causal link between the activity of the sponsored contractor and the consequent damage. Nevertheless, the Chamber is of the view that, in order for the sponsoring State's liability to arise, there must be a causal link between the failure of that State and the damage caused by the sponsored contractor.

. . . .

V. Exemption from liability

185. The Chamber will now direct its attention to the meaning of the clause "shall not however be liable for damage" in article 139, paragraph 2, second sentence, and in Annex III, article 4, paragraph 4, second sentence, of the Convention.

186. This clause provides for the exemption of the sponsoring State from liability. Its effect is that, in the event that the sponsored contractor fails to comply with the Convention, the Regulations or its contract, and such failure results in damage, the sponsoring State cannot be held liable. The condition for exemption of the sponsoring State from liability is that, as specified in article 139, paragraph 2, of the Convention, it has taken "all necessary and appropriate measures to secure effective compliance" under article 153, paragraph 4, and Annex III, article 4, paragraph 4, of the Convention.

. . . .

VI. Scope of liability under the Convention

188. The Chamber will now deal with the scope of liability under article 139, paragraph 2, second sentence, of the Convention. This requires addressing several issues, namely, the standard of liability, multiple sponsorship, the amount and form of compensation and the relationship between the liability of the contractor and of the sponsoring State.

Standard of liability

189. With regard to the standard of liability, it was argued in the proceedings that the sponsoring State has strict liability, i.e., liability without fault. The Chamber, however, would like to point out that liability for damage of the sponsoring State arises only from its failure to meet its obligation of due diligence. This rules out the application of strict liability.

Multiple sponsorship

. . . .

192. Apart from the exception mentioned in paragraph 191, the provisions of article 139, paragraph 2, of the Convention and related instruments dealing with sponsorship do not differentiate between single and multiple sponsorship. Accordingly, the Chamber takes the position that, in the event of multiple sponsorship, liability is joint and several unless otherwise provided in the Regulations issued by the Authority.

Amount and form of compensation

. . . .

194. The obligation for a State to provide for a full compensation or restitute in integrum is currently part of customary international law. This conclusion was first reached by the Permanent Court of International Justice in the *Factory of Chorzow* case (PCJJ Series A, No. 17, p. 47). This obligation was further reiterated by the International Law Commission. According to article 31, paragraph 1, of the ILC Articles on State Responsibility: "The responsible State is under an obligation to make full reparation for the injury caused by the internationally wrongful act."

. . . .

Relationship between the liability of the contractor and of the sponsoring State

199. Concerning the relationship between the contractor's liability and that of the sponsoring State, attention may be drawn to Annex III, article 22, of the Convention. This provision reads as follows:

> The contractor shall have responsibility or liability for any damage arising out of wrongful acts in the conduct of its operations, account being taken of contributory acts or omissions by the Authority. Similarly, the Authority shall have responsibility or liability for any damage arising out of wrongful acts in the exercise of its powers and functions, including violations under article 168, paragraph 2, account being taken of contributory acts or omissions by the contractor. Liability in every case shall be for the actual amount of damage.

200. No reference is made in this provision to the liability of sponsoring States. It may therefore be deduced that the main liability for a wrongful act committed in the conduct of the contractor's operations or in the exercise of the Authority's powers and functions rests with the contractor and the Authority, respectively, rather than with the sponsoring State. In the view of the Chamber, this reflects the distribution of responsibilities for deep seabed mining activities between the contractor, the Authority and the sponsoring State.

. . . .

202. If the contractor has paid the actual amount of damage, as required under Annex III, article 22, of the Convention, in the view of the Chamber, there is no room for reparation by the sponsoring State.

203. The situation becomes more complex if the contractor has not covered the damage fully. It was pointed out in the proceedings that a gap in liability may occur if, notwithstanding the fact that the sponsoring State has taken all necessary and appropriate measures, the sponsored contractor has caused damage and is unable to meet its liability in full. It was further pointed out that a gap in liability may also occur if the sponsoring State failed to meet its obligations but that failure is not causally linked to the damage. In their written and oral statements, States Parties have expressed different views on this issue. Some have argued that the sponsoring State has a residual liability, that is, the liability to cover the damage not covered by the sponsored contractor although the conditions for a liability of the sponsoring State under article 139, paragraph 2, of the Convention are not met. Other States Parties have taken the opposite position.

204. In the view of the Chamber, the liability regime established by article 139 of the Convention and in related instruments leaves no room for residual liability. As outlined in paragraph 201, the liability of the sponsoring State and the liability of the sponsored contractor exist in parallel. The liability of the sponsoring State arises from its own failure to comply with its responsibilities under the Convention and related instruments. The liability of the sponsored contractor arises from its failure to comply with its obligations under its contract and its undertakings there under. As has been established, the liability of the sponsoring State depends on the occurrence of damage resulting from the failure of the sponsored contractor. However, as noted in paragraph 182, this does not make the sponsoring State responsible for the damage caused by the sponsored contractor.

205. Taking into account that, as shown above in paragraph 203, situations may arise where a contractor does not meet its liability in full while the sponsoring State is not liable under article 139, paragraph 2, of the Convention, the Authority may wish to consider the establishment of a trust fund to compensate for the damage not covered. The Chamber draws attention to article 235, paragraph 3, of the Convention which refers to such possibility.

VII. Liability of sponsoring States for violation of their direct obligations

206. As stated in paragraph 121, the Convention and related instruments provide for direct obligations of sponsoring States. Liability for violation of such obligations is covered by article 139, paragraph 2, first sentence, of the Convention.

207. In the event of failure to comply with direct obligations, it is not possible for the sponsoring State to claim exemption from liability as article 139, paragraph 2, second sentence, of the Convention does not apply.

VIII. "Without prejudice" clause

208. The Chamber will now consider the impact of international law on the deep seabed liability regime. Articles 139, paragraph 2, first sentence, and 304 of the Convention, state that their provisions are "without prejudice" to the rules of international law (see paragraph 169). It remains to be considered whether such statement may be used to fill a gap in the liability regime established in Part XI of the Convention and related instruments.

209. As already indicated, if the sponsoring State has not failed to meet its obligations, there is no room for its liability under article 139, paragraph 2, of the Convention even if activities of the sponsored contractor have resulted in damage. A gap in liability which might occur in such a situation cannot be closed by having recourse to liability of the sponsoring State under customary international law. The Chamber is aware of the efforts made by the International Law Commission to address the issue of damages resulting from acts not prohibited under international law. However, such efforts have not yet resulted in provisions entailing State liability for lawful acts. Here again (see paragraph 205) the Chamber draws the attention of the Authority to the option of establishing a trust fund to cover such damages not covered otherwise.

. . . .

Question 3

212. The third question submitted to the Chamber is as follows :

> *What are the necessary and appropriate measures that a sponsoring State must take in order to fulfill its responsibility under the Convention, in particular Article 139 and Annex III, and the 1994 Agreement?*

I. General aspects

213. The focus of Question 3, as of Questions 1 and 2, is on sponsoring States. The Question seeks to find out the "necessary and appropriate measures" that the sponsoring State "must" take in order to fulfill its responsibility under the Convention, in particular article 139 and Annex III, and the 1994 Agreement. The starting point for this inquiry is article 153 of the Convention, since it introduces for the first time the concept of the sponsoring State and the measures that it must take. Article 153 does not specify the measures to be taken by the sponsoring State. It makes a cross reference to article 139 of the Convention for guidance in the matter.

214. Article 139, paragraph 2, of the Convention provides that the sponsoring State shall not be liable for damage caused by any failure to comply with Part XI of the Convention by an entity sponsored by it under article 153, paragraph 2(b), of the Convention, "if the State Party has taken all necessary and appropriate measures to secure effective compliance under article 153, paragraph 4, and Annex III, article 4, paragraph 4."

215. Article 139, paragraph 2, of the Convention does not specify the measures that are "necessary and appropriate." It simply draws attention to article 153, paragraph 4, and Annex III, article 4, paragraph 4, of the Convention. The relevant part of Annex III, article 4, paragraph 4, reads as follows:

> A sponsoring State shall not, however, be liable for damage caused by any failure of a contractor sponsored by it to comply with its obligations if that State Party has adopted laws and regulations and taken administrative measures which are, within the framework of its legal system, reasonably appropriate for securing compliance by persons under its jurisdiction.

216. Although the terminology used in these provisions varies slightly, they deal in essence with the same subject matter and convey the same meaning. Annex III, article 4, paragraph 4, of the Convention contains an explanation of the words "necessary and appropriate measures" in article 139, paragraph 2, of the Convention.

217. Under these provisions, in the system of the responsibilities and liability of the sponsoring State, the "necessary and appropriate measures" have two distinct, although interconnected, functions as set out in the Convention. On the one hand, these measures have the function of ensuring compliance by the contractor with its obligations under the Convention and related instruments as well as under the relevant contract. On the other hand, they also have the function of exempting the sponsoring State from liability for damage caused by the sponsored contractor, as provided in article 139, paragraph 2, as well as in Annex III, article 4, paragraph 4, of the Convention. The first of these functions has been illustrated in the reply to Question 1, in connection with the due diligence obligation of the sponsoring State to ensure compliance by the sponsored contractor, while the second has been partially addressed in the reply to Question 2 and will be further addressed in the following paragraphs.

II. Laws and regulations and administrative measures

218. Annex III, article 4, paragraph 4, of the Convention requires the sponsoring State to adopt laws and regulations and to take administrative measures. Thus, there is here a stipulation that the adoption of laws and regulations and the taking of administrative measures are necessary. The scope and extent of the laws and regulations and administrative measures required depend upon the legal system of the sponsoring State. The ad option of laws and regulations is prescribed because not all the obligations of a contractor may be enforced through administrative measures or contractual arrangements alone, as specified in paragraphs 223 to 226.

. . . .

III. Compliance by means of a contract?

223. It is the requirement in Annex III, article 4, paragraph 4, of the Convention, that the measures to be taken by the sponsoring State should be in the form of laws and regulations and administrative measures. This

means that a sponsoring State could not be considered as complying with its obligations only by entering into a contractual arrangement, such as a sponsoring agreement, with the contractor. Not only would this be incompatible with the provision referred to above but also with the Convention in general and Part XI thereof in particular.

224. Mere contractual obligations between the sponsoring State and the sponsored contractor may not serve as an effective substitute for the laws and regulations and administrative measures referred to in Annex III, article 4, paragraph 4, of the Convention. Nor would they establish legal obligations that could be invoked against the sponsoring State by entities other than the sponsored contractor.

. . . .

IV. Content of the measures

227. The Convention leaves it to the sponsoring State to determine what measures will enable it to discharge its responsibilities. Policy choices on such matters must be made by the sponsoring State. In view of this, the Chamber considers that it is not called upon to render specific advice as to the necessary and appropriate measures that the sponsoring State must take in order to fulfill its responsibilities under the Convention.

. . . .

240. Under Annex III, article 21, paragraph 3, of the Convention, the rules, regulations and procedures concerning environmental protection adopted by the Authority are used as a minimum standard of stringency for the environmental or other laws and regulations that the sponsoring State may apply to the sponsored contractor. It is implicit in this provision that sponsoring States may apply to the contractors they sponsor more stringent standards as far as the protection of the marine environment is concerned.

241. Article 209, paragraph 2, of the Convention is based on the same approach. According to this provision, the requirements contained in the laws and regulations that States adopt concerning pollution of the marine environment from activities in the Area "undertaken by vessels, installations, structures and other devices flying their flag or of their registry or operating under their authority . . . shall be no less effective than the international rules, regulations, and procedures" established under Part XI, which consist primarily of the international rules, regulations and procedures adopted by the Authority.

242. For these reasons,

THE CHAMBER,

1. Unanimously,

   Decides that it has jurisdiction to give the advisory opinion requested.

2. Unanimously,

Decides to respond to the request for an advisory opinion.

3.   Unanimously,

Replies to Question 1 submitted by the Council as follows:

Sponsoring States have two kinds of obligations under the Convention and related instruments:

A.   The obligation to ensure compliance by sponsored contractors with the terms of the contract and the obligations set out in the Convention and related instruments.

This is an obligation of "due diligence." The sponsoring State is bound to make best possible efforts to secure compliance by the sponsored contractors.

B.   Direct obligations with which sponsoring States must comply independently of their obligation to ensure a certain conduct on the part of the sponsored contractors.

4.   Unanimously,

Replies to Question 2 submitted by the Council as follows:

The liability of the sponsoring State arises from its failure to fulfil its obligations under the Convention and related instruments. Failure of the sponsored contractor to comply with its obligations does not in itself give rise to liability on the part of the sponsoring State.

The conditions for the liability of the sponsoring State to arise are:

(a)   failure to carry out its responsibilities under the Convention; and

(b)   occurrence of damage.

5. Unanimously,

Replies to Question 3 submitted by the Council as follows:

The Convention requires the sponsoring State to adopt, within its legal system, laws and regulations and to take administrative measures that have two distinct functions, namely, to ensure compliance by the contractor with its obligations and to exempt the sponsoring State from liability.

The scope and extent of these laws and regulations and administrative measures depends on the legal system of the sponsoring State.

Such laws and regulations and administrative measures may include the establishment of enforcement mechanisms for active supervision of the activities of the sponsored contractor and for co-ordination between the activities of the sponsoring State and those of the Authority.

NOTES AND QUESTIONS

1.   The ITLOS Advisory Opinion was well-received especially because all three questions were answered unanimously by the court. Was the court correct in

interpreting the standard for compliance to be due diligence instead of strict liability? Was the court correct in stating that the obligations of both kinds — due diligence and direct obligations — apply equally to developed and developing states? What is the relationship between the due diligence and the direct obligations?

2. How does the standard of liability for sponsoring states differ from the standard of liability for the sponsored contractor?

3. How do you evaluate the care with which the Authority is preparing for exploitation of the resources of the deep seabed? Do you think the Authority is doing enough to protect marine ecosystems and the marine environment?

Section V. OPERATIONAL SHIP POLLUTION

The safe operation of ships is comprehensively addressed by IMO conventions. The relevant IMO conventions in this regard are listed in section II of this chapter. Several IMO conventions deal specifically with various forms of operational ship pollution. Two conventions deal with particular environmental problems of shipping: (1) the International Convention on the Control of Harmful Antifouling Systems on Ships (Antifouling Convention) (2001), which prohibits the use of harmful organotins (listed in Annex I of the convention) in antifouling paints used on ships, and (2) the International Convention for the Control and Management of Ships' Ballast Water and Sediments (Ballast Water Convention) (2004), which seeks to prevent, minimize, and ultimately eliminate the transfer of harmful aquatic organisms and pathogens through the control and management of ships' ballast water and sediments. The Antifouling Convention entered into force in 2008; the Ballast Water Convention is not yet in force. The United States ratified the Antifouling Convention in 2012.

The principal IMO convention dealing with operational ship pollution is the International Convention for the Prevention of Pollution from Ships (London, 1973 and 1978), which is known as MARPOL 73/78. MARPOL consists of two types of regulations. First, technical regulations cover the design and construction of ships and their onboard equipment. For example, after the Exxon Valdez oil spill in 1989, MARPOL was amended to require double-hull construction for new oil tankers (Regulation 13F), and single-hull tankers were required to be phased out (Regulation 13G). Second, MARPOL sets out discharge standards and regulations governing the discharge of certain categories of substances from ships.

MARPOL's operational pollution standards are contained in Annexes I to VI, as follows:

ANNEX I: PREVENTION OF POLLUTION BY OIL
Entry into force: 2 October 1983

The 1973 Convention maintained the oil discharge criteria prescribed in the 1969 amendments to the 1954 Oil Pollution Convention, without substantial changes, namely:

Operational discharges of oil from tankers are allowed only when all of the following conditions are met:

1. the total quantity of oil which a tanker may discharge in any ballast voyage whilst under way must not exceed 1/15,000 of the total cargo carrying capacity of the vessel;

2. the rate at which oil may be discharged must not exceed 30 litres per mile travelled by the ship; and

3. no discharge of any oil whatsoever must be made from the cargo spaces o f a tanker within 50 miles of the nearest land.

An oil record book is required, in which is recorded the movement of cargo oil and its residues from loading to discharging on a tank-to-tank basis.

In addition, in the 1973 Convention, the maximum quantity of oil permitted to be discharged on a ballast voyage of new oil tankers was reduced from 1/15,000 of the cargo capacity to 1/30,000 of the amount of cargo earned. These criteria applied equally both to persistent (black) and non-persistent (white) oils.

As with the 1969 OILPOL amendments, the 1973 Convention recognized the "load on top" (LOT) system which had been developed by the oil industry in the 1960s. On a ballast voyage the tanker takes on ballast water (departure ballast) in dirty cargo tanks. Other tanks are washed to take on clean ballast. The tank washings are pumped into a special slop tank. After a few days, the departure ballast settles and oil flows to the top. Clean water beneath is then decanted while new arrival ballast water is taken on. The upper layer of the departure ballast is transferred to the slop tanks. Alter further settling and decanting, the next cargo is loaded on top of the remaining oil in the slop tank, hence the term load on top.

A new and important feature of the 1973 Convention was the concept of "special areas" which are considered to be so vulnerable to pollution by a oil that oil discharges within them have been completely prohibited with minor and well-defined exceptions. The 1973 Convention identified the Mediterranean Sea, the Black Sea, and Baltic Sea, the Red Sea and the Gulf area as special areas. All oil-carrying chips are required to be capable of operating the method of retaining oily wastes on board through the "load on top" system or for discharge to shore reception facilities.

This involves the fitting of appropriate equipment, including an oil-discharge monitoring and control system, oily-water separating equipment and a fitting system, slop tanks, sludge tanks, piping and pumping arrangements.

New oil tankers (i.e. those for which the building contract was placed after 31 December 1975) of 70,000 tons deadweight and above, must be fitted with segregated ballast tanks large enough to provide adequate operating draught without the need to carry ballast water in cargo oil tanks.

Secondly, new oil tankers are required to meet certain subdivision and damage stability requirements so that, in any loading conditions, they can survive after damage by collision or stranding.

The Protocol of 1978 made a number of changes to Annex I of the parent convention. Segregated ballast tanks (SBT) are required on all new tankers of

20,000 dwt and above (in the parent convention SBTs were only required on new tankers of 70,000 dwt and above). The Protocol also required SBTs to be protectively located — that is, they must be positioned in such a way that they will help protect the cargo tanks in the event of a collision or grounding.

Another important innovation concerned crude oil washing (COW), which had been developed by the oil industry in the 1970s and offered major benefits. Under COW, tanks are washed not with water but with crude oil — the cargo itself. COW was accepted as an alternative to SBTs on existing tankers and is an additional requirement on new tankers.

For existing crude oil tankers (built before entry into force of the Protocol) a third alternative was permissible for a period of two to four years after entry into force of MARPOL 73/78. The dedicated clean ballast tanks (CBT) system meant that certain tanks are dedicated solely to the carnage of ballast water. This was cheaper than a full SBT system since It utilized existing pumping and piping, but when the period of grace has expired other systems must be used.

Drainage and discharge arrangements were also altered in the Protocol, regulations for improved stopping systems were introduced.

Some oil tankers operate solely in specific trades between ports which are provided with adequate reception facilities. Some others do not use water as ballast. The TSPP Conference recognized that such ships should not be subject to all MARPOL requirements and they were consequently exempted from the SBT, COW and CBT requirements. It is generally recognized that the effectiveness of international conventions depends upon the degree to which they are obeyed and this in turn depends largely upon the extent to which they are enforced. The 1978 Protocol to MARPOL therefore introduced stricter regulations for the survey and certification of ships.

The 1992 amendments to Annex I made it mandatory for new oil tankers to have double hulls — and it brought in a phase-in schedule for existing tankers to fit double hulls, which was subsequently revised in 2001 and 2003.

ANNEX II: CONTROL OF POLLUTION BY NOXIOUS LIQUID SUBSTANCES
Entry into force: 6 April 1987

Annex II details the discharge criteria and measures for the control of pollution by noxious liquid substances carried in bulk.

Some 250 substances were evaluated and included in the list appended to the Convention. The discharge of their residues is allowed only to reception facilities until certain concentrations and conditions (which vary with the category of substances) are complied with.

In any case, no discharge of residues containing noxious substances is permitted within 12 miles of the nearest land. More stringent restrictions apply to the Baltic and Black Sea areas.

ANNEX III: PREVENTION OF POLLUTION BY HARMFUL SUBSTANCES IN PACKAGED FORM
Entry into force: 1 July 1992

The first of the convention's optional annexes. States ratifying the Convention must accept Annexes I and II but can choose not to accept the other three — hence they have taken much longer to enter into force.

Annex III contains general requirements for the issuing of detailed standards on packing, marking, labeling, documentation, stowage, quantity limitations, exceptions and notifications for preventing pollution by harmful substances.

The International Maritime Dangerous Goods (IMDG) Code has, since 1991, included marine pollutants.

ANNEX IV: PREVENTION OF POLLUTION BY SEWAGE FROM SHIPS
Entry into force: 27 September 2003

The second of the optional Annexes, Annex IV contains requirements to control pollution of the sea by sewage. A revised Annex was adopted in 2004.

ANNEX V: PREVENTION OF POLLUTION BY GARBAGE FROM SHIPS
Entry into force: 31 December 1988

This deals with different types of garbage and specifies the distances from land in the manner in which they may be disposed of. The requirements are much stricter in a number of "special areas" but perhaps the most important feature of the Annex is the complete ban imposed on the dumping into the sea of all forms of plastic.

ANNEX VI: PREVENTION OF AIR POLLUTION FROM SHIPS
Entry into force: 19 May 2005

The regulations in this annex set limits on sulphur oxide and nitrogen oxide emissions from ship exhausts and prohibit deliberate emissions of ozone depleting substances.

Enforcement

Any violation of the MARPOL 73/78 Convention within the jurisdiction of any Party to the Convention is punishable either under the law of that Party or under the law of the flag State. In this respect, the term "jurisdiction" in the convention should be construed in the light of international law in force at the time the Convention is applied or interpreted.

With the exception of very small vessels, ships engaged on international voyages must carry on board valid international certificates which may be accepted at foreign ports as prima facie evidence that the ship complies with the requirements of the Convention.

If, however, there are clear grounds for believing that the condition of the ship or its equipment does not correspond substantially with the particulars of the certificate, or if the ship does not carry a valid certificate, the authority carrying out the inspection may detain the ship until it is satisfied that the ship can proceed to sea without presenting unreasonable threat of harm to the marine environment.

Under Article 17, the Parties to the Convention accept the obligation to promote, in consultation with other international bodies and with the assistance of UNEP, support for those Parties which request technical assistance for various purposes, such as training the supply of equipment, research, and combating pollution.

INTERNATIONAL MARITIME ORGANIZATION
Vessel Discharge Regulations

Annex I (oil)

TABLE I **OIL TANKERS OF ALL SIZES** **Control of discharge of oil from tank areas including cargo pump room**	
Within special areas OR outside special areas, within 50 nautical miles (nm) from the nearest land	ANY DISCHARGE IS PROHIBITED, except clean or segregated ballast
Outside special areas, more than 50 nm from the nearest land	ANY DISCHARGE IS PROHIBITED, except clean or segregated ballast, or when: 1. the tanker is proceeding en route, and 2. the instantaneous rate of discharge of oil does not exceed 30 litres/nm, and 3. the total quantity of oil discharged into the sea does not exceed - 1/15,000 (for existing tankers) and/ - 1/30,000 (for new tankers) of the total quantity of the cargo which was carried on the previous voyage, and 4. the tanker has in operation a monitoring and control system for the discharge of oil, and slop tank arrangements as required by Regulation 15.

TABLE II	
OIL TANKERS OF ALL SIZES OTHER SHIPS OF 400 GRT AND ABOVE	
Control of discharge of oil from machinery spaces	
Within special areas	ANY DISCHARGE IS PROHIBITED, except when 5. the ship is proceeding en route, and 6. the oil content of the effluent without dilution does not exceed 15 ppm, and 7. the ship has in operation oil filtering equipment with automatic 15 ppm stopping device, and 8. bilge water is not mixed with oil cargo residue or cargo pump room bilges (on oil tankers)
Outside special areas	ANY DISCHARGE IS PROHIBITED, except when 1. the ship is proceeding en route 2. the oil content of the effluent is less than 15 ppm, and 3. the ship has in operation an oil discharge monitoring and control systems, oily-water separating or filtering equipment of other installation required by Regulation 16, and 4. bilge water is not mixed with oil cargo residue or cargo pump room bilges (on oil tankers) Note: Oily mixtures which are not mixed with oil cargo residue or cargo pump room bilges, and where the oil content of the effluent without dilution does not exceed 15 ppm may be discharge outside special areas without any additional restrictions.

TABLE III	
SHIPS BELOW 400 GRT OTHER THAN OIL TANKERS	
Control of discharge of oil from machinery spaces	
Within special areas	ANY DISCHARGE IS PROHIBITED, except when the oil content without dilution does not exceed 15 ppm

Outside special areas	ANY DISCHARGE IS PROHIBITED, except when the Flag State considers that all the following conditions are satisfied as far as practicable and reasonable: 1. the ship is proceeding en route, and 2. the oil content of the effluent is less than 15 ppm, and 3. the ship has in operation suitable equipment as required by Regulation 16 Note: Oily mixtures where the oil content of the effluent without dilution does not exceed 15 ppm may be discharged without any additional restrictions.

Annex II (noxious liquid substances in bulk)

1. General

Division of noxious substances into 4 categories:

Category	Hazard to marine resources	Harm to amenities or other legitimate uses of the sea
A	Major hazard	Serious harm
B	Hazard	Harm
C	Minor hazard	Minor harm
D	Recognizable hazard	Minimal harm

Group	In all areas	
A, B and C	- ship is proceeding en route - minimum speed 7 knots (self-propelled) or 4 knots (not self-propelled) - at least 12 nautical miles from the nearest land - discharge below the waterline - minimum water depth 25 metres	
And	Outside special areas	Within special areas
A	Maximum concentration of tank washings 0.1 percent by weight	Maximum concentration of tank washings 0.05 percent by weight

	-	per tank max. 1 cubic metre or 1/3,000 of the tank capacity in cubic metres	-	The tank has been precleaned, and the washings have been discharge to a reception facility
	-	concentration of the substance in the wake astern of the ship max. 1 ppm	-	concentration of the substance in the wake astern of the ship max. 1 ppm
C	-	per tank max. 3 cubic metres or 1/1,000 of the tank capacity in cubic metres	-	per tank max. 1 cubic metre or 1/3,000 of the tank capacity in cubic metres
	-	concentration of the substance in the wake astern of the ship max. 10 ppm	-	concentration of the substance in the wake astern of the ship max. 1 ppm
D	In all areas - Ship is proceeding en route - Minimum speed 7 or 4 knots - At least 12 nautical miles from the nearest land - Max. one part of the substance in ten parts of water			

1. Discharge of cargo residues

   • Special Areas

      – Baltic Sea

      – Black Sea

      – Antarctica

Annex IV (sewage from ships)

   • In force since 27 September 2003-10-29

The discharge regulations in Annex IV MARPOL have been implemented

   – for the Baltic Sea area under German jurisdiction by the 1st Amendment to the Ordinance for the Protection of the Baltic Sea

   – and for the North Sea area under German jurisdiction by the Ordinance of the Prevention of Pollution of the North Sea by Sewage from Ships.

1. Discharge regulations

Sewage		
From treatment plants	Comminuted and disinfected	Untreated

- treatment plant has been approved by the administration	- treatment plant has been approved by the administration	- retained in holding tanks
		- at least 12 nautical miles from the nearest land
		- discharge rate approved by the administration
- no visible floating solids or discoloration of surrounding water	- at least 4 nautical miles from the nearest land	- ship is proceeding en route
		- minimum speed 4 knots

UNITED STATES ENVIRONMENTAL PROTECTION AGENCY OFFICE OF TRANSPORTATION AND AIR QUALITY, INTERNATIONAL MARITIME ORGANIZATION ADOPTS PROGRAM TO CONTROL AIR EMISSIONS FROM OCEANGOING VESSELS (OGVs)
EPA420-F-08-033 (Oct. 2008)

What did the IMO do?

The IMO adopted a comprehensive program of engine and fuel standards, detailed in amendments to Annex VI to the International Convention for the Prevention of Pollution from Ships (also called MARPOL), that closely matches a proposal submitted by EPA and its Federal partners to the IMO last year.

Like the original Annex VI program, the new standards are geographically-based. That is, ships operating in areas with air quality problems, designated as Emission Control Areas (ECAs), are required to meet tighter emission limits. Beginning in 2015, new and existing ships operating in ECAs will be required to use fuel with no more than 1,000 parts per million (ppm) sulfur, or a 98% reduction from today's global cap. Beginning in 2016 new ships operating in ECAs must also have advanced-technology engines designed to cut emissions of ozone-forming oxides of nitrogen (NOX) by roughly 80%. The new fuel standards will phase in over time beginning with an interim fuel sulfur standard in 2010. The IMO did not designate any new emission control areas in this action. Countries will need to seek such a designation in order to realize fully the benefits of this program. the EPA is working closely with all parts of the Federal Government to prepare an application for ECA status for our coasts and will submit that application to IMO as soon as possible.

Emissions from ships operating outside of designated ECAs will be reduced through engine and fuel standards. OGVs everywhere will be required to use fuel with at most 5,000 ppm sulfur, or a 90% reduction from today's global cap. This fuel standard will begin in 2020, pending a fuel availability review in 2018. The engine standards will apply to new engines in 2011, and to existing engines as certified low-emission kits become available, beginning in 2011.

What ships are affected?

The new international standards contained in the Annex VI amendments apply to all new marine diesel engines above 130 kW (175 hp) and all marine diesel fuels. For vessels flagged and registered in the United States. EPA's clean diesel engine and fuel standards (www.epa.gov/otaq/marine.htm#2008final) will apply for all but the very largest new marine diesel engines (those above 30 liters per cylinder displacement). For engines above 30 liters per cylinder and for residual fuels, the new Annex VI standards will apply.

Most importantly, the new international standards will apply to all new marine diesel engines and fuels on foreign vessels that operate near America's coasts and ports. These foreign flagged vessels account for the vast majority of OGV traffic in the U.S.

How do oceangoing vessels harm U.S. air quality?

Oceangoing vessels dock at over a hundred ports in the U.S., including some along navigable waterways in the nation's interior. More than 40 of these ports are in metropolitan areas that do not meet the National Ambient Air Quality Standards (www.epa.gov/air/criteria.html). These vessels also travel along our populated coasts and waterways. Most have, at best, very modest air pollution controls and many have no controls at all, emitting pollutants at levels (measured in grams per horsepower-hour) typical of highway trucks built before the 1980s. Furthermore, these emissions of particulate matter (PM), sulfur oxides ("SOx"), hydrocarbons, and NOx can degrade air quality for people living hundreds of miles downwind.

We have estimated that in 2001 marine diesel engines with per-cylinder displacement of 30 liters or more (a group roughly corresponding to the engines covered by the new IMO standards) contributed 6% of the NOx coming from all mobile sources in the U.S., as well as 10% of the PM, and 40% of the SOx. We further estimate that without new emission controls, these contributions would have increased by 2030 to 34% of the NOx coming from all mobile sources in the U.S., 45% of the PM, and 94% of the SOx. Percent contributions from these marine engines in some port cities with poor air quality range much higher.

What will this program mean for the environment?

The final ECA standards will achieve reductions from current Tier 1 engine emission levels (www.epa.gov/otaq/oceanvessels.htm#tier1) of 80%, 85%, and 95% for NOx, PM, and SOx, respectively. Considering the large contribution OGVs make to U.S. air quality problems, especially in port cities, the health benefits from these emission reductions will be very substantial. We anticipate many billions of dollars of health and welfare benefits in the U.S. from this program if an BCA designation is made for U.S. coastlines.

Why is the IMO process important?

In today's global economy, the number of ships doing business at U.S. ports is increasing at a rapid rate. Very few of these ships are U.S.-flagged, and the fuel they burn when entering U.S. waters has typically been obtained elsewhere, at ports all over the world. This new IMO program directly addresses emissions from these foreign-flagged vessels. It requires them to meet stringent standards whenever they operate in designated ECAs.

What are the new standards?

The ECA fuel sulfur standards are:

– 10,000 ppm starting July 2010.

– 1,000 ppm starting January 2015.

The global fuel sulfur standards are:

– 35,000 ppm starting January 2012.

– 5,000 ppm starting January 2020 (subject to a review in 2018, but no delay past 2025).

The engine emission standards vary with rated engine speed according to a formula. See "Where can I get more information" below for details. Percent reductions from the existing Tier 1 standards are provided below:

The ECA engine emission standards are:

– Tier 3 for new engines: 80% NOx reduction starting January 2016 (based on the use of advanced catalytic after treatment systems).

The global engine emission standards are:

– Tier 2 for new engines: 20% NOx reduction starting January 2011.

– Tier 1 for existing engines: 15–20% NOx reduction from current uncontrolled levels. Manufactures may begin certifying systems (sets of upgraded replacement parts) starting in 2010. Installation will occur at a vessel's first "renewal survey" following the Tier 1 certification applicable to the vessel's engines. A renewal survey is a major inspection and maintenance activity, typically done every 5 years.

PROBLEM 7-6
ENFORCING MARPOL SHIP POLLUTION STANDARDS

The cargo ship Flying Dutchman has come into port in Nation A, about one month after leaving its home port of Genoa, Italy and after making port calls in Kingston, Jamaica and Havana, Cuba. The Flying Dutchman is owned by the Greek Shipping Company, based in Athens, Greece, and is under charter to the Latina Shipping Company based in Genoa. The master of the Flying Dutchman is Greek, an employee of the Greek Shipping Company, and the crew members carry Indonesian passports. The Flying Dutchman is registered and flies the flag of Liberia. Nation A is a party to the UNCLOS 1982 and MARPOL 73/78.

A tip has come to Coast Guard in Nation A that the Flying Dutchman has discharged oil, raw sewage, and garbage in violation of MARPOL standards. It is understood that the master routinely falsifies entries on the ship's oil record book and other documents to conceal the violations.

One hour after the Flying Dutchman entered port, the authorities of Nation A arrested the vessel as well as the master and the crewmembers, charging them with violating international pollution standards as implemented in the national laws of Nation A. The violations carry both possible criminal and civil penalties.

1. UNCLOS provides for enforcement of international pollution standards by the flag state (Article 217), the port state (Article 218), and the coastal state (Article 220). Problem 7-6 concerns port state enforcement of MARPOL standards. Under UNCLOS Article 218, does Nation A have authority to enforce MARPOL standards under international law? Does Nation A have authority to institute a proceeding concerning discharges of oil and other substances in the EEZ or territorial sea of Jamaica or Cuba? Does Nation A have any obligation to notify authorities in Liberia (the flag state) and other states such as Jamaica and Cuba?

2. In the proceedings instituted by Nation A, what are its obligations under international law? Consider UNCLOS Articles 223 and 231.

3. May Nation A impose criminal penalties such as imprisonment against the master and crew members of the Flying Dutchman? *See* UNCLOS Article 230.

4. Can authorities of Nation A detain the Flying Dutchman in port indefinitely? Can the ship be confiscated? Is there an obligation to release the master and crew members upon the posting of a reasonable bond? *See* UNCLOS Article 226.

5. Suppose the flag state, Liberia, institutes proceedings against the Flying Dutchman in Monrovia, Liberia. What are the obligations of Nation A? *See* UNCLOS Article 228.

NOTE

MARPOL 73/78 has been amended some 30 times since 1978. Amendments may be easily adopted using a "tacit acceptance" procedure whereby the amendments enter into force automatically on a specific date unless an agreed number of states object by an agreed date. 149 states, including the United States, are parties to MARPOL 73/78, although the U.S. has not accepted optional Annex IV. The domestic law whereby the U.S. has implemented MARPOL 73/78 is the Act to Prevent Pollution from Ships, 33 U.S.C. § 1901 et seq.

MARPOL is aggressively enforced by the U.S. Coast Guard, as is shown by the following case.

UNITED STATES v. PEÑA
684 F.3d 1137 (11th Cir. 2012)

Before DUBINA, CHIEF JUDGE, ANDERSON and KLEINFELD, CIRCUIT JUDGES.

ANDERSON, CIRCUIT JUDGE:

This case presents an issue of first impression in this Circuit and, to the best of our knowledge, in the country. We are asked to determine whether the United States has jurisdiction to prosecute a nominated surveyor — i.e., a person who conducts a MARPOL survey on behalf of a foreign nation — for knowingly violating the MARPOL treaty while aboard a foreign vessel docked in the United States. Defendant Hugo Peña argues that under MARPOL it is the responsibility of the Flag State to conduct surveys and issue certificates, and therefore only the Flag State has jurisdiction to prosecute a surveyor for failure to conduct a proper MARPOL survey. We disagree. After thorough review of the relevant treaty and U.S. law, we hold that the United States has jurisdiction to prosecute surveyors for MARPOL violations committed in U.S. ports. Furthermore, under our lenient standards of review for issues raised for the first time on appeal, we find no reversible error in the indictment or jury instructions. Finally, we affirm the district court's denial of judgment of acquittal. Accordingly, we affirm Peña's conviction.

I. BACKGROUND

A. Background Law

MARPOL is the common name for the International Convention for the Prevention of Pollution from Ships, Nov. 2, 1973, as modified by the Protocol of 1978, opened for signature Feb. 17, 1978. 1340 U.N.T.S. 62 [hereinafter MARPOL]. This multilateral maritime treaty aims "to achieve the complete elimination of intentional pollution of the marine environment by oil and other harmful substances and the minimization of accidental discharge of such substances." *Id.* at 184. MARPOL is not a self-executing treaty; instead, each party agrees to "give effect" to it by establishing rules for ships that fly its flag, certifying that such ships comply with the treaty rules, and sanctioning those ships that violate the treaty. MARPOL arts. 1(1), 4(1), 5(1); *see United States v. Ionia Mgmt. S.A.*, 555 F.3d 303, 307 (2d Cir. 2009). As relevant to this case, both the United States and the Republic of Panama are signatories to the treaty. The Act to Prevent Pollution from Ships ("APPS"), 33 U.S.C. § 1901 et seq., implements MARPOL and authorizes the U.S. Coast Guard to issue regulations implementing the requirements of the treaty. *See* 33 U.S.C. § 1903(c)(1); 33 C.F.R. § 151.01 et seq.

Annex I to MARPOL sets forth regulations for the prevention of pollution by oil from ships. Annex I prohibits a ship from dumping its bilge water into the ocean unless the oil content of that water has been reduced to less than 15 parts per million ("ppm"). Reg. 15.2, Resolution MEPC.117(52), Amendments to the Annex of the Protocol of 1978 Relating to the International Convention for the Prevention of Pollution from Ships, 1973, Oct. 15, 2004 (entered into force Jan. 1, 2007) [hereinafter Annex I]. To reduce the oil content to permissible levels, the bilge water must be pumped through a piece of equipment that filters the oil out of the water, commonly called an "oily water separator." See id. reg. 14.6. Annex I requires all ships of 400 gross tonnage and above to have a functioning oily water separator and to use it to filter the bilge water before it is discharged into the ocean. *Id.* regs. 14.1, 15.2. If a ship's bilge water is not filtered through an oily water separator to reduce the oil content to permissible levels, then the bilge water must be collected and retained in tanks on the ship and discharged at a proper facility once the ship arrives in port. *Id.* reg. 15.9.

It is the responsibility of the "Flag State" to certify that ships sailing under its authority (or "flag") comply with international laws such as MARPOL. *Id.* regs. 6.3.1, 6.3.4. With respect to the prevention of oil pollution, the Flag State conducts an inspection, or "survey," and certifies the ship's compliance by issuing an International Oil Pollution Prevention ("IOPP") Certificate. *Id.* regs. 6.1, 6.3.1, 7.

The Flag State may delegate the authority to conduct the survey and to issue the IOPP Certificate to a recognized "classification society," which is an organization that inspects the vessels and issues the certificates on the Flag State's behalf. *Id.* reg. 6.3.1. The person employed by the classification society to conduct the survey and issue the certificate on behalf of the Flag State is known as a "surveyor." *Id.*

A surveyor nominated by a foreign nation has the following duties under MARPOL. First, when conducting 3 an "initial survey" of a ship, he shall conduct a complete survey of the structure and equipment "such as to ensure that the structure, equipment, systems, fittings, arrangements and material fully comply with the applicable requirements" of Annex I. *Id.* reg. 6.1.1. Similarly, when conducting a "renewal survey," he shall "ensure that the structure, equipment, systems, fittings, arrangements and material fully comply with the applicable requirements" of Annex I. *Id.* reg. 6.1.2. After conducting an initial or renewal survey in accordance with the provisions of Regulation 6, the surveyor shall issue or endorse an IOPP Certificate. *Id.* reg. 7. When the nominated surveyor determines that the condition of the ship does not correspond to the IOPP Certificate or is not fit to go to sea, he shall immediately ensure that corrective action is taken and shall in due course notify the Flag State. *Id.* reg. 6.3.3. If corrective action is not taken, he shall withdraw the IOPP Certificate and notify the Flag State as well as the authorities of the Port State. *Id.* Upon receiving, from the master or owner of a ship, a report of an accident or defect, the nominated surveyor shall investigate to determine if a survey is necessary and shall ascertain that the master or owner has also reported to the appropriate authorities of the Port State. *Id.* reg. 6.4.3.

The IOPP Certificate must be maintained by the ship's master on board the vessel. *See* MARPOL art. 5(2). If a ship does not have a valid IOPP Certificate on board, it is not permitted to set sail or enter the ports of other signatory nations. *See id.*

"Port States" — nations visited by commercial ships — may inspect the vessels entering their waters and ports to ensure compliance with MARPOL regulations. Id. arts. 5(2), 6(2). An inspection of a foreign vessel by a Port State is called a "port state control examination." In the United States, the Coast Guard is charged with conducting port state control examinations to ensure that all commercial vessels entering the United States comply with MARPOL. 33 C.F.R. § 151.23.

B. Factual and Procedural History

On May 4, 2010, the Coast Guard conducted an unannounced port state control examination of the motor vessel Island Express I ("Island Express"), which was docked at a port just south of Fort Lauderdale, Florida. The ship was in the process of changing its flag from St. Kitts and Nevis to Panama. The Coast Guard inspected the ship's documents, including its IOPP Certificate. The IOPP Certificate, dated April 15, 2010, stated that it was issued in Fort Lauderdale, Florida, by the classification society Universal Shipping Bureau on behalf of the Republic of Panama. Hugo Peña was the "attending surveyor" who conducted the April 15, 2010, survey and signed the IOPP Certificate.

As stated on the top of the Certificate itself, Peña issued the IOPP Certificate "under the provisions of" MARPOL. On the first page of the IOPP Certificate, Peña expressly certified: (1) that the ship had been surveyed in accordance with Regulation 44 of Annex I of MARPOL; and (2) that the survey showed that the structure, equipment, systems, fittings, arrangement, and material of the ship and the condition thereof were in all respects satisfactory and that the ship complied with the applicable requirements of Annex I. Peña further certified that the Island Express was equipped with "[o]il filtering (15 ppm) equipment with alarm and automatic stopping device." Finally, Peña certified that the IOPP Certificate was "correct in all respects." Peña did not note any conditions or deficiencies on the IOPP Certificate indicating any violations on the Island Express.

Upon further inspection, the Coast Guard examiner discovered that the oily water separator did not operate at all and that the ship did not have a bilge holding tank for storing its bilge water for later disposal at a port facility. Instead, the ship had a makeshift system of pumps and rubber tubes designed to pump oily waste from the ship's bilge directly up to the main deck of the ship, where it could flow overboard into the ocean. Although this system of portable pumps and tubes was not part of the ship's standard equipment or an approved modification, Peña made no mention of the pumps and tubing in the IOPP Certificate that he had issued just nineteen days earlier. Furthermore, Peña had not attached any conditions to the IOPP Certificate requiring the repair of the oily water separator or the proper management of the ship's bilge water.

When questioned by the Coast Guard examiners, Peña admitted that he had not tested the oily water separator when he conducted the April 15 survey because the ship's chief engineer had told him that it did not work. Peña further admitted that he had authorized the chief engineer to place portable pumps in the bilge and pump bilge water directly overboard, but only in an emergency. Finally, he acknowledged that the only condition he had issued for the Island Express was for an unrelated crack in the forward bulkhead.

Peña was indicted for: (1) conspiring with the owner and operators of the Island Express to knowingly fail to maintain an accurate oil record book on board the vessel, in violation of 33 U.S.C. § 1908(a), 33 C.F.R. § 151.25, and MARPOL, Annex I, Regulation 17 ("Count 1"); (2) knowingly violating MARPOL by failing to conduct a complete survey of the Island Express, in violation of 33 U.S.C. § 1908(a) and MARPOL, Annex 1, Regulation 6 ("Count 27"); and (3) in a matter within the jurisdiction of the United States Coast Guard, knowingly and willfully making a materially false, fictitious, and fraudulent statement, by certifying that the structure, equipment, systems, fittings, arrangements, and material of the Island Express and its condition were in compliance with Annex I of MARPOL, in violation of 18 U.S.C. § 1001(a)(2) ("Count 28").

At trial, the district court granted Peña's motion for judgment of acquittal on the conspiracy count but denied the motion as to Counts 27 and 28. The jury found Peña guilty of Counts 27 and 28, and the district court sentenced Peña to a term of five years' probation. Peña now appeals that conviction, arguing: (1) that the United States lacks jurisdiction to prosecute Peña for failure to conduct a MARPOL survey of a Panamanian-flagged vessel; (2) that there is no crime under U.S. law for knowingly violating MARPOL by failing to conduct a complete survey of a vessel, because there is no legal duty to do so; (3) that Count 27 of the indictment was fundamentally defective because it failed to allege that Peña had a legal duty to conduct a MARPOL survey; (4) that the district court's jury instructions pertaining to Count 27 amounted to plain error; (5) that the district court should have granted Peña's motion for judgment of acquittal on Count 27; and (6) that the district court should have granted his motion for judgment of acquittal on Count 28.

II. DISCUSSION

A. Jurisdiction

Peña argues that under MARPOL it is the responsibility of the Flag State to conduct surveys and to issue IOPP Certificates, and therefore only the Flag State has jurisdiction to prosecute a surveyor for failure to conduct a proper MARPOL survey. According to Peña's argument, Panama had sole jurisdiction to prosecute Peña because the Island Express was a Panamanian-flagged vessel, and therefore, the United States had no jurisdiction to prosecute Peña for failing to conduct a complete MARPOL survey of the Island Express. We disagree.

"[D]istrict courts . . . have original jurisdiction . . . [over] all offenses against the laws of the United States." 18 U.S.C. § 3231. Where the Government charges a defendant with an offense against the laws of the United States, the district court has authority to adjudicate whether the defendant violated that law, unless there is a separate limit on subject matter jurisdiction. *United States v. De La Garza*, 516 F.3d 1266, 1271 (11th Cir. 2008). "Congress . . . can create additional statutory hurdles to a court's subject matter jurisdiction through separate jurisdictional provisions found in the substantive criminal statute itself under which a case is being prosecuted." Unites Stated v. Tinoco, 304 F.3d 1088, 1104 n.18 (11th Cir. 2002).

The Government charged Peña with an offense against a law of the United States. Specifically, Peña was charged with a violation of the APPS, 33 U.S.C. § 1908(a), which provides: "A person who knowingly violates the MARPOL Protocol, . . . [the APPS], or the regulations issued thereunder commits a class D felony." 33 U.S.C. § 1908(a). Thus, the district court had jurisdiction to adjudicate the offense unless there was a separate limit on subject matter jurisdiction.

Congress created two express limitations to the application of the APPS. First, the APPS and its implementing regulations apply to violations of MARPOL occurring on foreign-flagged ships only "while [the ships are] in the navigable waters of the United States." 33 U.S.C. § 1902(a)(2); see Ionia Mgmt., 555 F.3d at 307; United States v. Abrogar, 459 F.3d 430, 435 (3d Cir. 2006) (finding that "under the APPS and accompanying regulations, Congress and the Coast Guard created criminal liability for foreign vessels and personnel only for those substantive violations of MARPOL that occur in U.S. ports or waters"). It is undisputed that the conduct at issue in this case occurred at a port in Florida. Thus, the first limitation provides no bar to jurisdiction in this case. The second limitation imposed by Congress is that "[a]ny action taken under [the APPS] shall be taken in accordance with international law." 33 U.S.C. § 1912. As we explain below, the U.S. government's jurisdiction to prosecute violations of domestic law committed in U.S. ports is in accordance with well-established international law. See United States v. Jho, 534 F.3d 398, 409 (5th Cir. 2008) ("Neither [the United Nations Convention on the Law of the Seas] nor the law of the flag doctrine encroaches on the well-settled rule that a sovereign may exercise jurisdiction to prosecute violations of its criminal laws committed in its ports.").

A foreign commercial ship at a U.S. port is subject to the jurisdiction of the United States. Mali v. Keeper of the Common Jail, 120 U.S. 1, 11, 7 S. Ct. 385, 387 (1887); see Cunard S.S. Co. v. Mellon, 262 U.S. 100, 122, 43 S. Ct. 504, 507 (1923) (noting that it is "settled in the United States and recognized elsewhere that the territory subject to its jurisdiction includes . . . the ports"). "The jurisdiction of the nation within its own territory is necessarily exclusive and absolute." Cunard, 262 U.S. at 124, 43 S. Ct. at 507 (quotation omitted). "All exceptions, therefore, to the full and complete power of a nation within its own territories, must be traced up to the consent of the nation itself." Id., 43 S. Ct. at 508 (quotation omitted). The United States "may out of considerations of public policy choose to forego the exertion of its jurisdiction or to exert the same in only a limited way, but this is a matter resting solely within its discretion." Id., 43 S. Ct. at 507. Thus, the United States "has exclusive jurisdiction to punish offenses against its law committed within its borders, unless it expressly or impliedly consents to surrender its jurisdiction." Wilson v. Girard, 354 U.S. 524, 529, 77 S. Ct. 1409, 1412 (1957) (per curiam).

Jurisdiction over foreign vessels in port is frequently limited by treaty agreement. RESTATEMENT (THIRD) OF FOREIGN RELATIONS LAW § 512 cmt. 5 (1987); see Mali, 120 U.S. at 11, 7 S. Ct. at 387 (noting that it is "part of the law of civilized nations that, when a merchant vessel of one country enters the ports of another for the purposes of trade, it subjects itself to the law of the place to which it goes, unless, by treaty or otherwise, the two countries have come to some different understanding or agreement"). Article 4 of the MARPOL Convention makes clear that, for violations that occur within the jurisdiction of the Port State, the Port State and the Flag State have concurrent jurisdiction. Article 4(1) provides: "Any violation of the requirements of the present Convention shall be prohibited and sanctions shall be established therefor under the law of the Administration of the ship concerned wherever the violation occurs." 1340 U.N.T.S. at 185. Article 4(2) of the Convention provides:

> Any violation of the requirements of the present Convention within the jurisdiction of any Party to the Convention shall be prohibited and sanctions shall be established therefor under the law of that Party. Whenever such a violation occurs, that Party shall either: (a) Cause proceedings to be taken in accordance with its laws; or (b) Furnish to the Administration of the ship such information and evidence as may be in its possession that a violation has occurred.

Id. at 186. Therefore, by signing the MARPOL treaty, the United States consented to surrender its exclusive jurisdiction over violations within its ports, but it still maintained concurrent jurisdiction to sanction violations of the treaty according to U.S. law.

33 U.S.C. § 1907(a) and (b) of the APPS essentially codify the provisions of Articles 4(1) and 4(2), and § 1908(a) establishes the sanctions required in Article 4. Section 1907(a) makes it "unlawful to act in violation of the MARPOL Protocol" and requires the Secretary to "cooperate with other parties to the MARPOL Protocol . . . in the detection of violations and in enforcement of the MARPOL Protocol;" to "use all appropriate and practical measures of detection and environmental monitoring;" and to "establish adequate procedures for reporting violations and accumulating evidence." 33 U.S.C. § 1907(a). Section 1907(b) further provides: "Upon receipt of evidence that a violation has occurred, the Secretary shall cause the matter to be investigated. . . . Upon completion of the investigation, the Secretary shall take the action required by the MARPOL Protocol . . . and whatever further action he considers appropriate under the circumstances." Id. § 1907(b). We find nothing in Article 4 or the APPS that provides express or implied consent to surrender the United States' concurrent jurisdiction over violations of the APPS occurring on foreign ships while docked at U.S. ports. *See Wilson*, 354 U.S. at 529, 77 S. Ct. at 1412.

Pursuant to Article 4 of MARPOL, the United States shares concurrent jurisdiction with the Flag State over MARPOL violations occurring on foreign-flagged ships in U.S. ports. Furthermore, 18 U.S.C. § 3231 and 33 U.S.C. §§ 1907 and 1908 give U.S. district courts jurisdiction over violations of MARPOL committed on foreign-flagged ships in U.S. ports, and Congress has neither explicitly nor implicitly surrendered complete jurisdiction to the Flag State. Thus, we conclude that the United States had jurisdiction to prosecute Peña, a surveyor of a foreign-flagged ship, for a knowing violation of MARPOL committed on a foreign-flagged ship at a U.S. port.

B. Sufficiency of the Indictment

We review de novo the sufficiency of an indictment. *United States v. Wayerski*, 624 F.3d 1342, 1349 (11th Cir. 2010). Substantively, for an indictment to be sufficient, it must: (1) present the essential elements of the charged offense; (2) provide the accused notice of the charge he must defend against; and (3) enable the accused to rely upon any judgment under the indictment for double jeopardy purposes. *United States v. Woodruff*, 296 F.3d 1041, 1046 (11th Cir. 2002). "In determining whether an indictment is sufficient, we read it as a whole and give it a common sense construction." *United States v. Jordan*, 582 F.3d 1239, 1245 (11th Cir. 2009) (per curiam) (quotations omitted). "A criminal conviction will not be upheld if the indictment upon which it is based does not set forth the essential elements of the offense." *United States v. Fern*, 155 F.3d 1318, 1324–25 (11th Cir. 1998). "If an indictment specifically refers to the statute on which the charge was based, the reference to the statutory language adequately informs the defendant of the charge." *Id.* at 1325.

However, when a defendant challenges the adequacy of an indictment for the first time on appeal, "this Court must find the indictment sufficient unless it is so defective that it does not, by any reasonable construction, charge an offense for which the defendant is convicted." *United States v. Gray*, 260 F.3d 1267, 1282 (11th Cir. 2001) (quotations omitted). Thus, in some instances, an element may be inferred from the express allegations of the indictment. *Id.* at 1283. "Practical, rather than technical, considerations govern the validity of an indictment. Minor deficiencies that do not prejudice the defendant will not prompt this court to reverse a conviction." *United States v. Adams*, 83 F.3d 1371, 1375 (11th Cir. 1996) (per curiam) (quotations and alteration omitted). Where the defendant suffers no actual prejudice as a result of the indictment, and the indictment provides facts and the specific statute under which the defendant is charged, the court will find the indictment sufficient. *Id.*

We readily conclude that Peña suffered no actual prejudice as a result of the indictment. Peña argues on appeal that Count 27 of the indictment was insufficient because it failed to allege that Peña had a legal duty to conduct a complete survey of the vessel. We disagree. The indictment was sufficient to charge Peña with the offense for which he was convicted, especially in light of our lenient standard of review for sufficiency challenges raised for the first time on appeal. Count 27 alleges that Peña knowingly violated MARPOL by failing to conduct a survey, which necessarily implies that he had a duty to conduct the survey in the first place. Moreover, it is clear from the references to MARPOL and Regulation 6, and from the context revealed by other allegations of the indictment, that Count 27 charges Peña with failing to conduct the survey that is required prior to issuing the IOPP Certificate.

Peña further argues that Count 27 of the indictment is defective because it alleged the wrong standard for a survey conducted due to a change of flags under Annex 1, Regulation 10.9.3. Peña argues that although Count 27 charges him with failure to conduct a "complete survey . . . such as to ensure that the structure, systems, arrangements, and material of the ship fully complied with MARPOL," such a survey is only required for the initial MARPOL survey. He contends that, for a change of flags, Regulation 10.9.3 requires only compliance with Regulations 6.4.1 and 6.4.2, which do not require a complete survey.

We find Peña's argument wholly without merit. The owner of the vessel was in the process of changing its flag to that of Panama. In such circumstance, Regulation 10.9.3 provides that the prior certification ceases to be valid, that a "new certificate" has to be issued, and that before issuing the new certificate the Flag State must be fully satisfied "that the ship is in compliance with the requirements of [R]egulations 6.4.1 and 6.4.2 of this Annex." Annex I reg. 10.9.3. Because the original IOPP Certificate becomes invalid upon the re-flagging of a ship, a new IOPP Certificate must be issued. Regulation 7 prescribes the requirements for the issuance of an IOPP Certificate. Therefore, a surveyor issuing a new certificate upon the re-flagging of a ship must comply with Regulation 7, in addition to Regulations 6.4.1 and 6.4.2.

Regulation 7.1 provides that an IOPP Certificate shall be issued "after an initial or renewal survey in accordance with the provisions of [R]egulation 6 of this Annex." *Id.* reg. 7.1. In other words, Regulation 7 expressly provides that any certificate — therefore including the new certificate required by Regulation 10.9.3 upon re-flagging — may only be issued after either an initial or a renewal survey in accordance with Regulation 6. Thus, a surveyor must conduct either an initial or a renewal survey prior to issuing a new IOPP Certificate to a newly-flagged ship. Either type of survey "shall be such as to ensure that the structure, equipment, systems, fittings, arrangements and material fully comply with the applicable requirements of this Annex." *Id.* regs. 6.1.1, 6.1.2. Therefore, prior to issuing an IOPP Certificate to a re-flagged vessel, a surveyor must conduct a survey that is "such as to ensure that the structure, equipment, systems, fittings, arrangements and material fully comply with the applicable requirements" of Annex I of MARPOL. *Id.* This, of course, is the precise language of Count 27 (which tracked the language of Regulations 6.1.1 and 6.1.2). Thus, Peña's argument that Count 27 is defective is wholly without merit.

Although we believe that the above interpretation is the most plausible construction of the regulations, because of our lenient standard of review we are not required to definitively establish the precise interpretation of Regulation 10.9.3 in this case. For the reasons that follow, even if Regulation 10.9.3 were construed as requiring compliance with only Regulations 6.4.1 and 6.4.2, under the narrow language of those regulations, the indictment would not be "so defective that it does not, by any reasonable construction, charge an offense for which the defendant is convicted." *Gray*, 260 F.3d at 1282.

Regulation 10.9.3 provides, in pertinent part:

> A certificate issued under [R]egulation 7 . . . shall cease to be valid . . . upon transfer of the ship to the flag of another State. A new certificate shall only be issued when the Government issuing the new certificate is fully satisfied that the ship is in compliance with the requirements of [R]egulations 6.4.1 and 6.4.2 of this Annex.

Annex I reg. 10.9.3 (emphasis added). Regulation 6.4.1 provides:

> The condition of the ship and its equipment shall be maintained to conform with the provisions of the present Convention to ensure that the ship in all respects will remain fit to proceed to sea without presenting an unreasonable threat of harm to the marine environment.

Thus, a nominated surveyor — who issues the IOPP Certificate on behalf of "the Government issuing the new certificate" — must be "fully satisfied," *id.* reg. 10.9.3, that "the ship and its equipment . . . conform with the provisions of [Annex I] to ensure that the ship in all respects will remain fit to proceed to sea without presenting an unreasonable threat of harm to the marine environment," *id.* reg. 6.4.1. Under MARPOL, the only way for a surveyor to be "fully satisfied" that the ship conforms with the provisions of Annex I is to conduct a survey as described in Regulation 6.1.

Indeed, this is even clearer from Regulation 6.4.2, the requirements of which also must be met under the narrow language of Regulation 10.9.3. Regulation 6.4.2 specifically references the survey described in Regulation 6.1. Regulation 6.4.2 provides:

> After any survey of the ship under paragraph 1 of this regulation has been completed [*i.e.*, the survey described in Regulation 6.1], no change shall be made in the structure, equipment, systems, fittings, arrangements or material covered by the survey, without the sanction of the Administration, except the direct replacement of such equipment and fittings.

Again, the only way to be "fully satisfied" that there has been no change in the "structure, equipment, systems, fittings, arrangements or material" of the re-flagged vessel is to conduct a survey of those parts of the vessel, the very parts required under Regulation 6.1 to be surveyed, and the very parts Peña was charged in the indictment with having failed to survey. In other words, Regulation 10.9.3's reference to Regulation 6.4.2, which in turn references Regulation 6.1, indicates that a survey in compliance with Regulation 6.1 must be performed upon the reflagging of a ship. Thus, even if the narrow language of Regulation 10.9.3 — independent of Regulation 7 — solely governs the issuance of an IOPP Certificate upon the re-flagging of a vessel, the survey requirements of Regulation 6 must still be performed prior to issuing the IOPP Certificate.

Because Peña did not challenge the indictment prior to this appeal, we must find the indictment sufficient "unless it is so defective that it does not, by any reasonable construction, charge an offense for which" Peña was convicted. *Gray*, 260 F.3d at 1282. Under either reading of the treaty described above — that is, that the re-flagging of a ship is governed by Regulations 10.9.3, 7, and 6; or that the reflagging is governed only by the narrow language of Regulations 10.9.3, 6.4.1, and 6.4.2 — a surveyor is required to conduct a survey of the ship such as to ensure that the ship fully complies with MARPOL. The indictment charged Peña with failing to conduct a survey "such as to ensure that the structure, equipment, systems, arrangements, and material of the ship fully complied with MARPOL, in violation of [33 U.S.C. § 1908(a)] and MARPOL, Annex I, Regulation 6." We readily conclude that, under our lenient standard of review, the indictment was sufficient.

[The Court's discussion of the Jury Instruction and the Denial of Judgment of Acquittal on Counts 27 and 28 is omitted.]

NOTES AND QUESTIONS

1. *MARPOL enforcement*. MARPOL and APPS standards apply to U.S.-flag ships anywhere in the world, but enforcement against foreign-flag ships is based on coast-state and port-state enforcement for substantial violations of MARPOL that occur in U.S. ports or waters. In cases of discharges in violation of MARPOL by foreign-flag vessels, it may be difficult to prove exactly where the discharge took place and if it occurred in an area subject to U.S. jurisdiction. *See generally, United States v. Abrogar*, 459 F.3d 430, 435 (3d Cir. 2006). In order to clear this hurdle, MARPOL offenses by foreign-flag vessels are typically prosecuted as record-keeping violations. If such discharges occurred and they were not properly logged in the ship's Oil Record Book (ORB), criminal liability may attach pursuant to 33 U.S.C. § 1908(a). A foreign-flag ship's ORB must not be knowingly inaccurate upon entering the ports or navigable waters of the United States. *See United States v. Ionia Management, S.A.*, 555 F.3d 303 (2d Cir. 2009). In the *Peña* case, criminal liability attached to the surveyor employed by the foreign-flag vessel. Is this good policy, or should liability be based only upon finding a direct violation of a MARPOL effluent standard?

2. *Enforcement against foreign shipowners*. In cases involving foreign-flag ships, the shipowners are typically located outside the U.S. Is it fair to arrest and prosecute the master or members of the crew, who may be poorly educated and have meager financial means, while the foreign shipowner cannot be brought before the court? In fact, the APPS also permits civil penalties to be levied against the vessel and shipowner, and the vessel in question may be arrested and kept in port pending payment of the fines levied. Moreover, the Coast Guard may arrest the ship and the crewmembers and require them to stay in port indefinitely pending investigation of the incident. This will be quite costly to the foreign shipowners. In *Giuseppe Bottigliere Shipping Co. S.P.A. v. United States*, 843 F. Supp. 2d (S.D. Ala. 2012), the Coast Guard discovered a "magic pipe" aboard an Italian-owned cargo vessel arrived at the port of Mobile, Alabama, and arrested the ship and the crew, pending its ongoing investigation of illegal activity. The Coast Guard delivered a letter to the vessel stating that "there is reasonable cause to believe that the vessel, its owner, operator, person in charge, or crew members may be subject to a fine or criminal penalty" and further stated that "when [our] investigation is complete, we will request that CBP [U.S. Customs and Border Protection] grant departure clearance for the vessel." (Ibid. at 1244).

This detention of the vessel cost the owners $15,000 per day in lost hire as well as the wages and expenses of the idle crewmembers during the time for investigation. What can the shipowner do to regain its ship? Under APPS section 1908(e), clearance may be granted for the vessel under investigation upon the filing of a bond or other surety. In the *Bottigliere* Case, the Coast Guard not only required a bond in the amount of $700,000, but also required the shipowner to guarantee payment of the wages and hotel expenses of the crew members during the ongoing investigation of the matter. The shipowner regarded these terms to be unreasonable, but they were upheld by the court, which outlined the shipowner's options as follows: (1) "accede to the demands of the Coast Guard, even though it thinks them unreasonable;" (2) "request reconsideration and/or appeal the surety agreement terms;" or (3) "provide the Coast Guard and Attorney General with the 60-day notice for judicial review under 33 U.S.C. § 1910(b)(1) and initiate judicial review proceedings under the APPS, with a view to seeking relief . . . and/or recovering damages under section 1904(h) for what it perceives as the unreasonable detention or delay of the vessel." (Ibid. at 1253). How realistic are these options?

3. *Discharge of sewage from vessels*. Although the United States is not a party to MARPOL Annex IV, the United States regulates the discharge of sewage from vessels under section 312 of the U.S. Clean Water Act, 33 U.S.C. § 1322. The regulations for marine sanitation devices (MSDs) are contained in 33 CFR Part 159. Under these provisions different marine sanitation devices are specified for different categories of vessels. Both commercial and recreational vessels with installed toilets must comply with specified standards for MSDs that are designed either to hold sewage for shore-based disposal or to treat sewage prior to discharge. In addition, the Coast Guard enforces MARPOL Annex IV standards against foreign vessels in U.S. ports or waters. U.S.-flagged ships that call in ports abroad should have a certificate demonstrating compliance with Annex IV to avoid possible port state detention while abroad. See U.S. Coast Guard Navigation and Vessel Inspection Circular (NVIC) No. 1-091, on-U.S. voluntary compliance with the revised MARPOL Annex IV effluent and performance standards that entered into force January 1, 2010.

4. *Garbage and plastics*. MARPOL Annex V requires every vessel of 12 meters or more to display instructions to inform the ship's crew and passengers regarding garbage disposal requirements. Garbage on ships in classified into six categories: plastics; floating dunnage, lining and packing material; ground-down paper products, rags, glass, metal bottles, and crockery; food waste; incinerator ash; and normal paper products, rags, oily rags and metal scrap. Annex IV prohibits disposal of plastic anywhere at sea. No form of garbage may be disposed in coastal areas or designated special areas. Special areas include the Mediterranean Sea, the Baltic Sea, the Black Sea, the Gulf Areas, the Antarctic Area, the Red Sea Area, the North Sea Area, and the Wider Caribbean Region. Annex V requires governments to provide facilities at ports and terminals for the reception of garbage. The requirements of MARPOL Annex V that came into effect on January 1, 2013, are summarized in the following table:

SUMMARY OF RESTRICTIONS TO THE DISCHARGE OF GARBAGE INTO THE SEA UNDER REGULATIONS 4, 5, AND 6 OF MARPOL ANNEX V (extract from resolution MEPC 219(63))

Garbage type[1]	All ships except platforms4		Offshore platforms located more than 12 nm from nearest land and ships when alongside or within 500 metres of such platform[4] regulations[5]
	Outside special areas Regulation[4] (Distances are from the nearest land)	Within special areas Regulation[6] (Distances are from nearest land or nearest ice-shelf)	
Food waste comminuted or ground[2]	≥ 3 nm, en route and as far as practicable	≥ 12 nm, en route and as far as practicable[3]	Discharge permitted
Food waste comminuted or ground	≥ 12 nm, en route and as far as practicable	Discharge prohibited	Discharge prohibited
Cargo residues [5,6] not contained in washwater	≥ 12 nm, en route and as far as practicable	Discharge permitted	Discharge permitted
Cargo residues [5,6] contained in washwater		≥ 12 nm, en route and as far as practicable (subject to conditions in regulation 6.1.2)	Discharge permitted
Cleaning agents and additives[6] contained in cargo hold washwater	Discharge permitted	≥ 12 nm, en route and as far as practicable (subject to conditions in regulation 6.1.2)	Discharge permitted
Cleaning agents and additives[6] in deck and external surfaces washwater		Discharge permitted	
Animal Carcasses (should be split or otherwise treated to ensure the carcasses will sink immediately)	Must be en route and as far from the nearest land as possible. Should be > 100 nm and maximum water depth	Discharge permitted	Discharge permitted

All other garbage including plastics, synthetic ropes, fishing gear, plastic garbage bags, incinerator ashes, clinkers, cooking oil, floating dunnage, lining and packing materials, paper, rags, glass, metal, bottles, crockery and similar refuse	Discharge prohibited	Discharge permitted	Discharge permitted

1   When garbage is mixed with or contaminated by other harmful substances prohibited from discharge or having different discharge requirements, the more stringent requirements shall apply.

2   Comminuted or ground food wastes must be able to pass through a screen with mesh no larger than 25 mm.

3   The discharge of introduced avian products in the Antarctic area is not permitted unless incinerated, autoclaved or otherwise treated to be made sterile.

4   Offshore platforms located 12 nm from nearest land and associated ships include all fixed or floating platforms engaged in exploration or exploitation or associated processing of seabed mineral resources, and all ships alongside or within 500 m of such platforms.

5   Cargo residues means only those cargo residues that cannot be recovered using commonly available methods for unloading.

6   These substances must not be harmful to the marine environment

The revised MARPOL Annex V requires among others, the following new/ revised requirements for garbage management plan and garbage record book:

1. The Garbage Management Plan is now required for every ship of 100 gt and above (previously 400gt and above), every ship which is certified to carry 15 or more persons and fixed or floating platforms which are engaged in the exploration, exploitation or associated offshore processing of sea-bed mineral resource.

The Garbage Management Plan shall be based on the 2012 guidelines — see the below attached resolution MEPC.220(63) — adopted by the Marine Environment Protection Committee of the Organization. This will revoke the Guidelines for the Development of Garbage Management Plans (resolution

MEPC.71 (38)), upon the entry into force of the revised MAR POL Annex V (i.e. 1 January 2013).

2. The garbage record book and the record of garbage discharges have been revised. The Garbage Record Book, whether as a part of the ship's official log-book or otherwise, shall be in the form specified in the appendix to the revised Annex V as per resolution MEPC 201(62).

5. *Air pollution from ships*. Updated IMO air pollution from ships regulations are set out in the foregoing U.S. EPA notice of October 2008. In the United States these regulations are enforced by the U.S. EPA and the Coast Guard, and violators may be liable for criminal and civil penalties. Note how the standards for air emissions and fuel requirements become progressively more stringent. The regulations governing ship emissions may be found in 40 CFR Part 1043 and Part 80, subpart I. The U.S. Clean Air Act authorizes federal regulation, and explicitly preempts state regulation of air pollution emissions from "new motor vehicles and new motor vehicle engines." 42 U.S.C. § 7521(a) (1), 7543(a). One state is exempted from this preemption — California. *See* 42 U.S.C. § 7543 (b)(1). However, 1990 amendments to the Clean Air Act require California to seek authorization from the EPA to enforce its separate state regulations relating to "non-road vehicles or engines." 42 U.S.C. § 7543(e)(2). Other states can adopt regulations identical to California's approved by the EPA. In 2007, the California Air Resources Board (CARB) began enforcing new state marine vessel rules regarding the emissions of particulate matter, nitrogen oxide and sulfur oxide from ocean-going vessels on all waters within 24 nautical miles of the California coast. Cal. Code Regs. (CCR) Tit. 13, sec. 2299. In *Pacific Merchant Shipping Association v. Goldstene*, 517 F.3d 1108 (9th Cir. 2008), the court ruled that these California standards were emission standards relating to non-road engines requiring advance EPA approval, and, since California had neither sought nor obtained approval by the EPA for these emission standards, they were preempted by the Clean Air Act. In 2009, CARB promulgated new Vessel Fuel Rules (13 CCR sec. 2299.2 and 19 CCR sec. 93118) that vessel operators in California waters must meet in order to reduce particulate matter, nitrogen oxide and sulfur oxide emissions by about 90 %, essentially accomplishing the same purposes as the repudiated emissions rules. In *Pacific Merchant Shipping Association v. Goldstene*, 659 F. 3d 1154 (9th Cir. 2011), since the Vessel Fuel Rules did not require advance approval by the EPA, the court considered whether the rules were preempted through (1) statutory preemption by the U.S. Submerged Lands Act; (2) admiralty preemption; or (3) implied field preemption. The court also considered whether the Vessel Fuel Rules were inconsistent with the Dormant Commerce Clause doctrine. The court rejected all these challenges and upheld the Vessel Fuel Rules. Although the 24 mile enforcement area under California law is broader than the three-mile grant to the state under the Submerged Lands Act, the court ruled that the Vessel Fuel Rules do not make any territorial claim, and that prior Supreme Court cases recognize the right of states to legislate extraterritorially under their historic police powers. The court also rejected admiralty preemption on the ground that the Vessel Fuel Rules contain a sunset clause that will lead them to expire when MARPOL Annex VI is fully phased in. The court also rejected the Dormant Commerce Clause challenge on the ground that the federal interest in uniformity is "rather attenuated" in the field of air pollution and environmental degradation.

6. ***Regulation of ships' ballast water, bilge water, and graywater.*** Discharges of waters from ships were long exempt from the permitting requirements of the U.S. Clean Water Act. 40 CFR sec. 122.3(a) excluded from permitting discharges incidental to the normal operation of a vessel. This exemption regulation was challenged and overturned in *Northwest Environmental Advocates v. Environmental Protection Agency*, 537 F.3d 1006 (9th Cir. 2008), which ruled that all vessel discharges — ballast water, bilge water, graywater, and deck runoff water — are subject to EPA permitting under the Clean Water Act. [ballast water is water that is taken on or released by cargo vessels to compensate for changes in the vessels' weights as cargo is taken on or discharged; bilge water is the water that collects in ships' bilges, their lowest parts; graywater is wastewater from showers, sinks, and kitchens]. Ballast water is a particular problem because it may contain aquatic invasive species that cause millions of dollars in damages to fisheries, recreation, and public infrastructure. Ballast water discharges are now subject to meeting the requirements under a General Permit under the Clean Water Act NPDES Program and the Non-Indigenous Aquatic Nuisance Prevention and Control Act, 16 U.S.C. § 4701 et seq. The new regulations, contained in 33 CFR Part 151 and 46 CFR 162, require flushing and exchange of ballast water by vessels in Pacific-near-shore voyages and salt water flushing of ballast water tanks that are empty or contain only un-pumpable residual ballast water. The EPA is also investigating the feasibility of ballast water treatment systems for future possible application. Some states, notably Alaska, prohibit the discharge of ballast water in their territorial waters. *See Chevron USA, Inc. v Hammond*, 726 F.2d 483 (9th Cir. 1984).

Section VI.   OCEAN DUMPING

Until the early 1970s, the oceans of the world were treated as convenient receptacles for the worst types of waste materials: toxic chemicals, radioactive waste, hazardous waste, garbage, and other unwanted items of every kind. In 1972, a multilatural convention, the London Convention on the Prevention of Marine Pollution by Dumping of Wastes and Other Matter, finally limited intentional dumping of wastes at sea. The mechanism employed by the 1972 London Convention was to prohibit the dumping of certain listed materials, and to allow dumping for non-listed materials through national permitting programs.

The United States is a party to the 1972 London Dumping Convention, and has implemented the Convention by enacting the Ocean Dumping Act, 33 U.S.C. § 1401 et seq. This Act prohibits persons and U.S. flag vessels from transporting any materials from the United States for the purpose of dumping into ocean waters without a permit. Furthermore, no person from outside the United States may dump any material into the United States territorial sea or contiguous zone without a permit. Permits for dumping are issued by the U.S. Environmental Protection Agency, except the U.S. Army Corps of Engineers has authority to issue permits for the dumping of dredged materials. In determining whether to grant a permit, the EPA and the Corps are required to evaluate the following criteria: the need for the proposed dumping; the effect of the dumping on human health and welfare; the impact of the dumping on fisheries and resources; the effect on marine ecosystems; the persistence and permanence of the dumped materials; the effect of particular volumes and concentrations of the materials; the appropriateness of the location; whether recycling or other methods of disposal are available; and the effect of the dumping on alternative uses of the oceans. 33 U.S.C. § 1412.

In 1996, because of widespread concern that the 1972 Dumping Convention was not strict enough, a Protocol was agreed that essentially replaces the earlier treaty. The 1996 Protocol to the London Convention on Prevention of Marine Pollution by Dumping of Wastes and Other Matter was agreed on November 7, 1996, and entered into force for 49 parties on March 24, 2006. The United States has signed but not ratified this Protocol, so U.S. law still reflects the earlier Convention. The distinctive.feature of the 1996 Protocol, which is partially reproduced below, is the "reverse list" approach: rather than prohibiting the dumping of specifically listed substances, the 1996 Protocol prohibits dumping of any substance other than those specifically listed in Annex I.

1996 PROTOCOL TO THE CONVENTION ON THE PREVENTION OF MARINE POLLUTION BY DUMPING OF WASTES AND OTHER MATTER, 1972

The Contracting Parties to this Protocol,

. . .

Have agreed as follows:

ARTICLE 3
GENERAL OBLIGATIONS

1. In implementing this Protocol, Contracting Parties shall apply a precautionary approach to environmental protection from dumping of wastes or other matter whereby appropriate preventative measures are taken when there is reason to believe that wastes or other matter introduced into the marine environment are likely to cause harm even when there is no conclusive evidence to prove a causal relation between inputs and their effects.

2. Taking into account the approach that the polluter should, in principle, bear the cost of pollution, each Contracting Party shall endeavour to promote practices whereby those it has authorized to engage in dumping or incineration at sea bear the cost of meeting the pollution prevention and control requirements for the authorized activities, having due regard to the public interest.

3. In implementing the provisions of this Protocol, Contracting Parties shall act so as not to transfer, directly or indirectly, damage or likelihood of damage from one part of the environment to another or transform one type of pollution into another.

4. No provision of this Protocol shall be interpreted as preventing Contracting Parties from taking, individually or jointly, more stringent measures in accordance with international law with respect to the prevention, reduction and where practicable elimination of pollution.

ARTICLE 4
DUMPING OF WASTES OR OTHER MATTER

1. 1. Contracting Parties shall prohibit the dumping of any wastes or other matter with the exception of those listed in Annex l.

    2. The dumping of wastes or other matter listed in Annex 1 shall require a permit. Contracting Parties shall adopt administrative or legislative measures to ensure that issuance of permits and permit conditions comply with provisions of Annex 2. Particular attention shall be paid to opportunities to avoid dumping in favour of environmentally preferable alternatives.

2. No provision of this Protocol shall be interpreted as preventing a Contracting Party from prohibiting, insofar as that Contracting Party is concerned, the dumping of wastes or other matter mentioned in Annex 1. That Contracting Party shall notify the Organization of such measures.

ARTICLE 5
INCINERATION AT SEA

Contracting Parties shall prohibit incineration at sea of wastes or other matter.

ARTICLE 6
EXPORT OF WASTES OR OTHER MATTER

Contracting Parties shall not allow the export of wastes or other matter to other countries for dumping or incineration at sea.

ARTICLE 8
EXCEPTIONS

1. The provisions of articles 4.1 and 5 shall not apply when it is necessary to secure the safety of human life or of vessels, aircraft, platforms or other man-made structures at sea in cases of force majeure caused by stress of weather, or in any case which constitutes a danger to human life or a real threat to vessels, aircraft, platforms or other man-made structures at sea, if dumping or incineration at sea appears to be the only way of averting the threat and if there is every probability that the damage consequent upon such dumping or incineration at sea will be less than would otherwise occur. Such dumping or incineration at sea shall be conducted so as to minimize the likelihood of damage to human or marine life and shall be reported forthwith to the Organization.

2. A Contracting Party may issue a permit as an exception to articles 4.1 and 5, in emergencies posing an unacceptable threat to human health, safety, or the marine environment and admitting of no other feasible solution. Before

doing so the Contracting Party shall consult any other country or countries that are likely to be affected and the Organization which, after consulting other Contracting Parties, and competent international organizations as appropriate, shall, in accordance with article 18.1.6 promptly recommend to the Contracting Party the most appropriate procedures to adopt. The Contracting Party shall follow these recommendations to the maximum extent feasible consistent with the time within which action must be taken and with the general obligation to avoid damage to the marine environment and shall inform the Organization of the action it takes. The Contracting Parties pledge themselves to assist one another in such situations.

3. Any Contracting Party may waive its rights under paragraph 2 at the time of, or subsequent to ratification of, or accession to this Protocol.

ARTICLE 9
ISSUANCE OF PERMITS AND REPORTING

1. Each Contracting Party shall designate an appropriate authority or authorities to:

   1. issue permits in accordance with this Protocol;

   2. keep records of the nature and quantities of all wastes or other matter for which Jumping permits have been issued and where practicable the quantities actually dumped and the location, time and method of dumping; and

   3. monitor individually, or in collaboration with other Contracting Parties and competent international organizations, the condition of the sea for the purposes of this Protocol.

ANNEX 1

WASTES OR OTHER MATTER THAT
MAY BE CONSIDERED FOR DUMPING

1. The following wastes or other matter are those that may be considered for dumping being mindful of the Objectives and General Obligations of this Protocol set out in articles 2 and 3:

   1. dredged material;

   2. sewage sludge;

   3. fish waste, or material resulting from industrial Fish processing operations;

   4. vessels and platforms or other man-made structures at sea;

   5. inert, inorganic geological material;

   6. organic material of natural origin;

   7. bulky items primarily comprising iron, steel, concrete and similarly unharmful materials for which the concern is physical impact, and

limited to those circumstances where such wastes are generated at locations, such as small islands with isolated communities, having no practicable access to disposal options other than dumping; and

8. Carbon dioxide streams from carbon dioxide capture processes for sequestration.

2. The wastes or other matter listed in paragraphs 1.4 and 1.7 may be considered for dumping, provided that material capable of creating floating debris or otherwise contributing to pollution of the marine environment has been removed to the maximum extent and provided that the material dumped poses no serious obstacle to fishing or navigation.

3. Notwithstanding the above, materials listed in paragraphs 1.1 to 1.8 containing levels of radioactivity greater than de minimis (exempt) concentrations as defined by the IAEA and adopted by Contracting Parties, shall not be considered eligible for dumping; provided further that within 25 years of 20 February 1994, and at each 25 year interval thereafter, Contracting Parties shall complete a scientific study relating to all radioactive wastes and other radioactive matter other than high level wastes or matter, taking into account such other factors as Contracting Parties consider appropriate and shall review the prohibition on dumping of such substances in accordance with the procedures set forth in article 22.

4. Carbon dioxide streams referred to in paragraph 1.8 may only be considered for dumping, if:

1. disposal is into a sub-seabed geological formation; and

2. they consist overwhelmingly of carbon dioxide.

NOTES AND QUESTIONS

1. *The reverse list approach*. Is the reverse list approach better than the 1972 Convention's approach of forbidding the dumping of listed substances?

2. *Ocean carbon sequestration*. Does the 1996 Protocol allow ocean carbon sequestration — the storage of carbon dioxide beneath the sea? Is this a good idea? Will ocean carbon sequestration help combat climate change?

3. *Radioactive wastes*. To what extent can radioactive waste be dumped into the sea? Can low level radioactive waste (equipment and clothing) be dumped?

4. *Offshore oil and gas operations*. Does the 1996 Protocol unduly interfere with seabed mining or offshore oil and gas operations? Article I (4.3) provides that "the disposal of wastes or other matter directly arising from, or related to the exploration, exploitation and associated off-shore processing of seabed mineral resources is not covered by the provisions of this Protocol."

5. *Dumping of sewage, sludge, and medical wastes*. Does the Protocol permit ocean dumping of sewage, sludge, and medical waste? Congress banned the dumping of these wastes after December 31, 1991. *See* 33 U.S.C. § 1414b (a)(l)(B).

6. *Dumping of dredge spoil*. Does the Protocol allow dumping of dredge spoil?

7. *Incineration at sea.* Does the Protocol permit incineration of wastes at sea? Article I (5.2) provides that "incineration at sea" does not include "the incineration of wastes or other matter on board a vessel, platform, or other man-made structure at sea if such wastes or other matter were generated during the normal operation of that vessel, platform, or other man-made structure at sea."

8. *Exceptions.* Are the exceptions in the 1996 Protocol too broad or are they reasonable?

9. *Precautionary and polluter pays principles.* Are these two principles part of the 1996 Protocol? Are they meaningful in this context or just window dressing?

10. *U.S. Ratification.* Should the United States ratify the 1996 Protocol? In 2008 the Bush Administration submitted the Protocol to the U.S. Senate for ratification, but no action has been taken. What are the advantages of ratification for the United States as opposed to unilateral action?

PROBLEM 7-7
STORING CARBON DIOXIDE UNDER THE SEABED TO COMBAT CLIMATE CHANGE

Nation *B* has embarked on a program to aggressively decrease carbon emissions to combat climate change. The method Nation *B* is relying upon to accomplish this is carbon capture and sequestration, a variety of technologies that involve capturing carbon dioxide from electric generating facilities and industrial processes, compressing the gases captured into liquids, transporting the liquid CO2 by pipeline to an underground storage facility, where the CO2 is injected deep into an impermeable geologic formation where it will be permanently stored and sequestered from the environment. Since Nation *B* has limited capacity to store CO2 on its territory, it is proposing to sequester and store CO2 in the seabed offshore in its EEZ. Nation *B* has, for this purpose, identified 3 sites that it deems suitable for long-term carbon storage and sequestration.

Nation *B* is a party to the London Dumping Convention and its 1996 Protocol. In 2006, Annex I of the 1996 Protocol was amended as follows:

AMMENDMENT TO ANNEX 1 TO THE LONDON PROTOCOL

1.8 Carbon dioxide streams from carbon dioxide capture processes for sequestration

. . . .

    4. Carbon dioxide streams referred to in paragraph 1.8 may only be considered for dumping, if:

        1. disposal is into a sub-seabed geological formation; and

        2. they consist overwhelmingly of carbon dioxide. They may contain incidental associated substances derived from the source material and the capture and sequestration processes used; and

        3. no wastes or other matter are added for the purpose of disposing of those wastes or other matter.

What criteria must Nation *B* satisfy in order to carry out its carbon capture and sequestration program in its EEZ? Is an aggressive carbon capture and sequestration program the answer to preventing climate change? Consider the costs and risks involved in (1) capturing and compressing CO_2; (2) transporting CO_2; and (3) injecting CO_2 deep into the earth. What assurances are there that the "impermeable" rock formations into which CO_2 is injected will not leak in the future?

Section VII. MARINE CASUALTIES AND LIABILITY FOR DAMAGES

Over the past 60 years international law has created a framework to deal with marine casualties involving accidental spills of oil or hazardous substances. Much of this legal architecture was erected in response to spectacular and tragic events. For example, on March 18, 1967, the tanker Torrey Canyon ran aground on Seven Stones reef near the Isles of Scilly in the United Kingdom. In a largely futile effort to minimize the damage from spilled oil, the U.K. destroyed the tanker without the permission of the flag state. Two years later the Brussels Convention Relating to Intervention on the High Seas in Cases of Oil Pollution Casualties (1969), was concluded, which permits states (Article 1) to take "such measures on the high seas as may be necessary to prevent, mitigate, or eliminate grave and imminent danger to their coast line or related interests from pollution or threat of pollution of the sea by oil, following upon a marine casualty."[20] The wreck of the Torrey Canyon and the subsequent pollution caused the International Maritime Organization (IMO) to convene diplomatic conferences that adopted two landmark treaties creating an international regime to compensate for damages from oil spills into the sea : the International Convention on Civil Liability for Oil Pollution Damage (1969) (the CLC or Civil Liability Convention), and the International Convention on the Establishment of an Oil Pollution Fund (1971) (the Fund Convention). In the United States, the wreck of the Exxon Valdez, an oil tanker that spilled an estimated 11 million gallons of crude oil in Prince William Sound, Alaska, polluted the sea and some 1300 miles of coastline. In response to this casualty the United States enacted the Oil Pollution Act 1990 (OPA), which imposes strict liability for damages upon "responsible parties" in cases of spills of oil into the navigable waters of the United States or its Exclusive Economic Zone. (33 U.S.C. § 2701 et seq.). There was also an international response to the spill of the Exxon Valdez: IMO sponsored an international conference that adopted the International Convention on Oil Pollution Preparedness, Response, and Cooperation (1990) (OPRC), which entered into force in 1995.[21]

The focus of this section is to explore liability for accidental oil spill maritime pollution under the U.S. OPA 90 as compared with liability under the international law regime, the CLC and Fund Conventions. As a vehicle for making this comparison, consider the following problem:

---

[20] The Intervention Convention was transposed into U.S law by Congress. 33 U.S.C. § 1471 et seq.

[21] *See also* the Protocol to OPRC Relating to Hazardous and Noxious Substances (the OPRC-HNS Protocol) of 2000 (not in force).

PROBLEM 7-8
AN INTERNATIONAL OIL TANKER CASUALTY

On July 14, 1996, the 500,000 ton *S.S. Persian Festiva* collided in a fog with the *S.S. Multi-Media Transport Festoon*. The *Persian Festiva* is a Liberian registered supertanker, owned by the Festiva Ltd., a Liberian subsidiary of a major United States shipping company. The Multi-Media Transportation Company's *Festoon* is a United States registered container vessel. The collision happened in the Pacific Ocean exactly 198-nautical-miles from the United States' baseline from which the U.S. territorial sea is measured. It is substantially further from the baselines of other states. This location is generally west of the boundary between Canada and the United States at the Dixon Entrance. The *Persian Festiva* supertanker was en route from the Persian Gulf to deliver more than 175,000 tons of crude oil at a Canadian port. It was constructed in 1992 without a double hull.

The collision was the result of a design flaw in the supertanker radar system, which prevented it from showing the necessary information regarding the *S.S. Festoon* in order to determine that the vessels were on a collision course. At the time of the accident a qualified member of the crew was watching the radar screen. Neither the members of the crew nor the owner, however, was aware of the flaw before the accident. The supertanker was piloted by the captain, Mohammed Khori, a Liberian national. The United States Coast Guard later determined that Khori was drunk at the time of the collision. He had a history of drinking on the job. The owner of the supertanker was aware of this and had ordered Khori to stop consuming alcohol when aboard his vessel. Khori was also required to attend a month-long program designed to stop employees from drinking on the job. He attended this program and the instructor reported that he had successfully completed it. The owners had no information suggesting that after he completed the program he continued drinking alcohol on the job. When the lookout on the supertanker heard the fog horn of the freighter, it was too close for the supertanker to alter its course, direction, or speed in order to avoid a collision. The collision punctured one of the holds of the supertanker that contained crude oil. As a result, 20% of the crude oil carried by the vessel spilled into the ocean and spread over a large area of the sea. An ocean current in the area carried some of the discharge into the Canadian 12-nautical-mile territorial sea. That oil caused injuries to the living natural resources in the area. The supertanker crew was able to seal the hole in the vessel and stop the remaining oil in the vessel from discharging.

The United States Coast Guard was notified of the collision and arrived on the scene. It deployed equipment to clean up as much of the crude oil in the sea as possible. Unfortunately, due to the sea conditions and delays in getting the clean up equipment to the area, much of the oil could not be recaptured. The effect of the spill was devastating to the near shore areas of Canada. Thousands of seabirds and sea otters were killed, and the marine ecosystem was severely damaged. Although no humans were physically injured, damage to public and private property was extensive. In addition, the spill had significant adverse effects on the tourist and fisheries industries in the affected areas.

The U.S. Coast Guard arrested the supertanker and ordered it into the port of Seattle, Washington, in the United States. By service on the captain and arrest of the vessel, the United States commenced an action in the United States District Court in Seattle against the vessel, the captain, the owners of the supertanker *Festiva* and Liberia. The United States sought to recover the cost of the cleanup, compensation for damages to the environment of the United States Exclusive Economic Zone and of the high seas beyond the zone. This included damages to the living natural resources located in the seas and the seabed caused by the spill. Multi-Media Transportation Company, the owner of the *S.S. Festoon* joined the suit claiming monetary compensation for damages to the freighter and its cargo caused by the collision. Claims were also brought in the District Court case against the supertanker and the owner of the vessel company by Canada and by the owners of Canadian property damaged by the spill. The Canadian fishermen and Canadian tourist companies, which suffered losses as a result of the spill, also brought claims.

Subsequent to the collision, the supertanker and its cargo were valued at US $10 million. The total liability insurance carried by the vessel was US $15 million. Persian Gulf Oil Company, the owner of the oil aboard the *Persian Festiva*, is a wholly-owned subsidiary of a large and wealthy U.S. corporation. The United States damages claim is for US $30 billion, the Multi-Media Transportation Company's claim is for US $5 million, and Canada's claim is for US $10 billion in losses. The Canadian property owners claimed US $15 billion; and the fishermen and Canadian tourist companies claimed US $5 billion in losses. Additional claimants may come forward as well.

The owners of the supertanker and the Government of Liberia claim that the United States violated public international law when it arrested the captain, the vessel, and brought suit against the vessel and Liberia. They maintain that compensation is not owed for the damages. This position was put forward in a diplomatic note delivered to the United States State Department and filed in the pending United States District Court action. Canada and Liberia are parties to the 1982 United Nations Convention on the Law of the Sea, and they have made the relevant provisions of that Convention applicable to their flag vessels.

The United States was not a party to the Convention at the time of the incident.

PRELIMINARY CONSIDERATIONS

This realistic hypothetical problem poses a number of important non-environmental law questions. We consider these briefly before focusing on the liability and environmental issues involved. Preliminary questions that will come up are the following:

1. *Violation of international law.* Did the United States' actions violate international law? Although the U.S. was not a party to the UNCLOS at the time of the casualty, the provisions of UNCLOS, which the U.S. will claim as applicable customary law rules, are essential to answering this question. Compare UNCLOS Articles 97, which concerns arrest of the ship and disciplining the master and crew with respect to a ship on the high seas, with UNCLOS Articles 56 (the rights of the coastal state in the EEZ), 211 (pollution from vessels) 220 (enforcement by coastal states) and Article 292 (prompt release of master and crew).

2. *Jurisdiction.* Under the Constitution of the United States, the judicial power of United States (federal) courts extends to "all Cases of admiralty and maritime jurisdiction." (Art. III, sec. 2). Federal court jurisdiction over admiralty and maritime cases is codified in 28 U.S.C. § 1333. There is a separate provision for "special maritime and territorial jurisdiction of the United States" in criminal cases. 18 U.S.C. § 7.

3. *Collision damages and limitation of liability.* It appears that American law would apply to the collision itself. U.S. maritime law imposes liability for collision damages on proof of negligence or fault, and damages are apportioned between the vessels involved in a collision on the basis of comparative negligence or fault. *United States v. Reliable Transfer Co.*, 421 U.S. 397 (1975). Would Multi-Media Transp. Co. be able to claim collision damages from the owners of the *S.S. Persian Festiva?* Limitation of liability is an important principle of shipping law. The United States law on limitation is the Limitation of Shipowners' Liability Act, 46 U.S.C. § 30501 et seq, which allows a shipowner involved in a casualty to file a petition for exoneration or limitation of liability within six months after receiving written notice of a claim in a marine casualty. If limitation is upheld, all claims for damages must be filed in a single court proceeding, and liability is limited to the value of the vessel after the casualty plus pending freight. 46 U.S.C. § 30505. Limitation may be "broken," denied by the court, if the "privity or knowledge" — the fault — of the master or crew that caused the casualty, can be imputed to the shipowner. How would apportionment of damages and limitation of liability be handled in this case?

4. *Cargo owners.* The owners of cargo aboard both ships would have claims; these damages would be included as collision damages and liability ultimately would be apportioned according to comparative fault. *See, e.g., Allied Chemical Corp. v. Hess Tankship Co.*, 661 F.2d 1044 (5th Cir. 1981)

5. *Likely claimants for damages resulting from the oil spill.* Who are the likely claimants in this case? In addition to the parties involved in the collision, likely claimants will include: (1) the United States; (2) the State of Alaska; (3) Canada; and (4) private claimants from both the United States and Canada, including commercial and recreational fishermen, owners of contaminated boats and shore property, tackle and bait shops, shore motels and restaurants, marinas and boat rental shops, wholesale and retail seafood enterprises, and commercial shipping unable to transit the area contaminated by the spill.

6. *Likely defendants.* Who are the likely defendants in this case?

APPLICABLE LAW

We analyze the applicability of two legal regimes with respect to this case. Some 105 states are parties to the international regime on civil liability for oil pollution damage, the CLC and Fund Conventions. The original CLC and Fund Conventions were replaced by a 1992 Protocol, which established a new international liability regime known as the 1992 CLC and Fund Conventions. An agreement in 2000 increased the limits of liability of the 1992 CLC and Fund Conventions, and in 2003, a Supplementary Fund was added, accepted at this writing by 27 states.

Canada is a party to the 1992 CLC and Fund Conventions.

The United States is not a party to the 1992 CLC or Fund Conventions' regime, and has enacted its own national law on oil spill damages, the OPA 90.

The full CLC and Fund Conventions are reprinted in the **Document Supplement**. The following materials provide a comparison of the two liability regimes.

INTERNATIONAL CONVENTION ON CIVIL LIABILITY FOR OIL POLLUTION DAMAGE (CLC)

Adoption: 29 November 1969; Entry into force: 19 June 1975; replaced by 1992 Protocol:

Adoption: 27 November 1992; Entry into force: 30 May 1996

The Civil Liability Convention was adopted to ensure that adequate compensation is available to persons who suffer oil pollution damage resulting from maritime casualties involving oil-carrying ships.

The Convention places the liability for such damage on the owner of the ship from which the polluting oil escaped or was discharged.

Subject to a number of specific exceptions, this liability is strict; it is the duty of the owner to prove in each case that any of the exceptions should in fact operate. However, except where the owner has been guilty of actual fault, they may limit liability in respect of any one incident.

The Convention requires ships covered by it to maintain insurance or other financial security in sums equivalent to the owner's total liability for one incident.

The Convention applies to all seagoing vessels actually carrying oil in bulk as cargo, but only ships carrying more than 2,000 tons of oil are required to maintain insurance in respect of oil pollution damage.

This does not apply to warships or other vessels owned or operated by a State and used for the time being for Government non-commercial service. The Convention, however, applies in respect of the liability and jurisdiction provisions, to ships owned by a State and used for commercial purposes. The only exception as regards such ships is that they are not required to carry insurance. Instead they must carry a certificate issued by the appropriate authority of the State of their registry stating that the ship's liability under the Convention is covered.

The Convention covers pollution damage resulting from spills of persistent oils suffered in the territory (including the territorial sea) of a State Party to the Convention. It is applicable to ships which actually carry oil in bulk as cargo, i.e. generally laden tankers. Spills from tankers in ballast or bunker spills from ships other than other than tankers are not covered, nor is it possible to recover costs when preventive measures are so successful that no actual spill occurs. The shipowner cannot limit liability if the incident occurred as a result of the owner's personal fault.

The Protocol of 1976, which entered into force in 1981, provided for the applicable unit of account used under the convention to be based on the Special Drawing Rights (SDR) as used by the International Monetary Fund (IMF), replacing the "Poincare franc," based on the "official" value of gold, as the applicable unit of account.

The Protocol of 1984 set increased limits of liability but was superseded by the 1992 Protocol.

The Protocol of 1992 changed the entry into force requirements by reducing from six to four the number of large tanker-owning countries that were needed for entry into force.

The compensation limits were set as follows:

- For a ship not exceeding 5,000 gross tonnage, liability is limited to 3 million SDR

- For a ship 5,000 to 140,000 gross tonnage: liability is limited to 3 million SDR plus 420 SDR for each additional unit of tonnage

- For a ship over 140,000 gross tonnage: liability is limited to 59.7 million SDR.

The 1992 protocol also widened the scope of the Convention to cover pollution damage caused in the exclusive economic zone (EEZ) or equivalent area of a State Party. The Protocol covers pollution damage as before but environmental damage compensation is limited to costs incurred for reasonable measures to reinstate the contaminated environment. It also allows expenses incurred for preventive measures to be recovered even when no spill of oil occurs, provided there was grave and imminent threat of pollution damage.

The Protocol also extended the Convention to cover spills from sea-going vessels constructed or adapted to carry oil in bulk as cargo so that it applies to both laden and unladen tankers, including spills of bunker oil from such ships.

Under the 1992 Protocol, a shipowner cannot limit liability if it is proved that the pollution damage resulted from the shipowner's personal act or omission, committed with the intent to cause such damage, or recklessly and with knowledge that such damage would probably result.

The 2000 Amendments

Adoption: 18 October 2000

Entry into force: 1 November 2003

The amendments raised the compensation limits by 50 percent compared to the limits set in the 1992 Protocol, as follows:

- For a ship not exceeding 5,000 gross tonnage, liability is limited to 4.51 million SDR (US $5.78 million)

- For a ship 5,000 to 140,000 gross tonnage: liability is limited to 4.51 million SDR plus 631 SDR for each additional gross tonnage over 5,000

- For a ship over 140,000 gross tonnage: liability is limited to 89.77 million SDR

Special Drawing Rights

The daily conversion rates for Special Drawing Rights (SDRs) can be found on the International Monetary Fund website at http//www.imf.org.

INTERNATIONAL CONVENTION ON THE ESTABLISHMENT OF AN INTERNATIONAL FUND FOR COMPENSATION FOR OIL POLLUTION DAMAGE

Adoption: 18 December 1971; Entry into force: 16 October 1978; superseded by 1992 Protocol:

Adoption: 27 November 1992; Entry into force: 30 May 1996

Although the 1969 Civil Liability Convention provided a useful mechanism for ensuring the payment of compensation for oil pollution damage, it did not deal satisfactorily with all the legal, financial and other questions raised during the Conference adopting the CLC Convention. The 1969 Brussels Conference considered a compromise proposal to establish an international fund, to be subscribed to by the cargo interests, which would be available for the dual purpose of, on the one hand, relieving the shipowner of the burden by the requirements of the new convention and, on the other hand, providing additional compensation to the victims of pollution damage in cases where compensation under the 1969 Civil Liability Convention was either inadequate or unobtainable.

The Conference recommended that IMO should prepare such a schema and the International Convention on the Establishment of an International Fund for Compensation for Oil Pollution Damage was adopted at a Conference held in Brussels in 1971. It is supplementary to the Civil Liability Convention.

The purposes of the Fund Convention are:

To provide compensation for pollution damage to the extent that the protection afforded by the 1969 Civil Liability Convention is inadequate.

To give relief to shipowners in respect of the additional financial burden imposed on them by the 1969 Civil Liability Convention, such relief being subject to conditions designed to ensure compliance with safety at sea and other conventions.

To give effect to the related purposes set out in the Convention.

Under the first of its purposes, the Fund is under an obligation to pay compensation to States and persons who suffer pollution damage, if such persons are unable to obtain compensation from the owner of the ship from which the oil escaped or if the compensation due from such owner is not sufficient to cover the damage suffered.

Under the Fund Convention, victims of oil pollution damage may be compensated beyond the level of the shipowner's liability. However, the Fund's obligations are limited. Where, however, there is no shipowner liable or the shipowner liable is unable to meet their liability, the Fund will be required to pay the whole amount of compensation due. Under certain circumstances, the Fund's maximum liability may increase.

With the exception of a few cases, the Fund is obliged to pay compensation to the victims of oil pollution damage who are unable to obtain adequate or any compensation from the shipowner or his guarantor under the CLC Convention.

The Fund is not obliged to indemnify the owner if damage is caused by his wilful misconduct or if the accident was caused, even partially, because the ship did not comply with certain international conventions.

The Convention contains provisions on the procedure for claims rights and obligations and jurisdiction.

Contributions to the Fund should be made by all persons who receive oil by sea in Contracting States.

Protocols to the 1971 convention were adopted in 1976 and 1984, but were superseded by the 1992 Protocol.

The 1971 convention ceased to be in force from 24 May 2002.

The Protocol of 1992
Adoption: 27 November 1992
Entry into force: 30 May 1996

As was the case with the 1 992 Protocol to the CLC Convention, the main purpose of the Protocol was to modify the entry into force requirements and increase compensation amounts.

The scope of coverage was extended in line with the 1992 CLC Protocol.

The 1992 Protocol established a separate, 1992 International Oil Pollution Compensation (IOPC) Fund, known as the 1992 Fund, which is managed in London by a Secretariat.

Under the 1992 Protocol, the maximum amount of compensation payable from the Fund for a single incident, including the limit established under the 1992 CLC Protocol, is 135 million SDR.

However, if three States contributing to the Fund receive more than 600 million tonnes of oil per annum, the maximum amount is raised to 200 million SDR.

Protocol of 2000
Adoption: 27 September 2000
Entry into force: 27 June 2001

The purpose of the 2000 Protocol has been to terminate the 1971 Fund Convention.

According to the Protocol, the 1971 Fund Convention ceases to be in force on the date when the number of Contracting States falls below twenty-five. This happened on 24 May 2002, because of the denunciations by States Parties to Fund 1971 in favor of their membership of Fund 1992.

The 2003 Protocol (supplementary fund)
Adoption: 16 May 2003
Entry into force: 3 March 2005

The 2003 Protocol establishing an International Oil Pollution Compensation Supplementary Fund was adopted by a diplomatic conference held at IMO Headquarters in London.

The aim of the established Fund is to supplement the compensation available under the 1992 Civil Liability and Fund Conventions with an additional, third tier of compensation. The Protocol is optional and participation is open to all States Parties to the 1992 Fund Convention.

The total amount of compensation payable for any one incident will be limited to a combined total of 750 million Special Drawing Rights (SDR) including the amount of compensation paid under the existing CLC/Fund Convention.

The supplementary fund will apply to damage in the territory, including the territorial sea, of a Contracting State and in the exclusive economic zone of a Contracting State.

Annual contributions to the Fund will be made in respect of each Contracting State by any person who, in any calendar year, has received total quantities of oil exceeding 150,000 tons. However, for the purposes of the Protocol, there is a minimum aggregate receipt of 1,000,000 tons of contributing oil in each Contracting State.

The Assembly of the Supplementary Fund will assess the level of contributions based on estimates of expenditure (including administrative costs and payments to be made under the Fund as a result of claims) and income (including surplus funds from previous years, annual contributions and any other income).

Amendments to the compensation limits established under the Protocol can be adopted by a tacit acceptance procedure, so that an amendment adopted in the Legal Committee of IMO by a two-thirds majority of Contracting States present and voting, can enter into force 24 months after its adoption.

The IOPC Funds and IMO

Although the Funds were established under Conventions adopted under the auspices of IMO, they are completely independent legal entities.

Unlike IMO, the IOPC Funds are not United Nations (UN) agencies and are not part of the UN system. They are intergovernmental organizations outside the UN, but follow procedures which are similar to those of the UN. Only States can become Members of the IOPC Funds.

To become a member of the Fund, a State must accede to the 1992 Civil Liability Convention and to the 1992 Fund Convention by depositing a formal instrument of accession with the Secretary-General of IMO. These Conventions should be incorporated into the national law of the State concerned.

See the IOPC Funds website at http://www.iopcfund.org/.

Special drawing rights

The daily conversion rates for Special Drawing Rights (SDRs) can be found on the International Monetary Fund website at http://www.imf.org/.

NOTES AND QUESTIONS

1. Under the CLC, liability for damages in cases of tanker oil spills is channeled to the registered owner of the vessel (CLC Art. III). The Fund Convention was concluded to complement the CLC by creating a compensation fund (created by levies on oil companies and member states) that imposes supplemental liability on oil cargo owners. Currently there are three separate funds each with different parties and each responsible to its assembly of parties. Liability under the CLC and the Fund regimes is strict but limited: the maximum available for any one incident is 750 million SDRs. (An SDR is a weighted average of a basket of national currencies including the U.S. dollar, the euro, the British pound sterling, and the Japanese yen).

2. Under the CLC, the owner of any ship registered in a contracting state and carrying more than 2000 tons of oil in bulk as cargo must maintain insurance or other financial security covering liability up to the applicable limits of the CLC. A direct action for compensation may be maintained against the insurer. CLC Art. VII.

3. Damages recoverable under the CLC and the Fund Convention[22] include:

- Property damage
- Costs of response and clean up both onshore and offshore
- Economic losses by fishers
- Certain economic losses of the tourism industry
- Cost of reinstatement of the affected environment

4. Claims for compensation must be filed within three years of the date the damage was suffered and may only be brought in the state in which the damage occurred.[23] In the first instance, the national court will establish the limitation amount under the CLC (an amount ultimately paid by the liability insurer), and the claims will be paid out of this amount. If the claims exceed the limit under the CLC, the applicable fund or funds will become involved to pay remaining claims. Under the Fund Convention, an international organization, the International Oil Pollution Compensation Funds (IOPC Funds) is the agency that handles these claims. Since its establishment in 1978, as of this writing, the IOPC Funds have handled 145 oil

---

[22] *See* INTERNATIONAL OIL POLLUTION COMPENSATION (IOPC) CLAIMS MANUAL 23–37 (2008).

[23] CLC Art. VIII.

pollution incidents in which payments from the funds have come into play.[24] Claims against the IOPC Fund may be filed at the IOPC office in London, but the IOPC will commonly open one or more claims' offices in the country where the damage occurred. The IOPC claim process is an out-of-court settlement process in which claims are processed according to criteria set out in the IOPC Claims Manual.[25] If a claimant is turned down by the IOPC, he or she may file a claim against the IOPC in national court. In most cases the national court will uphold the IOPC determination, although there are several celebrated cases in which national courts awarded damages against the IOPC. For example, in the case of the oil spill by the tanker *Patmos*, a claim by the Italian state for environmental damages because the "loss of enjoyment suffered by the community," was admitted by an Italian Court of Appeal,[26] damages were awarded against the shipowner after being denied by the IOPC Funds.[27]

5.   Note that the CLC and the Fund Convention apply only to spills from ships carrying oil as cargo. A separate international convention, the International Convention on Civil Liability for Bunker Oil Pollution Damage (2001) establishes strict liability for damages in cases of bunker oil spills from non-tankers, and requires ships over 1000 gross tons to maintain insurance or other financial security, but the ship involved may limit liability under the Convention on Limitation of Liability for Maritime Claims (1976) and its 1996 Protocol. Some 47 parties have adhered to the Bunker Oil Convention. Because shipowners may limit liability under the Limitation Convention (which does not apply to limit liability under the CLC or the Funds regime), in the event of a major spill of bunker oil, the damages will greatly exceed the shipowner's liability. See the Case of the Rena, High Court of New Zealand, CIV-2012-470-838, [2013] NZHC 500 (2013). Neither the CLC/Fund regime nor the Bunker Oil Convention apply to damages from spills of hazardous substances. The Hazardous and Noxious Substances Convention (HNS Convention) (1996) was concluded to establish an international compensation regime for spills of hazardous and noxious substances, but the HNS Convention is not yet in force. No international convention presently covers spills or emissions of oil from offshore oil and gas drilling activities, such as the accident that occurred in 2010 at the BP Macondo Well that polluted the Gulf of Mexico.

---

[24]   *See* http://www.iopcfunds.org.

[25]   IOPC Claims Manual, op. cit. at 2–4.

[26]   Patmos incident (1985), reported in International Oil Pollution Compensation Fund Annual Report, 1989, pp. 18–22.

[27]   Under the international regimes, the CLC and the Funds, recovery of environmental damages are limited in two ways. First, IOPC Fund Resolution 3, First Extra Sess., Oct. 17, 1980, FUND/A/ES.1/13, adopted by the Funds' Assembly, states that "assessment of compensation to be paid by the Fund is not to be made on the basis of an abstract quantification of damage calculated in accordance with theoretical models." Second, the CLC Protocol, Art. 1(2) limits damages as follows: "compensation for impairment of the environment shall be limited to costs of reasonable measures of reinstatement actually undertaken or to be undertaken."

NOTE ON COLLATERAL ACTIONS TO OVERCOME LIMITS UNDER THE INTERNATIONAL LIABILITY REGIMES

Suppose the damage from an oil spill is in excess of the limits applicable under the international liability regime; is there any way persons damaged by the oil pollution incident can bring collateral actions to recover further damages? This problem was raised in connection with the wreck of the oil tanker *Erika* off the west coast of France in 1999. The *Erika* was a Malta-registered tanker whose principal owner as a shareholder in a Maltese company was an Italian national, Giuseppe Savarese, living in London. The classification society that approved the seaworthiness of the *Erika* was an Italian company, Registro Italiano Navale (RINA). The *Erika* foundered in international waters but sank within the French Exclusive Economic Zone (EEZ), spilling tons of oil into the sea causing the death of tens of thousands of seabirds and other marine life and polluting over 400 kilometers of pristine beaches and shorelands in Brittany and the Vendee region of France. The wreck of the *Erika* was found to have been caused by a combination of bad weather and corrosion of the vessel's structures. At the time of the spill the *Erika* was under time charter to Total, S.A., a French multinational oil company. The *Erika* was laden with some 30,884 metric tons of grade 2 fuel oil at the time of the casualty. The shipowner's limit of liability under the CLC Convention based on the vessel's tonnage was 13 million euros. Thus the IOPC was called upon to pay excess damages. At the time of the spill the IOPC limit was 185 million euros so the damages to individuals and French local governments (communes) as well as for response, clean-up and environmental damages were greatly in excess of the limits provided under the IOPC.

Note that the CLC channels liability for an oil spill to the shipowner; the cargo owner as time or voyage charterer does not have liability under the international regime.

The spill of the *Erika* sparked three extremely interesting collateral actions:

1.   The Italian classification society, RINA, filed suit in the Tribunal of Syracuse, Sicily, against the French state and Total, asking for a declaratory judgment that it had no liability in the matter. On appeal the Italian Corte di Cassazione, the Italian Supreme Court, ruled that Italian courts did not have jurisdiction since 1992 CLC, Article IX(l) establishes exclusive jurisdiction in the courts in t h e state where the damage occurred. Corte di Cassazione No. 14769, Sezione Unite, Judgment of 17 October 2002.

2.   The French commune (local government) of Mesquer filed an action for damages in a French court against Total, S.A., the cargo owner/charterer of the *Erika*, praying for damages on the theory that oil spilled into the sea becomes "waste" under the laws of France and the European Union, and that under these laws, Total, as the owner of the "waste," has the duty to bear the full cost of clean-up and damages. When the case reached the Supreme Court of France, the judges of that court, the Cour de Cassation, referred the question of whether spilled oil constitutes waste to the European Court of Justice (ECJ) to answer the question under European law. In 2008, the ECJ, in Case C-188/07, *Commune de Mesquer v. Total France, S.A.*, [2008] ECRI 4501, ruled that, indeed, hydrocarbons accidentally

spilled into the sea constitute "waste" within the meaning of European Union Council Directive 75/442, and in accordance with the "polluter pays" principle, Total, as generator of the waste, is fully liable for damages if it has contributed by its conduct to the risk that pollution caused by the shipwreck will occur. Under this ruling Total, as the cargo owner, may have virtually unlimited liability for further damages.

3.   French prosecutors filed criminal actions in a Paris court against several defendants in connection with the *Erika* spill, and in 2008, the trial court rendered guilty verdicts against Total, Giuseppe Savarese, the principal shareholder of the shipowning company, Antonio Pollara, the ship's master, and RINA, the classification society. *Procès Erika*, Jugement du Tribunal Correctionnel de Paris (Grande Instance), 16 Jan. 2008. The court levied a criminal fine of 375 million euros against Total. In addition, under French law, as is typical of civil law countries, victims of crimes may join the criminal proceedings and recover damages [see the Code Penal de France, Arts. 85 and 86]. Some 200 French communes and French environmental organizations joined the criminal action, and the court declared that under French law the four convicted defendants were liable for civil compensatory damages in the amount of 200.6 million euros. The two amounts levied — the 375 million euro criminal fine and the 200.6 million euro civil damages — were in addition to a mounts voluntarily paid already by Total and RINA, 171 million euros and 30 million euros, respectively. The trial court's judgment was upheld by the French Court of Appeal in 2010 [*Affaire Erika*, Judgment of the Cour d'Appel de Paris, 30 March 2010], and was appealed to the Supreme Court, the Cour de Cassation. Most observers expected the Cour de Cassation to nullify the judgment, especially after the Court's Advocate General, which Cour de Cassation follows most of the time, ruled in an "Avis," on May 24, 2012, that French courts had no criminal or civil jurisdiction in the matter. As to the criminal liability, the Advocate General held that French criminal jurisdiction under the Code Penal, Art. 113-2, is territorial and that this included only French territory and the French territorial sea, not the French Exclusive Economic Zone. He further ruled that in the area of the EEZ the flag state, Malta, had exclusive criminal jurisdiction. As to the civil liability of the defendants, the Advocate General held that the CLC and Fund Conventions as accepted by France provided exclusive jurisdiction and that collateral civil actions for damages were excluded under French law. Nonetheless, on September 25, 2012, the Cour de Cassation handed down a 330 page opinion fully upholding the criminal convictions and the criminal and civil liability rendered by the trial court. The Cour de Cassation ruled that the court had jurisdiction under French criminal law over pollution incidents occurring in the French EEZ based on the provisions of UNCLOS (*see* Articles 27, 28, 56, 97, 211, and 220). The court upheld civil jurisdiction for damages under a theory of "prejudice ecologique" which could be the basis for civil damages rendered to victims of crimes resulting from an oil spill incident. Cour de Cassation, Chambre criminelle, Arret no. 3439 of 25 September 2012,   available   at   http://www.courdecassation.fr/IMG/// Crim_arret3439_20120925.pdf, accessed 23 November 2012.

This case may soon enter a new phase: the lawyers for Total have announced that they intend to seek review of the judgment of the Cour de Cassation in the European Court of Human Rights.

In the case of the *Prestige*, a tanker which sank some 30 kilometers off Cape Finisterre, Galicia, Spain in 2002, fouling much of the Spanish coast and wreaking havoc with the fishing industry, the Spanish government in 2003, filed suit against the U.S. classification society, Houston-based American Bureau of Shipping (ABS), that had approved the seaworthiness of the *Prestige* and had certified the vessel as fit to carry fuel cargos.

The United States District Court for the Southern District of New York granted summary judgment in favor of ABS on the ground that under the CLC, Spain was the exclusive forum for the assertion of pollution claims concerning the spill. *Reino de Espana v. American Bureau of Shipping*, 528 F. Supp. 2d 455 (S.D.N.Y. 2008). After this judgment was reversed by the Court of Appeals on the ground that an international treaty to which the U.S. is not a party cannot divest the U.S. federal courts of subject matter jurisdiction [Summary Order of the United States Court of Appeals of the Second Circuit, 12 June 2009], the District Court again granted summary judgment in favor of ABS on the substantive ground that a classification society's services; which involve conducting an inspection of a vessel for the owner, do not constitute a "global guarantee" to third parties concerning a vessel's seaworthiness. *Reino de España v. American Bureau of Shipping*, 729 F. Supp. 2d 635 (S.D.N.Y. 2010). The Court of Appeals affirmed this decision but on different grounds. The Court of Appeals refused to decide whether a classification society may be liable in tort to third parties for negligent or for reckless conduct in connection with the classification of vessels. Instead, the Court, after a choice of laws analysis holding that the question of liability was governed by the maritime law of the United States, ruled that Spain had not introduced sufficient evidence to prove its allegation that ABS had acted recklessly, and, consequently, a jury could not conclude that the failure of ABS had led to the damages incurred by the spill of oil from the Prestige. *Reino de España v. American Bureau of Shipping*, 691 F.3d 461 (2d Cir. 2012). Did the lawyers for Spain make a tactical error in not alleging that ABS was liable for simple negligence?

UNITED STATES OIL POLLUTION ACT OF 1990
(OPA 90)
33 U.S.C. § 2701 et seq.

[OPA 90 imposes strict liability for damages resulting from an oil spill on "responsible parties" who are defined as, for vessels, the owner, operator, or demise charterer (and the owner of the oil for single hull tankers); for offshore facilities, the lessee or permittee and the holder of the right of use; for onshore facilities, the owner and the operator; for pipelines, the owner and operator; and for deep water ports, the licensee. 33 U.S.C. § 2701 (32). Oil spill liability is triggered by any discharge of oil that produces "sheen" on the water; a sheen is an iridescent appearance on the surface of the water. 40 C.F.R. § 110. OPA 90 also establishes an Oil Spill Liability Trust Fund, which is available to pay claims up to $1 billion per incident if a claim is not paid after first being presented to a responsible party or if the responsible party is entitled to a defense or if the liability limit under the statute has been reached. 33 U.S.C. § 2708. The principal liability provisions of OPA 90 are as follows.]

§ 2702.   Elements of liability

(a) In general. Notwithstanding any other provision or rule of law, and subject to the provisions of this Act. each responsible party for a vessel or a facility from which oil is discharged, or which poses the substantial threat of a discharge of oil, into or upon the navigable waters or adjoining shorelines or the exclusive economic zone is liable for the removal costs and damages specified in subsection (b) that result from such incident

(b) Covered removal costs and damages.

(1) Removal costs. The removal costs referred to in subsection (a) are—

(A) all removal costs incurred by the United States, a State, or an Indian tribe under subsection (c), (d), (e), or (I) of section 311 of the Federal Water Pollution Control Act (33 U.S.C. 1321), as amended by this Act, under the Intervention on the High Seas Act (33 U.S.C. 1–171 et seq.), or under State law; and

(B) any removal costs incurred by any person for acts taken by the person which are consistent with the National Contingency Plan.

(2) Damages. The damages referred to in subsection (a) are the following:

(A) Natural resources. Damages for injury to, destruction of, loss of, or loss of use of, natural resources, including the reasonable costs of assessing the damage, which shall be recoverable by a United States trustee, a State trustee, an Indian tribe trustee, or a foreign trustee.

(B) Real or personal property. Damages for injury to, or economic losses resulting from destruction of real or personal property, which shall be recoverable by a claimant who owns or leases that property.

(C) Subsistence use. Damages for loss of subsistence use of natural resources, which shall be recoverable by any claimant who so uses natural resources which have been injured, destroyed, or lost. without regard to the ownership or management of the resources.

(D) Revenues. Damages equal to the net loss of taxes, royalties, rents, fees, or net profit shares due to the injury, destruction, or loss of real property, personal property, or natural resources, which shall be recoverable by the Government of the United States, a State, or a political subdivision thereof.

(E) Profits and earning capacity. Damages equal to the loss of profits or impairment of earning capacity due to the injury, destruction, or loss of real property, personal property, or natural resources. which shall be recoverable by any claimant

(F) Public services. Damages for net costs of providing increased or additional public services during or after removal activities, including protection from fire, safety, or health hazards, caused by a discharge of oil, which shall be recoverable by a State, or a political subdivision of a State.

(c) Excluded discharges. This title does not apply to any discharge—

(1) permitted by a permit issued under Federal, State, or local law;

(2) from a public vessel; or

(3) from an onshore facility which is subject to the Trans-Alaska Pipeline Authorization Act (43 U.S.C. 1651 et seq.).

(d) Liability of third parties.

(1) In general.

(A) Third party treated as responsible party. Except as provided in subparagraph (B), in any case in which a responsible party establishes that a discharge or threat of a discharge and the resulting removal costs and damages were caused solely by an act or omission of one or more third parties described in section 1003(a)(3) [33 USCS § 2703(a)(3)] (or solely by such an act or omission in combination with an act of God or an act of war), the third party or parties shall be treated as the responsible party or parties for purposes of determining liability under this title.

(B) Subrogation of responsible party. If the responsible party alleges that the discharge or threat of a discharge was caused solely by an act or omission of a third party, the responsible party—

(i) in accordance with section 1013 [33 USCS § 2713] shall pay removal costs and damages to any claimant; and

(ii) shall be entitled by subrogation to all rights of the United States Government and the claimant to recover removal costs or damages from the third party or the Fund paid under this subsection.

(2) Limitation applied.

(A) Owner or operator of vessel or facility. If the act or omission of a third party that causes an incident occurs in connection with a vessel or facility owned or operated by the third party, the liability of the third party shall be subject to the limits provided in section 1004 [33 USC § 2704] as applied with respect to the vessel or facility.

(B) Other cases. In any other case, the liability of a third party or parties shall not exceed the limitation which would have been applicable to the responsible party of the vessel or facility from which the discharge actually occurred if the responsible party were liable.

§ 2703.   Defenses to liability

(a) Complete defenses. A responsible party is not liable for removal costs or damages under section 1002 [33 USCS § 2702] if the responsible party establishes, by a preponderance of the evidence, that the discharge or substantial threat of a discharge of oil and the resulting damages or removal costs were caused solely by—

(1) an act of God;

(2) an act of war;

(3) an act or omission of a third party, other than an employee or agent of the responsible party or a third party whose act or omission occurs in connection with any contractual relationship with the responsible party (except where the sole contractual arrangement arises in connection with carriage by a common carrier by rail), if the responsible party establishes, by a preponderance of the evidence, that the responsible party—

(A) exercised due care with respect to the oil concerned, taking into consideration the characteristics of the oil and in light of all relevant facts and circumstances; and

(B) took precautions against foreseeable acts or omissions of any such third party and the foreseeable consequences of those acts or omissions; or (4) any combination of paragraphs (1), (2), and (3).

(b) Defenses as to particular claimants. A responsible party is not liable under section 1002 [33 USCS § 2702] to a claimant, to the extent that the incident is caused by the gross negligence or willful misconduct of the claimant.

(c) Limitation on complete defense. Subsection (a) does not apply with respect to a responsible party who fails or refuses—

(1) to report the incident as required by law if the responsible party knows or has reason to know of the incident;

(2) to provide all reasonable cooperation and assistance requested by a responsible official in connection with removal activities; or

(3) without sufficient cause, to comply with an order issued under subsection (c) or (e) of section 311 of the Federal Water Pollution Control Act (33 U.S.C. 1321), as amended by this Act, or the Intervention on the High Seas Act (33 U.S.C. 1471 et seq.).

§ 2704. Limits on liability

(a) General rule. Except as otherwise provided in this section, the total of the liability of a responsible party under section 1002 [33 USCS § 2702] and any removal costs incurred by, or on behalf of the responsible party, with respect to each incident shall not exceed—

(1) for a tank vessel, the greater of—

(A) $ 1,200 per gross ton; or

(B)   (i) in the case of a vessel greater than 3,000 gross tons, $ 10,000,000; or

(ii) in the case of a vessel of 3,000 gross tons or less, $ 2,000,000;

(2) for any other vessel, $ 600 per gross ton or $ 500,000. whichever is greater;

(3) for an offshore facility except a deep water port, the total of all removal costs plus $ 75,000,000; and

(4) for any onshore facility and a deep water port, $ 350,000,000.

. . . .

(c) Exceptions.

(1) Acts of responsible party. Subsection (a) does not apply if the incident was proximately caused by—

(A) gross negligence or willful misconduct of, or

(B) the violation of an applicable Federal safety, construction, or operating regulation by, the responsible party, an agent or employee of the responsible party, or a person acting pursuant to a contractual relationship with the responsible party.

§ 2707.   Recovery by foreign claimants

(a) Required showing by foreign claimants.

(1) In general. In addition to satisfying the other requirements of this Act, to recover removal costs or damages resulting from an incident a foreign claimant shall demonstrate that—

(A) the claimant has not been otherwise compensated for the removal costs or damages: and

(B) recovery is authorized by a treaty or executive agreement between the United States and the claimant's country, or the Secretary of State, in consultation with the Attorney General and other appropriate officials, has certified that the claimant's country provides a comparable remedy for United States claimants.

(2) Exceptions. Paragraph (l) (B) shall not apply with respect to recovery by a resident of Canada in the case of an incident described in subsection (b)(4).

(b) Discharges in foreign countries. A foreign claimant may make a claim tor removal costs and damages resulting from a discharge, or substantial threat of a discharge, of oil in or on the territorial sea, internal waters, or adjacent shoreline of a foreign country, only if the discharge is from—

(1) an Outer Continental Shelf facility or a deepwater port;

(2) a vessel in the navigable waters;

(3) a vessel carrying oil as cargo between 2 places in the United States; or

(4) a tanker that received the oil at the terminal of the pipeline constructed under the Trans-Alaska Pipeline Authorization Act(43 U.S.C. 1651 et seq.), for transportation to a place in the United States, and the discharge or threat occurs prior to delivery of the oil to that place.

(c) Foreign claimant defined. In this section, the term "foreign claimant" means—

(1) a person residing in a foreign country;

(2) the government of a foreign country; and

(3) an agency or political subdivision of a foreign country.

§ 2713.   Claims procedure

(a) Presentation. Except as provided in subsection (b), all claims for removal costs or damages shall be presented first to the responsible party or guarantor of the source designated under section 1014(a) [33 USC § 2714(a)].

(b) Presentation to Fund.

(1) In general. Claims tor removal costs or damages may be presented first to the Fund—

(A) if the President has advertised or otherwise notified claimants in accordance with section 10l4(c) [33 USC § 2714(c)];

(B) by a responsible party who may assert a claim under section 1008 [33 USC § 2708]:

(C) by the Governor of a State for removal costs incurred by that State: or

(D) by a United States claimant in a case where a foreign offshore unit has discharged oil causing damage for which the Fund is liable under section 1012(a) [33 USC § 2712(a)].

(2) Limitation on presenting claim. No claim of a person against the Fund may be approved or certified during the pendency of an action by the person in court to recover costs which are the subject of the claim.

(c) Election. If a claim is presented in accordance with subsection (a) and—

(1) each person to whom the claim is presented denies all liability for the claim, or

(2) the claim is not settled by any person by payment within 90 days after the date upon which (A) the claim was presented, or (B) advertising was begun pursuant to section 1014(b) [33 USC § 2714(b)], whichever is later, the claimant may elect to commence an action in court against the responsible party or guarantor or to present the claim to the Fund.

(d) Uncompensated damages. If a claim is presented in accordance with this section, including a claim for interim, short-term damages representing less than the full amount of damages to which the claimant ultimately may be entitled, and full and adequate compensation is unavailable, a claim for the uncompensated damages and removal costs may be presented to the Fund.

(e) Procedure for claims against Fund. The President shall promulgate, and may from time to time amend, regulations for the presentation, filing, processing, settlement, and adjudication of claims under this Act against the Fund.

§ 2718.   Relationship to other law

(a) Preservation of State authorities; Solid Waste Disposal Act. Nothing in this Act or the Act of March 3, 1851 shall—

(1) affect, or be construed or interpreted as preempting, the authority of any State or political subdivision thereof from imposing any additional liability or requirements with respect to—

(A) the discharge of oil or other pollution by oil within such State; or

(B) any removal activities in connection with such a discharge; or

(2) affect, or be construed or interpreted to affect or modify in any way the obligations or liabilities of any person under the Solid Waste Disposal Act(48 U.S.C. 6901 et seq.) or State law, including common law.

(b) Preservation of State funds. Nothing in this Act or in section 9509 of the Internal Revenue Code of 1986 (26 U.S.C. 9509) shall in any way affect, or be construed to affect, the authority of any State—

(1) to establish, or to continue in effect, a fund any purpose of which is to pay for costs or damages arising out of, or directly resulting from, oil pollution or the substantial threat of oil pollution; or

(2) to require any person to contribute to such a fund.

(c) Additional requirements and liabilities; penalties. Nothing in this Act, the Act of March 3, 1851 (46 U.S.C. 183 et seq.), or section 9509 of the Internal Revenue Code of 1986 (26 U.S.C. 9509), shall in any way affect, or be construed to affect, the authority of the United States or any State or political subdivision thereof—

(1) to impose additional liability or additional requirements; or

(2) to impose, or to determine the amount of, any fine or penalty

(whether criminal or civil in nature) for any violation of law; relating to the discharge, or substantial threat of a discharge, of oil.

§ 2751.   Savings provisions

. . . .

(e) Admiralty and maritime law. Except as otherwise provided in this Act, this Act does not affect—

(1) admiralty and maritime law; or

(2) the jurisdiction of the district courts of the United States with respect to civil actions under admiralty and maritime jurisdiction, saving to suitors in all cases all other remedies to which they are otherwise entitled.

IN RE OIL SPILL BY THE OIL RIG DEEPWATER HORIZON
808 F. Supp. 2d 943 (E.D. La. 2011)

[This case is the first published decision by the Court handling the multi-district litigation arising from the explosion, fire, and subsequent release of an estimated 4.9 million barrels (205.8 million gallons) of oil in the Gulf of Mexico in 2010].

ORDER AND REASONS

[As to Motions to Dismiss the B1 Master Complaint]

BARBIER, DISTRICT JUDGE.

This multi-district litigation ("MDL") consists of hundreds of consolidated cases, with thousands of claimants, pending before this Court. These cases arise from the April 20, 2010 explosion, tire, and sinking of the DEEPWATER HORIZON mobile offshore drilling unit ("MODU"), which resulted in the release of millions of gallons of oil into the Gulf of Mexico before it was finally capped approximately three months later. The consolidated cases include claims for the death of eleven individuals, numerous claims for personal injury, and various claims for environmental and economic damages.

In order to efficiently manage this complex MDL, the Court consolidated and organized the various types of claims into several "pleading bundles." The "B1" pleading bundle includes all claims for private or "non-governmental economic loss and property damages." There are in excess of 100,000 individual claims encompassed within the B1 bundle.

PROCEDURAL HISTORY

In the B1 Master Complaint, the [plaintiffs' steering committee] identifies a number of categories of claimants seeking various types of economic damages, including Commercial Fishermen Plaintiffs, Processing and Distributing Plaintiffs, Recreational Business Plaintiffs, Commercial Business Plaintiffs, Recreation Plaintiffs, Plant and Dock Worker Plaintiffs, Vessel of Opportunity ("VoO") Plaintiffs, Real Property Plaintiffs, Real Property/Tourism Plaintiffs, Banking/Retail Business Plaintiffs, Subsistence Plaintiffs, Moratorium Plaintiffs, and Dealer Claimants.

Plaintiffs named the following as Defendants in their B1 Master Complaint: BPExploration & Production Inc., BP America Production Company and BP p.l.c. (collectively "BP"); Transocean Ltd., Transocean Offshore, Transocean Deepwater, Transocean Holdings (collectively "Transocean"); Halliburton; Cameron; Weatherford; Anadarko, Anadarko E & P (collectively "Anadarko"); MOEX Offshore, MOEX USA (collectively "MOEX"). All of the Defendants have filed Motions to Dismiss.

Plaintiffs allege claims under general maritime law, the Oil Pollution Act of 1990 ("OPA"), 33 U.S.C. § 2701 et seq., and various state laws. Under general maritime law, Plaintiffs allege claims for negligence, gross negligence, and strict liability for manufacturing and/or design defect. Under various state laws, Plaintiffs allege claims for nuisance, trespass, and fraudulent concealment, and they also allege a claim for strict liability under the Florida Pollutant Discharge Prevention and Control Act, Fla. Stat. § 376.011 et seq. Additionally, Plaintiffs seek punitive damages under all claims and request declaratory relief regarding any settlement provisions that purport to affect the calculation of punitive damages.

PARTIES' ARGUMENTS AND DISCUSSION

The subject Motions to Dismiss go to the heart of Plaintiffs' claims in this case. Various Defendants advance somewhat different arguments as to why some or all of the B1 bundle claims should be dismissed. At bottom, however, all Defendants seek dismissal of all non-OPA claims for purely economic damages resulting from the oil spill.[28] Essentially, Defendants move to dismiss all claims brought pursuant to either general maritime law or state law. All parties advance a number of arguments regarding the law that should apply to the Plaintiffs' claims for economic loss.

Vessel status

Although it was unclear prior to oral argument, it is now apparent that only Defendant Cameron suggests that the DEEPWATER HORIZON MODU was not a vessel in navigation at the time of the casualty on April 20, 2010. Plaintiffs and all other Defendants agree that the DEEPWATER HORIZON MODU was at all material times a "vessel" as that term is defined and understood in general

---

[28] Additionally, Defendants move to dismiss all OPA claimants who have not complied with OPA's "presentment" requirement. They also question whether Plaintiffs can properly sue parties under OPA who have not been named as "Responsible Parties," as well as whether VoO Claimants and Moratorium Claimants have stated viable OPA claims.

maritime law. Cameron argues that although the DEEPWATER HORIZON may have been a vessel during the times it was moved from one drilling location to another, at the time of the casualty it was stationary and physically attached to the seabed by means of 5,000 feet of drill pipe. Cameron relies on a line of cases beginning with *Rodrigue v. Aetna Casualty Co.*, 395 U.S. 352, 89 S. Ct. 1835, 23 L. Ed. 2d. 360 (1969), for the proposition that a drilling platform permanently or temporarily attached to the seabed of the Outer Continental Shelf is considered an "fixed structure" and not a vessel. Accordingly, argues Cameron, admiralty jurisdiction is absent and general maritime law does not apply.

The Court is not persuaded by Cameron's arguments. Under clearly established law, the DEEPWATER HORIZON was a vessel, not a.fixed platform. Cameron's arguments run counter to longstanding case law which establishes conclusively that the Deepwater Horizon, a mobile offshore drilling unit, was a vessel.

In the seminal case of Offshore Co. v. Robison, the Fifth Circuit held that a "special purpose vessel, a floating drilling platform" could be considered a vessel. 266 F.2d 769, 779 (5th Cir. l959). Specifically, the defendants in that case, who claimed that the floating platform should not be considered a vessel, argued that "[t]he evidence shows that Offshore 55 was a platform designed and used solely for the purpose of drilling oil wells in offshore waters-in this instance, the Gulf of Mexico, that the platform was not self-propelled and when moved from one well to another, two large tugs were used. Further, when an oil well was being drilled the platform was secured to the bed of the Gulf in an immobilized position with the platform itself raised forty to fifty feet above the water level . . . . " Id. at 773 n.3. Nonetheless, the Fifth Circuit held that such a "floating drilling platform" can be a vessel, though secured to the seabed while drilling a well.

Cameron argues that its blowout preventer ("BOP") was physically attached to the wellhead, located on the seabed some 5,000 feet below the surface of the water, and that the oil spill occurred at the wellhead, not from the DEEPWATER HORIZON. This does not persuade the Court to reach a different conclusion. The B1 Master Complaint alleges that both the BOP and the drill string were part of the vessel's gear or appurtenances. Maritime law "ordinarily treats an 'appurtenance' attached to a vessel in navigable waters as part of the vessel itself." *Grubart, Inc. v. Great Lakes Dredge & Dock Co.*, 513 U.S. 527, 535, 115 S. Ct. 1043, 130 L. Ed. 2d 1024 (1995).

Admiralty jurisdiction

The test for whether admiralty jurisdiction exists in tort cases was outlined by the Supreme Court in *Grubart, Inc. v. Great Lakes Dredge & Dock Co.*:

> [A] party seeking to invoke federal admiralty jurisdiction pursuant to 28 U.S.C. § 1333(1) over a tort claim must satisfy conditions both of location and of connection with maritime activity. A court applying the location test must determine whether the tort occurred on navigable water. The connection test raises two issues. A court, first, must assess the general features of the type of incident involved to determine whether the incident has a potentially disruptive impact on maritime commerce. Second, a court

must determine whether the general character of the activity giving rise of the incident shows a substantial relationship to traditional maritime activity.

513 U.S. 527, 534, 115 S. Ct. 1043, 130 L. Ed. 2d 1024 (1995) (citations and internal quotations omitted).

The location test, which is satisfied when the tort occurs on navigable water, is readily satisfied here. The B1 Master Complaint alleges that the blowout, explosions, fire, and subsequent discharge of oil, occurred on or from the DEEPWATER HORIZON and its appurtenances, which was operating on waters overlying the Outer Continental Shelf; i.e., navigable waters. The connection test is also met. First, there is no question that the explosion and resulting spill caused a disruption of maritime commerce, which exceeds the "potentially disruptive" threshold established in *Grubart*. Second, the operations of the DEEPWATER HORIZON bore a substantial relationship to traditional maritime activity. *See Theriot v. Bay Drilling Corp.*, 783 F.2d 527, 538–39 (5th Cir. 1986) ("oil and gas drilling on navigable waters aboard a vessel is recognized to be maritime commerce"). Further, injuries incurred on land (or in the seabed) are cognizable in admiralty under the Admiralty Extension Act, 46 U.S.C. § 30101.

This case falls within the Court's admiralty jurisdiction. With admiralty jurisdiction comes the "application, of substantive admiralty law." Grubart, 513 U.S. at 545, 115 S.Ct. 1043. "[W]here OCSLA and general maritime law both could apply, the case is to be governed by maritime law." *Tenn. Gas Pipeline v. Houston Cas. Ins. Co.*, 87 F.3d 150, 154 (5th Cir. 1996).

Plaintiffs' state law claims

Plaintiffs designated their B1 Master Complaint as "an admiralty or maritime case" under Rule 9(h) of the Federal Rules of Civil Procedure. Although Plaintiffs acknowledge that admiralty jurisdiction applies to this case, they insist that substantive maritime law does not preempt their state-law claims because state law can "supplement" general maritime law, either where there is a substantive gag in maritime law or where there is no conflict with maritime law. Plaintiffs also argue that OPA contains a state-law savings provision, which preserves these claims.

The focus turns, then, to the relationship between federal maritime law and state law. As mentioned, with admiralty jurisdiction comes substantive maritime law. This means that general maritime law — an amalgam of traditional common law rules, modifications of those rules, and newly created rules — applies to this matter to the extent it is not displaced by federal statute. *E. River S.S. Corp. v. Transamerica Delaval Inc.*, 476 U.S. 858, 864, 106 S. Ct. 2295, 90 L. Ed. 2d 865 (1986) This framework, established by the Constitution[29], intends that a consistent, uniform system will govern maritime commerce. *See The Lottawanna*, 88 U.S. 558, 557, 21

---

[29] Article III. § 2 extends the judicial power to "all cases of admiralty and maritime jurisdiction." Congress legislates in this area by virtue of the Interstate Commerce Clause and Necessary and Proper Clause. U.S. Const. Art. I. § 8. The Supremacy Clause, Article VI, ensures federal maritime law supersedes state law. *See* 1 Thomas J. Schoenbaum, Admiralty and Maritime Law §§ 4-1 to 4-2 (4th ed. 2004).

Wall. 558, 22 L. Ed. 654 (1874) ("It certainly could not have been the intention to place the rules and limits of maritime law under the disposal and regulation of the several States, as that would have defeated the uniformity and consistency at which the Constitution aimed on all subjects of a commercial character affecting the intercourse of the States with each other or with foreign states."). Admiralty does not entirely exclude state law, however, and States may "create rights and liabilities with respect to conduct within their borders, when the state action does not run counter to federal laws or the essential features of an exclusive federal jurisdiction." *Romero v. Int'l Terminal Operating Co.*, 358 U.S. 354, 375 n.42, 79 S. Ct. 468, 3 L. Ed. 2d 368 (1959) (emphasis added; internal quotations and citations omitted).

But this case does not concern conduct within state borders (waters). This casualty occurred over the Outer Continental Shelf-an area of "exclusive federal jurisdiction" — on waters deemed to be the "high seas." 43 U.S.C. § 1332(2), 1333(a)(1)(A). The Admiralty Extension Act, though not itself a grant of exclusive jurisdiction, see *Askew, infra*, nevertheless ensures that damages incurred on land are cognizable in admiralty. *See Grubart*, 513 U.S. at 531, 115 S. Ct. 1043. Citizens from multiple states have alleged damage, and multiple states' laws are asserted. While it is recognized that States have an interest to protect their citizens, property, and resources from oil pollution, to subject a discharge to the varying laws of each state into which its oil has flowed would contravene a fundamental purpose of maritime law: "[t]o preserve adequate harmony and appropriate uniform rules relating to maritime matters." *Kwickerbocker Ice Co., see supra* note 7. Thus, to the extent state law could apply to conduct outside state waters, in this case it must "yield to the needs of a uniform federal maritime law." Romero, 358 U.S. at 373, 79 S. Ct, 468 (citing S. Pac. Co. v. Jensen, 244 U.S. 205, 37 S. Ct. 524, 61 L. Ed. 1086 (1916)).

Plaintiffs' contention that OPA's savings' provisions preserves its state-law claims is also unavailing. These provisions state:

(a) Preservation of State authorities; Solid Waste Disposal Act Nothing in this Act or the Act of March 3, 1851 shall—

(1) affect, or be construed or interpreted as preempting, the authority of any State or political subdivision thereof from imposing any additional liability or requirements with respect to—

(A) the discharge of oil or other pollution by oil within such State; or

(B) any removal activities in connection with such a discharge; or

(2) affect, or be construed or interpreted to affect or modify in any way the obligations or liabilities of any person under the Solid Waste Disposal Act (42 U.S.C. 6901 et seq.) or State law, including common law.

. . .

(c) Additional requirements and liabilities; penalties

Nothing in this Act, the Act of March 8, 1851 (46 U.S.C. 183 et seq.), or section 9509 of title 26, shall in any way affect, or be construed to affect, the authority of the United States or any State or political subdivision thereof—

(1) to impose additional liability or additional requirements; or

(2) to impose, or to determine the amount of, any fine or penalty (whether criminal or civil in nature) for any violation of law;

relating to the discharge, or substantial threat of a discharge, of oil.

33 U.S.C. § 2718. These provisions evince Congress' intent to preserve the States' police power to govern pollution discharges within their territorial waters. The Court does not read as them giving States the power to govern out-of-state conduct affecting multiple states. "The usual function of a saving clause is to preserve something from immediate interference-not to create; and the rule is that expression by that the Legislature of an erroneous opinion law claim concerning law does not alter it." *Knickerbocker Ice*, 253 U.S. at 162, 40 S. Ct. 488. In other words, although Congress has expressed its intent to not preempt state law, this intent does not delegate to the States a power that the Constitution vested in the federal government.

This conclusion is consistent with the Supreme Court's rationale in International Paper Co. v. Ouellette, 479 U.S. 481, 107 S. Ct. 805, 93 L. Ed. 2d 883 (1987). There the Court addressed the question of whether the [Clean Water] Act preempts a common-law nuisance suit filed in a Vermont court under Vermont law, when the source of the alleged injury is located in New York." *Id.* at 483, 107 S. Ct. 805. The Clean Water Act ("CWA") contained two provisions relating to state-law remedies:

Except as expressly provided . . . nothing in this chapter shall . . . be construed as impairing or in any manner affecting any right or jurisdiction of the States with respect to the waters (including boundary waters) of such States.

Nothing in this section [Citizen Suits] shall restrict any right which any person (or class of persons) may have under any statute or common law to seek enforcement of any effluent standard or limitation or to seek any other relief . . . .

Id. at 485, 107 S. Ct. 805 (quoting 33 U.S.C. §§ 1370, 1365(e)). Notwithstanding these provisions, the Ouellette Court determined that ". . . when a court considers a state law claim concerning interstate water pollution that is subject to the CWA, the court must apply the law of the State in which the point source is located." *Id.* at 187, 107 S. Ct. 805. According to the Court, "[a]pplication of an affected State's law to an out-of-state source would . . . undermine the important goals of efficiency and predictability in the permit system." *Id.* at 496, 107 S. Ct. 805. The Court also noted that prohibiting an action under the affected State's laws did not leave the plaintiffs without a remedy as they could avail themselves of either the source State's law or the CWA's citizen suit provision. *Id.* at 497–98 & n.18, 107 S.Ct. 805. Although this matter may not immediately concern a permitting process, similar goals exist in maritime law (uniformity), as discussed above. Thus, just as the Supreme Court limited the state-law claims preserved by the CWA savings clause, this Court finds it appropriate to limit state-law claims purportedly saved by OPA.

General maritime law claims

Defendants seek to dismiss all general maritime claims, contending that when Congress enacted OPA, it displaced pre-existing federal common law, including general maritime law, for claims covered by OPA. Defendants argue that OPA provides the sole remedy for private, nongovernmental entities asserting economic loss and property damage claims. They urge that when Congress enacts a comprehensive statute on a subject previously controlled by federal common law, the federal statute controls and displaces the federal common law. Defendants further argue that under OPA, Plaintiffs are allowed to pursue their claims for economic damages solely against the designated "Responsible Party" and that OPA does not allow claims directly against non-Responsible Parties.

Prior to the enactment of OPA in 1990, a general maritime negligence cause of action was available to persons who suffered physical damage and resulting economic loss resulting from an oil spill. General maritime law also provided for recovery of punitive damages in the case of gross negligence, *Exxon Shipping Co. v. Baker*, 554 U.S. 471, 128 S. Ct. 2605, 171 L. Ed. 2d 570 (2008), and strict product liability for defective products, *E. River S.S. Corp.*, 476 U.S. 858, 106 S. Ct. 2295 (1986). However, claims for purely economic losses unaccompanied by physical damage to a proprietary interest were precluded under *Robins Dry Dock & Repair Co. v. Flint*, 275 U.S. 303, 48 S. Ct. 134, 72 L. Ed. 290 (1927). The Fifth Circuit has continuously reaffirmed the straightforward application of the Robins Dry Dock rule, explaining that "although eloquently criticized for its rigidity, the rule has persisted because it offers a bright-line application in an otherwise murky area." *Mathiesen v. M/V Obelix*, 817 F.2d 345, 346–47 (5th Cir. 1985) (citing *Louisiana v. M/V Testbank*, 752 F.2d 1019 (5th Cir. 1985)); *see also Wiltz v. Bayer CropScience, Ltd.*, 645 F.3d 690 (5th Cir. 2011); *Catalyst Old River Hydroelectric Ltd. v. Ingram Barge Co.*, 639 F.3d 207 (5th Cir. 2011) (both reaffirming the applicability of Robins Dry Dock).

One relevant exception to the Robins Dry Dock rule applies in the case of commercial fishermen. *See Louisiana v. M/V Testbank*, 524 F. Supp. 1170, 1173 (E.D. La. 1981) ("claims for [purely] economic loss [resulting from an oil spill and subsequent river closure) asserted by the commercial oystermen, shrimpers, crabbers, and fishermen raise unique considerations requiring separate attention . . . seamen have been recognized as favored in admiralty and their economic interests require the fullest possible legal protection."). A number of other courts have recognized that claims of commercial fishermen are suigeneris because of their unique relationship to the seas and fisheries, treating these fishermen as akin to seamen under general maritime law. *See Yarmouth Sea Prods. Ltd. v. Scully*, 131 F.3d 389 (4th Cir. 1997); *Union Oil Co. v. Oppen*, 501 F.2d 558 (9th Cir. 1974).

Accordingly, long before the enactment of OPA, this was the state of general maritime law. Persons who suffered physical damage to their property as well as commercial fisherman had a cause of action under general maritime law to recover losses resulting from unintentional maritime torts. In the case of gross negligence or malicious, intentional conduct, general maritime law provided a claim for punitive or exemplary damages. *Baker*, 554 U.S. 471, 128 S. Ct. 2605. And, in the case of a defective product involved in a maritime casualty, maritime law imposed strict liability. *E. River S.S. Corp.*, 476 U.S. 858, 106 S. Ct. 2295 (1986).

In the wake of the EXXON VALDEZ spill in 1989, there were large numbers of persons who suffered actual economic losses but were precluded from any recovery by virtue of the Robins Dry Dock rule. At that time, an oil spill caused by a vessel on navigable water was governed by a web of different laws, including general maritime law, the CWA, and the laws of states affected by the spill in question. Various efforts had been made in the past to enact comprehensive federal legislation dealing with pollution from oil spills. With impetus from the EXXON VALDEZ incident, Congress finally enacted OPA in 1990.

OPA is a comprehensive statute addressing responsibility for oil spills, including the cost of cleanup, liability for civil penalties, as well as economic damages incurred by private parties and public entities. Indeed, the Senate Report provides that the Act "builds upon section 3111 of the Clean Water Act to create a single Federal law providing cleanup authority, penalties, and liability for oil pollution." S. Rep. 101-94 (1989), 1990 U.S.C.C.A.N. 722, 730. One significant part of OPA broadened the scope of private persons who are allowed to recover for economic losses resulting from an oil spill. OPA allows recovery for economic losses "resulting from" or "due to" the oil spill, regardless of whether the claimant sustained physical damage to a proprietary interest. OPA allows recovery for "[d]amages equal to the loss of profits or impairment of earning capacity due to the injury destruction, or loss of real property, or natural resources, which shall be recoverable by *any claimant*." 33 U.S.C. § 2702(b)(2)(E) (emphasis added). Furthermore, the House Report noted that "[t]he claimant need not be the owner of the damaged property or resources to recover for lost profits or income." H.R. Conf. Rep. 101-653 (1990), 1990 U.S.C-.C.A.N. 779, 781.

Clearly, one major remedial purpose of OPA was to allow a broader class of claimants to recover for economic losses than allowed under general maritime law. Congress was apparently moved by the experience of the Alaskan claimants whose actual losses were not recoverable under existing law. Another obvious purpose of OPA was to set up a scheme by which a "Responsible Party" (typically the vessel or facility owner) was designated and made strictly liable (in most instances) for cleanup costs and resulting economic damages. The intent is to encourage settlement and reduce the need for litigation. Claimants present their claims to the Responsible Party, who pays the claims and is then allowed to seek contribution from other allegedly liable parties. 33 U.S.C. § 2709, 2710, 2713. If the Responsible Party refuses or fails to pay a claim after ninety days, the claimant may either pursue its claim against the government-created Oil Spill Liability Trust Fund or file suit in court. *Id.* 2713. There was much debate in Congress about whether or not this new federal statute should completely preempt or displace other federal or state laws. Ultimately, the statute included two "saving" provisions, one relating to general maritime law[30] and the other to state laws (discussed above). The question arises in this case as to whether, or to what extent, OPA has displaced any claims

---

[30] "Except as otherwise provided in this Act, this Act does not affect — (1) admiralty and maritime law; or (2) the jurisdiction of the district courts of the United States with respect to civil actions under admiralty and maritime jurisdiction, saving to suitors in all cases all other remedies to which they are otherwise entitled." 33 USC sec. 2751(c).

previously existing under general maritime law, including claims for punitive damages.

Only a handful of courts have had the opportunity to address whether OPA displaces general maritime law. For example, the *First Circuit in South Port Marine, LLC v. Gulf Oil Limited Partnership*, 234 F.3d 58 (1st Cir. 2000), held that punitive damages were not available under OPA. The First Circuit began by noting that in enacting OPA "Congress established a comprehensive federal scheme for oil pollution liability" and "set[ ] forth a comprehensive list of recoverable damages." *Id.* at 64. "Absent from that list of recoverable damages is any mention of punitive damages." *Id.*

The First Circuit found that the Supreme Court decision of *Miles v. Apex Marine*, 498 U.S. 19, 111 S. Ct. 317, 112 L. Ed. 2d 275 (1990), led to the conclusion that OPA did not allow for punitive damages. "The Court [in Miles] refused to allow recovery for loss of society when such damages were not provided in [Death on the High Seas Act], reasoning that in an 'area covered by statute, it would be no more appropriate to prescribe a different measure of damage than to prescribe a different statute of limitations, or a different class of beneficiaries.' " *Id.* at 65–66 (internal citations omitted). Likewise, the First Circuit determined that OPA's absence of an allowance for punitive damages was conclusive. In *Clausen v. M/V New Carissa* the district court adopted the First Circuit's rationale and held that punitive damages were not allowable under OPA. 171 F. Supp. 2d 1127 (D. Or. 2001).

In *Gabarick v. Laurin Maritime (America) Inc.*, 623 F. Supp. 2d 741, 747 (E.D. La. 2009), the district court determined that OPA preempted maritime law claims for economic loss, using the four factors articulated in *United States v. Oswego Barge Corp.* 664 F.2d 327 (2d Cir. 1981), to analyze whether OPA displaced general maritime law: "(1) legislative history; (2) the scope of legislation; (3) whether judge made law would fill a gap left by Congress's silence or rewrite rules that Congress enacted; and (4) likeliness of Congress's intent to preempt long established and familiar principles of the common law or the general maritime law."

However, more recent Supreme Court precedents cause this Court to question the notion that long-standing federal common law can be displaced by a statute that is silent on the issue. *See Exxon Shipping Co. v. Baker*, 554 U.S. 471, 128 S. Ct. 2605, L. Ed. 2d 570 (2008) (holding that the CWA did not displace a general maritime remedy for punitive damages) and *Atlantic Sounding Co. v. Townsend*, 557 U.S. 404, 129 S. Ct. 2561, 174 L. Ed. 2d 382 (2009) (holding that the Jones Act did not displace the availability of punitive damages for a seaman's maintenance and cure claim).

In *Baker*, the Court employed a three-part analysis to determine if a statue preempts or displaces federal common law. First, is there a clear indication that Congress intended to occupy the entire field? Second, does the statute speak directly to the question addressed by the common law? Third, will application of common law have a frustrating effect on the statutory remedial scheme? 554 U.S. at 489, 128 S. Ct. 2605. The question presented in *Baker* was whether the CWA preempted or displaced general maritime punitive damages for economic loss. The Court first stated that it saw no clear indication of congressional intent to occupy the entire field of pollution remedies. Next, the Court noted that the CWA made no mention of punitive damages, and that "[i]n order to abrogate a common-law principle, the statute must speak directly to the question addressed by the common law." Finally, the Court did not perceive that punitive damages for private harms would have any frustrating effect on the CWA remedial scheme. Accordingly, the Court concluded that the CWA did not preempt punitive damages under general maritime law.

In *Townsend*, the Supreme Court revisited its prior holding in *Miles v. Apex Marine*, 498 U.S. 19, 111 S. Ct. 317, 112 L. Ed. 2d 275 (1990), on which the *South Port Marine* Court hinged its analysis. The *Townsend* Court explained that *Miles* did not allow punitive damages for wrongful death claims because it was only as a result of federal legislation that a wrongful death cause of action existed. 129 S. Ct. at 2572–73. Accordingly, "to determine the remedies available under the common-law wrongful-death action, 'an admiralty court should look primarily to these legislative enactments for policy guidance.' It would have been illegitimate to create common law remedies that exceeded those remedies statutorily available under the Jones Act and DOHSA." *Id.* at 2572 (citing *Miles*, 498 U.S. at 27, 111 S. Ct. 317). The Court contrasted the situation in *Miles* with the question before it in *Townsend*, and it concluded that "both the maritime cause of action (maintenance and cure) and the remedy (punitive damages) were well established before the passage of the Jones Act." *Id.* In other words, the Court limited the application of *Miles* when it concluded that punitive damages were available to the seaman asserting a cause of action for maintenance and cure.

The B1 Master Complaint alleges economic loss claims on behalf of various categories of claimants, many of whom have not alleged physical injury to their property or other proprietary interest. Pre-OPA, these claimants, with the exception of commercial fishermen, would not have had a viable cause of action and would be precluded from any recovery by virtue of *Robins Dry Dock*. Accordingly, claims under general maritime law asserted by such claimants are not plausible and must be dismissed.

However, the Court finds that the B1 Master Complaint states a viable cause of action against the non-Responsible Parties under general maritime law on behalf of claimants who either allege physical damage to a proprietary interest and/or qualify for the commercial fishermen exception to *Robins Dry Dock*. In brief, these claims are saved and not displaced by OPA for the following reasons.

First, when reading OPA and its legislative history, it does not appear that Congress intended to occupy the entire field governing liability for oil spills, as it included two savings provisions-one that preserved the application of general maritime law and another that preserved a State's authority with respect to discharges of oil or pollution within the state. 33 U.S.C. §§ 2718, 2751.

Second, OPA does not directly address or speak to the liability of non-Responsible Parties to persons who suffer covered losses. Although OPA contains provisions regarding the Responsible Party's ability to seek contribution and indemnification, *Id.* §§ 2709, 2710, it is silent as to whether a claimant can seek redress directly from non-Responsible Parties. Prior to OPA's enactment, commercial fisherman and those who suffered physical damage had a general maritime law cause of action against these individuals.

Third, there is nothing to indicate that allowing a general maritime remedy against the non-Responsible Parties will somehow frustrate Congress' intent when it enacted OPA. Under OPA, a claimant is required to first present a claim to the Responsible Party. If the claim is not paid within ninety days, the claimant may file suit or file a claim against the Oil Spill Liability Trust Fund. A Responsible Party is strictly liable and damages are capped unless there is gross negligence or violation of a safety statute or regulation that proximately caused the discharge. To allow a general maritime claim against the Responsible Party would serve to frustrate and circumvent the remedial scheme in OPA.

Thus, claimants' maritime causes of action against a Responsible Party are displaced by OPA, such that all claims against a Responsible Party for damages covered by OPA must comply with OPA's presentment procedure. However, as to the non-Responsible Parties, there is nothing in OPA to indicate that Congress intended such parties to be immune from direct liability to persons who either suffered physical damage to a proprietary interest and/or qualify for the commercial fishermen exception. Therefore, general maritime law claims that existed before OPA may be brought directly against non-Responsible parties.

Claims for punitive damages

OPA is also silent as to the availability of punitive damages Plaintiffs who could assert general maritime claims pre-OPA enactment may plausibly allege punitive damages under general maritime for several reasons. First, "[p]unitive damages have long been available at common law" and "the common-law tradition of punitive damages extends to maritime claims." *Townsend*, 129 S. Ct. at 2569. Congress has not occupied the entire field of oil spill liability in light of the OPA provision preserving admiralty and maritime law, "[e]xcept as otherwise provided." 0PA does not mention punitive damages; thus, while punitive damages are not available under OPA, the Court does not read OPA's silence as meaning that punitive damages are precluded under general maritime law. Congress knows how to proscribe punitive damages when it intends to, as it did in the commercial aviation exception under the Death on the High Seas Act, 46 U.S.C. § 30307(b) ("punitive damages are not recoverable").

There is also nothing to indicate that allowing a claim for punitive damages in this context would frustrate the OPA liability scheme. As stated above, claims against the Responsible Party must comply with OPA's procedure, regardless of whether there is also cause of action against the Responsible Party under general maritime law. However, the behavior that would give rise to punitive damages under general maritime law — gross negligence — would also break OPA's limit of liability. *See* 33 U.S.C. § 2704(a). Thus, the imposition of punitive damages under general maritime law would not circumvent OPA's limitation of liability.

Finally on this issue, the Court notes Justice Stevens' concurrence in Baker in which he wrote that the Trans-Alaska Pipeline Authorization Act ("TAPAA") which provided "the liability regime governing certain types of Alaskan oil spills, imposing strict liability but also capping recovery." "did not restrict the availability of punitive damages." 554 U.S. at 518, 128 S. Ct. 2605. Although the issue of whether TAPAA precluded an award of punitive damages was not squarely before the Court's conclusion. OPA, like TAPAA creates a liability regime governing oil spills, impose strict liability on the Responsible Parties, includes liability limits, and is silent on the issue of punitive damages.

Thus, OPA does not displace general maritime law claims for those Plaintiffs who would have been able to bring such claims prior to OPA's enactment. These Plaintiffs assert plausible claims for punitive damages against Responsible and non-Responsible parties.

Negligence claims against Anadarko and MOEX

Anadarko and MOEX, the non-operating lessees for the Macondo well, have joined in the arguments made by other Defendants.[31] However, these two Defendants advance additional, independent reasons supporting their Motions to Dismiss. In essence, Defendants argue that under the Joint Operating Agreement ("JOA") existing between BP and themselves, BP was the operating partner, responsible for the drilling of the Macondo well. Anadarko or MOEX had no personnel present aboard the DEEPWATER HORIZON and assert they had no right to control BP's conduct.

Ainsworth v. Shell Offshore, Inc. lays out the analysis for evaluating Plaintiffs' negligence claim against *Anadarko and MOEX*. 829 F.2d 548 (5th Cir. 1987). "[A] principal generally is not liable for the offenses an independent contractor commits in the course of performing its contractual duties." *Id.* at 549. There are two recognized exceptions to this general principle, in the case of an ultra-hazardous activity, or when the principal retains or exercises operational control. *Id.* at 550. Offshore drilling operations are not considered ultra-hazardous. *Id.* As to operational control, the Court in *Ainsworth* did not find that this exception was met even when the principal had a company man present on the platform. In this case, it is not alleged that either Anadarko or MOEX had anyone resent on the DEEPWATER HORIZON. Under the JOA, BP was solely responsible for the drilling operations. Any access to information that Anadarko and MOEX may have had did not give rise to a duty to intercede in an independent contractor's operations-especially because Plaintiffs have not alleged in their Complaint that Non-Operating Defendants had access to any information not already available to BP and Transocean personnel either onshore or on the rig.

Plaintiffs attempt to avoid dismissal by suggesting that they do not argue for vicarious liability of the Non-Operating Defendants, but rather that Anadarko and MOEX were directly negligent. However, adding a "direct-duty" label to their claims does not add merit to them. *See Dupre v. Chevron U.S.A. Inc.*, 913 F. Supp. 473, 483 (E.D. La. 1996) (rejecting plaintiffs' attempt to disguise a vicarious liability claim as one of direct duty because doing so "would amount to an end-run around a large body of Fifth Circuit precedent finding no 'operational control' despite some knowledge of risk or involvement with safety issues and the presence of 'company men' on the contractor's rig"). Simply put, Plaintiffs have failed to allege a plausible general maritime negligence claim against the two Non-Operating Defendants. All

---

[31] Although minority interest lessees, Anadarko and MOEX contest their status as responsible Parties. Neither has been formally named as a Responsible Party at this time.

general maritime negligence claims against Anadarko and MOEX must be dismissed.[32]

Presentment under OPA

Defendants also seek to dismiss all OPA claims because the B1 Master Complaint does not properly allege that the B1 Claimants have complied with the "presentment" requirements of OPA. Defendants argue that presentment to the Responsible Party is either a jurisdictional requirement or, alternatively, a mandatory condition precedent before filing suit.

The Court finds that the text of OPA clearly requires that OPA claimants must first "present" their OPA claim to the Responsible Party before filing suit. The "Claims Procedure" section of OPA reads:

(a) Presentation

Except as provided in subsection (b) of this section, all claims for removal costs or damages shall be presented first to the responsible party or guarantor of the source designated under section 2714(a) of this title. . . .

(c) If a claim is presented in accordance with subsection (a) of this section and—

(1) each person to whom the claim is presented denies all liability for the claim, or

(2) the claim is not settled by any person by payment within 90 days after the date upon which

(A) the claim was presented, or

(B) advertising was begun pursuant to section 2714(b) of this title, whichever is later,

the claimant may elect to commence an action in court against the responsible party or guarantor or to present the claim to the Fund.

33 U.S.C. § 2713 (emphasis added).

The text of the statute is clear. Congress intended presentment to be a mandatory condition precedent to filing suit. *See Boca Ciega Hotel, Inc. v. Bouchard Transp. Co., Inc.,* 51 F.3d 235 (11th Cir. 1995) (presentment is a mandatory condition precedent to filing suit under OPA); Gabarick v. Laurin Maritime (America), Inc., 2009 U.S. Dist. LEXIS 20974, . . . (E.D. La. 2009) (noting that the purpose of the claim presentation procedure is to promote settlement and avoid litigation).

In summary on this issue, the Court finds that presentment is a mandatory condition precedent with respect to Plaintiffs' OPA claims.[33] The Court finds that

---

[32] Because it is plausible that Anadarko and MOEX will be found to be Responsible Parties and thus liable under OPA, OPA claims are not dismissed.

[33] Of course, there is no presentment requirement for Plaintiffs to pursue any general maritime law

Plaintiffs have sufficiently alleged presentment in their B1 Master Complaint, at least with respect to some of the Claimants. For the reasons stated above, the Court does not intend to engage in the process of sorting through thousands of individual claims at the present time to determine which claims have or have not been properly presented.[34]

NOTE

On October 1, 2012, the District Court, Judge Carl Barbier, issued a ruling in the *Deepwater Horizon Oil Spill* case involving three classes of claimants. *See In re Oil Spill by the Oil Rig "Deepwater Horizon,"* 902 F. Supp. 2d 808 (E.D. La. 2012). The first class of plaintiffs, known as "Pure Stigma" claimants, were owners, lessors and lessees of real property who alleged they suffered damages from the Gulf of Mexico oil spill in the form of a reduction in their property values. The properties of these claimants were not physically touched by the oil and were not sold. The court ruled that these claimants failed to state a claim under OPA, federal maritime or state law, and the defendants' motions to dismiss were granted by the court. Consider OPA sections 2702 (b)(2)(B) and (E). Was the court's ruling correct?

A second class of claimants, known as BP Dealer claims, were claimants who alleged that they were in the business of marketing BP branded fuels and that they lost money because of consumer animosity toward BP after the spill. The court ruled that these BP Dealer claims were not viable under state or general maritime law and also were not viable under OPA subsections (B) or (E). Was this correct? The ruling under subsection (B) was based on the fact that the BP Dealers' property was not physically touched by the oil; the ruling under subsection (E) was based on the lack of any causal role the destruction of resources or property played in producing the damages.

The third class of claimants, known as Recreation Claimants, were recreational fishermen, recreational divers, beachgoers, and recreational boaters that alleged they suffered damages to their enjoyment of life from their inability to use portions of the Gulf of Mexico for recreational and amusement purposes. The court dismissed these claims as well under OPA as well as state and maritime law. Was this the correct ruling?

What about claimants whose property lost value because of the spill and who sold their property for the diminished value? What about the real estate brokers involved in these transactions who suffered reduced profits in these sale transactions?

NOTES AND QUESTIONS

1. *Applicability*. Compare the applicability of the CLC and OPA. While the

---

claims which survive the present Motions to Dismiss.

[34] The Court does not decide today what constitutes "presentment." OPA requires a claimant to present his or her claim for a "sum certain" to the Responsible Party. How this requirement can be applied in the context of the BP oil spill is unclear. The long term effects on the environment and fisheries may not be known for many years.

CLC applies only to spills from ships which carry oil in bulk as cargo — laden tankers. What about OPA? Would any international liability regime apply to a discharge from an offshore oil or gas facility such as the rig Deepwater Horizon?

2. **Bunker oil spills.** In 2001, the International Convention on Civil Liability for Bunker Oil Pollution Damage was promulgated by IMO. This Convention entered into force in 2008; the U.S. is not a party. Does OPA cover bunker oil spills?

3. **Liability.** Who is liable for damages under the CLC? Who is liable under OPA?

4. **Defenses and exclusions to liability.** Are any exclusions or defenses to liability applicable under the CLC or OPA?

5. **Limitation of Liability.** For the owners of the *SS Persian Festiva*, what liability limits apply under OPA? Under the CLC? Under what conditions can the limits under OPA be disregarded? *See* OPA section 2704(c).

6. **Limitation of Shipowners' Liability Act.** Can the owners of the 55 Persian Festiva invoke the U.S. Limitation of Shipowners' Liability Act to further limit liability under OPA 90? In international law shipowners enjoy the right to limit liability for certain damages under the International Convention on Limitation for Liability for Maritime Claims (1957, 1976, and 1996), but Article 3 of this Convention, Article 3, excludes limitation for pollution claims.

7. **Categories of recoverable damages.** What categories of damages are recoverable under the CLC? Under OPA?

8. **Elements of proof for each damage category.** Read OPA section 2702 with care. Section 2702(a) requires proof that all removal costs and damages claimed "result from" the oil pollution incident. Moreover, each subsection of section 2702(b) contains additional elements of proof that must be carried by claimants. Parse each of these subsections for the additional elements of liability.

9. **Clean-up and removal responsibility.** The International Convention on Oil Pollution Preparedness, Response, and Cooperation (OPRC) of 1990 requires states to have oil spill response and clean-up plans in place. In the United States the U.S. Coast Guard has this responsibility. The U.S. and Canada have concluded a n agreement to create a Canada-US Joint. Marine Pollution Contingency Plan for response to a transborder spill of oil or a hazardous substance. *See* http://www.uscg.mil, accessed 20 November 2012.

10. **Spills of hazardous and noxious substances.** In United States law, a separate liability regime, the Comprehensive Environmental Response, Compensation, and Liability Act, 42 U.S.C. § 9601 et seq., permits recovery of response costs and damages from responsible parties in cases of spills of hazardous or noxious substances. On the international level, IMO has promulgated an International Convention on Liability and Compensation for Damage in Connection with the Carriage of Hazardous and Noxious Substances (1996) (HNS Convention), but the HNS Convention has not received the number of ratifications needed to come into force.

11. *Damage recovery by Canadian claimants*. Canada is a party to the CLC and Fund Conventions as incorporated into Canadian law by the Marine Liability Act (S.C. 2001, C. 6), section 5 1. Under Canadian law and the Conventions, a four tier liability scheme will apply. First, under the CLC as amended, SDR 89.77 million in Canadian dollars will be available to pay claims. This sum will typically be covered by compulsory insurance carried by the ship, so that in practice this amount will be paid by the insurer, a protection and indemnity (P&I) club. Second, if outstanding claims exceed this sum, the second tier of money available to pay claims is the International Oil Pollution Compensation Fund (IOPC Fund) created under the Fund Convention. The maximum amount available under the IOPC is SDR 203 million, inclusive of the tier one compensation. Third, Canada is a party to the Supplemental Fund Agreement of 2003, which provides an additional amount up to a maximum of SDR 750 million, inclusive of the compensation available under tiers one and two. Under Canadian law a fourth tier of compensation is available: Canada's Ship Source Compensation Fund provides a maximum of Canada $155 million when funding from the first three liability tiers is exhausted, exclusive of the funding from tiers one, two and three. The fund's administrator must attempt to recover reimbursement to this fund by the responsible party. Canada would set up a claim procedure to which Canadian claimants would apply that would be separate from the claim procedure in the United States under OPA.

12. *Damage recovery by U.S. claimants*. Under OPA U.S. claimants must first present their claims to the responsible party or parties. In the case of the *SS Persian Festiva*, the maximum amount available to pay claimants (unless the limit can be broken) is $600 million. OPA requires that ships carry mandatory insurance to pay claims. 33 U.S.C. § 2716. Claims not paid within 90 days by the responsible parties may be presented to the U S Oil Pollution Liability Trust Fund, which may pay claims up to a maximum of $1 billion per incident. (26 U.S.C. § 9509(c)).

13. *State law liability*. OPA section 2718 is a savings clause for state law. Do you agree with the Deepwater Horizon court's ruling that state law did not apply in that case?

14. *Liability under the general maritime law*. The general maritime law provides a cause of action for damages caused by negligent conduct. There are important differences between liability under OPA and liability under the general maritime law, such as the applicability of the *Robins Dry Dock* ruling. Do you agree with the court's analysis regarding the OPA savings clause section 2751 (e) and the issue of preemption of the general maritime law by OPA?

15. *Punitive damages*. Are punitive damages available under OPA or the general maritime law? In the final episode of the litigation sparked by the wreck of the *Exxon Valdez, Exxon Shipping Co. v. Baker*, 554 U.S. 471 (2008), punitive damages are available under the general maritime law but are limited to a 1 to 1 ratio with compensatory damages.

16. *Recovery by Canadian claimants under OPA*. Note that OPA section 2707 permits recovery by foreign claimants. What are the conditions to such recovery? Before OPA was enacted, the United States reimbursed Canada for damages incurred in a transboundary oil spill in St. Lawrence Seaway. *See United States v. Oswego Barge Corp.*, 664 F.2d 327 (2d Cir. 1981).

17. *OPA claim procedure.* The claim procedure under OPA requires present-ment of claims to the responsible parties and filing claims in court. In the Deepwater Horizon litigation, most claims were consolidated by the Judicial Panel on Multidistrict Litigation in the Eastern District of Louisiana, which divided the various claims into pleading "bundles." Both individual and class action claims may be filed. The Deepwater Horizon claims are also being handled in an extrajudicial forum. After a meeting with President Barack Obama in June 2010, BP agreed to create a fund of $20 billion to compensate victims of the disaster and to disburse this money through a specially created entity, the Gulf Coast Claims Facility (GCCF), which is constituted as "an independent claims facility for the submission and resolution of claims of individuals and businesses for costs and damages incurred as a result of discharges due to the Deepwater Horizon incident." See http:/www.gulfcoastclaimsfacility.com, accessed 20 November 2012. BP has designated Kenneth Feinberg, Esq. as claims administrator of this $20 billion fund. Mr. Feinberg is fully responsible for the administration and disbursement of the fund and is charged to act independently of BP. Claims are processed by the GCCF according to rules devised by the administrator. Claimants may file claims both with the GCCF and the court, but a claimant can accept only one avenue of compensa-tion.

18. *Claim procedure under the international regime.* By contrast, the claims procedure of the international regime is left to national courts; a claim may be filed only in the state in which the damage occurs. Once the CLC fund established in the national courts is exhausted, the IOPC Fund will establish local offices in the country involved to pay claims. The IOPC claims process is essentially an out-of-court settlement in which claims are handled according to criteria in the IOPC Claims Manual, adopted by the Fund's Assembly of Parties.

19. *Pure economic loss damages.* Many of the claimants in the *SS Persian Festiva* hypothetical problem will present claims for purely economic losses without any accompanying proprietary damages. Many of these losses will be very real: commercial fishermen who cannot fish; motels and restaurants and other marine-dependent businesses will suffer financial hardship. American law has long applied a bright-line, no recovery-rule for purely economic losses under the authority of the decision of the Supreme Court in *Robins Dry Dock v. Flint*, 275 U.S. 303 (1927), and this holding is widely applied under the general maritime law[35] and state law.[36] What is the status of the Robins Dry Dock rule under OPA according to the court's opinion in the *Deepwater Horizon* case? But what is the limit to recovery for purely economic losses? Is the court's ruling too broad? One way the court could have limited recovery of purely economic losses would be the following: Under OPA section 2702, two levels of proof are required to recover purely economic losses. A first level of proof is required by section 2702(a), which requires that the losses must "result from" the pollution incident. This language should be interpreted as a requirement of proximate as well as actual causation that must be proved as a condition to liability. If we interpret section 2702(a) as requiring proof of proximate

---

[35] *See, e.g., Louisiana ex rel. Guste v. M/V Testbank*, 752 F.2d 1019 (5th Cir. 1985) (en banc); *Taira Lynn Ltd. No. 5 v. Jays Seafood, Inc.*, 444 F.3d 371 (5th Cir. 2006).

[36] DAN B. DOBBS, THE LAW OF TORTS sec. 452, at 1282 (2000).

causation, we limit the open-endedness of recovery for purely economic losses. A second level of proof is required to recover economic loss damages under section 2702 (b)(2)(E): the claimant must prove that the loss is "due to the injury, destruction, or loss of real property, personal property, or natural resources." Should this "due to" language be interpreted to require a claimant to prove ownership of the damaged property or natural resources? This is the key issue — Robins Dry Dock says yes; the court in the *Deepwater Horizon* opinion says no. Which is correct? The problem is that if we answer this question "no" do we compensate all purely economic losses in the case of an oil spill? If we interpret section 2702(a) to require economic loss claimants under section 2702(b)(2)(E) to prove proximate causation, we limit purely economic loss recovery to those claimants who can show foreseeability and pass other proximate cause tests. How does the international law regime handle purely economic losses? According to the Claims Manual of the IOPC, the Fund evaluates economic losses according to the following criteria:

- The geographical proximity of the claimant's business activity to the contaminated area;

- The degree to which the claimant's business is economically dependent on the affected coastline;

- The extent to which the claimant had alternative sources of supply or business opportunities; The extent to which the claimant's business forms an integral part of the economic activity of the area affected by the spill.

Thus the Fund pays economic claims on a selective basis. Are these similar to proximate cause criteria that an American court may well use?

20.   *Criminal, administrative, and civil penalties*. The U.S. Clean Water Act authorizes the imposition of substantial criminal, administrative and civil penalties in a case of an oil spill or a spill of a hazardous substance. 33 U.S.C. § 1319 to 1321. In the *Deepwater Horizon* case, a settlement was reached on November 15, 2012, on criminal penalties against BP, which pleaded guilty to 14 criminal counts and agreed to pay the sum of $4 billion over five years. Two BP supervisors were also indicted for manslaughter because of the deaths of 11 workers on the Deepwater Horizon rig. BP and other companies involved are being sued by the U.S. Department of Justice for liability for civil penalties of up to $20 billion.

NOTES ON NATURAL RESOURCE DAMAGES

Both United States law and international law provide for the recovery of damages to natural resources, but the process of recovery and measurement differs greatly.

1.   *United States law*. In the United States, both OPA 90 [33 U.S.C. § 2702] and CERCLA [42 U.S.C. § 9607(f)(1)] provide for recovery of natural resource damages. OPA defines natural resources broadly as including, "land, fish, wildlife, biota, air, water, ground water, drinking water supplies, and other resources belonging to, or otherwise controlled by the United States (including the resources of the exclusive economic zone), any State, or local government or Indian tribe or foreign government." Sec. 2701(20). Only government entities designated by the President or authorized officials as trustees — federal, state, tribal, and foreign — may recover such natural resource damages. *See* sec. 2702(b) and sec. 2706(b)(1)–(5). The responsibilities of trustees are set out in Sec. 2706 (c) and 40 C.F.R. § 300.615. Liability for natural resource damages is strict, joint and several and is placed upon the responsible parties. Sec. 2702(a). Note that natural resource liability under OPA is limited to the amounts specified under the Act, but the limits do not apply if the incident was proximately caused by gross negligence or willful misconduct or violation of a federal safety regulation. Sec. 2704.

Note that the standard of liability for natural resource damages as set out in sections 2702(a) and (b)(2). Section 2702(a) requires that the damages must "result from" the pollution incident.

OPA regulations (15 CFR Part 990) provide a three step process for determining natural resource damages as detailed in the Flow Chart of the NRDA Process: a Preassessment Phase, a Restoration Planning Phase, and a Restoration implementation Phase.

In the Preassessment Phase the trustees must determine the scope of their jurisdiction under OPA and decide if it is appropriate to try to restore the damages resources. The trustees determine whether there are injuries to natural resources that have not been remedied and whether there are feasible restoration actions available to fix the injuries. 15 CFR Subpart D.

In the Restoration Planning Phase the trustees prepare a Notice of Intent to Conduct Restoration, which is delivered to the responsible parties and, after injury identification and quantification and consideration of alternative options for restoration, a Final Restoration Plan is adopted after public review and comment. Restoration alternatives are evaluated on the basis of their cost, the extent to which they meet the goal of returning the resources to their baseline condition, the likelihood of success, the extent to which future injury will be avoided, the extent to which the option benefits multiple resources, and their effect on public health. 15 C.F.R. § 990.54.

In the Restoration Implementation Phase the trustees implement the designated restoration plan and monitor its effectiveness. Restoration can include restoring, replacing, rehabilitating, or acquiring the equivalent of the natural resources harmed or destroyed by the pollution incident. 15 C.F.R. § 990.30. Two kinds of restoration are called for: (1) primary restoration is restoring the resource where the injury occurred; (2) compensatory restoration is action or payment to make up for the interim or permanent loss of a resource. OPA regulations also permit emergency restoration actions and early restoration actions. These are forms of compensatory restoration that may be necessary or advisable to carry out actions designed to restore habitat, shore lines, marine ecosystems or to enhance human uses of the polluted area without waiting for the adoption of the Final Restoration Plan. 15 CFR sec. 990. 26. In the case of the BP Deepwater Horizon incident, BP agreed to make available the sum of $1 billion for early restoration activities in the affected area of the Gulf of Mexico. See Press Release of April 21, 2011, http://www.restorethegulf.gov/release, accessed 12 November 2012. The responsible parties must pay the cost of both primary and compensatory restoration as detailed in the Final Restoration Plan. On judicial or administrative review, the

Final Restoration Plan benefits from a rebuttable presumption of validity. Sec. 2706(e)(2).

Natural resource damages recoverable from the responsible parties under OPA include: (1) the cost of restoring, rehabilitating, replacing, or acquiring the equivalent of the damaged natural resources; (2) the diminution of value of those natural resources pending restoration; and (3) the reasonable cost of assessing those damages. Sec. 2706(d). Upon completion of the Final Restoration Plan, trustees may present a demand for compensation to the responsible parties, who must respond to this demand within 90 days. 15 CFR sec. 990.62. If the responsible parties for some reason cannot be made to pay, the bill for NRDA can be presented to the Oil Pollution Liability Trust Fund. Sec. 2712.

Because most NRDA cases have been settled before trial, reported cases on natural resource damages are rare. A leading case that antedates OPA is *Puerto Rico v. SS Zoe Colocotroni*, 456 F. Supp. 1327, *aff'd in part*, 628 F.2d 652 (1st Cir. 1980). In this case, involving a spill of some 5000 tons of crude oil in the Bahia Sucia, a local bay, the Court of Appeals ruled that the correct standard for the recovery of natural resource damages is "the cost reasonably to be incurred by the sovereign or its designated agency to restore or rehabilitate the environment of the affected area to [its] pre-existing condition, or as close thereto as is feasible without grossly disproportionate expenditures." The court also ruled that the common law rule measuring damages as the difference in monetary value of the property before and after the event causing the injury was inadequate. However, the court also rejected the lower court's use of replacement value of non-commercially valued organisms as a measure of damages because these creatures "would replenish themselves naturally if and when restoration — either artificial or natural — took place."

Thus the correct measure of damages for primary restoration appears to be the reasonable cost of implementing the selected option of restoration or rehabilitation of the resources or of acquiring equivalent resources. The most controversial aspect of NRDA is the problem of valuing the diminution of value of the resources pending restoration — compensatory restoration. How should these losses be measured? OPA regulations require a method called "resource scaling": the trustees determine the scale of actions required to make the environment whole. Using resource-to-resource and service-to-service scaling an estimate can be made of the cost of producing the natural habitat and the services that are equivalent to those that have been lost. 15 C.F.R. § 990.53. If, however, resource scaling is deemed insufficient or infeasible, a second option is "valuation scaling" — an attempt to measure the value of the lost habitat and services. Valuation scaling opens the door to unconventional and controversial valuation techniques such as "contingent valuation" (CVM). CVM uses personal interviews, telephone interviews, and mail surveys to ask individuals their willingness to pay for a given resource contingent on the existence of a hypothetical situation: for example, how much would you expect to pay to assure the preservation of the native bird life in a given coastal marsh. CVM is defended by environmentalists as a method of measuring the immeasurable: the "non-use value," "passive value," "inherent value" or "existence value" of natural resources. *See* Frank B. Cross, *Natural Resource Damage Valuation*, 42 VAND. L. REV. 269 (1989). But many criticize CVM as producing wildly inaccurate estimates of value because individuals are asked to respond to hypothetical situations about which they have little information or experience. *See* Charles J. Di Bona (President of the American Petroleum Institute), 1992 Issues in Science and Technology SO.

The debate over CVM is unresolved, but no court seems to have accepted CVM as a measurement technique. In *State of Ohio v. Department of the Interior*, 880 F.2d 432 (D.C. Cir. 1989), a case involving judicial review of the NRDA rules adopted under CERCLA, the court did not invalidate the regulations permitting the use of CVM and other hypothetical valuation techniques, but invalidated a rule requiring the trustees to choose between "the lesser of" restoration cost and diminution of use and non-use values, because this "lesser of" rule violated the intent of the Congress to prefer restoration. In *General Electric Co. v. U.S. Department of Commerce*, 128 F.3d 767 (D.C. Cir. 1997), the court largely rejected an industry attempt to invalidate the OPA CVM regulations, so both the OPA a n d CERCLA regulations as they now stand have survived court challenges. However, several courts specifically confronted with CVM have rejected CVM surveys as speculative and unreliable. For example, in *United States v. Montrose Chemical Corp.*, No. CV 90-3122-R (C.D. Cal. Apr. 17, 2000) (No. 1914), the court excluded a CVM survey offered by the government to measure lost existence values with regard to two species of birds (bald eagles and peregrine falcons) and two species of fish (white croaker and kelp bass). *See also Idaho v. Southern Refrigerated Transp., Inc.*, 1991 U.S. Dist. Lexis 1869 (D. Idaho Jan. 24, 1991).

Thus the measurement of this statutorily mandated damage category is open to question.

2. *International law*. The CLC and the Fund Convention liability regimes sharply restrict the recovery of natural resource damages. In 1980, the Funds' Assembly adopted Resolution 3 [FUND/A/ES. 1/13], which states: "the assessment of compensation to be paid by the Fund is not to be made on the basis of an abstract quantification of damage calculated in accordance with theoretical models." This resolution was inspired by the fact that, following the grounding of the tanker *Antonio Gramsci* in the Baltic Sea, the Soviet government claimed environmental damages based on the formula — 2 Russian rubles per cubic meter of polluted waters. In addition, the 1992 CLC and Fund Conventions provide that "compensation for impairment of the environment shall be limited to costs of reasonable measures of reinstatement actually undertaken or to be undertaken." CLC Art. 1(6) and Fund Convention Art. 1(2).

Despite these limits, famous cases have found ways to grant more generous natural resource damages. In 1985, when the tanker *Patmos* sank off the coast of Calabria (Italy), and the IOPC rejected claims for natural resource damages, the Italian government brought suit in the Italian courts against the IOPC and the tanker's insurer, the UK P&I club. The court of first instance rejected the claim, but this decision was reversed by the Court of Appeal, which interpreted the CLC 1969 Art. 1(6) to allow equitable claims for damage to the environment which may be established by a panel of experts. Although the experts appointed by the court found damages to fishing activities in the amount of British Pounds Sterling (BPS) 465,000 (about $700,000), the court without explanation awarded a final judgment of BPS 827,000. Tribunal of Messina, Judgment of 24 June 1985 [1986] Dir. Mar. 439 and IOPC Annual Report 1990, p. 23–27. In the case of the tanker *Haven*, which in

1991, caught fire and spilled some 10,000 tons of oil into the Gulf of Genoa (Italy), the IOPC also rejected natural resource damages, sparking a suit by Italian government. In the event, the Court of First Instance interpreted the CLC and Fund Conventions to permit natural resource damages and awarded 40 million lire in damages (about $20 million), a decision which the IOPC termed "absurd." [FUND/EXC48/4 (1996)]. See Tribunal of Genoa, Judgment of 29 May 1991 [1991 Dir. Mar. 793.] On appeal the Italian government claimed that the damages should be increased to 883,435 million lire. In the end, the shipowner and the UK P&l Club, the insurer, made an ex gratia payment of 25 million lire in addition to the 40 million lire in damages to the Italian government to settle the case. *See* IOPC Annual Report 1999, para. 10.2.

3. ***Canadian law***. Canada is a party to the 1992 CLC and Fund Conventions and, accordingly, Section 51(2) of the Canada Marine Liability Act (S.C. 2001, c. 6) provides that natural resource damages are limited to the "costs of reasonable measures of reinstatement actually undertaken or to be undertaken." However, in the *Canfor* case, *British Columbia v. Canadian Forest Products, Ltd.*, 2004 SCC 38, [2004] 2 SCR 74, the Supreme Court of Canada ruled that in principle environmental damages may be recovered by the Canadian government for damage to publicly owned natural resources beyond the commercial value of the resources involved. The *Canfor* case was a non-maritime tort action for damages brought by the government of British Columbia seeking compensation from a company responsible for causing a forest fire that destroyed about 1,500 hectares of public forest lands. Although the claim for environmental damages was dismissed, the court did so for lack of evidence and stated that British Columbia could have obtained the damages sought had it provided proper pleading and evidence. The court did not provide any guidance on how natural resource damages should be measured.

In the case of Problem 7-8 would you advise the Canadian government to sue in tort under Canadian law to recover natural resource damages in excess of those permitted under international law?

Could the government of Canada use OPA 90 to recover a greater amount of natural resource damages than that permitted under international law? *See* OPA section 2707.

Section VIII. MARINE FISHERIES

A. Fishery Resources

Exploitation of the world's marine fisheries has increased dramatically, from 16.8 million tons in 1950, to a peak of 86.5 million tons in 1996, then leveling off to a current rate of about 80 million tons per year at the present time. Virtually all of the world's stocks of the top ten species of fish, which account for about 30% of marine capture fish production, are fully exploited; some 29.9% of fishery stocks are overexploited, producing lower yields than their biological and ecological potential and therefore require strict management to restore their full potential. World trade in fish products has also grown exponentially, setting a record at U S $111.8 billion in 2010, and increasing at a rate of some 15% per year. The total number of fishing vessels in the world is estimated at about 4.36 million, and fisheries and aquaculture provide employment for an estimated 54.8 million people engaged in the primary sector of fishing.[37]

Marine fisheries constitute a classic common resource. Fishery resources may be exploited by everyone so that individuals reap the benefit of the resource without regard to the cost of depletion of the resource until the resource is degraded for all. This is what is known as the "tragedy of the commons." *See* Garrett Hardin, *The Tragedy of the Commons*, 162 SCIENCE 143–48 (1968). In addition, fishing is commonly subsidized by many nations. Fisheries subsidies are estimated by the World Trade Organization to amount to between USD 14 to 20.5 per year, about 20 to 25% of global fishing revenues.[38] Subsidies obviously encourage overexploitation of fish stocks. The Doha Development Agenda, an international trade negotiation initiated in 2001 by the WTO seeks to reduce or eliminate fishing subsidies, but no agreement on this issue has been reached.

Global marine fishery production has reached or exceeded its maximum potential, and careful management of fish stocks is essential just to maintain the present rate of exploitation. It is essential to establish sustainable management of all fisheries and to eliminate the causes of unsustainable fisheries, such as illegal fishing, inadequate or ineffectively implemented conservation and management measures, disregard for the interdependency of marine living resources, and environmental degradation. Customary and treaty law have developed sophisticated legal regimes governing fisheries, which we cover in this section.

The international law of fisheries management adopts a sectoral approach that specifies different management regimes for areas of national jurisdiction, the exclusive economic zones and archipelagic waters, on the one hand, and the high seas, on the other. In addition, regional fisheries management organizations (RFMOs) are now at the heart of the fight to achieve sustainable fisheries under international law.

B. UNCLOS Provisions

The provisions of UNCLOS provide the framework for fisheries management under international law. UNCLOS contains provisions addressing fishing in national EEZs and on the High Seas; UNCLOS also addresses particular fishing stocks that range over both of these zones. Note especially the following provisions.

1) EEZ provisions:

- Article 56 grants extensive rights over fishing to the coastal state within its EEZ. Extensive enforcement powers are granted to the coastal state by Article 73.

- Article 61 imposes duties of conservation on coastal states. What are the contours of these duties?

---

[37] UNITED NATIONS FOOD AND AGRICULTURE ORGANIZATION, WORLD REVIEW OF FISHERIES AND AQUACULTURE, 2012, at 3–10.

[38] *See* http://www.wto.org/english/tratop_e/rulesneg_e/fish.

- Article 62 provides for coastal state "utilization" of living resources within its EEZ and states the objective of "optimal utilization." Under this article the coastal state exercises extensive powers to limit foreign fishing within its EEZ. Can a coastal state exclude foreign fishing altogether?

- Articles 69–71 concern the rights of land-locked and geographically disadvantaged states to fish in the EEZs of coastal states.

2) Certain articles of UNCLOS address particular stocks of fish without regard to what maritime zone they are found:

- Article 64 concerns highly migratory species. Note that these species are defined in UNCLOS Annex I.

- Article 65 concerns marine mammals.

- Article 66 deals with anadromous stocks.

- Article 67 deals with catadromous stocks

- Articles 68 and 77 concern sedentary species.

3) Certain UNCLOS provisions concern fishing on the High Seas:

- Article 87 concerns freedom to fish on the High Seas.

- Article 116 qualifies the freedom to fish on the High Seas. What are these qualifications?

- Article 117 requires states to take measures requiring their nationals to conserve the living resources of the High Seas.

- Article 118 requires states to enter into cooperative arrangements for the conservation of the living resources of the High Seas.

- Article 119 states particular criteria for conservation of the living resources of the High Seas. What are these criteria?

- Article 120 states that Article 65 concerning marine mammals also applies to the conservation and management of marine mammals on the High Seas.

4) One provision of UNCLOS — Article 63 — applies specifically to so-called "straddling stocks" of fisheries — fisheries stocks that range over one or more EEZs or over EEZs and the High Seas.

C. National Fisheries Management Systems

Under UNCLOS the territorial sea and archipelagic waters are part of the territory of a coastal state. Foreign vessels exercising the right of innocent passage are not allowed to engage in fishing activities. Nevertheless, even in these national zones coastal states must take into account Article 193 of UNCLOS, which recognizes the sovereign right to exploit natural resources, but imposes a duty "to protect and preserve the marine environment."

The main international regime for exploitation, management and conservation of marine living resources under UNCLOS is the exclusive economic zone (EEZ). Within this 200 nautical mile zone the coastal state is recognized to have sovereign rights over all living resources without exception.

International law standards under UNCLOS governing the coastal state's management of fishery resources in its EEZ are set out in Articles 61 and 62. Read these provisions carefully. Is the coastal state obliged to maximize the production of its coastal fisheries? Is there a contradiction between Article 61, which requires maximum sustainable yield, and Article 62, which requires optimum utilization? What limits are there on the coastal state's freedom to determine harvesting capacity? Is the coastal state required to provide access to its EEZ fisheries to fishing vessels from other states? To what extent does the coastal state have a duty to cooperate with other states in setting the harvesting capacity in its EEZ?

What limits are there on the coastal state's ability to specify conservation measures and other restrictions on fishing? What are the duties of a flag state whose vessels operate in the exclusive economic zone of other states? See Article 58. Do coastal states have a duty to cooperate with other states with regard to fishing in their EEZs? See Article 63 (1) and Article 64.

The substance of each state's regulation of fisheries in its EEZ is up to national law. Fishery regulation in the United States is a cooperative effort under federal and state law. The states have jurisdiction over fisheries to the 3 nautical-mile limit (9 nautical miles offshore Texas and offshore Florida in the Gulf of Mexico). Federal regulation of fisheries in the remainder of the U.S. EEZ is authorized under the Magnuson Fishery Conservation and Management Act, 16 U.S.C. § 1801 et seq. The Magnuson Act delegates fishery management to eight regional fishery councils: the North Pacific Council; the Pacific Council; the Western Pacific Council; the New England Council; the Mid-Atlantic Council; the South Atlantic Council; the Caribbean Council; and the Gulf of Mexico Council. Fisheries regulation in the United States concentrates on regulations concerning particular species or groups of species of fish and setting seasonal limits, gear restrictions, size limits, catch limits, and designating marine protected areas closed to certain fishing. Federal fisheries laws are enforced by the United States Coast Guard. The regional fisheries councils are coordinated by the National Marine Fisheries Service (NMFS) of the National Oceanic and Atmospheric Administration of the U.S. Department of Commerce. Each year the NMFS reports to Congress on the state of U.S. fisheries. In its 2011 report, Status of Stocks 2011: Annual Report to Congress on the Status of U.S. Fisheries, the NMFS concluded that 174 fishing stocks (79%) are not overfished, while 45 fishing stocks (21%) are overfished.

A quite different form of fishery regulation is exemplified by New Zealand fishery law.[39] New Zealand's extensive EEZ is divided into 10 different regional zones. In each of these zones, New Zealand law, the Fisheries Act of 1996, establishes a quota management system, which covers some 95% of commercially valuable species of fish (96 different species and 628 different stocks). The first step in this system is that biological studies of a particular fish stock establish the stock's maximum sustainable yield (MSY) for the year in question. Second, using MSY data, the Primary Industries Ministry establishes an annual total allowable

---

[39] *See* OECD Country Note on National Fisheries Management Systems, New Zealand, *available at* http://www.oecd.org/newzealand.

catch (TAC) for each fish stock. Third, a portion of this TAC is allocated to recreational fishers and to native Maori groups under the Maori Fisheries Act 2004. The remainder of the quota after this allocation becomes the total allowable commercial catch (TACC). This TACC is then allocated to fishing individuals and companies as Individual Transferable Quotas (ITQs), which provide an annual catch entitlement (ACE) for each individual for each stock in question. This ACE, which is allocated on the basis of historical fishing factors, is freely transferable; transfers are recorded in a public registry. An ITQ holder can sell all or part of his ACE or purchase additional ACEs. Commercial and recreational fishers must obtain a fishing license to participate in this scheme. Fishing vessels must also be registered. The system is enforced through a "catch balancing regime" that requires fishers who catch more than their allocated ITQ to pay a civil penalty. Criminal penalties are provided for fishing without a license or for using an unregistered vessel. The New Zealand fisheries authorities state that they use the same methods as developed in the United States to measure overfishing, and according to these methods, 15% of New Zealand stocks are overfished, a slightly better record than in the United States.

Do you think the New Zealand fisheries regulation scheme is superior to that of the United States? What method do you think is best?

Consider the following problem.

PROBLEM 7-9
FISHERY MISMANAGEMENT IN THE EXCLUSIVE ECONOMIC ZONE

States A and B are both parties to UNCLOS and are geographically adjacent coastal states, sharing a large and productive coastal fishery that is continuous in each of their respective exclusive economic zones. In State B fishery management administration is dominated by commercial and sport fishing interests and these interests, have successfully resisted all efforts to manage fishing within the EEZ of State B that would have assured the survival of a commercially valuable stock of flounder, a groundfish that does not migrate long distances. Furthermore, since ratifying UNCLOS, State B has maintained that it has the capacity to exploit all of the fishing stocks in its EEZ, and State B grants fishing permits and licenses only to nationals of State B.

State A and State B have agreed on the delimitation of their lateral maritime boundary line. State B aggressively enforces this boundary line, and on two occasions, coast guard boats authorized by the government of State B have fired on fishing vessels from State A that have inadvertently crossed over the maritime boundary line by a few meters. On the second occasion three fishermen from State A suffered serious injuries. On a third occasion, a fishing boat from State A was confiscated by authorities from State B, and the master of the vessel was convicted of violations of State B's criminal laws and sentenced to a term in prison.

State A manages the fishing stocks within its EEZ on the basis of maximum sustainable yield. State A strictly enforces Fisheries regulations, which include the licensing of fishing boats and fishing personnel, catch and seasonal limits, and the regulation of fishing methods and equipment. None of State A's fishing stocks are considered overexploited, and the flounder fishery in State *A* is still productive. However, State *A* has received information from experts that the flounder stock in State *B* is on the verge of collapse and that the collapse of this fishery in State B will have a negative impact on the founder fishery in State *A*, particularly in the maritime boundary region. State *A* is also concerned by the use of force by State *B* to defend its maritime boundary line. State *A* also believes that, if State *B* properly managed its flounder fishing stocks, it would have excess capacity, so that access by non-State *B* nationals, including fishers from State *A*, to exploit State *B*'s flounder fishery would be feasible.

State *A* is contemplating bringing an action for dispute settlement against State *B*. Both State *A* and State *B* have selected the arbitration proceedings of UNCLOS Article 287, para. 1(c), as the applicable forum for compulsory dispute settlement under UNCLOS.

1.   Is compulsory arbitration in accordance with UNCLOS Annex VII the applicable dispute settlement forum? If not, what is the applicable forum, if any?

2.   What if States *A* and *B* desire this dispute to be decided by the International Tribunal for the Law of the Sea. Does ITLOS have jurisdiction?

3.   What is the scope of the dispute forum's jurisdiction? Can the dispute forum decide only questions relating to UNCLOS, or can it also decide additional questions of the international use of force?

4.   Before State *A* brings its action before a dispute settlement forum established by UNCLOS, must it exhaust domestic remedies that might be available under the domestic law of State *B*?

5.   Should State *A* ask the dispute settlement forum for provisional measures under UNCLOS Article 290?

6.   State *A* would like to introduce certain scientific evidence by its experts in order to prove violations of good fisheries practices by State *B*. Can scientific evidence be introduced and considered by the dispute settlement tribunal?

7.   States *C* and *D*, also parties to UNCLOS, may be interested in the outcome of this case. Can third party states intervene in this dispute settlement proceeding? Can private industry parties from State B intervene?

8.   What are the criteria for enforcing access and the requirements of the coastal state in its EEZ? Did State *B* violate UNCLOS Article 73 or Article 292 in taking enforcement measures?

9.   How should this case be decided on the merits? Can the Court compel State *B* to offer access to its flounder fishery to nationals from State *A*?

10.   Is the obligation to cooperate in Article 63, para. 1 enforceable?

11.   What remedies are available? State *A* would like to obtain injunctive relief as well as damages from State *B*.

D. High Seas Fisheries

1. UNCLOS provisions and Supplemental Fisheries Agreements

Beyond the exclusive economic zones lie the High Seas, which, even with the expansive EEZs of coastal states, cover about 70 percent of the world's ocean areas. In this section we take up the problem of fishing on the high seas.

Article 87 of UNCLOS provides that all states are free to fish on the High Seas, but Article 116 states that this freedom is not absolute, but is subject to important conditions and limitations:

1. The state's treaty obligations;

2. The rights and duties of coastal states as provided in UNCLOS Articles 63, para. 2, and Articles 64 to 67; and

3. The provisions of Articles 117 to 120.

These three categories of obligations require comment.

(i) Treaty obligations. In the last twenty-five years important treaties have been concluded with regard to fishing on the High Seas. These treaty obligations are intended to supplement and to reinforce the general provisions of UNCLOS.

- **The Agreement to Promote Compliance with International Conservation and Management Measures by Fishing Vessels on the High Seas (1993, in force, 2003) (Compliance Agreement).**

The Compliance Agreement was adopted under the auspices of the Food and Agriculture Organization (FAO) as part of the FAO's work on a Code of Conduct for Responsible Fisheries. Unlike the Code, which is voluntary, the Compliance Agreement is a legally binding treaty. The Compliance Agreement, which is reprinted in the **Document Supplement**, defines with particularity the responsibility of flag states with respect to fishing vessels on the High Seas that fly their flag. Article III, the heart of the Agreement, obligates flag states to take "such measures as may be necessary" to ensure that their fishing vessels do not undermine international fishery conservation and management measures. Article III (3) deals somewhat obliquely with the issue of reflagging, the practice of changing the national registration of a fishing vessel as a means of avoiding compliance with international conservation and management measures. This article provides that "No Party shall authorize any fishing vessel entitled to fly its flag to be used to fish on the high seas unless the Party is satisfied that it is able, taking into account the links that exist between it and the fishing vessel concerned, to exercise effectively its responsibilities under this Agreement in respect of that fishing vessel." This provision is intended to discourage states from accepting vessel reflagging. The Compliance Agreement also sets out obligations requiring monitoring and exchange of information; international cooperation; and dispute settlement. The Compliance Agreement is the first global agreement on flag state responsibility. Article IX on Settlement of Disputes does not entail mandatory dispute settlement, and this article seems to detract from the UNCLOS provisions on dispute settlement and contributes to the fragmentation of the legal regime governing fishing activities.

- **The Agreement for the Implementation of the Provisions of the United Nations Convention on the Law of the Sea of 10 December 1982 Relating to the Conservation and Management of Straddling Fish Stocks and Highly Migratory Fish Stocks (1995, in force 2001). (Fish Stocks Agreement or Straddling Stocks Agreement).**

The Fish Stocks Agreement is intended to promote the enforcement of conservation and management measures with respect to fishing activities on the High Seas with respect to straddling stocks — fish stocks that range over zones of national jurisdiction and the High Seas, as well as highly migratory fish stocks, which are listed in Annex I of UNCLOS. The Fish Stocks Agreement provides an elaborate list of obligations that the flag state must observe, and, consistently with the UNCLOS, confirms and strengthens the principle of exclusive flag state jurisdiction on the High Seas as set forth in UNCLOS Articles 91 and 94.

- **The Agreement on Port State Measures to Prevent, Deter, and Eliminate Illegal, Unreported and Unregulated Fishing (2009, not in force) (Port State Measures Agreement).**

The Port State Measures Agreement was formulated and adopted under the auspices of the FAO in order to bolster port state enforcement of illegal, unreported, and unregulated (IUU) fishing. This treaty retains enforcement authority in flag states, but authorizes port inspection and port states may deny the use of their ports to offending vessels.

(ii) UNCLOS Article 63, para. 2 and Articles 64 to 67.

Note that coastal states are recognized as having special rights and duties with respect to straddling stocks (Art. 63, para. 2); highly migratory species (Art. 64); marine mammals (Art. 65); anadromous stocks (Art. 66); and catadromous stocks (Art. 67). To what extent does the Fish Stocks Agreement supplement these provisions?

(iii) UNCLOS Articles 117 to 120.

These provisions require states to cooperate with respect to adopting conservation and management measures applicable to fishing on the High Seas, to cooperate with regional fisheries management organizations, to use best scientific information in formulating conservation and management measures, and to apply those measures to their nationals.

NOTE ON INTERNATIONAL AGREEMENTS GOVERNING DRIFTNET FISHING ON THE HIGH SEAS

Driftnets are a form of net that traps fish by their gills, a technology that goes back thousands of years. Until the 1950s the size of driftnets was limited by the weight of the natural fibres (hemp or cotton) from which they were made. Driftnets became much larger, however, with the advent of synthetic fibres and efficient winches. By the 1960s driftnets that were 10 to 60 kilometers in length were deployed in many areas of the world, permitting fishers to gather a large catch of fish, particularly in pelagic areas. Environmental concern over driftnets has centered on the size and scope of their take and on the fact that their catch is indiscriminate, including many non-target species, marine mammals, and seabirds, which are gathered up and simply discarded. Driftnets lost or abandoned at sea last indefinitely, causing environmental disruption. At its peak in the 1980s, over 1000 vessels from many countries were operating, each night setting some 30,500 kilometers of driftnets in the world's oceans.

In the late 1980s and early 1990s, the United Nations General Assembly passed a series of resolutions calling for the end of pelagic driftnets longer than 2.5 kilometers. In 1989, the UN General Assembly adopted Resolution 44/225, which called for a moratorium on the use of large-scale driftnets beyond the exclusive economic zone of any nation by June 30, 1992; and in 1992, the UN General Assembly adopted Resolution 46/215 (31 ILM 241), which is reprinted in the **Document Supplement**, calling for a global moratorium on all large-scale driftnet fishing on the High Seas of the world's oceans and seas by 31 December 1992. These UN resolutions were non-binding, but in 1989, fifteen South Pacific nations adopted the Convention for the Prohibition of Fishing with Long Drift Nets in the South Pacific (Wellington Convention, 1989), which commits the parties to undertake measures to combat driftnet fishing, including prohibiting the landing or processing of driftnet catches within their territory, prohibiting the importation of driftnet caught fish products, and restricting port access to driftnet vessels. Protocol I of the Wellington Convention commits parties that fish in the South Pacific region to prevent their nationals and vessels from using driftnets in the Convention area; Protocol II obligates parties to prohibit the use of driftnets in all areas under their fishery jurisdiction.

The United States, which joined the Wellington Convention in 1992, enacted in 1990 amendments to the 1987 Driftnet Impact Monitoring, Assessment, and Control Act of 1987, that authorizes the U.S. Secretary of State to seek to conclude international agreements that enforce a global ban on large-scale driftnet fishing. A key provision of such agreements is the right of the U.S. Coast Guard to board and inspect vessels flying foreign flags on the High Seas that may be in violation of the global ban. See 16 U.S.C. § 1826. The global ban on large-scale driftnets is a major environmental success story. Virtually all states accepted the 1992 ban, and, as of 2012, large-scale driftnet fishing on the High Seas has been eliminated except for sporadic illegal activities. See 2011 Report of the Secretary of Commerce to the Congress of the United States Concerning U.S. Actions Taken on Foreign Large-Scale High Seas Driftnet Fishing (U.S. Department of Commerce, 2011).

Questions:

1. Critics have charged that the moratorium on driftnet fishing was enacted without proper scientific data. See, e.g., William Burke, Mark Freeberg, and Edward Miles, United Nations Resolution on Driftnet Fishing: An Unsustainable Precedent for High Seas and Coastal Fisheries Management, 25 OCEAN DEV, & INT'L L. 127, 128–34 (1994) ["the U.S. position . . . was based primarily on emotion and hyperbole rather than scientific data and interpretations."]. Do you agree? Should such a global moratorium be

enacted only after compiling adequate scientific data and cost and benefit studies? Is there a basis in the provisions of UNCLOS to justify the global ban? See Articles 116 to 119.

2. The definition of large-scale driftnets that are subject to the moratorium under international and U.S. law are driftnets 2.5 km. in length or more. *See* 16 U.S.C. § 1802 (25). Is this distinction justified?

3. Within national EEZs, states are free to allow or to prohibit driftnet fishing. Many nations, but not all, have banned or restricted driftnet fishing within their EEZs. In the U.S., driftnets must be limited to nets not longer than 100 yards (914 meters). Should driftnet fishing be banned in the world's EEZs?

2. Regional Fisheries Management Organizations (RFMOs)

UNCLOS Article 117 to 119 requires states to cooperate regarding the conservation of High Seas fisheries. Regional Fisheries Management Organizations are international organizations dedicated to sustainable management of High Seas fisheries or highly migratory species of fish. Some 44 RFMOs cover all species of highly migratory species and geographically cover virtually all areas of the High Seas. Although a few RFMOs are purely advisory, most have management and even enforcement powers. RFMOs also engage in scientific research and fishery development. RFMOs play an increasingly important role in the conservation of highly migratory stocks and High Seas fisheries.

Regional Fisheries Management Organizations are now at the heart of international fisheries management. While some RFMOs are advisory, most have management powers and make three types of decisions: (1) establishing fishing limits — total allowable catches, maximum number of vessels, and the duration and location of fishing; (2) establishing technical measures — how fishing activities are to be carried out, permitted gear and the technical control of vessels and equipment; and (3) conducting control measures — monitoring and surveillance of fishing activities.

Many interesting and important problems arise in connection with the operation of RFMOs. Some of these are the following:

1. Investment. To achieve optimum utilization of a fishery resource, positive investment may be necessary. The most obvious form of investment in a renewable resource is to ensure that the harvest rate is below the net natural growth rate. Such investment will build (or rebuild) the resource. Many of the world's fisheries now are overexploited and require such investment in order to produce optimum returns in the future.

2. Some Conditions for Effective Cooperation.

   ▪ The game theory of cooperative games assumes that all players are coldly rational and that altruism has no role. Under these conditions, game theory holds that the difficulty of achieving a stable cooperative management regime will increase with the number of participants. Not only is cooperation more difficult to achieve with more players, but within the players, coalitions will almost inevitably form. Stability and cooperation may be disrupted if an individual or sub-coalition has an incentive to compete against the rest. An essential aspect of avoiding disruptive competition, whether by an individual member or a membership coalition, is to assure now and in the future that each individual participant's and each sub-coalition's economic return from cooperation is at least as great as it would receive by acting competitively. In addition, it is important that allocation issues be resolved satisfactorily and equitably.

■ In order to foster effective cooperation, non-compliance — the willful violation of cooperative management arrangements — must be aggressively combated. If noncompliance is widespread, the cooperative ethic necessary to the regime will break apart.

■ Effective cooperation will require addressing "free rider" problems. The burdens of the regime must be shared equally among all members and non-members must not be allowed to share the benefits. An obvious aspect of the "free rider" problem is the "new member" problem. Should a new member be admitted after much investment effort by charter members has created a valuable resource? When a new member joins an RFMO the temptation is to increase the existing allowable catch in order to accommodate the new member without decreasing the shares of existing members. This solves nothing and only masks the cost to existing members of admitting a new member. The best way of solving the "new member" problem is to require new members to pay a price of admission, for example, by purchasing quotas of existing members. See Recommended Best Practices for Regional Fisheries Management Organizations (Chatham House, 2007) p. 16–17.

• Effective cooperation requires that the RFMO be resilient over time so that it may survive the political, economic or environmental shocks that inevitably may arise. To the extent that the possibility of such change can be foreseen, it may be possible to build into an agreement automatic mechanisms of adjustment to changing conditions.

• Cooperative resource management requires productive bargaining among the participants. Bargaining can be facilitated by keeping the scope for bargaining as broad as possible. For example, in the fisheries context, negotiations over allocations among cooperating states should not be confined to shares of allowable catch; cooperation can be facilitated by supplementing such allocations with, *inter alia*, access arrangements and quota trading.

3. The Consequences of Ineffective Cooperation. Game theory tells us much about the consequences of non-cooperation with respect to a resource. When applied to fisheries, non-cooperation carries the risk of what is known as the "prisoners' dilemma" outcome. This term comes from a story developed to illustrate the point that, under conditions of non-cooperation, the participants (players) will be driven to adopt strategies that they know

will produce inferior results. For example, consider a transboundary stock of fish shared by two coastal states. If they do not engage in cooperative management each will inevitably deplete the resource, since neither party will have an incentive to "invest" in the resource, because the benefits of such investment would accrue to the other "free rider" state.

For a good overview of RFMOs, see http://www.fao.org/fishery/ri b/search.

E. Straddling Fish Stocks

Straddling fish stocks are stocks covered by UNCLOS Article 63: a situation where the same stocks or stocks of associated species occur both within the exclusive economic zone and in areas beyond and adjacent to this zone. Many commercially valuable fish stocks are highly migratory or straddling stocks that range over the high seas and exclusive economic zones. In such cases a coastal state that adopts and enforces conservation measures within its own EEZ must stand by helplessly as foreign fishing vessels line up just beyond the EEZ and fish indiscriminately. What can or should the coastal state do in such a case? There may be overwhelming political and economic pressure on the coastal state to take unilateral action, such as a declaration of extension of its EEZ beyond 200 miles (a clear violation of UNCLOS Article 89) or seizure of offending foreign vessels on the High Seas.

UNCLOS deals only obliquely with the highly migratory stocks and the straddling stocks problems. The international furor over highly migratory and straddling stocks resulted in the new agreements detailed above, especially the Fish Stocks Agreement and the Compliance Agreement. Do these agreements solve all the problems? Let us consider three famous cases that were never decided on their merits: (1) the Case of the Estai; (2) the Swordfish Stocks dispute between Chile and the European Union; and (3) the Case of the Bering Sea Doughnut Hole.

PROBLEM 7-10
THE CASE OF THE *ESTAI*

The case of the *Estai*, a Spanish fishing vessel, arose during the so-called "turbot war," a dispute over fishing for turbot (Reinharditus hippoglossoides) in the Northwest Atlantic Ocean. At this time, the early 1990s, the European Union quota for the catch of turbot was about five times above the quota established by the Northwest Atlantic Fisheries Organization (NAFO), a RFMO established in 1978. Out of desperation, Canada seized the *Estai* on the High Seas just outside Canada's EEZ in 1995 under the authority of the Canadian Coastal Fisheries Protection Act (1994), which authorized Canadian authorities to take urgent action necessary to protect fishing stocks on the Grand Banks off Newfoundland. The seizure of the *Estai* caused a major international crisis. Spain and the EU charged Canada with violating international law. Canada pleaded necessity. After the arrest Spain commenced proceedings against Canada in the International Court of Justice. However, the ICJ, in an important decision on jurisdiction and admissibility, ruled that Canada's optional clause declaration[40] excluded the ICJ's jurisdiction. *Estai* case [1998] ICJ Rep. 431 [87]. Although the *Estai* case was never decided on the merits, the case was an important catalyst that led to adoption of the Fish Stocks Agreement later in 1995.

1.   Why was this dispute not handled under the compulsory procedures established by Part XV of the UNCLOS? (Canada ratified UNCLOS in 2003).

2.   If the ICJ or an international tribunal had had jurisdiction, how would the Case of the *Estai* have been decided on the merits? Consider UNCLOS Articles 63 para. 2, 64, 87, 89, 90, 116, 117, 118, 119.

3.   Suppose it were proved that the *Estai*, just before the seizure, was fishing illegally just inside Canada's EEZ; would Canada have a right to seize the vessel? *See* UNCLOS Article 111.

4.   Suppose the Fish Stocks Agreement had been in force when the turbot war and the *Estai* incident arose; how would the matter likely have been handled under the Fish Stocks Agreement?

PROBLEM 7-11
THE SWORDFISH DISPUTE
EUROPEAN UNION (EU) v. CHILE
INTERNATIONAL TRIBUNAL FOR THE LAW OF THE SEA,
DISPUTE NO. 7

During the 1990s, the EU and Chile were engaged in a dispute over what Chile considered as overexploitation of swordfish on the High Seas just outside Chile's EEZ in the southern Pacific Ocean. After many years of fruitless discussions, Chile barred EU vessels from unloading swordfish in its ports. Swordfish (Xiphias gladius), a highly prized commercial fish species, migrate freely through the vast waters of the Pacific Ocean. The EU vessels fishing for swordfish seek to land the fish in Chilean ports so that they can be exported to international markets, mainly to the United States. This unilateral measure sparked two legal actions:

1.   The EU filed a complaint against Chile at the World Trade Organization charging that Chile's action was in violation of Articles V and XI of the General Agreement on Tariffs and Trade (GATT).

2.   Chile brought a n action against the EU in the International Tribunal for the Law of the Sea (ITLOS), charging the EU with violations of UNCLOS Articles 64 (requiring cooperation to assure the conservation of highly migratory fish species), 116–119 (conservation of living resources of the High Seas), and 300 (calling for good faith and no abuse of right). The EU countered with charging Chile with violating UNCLOS Articles 87 (freedom of the High Seas) and 89 (prohibiting any state from subjecting any part of the High Seas to its sovereignty).

---

[40] At the time, Canada's Declaration under Art. 36(2) of the Statute of the International Court of Justice excluded from the Court's jurisdiction "disputes arising out of or concerning conservation and management measures taken by Canada with respect to fishing vessels in the NAFO regulatory area, as defined in the Convention . . . and the enforcement of such measures."

In 2001, the EU and Chile reached a preliminary agreement to settle their dispute, and the ITLOS suspended the proceedings in the dispute. In 2010, Chile and the EU concluded a final agreement ending the dispute. See Understanding Concerning the Conservation of Swordfish Stocks in the South Eastern Pacific Ocean, Official Journal of the European Union, L 155/3 (22 June 2010). This Understanding opens Chilean ports to fishing vessels from the EU, but obligates both parties to enforce strict conservation and management measures relating to swordfish. The Understanding establishes an EU/Chile Bilateral Scientific and Technical Committee, requires full exchanges of information, and requires the parties to manage catch levels of swordfish at or near maximum sustainable yield levels with the objective of maintaining the sustainability of the resources and safeguarding the marine ecosystem. The parties committed to applying a precautionary approach to fishing and to take steps to develop a multilateral conservation forum for the South Pacific. On 16 December 2009, at the request of the parties, the ITLOS removed the case from the ITLOS list of cases. See Order 2009/1, International Tribunal for the law of the Sea, Case Concerning the Conservation and Sustainable Exploitation of Swordfish Stocks in the South-Eastern Pacific Ocean (Chile v. European Union), 16 December 2009.

Question: if the ITLOS proceeding had not been settled, how would the ITLOS have decided the case?

PROBLEM 7-12
THE CASE OF THE BERING SEA DOUGHNUT HOLE

In the Aleutian Basin of the Bering Sea is the so-called "doughnut hole," an area of ocean that is High Seas surrounded by the EEZs of Russia and the United States (Alaska). Because of a combination of natural factors, this area of the Bering Sea is one of the most productive fisheries in the world. The doughnut hole comprises about 10% of the Bering Sea, and was treated as a "global commons" by factory fishing ships from Japan, Taiwan, Russia, Poland, Korea, and the U.S. until the early 1990s. As a result of unregulated fishing, the fish stocks — principally Walleye pollock (Theragra chalcogramma) — crashed in 1992 to just 10% of their historic levels. Pollock, which at one time constituted over 50% of the seafood consumed in the U.S., are classic straddling stocks, most of which breed in the U.S. EEZ. In 1992, the principal fishing nations concerned declared a two year moratorium on fishing in the doughnut hole to allow fish stocks to recover.

1. What are the obligations of the fishing nations with respect to the doughnut hole under international law? Consider UNCLOS Article 116 (b): do high seas fishing nations have obligations toward coastal states? How would you define the scope of the obligations under this article?

2. How can UNCLOS Article 116 (b) be made effective? Consider UNCLOS Articles 117 to 119.

3. Consider UNCLOS Article 119 para. 2, which suggests the creation of a competent international organization.

4. In 1994, the Convention on the Conservation and Management of Pollock Resources in the Central Bering Sea was concluded [reprinted in the **Document Supplement** and in 34 ILM 67 (1995)].The parties to this

Convention are: Canada, China, Japan, Korea, Poland, Russia, and the United States. Read carefully the provisions of the Convention, which seeks to maintain catches of pollock at optimum levels that do not exceed the maximum sustainable yield, requires exchanges of data and information, and provides a forum for the establishment of necessary conservation and management measures. Does this Convention solve the problem of the doughnut hole? As of this writing, the fishing resources of the doughnut hole have not fully recovered. *See* Kevin M. Bailey, *An Empty Donut Hole: The Collapse of a Great North American Fishery* (2011), *available at* http://www.ecologyandsociety.org, accessed 3 December 2012.

NOTE ON THE IMPACT OF THE 1995 FISH STOCKS AGREEMENT ON THE MANAGEMENT OF STRADDLING STOCKS

A major accomplishment in dealing with the problems associated with straddling stocks was the adoption of the Fish Stocks Agreement of 1995. The Fish Stocks Agreement is reprinted in the **Document Supplement**. Read this Agreement and answer the following questions:

1.　Note that the Fish Stocks Agreement is designed to implement, not to replace, the provisions of UNCLOS, most importantly Article 63(2) of UNCLOS, which only requires parties to "seek to agree" on measures to conserve straddling stocks. The Fish Stocks Agreement also implements UNCLOS Article 64 on highly migratory fish stocks.

2.　What is the objective of the Fish Stocks Agreement? *See* Article 2.

3.　Note the management principles in Articles 5 and 6.

4.　Note how the management of straddling stocks and highly migratory stocks is stated differently in the compatibility Article 7.

5.　Articles 8 to 16 are designed to reform and strengthen the role of RFMOs.

6.　How is the problem of fishing by non-parties to RFMOs handled? See Article 8(4). See also Article 17 and 33. How can the Fish Stocks Agreement create obligations for non-party states?

7.　Articles 18 and 19 place obligations on flag states in order to strengthen flag state enforcement.

8.　Article 20 calls for cooperation in enforcement between flag states, coastal states and regional and subregional organizations.

9.　Articles 21 and 22 create a new kind of enforcement by "inspecting states." What is the authority of an "inspecting state"? What is the limit of this authority?

10.　Article 23 concerns the role of port states.

11.　Articles 24 to 26 is designed to strengthen the role of developing countries.

12.　Articles 27 to 32 deal with settlement of disputes.

PROBLEM 7-13
MANAGING THE DOUGHNUT HOLE AGREEMENT

Under the Convention on the Conservation and Management of Pollock Resources in the Central Bering Sea, (1994) (Bering Sea Convention), Canada, China, Japan, Korea, Poland, Russia, and the United States have agreed to manage pollock and other fish stocks in the doughnut hole area of the Bering Sea according to a scheme that allocates the Allowable Harvest Level (AHL) among the parties to the Convention. Each year an Annual Conference of the Parties to the Bering Sea Convention establishes an AHL for fish stocks in the doughnut hole as well as Individual National Quotas (INQ) for each of the parties. (See Bering Sea Convention, Article VIII).

A South Korean corporation operates a vessel, the *Daemon Ho*, that has fished in the doughnut hole on numerous occasions. The South Korean company has recently established a wholly-owned Panamanian subsidiary company and has transferred the *Daemon Ho* to that company. In addition, the home port and registration of the *Daemon Ho* was changed to Panama. The *Daemon Ho* now flies the flag of Panama, although its captain and several crewmembers are Korean. Fish captured by the Daemon Ho are usually offloaded in Korean ports. Once a year, the *Daemon Ho* puts into port in Panama for routine inspection and repairs.

The *Daemon Ho* recently returned to the doughnut hole to fish for pollock under a new flag (Panama) and under a new name, the *Panamanian Estralla*. The parties to the Bering Sea Convention have invited Panama to join the Convention and to negotiate a quota allocation for pollock and other fish, but Panama has refused, stating that, under the law of the sea, the doughnut hole is part of the High Seas, and that vessels flying its flag have the right to fish the resources of the High Seas without limitation. The parties to the Bering Sea Convention have issued a joint statement demanding that the *Panamanian Estralla* cease to fish in the doughnut hole. Panama, however, rejected this statement. Recently, the U.S. Coast Guard, after finding the *Panamanian Estralla* fishing illegally in the doughnut hole, confiscated its catch and forced it to leave the area.

Panama has protested this action as a violation of its rights under international law. Panama argues that as a non-party to the Bering Sea Convention, it is not bound by its provisions and its vessels are free to fish on the High Seas. Panama has also refused to become a party to the Fishing Stocks Agreement in order to be able to fully assert its rights as a party to the UNCLOS, which it has accepted.

Panama and the United States have recently concluded an agreement to submit the dispute over the rights of its vessels to fish in the Doughnut Hole to the International Court of Justice.

How should the ICJ rule on the following questions:

1. What rights, if any, does the *Panamanian Estralla* have to fish in the Doughnut Hole under UNCLOS? Consider UNCLOS Articles 116, 117, 118, and 119.

2. Even though Panama is not a party to the Fish Stocks Agreement, is this Agreement relevant to resolving the present dispute? Consider Part IV of the Fish

Stocks Agreement.

3.   Did the U.S. Coast Guard have the right to stop the vessel from fishing in the area, to confiscate its catch, and to force it to leave? Consider Article 21 of the Fish Stocks Agreement and Article XII of the Bering Sea Convention.

4.   Is the United States required to consider the *Panamanian Estralla* a Panamanian flag vessel? Consider UNCLOS Article 91. Consider also Article II of the Compliance Convention, which Panama has accepted as a State Party. Does South Korea have any duties under international law with respect to the reflagging of the *Panamanian Estralla*? *See* the Bering Sea Convention, Article XII, para. 4.

5.   How can non-parties be accommodated and allowed to fish under the Bering Sea Convention? Is there any mechanism in the Convention for non-party fishing? *See* Article XII.

F.   Highly Migratory Species of Fish.

Although most of the problems associated with the international law of highly migratory species are also true with respect to straddling stocks, and we have already considered one case of a highly migratory species, the *Swordfish* case, the importance of one case, the Southern Bluefin Tuna Case, and one particular class of highly migratory species, the eight species of tuna, demand fuller treatment.

Perhaps the most important and prized fish in the world is the regal Southern Bluefin Tuna, one specimen of which reportedly sold in January 2012, for US$ 736,000 at the Tsukiji fish market in Japan. As a result of relentless fishing pressures on the Bluefin tuna stock and, indeed, on all tuna stocks, the eight species of tuna are becoming very uncommon and, according to experts, five of the eight are in danger of extinction. *See More than half of tuna species at risk of extinction*, THE GUARDIAN, July 7, 2011, *available at* http://www.guardian.co.uk/environment/2011/jul/07tuna. Yet state parties to the Convention on International Trade in Endangered Species of Wild Fauna and Flora (CITES) have rejected all attempts to list species of tuna as Appendix I endangered species, which would end their exploitation.

SOUTHERN BLUE FIN TUNA CASES
NEW ZEALAND v. JAPAN;
AUSTRALIA v. JAPAN
International Tribunal for the Law of the Sea, Cases 3 And 4 (27 August 1999)

Requests for Provisional Measures

ORDER

[The Southern Bluefin Tuna Cases arose because of a breakdown in cooperation among the founding members of the 1993 Convention for the Conservation of Southern Bluefin Tuna (CCSBT), which was concluded to "ensure, through appropriate management, the conservation and optimum utilization of Southern Bluefin Tuna" (Art. 3). The CCSBT establishes the Commission for the Conservation of Southern Bluefin Tuna (C-CCSBT) to manage catches by member states by setting, by consensus, the total allowable catch (TAC) for Southern Bluefin Tuna (Thunnus maccayii) as well as individual national allocations. The parties to the CCSBT disagreed as to the current state of the fishery and the future prospects for recovery of stocks. Southern Bluefin Tuna are a highly migratory species at the top of the marine food chain. They are pelagic fish that spawn in the waters south of Indonesia and range over the High Seas and EEZs of many states. These stocks are long-lived and late breeders, and are mainly fished on the High Seas. In 1989, New Zealand, Australia and Japan had agreed on a TAC of 11,750 tonnes. From 1994 onward, Japan insisted on increasing this TAC, but the other two states disagreed. Japan then took unilateral action to establish its own fishing program for Southern Bluefin Tuna. New Zealand and Australia, on July 15, 1999, requested the establishment of an arbitral tribunal under Annex V II of the UNCLOS to hear the merits of t h e dispute between the parties. Both New Zealand and Australia maintain that Japan, by unilaterally designing and implementing its own experimental fishing program, was in violation of several provisions of the UNCLOS, including Articles 64, 117, 118, and 119. Pending the establishment of the Annex VII Tribunal, New Zealand and Australia sought provisional measures at the ITLOS in order to halt Japan's unilateral program. In August 1999, the ITLOS unanimously found that the Annex VII Tribunal to be established would have jurisdiction over the dispute.

ITLOS went on to order, by 18 votes to 4, that catches of tuna be maintained at 11,750 tonnes, and by 20 votes to 2, ordered that none of the parties engage in an experimental fishing program].

40. Considering that. before prescribing provisional measures under article 290, paragraph 5. of the Convention the Tribunal must satisfy itself that prima facie the arbitral tribunal would have jurisdiction;

41. Considering that Australia and New Zealand have invoked as the basis of jurisdiction of the arbitral tribunal article 288, paragraph l, of the Convention which re ads as follows:

> A court or tribunal referred to in article 287 shall have jurisdiction over any dispute concerning the interpretation or application of this Convention which is submitted to it in accordance with this Part;

42. Considering that Japan maintains that the disputes are scientific rather than legal;

43. Considering that, in the view of the Tribunal, the differences between the parties also concern points of law;

44. Considering that, in the view of the Tribunal, a dispute is a "disagreement on a point of law or fact, a conflict of legal views or of interests" (Mavrommatis Palestine Concessions. Judgment No. 2. 1924, P. C.J.J., Series A. No. 2. p. 11), and "[i]t must be shown that the claim of one party is positively opposed by the other" (South West Africa, Preliminary Objections, Judgment, I.C.J. Reports 1962, p.328);

45. Considering that Australia and New Zealand allege that Japan, by unilaterally designing and undertaking an experimental fishing programme, has failed to comply with obligations under articles 64 and 116 to 119 of the Convention on the Law of the Sea, with provisions of the Convention for the Conservation of Southern Bluefin Tuna of 1993 (hereinafter "the Convention of 1993") and with rules of customary international law:

46. Considering that Japan maintains that the dispute concerns the interpretation or implementation of the Convention of 1993 and does not concern the interpretation or application of the Convention on the Law of the Sea;

47. Considering that Japan denies that it has failed to comply with any of the provisions of the Convention on the Law of the Sea referred to by Australia and New Zealand;

48. Considering that, under article 64, read together with articles 116 to 119, of the Convention, States Parties to the Convention have the duty to cooperate directly or through appropriate international organizations with a view to ensuring conservation and promoting the objective of optimum utilization of highly migratory species;

49. Considering that the list of highly migratory species contained in Annex I to the Convention includes southern bluefin tuna: thunus maccoyii;

50. Considering that the conduct of the parties within the Commission for the Conservation of Southern Bluefin Tuna established in accordance with the Convention of 1993, and in their relations with non-parties to that Convention is relevant to an evaluation of the extent to which the parties are in compliance with their obligations under the Convention on the Law of the Sea;

51. Considering that the fact that the Convention of 1993 applies between the parties does not exclude their right to invoke the provisions of the Convention on the Law of the Sea in regard to the conservation and management of southern bluefin tuna;

52. Considering that, in the view of the Tribunal, the provisions of the Convention on the Law of the Sea invoked by Australia and New Zealand appear to afford a basis on which the jurisdiction of the arbitral tribunal might be founded;

53. Considering that Japan argues that recourse to the arbitral tribunal is excluded because the Convention of 1993 provides for a dispute settlement procedure;

54. Considering that Australia and New Zealand maintain that they are not precluded from having recourse to the arbitral tribunal since the Convention of 1993 does not provide for a compulsory dispute settlement procedure entailing a binding decision as required under article 282 of the Convention on the Law of the Sea;

55. Considering that, in the view of the Tribunal, the fact that the Convention of 1993 applies between the parties does not preclude recourse to the procedures in Part XV, section 2, of the Convention on the Law of the Sea;

56. Considering that Japan contends that Australia and New Zealand have not exhausted the procedures for amicable dispute settlement under Part XV, section 1,

of the Convention, in particular article 281, through negotiations or other agreed peaceful means, before submitting the disputes to a procedure under Part XV, section 2, of the Convention;

57. Considering that negotiations and consultations have taken place between the parties and that the records show that these negotiations were considered by Australia and New Zealand as being under the Convention of 1993 and also under the Convention on the Law of the Sea;

58. Considering that Australia and New Zealand have invoked the provisions of the Convention in diplomatic notes addressed to Japan in respect of those negotiations;

59. Considering that Australia and New Zealand have stated that the negotiations had terminated;

60. Considering that, in the view of the Tribunal, a State Party is not obliged to pursue procedures under Part XV, section 1, of the Convention when it concludes that the possibilities of settlement have been exhausted;

61. Considering that, in the view of the Tribunal, the requirements for invoking the procedures under Part XV, section 2. of the Convention have been fulfilled;

62. Considering that, for the above reasons, the Tribunal finds that the arbitral tribunal would prima facie have jurisdiction over the disputes;

63. Considering that, according to article 290, paragraph 5, of the Convention, provisional measures may be prescribed pending the constitution of the arbitral tribunal if the Tribunal considers that the urgency of the situation so requires;

64. Considering, therefore, that the Tribunal must decide whether provisional measures are required pending the constitution of the arbitral tribunal;

65. Considering that, in accordance with article 290, paragraph 5, of the Convention, the arbitral tribunal. Once constituted, may modify, revoke or affirm any provisional measures prescribed by the Tribunal;

66. Considering that Japan contends that there is no urgency for the prescription of provisional measures in the circumstances of this case;

67. Considering that, in accordance with article 290 of the Convention, the Tribunal may prescribe provisional measures to preserve the respective rights of the parties to the dispute or to prevent serious harm to the marine environment;

68. Considering that Australia and New Zealand contend that by unilaterally implementing an experimental fishing programme Japan has violated the rights of Australia and New Zealand under articles 64 and 116 to 119 of the Convention;

69. Considering that Australia and New Zealand contend that further catches of southern bluefin tuna, pending the of the matter by an arbitral tribunal, would cause immediate harm to their rights;

70. Considering that the conservation of the living resources of the sea is an element in the protection preservation of the marine environment;

71. Considering that there is no disagreement between the parties that the stock

of southern bluefin tuna is serve depleted and is at its historically lowest levels and that this is a cause for serious biological concern;

72. Considering that Australia and New Zealand contend that, by unilaterally implementing an experimental programme, Japan has failed to comply with its obligations under articles 64 and 118 of the Convention; which the parties to cooperate in the conservation and management of the southern bluefin tuna stock, and that the act of Japan have resulted in a threat to the stock;

73. Considering that Japan contends that the scientific evidence available shows that the implementation experimental fishing programme will cause no further threat to the southern bluefin tuna stock and that experimental fishing programme remains necessary to reach a more reliable assessment of the potential of the stock to recover;

74. Considering that Australia and New Zealand maintain that the scientific evidence available shows that the southern bluefin tuna taken under the experimental fishing programme could endanger the existence of the stock;

75. Considering that the Tribunal has been informed by the parties that commercial fishing for southern bluefin is expected to continue throughout the remainder of 1999 and beyond;

76. Considering that the catches of non-parties to the Convention of 1 993 have increased considerably since 1991;

77. Considering that, in the view of the Tribunal, the parties should in the circumstances act with prudence caution to ensure that effective conservation measures are taken to prevent serious harm to the stock the bluefin tuna;

78. Considering that the parties should intensify their efforts to cooperate with other participants in the fishery southern bluefin tuna with a view to ensuring conservation and promoting the objective of optimum utilization of the stock;

79. Considering that there is scientific uncertainty regarding measures to be taken to conserve the stock of southern bluefin tuna and that there is no agreement among the parties as to whether the conservation measures taken have led to the improvement in the stock of southern bluefin tuna;

80. Considering that, although the Tribunal cannot conclusively assess the scientific evidence presented by the parties, it finds that measures should be taken as a matter of urgency to preserve the rights of the parties and to a further deterioration of the southern bluefin tuna stock;

81. Considering that, in the view of the Tribunal, catches taken within the framework of any experimental fish programme should not result in total catches which exceed the levels last set by the parties for each of them, under agreed criteria;

82. Considering that, following the pilot programme which took place in 1998, Japan's experimental fishing currently designed consists of three annual programmes in 1999, 2000 and 2001;

83. Considering that the Tribunal has taken note that, by the statement of its

Agent before the Tribunal on 20 August 1999, Japan made a "clear commitment that the 1999 experimental fishing programme will end by 31 August;"

84. Considering, however, that Japan has made no commitment regarding any experimental fishing programme 1999;

85. Considering that, for above reasons in the view of the Tribunal, provisional measures are appropriate under the circumstances;

86. Considering that, in accordance with article 89, paragraph 5, of the Rules, the Tribunal may prescribe measures different in whole or in part from those requested;

87. Considering the binding force of the measures prescribed and the requirement under article 290, paragraph 6, of the Convention that compliance with such measures be prompt;

88. Considering that, pursuant to article 95, paragraph 1, of the Rules, each party is required to submit to the Tribunal a report and information on compliance with any provisional measures prescribed;

89. Considering chat it may be necessary for the Tribunal to request further information from the parties on the implementation of provisional measures and that it is appropriate that the President be authorized to request such information in accordance with article 95, paragraph 2, of the Rules;

I. For these reasons,

THE TRIBUNAL.

    1. Prescribes, pending a decision of the arbitral tribunal. the following measures:

By 20 votes to 2.

    a) Australia, Japan and New Zealand shall each ensure that no action is taken which might aggravate or extend the disputes submitted to the arbitral tribunal;

IN FAVOUR:	President Mensah Vice-President Wolfrum; Judges Zhao. Caminos, Maroita Rangel. Yankov, Yamamoto. Kolodkin, Park. Bamela Engo, Nelson, Chandra Sekhara Rao, A Kl. Anderson, Warioba, Laing, Treves, Marsit, Ndiaye; Judge ad hoc Shearer;
AGAINST:	Judges Vukas, Eiriksson.

By 18 votes to 4

(c) Australia, Japan and New Zealand shall ensure, unless they agree otherwise, that their annual catches do not exceed the annual national allocations at the levels last agreed by the parties of 5,265 tonnes. 6,065 tonnes and 420 tonnes. respectively; in calculating the annual catches for 1999 and 2000, and without prejudice to any decision of the arbitral tribunal account shall be taken of the catch during 1999 as part of an experimental fishing programme:

IN FAVOUR: President MENSAH; Vice-President WOLFRUM; Judges CAMINOS, MAST RANGEL, YANKOV, KOLODKIN, PARK, BAMELA ENGO, NELSON CHANDRASEKHARA RAO, AKL. ANDERSON, LAING,. TREVES, MARS, EIRIKSSON, NDIA YE; Judge ad hoc SHEARER;

AGAINST: Judges ZHAO, YAMAMOTO, YUKAS, W ARIOBA.

By 20 votes to 2,

(d) Australia, Japan and New Zealand shall each refrain from conducting an experimental fishing programme involving the taking of a catch of southern bluefin tuna, except with the agreement of the other parties unless the experimental catch is counted against its annual national allocation as prescribed in subparagraph (c);

IN FAVOUR: President MENSAH; Vice-President WOLFRUM; Judges ZHAO, CAMINOS, MAROTT, RANGEL, YANKOV, KOLODKIN, PARK, BAMELA ENGO, NELSON CHANDRASEKHARA RAO, AKL, ANDERSON. WARIOBA, LAING, TREVE MARSIT, EIRIKSSON, NDIAYE; Judge ad hoc S HEARER

AGAINST: Judges YAMAMOTO, VUKAS

By 21 votes to 1.

(e) Australia, Japan and New Zealand should resume negotiations without delay with a view to reaching agreement on measures for the conservation and management of southern bluefin tuna;

IN FAVOUR: President MENSAH; Vice- President WOLFRUM; Judges ZHAO, CAMINOS, MAROTT RANGEL, YANKOV, YAMAMOTO, KOLODKLN, PARK BAMELA ENGO, NELSON CHANDRASEKHARA RAO, AKL, ANDERSON, WARIOBA, LAING, TREVES MARSIT, EIRKSSON, NDIAYE; Judge ad hoc SHEARER;

AGAINST: Judge VUKAS.

By 20 votes to 2

(f) Australia, Japan and New Zealand should make further efforts to reach agreement with other States and fishing entities en gaged in fishing for southern bluefin tuna, with a view to ensuring conservation and promoting the objective of optimum utilization of the stock;

IN FAVOUR: President MENSAH; Vice-President WOLFRUM; Judges ZHAO, CAMINOS, MAROTTA RANGEL, YANKOV, YAMAMOTO. KOLODKIN, PARK, BAMELA ENGO, NELSON, CHANDRASEKHARA RAO, AKL, ANDERSON, LAING, TREVES, MARSIT, EIRIKSSON, NDIAYE; Judge ad hoc SHEARER;

AGAINST: Judges Vukas, Warioba

SOUTHERN BLUEFIN TUNA CASES
NEW ZEALAND v. JAPAN
AUSTRALIA v. JAPAN

Arbitral Panel Established under Annex VII of the United Nations
Convention on the Law of the Sea, United Nations Reports of International
Arbitration Awards, Award on Jurisdiction and Admissibility Decision of 4
August 2000, Vol. XXIII, at 1–57

Background to the Current Proceedings

21. Southern Bluefin Tuna (Thunnus maccoyi, hereafter sometimes designated
"SBT") is a migratory species of pelagic fish that is included in the list of highly
migratory species set out in Annex I of the United Nations Convention on the Law
of the Sea. Southern Bluefin Tuna range widely through the oceans of the Southern
Hemisphere, principally the high seas, but they also traverse the exclusive economic
zones and territorial waters of some States, notably Australia, New Zealand and
South Africa. They spawn in the waters south of Indonesia. The main market for the
sale of Southern Bluefin Tuna is in Japan, where the fish is prized as a delicacy for
sashimi.

22. It is common ground between the Parties that commercial harvest of
Southern Bluefin Tuna began in the early 1950s and that, in 1961, the global catch
peaked a t 81,000 metric tons ("mt"). By the early 1980s, the SBT stock had been
severely overfished; it was estimated that the parental stock had declined to 23-30%
of its 1960 level. In 1982, Australia, New Zealand and Japan began informally to
manage the catching of SBT. Japan joined with Australia and New Zealand in 1985
to introduce a global total allowable catch (hereafter, "TAC") for SBT, initially set
at 38,650 mt. In 1989, a TAC of 11,750 tons was agreed, with national allocations of
6,065 tons to Japan, 5,265 tons to Australia and 420 tons to New Zealand; Japan, as
the largest harvester of SBT, sustained the greatest cut. But the SBT stock
continued to decline. In 1997, it was estimated to be in the order of 7–15% of its 1960
level. Recruitment of SBT stock — the entry of new fish into the fishery — was
estimated in 1998 to be about one third of the 1960 level. The institution of total
allowable catch restrictions by Japan, Australia and New Zealand to some extent
has been offset by the entry into the SBT fishery of fishermen from the Republic of
Korea, Taiwan and Indonesia, and some flag-of-convenience States. Whether, in
response to TAC restrictions, the stock has in fact begun to recover is at the core
of the dispute between Australia and New Zealand, on the one hand, and Japan, on
the other. They differ over the current state and recovery prospects of SBT stock
and the means by which scientific uncertainty in respect of those matters can best
be reduced.

. . . .

49. From the record placed before the Tribunal by both Parties, it is clear that the most acute elements of the dispute between the Parties turn on their inability to agree on a revised total allowable catch and the related conduct by Japan of unilateral experimental fishing in 1998 and 1999, as well as Japan's announced plans for such fishing thereafter. Those elements of the dispute were clearly within the mandate of the Commission for the Conservation of Southern Bluefin Tuna. It was there that the Parties failed to agree on a TAC. It was there that Japan announced in 1998 that it would launch a unilateral experimental fishing program; it was there that that announcement was protested by Australia and New Zealand; and the higher level protests and the diplomatic exchanges that followed refer to the Convention for the Conservation of Southern Bluefin Tuna and to the proceedings in the Commission. The Applicants requested urgent consultations with Japan pursuant to Article 16(1) of the Convention, which provides that, "if any dispute arises between two or more of the Parties concerning the interpretation or implementation of this Convention, those Parties shall consult among themselves with a view to having the dispute resolved . . . ." Those consultations took place in 1998, and they were pursued in 1999 in the Commission in an effort to reach agreement on a joint EFP. It was in the Commission in 1999 that a proposal by Japan to limit its catch to 1800 mt. under the 1999 EFP was made, and it was in the Commission that Australia indicated that it was prepared to accept a limit of 1500 mt. It was in the Commission that Japan stated, on May 26 and 28, 1999 that, unless Australia and New Zealand accepted its proposals for a joint EFP, it would launch a unilateral program on June 1. Proposals for mediation and arbitration made by Japan were made in pursuance of provisions of Article 16 of the CCSBT. In short, it is plain that all the main elements of the dispute between the Parties had been addressed within the Commission for the Conservation of Southern Bluefin Tuna and that the contentions of the Parties in respect of that dispute related to the implementation of their obligations under the 1993 Convention. They related particularly to Article 8 (3) of the Convention, which provides that, "For the conservation, management and optimum utilization of southern bluefin tuna: (a) the Commission shall decide upon a total allowable catch and its allocation among the Parties . . ." and to the powers of a Party in a circumstance where the Commission found itself unable so to decide.

50. There is in fact no disagreement between the Parties over whether the dispute falls within the provisions of the 1993 Convention. The issue rather is, does it also fall within the provisions of UNCLOS? The Applicants maintain that Japan has failed to conserve and to cooperate in the conservation of the SBT stock, particularly by its unilateral experimental fishing for SBT in 1998 and 1999. They find a certain tension between cooperation and unilateralism. They contend that Japan's unilateral EFP has placed it in breach of its obligations under Articles 64, 116, 117, 118 and 119 of UNCLOS, for the specific reasons indicated earlier in this Award (in paragraphs 33 and 41). Those provisions, they maintain, lay down applicable norms by which the lawfulness of Japan's conduct can be evaluated. They point out that, once the dispute had ripened, their diplomatic notes and other demarches to Japan made repeated reference to Japan's obligations not only under the 1993 Convention but also under UNCLOS and customary international law.

51. Japan for its part maintains that such references were belated and were made for the purpose of permitting a request to ITLOS for provisional measures. It contends that the invoked articles of UNCLOS are general and do not govern the particular dispute between the Parties. More than that, Japan argues that UNCLOS is a framework or umbrella convention that looks to implementing conventions to give it effect; that Article 64 provides for cooperation "through appropriate international organizations" of which the Commission is an exemplar; that any relevant principles and provisions of UNCLOS have been implemented by the establishment of the Commission and the Parties' participation in its work; and that the *lex specialis* of the 1993 Convention and its institutional expression have subsumed, discharged and eclipsed any provisions of UNCLOS that bear on the conservation and optimum utilization of Southern Bluefin Tuna. Thus Japan argues that the dispute falls solely within the provisions of the 1993 Convention and in no measure also within the reach of UNCLOS.

52. The Tribunal does not accept this central contention of Japan. It recognizes that there is support in international law and in the legal systems of States for the application of a lex specialis that governs general provisions of an antecedent treaty or statute. But the Tribunal recognizes as well that it is a commonplace of international law and State practice for more than one treaty to bear upon a particular dispute. There is no reason why a given act of a State may not violate its obligations under more than one treaty. There is frequently a parallelism of treaties, both in their substantive content and in their provisions for settlement of disputes arising thereunder. The current range of international legal obligations benefits from a process of accretion and cumulation; in the practice of States, the conclusion of an implementing convention does not necessarily vacate the obligations imposed by the framework convention upon the parties to the implementing convention. The broad provisions for the promotion of universal respect for and observance of human rights, and the international obligation to co-operate for the achievement of those purposes, found in Articles 1, 55 and 56 of the Charter of the United Nations, have not been discharged for States Parties by their ratification of the Human Rights Covenants and other human rights treaties. Moreover, if the 1993 Convention were to be regarded as having fulfilled and eclipsed the obligations of UNCLOS that bear on the conservation of SBT, would those obligations revive for a Party to the CCSBT that exercises its right under Article 20 to withdraw from the Convention on twelve months notice? Can it really be the case that the obligations of UNCLOS in respect of a migratory species of fish do not run between the Parties to the 1993 Convention but do run to third States that are Parties to UNCLOS but not to the 1993 Convention? Nor is it clear that the particular provisions of the 1993 Convention exhaust the extent of the relevant obligations of UNCLOS. In some respects, UNCLOS may be viewed as extending beyond the reach of the CCSBT. UNCLOS imposes obligations on each State to take action in relation to its own nationals: "All States have the duty to take . . . such measures for their respective nationals as may be necessary for the conservation of the living resources of the high seas" (Article 117). It debars discrimination "in form or fact against the fishermen of any State" (Article 119). These provisions are not found in the CCSBT; they are operative even where no TAC has been agreed in the CCSBT and where co-operation in the Commission has broken down. Article 5 (1) of the CCSBT provides that, "Each Party shall take all action necessary to ensure the

enforcement of this Convention and compliance with measures which become binding . . . ." But UNCLOS obligations may be viewed not only as going beyond this general obligation in the foregoing respects but as in force even where "measures" being considered under the 1993 Convention have not become binding thereunder. Moreover, a dispute concerning the interpretation and implementation of the CCSBT will not be completely alien to the interpretation and application of UNCLOS for the very reason that the CCSBT was designed to implement broad principles set out in UNCLOS. For all these reasons, the Tribunal concludes that the dispute between Australia and New Zealand, on the one hand, and Japan on the other, over Japan's role in the management of SBT stocks and particularly its unilateral experimental fishing program, while centered in the 1993 Convention, also arises under the United Nations Convention on the Law of the Sea. In its view, this conclusion is consistent with the terms of UNCLOS Article 311(2) and (5), and with the law of treaties, in particular Article 30(3) of the Vienna Convention on the Law of Treaties.[41]

53. This holding, however, while critical to the case of the Applicants, is not dispositive of this case. It is necessary to examine a number of articles of Part XV of UNCLOS. Article 286 introduces section 2 of Part XV, a section entitled, "Compulsory Procedures Entailing Binding Decisions." Article 286 provides that, "Subject to section 3, any dispute concerning the interpretation or application of this Convention shall, where no settlement has been reached by recourse to section 1, be submitted at the request of any party to the dispute to the court or tribunal having jurisdiction under this section." Article 286 must be read in context, and that qualifying context includes Article 281(1) as well as Articles 279 and 280. Under Article 281(1), if the States which are parties to a dispute concerning the interpretation or application of UNCLOS (and the Tribunal has just held that this is such a dispute) have agreed to seek settlement of the dispute "by a peaceful means of their own choice," the procedures provided for in Part XV of UNCLOS apply only (a) where no settlement has been reached by recourse to such means and (b) the agreement between the parties "does not exclude any further procedure."

54. The Tribunal accepts Article 16 of the 1993 Convention as an agreement by the Parties to seek settlement of the instant dispute by peaceful means of their own choice. It so concludes even though it has held that this dispute, while centered in the 1993 convention, also implicates obligations under UNCLOS. It does so because the Parties to this dispute — the real terms of which have been defined above — are the same Parties grappling not with two separate disputes but with what in fact is a single dispute arising under both Conventions. To find that, in this case, there is a dispute actually arising under UNCLOS which is distinct from the dispute that arose under the CCSBT would be artificial.

55. Article 16 is not "a" peaceful means; it provides a list of various named procedures of peaceful settlement, adding "or other peaceful means of their own choice." No particular procedure in this list has thus far been chosen by the Parties

---

[41] Article 30(3) of the Vienna Convention on the Law of Treaties provides: When all the parties to an earlier treaty are parties also to the later treaty but the earlier treaty is not terminated or suspended in operation under Article 59, the earlier treaty applies only to the extent that its provisions are compatible with those of the later treaty.

for settlement of the instant dispute. Nevertheless — bearing in mind the reasoning of the preceding paragraph — the Tribunal is of the view that Article 16 falls within the terms and intent of Article 281(1), as well as Article 280. That being so, the Tribunal is satisfied about fulfillment of condition (a) of Article 281(1). The Parties have had recourse to means set out in Article 16 of the CCSBT. Negotiations have been prolonged, intense and serious. since in the course of those negotiations, the Applicants invoked UNCLOS and relied upon provisions of it, while Japan denied the relevance of UNCLOS and its provisions, those negotiations may also be regarded as fulfilling another condition of UNCLOS, that of Article 283, which requires that, when a dispute arises between States Parties concerning UNCLOS' interpretation or application, the parties to the dispute shall proceed expeditiously to an exchange of views regarding its settlement by negotiation or other peaceful means. Manifestly, no settlement has been reached by recourse to such negotiations, at any rate, as yet. It is true that every means listed in Article 16 has not been tried; indeed, the Applicants have not accepted proposals of Japan for mediation and for arbitration under the CCSBT, essentially, it seems, because Japan was unwilling to suspend pursuance of its unilateral EFP during the pendency of such recourse. It is also true that Article 16(2) provides that failure to reach agreement on reference of a dispute to the International Court of Justice or to arbitration "shall not absolve parties to the dispute from the responsibility of continuing to seek to resolve it by any of the various peaceful means referred to in paragraph 1 above." But in the view of the Tribunal, this provision does not require the Parties to negotiate indefinitely while denying a Party the option of concluding, for purposes of both Articles 281(1) and 283, that no settlement has been reached. To read Article 16 otherwise would not be reasonable.

56. The Tribunal now turns to the second requirement of Article 281(1): that the agreement between the parties "does not exclude any further procedure." This is a requirement, it should be recalled, for applicability of "the procedures provided for in this Part," that is to say, the "compulsory procedures entailing binding decisions" dealt with in section 2 of UNCLOS Part XV. The terms of Article 16 of the 1993 Convention do not expressly and in so many words exclude the applicability of any procedure, including the procedures of section 2 of Part XV of UNCLOS.

57. Nevertheless, in the view of the Tribunal, the absence of an express exclusion of any procedure in Article 16 is not decisive. Article 16(1) requires the parties to "consult among themselves with a view to having the dispute resolved by negotiation, inquiry, mediation, conciliation, arbitration, judicial settlement or other peaceful means of their own choice." Article 16(2), in its first clause, directs the referral of a dispute not resolved by any of the above-listed means of the parties' "own choice" for settlement "to the International Court of Justice or to arbitration" but "with the consent in each case of all parties to the dispute." The ordinary meaning of these terms of Article 16 makes it clear that the dispute is not referable to adjudication by the International Court of Justice (or, for that matter, ITLOS), or to arbitration, "at the request of any party to the dispute" (in the words of UNCLOS Article 286). The consent in each case of all parties to the dispute is required. Moreover, the second clause of Article 16(2) provides that "failure to reach agreement on reference to the International Court of Justice or to arbitration shall not absolve the parties to the dispute from the responsibility of continuing to seek

to resolve it by any of the various peaceful means referred to in paragraph 1 above." The effect of this express obligation to continue to seek resolution of the dispute by the listed means of Article 16(1) is not only to stress the consensual nature of any reference of a dispute to either judicial settlement or arbitration. That express obligation equally imports, in the Tribunal's view, that the intent of Article 16 is to remove proceedings under that Article from the reach of the compulsory procedures of section 2 of Part XV of UNCLOS, that is, to exclude the application to a specific dispute of any procedure of dispute resolution that is not accepted by all parties to the dispute. Article 16(3) reinforces that intent by specifying that, in cases where the dispute is referred to arbitration, the arbitral tribunal shall be constituted as provided for in an annex to the 1993 Convention, which is to say that arbitration contemplated by Article 16 is not compulsory arbitration under section 2 of Part XV of UNCLOS but rather autonomous and consensual arbitration provided for in that CCSBT annex.

59. For all these reasons, the Tribunal concludes that Article 16 of the 1993 Convention "exclude[s] any further procedure" within the contemplation of Article 281(1) of UNCLOS.

65. It follows from the foregoing analysis that this Tribunal lacks jurisdiction to entertain the merits of the dispute brought by Australia and New Zealand against Japan. Having reached this conclusion, the Tribunal does not find it necessary to pass upon questions of the admissibility of the dispute, although it may be observed that its analysis of provisions of UNCLOS that bring the dispute within the substantive reach of UNCLOS suggests that the dispute is not one that is confined to matters of scientific judgment only. It may be added that this Tribunal does not find the proceedings brought before ITLOS and before this Tribunal to be an abuse of process; on the contrary, as explained below, the proceedings have been constructive.

66. In view of this Tribunal's conclusion that it lacks jurisdiction to deal with the merits of the dispute, and in view of the terms of Article 290(5) of UNCLOS providing that, "Once constituted, the tribunal to which the dispute has been submitted may modify, revoke or affirm those provisional measures . . . ," the Order of the International Tribunal for the Law of the Sea of August 27, 1999, prescribing provisional measures, shall cease to have effect as of the date of the signing of this Award.

NOTES AND QUESTIONS

1.   Do you agree with the narrow approach taken by the arbitral panel (4 votes to 1) to jurisdiction and dispute settlement under Part XV of UNCLOS? Do you agree with the arbitral tribunal's interpretation of UNCLOS Article 281? Would not the tribunal's broad reading of Article 281 catch all dispute resolution procedures in parallel international instruments rather than being limited to specific agreements to seek a settlement of an UNCLOS dispute outside the framework of Part XV? In relation to the second requirement of Article 281, the tribunal ruled that Article 16 of the CCSBT "exclude[d] any further procedure" and therefore rendered Part XV of UNCLOS inoperable. Do you agree? Consider the full text of Article 16:

1. If any dispute arises between two or more of the Parties concerning the interpretation or implementation of this Convention, those Parties shall consult among themselves with a view to having the dispute resolved by negotiation, inquiry, mediation, conciliation, arbitration, judicial settlement or other peaceful means of their own choice.

2. Any dispute of this character not so resolved shall, with the consent in each case of all parties to the dispute, be referred for settlement to the International Court of Justice or to arbitration; but failure to reach agreement shall not a solve parties to the dispute from the responsibility of continuing to seek to resolve it by any of the various peaceful means referred to in paragraph 1 above.

3. In cases where the dispute is referred to arbitration, the arbitral tribunal shall be constituted as provided in the Annex to this Convention. The Annex forms and integral part of this Convention.

2. The Southern Bluefin Tuna Case was the very first arbitration under Annex VII of the UNCLOS. What are the implications of the case for the dispute settlement provisions of UNCLOS? Are not the dispute settlement provisions of UNCLOS, which were intended to be compulsory, in fact highly vulnerable to displacement?

3. The Southern Bluefin Tuna Award casts doubt on the correctness of the adjudications of the ITLOS and the acumen and expertise of the ITLOS judges. Should the arbitration panel have given more deference to the decision of the ITLOS? Did the ITLOS make a mistake in formulating the findings in its Order in conclusory fashion without any accompanying legal analysis?

4. Tim Stephens of the University of Sydney, in his book, International Courts and Environmental Protection (Cambridge: Cambridge University Press, 2009), p. 228, states that "The practical effect of the Southern Bluefin Tuna Award is to allow unsustainable high seas fishing to continue while precluding direct enforcement of the duty of all states to conserve and manage living [marine] resources." Do you agree?

5. Is the result in these cases indicative of the fragmentation in the governance of international environmental disputes? International environmental disputes are subject to a jurisdictional patchwork that is without any systematic organization. How can this problem be overcome? Should there be a supreme international environmental appeals court of some kind?

Section IX. WHALES AND MARINE MAMMALS

UNCLOS Article 65 requires states to "cooperate with a view to the conservation of marine mammals and in the case of cetaceans shall in particular work through the appropriate international organizations for their conservation, management and study." The conservation of many marine mammals, such as seals, sea lions and polar bears is left to national laws; some nations, such as the United States[42] and

---

[42] Marine Mammal Protection Act, 16 U.S.C. § 1361 et seq.

New Zealand[43], have passed Marine Mammal Protection Acts, granting these animals total protection within their nation al territories. Whales are covered by an important international instrument, the International Convention for the Regulation of Whaling (1946), which is reprinted in the **Document Supplement**. Eighty-nine state parties have accepted the Whaling Convention, whose principal body is the International Whaling Commission (IWC), which meets at least once each year. The IWC's work includes the regulation of whaling and the promotion of conservation initiatives. The only quotas presently set by the Commission concern Aboriginal Subsistence Whaling. The IWC is also responsible for setting quotas for commercial whaling, but since 1985, those quotas have been set at zero. On the Commission, each member of the Convention has one vote. Decisions of the Commission are taken by majority vote, except that a three-fourths majority of those members voting is required for action relating to Article V of the Convention: conservation and utilization of whale resources, protected species, open and closed seasons, open and closed waters, sanctuary areas, size limits, time, method and intensity of whaling, types and specification of equipment and gear, methods of measurement, and catch returns and other statistical records. Even in the case of the adoption of a regulation concerning one of these matters, any party can utilize an objection procedure in Article V para. 3 so that it will not be bound by a decision of the Commission. Article VIII permits a party to the Convention to grant to any of its nationals a special permit to kill, take and treat whales for purposes of scientific research, "subject to . . . conditions as the Contracting Government thinks fit."

In 1982 the IWC adopted a commercial whaling moratorium effective from the 1985/86 season that is in effect today. However, Norway and Iceland take whales commercially, having invoked the objection procedure against the moratorium. The IWC has established two whale sanctuaries: the Indian Ocean Sanctuary and the waters of the Southern Ocean around Antarctica. Japan for many years has authorized the taking of whales under the Research Permit Article VIII of the Convention. South Korea has announced that it will resume whaling under this article as well. In 2005, Japan announced its intention to take a maximum of 850 minke whales and 10 fin whales per year under its JARPA II whale research program.

NOTE ON THE INTERNATIONAL CONVENTION FOR THE REGULATION OF WHALING (1946)

The International Convention for the Regulation of Whaling (ICRW) (1946) is reprinted in the **Document Supplement**. 89 nations are parties to this Convention. Read the provisions of this Convention and consider the following questions:

1.   What is the coverage of the ICRW? Does it concern all cetaceans (some 80 species) or just 13 species of "great" whales? Does it concern especially endangered species?

2.   What is the objective of the ICRW? Is the objective preservation of cetaceans

---

[43] Marine Mammals Protection Act, NZ Public Law No. 80 (1978).

or to ensure their future economic exploitation?

3. How are decisions taken by the International Whaling Commission? *See* Article III.

4. Can state-parties be bound by decisions of the Commission against their will? See Article V.

5. Article VIII concerns "research" whaling. Is research whaling defined? What is research whaling?

6. How are disputes relating to whaling settled under the Convention?

7. Two states engage in commercial whaling within their EEZs: Norway and Iceland. Only Japan carries out extensive "research" whaling under Article VIII. Why do you think Japan characterizes its whaling as "research" whaling? Whale products are commonly sold commercially in Japan.

8. The United States and many other nations have singled out Japan for criticism over its whaling activities. Under the U.S. Marine Mammal Protection Act,[44] the United States prohibits not only the taking of whales within its EEZ, but also prohibits the importation of marine mammals and marine mammal products into the United States. Under the U.S. Endangered Species Act, the United States prohibits imports of products derived from whales that are on the endangered species list.[45] The United States has also announced that it will not enter into any Governing International Fishing Agreement (GIFA) with Japan. Since a GIFA is a prerequisite for fishing in the U.S. EEZ, this action effectively bars Japanese vessels from fishing in U.S. waters. However, Japan has already been barred from fishing in U.S. waters by the action of U.S. fisheries councils and has not sought to fish in U.S. waters since 1988.[46] Under the Pelly Amendment of 1971, 22 U.S.C. § 1978, if the Secretary of Commerce certifies to the President that nationals of a foreign state are diminishing the effectiveness of an international fishery conservation program, the President has discretion to ban the importation of fishery products from that state. The Pelly Amendment was invoked against Japan by the Department of Commerce in 2000, but President Clinton declined to invoke trade sanctions.[47]

9. Japan's whaling activities in the southern ocean have generated particular controversy as is evident in the following case:

---

[44] 16 U.S.C. § 1361 et seq.

[45] 16 U.S.C. § 1538(a)(1)(A).

[46] *See*, Note, *U.S. Sanctions against Japan for Whaling*, 95 Am. J. Int'l L. 149 (2001).

[47] *Id.*

INSTITUTE OF CETACEAN RESEARCH v. SEA SHEPHERD CONSERVATION SOCIETY

725 F.3d 940 (9th Cir. 2013)

KOZINSK, CHIEF JUDGE:

You don't need a peg leg or an eye patch. When you ram ships; hurl glass containers of acid; drag metal-reinforced ropes in the water to damage propellers and rudders; launch smoke bombs and flares with hooks; and point high-powered lasers at other ships, you are, without a doubt, a pirate, no matter how high-minded you believe your purpose to be.

Plaintiffs-Appellants (collectively, "Cetacean") are Japanese researchers who hunt whales in the Southern Ocean. The United States, Japan and many other nations are signatories to the International Convention for the Regulation of Whaling art. VIII, Dec, 2, 1946, 62 Stat. 1716, 161 U.N.T.S. 74, which authorizes whale hunting when conducted in compliance with a research perm it issued by a signatory. Cetacean has such a permit from Japan. Nonetheless, it has been hounded on the high seas for years by a group calling itself Sea Shepherd Conservation Society and its eccentric founder, Paul Watson (collectively "Sea Shepherd"). Sea Shepherd's tactics include all of those listed in the previous paragraph.

Cetacean sued under the Alien Tort Statute, 2 8 U.S.C. § 1350, for injunctive and declaratory relief. The statute provides a cause of action for "a tort . . . committed in violation of the law of nations or a treaty of the United States." 28 U.S.C. § 1350. Cetacean argues that Sea Shepherd's acts amount to piracy and violate international agreements regulating conduct on the high seas. The district court denied Cetacean's request for a preliminary injunction and dismissed its piracy claims. We have jurisdiction over the order denying the injunction pursuant to 28 U.S.C. § 1292 (a). We also have jurisdiction to review the dismissal of the piracy claims because the district court's reasoning for dismissing them is "inextricably intertwined with" its reasons for denying the preliminary injunction. *Smith v. Arthur Andersen LLP*, 421 F.3d 989, 998 (9th Cir. 2005) (internal quotation marks omitted).

I. DISMISSAL OF THE PIRACY CLAIMS

We review the district court's dismissal of Cetacean's piracy claims de novo. "[The definition of piracy under the law of nations . . . [is] spelled out in the UNCLOS, as well as the High Seas Convention," which provide almost identical definitions. *United States v. Dire*, 680 F.3d 446, 469 (4th Cir. 2012); see United Nations Convention on the Law of the Sea ("UNCLOS"), art. 101, Dec. 10, 1982, 1833 U.N.T.S. 397; Convention on the High Seas, art. 15, Apr. 29, 1958, 13 U.S.T. 2312, 450 U.N.T.S. 82. The UNCLOS defines "piracy" as "illegal acts of *violence* or detention, or any act of depredation, committed for private ends by the crew or the passengers of a private ship . . . and directed . . . on the high seas, against another ship . . . or against persons or property on board such ship." UNCLOS art. 101 emphasis added); see also Convention on the High Seas art. 15.

The district court's analysis turns on an erroneous interpretation of "private ends" and "violence." The district court construed "private ends" as limited to those pursued for "financial enrichment." But the common understanding of "private" is far broader. The term is normally used as an antonym to "public" (*e.g.*, private attorney general) and often refers to matters of a personal nature that are not necessarily connected to finance (e.g., private property, private entrance, private understanding and invasion of privacy). See Webster's New Int'l Dictionary 1969 (2d. ed. 1939) (defining "private" to mean "[b]elonging to, or concerning, an individual person, company, or interest").

We give words their ordinary meaning unless the context requires otherwise. The context here is provided by the rich history of piracy law, which defines acts taken for private ends as those not taken on behalf of a state. See Douglas Guilfoyle, Piracy Off Somalia : UN Security Council Resolution 1816 and IMO Regional Counter Piracy Efforts, 57 Int'l & Comp. L.Q. 690, 693 (2008) (discussing the High Seas Convention); Michael Bahar, Attaining Optimal Deterrence at Sea: A Legal and Strategic Theory for Naval Anti-Piracy Operations, 40 VAND. J. TRANSNAT'L L. 1, 32 (2007); *see also Harmony v. United States*, 43 U.S. (2 How.) 210, 232 (1844) ("The law looks to [piracy] as an act of hostility . . . being committed by a vessel not commissioned and engaged in lawful warfare."). Belgian courts, perhaps the only ones to have previously considered the issue, have held that environmental activism qualifies as a private end. See Cour de Cassation [Cass.] [Court of Cassation] *Castle John v. NV Mabeco*, Dec. 19, 1986, 77 I.L.R. 537 (Belg.). This interpretation is "entitled to considerable weight." Abbott v. Abbott, 130 S. Ct. 1983, 1993 (2010) (internal quotation marks omitted). We conclude that "private ends" include those pursued on personal, moral or philosophical grounds, such as Sea Shepherd's professed environmental goals. That the perpetrators believe themselves to be serving the public good does not render their ends public. The district court's interpretation of "violence" was equally off-base. Citing no precedent, it held that Sea Shepherd's conduct is not violent because it targets ships and equipment rather than people. This runs a foul of the UNCLOS itself, which prohibits "violence . . . against another ship" and "violence . . . against persons or property." UNCLOS art. 101. Reading "violence" as extending to malicious acts against inanimate objects also comports with the commonsense understanding of the term, see Webster's New Int'l Dictionary 2846, as when a man violently pounds a table with his fist. Ramming ships, fouling propellers and hurling fiery and acid-filled projectiles easily qualify as violent activities, even if they could somehow be directed only at inanimate objects.

Regardless, Sea Shepherd's acts fit even the district court's constricted definition. The projectiles directly endanger Cetacean's crew, as the district court itself recognized. And damaging Cetacean's ships could cause them to sink or become stranded in glacier- filled, Antarctic waters, jeopardizing the safety of the crew.

The activities that Cetacean alleges Sea Shepherd has engaged in are clear instances of violent acts for private ends, the very embodiment of piracy. The district court erred in dismissing Cetacean's piracy claims.

II. PRELIMINARY INJUNCTION

"A plaintiff seeking a preliminary injunction must establish [1] that he is likely to succeed on the merits, [2] that he is likely to suffer irreparable harm in the absence of preliminary relief, [3] that the balance of equities tips in his favor, and [4] that an injunction is in the public interest." *Winter v. Natural Res. Def. Council Inc.*, 555 U.S. 7, 20 (2008). We review the district court's denial of the preliminary injunction for abuse of discretion. *Harris v. Bd. of Supervisors, L.A. Cnty.*, 366 F.3d 754, 760 (9th Cir. 2004). "A district court would necessarily abuse its discretion if it based its ruling on an erroneous view of the law or on a clearly erroneous assessment of the evidence."

A. Likelihood of Success

Cetacean sought its injunction pursuant to three international agreements: the Convention for the Suppression of Unlawful Acts Against the Safety of Maritime Navigation ("SUA Convention"), art. 3, Mar. 10,1988, S. Treaty Doc. No. 101-1, 1678 U.N.T.S. 222, the UNCLOS and the Convention on the International Regulations for Preventing Collisions at Sea ("COLREGS"), Oct. 20, 1972, 28 U.S.T. 3459, 1050 U.N.T.S. 18.

1. The SUA Convention

The SUA Convention prohibits acts that endanger, or attempt to endanger, the safe navigation of a ship. SUA Convention art. 3. Cetacean presented uncontradicted evidence that Sea Shepherd's tactics could seriously impair its ability to navigate. The district court nonetheless concluded that, since Sea Shepherd has not yet disabled any of Cetacean's ships, it's unlikely it would succeed in the future. This was clear error. The district court overlooked the actual language of the Convention, which prohibits "endanger[ing]" safe navigation. Id. This requires only that Sea Shepherd create dangerous conditions, regardless of whether the harmful consequences ever come about. As to whether Sea Shepherd's tactics actually are dangerous, the record disc loses that it has rammed and sunk several other whaling vessels in the past.

The district court also erred by failing to recognize that Sea Shepherd, at the very least, attempted to endanger the navigation of Cetacean's ships. An attempt is sufficient to invoke the SUA Convention, even if unsuccessful. Sea Shepherd's repeated claims that its efforts are merely "symbolic" and "employed so as to ensure maximum safety" are disingenuous. How else can it explain that it has switched to metal-reinforced prop- fouling ropes? Reinforced ropes carry the same symbolic meaning as normal ropes, but they are far more destructive. Nor does symbolism require Sea Shepherd to bring its ships dangerously close to Cetacean's. The district court's conclusion that Cetacean wasn't likely to succeed on its SUA Convention claims rested on an implausible determination of the facts and an erroneous application of law; it was an abuse of discretion.

2. The UNCLOS

For the reasons explained above, Part I, supra, the district court erred in its assessment of Cetacean's UNCLOS piracy claims, and consequently abused its discretion in assessing the likelihood of success on these claims.

3. The COLREGS

The district court did find that Cetacean is likely to succeed on the merits of its claims under the COLREGS. The COLREGS state obligatory and universal norms for navigating ships so as to avoid collision. *Crowley Marine Services, Inc. v. Maritrans, Inc.*, 530 F.3d 1169, 1172–73 (9th Cir. 2008). Sea Shepherd deliberately navigates its ships dangerously close to Cetacean's ships. The district court's finding that this is likely a violation of the COLREGS is adequately supported by the record.

B. LIKELIHOOD OF IRREPARABLE HARM

The district court determined that "injury is possible, but not likely," even though it found that the projectiles Sea Shepherd launches at Cetacean's ships "are an obvious hazard to anyone who [sic] they might hit" and that Sea Shepherd navigates its ships "in such a way that a collision is highly likely." Sea Shepherd itself adorns the hulls of its ships with the names and national flags of the numerous whaling vessels it has rammed and sunk. *See* Appendix. The district court's observation that Cetacean hasn't yet suffered these injuries is beside the point. Cetacean's uncontradicted evidence is that Sea Shepherd's tactics could immobilize Cetacean's ships in treacherous Antarctic waters, and this is confirmed by common sense: A dangerous act, if committed often enough, will inevitably lead to harm, which could easily be irreparable.

C. BALANCE OF EQUITIES

The district court correctly found that the balance of equities favors Cetacean. As it noted, "[a]bsent an injunction, the whalers will continue to be the victims of Sea Shepherd's harassment," but "Sea Shepherd . . . points to no hardship that it will suffer if the court imposes an injunction."

D. PUBLIC INTEREST

"The public interest inquiry primarily addresses impact on non-parties rather than parties." *Bernhardt v. L.A. Cnty.*, 339 F.3d 920, 931 (9th Cir. 2003) (internal quotation marks omitted). This is particularly the case where "the impact of an injunction reaches beyond the parties, carrying with it a potential for public consequences." Stormans, Inc. v. Selecky, 586 F.3d 1109, 1139 (9th Cir. 2009). The primary public interests at issue here are the health of the marine ecosystem, Winter, 555 U.S. at 25–26; see also *Earth Island Inst. v. U.S. Forest Serv.*, 442 F.3d 1147, 1177 (9th Cir. 2006), and the safety of international waterways.

Where a valid law speaks to the proper level of deference to a particular public interest, it controls. Our laws defining the public interest in regards to whaling are the Whaling Convention Act and the Marine Mammal Protection Act, both of which permit whaling pursuant to scientific permits issued under the Whaling Convention. 16 U.S.C. § 1372; 16 U.S.C. § 916c. Cetacean's activities are covered by such a permit and thus are consistent with congressional policy as to the marine ecosystem.

Our laws also reflect a strong public interest in safe navigation on the high seas. As already discussed, Sea Shepherd's activities clearly violate the UNCLOS, the SUA Convention and the COLREGS; as such, they are at loggerheads with the public interest of the United States and all other seafaring nations in safe navigation of the high seas.

The district court also considered the interest in keeping U.S. courts out of the international political controversy surrounding whaling. But enjoining piracy sends no message about whaling; it sends the message that we will not tolerate piracy. This is hardly a controversial view, as evidenced by a joint statement from the United States, Australia, the Netherlands and New Zealand condemning dangerous activities in the Southern Ocean. Joint Statement on Whaling and Safety at Sea from the Governments of Australia, the Netherlands, New Zealand, and the United States: Call for Responsible Behavior in the Southern Ocean Whale Sanctuary (Dec. 13, 2011), available at http://www.state.gov/r/pa/prs/ps/2011/12/178704. htm. Refusing the injunction sends the far more troublesome message that we condone violent vigilantism by U.S. nationals in international waters.

The district court also rejected Cetacean's claims on international comity grounds. While there is a public interest in maintaining harmonious international relations, it's not a factor here. An Australian court has entered default judgment against Cetacean, purporting to enjoin it from whaling in Antarctic coastal waters over which Australia claims sovereignty. The district court's deference to Australia's judgment in that case was an abuse o f discretion. To begin, the district court misunderstood the Australian judgment, which addressed the legality of Cetacean's activities, not Sea Shepherd's. Whatever the status of Cetacean's whaling under Australian law, it gives Sea Shepherd no license to engage in piracy. It is for Australia, not Sea Shepherd, to police Australia's court orders.

Additionally, comity applies only if the foreign court has competent jurisdiction. But the United States doesn't recognize Australia's claims of sovereignty over Antarctic waters. See Note from U.S. Deputy Representative to the United Nations, to Secretary-General of the United Nations (Dec. 3, 2004); Note from Embassy of the United States, to Australian Department of Foreign Affairs and Trade (Mar. 31, 1995). By according comity to Australia's judgment, we would implicitly recognize Australia's jurisdiction, in contravention of the stated position of our government. The conduct of foreign affairs is within the exclusive province of the Executive, and we must defer to its views, see *Williams v. Suffolk Ins. Co.*, 38 U.S. (13 Pet.) 415, 420 (1839); *cf. Mingtai Fire Ins. Co. v. United Parcel Serv.*, 177 F.3d 1142 1147 (9th Cir. 1999).

E. UNCLEAN HANDS

An injunction is an equitable remedy. *Winter*, 555 U.S. at 32. While the Winter factors "are pertinent in assessing the propriety of any injunctive relief," id., traditional equitable considerations such as laches, duress and unclean hands may militate against issuing an injunction that otherwise meets Winter's requirements. Here, however, the district court abused its discretion in denying the injunction based on unclean hands.

The district court held that Cetacean's hands are unclean because, "[i] n flouting the Australian injunction, the whalers demonstrate their disrespect for a judgment of a domestic court." Because neither the United States nor Japan recognizes Australia's jurisdiction over any portion of the Southern Ocean, Cetacean owes no respect to the Australian order. Moreover, the unclean hands doctrine requires that the plaintiff have "dirtied [his hands] in acquiring the right he now asserts, or that the manner of dirtying renders inequitable the assertion of such rights against the defendant." *Republic Molding Corp. v. B. W. Photo Utils.*, 319 F. 2d 347, 349 (9th Cir. 1963). Cetacean has done nothing to acquire the rights to safe navigation and protection from pirate attacks; they flow automatically from customary international law and treaties. Nor is there anything remotely inequitable in seeking to navigate the sea lanes without interference from pirates.

*   *   *

The district court's orders denying Cetacean's preliminary injunction and dismissing its piracy claims are *REVERSED*. The preliminary injunction we issued on December 17, 2012, *Inst. of Cetacean Research v. Sea Shepherd Conservation Soc'y*, 702 F.3d 573 (9th Cir. 2012), will remain in effect until further order of this court. The district judge's numerous, serious and obvious errors identified in our opinion raise doubts as to whether he will be perceived as impartial in presiding over this high-profile case. The appearance of justice would be served if the case were transferred to another district judge, drawn at random, and we so order in accordance with the standing orders of the Western District of Washington. The panel retains jurisdiction over any further appeals or writs involving this case.

NOTE AND QUESTION

What impact will an injunction issued by a U.S. court have on the Sea Shepherd? On March 20, 2013, three Sea Shepherd vessels, the *Steve Irwin*, the *Bob Barker*, and the *Sam Simon*, returned to port in Australia claiming "victory" over Japan in the whaling wars. The group announced that the Japanese whaling vessel, *Nissin Maru*, had only captured about 75 whales, far fewer than its announced intentions.

Paul Watson, the founder of Sea Shepherd, was at an undisclosed location reportedly aboard the vessel *Brigitte Bardot*, seeking a guarantee that he may come into Australia without being arrested. Watson is under indictment in Japan and was arrested by Costa Rica in 2002 on charges relating to a confrontation with a shark-finning operation. Watson skipped bail after being arrested in Germany in 2012, and is wanted under an Interpol Red Notice. On March 22, 2013, Sea Shepherd filed suit in the Netherlands against Japan, charging piracy and attempted manslaughter in connection with various confrontations at sea in early 2013.

DISPUTE CONCERNING JAPAN'S JARPA II PROGRAM OF "SCIENTIFIC WHALING" (AUSTRALIA v. JAPAN)

International Court of Justice, Australia's Application Instituting Proceedings (31 May 2010)

[Australia's Application formally instituting suit against Japan in the International Court of Justice brings to a head the longstanding dispute between Australia and Japan concerning Japan's annual whale hunt in the Southern Pacific Ocean. In 2012, New Zealand formally intervened in the Case on the side of Australia. In its pleading, New Zealand stated that "As a member of the International Whaling Commission, New Zealand has an interest in ensuring that the IWC works effectively and that the International Whaling Convention is properly interpreted and applied. New Zealand has worked hard with Japan to try and find a permanent solution to whaling in the Southern Ocean. The government will use all avenues possible to bring to a halt Japanese whaling in the Southern Ocean."].

To the Registrar, International Court of Justice.

The undersigned being July authorized by the Government of Australia:

Introduction

1. On behalf of the Government of Australia and pursuant to Article 36, paragraphs 1 and 2 and Article 40 of the Statute of the Court and Article 38 of the Rules of Court, I have the honour to submit to the Court the present Application instituting proceedings against the Government of Japan.

2. The present Application concerns Japan's continued pursuit of a large-scale program of whaling under the Second Phase of its Japanese Whale Research Program under Special Permit in the Antarctic ("JARPA II"), in breach of obligations assumed by Japan under the International Convention for the Regulation of Whaling ("ICRW"), as well as its other international obligations for the preservation of marine mammals and the marine environment.

3. Australia has consistently opposed Japan's JARPA II program, both through individual protests and demarches and through relevant international forums, including the International Whaling Commission ("IWC").

The Court's Jurisdiction

4. The Court has jurisdiction over the present dispute in accordance with the provisions of Article 36, paragraph 2 of its Statute, by virtue of the operation of the declarations of acceptance made respectively by Australia, dated 22 March 2002 and by Japan, dated 9 July 2007.

Content of the Dispute

Japan's obligations under the ICRW

5. In 1982 the IWC adopted under Article V (1)(e) of the ICRW a "moratorium" on whaling for commercial purposes fixing the maximum catch of whales to be taken in any one season at zero. This was brought into effect by the addition of paragraph 10 (e) to the Schedule to the ICRW which provides that:

> "catch limits for the killing for commercial purposes of whales from all stocks for the 1986 coastal and the 1985-1986 pelagic seasons and thereafter shall be zero. This provision will be kept under review based upon the best scientific advice . . ."

Japan objected to paragraph 10 (e) within the prescribed period but subsequently withdrew its objection.

6. In 1994 the IWC adopted under Article V (1)(c) of the ICRW the Southern Ocean Sanctuary. This was brought into effect by the addition of paragraph 7 (b) of the Schedule to the ICRW which provides that:

> "commercial whaling. whether by pelagic operations or from land stations, is prohibited in a region designated as the Southern Ocean Sanctuary. This Sanctuary comprises the waters of the Southern Hemisphere southwards of the following line: starting from 40 degrees S, 50 degrees W: thence due east to 20 degrees E: thence due south to 55 degrees S: thence due east to 130 degrees E; thence due north to 40 degrees S: thence due east to 130 degrees W; thence due south to 60 degrees S: thence due east to 50 degrees W: thence due north to the point of beginning. This prohibition applies irrespective of the conservation status of baleen and toothed whale stocks in this Sanctuary, as may from time to time be determined by the Commission . . ."

Japan objected to paragraph 7 (h) within the prescribed period in relation to Antarctic minke whale stocks and has not subsequently withdrawn its objection.

7. Under the Schedule to the ICRW, Japan is therefore obliged:

   (a) by paragraph 10 (e), to refrain from killing all whale stocks for commercial purposes: and

   (b) by paragraph 7 (b), to refrain from commercial whaling in the Southern Ocean Sanctuary for all whale stocks other than minke whale stocks.

8. In accordance with Article 26 of the Vienna Convention on the Law of Treaties and with customary international law, Japan is obliged to perform those obligations in good faith.

Conduct of Japan

9. Following the introduction of the moratorium, Japan ostensibly ceased whaling for commercial purposes. But at virtually the same time Japan launched the "Japanese Whale Research Program under Special Permit in the Antarctic"

("JARPA I")[48] which it purported to justify by reference to Article VIII of the [ICRW, under which a Contracting Government may issue special permits to its nationals authorizing that national to "kill, take and treat whales for the purposes of scientific research . . ." (emphasis added).

10. JARPA I commenced in the 1987–1988 season and continued until the 2004–2005 season. The focus of JARPA I was the killing and taking of Antarctic minke whales (Balaenoptera honuerensis) within the Southern Ocean Sanctuary. Approximately 6,800 Antarctic minke whales were killed in Antarctic waters under JARPA I. This compares with a total of 840 whales killed globally by Japan for scientific research in the 31-year period prior to the moratorium. Whale meat caught during JARPA I was taken to Japan where it was placed on commercial sale.

11. JARPA II commenced in the 2005–2006 season with a two-year feasibility study. The full-scale JARPA II then commenced in the 2007–2008 season. Although Japan has purported to justify JARPA II by reference to the special permit provision in Article VIII of the ICRW, the scale of killing, taking and treating carried out under this program greatly outweighs any previous practice undertaken on the basis of scientific permits in the history of the IWC.

12. The focus of JARPA II is on the killing and taking not only of Antarctic minke whales but also of fin whales (Balaenoptera physalus), humpback whales (Megaptera novaeangliae) and possibly other species within the Southern Ocean Sanctuary. During the feasibility stage of JARPA II (2005–2006/2006–2007). 1364 Antarctic minke whales and 13 fin whales were killed; 551 Antarctic minke whales were killed during the 2007–2008 season; and 680 Antarctic minke whales and one fin whale were killed during the 2008–2009 season. Media reports suggest 506 Antarctic minke whales and one fin whale were killed in the 2009–2010 season, but these data have yet to be formally reported to the IWC. Whale meat caught during JARPA II has been taken to Japan where it has been placed on commercial sale. Japan maintains an annual quota for future seasons of JARPA II of 850 ± 10 % Antarctic minke whales. 50 fin whales and 50 humpback whales. Despite this annual quota, Japan has refrained from killing humpback whales as part of the JARPA II program.

13. In brief, the status of the whale stocks which are the principal focus of JARPA II is as follows:

14. *Minke whales*. There appears to have been a substantial decrease in the abundance estimates of Antarctic minke whales. This is evident from the data collected by the two, decadal long, circumpolar surveys conducted between 1985–1986 and 2003–2004 (CPII and CPIII). The several methods that have been presented to the Scientific Committee of the IWC all suggest a substantial decrease in the abundance estimates of Antarctic minke whales during the period of the surveys. The population structure of the Antarctic minke whales remains unknown, so there is a risk of depletion of small stocks.

15. *Fin whales*. Virtually nothing is known about the abundance or recovery of fin

---

[48] The whaling program is conducted pursuant to permits granted by the Japanese Government to the Institute of Cetacean Research, an organization established under Japanese law.

whales in the Southern Hemisphere and there is no assessment of these stocks underway by the Scientific Committee of the IWC. Following massive takings (750,000 between 1904 and 1979 in the Southern Hemisphere alone), fin whales were classified in the 1970s as protected stocks under the ICRW and have also been classified as "endangered" (at a very high risk of extinction) by the International Union for the Conservation of Nature (IUCN). Of the three species targeted by JARPA II, this is the one about which the least is known, but it is probable that they are still severely depleted relative to the pre-1904 population. There are limited indications of some recovery in population numbers in the Southern Hemisphere but no agreed population estimate exists. Also, the population structure of the Southern Hemisphere fin whales remains unknown. Accordingly, there is a risk of the depletion of small stocks.

16. *Humpback whales.* There are indications of recovery in some breeding stocks of humpback whales, including some stocks known to feed in Antarctic Areas IV and V (the regions of the JARPA II catches). However, ongoing research in Oceania indicates that some areas that had reasonably high numbers of whales (*e.g.*, New Zealand, New Caledonia, and Fiji), today have very few whales. Some of these depleted populations show little sign of recovery, and whales from these areas migrate into the JARPA II whaling grounds. Due to the mixing of highly depleted and less depleted breeding stocks on the feeding grounds, it is impossible to target only whales from less depleted breeding stocks in the Antarctic region. Whilst the JARPA II program has not yet killed any humpback whales, they remain listed on the description of the plan.

Refusal of Japan to Accept Recommendations of the IWC

17. Under Article VI of the ICRW the IWC may from time to time make recommendations to any or all parties on any matters which relate to whales or whaling and to the objectives and purposes of the ICRW which include, first and foremost, "safeguarding for future generations the great natural resources represented by the whale stocks."

18. The IWC has made numerous recommendations to Japan that it not proceed with JARPA II. It has done so against the background of earlier recommendations that special permit whaling must meet critically important research needs (1987): that it be conducted in a manner consistent with the Commission's conservation policy and ensure that the recovery of populations is not impeded (1987); that it only be permitted in exceptional circumstances (1995, 1998, 1999); that it be conducted using non-lethal techniques (1995–1999); and that it ensure the conservation of whales in sanctuaries (1995–1998).

19. In 2003 the IWC called on Japan to halt the JARPA program, or to revise it so that it is limited to non-lethal research methodologies. It recommended that no additional JARPA programs be considered until the Scientific Committee of the IWC had, amongst other things, completed an in-depth review of the results of sixteen years of JARPA, and further recommended that any such programs be limited to non-lethal research.

20. In 2005 the IWC:

"STRONGLY URGED the Government of Japan to withdraw its JARPA II proposal or to revise it so that any information needed to meet the stated objectives of the proposal is obtained using non-lethal means."

21. In 2007 the IWC:

"CALLED UPON the Government of Japan to suspend indefinitely the lethal aspects of JARPA II conducted within the Southern Ocean Whale Sanctuary."

22. Japan has refused to comply with any of these recommendations.

IWC Negotiations

23. In 2008 the IWC established a Small Working Group on the Future of the IWC, comprising 33 countries (including Australia and Japan), whose mandate included consideration of the issue of special research permits. In 2009, the IWC noted that the Small Working Group had not been able to reach its goal of agreeing a package or packages on the future of the IWC by IWC61 (2009). The IWC agreed "to intensify its efforts to conclude a package or packages by IWC62 (2010) at the latest," reconstituted the Small Working Group for a further year and formed a core Support group of 12 key countries (including Australia and Japan) to assist the Chair of the IWC in discussions on the Future of the IWC and to prepare material for submission to the Small Working Group, on the firm understanding that "nothing is agreed until everything is agreed."

24. The first product of Support Group negotiations, the draft "Consensus Decision to Improve the Conservation of Whales," was presented as an incomplete draft to the meeting of the Small Working Group in March 2010 under cover of the Chair's Report to the Small Working Group on the Future of the IWC.

25. The draft Consensus Decision addressed the taking of whales allegedly pursuant to Article VIII in the following terms:

"The Commission will continue to address the different views that exist amongst the members on key issues regarding whales and whaling; including research by special permit. . . . Proposals will be developed to address these issues for consideration during the initial five years of the arrangement."

26. In March 2010, Australia tabled a proposal in the small Working Group which, in addressing its concerns with the draft Consensus Decision, identified as one of its four major priorities that:

"Australia needs to see an immediate end to unilateral so-called "scientific" whaling purportedly conducted under Article VIII of the ICRW. From the outset, Australia has been clear that we consider any new approach must include an agreement to bring an immediate end to this form of whaling and must put in place a mechanism and timetable to address the reform of Article VIII of the ICRW to permanently end this practice."

27. The Support Group was unable to reach consensus on the draft Consensus Decision. On 22 April 2010 the IWC Chair and Vice-Chair produced a "compromise

text" for consideration by member Governments at IWC62 in June 2010, emphasizing that the proposed "Consensus Decision" it contained "does not represent an agreed approach of the Support Group or the SWG."

28. Under that proposal, whaling by special permit would be suspended for ten years and a Working Group would be established to continue to examine a number of issues, including research conducted by special permit. It would report omits progress to the Commission by 2013.

29. While Japan indicated a willingness to negotiate on the numbers and species targeted by its programs in the context of a negotiated package, it continued to reiterate the "scientific" justification for JARPA II and it purported legality under international law. It has become clear that current and proposed IWC processes cannot resolve the key legal issue that is the subject of the dispute between Australia and Japan, namely the legality of large-scale "special permit" whaling under JARPA II.

Refusal of Japan to Comply with other Bilateral and Multilateral Requests

30. Australia has consistently raised, both within and outside the IWC, its concerns over the JARPA II program, asking Japan on several occasions to withdraw or substantially revise it.

31. On 21 December 2007, Australia together with 29 other countries and the European commission sent an Aide Memoire to the Government of Japan to inform Japan of its "strong objection to the resumption of the second Japanese Whale Research Program under Special Permit in the Antarctic (JARPA II) . . . ." The Aide Memoire (reproduced at Annex 1) concluded by urging "Japan to join the international community and cease all its lethal scientific research on whales and assure the immediate return of the vessels which are implementing JARPA II."

32. Japan responded that it was fully aware of the strong reaction of the international community to its scientific whaling program and in particular it's proposed take of humpback whales. Japan states that the purpose of the program was to undertake research on the appropriate means of managing whaling and was in line with the relevant international conventions. Japan indicated that, while it would not change its research program, it would postpone its plans to hunt humpback whales as long as the process of "normalization" in the IWC proceeded.

33. Australia has appointed a Special Envoy on Whale conservation whose role is to engage with Japan, as well as other important IWWC partners, with a view to progressing Australia's position on Japan's special permit whaling programs. Discussions held by the Special Envoy with the Government of Japan have not resulted in any substantial modification or termination of the whaling program. Indeed Japan continues to reiterate the "scientific" justification for the JARPA II and its legitimacy under international law.

34. The focus of the present dispute is the conduct of Japan in proposing and implementing the JARPA II "scientific whaling" program in the Southern Ocean as described above. But it is relevant to note that Japan is also conducting, since 2000, a similar northern hemisphere program ("JARPN II"), which presents analogous

issues. Australia considers that the JARPN II also breaches Japan's international obligations.

Obligations Breached by Japan

35. In proposing and implementing JARPA II, Japan has breached and is continuing to breach its international obligations.

36. In particular, Japan has breached and is continuing to breach the following obligations under the ICRW:

(a)   the obligation under paragraph 10 (e) of the Schedule to the ICRW to observe in good faith the zero catch limit in relation to the killing of whales for commercial purposes; and

(b)   the obligation under paragraph 7 (b) of the Schedule to the ICRW to act in good faith to refrain from undertaking commercial whaling of humpback and fin whales in the Southern Ocean Sanctuary.

37. Moreover, having regard to the scale of the JARPA II program, to the lack of any demonstrated relevance for the conservation and management of whale stocks, and to the risks presented to targeted species and stocks, the JARPA II program cannot be justified under Article VIII of the ICRW.

38. Further, Japan has breached and is continuing to breach, *inter alia*, the following obligations:

(a)   under the Convention on International Trade in Endangered Species of Wild Fauna and Flora ("CITES")[49], the Fundamental Principles contained in Article II in relation to "introduction from the sea" of an Annex I listed specimen other than in "exceptional circumstances," and the conditions in Article III (5) in relation to the proposed taking of humpback whales under JARPA II; and

(b)   under the Convention on Biological Diversity, the obligations to ensure that activities within their jurisdiction or control do not cause damage to the environment of other States or of areas beyond the limits of national jurisdiction (Article 3), to co-operate with other Contracting Parties, whether directly or through a competent international organization (Article 5), and to adopt measures to avoid or minimize adverse impacts on biological diversity (Article 10 (h)).

39. These provisions are to be interpreted and applied in the light of each other, and of Japan's obligations under customary international law.

Remedies Sought By Australia

40. For these reasons, and reserving the right to supplement, amplify or amend the present Application, Australia requests the Court to adjudge and declare that Japan

---

[49] While all three whale species targeted by JARPA II are listed in Annex I of CITES, Japan has entered reservations as to minke and fin whales. Ed. Note: Annex I of CITES includes "all species threatened with extinction which are or may be affected by trade."

is in breach of its international obligations in implementing the JARPA II program in the Southern Ocean.

41. In addition, Australia requests the Court to order that Japan:

(a) cease implementation of JARPA II;

(b) revoke any authorizations, permits or licenses allowing the activities which are the subject of this application to be undertaken; and

(c) provide assurances and guarantees that it will not take any further action under the JARPA II or any similar program until such program has been brought into conformity with its obligations under international law.

NOTES AND QUESTIONS

Consider the allegations in Australia's Application to the ICJ. What result? For analysis, see Donald K. Anton, *Dispute Concerning Japan's JARPA II Program of "Scientific Whaling" (Australia v. Japan)* 14ASIL INSIGHT, (July 3, 2010), *available at* http://www.asil.org/insight.

(i) Jurisdictional Issues

1. Does the ICJ have jurisdiction over this dispute? Both Australia and Japan have accepted the "compulsory" jurisdiction of the ICJ under the "optional clause" of the Statute of the International Court of Justice, Art. 36 (2).

AUSTRALIA

22 March 2002

The Government of Australia declares that it recognises as compulsory ipso facto and without special agreement, in relation to any other State accepting the same obligation, the jurisdiction of the International Court of Justice in conformity with paragraph 2 of Article 36 of the Statute of the Court, until such time as notice may be given to the Secretary-General of the United Nations withdrawing this declaration. This declaration is effective immediately.

This declaration does not apply to:

(a) any dispute in regard to which the parties thereto have agreed or shall agree to have recourse to some other method of peaceful settlement;

(b) any dispute concerning or relating to the delimitation of maritime zones, including the territorial sea, the exclusive economic zone and the continental shelf, or arising out of, concerning, or relating to the exploitation of any disputed area of or adjacent to any such maritime zone pending its delimitation;

(c) any dispute in respect of which any other party to the dispute has accepted the compulsory jurisdiction of the Court only in relation to or for the purpose of the dispute; or where the acceptance of the Court's compulsory jurisdiction on behalf of any other party to the dispute was deposited less than 12 months prior to the filing of the application bringing the dispute before the Court.

DONE at Canberra this 21st day of March, two thousand and two.

(Signed) Alexander John Gosse Downer,

Minister for Foreign Affairs of Australia

JAPAN

9 July 2007

"I have the honour, by direction of the Minister for Foreign Affairs, to declare on behalf of the Government of Japan that, in conformity with paragraph 2 of Article 36 of the Statute of the International Court of Justice, Japan recognizes as compulsory ipso facto and without special agreement, in relation to any other State accepting the same obligation and on condition of reciprocity, the jurisdiction of the International Court of Justice, over all disputes arising on and after 15 September 1958 with regard to situations or facts subsequent to the same date and being not settled by other means of peaceful settlement.

This declaration does not apply to disputes which the parties thereto have agreed or shall agree to refer for final and binding decision to arbitration or Judicial settlement.

This declaration does not apply to any dispute in respect of which any other party to the dispute has accepted the compulsory jurisdiction of the International Court of Justice only in relation to or for the purpose of the dispute; or where the acceptance of the Court's compulsory jurisdiction on behalf of any other party to the dispute was deposited or ratified less than twelve months prior to the filing of the application bringing the dispute before the Court.

This declaration shall remain in force for a period of five years and thereafter until it may be terminated by a written notice."

New York, 9 July 2007

(Signed) Kenzo Oshima

Permanent Representative of Japan to the United Nations

Note that, although Australia has proclaimed an EEZ around its claimed territory in Antarctica,[50] Australia's Application to the ICJ does not allege that Japan has violated its national fishing or conservation regulations. Australia's claim to an Antarctic EEZ is very controversial and is disputed by many countries. Under the Antarctic Treaty of 1959, the continent of Antarctica is open to all for observation

---

[50] Seas and Submerged Lands Act of 1973 Proclamation, Commonwealth of Australia Gazette (Special), No. S290, 29 July 1994. (1994).

and scientific research (Article VII). Article IV (1) of the Antarctic Treaty provides, however, that "Nothing [in this] treaty shall be interpreted as . . . a renunciation . . . of . . . a claim to sovereignty" over any portion of Antarctica. However, Article IV(2) of this treaty forbids any enlargement of an existing claim. Thus, the Antarctic Treaty is ambiguous about the existence of an EEZ. The concept of a 200 mile EEZ was not accepted in international law in 1959, so it can be argued that Australia's claim is an enlargement of its sovereignty claim. Australia's entitlement to an Antarctic EEZ is accepted in Australian domestic law, and Australia's declaration of a whale sanctuary within its claimed EEZ in implementation of the IWC's Proclamation of a Southern Ocean Whale Sanctuary is accepted by Australian courts. In 2008, the Federal Court of Australia issued declaratory relief and an injunction against Kyodo Senpaku Kaisha Ltd, a Japanese whaling company operating in the Southern Ocean within the claimed Australian EEZ. *See Humane Society International Inc. v. Kyodo Senpaku Kaisha Ltd.*, [2008] FCA 3 (15 Jan. 2008). The result in this case is both praised and criticized. Compare Donald K. Anton, False Sanctuary: the Australian Antarctic Whale Sanctuary and Long-Term Stability in Antarctica, Cornell Law School Berger International Speaker Papers (9-19-2008); and Chris McGrath, Australia can lawfully stop whaling within its Antarctic EEZ, EDO NSW Seminar, Sydney, 21 February 2008.

Australia did not invoke the Antarctic Treaty for dispute settlement since the relevant provision, Article XI does not provide for compulsory jurisdiction. And of course the International Whaling Convention itself does not have any provision for dispute settlement.

Why did Australia not invoke dispute settlement under UNCLOS? *See* Article 297(3).

(ii) Merits Issues

2.   Read carefully the provisions of the International Convention on the Regulation of Whaling (ICRW), which is reprinted in the **Document Supplement**. Now read the allegations contained in paragraphs 5, 6, 7, and 8 of Australia's Application. Are these allegations common ground, or will Japan dispute these allegations? Consider Australia's use of the terms "ostensibly" and "purported" in these allegations.

3.   *The Conduct of Japan.* The allegations in paragraphs 9 to 16 are primarily factual assertions. Under the ICJ's Rules of Court (1978), parties may attach to their pleadings certified copies of documents in support of their allegations. (Art. SO). Parties may also introduce evidence through witnesses and experts. (Art. 57). The Court may ask the parties to provide additional evidence or explanations. (Arts. 62 and 67). The Court may also request information from any "public international organization." (Art. 69). The ICJ may want to ask the IWC or outside experts for information dealing with paragraphs 14, 15, and 16 of the Application.

4.   *The JWC recommendations and negotiations with Japan.* Paragraphs 17 to 34 detail the history of recommendations and negotiations with Japan.

5.   *Breaches of obligations by Japan.* Australia alleges two breaches of specific obligations contained in the Schedule to the ICRW. The crux of the dispute between

Australia and Japan is that Japan is conducting commercial whaling under the guise of research whaling. Why did Australia not allege a violation of ICRW Article VIII? Australia alleges only that the JARPA II program "cannot be justified under Article VIII." In light of the importance of this allegation, should Australia have provided more details as to why Article VIII is insufficient to justify Japan's conduct.

6. *Abuse of rights*. UNCLOS Article 300 prohibits "abuse of rights" and requires good faith. Why did Australia not allege an abuse of rights? The prohibition against abuse of rights is also a norm under customary international law. See Michael Byers, *Abuse of Rights: An Old Principle, A New Age*, 47 McGILL L. J. 389, 427–429 (2002); Gillian Triggs, *Japanese Scientific Whaling: An Abuse of Right or Optimum Utilization?*, 5 ASIAN-PACIFIC J. ENVT'L L. 33 (2002). How will this issue be decided? Will the outcome of the case turn on the evidence adduced by the parties as to the nature of scientific research with respect to whales? Is the matter of scientific research to be judged by objective criteria or is this matter up to the subjective determination of each individual party to the ICRW?

7. *Convention on International Trade in Endangered Species (CITES)*. Minke, Fin and Humpback whales are listed in Appendix I of CITES. Article 11(1) of CITES states that trade in an Appendix I endangered species "must be subject to particularly strict regulation in order not to endanger further their survival and must only be authorized in exceptional circumstances." Article III(5) of CITES states that the "introduction from the sea" of an Appendix I species may only be done with a Certificate from an appropriate scientific authority that certifies that three conditions have been met: (1) the action will not be detrimental to the survival of the species; (2) the recipient of the specimen is equipped to house and care for the specimen; and (3) the specimen will not be used for commercial purposes. Are these provisions applicable to the JARPA II program?

8. The Convention on Biological Diversity. Both of the obligations cited in the Australia Application are qualified by the phrase: "as far as possible and appropriate." Are these soft law obligations enforceable?

(iii) Remedies

9. *Remedies*. How do you evaluate the remedies asked by Australia? If the suit is successful, will whaling be ended in the Southern Ocean?

10. *Amendment of the ICRW*. How do you evaluate the ICRW as a legal instrument? What amendments would you suggest? A dispute resolution procedure? A compliance procedure? Should enforcement of the Convention be left to the individual parties or be within the remit of the IWC?

NOTES ON THE OUTCOME OF THE JARPA II WHALING CASE

On 31 March 2014, the International Court of Justice (ICJ) handed down its opinion in the case, *Australia v. Japan* (New Zealand intervening).

1. *Jurisdiction.* The basis of the ICJ's jurisdiction was the declarations made by both parties under Article 36, paragraph 2, of the Court's Statute. Japan disputed the Court's jurisdiction, arguing that the dispute falls within Australia's reservation (b). The Court rejected this argument, holding that for this reservation to apply there must be a dispute concerning maritime delimitation between the parties. The Court ruled that there is no pending maritime delimitation dispute between the parties in the Antarctic Ocean.

2. ***Interpretation of Article VIII, paragraph 1 of the ICRW***. The Court stated that its standard of review and its task was to make an objective assessment of the reasonableness of Japan's authorization of scientific whaling under JARPA II in the light of the phrase "for purposes of scientific research" in Article VIII. The Court did not consider it necessary to provide a definition of "scientific research; rather it focused on the meaning of the term "for purposes of." The Court framed the issue as to whether the design and implementation of JARPA II are reasonable in relation to its stated research objectives.

3. ***Application of Article VIII, paragraph 1, to JARPA II***. The stated research objective of JARPA II is to demonstrate that the commercial hunting of whales is environmentally sustainable. The Court accepted the scientific research purpose of JARPA II; but the Court ruled that "the evidence does not establish that the programme's design and implementation are reasonable in relation to achieving its stated objectives." In this regard the Court pointed to (1) the use of lethal methods; (2) the scale of the use of lethal methods; (3) the fact that Japan launched JARPA II without waiting for the final review of the Scientific Committee of the IWC; (4) the open-ended time frame of the program; (5) its limited scientific output to date; and (6) the lack of cooperation with other scientific research programs in the Antarctic Ocean.

4. ***Violations of the Schedule***. The Court ruled that all whaling that falls outside Article VIII, paragraph 1, other than aboriginal subsistence whaling, is subject to paragraphs 7(b), 10(d) and 10(e) of the Schedule. The Court concluded that Japan accordingly has violated the IWC moratorium on commercial whaling; the factory ship moratorium; and the prohibition of commercial whaling in the Southern Ocean Sanctuary.

5. ***Remedies.*** The Court ordered that Japan revoke any extant authorization, permit or license to kill, take or treat whales in relation to JARPA II, and to refrain from granting any additional permits in pursuance of that program.

Japan has announced that it intends to comply with the Court's judgment. The Court's ruling applies only to the Antarctic Ocean, and Japan intends to resume whaling in the North Pacific, where it takes about 60 whales per year. Japan also intends to pursue a revised research program in the Antarctic Ocean. Norway and Iceland together kill about 550 minke whales in the Northeast Atlantic each year.

Consumption of whale meat in Japan has greatly declined in recent years, but some still consider it a delicacy. Because of low demand, the JAPAN TIMES reported (April 2, 2014) that unsold whale meat from the JARPA II hunt is piling up in warehouses in Japan.

Section X.   MARINE ECOSYSTEMS, BIODIVERSITY, AND MARINE PROTECTED AREAS

The marine ecosystems of the world are rich and varied. The United Nations Environment Programme[51] has identified 64 Large Marine Ecosystems (LME) adjacent to continental areas that are rich in biological productivity and biodiversity. These ecosystems produce about 95% of the world's annual marine fisheries catch and contribute an estimated $12.6 trillion in goods and services annually to the world's economy. LMEs have distinct bottom topography, oceanographic features such as currents or water circulation, biological productivity, and biodiversity, and are usually areas encompassing 200 000 square kilometers or more. Within each of these large ecosystems are hundreds of diverse types of additional ecosystems, each with its own distinctive hydrography, oceanography, and trophic relationships. All of these ecosystems are vulnerable to degradation through human activities, such as fishing down food webs, pollution, offshore resource exploitation, and shipping activities. In recent years there is a growing movement to take concrete steps to preserve sensitive marine ecosystems from degradation.

Many policy instruments call for ecosystem-based action to protect marine areas from degradation.

- UNCLOS Article 194, para. 5 provides that measure to protect the marine environment" shall include those necessary to protect and preserve rare or fragile ecosystems as well as the habitat of depleted, threatened or endangered species and other forms of marine life."

- Agenda 21, the Action Programme adopted in Rio de Janeiro by the United Nations Conference on Environment and Development in 1992, provides that "States should identify marine ecosystems exhibiting high levels of biodiversity and productivity and other critical habitat areas and provide necessary limitations on use in these areas, through . . . the designation of protected areas." (para. 17.86).

- The Plan of Implementation of the World Summit on Sustainable Development (Johannesburg, 2002) confirmed the need for "the establishment of marine protected areas consistent with international law." (para. 32, c).

- The UN Food and Agriculture Organization International Guidelines for the Management of Deep-Sea Fisheries in the High Seas (2008) call for conservation management measures to achieve long-term conservation and sustainable use of deep-sea fish stocks that ensure adequate protection for marine ecosystems. (para. 70).

- The 2010 Conference of the Parties to the United Nations Convention on Biological Diversity adopted a recommendation that encourages parties to establish marine protected areas for conservation and management of biodiversity. (Decision X/31).

---

[51] The UNEP Large Marine Ecosystems Report: UNEP Regional Seas Programme Report and Studies No. 182 (UNEP, 2008).

MAP OF LARGE MARINE ECOSYSTEMS (LMEs) WITHIN AND ADJACENT TO DESIGNATED REGIONAL SEAS

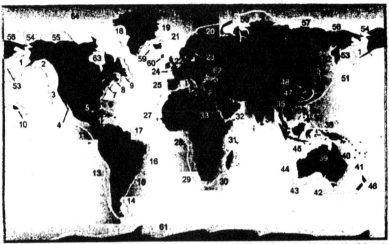

Regional Seas, West to East: North-East Pacific • South-East Pacific • Wider Caribbean • South-West Atlantic • West & Central Africa Mediterranean • Black Sea • Eastern Africa • Red Sea & Gulf of Aden • ROPME Sea Area • South Asian Seas • East Asian Seas • North-West Pacific • South Pacific **Partner programmes:** Arctic • North-East Atlantic • Baltic Sea • Caspian Sea • Antarctic

1 East Bering Sea	17 North Brazil Shelf	33 Red Sea	49 Kuroshio Current
2 Gulf of Alaska	18 West Greenland Shelf	34 Bay of Bengal	50 Sea of Japan / East Sea
3 California Current	19 East Greenland Shelf	35 Gulf of Thailand	51 Oyashio Current
4 Gulf of California	20 Barents Sea	36 South China Sea	52 Okhotsk Sea
5 Gulf of Mexico	21 Norwegian Sea	37 Sulu-Celebes Sea	53 West Bering Sea
6 Southeast US Continental Shelf	22 North Sea	38 Indonesian Sea	54 Chukchi Sea
7 Northeast US Continental Shelf	23 Baltic Sea	39 North Australian Shelf	55 Beaufort Sea
8 Scotian Shelf	24 Celtic Biscay Shelf	40 Northeast Australian Shelf	56 East Siberian Sea
9 Newfoundland-Labrador Shelf	25 Iberian Coastal	– Great Barrier Reef	57 Laptev Sea
10 Insular Pacific Hawaiian	26 Mediterranean Sea	41 East-Central Australian Shelf	58 Kara Sea
11 Pacific Central-American Coastal	27 Canary Current	42 Southeast Australian Shelf	59 Iceland Shelf
12 Caribbean Sea	28 Guinea Current	43 Southwest Australian Shelf	60 Faroe Plateau
13 Humboldt Current	29 Benguela Current	44 West-Central Australian Shelf	61 Antarctic
14 Patagonian Shelf	30 Agulhas Current	45 Northwest Australian Shelf	62 Black Sea
15 South Brazil Shelf	31 Somali Coastal Current	46 New Zealand Shelf	63 Hudson Bay
16 East Brazil Shelf	32 Arabian Sea	47 East China Sea	64 Arctic Ocean
		48 Yellow Sea	

Fig.1. Large Marine Ecosystems are areas of the ocean characterized by distinct bathymetry, hydrography, productivity, and trophic interactions. They annually produce 95% of the world's fish catch. They are national and regional focal areas of a global effort to reduce the degradation of linked watersheds, marine resources, and coastal environments from pollution, habitat loss, and over-fishing.

• The United Nations General Assembly adopted in 2010 Resolution 65/37 on "Oceans and the Law of the Sea" stressing the need for states to "intensify their effort" to conserve vulnerable marine ecosystems.

PROBLEM 7-14
Designating Marine Protected Areas

State *A*, an island state with a large territorial sea and exclusive economic zone, is active in assuring the protection of marine ecosystems within its jurisdiction. The legislature of State *A* has passed a Marine Sanctuaries Act under which defined areas of the ocean located in its territorial sea or EEZ may be formally designated as qualifying to be one of the following categories:

- A Marine Managed Area (MMA). A MMA is a named, discrete geographic marine or estuarine area designated by law and intended to protect, conserve, or otherwise manage a variety of resources and their uses.

- A Marine Reserve (MR). A MR is a discrete marine or estuarine area that is designated so the managing agency can achieve one or more of the following:

  1. Protect or restore rare, threatened, or endangered native plants, animals or habitats in marine areas;

  2. Protect or restore outstanding, representative, or imperiled marine species, communities, habitats and ecosystems;

  3. Protect or restore diverse gene pools; or

  4. Contribute to the understanding and management or marine resources and ecosystems by providing the opportunity for scientific research in outstanding marine habitats or ecosystems.

- A Marine Park (MP). A MP is a designated marine or estuarine area that possesses unique or distinctive characteristics and opportunities for spiritual, scientific, educational and recreational opportunities.

- A Marine Protected Area (MPA). An MPA is a designated marine or estuarine area that contains cultural objects of historical, archaeological and scientific interest or outstanding geological features.

State *A* has designated areas within its territorial sea and EEZ in all four of these categories together with management regulations for each area and is enforcing these under its national law.

Questions:

1. State *A* would like to gain international recognition for the areas it has designated under its national law. What avenues are open under international law to preserve and protect marine areas of these types?

2. State *A* is concerned about marine areas beyond national jurisdiction. State *A* is in the forefront of adopting restrictions prohibiting its own nationals from exploiting or disrupting areas beyond national jurisdiction that have unique gene pools, ecosystems, or geological or cultural characteristics. Is there any mechanism under international law to protect areas of the seas beyond national jurisdiction?

Consider the following Document:

ASSEMBLY OF THE INTERNATIONAL MARITIME ORGANIZATION RESOLUTION A.982(24)

Revised Guidelines for the Identification and Designation of Particularly Sensitive Sea Areas Adopted on 1 December 2005

1 INTRODUCTION

1.1 The Marine Environment Protection Committee (MEPC) of the International Maritime Organization (IMO) began its study of the question of Particularly Sensitive Sea Areas (PSSAs) in response to a resolution of the International Conference on Tanker Safety and Pollution Prevention of 1978. The discussions of this concept from 1986 to 1991 culminated in the adoption of Guidelines for the Designation of Special Areas and the Identification of Particularly Sensitive Sea Areas by Assembly resolution A. 720(17) in 1991. In a continuing effort to provide a clearer understanding of the concepts set forth in the Guidelines, the Assembly adopted resolutions A.885(21) and A.927(22). This document is intended to clarify and, where appropriate, strengthen certain aspects and procedures for the identification and designation of PSSAs and the adoption of associated protective measures. It sets forth revised Guidelines for the Identification and Designation of Particularly Sensitive Sea Areas (the Guidelines or PSSA Guidelines).

1.2 A PSSA is an area that needs special protection through action by IMO because of its significance for recognized ecological, socio-economic, or scientific attributes where such attributes may be vulnerable to damage by international shipping activities. At the time of designation of a PSSA, an associated protective measure', which meets the requirements of the appropriate legal instrument establishing such measure, must have been approved or adopted by IMO to prevent, reduce, or eliminate the threat or identified vulnerability. Information on each of the PSSAs that has been designated by IMO is available at www.imo.org.

1.3 Many international and regional instruments encourage the protection of areas important for the conservation of biological diversity as well as other areas with high ecological, cultural, historical/archaeological, socio-economic or scientific significance. These instruments further call upon their Parties to protect such vulnerable areas from damage or degradation, including from shipping activities.

1.4 The purpose of these Guidelines is to:

1. provide guidance to IMO Member Governments m the formulation and submission of applications for designation of PSSAs;

2. ensure that in the process all interests — those of the coastal State, flag State, and the environmental and shipping communities — are thoroughly considered on the basis of relevant scientific, technical, economic, and environmental information regarding the area at risk of damage from international shipping activities and the associated protective measures to prevent, reduce, or eliminate that risk; and

3. provide for the assessment of such applications by IMO.

1.5 Identification and designation of any PSSA and the adoption of associated protective measures require consideration of three integral components: the particular attributes of the proposed area, the vulnerability of such an area to damage by international shipping activities, and the availability of associated protective measures within the competence of IMO to prevent, reduce, or eliminate risks from these shipping activities.

3 PROCESS FOR THE DESIGNATION OF PARTICULARLY SENSITIVE SEA AREAS

3.1 The IMO is the only international body responsible for designating areas as Particularly Sensitive Sea Areas and adopting associated protective measures. An application to IMO for designation of a PSSA and the adoption of associated protective measures, or an amendment thereto, may be submitted only by a Member Government. Where two or more Governments have a common interest in a particular area, they should formulate a coordinated proposal. The proposal should contain integrated measures and procedures for co-operation between the jurisdictions of the proposing Member Governments.

3.2 Member Governments wishing to have IMO designate a PSSA should submit an application to MEPC based on the criteria outlined in section 4, provide information pertaining to the vulnerability of this area to damage from international shipping activities as called for in section 5, and include the proposed associated protective measures as outlined in section 6 to prevent, reduce or eliminate the identified vulnerability. Applications should be submitted in accordance with the procedures set forth in section 7 and the rules adopted by IMO for submission of documents.

4 ECOLOGICAL, SOCIO-ECONOMIC, OR SCIENTIFIC CRITERIA FOR THE IDENTIFICATION OF A PARTICULARLY SENSITIVE SEA AREA

4.1 The following criteria apply to the identification of PSSAs only with respect to the adoption of measures to protect such areas against damage, or the identified threat of damage, from international shipping activities.

4.4 In order to be identified as a PSSA, the area should meet at least one of the criteria listed below and information and supporting documentation should be provided to establish that at least one of the criteria exists throughout the entire proposed area, though the same criterion need not be present throughout the entire area. These criteria can be divided into three categories: ecological criteria; social, cultural, and economic criteria; and scientific and educational criteria.

Ecological criteria

    4.4.1   Uniqueness or rarity — An area or ecosystem is unique if it is "the only one of its kind." Habitats of rare, threatened, or endangered species that occur only in one area are an example. An area or ecosystem is rare if it only occurs in a few locations or has been seriously depleted across its range. An ecosystem may extend beyond country borders, assuming regional or international significance. Nurseries or certain feeding, breeding, or spawning areas may also be rare or unique.

    4.4.2   Critical habitat — A sea area that may be essential for the survival, function, or recovery of fish stocks or rare or endangered marine species, or for the support of large marine ecosystems.

4.4.3   Dependency — An area where ecological processes are highly dependent on biotically structured systems (e.g., coral reefs, kelp forests, mangrove forests, seagrass beds). Such ecosystems often have high diversity, which is dependent on the structuring organisms. Dependency also embraces the migratory routes of fish, reptiles; birds, mammals, and invertebrates.

4.4.4   Representativeness — An area that is an outstanding and illustrative example of specific biodiversity, ecosystems, ecological or physiographic processes, or community or habitat types or other natural characteristics.

4.4.5   Diversity — An area that may have an exceptional variety of species or genetic diversity or includes highly varied ecosystems, habitats, and communities.

4.4.6   Productivity — An area that has a particularly high rate of natural biological production. Such productivity is the net result of biological and physical processes which result in an increase in biomass in areas such as oceanic fronts, upwelling areas and some gyres.

4.4.7   Spawning or breeding grounds — An area that may be a critical spawning or breeding ground or nursery area for marine species which may spend the rest of their life-cycle elsewhere, or is recognized as migratory routes for fish, reptiles, birds, mammals, or invertebrates.

4.4.8   Naturalness — An area that has experienced a relative lack of human-induced disturbance or degradation.

4.4.9   Integrity — An area that is a biologically functional unit, an effective, self-sustaining ecological entity.

4.4.10 Fragility — An area that is highly susceptible to degradation by natural events or by the activities of people. Biotic communities associated with coastal habitats may have a low tolerance to changes in environmental conditions, or they may exist close to the limits of their tolerance (e.g., water temperature, salinity, turbidity or depth). Such communities may suffer natural stresses such as storms or other natural conditions (e.g., circulation patterns) that concentrate harmful substances in water or sediments, low flushing rates, and/or oxygen depletion. Additional stress may be caused by human intluences such as pollution and changes in salinity. Thus, an area already subject to stress from natural and/or human factors may be in need of special protection from further stress, including that arising from international shipping activities.

4.4.11 Bio-geographic importance — An area that either contains rare bio-geographic qualities or is representative of a bio-geographic "type" or types, or contains unique or unusual biological, chemical, physical, or geological features.

Social, cultural and economic criteria

4.4.12 Social or economic dependency — An area where the environmental quality and the use of living marine resources are of particular social or economic importance, including fishing, recreation, tourism, and the livelihoods of people who depend on access to the area.

4.4.13   Human dependency — An area that is of particular importance for the support of traditional subsistence or food production activities or for the protection of the cultural resources of the local human populations.

4.4.14   Cultural heritage — An area that is of particular importance because of the presence of significant historical and archaeological sites.

Scientific and educational criteria

4.4.15   Research — An area that has high scientific interest.

4.4.16   Baseline for monitoring studies — An area that provides suitable baseline conditions with regard to biota or environmental characteristics, because it has not had substantial perturbations or has been in such a state for a long period of time such that it is considered to be in a natural or near-natural condition.

4.4.17   Education — An area that otters an exceptional opportunity to demonstrate particular natural phenomena.

4.5 In some cases a PSSA may be identified within a Special Area and vice versa. It should be noted that the criteria with respect to the identification of PSSAs and the criteria for the designation of Special Areas are not mutually exclusive.

6 ASSOCIATED PROTECTIVE MEASURES

6.1 In the context of these Guidelines, associated protective measures for PSSAs are limited to actions that are to be, or have been, approved or adopted by IMO and include the following options:

6.1.1   designation of an area as a Special Area under MARPOL Annexes I, II or V, or a SO3 emission control area under MARPOL Annex VI, or application of special discharge restrictions to vessels operating in a PSSA. Procedures and criteria for the designation of Special Areas are contained in the Guidelines for the Designation of Special Areas set forth in annex I of Assembly resolution A.927(22). Criteria and procedures for the designation of SO_3 emission control areas are found in Appendix 3 to MARPOL Annex VI;

6.1.2   adoption of ships' routing and reporting systems near or in the area, under the International Convention for the Safety of Life at Sea (SOLAS) and in accordance with the General Provisions on Ships' Routeing and the Guidelines and Criteria for Ship Reporting Systems. For example, a PSSA may be designated as an area to be avoided or it may be protected by other ships' routing or reporting systems; and

6.1.3   development and adoption of other measures aimed at protecting specific sea areas against environmental damage from ships, provided that they have an identified legal basis.

6.2 Consideration should also be given to the potential for the area to be listed on the World Heritage List, declared a Biosphere Reserve, or included on a list of areas of international, regional, or national importance, or if the area is already the subject of such international, regional, or national conservation action or agreements.

6.3 In some circumstances, a proposed PSSA may include within its boundaries a buffer zone, in other words, an area contiguous to the site-specific feature (core area) for which specific protection from shipping is sought. However, the need for such a buffer zone should be justified in terms of how it would directly contribute to the adequate protection of the core area.

7 PROCEDURE FOR THE DESIGNATION OF PARTICULARLY SENSITIVE SEA AREAS AND THE ADOPTION OF ASSOCIATED PROTECTIVE MEASURES

7.1 An application for PSSA designation should contain a proposal for an associated protective measure that the proposing Member Government intends to submit to the appropriate IMO body. If the measure is not already available under an IMO instrument, the proposal should set forth the steps that the proposing Member Government has taken or will take to have the measure approved or adopted by IMO pursuant to an identified legal basis (*see* paragraph 7.5.2.3).

7.2 Alternatively, if no new associated protective measure is being proposed because IMO measures are already associated with the area to protect it, then the application should identify the threat of damage or damage being caused to the area by international shipping activities and show how the area is already being protected from such identified vulnerability by the associated protective measures. Amendments to existing measures may be introduced to address identified vulnerabilities.

7.3 In the future, additional associated protective measures may also be introduced to address identified vulnerabilities.

7.4 The application should first clearly set forth a summary of the objectives of the proposed PSSA designation, the location of the area, the need for protection, the associated protective measures, and demonstrate how the identified vulnerability will be addressed by existing or proposed associated protective measures. The summary should include the reasons why the associated protective measures are the preferred method for providing protection for the area to be identified as a PSSA.

7.5 Each application should then consist of two parts.

7.5.1   Part I — Description, significance of the area and vulnerability

1.   Description — a detailed description of the location of the proposed area, along with a nautical chart on which the location of the area and any associated protective measures are clearly marked, should be submitted with the application.

2.   Significance of the area — the application should state the significance of the area on the basis of recognized ecological, socio-economic, or scientific attributes and should explicitly refer to the criteria listed above in section 4.

3. Vulnerability of the area to damage by international shipping activities — the application should provide an explanation of the nature and extent of the risks that international shipping activities pose to the environment of the proposed area, noting the factors listed in section 5. The application should describe the particular current or future international shipping activities that are causing or may be expected to cause damage to the proposed area, including the significance of the damage and degree of harm that may result from such activities, either from such activity alone or in combination with other threats.

7.5.2 Part II — Appropriate associated protective measures and IMO's competence to approve or adopt such measures

1. The application should identify the existing and/or proposed associated protective measures and describe how they provide the needed protection from the threats of damage posed by international maritime activities occurring in and around the area. The application should specifically describe how the associated protective measures protect the area from the identified vulnerability.

2. If the application identies a new associated protective measure, then the proposing Member Government must append a draft of the proposal which is intended to be submitted to the appropriate Sub-Committee or Committee or, if the measures are not already available in an IMO instrument, information must be provided with regard to its legal basis and/or the steps that the proposing Member Government has taken or will take to establish the legal basis.

3. The application should identify the legal basis for each measure. The legal bases for such measures are:

   (I)   any measure that is already available under an existing IMO instrument; or

   (II) any measure that does not yet exist but could become available through amendment of an IMO instrument or adoption of a new IMO instrument. The legal basis for any such measure would only be available after the IMO instrument was amended or adopted, as appropriate; or

   (III) any measure proposed for adoption in the territorial sea., or pursuant to Article 211(6) of the United Nations Convention on the Law of the Sea where existing measures or a generally applicable measure (as set forth in subparagraph (ii) above) would not adequately address the particularized need of the proposed area.

4. These measures may include ships' routing measures; reporting requirements discharge restrictions; operational criteria; and prohibited activities, and should be specifically tailored to meet the need of the area to prevent, reduce, or eliminate the identified vulnerability of the area from international shipping activities.

5. The application should clearly specify the category or categories o f ships to which the proposed associated protective measures would apply, consistent with the provisions of the United Nations Convention on the Law of the Sea, including those related to vessels entitled to sovereign immunity, and other pertinent instruments.

8 CRITERIA FOR ASSESSMENT OF APPLICATIONS FOR DESIGNATION OF PARTICULARLY SENSITIVE SEA AREAS AND THE ADOPTION OF ASSOCIATED PROTECTIVE MEASURES

8.1 IMO should consider each application, or amendment thereto, submitted to it by a proposing Member Government on a case-by-case basis to determine whether the area fulfills at least one of the criteria set forth in section 4, the attributes of the area meeting section 4 criteria are vulnerable to damage by international shipping activities as set forth in section 5, and associated protective measures exist or are proposed to prevent, reduce, or eliminate the identified vulnerability.

8.2 In assessing each proposal, IMO should in particular consider:

1. the full range of protective measures available and determine whether the proposed or existing associated protective measures are appropriate to prevent, reduce, or eliminate the identified vulnerability of the area from international shipping activities;

2. whether such measures might result in an increased potential for significant adverse effects by international shipping activities on the environment outside the proposed PSSA; and

3. the linkage between the recognized attributes, the identified vulnerability, the associated protective measure to prevent, reduce, or eliminate that vulnerability, and the overall size of the area, including whether the size is commensurate with that necessary to address the identified need.

8.3 The procedure for considering a PSSA application by IMO is as follows:

1. the MEPC should bear primary responsibility within IMO for considering PSSA applications and all applications should first be submitted to the MEPC:

    1. the Committee should assess the elements of the proposal against the Guidelines and, as appropriate, should establish a technical group, comprising representatives with appropriate environmental, scientific, maritime, and legal expertise;

    2. the proposing Member Government is encouraged to make a presentation of the proposal, along with nautical charts and other supporting information on the required elements for PSSA designation;

    3. any technical group formed should prepare a brief report to the Committee summarizing their findings and the outcome of its assessment; and

    4. the outcome of the assessment of a PSSA application should be duly reflected in the report of the MEPC;

2. if appropriate following its assessment, the MEPC should designate the area "in principle" and inform the appropriate Sub-Committee, Committee (which could be the MEPC itself), or the Assembly that is responsible for addressing the particular associated protective measures proposed for the area of the outcome of this assessment;

3. the appropriate Sub-Committee or Committee which has received a submission by a proposing Member Government for an associated protective measure should review the proposal to determine whether it meets the procedures, criteria, and other requirements of the legal instrument under which the measure is proposed. The Sub-Committee may seek the advice of the MEPC on issues pertinent to the application;

4. the MEPC should not designate a PSSA until after the associated protective measures are considered and approved by the pertinent Sub-Committee, Committee, or Assembly. If the associated protective measures are not approved by the pertinent IMO body, then the MEPC may reject the PSSA application entirely or request that the proposing Member Government submit new proposals for associated protective measures. A proper record of the proceedings should be included in the report of the MEPC;

5. for measures that require approval by the Maritime Safety Committee (MSC), the Sub-Committee should forward its recommendation for approval of the associated protective measures to the MSC or, if the Sub-Committee rejects the measures, it should inform the MSC and MEPC and provide a statement of reasons for its decision. The MSC should consider any such recommendations and, if the measures are to be adopted, it should notify the MEPC of its decision;

6. if the application is rejected, the MEPC shall notify the proposing Member Government, provide a statement of reasons for its decision and, if appropriate, request the Member Government to submit additional information; and

7. after approval by the appropriate Sub-Committee, Committee, or. where necessary, the Assembly of the associated protective measures, the MEPC may designate the area as a PSSA.

9 IMPLEMENTATION OF DESIGNATED PSSAs AND THE ASSOCIATED PROTECTIVE MEASURES

9.1 When a PSSA receives final designation, all associated protective measures should be identified on charts in accordance with the symbols and methods of the international Hydrographic Organization (IHO).

9.2 A proposing Member Government should ensure that any associated protective measure is implemented in accordance with international law as reflected in the United Nations Convention on the Law of the Sea.

9.3 Member Governments should take all appropriate steps to ensure that ships flying their flag comply with the associated protective measures adopted to protect the designated PSSA. Those Member Governments which have received information of an alleged violation of an associated protective measure by a ship t1ying their flag should provide the Government which has reported the offence with the details of any appropriate action taken.

NOTES AND QUESTIONS

1. *Designated PSSAs*. The following PSSAs have been designated under the IMO procedure:

- The Great Barrier Reef, Australia; this designation was extended in 2005 to include the Torres Strait (Australia and Papua New Guinea)
- The Sabana-Camaguey Archipelago in Cuba
- Malpelo Island Columbia
- The sea around the Florida Keys, USA
- The Wadden Sea, Denmark, Germany and Netherlands
- Paracas National Reserve, Peru
- Western European Waters
- Canary Islands, Spain
- The Galapagos Archipelago, Ecuador
- The Baltic Sea Area, Denmark, Estonia, Finland, Germany, Lithuania, Poland, and Sweden
- The Papahanaumokuakea Marine National Monument, USA
- The Strait of Bonifacio, France and Italy

2. *Is the IMO procedure too limited and cumbersome?* IMO protects PSSAs primarily through ship routing measures. If State A wishes to enforce stringent and detailed management measures in its PSSAs, does it risk violating the provisions of UNCLOS applicable to EEZs and its territorial sea?

3. An ecosystems approach to the management of marine areas requires an understanding of the physical and biological characteristics of the particular area and the interconnections among living and non-living systems as well as human and economic and social systems that impact these resources. The ecosystem approach contrasts with a more narrowly focused management strategy that focuses on single species or short-term, sectoral, thematic approaches to management. From a fisheries perspective, the ecosystem approach requires sustaining the ecosystems that produce the fish. Is an ecosystem approach to management of marine areas compatible with UNCLOS?

4. Suppose one of the areas in its EEZ State A wishes to protect consists of an underwater shipwreck that is the remains of a ship that sank during an eighteenth century war. State A wishes to protect this site from international salvors who might dive on the wreck to extract valuable cultural objects. Can this site be protected under international law? See also the UNESCO Convention on Protection of the Underwater Cultural Heritage (2001).

5. *United States law*. The United States has enacted the Marine Sanctuaries Act, 16 U.S.C. § 1431 et seq., under which the Secretary of Commerce may designate certain areas of its territorial sea or EEZ as National Marine Sanctuaries. At present the National Marine Sanctuary Program includes 13 marine sanctuaries and one marine national monument.

- Channel islands (Cal.)
- Cordell Bank (Cal.)
- Fagatele Bay (Alaska)
- Florida Keys (Fl.)
- Flower Garden Banks (Tx.)
- Gray's Reef (Ga.)
- Gulf of the Farallones (Cal.)
- Hawaiian Islands Humpback Whale Sanctuary (Hawaii)
- Monitor (Civil War ship) Marine Sanctuary
- Monterrey Bay (Cal.)
- Olympic Coast (Wash.)
- Papahanaumokuakea Marine National Monument (Hawaii)
- Stellwagen Bank (Ma.)
- Thunder Bay (Mich.)

6. *Developing countries*. Beginning in the 1990s, developing countries approached the Global Environment Facility (GEF) for funding and technical assistance to improve the management of Large Marine Ecosystems, including those shared with neighboring nations. The GEF is supporting several hundred marine projects in 156 developing countries. *See* ALFRED M. DUDA AND KENNETH SHERMAN, A NEW IMPERATIVE FOR IMPROVING THE MANAGEMENT OF LARGE MARINE ECOSYSTEMS, OCEAN & COASTAL MANAGEMENT 45 (2002) 797–833.

7. *Marine protected areas and biodiversity beyond national jurisdiction*. What legal framework exists to conserve marine ecosystems and marine biodiversity on the High Seas and other marine areas beyond national jurisdictions? Consider UNCLOS Articles 86 and 87; is there any authority for marine protected areas? Consider also the provisions of UNCLOS dealing with the "Area," especially Article 136, which states that the Area and its resources are the common heritage of mankind. This concept constitutes a "third way" that is neither sovereignty nor complete freedom of action. Does this concept provide a basis for marine protected areas or for protecting the genetic resources of areas beyond national jurisdictions from indiscriminate exploitation? Note that Article 133 of UNCLOS defines the resources of the area to include only non-living resources. UNCLOS does not provide any specific regime for either the preservation or the exploitation of marine genetic resources. Professor Tullio Scovazzi has stated that the fact that there is no specific UNCLOS regime for biological resources in areas beyond national jurisdictions constitutes a legal "gap" in UNCLOS. He recommends filling this legal gap by approving a third Implementation Agreement (to go along with the 1994 Part XI Agreement on Seabed Mining and the 1995 Fish Stocks Agreement) that would create a new regime to cover this issue, which was not foreseen at the time of the conclusion of UNCLOS. *See* Tullio Scovazzi, *The Conservation and Sustainable Use of Marine Biodiversity, including Genetic Resources*, in AREAS BEYOND NATIONAL JURISDICTION: A LEGAL PERSPECTIVE (2012), *available at* http://www.un.org/Oepts/los/consultative_process/ICP12_Presentation.pdf. *See also* Tullio Scovazzi, *Marine Protected Areas on the High Seas: Some Legal and Policy Considerations* (World Parks Congress, Durban South Africa, 2003); and IUCN, *Elements of a Possible Implementation Agreement to UNCLOS for the Conservation and Sustainable Use of Marine Biodiversity in Areas beyond National Jurisdiction*, Marine Series No. 4 (2012).

Chapter 8

BIOLOGICAL DIVERSITY

Section I. INTRODUCTION

According to a recent U.S. Geological Survey study,[1] amphibians — frogs, toads and salamanders — continue to vanish from the American landscape at an alarming pace. More than 40 species of frogs are declining at a rate of 2.7% per year. This decline has persisted at least since 1989. A prominent scientist, Edward O. Wilson, has stated that the world may be entering a wave of mass extinction of species of living things: by some estimates the world is losing 27,000 species each year, which translates into 74 species lost every day, a rate of extinction about a thousand times greater than the "natural" rate of extinction evidenced in the fossil record.[2]

This chapter[*] covers the major treaties and other international instruments designed to address the problem of the diminution of biological diversity on the Earth. In this introductory section we address certain preliminary questions: (1) What do we mean by biological diversity (often shortened to "biodiversity")? (2) How do we measure biological diversity? (3) Why should we care about biological diversity — why is it important? What values are associated with biological diversity? (4) What are the threats to biological diversity and the causes of losses such as those described above?

A. The Meaning of Biological Diversity

Biological diversity (often shortened to biodiversity) is a term used to describe the variation of life forms found on Earth or within smaller sub-units like ecosystems and species. This description includes both the diversity across different species and subtle variations within species themselves. The term biological diversity is used also to describe the various ecosystems where living organisms may be found. Thus, the term biological diversity commonly refers to the diversity of species within larger ecosystems. The study of biodiversity is, in essence, the study of food webs and their related ecosystems; functional biodiversity acknowledges that species fulfill certain roles (called "niches") within their biological communities (ecosystems) and that the niches of all living things

---

[1] Michael J. Adams et al., *Trends in Amphibian Occupancy in the United States*, 2013 Plos One Online Journal, posted May 22, 2013, *available at* http://www.plosone.org/article/info%3Adoi%2F10.1371%2Fjournal.pone.0064347, accessed 24 May 2013.

[2] E.O. Wilson, The Diversity of Life 280 (1992).

[*] The authors wish to acknowledge the preliminary research done for this chapter by Jessica L. Montgomery.

are interconnected with other living things and with the non-living environment.[3]

Plants and animals have evolved over hundreds of millions of years into a highly interrelated and diverse web of genetic varieties, species and ecosystems. From an anthropocentric perspective, this diversity is important because civilization — whether urban, rural, industrial or non-industrial — relies on diverse natural resources to meet its ever-expanding and constantly changing societal needs. Various plant and animal species constitute all of society's food supply and most of society's raw materials. This includes genetic materials for agricultural, medicinal, industrial, and technological development and advancement. Aesthetically, nature's diversity is a source of beauty and enjoyment which throughout the ages has inspired civilization's artistic, scientific, and spiritual creativity. Moreover, diversity of plant and animal species is essential to maintaining Earth's delicate ecological balance. Species that may not be "useful" to civilization are nonetheless important components of Earth's ecosystems. Therefore maintaining and supporting such diversity is crucial not only for meeting the immediate needs of humanity, but for sustaining Earth's life support systems.

For several decades, scientists and environmentalists have shared a widespread interest in the conservation and promotion of biological diversity. Biological diversity may be defined as the variety and variability that exists among living organisms and the ecological complexes in which they occur, including the total number of species worldwide or within a given ecosystem, the variability of habitats which sustain species diversity, as well as the degree of genetic variability within each species. *See e.g.*, Jeffrey A. McNeely et al., *Conserving the World's Biological Diversity* (1990). Biodiversity is defined in Article 2 of the United Nations Convention on Biological Diversity (1992) as "[t]he variability among living organisms from all sources including, *inter alia*, terrestrial, marine and other aquatic ecosystems and the ecological complexes of which they are part: this includes diversity within species, between species, and of ecosystems."

Unfortunately, the scientific community still does not have scientific data regarding the precise number of species currently in existence, the number of species which are in imminent danger of extinction, or the number of species the Earth has already lost. A 2011 United Nations Environment Program study[4] estimates that there are currently 8.7 million living species on Earth, approximately 6.5 million on land and 2.2 million in water. Most of these species are relatively small, like insects. This study also maintains that 81% of land-dwelling species and 91% of sea-dwelling species have not yet been identified or catalogued. The scientific community's lack of knowledge about the full range of species on Earth means that we lack the ability to understand fully the individual, interactive, and interdependent roles which species play in performing and preserving basic

---

[3] *See generally* Robert K. Colwell, *Biodiversity: Concepts, Patterns and Measurement, in* S.A. LEVIN (ed), THE PRINCETON GUIDE TO ECOLOGY 257–63 (Princeton: Princeton University Press, 2009).

[4] *How Many Species on Earth?*, UNEP NEWS CENTRE, August 24, 2011, *available at* http://www.unep.org/NEWSCENTRE/Default.aspx?DocumentID=2649&ArticleID=8838. *See also* Camilo Mora et al., *How Many Species Are There on Earth and in the Ocean?*, 9(8) PLOS BIOLOGY ONLINE (2011), *available at* http://www.unep.org/NEWSCENTRE/Default.aspx?DocumentID=2649&ArticleID=8838, accessed 24 August 2011.

ecosystem functions. Without this knowledge it is difficult to predict and to prevent ecosystem to collapse. Before addressing the potential legal solutions to diversity loss, it is first important to understand the basic concepts of biodiversity, its measurement, and the causes of biodiversity loss.

It is important to realize that species diversity is not the only concept of biological diversity. Biodiversity may be described in terms of three fundamental biological concepts: (1) genetic diversity; (2) species diversity; and (3) ecosystem diversity.

Genetic diversity refers to the sum of genetic information contained in the genes of individual living things. Every living thing is a repository of an immense amount of genetic information, ranging from about 1000 in simple bacteria to more than 400,000 in more complex organisms. Even among the same species, no two individuals are genetically identical. The implications of genetic diversity mean that even where a species is saved from extinction, if it exists in reduced numbers, there is a loss of genetic and therefore biological diversity. Moreover, this loss is irreversible because, even if the species later expands in numbers, the resultant population will be more genetically uniform than the previous one. Thus, preserving genetic diversity within species means that preservation of populations of organisms within species is of great importance.

Species diversity is the most commonly understood type of biodiversity. A species is a population of living organisms within which gene flows occur under natural conditions. Within a species all normal individuals are capable of breeding with other individuals of the same species through sexual or asexual reproduction methods. By definition therefore, members of one species do not breed freely with members of another species. But species are not stable; new species may be established through polyploidy, the multiplication of gene-bearing chromosomes or by geographic speciation, the process by which isolated populations diverge through being subjected to different environmental conditions over time. A species is the lowest level of classification in the system used by scientists to classify living organisms. The main categories of the commonly used system of classification are: species; genus; family; order; class; phylum; and kingdom.

Ecosystem diversity refers to the variety of habitats, biotic communities, and ecological processes in the biosphere. What is an ecosystem is an open term; an ecosystem may be as small as a glass-enclosed terrarium or as large as the Earth itself. An ecosystem is a linked system of biological processes enclosing the interrelationships of living organisms with each other and with the associated non-living environment. Ecosystems are usually defined and determined by food and trophic interrelationships. A broad classification of the major ecosystems of the world is:

Tropical forests

Temperate forests

Boreal Forests

Tropical grasslands and savannahs

Temperate grasslands

Mountain grasslands and savannahs

Mediterranean shrubs

Deserts

Tundra

Estuarine and mangrove wetlands

Fresh-water wetlands

Marine ecosystems

Within each of these ecosystem classifications there are a variety of sub-ecosystems.

A key concept of an ecosystem is the interdependence of the living organisms and the non-living environment in which they exist. All species within a food web of an ecosystem are connected, and the removal or diminution of any one species may cause related populations and thus the whole ecosystem to break down or be diminished. Similarly, the disruption of the non-living part of an ecosystem will tend to disrupt the entire system as the disruption ripples through the entire interdependent system. Thus the removal of a predator or the introduction of a new species, the diminution of an essential nutrient or water supply have the potential to destroy biodiversity. Often, therefore, ecosystem biodiversity is disrupted unintentionally by actions taken when the functioning of ecosystems in which they are taken are not fully understood.

Six general rules of ecosystem dynamics linking environmental processes and biodiversity are as follows:

- The mix of species making up communities and ecosystems changes continuously.

- Species diversity increases with the environmental heterogeneity of habitats (a habitat is an area or environment where a species or ecological community normally occurs).

- Habitat "patchiness" influences not only the composition of species but also the interactions among species.

- Periodic natural disturbances of habitats may increase species richness by keeping an array of habitats in various successional states.

- Both size and isolation of habitats influence species richness as can the extent of transition zones between habitats.

- Certain "keystone" species have disproportionate influences on the characteristics of an ecosystem. A keystone species is one whose loss would cause a fundamental shift in the ecological processes of the community.

B. Measurement of Biological Diversity

At its most basic level, species diversity is measured by examining the abundance of different species represented in a given dataset. New technological and scientific developments, such as horizon-scanning and scenario planning approaches, have made it more feasible to track species diversity and to assess and prevent diversity loss. However, scientists have been measuring biodiversity for a long time without the aid of such sophisticated technological models. An indicator of biological diversity is species richness. Species richness — a term used to describe the number of species in a taxon, biological community, habitat or ecosystem — has historically been measured using data collected from the political units claiming sovereignty over such habitats or ecosystems.[5] Measuring biodiversity and species richness can be a complicated task. For example, the presence of some species even within a relatively small test area may be difficult if the organisms are difficult to detect. Lack of knowledge and lack of access may also pose burdens to scientific research of biodiversity. In sum, there are varied ways in which the scientific community calculates biodiversity. Across these varied methods of measurement, three lines of inquiry tend to be of primary importance: i) the number of species in a given unit; ii) the relative abundance of different species in that unit; and iii) the genetic variations between the species in that unit.

Measuring species diversity is the most common type of biodiversity measurement. For example, in the study on the decreasing numbers of amphibians referenced at the beginning of this section, scientists from the U.S. Geological Survey collected and examined data from 34 watery and swampy areas ranging from the Sierra Nevada mountains to Louisiana and Florida over nine years.

Measuring genetic diversity is much more complex than measuring species diversity. Genetic differences between populations can be determined in three fundamental ways: by measuring phenetic diversity, allelic frequencies, or DNA sequences.

Phenetic diversity is measured by examining phenotypes by comparing individuals of the same species that share the same characteristics. Phenotypes are individuals that share the same traits. For example, the various color patterns of Siamese cats may be cataloged and classified. Measuring phenetic diversity may be associated with assessing the ecological or practical utility of the trait in question. Measurement of phenotypes typically ignores or excludes measurement of their genetic basis.

Allelic diversity refers to the fact that the same gene can exist in a number of different variants and these variants are called allelic. Allelic diversity involves a process called protein electrophoresis, which analyzes the migration of enzymes under the influence of an electric field. Several different indexes and coefficients are then applied to the measurements to assess genetic distance and the allelic variation.

DNA sequence variation involves sequencing a portion of DNA using the polymerase chain reaction technique so that examining as little as one cell may allow such sequencing and comparisons may be made between individuals of the same species.

Measurement of biotic community and ecosystem diversity involves identifying a particular ecosystem and analyzing such factors as the pattern of habitats in the

---

[5] Colwell, *Biodiversity*, op. cit. at 263.

ecosystem; the relative abundance of the species present; the age structure of populations; the trophic structure; and other matters.

NOTES AND QUESTIONS

1. *Measuring biological diversity.* What does it really mean to measure biological diversity? Is biological diversity a quantifiable concept? To what extent will the continued monitoring, indexing, and categorizing of biodiversity further our understanding of the role it plays in preserving Earth's ecological balance?

2. *Estimating diversity.* Because so little is known of many species, and of the genetic attributes of species populations, scientists have adopted indirect methods to estimate changes in species diversity. Three methods are common. The first involves listing species known to be threatened with extinction. These species are then monitored and specific measures are taken for their protection. While this approach is widely used in developed countries, it has obvious problems for developing countries that are poorer in financial and technical resources and richer in biodiversity. A second method involves monitoring populations of relatively well known "indicator species" in areas where habitats have been altered. Changes in indicator species allow inferences to be made about changes in other related species existing within the same ecosystem. Indicator species usually include large mammals, butterflies, flowering plants, and birds. Finally, mathematical models of species-area relationships are increasingly being used to project extinction numbers likely to result from various levels of habitat reduction. *See* U.S. Congress, *Office of Technology Assessment, Technologies to Maintain Biological Diversity* 68–75 (OTA-F-330) (1987).

3. *Genetic diversity.* What is genetic diversity? What role does genetic diversity play in global agriculture? Specifically, how does genetic diversity foster greater food crop security? What is the relationship between the population size of a species and its genetic diversity? Understanding biodiversity loss requires that we able to measure and assess biodiversity levels. Yet there is a continuing lack of consensus about how biodiversity should be measured. What are some of the techniques currently used for measuring genetic diversity?

4. *Species diversity.* What is a "species"? Which areas of the world have the highest levels of species diversity? How do we differentiate between different species? Professor Edward O. Wilson of Harvard University, a noted biologist and biodiversity specialist, offers the following:

> [S]pecies are regarded conceptually as a population or series of populations within which free gene flow occurs under natural conditions. This means that all the normal, physiologically competent individuals at a given time are capable of breeding with all the other individuals of the opposite sex belonging to the same species or at least that they are capable of being linked genetically to them through chains of other breeding individuals. By definition they do not breed freely with members of other species.

Edward O. Wilson, *The Current State of Biological Diversity*, in E.O. WILSON (ed.), BIODIVERSITY 5–7 (1988).

Scientists acknowledge significant doubt about existing levels of species diversity. In light of this uncertainty, how can we develop coherent policies to protect biodiversity? What impact might this have on decisions to protect species diversity? For example, should we seek to target known threatened species or to focus on broader measures such as ecosystem protection.

5. *Ecosystem diversity.* What is ecosystem diversity? Ecologists acknowledge that there are no unambiguous boundaries delineating ecosystems. How might this affect attempts to protect genetic and species biodiversity at an ecosystem level? What are the relationships between ecosystem, genetic and species diversity?

6. *Cultural diversity.* The World Resources Institute has argued that loss of biodiversity "both stems from and invites the loss of cultural diversity." This implies a positive relationship between cultural diversity and biological diversity. Is this correct? How might cultural diversity and biological diversity interrelate? What are the policy implications of any such link? *See* World Resources Institute, The World Conservation Union (IUCN), United Nations Environment Program, GLOBAL BIODIVERSITY STRATEGY: POLICY-MAKER'S GUIDE 7–9 (1992).

C. The Importance of Biological Diversity

Why should it matter if biological diversity is diminished in the world? While superficially we seem independent of the wild creatures of the world, in reality we are highly dependent on the features of the natural world, including living organisms, for our survival and prosperity.

Ten reasons are often given for valuing biological diversity:

1. Agriculture and food security. About 20 species of plants provide 90% of the world's food. All these species once existed and typically still exist in the wild. All major food crops depend on the introduction of new strains from the wild to cope with evolving diseases and pests.

2. Medicines. Some 40% of prescriptions dispensed in the United States are from substances originally derived from plants, animals, or microorganisms. We depend on such biota for future drugs and cures.

3. Natural resources. Society derives most of life's necessities — food, raw materials, clothing — from the natural world. Thousands of products are dependent for their manufacture on genetic capital and the diversity of life on the planet.

4. Ecosystem services. We are dependent on the functioning of healthy ecosystems for a variety of essential services we take for granted. For example, trees, plants, and lowly algae replenish the atmosphere with oxygen; forests create rainfall patterns we depend upon; wetlands filter pollutants from drinking water and are nurseries for fisheries.

5. Education. Human beings have a natural desire for knowledge. This includes exploring the natural world. For example, there may be millions of undiscovered new species of living organisms.

6. Aesthetics. Humans are drawn to natural places to provide beauty that enriches our lives.

7. Wonder. We are awed by the variety and complexity of the natural world. This source of wonder must be preserved for future generations.

8. Ethics. Humans have an ethical obligation to respect other organisms living on the planet and the natural world.

9. Heritage. The existence of natural landscapes and natural places has shaped our cultures and our ways of thinking. We have an obligation to pass these experiences on to future generations.

10. Precaution. Destruction of biodiversity and the natural world poses risks that we do not fully understand or appreciate. We have an obligation to use precaution to minimize these risks.

Biodiversity is essential to the proper functioning of human societies. We rely upon the variety and variability of biological resources for scientific and technological advancements in areas such as agriculture, pest control, pharmaceuticals, disease prevention, raw materials for industrial development, pollution control, and hazardous waste remediation. At a more basic level, diverse biological resources are also necessary for the preservation of Earth's ecosystems. As noted by the World Commission on Environment and Development, "[t]he diversity of species is necessary for the normal functioning of ecosystems and the biosphere as a whole." OUR COMMON FUTURE 13 (1987). Paul and Anne Ehrlich argue that "the most anthropocentric reason for preserving diversity is the role that micro-organisms, plants and animals play in providing free ecosystem services, without which society in its present form could not persist." P. EHRLICH & A. EHRLICH, EXTINCTION: THE CAUSES AND CONSEQUENCES OF THE DISAPPEARANCE OF SPECIES 21–22 (1981). These "free ecosystem services" include recycling water and nutrients, purifying contaminated soil, water and air, affixing minerals to plant roots, and integrating protective habitat structures. All of these functions are essential to the sustenance of living organisms and the continued survival of species. According to the Ehrlichs, "the basic point is that organisms, most of which are obscure to biologists, play roles in ecological systems that are essential to civilization." *Id.* at 24.

Conservation of biological diversity is especially important in tropical regions where forests, coral reefs, marine environments, and other ecosystems may support as much as 80% of the world's species. Loss of biological diversity adversely impacts the future availability of these resources, especially those that remain untapped, and also affects the availability of as yet undiscovered scientific treasures, such as "miracle drugs" which might cure cancer or prevent the spread of HIV/AIDS.

Given biodiversity's importance, the loss of biological diversity carries serious implications. As the NGO Worldwatch points out, "when local populations of plants or animals are wiped out, the genetic diversity within each species that provides the capacity to adapt to environmental changes is diminished . . . [and] as species disappear, the intricate links between the species their biological and behavioral associations are sundered." E. Wolf, *On the Brink of Extinction: Conserving the Diversity of Life* 6 (Worldwatch Paper No. 78, 1987).

Acknowledging the importance of biodiversity does not in itself provide us with an analytical framework for deciding how we should go about conserving it, including how we should assess and implement conservation priorities. Yet how we value biodiversity will ultimately shape the policies, legal instruments, and programs we design and implement to protect it. In this Chapter, we explore the importance of biodiversity and the techniques and approaches we might use to assess its value and protect its future.

NOTES AND QUESTIONS

1. *Competing values.* Biodiversity has a myriad of values. It provides benefits directly through the availability of genetic material for use in crop development and the creation of new drugs, and it provides benefits indirectly by supporting and maintaining the ecosystems on which we rely. Some aspects of biodiversity's value are less tangible, including the value we place on the existence of species and the options this provides us for the future. Even less tangible is the notion that biodiversity or its components have "inherent rights" and should therefore be preserved. These values and others are expressly recognized in the first two paragraphs of the preamble to the UN Convention on Biological Diversity (1992), which provides that states party to the treaty are "[c]onscious of the intrinsic value of biological diversity and of the ecological, genetic, social, economic, scientific, educational, cultural, recreational, and aesthetic values of biological diversity and its components," as well as "the importance of biological diversity for evolution and for maintaining life sustaining systems of the biosphere." *Convention on Biological Diversity*, Preamble paras. 1–2, 1760 U.N.T.S. 79 (1992).

In light of these many sources of value, how can we assess the importance of biodiversity conservation relative to other goals, such as the development of a rainforest for timber or agriculture, or other more general policies such as poverty alleviation and liberalized international trade?

2. *Scientific uncertainty.* Although the existence, nature, and functions of many species still remain a mystery, the scientific community insists that the measurable rate of erosion to biodiversity is steadily increasing, and that the international community must design and implement conservation programs to slow down this process. Can we safely design and implement conservation programs in the face of such overwhelming scientific uncertainty? If so, how do we prioritize conservation targets? How can we ensure that countries, especially developing countries, are able to invest in those conservation programs which have the greatest likelihood of preserving the greatest number of biodiversity's "most important" components without suffering severe economic hardship and detriment to their own sustainable economic growth?

3. *Economic value.* Economists use "willingness to pay" as a proxy for how much people value an asset: The more a person cares about the asset the more he or she would be willing to pay for it. Normally willingness to pay is disclosed by the prices people pay for goods traded in the market-place. However environmental goods are rarely traded in well-functioning markets and consequently economists have developed a number of surrogate techniques, such as contingent valuation, hedonic pricing, and travel cost valuation, in order to determine people's "willing-

ness to pay" in such contexts. Do you think that these measures are likely to give an accurate indication of people's preferences for the conservation or use of environmental assets? How might willingness to pay be affected by the size of a person's income?

Consider the following remarks from Professor Ehrenfeld:

> In the long run, basing our conservation strategy on the economic value of diversity will only make things worse, because it keeps us from coping with the root cause of the loss of diversity. It makes us accept as givens the technological/socioeconomic premises that make biological impoverishment of the world inevitable. If I were one of the many exploiters and destroyers of biological diversity, I would like nothing better than for my opponents, the conservationists, to be bogged down over the issue of valuing. As shown by the example of the faltering new search for drugs in the tropics, economic criteria of value are shifting, fluid, and utterly opportunistic in their practical application.
>
> This is the opposite of the value system needed to conserve biological diversity over the course of decades and centuries. Value is an intrinsic part of diversity; it does not depend on the properties of the species in question, the uses to which particular species may or may not be put, or their alleged role in the balance of global ecosystems. For biological diversity, value is. Nothing more and nothing less. No cottage industry of expert evaluators is needed to assess this kind of value. David Ehrenfeld, *Why Put a Value on Biodiversity*? in BIODIVERSITY 211 (E.O. Wilson ed., National Academy Press 1988).

4. *Intrinsic value.* Deep ecologist and feminist theorists have criticized the economic approach to valuing biodiversity as being too focused on meeting the needs and interest of human kind without effectively considering the intrinsic value of its components. What is intrinsic value and how might we get an idea of its quality and quantum? Is it sufficient to say merely that it "is"? And if so, how can we compare this intrinsic value to other sources of value when making actual decisions about actual biological resource conservation? Is acknowledging intrinsic value really inconsistent with using economic approaches to the valuation of environmental resources as suggested by David Ehrenfeld?

5. *Ecosystem services.* Traditionally, concern about biodiversity loss has been focused on species threatened with extinction. These species are often high-profile and charismatic, and their plight quickly evokes public support for their protection. However many of the "ecosystem support services" are provided by far less publicly sympathetic creatures: microorganisms invisible to the human eye and often not well understood by scientists. How can we value these microorganisms within an economic framework? What other ways might we use to ensure that the value of these organisms is considered when deciding about polices to conserve biodiversity?

D. Threats to Biological Diversity and Causes of Loss

The threats and causes of loss of biological diversity are associated with the growth of human populations and the over-exploitation of natural resources. The chief cause of loss of biodiversity is loss and degradation of habitats and ecosystems all over the world. Additional causes of loss include pollution, overfishing, climate change, and the introduction of invasive alien species into native ecosystems.

As the world population continues to increase, human activities such as agricultural cultivation, deforestation, urban development, and industrial expansion have altered and adversely impacted the natural environment. The World Conservation Union (WCU) and the Conservation Measures Partnership (CMP) have compiled a list of what they believe are the primary threats to biodiversity.[6] Included in the list are residential and commercial development, agriculture and aquaculture, energy production and mining, transportation and service corridors, biological resource use (such as hunting and harvesting), non-consumptive human intrusions and disturbances (such as military activity and outdoor recreation), natural system modifications (such as fire suppression or modification of water flow patterns), introduction of invasive species, pollution, geological events and climate change. Many of these causes of biodiversity loss can be attributed to human activity.

A report[7] prepared for the Conference of the Parties of the U.N. Convention on Biological Diversity meeting, asserts that the continuing loss of biodiversity is likely to result in such consequences as water scarcity and declining agricultural productivity, but focusing resources on the protection of biodiversity can produce a more stable natural environment capable of providing society with tangible benefits. For example, the report states that focusing resources on the conservation of fish stocks which could cost from $800 million to $3 billion a year from 2013 until 2012 — could rehabilitate global fisheries to the extent of being $50 billion per year more profitable.

NOTES AND QUESTIONS

1. *Population.* Many drivers of biodiversity loss, such as habitat destruction and agriculture, are linked to the expansion of the human population in recent decades. Does the value of reproductive rights outweigh the value of biodiversity? Are these two interests irreconcilable?

2. *Agriculture.* Modern agriculture, involving the specialization of crops and the standardization of agricultural techniques, has been blamed for much biodiversity loss. Ironically, the use of improved genetic varieties causes biodiversity loss as the improved variety breeds with its wild cousins. This loss of biodiversity has an

---

[6] Salefsky et al., *A Standard Lexicon for Biodiversity Conservation: Unified Classifications of Threats and Actions* 22:4 CONSERVATION BIOLOGY 897 (2008).

[7] *Biodiversity Targets: A First Assessment of the Resources Required for Implementing the Strategic Plan for Biodiversity 2011–2020* (2010), *available at* http://www.cbd.int/doc/meetings/fin/hlpgar-sp-01/official/hlpgar-sp-01-01-report-en.pdf, accessed 4 August 2013.

adverse effect on agriculture as maintaining genetic diversity is essential to developing new crop strains in the future, to combating pests and disease and therefore to the long term stability and viability of global agriculture. Why might these apparent conflicts arise? Should we be willing to accept a slight loss of biodiversity to get greater crop output? Does loss of biodiversity in this way shift risk to future generations by increasing the risk of major crop failures, and by losing options for future crop development?

3. *Forests.* Forests are home to a rich variety of species, provide valuable ecosystem services, and sustain livelihoods of many indigenous peoples. A 2006 report from the U.N. Food and Agriculture Organization (FAO) estimated that roughly 13 million hectares of the world's forests are cut down every year. While the planting of new trees has offset the total amount of forests lost to land conversion, the report estimates that 3% of the world's forests were lost between 1990 and 2005. Further, it estimated that 2,000 square kilometers of forest are still lost each day. The most common driver of deforestation is agriculture — primarily crop growth and livestock grazing, UNEP, FAO & UNEP, Vital Forest Graphics (2009), *available at* http://grida.no/_res/site/file/publications/vital_forest_graphics.pdf

Section II. THE UNITED NATIONS CONVENTION ON BIOLOGICAL DIVERSITY

A. Introduction

Until the 1990s, biodiversity conventions were regional agreements that afforded protections for wildlife and required action by state-parties to protect wildlife habitats. For example, the Bonn Convention on the Conservation of Migratory Species of Wild Animals (1979) requires concerted action by all states through which migratory species travel to safeguard habitat, regulate hunting, and ameliorate degradation of feeding sites. The Treaty of Amazonian Cooperation (1978) aims to promote harmonious development of the Amazon region. The Bern Convention on the Conservation of European Wildlife and Natural Habitats (1979) requires action by parties to safeguard natural habitats, The Apia Convention on the conservation of Nature in the South Pacific (1976) focuses on the creation of protected areas. The ASEAN Convention on the Conservation of Nature and Natural Resources (1985) contains many substantive obligations but never entered into force. The Convention on Nature Protection and Wildlife Preservation in the Western Hemisphere (1940) requires parties to comprehensively protect all species of native fauna and flora and their natural habitats. With the exception of the Bern Convention, these conventions have been largely ineffective; they were largely ignored by the parties after their conclusion. Because there was no follow-up and no institutional structures created, their pious pronouncements went largely unfulfilled. When it came to creating a new regime to protect global biodiversity, therefore, a new departure was needed.

The centerpiece of the international legal regime to conserve biological diversity is the United Nations Convention on Biological Diversity (UNCBD), which was concluded in Rio de Janeiro at the 1992 United Nations Conference on Environment and Development. The provisions of the UNCBD reflect hard bargaining and much work reflected in such documents as the World Conservation Strategy (1980) and Caring for the Earth (1991), advocating that biodiversity must be conserved for reasons of both ethics and economic necessity. The UNCBD is a framework convention with many obligations framed in general terms and with qualifiers. Goals and policies predominate, not hard and precise obligations. The Secretariat of the UNCBD is based in Montreal and operates under the auspices of the U.N. Environmental Program. The Conference of the Parties, which meets annually, has adopted significant protocols that we study in this section.

Currently the UNCBD has been ratified by 193 parties so it is a virtually universal environmental convention. The only important country that is not a party is the United States, which has signed but has not ratified the convention.

PROBLEM 8-1
ANALYSIS OF THE UNCBD: SHOULD THE UNITED STATES BECOME A PARTY?

You are a staff member for the Committee on Foreign Relations of the United States Senate. The chairman of the committee has asked you to analyze the UNCBD and to report on whether the United States should become a party to this convention.

Read carefully the provisions of the convention, which is set out in the **Document Supplement**. Consider the following matters:

1. Note that Article 1 sets out three objectives: conservation, sustainable use, and fair and equitable sharing of the benefits arising out of the utilization of genetic resources. Article 2 defines genetic resources and sustainable use, but there is no definition of conservation. Why not? A point of debate leading up to the Convention was whether to include sustainable use as a matter separate from conservation of natural resources. Was it good policy to separate these two matters? How do the sustainable use and equitable sharing objectives contribute to the preservation of biodiversity?

2. What is the point of Articles 3 and 4? Which of the objectives is especially relevant to Articles 3 and 4?

3. Article 5 is a general requirement to cooperate.

4. Article 6 contains two separate obligations. How precise are these obligations?

5. Article 7 contains four separate obligations relating to identification and monitoring of biodiversity.

6. Article 8 places in-situ conservation at the heart of the effort to preserve biodiversity. Note that these obligations require implementation at the national level through legislation and administration.

7. Note in particular Article 8(g), the requirement to manage risks associated with the use and release of living modified organisms. What is the point of this provision? In response to this provision, the Conference of the Parties adopted the Cartagena Protocol on Biosafety in 2000.

8. Note Article 8(j). What is the purpose of this provision?

9. Article 9 concerns ex-situ conservation. What do these five obligations entail?

10. Article 10 covers some specifics with respect to sustainable use of biological resources.

11. Article 11 requires the use of incentive measures to promote the conservation and sustainable use objectives.

12. Articles 12 and 13 cover, respectively, research and training and public education and awareness.

13. Article 13 is a requirement to employ environmental impact assessment and mitigation of adverse impacts in connection with development projects.

14. Article 14 (2) provides for the future conclusion of an agreement to restore and compensate damage to biodiversity. As we shall see, this has been partially accomplished in the form of the Nagoya-Kuala Lumpur Supplementary Protocol on Liability and Redress to the Cartagena Protocol on Biosafety (2010).

15. Articles 15, 16, and 19 relate specifically to the objective of sharing of the benefits from the utilization of genetic resources.

16. Articles 17 and 18 require exchange of information and technical and scientific cooperation.

17. Article 20 and 21 deal with financial matters.

18. Article 22 covers the relationship with other conventions.

19. Article 23, 24, and 25 create the convention's permanent institutions.

20. Article 26 requires periodic reports.

21. Article 27 covers settlement of disputes.

22. Articles 28, 29, and 30 deal with the adoption of protocols and amendments and annexes.

23. Note that the UNCBD contains many provisions designed to accommodate specific concerns of developing countries, such as provisions relating to the sustainable use of natural resources; sharing of benefits from exploiting genetic resources, and protection of traditional knowledge. The financial provisions of the UNCBD also call for transfers of money from developed to developing states.

Why do you think the United States did not become a party to the UNCBD? Would you favor the United States becoming a party?

B. Conservation of Biological Diversity

One part of the UNCBD concerns conservation of biological diversity. Articles 6 and 8 to 11 are especially relevant to this concern. The United States at the federal level has no coordinated program or mandate to conserve biological diversity. If the United States were to become a party to the UNCBD, new national laws would be required to implement the obligations relating to biodiversity and the obligation to establish a national program of action. What would be required? Note that the

UNCBD is flexible as to specific requirements.

PROBLEM 8-2
UNITED STATES IMPLEMENTATION OF A POLICY TO CONSERVE BIODIVERSITY

Suppose the United States were to ratify the UNCBD. What national policy should be adopted to implement the UNCBD obligations to conserve biodiversity? Consider the policies adopted by two entities — Australia and the European Union.

AUSTRALIA'S BIODIVERSITY CONSERVATION STRATEGY EXECUTIVE SUMMARY

http://www.environment.gov.au/resource/australias-biodiversity-conservation-strategy-0

Australia's biodiversity Conservation Strategy 2010–2030 (referred to as 'the strategy') is a guiding framework for conserving our nation's biodiversity over the coming decades.

The vision of this Strategy is that Australia's biodiversity is healthy and resilient to threats, and valued both in its own right and for its essential contribution to our existence.

Biodiversity, or biological diversity, is the variety of all life forms. There are three levels of biodiversity:

- genetic diversity — the variety of genetic information contained in individual plants, animals and micro-organisms
- species diversity — the variety of species
- ecosystem diversity — the variety of habitats, ecological communities and ecological processes

Biodiversity occurs in all environments on Earth — terrestrial, aquatic and marine.

Biodiversity is not static; it is constantly changing. It can be increased by genetic change and evolutionary processes, and it can be reduced by threats which lead to population decline and extinction. Biodiversity in Australia is currently declining because of the impacts of a range of threats.

Conserving biodiversity is an essential part of safeguarding the biological life support systems on Earth. All living creatures, including humans, depend on these life support systems for the necessities of life. For example, we need oxygen to breathe, clean water to drink, fertile soil for food production and physical materials for shelter and fuel. These necessities can be described collectively as ecosystem services. They are fundamental to our physical, social, cultural and economic well-being.

Ecosystem services are produced by the functions that occur in healthy ecosystems. These functions are supported by biodiversity and its attributes, including the number of individuals and species, and their relative abundance, composition and interactions. Ecosystem services can be divided into four groups:

- provisioning services (e.g., food, fiber, fuel, fresh water)
- cultural services (e.g., spiritual values, recreation and aesthetic values, knowledge systems)
- supporting services (e.g., primary production, habitat provision, nutrient cycling, atmospheric oxygen production, soil formation and retention)
- regulating services (e.g., pollination, seed dispersal, climate regulation, pest and disease regulation, water purification).

Ecosystem resilience is the capacity of an ecosystem to respond to changes and disturbances, yet retain its basic functions and structures. The resilience of ecosystems in Australia is currently being reduced by a number of threats, including:

- habitat loss, degradation and fragmentation
- invasive species
- unsustainable use and management of natural resources
- changes to the aquatic environment and water flows
- changing fire regimes
- climate change.

For ecosystems to be resilient to these and other threats, they need a healthy diversity of individuals, species and populations.

The Strategy is a guiding framework for biodiversity conservation over the coming decades for all sectors — government, business and the community. The Strategy sets out priorities which will direct our efforts to achieve healthy and resilient biodiversity and provide us with a basis for living sustainably.

This Strategy is divided into three sections:

Setting the content

Priorities for action

Implementation and action.

The Setting the Content section describes the crisis of biodiversity decline that we face, and outlines why we must change our current practices and adopt more sustainable economies and lifestyles. It also outlines developments from Australia's first biodiversity conservation strategy in 1996, The National Strategy for the Conservation of Australia's Biological Diversity (DEST 1996), to the present.

The Priorities for action section identifies three national priorities for action to help stop the decline in Australia's biodiversity.

These priorities for action are:

1. Engaging all Australians in biodiversity conservation through:
   - mainstreaming biodiversity
   - increasing indigenous engagement
   - enhancing strategic investments and partnerships.

2. Building ecosystem resilience in a changing climate by:
   - protecting diversity
   - maintaining and re-establishing ecosystem functions
   - reducing threats to biodiversity.
3. Getting measurable results through:
   - improving and sharing knowledge
   - delivering conservation initiatives efficiently
   - implementing robust national monitoring, reporting and evaluation.

Each of the priorities for action is supported by subpriorities, outcomes, measurable targets and actions which collectively provide a strategic focus for our efforts.

The Implementation and Action section provides detail on implementation and identifies a series of actions that will help to achieve our outcomes and targets. These actions will be variously carried out at national, state, regional and local levels. The actions are an indicative set, acknowledging that as we progress our biodiversity conservation efforts, we will need to adapt our approaches and develop new actions to help achieve our outcomes and targets. The section also sets out arrangements for monitoring and reporting on implementation of the Strategy, and evaluation the effectiveness of our efforts.

The Strategy functions as a policy 'umbrella' over other more specific national frameworks. These include:

- National Framework for the Management and Monitoring of Australia's Native Vegetation (NRMMC 1999)
- The Australian Weeds Strategy (NRMMC 2007a)
- Australian Pest Animal Strategy (NRMMC 2007b)
- Australia's Strategy for the National Reserve System 2009–2030 (National Reserve System Task Group 2009).

It is also a guiding policy framework for the diverse mix of Australian, state, territory and local government and private sector approaches to biodiversity conservation.

Implementing this Strategy will involve updating existing programs and setting clear priorities for new investment to fill gaps and address emerging issues. Success will require increased integration of efforts within and between governments and between the public and private sectors. With this in mind, the first priority for action highlights the importance of engaging the private sector in conserving biodiversity and working with stakeholders who may be adversely affected by change.

The Natural Resource Management Ministerial Council (NRMMC) has overall responsibility for the Strategy and will monitor its implementation. The NMMC will formally review the Strategy in 2015.

The Strategy contains 10 interim national targets for the first five years. All governments will continue to work in the early years of the Strategy to evaluate the suitability of these targets for progressing implementation to meet the three priorities for action.

In the 2015 review, NRMMC will assess progress in implementing the Strategy, including against the national targets. The review will also consider whether the targets or other elements of the Strategy should be amended.

The 10 national targets are as follows:

1. By 2015, achieve a 25% increase in the number of Australians and public and private organizations who participate in biodiversity conservation activities.

2. By 2015, achieve a 25% increase in employment and participation of indigenous peoples in biodiversity conservation.

3. By 2015, achieve a doubling of the value of complementary markets for ecosystem services.

4. By 2015, achieve a national increase of 600,000 km^2 of native habitat managed primarily for biodiversity conservation across terrestrial, aquatic and marine environments.

5. By 2015, 1,000 km^2 of fragmented landscapes and aquatic systems are being restored to improve ecological connectivity.

6. By 2015, four collaborative continental-scale linkages are established and managed to improve ecological connectivity.

7. By 2015, reduce by at least 10% the impacts of invasive species on threatened species and ecological communities in terrestrial, aquatic and marine environments.

8. By 2015, nationally agreed science and knowledge priorities for biodiversity conservation are guiding research activities.

9. By 2015, all jurisdictions will review relevant legislation, policies and programs to maximize alignment with Australia's Biodiversity Conservation Strategy.

10. By 2015, establish a national long-term biodiversity monitoring and reporting system.

THE EUROPEAN UNION'S BIOLOGICAL DIVERSITY STRATEGY, EUROPEAN PARLIAMENT RESOLUTION OF 20 APRIL 2012
OJC 50 E, 21.2. 2012, at 19

The European Parliament,

– having regard to the communication from the Commission entitled 'Our life insurance, our natural capital: an EU biodiversity strategy to 2020' (COM(2011)0244),

– having regard to the 2050 vision and the 2020 headline target adopted by the EU Heads of State and Government in March 2010,

- having regard to the Environment Council conclusions of 21 June and 19 December 2011 on the 'EU Biodiversity Strategy to 2020',

- having particular regard to the outcome of the 10th Conference of the Parties (COP 10) to the UN Convention on Biological Diversity (CBD), in particular Strategic Plan for Biodiversity 2011–2020 and the Aichi targets, the Nagoya Protocol on Access to Genetic Resources and the Fair and Equitable Sharing of Benefits Arising from their Utilization, and the strategy to mobilize resources for global biodiversity,

Notes that out natural heritage is a major ecological asset which is fundamental to human well-being; takes the view that all Member States should cooperate and coordinate their efforts in order to ensure more effective use of natural resources and avoid net losses in terms of biodiversity and ecosystem services in both rural and urbanized areas;

Targets — mainstreaming biodiversity in all EU policies

Highlights the importance of mainstreaming biodiversity protection and conservation in the development, implementation and funding of all other EU policies — including those on agriculture, forestry, fisheries, regional development and cohesion, energy, industry, transport, tourism, development cooperation, research and innovation — in order to make the EU's sectoral and budgetary policies more coherent and ensure that it honors its binding commitments on biodiversity protection;

Underlines that the EU Biodiversity Strategy should be fully integrated into the strategies for the mitigation of, and adaption to, climate change;

Recalls that the precautionary principle constitutes a legal basis to be applied in all legislation and decisions affecting biodiversity;

Stresses that protecting, valuing, mapping and restoring biodiversity and ecosystem services is essential in order to meet the goals of the Roadmap to a Resource-Efficient Europe, and calls on the Commission and the Member States to consider, as part of specific measures, presenting a timetable for mapping and assessing ecosystem services in the EU which will enable targeted an deficient measures to be taken to halt the degradation of biodiversity and ecosystem services;

Emphasizes that the loss of biodiversity has devastating economic costs for society which until now have not been integrated sufficiently into economic and other policies; urges the Commission and the Member States, therefore, to value ecosystem services and to integrate these values into accounting systems as a basis for more sustainable policies; takes the view that any economic model that disregards the proper preservation of biodiversity is no viable; also stresses that actions to restore ecosystems and biodiversity have significant potential to create new skills, jobs and business opportunities;

Conserving and restoring nature

Emphasizes the need to halt the deterioration in the status of all species and habitats covered by EU nature conservation legislation and achieve a significant and measurable improvement in their status at EU level; stresses that this should take the form of an improvement in at least one of the parameters for conservation status defined in Article 1 of the Habitats Directive, without any deterioration in the other parameters;

Calls on the commission and the Member States to undertake to adopt integrated strategies in order to identify each geographical area's natural values and the features of its cultural heritage, as well as the conditions necessary for maintaining them;

Emphasizes that biodiversity objectives need to be implemented through concrete action in order to be effective; regrets that; in spite of the action taken to combat biodiversity loss, in the EU only 17% of habitats and species and 11% of key ecosystems protected under EU legislation are in a favorable state; calls on the Commission to analyze, as a matter of urgency, why current efforts have not yet succeeded and to consider whether other, potentially more effective instruments are available;

Stresses that, in order to establish a clear pathway to achieving the 2050 vision, at least 40% of all habitats and species must have a favorable conservation status by 2020; recalls that, by 2050, 100% (or almost 100%) of habitats and species must have a favorable conservation status;

Expresses concern at the increasing deterioration of essential habitats, such as wetlands, which should be treated as a priority and addressed by means of urgent measures that actually correspond to the special protection status granted to them by the EU;

Calls on the Commission and the Member States to ensure proper conservation of the Natura 2000 network through adequate funding for those sites; calls, in particular, on the member States to develop binding national instruments in cooperation measures and state the relevant planned source of financing (whether from EU funds or Member States' own budgets);

Calls on the Commission to increase its capacity to process and investigate effectively complaints and infringements connected with the proper implementation of the Birds and Habitats Directives, and to develop adequate guidance for the Member States with regard to monitoring on-the-ground implementation of those directives; calls on the Commission, furthermore, to incorporate measures to enhance the implementation and joint enforcement of the Birds and Habitats Directives into its current work on improving the implementation and inspection of environmental legislation;

Maintain and restore ecosystems and their services

Notes the requirement under the CBD to restore 15% of degraded ecosystems by 2020; regards this as a minimum, however, and wishes the EU to set a considerably higher restoration target reflecting its own more ambitious headline target and its 2050 vision, taking into account country-specific natural conditions; urges the Commission to define clearly what is meant by 'degraded ecosystems' and to set a baseline against which progress can be measured;

Urges the Commission to adopt a specific Green Infrastructure Strategy by 2012 at the latest, with biodiversity protection as a primary objective; underlines that this strategy should address objectives relating to urban as well as rural areas, *inter alia* in order better to fulfill the provisions of Article 10 of the Habitats Directive;

Emphasizes that the creation of natural environments should not be limited to designated areas alone, but should also be encouraged in different places — for instance in cities, along highways and railroads and at industrial sites — in order to develop a truly green infrastructure;

Urges the Commission to develop an effective regulatory framework based on the 'No Net Loss' initiative, taking into account the past experience of the Member States while also utilizing the standards applied by the Business and Biodiversity Offsets Program; notes, in this connection, the importance of applying such an approach to all EU habitats and species not covered by EU legislation;

Calls on the Commission to devote particular attention to species and habitats whose 'functions' are of priceless economic value, since efforts to preserve biodiversity in the future will be directed at those areas that will produce economic benefits over a short period of time, or be expected to do so;

Recognizes that biodiversity and ecosystem services provide significant non-monetized benefits to industries and other economic actors; invites organizations representing the private sector to put forward proposals on how best to preserve and restore biodiversity on a meaningful scale;

Agriculture

Recalls that over half of the EU's territory is managed by farmers, that farmland delivers important ecosystem services and has considerable socio-economic value, and that funding for the CAP [Common Agricultural Policy] represents a significant part of the EU budget; stresses that the CAP is not confined to the aim of food provision and rural development, but is a crucial tool for biodiversity, conservation, mitigation of climate change, and maintenance of ecosystem services; notes that the CAP already includes measures aimed at environmental protection, such as decoupling, cross-compliance and agri-environment measures; considers it regrettable, however, that these measures have so far failed to halt the overall decline in biodiversity in the EU and that farmland biodiversity is in continued decline; calls, therefore, for a reorientation of the CAP towards the provision of compensation to farmers for the delivery of public goods, since the market is currently failing to integrate the economic value of the important public goods agriculture can deliver;

Emphasizes the connection between water management and biodiversity as an essential component for sustaining life and for sustainable development;

Stresses the need to move from a means-based approach to a results-based approach in order to assess the effectiveness of the instruments applied;

Calls for the greening of Pillar I of the CAP in order to ensure the conservation of biodiversity in the wider farmed landscape, improve connectivity and adapt to the effects of climate change; welcomes the Commission's CAP reform proposal, which provides for a 'greening' of the CAP through the allocation of Pillar I payments to a package of basic good practices applied at farm level, including crop rotation and diversification, permanent pasture and a minimum 'ecological focus area'; underlines that such greening measures need to be workable and must not create unnecessary bureaucracy; reiterates its call for area-based support for the Natura 2000 network under the direct payment scheme; believes that resource-efficient, environment-and climate-friendly agricultural practices will ensure both the sustainability of agricultural businesses and long-term food security, and recognizes that the CAP should play a significant role in achieving this;

Calls for 'greening' practices to be geared to agricultural diversity in the various Member States, taking into account, for example, the specific situation of Mediterranean countries, which is not addressed by the proposed thresholds in relation to the diversification of crops and land of ecological importance; notes that assembled crops, permanent crops (olive groves, vineyards, apple orchards and rice crops) are some examples of practices that should be compatible with 'greening', given the high ecological and conservation value of some of these agricultural systems;

Maintains that assistance to public and private actors working to protect forest biodiversity in terms of species, habitats and ecosystem services must be increased under the new CAP, and eligibility extended to areas connecting Natura 2000 sites;

Calls for all CAP payments, including those made from 2014, to be underpinned by robust cross-compliance rules which help to preserve biodiversity and ecosystem services, covering the Birds and Habitats Directives (without watering down the current standards applicable from 2007 to 2013), pesticides and biocides legislation and the Water Framework Directive; calls for simple and transparent rules for those affected;

Forestry

Calls for specific action with a view to achieving Aichi Target 5, whereby the rate of loss of all natural habitats, including forests, should be at least halved by 2020 and where feasible brought close to zero, and degradation and fragmentation significantly reduced;

Calls on the Commission, once the study on the impact of European consumption on deforestation has been completed, to follow up its findings with new policy initiatives addressing the types of impact identified;

Calls on the Member States to adopt and implement forest management plans taking account of appropriate public consultation, including effective measures for the conservation and recovery of protected species and habitats and related ecosystem services;

Urges the Member States and the Commission to encourage the adoption of forest management plans, *inter alia* through rural development measures and the LIFE+ program; stresses the need for forest management plans to include special biodiversity measures, notably specific measures for the conservation of protected species and natural habitats in order to improve their status, both within and beyond Natura 2000 areas;

Urges the Member States to design their forestry policies in such a way as to take full account of the importance of forests in protecting biodiversity, in preventing soil erosion, in carbon sequestration and air purification and in maintaining the water cycle;

Urges the Member States to ensure that forest fire prevention schemes in their forest management plans include ecosystem-based measures designed to make forest more resilient to fires;

Fisheries

Welcomes the Commission's proposals for the reform of the CFP [Common Fisheries Policy], which should guarantee the implementation of the ecosystem approach and the application of updated scientific information serving as the basis for long-term management plans for all commercially exploited fish species; emphasizes that only by securing the long-term sustainability of fish stocks can we ensure the economic and social viability of the European fisheries sector;

Stresses that no one country can deal with the problem of biodiversity loss, particularly in marine ecosystems, and that the Member State governments must cooperate and coordinate their efforts more effectively in order to address this global issue; emphasizes that strong implementation of biodiversity policy benefits both society and the economy;

Calls on the Commission and the Member States to implement marine protected areas in which economic activities, including fishing, are subject to strengthened ecosystem-based management, making it possible to reconcile preservation of the environment with the practice of sustainable fishing;

Stresses that there are still large gaps in knowledge regarding the state of marine ecosystems and fisheries resources, and calls for increased EU efforts in the area of marine research;

Requests the Commission and the Member States to consolidate their efforts in collecting scientific data on fish populations, where these are deficient, with the aim of offering more reliable scientific advice;

Calls on the Commission and the Member States to cooperate with a view to establishing a European Coastguard in order to boost common monitoring and inspection capacity and ensure enforcement;

Calls on the Commission and the Member States to step up their efforts to ensure that catches fall below Maximum Sustainable Yield (MSY) levels by 2015, and to take ecological considerations into account when defining MSYs; stresses, therefore, that a lack of adequate scientific data should not be used as an excuse for inaction, and that in such circumstances fishing mortality rates should be decreased on a precautionary basis; recalls the legal obligation — as set out in the Marine Framework Strategy Directive (MFSD) — to ensure that all commercially exploited fish stocks are within safe biological limits by 2020;

Points out that the commitment to maintain or restore fish stocks, by 2015, to levels above those able to produce the MSY, as provided for in the CFP reform package proposed by the Commission, was endorsed by heads of state and government at the Johannesburg World Summit on Sustainable Development in 2002;

Underlines that fisheries management should contribute to achieving favorable conservation status pursuant to the Birds and Habitats Directives and achieving the objective of Good Environmental Status (GES) under the MFSD; stresses that long-term management plans should be based on multiple species rather than single species, taking account of all aspects of fish populations — in particular size, age and reproductive status — in order better to reflect an ecosystem-based approach, and that strict timelines for their development should be set;

Invasive alien species

Calls on the Commission and the Member States to ensure that measures are taken to prevent both the entry of new invasive alien species into the EU and the spread of currently established invasive alien species to new areas; calls, in particular, for clear guidelines under the CAP Rural Development Regulation in order to ensure that afforestation does not harm biodiversity and to prevent the provision of financial support for the planting of invasive alien species; underlines the need for ambitious strategies and up-to-date inventories both at the EU level and in the Member States; takes the view that these strategies should not focus solely on those species considered to be a 'priority', as suggested in Target 5 of the Biodiversity Strategy; encourages the Commission, with a view to enhancing the knowledge base, to support similar activities to those supported under the DAISIE (Delivering Alien Invasive Species Inventories for Europe) project;

Climate change

Recalls the inter-linkages between biodiversity and the climate system; is mindful of the significant negative impact of climate change on biodiversity, an underlines the fact that biodiversity loss inherently exacerbates climate change on account of the degradation of the carbon sink provided by the natural environment; emphasizes the urgency of biodiversity protection, *inter alia* as a means of mitigating climate change and preserving natural carbon sinks;

NOTES AND QUESTIONS

1. The biological diversity strategies of Australia and the EU are different but quite similar in many respects. Do these strategies fulfill the obligations set out in the UNCBD Articles 6, 8, and 9? If the United States were to join the UNCBD, what specific biodiversity policies would you recommend?

2. As set out in the European Union's Biodiversity Action Plan (European Commission, 2010), the EU's strategy has ten objectives:

- Safeguarding the EU's most important habitats and species
- Conserving biodiversity in the wider EU countryside
- Conserving biodiversity in the wider EU marine environment
- Integrating biodiversity into land-use planning and development
- Reducing the impact of invasive alien species
- Strengthening international governance
- Strengthening support for biodiversity in EU external assistance
- Reducing substantially the impact of international trade
- Supporting biodiversity adaptation to climate change
- Improving our knowledge base

At the heart of the EU's biodiversity policy are the Habitats Directive (Council Directive 92/43/EC of 21 May 1992 on the conservation of natural habitats and of wild fauna and flora) and the Birds Directive (Council Directive 2009/147/EC on the conservation of wild birds). These two Directives form the basis for the establishment of a coherent network of Special Protection Areas (SPAs), comprising all the most suitable territories for wild fauna and flora. Since 1994, these SPAs are part of a wider EU ecological network known as NATURA 2000.

3.   To protect the natural heritage of Europe, 51 European countries are Parties to the Bern Convention on the Conservation of European Wildlife and Natural Habitats (1979, in force 1982). This Convention, which is sponsored by the Council of Europe, is intended to establish and promote pan-European cooperation in the area of nature conservation. The Bern Convention addresses both conservation of flora and fauna and endangered wildlife species protection. The Convention (Article 9) requires bi-annual reports to be filed by each of the parties. Groups of experts then discuss these reports and make appropriate recommendations; Parties are required to respond to such recommendations in follow-up reports. Citizens and NGOs as well as Bern Convention parties can also file a complaint against a party using the Bern Convention website (http://www.coe.int/t/dg4). Complaints are referred to International Standing Committee of Experts which has the authority to investigate and, if appropriate, make recommendations to the state concerned.

PROBLEM 8-3
THE DANUBE DELTA CASE

The Delta of the Danube — where the Danube River flows into the Black Sea — is one of the most important wildlife areas in Europe. The Danube Delta is regarded by experts as the most important wetland area in Europe as it is frequented by some 325 species of birds and 75 species of fish. Many of these species are listed in the World Wildlife Fund Red Book as endangered or threatened with extinction. The estuaries of the Danube in this area form the spawning ground for many commercially valuable fish species. The importance of the Danube Delta is internationally recognized: In 1998, UNESCO designated the Danube Delta as a Biosphere Reserve under UNESCO's Man and the Biosphere Programme. A part of the Delta was designated a "wetland of international importance" under the Ramsar Convention on Wetlands of International Importance in 1995. In 2000, the government of Ukraine decided to build a deep navigation canal through the heart of the Biosphere Reserve without an Environmental Impact Assessment and without disclosing any information about the project to the public or neighboring states. In 2003, a Joint Ramsar and UNESCO mission to the Danube Delta investigated the situation and filed a Report that construction of the canal through the Bystroe Mouth of the Danube River would represent the "worst possible option" in terms of the damage the canal would inflict on the natural environment.[8]

Several NGOs and the government of Romania filed complaints against Ukraine to block the construction of the Danube canal. The complaints charged that the Ukraine canal involves the following violations:

1. The Bern Convention Articles 4, 5, and 6. Article 4 requires parties to enact "appropriate and necessary legislative and administrative measures to ensure the conservation of habitats" of species of flora and fauna listed in Appendices I and II. Article 5 requires parties to enact "appropriate and necessary legislation and administrative measures" to protect flora listed in Appendix I; Article 6 requires parties to enact "appropriate and necessary legislative and administrative measures" to protect fauna listed in Appendix II. The Danube Delta contains several species of flora and fauna that are listed on Appendices I and II.

2. The Espoo Convention on Environmental Impact Assessment in a Transboundary Context. (*See* Ch. 2). [For the Report of the Espoo Convention Compliance Committee in this case, see http://www.unece.org/fileadmin/DAM/env/eia/implementation/implementation_committee.htm].

3. The Aarhus Convention on Access to Information and Public Participation in Decisionmaking and Access to Justice in Environmental Matters. (*See* Ch. 2).

   Do you think the complaints were valid? Did Ukraine comply with these Conventions? For a report on this case see http://www.coe.int/t/dg4/cultureheritage/nature/Bern/default_en.asp (the case files system).

HOW TO CONSERVE GLOBAL BIODIVERSITY: IDEAS AND OPTIONS

In the history of life on Earth the fossil record has disclosed five mass extinctions of living things: (1) the Ordovician-Silurian mass extinction, about 450 million years ago (MYA); (2) the Late Devonian mass extinction, about 375 to 359 MYA; (3) the Permian mass extinction, about 248 MYA; (4) the Triassic-Jurassic mass extinction, about 200 MYA; and (5) the Cretaceous-Tertiary (K-T) mass extinction, about 65 MYA. The latter event is most famous as it was caused primarily by a massive asteroid falling in what is now the Yucatán Peninsula in Mexico and resulted in the extinction of the dinosaurs. The causes and extent of the previous mass extinctions are debated among scientists. Many scientists now discuss whether the Earth will experience a sixth mass extinction of biodiversity, this one caused primarily by anthropogenic activities, our modern way of life.

---

[8] UNESCO (Man and the Biosphere Programme) and Ramsar Convention Mission Report Danube Biosphere Reserve, 27–31 October 2003, http://www.ramsar.org/cda/fr/ramsar-documents-rams-ram53/main/ramsar/1-31-112%5E22947_4000_1__.

The conservation of global biodiversity is an immense undertaking. Reversal of the trends of worldwide diminution of ecosystems and habitats and the accelerating extinction of species requires global cooperation and attention. Is it even possible to tackle the problem of conservation of biodiversity on a global scale?

What legal tools does the UNCBD create that will help attain the goal of conservation of biodiversity? Are these tools adequate?

Three basic strategies may be used to promote conservation of biodiversity. These three strategies are not mutually exclusive but may be employed simultaneously in complementary fashion.

1. A Comprehensive/Integrative (C&I) Strategy to Conserve Biological Diversity

A comprehensive/integrative strategy to preserve biodiversity relies on a multiplicity of tools and procedures to attack the problem. This is the strategy most commonly employed in national action plans adopted under the UNCBD. As exhibited by the strategies of Australia and the EU, a variety of approaches are employed, including establishing protected areas, creating incentives in the form of direct payments to the private sector, and integrating biodiversity planning and conservation with all forms of development planning. What are the strengths and weaknesses of this approach?

2. A "Hot Spots" Strategy

"Hot Spots" are biologically rich areas with high biodiversity and a large percentage of endemic species. The Hot Spot Strategy to conserve biodiversity would concentrate on identifying and protecting crucial ecosystems all over the world. The theory behind this strategy is that some areas and ecosystems are more important than others with respect to conservation of biodiversity and that money and attention should be concentrated on the areas that matter the most. The World Wildlife Fund's (WWF) Global 200 project undertook to analyze the major ecosystems of the world to identify those that exhibit exceptional biodiversity. The initial list of such ecosystems identified the following 21 hot spots:

- Tropical Andes Mountains
- Mediterranean Basin
- Madagascar/Indian Ocean Islands
- Central America
- Caribbean and South Florida
- Brazil's Atlantic Forest
- Indochina/Myanmar
- Philippines
- Polynesia/Micronesia
- New Caledonia
- New Zealand

- Southwest Australia

- California Floristic Area

- Western Ghats of India/Sri Lanka

- Sundaland (Indonesia)

- Wallacea (New Guinea)

- South Central China

- Cape of Good Hope (South Africa)

- West African Tropical Forests

- Central Chile

- Brazil's Amazon Rain Forest

After this initial identification, further analysis identified 238 specific areas within these categories that should be singled out for special protection on a priority basis. These areas include 142 terrestrial areas; 53 freshwater areas; and 43 marine areas. For the complete list and complete account of this process, see https://worldwildlife.org/publications/global-200; and D.M. Olson et al., *The Global 200: Priority Ecosystems for Global Conservation*, 89 (2) ANNALS OF THE MISSOURI BOTANICAL GARDEN 199–224 (2002). WWF has estimated that the hot spots identified could be conserved with the expenditure of about $30 billion.

3. Strategic Habitat Preservation

A third method of conserving biodiversity is to prioritize preservation of "strategic habitats." Strategic habitat preservation is a method that may be used not only for hot spots, but for any and all areas of the world to identify and prioritize the preservation of natural areas. Strategic habitat preservation involves the following steps: First, for the area in question, researchers must develop estimates of habitat availability using geographic information systems (GIS). Such information systems exist for many areas, such as NOAA's Landsat and other government services. Second, the GIS data is then compared with plant and animal occurrence information. Third, focal species of plants and animals are selected; these include not only rare or endangered species but also species whose occurrence is typically associated with habitats that support diverse populations. Fourth, after selecting population goals for each of the focal species, distribution maps are created for each focal species based on occurrence records and land cover data. Fifth, a determination is then made of focal species security — the necessary habitat to prevent extinction due to inbreeding depression over the short term. Sixth, strategic habitats for each of the focal species is selected using seven general guidelines: (1) strategic habitats should protect other rare species as well as the focal species in question; (2) strategic habitats should incorporate a mix of large and small preserves, as necessary to maintain geographic distribution and meet the needs of individual focal species; (3) wildlife corridors, preserves arranged as stepping stones, and other types of landscape linkages should be designed to meet the needs of focal species; (4) strategic habitats designed to foster movement must lie within frequently reported dispersal distances for the species in question; (5) corridors and other linkages should consider the size of the populations to be linked; (6) corridors and linkages should meet the needs of wide-ranging species as well as the needs of focal species with smaller area requirements; and (7) strategic habitats should be designed to maintain or expand existing core populations and ecological processes, but should acknowledge that not every individual of every population can be protected.

For an example of this method, see Randy S. Kautz and James A. Cox, *Strategic Habitats for Biodiversity Conservation in Florida*, 15 (1) CONSERVATION BIOLOGY 55–77 (2001). The authors carried out a strategic habitat analysis for the state of Florida to conclude that strategic habitats in Florida cover 1.65 million ha (12% of the land area of the state). Much of the lands and waters identified as strategic habitat in this study is in private ownership. To implement this strategy the private lands in question would either have to be acquired or incentives created to give the private owners reason to manage the lands to conserve biodiversity. The authors conclude that the acquisition of strategic habitat areas not in the public domain would cost approximately $8.2 billion (15% of the state of Florida's total budget in 2001) and $ 122 million per year to manage. Is strategic habitat preservation superior to "hot spot" preservation? Is either method feasible economically or politically?

C.   Access to Genetic Resources and Benefit Sharing

1.   The Provisions of the UNCBD

Perhaps the most controversial provisions of the UNCBD are those dealing with access to genetic resources and fair and equitable benefit sharing. Historically, companies and nations enjoyed open access to plants and animals as well as genetic resources around the world. The natural world could be freely scoured in order to collect raw material as needed to develop new drugs, food crops, or fibers. The development of the biotechnology industry placed such openness on a new level. Now a Brazilian fungus can be collected, patented and marketed to control fire ants; and chemicals extracted from the neem tree can be patented as a natural insecticide. Companies and developed nations sought to retain the traditional openness of access to genetic materials that might be useful in developing new products derived from biotechnology as well. But developing countries sought to profit from the new effort to commercialize genetic and biochemical resources. Developing countries argued that it was unfair for them to provide free access to their rich genetic resources without sharing in the benefits derived from them.

While developing countries argued that free access to their genetic resources amounted to bioimperialism, developed countries on behalf of their pharmaceutical and biotechnology companies argued that the raw genetic material is but a small beginning; the development of Bt corn (Bt stands for *bacillus thuringiensis*, a soil bacteria that is naturally toxic to insects) cost some $1.5 to $3 million. Since the development of a new product from genetic material typically takes years of effort and great expense, and since the genetic material is usually available in many different countries anyway, developing countries should not put a price on access.

Which side won this debate? Consider CBD Articles 3, 15, 16, and 19.

A further question is: does the third objective announced in UNCBD Article 1 — the fair and equitable sharing of benefits arising out of the utilization of genetic resources — contribute to the conservation of biodiversity? Or is this objective simply an add-on, a price for obtaining international cooperation from developing countries? Developing countries argue that this objective gives them a needed incentive to conserve the biodiversity within their borders. But will the commercial interest in biodiversity fuel increased investment in resource conservation? Will the institutions created to capture the benefits of biodiversity in developing countries contribute to their economic growth? The jury is still out on these questions.

The UNCBD provisions on access and benefit sharing (ABS) raise several important questions. Almost simultaneously with the conclusion of the UNCBD, the parties to the World Trade Organization (WTO), which include virtually all of the parties to the UNCBD, concluded the WTO Agreement on Trade Related Intellectual Property Rights (TRIPS), which entered into force in 1995. Article 27.2 of TRIPS requires that all WTO members recognize patents for the biological processes for the production of plants and animals. Thus, WTO members cannot exclude biotechnology from patentability.

Furthermore, although Article 15 (5) of UNCBD states that access to genetic resources shall be by "prior informed consent," WTO members are prohibited by the General Agreement on Tariffs and Trade (GATT) from imposing an export ban (GATT Art. XI) or any discriminatory provisions (GATT Art. I) in connection with an ABS agreement, although nothing in TRIPS or the GATT would prohibit an ABS agreement itself on mutually agreed terms.

How can rights under TRIPS be reconciled with the UNCBD if there is a conflict? *See* Articles 16(5) and Article 22 of the UNCBD.

2. The Nagoya Protocol

Because the ABS regime contained in Articles 15, 16, and 19 of the UNCBD was not widely observed due to vagaries in the language of these provisions, in 2010 the Conference of the Parties adopted the Nagoya Protocol on Access to Genetic Resources and the Fair and Equitable Sharing of Benefits Arising from their Utilization. The Nagoya Protocol will go into force upon its ratification by 50 parties, which is expected early in 2014. The purpose of the Nagoya Protocol is to provide much needed detailed provisions which will allow the ABS regime of the UNCBD to become fully operational.

The Nagoya Protocol is reprinted in the **Document Supplement**. Read the Protocol and consider especially the following provisions:

- Article 6 makes clear that parties must provide access to their genetic resources; parties must enact legislative and regulatory provisions providing access under clear rules and procedures.

- Article 5 and Annex II spell out the types of benefit-sharing required. The benefits involved may be monetary and non-monetary in nature. Moreover, Article 10 provides that "parties shall consider the need for and modalities of a global multilateral benefit sharing mechanism." Benefits under this mechanism "shall be used to support the conservation of biological diversity and the sustainable use of its components globally." This provision makes an explicit connection between ABS and conservation of biodiversity.

- Articles 13 to 17 provide details as to the application and approval process as well as the implementation of ABS agreements.

- Articles 18 to 20 concern the content and compliance with ABS agreements.

- Article 23 seeks to encourage transfer of technology, collaboration and cooperation.

Will the Nagoya Protocol successfully institute widespread compliance with ABS as envisioned by the UNCBD? Does the Protocol clear up possible conflicts with intellectual property rights under international law? Since the United States is not a party, will U.S. companies be able to ignore ABS requirements? *See* Article 24.

3.   Traditional Knowledge

Article 8(j) of the UNCBD requires parties to "respect, preserve and maintain" what is known as traditional knowledge — innovations and practices of indigenous and local communities (ILCs). This article also requires parties to promote the wider application of traditional knowledge with the approval and involvement of such ILCs and the sharing of benefits arising out of such utilization. Although the UNCBD does not define traditional knowledge, it is generally taken to mean the "knowledge, innovations and practices" developed by ILCs from experience gained over centuries and adapted to the local culture and environment, transmitted orally from generation to generation, and collectively owned. Such knowledge takes the form of stories, songs, folklore, proverbs, cultural values, beliefs, rituals, health and agricultural practices. Many developing countries protect traditional knowledge through national laws.

Such traditional knowledge may come into play in connection with the utilization of genetic resources either because traditional knowledge about a genetic resource and its utilization has spread beyond the original ILC group or because a scientist visiting the ILC finds out about it and appropriates it. Traditional knowledge often is not subject to protection under international and national intellectual property regimes because it has entered the public domain or because there is no specific person or company that is the originator or repository of the knowledge.

The Nagoya Protocol contains several provisions designed to protect traditional knowledge, going beyond the UNCBD. Note that the utilization of traditional knowledge, even when it is not subject to intellectual property protection, will trigger ABS obligations under the Nagoya Protocol. *See* Nagoya Protocol Articles 5 (2) and (5); 6(2) and (3); 7, 10–13, 16, and 22. The Protocol thus protects traditional knowledge under international law and requires benefit sharing with ILCs at least if associated with the utilization of genetic resources.

PROBLEM 8-4
BIOTECHNOLOGY IN BRAZIL

The Government of Brazil has recently encouraged the development of the State of Rondonia, which is located in the southwestern basin of the Amazon. Using World

Bank funds, Brazil has opened new agricultural lands throughout Rondonia's rainforest regions. INCRA, Brazil's federal land reform authority, will grant each family 350 hectares of rainforest land to homestead upon application. The opening of Rondonia's virgin rainforest lands to large-scale settlement has created numerous problems: massive cutting of the rainforest, depletion of water supplies and environmental amenities, illegal poaching of monkeys and other wildlife, and disruption of the lives of native communities, notably the Xytere Indians, a native people of the Amazon region.

Brazil and the State of Rondonia are encouraging private companies to invest in the region to boost local employment and to spur development. A large U.S. biotechnology company, BioTech Industries, is exploring the idea of establishing a research facility in Rodonia in order to hunt and collect golden-maned tamarins, wooleys, and various indigenous marmoset monkeys within the rainforest, to conduct field experiments and clinical trials with these primates, to collect biological and genetic samples, and to export certain data and samples to BioTech's laboratories in the United States for research and development. BioTech hopes to use the resultant genetic material yielded by the research for various diseases, including the AIDS virus.

BioTech executives have approached officials of the Rondonia state government about this idea for research and have been welcomed with open arms. Officials of the State of Rondonia are very anxious to receive BioTech's investment, and they are willing to approve BioTech's plans as submitted without requiring any application to the central government of Brazil and without charge or any *quid pro quo*. Rondonia's officials are even offering a tax exemption to BioTech if it chooses to locate a facility in the state.

BioTech's executives have recently been apprised of the UNCBD regime and the Nagoya Protocol that governs access to genetic resources and benefit sharing. BioTech's Brazilian lawyer has also told BioTech that the federal government of Brazil has recently enacted legislation that requires that any use of genetic resources in Brazil requires an application for access to the Brazil Genetic Heritage Council, and approval and authorization will be granted only after signing a contract for use of genetic heritage and benefit sharing. The approval process for such applications is quite onerous. Under Brazilian law the application must include such matters as a full explanation of the aims of the research or economic exploitation contemplated; the sites where the research will be conducted; the number and names of researchers involved; the methods of collection and exploitation; a formal commitment by the interested parties to provide evidence of the origin of the genetic samples taken; and many other matters. In addition, approval will involve a promise of both monetary benefits and non-monetary benefits to Brazil and indigenous people such as the Xytere Indians. Approval will also require BioTech to enter into an agreement to transfer the technology resulting from the research to the Brazil Genetic Heritage Council.

1. Should BioTech accept the deal offered by the State of Rondonia or must BioTech comply with Brazilian federal law in connection with its research? Does it make a difference that the United States is not a party to either the UNCBD or the Nagoya Protocol?

2. If BioTech chooses to comply with Brazilian federal law, what types of benefit-sharing should it be prepared to offer and agree to?

3. Is Brazil guilty of violating the conservation provisions of the UNCBD? Can a complaint be made against Brazil in any forum for violating these provisions?

4. Suppose Brazilian officials refuse to consider or process BioTech's ABS application on the ground that the United States is not a party to the relevant conventions? Would Brazil's actions violate international law?

4. Marine Biodiversity and Genetic Resources

The UNCBD and the Nagoya Protocol do not cover marine biodiversity beyond the limits of national jurisdiction, although the UNCBD Article 5 requires parties to "cooperate" with regard to conservation and sustainable use of ocean biota. The UN Convention on the Law of the Sea (UNCLOS), which we cover in Chapter 7 of this book, contains extensive protections for the marine environment, including marine biodiversity, in Part XII; but no provision of UNCLOS requires an access application or benefit sharing in connection with the utilization of genetic resources from areas beyond national jurisdiction. Should this gap be filled by an amendment to UNCLOS or by a new agreement?

The Parties to the UNCBD, by Decision II/10 taken at COP 2, adopted the so-called "Jakarta Mandate," which expresses deep concern at "serious threats to marine and coastal biological diversity" and calls for integrated marine and coastal management to address these problems as well as increased actions by Parties to strengthen their management of marine and coastal ecosystems.

D. Financing the Convention on Biological Diversity's Work

The Global Environment Facility (GEF) is an independent financial organization which provides grants to developing countries to help them meet international environmental obligations. GEF operates the financial mechanisms for several international conventions, including the Convention on Biological Diversity.[9] The UNCBD's Conference of Parties (COP) is responsible for setting policy and overseeing the utilization and management of financial resources in connection with the Convention.[10] GEF applies the UNCBD's relevant policies as guidelines[11] in accordance with a Memorandum of Understanding (MOU) between the Conference of Parties to the Convention on Biological Diversity and the Council of the Global Environment Facility. This MOU governs the relationship between the UNCBD and GEF. The MOU states that "GEF, in operating the financial

---

[9] *See, What is the GEF, Global Environment Facility?, available at* http://www.thegef.org/gef/whatisgef.

[10] Final Report of the Third Meeting of the Conference of the Parties to the Convention on Biological Diversity, III/8, UNEP/CBD/COP/3/38, p. 61–72, *available at* http://www.iisd.ca/biodiv/cop3/cop30008.htm.

[11] Most of the guidelines are contained in a Decision of COP 10: Decision X/24 (2010) — Guidance to the Financial Mechanism, Convention on Biological Diversity, *available at* http://www.cbd.int/financial/gef/guidance.

mechanism under the Convention, will finance activities that are in full conformity with the guidance provided by the Conference of the Parties" and requires the GEF Council to prepare and submit a report to the COP regarding the implementation of COP policies and any monitoring or evaluation of the activities undertaken.

The GEF thus fulfills the functions specified under UNCBD Articles 20 (Financial Resources) and Article 21 (Financial Mechanism).

The GEF, created in 1991 as a partnership of 182 nations, is the largest funding source projects to improve the global environment. The GEF is the designated financial mechanism and funding source for many international conventions and thus provides grants for projects relating to biodiversity, climate change, international waters, land degradation, the protection of the ozone layer, and measures to deal with persistent organic pollutants. The GEF is managed by several bodies, an assembly of the parties and a governing council of 32 members (16 from developing countries, 14 from developed countries, and 2 from countries with economies in transition), who function as the GEF's Board of Directors. The GEF is located in Washington DC.

The GEF is funded by 39 donor nations, which commit money every four years; the budget is US $4.34 billion for the period 2010 to 2014. The GEF also leverages funds from 10 other international development agencies, funds and banks. Only certain countries — developing countries — are eligible for GEF grants. Access to GEF is by application: to obtain financing, the proponent of a project in an eligible country contacts its country's operational focal point in the GEF, the person who is designated as responsible for GEF activities for that country. If the proposed action or project meets GEF guidelines, a Project Preparation Form is prepared and submitted to the GEF Secretariat for approval. Since its inception the GEF has funded over 1000 biodiversity projects in over 80 developing countries. Information is available at http://www.thegef.org.

E. Biosafety

Article 8(g) of the UNCBD obliges the parties to establish or maintain means to regulate, manage, or control the risks associated with the use and release of living modified organisms which may have adverse effects on biological diversity, sustainable use, or human health. Articles 19(3) and (4) look to the need for appropriate procedures, exchanges of information and a protocol to deal with biosafety, the need for safe transfer, handling, and use of living modified organisms.

The advancement of modern biotechnology has raised concerns among the scientific community, specifically involving the potentially adverse effects on biodiversity. For example, the presence of genetically modified organisms may hurt other organisms in shared habitats because of increased competitiveness. Similarly, inserted genetic material may be inadvertently transferred to other organisms through cross-pollination or other processes.[12]

---

[12] RUTH MACKENZIE ET AL., AN EXPLANATORY GUIDE TO THE CARTAGENA PROTOCOL ON BIOSAFETY 10 (2003).

An associated treaty to the Convention on Biodiversity is the Cartagena Protocol on Biosafety. As a supplement to the Convention, the Biosafety Protocol aims to protect biological diversity from the risks associated with the development of biotechnology. The Protocol achieves this goal principally through managing the trans-boundary movement of living modified organisms (LMOs), such as genetically modified crops or organisms. It uses an advance informed agreement (AIA) procedure to ensure that countries can make informed decisions about the import of LMOs. The Cartagena Protocol was adopted by the UNCBD COP on January 29, 2000 as a supplement to the Convention and entered into force on September 11, 2003, after it had received the necessary 50 instruments of ratification.

The governing body of Protocol is known as COP-MOP because, pursuant to Article 29 of the Protocol, the UNCBD COP meetings also serve as the designated Meetings of the Parties to the Protocol. COP-MOP reviews implementation of the Protocol and issues decisions to facilitate such implementation and to improve the Protocol's functioning. To date there have been six official COP-MOP meetings, the last being held in India in 2012. There are currently 164 Parties to the Protocol. The United States has not signed or ratified the Protocol.

The scope of the Protocol is limited to ". . . the transboundary movement, transit, handling and use of all living modified organisms that may have adverse effects on the conservation and sustainable use of biological diversity, taking also into account risks to human health."[13] However, the application of the Protocol in most instances does not apply to the movement of pharmaceuticals intended for human use.[14] The general obligations of Parties are laid out in Article 2, which requires that " '[e]ach Party . . . take necessary and appropriate legal, administrative and other measures to implement its obligations under this Protocol" and ". . . shall ensure that the development, handling, transport, use, transfer and release of any living modified organisms are undertaken in a manner that prevents or reduces the risks to biological diversity, taking also into account risks to human health."

Parties to the Protocol are entitled to make decisions about importing LMOs pursuant to the guidelines set forth in Article 15 and Annex III for scientific assessments. Parties are also permitted to consider socio-economic factors in making decisions on the importation of LMOs.[15] The Protocol also requires that Parties adopt measures for managing the risks identified with imported LMOs and take certain steps in the case of an inadvertent release of LMOs.[16] Information sharing is conducted through the Protocol's Biosafety Clearing House (BCH).[17]

The AIA procedure is primarily laid out in Articles 8, 9, 10, and 12. It applies "prior to the first intentional transboundary movement of living modified organisms for intentional introduction into the environment of the Party of import,"

---

[13] Art. 4.

[14] Art. 5.

[15] Art. 26.

[16] Arts. 16–17.

[17] Art. 20.

but does not apply to living modified organisms intended for use as feed or for processing or to organisms identified in COP-MOP decisions as not being likely to have adverse effects.[18] This system exists to ensure that Parties can adequately assess the risks associated with the importation of certain LMOs. The assessment is undertaken in four main steps. The exporting Party must send a notification to the importing Party containing certain information and the importing Party must reply with an acknowledgement of receipt of notification.[19] The importing Party then must reach a decision as to the import of the LMOs at issue.[20] Either Party may then initiate a review of this decision.[21]

PROBLEM 8-5
THE INTERNATIONAL GRAIN TRADE COALITION WRESTLES WITH BIOSAFETY

You are Washington DC counsel for a group of grain exporters known as the International Grain Trade Coalition (IGTC). The companies that are members of the IGTC are major grain and processed food exporters located in the United States and Canada. Although the United States has not ratified either the UNCBD or the Cartagena Protocol, Canada is a member of both regimes. Your members have asked you for legal advice concerning compliance with the Cartagena Protocol. You are asked to respond to the following questions: (Please refer to the text of the Cartagena Protocol, which is reprinted in the **Document Supplement**).

1. Where did this Cartagena Protocol come from? We hear that biosafety is a concern of the parties to the UN Convention on Biological Diversity, but we do not see any connection between biodiversity and biosafety. What is the connection? (Consult the Preamble to the Protocol).

2. Our members export grain seeds to be used for planting crops, grains to be used for human and animal feed as well as many varieties of processed foods. Virtually all of these exports contain materials that are the products of biotechnology. Most food crops in North America are produced from varieties of plants that are the products of biotechnological research. Does this Cartagena Protocol apply to all of our export activities? (Consult Article 4, which limits the scope of the Protocol to living modified organisms that may have adverse effects on the conservation and sustainable use of biodiversity).

3. There is no evidence that any of the products our members export — living or non-living — have any adverse effects. Are we in the clear? (Consult Articles 1, 2(4), and 10(6).

4. OK, but our members are weary of extra red tape in connection with their exporting. How does this Protocol affect our exporting activities? (Consult Articles 7, 8, 9, and 10).

---

[18] Art. 7.

[19] Arts. 8–9.

[20] Art. 10.

[21] Art. 12.

5. You mean we must obtain Advance Informed Agreement (AIA) for everything we export if it contains living modified organisms? (Consult Article 7, which provides for exemptions, notably for living modified organisms intended for direct use as food, feed, or for processing; and an exemption for living modified organisms identified in a decision of the Conference of the Parties as not being likely to have adverse effects. In addition, pharmaceuticals are also exempt under Article 5; and Article 6 exempts living modified organisms in transit and destined for contained use).

6. That is good news. Our members like the exemption for living modified organisms intended for food, feed, and processing. Of course, we may export a shipment of seeds that we think is intended for food, feed or processing, but it may end up planted for crops. What about that? (Consult Article 7, which makes the exporters' intention central to the exemption regardless of the ultimate use of the seeds exported. But note Articles 11, 19, and 20, as well as Annex II, which are relevant to transboundary movement of living modified organisms intended for direct use as food, feed, or for processing).

7. Our members are also concerned with labeling requirements. What new labeling is required for exports of our various commodities and products? (Consult Article 18).

8. Our members are quite familiar with the law of the World Trade Organization (WTO) concerning imports and exports. Under the WTO Agreement Sanitary and Phytosanitary (SPS) Measures Agreement, an importing country may not ban the import of any product without scientific evidence that it is harmful and without conducting a prior risk assessment. You are telling me that we may run into an import ban that is based on the precautionary principle. Doesn't this conflict with WTO law? (Consult the Preamble and point out that the Cartagena Protocol does have provisions for risk assessment and risk management, Articles 15 and 16; but a conflict may arise in the future because, while the SPS Agreement largely excludes the application of the precautionary principle, the Cartagena Protocol clearly embodies this principle).

9. Our members are also concerned with possible liability under international law. While we think our products are safe, is there a possibility we will be faced with lawsuits over damages allegedly caused by our exports of living modified organisms? (Consult the provisions of the Nagoya-Kuala Lumpur Supplementary Protocol on Liability and Redress to the Cartagena Protocol (2010), which is reprinted in the **Document Supplement**).

Section III. PROTECTION OF SPECIES DIVERSITY

A. Treaties to Conserve or Protect Migratory Birds and Other Species

Traditionally the common type of international agreement protecting biodiversity was aimed at protecting particular species or groups of species. A large number of such treaties protect or conserve marine species — marine mammals such as seals, whales, and dolphins (the U.S. comprehensively protects marine mammals under domestic law, the Marine Mammal Protection Act, 16 U.S.C. § 1361 *et seq.*), and fish such as salmon and bluefin tuna. We discuss these treaties in Chapter 7. A second important category of species conservation treaty is agreements to protect migratory birds. The United States has concluded a Convention Between the United States and Canada for the Protection of Migratory Birds (1916) (39 STAT. 1702; TS 628); a Convention Between the United States and the Union of Soviet Socialist Republics (now Russia) Concerning the Conservation of Migratory Birds and their Environment (1976) (TIAS 9073); a Convention between the United States and the United Mexican States for the Protection of Migratory Birds and Game Mammals (1936) (50 Stat. 1311; TS 912); and a Convention Between the United States and Japan for the Protection of Migratory Birds and Birds in Danger of Extinction (1972) (25 UST 3329; TIAS 7990). Third, the United States is a party to an Agreement to Protect Polar Bears (1973) (13 I.L.M. 13 (1974)) along with Canada, Denmark, Norway, and the USSR (now Russia).

B. The Convention on International Trade in Endangered Species of Wild Fauna and Flora (CITES)

1. How CITES Works

The primary mechanism for the regulation of international trade in endangered species is the Convention on International Trade in Endangered Species of Wild Fauna and Flora (CITES)[22], which was drafted in the 1960s, opened for signing in 1973, and entered into force in 1975. CITES is legally binding on Parties, but relies on the Parties themselves to implement the CITES framework in their respective jurisdictions. The system is largely reliant on self-policing, and trade suspensions are generally used to punish non-compliance with CITES policies. There are currently 177 Parties to CITES, with the U.S. being one of the first states to adopt the agreement. It is considered one of the strongest bodies of international environmental law to date. Approximately 5,000 animal and 29,000 plant species are listed as protected in CITES' Appendices. Some listed species include sea turtles, parrots, corals, and orchids. The Conference of the Parties (COP) serves as CITES' main governing body and holds regular meetings.

The main objective of CITES is to prevent the commercial over-exploitation of plant and animal species which are in danger of extinction. In its preamble, CITES

---

[22] See the website, http://www.cites.org.

goes beyond the economic perspective of most conservation treaties. "Conscious of the ever-growing value of wild fauna and flora from aesthetic, scientific, cultural, recreational and economic points of view," it recognizes that wild flora and fauna are an "irreplaceable part of the natural systems of the earth which must be protected for generations to come."

CITES provides three different categories of threatened species distinguished based on the degree of protection needed. Appendix I is a list of species considered in present danger of extinction. Species listed under this appendix are subject to a general ban on international trade, the object being to halt the international trade leading to overexploitation of these species. There are limited exceptions to this ban in order to permit, for example, the international transportation of living species or specimens for scientific purposes. Appendix II includes a list of species which, though not currently threatened with extinction, may face such danger if international trade is not strictly monitored and controlled. These species may be traded commercially if it would not be detrimental to the survival of the species. The Conference of Parties (COP), the decision-making body within CITES, meets every three years and uses a set of established biological and trade criteria to determine whether a species should be listed on either Appendix I or II. Listing requires a two-thirds vote (Article XV) and a Party who disagrees with an affirmative listing vote has 90 days to file a dissenting reservation. Appendix III lists species which may only be endangered within some territories and jurisdictions. Unlike Appendices I and II, Appendix III can be unilaterally amended by individual Parties.

The framework created by CITES is implemented at the domestic level by Parties, which are required by Article IX to designate Management and Scientific Authorities to grant permits or certificates on its behalf and perform other functions. Permits and certificates granted by such bodies, in line with Article VI, are to comply with the various requirements listed in CITES and its appendices. While some national laws are stricter than others, CITES requires at a minimum that listed species are not to be exported or imported by Parties without such permits or certificates being obtained and presented for clearance at the appropriate ports of entry or exit. As one might suspect, the bar for obtaining import and export permits and certificates is higher for Appendix I species and lower for Appendix II and Appendix III species. However, for all listed species, Management Authorities are instructed to take measures to ensure that the preparation and shipment of such species are undertaken in manner which minimizes the risk of injury, damage to health, or cruel treatment of the species.

CITES, which entered into force in 1975, currently has 177 parties and about 33,000 species of plants and animals are accorded some degree of protection under its provision, including about 900 species protected under Appendix I; and some 32,000 species listed on Appendices II and III. Parties to CITES are required to designate management and scientific authorities to carry out the functions specified in the treaty; the U.S. has designated the U.S. Fish and Wildlife Service as the lead CITES agency.

Since CITES regulates international trade, the problem arises whether its provisions are consistent with the international trade agreements administered by the World Trade Organization. This matter is covered in Chapter 5 of this book.

NOTES AND QUESTIONS

1. *CITES violations.* Assume that a Contracting Party violates CITES by illegally trading a listed species. Under CITES, how is the violator accountable for adverse impacts of its trading activity on the listed species in question? In other words, assuming such adverse impacts could be quantifiably measured, is the violator "liable" for the damage?

2. CITES attempts to control directly the activity of trading, not the adverse consequences of trade's impact-on certain species. In other words, CITES does not itself impose liability, fines, or sanctions against trade participants which might arguably cause adverse impacts on certain species. Consequently, CITES does not contain "compensation/restoration" provisions triggered by measurable consequences of international trade. Similarly, CITES also does not contain "response/ adaptation" requirements which respond to measurable impacts on certain species. For example, CITES does not require "responsible" Parties to incur response costs or to bear the cost of remedying adverse impacts on certain species.

3. *Incentives.* What incentives does CITES offer to Parties? Do CITES' provisions which require the dissemination of scientific and technological information create a financial "incentive" to Parties? What should be the primary motivators for encouraging state participation in an environmental treaty? States were urged to join CITES given the "ever-growing value of wild fauna and flora from aesthetic, scientific, cultural, recreational and economic points of view." However, from a more practical point of view, states — especially lesser developed countries — often need financial "carrots" before they will sign on to a treaty which requires them to adopt measures that place restraints on domestic economic development efforts.

4. *Dispute Resolution under CITES.* What if two parties differ in their interpretation of CITES provisions? How can the Parties resolve their dispute? Can the Parties ask the Secretariat for a formal interpretation of a disputed provision? The main objective of CITES is to discourage trade in species listed in the Appendices (*See* Article II, para. 4). Such trade is subject to "strict" regulation. However, trade is permissible among the Parties so long as the appropriate scientific and management authorities make certain determinations. Although CITES' primary implementation mechanism operates through the regulatory provisions of Articles III, IV, and V, these regulations do allow for wide discretion. Therefore, it appears that an implied "honor code" underlies CITES provisions, and that this implied aspect of CITES operates as the fundamental mechanism for achievement of the Treaty's objectives and full implementation of its provisions. This wide discretion also leaves much room for disagreement.

5. Article XVIII sets forth CITES' disputes resolution provisions. Paragraph 1 states that any dispute arising between or among Parties concerning interpretation or application of the Treaty should be negotiated between/among the Parties. If the Parties cannot resolve their dispute, paragraph 2 provides that the Parties can jointly submit their dispute to binding arbitration. If this is not successful, a Party can resort to more drastic tactics like denunciation. Many disputes and disagreements have occurred between CITES Parties, but the formal dispute resolution procedure has never been used.

6. The Parties may also ask the Secretariat for a recommendation, but this does not result in an authoritative interpretation. Of course, disputing Parties who agree to submit their dispute to binding arbitration will receive a binding authoritative interpretation of the disputed provision's meaning, but this interpretation is not necessarily authoritative outside the particular arbitration. Later parties could look to such decisions as persuasive authority.

7. *Regulation of Trade.* How does CITES promote organization and cooperation between the Parties to develop programs aimed at protecting listed species? Article III, IV, and V regulate trade in certain species by requiring the scientific and management authorities of import and export countries to coordinate their permitting processes. Article VIII, paras. 6, 7, and 8 encourage Parties to share information concerning species import and export activities by subjecting the Parties to record-keeping and reporting requirements, and to make such information available to the public. The procedural requirements of Articles XI, XV, XVI, XVII, and XVIII encourage the Parties to regularly meet and discuss the effectiveness of Treaty provisions, to resolve related disputes, and to negotiate improvements. For these reasons, CITES provides a fairly detailed blueprint for how the international community can and should cooperate to protect certain species of wild fauna and flora against over-exploitation through international trade.

8. *Shortcomings.* Although CITES stepped up the international community's conservation efforts by restricting trade in endangered species of plants and animals, CITES as a conservation instrument is limited in several key respects: 1) CITES protects only those plants and animals which have been identified and listed in its Appendices as either threatened or endangered; 2) CITES restricts only the international trade of listed plants and animals, and 3) CITES provides only vague restrictions on trade with non-Parties. CITES does not promote conservation of unlisted species. Additionally, CITES does not mandate how signatories use or exploit these resources outside the parameters of the trade restriction provisions. For example, bluefin tuna — a species that scientists agree is heavily overfished — is not listed and is therefore not regulated under CITES' trade restrictions. *See generally* Fiona Harvey, *Overfishing Causes Pacific Bluefin Tuna Numbers to Drop 96%*, THE GUARDIAN, Jan. 9, 2013. Also, CITES does not purport to regulate domestic trade in listed species. Conserving biodiversity may require the international community to adopt a broader, more far-reaching instrument which could ensure that all plants and animals are hunted, harvested and traded on a sustainable basis.

9. *Market forces.* By banning international trade in endangered species, CITES seeks to remove the economic incentives which are responsible for the over-exploitation of these species. This approach seeks to work through the economic system by raising the price of a species' product by reducing the size of the market in which it is sold, and by increasing the costs of supply through the criminalization of the production process. To what extent do the current developments in "sustainable use" under CITES reflect this approach? Do current attempts at "sustainable use" provide appropriate incentives for the conservation of endangered species? What are some of the problems with permitting the relisting of Appendix I species as Appendix II species to allow trade in commercially developed species?

10. *The SPAW Protocol.* The 1990 Protocol Concerning Specially Protected Areas of Wildlife (signed in Kingston, Jamaica on January 18, 1990) to the Convention for the Protection and Development of the Marine Environment of the Wider Caribbean Region (Cartagena Convention), is more far-reaching than CITES. The SPAW Protocol builds upon the Cartagena Convention requirements that the Contracting Parties establish regimes to protect and preserve rare and fragile ecosystems, as well as the habitats of threatened and endangered species of fauna and flora. In essence, the SPAW Protocol is a means for local implementation of these requirements in the Caribbean Region. The SPAW Protocol contains three Annexes listing endangered species within the Caribbean Region. The SPAW Protocol requires parties to establish protected areas (Article 4), and to undertake certain protection measures (Article 5) and planning and management measures (Article 6). Additionally, parties must adopt national measures to implement protection of listed flora and fauna (Article 10), and to regulate activities having adverse effects on protected species and their habitats, including the killing of or trade in these species. Similar to the 1991 Madrid Protocol to the Antarctic Treaty, the SPAW Protocol requires parties to perform environmental assessments on "industrial and other projects and activities that would have a negative environmental impact." The Protocol also obligates parties to publicize protected areas (Article 16), to conduct certain scientific and technical research (Article 17), to cooperate with implementing the Protocol (Article 18) and to submit reports on protected areas to the U.N. Environment Program (Article 19).

11. *A Ranching exception?* Is ranching permissible with respect to species listed in Appendix I? Read Articles III and VII (4) of CITES. What is the effect of the deemed transfer of "specimens bred in captivity for commercial purposes" from Appendix I to Appendix II? What are the restrictions on trade applicable to Appendix II species. Clearly the Conference of the Parties was relying on the deemed transfer provision in Article VII (4) to permit trade in "ranched" specimens. Is this trade consistent with CITES general use of bans to foreclose markets of Appendix I species? And are markets for Appendix I species really being foreclosed if we allow limited trade? Once on the market, how can we be certain that specimens were "bred in captivity" rather than taken illegally from the wild? See Article VII, which provides for the marking of specimens "where appropriate and feasible."

12. *Enforcement.* CITES leaves enforcement to the Parties. Enforcement of CITES is problematic. According to a 2013 Report[23] by the International Fund for Animal Welfare illegal wildlife trade is now worth $19 billion annually and is the fourth largest branch of illegal international trade. In the past decade, over 1000 forest rangers have been killed at the hands of poachers. In July 2013, President Obama issued Executive Order 13648 directing increased action by U.S. agencies to combat illegal wildlife trafficking. *See Note*, 107 Am. J. Int'l L. 924 (2013).

---

[23] *Criminal Nature* (2013), *available at* http://www.ifaw.org.

2. Sustainable Use Issues

Throughout its early history CITES was criticized for "following a narrow preservationist agenda [centered] on protecting charismatic species through trade-restrictive policies that disregard the livelihood strategies of communities living alongside wildlife."[24] However, in more recent years, CITES expanded its framework to facilitate increased input from local people, thus helping to bridge the gap between wildlife conservation and economic development. The concept of sustainable development is relatively unprecedented within the CITES context, and it still remains to be seen how exactly this new focus will influence policymaking. Parties seem to be somewhat divided on the issue — some view CITES as a means to prevent unsustainable species use; others see it as a means to ensure and facilitate the sustainable use of endangered species.

Scholars point to the increased participation of developing countries, particularly during the mid-1990s, to explain CITES' eventual recognition and appreciation of sustainable development as a part of its international conservation scheme.[25] As adopted by COP 14 in 2007, the CITES' Strategic Vision for 2008–2013 states that the primary purpose of CITES is to "[c]onserve biodiversity and contribute to its sustainable use by ensuring that no species of wild fauna or flora becomes or remains subject to unsustainable exploitation through international trade, thereby contributing to the significant reduction of the rate of biodiversity loss."[26] This statement indicates that the CITES framework is concerned with preventing the unsustainable trade of endangered species, but does not necessarily encourage the trade of endangered species even if undertaken in a sustainable manner. This may be a result of the fact that many Parties still define sustainable use in biological terms. COP 14 also saw the development of policies meant to assess the impacts of CITES conservation strategies on the livelihoods of direct resource users, local producers, and the poor, especially in developing countries.

The tension between economic development and species conservation was also evident at COP 15 (2010, Doha), where the proposed Appendix I listing of bluefin tuna received a less than welcome response from Japan. Consuming nearly 80% of the world's bluefin tuna, Japan voted against its listing despite wide agreement among scientists that bluefin met the criteria for an Article I species. Defending its vote, Japan cited the fact that bluefin is managed by another international body, though many argue that an Appendix I listing would not bar other organizations from continuing their management functions. Japan also claimed that the European Union, which supported listing bluefin under Appendix I, would unfairly benefit since trade between European Union countries is considered domestic and therefore does not fall within the auspices of CITES.

Perhaps the most important aspect of this tale is not the vote itself, but the changing dynamics and rising stakes implicit in the modem CITES framework. Japan brought a large delegation to COP 15 and flew in over 10 nondomestic

---

[24] Jose Octavio Velazquez Gomar and Lindsay C. Stringer, *Moving Toward Sustainablity: An Analysis of CITES' Conservation Policies*, 21 Env't Pol'y & Governance 240, 240 (2011).

[25] *Id.* at 249.

[26] Quoted *Id.* at 249.

fisheries ministers — mainly from African states in which it was financing projects-to ensure the vote went their way. These actions are indicative of a larger trend. Parties, cognizant of the effects species listings can have on their domestic economies, are increasingly represented at these meetings by members of trade and fisheries ministries as opposed to environment and wildlife officials. One can hardly blame Japan for wanting to protect its domestic producers and consumers, but what does this episode say about the effectiveness of the CITES framework? If a species as high-profile and overfished as bluefin tuna cannot find protection within the auspices of CITES, what future lies ahead for other commercially popular endangered species? *Fishy Business: How The Elephants' Success Hurt the Bluefin Tuna*, THE ECONOMIST, Mar. 25, 2010, *available at* http://www.economist.com/node/ 15767253. *See also Eaten Away: A Ban on the Trade in Bluefin Tuna Is Rejected*, THE ECONOMIST, Mar. 18, 2010, *available at* http://www.economist.com/node/ 15745509.

At the 16th Meeting of the Conference of Parties in Bangkok, held in March 2013, several commercially exploited marine species were voted into Appendix II of CITES. In particular, Appendix II listing was afforded to manta rays, oceanic whitetip sharks, porbeagle sharks, and three species of hammerhead sharks. This listing increases the protection afforded to such species, while still permitting legal and sustainable trade. Shark fins are prized in many Asian countries, where shark fin soup is enjoyed as a delicacy. The shark fin trade is extremely profitable, and fishermen have taken note. This has resulted in a significant and unsustainable decline in global shark populations. Manta rays, on the other hand, are often targeted for their gill plates. While the gill plate trade does not garner as much international attention as shark finning, many argue it is just as serious. Gill plates, used by manta rays to filter plankton out of the water column, are often used in Chinese traditional medicine to treat a variety of afflictions. As the bluefin tuna example demonstrated, listing commercially valuable species can be difficult. Conservationists, recognizing the importance of sharks and manta rays to ocean ecosystems, hope that the Appendix II listing will give these species the protection they need in order for their populations to rebound to sustainable levels. However, the fact that Parties can make reservations to new listing may limit the effect of this decision. Sharks and Manta Rays Receive Protection Under CITES, NOAA Fisheries, March 14, 2013, *available at* http://www.nmfs.noaa.gov/ia/slider_stories/ 2013/02/cites_cop16.html.

3. Implementation and Enforcement

As previously stated, CITES lays out requirements, policies and decisions which are to be implemented by Parties at the domestic level. Article XIV makes clear that Parties are free to adopt domestic measures which are stricter than those found within the CITES framework. In the United States, for example, CITES is implemented through the domestic Endangered Species Act (ESA) which was passed in 1973. Parties are also responsible for establishing domestic Management and Scientific Authorities to oversee the CITES permitting system. Since the system is heavily reliant on domestic implementation and enforcement, some argue that Parties may choose not to enforce trade restrictions that may adversely affect their domestic economies. Also, Parties with something to gain from the trade of listed species could strategically engage with non-Parties who have more lax regulations.

Parties to CITES are also permitted to make specific reservations if entered in accordance with Articles XXII, XV, and XVI. Reservations may be entered regarding any listed species, or any parts or derivatives listed in Appendix III. These Parties are essentially treated as non-Parties in relation to the portions of CITES which they have entered reservations against. For example, Japan, Norway, and Iceland have entered reservations to several species of whales, dolphins and porpoises listed in Appendices I and II.[27] Generally, a Party must enter a reservation within 90 days of becoming a Party or the adoption of an amendment to the Appendices (for example, the listing of a new species). While the reservation system may seem to defeat some of the core preservationist principles of CITES, the ability to opt-out is likely one of the reasons why CITES has such strong international membership. Recognizing the potential for implementation problems inherent in allowing reservations, COP adopted a Resolution at COP 14 which recommends that Parties who have made reservations to Appendix I listed species instead treat the species in question as if it were an Appendix II species. CITES also lists several exemptions to trade protection in Article VII. For example, certain trade restrictions may be waived for specimens that are part of a traveling zoo or collection, or that are bred in captivity for commercial purposes. It has been argued that illegal smugglers are often able to fraudulently claim these exceptions, but accurate numbers detailing this phenomenon are hard to come by.

The CITES Standing Committee, a part of the COP apparatus which provides policy guidance to the Secretariat regarding implementation issues, also recommends trade sanctions in some situations where noncompliance with CITES is discovered. Such recommendations are to be taken into account by domestic management authorities of other Parties in considering applications for permits or certificates. Most of the Parties currently subject to recommended trade sanctions are in Africa.

In 2011, four international organizations joined CITES to create the International Consortium on Combating Wildlife Crime (ICCWC) for the purpose of supporting national wildlife enforcement agencies and regional networks that protect natural resources. The organizations that make up ICCWC include: the CITES Secretariat, INTERPOL, the U.N. Office on Drugs and Crime, the World Bank, and the World Customs Organization. The ICCWC organizations recognize that perpetrators of wildlife crimes often face a low risk of detection and punishment and hope that, in joining together, this will no longer be the case. How successful this effort will be remains to be seen, although steps toward stronger enforcement of CITES are likely to strengthen the regime as a whole.

PROBLEM 8-6
PROTECTING ELEPHANTS

Both Asian and African species of elephants are protected under CITES and listed in Appendix I. African elephants receive special protection in the United

---

[27] Reservations entered by Parties, CITES website, http://www.cites.org/eng/app/reserve.php.

States under the African Elephant Conservation Act of 1989, 16 U.S.C. § 4201 *et seq.* Under CITES, populations of elephants in Namibia, Botswana, and Zimbabwe are listed in Appendix Ii to allow limited trade in those elephants. Listing the African elephant on Appendix I was very controversial when it occurred, but the CITES parties have accepted the listing with the three-country exception arrangement.

1. Jed, a law student, would like to buy a piece of worked ivory as a keepsake. On vacation in New York, he sees an ivory carving he would like to buy. If Jed purchases the ivory and brings it back to his home in California, has he violated CITES?

2. Jed would love to buy more ivory, especially what is known as raw ivory (ivory that is a tusk or a piece of a tusk that is unpolished or polished but unaltered and minimally carved). On vacation in Botswana, Jed sees raw ivory being sold at very reasonable prices on the streets of cities. Jed buys a piece of raw ivory. Can this piece be legally imported into the United States?

3. Jed has a piece of worked (carved) ivory that he inherited from his mother. He is sure that this ivory was originally acquired legally about 1965. Jed is going to China and needs some extra cash. He decides to take the ivory with him to China with the intention of selling it there. He has heard there is a great demand for ivory in China. Will this be consistent with CITES?

PROBLEM 8-7
PROTECTING POLAR BEARS

The United States implements its obligations under CITES primarily by means of two federal statutes, the Marine Mammal Protection Act (MMPA), 16 U.S.C. § 1361 *et seq.*, and the Endangered Species Act (ESA), 16 U.S.C. § 1531 *et seq.* The MMPA, 16 U.S.C. § 1371(a) places a general moratorium on the taking and importation of all marine mammals, regardless of the species scarcity or abundance. This moratorium, however, has several exceptions, including one that allows the importation of sport-hunted polar bear trophies. 16 U.S.C. § 1371(a)(1). Moreover, 16 U.S.C. § 1374(c)(5)(A) authorizes the Fish and Wildlife Service to issue a permit for the importation of polar bear parts (other than internal organs) taken in sport hunts in Canada and provides that the Service "shall" do so when certain criteria are satisfied.

A 2006 study estimated the number of remaining polar bears in the world at 20,000 to 25,000 in nineteen discrete population groups. On May 15, 2008, the Fish and Wildlife Service published a rule listing the polar bear as a threatened species under the ESA. *Determination of Threatened Status for the Polar Bear (Ursus maritimus) Throughout Its Range*, 73 Fed. Reg. 2812 (May 15, 2008). In the same rule, the Service determined that the listing had the effect of designating the polar bear as "depleted" under the MMPA, and that accordingly sections 101(a)(3)(B) and 102(b)(3) bar continued importation of sport-hunted polar bear trophies under that statute.

You are the attorney for two hunters who killed polar bears in Canada prior to the listing decision and now — after the effective date of the rule — wish to import polar bear skins and heads as trophies into the United States. The Service has written to your clients rejecting their import applications, explaining that "import of polar bear trophies from Canada is no longer available even if your bears were hunted prior to the effective date of the ESA listing."

What can you do to help your clients? (1) Should you challenge the listing as arbitrary and capricious? *See In re Polar Bear Endangered Species Act Listing*, 709 F.3d 1 (D.C. Cir. 2013). (2) What about the argument that listing under the ESA should not be carried over to the MMPA? But the MMPA, sections 1371(a)(5)(E)(i) and 1387(a)(2) refer to a species being "depleted" because of or on the basis of its listing as an endangered or threatened species under the ESA. (3) What about the argument that the MMPA authorization to import sport-hunted polar bear trophies applies even where the polar bear is designated as depleted under the MMPA? But the MMPA clearly bars importation of a depleted species with only an exception for scientific research and actions enhancing the survival of the species. 16 U.S.C. §§ 1371(a)(3)(B) and 1372(b). (4) What about arguing that the import restrictions apply only to polar bears taken after the species was designated as depleted? The statute, 16 U.S.C. § 1372(b)(3), prohibits importation of any marine mammal "taken from a species or population stock which the Secretary has, by regulation . . . designated as a depleted species or stock." *See In Re Polar Bear Endangered Species Act*, 720 F.3d 354 (D.C. Cir. 2013).

Section IV.   PROTECTION OF ECOSYSTEMS

A.   Wetlands

Wetlands are areas covered by water either permanently or seasonally. Some common wetland types include swamps, bogs, marshes, and fens. Wetlands are found all across the world and are important, highly diverse habitats. Not only do wetlands support a wide range of plant and animal life, wetlands perform important ecosystem services. For example, wetlands may improve water quality, protect against floods, stabilize shorelines, and recharge groundwater. Wetlands may also constitute a source of food for local communities. However, largely due to human activity and urbanization, many wetland ecosystems have been lost or degraded.

The Convention on Wetlands of International Importance — more commonly known as the Ramsar Convention — is an international treaty governing wetland use and conservation. Its mission is "the conservation and wise use of all wetlands through local and national actions and international cooperation, as a contribution towards achieving sustainable development throughout the world." The Convention contains a broad definition of wetlands, including "areas of marsh, fen, peatland or water, whether natural or artificial, permanent or temporary, with water that is static or flowing, fresh, brackish or salt, including areas of marine water the depth of which at low tide does not exceed six meters."

The centerpiece of the Ramsar Convention is its "Wise Use Concept," which emphasizes the importance of maintaining the ecological character of wetlands through the implementation of ecosystem approaches, within the context of sustainable development. The Ramsar Convention was adopted in 1971 and currently has 164 Contracting Parties. The United States is a Contracting Party and maintains 35 Ramsar sites. The Ramsar Convention has also been designated as the "lead implementation partner on wetlands" to the Convention on Biodiversity.

Article 2 of the Ramsar Convention requires Contracting Parties to designate wetland sites for inclusion in the List of Wetlands of International Importance. In practice, this is done using certain scientifically accepted criteria for identifying wetlands of International Importance. Wetlands designated in the List are to be significant in terms of ecology, botany, zoology, limnology, or hydrology. After the Secretariat acknowledges the status of a listed site, certification is sent to the administrative authority charged with implementing the Ramsar Convention in the Contracting Party's jurisdiction.

CONVENTION ON WETLANDS OF INTERNATIONAL IMPORTANCE ESPECIALLY AS WATERFOWL HABITAT
996 U.N.T.S. 245 (1971)

Article 2

1. Each Contracting Party shall designate suitable wetlands within its territory for inclusion in a List of Wetlands of International Importance, hereinafter referred to as "the List" which is maintained by the bureau established under Article 8. The boundaries of each wetland shall be precisely described and also delimited on a map and they may incorporate riparian and coastal zones adjacent to the wetlands, and islands or bodies of marine water deeper than six meters at low tide lying within the wetlands, especially where these have importance as waterfowl habitat.

2. Wetlands should be selected for the List on account of their international significance in terms of ecology, botany, zoology, limnology or hydrology. In the first instance wetlands of international importance to waterfowl at any season should be included.

3. The inclusion of a wetland in the List does not prejudice the exclusive sovereign rights of the Contracting Party in whose territory the wetland is situated.

4. Each Contracting Party shall designate at least one wetland to be included in the List when signing this Convention or when depositing its instrument of ratification or accession, as provided in Article 9.

5. Any Contracting Party shall have the right to add to the List further wetlands situated within its territory, to extend the boundaries of those wetlands already included by it in the List, or, because of its urgent national interests, to delete or restrict the boundaries of wetlands already included by it in the List and shall, at the earliest possible time, inform the organization or government responsible for the continuing bureau duties specified in Article 8 of any such changes.

6. Each Contracting Party shall consider its international responsibilities for the conservation, management and wise use of migratory stocks of

waterfowl, both when designating entries for the List and when exercising its right to change entries in the List relating to wetlands within its territory.

NOTES AND QUESTIONS

1. Under the Ramsar Convention, Contracting Parties are to promote the conservation of listed wetlands and the "wise use" of all other wetlands.[28] In this way, listed wetlands are afforded superior protection under this legal framework. Contracting Parties are also obligated to establish nature reserves in wetlands regardless of their inclusion in the Ramsar List. In terms of international cooperation, Article 5 states that Contracting Parties are required to "consult with each other about implementing obligations arising from the Convention especially in the case of a wetland extending over the territories of more than one Contracting Party or where a water system is shared by Contracting Parties." Additionally, Contracting Parties are instructed to coordinate their policies and regulations concerning wetlands conservation. Contracting Parties also have reporting responsibilities under the Ramsar Convention. Parties are to periodically report information from their jurisdictions to the Conference of the Contracting Parties and should report changes or threats to listed wetlands.

2. Some have criticized the Ramsar Convention for being too limited in scope.[29] While the Convention's terms focus on wetland conservation and wise use, the fact remains that activities far from wetlands can affect their health and viability. It has also been argued that the "Wise Use" concept has not been wholeheartedly embraced by the Contracting Parties, especially if there remains scientific uncertainty about the sustainability of certain human activities.[30] For example, many Parties maintain the right to conduct potentially unsustainable activities on wetlands, like grazing, introduced species, cropping, and peat mining. In cases where the scientific community has doubts about the sustainability of a given activity but lacks sufficient hard evidence, should continuation of such activities be accepted under the "Wise Use" banner?

3. The Conference of Contracting Parties has established a Compliance Committee for the Convention. If a Party to the Ramsar Convention wants to delete a recognized Wetland of International Importance from the List, what can the Compliance Committee do if other Contracting Parties oppose this action?

B. Forests

Forests perform three important ecological functions. First, forests support biodiversity by providing a habitat for a variety of species. Second, forests slow the process of climate change by limiting atmospheric concentrations of carbon dioxide. Lastly, forests play a significant role in maintaining and improving soil

---

[28] D. Farrier & L. Tucker, *Wise Use of Wetlands Under the Ramsar Convention: A Challenge for Meaningful Implementation of International Law*, 12 J. OF ENVTL L. 21, 24 (2000).

[29] *Id.* at 22.

[30] *Id.* at 33.

quality. As a result, forest conservation is a vital part of global efforts to support biodiversity and mitigate climate change. PHILIPPE SANDS, PRINCIPLES OF INTERNATIONAL ENVIRONMENTAL LAW 545–51 (2d ed. 2003).

The world's total forest area is approximately four billion hectares, making up roughly 30% of global land area. Some forest area is lost from natural causes, like drought. However, much of the forest loss in the world today is a result of logging, overgrazing, and environmental mismanagement. A U.N. Food and Agriculture (FAO) report published in 2010 revealed that while global deforestation has decreased over the past decade, deforestation rates are still alarmingly high in certain regions. In the 1990s, an estimated 16 million hectares of forests were lost or destroyed per year, compared with an estimated 13 million hectares per year between 2000 and 2010.[31] This decline can be attributed to several factors, including tree planting programs in countries like China, India, and the United States. Also, several countries with the high deforestation rates in the 1990s — such as Brazil and Indonesia — have significantly reduced their rates of forest loss. The FAO report found that deforestation rates were highest in South American and African countries. Although the world saw less deforestation in the 2000–2010 period, a trend the FAO partly attributes to international conservation efforts, it is important to note that the net forest area lost was still equivalent to the size of Costa Rica. In 2014, deforestation continues at a rate of about 13 million hectares per year.[32]

The Convention on Biological Diversity (CBD) calls on Parties to establish biologically and geographically representative networks of protected areas relative to forest types. Parties are to ensure that at least 10% of each of the world's forest types is "effectively conserved." Some have criticized this 10% threshold as being arbitrary and unhelpful — this number is not based on biological evidence and does not guarantee that high priority forest areas are protected.[33] Conserving 10% of ecologically distinct forest areas does not necessarily conserve 10% of biodiversity within the world's forests. Some forest types, like tropical forests, support more biodiversity than others. Moreover, studies have shown that Parties are having trouble achieving the 10% threshold. Since the 10% figure was a compromise reached by the Parties after prolonged negotiations, some may consider it better than nothing. Still, it has been suggested that systematic conservation planning on a regional scale would be more effective because such a system could act with increased precision and efficiency for more targeted results.

The Convention on the International Trade in Endangered Species (CITES) also gives some protection to forests. At the 16th Conference of Parties, held in Bangkok in 2013, several tree species were added to CITES' appendices. Rosewood, mahogany, and ebony trees were among those listed as protected species. These trees have been particularly targeted by the logging trade in recent

---

[31] World deforestation decreases, but remains alarming to many countries: FAO publishes key findings of global forest resources assessments, Food and Agriculture Organization of the United Nations, March 25, 2010, *available at* http://www.fao.org/news/story/en/item/40893/icode/.

[32] *Id.*

[33] Schmitt et al., *Global Analysis of the Protection Status of the World's Forests*, 142 BIOLOGICAL CONSERVATION 2122 (2009).

years. Ebony and rosewood, for example, are used to make up-market furniture and musical instruments. Because this timber can fetch top-dollar in the international market, especially in Asian countries, these trees have become a target for organized criminal enterprises. CITES listing could make a positive difference for these tree species, but if exporting countries are more interested in short-term profits than in long-term conservation goals, then enforcement could be a challenge.

The International Tropical Timber Agreement (ITTA), adopted in 1994 and amended in 2006, is another binding international agreement relating to forest conservation. Its primary objective is to promote the sustainable management of tropical timber producing forests. In this way, the ITTA functions as both a conservation and a trade agreement. The International Tropical Timber Organization (ITTO), created in the late 1980s, helps Parties fulfill their obligations within the ITTA. The 2006 version of the ITTA contains provisions on sustainable management of tropical forests, information sharing, and annual reporting. Many of the ITTA's objectives are to be fulfilled through policy work, international consultation, and projects undertaken by the lTTO and ITTA Parties. The ITTA, which is based in Yokohama, Japan, has over 60 members, including the United States.

In 1992, at the United Nations Conference on Environment and Development, the delegates adopted a "Non-Legally Binding Authoritative Statement of Principles for a Global Consensus on the Management, Conservation and Sustainable Development of All Types of Forests" (1992 Forest Principles).[34] The 1992 Forest Principles make recommendations for the forest conservation and sustainable forestry. There was much tension in the negotiation of this document between developing and developed nations. Developing nations claimed that without increased foreign aid it would be impossible for them to take the conservation decisions proposed. Because the developed nations were unwilling to make such foreign aid commitments, the 1992 Forest Principles are less ambitious than they otherwise might have been. Nonetheless, critics have said that the Principles themselves are poorly drafted and are of little practical assistance in terms of international forest conservation.

Thus, there is no extant international regime governing forest conservation or preventing deforestation. In Chapter 4, we studied a new effort known as REDD-Plus (Reducing Emissions from Deforestation and Forest Degradation) being developed under the Climate Change regime. REDD-Plus is based upon creating incentives for developing countries to manage their forests sustainably by instituting a system of "results-based financing."

C. World Heritage

International agreements for the conservation of cultural and natural heritage also tend to be broad enough in scope to contribute to the preservation of biodiversity. For example, the 1972 Convention Concerning the Protection of the World Cultural and Natural Heritage (World Heritage Convention) defines

---

[34] Report of the United Nations Conference on Environment and Development, Annex III (1992).

"natural heritage" to include "natural features consisting of physical and biological formations or groups of such formations, which are of outstanding universal value from the aesthetic or scientific point of view . . ."

The World Heritage Convention requires Parties to integrate protection of natural heritage into domestic planning programs, conduct scientific and technical studies as needed to enable the proper protection and conservation of natural heritage, and to take appropriate legal or financial measures to preserve or rehabilitate natural heritage. The World Heritage Committee, which meets annually and consists of 21 elected members, is charged with administering the World Heritage Convention.

Parties to the World Heritage Convention delineate their own cultural and natural heritage sites. These sites constitute a "world heritage" for the international community, but are left to the protection of individual Parties. The United States has designed over 20 World Heritage sites. One of these sites, Redwoods National Park, is a habitat for species such as the bald eagle and the endangered California brown pelican. Other famous areas listed as World Heritage Sites are the Great Barrier Reef in Australia and the Galapagos Islands in Ecuador.

While urged to conserve these sites to the fullest extent by the treaty, ultimately Parties retain jurisdiction over the sites and may administer them as they see fit. Some Parties, such as Australia, have interpreted the obligations in the World Heritage Convention to be legally binding to the extent that they could prohibit domestic actions which could adversely affect designated sites. (*See* Ch. 2). Other Parties regard the obligations of the World Heritage Convention as only statements of intention and aspirational guides.

Section V. COMBATTING DESERTIFICATION

Desertification is the development of desert-like conditions in regions that have minimal rainfall coupled with human disturbances, such as deforestation, overgrazing, and poorly managed agriculture. Dryland ecosystems, which characterize as much as one-third of land ecosystems, are especially vulnerable to human over-exploitation. The problem of desertification is widespread: all areas with a ratio within the range of 0.5 to 0.65, annual precipitation to annual evaporation, are potentially affected. Especially vulnerable are areas in Africa, Asia, Latin America and the Caribbean, the northern Mediterranean, and central and Eastern Europe.

In 1992, during the United Nations Conference on Environment and Development, desertification, along with loss of biodiversity and climate change, was identified as presenting the greatest challenge to sustainable development. Desertification causes degradation of dryland ecosystems along with human impoverishment. The consequences of desertification include forced migration, impoverishment of populations, and food shortages. Desertification therefore adversely affects the functioning of ecosystems and biological diversity, accompanied by direct adverse impacts on human populations.

A.   The Desertification Convention

In 1994, an international conference concluded the United Nations Convention to Combat Desertification in Countries Experiencing Serious Drought and/or Desertification, Particularly in Africa (UNCCD). The UNCCD, which has 194 parties (including the United States), is a legally binding international instrument designed to take actions to combat desertification and to rehabilitate affected regions and ecosystems.

The UNCCD is reprinted in the **Document Supplement** of this book. Read the Convention and answer the following questions:

1.   What are the objectives of the Convention? (Art. 2).

2.   What state-parties are eligible for assistance in implementing these objectives? (Art. 4).

3.   What are the obligations of developed state-parties? (Art. 6).

4.   Is the UNCCD related to other UN conventions? (Art. 8).

5.   What is the basic mechanism used to implement the UNCCD? (Arts. 9–19).

6.   How is the Convention financed? (Arts. 20–21). The Global Environment Fund is designated as the lead funding agency for desertification projects.

7.   What institutions are created by the Convention? (Arts. 22–25).

Note that the UNCCD contains five separate annexes for regional implementation. Annex I is the Regional Implementation Annex for Africa; Annex II is the Regional Implementation Annex for Asia; Annex III is the Regional Implementation Annex for Latin America and the Caribbean; Annex IV is the Regional Implementation Annex for the Northern Mediterranean; and Annex V is the Regional Implementation Annex for Central and Eastern Europe.

B.   How Can Desertification Be Prevented or Reversed?

Prevention of desertification involves implementing proper land and water management techniques, measures that protect soils from erosion, salinization, and other forms of soil degradation. Prevention involves stopping overgrazing, overexploitation of vegetative cover, trampling of soils, and unsustainable irrigation practices. Protection of existing vegetative cover is usually the key to protecting against land degradation and desertification.

Reversal of land degradation is more expensive than prevention techniques. The restoration of dryland ecosystem services requires a combination of policies and technologies with the close cooperation of local communities. Frequently soil organic matter must be restocked and countererosion must be taken such as terracing and planting of trees, grasses or shrubs. Community involvement in this process is essential.

The following is a case study of land rehabilitation prepared by the UNCCD Secretariat.

COMBATTING DESERTIFICATION AND LAND DEGRADATION: PROVEN PRACTICES FROM ASIA AND THE PACIFIC
UNCCD, October 2011

[China is suffering from serious land desertification that affects some 27% of its total land territory. Overgrazing, cutting trees and shrubs, poor agricultural practices, the blind collection of herb medicines, and mismanagement of water supplies are the leading causes of land degradation. Crucial to the success of land rehabilitation in China has been (1) direct payments to farmers in return for environmental services; (2) integration of ecology service and economic benefits; (3) property rights that incentivize long-term management; and (4) a voluntary-based participation process].

Case study in Hangjinhouqi County, Inner Mongolia

Hangjinhouqi County is one of the project counties of the State Grain for Green Program in Bayannuur City, Inner Mongolia. The project area is located in irrigation area of the Yellow River, the east periphery of the Ulan Buh Desert. It is an important national agricultural base and is characterized by an arid climate. Natural vegetation of the area is rarely seen, and tree-bush plantation consists of Populus spp. Sophora japonica, Ulmus spp., Elaiagnus angustifolia, and Tarimax spp. Long-term careless agricultural activities have caused decline of land productivity. Salinization, alkalization and sand movement/fixed dune reactivation are intensified increasingly and becoming major constraints of local economic development and sustainable land management.

In 2000, the Central Government initiated the project of conversion of steep slope cropping and dry farming along foothills in desertification-prone land areas or affected regions to woodland, bush land or revegetated and replanted lands and grassland with aims to halt the cultivation of severely degraded mountainous cropping land and dry farming lands, restore vegetation cover by planting trees and forage/fodders (herbage], to improve the ecosystem services. Food and cash subsidies are set in line with the policy that annual food supply of 1.50 tons/ha is provided to the contracted householders for compensating their potential loss of stopping steep slope and dry farming and 750 RMB Yuan/ha/per year (1 US$=8.2 RMB Yuan in 2000] cash subsidy is provided for family consumption. However, the government provides seeds or tree seedlings and 300 RMB Yuan/ha for maintaining (tending] and daily management of the contracted areas during the implementation of the "Grain for Green Project."

Technical components: In consideration of the long-term livelihood and ecology service, integrative planting model of mixed trees and perennial forage/fodder was selected as dominant model in the Grain for Green Program in Hangjinhouqi County.

Major technical components include: (1) tree (forage/fodder) species selection — for trees Populus popularis and Populus albavar. pyramidalis; and forage/fodder of high quality leguminous plants such as Medicago sativa; (2) planting scheme — using the two-row belt scheme with row/plant spacing of 2m and belt spacing of 8m;

inter-cropping forage/fodder such as Medicago sativa between belts; (3) soil preparation - carrying out complete soil preparation using machines to loosen soil layers in the first year at depth of 35cm; pit soil preparation for tree planting with a specification of 50X50X50cm; (4) seedlings — selecting healthy winter-stored seedlings with basal diameter > 3cm; removing all side branches and soaking the seedlings for 2–4 days with fresh water before planting; (5) plantation — To be carried out in May and irrigated with sufficient water immediately after planting; (6) Maintenance — watered once each month in late May, June, July, and October; disease and insect control twice a year, including beetles and Tettigella viridis, and prevent animal browsing and human damage. After the plantation, Medicago sativa seeds are sown between tree belts at a row spacing of 30cm and seed quantity of 15kg/ha.

The overall benefits of this approach include: (1) inter-cropping of trees and forage/fodder is good for tree growth; Medicago sativa as a perennial plant covers land surface and holds soil in all seasons and increases vegetation coverage with trees, with significant results for reducing wind erosion and stabilizing shifting sands; (2) land re-vegetation brings about economic benefits. It is estimated that the one ha of inter-cropping of tree-forage/fodder will cost 3,228 RMB Yuan, excluding manual-labor. The total inputs for one ha is as follows: tree seedlings 2,778 RMB Yuan; Medicago sativa seed 300 RMB Yuan, water and fertilizers 150 RMB Yuan. However, the approximately estimated output or annual income is 8,100 RMB Yuan, including the profits from Medicago sativa, fodder production 1,200 RMB Yuan from timber production. The total annual net profit is 6,072 RMB Yuan/ha; and (3) surplus rural labor can be employed as odd jobbers for urbanization, manufacturing, breeding poultry and livestock and offering service industry.

The Project was implemented under overall arrangements of the county government and technical guidance and operational organization by the Forestry Section of the County. Major steps included: (1) The County Government was responsible for technical and coordination meetings participated by all relevant officers and technicians; (2) forestry offices organized the technical staff to design and submit operational plans; (3) township administrations organized farmers to learn the related policies and, on a voluntary basis in accordance with the conditions on land to be converted, to determine the size of land for conversion; (4) Farmers planted trees and forage/fodder based on technical schemes provided by forestry offices; (5) forestry offices inspected the reafforestation and/or replantation, and advised food supplies offices to make payment to contracted farmers either in cereal/grain or cash equivalent (township administrations are authorized to make payment in cash).

This project to convert steep slope farming and dry farming on foothills to woodlands/bush lands and tree plantations was warmly welcomed and well operated by farmers and local communities, and promoted by the County, township administrations and forestry offices. Ecological service and economic benefits from implementation of the project are significant and were welcomed by farmers and the public. As of 2009, the County has converted 40,000 ha of steep slope cropping lands and dry farming lands on foothills to woodland, bush lands and tree plantations, and farmers received 96 million RMB Yuan in subsidized food/cereal/grain and cash.

Conclusion

The case of Hangjinhouqi County proves that the joint-function of a well-selected model of inter-cropping of the trees and grass/fodder, policy incentives of Grain for Green subsidies, and well- organized implementation of the project has played effective effects in accelerating re-vegetation and replanting of an area of the Yellow River Basin and in adjusting and optimizing rural production structure, and offering lessons and experiences of demonstration and pilot project implementation and management to the similar projects in other Western China regions.

C.　Implementation of the UNCCD

At the eighth meeting of the Conference of the Parties to the UNCCD (COP-8), in Madrid in 2007, the state-parties adopted a 10-year strategic plan covering the years 2008 to 2018. In addition, in September 2011, a high-level meeting of UNCCD member states was convened in New York to discuss and to reaffirm the commitment to the UNCCD goals and objectives. The outcome of this meeting was UN General Assembly Resolution 65/160, which affirms the 10-year strategic plan and which urges a higher priority for its implementation.

UNITED NATIONS CONVENTION TO COMBAT DESERTIFICATION

Ten Year Strategic Plan to Enhance Implementation of the Convention (2008-2018) , Decision 3/COP 8, Adopted by the Parties at Conference of the Parties 8, Madrid, September 2008

I. Introduction

1. Developed as a result of the Rio Summit, the United Nations Convention to Combat Desertification (UNCCD) is a unique instrument that has brought attention to land degradation in the drylands where exist some of the most vulnerable ecosystems and people in the world. Ten years after its coming into force, the UNCCD benefits from universal membership and is increasingly recognized as an instrument which can make a lasting contribution to the achievement of sustainable development and poverty reduction globally.

2. After a decade of implementation, it is recognized that limiting factors have prevented optimal deployment of the Convention. Chief among these factors are insufficient financing compared to its two Rio sister conventions, a weak scientific basis, insufficient advocacy and awareness among various constituencies, institutional weaknesses and difficulties in reaching consensus among Parties.

3. Also, the UNCCD operates today in an environment that has evolved considerably since when it was first negotiated and it faces different opportunities and constraints which will condition its implementation in the forthcoming decade.

4. For one thing, the policy environment has changed considerably since Rio with the adoption of the Millennium Development Goals (MDGs), the outcomes of the World Summit on Sustainable Development (WSSD), increased support to Africa and the least developed countries, stronger commitment for climate change

mitigation and adaptation, prospects of global agricultural trade liberalization, and growing numbers of environmental refugees and migrants shedding new light on the impacts of poverty and environmental degradation.

5. The scientific environment has also evolved with the work of the Millennium Assessment (MA) on dryland ecosystems, which has contributed to improved understanding of the biophysical and socio-economic trends relating to land degradation in global drylands, and their impacts on human and ecosystem well-being. The MA has also contributed to mapping out key gaps in data and knowledge on dryland ecosystems and people.

6. The financing environment has also changed profoundly in the last decade, with the Global Environment Facility (GEF) becoming a financial mechanism of the Convention, official development assistance (ODA) flows increasing again after a decade of stagnation, and declining resources for rural development and agriculture. Donors have refocused their financing strategies to support country-driven priorities, based on Poverty Reduction Strategy Papers (PRSPs) and other country-led development planning instruments. Lastly, various innovative financing instruments have come to life, including payments for ecological services and carbon finance.

7. This new environment provides the starting point for this strategic plan along with an assessment of the successes and limiting factors of the Convention as it enters its second decade. This strategic plan provides a unique opportunity to address some of the Convention's key challenges, to capitalize on its strengths, to seize opportunities provided by the new policy and financing environment, and to create a new, revitalized common ground for all UNCCD stakeholders.

II. The vision

8. The aim tor the future is to forge a global partnership to reverse and prevent desertification/land degradation and to mitigate the effects of drought in affected areas in order to support poverty reduction and environmental sustainability.

III. Strategic objectives and expected impacts

9. The following "strategic objectives" will guide the actions of all UNCCD stakeholders and partners in the period 2008–2018, including raising political will. Meeting these long-term1 objectives will contribute to achieving the abovementioned vision. The expected impacts" are the long-term effects intended by the strategic objectives.

Strategic objective 1: To improve the living conditions of affected populations

Expected impact. People living in areas affected by desertification/land degradation and drought to have an improved and more diversified livelihood base and to benefit from income generated from sustainable land management.

Strategic objective 2: To improve the condition of affected ecosystems

Expected impact. Land productivity and other ecosystem goods and services in affected areas are enhanced in a sustainable manner contributing to improved livelihoods. The vulnerability of affected ecosystems to climate change, climate variability and drought is reduced.

Strategic objective 3: To generate global benefits through effective implementation of the UNCCD

Expected impact. Sustainable land management and combating desertification/land degradation contribute to the conservation and sustainable use of biodiversity and the mitigation of climate change.

Strategic objective 4: To mobilize resources to support implementation of the Convention through building effective partnerships between national and international actors

IV. The mission

10. To provide a global framework to support the development and implementation of national and regional policies, programs and measures to prevent, control and reverse desertification/land degradation and mitigate the effects of drought through scientific and technological excellence, raising public awareness, standard setting, advocacy and resource mobilization, thereby contributing to poverty reduction.

V. Operational objectives and expected outcomes

11. The following "operational objectives" will guide the actions of all UNCCD stakeholders and partners in the short and medium term with a view to supporting the attainment of the above-mentioned vision and strategic objectives. The "outcomes" are the short and medium-term effects intended by the operational objectives.

Operational objective 1: Advocacy, awareness raising and education

To actively influence relevant international, national and local processes and actors in adequately addressing desertification/land degradation and drought-related issues.

Operational objective 2: Policy framework

To support the creation of enabling environments for promoting solutions to combat desertification/land degradation and mitigate the effects of drought.

Operational objective 3: Science, technology and knowledge

To become a global authority on scientific and technical knowledge pertaining to desertification/land degradation and mitigation of the effects of drought.

Operational objective 4: Capacity-building

To identify and address capacity-building needs to prevent and reverse desertification/land degradation and mitigate the effects of drought.

Operational objective 5: Financing and technology transfer

To mobilize and improve the targeting and coordination of national, bilateral and multilateral financial and technological resources in order to increase their impact and effectiveness.

VI. Implementation framework

12. This section defines the roles and responsibilities of the various UNCCD institutions, partners and stakeholders in meeting the above-mentioned objectives.

A. The Committee on Science and Technology (CST)

13. Operational objective 3 on science, technology and knowledge is a central component of the strategic plan. The CST is given primary responsibility to fulfill this objective as well as a support role for implementing operational objective 1. In order to fulfill this mandate, the CST shall be strengthened to assess, advise and support implementation, on a comprehensive, objective, open and transparent basis, of the scientific, technical and socio-economic information relevant to understanding the causes and impacts of desertification/land degradation, and shall inform COP decisions.

B. The Committee for the Review of the Implementation of the Convention (CRIC)

15. The CRIC plays a central role in reviewing the implementation of the strategic plan through an effective reporting process and documenting and disseminating best practices from experience in implementing the Convention, thereby bringing a crosscutting contribution to all operational objectives. Overall, the CRIC shall be strengthened to improve feedback loops to measure progress and support continuous improvement in implementing the strategic plan.

C. The Global Mechanism (GM)

17. Operational objective 5 on financing and technology transfer is a central component of the strategic plan. The GM has a control responsibility in contributing to this objective, given its mandate to increase the effectiveness and efficiency of existing financial mechanisms and to mobilize and channel substantial financial resources. The GM also has a support role for operational objectives 1 and 2. In order to fulfill its role, the GM shall strengthen its capacity to mobilize existing as well as fresh sources of finance and to facilitate access to technology.

D. The Secretariat

Successful implementation of this strategic plan requires a strengthening of the core servicing, advocacy and agenda-setting and representation functions of the UNCCD secretariat — with commensurate capacity and resources — in order to support Parties, the COP and the subsidiary bodies of the Convention in fulfilling their respective roles. The secretariat has a lead role for operational objective 1 and specific outcomes of operational objectives 2 and 3 as well as a support role in other operational objectives.

PROBLEM 8-8
FORMULATING A NATIONAL ACTION PLAN (NAP)

You are a consultant to a major developing country that is a party to the UNCCD. You are asked to help formulate a new NAP that will conform to the 10-year strategic strategy adopted by COP-8 of the UNCCD members. NAPs are formulated through a participatory approach involving various stakeholders, relevant government agencies, scientific institutions and local communities. They spell out practical steps and measure to be taken to combat desertification and to rehabilitate ecosystems. The Secretariat of the UNCCD urges that relevant parties align their NAPs with the UNCCD's current 10-year strategy. The Secretariat of the UNCCD, located in Bonn, Germany, recommends the following steps in the formulation and alignment process: (Source: Dr. Richard A. Byron-Cox, rbyroncox@unccd.int).

1. Preliminary organization (designating the relevant agency)
2. The initial plan of activities
3. Public involvement
4. Initiating the alignment
5. Preparing the NAP
6. National review of the draft NAP
7. Expert/technical review
8. Finalization and national approval
9. Official adoption
10. Publication and circulation of the NAP

Chapter 9

THE POLAR REGIONS

Section I. ANTARCTICA

A. Introduction

Antarctica hosts one of Earth's most fragile ecosystems: a vast, cold and dry continent hospitable to only a few hardy, sea-nourished species. Moreover, the Antarctic ecosystem is vital to the planet's health. Changes to Antarctica's climate may cause a variety of catastrophic effects including depleting the ozone layer, raising sea levels, and altering the global climate. Antarctica provides an almost entirely unsullied environment for studying such global environmental problems. As the last continent to experience human contact and a region still largely uncorrupted by human activity, Antarctica is Earth's largest remaining wilderness.

The Antarctic Treaty System (ATS) is the most important body of international law governing the Antarctic region today. The original impetus to create the ATS was to defuse potentially violent conflicts between 12 states[1] with competing claims to sovereignty over portions of the continent. Reacting to transparently veiled threats of war, nations with an interest in Antarctica signed the Antarctic Treaty (AT) in December 1959. In signing this treaty, the parties agreed to "freeze" their territorial claims without prejudice and to use the continent solely for peaceful purposes, prohibiting military activities and the dumping of nuclear waste while encouraging scientific research.

The Antarctic Treaty forms the foundation and framework of the ATS which, In addition to demilitarization, governs usage of the continent and its interdependent ecosystems. This framework continues to develop, largely through multilateral agreements adopted at Antarctic Treaty Consultative Meetings (ATCM). The ATS provides an excellent example of nations joining together to build a richly constructive international regime for the benefit of the environment, though the system is far from being perfect.

In order to properly evaluate the strengths and weaknesses of the international legal regime as it relates to Antarctica, one must become familiar with Antarctica's biophysical environment. Antarctica is the most remote and inhospitable continent on Earth. With temperatures as low as 130°F below zero, wind speeds up to 200 mph and only 2.4% of the continent free of ice at any given time, Antarctica

---

[1] The original signatories included Argentina, Australia, Chile, Belgium, France, Japan, New Zealand, Norway, the United States, South Africa, the Union of Soviet Socialist Republics, and the United Kingdom. As of 2013, there are 50 signatories to the Antarctic Treaty.

sustains no natural human settlements. Despite having a land mass of 5.4 million square miles, Antarctica's climate inhibits vegetation growth, leaving its landscape relatively barren. Further, it is considered one of the driest deserts on Earth.

Antarctica's inhospitable climate aside, scientists assert that the continent is essential to the global environment because of the resources and processes its natural ecosystems provide. Its icy land mass reflects sunlight away from Earth and back into space. Cold water and icebergs surrounding the continent move north and combine with warm equatorial waters, producing currents, clouds and a variety of global weather patterns. Its seas are full of life, from carbon-dioxide absorbing phytoplankton to whales and seals. Many species of birds and mammals are also unique to the Antarctica.

Antarctica is an ideal place to carry out scientific research because of its undisturbed environment and relative inaccessibility. Moreover, research in Antarctica has promoted cooperation and understanding between states which may otherwise be hostile toward each other, particularly during the Cold War. Perhaps more importantly, scientific research carried out in Antarctica has expanded our understanding of planetary health. Antarctica is seen by scientists as a sort of early warning system for the climate. In the 1980s, for example, satellite observations of Antarctica first revealed disturbing reductions in upper stratospheric ozone in the atmosphere, and with it, a reduction in our protection from the Sun's unfiltered and harmful ultraviolet radiation.

Antarctica has much to teach us about climate change. Evidence of climates past, like trapped bubbles of atmospheric gases, can be found buried beneath thick layers of Antarctic ice. Such evidence can help scientists predict — and ultimately thwart — various threats posed by global warming. Moreover, the ice cap itself may play a significant long-term role in determining the Earth's future climate. Indeed, scientists estimate that 70% of the world's fresh water is locked away in Antarctica's icecaps; if it were to melt, sea levels might rise by 200 feet, inundating coastal lands and potentially major cities.[2]

Finally, Antarctica has bountiful untapped natural resources. Although many of these resources are not economically viable to exploit at present, increasing global scarcity will make their use more attractive in the future. Indeed, some experts assert that decreasing global oil reserves are quickly increasing pressure to conduct oil exploration in Antarctica. It is here that international law has a role to play — to ensure that resource use and extraction do not compromise the Antarctic nor the global environment.

1. Geography and Climate

Antarctica, an estimate 600 miles from its closest neighbor South America, is the most isolated place on earth. It is the fifth largest continent and accounts for nearly 10% of the Earth's land mass. Its total surface area is approximately 5.5 million square miles, through it varies seasonally as a result of sea ice that forms at its

---

[2] *Antarctica, the Environment*, National Science Foundation, *available at* http://www.nsf.gov/pubs/ 1997/antpanel/3enviro.htm.

periphery. More than 98% of Antarctica is covered with ice at any given time, yet it has extremely low annual precipitation.

The ice covering Antarctica is one mile deep on average. The continent's interior, with temperatures averaging -57°C (-70°F), is uninhabitable. Temperatures along the coast tend to be warmer. The surrounding Antarctic Ocean supports a rich array of fauna including: whales, seals, fish, penguins, birds, and krill. However, the continent's cold desert climate is inhospitable to vegetation. Antarctica has no trees and few species of vegetation — largely moss, lichen, and algae. The severity of these conditions makes Antarctic the world's most pristine and isolated laboratory for scientific research.

2. Population

Antarctica has no native population. Its year-round population generally consists of a few thousand scientists studying meteorology, seismology, glaciology, virology, and geomagnetism. Commercial tourism has also been increasing in recent years, threatening adverse environmental impacts if not properly regulated.

3. Environmental Concerns

As with the high seas and Earth's atmosphere, the international community largely treats Antarctica as a "global commons." As global demand for seafood rises, the marine life off the coast of Antarctica is increasingly targeted by the world's commercial fisheries. There have been several proposals to create new marine protected areas (MPAs) in key areas of the Antarctic Ocean, such as in the Ross Sea, but disagreements within the Commission for the Conservation of Antarctic Marine Living Resources (CCAMLR) — a part of the Atlantic Treaty System — have thus far prevented their creation. A number of MPAs have previously been created in the Antarctic Ocean, however many experts insist that without a comprehensive network of MPAs, biodiversity and marine ecosystems are still at risk.

Aside from hunting and fishing, other environmental concerns remain. Like the rest of the plant, Antarctica is affected by climate change and ozone depletion. The loss of ice associated with climate change has the potential to raise sea levels and damage native wildlife populations. Increased tourism and scientific travel to the area has resulted in increased pollution. These concerns are escalated by the fact that over half the fresh water on the planet is housed within the Antarctic ice shelf.

a)   Ozone Depletion and Climate Change

The ozone layer shields Earth's inhabitants from the sun's harmful ultraviolent light. The most drastic destruction of the Earth's ozone layer, likely caused by human activity over the past several decades, has been over Antarctica. Ozone depletion is exacerbated in Antarctica because the cold temperatures in the region facilitate chemical reactions — mainly involving the release and subsequent breaking apart of chlorine gas — which ultimately lead to more ozone destruction than would occur in warmer climates.[3] As such, in warmer years there is less ozone depletion in the Antarctic region.

The ozone hole over Antarctica fluctuates in size every year and generally persists for 3–4 months at a time. The ozone hole was measured at approximately 10.6 million square miles in 2006, its largest ever recorded size.[4] After the adoption of the Montreal Protocol in the 1990s, a treaty intended to limit the use of substances thought to be responsible for ozone depletion, levels of such substances in the atmosphere have decreased and the ozone layer is on its way to recovery. While this is a positive development made possible by international cooperation, because some of these substances can remain in the atmosphere for 40 years or longer, the continued shrinking of the hole in the ozone layer may be a slow and unsure process largely dependent on weather patterns and human restraint.

There remain concerns about the combined effect of the ozone hole and global warming. Since ozone depletion results in increased levels of solar radiation passing through the atmosphere, it is possible that because of accumulating greenhouse gases this radiation will be trapped in the form of heat and eventually cause a large-scale melting of the Antarctic ice sheet. This effect could result in dramatically higher sea levels and other adverse environmental consequences.

b)   A Melting Ice Shelf

Concerns about melting Antarctic sea ice was first realized in 2002 and 2003 when two large ice shelves — one as large as 3,250 square kilometers — broke apart and splintered into numerous smaller icebergs. Research has shown that warm ocean currents, likely a result of climate change, are responsible for the melting and breaking apart of these large ice shelves. This phenomenon could have far-reaching consequences as the amount of ice in the Antarctic region capable of being melted by a warming planet would significantly contribute to sea level rises, potentially inundating coastal communities. As stated previously, such melting may also create a potentially disastrous feedback loop. Melting in the Antarctic decreases reflective surfaces with which to deflect the sun's rays, trapping more heat on Earth and hastening global warming. Also, the thawing of Antarctic permafrost may release harmful amounts of methane into the atmosphere which could further accelerate the rate of climate change.

c)   Krill

Krill is the foundation of the vast Antarctic marine ecosystem. It is the primary food source for the region's whales, fish, seals, and penguins. Krill is also a potential major feedstock in global agriculture, being easily harvested and high in protein and vitamins. *See* William M. Hamner, *Krill: Untapped Bounty from the Sea*, 165 NATIONAL GEOGRAPHIC 626 (1984).

---

[3] *Science on the Edge*, National Science Foundation, *available at* https://www.nsf.gov/about/history/nsf0050/arctic/arctic.htm.

[4] *NASA and NOAA announce Ozone Hole Is a Double Record Breaker*, *available at* http://www.nasa.gov/vision/earth/lookingatearth/ozone_record.html.

Scientists fear the krill population, and specifically the Antarctic krill population, may be in danger.[5] Algal blooms caused by ozone depletion and water pollution choke out essential light and nutrients. Further, increasing water temperatures mean that phytoplankton that Antarctic krill depend on for sustenance, which largely grow on the underside of ice mats, appear in smaller numbers. Without krill, Antarctica's rich sea life would vanish and a potential world food source could be lost.

B. The Antarctic Treaty System: Security, Peace and Preservation of Sovereign Claims

As discussed above, the Antarctic Treaty (AT) and the subsequently developed Antarctic Treaty System (ATS) form the primary international legal framework governing Antarctica. These agreements have several overriding goals: maintaining peace, promoting scientific exploration, encouraging increased transparency, and assuring environmental stewardship in the Antarctic region. The territory covered by the Antarctic Treaty is stated in Article VI of the Antarctic Treaty as being "the area south of 60° south latitude, including all ice shelves." However, that article also makes clear that the Antarctic Treaty does not create or alter any rights regarding the high seas within that boundary.

The ATS includes the Antarctic Treaty as its foundational basis along with several other agreements, mostly recommendations adopted at yearly Antarctic Treaty Consultative Meetings (ATCM) which will be discussed later in this chapter. Several of those agreements are notable, including the Agreed Measures for the Conservation of Antarctic Fauna and Flora, the Convention for the Conservation of Antarctic Marine Living Resources, and the Protocol on Environmental Protection to the Antarctic Treaty (Madrid Protocol).

1. The Antarctic Treaty

In response to mounting conflicting territorial claims and global desires to conduct scientific research on Antarctica, the Antarctic Treaty was signed in Washington D.C. by 12 states on December 1, 1959.[6] The original signatories included the United States, South Africa, the Union of Soviet Socialist Republics, Japan, Belgium, the United Kingdom, Norway, New Zealand, France, Chile, Australia, and Argentina — the signatories all being territorial claimants or interested parties. The Antarctic Treaty went into effect on June 23, 1961 with the original signatories named Consultative Parties with rights to participate in Antarctic Treaty Consultative Meetings under Article IX. By 2012, 50 states had become members, with 28 of those states holding Consultative Party status. Any state which is a member of the United Nations, or other states which are invited to accede by all Consultative Parties, may accede to the Antarctic Treaty.[7]

---

[5] Jessica Marshall, *Penguin, Krill Populations in Freefall*, Discovery News, April 11, 2011, *available at* http://news.discovery.com/animals/chinstrap-adelie-penguins-krill-110411.htm.

[6] Antarctic Treaty, 407 U.N.T.S. 71.

[7] Antarctic Treaty, Art. XIII.

MAP OF THE ANTARCTIC REGION

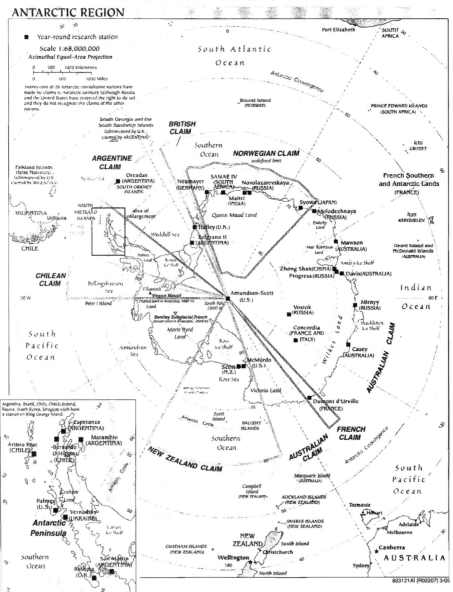

The Antarctic Treaty (1) puts territorial claims in abeyance; (2) bars new territorial claims; (3) prohibits the establishment of military bases, the testing of weapons, nuclear explosions, and the disposal of radioactive waste; and (4) authorizes scientific research by all interested parties. The Antarctic Treaty began an ongoing process of decision-making regarding Antarctica under which more than 100 resolutions and regulations have been agreed by the Contracting Parties.[8]

---

[8] *See generally* Emilio J. Sahurie, The International Law of Antarctica (1992).

The Antarctic Treaty is made up of 14 articles, the substantive portions of which are summarized here. Article I of the Atlantic Treaty prohibits military activity and reserves the use of Antarctica for peaceful purposes. Article II establishes scientific freedom and encourages scientific cooperation among nations. Article III provides for the sharing of information collected by member states regarding research and scientific program plans research results and scientific personnel. Article IV freezes territorial claims with regard to the region. Article V bans nuclear testing and regulates the use of nuclear power. Article VI establishes the territory covered by the Treaty. Article VII governs the designation and regulation of observers. Article VIII states that observers, scientific personnel, and staff members of such persons are subject only to the jurisdiction of the member country of which they are a citizen. Article IX creates the blueprint for Atlantic treaty Consultative Meeting. Article X discourages activities contrary to the spirit of the Treaty. Article XI controls dispute resolution, requiring that member states first attempt to settle disputes regarding the Treaty amongst themselves through various peaceful means, and suggesting that disputes which cannot be settled through these means be referred to the International Court of Justice. Article XIII and XIV provide for ratification and deposit.

NOTES AND QUESTIONS

1. *Scope*. What were the primary concerns of the drafters of the Antarctic Treaty? The absence of express language addressing environmental protection suggests the Antarctic Treaty was not adopted to protect the environment. The only language relating to the environment is Article IX's list of issues to be addressed through the consultative process which includes "preservation and conservation of living resources in Antarctica." This provision may have been an acknowledgement of the over exploited whaling stock in Antarctica's Southern sea. Can you tell whether the language was meant to be aspirational? Should Article IX language be interpreted more broadly to include preservation and conservation of the physical environment? What problems does such an interpretation raise?

2. *The Antarctic Treaty system*. Subsequent treaties and state practice have broadened the Antarctic Treaty System to encompass environmental protection. Was this the drafters' intent? Is this gradual broadening of environmental regulations an effective approach? Would the alternative of strict measures sacrifice compliance? The Antarctic Treaty and subsequent related agreements and legal documents comprise the Antarctic Treaty System. Beginning with a general, though incomplete, framework and supplementing it with more specific agreements allows for evolution within the general structure as understanding of the regulatory needs and achievable means changes. Contentious issues and even irreconcilable ones, such as territorial claims, can be addressed without paralyzing the entire legal framework. However, without pressure to compromise, important gaps may remain unresolved. Consider the absence of a true liability regime and the uncompensated harm that remains unaddressed due to such a gap.

2. Antarctic Treaty Consultative Parties and Consultative Meetings

Consultative Meetings are established in Article IX of the Antarctic Treaty, which is reproduced below. Much of the action in the Antarctic Treaty System stems from its Consultative Meetings, which now take place annually for the purpose of exchanging information, engaging in discussion, and taking collective action on important issues facing the Antarctic region. Decision-making power at these meetings is reserved for Consultative Parties, of which there are currently 28. Consultative Parties include the original 12 signatories to the Antarctic Treaty and any other member state determined by the Consultative Parties to have demonstrated an interest in Antarctica by conducting substantial scientific research in the region.[9]

THE ANTARCTIC TREATY
December 1, 1959, 407 U.N.T.S. 71
Article IX

1. Representatives of the Contracting Parties named in the preamble to the present Treaty shall meet at the City of Canberra within two months after date of entry into force of the Treaty, and thereafter at suitable intervals and places, for the purpose of exchanging information, consulting together on matters of common interest pertaining to Antarctic, and formulating and considering, and recommending to their Governments, measure in furtherance of the principles and objectives of the Treaty including measures regarding:

   (a) use of Antarctica for peaceful purpose only;

   (b) facilitation of scientific research in Antarctica;

   (c) facilitation of international scientific cooperation in Antarctica;

   (d) facilitation of the exercise of the rights of inspection provided for in Article VII of the Treaty;

   (e) questions relating to the exercise of jurisdiction in Antarctica;

   (f) preservation and conservation of living resources in Antarctica.

2. Each Contracting Party which has become a party to the present Treaty by accession under Article XIII shall be entitled to appoint representatives to participate in the meeting referred to in paragraph 1 of the present Article, during such time as that Contracting Party demonstrates its interest in Antarctica by conducting substantial scientific research activity there, such as the establishment of a scientific station or the dispatch of a scientific expedition.

3. Reports from the observers referred to in Article VII of the present Treaty shall be transmitted to the representatives of the Contracting

---

[9] The Operation of the Antarctic Treaty System, U.S. Department of State, *available at* http://www.state.gov/documents/organization/15273.pdf.

Parties participating in the meetings referred to in paragraph 1 of the present Article.

4. The measures referred to in paragraph 1 of this Article shall become effective when approved by all the Contracting Parties whose representatives were entitled to participate in the meetings held to consider those measures.

5. Any or all of the rights established in the present Treaty may be excised as from the date of entry into force of the Treaty whether or not any measures facilitating the exercise of such rights have been proposed, considered or approved as provided in this Article.

NOTES

Non-Consultative parties are permitted to attend Consultative Meetings and give input, but lack decision-making authority. Observers appointed by Consultative Parties and their representatives, including the Scientific Committee on Antarctic Research (SCAR) and the Commission for the Conservation of Antarctic Marine Living Resources (CCAMLR), are also invited to participate in Consultative Meetings. Thirty-five Consultative meetings have been held since 1961, taking place all over the world.[10]

In 1995 the Antarctic Treaty Consultative Meeting's deliberations[11] resulted in clarification of several ATS procedural terms. A *measure* was redefined as "[a] text which contains provisions intended to be legally binding once it has been approved by all the Antarctic Treaty Consultative Parties." *Decisions* were defined as acts "taken by an Antarctic Treaty Consultative Meeting on an internal organizational matter [which] will be operative at adoption or at such other time." On the other hand, "[a] hortatory text adopted at an Antarctic Treaty Consultative Meeting will be contained in a resolution." The Rules of Procedure which govern Consultative Meetings were most recently amended in 2011.[12] These rules state that procedural decisions made at Consultative Meetings shall pass if adopted by a majority of present Consultative Parties, each of which receives one vote. However, amendments to the 2011 Rules of Procedure require a two-thirds vote of the Consultative Parties.

Special Consultative Meetings may also be arranged if deemed necessary by the Consultative Parties. Many of these have taken place over the past three decades. Measures adopted at Special Consultative Meetings are limited to the specific purpose of the meeting and are only binding on participating governments. Meetings of Experts are also held on occasion for the purpose of preparing reports, generally for use at Consultative Meetings.[13]

---

[10] *Id.*

[11] Decision 1 (1995), Measures, Decisions and Resolutions, *available at* http://www.State.gov/documents/organization/15273.pdf.

[12] Antarctic Treaty Revised Rules of Procedure (2011), *available at* http://www.ats.aq/documents/recatt/Att468_e.pdf.

[13] The Operation of the Antarctic Treaty System, op. cit. *supra.*

QUESTIONS

1. *Consultative Party status*. Consider the provision in Article IX.2 that specifies that an acceding party ". . . shall be entitled to appoint representatives to participate in the [consultative] meetings . . . during such times as that Contracting party demonstrates its interest in Antarctica by conducting substantial research activity there . . . ." This has been interpreted to mean that consultative status is revoked when a party ceases to conduct substantial research activity in Antarctica, though this does not seem to apply to the original signatories. What is the justification for this discrimination? In 1977, Poland was the first acceding state to be granted Consultative Party status. Consultative parties have reserved the right to examine whether an acceding state's action qualifies under Article IX.2.

What constitutes substantial scientific research for purposes of qualifying for consultative status? This, too, is not expressly addressed in the Treaty. What should constitute such research? If activity must be scientific and based in Antarctica, marine research alone probably does not suffice. The Treaty requires state activity; does that mean a private expedition is also insufficient? What about a private expedition commissioned but only partly funded by a state? Would the high cost of consultative status preclude participation by less affluent nations? Is this politically acceptable?

2. *Non-Parties*. Non-Treaty parties have criticized the secrecy of Consultative Meetings in the past. What are the justifications for secrecy? While the confidentially of discussions and negotiations is a widely followed practice in territorial affairs, some argue that the Antarctic Treaty System's secrecy is excessive, even by generous international standards. In response to criticism, the Consultative Parties granted the non-Consultative Parties (NCP) at the 12th Consultative Meeting in 1983 observer status at future Consultative Meetings. The 2011 Rules of Procedure also make provisions for the attendance of non-Consultative Parties and state that "[t]he opening plenary session shall be held in public, other sessions shall be held in private, unless the Meeting shall determine otherwise."

3. *Application procedure for Consultative Party status*. Although the treaty itself does not provide much guidance on how a member gains Consultative Party status, later decisions of the Consultative Meeting have illuminated this procedure somewhat. Article 22 of the 1991 Madrid Protocol (also part of the Antarctic Treaty System) states that Consultative Parties shall not grant such status to other Treaty members unless those members first ratified, approved, or acceded to the Madrid Protocol. At a 1997 Consultative Meeting, it was further clarified that members applying for Consultative Party status are required to provide specific information concerning their scientific activities in Antarctica and may be asked to declare their intent to approve specific Recommendations (now "measures"). Qualification for Consultative Party status is generally considered at Special Consultative Meetings. The grant of Consultative Party status is typically embodied in "decisions" of Consultative Meetings. There are also informal requirements that members may need to fulfill in order to be considered for Consultative Party status, such as contributing to the Scientific Committee on Antarctic Research (SCAR) and participating in the Convention on the Conservation of Antarctic Marine Living Resources (CCAMLR).

4. *Reform*. Some wonder whether the Consultative Meeting apparatus is effective. Critics of the current mechanism argue there is a need for a more formal bureaucratic structure to respond adequately to demands, which are themselves increasingly specialized. Does the secrecy of meeting conflict with the spirit of cooperation and openness in Antarctica? Is it unfair to the non-treaty parties? Does it prevent or inhibit adequate consideration of the many environmental and developmental issues that concern the Antarctic? If so, how could you change it?

PROBLEM 9-1
AUSTRALIA ENFORCES ENVIRONMENTAL RESTRICTIONS IN ITS ANTARCTIC TERRITORY

Australia is one of seven countries (New Zealand, United Kingdom, France, Norway, Argentina, and Chile are the others) that have long-standing territorial claims in Antarctica. Many of these claims overlap. The Australian Antarctic Territory (AAT) covers a large sector (42%) of the Antarctic continent lying south of 60 degrees S latitude to the South Pole and between the 160th degree E longitude and the 45th degree E longitude. Under Australian domestic law, the AAT is an External Territory: the Australian Antarctic Territory Acceptance Act of 1954 provides for the government of the AAT and applies Australian law to the AAT. Australia's sovereignty over the AAT is officially recognized only by the UK, France, Norway, and New Zealand. The United States, Russia, China, and Japan have protested Australia's claim

Under the Antarctic Treaty system (ATS), there are now 28 Consultative Parties (the original 12 parties plus 16 additional parties that have Consultative status on the basis that they do substantial research in Antarctica). In addition, 22 Non-Consultative Parties have acceded to the ATS; they may attend the Consultative Meetings but cannot participate in decision making. *See* http://www.ats.aq.

Japan, one of the Consultative Parties to the ATS, is active in carrying out research on the continent and in the surrounding waters. A Japanese vessel, the *Mifune Maru*, has entered the Southern ocean and is now carrying out what it terms "research" operations on whales and dolphins. Although these operations are designated as "research," in fact the *Mifune Maru* is catching whales and dolphins for commercial purposes as the meat is shipped back to Japan for commercial sale. In addition, the *Mifune Maru* has landed parties on the Antarctic shore and offshore island and, in the guise of "research," Japanese nationals have killed numerous seabirds and disturbed their nesting sites.

The killing of seabirds has occurred on lands that are claimed by Australia and to which Australia applies its domestic laws. Under Australian law, the killing of seabirds or the disturbance of their nesting area is illegal and is punishable by fines and imprisonment.

The whaling activities of the *Mifune Maru* are occurring in the seas offshore Antarctica that are area of the Exclusive Economic Zone (EEZ) — a zone 200 nautical miles offshore measured from the baseline of the continent — claimed by Australia. Within Australia's Antarctic EEZ it is illegal to kill or disturb marine mammals.

1. May Australia enforce its domestic laws against Japanese nationals in the AAT and the waters of its EEZ? Consider carefully the language of Article IV of the Antarctic Treaty. In addition, Article VIII.1 of the Treaty exempts certain foreign nationals from the jurisdiction of parties' territorial claims. Does this mean that foreign nationals not within the scope of the Article VIII.1 exemption are subject to Australia's jurisdiction? A committee of the Australian House of Representatives has ruled that foreign nationals are subject to Australian law in the AAT. See House of Representatives Standing Committee on Legal and Constitutional Affair, *Australian Law in Antarctica: The Report of the Second Phase of an Inquiry into the Legal Regimes of Australia's External Territories and the Jervis Bay Territory* (AGPS, Canberra, 1992). However, the Australian government has generally avoided enforcing Australian domestic law against foreign nationals in the AAT.

2. Is Australia's claim to an EEZ consistent with Article IV of the Antarctic Treaty? Note that the concept of an EEZ came into being only with the UN Convention on the Law of the Sea (1982). Note in this regard the last sentence in Article IV.2. Does Australia's EEZ claim contravene this provision? Australia argues that it does not because the claim to an EEZ is not a claim to territorial sovereignty, but only an assertion of sovereign rights under international law. Do you think this distinction is sound?

3. The Australian courts have accepted that Australia has a legally enforceable EEZ in connection with its AAT, and the Federal Court has declared Japanese whaling unlawful under Australia's Environmental Protection and Biodiversity Conservation Act of 1999, and has issued an injunction restraining Japanese whaling. *Humane Society International, Inc. v. Kyodo Senpaku Kaisha Ltd.* [2008] FCA 3. The Australian government has not enforced this injunctive relief.

4. Both Japan and Australia are Consultative Parties to the ATS, so consider Article XI, the dispute settlement provision of the Antarctic Treaty. Can this dispute be settled by the Consultative Parties under this provision or by reference to the International Court of Justice? (In fact, Australia has sued Japan in the ICJ over illegal whaling, but on different grounds, we cover this in Chapter 7).

5. Is scientific research defined in the Antarctic Treaty? Can environmentally disruptive activities be carried out with impunity under the guise of "research"? Does this demonstrate the need for additional environmental international agreements under the ATS?

C. Scientific Research, Environmental Stewardship and Species Protection

One of the strongest critiques of the Antarctic Treaty System through its history has been that it provides insufficient protection for the Antarctic environment. Initial measures to solve this problem were embodied in the Agreed Measures for the Conservation of Antarctic Fauna and Flora of 1964 (the Agreed

Measures)[14] and the Convention for Conservation of Antarctic Seals (CCAS). Later the Convention for the Conservation of Antarctic Marine Living Resources (CCAMLR) was negotiated which explicitly introduced an ecosystem-based approach to Antarctic management and expanded boundary protection beyond the Antarctic Treaty's imprecise 60° south latitude line. However, scarcity of key scientific knowledge and CCAMLR's reliance on individual nations for data and enforcement have limited its effectiveness. Perhaps most importantly, in 1998 the Protocol on Environmental Protection to the Antarctic Treaty, commonly known as the Madrid Protocol or the Environmental Protocol, went into force. The Madrid Protocol is arguably the most comprehensive agreement covering the Antarctic environment, complete with five annexes covering topics such as marine pollution, flora and fauna, environmental impact assessments, waste management, and protected areas.

Before continuing with this section, review the following: the Agreed Measures for the Conservation of Antarctic Fauna and Flora in the Supplement, focusing on Articles I, IV and VI through IX; the Convention for the Conservation of Antarctic Seals, focusing on Articles 2 and 5; and the Convention for the Conservation of Antarctic Marine Living Resources, focusing on Articles I, II, VI, IX, X, and XXIII. Also examine Antarctic Treaty Article V.

NOTES AND QUESTIONS

1. *Monitoring and inspection*. Antarctic Treaty Article VII provides for self-policing by the Antarctic Treaty Consultative Parties. The AT authorizes "observers" designated by the Consultative Parties to conduct inspections of all stations, their installations and equipment, and all ships and aircraft at points of embarkation in Antarctica. Ships at sea are likely not covered by these provisions since the high seas rights of Parties are retained. The original Consultative Parties deemed such inspections essential to the successful implementation of the AT. However, questions have long been raised as to whether the inspection system has been effective in practice. *See* F.M. AUBURN, ANTARCTIC LAW & POLITICS 110–115 (1982); GILLIAN TRIGGS, INTERNATIONAL LAW AND AUSTRALIAN SOVEREIGNTY IN ANTARCTICA 157 (1986).

Official inspections tend to be infrequent. In the period between 1959 and 2001, only 36 official inspections took place. Since 1959, official inspections have been on an upward trend-if only slightly. Likewise the number of inspected sites, mostly in the Antarctic Peninsula, has risen in this period as well. This uptick in inspections was likely influenced by the negotiations surrounding the Convention on the Regulation of Antarctic Mineral Resource Activities (CRAMRA) in the late 1980s. The Parties carrying out a majority of these official inspections include the United States, the United Kingdom, Argentina, Australia and New Zealand. Antarctic and Southern Ocean Coalition/United Nations Environment Programme, *A Review of Inspections Under Article 7 of the Antarctic Treaty and Article 14 of Its Protocol*

---

[14] At the 2011 ATC Meeting in Buenos Aires, the Agreed Measures were declared "no longer current. *See* http://www.ats.aq/e/ep_faflo.htm.

on Environmental Protection 3–9 (June 2003) (submitted to XXVI ATCM in Madrid, Spain).

Historically, Parties have formally reported few violations under the Treaty's inspection procedures. In contrast, NGOs like Greenpeace International have reported many violations during private inspections of scientific station and bases. For example, even after an inspection, neither the United States nor Australia reported any concern regarding the environmental impact of construction at a French airstrip at Pointe Geologie in the late 1980s. Once construction began, it was reported that penguins were killed when construction workers used dynamite to level islets on the site. Eggs were crushed and birds were allegedly removed by truck from their nesting area. Article IV of the Agreed Measures for the Conservation of Antarctic Fauna and Flora states that "[e]ach Participating Government shall prohibit within the Treaty Area the killing, wounding, capturing or molesting of any native mammal or native bird, or any attempt at any such act, except in accordance with a permit." Was the construction of the French airstrip a violation of ATS? If so, what could Parties have done? What should the Parties have done? Could one Party alone be effective?

2. Enforcement. The Consultative Parties made no official response to the French airstrip incident. Only New Zealand and Australia privately expressed their concern to the French. The absence of a formal response by the Parties prompted the Antarctic and Southern Ocean Coalition (ASOC), another NGO, to draw the following conclusion: "The handling of this case raises a question of credibility for the Antarctic Treaty System. If member governments fail to take any collective action-even to investigate allegations of a breach, the public can have little confidence in the commitments of governments pursuant to the Antarctic Treaty and related instruments." ASOC, *Background Paper on the French Airfield at Pointe Geologie*, ANTARCTICA (Mar. 1, 1985). Do you agree with ASOC's assessment? Why did Parties choose not to take action? Has the French airstrip case exposed the ineffectiveness of the environmental protections of the existing Treaty regime? Christopher Joyner, a leading expert on international law in Antarctica, asserts that "[o]pposition to the Pointe Geologie airstrip on environmental grounds carries relatively few political costs for the Consultative Parties, yet they are nonetheless unwilling to oppose it. What will happen to environmental concerns when opportunities for potentially large economic gains are made plainly available for governments willing to exploit the Antarctic environment?" Christopher C. Joyner, *Protection of the Antarctic Environment: Rethinking the Problems and Prospects*, 19 CORNELL INT'L L.J. 259 (1986). Is the answer self-evident? Alternatively, might one argue that the ATS framework is nevertheless effective because of relatively high levels of compliance? Does that compliance derive from the political pressure member states may place on malefactors? Or is the high degree of compliance a product of the Parties' lack of interest combined with their own occasional need to violate the AT? What, if any, modifications to the ATS would you propose to make it more effective? What consequences would those modifications have on the scope of commitments? Would the Consultative Parties accept a centralized review mechanism to oversee national activities affecting the Antarctic environment? How would such a mechanism have responded to the French airstrip case?

Joyner proposes the creation of an Antarctic Environmental Protection Agency (AEPA), an independent institution within the Antarctic Treaty System responsible for protecting Antarctica's environment. The AEPA would evaluate proposed activities within the ATS area, devise environmental regulations, and monitor and report on compliance. The AEPA could be modeled on similar national organizations. But Joyner warns of the danger of politicization of the agency, which could compromise effectiveness. Christopher Joyner, *Protection of the Antarctic Environment: Rethinking the Problems and Prospects*, 19 CORNELL INT'L L.J. 259, 270 (1986). Would such an agency be effective without the power to sanction violators? What other problems might it face?

3. ***Other instances of noncompliance***. Under Article VIII of the Agreed Measures for the Conservation of Antarctic Fauna and Flora of 1964 (the Agreed Measures), areas of outstanding scientific interest are designated as "Specially Protected Area" (SPAs) to preserve their unique natural ecological systems. The collection of native plants and operation of vehicles are prohibited in such areas. In 1964, the Fildes Peninsula — a biologically diverse region with numerous small lakes which are ice free during the summer — was designated an SPA under the Agreed Measures Agreement. In February 1968, the Soviet Union established a scientific base in the middle of the Fildes Peninsula, clearly inconsistent with the purposes of a SPA designation. Notably, the Soviet Union had not approved Recommendation IV-12 establishing the SPA or Recommendation IV-20, making the Agreed Measures akin to interim guidelines. Since the existence of the Soviet base made travel and disturbances in the adjacent environment inevitable, the extensive Fildes Peninsula SPA was reduced in 1968 to a small lake and the surrounding 100 meters of land. Following Soviet precedent, Chile also set up a scientific base on the Fildes Peninsula, further aggravating the environmental damage to the land and lakes from vehicle traffic and pollution. SPA designation was terminated in 1975 and instead the Fildes Peninsula was deemed a "Site of Special Scientific Interest" (SSSI), mandating a lower level of protection. *See* F.M. Auburn, *The Antarctic Environment*, in THE YEARBOOK OF WORLD AFFAIRS 249, 259 (1981). What message did this send to other Parties? Why do you think this course of action was chosen as opposed to other?

4. ***Liability***. Article 16 of the Protocol directs the parties to "elaborate rules and procedures relating to liability for damage arising from activities taking place in the Antarctic Treaty area and covered by this Protocol." Is the Protocol ineffective until such a liability regime exists? Will parties obey the Protocol if there are no costs for violating it yet there are financial incentives to engage in activities that might violate the Protocol? Does a liability system conflict with an environmental protection system by implicitly allowing resource exploitation at a predeterminable price? *See* Rowana Whalen, *Antarctica Talks Deadlocked by World Parks Debates*, REUTER LIBR., Oct. 19, 1989.

Some officials argue a liability system would require resolution of the territorial disputes, reasoning there could not be a plaintiff without a sovereign nation whose territory or interests had been violated. How could this problem be remedied? Some scholars have proposed that Parties could create a trust to stand in for any and all potential claimants. Would the risk of liability make research cost prohibitive, or is an enforceable environmental protection regime essential to safeguard the pristine environment that gives Antarctica unique value to researchers? What other arguments can be made for and against a liability regime?

5. *Other perspectives.* Consider also the perspective of developing nations whose people suffer from inadequate nutrition, polluted water and preventable diseases. Why should Antarctica be preserved for future generations when its resources may be used to provide the survival needs of people living today? Has environmentalism gone too far by ignoring urgent immediate needs for the speculative benefit of future ones?

1. Convention for the Conservation of Antarctic Seals

The Convention for the Conservation of Antarctic Seals (CCAS) is a freestanding agreement within the Antarctic Treaty System framework. In response to the depletion of fur seal populations in other parts of the world, and in recognition of the fact that the Antarctic Treaty and the Agreed Measures asserted no jurisdiction over the high seas around Antarctica, the Convention for the Conservation of Antarctic Seals was developed to facilitate the scientific study and the protection of seal populations living in Antarctic waters. The convention was opened for signature in 1972 and subsequently entered into force on March 11, 1978. The parties to the Convention include: Argentina, Australia, Belgium, Brazil, Canada, Chile, France, Germany, Italy, Japan, Norway, Poland, Russia, South Africa, the United Kingdom, and the United States. While New Zealand signed the Convention in 1972, it has yet to ratify it.

The Convention recognizes the value in protecting seal populations from commercial overexploitation both for purposes of scientific study and maintaining a balanced marine environment in the seas surrounding Antarctica. Article I extends jurisdiction to the seas south of 60° south latitude and lists six types of seal species covered by the Convention. Article II states that seals covered by the Convention shall not be killed or captured within the relevant jurisdiction by nationals or vessels of contracting parties, except as permitted by the Convention. Article II also states that contracting parties must adopt appropriate laws and regulations to facilitate the implementation of the Convention.

The Convention creates the foundation for a permitting system for the kill or capture of seals in the Antarctic region and provides for the exchange of information and scientific advice. The annex to the Convention sets limits on permissible yearly catch rates and establishes closed seasons, sealing zones, and seal reserves. The Annex also specifies which information must be shared and in what manner. Generally, contracting parties must provide each other with certain statistical information about seals caught or killed at least once per year. The Report of the 1988 Meeting to Review the Operation of the Convention for the Conservation of Antarctic Seals, conducted in London, expanded the protection given to certain seals and further clarified information sharing requirements, among other things.

The Convention has enjoyed relative success since its inception. Many of the seal species protected under its auspices, most notable Antarctic fur seals, have recovered from near-extinction and today maintain self-sustaining populations. However these positive outcomes are not solely the result of the Convention. Instead, they reflect the effects of a variety of conservation approaches — including the protection of krill populations, discussed below — which come together for the benefit of Antarctica's marine environment.

2. Convention on the Conservation of Antarctic Marine Living Resources (CCAMLR)

The Convention on the Conservation of Antarctic Marine Living Resources (CCAMLR) was signed on May 20, 1980 in Canberra and subsequently entered into force on April 7, 1982. The creation and adoption of CCAMLR were fueled by concerns that the Antarctic marine ecosystem could be adversely affected by the overexploitation of krill populations in the Antarctic Ocean. After all, krill are an important food source for fish, seals, whales, and other species found in Antarctic waters.

CCAMLR extends protection "to the Antarctic marine living resources of the area south of 60° south latitude and to the Antarctic marine living resources of the area between that latitude and the Antarctic Convergence which forms part of the Antarctic marine ecosystem." Antarctic marine living resources are defined by CCAMLR as "the population of fin fish, mollusks, crustaceans and all other species of living organisms, including birds, found south of the Antarctic Convergence." CCAMLR coverage excludes whales and seals, however, which are the subject of other international agreements.

The Convention is composed of 33 articles and an annex. Article VII establishes the Commission for the Conservation of Antarctic Marine Living Resources. The Commission handles the financial and administrative need of CCAMLR and meets annually. The commission has the power to adopt conservation measures consistent with CCAMLR and to facilitate research into the Antarctic marine ecosystem, among other things. Essentially, through its acts, the Commission gives life to the goals and purposes stated in CCAMLR. Contracting parties are deemed members of the Commission. Article XII states that "[d]ecisions of the Commission on matters of substance shall be taken by consensus. The question of whether a matter is one of substance shall be treated as a matter of substance." CCAMLR also establishes a Scientific Committee on Antarctic Research (SCAR) in Article XIV which is a consultative body to the Commission and composed of representatives of Commission members. Its basic function is to provide scientific information and advice to the Commission. CCAMLR also provides for cooperation with other international bodies, such as the Antarctic Treaty Consultative Parties and the United Nations.

The primary objective of CCAMLR is to ensure the rational and sustainable use of Antarctic marine species, thus maintaining balance in the Antarctic marine ecosystem.[15] It accomplishes this objective by, among other things, requiring that harvesting and associated activities in the covered area comply with CCAMLR's requirements. The Commission has the power to make decisions regarding fisheries

---

[15] *See* Constable et al., *Managing Fisheries to conserve the Antarctic Marine Ecosystem: Practical Implementation of the Convention on the Conservation of Antarctic Marine Living Resources*, 57 J. OF MARINE SCIENCES 778 (2012).

management, based on scientific evidence, which are binding on all CCAMLR signatories.

CCAMLR also acts through its Ecosystem Monitoring Program (CEMP), created in 1986. CEMP is limited in scope and focuses its activities on key areas and species. Monitoring is meant to ensure that commercial harvesting of Antarctic marine life complies with CCAMLR, and more broadly, determines the effect of fishing on target, dependent, and associated species. CEMP also strives to distinguish between ecosystem changes due to fishing versus those due to environmental variability. Species currently monitored, referred to as "indicator species," include the black-browed albatross, Antarctic petrel, and macaroni penguin.[16]

NOTES AND QUESTIONS

1. *CCAMLR's effectiveness*. One criticism of the CCAMLR is that its consensus-based method of decision-making hinders progress on any issues which may be controversial to any single member. Another criticism is the lack of enforcement mechanisms. One notable and persistent problem which encompasses both criticisms is illegal, unreported and unregulated (IUU) fishing.[17]In the 1990s, the tooth fish (commonly known as Chilean sea bass) population was being harvested at a rate of approximately six times the catch reported by member states. Fetching a high price on the market, this overexploitation nearly collapsed Antarctic tooth fish fisheries. Tooth fish are just one of several Antarctic marine stocks that have suffered as a result of overfishing. A Catch Documentation System (CDS) was implemented for tooth fish in 1999, which collected data on tooth fish populations and monitored imports and exports of tooth fish to establish compliance — or lack thereof — with CCAMLR and related provision. Twenty-one member states and three non-members have implemented CDS. While those associated with CDS claim it has been effective, tooth fish populations in the Antarctic are still in danger of being overfished. It is argued by some that the desires of certain member nations to continue benefitting from IUU fishing of tooth fish has prevented the Commission from taking more drastic action to address this problem. For an expanded discussion of the CCAMLR, see STUART KAYE, INTERNATIONAL FISHERIES MANAGEMENT (2001), chapters 10–11. This text includes analysis of the "CCAMLR crisis" concerning the decline of the Patagonian tooth fish. *Id.* at 424–33.

The CCAMLR has also been criticized for failure to achieve its stated goals. *See* WILLIAM T. BURKE, THE NEW INTERNATIONAL LAW OF FISHERIES 114–115 (1994); B. A. Boczek, *The Protection of the Antarctic Ecosystem: A Study in International Environmental Law*, 13 OCEAN DEV. & INT'L L. 380–81 (2001). Danger of the overexploitation of krill was a key motivator behind the negotiation of CCAMLR and its prompt implementation, yet the parties adopted no conservation measures to protect krill until 1991 due to the opposition of two krill-fishing states, Russia and Japan. The consensual decision-making process also hindered the effectiveness of SCAR. Russia viewed SCAR as a political forum while the United States, British

---

[16] CCAMLR Ecosystem Monitoring Program, http://www.ccamlr.org/en/science/ccamlr-ecosystem-monitoring-program-cemp.

[17] Illegal, Unreported, and Unregulated Fishing, http://www.ccamlr.org/en/compliance/compliance.

and Australia expected it to provide objective analysis of the Antarctic marine ecosystem. Moreover, even if the parties could agree to conservation measures, the treaty lacks an effective enforcement and liability procedure. What sort of changes in the treaty regime would solve this problem? Would such a change affect the range of commitments the parties might be willing to make under this treaty? Would a stronger dispute resolution mechanism decrease the parties' willingness to expand this commitment? Would it be better to have fewer commitments, but strong enforcement of those commitments?

2. *Biodiversity.* CCAMLR's innovative ecosystem approach seems to recognize the interdependence of species, but can it be interpreted to protect species not directly covered by the treaty? Since all species are part of the food chain and the destruction of any one species may adversely affect others, can the treaty be stretched to include all species? What are the limits to this scope? How does CCAMLR affect resources, such as seals and whales, which are covered by other international agreements, the Convention for the Conservation of Antarctic Seals (CCAS) and the International Convention for the Regulation of Whaling (ICRW)? CCAMLR is plagued with structural flaws which undermine its ecosystem-based approach to marine resource preservation. The Commission lacks an independent data gathering capacity, and therefore must rely on member states, usually fishing states, for information relating to the ecosystem. This dependence creates an incentive for fishing states to withhold information about endangered fishing stocks that might lead the Commission to impose catch limits. How would you modify this treaty to rectify this problem? Is NGO participation adequate? If not how might it be expanded? What would be the reaction of the member states to your proposals? What problems might arise if you modify the information gathering and dissemination process?

3. *Enforcement and flag state jurisdiction.* In CCAMLR, flag states (states under whose laws vessels are registered or licensed) are responsible for taking action to remedy or to punish breaches in connection with their vessels. However, not all vessels traveling through the Antarctic region belong to the Antarctic Treaty System. In 2001, several states outside of the Antarctic Treaty System, including Belize and Indonesia, were identified as harvesting and importing tooth fish. The CCAMLR Commission could only take limited action in the form of persuading the offending states to participate in the CCAMLR conservation scheme. Among other issues, problems tend to arise when nationals of an Antarctic Treaty System state reflag their vessels in order to avoid such international law obligations. For more information on flag state jurisdiction as it relates to the Antarctic Treaty System and an argument for a new enforcement mechanism, see Martin Lishexian Lee, *A Case for World Government of the Antarctic*, 9 Gonz. J. Int'l L. 73 (2005), *available at* http://www.acrossborders.com. Would an on-the-spot enforcement procedure be more effective? Would states agree to this?

4. *Krill.* In recent years Japanese, Russian and Polish fleets have increasingly been harvesting krill. Krill is an essential link in the Antarctic marine living food chain. At the base of the food chain, vitality of krill stocks affects the survival of all marine life, including whales, seals, birds, fish, and squid. *See* R.P. J Hewitt *et al.*, *Setting a Precautionary Catch Limit for Antarctic Krill*, 15(3) Oceanography 26–33 (2002). Despite krill's importance to the Antarctic ecosystem, much about the

species is still unknown, making krill harvests potentially dangerous. Intensive harvesting could result in: 1) an increase in competing species; 2) interference with the recovery of the depleted whale stocks; 3) depletion of other dependent species, such as seals, birds, fish, and squid; and 4) depletion of the krill stock itself. George Knox, *The Living Resources of the Southern Ocean: A Scientific Overview*, in ANTARCTIC RESOURCES POLICY: SCIENTIFIC, LEGAL AND POLITICAL ISSUES 21, 53 (Francisco Orrego Vicuna ed. 1983). In light of the lack of knowledge about krill, how can the stock be protected in a manner that reflects the dual interest of environmental protection and rational harvesting? How can CCAMLR's aim of maintaining the ecological balance between harvested species and their dependent predators be achieved? Is this possible considering the many unknown variables? *See* David M. Edwards and John A. Heap, *"Convention on the Conservation of Antarctic Marine Living Resources" A Commentary*, 20 POLAR RECORD 353, 354–55 (1981); Stephen Nicol, *CCAMLR and its Approaches to Management of the Krill Fishery*, 27 POLAR RECORD 229, 229 (1991).

5. ***The scope of CCAMLR.*** The CCAMLR only applies to Antarctic marine living resources not to all activities which take place within the covered area. Consider the express language of the various treaties on the area of application and subsequent state practice. Should the jurisdiction vary depending on the purpose of the particular treaty provisions? What problems, if any, do these differing jurisdictional definitions create?

PROBLEM 9-2
MANAGEMENT AND ENFORCEMENT PROBLEMS IN THE SOUTHERN OCEAN

The area of competence of CCAMLR is the southern ocean surrounding Antarctica, approximately 15% of the world's oceans. The Commission established under Article VII of CCAMLR is responsible for the conservation and management of marine living resources in this area. Note, however, Article VI, which effectively takes away authority to manage whaling or seals because these animals are the subjects of prior international agreements, the Convention for the Conservation of Antarctic Seals (1972) and the international Convention for the Regulation of Whaling (1946). Twenty-four states and the European Union are members of the Commission. An additional 11 states have acceded to CCAMLR but are not members of the Commission. The Commission's Secretariat is located in Hobart, Tasmania.

The Commission is particularly concerned with three types of living resources: krill, because they are the basis of the Antarctic food chain; icefish; and tooth fish. The Commission has authority to adopt Conservation Measures that are binding on all members and apply within CCAMLR's convention area. These Conservation Measures are published in an annual Schedule of Conservation Measures in Force. In addition, the Commission adopts non-binding resolutions which are designed to complement the binding measures. The Conservation Measures fall into four different categories: (1) compliance, (2) general fishery matters; (3) fishery regulations; and (4) protected areas. (*See* CCAMLR Article IX).

Read the provisions of CCAMLR in the **Document Supplement** and answer the following questions:

1. An argument has erupted between parties-members of the Commission over Conservation Measures application to tooth fish. One member argues that scientific data collected over the past five years show tooth fish populations to be stable. This member argues that the annual quota of tooth fish that may be harvested may be increased. Other members of the Commission argue that there is scientific evidence that removal of a greater number of tooth fish from the ecosystem would have an adverse effect on non-commercial species of fish and other birds and animals in the marine ecosystem. What should the Commission decide? (*See* Article II.3).

2. Several of the Commission members advocate that Conservation Measures be adopted that safeguard the general environment of certain areas during fishing. They also argue in favor of measures that minimize the mortality of seabirds and marine mammals during fishing operations. Other members argue that such general measures go beyond the legal authority accorded to the Commission. What do you think? (*See* Article IX.2).

3. A key component of the Commission's work is the formulation of Fishery Plans. Each plan provides a comprehensive summary of information on a fishery, including detailed regulatory requirements (harvest controls, notification requirements, a research and fishery operations plan, and a data collection plan). The Scientific Committee established by Article XIV is responsible for advising the Commission on conservation measures. To what extent does the Commission have to accede to the advice of the Scientific Committee? (*See* Article IX.4)

4. How are decisions taken by the Commission? Must there be unanimous agreement? (*See* Article XIII).

5. When do conservation Measures become binding upon members? Can a member that disagrees with a particular Conservation Measure opt out of the obligation to comply? (*See* Article IX.6)

6. One of the key flag states for fishing vessels, Panama, has acceded to CCAMLR. Thus CCAMLR Conservation Measures are binding on Panamanian flag vessels. But many potential flag states are not members of CCAMLR. What is to prevent a fishing vessel that wants to fish in the Southern Ocean from obtaining a flag of convenience from a nation not a member of CCAMLR? Can such a vessel fish without regard to the CCAMLR regulations? Several measures have been instituted to enforce CCAMLR Conservation Measures among both parties and non-parties. A catch documentation scheme is now operational for tooth fish; a centralized vessel monitoring system has been implemented; lists of vessels engaged in illegal, unreported and unregulated (IUU) fishing are routinely compiled; and port and coastal states have been enlisted against IUU fishing. (*See also* Articles XXI, XXII, and XXIV)

7. The Commission has adopted as Conservation Measure 91-04 (2011), a General Framework for the Establishment of CCAMLR Marine Protected Areas. The United States, supported by New Zealand, submitted the

following Proposal for the Ross Sea Region Marine Protected Area:

A PROPOSAL FOR THE ROSS SEA REGION MARINE PROTECTION AREA DELEGATION OF THE UNITED STATES
7 September 2012

Abstract

1. The delegation of the United States proposes the establishment by the Commission for the Conservation of Antarctic Living Marine Resources (Commission or CCAMLR) of a marine protected area (MPA) in the Ross Sea Region ("Ross Sea Region Marine Protected Area"). In 2010, the Commission endorsed the Scientific Committee's work program to develop a representative system of Antarctic MPAs with the aim of conserving marine biodiversity in the Convention Area. Consistent with this goal and to safeguard the exceptional ecological value and scientific importance of the Ross Sea Region for current and future generations, our delegation proposes to establish this MPA to conserve marine living resources, preserve ecological structure and function, protect vital ecosystem processes and areas of ecological significance, and maintain a reference area for scientific research and monitoring. This proposal is consistent with Conservation Measure 91-04 (2011) and the scientific conclusions and processes, endorsed by the Scientific Commission, from which the United States developed its original MPA scenario for the Ross Sea Region.

Background

2. Since 2005, the Commission has undertaken significant scientific analyses and planning toward the implementation of MPAs in the Convention Area. These efforts have progressed in accordance with the decision at the 2002 World Summit of Sustainable Development to achieve a representative network of MPAs by 2012. The Commission's work to establish MPAs in the Convention Area is further supported in the recent decision of the 2012 United Nations Conference on Sustainable Development, which noted the importance of conserving, by 2020, 10 percent of coastal and marine areas, especially areas important for biodiversity and ecosystem services, through representative and well-connected systems of protected areas. The Commission recognizes MPAs for, among other attributes, their important role in facilitating research and monitoring of Antarctic marine living resources and as a tool for contributing to sustained ecosystem structure and function, maintain the ability to adapt in the face of climate change.

3. To conserve the significant marine biodiversity of the Convention Area, in 2010 the Commission endorsed the Scientific Committee's work program to develop a representative system of Antarctic MPAs. The Commission's Committee to a system of MPAs further implements Article IX.2 (f) and 2(g) of the CAMLR Convention where the Commission may adopt conservation measures, formulated on the basis of the best scientific evidence available, designating open and closed seasons for harvesting and the opening and closing of areas, regions or sub-regions for the purpose of scientific study or conservation, including special areas for protection and scientific study. The Commission's first, and to date only, MPA was designated in 2009 in the South Orkney Islands region, and came

into force in 2010. In 2011, to facilitate efforts to further develop its representative system of MPAs, the Commission adopted Conservation Measure 91-04 (2011), which provides a general framework for the establishment of CCAMLR MPAs, including overarching MPA objectives, key elements and delimitation of MPA conservation measures, and requirements for management and research and monitoring plans.

4. Recognizing the remarkable ecological and scientific importance of the Ross Sea Region, the United States now proposes the establishment of the Ross Sea Region Marine Protected Area. The Ross Sea Region is among the best studied areas of high-latitude continental shelf ocean in the Southern hemisphere. The existing high level of scientific understanding and information about the Ross Sea Region make it a uniquely desirable candidate for protection. Such protection would safeguard this extremely valuable scientific reference area for research and monitoring, particularly as it relates to long-term climate and other environmental change. The existing long-term datasets on the region's geology, oceanography, climatology and biology provide a robust characterization of a region with tremendous ecological value, biological productivity and biodiversity. The Ross Sea continental shelf is known to encompass the most productive ecosystems of the Southern Ocean, generating abundant marine life, and it is one of the few places in the world that retains its full community of top-level predators. Indeed, for its unique scientific, biodiversity, and ecosystem values, the Ross Sea Region is among the most pristine natural regions in the world and of tremendous conservation and scientific value to current and future generations.

5. This MPA proposal is consistent with Conservation Measure 91-04 (2011), the MPA planning domains endorsed by the Commission in 2011, and the Commission's precautionary approach to management. The proposal further reflects the scientific conclusions and processes, endorsed by the Scientific Committee, from which the United States developed its original MPA scenario for the Ross Sea Region. The Ross Sea Region Marine Protected Area proposal is based on a substantial body of interdisciplinary research, extensive consultations with scientists and stakeholders, and in-depth bilateral and multilateral discussion in various CCAMLR fora.

6. The proposed Ross Sea Region MPA encompasses key areas of the Ross Sea Region marine environment that both correspond and contribute to achieving the MPAs conservation and science objectives, which are:

a) to conserve ecological structure and function throughout the Ross Sea Region, at all levels of biological organization, by prohibiting fishing in habitats that are important to native mammals, birds, fishes, and invertebrates;

b) to provide a reference area, in which fishing is prohibited, to better gauge the ecosystem effects on climate change and fishing and to provide other opportunities for better understanding the Antarctic marine ecosystem; and

c) to promote research and other scientific activities (including monitoring) focused on marine living resources.

7. The United States likewise recognizes the interest of many CCAMLR Members in commercial fishing in the Ross Sea Region, and the utility of continuing tooth fish tagging research to inform stock assessment. In designing the proposal, our delegation sought to maximize the achievement of objectives for

scientific research, ecosystem protection, and marine living resource conservation, where conservation includes rational use. To this end, the MPA proposal leaves the vast majority of main tooth fish fishing grounds in the Ross Sea Region open to fishing. The proposal further would allow total allowable catch to be reallocated between existing management units (Small Scale Research Units), potentially displaced fishing effort to be redistributed with few anticipated impacts to fishing operations, and research fishing to be conducted within the MPA.

8.   Our proposal further accommodates Members' interests in commercial fishing in the Ross Sea Region by including zones designed to achieve protection and scientific objectives while still allowing some fishing to occur in certain areas within the MPA. Specifically, our proposal comprises three zones — the North Central Zone, the Western Zone and the Southern Zone — designed to respond to Members' comments on our initial MPA scenario for the Ross Sea Region presented in SC-CAMLR-XXX/9.

9.   First, some Members recommended that we consider seasonal closures to achieve protection objectives for spawning tooth fish associated with the seamounts north of about 65°S. In response to this suggestion our proposal includes the North Central Zone where directed fishing for tooth fish is allowed subject to specific season and gear restrictions, the latter of which is intended to minimize risks to vulnerable benthic communities.

10. Second, to accommodate Members who may be interested in krill fishing, our proposal includes the Western Zone in which krill fishing would be permitted pursuant to Conservation Measure 51-04 (2011). The United States considers that such fishing would pose minimal risk to the ecosystem in the Western Zone and provide critical data for understanding the dynamics and role of krill in this area of the Ross Sea Region.

11. Finally, our proposal would establish the Southern Zone in which research fishing is the only type of fishing that would be permitted, and such fishing must be approved, in advance, by the Commission on a case-by-case basis if planned catches exceed threshold established in Conservation Measure 24-01 (2011). The United States recognizes the importance of research fishing and considers that commercial fishing in this zone would undermine its ability to serve as a scientific reference area to support research aimed at understanding the ecosystem effects of climate change and fishing by contrasting ecosystem structure and function in the Southern Zone with that in fishing grounds outside the MPA.

12. It is our view that the proposed Ross Sea Region Marine Protected Area would mark a major achievement toward meeting the Commission's goal of developing a representative system of Antarctic MPAs with the aim of conserving marine biodiversity in the Convention Area.

13. The delegation of the United States invites all Members to consider the following Conservation Measure to establish the Ross Sea Region Marine Protected Area for the purpose of achieving the conservation of Antarctic marine living resources, where conservation includes rational use.

MAP OF THE THREE ZONES (WESTERN, NORTH CENTRAL, AND SOUTHERN) CONSTITUTING THE PROPOSED ROSS SEA REGION MARINE PROTECTED AREA

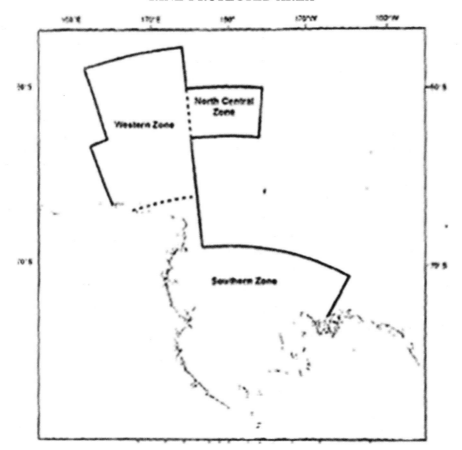

Do you think this proposal should be approved? At the CCAMLR Meeting of Parties in October 2013, the United States' Proposal failed to win the required unanimous approval for the Marine Protected Area in the Ross Sea. The United States and New Zealand plan to continue their efforts to make this designation. See the account of the October meeting in Note, 107 AM. J. INT'L L. 928–29 (2013).

3. Protocol on Environmental Protection (The Madrid Protocol)

The Protocol on Environmental Protection to the Antarctic Treaty, commonly known as the Madrid Protocol, is a key component of the Antarctic Treaty System. The Madrid Protocol was signed in Madrid on October 4, 1991 and subsequently entered into force on January 14, 1998. It has been ratified by 27 states, including the United States, China, Germany, Argentina, Japan, and South Korea. Another 16 states have signed the Protocol but have yet to ratify it, including Canada, Greece, Turkey, and Switzerland. The Protocol seeks to ensure that activities in Antarctica conform to the principles of the Antarctic Treaty, reaffirm the status of the Antarctica as a special Conservation Area, and build a further framework for the protection of the Antarctic Environment with regard to its dependent and associated ecosystem. The Protocol also prohibits mineral resource activities for purposes other than scientific research. Further, Article 25 of the Protocol states that the Article 7 mining ban cannot be repealed unless a future treaty establishes a binding regulatory framework for such activity. The scope of the Protocol is limited to "The area to which the provisions of the Antarctic Treaty apply in accordance with Article VI of that Treaty."

The Protocol (Art. 2) designates Antarctica as a natural reserve "devoted to peace and science," prohibits mining, requires environmental impact assessments before certain activities may be undertaken, mandates the creation of contingency plans in case of environmental emergencies, and creates an expert advisory board — the Committee for Environmental Protection (CEP) — to advise to Antarctic Treaty Consultative Meeting. To facilitate this process, CEP holds annual meetings in conjunction with the Antarctic Treaty Consultative Meeting.

The parties designed the Protocol so it could only be modified by the consensus of all Antarctic Treaty Consultative Parties. Article 4 of the Protocol clarifies that it is meant to supplement the Antarctic Treaty, not to modify or amend it. Article 5 states that signatories to the Protocol shall

> consult and co-operate with the contracting parties to the other international instruments in force within the Antarctic Treaty System and their respective institutions with a view to ensuring the achievement of the objectives and principles of this protocol and avoiding any interference with the achievement of the objectives and principles of those instruments . . . .

Thus, the text of the Protocol makes clear that it is meant to provide depth and reach to the agreements and institutions already existing within the Antarctic Treaty System framework. Article 6 of the Protocol envisions a cooperative system where member states assist one another in the planning and conduct of activities and programs in the Antarctic. It also provides that member states are to jointly "carry out such steps as may be agreed upon at Antarctic Treaty Consultative Meeting." Moreover, participants at Antarctic Treaty Consultative Meeting are given the responsibility of defining the general policies for the protection of the Antarctic Environment in accordance with the Protocol and adopting measures under Article IX of the Antarctic Treaty in order to implement the protocol. In carrying out these tasks, the participants are to draw on the information and advice provided by CEP and SCAR at the Consultative Meeting.

The Protocol contains six annexes, four of which were adopted along with the protocol in 1991. Annexes V and VI were adopted at a subsequent Antarctic Treaty Consultative Meeting. Annex I concerns environmental impact assessments activities undertaken in the covered area are to be assessed based on their impacts on the environment, with high level impact activities requiring a comprehensive environment evaluation and CEP comment period before proceeding. Annex II pertains to the conservation of Antarctic flora and fauna and updates the existing rules regarding the protection of plants and animals in the covered area. Annex III concerns waste disposal and management, distinguishes between waste which may and may not be disposed of within the covered area, and requires the development of waste management plans. Annex IV covers marine pollution and includes provisions regarding discharge from marine vessels and the disposal of plastics at sea. Annex V introduces a renewed "Protected Area" System composed of Antarctic Specially Protected Areas and Antarctic Specially Managed Areas. Annex VI provides for liability in instances of environmental emergency. It also formulates rules regarding the prevention and subsequent responsibility for dealing with the effects of environmental emergencies arising from activities in the covered area.

The provisions of the protocol are largely self-enforcing. Article 13 establishes that member states shall take "appropriate measures" to ensure compliance with the protocol, exert "appropriate effort" to ensure that no one engages in activities which conflict with the protocol, and alert other member of activities which interfere with protocol's implementation and objectives. Article 14 provides for inspections carried out by observers arranged by Antarctic Treaty Consultative Parties.

NOTES AND QUESTIONS

1. ***The Protocol and the Antarctic Treaty System.*** What powers and rights does the Protocol give nations and NGOs that the previous agreements did not? How does the Protocol work, or fail to work, in conjunction with the Antarctic Treaty and CCAMLR?

2. ***Environmental impact assessments.*** Is the Protocol's environmental impact assessment regime meaningful? By what standard is it determined that a proposed activity will have less than a "minor" or "transitory" impact on the environment? *See* Article 8.1 and Annex 1. Given the importance of the initial assessment, which will determine the amount of scrutiny a proposed activity will receive, how will the Protocol protect against activities that are intentionally or mistakenly characterized as having only "minor" or "transitory" impact?

Does the Protocol identify who determines whether a particular activity will proceed once an impact assessment has been made? The Protocol only provides that the decision is to be based upon a Comprehensive Environmental Evaluation (CEE). *See* Annex I, Art. 4. In practice, drafts of the CEEs are examined by the Committee for Environmental Protection and then by the Antarctic Treaty Consultative Meeting with the Committee's recommendations. It appears that the Committee only advises on the evaluation, which presumably the individual nation itself makes. Art. 12.1 (1). The decision whether or not to proceed remains with the individual nation. Is this an effective process? How could this process be improved? What might explain the absence of an independent body authorized to make binding decisions? Even if the Consultative Parties were reluctant to give up their formal rights to make the decision whether to proceed, would an independent evaluation by a body, such as the Committee for Environmental Protection, enhance the credibility of the process? Some scholars assert that nations would be reluctant to ignore a Committee determination that a proposed activity should not proceed. Do you agree?

3. ***The Protocol and CRAMRA.*** It appears that the structure and working of Article 3, which states the Protocol's environmental principles, is drawn from

Article 4 of the 1988 Convention on the Regulation of Antarctic Mineral Resource Administration (CRAMRA), which never entered into force and will be examined in the next section. *See* David Lysons, *Environmental Impact Assessment in Antarctica Under the Protocol on Environmental Protection*, 29 POLAR RECORD 111, 116 (1993).

4.   *Oversight.* Article 3(4)(b) provides activities must be "modified, suspended or canceled if they result in or threaten to result in impacts upon the Antarctic environment or dependent or associated ecosystems inconsistent with those principles [of the Protocol]." Who is supposed to make that determination? Does the Protocol provide any guidance? If it is against the country engaging in the activity, how effective do you think this provision is likely to be? What if a country makes a determination about its activities with which other countries disagree?

5.   *Unpredicted impacts.* Consider CRAMRA's provision covering unpredicted impacts. Under Article 51(1), the Regulatory Committee would have required to suspend, modify, or cancel an activity if it "has resulted or is about to result in impacts on the Antarctic environment or dependent or associated ecosystems, beyond those judged acceptable." Why did the drafters of the protocol not include a similar provision that identifies an independent body with the responsibility of assuring compliance?

D.   Mineral Resource Regulation

Antarctica's geological features make mineral exploration difficult and costly. A lack of scientific research means it is unclear how great Antarctica's mineral resource potential may be. Some experts believe that Antarctica may have an abundance of minerals — especially on the eastern portion of the continent — though thick ice sheets, icebergs, cold temperatures, and the remoteness of Antarctica make such mineral exploration a tough endeavor. Iron oxide and coal are the primary minerals thus far identified in Antarctica through scientific studies. At present it is not economically viable to engage in commercial exploration and exploitation of Antarctica's mineral resources, but the prospect of future commercial viability and the potentially disastrous environmental damage such activities could cause gives this issue great importance.

The Antarctic Treaty is largely silent on the subject of mineral exploration and exploitation. At the Treaty's inception it was thought to be too soon to decide such matters, especially given their contentious nature. It was later concluded amongst the Consultative Parties that the establishment of a regime governing mineral resources would be useful. At the Eighth Antarctic Treaty Consultative Meeting (Oslo, 1975), the Ninth Antarctic Treaty Consultative Meeting (London 1977), and the Tenth Antarctic Treaty Consultative Meeting (Washington, D.C., 1979), SCAR presented an important series of reports about the various potential risks and effects of Antarctic mineral exploration and exploitation. These reports indicated, among other things, that while mineral exploration and exploitation in the Antarctic region carried grave risks such activities need not necessarily be banned entirely. With the possibility of mineral exploration and exploitation left open, especially considering that future scientific gains could conceivably make these processes more feasible and less damaging to the environment, the Consultative

Parties pressed on to create an appropriate legal regime governing Antarctic mineral resources.

The Convention on the Regulation of Antarctic Mineral Resource Administration (CRAMRA) was meant to be that legal regime. However, while the Consultative Parties agreed on the need for action, they did not agree on much else. The negotiations leading up to CRAMRA were drawn out over six years until it was finally concluded in Wellington, New Zealand in 1988. One of the most controversial subjects in this negotiation involved creating a means of allocating property rights in connection with mineral exploitation for the purpose of providing assurance to commercial investors.[18] While a compromise was ultimately reached in 1988, France and Australia's refusal to sign CRAMRA sent the parties back into negotiation which were ultimately unsuccessful.

While CRAMRA would have permitted mineral exploration and exploitation — albeit in a heavily regulated framework — the Parties eventually adopted the Madrid Protocol which bans any mineral activity in Antarctic's unrelated to scientific research.

NOTES AND QUESTIONS

1. *France, Australia, and CRAMRA.* Why did France and Australia refuse to sign CRAMRA? The former Australian, Prime Minister, Bob Hawks, has said that "[m]ining in Antarctica just seemed absurd to me . . . [t]here was an unequalled opportunity for our scientists to measure the past and the present with a view to protecting the future. And to allow anything to compromise that capacity was, in our view, criminal." The former French Prime Minister, Michel Rocard, had similar sentiments: "[o]ur aim was to destroy the mining treaty, and throw it away . . . [t]he rest of the world was surprised, but I think we did a good job." Indeed, the two countries as recently as 2011 have called for a strengthening of the Antarctic Treaty System in order to ensure the ban on exploration and exploitation of mineral resources is respected.

2. *CRAMRA's legacy.* Although CRAMRA will likely never enter into force, many consider it an important model for environmental regulation. *See* DONALD R. ROTHWELL, THE POLAR REGIONS AND THE DEVELOPMENT OF INTERNATIONAL ENVIRONMENT LAW 133–39 (1996). The key weakness in the Madrid Protocol is the possibility that the moratorium on mineral extraction may be discontinued or, more likely, disregarded in the face of an energy crisis. Should CRAMRA be reconsidered as a regulatory structure or should key provisions of it be transplanted into the Protocol? Which provisions, if any, would you enact? Which would you modify and why?

3. *CRAMRA and development.* Developing countries were another source of severe criticism of CRAMRA, but with a very different outlook than Australia and France, whose concerns were primarily environmental. From the onset of negotia-

---

[18] *Antarctic Treaty Handbook: Regulation of Antarctic Mineral Resources Activities* (United States State Department, 1990). *See* Dianne Nicol & Julia Jabour-Green, *Bioprospecting in Areas Outside National Jurisdiction: Antarctica and the Southern Ocean*, 4 MELB. J. INT'L L. 76, 82 (2003).

tion, they resented the presumed control of mineral resources by the elitist original Consultative Parties. Ellen S. Tenenbaum, *A World Park in Antarctica: The Common Heritage of Mankind*, 10 VA. ENVTL. L.J. 109, 109–10 (1990); *1984 Annual Review of United Nations Affairs* 371–74 (D. Lincoff ed.). How would you propose Earth's numerous countries divide up the benefits of income from mining in Antarctica? By equal shares to each nation? Should the Consultative Parties receive a larger share because of their long history of scientific research in the region?

4. *Russia's role.* The Madrid Protocol prohibits mining in the covered area. However, this provision is subject to amendment or repeal in 2048. At the Thirty-Fourth Antarctic Treaty Consultative Meeting (Buenos Aires, 2011), Russia introduced a plan detailing its proposed activities in Antarctica spanning 2011–2030, which included mineral, hydrocarbon, and natural resource exploration. Should the Consultative Parties be concerned? What would happen if Russia carries out its intended mineral exploration in conflict with Article 7 of the Madrid Protocol?

5. *The "walkout clause" of the Madrid Protocol.* The Protocol imposes a 50-year ban on mining in Antarctica. However, this provision as originally presented was unacceptable to the United States. The earlier provision stated that unanimous approval of Consultative Parties would be necessary in order to lift the ban after the fifty-year period had expired. The United States believed this would foreclose any possibility of mining in the future — a restriction the United States refused to be bound by. Through further negotiations the provision was changed to permit an end to the mining ban by a three-fourths vote. In addition, a "walkout clause," as it is commonly called, was added to Article 25 of the Protocol. It states that if a majority approved amendment to allow mining has not been ratified within three years of being submitted to all voting nations for approval, then any voting nation can subsequently give notice to withdraw from the mining prohibition of the protocol. Actual mining operations could then begin two years after notification of withdrawal. There has been much criticism of the walkout clause, generally arguing that it significantly reduces the Protocol's relevance. *See* William Welch, *The Antarctic Treaty System: Is It Adequate to Regulate or Eliminate the Environmental Exploitation of the Globe's Last Wilderness?*, 14 HOUS. J. INT'L L. 597 (1992). Was this a good compromise?

E. Oil Spills and Waste Management

As human activity in Antarctica increases, so does the potential for oil spills. This is especially true as many tourist vessels traveling through the region may not be properly equipped to operate in the ice-filled Antarctic Ocean.[19] While oil spills are always detrimental to the natural environment, oil spills in Antarctica tend to be especially problematic. The remote location and tumultuous weather patterns of Antarctica complicate even the most sophisticated clean-up efforts. In May 2012 a Brazilian vessel, The Endless Sea, which was carrying approximately 2,000 gallons of oil became trapped in Antarctic ice and sank in 39 feet of water.[20] The vessel was

---

[19] For expanded information on tourism, see Asia N. Wright, *Southern Exposure: Managing Sustainable Cruise Ship Tourism in Antarctica*, 39 CAL. W. INT'L L.J 43 (2008).

[20] *Wrecked Brazilian Ship Leaking Oil in Antarctica*, USA TODAY, May 9, 2012, at 1.

leaking fuel when it sank, but the extent of the damage was initially hard to ascertain and reparative measures were difficult to implement as a result of the cold and stormy weather. In fact, it was not until the end of the Antarctic winter that a comprehensive clean-up could be carried out. The worst Antarctic oil spill to date occurred in 2007 when a Canadian tourist vessel registered to Liberia (a non-ATS nation), the *MS Explorer*, struck ice off the coast of Antarctica near the Shetland Islands.[21] The *MS Explorer* was carrying approximately 50,000 gallons of diesel, 6,300 gallons of lubricant, and 260 gallons of gasoline when it sank. Poor weather conditions posed serious challenges to containment of the spill, which stretched over a mile of ocean and polluted the route to the breeding grounds of Antarctic, Papua, and Adelie penguins. The spill likely also affected other fauna living in the area, including krill, plankton, sea lions, and sea birds.

At the Thirtieth Antarctic Treaty Consultative Meeting (New Delhi, 2007), the United States and England raised the subject of increasing tourism in Antarctica and cautioned that Consultative Parties ought to take a hard look at vessel safety issues.[22] This, of course, was before the sinking of the *MS Explorer*. Part of the problem with increased tourism is the fact that many tourist vessels traveling to and from Antarctica have minimal or nonexistent ice reinforcement.[23] Although these ships tend to stay far offshore or travel in warmer months in order to avoid sea ice, this strategy is not always effective. Also, some tourist vessels may feel pressured into making riskier trips to remain economically competitive.

In contrast to oil spills, most pollution occurring in the waters around Antarctica is more discrete. Marine vessels expel several types of waste as part of their normal functioning, including sewage (toilet waste), solid waste (such as plastic), gray water (waste water from sinks, laundry, etc.), air emissions (pollutants from engines, such as carbon dioxide), hazardous waste, ballast water (seawater taken on during loading), and oily bilge water (a byproduct of operation of the vessel's machinery).[24] A small cruise ship carrying 1,400 passengers may produce several tons of waste in a single day.[25] Also, many items may accidentally fall from ship or be washed off the vessel — or may be deliberately thrown overboard — resulting in the accumulation of marine debris. Some common examples of this marine debris include fishing nets, bait boxes, trash, and plastic bags.[26]

Waste is also created on the Antarctic continent itself, mostly as a result of the scientific bases and personnel who are positioned there. Annex III of the Madrid Protocol governs waste management and disposal. It provides that waste should be removed from the Antarctic Treaty Area to the maximum extent practicable by the generator of such waste. Annex III also provides for waste disposal by incineration and limited disposal of sewage and liquid wastes into the sea. Parties are to create

---

[21] Ian Austin, *For Cruise Ships, Antarctica Presents Murky Waters*, N.Y. TIMES, Nov. 26, 2007, at 1.

[22] Austin, op. cit.

[23] *Id.*

[24] Wright, op. cit. at 58–59.

[25] *Id* at 59.

[26] U.S. EPA, *Prevention, Control and Reduction of Vessel Waste*, *available at* http://water.epa.gov/type/oceb/marinedebris/prevention_vessel.cfm.

their own waste management plans and are expected to share such plans with other parties annually. In addition, parties are to send information related to waste management plans to the Committee for Environmental Protection, which may offer suggestions. The Annex also states that it does not apply in cases of emergency such as when human life is at risk. Further, Article 15 of the Madrid Protocol requires member states to prepare contingency plans for the handling of emergencies such as oil or waste spills.

In accordance with Annex III of the Madrid Protocol, Parties create and administer their own Waste Management Systems. The field manual[27] for the United States Antarctic Program details the United States' policies on waste management. It states that "[i]n general, everything taken into the field must be brought out. This includes food containers, empty fuel drums, toilet paper, urine, human solid waste, used dish water, and everything else that is brought into the field. All hazardous waste generated on Antarctica or encountered in the field must be returned to the United States by vessel. This is generally accomplished by placing waste on the resupply vessels which travel from the United States to Antarctica and back every year. Waste returned on these ships is to be segregated in accordance with stated procedures and established categories. United States to Antarctica personnel going into the field must have spill response training and be equipped with spill-response kits."[28] The United States also has spill response teams based in Antarctica who are equipped to deal with more serious spills. Other countries have similar waste management programs. For example, the British Antarctic Survey (BAS) also states that waste produced by BAS personnel and programs must be removed from the Continent, with limited exceptions.

NOTES

1. *Flags of convenience*. The practice of registering ships to other states and thereby submitting to the jurisdiction of those states is more common than one might think. There are numerous reasons that ship owners fly a so-called "Flag of Convenience," including reduced operating costs and minimized legal responsibilities. Liberia, the state under which the Canadian *MS Explorer* vessel was flagged, has one of the largest ship registries in the world. The Liberian Registry,[29] which is administrated by a corporation owned and operated in the United States, is the second largest vessel registry in the world, representing 11% of the world's ocean going ships. Other popular registries are those of Panama and the Marshall Islands. Neither Liberia, Panama nor the Marshall Islands are signatories to the Antarctic Treaty or the Madrid Protocol. For an expanded discussion of the dangers Flags of Convenience pose to the environment, see Scott P. Wilson, *Flags of Convenience Shield Polluters in Battle to Protect Seas*, 455 NATURE 1029 (2008).

2. *After the MS Explorer oil spill*. Argentina's first response after the *MS Explorer* spill was to push for further international regulation of Antarctic tourism.

---

[27] Field Manual for the United States Antarctic Program, ch. 15, *available at* http://www.usap.gov.

[28] *Id* at 173.

[29] About the Liberian Registry, *available at* http://www.liscr.com/liscr/AbouttheLiberianRegistry/tabid/197/Default.aspx.

Argentina also sought to sue the Canadian travel company that operated the vessel. Simultaneously, Chile spent over $50 million in an attempt to disperse the fuel which had leaked from the vessel.

3. *Tourist vessels in the Antarctic*. While tourism in Antarctica used to entail traveling on research vessels to observe penguins, today tourists can choose to travel on luxurious yachts and cruise ships. Most tourists make the trek to Antarctica aboard small and medium sized vessels, though the number of tourists opting for large cruise ships is quickly increasing. Many of these tourist vessels are ill-equipped to deal with the harsh conditions of Antarctic sea travel, posing serious environmental risks as demonstrated in the *MS Explorer* incident. Asia N. Wright, *Southern Exposure: Managing Sustainable Cruise Ship Tourism in Antarctica*, 39 CAL. W. INT'L L.J. 43, 58–59 (2008).

4. *The actual state of waste management in Antarctica*. The Madrid Protocol establishes the framework for waste management in Antarctica, leaving the finer details to individual members. How has this system fared in reality? Some have claimed that the self-administration of Waste Management has let to disastrous results. *See* KEITH SUTER, ANTARCTICA: PRIVATE PROPERTY OR PUBLIC HERITAGE?, 108–10 (1991). Suter noted observations that the United States base at McMurdo Sound, operated by the United States National Science Foundation, looks like "a dusty mining camp in the old west . . ." with junk being tossed into coastal waters and rubbish being openly burned. Both practices are prohibited in the United States. With increasing tourism and travel to Antarctica, the waste management problem is expected to increase.

F. Regulation of Tourism

Tourism to Antarctica remained in the low thousands until the mid-1990s when it spiked.[30] There has been an upward trend ever since. It is estimated that over 26,500 tourists travelled to Antarctica between 2011 and 2012.[31] Of these tourists, most came from the United States, Australia, and Europe.[32] Tourists travelling to Antarctica in the past several years generally chose trips on seaborne vessels with landings on the Antarctic continent, but many tourists choose to travel to Antarctica by ship without ever stepping foot on land.[33]

Tourism is permissible activity under the Antarctic Treaty, though the treaty itself does not purport to regulate tourism. In contrast, the Madrid Protocol contains several provisions relating to tourist activities. However, the management of tourism in Antarctica is largely left to the tourist industry itself. The International Association of Antarctica Tour Operators (IAATO), an industry group for Antarctic tourism has taken a leading role in establishing procedures and

---

[30] Brian Witte, *Calls for Regulation of Rising Antarctic Tourism*, USA TODAY, Aug. 17, 2006, at 1.

[31] Antarctica Tourism Fact Sheet 2012–13, IATTO, *available at* http://www.iatto.org/documents/10157/15716.

[32] *Id.*

[33] Antarctica Tourism Fact Sheet, op. cit. supra.

guidelines for Antarctic tourism.[34] These guidelines include restrictions on the number of people permitted ashore, staff-to-passenger ratios on tours, site and activity specific guidelines, reporting measures, and the required creation of contingency and emergency evacuation plans.[35] IAATO has instituted a mandatory briefing requirement in order to implement the ATCM Recommendation XVIII-1, titled *Guidance for those Organizing and Conducting Tourism and Non-Governmental Activities in the Antarctic*, which requires things such as conducting assessments of the potential environmental impacts of planned activities.[36]

IATTO's stated goal is to facilitate tourism while preserving Antarctica's pristine environment. IAATO is made up of voluntary members, including travel agencies, ship- and land-based operators, and others, who meet at least once a year to review, create, and amend the organization's policies and regulations. Moreover, IAATO representatives often attend Antarctic Treaty Consultative Meetings.[37] Some have argued that the IAATO Management System has developed so rapidly because the organization exists outside the ATS and is unfettered by its consensual decision-making system.[38]

While law regarding Antarctic tourism is in short supply, states do often issue guidelines to be used by their tourists. For example, Australia's "Visitor Guidelines" incorporate the recommendations arising from Antarctic Treaty Consultative Meeting XVIII (Kyoto, 1994) and include sections related to Antarctic wildlife, protected areas, safety, and waste disposal.[39] The guidelines instruct visitors to respect scientific research facilities, comply with smoking restrictions, keep a safe distance from wildlife, refrain from bringing non-native plants and animals onto the continent, and more. However, this public-private management system still faces significant and mounting challenges. While the tourist industry has created its own set of best practices, it is not a substitute for government and ATS regulation. Unfortunately this regulation lags behind, in large part due to gridlock in ATS decision-making mechanisms. Many tourist operators understand that Antarctic tourism is dependent on the preservation of the Antarctic environment and will therefore comply with established guidelines out of self-interest. However, without legal oversight and jurisdiction it is not always possible to deter or punish those who refuse to comply.[40] This is especially troublesome in instances like the *MS Explorer* oil spill where the presence of tourist vessels not particularly well-suited to navigate Antarctic waters results in serious ecological damage.

---

[34] *See* "What is IATTO," *available at* http://www.iatto.org.

[35] *Id.*

[36] Denise Landau, *International Cooperation and Management of Tourism: A World Within a World*, in ANTARCTICA, SCIENCE, AND THE GOVERNANCE OF INTERNATIONAL SPACES 241–44 (Berkman et al. eds., Smithsonian Institution, 2009).

[37] *Id.*

[38] *Id.*

[39] *See* Visitor Guidelines, Australia Antarctic Division, *available at* http://www.antarctica.gov.au/about-antarctica/tourism.

[40] *Id.* at 243–44.

NOTES AND QUESTIONS

1. ***The future of Antarctic management***. What does the future hold for Antarctica? Commentators have had continuing exchanges on the "what if" possibilities for nearly a century. *See e.g.*, SMEDAL, ACQUISITION OF SOVEREIGNTY OVER POLAR REGION (1931); CHRISTIE, THE ANTARCTIC PROBLEM (1951; Balch, *The Arctic and Antarctic Regions and the Law of Nations*, 4 AM. J. INT'L L. 265 (1910); Jessup, *Sovereignty in Antarctica*, 41 AM. J. INT'L L. 265 (1947); Jessup, *Sovereignty in Antarctica*, 41 AM. J. INT'L L. 117 (1947); Daniel, *Conflict of Sovereignties in Antarctica*, 3 Y.B. WORLD AFF. 241 (1949); Hayton, *The Nations and Antarctica*, 10 OESTERREICHISCHE ZEITSCHRIFT FUR OFFENTLICHES RECHT 368 (1960); *Antarctica's Future*, N.Y. TIMES, Apr. 16, 1947, p.24.

Today, one possible next step is the establishment of alternative international management systems for Antarctica. The two principal suggestions in circulation are: i) United Nations' involvement, and ii) establishment of an Antarctic World Park. Another possible step into the future would be to declare Antarctica the "Common Heritage of Humankind," although as the notes below indicate the doctrine of Common Heritage is not as strong today as it was before developments in the Law of the Sea in the 1990s. In general, in order for territory to be denominated Common Heritage four conditions must prevail: i) the territory must be limited to peaceful uses, ii) it must not be subject to territorial acquisition by states, iii) some form of international management should prevail, and iv) the benefits and burdens of exploiting the territory are to be shared internationally.

2. ***Tourists and the treaty***. The Antarctic Treaty Consultative Parties have asserted tourists are subject to the Protocol, yet they have established no system of tourist regulation. SCAR bulletin No. 104, 28 Polar Record 92 (1992). How can tourists be subject to ATS? By virtue of their state of origin or the nation where the commercial cruise is registered? *See* Debra Enzen-Bacher, *Tourists in Antarctica: Number and Trends*, 28 POLAR RECORD 17, 19 (1992). Should the Parties create a formal regime to regulate tour operators? What form would such a regime take? How would it be enforced? Who would be subject to it? Colin Harris has suggested establishing a renewable license system for tour operators. Licenses would be renewed subject to compliance with rules and payment of fees. The fees could fund a tourist education system and mechanisms to protect areas of high use against wear and destruction. Colin M. Harris, *Environmental Management on King George Island, South Shetland Islands, Antarctica*, 27 POLAR RECORD 313, 322 (1991). Would this be more effective than the current governance structure which is largely managed by private interests? Why or why not?

PROBLEM 9-3
VISITING ANTARCTICA

Joe and Mary (brother and sister) have just graduated from college and they long to fulfill their dream of visiting Antarctica. Both are American citizens and come from wealthy families. Their parents have promised that as a graduation present they would finance a trip by both to Antarctica. Joe and Mary are aware that tour operators provide boat trips to Antarctica, but both siblings long to go on their own in order to be free to do what they want and to stay a longer period of time. They have contacted a private yacht company in Ushuaia, Argentina that is willing to transport them to the Antarctic Peninsula, where they will find abundant wildlife and many sites of historic and scientific interest. Mary is an extreme sports fanatic and wants to take her cross-country skis on a marathon trip. Joe likes nature and looks forward to bird watching and wildlife viewing.

Joe and Mary have made plans to go to Antarctica in late November, flying to Buenos Aires and then to Ushuaia and boarding their private yacht for the scientific trip to the Antarctic Peninsula by way of the beautiful South Shetland Islands. As they were planning their trip, a law student friend told them that she had heard there may be some legal restrictions to activities in Antarctica that they better find out about. Joe and Mary have done some research and are quite appalled by all the "red tape" necessary to fulfill their plan.

The first thing Joe and Mary discovered in their research was an international agreement — the Protocol on Environmental Protection to the Antarctic Treaty (1991). (This Protocol is reprinted in the **Document Supplement** to this book).

1. The Environment Protocol (also called the Madrid Protocol) has the purpose of enhancing protection of the Antarctic environment and associated ecosystems (Preamble).

2. The Protocol designates Antarctica as a "natural reserve" (Article 2) and a Special Conservation Area (Preamble).

3. Antarctica is governed by a set of special environmental principles set out in Article 3.

4. The governance of Antarctica under the Environmental Protocol is set by an Environmental Committee (Articles 11 and 12).

5. The Environmental Protocol deals not only with a 50 year moratorium on mineral resource activities (Articles 7 and 25) but also with six matters set out in annexes to the Protocol:

   Annex I. Environmental Impact Assessment

   Annex II. Conservation of Antarctic Fauna and Flora

   Annex III. Waste Disposal and Waste Management

   Annex IV. Prevention of Marine Pollution

   Annex V. Special Area Protection and Management

   Annex VI. Liability Arising from Environmental Emergencies (not yet in force)

6. There is no independent enforcement power under the Protocol. Enforcement of environmental restrictions is up to the parties (Articles 13 and 14).

7. As American nationals, Joe and Mary are subject to United States' laws enforcing the Protocol. The United States has enacted the Antarctic Conservation Act of 1978, as amended by the Antarctic Science, Tourism, and Conservation Act of 1996, 16 U.S.C. §§ 2401 to 2413, implemented by associated regulations, 45 CFR Parts 670 (Conservation of Antarctic animals and Plants); 671 (Waste Regulation); 672 (Enforcement and Hearing Procedures); and 673 (Antarctic Non-Governmental Expeditions).

These laws and regulations are set out in the **Document Supplement**. These laws apply to

- The area south of 60 degrees latitude

- U.S. citizens in Antarctica

- U.S. corporations or other legal entities that organize expeditions into Antarctica

- U.S. persons wherever located and foreign persons while in the United States who import certain Antarctic animals or plants.

The National Science Foundation is the agency of the U.S. government that funds and manages the U.S. Antarctic law and programs.

8. Violations of the law carry a penalty of up to $25,000 and 1 year imprisonment.

9. Will Joe and Mary need an NSF permit to visit Antarctica?

10. Will Joe and Mary need a special permit to visit certain natural areas in Antarctica? What risks do they run by visiting nesting areas or colonies of birds and animals?

11. What waste disposal requirements apply?

12. Is special permission needed to visit certain Specially Protected Areas and Specially Managed Areas of Antarctica?

Section II. THE ARCTIC

A. Overview

The precise boundaries of the Arctic are a subject of debate, however the most common definition is that the Arctic encompasses the region north of the Arctic Circle which lays at 66° 32 minutes north latitude.[41] Additionally the Bering Sea is considered — at least by the United States — to be part of the Arctic despite the fact that it extends outside the southern boundary set by the Arctic Circle.[42] Some also define the Arctic as the region extending beyond the northern limit of upright tree growth or the northern region where average daily temperatures are 10° Celsius or below.[43] Regardless of its precise boundaries, the Arctic is a large region — approximately 6% of the Earth's surface area — which includes the Arctic Ocean and parts of the United States, Canada, Russia, Norway, Greenland, Finland, Iceland, and Sweden. At the top of the Arctic is the North Pole, a point which sits in the middle of the largely ice-covered Arctic Ocean.

Similar to Antarctica, the Arctic is a haven for scientific research because of its remote and relatively unspoiled environment. The Arctic is home to several permanent research facilities, though many scientists today also utilize satellites and automated instruments that do not require scientific personnel to be on site.

---

[41] Arctic Theme Page, NOAA, *available at* http://www.arctic.noaa.gov/faq.html.

[42] *Id.*

[43] *Id.*

Despite its secluded location, the Arctic region is not unaffected by human activity, even activities taking place in other parts of the world. Industrial pollutants and toxic metals produced elsewhere can be carried in the atmosphere and deposited in the Arctic. The effects of climate change are also felt in the Arctic which in the past years has seen record lows in snow and sea ice extent and record highs in duration of melting. Melting sea ice in the Arctic has wide-ranging implications.[44] Such melting can raise global sea levels and alter ocean currents; it also means that the Earth can absorb more of the Sun's rays. However, such melting also increases the economic viability of the region as will be discussed below.

Unlike Antarctica, the Arctic has a native human population dating back hundreds of years. Today this population mainly consists of indigenous people, such as the Inuit. These Arctic dwellers have equipped themselves to live in a hostile environment with near constant darkness and below freezing temperatures in winter months. Their diet is largely made up of locally sourced foods like fish, whales, deals, caribou, plants, and berries. However scientific research, commercial resource exploration, and growing tourism have begun to westernize life in many places in the Arctic.[45]

---

[44] Arctic Sea Ice, NRDC, *available at* http://www.nrdc.org/globalwarming/qthinice.asp.

[45] Arctic Theme Page, op. cit., supra.

MAP OF THE ARCTIC REGION

B.   The Arctic Legal Regime

The international legal framework of the Arctic lacks the development and comprehensive nature of its southern counterpart. At present it is a patchwork of regional and issue-specific treaties, cooperative associations, national law enacted by Arctic-adjacent states, and rising territorial tensions. As the effects of climate change continue to shape the Arctic landscape, new questions of governance and resource management are sure to arise. Wide-scale melting of ice makes the Arctic more accessible for more purposes, including commercial travel, resource extraction, and tourism. These activities are likely to have significant environmental impacts on the region's ecosystems. Whether the existing framework is sufficient to meet these new challenges remains to be seen. The main components of the Arctic legal regime and the issues presented by a warming planet are discussed below.

1. Regulation of Arctic Waters

Arctic governance is complicated by the fact that many states disagree about the outer limits of the Arctic region. Nevertheless, the 1982 United Nations Convention on the Law of the Sea ("UNCLOS")[46] is the primary legal framework through which Arctic waters are managed. UNCLOS entered into force in 1994 and covers a multitude of issues relating to the world's oceans. UNCLOS Article 76 provides formulas for determining the outer limits of national claims to continental shelves; but the issues relating to continental shelves in Arctic waters are unresolved.

UNCLOS owes its origin to the Third United Nations Conference on the Law of the Sea, where, in response to Malta's Ambassador's call to the United Nations in 1967, to create an effective International regime for the oceans, United Nations' members joined together to write a comprehensive agreement to manage the world's oceans. The Third United Nations Conference on the Law of the Sea convened in 1973 and drew to a close in 1982 when UNCLOS was formally adopted.

In total UNCLOS contains 320 articles, nine Annexes, and two implementing agreements: The Part XI Deep-Sea Mining Agreement and the 1995 Fish Stocks Agreement. The Treaty governs such diverse issues as environmental protection, scientific research, technology transfer, territorial boundaries, and dispute resolution. Specifically, UNCLOS Article 234 vests authority in coastal states to regulate certain human activities in ice-covered waters within their Exclusive Economic Zones (EEZs). Canada, for example, subsequently enacted the Arctic Water Pollution Prevention Act (AWPPA), an act aimed at curbing pollution in Canadian Arctic waters.[47] Article 56 of UNCLOS states that within their respective EEZs coastal states have exclusive rights to explore, exploit, and manage the natural resources of seabed areas and waters contiguous to the seabed, giving Arctic states special jurisdiction over vast swathes of Arctic waters.[48]

Although first meeting of the Third United Nations Conference on the Law of the Sea took place in New York, the United States did not actually sign UNCLOS until 1994 and has yet to ratify it. The United States' concerns about UNCLOS have largely centered on economic concerns relating to seabed mining and fears that ratification may abrogate the country's sovereignty. The United States applies most of UNCLOS' provisions as customary international law.[49] The United States' non-participation in UNCLOS means, however, that the UNCLOS dispute settle-

---

[46] United Nations Convention on the Law of the Sea, done at Montego Bay, Dec. 10, 1982, in force Nov. 16, 1994, 1833 U.N.T.S. 243.

[47] Transport Canada, Arctic Waters Pollution Prevention Act, Government of Canada, *available at* http://www.tc.gc.ca/eng/marinesafety/debs-arctic-acts-regulations-awppa-494.htm.

[48] The United Nations Convention on the Law of the Sea: A Historical Perspective (2013), *available at* http://www.un.org/depts/los/convention_agreements/convention_historical_perspective.htm.

[49] Thomas Wright, Outlaw of the Sea, Foreign Affairs, Aug. 7, 2012, *available at* http://www.foreignaffairs.com/articles/137815/thomas-wright/outlaw-of-the-sea.

ment mechanisms do not control disputes over arctic waters where the United States is a party to such dispute.

The regulation of Arctic waters is becoming increasingly important. As ice continues to melt at unprecedented rates, new shipping lanes are opening and valuable natural resources are becoming more accessible.[50] Climatic changes in the Arctic have eased travel through the Northwest Passage, a direct shipping lane through parts of the Canadian Arctic, making ocean travel from Asia to Europe significantly quicker and less costly.[51] Canada has asserted rights over parts of the Northwest Passage, whereas the United States and Europe claim it lies in international waters. Although UNCLOS gives international vessels the right of innocent passage through waterways joining two high seas, it remains unclear under UNCLOS whether the Northwest Passage should be considered an "international strait."[52] Concerns have also been raised by various shipping companies that ineffective Canadian emergency response mechanisms make it difficult for vessels traveling through the Northwest Passage to obtain insurance for such trips. In response the United States has itself pledged to increase its presence and capabilities in the Arctic.[53]

Increased traffic in Arctic waters increases the potential for marine pollution. Mechanisms must be instituted to delegate responsibility for environmental stewardship in Arctic waters. UNCLOS alone is not up to this task; regional agreements and organizations are better able to take into account varying regional conditions. UNCLOS is also criticized for containing regulatory and governance gaps, particularly in the fields of bio-prospecting, tourism and seabed construction.[54]

2.   The Ilulissat Declaration

The Ilulissat Declaration[55] was signed by the United States, Canada, Denmark, Norway, and Russia in 2008, at the Arctic Oceans States Conference in Ilulissat, Greenland. This Declaration recognizes the effects of climate change in the Arctic, notes the need for strengthened management of the region, commits to protection and responsible use of the Arctic marine environment, and emphasizes that there is no need for a "new comprehensive international legal regime to govern the Arctic Ocean." It also reaffirms the Arctic states' adherence to existing international law governing the region, such as UNCLOS. The text of the declaration is reproduced

---

[50] Mark Jarashow, Michael B. Runnels, and Tait Svenson, *UNCLOS and the Arctic: The Path of Least Resistance*, 30 FORD. INT'L L.J. 1587, 1588 (2006).

[51] John Roach, *Arctic Melt Opens Northwest Passage*, NATIONAL GEOGRAPHIC NEWS, Sept. 17, 2007, *available at* http://www.nationalgeographic.com/news.

[52] Jarashow, op cit. supra at 1596.

[53] Grant Laten, *A New Look at Northwest Passage Sovereignty, Center for Strategic and International Studies*, July 28, 2010, *available at* http://www.csis.org/blog/new-look-northwest-passage-sovereignty.

[54] Timo Koivurova and Erik J. Molenaar, *International Governance and Regulation of the Marine Arctic*, World Wildlife Fund, Jan. 2009, *available at* http://www.wwf.se/source.php/1223579/International%20Governance%20and%20Regulation%20of%20the%20Marine%20Arctic.pdf.

[55] *Ilulissat Declaration*, May 28, 2008, *available at* http://www.oceanlaw.org/downloads/arctic/Ilulissat_Declaration.pdf.

below. When reading the text, consider the following questions: What are the Declaration's primary objectives? Does the Declaration evidence an attempt by the Arctic coastal states to assert primacy over Arctic waters? Why would the United States join the Declaration yet refuse to ratify UNCLOS? Why were only five of the eight Arctic states, parties to the Declaration?

THE ILULISSAT DECLARATION[56]
May 28, 2008

At the invitation of the Danish Minister for Foreign Affairs and the Premier of Greenland, representatives of the five coastal states bordering on the Arctic Ocean — Canada, Denmark, Norway, the Russian Federation and the United States of America — met at the political level on 28 May 2008 in Ilulissat, Greenland, to hold discussions. They adopted the following declaration:

The Arctic Ocean stands at the threshold of significant changes. Climate change and the melting of ice have a potential impact on vulnerable ecosystems, the livelihoods of local inhabitants and indigenous communities, and the potential exploitation of natural resources.

By virtue of their sovereignty, sovereign rights and jurisdiction in large areas of the Arctic Ocean the five coastal states are in a unique position to address these possibilities and challenges. In this regard, we recall that an extensive international legal framework applies to the Arctic Ocean as discussed between our representative at the meeting in Oslo on 15 and 16 October 2007, at the level of senior officials. Notably, the law of the sea provides for important rights and obligations concerning the delineation of the outer limits of the continental shelf, the protection of the marine environment, including ice-covered areas, freedom of navigation, marine scientific research, and other uses of the sea. We remain committed to this legal framework and to the orderly settlement of any possible overlapping claims.

This framework provides a solid foundation for responsible management by the five coastal States and other users of this Ocean through national implementation and application of relevant provisions. We therefore see no need to develop a new comprehensive international legal regime to govern the Arctic Ocean. We will keep abreast of the developments in the Arctic Ocean and continue to implement appropriate measures.

The Arctic Ocean is a unique ecosystem, which the five coastal states have a stewardship role in protecting. Experience has shown how shipping disasters and subsequent pollution of the marine environment may cause irreversible disturbance of the ecological balance and major harm to the livelihoods of local inhabitants and indigenous communities. We will take steps in accordance with international law both nationally and in cooperation among the five states and other interested parties to ensure the protection and preservation of the fragile marine environment of the Arctic Ocean. In this regard we intend to work together including through the International Maritime Organization to strengthen existing measures and develop new measures to improve the safety of maritime navigation and prevent or reduce

---

[56] *Available at* http://www.oceanlaw.org.

the risk of ship-based pollution in the Arctic Ocean.

The increased use of Arctic waters for tourism, shipping, research and resource development also increases the risk of accidents and therefore the need to further strengthen search and rescue capabilities and capacity around the Arctic Ocean to ensure an appropriate response from states to any accident. Cooperation, including on the sharing of information, is a prerequisite for addressing these challenges. We will work to promote safety of life at sea in the Arctic Ocean including through bilateral and multilateral arrangements between or among relevant states.

The five coastal states currently cooperate closely in the Arctic Ocean with each other and with other interested parties. This cooperation includes the collection of scientific data concerning the continental shelf, the protection of the marine environment and other scientific research. We will work to strengthen this cooperation, which is based on mutual trust and transparency, *inter alia*, through timely exchange of data and analyses.

The Arctic Council and other international fora, including the Barents Euro-Arctic Council, have already taken important steps on specific issues, for example with regard to safety of navigation, search and rescue, environmental monitoring and disaster response and scientific cooperation, which are relevant also to the Arctic Ocean. The five coastal states of the Arctic Ocean will continue to contribute actively to the work of the Arctic Council and other relevant International fora.

3. The Arctic Environmental Protection Strategy and the Arctic Council

In 1987, Mikhail Gorbachev, Secretary General of the Soviet Union until 1991, urged the Arctic states to take multilateral action to address key Arctic issues like environmental protection.[57] In the same spirit, the United States, Canada, Denmark, Finland, Iceland, Sweden, the Soviet Union, and Norway engaged in a series of meetings in the late 1980s and early 1990s, eventually resulting in the drafting and signing of the Rovaniemi Declaration. This Declaration established the "Arctic Environmental Protection Strategy" (AEPS), an ambitious but non-binding commitment among the eight Arctic states to protect the Arctic Environment.

THE ROVANIEMI DECLARATION ON THE PROTECTION OF THE ARCTIC ENVIRONMENT
June 14, 1991

We, the representatives of the Governments of Canada, Denmark, Finland, Iceland, Norway, Sweden, the Union of Soviet Socialist Republics and the United States of America;

Meeting at Rovaniemi, Finland for the First Ministerial Conference on the Protection of the Arctic Environment;

---

[57] Timo Koivurova and David Vanderzwang, *The Arctic Council at 10 Years: Retrospect and Prospects*, 40 UBC L. Rev. 121, 123 (2007).

Deeply concerned with threats to the Arctic environment and the impact of pollution on fragile arctic ecosystems;

Acknowledging the growing national and international appreciation of the importance of Arctic ecosystems and an increasing knowledge of global pollution and resulting environmental threats;

Resolving to pursue together in other international environmental fora those issues affecting the Arctic environment which require broad international cooperation;

Emphasizing our responsibility to protect and preserve the Arctic environment and recognizing the special relationship of the indigenous peoples and local populations to the Arctic and their unique contribution to the protection of the Arctic environment;

Hereby adopt the Arctic Environment Protection Strategy and commit ourselves to take steps towards its implementation and consider its further elaboration.

We commit ourselves to a joint action plan of the Arctic Environmental Protection Strategy which includes:

- Assessment of potential environment impacts of development activities:
- Full implementation and consideration of further measures to control pollutants and reduce their adverse effects to the Arctic;

We intend to assess on a continuing basis the threats to the Arctic environment through the preparation and updating of reports on the state of the Arctic environment, in order to propose further cooperative action;

We also commit ourselves to implement the following measures of the strategy:

- Arctic Monitoring and Assessment Programme (AMAP) to monitor the levels of, and assess the effects of, anthropogenic pollutants in all components of the Arctic environment. To this end, an Arctic Monitoring and Assessment Task Force will be established. Norway will provide for an AMAP secretariat:
- Protection of the marine environment in the Arctic, to take preventive and other measures directly or through competent international organizations regarding marine pollution in the Arctic irrespective of origin;
- Emergency prevention, preparedness and response in the Arctic, to provide a framework for future cooperation in responding to the threats of environmental emergencies;
- Conservation of Arctic flora and fauna, to facilitate the exchange of information and coordination or research on species and habitats of flora and fauna. Information and coordination of research on species and habitats of flora and fauna.

We agree to hold regular meeting to assess the progress made and to coordinate actions which will implement and further develop the Arctic Environmental Protection Strategy.

We agree to continue to promote cooperation with the Arctic indigenous peoples and to invite their organizations to future meetings as observers . . .

Wherefore, we, the undersigned representatives of our respective governments, recognizing its political significance and environmental importance, and intending to promote its results, have signed this Declaration,

NOTE ON THE ARCTIC ENVIRONMENTAL PROTECTION STRATEGY

The Arctic Environmental Protection Strategy (AEPS), a non-binding agreement among the Arctic states to protect the Arctic environment, was begun in 1989 on the initiative of Finland and was formally approved in the Rovaniemi Declaration in 1991. An overriding goal of the AEPS is to protect the Arctic environment from pollution. The AEPS focused on several problems as primary action-points: acidification, radioactivity, noise, heavy metals, oil pollution, and persistent organic contaminants. The AEPS established working groups organized around monitoring and assessment, protection of the marine environment, emergency prevention and response, and conservation of Arctic flora and fauna. Provisions were made for the participation of non-Arctic states, international organizations, and Arctic indigenous peoples, who were given the legal status of observers. The AEPS, after several meetings, was absorbed into the Arctic Council in 1996.

In September of 1996 the Arctic states — Canada, Denmark (representing Greenland and the Faroe Islands), Finland, Iceland, Norway, Russia, Sweden, and the United States — signed the Arctic Council Declaration ("Ottawa Declaration"), creating the Arctic Council. The Arctic Council took over the roles and functions of the AEPS (including adopting but reorganizing its working groups) and significantly expanded its reach. Instead of being a forum dedicated to environmental issues, the Arctic Council is concerned more broadly with "common Arctic issues."[58]

The Arctic Council is composed of members, permanent participants, and observers.[59] The members are the eight Arctic nations who signed the Arctic Council Declaration. Permanent participants include certain organizations representing Arctic indigenous peoples. Such organizations are granted consultation rights to be exercised in the context of the Council's decision-making process. An indigenous peoples secretariat has also been established to support the activities and involvement of permanent participants. Observer status in the Arctic Council is available to qualifying non-Arctic states, non-governmental organizations, and inter-governmental and inter-parliamentary organizations. The Council has set forth several guidelines to be used in determining the suitability of states and organizations to obtain observer status: acceptance and support of the Arctic Council's objectives, recognition of Arctic states' sovereignty and jurisdiction in the region, respect of indigenous peoples in the Arctic, acceptance of UNCLOS' application in Arctic waters, demonstration of interest and expertise relevant to the Arctic Council's work, and an ability and interest to move the work of the Arctic Council forward. Observers can attend Arctic Council meetings and make relevant contributions. They may also participate in the Council's working groups and may propose projects through members or permanent participants, though there are

---

[58] *See* Koivurova and Vanderzwang, op. cit. *supra*.

[59] See the Council's web site, http://www.arctic-council.org.

limits on the amount of funding observers may contribute to such projects. Current observers to the Arctic Council include France, Germany, Spain, the United Nations Development Program, the United Nations Environment Program, the Nordic Council of Ministers, and the World Wildlife Fund for Nature-Global Arctic Program. Several Asian countries, such as China and Japan, and organizations like Greenpeace and the Association of Oil and Gas Producers currently have pending applications for observer status.[60] Only the eight Arctic Council Members have decisionmaking authority; decisions are taken by consensus.

The Arctic Council's activities are accomplished through its six working groups: the Arctic Contaminants Action Program (ACAP), the Arctic Monitoring and Assessment Program (AMAP), the Conservation of Arctic Flora and Fauna Program (CAFF), the Emergency Prevention, Preparedness and Response Program (EPPR), the Protection of the Arctic Marine Environment Program (PAME), and the Sustainable Development Working Group (SDWG). Membership in working groups consists of researchers and representatives of sectorial ministries and government agencies. For example, the Environmental Protection Agency (EPA) is tasked with representing the United States in ACAP. The working groups have their own individualized mandates, are overseen by a Chair and Management Board, and are supported by a Secretariat. Management Boards typically include representatives from various national government agencies of member states and representatives of the permanent participants. Decisions of working groups are made by consensus.

In May of 2011 the Arctic Council met in Greenland at its seventh Ministerial Meeting and adopted a legally binding agreement on Arctic search and rescue as a part of the Nuuk Declaration. This search and rescue agreement, the Agreement on Cooperation in Aeronautical and Maritime Search and Rescue in the Arctic, requires each member of the Arctic Council to "promote the establishment, operation and maintenance of an adequate, effective search and rescue capability within its area . . . ." The Nuuk Declaration addresses climate change and the environment and emphasizes the Arctic states' dedication to environmental protection, particularly with regard to black carbon emissions, and reconfirms the states' commitment to reducing the impact of human activity on the Arctic environment. The states also agreed to establish an expert group on Arctic ecosystems-based management, to create a permanent secretariat in Norway, and to make progress on an Arctic marine oil pollution preparedness and response agreement. Some believe that the Arctic Council's creation of a permanent secretariat and the adoption of a legally binding agreement signal increasing acceptance of multilateral pre-crisis action among the Arctic states, which could open the doors to future agreements on environmentally significant subjects such as resource extraction and marine pollution.

The Arctic Council has been both praised and criticized since its creation. Its proponents claim that the Council has fostered substantial international cooperation for the benefit of the environment without a legal mandate. However, it has also been argued that the non-binding nature of the organization also means that many of the Council's objectives and commitments might not be incorporated into national

---

[60] *Id.*

laws and are therefore weak. Similarly, the Council's system of consensual decision-making has provoked criticisms, namely that the Council is not doing as much as it could. Some have also argued that local governments within Arctic regions should be granted more power in the Council because their location gives them a disproportionate stake in outcomes. The Arctic Council's critics and proponents both make valid points. The Arctic Council has been successful in a myriad of ways — collecting data, lobbying for Arctic environmental protection and empowering indigenous peoples. However the Council, like many other international organizations, occasionally has trouble enforcing the obligations its members have agreed upon. An example can be found in the Council's EIA Guidelines, a set of instructions adopted at a 1997 meeting meant to standardize the way environmental impact assessments are conducted in the Arctic, which were all but forgotten after their adoption. It remains to be seen whether the Arctic Council can respond to the many challenges that beset the Arctic, exacerbated by climate change.

QUESTIONS

Non-Arctic nations. Many non-Arctic states, such as China and Japan, have interests in the Arctic yet are not a part of the Arctic Council. Many of these interests are economic in nature and involve natural resource extraction and the use of Arctic shipping routes. China also has scientific and administrative interests in the Arctic, as evidenced by the establishment of the Chinese Administration on Arctic and Antarctic Administration (CAAAA) in 1981 and the 1988 founding of the Chinese Journal of Polar Research by the Chinese Academy of Sciences. China has a permanent research station, named Yellow River, in the Arctic and has conducted several Arctic missions in the past two decades. China asserts that climatic changes in the Arctic have the potential to cause extreme and destructive weather patterns which affect the country, and therefore it should be involved in any international dialogue and policymaking affecting the Arctic region. However, China is not a member of the Arctic Council and its application for Observer status has not yet been accepted. This is also the case with many other states with interests in the Arctic. In the meantime China has negotiated several bilateral treaties with Arctic states such as Iceland and Denmark and is investing in joint energy, minerals exploitation, and Arctic navigation projects. Olga Alexeeva & Frederic Lasserre, *China and the Arctic*, ARCTIC YEARBOOK 2012, at 81–89. Should countries such as China that are not Arctic-adjacent be granted membership in the Arctic Council? Will bilateral treaties negotiated by non-Arctic states complicate the functioning of the Arctic Council?

C.   Arctic Marine Life and Fisheries

Overfishing is problematic both in itself and because of the wide-ranging effects it can have on the marine ecosystem as a whole. In the case of Arctic waters, this is an ecosystem which is not well understood. The overfishing of one species is likely to have effects on others, particularly on species higher in the food chain which may not have alternative food sources. In the Arctic, Pollock and other fish serve as a crucial food source for sea lions, seals, bears, sea birds, and other species. However, overfishing is not the only threat to Arctic marine life; Arctic mining also poses a risk to the Arctic marine ecosystem. For example, the proposed Pebble Mine in Alaska has been controversial, as many assert the operation will leak toxic waste into bays which house salmon, whales, walruses, and other species. Climate change and shipping traffic are also adversely affecting the viability of Arctic fisheries. Global warming has caused sea acidification which is harmful to plankton populations. This is particularly troublesome since plankton form the base of the Arctic food chain. Moreover, many marine mammals, such as seals and polar bears, depend on sea ice for survival, and its rapid melting is endangering such populations. The presence of more vessel traffic in Arctic waters also means the potential for more shipwrecks, pollution, and oil spills.

The high seas, areas such as the central Arctic Ocean, are generally open to commercial fishing. Pursuant to UNCLOS, states may negotiate regional fisheries' management agreements to administer commercial fishing in such regions. This has been done in the Bering Sea, but not in the central Arctic Ocean. Without a comprehensive multilateral agreement on fishing in the central Arctic Ocean, there is danger of overexploiting its resources.

The following subsections discuss fisheries and their management in central and western Arctic waters.

1. The Central Arctic Ocean "Doughnut Hole"

At the top of the Arctic beyond the EEZs of circumpolar states lies an area of ocean called the central Arctic "doughnut hole," This swathe of ocean is approximately 1.1 million square miles (2.8 million square kilometers), where fishing is largely unregulated. The development of central Arctic fisheries beyond the bounds of circumpolar EEZs is relatively new because the area has traditionally been covered by thick sea ice. However as sea ice continues to melt at alarming rates, the commercial fishing industry has taken notice. This shift has caused scientists and others to call for the development of an international fisheries agreement to protect the central Arctic Ocean, commonly referred to as the "Arctic doughnut hole." This concern seems to be warranted. The Bering Sea "doughnut hole," an area lying beyond circumpolar EEZ boundaries in the western Arctic, experienced aggressive overfishing before a 1994 treaty was negotiated to manage the region's Pollock fisheries. Currently the Bering Sea houses some of the largest and most profitable fisheries in the world, including several varieties of crab, salmon, Pollock, and groundfish. The region still experiences illegal fishing and Pollock stocks in the central Bering Sea have yet to fully recover, but the situation is not as dire as it was pre-1994.

A small portion of the central Arctic "doughnut hole" is managed by the Northeast Atlantic Fisheries Commission (NEAFC) and regulations created pursuant to that body. But the covered area is less than 10% of the total "doughnut hole" and is currently still inaccessible to commercial fishing. Because many Arctic fish stocks are migratory, the marine ecosystem is still potentially in danger if a multilateral management system covering the entire central Arctic "doughnut hole" is not soon implemented.

Many believe that a commercial fishery in the central Arctic Ocean is feasible so long as a proper management system is created to administer it. At present, many scientists believe that "[t]he science community currently does not have sufficient biological information to understand the presence, abundance, structure, movements, and health of fish stocks and the role they play in the broader ecosystem of the Arctic Ocean." The absence of such data means that even if a management system is created, it may not have the information and tools necessary to perform its management functions. As a result many scientists are calling for a moratorium on commercial fishing operations in the central Arctic Ocean until such time as the scientific community can determine sustainable catch levels and a functioning management system can be established. Some Arctic states seem to agree with this conclusion. For example, the United States' Arctic Fishery Management Plan, established in 2008 and approved in 2009, prohibits commercial fishing in large areas of Arctic waters in order to allow scientists time to further study the Arctic marine environment. The Plan limits commercial fishing in United States' waters north of the Bering Strait, an area which is not currently at risk of overfishing because of limited accessibility due to sea ice, but with rising temperatures may soon be the target of those fishing for Pollock and snow crab. Other Arctic states, like Norway, have similar regulations. Increased accessibility is not the only draw to this region; warming temperatures in southern Arctic waters are causing some stocks to move north into the central Arctic Ocean. Environmentalists hope that the use of such preventative measures will prevent a stock depletion crisis as witnessed in the Bering Sea before fisheries regulation was enacted in the region.

2. The Bering Sea "Doughnut Hole"

The Bering Sea lies between the United States and Russia. Portions of the sea are within United States and Russian EEZs. In between the EEZs is the Bering Sea "doughnut hole," international waters which before 1994 had no multilateral fisheries management mechanism. In the 1970s and 1980s the Bering Sea suffered rampant overfishing, mostly at the hands of commercial fishing operations from Asia. Pollock stocks were severely depleted as a result. In response to this overexploitation, the United States, Russia, Japan, South Korea, Poland, and China signed the Convention on the Conservation and Management on Pollock Resources in the Central Bering Sea (1994) and provided for the establishment of Pollock harvest levels, annual meetings and committees. The Agreement's objectives were to establish an international management regime for Pollock resources in the central Bering Sea, restore and maintain Pollock resources in the region, cooperate in the scientific study of marine resources in the central Bering Sea, and establish a forum which could be used to implement conservation and management measures. It also contained several substantive measures, such as the requirement that vessels flagged under a state party to the Agreement that intend to fish for Pollock in the central Bering Sea notify other Parties 18 hours prior to entry. As of the 16th Annual Conference, which took place in 2011, the Allowable Harvest Level (AHL) for Pollock in the central Bering Sea was set at zero. Pollock stock have not fully recovered from the overfishing of decades past, though it is likely that the AHL for Pollock — and individual national quotas pursuant to the AHL — will be raised (if only slightly) for 2013.

NOTES AND QUESTIONS

1. *Antarctic and Arctic ecosystems.* In both areas, Pollock and krill are central members of a narrow food chain, the disruption of which would seriously threaten the viability of other fauna. The marine living resources in both regions have been adversely affected by over-exploitation of finfish and Pollock. The regulatory regimes also share common features: decision-making by consensus, a discretionary membership process, and the attempt to enhance the effectiveness of the regime by encouraging third parties to comply with its provisions. Stuart Kaye asserts that "these similarities are superficial" and in fact there are "fundamental differences in attitude and approach." Stuart Kaye, *Legal Approaches to Polar Fisheries Regimes: A Comparative Analysis of the Convention for the Conservation of Antarctic Marine Living Resources and the Bering Sea Donut Hole Convention*, 26 CAL. W. INT'L L.J. 75, 107 (1995). What are the main differences between the Doughnut Hole Convention and the CCAMLR? What do you think accounts for those differences? Different environmental problems? Territorial issues? Different countries?

2. *The Bering Sea and geopolitics.* According to Stuart Kaye, the Bering Sea was an important theater for potential superpower conflict. This alone was sufficient to stifle most attempts at Arctic regional cooperation. The actual formation of a regime required an environmental disaster that practically destroyed all parties' interests before national self-interest was perceived to be best served by negotiation. Why were the superpowers able to cooperate in Antarctica, but unable in the Arctic? Can other factors explain the different outcomes?

Kaye asserts that "the most significant difference between the Arctic and the Antarctic is to be found in the influence of epistemic communities in the Negotiations of the regimes, and the continuing impact of these communities over time . . . The objectives of CCAMLR reflect a scientists' view of how environmental management should take place." This explains the ecosystem approach in contrast to the maximum sustainable yield approach of the Bering Sea "doughnut hole" convention, which reflects the interests of the national fishing lobbies. Kaye concludes that, "[u]ltimately what stifles the cooperation in the Arctic is sovereignty. In the Antarctic, the political environment is 'sovereignty-neutral.' Claimant states in Antarctica could and have claimed EEZs for their territories, but most fishing states would simply ignore them. A cooperative regime was the only way to protect the resources." In contrast, the EEZs in the Arctic are claimed by coastal states and they are recognized by other fishing states. The coastal states would not relinquish any sovereign rights to a multilateral or international management system regulating the EEZS.

Thus, the Convention could only regulate the area of the hole. Does this mean that the Bering Sea "doughnut hole" convention is ineffective? In comparison, is CCAMLR a success? Could enforcement provisions of the "doughnut hole" convention be utilized in CCAMLR or incorporated as a basic principle of the Antarctic Treaty System? What effect would they have on the range of commitments the parties consent to undertake in CCAMLR? What effect would they have on the process for adding new commitments and on the number of parties?

D.   The Kiruna Declaration

KIRUNA DECLARATION
On the occasion of the Eighth Ministerial Meeting
of the Arctic Council
15 May 2013

We, the Ministers representing the eight Arctic States, joined by the representative of the six permanent participants organizations of the Arctic Council, have gathered in Kiruna, Sweden, at the conclusion of the first cycle of Chairmanship for the Eighth Ministerial meeting of the Arctic Council,

Recognizing the importance of maintaining peace, stability, and constructive cooperation in the Arctic,

Recognizing the importance of the sustainable use of resources, economic development and environmental protection,

Recognizing that the Arctic is first and foremost an inhabited region with diverse economies, cultures and societies, further recognizing the rights of the indigenous peoples and interests of all Arctic inhabitants, and emphasizing that a fundamental strength of the Council is the unique role played by Arctic indigenous peoples,

Expressing concern that global emissions of greenhouse gases are resulting in rapid changes in the climate and physical environment of the Arctic with widespread effects for societies and ecosystems and repercussions around the world, reiterating the urgent need for increased national and global actions to mitigate and adapt to climate change,

Noting the substantial progress we have made to strengthen our cooperation and acknowledging the leadership of the Arctic Council in taking concrete action to respond to new challenges and opportunities,

PROTECTING THE ARCTIC ENVIRONMENT

Announce the Agreement on Cooperation on Marine Oil Pollution Preparedness and Response in the Arctic, the second legally binding agreement negotiated under the auspices of the Arctic Council, and **encourage** future national, bi-national and multinational contingency plans, training and exercise, to develop effective response measures,

Recognize that effective prevention, including related containment practices, is critical to ensuring the protection of the Arctic marine environment from oil pollution incidents, welcome the Recommended Practices in the Prevention of Arctic Marine Oil Pollution Project reports and recommendations to Ministers, and encourage Arctic States to pursue further work in the recommended areas,

Decide to establish a Task Force to develop an Arctic Council action plan or other arrangement on oil pollution prevention, and to present the outcomes of its work and any recommendations for further action at the next Ministerial meeting in 2015,

Recognize the value of sustaining Arctic ecosystems and biodiversity and that the

Arctic environment needs to be protected as a basis for sustainable development, prosperity, lifestyles and human well-being, and **commit** to pursue the conservation and sustainable use of Arctic biological resources,

Note with concern that Arctic biodiversity is being degraded and that climate change is the most serious threat, **welcome** the Arctic Biodiversity Assessment, the first Arctic-wide comprehensive assessment of status and emerging trends in Arctic biodiversity, **approve** its recommendations and **encourage** Arctic States to follow up on its recommendations, and **instruct** Senior Arctic Officials to ensure that a plan for further work under the Arctic Council to support and implement its recommendations is developed, and that a progress report is delivered to the next ministerial meeting,

Encourage Arctic States to take decisive action to help sustain Arctic biodiversity and implement internationally agreed biodiversity objectives, to cooperate on adaptive management strategies for vulnerable species and ecosystem, and to continue existing Arctic biodiversity research and monitoring efforts through the Circumpolar Biodiversity Monitoring Program,

Welcome the Arctic Ocean Acidification assessment, **approve** its recommendations, **note** with concern the potential impacts of acidification on marine life and people that are dependent on healthy marine ecosystems, **recognize** that carbon dioxide emission reductions are the only effective way to mitigate ocean acidification, and **request** the Arctic States to continue to take action on mitigation and adaption and to monitor and assess the state of Arctic Ocean acidification,

Recognize the important ongoing work in the international Maritime Organization to develop a mandatory Polar Code on shipping and **decide** to strengthen our collaboration in that work toward its expeditious completion,

Welcome the Arctic Ocean Review report, undertaken to provide guidance to Arctic States on strengthening governance in the Arctic through a cooperative, coordinated and integrated approach to the management of the Arctic marine environment, approve its recommendations and request appropriate follow-up actions, and report on progress at subsequent ministerial meetings,

Recognize that there are further persistent organic pollutants to be addressed that pose threats to human health and the environment in the Arctic, **encourage** Arctic States to continue monitoring and assessment activities and enhance their effort to meet the objectives of Stockholm convention, and **welcome** the completion of the successful demonstration project preventing the release of 7000 tons of obsolete pesticides into the Arctic environment, and look forward to further activities in this area,

Note the work of the Arctic Council in raising global awareness and understanding of the impacts of mercury on the health of people and wildlife in the Arctic, **welcome** the Minamata Convention on Mercury, **appreciate** the reference to the particular vulnerabilities of Arctic ecosystems and indigenous communities, **encourage** its swift entry into force along with robust use and emission reduction actions, and **pledge** to assist the evaluation of its effectiveness through continued monitoring and assessments,

Welcome the report on Ecosystem Based Management, **approve** the definition, principles and recommendations, **encourage** Arctic States to implement recommendations both within and across boundaries, and **ensure** coordination of approaches in the work of the Arctic Council's Working Groups,

Agree that cooperation in scientific research across the circumpolar Arctic is of great importance to the work of the Arctic Council, and **establish** a Task Force to work towards an arrangement on improved scientific research cooperation among the eight Arctic States,

STRENGTHENING THE ARCTIC COUNCIL

Adopt the statement "Vision for the Arctic,"

Welcome the establishment of the Arctic Council Secretariat in Tromsø, Norway, **note** the Host Country agreement signed between the Government of Norway and the Director of the Arctic Council Secretariat, **approve** its Terms of Reference, staff rules, financial rules, roles and responsibilities of the director, and budget for 2013, and **instruct** Senior Arctic Officials to approve a budget for 2014–2015,

Approve the revised Arctic Council Rules of Procedure,

Note the Chair's conclusions from the Arctic Environment Ministers Meeting in February 2013, and **welcome** further high-level engagement and meetings,

Welcome China, India, Italy, Japan, Republic of Korea and Singapore as new Observer States, and **take note** of the adoption by Senior Arctic Officials of an Observer manual to guide the Council's subsidiary bodies in relation to meeting logistics and the roles played by Observers,

The Arctic Council receives the application of the EU for observer status affirmatively, but defers a final decision on implementation until the Council ministers are agreed by consensus that the concerns of Council members, addressed by the President of the European Commission in his letter of 8 May are resolved, with the understanding that the EU may observe Council proceedings until such time as the Council acts on the letter's proposal,

Acknowledge that the work of the Arctic Council continues to evolve to respond to new challenges and opportunities in the Arctic, request Senior Arctic Officials to recommend ways and means to strengthen how the work of the Arctic Council is carried out, including identifying opportunities for Arctic States to use the Council's work to influence and shape action in other regional and international fora as well as identifying approaches to support the active participation of permanent participants, and to present a report on their work at the next Ministerial meeting in 2015,

Acknowledge the decision of the permanent participants to relocate the Indigenous Peoples Secretariat to Tromsø, Norway,

Adopt the Senior Arctic Officials Report to Ministers, including its working group work plans, and instruct Senior Arctic Officials to review and adjust the mandates and work plans of the Arctic Council working groups and other subsidiary bodies, and establish new ones, if appropriate, and to follow up on the recommendations agreed to by the Arctic Council,

Thank the Kingdom of Sweden of its Chairmanship of the Arctic Council during the period 2011–2013, concluding the first round of eight Arctic States chairmanships, and Welcome the offer of Canada to chair the Arctic Council during the period 2013–2015 and to host the Ninth Ministerial meeting in 2015

Vision for the Arctic

We, the eight Arctic States together with the six Arctic Indigenous Peoples' Organizations, have met today at the end of the first round of eight successive chairmanships of the Arctic Council.

We have many accomplishments to celebrate since the signing of the Ottawa Declaration in 1996, and it is timely for us to set out a vision for the future of our region.

Guided by the Ottawa Declaration, the Arctic Council has become the pre-eminent high-level forum of the Arctic region and we have made this region into an area of unique international cooperation.

We have achieved mutual understanding and trust, addressed issues of common concern, strengthened our co-operation, influenced international action, established a standing secretariat and, under the auspices of the Council, Arctic States have concluded legally binding agreements. We have also demonstrated the importance of science and traditional knowledge for understanding our region and for informed decision-making in the Arctic.

The Arctic is changing and attracting global attention and as we look to the future, we will build on our achievements and will continue to cooperate to ensure that Arctic voices are heard and taken into account in the world.

A peaceful Arctic

The further development of the Arctic region as a zone of peace and stability is at the heart of our efforts. We are confident that there is no problem that we cannot solve together through our cooperative relationships on the basis of existing international law and good will. We remain committed to the framework of the Law of the Sea, and to the peaceful resolution of disputes generally.

The Arctic Home

We are committed to demonstrating leadership in regional and global forums to address challenges affecting our home. The well-being of all Arctic people is fundamental as the region develops.

We will continue to exercise our responsibility for safeguarding indigenous peoples' rights, including by creating conditions for the preservation and development of social structures, cultural traditions, languages and means of subsistence.

A prosperous Arctic

The economic potential of the Arctic is enormous and its sustainable development is key to the region's resilience and prosperity. Transparent and predictable rules and continued cooperation between Arctic States will spur economic development, trade and investments.

We will continue to work cooperatively to support the development of sustainable Arctic economies to build self-sufficient, vibrant and healthy Arctic communities for present and future generations.

Economic cooperation will be on the top of our agenda.

A safe Arctic

To meet the needs of an ever-changing Arctic we will further strengthen our cooperation in the fields of environmental and civil security. Aware the maritime safety requires broad regional and international cooperation, we will continue to develop best practices and other measures for the Arctic region.

A healthy Arctic environment

We recognize the uniqueness and fragility of the Arctic environment, and the critical importance of healthy environments to sustainable communities. We are aware that the Arctic environment continues to be affected by events outside for the region, in particular climate change, and that resulting changes in the Arctic have global repercussions.

We are concerned with growing effects of climate change, and the local and global impacts of large-scale melting of the Arctic snow, ice and permafrost. We will continue to take action to reduce emissions of greenhouse gases and short-lived climate pollutants, and support action that enables adaptation.

We will strengthen our work, both within the Arctic and globally, to address the environmental challenges facing the region. We remain committed to managing the region with an ecosystem-based approach which balances conservation and sustainable use of the environment.

Arctic Knowledge

We will continue to deepen the knowledge and understanding of the Arctic, both inside and outside the region, and to strengthen Arctic research and transdisciplinary science, encourage cooperation between higher education institutions and society, and synergies between traditional knowledge and science.

A strong Arctic Council

Membership in the Arctic Council is and will remain for the Arctic States with the active participation and full consultation of the Arctic Indigenous Peoples Organizations. Decisions at all levels in the Arctic Council are the exclusive right and responsibility of the eight signatories to the Ottawa Declaration.

The Arctic Council is open to observers who can contribute to the work of the Arctic Council and share the commitment of the Arctic States to the peaceful resolution of disputes and abide by the criteria for observers established by the Arctic Council.

As we embark on the second round of chairmanships, we will continue our work to strengthen the Arctic Council to meet new challenges and opportunities for cooperation, and pursue opportunities to expand the Arctic Council's role from policy-shaping to policy-making.

The founding values, objectives and commitments of the Arctic Council will continue to be the North Star to guide our cooperation.

NOTES AND QUESTIONS

1.   A concrete step of cooperation in the Arctic Council was the signing in May of 2013 of an Agreement on Cooperation on Marine Oil Pollution Preparedness and Response to the Arctic. This agreement is reprinted in the **Document Supplement** to this book. Under this agreement, what is required of Arctic member states? Who bears the cost of an oil spill in the Arctic? Is there any liability under international law placed upon the responsible parties?

2.   The cooperative tone of the Arctic council declarations belies the fact that the Arctic is replete with unresolved disputes and controversies. For example, the eight states bordering the Arctic have made claims to continental shelves off their shores. Many of these claims overlap. A second important controversy involves Canada's claim to the "northwest passage" through the arctic archipelago. Canada draws straight baselines enclosing this archipelago and claims the passage as internal waters. The United States and other nations dispute Canada's claim. Canada and the United States also have not settled their lateral maritime boundary in the Beaufort Sea. As the Arctic warms and becomes ice-free during summer months, shipping and resource exploitation will increase, presenting new challenges. Will the Arctic Council be up to meeting these challenges?

Chapter 10

THE ENVIRONMENTAL RESPONSIBILITY OF NON-STATE ACTORS

In this chapter we cover environmental responsibility under international law of non-state actors, intergovernmental organizations, non-governmental organizations (NGOs), and individual legal persons, business and industrial organizations. In Chapter 3, we placed particular emphasis on the environmental responsibility of states because for the past 70 years or more, much work by international bodies was done to define state responsibility, and this effort continues. By contrast, the environmental responsibility of non-state actors has not received great attention, but this is changing due to efforts by the Organization for Cooperation and Development (OECD), with the publication of the 2011 OECD Guidelines for Multilateral Enterprises, and the United Nations, with the 2011 adoption by the Human Rights Council of the "Protect, Respect and Remedy" Framework for Business and Human Rights.

We first turn to the environmental responsibility of intergovernmental organizations.

Section I. INTERNATIONAL ORGANIZATIONS

A. Introduction

International organizations — by which we mean organizations whose membership is limited to states — play a leading role in both environmental and developmental activities around the world. Such organizations exist at the global, regional, and sub-regional levels. They may have a broad or narrow mission, depending on their constituent charter. They exercise administrative, judicial, and even legislative functions with respect to the matters within their authority. Perhaps the most important category, or at least the most influential, of international organizations are the global and regional organizations of the United Nations system and its specialized agencies. There are also many regional organizations outside the U.N. system and many *ad hoc* organizations established by environmental and other treaties.

Some international organizations have specific environmental responsibilities. Many other international organizations have developmental missions and their environmental responsibilities are more oblique. In this Chapter we focus on the World Bank as a prototypical intergovernmental organization whose immense responsibilities and activities have made it particularly controversial. Note that the meaning of "responsibility" is broader than the doctrine of state responsibility and the duty to make reparations for the breach of international obligations (although accountability and damages may be involved). Here, we are primarily concerned with the duties imposed on international organizations to protect the environment and conserve natural resources, as well as the process by which these organizations develop and apply international environmental rules. Secondarily we consider the accountability of international organizations for environmental harm their actions or decisions may occasion.

B. The Example of the World Bank

The World Bank, which arose out of the 1944 Bretton Woods Conference and was officially created in 1945, currently has 188 member countries and consists of five groups: (1) the original International Bank for Reconstruction and Development, which directs loans toward developing countries; (2) the International Finance Corporation, which assists economic development in the private sector of less developed countries; (3) the International Development Association, which makes loans to the poorest countries on very favourable terms; (4) the International Centre for the Settlement of Investment Disputes, which offers arbitration to settle disputes; and (5) the Multilateral Investment Guarantee Agency, which guarantees certain investments in developing countries. In its early history, protection of the environment played no formal role in its financing and development projects. This changed with the growth of environmental consciousness in the 1960s, and in 1971, the Bank established an Office of Environmental Affairs. In 1989, the Bank issued an Operational Directive on Environmental Assessment (ODEA) that mandated and standardized a process in which all projects financed by the Bank undergo an environmental assessment.

Despite the regularization of environmental assessments of investment and development projects funded by the Bank, critics charged that the Bank was giving protection of the environment short shrift. The most severe critic of the Bank was Bruce Rich, whose book, Mortgaging the Earth: The World Bank, Environmental Impoverishment, and the Crisis of Development (1994) took the Bank to task for environmental insensitivity. Rich's book cites examples, such as the Pak Mun Dam in Thailand, which, he charged, did not perform as advertised and had devastating consequences for the environment and indigenous people.

In 1993, World Bank Executive Directors, stung by critics like Rich, created a three-member body called the World Bank Inspection Panel, whose job is to make an outside, objective evaluation of controversial Bank projects. Individuals or communities affected by a Bank funded project can request the Inspection Panel to investigate whether the Bank has in fact observed environmental and public health standards. *See* World Bank Inspection Panel, *International Bank for Reconstruction and Development* (IBRD) Resolution No. IBRD 93-10; *International Development Association* (IDA) Resolution No. IDA 93-6, reprinted in 34 I.L.M. 503 (1995). The purpose of the Inspection Panel is to promote accountability at the World Bank, to give people affected by the Bank's projects a greater voice, and to foster redress where warranted. The Panel assesses allegations of harm to people or the environment and reviews whether the Bank has adhered to its own operational policies and procedures. The jurisdiction of the Panel extends to IBRD and IDA projects. Complaints related to projects supported by other parts of the Bank are dealt with by the Office of Compliance Advisor Ombudsman of the Bank. The members of the Inspection Panel are appointed by the Executive Directors of the Bank for five-year, non-renewable terms. The Panel is assisted by a permanent Secretariat. The Panel may also consult outside experts.

For a history of the formation of the World Bank Inspection Panel and its work, the reader may consult the World Bank publication: *The Inspection Panel at 15 Years* (Washington DC: World Bank, 2009.

THE WORLD BANK INSPECTION PANEL PROCESS
http://web.worldbank.org/website/external/extinspectionpanel/0,,content
MDK:20173251~menuPK:568196~pagePK:64129751~pi
PK:64128378~theSitePK:380794,00.html

The World Bank Inspection Panel process begins when it receives a Request for Inspection from a party of two or more Requesters, claiming that the Bank has violated its policies and procedures. Most of the Requests submitted have concerned some of the Bank's safeguard policies, such as the policies on environmental assessment, involuntary resettlement, or indigenous people.

Once the Panel has received and registered a Request for Inspection, the Eligibility Phase of the Inspection Process commences. Beginning on the day of registration the World Bank's Management has 21 business days to provide the Panel with evidence that it complied or intends to comply with the relevant policies and procedures. After receiving Management's response the Panel has 21 business days to determine the eligibility of the Request.

Once it determines that the eligibility criteria have been met, and after having reviewed the Request, the Management Response to the Request, and additional related facts it may have observed during a field visit, the Panel may make a recommendation to investigate, not to investigate, or, as in some previous cases, to postpone its recommendation to a later date allowing for Management and the Requesters to resolve their differences. In such cases, the Panel has promoted problem solving between Management and the Requesters to help concerns receive an earlier and accepted resolution.

An investigation is not automatic, and can only be authorized by the Board of Executive Directors. If the Board approves an investigation, the next step is the substantive phase of the inspection process when the Panel evaluates the merits of the Request. In the investigation phase, the Panel is focused on fact finding and verification. It visits the borrowing country and meets with the Requesters and other affected people, as well as with a broad array of people from whom it can learn in detail about the issues, concerns, the project's status, and potential harmful effects. The investigation phase may take a few months, or more in complex cases.

Once the investigation phase is complete, the Panel submits its Investigation Report to the Board of Executive Directors of the Bank copying Bank Management. Bank Management then has six weeks to submit to the Board its Report and Recommendation in response to the Panel's findings. The Board meets to consider both the Panel's Investigation Report and Management's recommendations, and —

decides whether to approve the Management's recommendations which are intended to bring the Project into compliance in accordance with Bank policies and procedures. The Board may, at this stage, ask the Panel to verify whether Management conducted appropriate consultations with the Requesters and affected people prior to approving Management's recommendations for remedial measures.

PROBLEM 10-1
THE LAKE TITICACA (BOLIVIA) TO PUERTO MALDONADO (PERU) HIGHWAY

The World Bank has long been involved in infrastructure development projects in Latin America. A principal component of international poverty reduction policies in Latin America is the Initiative for the Integration of the Infrastructure of South America (IIRSA) established in 2000 by 12 South American governments. The purpose of IIRSA is the improvement of the economic, social, and cultural integration of South America. At the request of the governments of Bolivia and Peru, the IBRD has approved a loan of $3.6 billion to fund the construction of a modern, limited access highway from Lake Titicaca in Bolivia to Puerto Maldonado in Peru. This highway — known as the Bolivia/Peru Highway Project — would traverse a dense rain forest and the majestic Andes Mountains and would pass close to several sites famed for Inca remains. Small towns in eastern Peru would be connected for the first time to markets in Bolivia, and the road will benefit mining, tourism, and agricultural interests in the region. The new road will also connect Bolivia to the newly constructed Inter-Oceanic Highway completed in 2013 that connects cities on the Atlantic coast of Brazil, including Rio de Janeiro and Santos, to two port cities on the Pacific Ocean in Peru, San Juan and Ilo.

The World Bank Inspection Panel has received a Request for Inspection related to the Highway Project from residents of Franck, a town located in the path of the road as well as the Peruvian branch of the Sierra Club, alleging the road may cause harm through destruction of Incan burial sites and other Incan remains; opening the region to unregulated logging of the rain forest; and opening the area to unregulated gold mining operations that use mercury and other dangerous chemicals. The forest of the area near Puerto Maldonado is almost pristine and includes the Altos Puros National Park embracing the headwaters of the Puros River, a major tributary of the Amazon River. The Bolivia/Peru Highway Project would thus increase the danger of degradation of the Amazonia region of South America.

What is the process by which the Inspection Panel should consider this Request?

What substantive measures might the Panel consider in this case?   .

Does the Panel have the power to stop or demand modifications of the Project in order to safeguard the environment?

BACKGROUND: THE POLONOROESTE PROJECT
AND THE INTEROCEANIC HIGHWAY

In the 1980s the World Bank was involved in funding several infamous projects that had a devastating impact on the environment. One of these was the Polonoroeste Highway Project in the Brazilian state of Rondônia. From 1981 to 1983, the IBRD approved over $457 million in loans to Brazil for the construction of a 1600 kilometer highway running from the city of Cuiabá in the Brazilian state of Mato Grosso to Porto Velho in the Brazilian state of Rondônia. This highway was approved for the purpose of opening up sparsely populated areas of the Amazon rain forest to increase access to natural resources and to create new agricultural lands. The Polonoroeste Project was intended to be a model of sustainable regional development in rain forest areas. But from the beginning this Project was beset with poor planning, overlooked assessments of project impacts and a lack of oversight and supervision. The result was disaster.[1] The Brazilian government planned and approved new settlements without taking into consideration soils, water and slope conditions; much of the new land had poor soils unsuitable for agriculture; property boundaries neglected the rights of indigenous populations; and a new extractive economic ethic was established based on logging, cattle ranching, and mining. New people poured into the region: the population of about 71,000 in the mid-1970s surged to more than 1.6 million in 1995. New, deadly diseases ravaged particularly the indigenous population and thousands died. The President of the Bank, Barber Conable, in 1987, leveled special criticism, stating:

> [The Polonoroeste Project] is a sobering example of an environmentally sound effort which went wrong. The Bank misread the human, institutional and physical realities of the jungle and the frontier. In some cases the dynamics of the frontier got out of control. Protective measures to shelter fragile land and tribal people were included; they were not, however, carefully timed or adequately monitored"[2]

The Bank then took the extraordinary step of suspending funding of the Polonoroeste Project. Nevertheless the Cuiabá to Porto Velho highway was finished in early 1991, and this highway became an essential link in an even bigger project long envisioned by certain South American leaders: the completion of a highway across the heart of South America connecting cities on the Pacific and the Atlantic Ocean. This latter project, the Inter-Oceanic Highway, was completed in 2013.

---

[1] *See The Polonoroeste Road Project in Brazil's Amazon*, London School of Economics, Grantham Research Institute on Climate Change and the Environment, Paper No. 55 (2011).

[2] *Id.* at 6.

FIGURE 1. THE INTEROCEANIC HIGHWAY

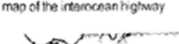

The Amazon watershed and its rain forest cover some 2.1 million square miles in nine South American countries. About 60% of the Amazon rain forest lies in Brazil's region known as Amazonia, covering 58 percent of Brazil's surface area. This forest is the greatest repository of biological diversity on Earth and constitutes over half of the planet's remaining tropical forests. Yet the rain forest in Brazil and other South American countries is disappearing at an alarming rate. For example, in the state of Rondônia, the site of the Polonoroeste Highway Project, the rain forest was largely intact in 1975: only 1.73% of the forest area had disappeared. But in 2003, satellite images showed that over one-third of the rain forest was gone, due to logging, land use transformations and uncontrolled burning.[3] Destruction of the rain forest is continuing; government policies that involve opening up interior lands and subsidization of economic pursuits such as ranching, farming, and mining are

---

[3] Luciana de Souza and Peter H. Verburg, *Combining Remote Sensing and Household Life Data for Regional Scale Analysis of Land Cover Change*, 10 REGIONAL ENVIRONMENTAL CHANGE 371–86 (2010).

important causes of this destruction.[4]

What will be the impact of the new Inter-Oceanic Highway? It is now possible to travel by road from Sao Paolo or Rio de Janeiro to Lima, Peru. Brazil's burgeoning trade with China and other Asian countries now will flow through Peru's port cities.

How should the World Bank respond to these new realities? Does the Inspection Panel have authority to consider these problems? How can we assure that the new cross-continent road will not lead to serious social and environmental impacts — overexploitation of natural resources, the introduction of diseases, and environmental degradation?

In Chapter 4, we considered the problem of climate change and the new REDD+ program to prevent deforestation in return for payments by advanced countries and non-governmental organizations. Peru, Bolivia, and Brazil are members of the World Bank's Forest Carbon Partnership Facility (FCPF), a fund which provides incentives to countries that reduce deforestation and forest degradation. Is this the answer?

The World Bank Inspection Panel has considered one case related to development in Brazil's Amazon region. In early 1992, the IBRD approved funding for a project in the Brazilian state of Rondônia known as the Rondônia Natural Resources Management Project, which was known locally as PLANAFLORO. The components of this project were as follows:

WORLD BANK INSPECTION PANEL, RONDÔNIA NATURAL RESOURCES MANAGEMENT PROJECT
Case 4

The project assists the Government to: (a) institute a series of changes in policies so as to provide a coherent incentive framework for the sustainable development of Rondônia; (b) conserve the rich biodiversity of the State, while creating the basis for the sustainable utilization of its renewable natural resources for the direct economic benefit of the local population; (c) protect and enforce the borders of all conservation units, Amerindian reserves, public forests and extractive reserves, and control and prevent illegal deforestation, wood transport and forest fires; (d) develop integrated farming systems in areas suitable for permanent agriculture and agro-forestry, and systems for sustainable forest management and extraction of non-wood forest products in other areas which should remain under natural forest cover; (e) support priority investments in socio-economic infrastructure and services to implement the State's agro-ecological zoning; and lastly, (f) consolidate the technical operational capacity of state institutions. The project, implemented over a period of 5 years, supports priority environmental conservation, management and enforcement activities, and finances no new settlements or new roads.

Project Status	Closed
Region	Latin America And Caribbean

---

[4] See Dennis J. Mahar, Government Policies and Deforestation in Brazil's Amazon Region (Washington DC: World Bank, 1989).

Country/Area	Brazil
Major Sector (Sector) (%)	Agriculture, fishing, and forestry (General agriculture, fishing and forestry sector)
	Transportation (General transportation sector)
	Public Administration, Law, and Justice (Sub-national government administration)
	Finance (Micro- and SME finance)
	Water, sanitation and flood protection (General water, sanitation and flood protection sector)
Old Major Sector	N/A
Old Sector	N/A
Env Category	B
Project ID	P006454
Bank Team Lead (Last Name, First)	N/A
Approval Date	17-Mar-1992
Closing Date	30-Sep-2002
Borrower/Recipient	GOB
Implementing Agency	Sec. Reg. Dvt/Rondônia
Main Loan/Credit #	34440
IBRD Commitment *	167
IDA Commitment *	0
IBRD + IDA Commitment *	167
Grant Amount *	0
Total Project Cost*	228.9
Product Line	IBRD/IDA
Lending Instrument	Specific Investment Loan
Targeted Thematic Outcomes . . .	*Supporting this Broader Dev't Goal*

[The PLANAFLORO project experienced difficulties from the beginning. No single Rondônia agency was In charge, and a coordination problem existed between key state agencies, especially FUNAI, ITERON, and SEDAM.* A Request for Inspection of the project was filed with the World Bank Inspection Panel in 1995, and the Panel issued its Report in 1997.]

---

* Editors Note: FUNAI is the National Indigenous Peoples Foundation; ITERON is Rondônia's lands' agency; SEDAM is Rondônia's environmental agency.

WORLD BANK INSPECTION PANEL, REPORT ON PROGRESS REVIEW OF IMPLEMENTATION OF BRAZIL: RONDÔNIA NATURAL RESOURCES MANAGEMENT PROJECT
(Loan 3444-BR) Mar. 25, 1997

FINDINGS

○ Analysis of satellite imagery for the State of Rondônia done under the project demonstrates that contrary to project objectives, deforestation during the period 1993–1996 has increased considerably. This is the only data available on the rate of deforestation during PLANAFLORO execution. Continuous monitoring of deforestation and utilization of other methods to control deforestation on real-time should be a priority under a restructured phase.

○ Due to the inherent difficulties in achieving most of the environmental goals of the project, a potential restructuring should include conditions that provide for long-term solutions to existing problems, including legal safeguards against changing the characteristics and reducing the size of the protected areas. The State, Bank Management and NGOs have worked together to avoid adverse effects of legislation viewed by some as contrary to project objectives. Both local and international NGOs closely monitor this aspect.

○ Persistent invasions of indigenous and extractive areas have continued. The Panel found that there are illegal settlements and that legal problems remain with respect to the demarcations. Unless these border problems are addressed effectively the long-term sustainability of protected areas is in question. In those cases where settlements have been found illegal the invaders must be removed. This is unlikely to be possible unless SEDAM and ITERON capabilities are strengthened. The Panel has been informed that in the proposed project restructuring a number of conditions in relation to indigenous people will be included, for example:

  • Removal of illegal invaders from Uru-eu-wau-wau reserve by April 30, 1997.

  • FUNAI will announce its position on the legal dispute regarding the Burareiro settlements.

  • Removal of invaders from the Mequens reserve by October 30, 1997.

  • Demarcation of the Massaco indigenous reserve by November 30, 1997.

  • In the absence of criteria for allocation of PAIC [Community Initiatives Fund] resources, special efforts should be made to ensure that indigenous and other disenfranchised groups participate and have technical assistance in the development of economic alternatives and preparation of sub-projects, otherwise potential beneficiaries of this project component may be limited to those with technical capacity and current access to funds.

- It is critical that implementation of a realistic sustainable health plan for indigenous people be part of the restructured project.

- Management supervision of this multifaceted project has improved. Progress has been made during the past year to decentralize oversight to meet the serious supervision challenges. Management should be encouraged to continue with initiatives to achieve effective project management and supervision.

- With Bank assistance significant improvements have taken place in PLANAFLORO administration at the technical and accounting as well as the managerial level. The Bank and the restructured project should build on this increased implementation capacity.

- In spite of all project delays and difficulties, most critics recognize PLANAFLORO's potential to make a contribution to sustainable development. It is acknowledged that every effort should be made to achieve even the more modest objectives of the restructured project with respect to agro-ecological zoning and social/environmental objectives. Proper guarantees and conditionalities for critical missing or delayed actions should be established in amended legal documents.

NOTES AND QUESTIONS

The Request in the PLANAFLORO case was filed by 24 NGOs claiming to represent Rondônia residents, including small farmers, rubber-tappers, and indigenous communities. The Requesters alleged that a project designed to protect the local ecosystem was in fact having the opposite effect — the construction of roads was leading to deforestation and environmental degradation. The project's Management asserted that any harm was not due to any failure by the Bank but was the fault of the borrower. The Panel's Report confirmed that extensive environmental harm had been caused in the project area and that Management's failure to properly supervise the project "had undoubtedly contributed" to the damage. Inspection Panel Report, p. 8.

The Inspection Panel recommended "restructuring," but at this point what can be done? The real purpose of the project was poverty relief. The project involved providing funding to benefit local people. The project created income generating activities, health care, and infrastructure for Rondôniaa. The infrastructure component involved rehabilitating 3,900 km. of state and municipal roads and paving of 81 kms. as well as transport and maintenance activities. As a result of the project, 66,000 sq. kms., or about 30% of Rondônia's territory was designated conservation units or indigenous reserves. The Bank's Executive Board thanked the Panel for "invaluable insight and thorough assessment of the issues, which allowed the staff and Management to critically examine . . . the difficulties faced in the implementation of this complex operation." Inspection Report, Attachment 1, p. 2.

Before undertaking this project, should the Bank have recognized the difficulties and environmental degradation that later occurred? A weakness of the inspection process is that once a project is well underway, little can be done to mitigate the environmental problems once they have occurred. In some cases the Panel process can make only very marginal improvements. A more successful case was the Chad Petroleum Development and Pipeline Project, Inspection Panel Case 22:

On March 22, 2001, Mr. Ngarlejy Yorongar, on behalf of 120 residents of the Chad Cantons of Miandoum, Kome, Bero, Mbikou, Behedjia, and Beboni ("Requesters") submitted a Request for Inspection claiming that residents of the Project area and their environment would be harmed by the project. Among other things, Requesters alleged that the International Development Association had failed to prepare an adequate compensation plan and environmental assessment and had failed to consult properly with the communities.

The Panel registered the Request on April 11, 2001, and submitted its Report and Recommendation in favor of an inspection to the Board on September 12, 2001. The Board approved an investigation into the Project on October 1, 2001. The Panel investigated and then prepared and sent its Investigation Report to the Board on July 17, 2002. Management responded on August 21, 2002. The Board then approved Management's response on September 18, 2002.

A press release about the Inspection Panel Investigation Report said the Panel concluded that:

> Management was in compliance with several aspects of the Bank's environmental and social policies, such as Natural Habitats, Forests, Involuntary Resettlement and Pest Management. The Panel, however, found the Bank not in compliance with Environmental Assessment, such as the Bank's approach to the Project's spatial context and the need for requiring a 'Regional Environmental Assessment,' baseline data gathering and utilization in impact mitigation, consideration of environmental costs and benefits of alternatives and institutional capacity. The latter two aspects were also the basis for the Panel's finding of non-compliance with certain requirements under OP10.04 on Economic Evaluation and OD 4.15 on Poverty Reduction.

In its August 21 2002 response, Management agreed to prepare a Regional Development Plan, accelerate efforts to help the governments manage anticipated revenues and production processes, assist the governments with long-term financial planning to allow the Project to alleviate poverty and improve the environment, and to intensify monitoring and supervision of the Project.

The Board of Executive Directors then approved Management's response plan in September 2002.

1. In Problem 10-1, should the Bank extend financing for the Bolivia/Peru Highway Project? What problems should be anticipated in this venture? What mitigation efforts would you suggest?

2. In the 20 years 1993 to 2013, 83 Requests were handled by the World Bank Inspection Panel. The World Bank, through the Inspection Panel process, allows an objective, outside assessment of its activities. Should the Panel process be strengthened? In testimony before the U.S. House of Representatives Committee on Financial Services, June 18, 2008, Lori L. Udall, on behalf of the Bank Information Center and several environmental

NGOs, offered the following suggestions:

Since the establishment of the Panel in 1993, NGOs have warned that the Panel process does not allow enough access for claimants to have their concerns heard by management and the Board throughout the Panel process. These concerns have borne out in the intervening years.

Access to Information

The current Panel process has important weaknesses when the claimant is left out of the process and finds it difficult to get information or provide important comments or input. For example, after the claim is filed and the Panel site visit has been completed, the claimant has few opportunities for engagement in the process.

Importantly, claimants do not have access to management's initial response to their claim of harm until it is too late to respond. Further on in the process when the Panel issues its final report to the Board, Bank management receives a copy, and sends a response to the Board that makes recommendations for next steps called an "action plan."

Full Consultation with Claimants and Affected Stakeholders on Developing Actions Plans

In 1999, the World Bank Board mandated that Management should communicate to the Panel the outcome of its consultations with affected parties regarding the action plans, implicitly requiring Management to involve claimants in developing action plans regarding project remedies. The Board also gave the Panel a mandate to comment to the Board on whether the claimants were adequately consulted on the actions plans. Neither of these processes has developed adequately.

For years, NGO case studies have documented the absence of claimant involvement in developing action plans or remedies to bring the project back into compliance. For example in the Chad Cameroon Pipeline, the claimants whose livelihoods and environment were harmed by the pipeline said they were never consulted about the plans to improve compliance in the project, and thus the actions plan fell short of their needs.

Claimants usually have first-hand experience and knowledge to provide recommendations for remedial measures that would improve their own situation, but have generally been prevented by the process from doing this. As a result, Management produced action plans are usually the course followed by the Board.

Post-Inspection Follow-up and Monitoring

Since the establishment of the Panel, the World Bank Board has changed its position on whether the Panel should be empowered to monitor projects that have been the subject of a claim. In some of the early claims — such as the Rondônia Natural Resources Project in Brazil, the ltaparica

Resettlement and Irrigation Project, the Jamuna Multipurpose Bridge Project, and the Yacyreta Hydroelectric Project — the Panel was asked to monitor and review the implementation of the Bank's action plans. In some cases, the Panel was asked to monitor progress in lieu of a full investigation.

Leading up to the 1999 Board Review of the Panel many borrowing country Board members objected to the Panel returning to projects sites yet another time in order to monitor remedial actions. This resulted in the Board explicitly prohibiting the Panel from an oversight or monitoring role in management-generated action plans in the second clarification of the Panel's Resolution. However, the Board did not specifically prohibit the Panel from monitoring whether the project has returned to compliance with Bank policy.

Over the years, the lack of monitoring and follow-up has resulted in inadequate resolution of problems and policy violations in many problem projects. In some claims, such as Yacyreta Hydroelectric Project, Itaparica Resettlement, NTPC Power Generation Project, Bujagali Hydropower Project, and Brazilian Land Reform, the claimants have had no choice but to file additional claims to seek remedies for their problems and to request further policy compliance.

The Board has been left with overseeing implementation of remedies and ensuring that projects are being brought back into compliance, but the Board has no process for monitoring and has not appointed any independent panels to undertake this critical function. In some cases, the Board has asked Management to report back but this has no independent feature to it.

The current Bank Board may realize the limitations of not having an independent voice to follow-up on remedial actions and compliance. Recently it has requested the Panel to conduct follow-up fact finding in the Mumbai Urban Transport project and in the second Yacyreta Power project.

It has long been recognized by Panel claimants and advocacy NGOs that monitoring would be a logical and effective step to ensure that the issues that gave rise to the complaint are in fact being addressed. Follow-up and monitoring is also required in order for the Bank's Board to have independent information and to exercise effective oversight of management. Independent monitoring would also pressure the Bank's operations staff to fulfill their action plans.

C. The Environmental Liability of International Organizations

On May 30, 2011, the United Nations General Assembly "took note" of the International Law Commission's Draft Articles on the Responsibility of International Organizations. Under these Draft Articles (reprinted in the **Document Supplement**), an international organization incurs liability for damages in any case of a wrongful international act. The Draft Articles do not, however, define the precise environmental obligations of international organizations; the Draft Articles are secondary rules that impose liability assuming the violation of a primary international environmental obligation. Thus, for example, the International Maritime Organization would incur liability if one of its research vessels discharged oil into the sea in violation of international standards. But many uncertainties underlie the application of these Draft Articles; for example, would UNEP incur liability for non-compliance with the rules of the Montreal Protocol by one of the state-parties? Since there is virtually no state practice or *opinio juris* on the environmental liability of international organizations, the impact of these Draft Articles is uncertain.

The Draft Articles are very controversial. For analysis, see Noemi Gal-Or and Cedric Ryngaert, *From Theory to Practice: Exploring the Relevance of the Draft Articles on the Responsibility of International Organizations*, 13 GERMAN L.J. 511 (2012).

Section II. NON-GOVERNMENTAL ORGANIZATIONS (NGOs)

Non-governmental organizations have emerged as important actors in international environmental law. Both the Rio Declaration and Agenda 21 affirm the partnership role of NGOs and call for their "expanded role." Agenda 21 states:

> The organizations of the United Nations system and other intergovernmental organizations and forums, bilateral programs and the private sector, as appropriate, will need to provide increased financial and administrative support for non-governmental organizations and their self-organized networks, in particular those based in developing countries, contributing to the monitoring and evaluation of Agenda 21 programs, and provide training for non-governmental organizations . . . to enhance their partnership role in program design and implementation.

Agenda 21 also calls on the UN system to take measures to enhance the contribution of NGOs to policy design, decision making, and the implementation and evaluation of environmental programs. NGOs are increasingly taking part in interagency discussions and in UN conferences on environmental issues. Agenda 21 calls on governments to take "legislative measures necessary to enable the establishment by non-governmental organizations of consultant groups, and to ensure the right of non-governmental organizations to protect the public interest through legal action."

QUESTION

What strategies should NGOs employ to have an impact on the public interest in protecting the environment?

NOTES

1. ***Rights and duties.*** International instruments address the idea that individuals have a responsibility to protect the environment. Principle 1 of the Stockholm Declaration referred to man's "solemn responsibility" to protect the environment. The World Charter for Nature mentions the duty of "each person" to comply with its terms. However, these are non-binding instruments. As a general rule individuals and even transnational corporations do not have enforceable rights or duties under international environmental law. This section highlights areas of concern especially for transnational business entities.

2. ***Promoting compliance.*** Non-state actors — especially transnational business enterprises and non-governmental organizations (NGOs) — have forged three main avenues by which their participation in the international system promotes the compliance by states of international obligations.

First, under the right circumstances non-state actors may bring environmental claims in municipal systems. A recent example of potential access to domestic administrative and legal systems can be found in Article 6 of the North American Agreement on Environmental Cooperation (NAAEC) — the environmental "side agreement" to the North American Free Trade Agreement (NAFTA). Article 6(1) provides that each party to the Agreement shall ensure that "interested persons" have the right to request investigations of alleged violations of the agreement and that such requests are given due consideration. It is uncertain what qualifies a person as "interested" under Article 6, but it seems doubtful that nationality would be a factor in most, if any, circumstances. Thus, any "interested person" within the territory of any of NAFTA's parties can request that competent authorities investigate an alleged violation of an offending party's environmental laws. Additionally, Article 6(2) states "each Party shall ensure that persons with a legally recognized interest under its law in a particular matter have appropriate access to administrative, quasi-judicial or judicial proceedings for the enforcement of the Party's environmental laws and regulations." Of course, the municipal law of standing may still pose hurdles — in some cases insurmountable — to access to domestic courts granted by Article 6(2), and the provision's effectiveness may be limited.

Second, in some instances non-state actors can superintend state compliance with international environmental law by invoking international oversight of municipal environmental law. Such an approach is exemplified under Article 14 of NAAEC. Under Article 14, the Secretariat of the Commission for Environmental Cooperation (CEC) may consider a procedurally correct submission by any NGO or any person established or residing within the territory of any of NAFTA's parties that alleges that a party is failing to effectively enforce its environmental law. If warranted and approved by a two-thirds vote of the Council of the CEC, the Secretariat prepares a factual record concerning the submission for consideration by the parties.

Third, non-state actors have increasingly gained roles in promoting compliance with and implementation of international environmental law through partnerships with convention secretariats. For instance, non-state actors such as World Wide Fund for Nature (WWF) and the World Conservation Union (IUCN), and in particular their joint program TRAFFIC, have been instrumental in tracking illegal trade in endangered species regulated under the Convention on International Trade in Endangered Species of Flora and Fauna (CITES). TRAFFIC's activities, including its informative publications, have assisted the CITES secretariat and parties to the Convention to identify weaknesses in customs enforcement at the border in many countries, including the United States. TRAFFIC has also documented wildlife smuggling activities, located clandestine trade routes for illegal trade, and engaged in "undercover" investigations that have helped in the enforcement of CITES.

3. *Participation in international/environmental affairs.* Non-state participants in the international legal and political system serve a number of important roles, in addition to enforcement and compliance, including: (i) the identification of environmental problems requiring international cooperation for resolution, (ii) the proposal of scientific, policy and legal solutions to problems identified, and (iii) the direct participation — if not voting with states — in international negotiations touching international environmental obligations. Additionally, as Steve Charnovitz observes:

> In thinking about how to structure the NGO role for the maximum advantage of world public order, one should start with an understanding of what NGOs do. A useful framework is the seven decision functions identified [in Myres S. Mcdougal, Harold D. Lasswell, & W. Michael Reisman, *The World Constitutive Process of Authoritative Decision*, in INTERNATIONAL LAW ESSAYS: A SUPPLEMENT TO INTERNATIONAL LAW IN CONTEMPORARY PRACTICE (Myres S. McDougal & W. Michael Reisman eds., 1981) (defining private associations as groups not seeking power)]. They are: intelligence, promotion, prescription, invocation, application, termination, and appraisal. [Non-state actors] engage in all of these functions.
>
> The intelligence function involves the gathering, analysis, and dissemination of information relevant to decision making. . . . A current example is human rights reporting by NGOs. Because of the expertise of their personnel, many NGOs are well positioned to expand their influence through intelligence.
>
> The promotion function involves the advocacy of policy alternatives to authoritative decisionmakers either directly or indirectly through a broader public. Some historical examples are the efforts of the Red Cross to stimulate treaties on international humanitarian law, of literary societies to seek better copyright policies, and of the bird groups to advocate a migratory bird treaty. NGOs are extremely active today in the promotion function, particularly on the environment and on social development.
>
> The prescription function involves the designation of policies and the communication of authority and control intentions. A contemporary example of prescription occurred in 1995 when a group of environmental NGOs negotiated an understanding with Mexico to safeguard dolphins.
>
> The invocation function involves the characterization of behavior as deviating from prescribed policy and the assertion of control to abate the

deviation. . . . A recent example is the North American Agreement on Environmental Cooperation. This Agreement permits NGOs to submit petitions alleging that a government is failing to effectively enforce its environmental law. . . .

The application function involves giving effect to prescriptions in concrete disputes. NGOs are not typically involved in application. But there are at least two historical examples of it. First, worker and employer delegates to the [International Labor Organization (ILO)] conference may file complaints with the ILO Governing Body that can lead to the appointment of a Commission of Inquiry. Second, since 1923 the [International Chamber of Commerce (ICC)] has sponsored a Court of International Arbitration that settles commercial disputes, including those involving States or State enterprises. NGOs can also be active in promoting application by persuading governments or international agencies to seek authoritative judgments. For example, in 1993–94, NGOs pressed governments to urge the U.N. General Assembly to seek an advisory opinion from the International Court of Justice (ICJ) regarding the legality of the threat or use of nuclear weapons.

The termination function involves putting an end to prescriptions that do not contribute to the common interest. . . . NGOs are often catalysts in pressing for termination. . . . A modern example . . . is the Convention on the Regulation of Antarctic Mineral Resource Activities that, although adopted unanimously by governments in 1988, failed to come into force after protests by environmental groups caused some governments to back down.

The appraising function involves evaluating the degree to which the policies of an international system are achieved in fact. An early example is the criticism of the 1902 treaty on birds by the International Committee for Bird Preservation. Some current examples include reports by organizations like Worldwatch, Human Rights Watch, and Global Witness. Because international bureaucracies cannot easily evaluate themselves, the NGO role in this area is likely to expand.

This framework of decision functions is useful in showing the wide range of NGO activities. Because NGOs play multiple roles, the task of structuring their input is complex. Facilitating one function may hinder others. For example, intelligence and appraisal functions may be compromised by promotional activities. NGOs are likely to continue strengthening their activities in all seven areas.

*   *   *

There are several potential benefits of NGO involvement [in the international system]. First, NGO networks can deliver technical expertise on particular topics needed by government officials. Second, NGOs can facilitate a negotiation by giving politicians access to competing ideas from outside normal bureaucratic channels. Third, NGOs can help government officials test controversial proposals by providing rapid feedback. Fourth,

NGOs can help governments secure ratification or implementation of new treaties. Fifth, NGOs can vocalize the interests of persons not well represented in policymaking. Sixth, NGOs can help IGOs fulfill the role of being fiduciaries for future generations. The fact that some NGOs persist over decades shows that their programs have inter-generational authenticity. Seventh, NGO involvement may enhance the accountability of IGOs. Eighth, NGOs may enhance the accountability of governments by monitoring negotiating efforts. NGOs can also press compromises upon reluctant negotiators. Ninth, NGOs may strengthen international agreements by monitoring governmental compliance. Tenth, the consultation process may improve the behavior of NGOs by giving them a greater stake in policymaking.

Although there is universal agreement that NGO involvement in developing projects can be constructive, . . . [s]everal problems are raised. First, the vast number of NGOs makes deeper participation impractical. Second, because many NGOs are from industrial countries, they amplify certain views . . . that may not be reflective of the views of developing countries. NGOs from developing countries may also be less well-financed than their industrial country counterparts and therefore less able to participate effectively. Third, and more fundamentally, some government officials argue that NGO involvement in international organizations is unnecessary because NGOs can seek influence through their own governments.

Steve Charnovitz, *Two Centuries of Participation: NGOs and International Governance*, 18 Mich. J. Int'l L. 183, 271–75 (1997). In the twenty-first century, international law will become increasingly relevant to non-governmental persons, especially non-governmental organizations and transnational corporations. At present their international environmental obligations are quite diffuse. International law in this area is a work in progress.

Section III.   BUSINESS AND INDUSTRY

A.   Codes of Conduct and Environmental Management Systems

AGENDA 21, REPORT OF THE UNITED NATIONS CONFERENCE ON ENVIRONMENT AND DEVELOPMENT
A/Conf. 151/26/Rev. 1 (Vol. 1) (3–14 June 1992), Annex II, at 398

Chapter 30

STRENGTHENING THE ROLE OF BUSINESS AND INDUSTRY

Introduction

30.1. Business and industry, including transnational corporations, play a crucial role in the social and economic development of a country. A stable policy regime enables and encourages business and industry to operate responsibly and efficiently and to implement longer-term policies. Increasing prosperity, a major goal of the development process, is contributed primarily by the activities of business and industry. Business enterprises, large and small, formal and informal, provide major trading, employment and livelihood opportunities. Business opportunities available to women are contributing towards their professional development, strengthening their economic role and transforming social systems. Business and industry, including transnational corporations and their representative organizations should be full participants in the implementation and evaluation of activities related to Agenda 21.

30.2. Through more efficient production processes, preventive strategies, cleaner production technologies and procedures throughout the product life cycle, hence minimizing or avoiding wastes, the policies and operations of business and industry, including transnational corporations, can play a major role in reducing impacts on resource use and the environment. Technological innovations, development, applications, transfer and the more comprehensive aspects of partnership and cooperation are to a very large extent within the province of business and industry.

30.3. Business and industry, including transnational corporations, should recognize environmental management as among the highest corporate priorities and as a key determinant to sustainable, development. Some enlightened leaders of enterprises are already implementing "responsible care" and product stewardship policies and programs, fostering openness and dialogue with employees and the public and carrying out environmental audits and assessments of compliance. These leaders in business and industry, including transnational corporations, are increasingly taking voluntary initiatives, promoting and implementing self-regulation and greater responsibilities in ensuring their activities have minimal impacts on human health and the environment. The regulatory regimes introduced in many countries and the growing consciousness of consumers and the general public and enlightened leaders of business and industry, including transnational corporations, have all contributed to this. A positive contribution of business and industry, including transnational corporations, to sustainable development can increasingly be achieved by using economic instruments such as free market mechanisms in which the prices of goods and services should increasingly reflect the environmental costs of their input, production, use, recycling and disposal subject to country-specific conditions.

NOTES

1.   There have been several efforts to develop generally applicable policies and standards to govern the activities of transnational corporations. Guidelines for Multinational Enterprises were first adopted by the Organization for Economic Cooperation and Development (OECD) in 1976 (15 I.L.M. 967, 969) and were revised in 2000 (40 I.L.M. 237 (2001)) and again in 2011. The OECD Guidelines are recommendations addressed by governments to multinational enterprises. They provide voluntary principles and standards for responsible business conduct consistent with applicable laws. According to the OECD Guidelines:

> Enterprises should, within the framework of laws, regulations and administrative practices in the countries in which they operate, and in consideration of relevant international agreements, principles, objectives, and standards, take due account of the need to protect the environment, public health and safety, and generally to conduct their activities in a manner contributing to the wider goal of sustainable development. In particular, enterprises should:
>
> 1.   Establish and maintain a system of environmental management appropriate to the enterprise, including:
>
>   •   Collection and evaluation of adequate and timely information regarding the environmental, health, and safety impacts of their activities;
>
>   •   Establishment of measurable objectives and, where appropriate, targets for improved environmental performance, including periodically reviewing the continuing relevance of these objectives; and
>
>   •   regular monitoring and verification of progress toward environmental, health, and safety objectives or targets.
>
> 2.   Taking into account concerns about cost, business confidentiality, and the protection of intellectual property rights:
>
>   •   Provide the public and employees with adequate and timely information on the potential environment, health and safety impacts of the activities of the enterprise, which could include reporting on progress in improving environmental performance; and
>
>   •   Engage in adequate and timely communication and consultation with the communities directly affected by the environmental,

health and safety policies of the enterprise and by their implementation.

3. Assess, and address in decision-making, the foreseeable environmental, health, and safety-related impacts associated with the processes, goods and services of the enterprise over their full life cycle. Where these proposed activities may have significant environmental, health, or safety impacts, and where they are subject to a decision of a competent authority, prepare an appropriate environmental impact assessment.

4. Consistent with the scientific and technical understanding of the risks, where there are threats of serious damage to the environment, taking also into account human health and safety, not use the lack of full scientific certainty as a reason for postponing cost-effective measures to prevent or minimize such damage.

5. Maintain contingency plans for preventing, mitigating, and controlling serious environmental and health damage from their operations, including accidents and emergencies; and mechanisms for immediate reporting to the competent authorities.

6. Continually seek to improve corporate environmental performance, by encouraging, where appropriate, such activities as:

   • Adoption of technologies and operating procedures in all parts of the enterprise that reflect standards concerning environmental performance in the best performing part of the enterprise;

   • Development and provision of products or services that have no undue environmental impacts; are safe in their intended use; are efficient in their consumption of energy and natural resources; can be reused, recycled, or disposed of safely;

   • Promoting higher levels of awareness among customers of the environmental implications of using the products and services of the enterprise; and

   • Research on ways of improving the environmental performance of the enterprise over the longer term.

7. Provide adequate education and training to employees in environmental health and safety matters, including the handling of hazardous materials and the prevention of environmental accidents, as well as more general environmental management areas, such as environmental impact assessment procedures, public relations, and environmental technologies.

8. Contribute to the development of environmentally meaningful and economically efficient public policy, for example, by means of partnerships or initiatives that will enhance environmental awareness and protection.

The OECD Guidelines for Multinational Enterprises, available at http://www.oecd.org, are reprinted in the **Document Supplement**.

2. The United Nations Commission and Centre on Transnational Corporations has worked on the promulgation of a Code of Conduct for Transnational Corporations. The difficulty of coming to agreement on the norms of international law to be established under such a Code is typified by the following excerpt from the 1985 Report of the Centre on Transnational Corporations:

> There are at least two different schools of thought on this matter. The first maintains that the code should allow for the applicability of customary international legal principles in relevant areas to amplify or qualify the broad standards enunciated in the code. According to this view, the applicability of international law to the relations between States and transnational corporations is not limited to international obligations expressly founded on conventions, treaties or other international agreements. In addition, customary international law is seen as prescribing principles and rules with respect to such matters as jurisdiction over transnational corporations, permanent sovereignty of States over their natural wealth and resources, renegotiation of State contracts, nationalization and compensation, non-discriminatory treatment of transnational corporations, diplomatic protection of aliens and alien property, and procedures for the settlement of disputes between Governments and transnational corporations. It follows that the provisions of the code would not derogate from the application of those customary principles of international law, subject of course to the express undertakings of the States concerned under conventions, treaties and other international agreements concluded by such States. The proponents of this view accordingly maintain that the code ought to take into account the relevance of international law by incorporating stipulations with respect to its applicability to the relations between Governments and transnational corporations.

> The second school of thought questions the existence of universally recognized principles of customary international law governing the treatment of transnational corporations or foreign investors. Adherents to that school maintain that this area falls primarily within the purview of national law, subject to international legal norms and specific undertakings and obligations expressly stipulated in international instruments, such as codes of conduct and conventions, treaties and other international agreements, to which the States concerned have freely subscribed.

3. In 2000, the Office of the Secretary-General of the United Nations launched a new initiative, The Global Compact, to promote human rights, workers' rights, and the protection of the environment by multinational companies. The Global Compact attempts to bring multinational corporations into the fold of responsible international citizens. The Compact was launched in 1999 by Secretary General Kofi Annan and endorsed in his *Millennium Report* entitled, *We the Peoples: The Role of the United Nations in the Twenty-First Century, Report of the Secretary-General*, UN A/54/2000) (March 27, 2000). The Global Compact is sponsored by the International Labor Organization, the United Nations Environment Program and the Office of the United Nations High Commissioner for Human Rights. The Compact originally comprised nine principles (now 10) aimed at the promotion by corporations of equitable labor standards, respect for human rights generally and protection of the environment. Companies can join the Compact by addressing a letter to the Office of the U.N. Secretary-General and agreeing to implement the 10 principles:

Human Rights

Principle 1: Businesses should support and respect the protection of internationally proclaimed human rights; and

Principle 2: make sure that they are not complicit in human rights abuses.

Labor Standards

Principle 3: Businesses should uphold the freedom of association and the effective recognition of the right to collective bargaining;

Principle 4: the elimination of all forms of forced and compulsory labor;

Principle 5: the effective abolition of child labor; and

Principle 6: the elimination of discrimination in respect of employment and occupation.

Environment

Principle 7: Businesses should support a precautionary approach to environmental challenges;

Principle 8: undertake initiatives to promote greater environmental responsibility; and

Principle 9: encourage the development and diffusion of environmentally friendly technologies

Anti-Corruption

Principle 10: Businesses should work against all forms of corruption, including extortion and bribery

See further United Nations, The Global Compact: Corporate Citizenship in the World Economy (Global Compact Office, January 2003).

4.   Environmental reporting and "eco-audits" on a voluntary basis are quickly becoming the norm among transnational corporations. There are many national and industry-based voluntary codes of conduct. The Valdez Principles have been renamed the CERES Principles after their sponsor, the Coalition for Environmentally Responsible Economics (CERES). Another influential code is the International Chamber of Commerce's Business Charter for Sustainable Development, which calls for providing "appropriate information" to shareholders.

The European Union has adopted Regulation 1836/93 (EEC) which provides for voluntary eco-audits by participating companies that are willing to report on corporate environmental performance. In Australia, a number of states have enacted legislation that empowers state environmental protection authorities to require mandatory environmental audits for certain pollution license-holders in the case of poor environmental performance. *See e.g.*, Protection of the Environment (Operations) Act 1997 (New South Wales); Environment Protection Act 1970 (Victoria).

Are these codes of conduct useful? What are their advantages and disadvantages? Should they be compulsory?

5. The International Organization for Standardization (usually referred to as ISO) has published an international standard for environmental management systems (EMS). The goal of this international standard is to reduce environmental contamination and pollution through environmental management decisions. The publication of this document, ISO 14000, has had worldwide impact. Many transnational companies have announced their acceptance and implementation of IS 14000. The main topics of IS 14000 are summarized by Henry P. Baer, Jr.:

> The environmental management system advocated by ISO 14001 is organized into five areas: (1) definition of a corporate environmental policy; (2) formulation of a plan to implement the policy; (3) implementation and operation of the plan; (4) measurement, monitoring, and evaluation of environmental performance, and corrective action; and (5) review and continual improvement of the management systems. Viewed as an integrated system, the organizational framework of ISO 14001 will be an ongoing and evolving mechanism dependent on honest and in depth understanding of environmental goals, needs, and impacts, as well as the steps necessary to continually attain those goals. It will ensure that a company has a defined and acceptable system for compliance with all relevant legislation and regulations, and that the company is committed to continual improvement.
>
> The first step in designing an acceptable EMS is establishing a definition of environmental policies and principles. This must include a commitment to comply with all relevant international, federal, state, and local environmental regulations, along with any other requirements potentially affecting corporate action. It must include management's commitment and leadership to the environmental policy. Furthermore, the policy should be "appropriate to the nature, scale and environmental impacts of (the corporation's) activities, products or services" and include a commitment to continual improvement and pollution prevention. Lastly, it should be documented, communicated to all employees, and open to the public.

Henry P. Baer, Jr., *ISO 14000: Potential Compliance and Prevention Guidelines for EPA and DOJ*, 7 FORD. ENVTL J. 927, 937–38 (1996).

6. On July 6, 2011, the Human Rights Council of the United Nations General Assembly formally adopted the Report of the Special Representative of the Secretary-General on the issue of human rights and transnational corporations and other business enterprises. (The text of the Resolution of the Human Rights Council is reprinted in the **Document Supplement**). The Council has formed a Working Group to examine and promote the application of human rights norms to business enterprises. The Council's Guiding Principles on Business and Human Rights implement a "Protect, Respect and Remedy" framework that requires all states to ensure that businesses within their jurisdiction respect human rights norms, including those associated with environmental protection.

B. Enforcing Code of Conduct Norms

The OECD Guidelines for Multinational Enterprises include an implementation procedure to promote the effectiveness of the Guidelines. Countries adhering to the Guidelines must designate National Contact Points (NCPs) to which individuals and NGOs can bring comments and complaints. The function of the NCPs is to facilitate discussion and dispute settlement in matters concerning the Guidelines. The NCPs are also required to make reports to the investment Committee of the OECD regarding the matters it handles.

We set out the OECD Procedural Guidance on National Contact Points and the results of a complaint filed with the NCP of the U.K.

OECD, PROCEDURAL GUIDANCE

I. National Contact Points

The role of National Contact Points (NCPs) is to further the effectiveness of the Guidelines. NCPs will operate in accordance with core criteria of visibility, accessibility, transparency and accountability to further the objective of functional equivalence.

A. Institutional Arrangements

Consistent with the objective of functional equivalence and furthering the effectiveness of the Guidelines, adhering countries have flexibility in organizing their NCPs, seeking the active support of social partners, including the business community, worker organizations, other nongovernmental organizations, and other interested parties.

Accordingly, the National Contact Points:

1. Will be composed and organized such that they provide an effective basis for dealing with the broad range of issues covered by the Guidelines and enable the NCP to operate in an impartial manner while maintaining an adequate level of accountability to the adhering government.

2. Can use different forms of organization to meet this objective. An NCP can consist of senior representatives from one or more Ministries, may be a senior government official or a government office headed by a senior official, be an interagency group, or one that contains independent experts. Representatives of the business community, worker organizations and other non-governmental organizations may also be included.

3. Will develop and maintain relations with representatives of the business community, worker organizations and other interested parties that are able to contribute to the effective functioning of the Guidelines.

B. Information and Promotion

The National Contact Point will:

1. Make the Guidelines known and available by appropriate means, including through on-line information, and in national languages. Prospective investors (inward and outward) should be informed about the Guidelines, as appropriate.

2. Raise awareness of the Guidelines and their implementation procedures, including through cooperation, as appropriate, with the business community, worker organizations, other non-governmental organizations, and the interested public.

3. Respond to enquiries about the Guidelines from:

    a) other National Contact Points;

    b) the business community, worker organizations, other nongovernmental organizations and the public; and

    c) governments of non-adhering countries.

C. Implementation in Specific Instances

The National Contact Point will contribute to the resolution of issues that arise relating to implementation of the Guidelines in specific instances in a manner that is impartial, predictable, equitable and compatible with the principles and standards of the Guidelines. The NCP will offer a forum for discussion and assist the business community, worker organizations, other non-governmental organizations, and other interested parties concerned to deal with the issues raised in an efficient and timely manner and in accordance with applicable law. In providing this assistance, the NCP will:

1. Make an initial assessment of whether the issues raised merit further examination and respond to the parties involved.

2. Where the issues raised merit further examination, offer good offices to help the parties involved to resolve the issues. For this purpose, the NCP will consult with these parties and where relevant:

    a) seek advice from relevant authorities, and/or representatives of the business community, worker organizations, other nongovernmental organizations, and relevant experts;

    b) consult the NCP in the other country or countries concerned;

    c) seek the guidance of the Committee if it has doubt about the interpretation of the Guidelines in particular circumstances;

    d) offer, and with the agreement of the parties involved, facilitate access to consensual and non-adversarial means, such as conciliation or mediation, to assist the parties in dealing with the issues.

3. At the conclusion of the procedures and after consultation with the parties involved, make the results of the procedures publicly available, taking into account the need to protect sensitive business and other stakeholder

information, by issuing:

a)   a statement when the NCP decides that the issues raised do not merit further consideration. The statement should at a minimum describe the issues raised and the reasons for the NCP's decision;

b)   a report when the parties have reached agreement on the issues raised. The report should at a minimum describe the issues raised, the procedures the NCP initiated in assisting the parties and when agreement was reached. Information on the content of the agreement will only be included insofar as the parties involved agree thereto;

c)   a statement when no agreement is reached or when a party is unwilling t o participate in the procedures. This statement should at a minimum describe the issues raised, the reasons why the NCP decided that the issues raised merit further examination and the procedures the NCP initiated in assisting the parties. The NCP will make recommendations on the implementation of the Guidelines as appropriate, which should be included in the statement. Where appropriate, the statement could also include the reasons that agreement could not be reached.

The NCP will notify the results of its specific instance procedures to the Committee in a timely manner.

4.   In order to facilitate resolution of the issues raised, take appropriate steps to protect sensitive business and other information and the interests of other stakeholders involved in the specific instance. While the procedures under paragraph 2 are underway, confidentiality of the proceedings will be maintained. At the conclusion of the procedures, if the parties involved have not agreed on a resolution of the issues raised, they are free to communicate about and discuss these issues. However, information and views provided during the proceedings by another party involved will remain confidential, unless that other party agrees to their disclosure or this would be contrary to the provisions of national law.

5.   If issues arise in non-adhering countries, take steps to develop an understanding of the issues involved, and follow these procedures where relevant and practicable.

D. Reporting

1.   Each NCP will report annually to the Committee.

2.   Reports should contain information on the nature and results of the activities of the NCP, including implementation activities in specific instances.

II. Investment Committee

1.   The Committee will consider requests from NCPs for assistance in carrying out their activities, including in the event of doubt about the interpretation of the Guidelines in particular circumstances.

2. The Committee will, with a view to enhancing the effectiveness of the Guidelines and to fostering the functional equivalence of NCPs:

   a) consider the reports of NCPs;

   b) consider a substantiated submission by an adhering country, an advisory body or OECD Watch on whether an NCP is fulfilling its responsibilities with regard to its handling of specific instances;

   c) consider issuing a clarification where an adhering country, an advisory body or OECD Watch makes a substantiated submission on whether an NCP has correctly interpreted the Guidelines in specific instances;

   d) make recommendations, as necessary, to improve the functioning of NCPs and the effective implementation of the Guidelines;

   e) co-operate with international partners;

   f) engage with interested non-adhering countries on matters covered by the Guidelines and their implementation.

3. The Committee may seek and consider advice from experts on any matters covered by the Guidelines. For this purpose, the Committee will decide on suitable procedures.

4. The Committee will discharge its responsibilities in an efficient and timely manner.

5. In discharging its responsibilities, the Committee will be assisted by the OECD Secretariat, which, under the overall guidance of the Investment Committee, and subject to the Organization's Program of Work and Budget, will:

   a) serve as a central point of information for NCPs that have questions on the promotion and implementation of the Guidelines;

   b) collect and make publicly available relevant information on recent trends and emerging practices with regard to the promotional activities of NCPs and the implementation of the Guidelines in specific instances. The Secretariat will develop unified reporting formats to support the establishment and maintenance of an up-to-date database on specific instances and conduct regular analysis of these specific instances;

   c) facilitate peer learning activities, including voluntary peer evaluations, as well as capacity building and training, in particular for NCPs of new adhering countries, on the implementation procedures of the Guidelines such as promotion and the facilitation of conciliation and mediation;

   d) facilitate co-operation between NCPs where appropriate; and

   e) promote the Guidelines in relevant international forums and meetings and provide support to NCPs and the Committee in their efforts to raise awareness of the Guidelines among non-adhering countries.

REVISED FINAL STATEMENT ON COMPLAINT CONCERNING OIL MULTINATIONAL BP UNDER OECD GUIDELINES FOR MULTINATIONAL ENTERPRISES
Background and history (2011)

Summary

In March 2011, the UK Government ruled that the consortium led by oil multinational BP is breaking international corporate social responsibility rules in operating its Caspian BTC oil pipeline.

The ruling follows a Complaint lodged under the OECD Guidelines for Multinational Enterprises by six environment and human rights groups back in April 2003. The Revised Final Statement states that BP failed to investigate and respond to complaints from local people of intimidation by state security forces in Turkey guarding the pipeline.

The ruling sets a major precedent. In future, multinationals should take into account the human rights context in which they operate if they are to comply with the Guidelines.

The ruling potentially places BP in breach of its contracts with international financial institutions that backed the project with taxpayers' money in 2004. Although the OECD Guidelines are voluntary, BP gave a legally-binding commitment to these institutions that the BTC project would comply with them.

Background and Chronology of Complaint

The 1,760 kilometre-long Baku-Tbilisi-Ceyhan (BTC) oil pipeline runs from the offshore oil fields in the Caspian Sea near Baku in Azerbaijan, through Georgia's national park and close to the town of Tbilisi, finishing south of Ceyhan on the southern shores of Turkey on the Mediterranean at a tanker terminal, where the oil is loaded on to supertankers that transport the oil to Western Europe.

Construction of the pipeline by a consortium of oil companies, led by British oil multinational BP, started in May 2003 after 13 years of negotiations and preparations. The preparations laying the legal groundwork for the project included agreements between the consortium and the governments of the three countries (Host Government Agreements) signed in 1999 and consultations with the people over whose land the pipeline would cross to negotiate compensation.

In 2002, from June to September, local and international public interest groups conducted fact-finding missions to the pipeline areas in Azerbaijan, Georgia and Turkey. Their detailed reports indicated grave concerns about irregularities involving the consultation process about the pipeline's route and availability of documents; land expropriation and compensation; and intimidation over freedom of expression. Within Turkey, the reports noted particular issues affecting substantial numbers of Kurdish people.

2003

Just one month before construction started, in April 2003, six public interest organizations (including The Corner House) lodged a Complaint against BP alleging breaches of six OECD Guidelines for Multinational Enterprises intended to encourage "good corporate behaviour."

The Complaint alleged that the Consortium had:

- exerted undue influence on the regulatory framework;
- sought or accepted exemptions related to social, labour, tax and
- environmental laws;
- failed to operate in a manner contributing to the wider goals of sustainable development;
- failed to adequately consult with project-affected communities on pertinent matters; and
- undermined the host governments' ability to mitigate serious threats to the environment, human health and safety.

The UK's National Contact Point (NCP) — a government office established to promote adherence to the Guidelines — accepted the Complaint and asked BP to respond.

Under the OECD Guidelines (which are not legally-binding), the NCP does not act as a court of law and adjudicate over the rights and wrongs of actions, but aims instead to resolve Complaints by acting as a mediator between the parties involved and to issue forward looking statements outlining what action parties might take in future. As an NCP review stated subsequently, "It is the basic aim of the NCP process to attempt to bring parties together to resolve Complaints mutually." Information shared and correspondence between the parties and the National Contact Point cannot be disclosed to others without permission of the parties (for this reason, many documents referred to below are not publicly available).

2004

In March 2004, BP denied all the points made in the Complaint, which prompted the groups to submit to the NCP in November 2004 a detailed rebuttal of BP's response. The rebuttal included procedural concerns arising from the UK government (which would rule on the Complaint) now having a financial interest in the BTC pipeline since the UK's export credit agency, the Export Credits Guarantee Department (ECGD) announced in February 2004 support to the BTC Consortium worth £81,703,893 ($106 million), the largest guarantee issued in the 2003–04 financial year.

2005

The significant factual differences between BP and the groups that emerged from these exchanges, particularly over the impacts on local people, prompted the NCP to visit the region of the pipeline in the three countries from August–September

2005. His October 2005 report indicates that several villagers made specific complaints to him during his visit about their intimidation by Turkish state authorities.

The NCP hosted a dialogue meeting in October 2005 between the groups and BP to discuss the NCP's field visit and report. At this meeting, BP agreed to undertake its own field research to investigate the specific complaints made by villagers to the NCP during his field visit, and to report back in November 2005.

2006

BP sent a report back to the NCP in 2006 of its own investigations but refused to let the Complainants see it on grounds of confidentiality.

The NCP compiled a draft statement on the Complaint, which it circulated to the parties, who submitted their comments and corrections.

2007

Nevertheless, in August 2007, the National Contact Point issued a Final Statement on the Complaint, dismissing all the alleged breaches of the OECD Guidelines, making no recommendations for the future, not clarifying differences between factual information proved by the groups and that by BP, and not giving any reasons or justifications for its conclusions. It appeared to rely on the confidential BP report stating that the majority of claims raised by villagers with the NCP lacked any basis.

The groups appealed (via solicitors Leigh Day & Co) in September 2007 to the NCP's Steering Board, arguing that the Final Statement was procedurally flawed because it relied on the BP report that the company had refused to send to the organisations. (The OECD Guidelines stipulate that all information concerning a Complaint should be seen by both parties). The appeal argued that the NCP's involvement with them had been "one-sided, limited and partial, and wholly fails to meet basic standards of fairness or natural justice." It stated that the NCP had conducted itself throughout with "conspicuous unfairness," favouring the commercial organisations involved at every stage.

The NCP acknowledged "some procedural failings" and withdrew its August 2007 Final Statement in December of that year.

2008

In March 2008, the NCP agreed to a review of the whole Complaint process. In April 2008, the groups submitted a detailed report on the flawed and biased procedures the NCP had followed in handling the Complaint:
- the NCP had failed to engage critically with the issues or to justify positions taken in the Final Statement;
- there was improper interference and influence in the Complaint process by BP;

- the NCP failed to act fairly and misdirected itself on confidentiality;

- the NCP breached its undertakings to the groups to disclose a copy of the Final Statement prior to its publication for comment by all the parties involved;

- the NCP failed to disclose or assess the evidence received from third parties (such as other government departments, including information supplied by the Foreign Office on the lack of emergency oil response plans in Azerbaijan).

The NCP's Review Committee met in June 2008 and in July 2008 found that the UK NCP had indeed acted unfairly by not giving the complainants the opportunity to comment on the BP report. The Committee recommended that:

- the original Final Statement be withdrawn and reconsidered in the light of the review;

- BP be asked to reconsider consenting to share its 2006 report checking out the NCP's field visit with the Complainants;

- in the absence of such consent, the NCP consider to what extent it could rely on the report in reaching its final decision;

- the revised Final Statement set out in balanced terms the positions of the parties and the reasons for the UK NCP's conclusions on the points it considers relevant for its decision.

In October 2008, BP did finally agree to disclose the report to the Complainants — but refused to permit its disclosure to the Complainants' partner in Turkey to enable them to check its facts on-the-ground.

2009

In February 2009, the NCP facilitated mediation between the parties, which resulted in BP agreeing to its report being released to a Turkish-based human rights group that was mutually acceptable to all the parties involved.

The BP report stated that the complaints made by villagers to the NCP during his August 2005 visit had been investigated and resolved. The Complainants, through on-the-ground fact checking in Turky, including video testimonies from villagers, questioned the truth of such statements, resulting in several exchanges submitted to the NCP by the Complainants and by BP over several months.

(In February 2009, the groups drew up some "lessons learned" from their experience of the Complaint procedure and engagement with the NCP, which were submitted to the NCP and its governing structures.)

2011

The Revised Final Statement of 22 February 2011 (but released publicly on 9 March 2011) now accepts that BP breached the OECD Guidelines in its consultation and grievance process "the company failed to identify specific complaints of intimidation against affected communities by local security forces where the information was received outside of the formal grievance and monitoring channels, and, by not taking adequate steps in response to such complaints, failed to adequately safeguard against the risk of local partners undermining the overall consultation and grievance process."

The Revised Final Statement recommends that BP "consider and report on ways that it could strengthen procedures to identify and respond to reports of alleged intimidation by local pipeline security and other alleged breaches of the Voluntary Principles."

Both parties are asked to provide the UK NCP with a substantiated update within three months on the company's progress towards meeting the UK NCP's recommendation.

The ruling sets a major precedent. In future, to comply with the OECD's corporate social responsibility guidelines, multinationals will have to take into account the human rights context in which they operate, including the risk of intimidation, when designing and implementing corporate grievance mechanisms. Such mechanisms need to be robust enough that people can report intimidation without fearing further reprisals.

Given BP's legally-binding commitment in May 2003 to ensure that the BTC project complies with the OECD Guidelines, the ruling potentially places the company in breach of its contracts with the major international financial institutions (IFIs) that backed the project with taxpayers' money in 2004. In addition to the UK's export credit agency, these include the International Finance Corporation of the World Bank, the European Bank for Reconstruction and Development (EBRD) and other European and U.S. export credit agencies.

Even though the ruling states "the company's activities in this particular region were not in accordance with Chapter V paragraph 2(b) of the Guidelines," (p.2.), The Guardian newspaper reported that BP rejects the claim that the BTC project breached the OECD's Guidelines. BP "does not accept that in that area [of Turkey] BTC Co's activities were inconsistent with the OECD Guidelines," the company stated to the Business & Human Rights Resource Centre.

The Complaint in other countries

Back in April 2003, the Complaint was submitted not only to the UK's National Contact Point, but also to those of France, Germany, Italy, Belgium and the USA — all OECD member states — because their export credit agencies or banks had supported the BTC pipeline financially in some form.

Because the lead company in the BTC Consortium, BP, is British, the NCPs in the other countries collectively decided in 2004 that the UK would "take the lead" in handling the case. Despite this understanding, the UK NCP decided unilaterally in 2005 that it would deal only with the UK Complainants, thereby excluding others from participating in the process except as observers. The UK NCP did not communicate this decision to the other NCPs until January 2006 — at which point the Complaints in the other countries reverted to their national NCPs.

The Complaint continues to be assessed in Italy, although the Italian NCP has indicated it will take its lead from the UK, except in those areas where the Complaint has been expanded since it was originally submitted to include aspects relating to the Host Government Agreements. (Further information can be disclosed only when the Italian NCP has reached a final decision.)

The French and German NCPs have now rejected the Complaint, while no progress has been made in the USA. The Belgian NCP declared the Complaint against Belgian banks eligible to be considered under the OECD Guidelines, but forwarded it to the UK NCP on the grounds that the main actor in the BTC project, BP, is, a UK company, thereby closing the case in Belgium. But the UK NCP (unofficially) stated that it would not evaluate the role of the Belgian banks and thus the case remains in limbo.

NOTES AND QUESTIONS

1.   Note that although compliance with the OECD Guidelines is voluntary, BP undertook a contractual obligation to observe them. What may be the consequences of a breach of the Guidelines in this case?

2.   The National Contact Point for the United States is the U.S. Department of State:

> U.S. National Contact Point
> Bureau of Economic and Business Affairs
> Room 4950 Harry Truman Building
> U.S. Department of State
> 2201 C Street NW
> Washington, DC 20520
> Tel: 1-202-647-5686

3.   Is this procedure unduly burdensome for international business?

4.   The BTC pipeline officially opened with much fanfare in 2006. BP, the subject or the complaints, has a 30% stake in the consortium that built the pipeline. The pipeline saves at least 350 tanker trips per year through the Bosporus and the Dardanelles. In a follow-up Report in 2011, the UK National Contact Point noted that BP, in its Report on the alleged violation, stated that it did not accept the UK NCP's Finding that its activities were not in accordance with the Guidelines, but BP promised that its existing procedures would be examined with a view to strengthening its procedures in line with the UK NCP recommendation. *See* http://www.gov.uk/government/uploads/attachment_data/file/31751/11-1299-follow-up-1.

C. Environmental Liability

PROBLEM 10-2
A CHEMICAL PLANT EXPLOSION

Acme Corporation is a large, multinational chemical company incorporated in Delaware and headquartered in New York City. Acme manufactures a variety of chemicals that are very toxic but are used as raw materials to make a wide variety of useful products. Acme has located many of its manufacturing facilities in developing countries which welcome Acme's investment and whose people do not object to living close by a chemical manufacturing facility. Acme's international operations are all run through separate local companies that are wholly owned by Acme as the parent company. Acme's international operations are managed by American employees of Acme Delaware, but all plant workers are local employees.

On March 30, a terrible explosion ripped through Acme's chemical plant located in Kinshasa in the Democratic Republic of the Congo (DRC), killing 30 plant workers and injuring at least 123 people in the surrounding area. In addition, because the Acme plant is located on the Congo river, liquid chemicals flowed into the river, killing fish and poisoning the water supply for many people. In addition, smoke and fumes from the explosion drifted across the river sickening people in Brazzaville, the capital city of the Republic of the Congo. Acme immediately investigated this incident and has concluded that the explosion was caused by some careless local employees who were smoking cigarettes in a no smoking area. Acme's chemical plant, Acme Kinshasa, is owned and operated by Acme Ltd., a company incorporated under the laws of the DRC and a wholly-owned subsidiary of Acme Delaware.

What liability risks does this incident entail for Acme? Consider the following materials.

1. Liability under International Law

The first possibility is that Acme Delaware and Acme Kinshasa may be liable under international law since the Acme chemical explosion had a transboundary impact and polluted an international river, but neither Acme Delaware nor Acme Kinshasa is an "actor" under international law. As we saw in Chapter 3, international law imposes responsibility upon States, not upon private companies or individuals. International law can impose liability on individuals and private companies, but this requires the creation of a special regime to do so. In Chapter 3, we learned that some 15 international liability regimes have been concluded to impose liability upon private operators of certain facilities involved in incidents that cause transboundary harm or pollute the oceans. In fact, two of these Conventions are relevant to the Acme Chemical Plant explosion: *(1) the Lugano Convention on Civil Liability for Damage Resulting from Activities Dangerous to the Environment (1993) and (2) the Protocol on Civil Liability and Compensation for Damage Caused by the Transboundary Effects of Industrial Accidents on Transboundary Waters (2003).* Both of these Conventions are reprinted in the **Document Supplement**. What do these Conventions do? Would Acme Delaware and Acme Kinshasa have to pay damages under these Conventions? Note that both liability regimes would apply if they were duly ratified and in force. But neither Convention is in force.

Is this a gap in international law? Should multinational companies have general liability under international law for environmental and other harm? This matter was considered by the International Law Commission in the drafting of its Articles on State Responsibility, but was rejected as too much of a departure from current state practice. *See* Stephen McCaffrey, *The Work of the International Law Commission Relating to Transfrontier Environmental Harm*, 20 N.Y.U. J. OF INT'L L. & POL. 715, 720 (1988).

A related question, which harkens back to Chapter 3, is whether the Democratic Republic of the Congo as a State would be liable under international law for the transboundary damages caused by the Acme accident. What is the answer to this question?

Another question is whether there is any basis for holding the United States as the home country of Acme responsible for damages. Under current law is this possible? Some commentators have advocated that when an industrial accident occurs involving a multinational company using high-risk technology, the country of origin of the company should have state responsibility. Francesco Francioni argues that although in such a case there is no territorial link between the country and the accident, there is a legal and administrative link between the multilateral enterprise and its home country, and imposing responsibility on the home country should be done to assure greater supervision and administrative control of multinationals and due diligence by the home country. *See* Shinya Murase, *Perspectives from International Economic Law on Transnational Environmental Issues*, 253 RECEUIL DES COURS 287 (1995). Do you agree?

2. Liability Under the Home State or Host State Laws

If international law is not available in most cases for a major industrial accident causing transboundary harm, are the laws of the home state of the multinational business or the laws of the host state where the accident occurred available for victims to recover damages, including damage to the environment? Consider the following cases.

IN RE UNION CARBIDE CORP. GAS PLANT DISASTER
809 F.2d 195 (2d Cir. 1987)

MANSFIELD, CIRCUIT JUDGE:

This appeal raises the question of whether thousands of claims by citizens of India and the Government of India arising out of the most devastating industrial disaster in history — the deaths of over 2,000 persons and injuries of over 200,000 caused by lethal gas known as methyl isocyanate which was released from a chemical plant operated by Union Carbide India Limited (UCIL) in Bhopal, India — should be tried in the United States or in India. The Southern District of New York, John F. Keenan, Judge, granted the motion of Union Carbide Corporation (UCC), a defendant in some 145 actions commenced in federal courts in the United

States, to dismiss these actions on grounds of *forum non conveniens* so that the claims may be tried in India, subject to certain conditions. The individual plaintiffs appeal from the order and the court's denial of their motion for a fairness hearing on a proposed settlement. UCC and the Union of India (UOI), a plaintiff, cross-appeal. We eliminate two of the conditions imposed by the district court and in all other respects affirm that court's orders.

The accident occurred on the night of December 2–3, 1984, when winds blew the deadly gas from the plant operated by UCIL into densely occupied parts of the city of Bhopal. UCIL is incorporated under the laws of India. Fifty and nine-tenths percent of its stock is owned by UCC, 22% is owned or controlled by the government of India, and the balance is held by approximately 23,500 Indian citizens. The stock is publicly traded on the Bombay Stock Exchange. The company is engaged in the manufacture of a variety of products, including chemicals, plastics, fertilizers and insecticides, at 14 plants in India and employs over 9,000 Indian citizens. It is managed and operated entirely by Indians in India.

Four days after the Bhopal accident, on December 7, 1984, the first of some 145 purported class actions in federal district courts in the United States was commenced on behalf of victims of the disaster. On January 2, 1985, the Judicial Panel on Multidistrict Litigation assigned the actions to the Southern District of New York where they became the subject of a consolidated complaint filed on June 28, 1985.

In the meantime, on March 29, 1985, India enacted the Bhopal Gas Leak Disaster (Processing of Claims) Act, granting to its government, the UOI, the exclusive right to represent the victims in India or elsewhere. Thereupon the UOI, purporting to act in the capacity of parens patriae, and with retainers executed by many of the victims, on April 5, 1985, filed a complaint in the Southern District of New York on behalf of all victims of the Bhopal disaster, similar to the purported class action complaints already filed by individuals in the United States. The UOI's decision to bring suit in the United States was attributed to the fact that, although numerous lawsuits (by now, some 6,500) had been instituted by victims in India against UCIL, the Indian courts did not have jurisdiction over UCC, the parent company, which is a defendant in the United States actions. The actions in India asserted claims not only against UCIL but also against the UOI, the State of Madhya Pradesh, and the Municipality of Bhopal, and were consolidated in the District Court of Bhopal.

By order dated April 25, 1985, Judge Keenan appointed a three-person Executive Committee to represent all plaintiffs in the pre-trial proceedings. It consisted of two lawyers representing the individual plaintiffs and one representing the UOI. On July 31, 1985, UCC moved to dismiss the complaints on grounds of *forum non conveniens*, the plaintiffs' lack of standing to bring the actions in the United States, and their purported attorneys' lack of authority to represent them. After several months of discovery related to *forum non conveniens*, the individual plaintiffs and the UOI opposed UCC's motion. After hearing argument on January 3, 1986, the district court, on May 12, 1986, 634 F. Supp. 842, in a thoroughly reasoned 63-page opinion granted the motion, dismissing the lawsuits before it on condition that UCC:

(1) consent to the jurisdiction of the courts of India and continue to waive defenses based on the statute of limitations,

(2) agree to satisfy any judgment rendered by an Indian court against it and upheld on appeal, provided the judgment and affirmance "comport with the minimal requirements of due process," and

(3) be subject to discovery under the Federal Rules of Civil Procedure of the United States.

On June 12, 1986, UCC accepted these conditions subject to its right to appeal them; and on June 24, 1986, the district court entered its order of dismissal. In September 1986 the UOI, acting pursuant to its authority under the Bhopal Act, brought suit on behalf of all claimants against UCC and UCIL in the District Court of Bhopal, where many individual suits by victims of the disaster were then pending.

In its opinion dismissing the actions the district court analyzed the *forum non conveniens* issues, applying the standards and weighing the factors suggested by the Supreme Court in Gulf Oil Corp. v. Gilbert, 330 U.S. 501, 67 S. Ct. 839, 91 L. Ed. 955 (1947), and Piper Aircraft Co. v. Reyno, 454 U.S. 235, 102 S. Ct. 252, [70 L.Ed.2d 419](1981). At the outset Judge Keenan concluded, in accordance with the Court's expressed views in Piper that, since the plaintiffs were not residents of the United States but of a foreign country, their choice of the United States as a forum would not be given the deference to which it would be entitled if this country were their home. See Piper, 454 U.S. at 256, 102 S. Ct. at 266. Following the dictates of Piper, the district court declined to commit to compare the advantages and disadvantages to the respective parties of American versus Indian Laws or to determine the impact upon plaintiffs' claims of the laws of India, where UCC had acknowledged that it would make itself amenable to process, except to ascertain whether India provided an adequate alternative forum, as distinguished from no remedy at all. Judge Keenan reviewed thoroughly the affidavits of experts on India's law and legal system, which described in detail its procedural and substantive aspects, and concluded that, despite some of the Indian system's disadvantages, it afforded an adequate alternative forum for the enforcement of plaintiffs' claims.

As the district court found, the record shows that the private interests of the respective parties weigh heavily in favor of dismissal on grounds of *forum non conveniens*. The many witnesses and sources of proof are almost entirely located in India, where the accident occurred, and could not be compelled to appear for trial in the United States. The Bhopal plant at the time of the accident was operated by some 193 Indian nationals, including the managers of seven operating units employed by the Agricultural Products Division of UCIL, who reported to Indian Works Managers in Bhopal. The plant was maintained by seven functional departments employing over 200 more Indian nationals.

In short, the plant has been constructed and managed by Indians in India. No Americans were employed at the plant at the time of the accident. In the five years from 1980 to 1984, although more than 1,000 Indians were employed at the plant, only one American was employed there and he left in 1982. No American visited the plant for more than one year prior to the accident, and during the 5-year period before the accident the communications between the plant and the United States were almost non-existent.

We are concerned, however, that as it is written the district court's requirement that UCC consent to the enforcement of a final Indian judgment, which was imposed on the erroneous assumption that such a judgment might not otherwise be enforceable in the United States, may create misunderstandings and problems of construction. Although the order's provision that the judgment "comport with the minimal requirements of due process" (emphasis supplied) probably is intended to refer to "due process" as used in the New York Foreign Country Money Judgments Law and others like it, there is the risk that it may also be interpreted as providing for a lesser standard than we would otherwise require. Since the court's condition with respect to enforceability of any final Indian judgment is predicated on an erroneous legal assumption and its "due process" language is ambiguous, and since the district court's purpose is fully served by New York's statute providing for recognition of foreign-country money judgments, it was error to impose this condition upon the parties.

We also believe that the district court erred in requiring UCC to consent (which UCC did under protest and subject to its right of appeal) to broad discovery of it by the plaintiffs under the Federal Rules of Civil Procedure when UCC is confined to the more limited discovery authorized under Indian law.

Basic justice dictates that both sides be treated equally, with each having equal access to the evidence in the possession or under the control of the other. Application of this fundamental principle in the present case is especially appropriate since the UOI, as the sovereign government of India, is expected to be a party to the Indian litigation, possibly on both sides.

For these reasons we direct that the condition with respect to the discovery of UCC under the Federal Rules of Civil Procedure be deleted without prejudice to the right of the parties to have reciprocal discovery of each other on equal terms under the Federal Rules, subject to such approval as may be required of the Indian court in which the case will be pending. If, for instance, Indian authorities will permit mutual discovery pursuant to the Federal Rules, the district court's order, as modified in accordance with this opinion, should not be construed to bar such procedure. In the absence of such a court-sanctioned agreement, however, the parties will be limited by the applicable discovery rules of the Indian court in which the claims will be pending.

As so modified the district court's order is affirmed.

NOTE ON THE BHOPAL SETTLEMENT AND ITS TORTUOUS AFTERMATH

The Bhopal gas disaster is considered the world's worst industrial accident. The Bhopal gas disaster happened in 1984. The Indian government on behalf of all the Indian claimants entered into a financial settlement with Union Carbide in 1989; but litigation in both India and the United States has continued non-stop to this writing in 2014, with no end in sight.

No one knows the exact number of people killed and injured as a result of the Bhopal incident. The website www.bhopal.com, maintained by Union Carbide Corporation, states that "approximately" 3,800 people died and several thousand others experienced partial or total disabilities. Survivor organizations, of course, put the number of people killed and injured at much higher totals.

The precise cause of the incident has also never been determined. Various investigations found that a large quantity of water was introduced — by accident or on purpose — into a tank holding methyl isocyanate gas resulting in a chemical explosion, but the individuals responsible for this have never been identified.

At the time of the 1987 ruling by the Second Circuit Court of Appeals affirming the application of the doctrine of *forum non conveniens*, claims against UCC and UCIL were pending in India. In 1985, the Parliament of India enacted the Bhopal Gas Leak Disaster Act, which granted an exclusive right on the part of the Indian government to represent all claimants both within and outside India and directed the government to organize a plan for the registration and processing of victims' claims.

Litigation in India conducted by the Indian government reached the Indian Supreme Court in 1988 after rulings by the High Court of Madhya Pradesh. The Indian Supreme Court pressured both the government and UCC to enter into settlement talks. In 1989, what appeared to be a comprehensive settlement was reached and approved by the Supreme Court. Under the terms of the 1989 settlement, UCC and UCIL did not admit liability, but agreed to pay $470 million to the Indian government. (This was in addition to approximately $10 million voluntarily donated by UCC to various organizations for interim humanitarian aid). The settlement, which purported to end all UCC and UCIL civil and criminal liability, specified $44 million compensation for the survivors of the dead; $160 million for those permanently disabled; $60 million for those temporarily disabled; $50 million for those suffering various injuries; $16 million for specialized medical treatment and after-care; and $140 million for less serious injuries and property claims. This money was paid in full by UCC in February 1989. Various interests in India challenged the 1989 settlement and the constitutionality of the Gas Leak Disaster Act, but in 1991, the Indian Supreme Court rejected these challenges and affirmed the settlement.[5]

Subsequent to the 1989 settlement, two important corporate changes occurred. In 1994, the Indian government approved UCC's sale of its 50.9% stake in UCIL, reportedly so that the proceeds of the sale could be used to build a hospital. The reorganized UCIL business now operates in India under the ironic name, Eveready Industries, Ltd. The second change occurred in 2001, when Dow Chemical Company acquired control of UCC in a stock-purchase transaction.

Despite the 1989 settlement, legal proceedings have continued both in the United States and in India.

In the United States, a series of collateral class action and individual lawsuits were filed against UCC in New York federal courts asking for compensation under the Alien Tort Statute under nuisance laws, and under tort law asking for medical monitoring and environmental remediation of the Bhopal site. The plaintiffs focused

---

[5] M.J. Peterson, *Bhopal Plant Disaster*, Appendix F, p. 5, in INTERNATIONAL DIMENSIONS OF ETHICS EDUCATION IN SCIENCE AND ENGINEERING, Case Study Series (2008).

on post-leak contamination and additional uncompensated injuries as the basis for these lawsuits. These cases bounced back and forth between the U.S. district court and the U.S. Court of Appeals for the Second Circuit more than a score of times. Thus far the courts have denied relief, refusing to pierce the corporate veil between UCC and UCIL and upholding the validity of the 1989 settlement. *See Bano v. Union Carbide Corp.*, 273 F.3d 120 (2d Cir. 2001) and Bano case history, http://www.earthrights.org/print/787; *Sahu v. Union Carbide Corp.*, 475 F.3d 465 (2d Cir. 2007) and Summary Order of June 27, 2013, 2013 US App. LEXIS 13367 (4th Cir.), affirming 2012 US Dist. LEXIS 91066 (S.D.N.Y. 2012). But litigation in U.S. courts appears certain to continue as Indian activists have announced new efforts to hold not only UCC liable but also Dow Chemical as the successor owner of UCC. *See* Amnesty International News, *India: Court Decision requires Dow Chemical to respond to Bhopal Gas Tragedy*, 23 July 2013, http://www.amnesty.org, visited 3 January 2014.

Legal proceedings are continuing in India as well. On the civil side, the Indian Supreme Court has handled a series of filings by the Indian government as well as others to reopen the 1989 Bhopal settlement. Thus far the court has rejected all these petitions. *See* "SC refuses to open Bhopal case," May 11, 2011, Hindu Star Times, *available at* http://www.livemint.com, visited 4 January 2014. On the criminal side, in 2010, seven former executives of UCIL were convicted *in absentia* in the Bhopal district court of negligent homicide and given fines and jail sentences. Similar criminal charges are pending in Bhopal district court against UCC and its former CEO, Warren Anderson, who have refused to appear. The Indian government has filed a formal request for extradition with the U.S. State Department concerning these charges.

NOTES AND QUESTIONS

1. What is your opinion of the Bhopal settlement? Does it meet standards of corrective and distributive justice?

2. It appears that no UCC employee (and no American) was connected in any way with UCIL at the time of the Bhopal disaster. Moreover, UCIL and UCC were operated as independent legal entities. UCC management was clearly surprised, shocked, and dismayed by the disaster. But what do you make of the court's statement in the Bhopal case that for at least during the five-year period before the incident, communications between UCC and UCIL were "almost non-existent." Is it wise policy for a multinational company that is a majority owner of a foreign company to allow it extreme autonomy? Should a parent company in such a case incur liability for inadequate supervision, training, and oversight of the foreign company?

3. What law is applicable to a disaster such as occurred in Bhopal, India in 1984? At present national law — the law of the host country — applies. Is this sufficient? Although the Bhopal incident did not have transboundary impact, an industrial accident that causes deaths, injuries, and destruction across national boundaries can easily be imagined. In fact, such accidents occurred at the ICMESA plant in Seveso, Italy in 1976, and at the Sandoz plant near Basel, Switzerland in 1986. These accidents provided the impetus for lawmaking initiatives in European countries. The European Union has adopted a series of "Seveso Directives" that require standards for prevention, preparedness, and response to industrial accidents that apply in all 28 EU member states. The current Seveso Directive is Directive 2012/18/EU of 4 July 2012. In addition, the UN Economic Commission for Europe has adopted the 1992 (as amended 2008) Convention on the Transboundary Effects of Industrial Accidents (Helsinki, 1992) (in force 2000 for 41 parties), which adopts standards similar to the Seveso Directive for the wider European area. Two international instruments have been concluded that adopt international standards for liability of businesses involved in industrial accidents. The Convention on Civil Liability for Damage Resulting from Activities Dangerous to the Environment (Lugano, 1993) provides for recovery of damages from the parties responsible (persons or companies in control of the activity causing damage) for industrial accidents based on strict liability standards and including damages to the environment. In addition, a Protocol on Civil Liability for Damage and Compensation for Damage Caused by Transboundary Industrial Accidents on Navigable Waters was adopted in 2003, as a joint protocol to the Helsinki Convention and the Convention on the Protection and Use of Transboundary Waters (1992). However, neither convention allowing the recovery of damages is in force at present. Is it desirable to have international standards for damage liability and compensation in this area?

4. After conducting hearings on the Bhopal incident, the U.S. Congress enacted the Emergency Planning and Community-Right-to-Know Act (EPCRA), 42 U.S.C. §§ 11001–11050 in 1986. This law provides support for state and local government programs to inform the public and to have emergency plans in place to cope with possible industrial accidents. The EPCRA requires owners and operators of facilities in the U.S. that use hazardous substances (1) to notify local emergency planning committees of any releases of such substances; (2) to cooperate with local and state officials to prepare emergency contingency plans; (3) to make full disclosure regarding data and an inventory of chemicals being made or used; and (4) to submit annual reports on safety and release of chemicals. Thus, the Bhopal gas incident had a major impact in the United States.

We now turn to the question whether the U.S. Alien Tort Statute may be used to recover damages in international pollution and environmental damage cases. The Alien Tort Statute, 28 U.S.C. § 1350, reads as follows: "The district courts shall have original jurisdiction of any civil action by an alien for a tort only, committed in violation of the law of nations or a treaty of the United States."

KIOBEL v. ROYAL DUTCH PETROLEUM COMPANY
133 S. Ct. 1659 (2013)

[In this case the petitioners, Kiobel et al., Nigerian citizens residing in the United States, alleged that Royal Dutch Shell et al., two companies based in Europe, had aided and abetted the Nigerian government in committing human rights and environmental atrocities in Nigeria in violation of the law of nations. The Supreme Court initially granted Certiorari on the question whether a corporation can incur liability under the ATS. But after oral argument on this question, the Court directed the parties to brief a different question: "Whether and under what circumstances the ATS allows courts to recognize a cause of action for violations of the law of nations occurring within the territory of a sovereign other than the United States."]

CHIEF JUSTICE ROBERTS delivered the opinion of the Court.

The question here is not whether petitioners have stated a proper claim under the ATS, but whether a claim may reach conduct occurring in the territory of a foreign sovereign. Respondents contend that claims under the ATS do not, relying primarily on a canon of statutory interpretation known as the presumption against extraterritorial application. That canon provides that "when a statute gives no clear indication of an extraterritorial application, it has none." Morrison v. National Australia Bank, Ltd., 561 U.S. [247] (2010) [section 10(b) of the Securities Exchange Act cannot provide the basis for a cause of action to allow foreign plaintiffs to sue foreign and American defendants in connection with securities traded on foreign stock exchanges]. This presumption "serves to protect against unintended clashes between our laws and those of other nations which could result in international discord." [citations omitted]. We typically apply this presumption to discern whether an act of Congress regulating conduct applies abroad. [citations omitted]. [W]e think the principles underlying [this] canon of interpretation similarly constrain courts considering causes of action that may be brought under the ATS. Indeed, the danger of unwarranted judicial interference in the conduct of foreign policy is magnified in the context of the ATS, because the question is not what Congress has done but instead what courts may do.

[The Court's opinion points out that *Sosa v. Alvarez-Machain* (542 U.S. at 713) ruled that while extraterritoriality is a "merits question," the ATS is "strictly jurisdictional," and there is no indication in the text that Congress intended the ATS to have extraterritorial reach. "[T]he fact that the text reaches 'any civil action'. . . [does] not rebut the presumption against extraterritoriality."]

Nor does the historical background against which the ATS was enacted overcome the presumption against application to conduct in the territory of another sovereign. Two notorious episodes involving violations of the law of nations occurred in the United States shortly before passage of the ATS. Each concerned the rights of ambassadors and each involved conduct within the Union. In 1784, a French adventurer verbally and physically assaulted Francis Barbe Marbois — the Secretary of the French Legion — in Philadelphia. The assault led the French Minister Plenipotentiary to lodge a formal protest with the Continental Congress and threaten to leave the country unless an adequate remedy were provided. And in 1787, a New York constable entered the Dutch ambassador's house and arrested one of his domestic servants. At the request of Secretary of Foreign Affairs John Jay, the Mayor of New York City arrested the constable in turn, but cautioned that because "neither Congress nor our [State] Legislature have yet passed any act respecting a breach of the privileges of ambassadors, the extent of any available relief would depend on the common law. The two cases in which the ATS was involved shortly after its passage also concerned conduct within the territory of the United States. See Bolchos, 3 F. Cas. 810 (wrongful seizure of slaves from a vessel while in port in the United States); Moxon, 17 F. Cas. 942 (wrongful seizure in United States territorial waters).

The third example of a violation of a law of nations familiar to the Congress that enacted the ATS was piracy. Piracy typically occurs on the high seas, beyond the jurisdiction of the United States or any other country. Applying U.S. law to pirates, however, does not typically impose the sovereign will of the United States onto conduct occurring within the territorial jurisdiction of another sovereign, and therefore carries less direct foreign policy consequences. Pirates were fair game wherever found, by any nation, because they generally did not operate within any jurisdiction.

We therefore conclude that the presumption against extraterritoriality applies to claims under the ATS, and that nothing in the Statute rebuts that presumption. On these facts, all of the relevant conduct took place outside the United States. And even where the claims touch and concern the territory of the United States, they must do so with sufficient force to displace the presumption against extraterritorial application. Corporations are often present in many countries, and it would reach too far to say that mere corporate presence suffices.

[A concurring opinion was filed by JUSTICE KENNEDY, JUSTICE ALITO, with whom JUSTICE THOMAS joined, filed a concurring opinion holding that "a putative ATS cause of action will fall within the scope of the presumption against extraterritoriality — and will therefore be barred — unless the domestic conduct is sufficient to violate an international law norm that satisfies Sosa's requirements of definiteness and acceptance among civilized nations." A third concurring opinion was filed by JUSTICE BREYER, joined by JUSTICES GINSBURG, SOTOMAYOR, and KAGAN, holding that the presumption against extraterritorial application is not a helpful tool to resolve the jurisdictional issue. Rather JUSTICE BREYER would look to jurisdictional concepts under international law as expounded in the Restatement (Third) of Foreign Relations Law of the United States, sections 402 and 403. JUSTICE BREYER would limit the jurisdiction of the ATS to cases "where (1) the alleged tort occurs on American soil; (2) the defendant is an American national; or (3) the defendant's conduct substantially and adversely affects an important American national interest, and that includes a distinct interest in preventing the United States from becoming a safe harbor for a torturer or other common enemy of mankind."]

NOTES AND QUESTIONS

1.   The *Sosa* and *Kiobel* cases significantly cut back the application of the Alien Tort Statute. Is this a salutary development? How do you evaluate the three different interpretations of the ATS in the Kiobel case? There is a fundamental difference between Justices Roberts, Scalia, Kennedy, Alito, and Thomas, on the one hand, who focus on extraterritoriality — a "merits issue" and Justices Breyer, Ginsburg, Sotomayor, and Kagan, on the other hand, who focus on jurisdiction. Which interpretation is best?

2.   What is the future of the ATS after *Kiobel?* The question seems to be: What does it take to overcome the presumption articulated in the court's opinion?

3.   The *Kiobel* opinion leaves many questions surrounding the ATS unanswered, such as: (1) whether corporations may incur liability; (2) the existence and scope of a requirement to exhaust local remedies; (3) the viability of aiding and abetting

claims; (4) the liability of individual defendants; (5) the application of *forum non conveniens*; (6) the applicable substantive law; and (7) the appropriate deference to the U.S. executive's policy in a particular case.

4. For six essays on the future of the ATS after *Kiobel* by leading commentators on human rights law, see *Agora: Reflections on Kiobel*, 107 Am. J. Int'l L. 829–863 (2013).

TABLE OF CASES

[References are to pages]

[References are to pages]

INDEX

[References are to sections.]

[References are to sections.]

[References are to sections.]

[References are to sections.]